Selected Material from

Chemistry

Eighth Edition

Raymond Chang
Williams College

with

Brandon Cruickshank
Northern Arizona University

with Main Concepts and Practice Questions

by Peter M. Hierl

McGraw Hill **Custom Publishing**

Boston   Burr Ridge, IL   Dubuque, IA   Madison, WI   New York   San Francisco   St. Louis
Bangkok   Bogotá   Caracas   Lisbon   London   Madrid
Mexico City   Milan   New Delhi   Seoul   Singapore   Sydney   Taipei   Toronto

Selected Material from
Chemistry
Eighth Edition
with Main Concepts and Practice Questions

This book is a McGraw-Hill Custom Publishing textbook and contains select material from *Chemistry*, Eighth Edition by Raymond Chang with Brandon Cruickshank. Copyright © 2005, 2002, 1998, 1994, 1991, 1988, 1984, 1981 by The McGraw-Hill Companies, Inc. Reprinted with permission of the publisher. Many custom published texts are modified versions or adaptations of our best-selling textbooks. Some adaptations are printed in black and white to keep prices at a minimum, while others are in color.

1 2 3 4 5 6 7 8 9 0 QSR QSR 0 9 8 7 6 5

ISBN 0-07-323001-4

Editor: Barbara Duhon
Production Editor: Susan Culbertson
Printer/Binder: Quebecor World

IMPORTANT:

HERE IS YOUR REGISTRATION CODE TO ACCESS
YOUR PREMIUM McGRAW-HILL ONLINE RESOURCES.

MCGRAW-HILL

ONLINE RESOURCES

For key premium online resources you need THIS CODE to gain access. Once the code is entered, you will be able to use the Web resources for the length of your course.

If your course is using **WebCT** or **Blackboard**, you'll be able to use this code to access the McGraw-Hill content within your instructor's online course.

Access is provided if you have purchased a new book. If the registration code is missing from this book, the registration screen on our Website, and within your WebCT or Blackboard course, will tell you how to obtain your new code.

Registering for McGraw-Hill Online Resources

TO gain access to your MCGraw-Hill web
resources simply follow the steps below:

(1) USE YOUR WEB BROWSER TO GO TO: **www.mhhe.com/chang**

(2) CLICK ON **FIRST TIME USER**.

(3) ENTER THE REGISTRATION CODE* PRINTED ON THE TEAR-OFF BOOKMARK ON THE RIGHT.

(4) AFTER YOU HAVE ENTERED YOUR REGISTRATION CODE, CLICK **REGISTER**.

(5) FOLLOW THE INSTRUCTIONS TO SET-UP YOUR PERSONAL UserID AND PASSWORD.

(6) WRITE YOUR UserID AND PASSWORD DOWN FOR FUTURE REFERENCE.
KEEP IT IN A SAFE PLACE.

TO GAIN ACCESS to the McGraw-Hill content in your instructor's **WebCT** or **Blackboard** course simply log in to the course with the UserID and Password provided by your instructor. Enter the registration code exactly as it appears in the box to the right when prompted by the system. You will only need to use the code the first time you click on McGraw-Hill content.

Thank you, and welcome
to your MCGraw-Hill
online Resources!

HLWL-M9HV-FB7V-3SC5-CW3L

REGISTRATION CODE

Higher Education

* YOUR REGISTRATION CODE CAN BE USED ONLY ONCE TO ESTABLISH ACCESS. IT IS NOT TRANSFERABLE.

About the Author

Raymond Chang was born in Hong Kong and grew up in Shanghai, China, and Hong Kong. He received his B.Sc. degree in chemistry from London University, England, and his Ph.D. in chemistry from Yale University. After doing postdoctoral research at Washington University and teaching for a year at Hunter College of the City University of New York, he joined the chemistry department at Williams College, where he has taught since 1968.

Professor Chang has served on the American Chemical Society Examination Committee, the National Chemistry Olympiad Examination Committee, and the Graduate Record Examinations (GRE) Committee. He is an editor of *The Chemical Educator.* Professor Chang has written books on physical chemistry, industrial chemistry, and physical science. He has also coauthored books on the Chinese language, children's picture books, and a novel for juvenile readers.

For relaxation, Professor Chang maintains a forest garden; plays tennis, Ping-Pong, and the harmonica; and practices the violin.

Cover Image

The H^+ ion (proton) is hydrated to varying extents in aqueous solution. The diagram shows the top view of an electrostatic potential map of a H_3O^+ ion forming hydrogen bonds with three water molecules. The formula of this hydrated species is $H_9O_4^+$.

Contents in Brief

Contents

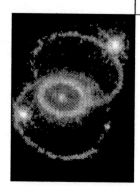

CHAPTER 1 CHEMISTRY: THE STUDY OF CHANGE 2

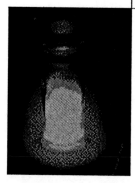

CHAPTER 2 ATOMS, MOLECULES, AND IONS 40

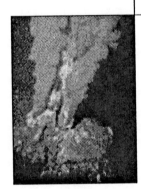

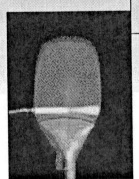

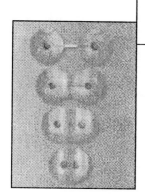

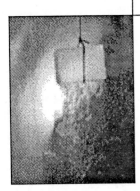

List of Applications

List of Animations

The animations listed here are correlated to *Chemistry* within each chapter in two ways. The first is the Interactive Activity Summary found in the opening pages of every chapter. Then within the chapter are icons letting the student and instructor know that an animation is available for a specific topic and where to find the animation for viewing. For the instructor, the animations are also available on the Chemistry Animations Library.

Chang Animations

Acid-base titrations (16.4)
Acid ionization (15.5)
Activation energy (13.4)
Alpha, beta, and gamma rays (2.2)
Alpha-particle scattering (2.2)
Atomic and ionic radius (8.3)
Base ionization (15.6)
Buffer solutions (16.3)
Cathode ray tube (2.2)
Chemical equilibrium (14.1)
Chirality (22.4 and 24.2)
Collecting a gas over water (5.6)
Dissolution of an ionic and a covalent compound (12.2)
Electron configurations (7.8)
Emission spectra (7.3)
Equilibrium vapor pressure (11.8)
Formal charge calculations (9.7)
Galvanic cells (19.2)
The gas laws (5.3)
Heat flow (6.4)
Hybridization (10.4)
Hydration (4.1)
Ionic versus covalent bonding (9.2)
Le Châtelier's principle (14.5)
Limiting reagent (3.9)
Making a solution (4.5)

Millikan oil drop (2.2)
Neutralization reactions (4.3)
Orientation of collision (13.4)
Oxidation-reduction reactions (4.4)
Packing spheres (11.4)
Polarity of molecules (10.2)
Precipitation reactions (4.2)
Preparing a solution by dilution (4.5)
Radioactive decay (23.3)
Sigma and pi bonds (10.5)
Strong electrolytes, weak electrolytes, and nonelectrolytes (4.1)
VSEPR (10.1)

McGraw-Hill Animations

Atomic line spectra (7.3)
Charles's law (5.3)
Cubic unit cells and their origins (11.4)
Dissociation of strong and weak acids (15.5)
Dissolving table salt (4.1)
Electronegativity (9.5)
Equilibrium (14.1)
Exothermic and endothermic reactions (6.2)
Formation of an ionic compound (9.2)
Formation of the covalent bond in H_2 (10.3)
Half-life (13.3)
Influence of shape on polarity (10.2)
Law of conservation of mass (2.1)
Molecular shape and orbital hybridization (10.4)
Nuclear medicine (23.7)
Operation of voltaic cell (19.2)
Oxidation-reduction reaction (4.4 and 19.1)
Phase diagrams and the states of matter (11.9)
Reaction rate and the nature of collisions (13.4)
Three states of matter (1.5)
Using a buffer (16.3)
VSEPR theory and the shapes of molecules (10.1)

Preface

The eighth edition of *Chemistry* continues the tradition of providing a firm foundation in chemical concepts and principles while presenting a broad range of topics in a clear, concise manner. My aims are to strike a balance between theory and application by incorporating real examples and to help students visualize the three-dimensional atomic and molecular structures that are the basis of chemical activity. An integral part of the text is to develop students' problem-solving and critical thinking skills.

Recent editions of *Chemistry* have witnessed the rapid advances in technology. While the textbook is still the best medium for students to use as they learn new concepts in chemistry, we employ many tools technology has to offer to help students visualize chemistry and explore ideas in an interactive environment. The integration of these tools in this textbook serves to inspire students in their learning process, and takes them beyond the confines of the traditional textbook.

Organization

The emphasis in this edition is on clarification. I have tried to present all processes in a step-by-step manner. You will find this style within the text of each chapter and also in the worked examples. I have reviewed and revised chapters based on the comments from reviewers and users. Some examples are shown next:

- Improved the treatment of limiting reagent (Section 3.9).

- Provided clearer explanation of atmospheric pressure (Section 5.2).

- Completely reorganized Chapter 6 so the topics flow in a more logical manner. In addition, the units for enthalpy change for chemical reactions (ΔH) are now given in kJ/mol. The same per mole unit is used for changes in entropy (ΔS) and Gibbs free energy (ΔG) in Chapter 18. As a result, the units are consistent in important thermodynamic equations such as Equation (18.14).

- Used radial probability plots to explain the shielding effect in Chapter 7.

- Clarified the influence of temperature on a reacting system at equilibrium in Chapter 14.

- Improved the treatment of acid strength, which now includes carboxylic acids in Chapter 15.

- Substantially revised the discussion of entropy and Gibbs free energy in Chapter 18.

- Added many new end-of-chapter problems and revised a number of others. As in previous editions, there is a good mix of easy, intermediate, and more challenging problems.

- Added two new Chemical Mysteries in Chapters 1 and 24.

Art

A completely new design can be seen throughout the eighth edition. As always, I strive for a clean but visual design. Each chapter opens with a two-page spread containing a photo with accompanying molecular models to illustrate the chemical or physical process at the molecular level.

Many of the line art drawings have a new look while still maintaining accurate chemical information.

Molecular art, created by the Spartan drawing program, is effective in emphasizing molecular geometry. Because I have also used *electrostatic potential maps* extensively to show charge distribution in molecules, a brief explanation of the meaning of these maps is in order. Imagine the situation in which a positive charge is brought toward a molecule. The interaction between this positive charge and some point in the molecule will be attractive if the point bears a negative charge. Conversely, the interaction will be repulsive if the point bears a positive charge. In this way, we can calculate such interactions over the entire molecule and present the results as a "map" according to the colors of the rainbow (red through blue tracks regions of greater negative charge to greater positive charge). The electrostatic potential map for a given molecule can be used to represent the charge distribution within the molecule, as illustrated in Figure 9.4 for hydrogen fluoride. These maps help students better understand the polarity of molecules, intermolecular forces, acid and base properties, and reaction mechanism.

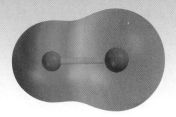

The electrostatic potential map of hydrogen fluoride (HF).

I have also added new molecular art to line drawings and photos and to a number of end-of-chapter problems. In addition, we have updated the photo program to complement the visual layout of the design.

Pedagogy

The development of problem-solving skills has always been a major objective of this text. Almost all of the Worked Examples in this new edition have been substantially revised. I have added a strategy step after stating the problem, followed by a step-by-step solution process, and, where appropriate, a check requesting the student to look at the answer to see if it makes sense. Additionally, marginal references enable students to apply new skills to other, similar problems at the end of the chapter. Each Worked Example is followed by a Practice Exercise that asks the students to solve a similar problem on their own. The answers to the Practice Exercises are provided after the end-of-chapter problems in each chapter.

As an instructor, I often tell my students that a good learning tool is to sketch out the inner workings of a problem. In some of the Worked Examples, I have included this type of drawing (for example, see Example 6.1 on p. 222). It is what a scientist would do as he or she works out a problem (sometimes called the back-of-the-envelope calculations).

Inside the front cover of this text you will see a periodic table. I have added the names of the elements under their chemical symbols in this table. Students will find that having the relevant information all at the same location is a real convenience.

Index to Important Figures and Tables

The back inside cover shows a list of important figures and tables with page references. This index makes it convenient for students to quickly look up information when solving problems or studying related subjects in different chapters.

Media

The Interactive Activity Summary in the chapter opening pages enables the student and instructor to see at a glance the media that can be incorporated into the learning process. Within the text, an icon shows the student where the concept of the animation or interactive is introduced. With the icon are directions to help the student locate the animations for viewing. For the instructor, there are also directions for finding the animation or interactive in the instructor materials.

Animations

With the creation of 11 NEW animations, we have a library of animations created to specifically support *Chemistry* by Chang. The animations visually bring to life the areas in chemistry that are difficult to understand by reading alone.

Simulations

NEW simulations enable the student to manipulate several variables. The student can "see" how changes affect the topic being studied. The seven topics include stoichiometry, gas laws, kinetics, equilibrium, acid/base, nuclear reactions and radioactivity, and electrochemical cell. The other set of interactives are simple and fun learning tools that encompass a broad range of topics. All of these interactives are marked by the Interactive Activity icon.

Example 6.1

A certain gas expands in volume from 2.0 L to 6.0 L at constant temperature. Calculate the work done by the gas if it expands (a) against a vacuum and (b) against a constant pressure of 1.2 atm.

Strategy A simple sketch of the situation is helpful here:

Opposing pressure
P

Gas

Initial volume	Final volume
2.0 L	6.0 L

$\Delta V = (6.0 - 2.0)\,L$
$= 4.0\,L$

(a) $P = 0$
(b) $P = 1.2\,atm$

The work done in gas expansion is equal to the product of the external, opposing pressure and the change in volume. What is the conversion factor between L · atm and J?

(Continued)

Interactives

The interactives are simple and fun learning tools that encompass a broad range of topics. All of these interactives are marked by the Interactive icon.

Online Learning Center

The student will find the animation center and interactive center in the Online Learning Center for *Chemistry*. Also located in the Online Learning Center are self-assessment quizzes, current news articles in chemistry and supporting sciences, as well as a library of links to help with difficult concepts or to do research for chemistry.

Instructor's Resources

Annotated Instructor's Edition

By Brandon Cruickshank (Northern Arizona University) and Raymond Chang. The Annotated Instructor's Edition includes all resources available to the instructor marked by icons located in the margins and other strategic locations of the text. Information about the integration of media (animations, interactives, Online Learning Center) and where to find them is provided. The difficulty level of the end-of-chapter problems and the various chemical disciplines that the problems relate to is indicated. You'll also find information on quality demonstration videos, tips for the instructor, and icons marking the digital assets available on the Digital Content Manager.

Instructor's Testing and Resource CD-ROM

Written by John Adams (University of Missouri). This manual contains over 2000 multiple-choice and short-answer questions. The questions, which are graded in difficulty, are comparable to the problems in the text and include multistep problems that require conceptual analysis. The Test Bank also includes over 200 algorithmic-based questions that instructors can edit to create their own test templates. The Test Bank is formatted for easy integration into the following course management systems: PageOut, WebCT, and Blackboard. The CD also contains the electronic file or the Instructor's Resource Manual with Solutions.

Online Learning Center

This comprehensive, book-specific website (www.mhhe.com/physsci/chemistry/chang) offers excellent tools for both the instructor and the student. Instructors can create an interactive course with the integration of this site, and a secured Instructor Center stores your essential course materials to save you preparation time before class. This center offers PowerPoint images, a PowerPoint lecture outline, Instructor's Manual and Instructor's Solution Manual, Chang animations, chemistry interactives, and more.

Instructor's Resource Manual with Solutions

By Brandon J. Cruickshank (Northern Arizona University) and Raymond Chang. This complete manual for teaching a general chemistry course is based on *Chemistry* and contains a brief summary of the contents of each chapter, along with learning goals and references to background concepts discussed in earlier chapters. Following this material is a complete listing of the more challenging problems in the chapter and the problems that are worked out in detail in the Student Solutions Manual. The solutions to all of the end-of-chapter problems, including those that are in the Solutions Manual, are then given. Finally, this resource contains discussion questions and tips, information on relevant applications, and references to other elements of the text package. You can access the manual on the Instructor's Testing and Resource CD-ROM or by opening the Instructor Center on the Online Learning Center.

Overhead Transparencies

Approximately 250 full-color text illustrations are reproduced on acetate for overhead projection.

Chang Animations

By Brandon Cruickshank (Northern Arizona University). Eleven *new* animations have been added to the current 28 animations. The animations are interactive and specifically support content and concepts in *Chemistry*. The interactive summary and the icons in the text show which concepts are animated. Animations can be used by both instructor and student in the Online Learning Center and are available on the Chemistry Animations Library for use in lecture and PowerPoint presentations.

Interactives

NEW for this edition are seven simulations that will be available in the Online Learning Center, enabling manipulation of variables for specific chemical concepts including stoichiometry, gas laws, kinetics, equilibrium, and acid/base.

Chemistry Animations Library

This instructor's CD-ROM enables you to use animations and simulations in your classroom in the way that works best for you. This multi-CD set includes over 300 animations that can be played directly from the CD or can be imported easily into your own lecture presentation. The animation library is fully searchable, and many animations are included at full-screen size.

Active Art

By Eric Johnson (Ball State University). **New** for this edition is Active Art, which presents key art pieces as a series of PowerPoint slides that illustrate difficult concepts in a step-by-step manner. Artwork is broken into small, digestible frames, enabling the instructor to bring each piece into lecture in whatever sequence or format is desired. The figures can be customized in almost any way imaginable. Because every Active Art image is completely ungroupable, any part of an Active Art slide can be used as a "chemical clipart" in any other PowerPoint presentation, or as a component in your own rendition of a figure. Active Art can be found on the Digital Content Manager under the Active Art folder for each chapter.

TextEdit Art

Also new to this edition, TextEdit Art allows an instructor to revise or delete labels on a figure as desired within PowerPoint for creating customized presentations or for use in tests. Labels can be moved, deleted, or revised; the leader lines can be moved or deleted separate from the image and labels; and images can be stretched or enlarged. TextEdit Art can be found on the Digital Content Manager.

PowerPoint Lecture Presentation

By J. David Robertson (University of Missouri). Instructors who adopt *Chemistry* will find that this presentation not only saves time but also enables them to create a visually stunning lecture presentation. The Web-based PowerPoint lecture includes notes for the entire course, visuals from the eighth edition, and animations embed-

ded at the appropriate points in the program. Use this complete lecture outline, or revise the lecture to fit your own course. The lecture presentation can be found on the Digital Content Manager or in the Instructor Center of the Online Learning Center.

Digital Content Library CD-ROM

This multimedia collection of visual resources enables instructors to utilize artwork from the text in multiple formats to create customized classroom presentations, visually based tests and quizzes, dynamic course website content, or attractive printed support material. The digital assets on this cross-platform CD-ROM are grouped by chapter within easy-to-use folders. Available are all figures, tables, many photographs, Active Art, TextEdit art, and the PowerPoint lecture presentation.

NetGrade

NetGrade is a robust Web-based electronic homework system that allows instructors to develop, publish, and deliver self-scoring algorithmic assignments. McGraw-Hill has provided question banks of the end-of-chapter problems, the majority of which are algorithmic, for Instructors to edit or use as is when creating assignments. You can create graded assessments (homework, quizzes, or exams), ungraded practice tests or quizzes, or tutorial assignments. Depending on the type of assessment, instant feedback and hints are provided.

Course Management Systems

The Test Bank questions and end-of-chapter problems are available in WebCT, Blackboard, and PageOut. Ask your sales representative how to receive material in the system of your choice.

Course-Specific PageOut

Designed specifically to help you with your individual course needs, PageOut will assist you in integrating your syllabus with *Chemistry* and state-of-the-art new media tools. At the heart of PageOut you will find integrated multimedia and a full-scale Online Learning Center. You can upload your original test questions and create your own custom designs. More than 60,000 professors have chosen PageOut to create customized course websites.

Primis LabBase

By Joseph Lagowski (University of Texas of Austin). More than 40 general chemistry experiments are available in this database collection of general lab experiments from the *Journal of Chemical Education* and experiments used by Professor Lagowski at the University of Texas at Austin, enabling instructors to customize their lab manuals.

General Chemistry Laboratory Manual

By Petra A. M. van Koppen (University of California, Santa Barbara). This is the definitive lab manual for the two-semester general chemistry course. The manual contains 21 experiments that cover the most commonly assigned experiments for the introductory chemistry course.

Cooperative Chemistry Laboratory Manual

By Melanie Cooper (Clemson University). This innovative guide features open-ended problems designed to simulate experience in a research lab. Working in groups, students investigate one problem over a period of several weeks, so that they might complete three or four projects during the semester, rather than one preprogrammed experiment per class. The emphasis here is on experimental design, analysis problem solving, and communication.

Student Resources

Student Solutions Manual

By Brandon J. Cruickshank (Northern Arizona University) and Raymond Chang. This supplement contains detailed solutions and explanations for all even-numbered problems in the main text. The manual also includes a detailed discussion of different types of problems and approaches to solving chemical problems, and tutorial solutions for many of the end-of-chapter problems in the text, along with strategies for solving them.

Student Study Guide

By Sharon Neal (University of Delaware). This valuable ancillary is designed to help students recognize their learning style; how to read, classify, and create a problem-solving list; and practice problem-solving skills. For each section of a chapter, the author provides study objectives and a summary of the corresponding text. Following the summary are sample problems with detailed solutions. Each chapter has true–false questions and a self-test, with all answers provided at the end of the chapter.

OLC (Online Learning Center)

This comprehensive, exclusive website provides a wealth of electronic resources for instructors and students alike. For students, the OLC features interactive quizzes, animation center, simulation center, and interactive center for each chapter of the text; key-term flashcards; Net-Tutor; and an interactive glossary with audio. You can also access the Essential Student Partner from the OLC. Log on with your passcode card at www.mhhe.com/physsci/chemistry/chang. The passcode card is available FREE with the purchase of a new textbook or you can purchase a card separately.

Chang Animations

By Brandon Cruickshank (Northern Arizona University). Eleven new animations have been added to the current 28 animations. The animations are interactive and specifically support content and concepts in *Chemistry*. The interactive summary and icons in the text show which concepts are animated. Animations can be used by both instructors and students in the Online Learning Center.

Simulations

NEW for this edition are seven simulations that will be available on the Online Learning Center. These simulations allow manipulation of variables for specific chemical concepts including stoichiometry, gas laws, kinetics, equilibrium, and acid/base.

Interactives

Also available are interactives that are simple and fun to help with learning many concepts.

Chang Chemistry Resource Card

Our resource card is an easy, quick source of information on general chemistry. The student will find the periodic table, basic tables, and key equations within reach without having to consult the text.

ChemSkill Builder

ChemSkill Builder is a highly regarded tutorial and electronic homework program that generates questions for students for every topic in the general chemistry course. The questions are presented in a randomized fashion with a constant mix of variables so that no two students will receive the same questions. The application provides feedback for students when incorrect answers are entered, and the answers can be submitted online to an instructor for grading.

Understanding Chemistry by Lovett/Chang

This brief text is specially written in a friendly and informative manner for easy learning of the most important chemical concepts. The authors break the information down into language for a nonscientist. Cartoons were created to provide a learning tool to remember basic concepts.

Essential Study Partner

By David Harwell (University of Hawaii at Manoa), Laura Muller (Wheaton College), Norbert Pienta (University of Iowa), Kathleen Robbins (University of Las Vegas–Nevada), and Brandon Cruickshank (Northern Arizona University). This online study partner engages, investigates, and reinforces what you are learning from your textbook. You will find the Essential Study Partner for *Chemistry* to be a complete, interactive student study tool packed with animations and learning activities. From quizzes to interactive diagrams, you will find that there has never been a better study partner to ensure the mastery of core concepts.

Schaum's Outline of College Chemistry

By Jerome Rosenberg (Michigan State University) and Lawrence Epstein (University of Pittsburgh). This helpful study aid provides students with hundreds of solved and supplementary problems for the general chemistry course.

Acknowledgments

Symposium Participants

I would like to thank the following individuals who participated in various McGraw-Hill symposia on general chemistry. Their insight into the needs of students and instructors were invaluable to me in preparing this revision.

John Adams *University of Missouri–Columbia*
Patricia Amateis *Virginia Tech University*
David R. Anderson *University of Colorado at Colorado Springs*
Ramesh D. Arasasingham *University of California–Irvine*
Tim T. Bays *U.S. Military Academy*
Don A. Berkowitz *University of Maryland*
Bob Blake *Texas Tech University*
Roberto Bogomolni *University of California–Santa Cruz*
Robert Bryant *University of Virginia*
Carolyn Collins *Community College of Southern Nevada*
David Coker *Boston University*
Brandon Cruickshank *Northern Arizona University*
William Durham *University of Arkansas*
Thomas Engel *University of Washington–Seattle*
Debra Feakes *Southwest Texas State University*
Sonya Franklin *University of Iowa*
Palmer Graves *Florida International University*
John M. Halpin *New York University*
John Hopkins *Louisiana State University–Baton Rouge*
Paul Hunter *Michigan State University*
Denley Jacobson *North Dakota State University*
Eric Johnson *Ball State University*
Brian Laird *University of Kansas*
Robley J. Light *Florida State University*
Jack Moore *University of Maryland–College Park*
Sharon Neal *University of Delaware*
Mark E. Noble *University of Louisville*
Sue Nurrenbern *Purdue University*
Maria Paukstelis *Kansas State University*
John Pollard *University of Arizona*
Bill Robinson *Purdue University*
Alan Stolzenberg *West Virginia University*
Greg Szulczewski *University of Alabama*
Jason Telford *University of Iowa*
Kathleen Trahanovsky *Iowa State University*
William C. Trogler *University of California–San Diego*
Petra Van Koppen *University of California–Santa Barbara*
Martin Vala *University of Florida*
Thomas Webb *Auburn University*
Troy Wood *SUNY Buffalo*
Kim Woodrum *University of Kentucky*

Reviewers

I would like to thank the following reviewers, whose comments were of great help to me in preparing this revision.

Joseph S. Alper *University of Massachusetts–Boston*
Don A. Berkowitz *University of Maryland*
Narayan G. Bhat *University of Texas–Pan American*
Suely Black *Norwalk State University*

Tim Brewer *Eastern Michigan University*
Brian Buffin *Western Michigan University*
Paul Charlesworth *Michigan Technological University*
David K. Erwin *Rose-Hulman Institute of Technology*
Michael F. Farona *University of North Carolina–Greensboro*
John M. Halpin *New York University*
Daniel T. Haworth *Marquette University*
James Hill *Cal State–Sacramento*
Carolyn Sweeney Judd *Houston Community College*
David Leddy *Michigan Technological University*
Gerhard Lind *Metropolitan State College of Denver*
M. C. (Mickey) McGaugh *Brazosport College*
Howard L. McLean *Rose-Hulman Institute of Technology*
Jalal Mondal *University of Texas–Pan American*
Richard S. Myers *Delta State University*
Anne-Marie Nickel *Milwaukee School of Engineering*
Gayle Nicoll *University of Nebraska–Lincoln*
Bruce Parkinson *Colorado State University*
Mark Perkovic *Western Michigan University*
Andrew Pierce *University of New Orleans*
Jeanette K. Rice *Georgia Southern University*
Rene Rodriguez *Idaho State University*
E. Alan Sadurski *Ohio Northern University*
Pete Smith *University of Georgia*
Jerry Suits *McNeese State University*
Kathleen Thrush *Villanova University*
Edmund L. Tisko *University of Nebraska–Omaha*
Anthony P. Toste *Southwest Missouri State University*
Richard Treptow *Chicago State University*
Bilin Paula Tsai *University of Minnesota–Duluth*
Sheryl A. Tucker *University of Missouri–Columbia*
Philip Watson *Oregon State University*
Christine R. Whitlock *Georgia Southern University*
Marcy Whitney *University of Alabama*
Milton Wieder *Metropolitan State College of Denver*
James Wingrave *University of Delaware*
Kim Woorum *University of Kentucky*
Linda Zarazna *American River College*
Lois Anne Zook *Delta State University*

Animations Reviewers

I would like to thank the following reviewers, whose comments were of great help in preparing the animations.

Robert Blake *Texas Tech University*
Lisa M. Goss *Idaho State University*
Palmer Graves *Florida International University*
Denley Jacobson *North Dakota State University*
John Pollard *University of Arizona*
Catherine Reck *Indiana University–Bloomington*
Alan Stolzenberg *West Virginia University*
Greg Szulczewski *University of Alabama*
Troy Wood *SUNY Buffalo*

Other Contributors

I would like to thank Brandon Cruickshank for his valuable contributions to this edition. His inputs in many areas have helped to improve the clarity and pedagogy of the text. I also thank Judith Kromm for her helpful comments on portions of the manuscript.

As always, I have benefited much from discussions with my colleagues at Williams College and correspondence with many instructors here and abroad.

It is a pleasure to acknowledge the support given to me by the following members of McGraw-Hill's College Division: Doug Dinardo, Tami Hodge, Kevin Kane, Jenni Lang, and Michael Lange. In particular, I would like to mention Gloria Schiesl for supervising the production, Stuart Paterson and David Hash for the book design, John Leland for photo research, and Jeffry Schmitt and Stacy Patch for the media. My publisher Kent Peterson and my editor Thomas Timp provided advice and support whenever I needed them. Finally, my special thanks go to Shirley Oberbroeckling, the developmental editor, for her care and enthusiasm for the project, and supervision at every stage of the writing of this edition. I am fortunate to work with such a dedicated and professional group of individuals.

Raymond Chang

Guided Tour

Text This guided tour to *Chemistry,* Eighth Edition, is designed to walk you through the features of our text and media.

Chapter Opening Pages

The chapter opening pages give the student and instructor the overall content that is discussed within the chapter at a quick glance.

The photo legend explains the connection between the photo and the molecules that are featured on the pages. The molecular models illustrate the chemical or physical process at the molecular level.

The Interactive Activity Summary gives a list of the media associated with the chapter. As the student moves through the chapter, the icon signals when and where to go for further understanding of the concept.

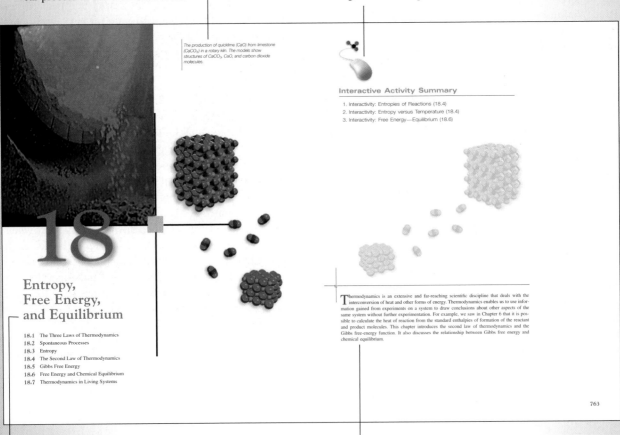

The production of quicklime (CaO) from limestone (CaCO₃) in a rotary kiln. The models show structures of CaCO₃, CaO, and carbon dioxide molecules.

Interactive Activity Summary

1. Interactivity: Entropies of Reactions (18.4)
2. Interactivity: Entropy versus Temperature (18.4)
3. Interactivity: Free Energy—Equilibrium (18.6)

18

Entropy, Free Energy, and Equilibrium

18.1 The Three Laws of Thermodynamics
18.2 Spontaneous Processes
18.3 Entropy
18.4 The Second Law of Thermodynamics
18.5 Gibbs Free Energy
18.6 Free Energy and Chemical Equilibrium
18.7 Thermodynamics in Living Systems

Thermodynamics is an extensive and far-reaching scientific discipline that deals with the interconversion of heat and other forms of energy. Thermodynamics enables us to use information gained from experiments on a system to draw conclusions about other aspects of the same system without further experimentation. For example, we saw in Chapter 6 that it is possible to calculate the heat of reaction from the standard enthalpies of formation of the reactant and product molecules. This chapter introduces the second law of thermodynamics and the Gibbs free-energy function. It also discusses the relationship between Gibbs free energy and chemical equilibrium.

763

The chapter outline provides the student and instructor with the main points that will be covered while studying the content within.

Finally, the opening text draws the student into the chapter and explains what will be learned.

Worked Examples

A main feature of all general chemistry textbooks is the worked examples. The student will find that in a select number of examples, the author has provided hand-drawn sketches showing how to reach the solution. Each sketch demonstrates how a chemist would work out an actual problem.

The author points out problems from the end of the chapter similar to the worked example for student reference.

Strategy In Lewis acid-base reactions, the acid is usually a cation or an electron-deficient molecule, whereas the base is an anion or a molecule containing an atom with lone pairs. (a) Draw the molecular structure for $C_2H_5OC_2H_5$. What is the hybridization state of Al in $AlCl_3$? (b) Which ion is likely to be an electron acceptor? An electron donor?

Solution (a) The Al is sp^2-hybridized in $AlCl_3$ with an empty $2p_z$ orbital. It is electron-deficient, sharing only six electrons. Therefore, the Al atom has a tendency to gain two electrons to complete its octet. This property makes $AlCl_3$ a Lewis acid. On the other hand, the lone pairs on the oxygen atom in $C_2H_5OC_2H_5$ make the compound a Lewis base:

(b) Here the Hg^{2+} ion accepts four pairs of electrons from the CN^- ions. Therefore Hg^{2+} is the Lewis acid and CN^- is the Lewis base.

Practice Exercise Identify the Lewis acid and Lewis base in the reaction

$$Co^{3+}(aq) + 6NH_3(aq) \rightleftharpoons Co(NH_3)_6^{3+}(aq)$$

Similar problem: 15.92.

The worked examples also include a strategy prior to the solution and, where appropriate, a check after the solution reminding the student to think about the reasonableness of his or her answer. Study of the worked examples helps the student develop problem-solving skills.

The Practice Problem that follows each worked example enables the student to check his or her ability to solve the type of problem illustrated in the Worked Example. Answers to the Practice Exercises can be found at the very end of the chapter, following the Questions and Problems.

Art

This edition has expanded use of the electrostatic potential maps that show the student charge distribution in molecules according to the colors of the rainbow (red through blue tracks regions of greater negative charge to greater positive charge). These maps will help the student understand the polarity of molecules, intermolecular forces, acid and base properties, and reaction mechanism.

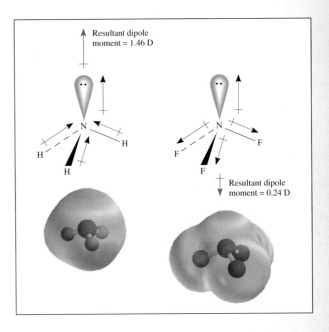

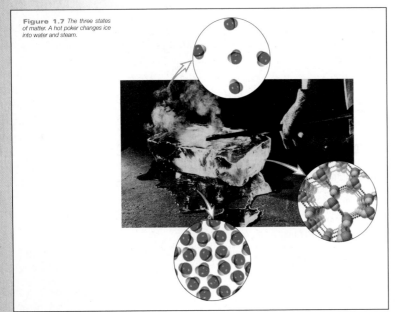

Figure 1.7 *The three states of matter. A hot poker changes ice into water and steam.*

To help the student visualize the progression of what is happening on a molecular level, certain concepts are shown from the macroscopic to the microscopic level.

A guide for the student, the periodic table icon illustrates the properties of elements according to their positions in the periodic table.

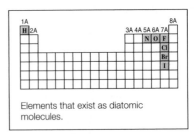

Elements that exist as diatomic molecules.

Media

Students

The Online Learning Center at www.mhhe.com/physsci/chemistry/chang is the doorway for the student to access the media for *Chemistry,* Eighth Edition, that is featured in the Interactive Activity Summary and pointed out in the text by the icon. The Online Learning Center also contains the self-assessment quizzes and various other study tools for the student.

The Interactive Center in the Online Learning Center hosts two different styles of interactives. One interactive is a simulation in which a student can control one or more variables that show different reactions. Another interactive is a simple manipulation of data that the student will use to learn specific concepts.

The Animation Center in the Online Learning Center hosts the animations created to help the student visualize difficult concepts in chemistry.

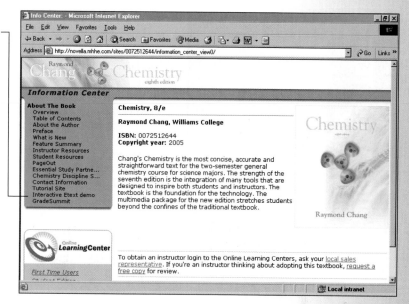

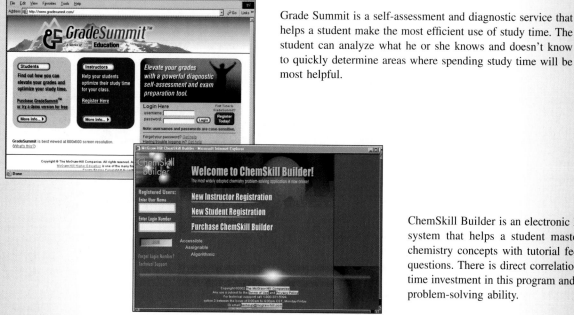

Grade Summit is a self-assessment and diagnostic service that helps a student make the most efficient use of study time. The student can analyze what he or she knows and doesn't know to quickly determine areas where spending study time will be most helpful.

ChemSkill Builder is an electronic homework system that helps a student master general chemistry concepts with tutorial feedback on questions. There is direct correlation between time investment in this program and increased problem-solving ability.

Instructor

The Animations Library is an instructor's CD-ROM enabling the instructor to use animations in the classroom in the way that works best for her or him. This multi-CD set includes over 300 animations and interactives that can be played directly from the CD or can be imported easily into the lecture presentation. The animation library is fully searchable, and many animations are included at full-screen size.

The Digital Content Manager is a multimedia collection of visual resources enabling instructors to utilize artwork from the text in multiple formats to create customized classroom presentations, visually based tests and quizzes, dynamic course website content, or attractive printed support material. The digital assets on this cross-platform CD-ROM are grouped by chapter within easy-to-use folders. Available are all figures, tables, many photographs, Active Art, and the PowerPoint lecture presentation.

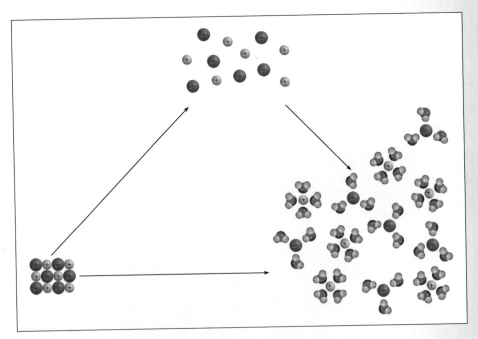

Active Art is a folder within the Digital Content Manager presenting key art pieces as a series of PowerPoint slides that illustrate difficult concepts in a step-by-step manner. Artwork is broken into small, digestible frames, enabling the instructor to bring each piece into lecture in whatever sequence or format is desired. The figures can be customized in almost any way imaginable.

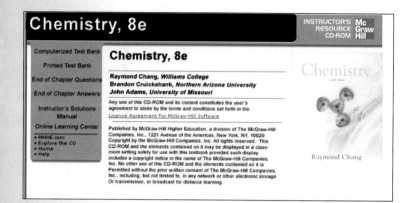

The Instructor's Testing and Resource CD is a cross-platform CD-ROM providing a wealth of resources. It includes a test bank utilizing Brownstone Diploma® testing software, which contains over 2000 multiple-choice, short-answer questions, and algorithmically based questions that instructors can edit to create their own test templates. Comparable to the problems in the text, the questions include multistep problems that require conceptual analysis. The CD also contains the electronic file of the Instructor's Resource Manual with Solutions.

Electronic Homework is available in a variety of programs and course management systems.

- ChemSkill Builder is an electronic homework program containing more than 1500 algorithmically generated questions, each with tutorial feedback. A record of student work is maintained in an online gradebook so that homework can be done at home, in a dorm room, or in a university lab.

- NetGrade is a robust Web-based electronic homework system that allows instructors to develop, publish, and deliver self-scoring algorithmic assignments. You can create graded assessments (homework, quizzes, or exams), ungraded practice tests or quizzes, or tutorial assignments.

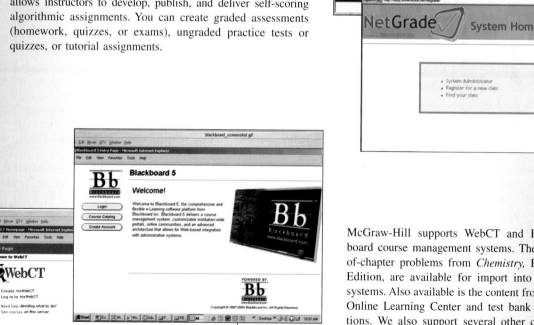

McGraw-Hill supports WebCT and Blackboard course management systems. The end-of-chapter problems from *Chemistry*, Eighth Edition, are available for import into these systems. Also available is the content from the Online Learning Center and test bank questions. We also support several other course management systems. Contact your sales representative for more details.

A Note to the Student

General chemistry is commonly perceived to be more difficult than most other subjects. There is some justification for this perception. For one thing, chemistry has a very specialized vocabulary. At first, studying chemistry is like learning a new language. Furthermore, some of the concepts are abstract. Nevertheless, with diligence you can complete this course successfully, and you might even enjoy it. Here are some suggestions to help you form good study habits and master the material in this text.

- Attend classes regularly and take careful notes.
- If possible, always review the topics discussed in class the same day they are covered in class. Use this book to supplement your notes.
- Think critically. Ask yourself if you really understand the meaning of a term or the use of an equation. A good way to test your understanding is to explain a concept to a classmate or some other person.
- Do not hesitate to ask your instructor or your teaching assistant for help.

The eighth edition tools for *Chemistry* are designed to enable you to do well in your general chemistry course. The following guide explains how to take full advantage of the text, technology, and other tools.

- Before delving into the chapter, read the chapter *outline* and the chapter *introduction* to get a sense of the important topics. Use the outline to organize your notetaking in class.
- Use the *Interactive Activity Icon* as a guide to review challenging concepts in motion. The animations and interactives are valuable in presenting a concept and enabling you to manipulate or choose steps so a full understanding can be reached.
- At the end of each chapter you will find key equations, a summary of facts and concepts, and a list of key words, all of which will help you review for exams.
- Definitions of the key words can be studied in context on the pages cited in the end-of-chapter list or in the glossary at the back of the book.
- Use the *Key-Word flashcards* on the website (Online Learning Center, or OLC) for more practice. The flashcards include audio, so you can test your pronunciation, too. The OLC houses an extraordinary amount of resources. Go to www.mhhe.com/physsci/chemistry/chang and click on the appropriate cover to explore chapter quizzes, the e-learning sessions, opportunities, the Essential Study Partner, and more.
- The *Essential Study Partner* is a tutorial that will help you review and test your understanding of each chapter.
- Careful study of the worked-out examples in the body of each chapter will improve your ability to analyze problems and correctly carry out the calculations needed to solve them. Also take the time to work through the practice exercise that follows each example to be sure you understand how to solve the type of problem illustrated in the example. The answers to the practice exercises appear at the end of the chapter, following the problems. For additional practice, you can turn to similar homework problems referred to in the margin next to the example.
- The questions and problems at the end of the chapter are organized by section. Generally the review questions do not require calculation. Their purpose is to help you check your understanding of new concepts introduced in the chapter. The problems enable you to test your analytical and computational skills. Even-numbered problems are similar in nature to the odd-numbered problems that precede them, except in the section titled "Additional Problems." The additional problems require that you decide how to approach the solution, and a number of them involve concepts from more than one section of the chapter. Although your instructor will most likely not assign all the problems for homework, it is to your advantage to work as many as necessary to assure yourself that you have mastered the chapter. Refer to the back of the book for answers to all even-numbered problems as well as to the problem-solving tutorials that are available in a separate Student Solutions Manual.
- For even more practice problems, use *ChemSkill Builder.* ChemSkill Builder is a problem-solving tutorial with hundreds of problems that include feedback.
- *Index to Important Figures and Tables* The back inside cover shows a list of important figures and tables with page references. This index is a convenient source for looking up information when you are solving problems or studying related subjects in different chapters.

If you follow these suggestions and stay up-to-date with your assignments, you should find that chemistry is challenging, but less difficult and much more interesting than you expected.

Raymond Chang

Chemistry

A view of Supernova 1987A. When all the fuel in a star is consumed, its core collapses and its outer layer explodes in a supernova. Elements through iron are formed in active stars and heavier elements are formed in supernovas. The models show the following elements: hydrogen, helium, oxygen, phosphorus, sulfur, and silver.

Chemistry
The Study of Change

Interactive Activity Summary

1. Substances and Mixtures (1.4)
2. Elements (1.4)
3. SI Base Units (1.7)
4. Unit Prefixes (1.7)
5. Density (1.7)
6. Accuracy and Precision (1.8)
7. Dimensional Analysis/Factor-Label Method (1.9)

Chemistry is an active, evolving science that has vital importance to our world, in both the realm of nature and the realm of society. Its roots are ancient, but as we will soon see, chemistry is every bit a modern science.

We will begin our study of chemistry at the macroscopic level, where we can see and measure the materials of which our world is made. In this chapter we will discuss the scientific method, which provides the framework for research not only in chemistry but in all other sciences as well. Next we will discover how scientists define and characterize matter. Then we will familiarize ourselves with the systems of measurement used in the laboratory. Finally, we will spend some time learning how to handle numerical results of chemical measurements and solve numerical problems. In Chapter 2 we will begin to explore the microscopic world of atoms and molecules.

The Chinese characters for chemistry mean "The study of change."

1.1 Chemistry: A Science for the Twenty-First Century

Chemistry is *the study of matter and the changes it undergoes.* Chemistry is often called the central science, because a basic knowledge of chemistry is essential for students of biology, physics, geology, ecology, and many other subjects. Indeed, it is central to our way of life; without it, we would be living shorter lives in what we would consider primitive conditions, without automobiles, electricity, computers, CDs, and many other everyday conveniences.

Although chemistry is an ancient science, its modern foundation was laid in the nineteenth century, when intellectual and technological advances enabled scientists to break down substances into ever smaller components and consequently to explain many of their physical and chemical characteristics. The rapid development of increasingly sophisticated technology throughout the twentieth century has given us even greater means to study things that cannot be seen with the naked eye. Using computers and special microscopes, for example, chemists can analyze the structure of atoms and molecules—the fundamental units on which the study of chemistry is based—and design new substances with specific properties, such as drugs and environmentally friendly consumer products.

As we enter the twenty-first century, it is fitting to ask what part the central science will have in this century. Almost certainly, chemistry will continue to play a pivotal role in all areas of science and technology. Before plunging into the study of matter and its transformation, let us consider some of the frontiers that chemists are currently exploring (Figure 1.1). Whatever your reasons for taking introductory chemistry, a good knowledge of the subject will better enable you to appreciate its impact on society and on you as an individual.

Health and Medicine

Three major advances in the past century have enabled us to prevent and treat diseases. They are public health measures establishing sanitation systems to protect vast numbers of people from infectious disease; surgery with anesthesia, enabling physicians to cure potentially fatal conditions, such as an inflamed appendix; and the introduction of vaccines and antibiotics that make it possible to prevent diseases spread by microbes. Gene therapy promises to be the fourth revolution in medicine. (A gene is the basic unit of inheritance.) Several thousand known conditions, including cystic fibrosis and hemophilia, are carried by inborn damage to a single gene. Many other ailments, such as cancer, heart disease, AIDS, and arthritis, result to an extent from impairment of one or more genes involved in the body's defenses. In gene therapy, a selected healthy gene is delivered to a patient's cell to cure or ease such disorders. To carry out such a procedure, a doctor must have a sound knowledge of the chemical properties of the molecular components involved. The decoding of the human genome, which comprises all of the genetic material in the human body and plays an essential part in gene therapy, relies largely on chemical techniques.

Chemists in the pharmaceutical industry are researching potent drugs with few or no side effects to treat cancer, AIDS, and many other diseases as well as drugs to increase the number of successful organ transplants. On a broader scale, improved understanding of the mechanism of aging will lead to a longer and healthier life span for the world's population.

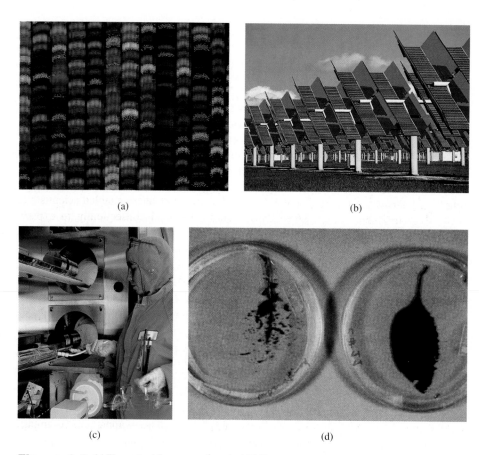

(a)   (b)

(c)   (d)

Figure 1.1 *(a) The output from an automated DNA sequencing machine. Each lane displays the sequence (indicated by different colors) obtained with a separate DNA sample. (b) Photovoltaic cells. (c) A silicon wafer being processed. (d) The leaf on the left was taken from a tobacco plant that was not genetically engineered but was exposed to tobacco horn worms. The leaf on the right was genetically engineered and is barely attacked by the worms. The same technique can be applied to protect the leaves of other types of plants.*

Energy and the Environment

Energy is a by-product of many chemical processes, and as the demand for energy continues to increase, both in technologically advanced countries like the United States and in developing ones like China, chemists are actively trying to find new energy sources. Currently the major sources of energy are fossil fuels (coal, petroleum, and natural gas). The estimated reserves of these fuels will last us another 50–100 years, at the present rate of consumption, so it is urgent that we find alternatives.

Solar energy promises to be a viable source of energy for the future. Every year Earth's surface receives about 10 times as much energy from sunlight as is contained in all of the known reserves of coal, oil, natural gas, and uranium combined. But much of this energy is "wasted" because it is reflected back into space. For the past 30 years, intense research efforts have shown that solar energy can be harnessed effectively in two ways. One is the conversion of sunlight directly to electricity using devices called *photovoltaic cells*. The other is to use sunlight to obtain hydrogen from water. The hydrogen can then be fed into a *fuel cell* to generate electricity.

Although our understanding of the scientific process of converting solar energy to electricity has advanced, the technology has not yet improved to the point where we can produce electricity on a large scale at an economically acceptable cost. By 2050, however, it has been predicted that solar energy will supply over 50 percent of our power needs.

Another potential source of energy is nuclear fission, but because of environmental concerns about the radioactive wastes from fission processes, the future of the nuclear industry in the United States is uncertain. Chemists can help to devise better ways to dispose of nuclear waste. Nuclear fusion, the process that occurs in the sun and other stars, generates huge amounts of energy without producing much dangerous radioactive waste. In another 50 years, nuclear fusion will likely be a significant source of energy.

Energy production and energy utilization are closely tied to the quality of our environment. A major disadvantage of burning fossil fuels is that they give off carbon dioxide, which is a *greenhouse gas* (that is, it promotes the heating of Earth's atmosphere), along with sulfur dioxide and nitrogen oxides, which result in acid rain and smog. (Harnessing solar energy has no such detrimental effects on the environment.) By using fuel-efficient automobiles and more effective catalytic converters, we should be able to drastically reduce harmful auto emissions and improve the air quality in areas with heavy traffic. In addition, electric cars, powered by durable, long-lasting batteries, should become more prevalent, and their use will help to minimize air pollution.

Materials and Technology

Chemical research and development in the twentieth century have provided us with new materials that have profoundly improved the quality of our lives and helped to advance technology in countless ways. A few examples are polymers (including rubber and nylon), ceramics (such as cookware), liquid crystals (like those in electronic displays), adhesives (used in your Post-It notes), and coatings (for example, latex paint).

What is in store for the near future? One likely possibility is room-temperature *superconductors*. Electricity is carried by copper cables, which are not perfect conductors. Consequently, about 20 percent of electrical energy is lost in the form of heat between the power station and our homes. This is a tremendous waste. Superconductors are materials that have no electrical resistance and can therefore conduct electricity with no energy loss. Although the phenomenon of superconductivity at very low temperatures (more than 400 degrees Fahrenheit below the freezing point of water) has been known for over 80 years, a major breakthrough in the mid-1980s demonstrated that it is possible to make materials that act as superconductors at or near room temperature. Chemists have helped to design and synthesize new materials that show promise in this quest. The next 30 years will see high-temperature superconductors being applied on a large scale in magnetic resonance imaging (MRI), levitated trains, and nuclear fusion.

If we had to name one technological advance that has shaped our lives more than any other, it would be the computer. The "engine" that drives the ongoing computer revolution is the microprocessor—the tiny silicon chip that has inspired countless inventions, such as laptop computers and fax machines. The performance of a microprocessor is judged by the speed with which it carries out mathematical operations, such as addition. The pace of progress is such that since their introduction, microprocessors have doubled in speed every 18 months. The quality of any microprocessor depends on the purity of the silicon chip and on the ability to add the desired amount of other substances, and chemists play an important role in the research and development of silicon chips. For the future, scientists have begun to explore the prospect of "molecular computing," that is, replacing silicon with molecules. The advantages are that certain molecules can be made to respond to light, rather than to electrons, so that we would have optical computers rather than electronic computers. With proper genetic engineering, scientists can synthesize such molecules using microorganisms instead of large factories. Optical computers also would have much greater storage capacity than electronic computers.

Food and Agriculture

How can the world's rapidly increasing population be fed? In poor countries, agricultural activities occupy about 80 percent of the workforce, and half of an average family budget is spent on foodstuffs. This is a tremendous drain on a nation's resources. The factors that affect agricultural production are the richness of the soil, insects and diseases that damage crops, and weeds that compete for nutrients. Besides irrigation, farmers rely on fertilizers and pesticides to increase crop yield. Since the 1950s, treatment for crops suffering from pest infestations has sometimes been the indiscriminate application of potent chemicals. Such measures have often had serious detrimental effects on the environment. Even the excessive use of fertilizers is harmful to the land, water, and air.

To meet the food demands of the twenty-first century, new and novel approaches in farming must be devised. It has already been demonstrated that, through biotechnology, it is possible to grow larger and better crops. These techniques can be applied to many different farm products, not only for improved yields, but also for better frequency, that is, more crops every year. For example, it is known that a certain bacterium produces a protein molecule that is toxic to leaf-eating caterpillars. Incorporating the gene that codes for the toxin into crops enables plants to protect themselves so that pesticides are not necessary. Researchers have also found a way to prevent pesky insects from reproducing. Insects communicate with one another by emitting and reacting to special molecules called pheromones. By identifying and synthesizing pheromones used in mating, it is possible to interfere with the normal reproductive cycle of common pests; for example, by inducing insects to mate too soon or tricking female insects into mating with sterile males. Moreover, chemists can devise ways to increase the production of fertilizers that are less harmful to the environment and substances that would selectively kill weeds.

1.2 The Study of Chemistry

Compared with other subjects, chemistry is commonly believed to be more difficult, at least at the introductory level. There is some justification for this perception; for one thing, chemistry has a very specialized vocabulary. However, even if this is your first course in chemistry, you already have more familiarity with the subject than you may realize. In everyday conversations we hear words that have a chemical connection, although they may not be used in the scientifically correct sense. Examples are "electronic," "quantum leap," "equilibrium," "catalyst," "chain reaction," and "critical mass." Moreover, if you cook, then you are a practicing chemist! From experience gained in the kitchen, you know that oil and water do not mix and that boiling water left on the stove will evaporate. You apply chemical and physical principles when you use baking soda to leaven bread, choose a pressure cooker to shorten the time it takes

Figure 1.2 *A badly rusted car. Corrosion of iron costs the U.S. economy tens of billions of dollars every year.*

to prepare soup, add meat tenderizer to a pot roast, squeeze lemon juice over sliced pears to prevent them from turning brown or over fish to minimize its odor, and add vinegar to the water in which you are going to poach eggs. Every day we observe such changes without thinking about their chemical nature. The purpose of this course is to make you think like a chemist, to look at the *macroscopic world*—the things we can see, touch, and measure directly—and visualize the particles and events of the *microscopic world* that we cannot experience without modern technology and our imaginations.

At first some students find it confusing that their chemistry instructor and text-book seem to be continually shifting back and forth between the macroscopic and microscopic worlds. Just keep in mind that the data for chemical investigations most often come from observations of large-scale phenomena, but the explanations fre-quently lie in the unseen and partially imagined microscopic world of atoms and molecules. In other words, chemists often *see* one thing (in the macroscopic world) and *think* another (in the microscopic world). Looking at the rusted car in Figure 1.2, for example, a chemist might think about the basic properties of individual atoms of iron and how these units interact with other atoms and molecules to produce the observed change.

1.3 The Scientific Method

All sciences, including the social sciences, employ variations of what is called the **scientific method,** *a systematic approach to research.* For example, a psychologist who wants to know how noise affects people's ability to learn chemistry and a chemist interested in measuring the heat given off when hydrogen gas burns in air would fol-low roughly the same procedure in carrying out their investigations. The first step is to carefully define the problem. The next step includes performing experiments, mak-ing careful observations, and recording information, or *data,* about the system—the part of the universe that is under investigation. (In the examples just discussed, the systems are the group of people the psychologist will study and a mixture of hydro-gen and air.)

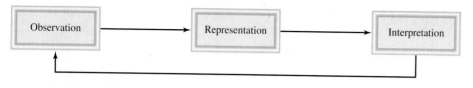

The data obtained in a research study may be both *qualitative, consisting of general observations about the system,* and *quantitative, comprising numbers obtained by various measurements of the system.* Chemists generally use standardized symbols and equations in recording their measurements and observations. This form of representation not only simplifies the process of keeping records, but also provides a common basis for communication with other chemists.

When the experiments have been completed and the data have been recorded, the next step in the scientific method is interpretation, meaning that the scientist attempts to explain the observed phenomenon. Based on the data that were gathered, the researcher formulates a *hypothesis, a tentative explanation for a set of observations.* Further experiments are devised to test the validity of the hypothesis in as many ways as possible, and the process begins anew. Figure 1.3 summarizes the main steps of the research process.

After a large amount of data has been collected, it is often desirable to summarize the information in a concise way, as a law. In science, a *law* is *a concise verbal or mathematical statement of a relationship between phenomena that is always the same under the same conditions.* For example, Sir Isaac Newton's second law of motion, which you may remember from high school science, says that force equals mass times acceleration ($F = ma$). What this law means is that an increase in the mass or in the acceleration of an object will always increase its force proportionally, and a decrease in mass or acceleration will always decrease the force.

Hypotheses that survive many experimental tests of their validity may evolve into theories. A *theory* is *a unifying principle that explains a body of facts and/or those laws that are based on them.* Theories, too, are constantly being tested. If a theory is disproved by experiment, then it must be discarded or modified so that it becomes consistent with experimental observations. Proving or disproving a theory can take years, even centuries, in part because the necessary technology may not be available. Atomic theory, which we will study in Chapter 2, is a case in point. It took more than 2000 years to work out this fundamental principle of chemistry proposed by Democritus, an ancient Greek philosopher. A more contemporary example is the Big Bang theory of the origin of the universe discussed on page 10.

Scientific progress is seldom, if ever, made in a rigid, step-by-step fashion. Sometimes a law precedes a theory; sometimes it is the other way around. Two scientists may start working on a project with exactly the same objective, but will end up taking drastically different approaches. Scientists are, after all, human beings, and their modes of thinking and working are very much influenced by their background, training, and personalities.

The development of science has been irregular and sometimes even illogical. Great discoveries are usually the result of the cumulative contributions and experience of many workers, even though the credit for formulating a theory or a law is usually given to only one individual. There is, of course, an element of luck involved in scientific discoveries, but it has been said that "chance favors the prepared mind." It takes an alert and well-trained person to recognize the significance of an accidental discovery and to take full advantage of it. More often than not, the public learns only of spectacular scientific breakthroughs. For every success story, however, there

CHEMISTRY IN ACTION

Primordial Helium and the Big Bang Theory

Where did we come from? How did the universe begin? Humans have asked these questions for as long as we have been able to think. The search for answers provides an example of the scientific method.

In the 1940s the Russian-American physicist George Gamow hypothesized that our universe burst into being billions of years ago in a gigantic explosion, or *Big Bang*. In its earliest moments, the universe occupied a tiny volume and was unimaginably hot. This blistering fireball of radiation mixed with microscopic particles of matter gradually cooled enough for atoms to form. Under the influence of gravity, these atoms clumped together to make billions of galaxies including our own Milky Way Galaxy.

Gamow's idea is interesting and highly provocative. It has been tested experimentally in a number of ways. First, measurements showed that the universe is expanding; that is, galaxies are all moving away from one another at high speeds. This fact is consistent with the universe's explosive birth. By imagining the expansion running backward, like a movie in reverse, astronomers have deduced that the universe was born about 13 billion years ago. The second observation that supports Gamow's hypothesis is the detection of *cosmic background radiation*. Over billions of years, the searingly hot universe has cooled down to a mere 3 K (or −270°C)! At this temperature, most energy is in the microwave region. Because the Big Bang would have occurred simultaneously throughout the tiny volume of the forming universe, the radiation it generated should have filled the entire universe. Thus the radiation should be the same in any direction that we observe. Indeed, the microwave signals recorded by astronomers are *independent* of direction.

The third piece of evidence supporting Gamow's hypothesis is the discovery of primordial helium. Scientists believe that helium and hydrogen (the lightest elements) were the first elements formed in the early stages of cosmic evolution. (The heavier elements, like carbon, nitrogen, and oxygen, are thought to have originated later via nuclear reactions involving hydrogen and helium in the center of stars.) If so, a diffuse gas of hydrogen and helium would have spread through the early

A color photo of some distant galaxy, including the position of a quasar.

universe before much of the galaxies formed. In 1995 astronomers analyzed ultraviolet light from a distant *quasar* (a strong source of light and radio signals that is thought to be an exploding galaxy at the edge of the universe) and found that some of the light was absorbed by helium atoms on the way to Earth. Because this particular quasar is more than 10 billion light years away (a light year is the distance traveled by light in a year), the light reaching Earth reveals events that took place 10 billion years ago. Why wasn't the more abundant hydrogen detected? A hydrogen atom has only one electron, which is stripped by the light from a quasar in a process known as *ionization*. Ionized hydrogen atoms cannot absorb any of the quasar's light. A helium atom, on the other hand, has two electrons. Radiation may strip a helium atom of one electron, but not always both. Singly ionized helium atoms can still absorb light and are therefore detectable.

Proponents of Gamow's explanation rejoiced at the detection of helium in the far reaches of the universe. In recognition of all the supporting evidence, scientists now refer to Gamow's hypothesis as the Big Bang theory.

are hundreds of cases in which scientists have spent years working on projects that ultimately led to a dead end, and in which positive achievements came only after many wrong turns and at such a slow pace that they went unheralded. Yet even the dead ends contribute something to the continually growing body of knowledge about the physical universe. It is the love of the search that keeps many scientists in the laboratory.

1.4 Classifications of Matter

We defined chemistry at the beginning of the chapter as the study of matter and the changes it undergoes. ***Matter*** is *anything that occupies space and has mass.* Matter includes things we can see and touch (such as water, earth, and trees), as well as things we cannot (such as air). Thus, everything in the universe has a "chemical" connection.

Chemists distinguish among several subcategories of matter based on composition and properties. The classifications of matter include substances, mixtures, elements, and compounds, as well as atoms and molecules, which we will consider in Chapter 2.

Substances and Mixtures

A ***substance*** is *a form of matter that has a definite (constant) composition and distinct properties.* Examples are water, ammonia, table sugar (sucrose), gold, and oxygen. Substances differ from one another in composition and can be identified by their appearance, smell, taste, and other properties.

A ***mixture*** is *a combination of two or more substances in which the substances retain their distinct identities.* Some familiar examples are air, soft drinks, milk, and cement. Mixtures do not have constant composition. Therefore, samples of air collected in different cities would probably differ in composition because of differences in altitude, pollution, and so on.

Mixtures are either homogeneous or heterogeneous. When a spoonful of sugar dissolves in water we obtain a ***homogeneous mixture*** in which *the composition of the mixture is the same throughout.* If sand is mixed with iron filings, however, the sand grains and the iron filings remain separate (Figure 1.4). This type of mixture is called a ***heterogeneous mixture*** because *the composition is not uniform.*

Any mixture, whether homogeneous or heterogeneous, can be created and then separated by physical means into pure components without changing the identities of the components. Thus, sugar can be recovered from a water solution by heating the solution and evaporating it to dryness. Condensing the vapor will give us back the water component. To separate the iron-sand mixture, we can use a magnet to remove

Interactivity: Substances and Mixtures
Online Learning Center, Interactives

Figure 1.4 *(a) The mixture contains iron filings and sand. (b) A magnet separates the iron filings from the mixture. The same technique is used on a larger scale to separate iron and steel from nonmagnetic objects such as aluminum, glass, and plastics.*

(a)　　　　(b)

TABLE 1.1	Some Common Elements and Their Symbols					
	Name	**Symbol**	**Name**	**Symbol**	**Name**	**Symbol**
	Aluminum	Al	Fluorine	F	Oxygen	O
	Arsenic	As	Gold	Au	Phosphorus	P
	Barium	Ba	Hydrogen	H	Platinum	Pt
	Bismuth	Bi	Iodine	I	Potassium	K
	Bromine	Br	Iron	Fe	Silicon	Si
	Calcium	Ca	Lead	Pb	Silver	Ag
	Carbon	C	Magnesium	Mg	Sodium	Na
	Chlorine	Cl	Manganese	Mn	Sulfur	S
	Chromium	Cr	Mercury	Hg	Tin	Sn
	Cobalt	Co	Nickel	Ni	Tungsten	W
	Copper	Cu	Nitrogen	N	Zinc	Zn

the iron filings from the sand, because sand is not attracted to the magnet [see Figure 1.4(b)]. After separation, the components of the mixture will have the same composition and properties as they did to start with.

Elements and Compounds

Interactivity: Elements
Online Learning Center,
Interactives

Substances can be either elements or compounds. An **element** is *a substance that cannot be separated into simpler substances by chemical means.* To date, 113 elements have been positively identified. Most of them occur naturally on Earth. The others have been created by scientists via nuclear processes, which are the subject of Chapter 23 of this text.

For convenience, chemists use symbols of one or two letters to represent the elements. The first letter of a symbol is *always* capitalized, but any following letters are not. For example, Co is the symbol for the element cobalt, whereas CO is the formula for the carbon monoxide molecule. Table 1.1 shows the names and symbols of some of the more common elements; a complete list of the elements and their symbols appears inside the front cover of this book. The symbols of some elements are derived from their Latin names—for example, Au from *aurum* (gold), Fe from *ferrum* (iron), and Na from *natrium* (sodium)—while most of them come from their English names. Appendix 1 gives the origin of the names and lists the discoverers of most of the elements.

Atoms of most elements can interact with one another to form compounds. Hydrogen gas, for example, burns in oxygen gas to form water, which has properties that are distinctly different from those of the starting materials. Water is made up of two parts hydrogen and one part oxygen. This composition does not change, regardless of whether the water comes from a faucet in the United States, a lake in Outer Mongolia, or the ice caps on Mars. Thus, water is a **compound,** *a substance composed of atoms of two or more elements chemically united in fixed proportions.* Unlike mixtures, compounds can be separated only by chemical means into their pure components.

The relationships among elements, compounds, and other categories of matter are summarized in Figure 1.5.

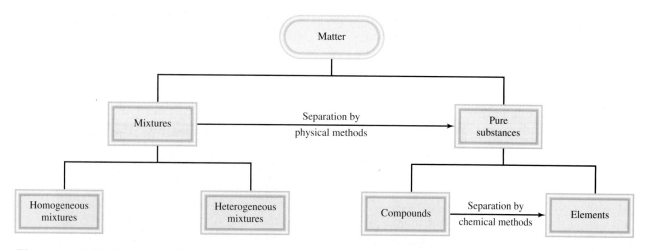

Figure 1.5 *Classification of matter.*

1.5 The Three States of Matter

All substances, at least in principle, can exist in three states: solid, liquid, and gas. As Figure 1.6 shows, gases differ from liquids and solids in the distances between the molecules. In a solid, molecules are held close together in an orderly fashion with little freedom of motion. Molecules in a liquid are close together but are not held so rigidly in position and can move past one another. In a gas, the molecules are separated by distances that are large compared with the size of the molecules.

The three states of matter can be interconverted without changing the composition of the substance. Upon heating, a solid (for example, ice) will melt to form a liquid (water). (The temperature at which this transition occurs is called the *melting point.*) Further heating will convert the liquid into a gas. (This conversion takes place at the *boiling point* of the liquid.) On the other hand, cooling a gas will cause it to condense into a liquid. When the liquid is cooled further, it will freeze into the solid

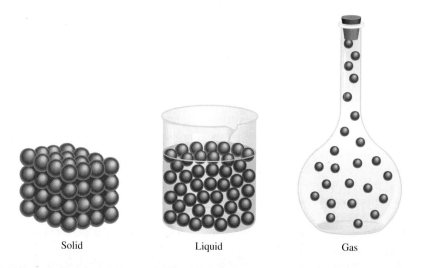

Solid   Liquid   Gas

Figure 1.6 *Microscopic views of a solid, a liquid, and a gas.*

Figure 1.7 *The three states of matter. A hot poker changes ice into water and steam.*

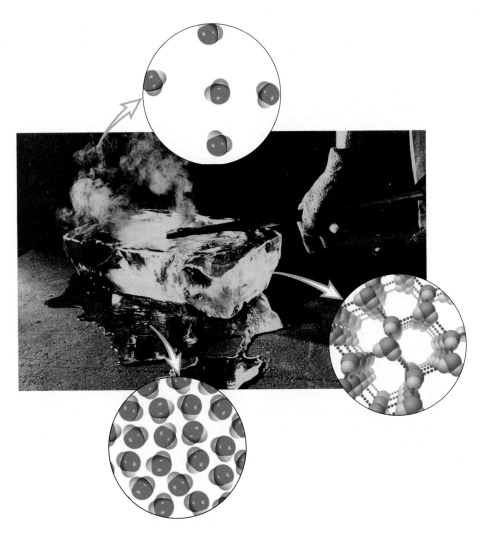

form. Figure 1.7 shows the three states of water. Note that the properties of water are unique among common substances in that the molecules in the liquid state are more closely packed than those in the solid state.

1.6 Physical and Chemical Properties of Matter

Substances are identified by their properties as well as by their composition. Color, melting point, and boiling point are physical properties. A ***physical property*** *can be measured and observed without changing the composition or identity of a substance.* For example, we can measure the melting point of ice by heating a block of ice and recording the temperature at which the ice is converted to water. Water differs from ice only in appearance, not in composition, so this is a physical change; we can freeze the water to recover the original ice. Therefore, the melting point of a substance is a physical property. Similarly, when we say that helium gas is lighter than air, we are referring to a physical property.

On the other hand, the statement "Hydrogen gas burns in oxygen gas to form water" describes a **chemical property** of hydrogen, because *in order to observe this property we must carry out a chemical change,* in this case burning. After the change, the original chemical substance, the hydrogen gas, will have vanished, and all that will be left is a different chemical substance—water. We *cannot* recover the hydrogen from the water by means of a physical change, such as boiling or freezing.

Every time we hard-boil an egg, we bring about a chemical change. When subjected to a temperature of about 100°C, the yolk and the egg white undergo changes that alter not only their physical appearance but their chemical makeup as well. When eaten, the egg is changed again, by substances in our bodies called *enzymes.* This digestive action is another example of a chemical change. What happens during digestion depends on the chemical properties of both the enzymes and the food.

All measurable properties of matter fall into one of two additional categories: extensive properties and intensive properties. The measured value of an **extensive property** *depends on how much matter is being considered.* **Mass,** which is *the quantity of matter in a given sample of a substance,* is an extensive property. More matter means more mass. Values of the same extensive property can be added together. For example, two copper pennies will have a combined mass that is the sum of the masses of each penny, and the length of two tennis courts is the sum of the lengths of each tennis court. **Volume,** defined as *length cubed,* is another extensive property. The value of an extensive quantity depends on the amount of matter.

The measured value of an **intensive property** *does not depend on how much matter is being considered.* **Density,** defined as *the mass of an object divided by its volume,* is an intensive property. So is temperature. Suppose that we have two beakers of water at the same temperature. If we combine them to make a single quantity of water in a larger beaker, the temperature of the larger quantity of water will be the same as it was in two separate beakers. Unlike mass, length, and volume, temperature and other intensive properties are not additive.

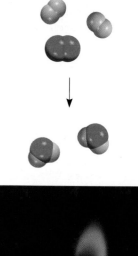

Hydrogen burning in air to form water.

1.7 Measurement

The measurements chemists make are often used in calculations to obtain other related quantities. Different instruments enable us to measure a substance's properties: The meterstick measures length or scale; the buret, the pipet, the graduated cylinder, and the volumetric flask measure volume (Figure 1.8); the balance measures mass; the thermometer measures temperature. These instruments provide measurements of **macroscopic properties,** which *can be determined directly.* **Microscopic properties,** *on the atomic or molecular scale, must be determined by an indirect method,* as we will see in Chapter 2.

A measured quantity is usually written as a number with an appropriate unit. To say that the distance between New York and San Francisco by car along a certain route is 5166 is meaningless. We must specify that the distance is 5166 kilometers. The same is true in chemistry; units are essential to stating measurements correctly.

SI Units

Interactivity: SI Base Units
Online Learning Center, Interactives

For many years scientists recorded measurements in *metric units,* which are related decimally, that is, by powers of 10. In 1960, however, the General Conference of Weights and Measures, the international authority on units, proposed a revised metric system called the **International System of Units** (abbreviated **SI,** from the French

Figure 1.8 *Some common measuring devices found in a chemistry laboratory. These devices are not drawn to scale relative to one another. We will discuss the uses of these measuring devices in Chapter 4.*

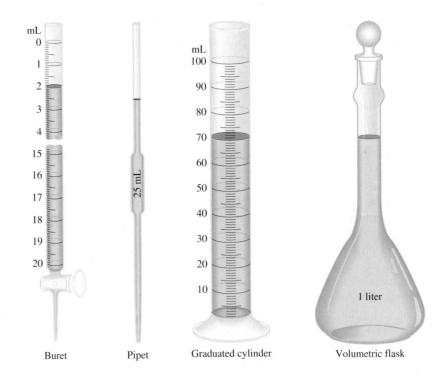

Buret   Pipet   Graduated cylinder   Volumetric flask

Interactivity: Unit
Prefixes
Online Learning Center,
Interactives

Système Internationale d'Unites). Table 1.2 shows the seven SI base units. All other units of measurement can be derived from these base units. Like metric units, SI units are modified in decimal fashion by a series of prefixes, as shown in Table 1.3. We will use both metric and SI units in this book.

Measurements that we will utilize frequently in our study of chemistry include time, mass, volume, density, and temperature.

Mass and Weight

The terms "mass" and "weight" are often used interchangeably, although, strictly speaking, they are different quantities. Whereas mass is a measure of the amount of matter in an object, **weight,** technically speaking, is *the force that gravity exerts on an object.* An apple that falls from a tree is pulled downward by Earth's gravity. The

TABLE 1.2

SI Base Units		
Base Quantity	**Name of Unit**	**Symbol**
Length	meter	m
Mass	kilogram	kg
Time	second	s
Electrical current	ampere	A
Temperature	kelvin	K
Amount of substance	mole	mol
Luminous intensity	candela	cd

TABLE 1.3

Prefixes Used with SI Units

Prefix	Symbol	Meaning	Example
Tera-	T	1,000,000,000,000, or 10^{12}	1 terameter (Tm) = 1×10^{12} m
Giga-	G	1,000,000,000, or 10^{9}	1 gigameter (Gm) = 1×10^{9} m
Mega-	M	1,000,000, or 10^{6}	1 megameter (Mm) = 1×10^{6} m
Kilo-	k	1,000, or 10^{3}	1 kilometer (km) = 1×10^{3} m
Deci-	d	1/10, or 10^{-1}	1 decimeter (dm) = 0.1 m
Centi-	c	1/100, or 10^{-2}	1 centimeter (cm) = 0.01 m
Milli-	m	1/1,000, or 10^{-3}	1 millimeter (mm) = 0.001 m
Micro-	μ	1/1,000,000, or 10^{-6}	1 micrometer (μm) = 1×10^{-6} m
Nano-	n	1/1,000,000,000, or 10^{-9}	1 nanometer (nm) = 1×10^{-9} m
Pico-	p	1/1,000,000,000,000, or 10^{-12}	1 picometer (pm) = 1×10^{-12} m

mass of the apple is constant and does not depend on its location, but its weight does. For example, on the surface of the moon the apple would weigh only one-sixth what it does on Earth, because the moon's gravity is only one-sixth that of Earth. The moon's smaller gravity enabled astronauts to jump about rather freely on its surface despite their bulky suits and equipment. Chemists are interested primarily in mass, which can be determined readily with a balance; the process of measuring mass, oddly, is called *weighing.*

The SI base unit of mass is the *kilogram* (kg), but in chemistry the smaller *gram* (g) is more convenient:

$$1 \text{ kg} = 1000 \text{ g} = 1 \times 10^{3} \text{ g}$$

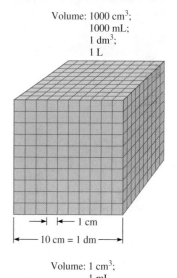

An astronaut jumping on the surface of the moon.

Volume

The SI unit of length is the *meter* (m), and the SI-derived unit for volume is the *cubic meter* (m³). Generally, however, chemists work with much smaller volumes, such as the cubic centimeter (cm³) and the cubic decimeter (dm³):

$$1 \text{ cm}^3 = (1 \times 10^{-2} \text{ m})^3 = 1 \times 10^{-6} \text{ m}^3$$
$$1 \text{ dm}^3 = (1 \times 10^{-1} \text{ m})^3 = 1 \times 10^{-3} \text{ m}^3$$

Another common unit of volume is the liter (L). A **liter** is *the volume occupied by one cubic decimeter.* One liter of volume is equal to 1000 milliliters (mL) or 1000 cm³:

$$1 \text{ L} = 1000 \text{ mL}$$
$$= 1000 \text{ cm}^3$$
$$= 1 \text{ dm}^3$$

and one milliliter is equal to one cubic centimeter:

$$1 \text{ mL} = 1 \text{ cm}^3$$

Figure 1.9 compares the relative sizes of two volumes. Even though the liter is not an SI unit, volumes are usually expressed in liters and milliliters.

Volume: 1000 cm³; 1000 mL; 1 dm³; 1 L

1 cm
10 cm = 1 dm

Volume: 1 cm³; 1 mL

1 cm

Figure 1.9 *Comparison of two volumes, 1 mL and 1000 mL.*

Interactivity: Density
Online Learning Center,
Interactives

Density

The equation for density is

$$\text{density} = \frac{\text{mass}}{\text{volume}}$$

or

$$d = \frac{m}{V} \tag{1.1}$$

where d, m, and V denote density, mass, and volume, respectively. Because density is an intensive property and does not depend on the quantity of mass present, for a given material the ratio of mass to volume always remains the same; in other words, V increases as m does.

The SI-derived unit for density is the kilogram per cubic meter (kg/m^3). This unit is awkwardly large for most chemical applications. Therefore, grams per cubic centimeter (g/cm^3) and its equivalent, grams per milliliter (g/mL), are more commonly used for solid and liquid densities. Because gas densities are often very low, we express them in units of grams per liter (g/L):

$$1 \text{ g/cm}^3 = 1 \text{ g/mL} = 1000 \text{ kg/m}^3$$
$$1 \text{ g/L} = 0.001 \text{ g/mL}$$

Examples 1.1 and 1.2 show density calculations.

Gold bars.

Similar problems: 1.21, 1.22.

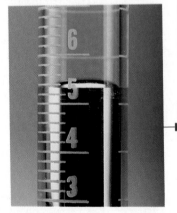

Mercury.

Example 1.1

Gold is a precious metal that is chemically unreactive. It is used mainly in jewelry, dentistry, and electronic devices. A piece of gold ingot with a mass of 301 g has a volume of 15.6 cm^3. Calculate the density of gold.

Solution We are given the mass and volume and asked to calculate the density. Therefore, from Equation (1.1), we write

$$d = \frac{m}{V}$$
$$= \frac{301 \text{ g}}{15.6 \text{ cm}^3}$$
$$= 19.3 \text{ g/cm}^3$$

Practice Exercise A piece of platinum metal with a density of 21.5 g/cm^3 has a volume of 4.49 cm^3. What is its mass?

Example 1.2

The density of mercury, the only metal that is a liquid at room temperature, is 13.6 g/mL. Calculate the mass of 5.50 mL of the liquid.

Solution We are given the density and volume of a liquid and asked to calculate the mass of the liquid. We rearrange Equation (1.1) to give

(Continued)

$$m = d \times V$$

$$= 13.6 \, \frac{g}{mL} \times 5.50 \, mL$$

$$= 74.8 \, g$$

Similar problems: 1.21, 1.22.

Practice Exercise The density of sulfuric acid in a certain car battery is 1.41 g/mL. Calculate the mass of 242 mL of the liquid.

Temperature Scales

Three temperature scales are currently in use. Their units are °F (degrees Fahrenheit), °C (degrees Celsius), and K (kelvin). The Fahrenheit scale, which is the most commonly used scale in the United States outside the laboratory, defines the normal freezing and boiling points of water to be exactly 32°F and 212°F, respectively. The Celsius scale divides the range between the freezing point (0°C) and boiling point (100°C) of water into 100 degrees. As Table 1.2 shows, the **kelvin** is *the SI base unit of temperature;* it is the *absolute* temperature scale. By absolute we mean that the zero on the Kelvin scale, denoted by 0 K, is the lowest temperature that can be attained theoretically. On the other hand, 0°F and 0°C are based on the behavior of an arbitrarily chosen substance, water. Figure 1.10 compares the three temperature scales.

Note that the Kelvin scale does not have the degree sign. Also, temperatures expressed in kelvins can never be negative.

The size of a degree on the Fahrenheit scale is only 100/180, or 5/9, of a degree on the Celsius scale. To convert degrees Fahrenheit to degrees Celsius, we write

$$?°C = (°F - 32°F) \times \frac{5°C}{9°F} \tag{1.2}$$

The following equation is used to convert degrees Celsius to degrees Fahrenheit:

$$?°F = \frac{9°F}{5°C} \times (°C) + 32°F \tag{1.3}$$

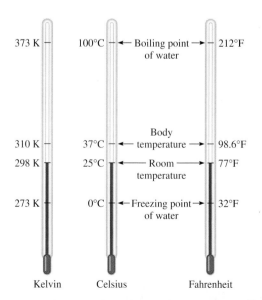

373 K — 100°C — ← Boiling point → 212°F
of water

310 K — 37°C — ← Body temperature → 98.6°F

298 K — 25°C — ← Room → 77°F
temperature

273 K — 0°C — ← Freezing point → 32°F
of water

Kelvin   Celsius   Fahrenheit

Figure 1.10 *Comparison of the three temperature scales: Celsius, Fahrenheit, and the absolute (Kelvin) scale. Note that there are 100 divisions, or 100 degrees, between the freezing point and the boiling point of water on the Celsius scale, and there are 180 divisions, or 180 degrees, between the same two temperature limits on the Fahrenheit scale. The Celsius scale was formerly called the centigrade scale.*

Both the Celsius and the Kelvin scales have units of equal magnitude; that is, one degree Celsius is equivalent to one kelvin. Experimental studies have shown that absolute zero on the Kelvin scale is equivalent to $-273.15°C$ on the Celsius scale. Thus we can use the following equation to convert degrees Celsius to kelvin:

$$? \text{ K} = (°C + 273.15°C) \frac{1 \text{ K}}{1°C} \tag{1.4}$$

We will frequently find it necessary to convert between degrees Celsius and degrees Fahrenheit and between degrees Celsius and kelvin. Example 1.3 illustrates these conversions.

The Chemistry in Action essay on page 21 shows why we must be careful with units in scientific work.

Solder is used extensively in the construction of electronic circuits.

Similar problems: 1.24, 1.25, 1.26.

Example 1.3

(a) Solder is an alloy made of tin and lead that is used in electronic circuits. A certain solder has a melting point of $224°C$. What is its melting point in degrees Fahrenheit? (b) Helium has the lowest boiling point of all the elements at $-452°F$. Convert this temperature to degrees Celsius. (c) Mercury, the only metal that exists as a liquid at room temperature, melts at $-38.9°C$. Convert its melting point to kelvins.

Solution These three parts require that we carry out temperature conversions, so we need Equations (1.2), (1.3), and (1.4). Keep in mind that the lowest temperature on the Kelvin scale is zero (0 K); therefore, it can never be negative.

(a) This conversion is carried out by writing

$$\frac{9°F}{5°C} \times (224°C) + 32°F = 435°F$$

(b) Here we have

$$(-452°F - 32°F) \times \frac{5°C}{9°F} = -269°C$$

(c) The melting point of mercury in kelvins is given by

$$(-38.9°C + 273.15°C) \times \frac{1 \text{ K}}{1°C} = 234.3 \text{ K}$$

Practice Exercise Convert (a) $327.5°C$ (the melting point of lead) to degrees Fahrenheit; (b) $172.9°F$ (the boiling point of ethanol) to degrees Celsius; and (c) 77 K, the boiling point of liquid nitrogen, to degrees Celsius.

1.8 Handling Numbers

Having surveyed some of the units used in chemistry, we now turn to techniques for handling numbers associated with measurements: scientific notation and significant figures.

CHEMISTRY IN ACTION

The Importance of Units

In December 1998 NASA launched the 125-million dollar Mars Climate Orbiter, intended as the red planet's first weather satellite. After a 416-million mi journey, the spacecraft was supposed to go into Mars' orbit on September 23, 1999. Instead, it entered Mars' atmosphere about 100 km (62 mi) lower than planned and was destroyed by heat. The mission controllers said the loss of the spacecraft was due to the failure to convert English measurement units into metric units in the navigation software.

Engineers at Lockheed Martin Corporation who built the spacecraft specified its thrust in pounds, which is an English unit. Scientists at NASA's Jet Propulsion Laboratory, on the other hand, had assumed that thrust data they received were expressed in metric units, as newtons. Normally, pound is the unit for mass. Expressed as a unit for force, however, 1 lb is the force due to gravitational attraction on an object of that mass. To carry out the conversion between pound and newton, we start with 1 lb = 0.4536 kg and from Newton's second law of motion,

$$\begin{aligned} \text{force} &= \text{mass} \times \text{acceleration} \\ &= 0.4536 \text{ kg} \times 9.81 \text{ m/s}^2 \\ &= 4.45 \text{ kg m/s}^2 \\ &= 4.45 \text{ N} \end{aligned}$$

because 1 newton (N) = 1 kg m/s^2. Therefore, instead of converting one pound of force to 4.45 N, the scientists treated it as 1 N.

The considerably smaller engine thrust expressed in newtons resulted in a lower orbit and the ultimate destruction of the spacecraft. Commenting on the failure of the Mars mission, one scientist said: "This is going to be the cautionary tale that will be embedded into introduction to the metric system in elementary school, high school, and college science courses till the end of time."

Artist's conception of the Martian Climate Orbiter.

Scientific Notation

Chemists often deal with numbers that are either extremely large or extremely small. For example, in 1 g of the element hydrogen there are roughly

$$602,200,000,000,000,000,000,000$$

hydrogen atoms. Each hydrogen atom has a mass of only

$$0.00000000000000000000000166 \text{ g}$$

These numbers are cumbersome to handle, and it is easy to make mistakes when using them in arithmetic computations. Consider the following multiplication:

$$0.0000000056 \times 0.0000000048 = 0.00000000000000002688$$

It would be easy for us to miss one zero or add one more zero after the decimal point. Consequently, when working with very large and very small numbers, we use a system called *scientific notation.* Regardless of their magnitude, all numbers can be expressed in the form

$$N \times 10^n$$

where N is a number between 1 and 10 and n, the exponent, is a positive or negative integer (whole number). Any number expressed in this way is said to be written in scientific notation.

Suppose that we are given a certain number and asked to express it in scientific notation. Basically, this assignment calls for us to find n. We count the number of places that the decimal point must be moved to give the number N (which is between 1 and 10). If the decimal point has to be moved to the left, then n is a positive integer; if it has to be moved to the right, n is a negative integer. The following examples illustrate the use of scientific notation:
(1) Express 568.762 in scientific notation:

$$568.762 = 5.68762 \times 10^2$$

Note that the decimal point is moved to the left by two places and $n = 2$.
(2) Express 0.00000772 in scientific notation:

$$0.00000772 = 7.72 \times 10^{-6}$$

Here the decimal point is moved to the right by six places and $n = -6$.

Any number raised to the power zero is equal to one.

Keep in mind the following two points. First, $n = 0$ is used for numbers that are not expressed in scientific notation. For example, 74.6×10^0 ($n = 0$) is equivalent to 74.6. Second, the usual practice is to omit the superscript when $n = 1$. Thus the scientific notation for 74.6 is 7.46×10 and not 7.46×10^1.

Next, we consider how scientific notation is handled in arithmetic operations.

Addition and Subtraction To add or subtract using scientific notation, we first write each quantity—say N_1 and N_2—with the same exponent n. Then we combine N_1 and N_2; the exponents remain the same. Consider the following examples:

$$(7.4 \times 10^3) + (2.1 \times 10^3) = 9.5 \times 10^3$$
$$(4.31 \times 10^4) + (3.9 \times 10^3) = (4.31 \times 10^4) + (0.39 \times 10^4)$$
$$= 4.70 \times 10^4$$
$$(2.22 \times 10^{-2}) - (4.10 \times 10^{-3}) = (2.22 \times 10^{-2}) - (0.41 \times 10^{-2})$$
$$= 1.81 \times 10^{-2}$$

Multiplication and Division To multiply numbers expressed in scientific notation, we multiply N_1 and N_2 in the usual way, but *add* the exponents together. To divide using scientific notation, we divide N_1 and N_2 as usual and subtract the exponents. The following examples show how these operations are performed:

$$(8.0 \times 10^4) \times (5.0 \times 10^2) = (8.0 \times 5.0)(10^{4+2})$$
$$= 40 \times 10^6$$
$$= 4.0 \times 10^7$$
$$(4.0 \times 10^{-5}) \times (7.0 \times 10^3) = (4.0 \times 7.0)(10^{-5+3})$$
$$= 28 \times 10^{-2}$$
$$= 2.8 \times 10^{-1}$$
$$\frac{6.9 \times 10^7}{3.0 \times 10^{-5}} = \frac{6.9}{3.0} \times 10^{7-(-5)}$$
$$= 2.3 \times 10^{12}$$

$$\frac{8.5 \times 10^4}{5.0 \times 10^9} = \frac{8.5}{5.0} \times 10^{4-9}$$
$$= 1.7 \times 10^{-5}$$

Significant Figures

Except when all the numbers involved are integers (for example, in counting the number of students in a class), it is often impossible to obtain the exact value of the quantity under investigation. For this reason, it is important to indicate the margin of error in a measurement by clearly indicating the number of *significant figures,* which are *the meaningful digits in a measured or calculated quantity.* When significant figures are used, the last digit is understood to be uncertain. For example, we might measure the volume of a given amount of liquid using a graduated cylinder with a scale that gives an uncertainty of 1 mL in the measurement. If the volume is found to be 6 mL, then the actual volume is in the range of 5 mL to 7 mL. We represent the volume of the liquid as (6 ± 1) mL. In this case, there is only one significant figure (the digit 6) that is uncertain by either plus or minus 1 mL. For greater accuracy, we might use a graduated cylinder that has finer divisions, so that the volume we measure is now uncertain by only 0.1 mL. If the volume of the liquid is now found to be 6.0 mL, we may express the quantity as (6.0 ± 0.1) mL, and the actual value is somewhere between 5.9 mL and 6.1 mL. We can further improve the measuring device and obtain more significant figures, but in every case, the last digit is always uncertain; the amount of this uncertainty depends on the particular measuring device we use.

Figure 1.11 shows a modern balance. Balances such as this one are available in many general chemistry laboratories; they readily measure the mass of objects to four decimal places. Therefore the measured mass typically will have four significant figures (for example, 0.8642 g) or more (for example, 3.9745 g). Keeping track of the number of significant figures in a measurement such as mass ensures that calculations involving the data will reflect the precision of the measurement.

Guidelines for Using Significant Figures We must always be careful in scientific work to write the proper number of significant figures. In general, it is fairly

Figure 1.11 *A common single-pan balance.*

easy to determine how many significant figures a number has by following these rules:

1. Any digit that is not zero is significant. Thus 845 cm has three significant figures, 1.234 kg has four significant figures, and so on.

2. Zeros between nonzero digits are significant. Thus 606 m contains three significant figures, 40,501 kg contains five significant figures, and so on.

3. Zeros to the left of the first nonzero digit are not significant. Their purpose is to indicate the placement of the decimal point. For example, 0.08 L contains one significant figure, 0.0000349 g contains three significant figures, and so on.

4. If a number is greater than 1, then all the zeros written to the right of the decimal point count as significant figures. Thus 2.0 mg has two significant figures, 40.062 mL has five significant figures, and 3.040 dm has four significant figures. If a number is less than 1, then only the zeros that are at the end of the number and the zeros that are between nonzero digits are significant. This means that 0.090 kg has two significant figures, 0.3005 L has four significant figures, 0.00420 min has three significant figures, and so on.

5. For numbers that do not contain decimal points, the trailing zeros (that is, zeros after the last nonzero digit) may or may not be significant. Thus 400 cm may have one significant figure (the digit 4), two significant figures (40), or three significant figures (400). We cannot know which is correct without more information. By using scientific notation, however, we avoid this ambiguity. In this particular case, we can express the number 400 as 4×10^2 for one significant figure, 4.0×10^2 for two significant figures, or 4.00×10^2 for three significant figures.

Example 1.4 shows the determination of significant figures.

Example 1.4

Determine the number of significant figures in the following measurements: (a) 478 cm, (b) 6.01 g, (c) 0.825 m, (d) 0.043 kg, (e) 1.310×10^{22} atoms, (f) 7000 mL.

Solution (a) Three, because each digit is a nonzero digit. (b) Three, because zeros between nonzero digits are significant. (c) Three, because zeros to the left of the first nonzero digit do not count as significant figures. (d) Two. Same reason as in (c). (e) Four, because the number is greater than one so all the zeros written to the right of the decimal point count as significant figures. (f) This is an ambiguous case. The number of significant figures may be four (7.000×10^3), three (7.00×10^3), two (7.0×10^3), or one (7×10^3). This example illustrates why scientific notation must be used to show the proper number of significant figures.

Similar problems: 1.33, 1.34.

Practice Exercise Determine the number of significant figures in each of the following measurements: (a) 24 mL, (b) 3001 g, (c) 0.0320 m^3, (d) 6.4×10^4 molecules, (e) 560 kg.

A second set of rules specifies how to handle significant figures in calculations.

1. In addition and subtraction, the answer cannot have more digits to the right of the decimal point than either of the original numbers. Consider these examples:

$$\begin{array}{r} 89.332 \\ + 1.1 \quad \longleftarrow \text{one digit after the decimal point} \\ \hline 90.432 \quad \longleftarrow \text{round off to } 90.4 \end{array}$$

$$
\begin{array}{l}
2.097 \\
\underline{-0.12} \quad \longleftarrow \text{two digits after the decimal point} \\
1.977 \quad \longleftarrow \text{round off to } 1.98
\end{array}
$$

The rounding-off procedure is as follows. To round off a number at a certain point we simply drop the digits that follow if the first of them is less than 5. Thus 8.724 rounds off to 8.72 if we want only two digits after the decimal point. If the first digit following the point of rounding off is equal to or greater than 5, we add 1 to the preceding digit. Thus 8.727 rounds off to 8.73, and 0.425 rounds off to 0.43.

2. In multiplication and division, the number of significant figures in the final product or quotient is determined by the original number that has the *smallest* number of significant figures. The following examples illustrate this rule:

$$
2.8 \times 4.5039 = 12.61092 \longleftarrow \text{round off to } 13
$$

$$
\frac{6.85}{112.04} = 0.0611388789 \longleftarrow \text{round off to } 0.0611
$$

3. Keep in mind that *exact numbers* obtained from definitions or by counting numbers of objects can be considered to have an infinite number of significant figures. If an object has a mass of 0.2786 g, then the mass of eight such objects is

$$
0.2786 \text{ g} \times 8 = 2.229 \text{ g}
$$

We do *not* round off this product to one significant figure, because the number 8 is 8.00000 . . . , by definition. Similarly, to take the average of the two measured lengths 6.64 cm and 6.68 cm, we write

$$
\frac{6.64 \text{ cm} + 6.68 \text{ cm}}{2} = 6.66 \text{ cm}
$$

because the number 2 is 2.00000 . . . , by definition.

Example 1.5 shows how significant figures are handled in arithmetic operations.

Example 1.5

Carry out the following arithmetic operations to the correct number of significant figures: (a) 11,254.1 g + 0.1983 g, (b) 66.59 L − 3.113 L, (c) 8.16 m × 5.1355, (d) 0.0154 kg ÷ 88.3 mL, (e) 2.64×10^3 cm + 3.27×10^2 cm.

Solution In addition and subtraction, the number of decimal places in the answer is determined by the number having the lowest number of decimal places. In multiplication and division, the significant number of the answer is determined by the number having the smallest number of significant figures.

(a)
$$
\begin{array}{r}
11{,}254.1 \text{ g} \\
+ \quad 0.1983 \text{ g} \\
\hline
11{,}254.2983 \text{ g}
\end{array} \longleftarrow \text{round off to } 11{,}254.3 \text{ g}
$$

(b)
$$
\begin{array}{r}
66.59 \text{ L} \\
- \quad 3.113 \text{ L} \\
\hline
63.477 \text{ L}
\end{array} \longleftarrow \text{round off to } 63.48 \text{ L}
$$

(c) 8.16 m × 5.1355 = 41.90568 m ⟵ round off to 41.9 m

(Continued)

(d) $\dfrac{0.0154 \text{ kg}}{88.3 \text{ mL}} = 0.000174405436 \text{ kg/mL}$ ⟵ round off to 0.000174 kg/mL

or 1.74×10^{-4} kg/mL

(e) First we change 3.27×10^2 cm to 0.327×10^3 cm and then carry out the addition (2.64 cm + 0.327 cm) $\times 10^3$. Following the procedure in (a), we find the answer is 2.97×10^3 cm.

Similar problems: 1.35, 1.36.

Practice Exercise Carry out the following arithmetic operations and round off the answers to the appropriate number of significant figures: (a) 26.5862 L + 0.17 L, (b) 9.1 g − 4.682 g, (c) 7.1×10^4 dm $\times 2.2654 \times 10^2$ dm, (d) 6.54 g ÷ 86.5542 mL, (e) $(7.55 \times 10^4$ m$) - (8.62 \times 10^3$ m$)$.

The preceding rounding-off procedure applies to one-step calculations. In *chain calculations,* that is, calculations involving more than one step, we use a modified procedure. Consider the following two-step calculation:

First step: A × B = C
Second step: C × D = E

Let us suppose that A = 3.66, B = 8.45, and D = 2.11. Depending on whether we round off C to three or four significant figures, we obtain a different number for E:

Method 1	Method 2
3.66 × 8.45 = 30.9	3.66 × 8.45 = 30.93
30.9 × 2.11 = 65.2	30.93 × 2.11 = 65.3

However, if we had carried out the calculation as 3.66 × 8.45 × 2.11 on a calculator without rounding off the intermediate result, we would have obtained 65.3 as the answer for E. In general, we will show the correct number of significant figures in each step of the calculation.

Accuracy and Precision

Interactivity: Accuracy and Precision
Online Learning Center, Interactives

In discussing measurements and significant figures it is useful to distinguish between accuracy and precision. **Accuracy** tells us *how close a measurement is to the true value of the quantity that was measured.* To a scientist there is a distinction between accuracy and precision. **Precision** *refers to how closely two or more measurements of the same quantity agree with one another* (Figure 1.12).

The difference between accuracy and precision is a subtle but important one. Suppose, for example, that three students are asked to determine the mass of a piece of copper wire. The results of two successive weighings by each student are

Figure 1.12 *The distribution of darts on a dart board shows the difference between precise and accurate. (a) Good accuracy and good precision. (b) Poor accuracy and good precision. (c) Poor accuracy and poor precision. The dots show the positions of the darts.*

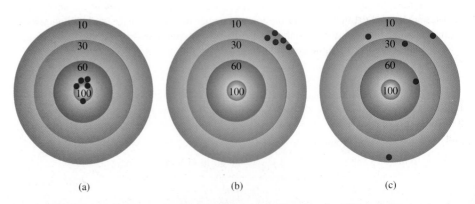

(a)   (b)   (c)

	Student A	Student B	Student C
	1.964 g	1.972 g	2.000 g
	1.978 g	1.968 g	2.002 g
Average value	1.971 g	1.970 g	2.001 g

The true mass of the wire is 2.000 g. Therefore, Student B's results are more *precise* than those of Student A (1.972 g and 1.968 g deviate less from 1.970 g than 1.964 g and 1.978 g from 1.971 g), but neither set of results is very *accurate*. Student C's results are not only the most *precise,* but also the most *accurate,* because the average value is closest to the true value. Highly accurate measurements are usually precise too. On the other hand, highly precise measurements do not necessarily guarantee accurate results. For example, an improperly calibrated meterstick or a faulty balance may give precise readings that are in error.

1.9 Dimensional Analysis in Solving Problems

Careful measurements and the proper use of significant figures, along with correct calculations, will yield accurate numerical results. But to be meaningful, the answers also must be expressed in the desired units. The procedure we use to convert between units in solving chemistry problems is called *dimensional analysis* (also called the *factor-label method*). A simple technique requiring little memorization, dimensional analysis is based on the relationship between different units that express the same physical quantity. For example, we know that the monetary unit "dollar" is different from the unit "penny." However, 1 dollar is *equivalent* to 100 pennies because they both represent the same amount of money; that is,

Interactivity: Dimensional Analysis/Factor-Label Method
Online Learning Center, Interactives

$$1 \text{ dollar} = 100 \text{ pennies}$$

This equivalence enables us to write a conversion factor

$$\frac{1 \text{ dollar}}{100 \text{ pennies}}$$

if we want to convert pennies to dollars. Conversely, the conversion factor

$$\frac{100 \text{ pennies}}{1 \text{ dollar}}$$

enables us to convert dollars to pennies. A conversion factor, then, is a fraction whose numerator and denominator are the same quantity expressed in different units.

    Now consider the problem

$$? \text{ pennies} = 2.46 \text{ dollars}$$

Because this is a dollar-to-penny conversion, we choose the conversion factor that has the unit "dollar" in the denominator (to cancel the "dollars" in 2.46 dollars) and write

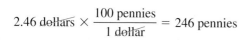

$$2.46 \text{ dollars} \times \frac{100 \text{ pennies}}{1 \text{ dollar}} = 246 \text{ pennies}$$

Note that the conversion factor 100 pennies/1 dollar contains exact numbers, so it does not affect the number of significant figures in the final answer.

Next let us consider the conversion of 57.8 meters to centimeters. This problem can be expressed as

$$? \text{ cm} = 57.8 \text{ m}$$

By definition,

$$1 \text{ cm} = 1 \times 10^{-2} \text{ m}$$

Because we are converting "m" to "cm," we choose the conversion factor that has meters in the denominator,

$$\frac{1 \text{ cm}}{1 \times 10^{-2} \text{ m}}$$

and write the conversion as

$$? \text{ cm} = 57.8 \text{ m} \times \frac{1 \text{ cm}}{1 \times 10^{-2} \text{ m}}$$
$$= 5780 \text{ cm}$$
$$= 5.78 \times 10^3 \text{ cm}$$

Note that scientific notation is used to indicate that the answer has three significant figures. Again, the conversion factor 1 cm/1 $\times$ 10^{-2} m contains exact numbers; therefore, it does not affect the number of significant figures.

In general, to apply dimensional analysis we use the relationship

$$\text{given quantity} \times \text{conversion factor} = \text{desired quantity}$$

and the units cancel as follows:

$$\text{given unit} \times \frac{\text{desired unit}}{\text{given unit}} = \text{desired unit}$$

In dimensional analysis the units are carried through the entire sequence of calculations. Therefore, if the equation is set up correctly, then all the units will cancel except the desired one. If this is not the case, then an error must have been made somewhere, and it can usually be spotted by reviewing the solution.

A Note on Problem Solving

At this point you have been introduced to scientific notation, significant figures, and dimensional analysis, which will help you in solving numerical problems. Chemistry is an experimental science and many of the problems are quantitative in nature. The key to success in problem solving is practice. Just as a marathon runner cannot prepare for a race by simply reading books on running and a pianist cannot give a successful concert by only memorizing the musical score, you cannot be sure of your understanding of chemistry without solving problems. The following steps will help to improve your skill at solving numerical problems.

1. Read the question carefully. Understand the information that is given and what you are asked to solve. Frequently it is helpful to make a sketch that will help you to visualize the situation.

2. Find the appropriate equation that relates the given information and the unknown quantity. Sometimes solving a problem will involve more than one step, and you may be expected to look up quantities in tables that are not provided in the problem. Dimensional analysis is often needed to carry out conversions.

3. Check your answer for the correct sign, units, and significant figures.

4. A very important part of problem solving is being able to judge whether the answer is reasonable. It is relatively easy to spot a wrong sign or incorrect units. But if a number (say 8) is incorrectly placed in the denominator instead of in the numerator, the answer would be too small even if the sign and units of the calculated quantity were correct.

5. One way to quickly check the answer is to make a "ball-park" estimate. The idea here is to round off the numbers in the calculation in such a way so as to simplify the arithmetic. This approach is sometimes called the "back-of-the-envelope calculation" because it can be done easily without using a calculator. The answer you get will not be exact, but it will be close to the correct one.

Example 1.6

A person's average daily intake of glucose (a form of sugar) is 0.0833 pound (lb). What is this mass in milligrams (mg)? (1 lb = 453.6 g.)

Strategy The problem can be stated as

$$? \text{ mg} = 0.0833 \text{ lb}$$

The relationship between pounds and grams is given in the problem. This relationship will enable conversion from pounds to grams. A metric conversion is then needed to convert grams to milligrams (1 mg = 1×10^{-3} g). Arrange the appropriate conversion factors so that pounds and grams cancel and the unit milligrams is obtained in your answer.

Solution The sequence of conversions is

$$\text{pounds} \longrightarrow \text{grams} \longrightarrow \text{milligrams}$$

Using the following conversion factors

$$\frac{453.6 \text{ g}}{1 \text{ lb}} \quad \text{and} \quad \frac{1 \text{ mg}}{1 \times 10^{-3} \text{ g}}$$

we obtain the answer in one step:

$$? \text{ mg} = 0.0833 \text{ lb} \times \frac{453.6 \text{ g}}{1 \text{ lb}} \times \frac{1 \text{ mg}}{1 \times 10^{-3} \text{ g}} = 3.78 \times 10^4 \text{ mg}$$

Check As a rough estimate, we note that 1 lb is roughly 500 g and that 1 g = 1000 mg. Therefore, 1 lb is roughly 5×10^5 mg. Rounding off 0.0833 lb to 0.1 lb, we get 5×10^4 mg, which is close to the preceding quantity.

Similar problem: 1.43.

Practice Exercise A roll of aluminum foil has a mass of 1.07 kg. What is its mass in pounds?

Conversion factors for some of the English system units commonly used in the United States for nonscientific measurements (for example, pounds and inches) are provided inside the back cover of this book.

As Examples 1.7 and 1.8 illustrate, conversion factors can be squared or cubed in dimensional analysis.

Example 1.7

An average adult has 5.2 L of blood. What is the volume of blood in m^3?

Strategy The problem can be stated as

$$? \, m^3 = 5.2 \, L$$

How many conversion factors are needed for this problem? Recall that 1 L = 1000 cm^3 and 1 cm = 1×10^{-2} m.

Solution We need two conversion factors here: one to convert liters to cm^3 and one to convert centimeters to meters:

$$\frac{1000 \, cm^3}{1 \, L} \quad and \quad \frac{1 \times 10^{-2} \, m}{1 \, cm}$$

Because the second conversion factor deals with length (cm and m) and we want volume here, it must therefore be cubed to give

$$\frac{1 \times 10^{-2} \, m}{1 \, cm} \times \frac{1 \times 10^{-2} \, m}{1 \, cm} \times \frac{1 \times 10^{-2} \, m}{1 \, cm} = \left(\frac{1 \times 10^{-2} \, m}{1 \, cm}\right)^3$$

This means that 1 cm^3 = 1×10^{-6} m^3. Now we can write

$$? \, m^3 = 5.2 \, \cancel{L} \times \frac{1000 \, cm^3}{1 \, \cancel{L}} \times \left(\frac{1 \times 10^{-2} \, m}{1 \, cm}\right)^3 = 5.2 \times 10^{-3} \, m^3$$

Check From the preceding conversion factors you can show that 1 L = 1×10^{-3} m^3. Therefore, 5 L of blood would be equal to 5×10^{-3} m^3, which is close to the answer.

Similar problem: 1.48(d).

Practice Exercise The volume of a room is 1.08×10^8 dm^3. What is the volume in m^3?

Example 1.8

The density of silver is 10.5 g/cm^3. Convert the density to units of kg/m^3.

Strategy The problem can be stated as

$$? \, kg/m^3 = 10.5 \, g/cm^3$$

Two separate conversions are required for this problem: g $\longrightarrow$ kg and $cm^3 \longrightarrow m^3$. Recall that 1 kg = 1000 g and 1 cm = 1×10^{-2} m.

Silver coin.

Solution In Example 1.7 we saw that 1 cm^3 = 1×10^{-6} m^3. The conversion factors are

$$\frac{1 \, kg}{1000 \, g} \quad and \quad \frac{1 \, cm^3}{1 \times 10^{-6} \, m^3}$$

Finally,

$$? \, kg/m^3 = \frac{10.5 \, \cancel{g}}{1 \, \cancel{cm^3}} \times \frac{1 \, kg}{1000 \, \cancel{g}} \times \frac{1 \, \cancel{cm^3}}{1 \times 10^{-6} \, m^3} = 10{,}500 \, kg/m^3$$
$$= 1.05 \times 10^4 \, kg/m^3$$

Check Because 1 m^3 = 1×10^6 cm^3, we would expect much more mass in 1 m^3 than in 1 cm^3. Therefore, the answer is reasonable.

Similar problem: 1.49.

Practice Exercise The density of the lightest metal, lithium (Li), is 5.34×10^2 kg/m^3. Convert the density to g/cm^3.

Key Equations

- $d = \dfrac{m}{V}$ (1.1)   Equation for density

- $?°C = (°F - 32°F) \times \dfrac{5°C}{9°F}$ (1.2)   Converting °F to °C

- $?°F = \dfrac{9°F}{5°C} \times (°C) + 32°F$ (1.3)   Converting °C to °F

- $? K = (°C + 273.15°C) \dfrac{1\,K}{1°C}$ (1.4)   Converting °C to K

Summary of Facts and Concepts

1. The study of chemistry involves three basic steps: observation, representation, and interpretation. Observation refers to measurements in the macroscopic world; representation involves the use of shorthand notation symbols and equations for communication; interpretations are based on atoms and molecules, which belong to the microscopic world.

2. The scientific method is a systematic approach to research that begins with the gathering of information through observation and measurements. In the process, hypotheses, laws, and theories are devised and tested.

3. Chemists study matter and the changes it undergoes. The substances that make up matter have unique physical properties that can be observed without changing their identity and unique chemical properties that, when they are demonstrated, do change the identity of the substances. Mixtures, whether homogeneous or heterogeneous, can be separated into pure components by physical means.

4. The simplest substances in chemistry are elements. Compounds are formed by the chemical combination of atoms of different elements in fixed proportions.

5. All substances, in principle, can exist in three states: solid, liquid, and gas. The interconversion between these states can be effected by changing the temperature.

6. SI units are used to express physical quantities in all sciences, including chemistry.

7. Numbers expressed in scientific notation have the form $N \times 10^n$, where N is between 1 and 10, and n is a positive or negative integer. Scientific notation helps us handle very large and very small quantities.

Key Words

Accuracy, p. 26
Chemical property, p. 15
Chemistry, p. 4
Compound, p. 12
Density, p. 15
Element, p. 12
Extensive property, p. 15
Heterogeneous
   mixture, p. 11

Homogeneous mixture,
   p. 11
Hypothesis, p. 9
Intensive property, p. 15
International System of
   Units (SI), p. 15
Kelvin, p. 19
Law, p. 9
Liter, p. 17

Macroscopic property,
   p. 15
Mass, p. 15
Matter, p. 11
Microscopic property, p. 15
Mixture, p. 11
Physical property, p. 14
Precision, p. 26
Qualitative, p. 9

Quantitative, p. 9
Scientific method, p. 8
Significant figures, p. 23
Substance, p. 11
Theory, p. 9
Volume, p. 15
Weight, p. 16

Questions and Problems

The Scientific Method

Review Questions

1.1   Explain what is meant by the scientific method.

1.2   What is the difference between qualitative data and quantitative data?

Problems

1.3   Classify the following as qualitative or quantitative statements, giving your reasons. (a) The sun is approximately 93 million mi from Earth. (b) Leonardo da Vinci was a better painter than Michelangelo. (c) Ice is less dense than water. (d) Butter tastes better than margarine. (e) A stitch in time saves nine.

1.4   Classify each of the following statements as a hypothesis, a law, or a theory. (a) Beethoven's contribution to music would have been much greater if he had married. (b) An autumn leaf gravitates toward the ground because there is an attractive force between the leaf and Earth. (c) All matter is composed of very small particles called atoms.

Classification and Properties of Matter

Review Questions

1.5   Give an example for each of the following terms: (a) matter, (b) substance, (c) mixture.

1.6   Give an example of a homogeneous mixture and an example of a heterogeneous mixture.

1.7   Using examples, explain the difference between a physical property and a chemical property.

1.8   How does an intensive property differ from an extensive property? Which of the following properties are intensive and which are extensive? (a) length, (b) volume, (c) temperature, (d) mass.

1.9   Give an example of an element and a compound. How do elements and compounds differ?

1.10 What is the number of known elements?

Problems

1.11 Do the following statements describe chemical or physical properties? (a) Oxygen gas supports combustion. (b) Fertilizers help to increase agricultural production. (c) Water boils below 100°C on top of a mountain. (d) Lead is denser than aluminum. (e) Uranium is a radioactive element.

1.12 Does each of the following describe a physical change or a chemical change? (a) The helium gas inside a balloon tends to leak out after a few hours. (b) A flashlight beam slowly gets dimmer and finally goes out. (c) Frozen orange juice is reconstituted by adding water to it. (d) The growth of plants depends on the sun's energy in a process called photosynthesis. (e) A spoonful of table salt dissolves in a bowl of soup.

1.13 Give the names of the elements represented by the chemical symbols Li, F, P, Cu, As, Zn, Cl, Pt, Mg, U, Al, Si, Ne. (See Table 1.1 and the inside front cover.)

1.14 Give the chemical symbols for the following elements: (a) potassium, (b) tin, (c) chromium, (d) boron, (e) barium, (f) plutonium, (g) sulfur, (h) argon, (i) mercury. (See Table 1.1 and the inside front cover.)

1.15 Classify each of the following substances as an element or a compound: (a) hydrogen, (b) water, (c) gold, (d) sugar.

1.16 Classify each of the following as an element, a compound, a homogeneous mixture, or a heterogeneous mixture: (a) seawater, (b) helium gas, (c) sodium chloride (table salt), (d) a bottle of soft drink, (e) a milkshake, (f) air in a bottle, (g) concrete.

Measurement

Review Questions

1.17 Name the SI base units that are important in chemistry. Give the SI units for expressing the following: (a) length, (b) volume, (c) mass, (d) time, (e) energy, (f) temperature.

1.18 Write the numbers represented by the following prefixes: (a) mega-, (b) kilo-, (c) deci-, (d) centi-, (e) milli-, (f) micro-, (g) nano-, (h) pico-.

1.19 What units do chemists normally use for density of liquids and solids? For gas density? Explain the differences.

1.20 Describe the three temperature scales used in the laboratory and in everyday life: the Fahrenheit scale, the Celsius scale, and the Kelvin scale.

Problems

1.21 Bromine is a reddish-brown liquid. Calculate its density (in g/mL) if 586 g of the substance occupies 188 mL.

1.22 The density of ethanol, a colorless liquid that is commonly known as grain alcohol, is 0.798 g/mL. Calculate the mass of 17.4 mL of the liquid.

1.23 Convert the following temperatures to degrees Celsius or Fahrenheit: (a) 95°F, the temperature on a hot summer day; (b) 12°F, the temperature on a cold winter day; (c) a 102°F fever; (d) a furnace operating at 1852°F; (e) −273.15°C (theoretically the lowest attainable temperature).

1.24 (a) Normally the human body can endure a temperature of 105°F for only short periods of time without permanent damage to the brain and other vital organs. What is this temperature in degrees Celsius? (b) Ethylene glycol is a liquid organic compound that is used as an antifreeze in car radiators. It freezes at −11.5°C. Calculate its freezing temperature in degrees Fahrenheit. (c) The temperature on the surface of the sun is about 6300°C. What is this temperature in degrees Fahrenheit? (d) The ignition temperature of paper is 451°F. What is the temperature in degrees Celsius?

1.25 Convert the following temperatures to kelvin: (a) 113°C, the melting point of sulfur, (b) 37°C, the normal body temperature, (c) 357°C, the boiling point of mercury.

1.26 Convert the following temperatures to degrees Celsius: (a) 77 K, the boiling point of liquid nitrogen, (b) 4.2 K, the boiling point of liquid helium, (c) 601 K, the melting point of lead.

Handling Numbers
Review Questions

1.27 What is the advantage of using scientific notation over decimal notation?

1.28 Define significant figure. Discuss the importance of using the proper number of significant figures in measurements and calculations.

Problems

1.29 Express the following numbers in scientific notation: (a) 0.000000027, (b) 356, (c) 47,764, (d) 0.096.

1.30 Express the following numbers as decimals: (a) 1.52×10^{-2}, (b) 7.78×10^{-8}.

1.31 Express the answers to the following calculations in scientific notation:
(a) $145.75 + (2.3 \times 10^{-1})$
(b) $79,500 \div (2.5 \times 10^2)$
(c) $(7.0 \times 10^{-3}) - (8.0 \times 10^{-4})$
(d) $(1.0 \times 10^4) \times (9.9 \times 10^6)$

1.32 Express the answers to the following calculations in scientific notation:
(a) $0.0095 + (8.5 \times 10^{-3})$
(b) $653 \div (5.75 \times 10^{-8})$
(c) $850,000 - (9.0 \times 10^5)$
(d) $(3.6 \times 10^{-4}) \times (3.6 \times 10^6)$

1.33 What is the number of significant figures in each of the following measurements?
(a) 4867 mi
(b) 56 mL
(c) 60,104 ton
(d) 2900 g
(e) 40.2 g/cm^3

(f) 0.0000003 cm
(g) 0.7 min
(h) 4.6×10^{19} atoms

1.34 How many significant figures are there in each of the following? (a) 0.006 L, (b) 0.0605 dm, (c) 60.5 mg, (d) 605.5 cm^2, (e) 960×10^{-3} g, (f) 6 kg, (g) 60 m.

1.35 Carry out the following operations as if they were calculations of experimental results, and express each answer in the correct units with the correct number of significant figures:
(a) 5.6792 m + 0.6 m + 4.33 m
(b) 3.70 g − 2.9133 g
(c) 4.51 cm × 3.6666 cm

1.36 Carry out the following operations as if they were calculations of experimental results, and express each answer in the correct units with the correct number of significant figures:
(a) 7.310 km ÷ 5.70 km
(b) $(3.26 \times 10^{-3} \text{ mg}) - (7.88 \times 10^{-5} \text{ mg})$
(c) $(4.02 \times 10^6 \text{ dm}) + (7.74 \times 10^7 \text{ dm})$

Dimensional Analysis
Problems

1.37 Carry out the following conversions: (a) 22.6 m to decimeters, (b) 25.4 mg to kilograms, (c) 556 mL to liters, (d) 10.6 kg/m^3 to g/cm^3.

1.38 Carry out the following conversions: (a) 242 lb to milligrams, (b) 68.3 cm^3 to cubic meters, (c) 7.2 m^3 to liters, (d) 28.3 μg to pounds.

1.39 The average speed of helium at 25°C is 1255 m/s. Convert this speed to miles per hour (mph).

1.40 How many seconds are there in a solar year (365.24 days)?

1.41 How many minutes does it take light from the sun to reach Earth? (The distance from the sun to Earth is 93 million mi; the speed of light = 3.00×10^8 m/s.)

1.42 A slow jogger runs a mile in 13 min. Calculate the speed in (a) in/s, (b) m/min, (c) km/h. (1 mi = 1609 m; 1 in = 2.54 cm.)

1.43 A 6.0-ft person weighs 168 lb. Express this person's height in meters and weight in kilograms. (1 lb = 453.6 g; 1 m = 3.28 ft.)

1.44 The current speed limit in some states in the United States is 55 miles per hour. What is the speed limit in kilometers per hour? (1 mi = 1609 m.)

1.45 For a fighter jet to take off from the deck of an aircraft carrier, it must reach a speed of 62 m/s. Calculate the speed in miles per hour (mph).

1.46 The "normal" lead content in human blood is about 0.40 part per million (that is, 0.40 g of lead per million grams of blood). A value of 0.80 part per million (ppm) is considered to be dangerous. How many grams of lead are contained in 6.0×10^3 g of blood (the amount in an average adult) if the lead content is 0.62 ppm?

1.47 Carry out the following conversions: (a) 1.42 light-years to miles (a light-year is an astronomical measure of distance—the distance traveled by light in a year, or 365 days; the speed of light is 3.00×10^8 m/s), (b) 32.4 yd to centimeters, (c) 3.0×10^{10} cm/s to ft/s.

1.48 Carry out the following conversions: (a) 185 nm to meters. (b) 4.5 billion years (roughly the age of Earth) to seconds. (Assume 365 days in a year.) (c) 71.2 cm^3 to m^3. (d) 88.6 m^3 to liters.

1.49 Aluminum is a lightweight metal (density = 2.70 g/cm^3) used in aircraft construction, high-voltage transmission lines, beverage cans, and foils. What is its density in kg/m^3?

1.50 The density of ammonia gas under certain conditions is 0.625 g/L. Calculate its density in g/cm^3.

Additional Problems

1.51 Give one qualitative and one quantitative statement about each of the following: (a) water, (b) carbon, (c) iron, (d) hydrogen gas, (e) sucrose (cane sugar), (f) table salt (sodium chloride), (g) mercury, (h) gold, (i) air.

1.52 Which of the following statements describe physical properties and which describe chemical properties? (a) Iron has a tendency to rust. (b) Rainwater in industrialized regions tends to be acidic. (c) Hemoglobin molecules have a red color. (d) When a glass of water is left out in the sun, the water gradually disappears. (e) Carbon dioxide in air is converted to more complex molecules by plants during photosynthesis.

1.53 In 2002, about 95.0 billion lb of sulfuric acid were produced in the United States. Convert this quantity to tons.

1.54 In determining the density of a rectangular metal bar, a student made the following measurements: length, 8.53 cm; width, 2.4 cm; height, 1.0 cm; mass, 52.7064 g. Calculate the density of the metal to the correct number of significant figures.

1.55 Calculate the mass of each of the following: (a) a sphere of gold with a radius of 10.0 cm [the volume of a sphere with a radius r is $V = (4/3)\pi r^3$; the density of gold = 19.3 g/cm^3], (b) a cube of platinum of edge length 0.040 mm (the density of platinum = 21.4 g/cm^3), (c) 50.0 mL of ethanol (the density of ethanol = 0.798 g/mL).

1.56 A cylindrical glass tube 12.7 cm in length is filled with mercury. The mass of mercury needed to fill the tube is 105.5 g. Calculate the inner diameter of the tube. (The density of mercury = 13.6 g/mL.)

1.57 The following procedure was used to determine the volume of a flask. The flask was weighed dry and then filled with water. If the masses of the empty flask and filled flask were 56.12 g and 87.39 g, respectively, and the density of water is 0.9976 g/cm^3, calculate the volume of the flask in cm^3.

1.58 The speed of sound in air at room temperature is about 343 m/s. Calculate this speed in miles per hour. (1 mi = 1609 m.)

1.59 A piece of silver (Ag) metal weighing 194.3 g is placed in a graduated cylinder containing 242.0 mL of water. The volume of water now reads 260.5 mL. From these data calculate the density of silver.

1.60 The experiment described in Problem 1.59 is a crude but convenient way to determine the density of some solids. Describe a similar experiment that would enable you to measure the density of ice. Specifically, what would be the requirements for the liquid used in your experiment?

1.61 A lead sphere has a mass of 1.20×10^4 g, and its volume is 1.05×10^3 cm^3. Calculate the density of lead.

1.62 Lithium is the least dense metal known (density: 0.53 g/cm^3). What is the volume occupied by 1.20×10^3 g of lithium?

1.63 The medicinal thermometer commonly used in homes can be read $\pm0.1°F$, whereas those in the doctor's office may be accurate to $\pm0.1°C$. In degrees Celsius, express the percent error expected from each of these thermometers in measuring a person's body temperature of 38.9°C.

1.64 Vanillin (used to flavor vanilla ice cream and other foods) is the substance whose aroma the human nose detects in the smallest amount. The threshold limit is 2.0×10^{-11} g per liter of air. If the current price of 50 g of vanillin is $112, determine the cost to supply enough vanillin so that the aroma could be detected in a large aircraft hangar with a volume of 5.0×10^7 ft^3.

1.65 At what temperature does the numerical reading on a Celsius thermometer equal that on a Fahrenheit thermometer?

1.66 Suppose that a new temperature scale has been devised on which the melting point of ethanol ($-117.3°C$) and the boiling point of ethanol (78.3°C) are taken as 0°S and 100°S, respectively, where S is the symbol for the new temperature scale. Derive an equation relating a reading on this scale to a reading on the Celsius scale. What would this thermometer read at 25°C?

1.67 A resting adult requires about 240 mL of pure oxygen/min and breathes about 12 times every minute. If inhaled air contains 20 percent oxygen by volume and exhaled air 16 percent, what is the volume of air per breath? (Assume that the volume of inhaled air is equal to that of exhaled air.)

1.68 (a) Referring to Problem 1.67, calculate the total volume (in liters) of air an adult breathes in a day. (b) In a city with heavy traffic, the air contains 2.1×10^{-6} L of carbon monoxide (a poisonous gas) per liter.

Calculate the average daily intake of carbon monoxide in liters by a person.

1.69 The total volume of seawater is 1.5×10^{21} L. Assume that seawater contains 3.1 percent sodium chloride by mass and that its density is 1.03 g/mL. Calculate the total mass of sodium chloride in kilograms and in tons. (1 ton = 2000 lb; 1 lb = 453.6 g.)

1.70 Magnesium (Mg) is a valuable metal used in alloys, in batteries, and in the manufacture of chemicals. It is obtained mostly from seawater, which contains about 1.3 g of Mg for every kilogram of seawater. Referring to Problem 1.69, calculate the volume of seawater (in liters) needed to extract 8.0×10^4 tons of Mg, which is roughly the annual production in the United States.

1.71 A student is given a crucible and asked to prove whether it is made of pure platinum. She first weighs the crucible in air and then weighs it suspended in water (density = 0.9986 g/mL). The readings are 860.2 g and 820.2 g, respectively. Based on these measurements and given that the density of platinum is 21.45 g/cm^3, what should her conclusion be? (*Hint:* An object suspended in a fluid is buoyed up by the mass of the fluid displaced by the object. Neglect the buoyance of air.)

1.72 The surface area and average depth of the Pacific Ocean are 1.8×10^8 km^2 and 3.9×10^3 m, respectively. Calculate the volume of water in the ocean in liters.

1.73 The unit "troy ounce" is often used for precious metals such as gold (Au) and platinum (Pt). (1 troy ounce = 31.103 g.) (a) A gold coin weighs 2.41 troy ounces. Calculate its mass in grams. (b) Is a troy ounce heavier or lighter than an ounce? (1 lb = 16 oz; 1 lb = 453.6 g.)

1.74 Osmium (Os) is the densest element known (density = 22.57 g/cm^3). Calculate the mass in pounds and in kilograms of an Os sphere 15 cm in diameter (about the size of a grapefruit). See Problem 1.55 for volume of a sphere.

1.75 Percent error is often expressed as the absolute value of the difference between the true value and the experimental value, divided by the true value:

$$\text{percent error} = \frac{|\text{true value} - \text{experimental value}|}{|\text{true value}|} \times 100\%$$

The vertical lines indicate absolute value. Calculate the percent error for the following measurements: (a) The density of alcohol (ethanol) is found to be 0.802 g/mL. (True value: 0.798 g/mL.) (b) The mass of gold in an earring is analyzed to be 0.837 g. (True value: 0.864 g.)

1.76 The natural abundances of elements in the human body, expressed as percent by mass, are: oxygen (O), 65 percent; carbon (C), 18 percent; hydrogen (H),

10 percent; nitrogen (N), 3 percent; calcium (Ca), 1.6 percent; phosphorus (P), 1.2 percent; all other elements, 1.2 percent. Calculate the mass in grams of each element in the body of a 62-kg person.

1.77 The men's world record for running a mile outdoors (as of 1997) is 3 min 44.39 s. At this rate, how long would it take to run a 1500-m race? (1 mi = 1609 m.)

1.78 Venus, the second closest planet to the sun, has a surface temperature of 7.3×10^2 K. Convert this temperature to °C and °F.

1.79 Chalcopyrite, the principal ore of copper (Cu), contains 34.63 percent Cu by mass. How many grams of Cu can be obtained from 5.11×10^3 kg of the ore?

1.80 It has been estimated that 8.0×10^4 tons of gold (Au) have been mined. Assume gold costs $350 per ounce. What is the total worth of this quantity of gold?

1.81 A 1.0-mL volume of seawater contains about 4.0×10^{-12} g of gold. The total volume of ocean water is 1.5×10^{21} L. Calculate the total amount of gold (in grams) that is present in seawater, and the worth of the gold in dollars (see Problem 1.80). With so much gold out there, why hasn't someone become rich by mining gold from the ocean?

1.82 Measurements show that 1.0 g of iron (Fe) contains 1.1×10^{22} Fe atoms. How many Fe atoms are in 4.9 g of Fe, which is the total amount of iron in the body of an average adult?

1.83 The thin outer layer of Earth, called the crust, contains only 0.50 percent of Earth's total mass and yet is the source of almost all the elements (the atmosphere provides elements such as oxygen, nitrogen, and a few other gases). Silicon (Si) is the second most abundant element in Earth's crust (27.2 percent by mass). Calculate the mass of silicon in kilograms in Earth's crust. (The mass of Earth is 5.9×10^{21} tons. 1 ton = 2000 lb; 1 lb = 453.6 g.)

1.84 The diameter of a copper (Cu) atom is roughly 1.3×10^{-10} m. How many times can you divide evenly a piece of 10-cm copper wire until it is reduced to two separate copper atoms? (Assume there are appropriate tools for this procedure and that copper atoms are lined up in a straight line, in contact with each other. Round off your answer to an integer.)

1.85 One gallon of gasoline in an automobile's engine produces on the average 9.5 kg of carbon dioxide, which is a greenhouse gas, that is, it promotes the warming of Earth's atmosphere. Calculate the annual production of carbon dioxide in kilograms if there are 40 million cars in the United States and each car covers a distance of 5000 mi at a consumption rate of 20 miles per gallon.

1.86 A sheet of aluminum (Al) foil has a total area of 1.000 ft^2 and a mass of 3.636 g. What is the thickness of the foil in millimeters? (Density of Al = 2.699 g/cm^3.)

1.87 Comment on whether each of the following is a homogeneous mixture or a heterogeneous mixture: (a) air in a closed bottle and (b) air over New York City.

1.88 Chlorine is used to disinfect swimming pools. The accepted concentration for this purpose is 1 ppm chlorine, or 1 g of chlorine per million grams of water. Calculate the volume of a chlorine solution (in milliliters) a homeowner should add to her swimming pool if the solution contains 6.0 percent chlorine by mass and there are 2.0×10^4 gallons of water in the pool. (1 gallon = 3.79 L; density of liquids = 1.0 g/mL.)

1.89 The world's total petroleum reserve is estimated at 2.0×10^{22} J (joule is the unit of energy where 1 J = 1 kg m^2/s^2). At the present rate of consumption, 1.8×10^{20} J/yr, how long would it take to exhaust the supply?

1.90 In water conservation, chemists spread a thin film of certain inert material over the surface of water to cut down the rate of evaporation of water in reservoirs. This technique was pioneered by Benjamin Franklin three centuries ago. Franklin found that 0.10 mL of oil could spread over the surface of water of about 40 m^2 in area. Assuming that the oil forms a *monolayer*, that is, a layer that is only one molecule thick, estimate the length of each oil molecule in nanometers. (1 nm = 1×10^{-9} m.)

1.91 Fluoridation is the process of adding fluorine compounds to drinking water to help fight tooth decay. A concentration of 1 ppm of fluorine is sufficient for the purpose. (1 ppm means one part per million, or 1 g of fluorine per 1 million g of water.) The compound normally chosen for fluoridation is sodium fluoride, which is also added to some toothpastes. Calculate the quantity of sodium fluoride in kilograms needed per year for a city of 50,000 people if the daily consumption of water per person is 150 gallons. What percent of the sodium fluoride is "wasted" if each person uses only 6.0 L of water a day for drinking and cooking? (Sodium fluoride is 45.0 percent fluorine by mass. 1 gallon = 3.79 L; 1 year = 365 days; 1 ton = 2000 lb; 1 lb = 453.6 g; density of water = 1.0 g/mL.)

1.92 A gas company in Massachusetts charges $1.30 for 15.0 ft^3 of natural gas. (a) Convert this rate to dollars per liter of gas. (b) If it takes 0.304 ft^3 of gas to boil a liter of water, starting at room temperature (25°C), how much would it cost to boil a 2.1-L kettle of water?

1.93 Pheromones are compounds secreted by females of many insect species to attract mates. Typically, 1.0×10^{-8} g of a pheromone is sufficient to reach all targeted males within a radius of 0.50 mi. Calculate the density of the pheromone (in grams per liter) in a circular air space having a radius of 0.50 mi and a height of 40 ft.

Answers to Practice Exercises

1.1 96.5 g. **1.2** 341 g. **1.3** (a) 621.5°F, (b) 78.3°C, (c) −196°C. **1.4** (a) Two, (b) four, (c) three, (d) two, (e) three or two. **1.5** (a) 26.76 L, (b) 4.4 g, (c) 1.6×10^7 dm^2, (d) 0.0756 g/mL, (e) 6.69×10^4 m. **1.6** 2.36 lb. **1.7** 1.08×10^5 m^3. **1.8** 0.534 g/cm^3.

CHEMICAL MYSTERY

The Disappearance of the Dinosaurs

Dinosaurs dominated life on Earth for millions of years and then disappeared very suddenly. To solve the mystery, paleontologists studied fossils and skeletons found in rocks in various layers of Earth's crust. Their findings enabled them to map out which species existed on Earth during specific geologic periods. They also revealed no dinosaur skeletons in rocks

formed immediately after the Cretaceous period, which dates back some 65 million years. It is therefore assumed that the dinosaurs became extinct about 65 million years ago.

Among the many hypotheses put forward to account for their disappearance were disruptions of the food chain and a dramatic change in climate caused by violent volcanic eruptions. However, there was no convincing evidence for any one hypothesis until 1977. It was then that a group of paleontologists working in Italy obtained some very puzzling data at a site near Gubbio. The chemical analysis of a layer of clay deposited above sediments formed during the Cretaceous period (and therefore a layer that records events occurring *after* the Cretaceous period) showed a surprisingly high content of the element iridium (Ir). Iridium is very rare in Earth's crust but is comparatively abundant in asteroids.

This investigation led to the hypothesis that the extinction of dinosaurs occurred as follows. To account for the quantity of iridium found, scientists suggested that a large asteroid several miles in diameter hit Earth about the time the dinosaurs disappeared. The impact of the asteroid on Earth's surface must have been so tremendous that it literally vaporized a large quantity of surrounding rocks, soils, and other objects. The resulting dust and debris floated through the air and blocked the sunlight for months or perhaps years. Without ample sunlight most plants could not grow, and the fossil record confirms that many types of plants did indeed die out at this time. Consequently, of course, many plant-eating animals perished, and then, in turn, meat-eating animals began to starve. Dwindling food sources would obviously affect large animals needing great amounts of food more quickly and more severely than small animals. Therefore, the huge dinosaurs, the largest of which might have weighed as much as 30 tons, vanished due to lack of food.

Chemical Clues

1. How does the study of dinosaur extinction illustrate the scientific method?

2. Suggest two ways that would enable you to test the asteroid collision hypothesis.

3. In your opinion, is it justifiable to refer to the asteroid explanation as the theory of dinosaur extinction?

4. Available evidence suggests that about 20 percent of the asteroid's mass turned to dust and spread uniformly over Earth after settling out of the upper atmosphere. This dust amounted to about 0.02 g/cm^2 of Earth's surface. The asteroid very likely had a density of about 2 g/cm^3. Calculate the mass (in kilograms and tons) of the asteroid and its radius in meters, assuming that it was a sphere. (The area of Earth is 5.1×10^{14} m^2; 1 lb = 453.6 g.) (Source: *Consider a Spherical Cow—A Course in Environmental Problem Solving* by J. Harte, University Science Books, Mill Valley, CA 1988. Used with permission.)

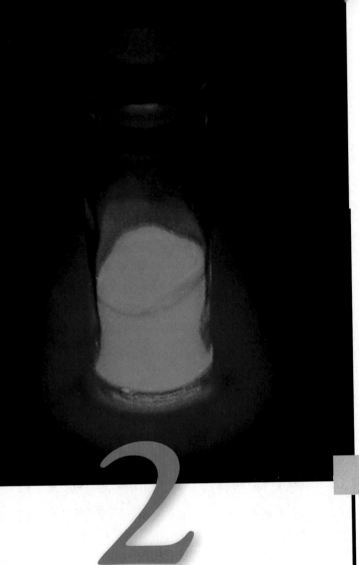

The glow from the radioactive decay of radium (Ra). Study of radioactivity helped to advance scientists' knowledge about atomic structure. The models show the nuclei of radium and its radioactive decay products—radon (Rn) and an alpha particle, which has two protons and two neutrons.

2

Atoms, Molecules, and Ions

Interactive Activity Summary

1. Animation: Cathode Ray Tube (2.2)
2. Animation: Millikan Oil Drop (2.2)
3. Animation: Alpha, Beta, and Gamma Rays (2.2)
4. Animation: α-Particle Scattering (2.2)
5. Interactivity: Build an Ionic Compound (2.6)
6. Interactivity: Build a Covalent Compound (2.7)

Since ancient times humans have pondered the nature of matter. Our modern ideas of the structure of matter began to take shape in the early nineteenth century with Dalton's atomic theory. We now know that all matter is made of atoms, molecules, and ions. All of chemistry is concerned in one way or another with these species.

2.1 The Atomic Theory

In the fifth century B.C. the Greek philosopher Democritus expressed the belief that all matter consists of very small, indivisible particles, which he named *atomos* (meaning uncuttable or indivisible). Although Democritus' idea was not accepted by many of his contemporaries (notably Plato and Aristotle), somehow it endured. Experimental evidence from early scientific investigations provided support for the notion of "atomism" and gradually gave rise to the modern definitions of elements and compounds. It was in 1808 that an English scientist and school teacher, John Dalton,[†] formulated a precise definition of the indivisible building blocks of matter that we call atoms.

Dalton's work marked the beginning of the modern era of chemistry. The hypotheses about the nature of matter on which Dalton's atomic theory is based can be summarized as follows:

1. Elements are composed of extremely small particles called atoms. All atoms of a given element are identical, having the same size, mass, and chemical properties. The atoms of one element are different from the atoms of all other elements.

2. Compounds are composed of atoms of more than one element. In any compound, the ratio of the numbers of atoms of any two of the elements present is either an integer or a simple fraction.

3. A chemical reaction involves only the separation, combination, or rearrangement of atoms; it does not result in their creation or destruction.

Figure 2.1 is a schematic representation of the first two hypotheses.

Dalton's concept of an atom was far more detailed and specific than Democritus'. The first hypothesis states that atoms of one element are different from atoms of all other elements. Dalton made no attempt to describe the structure or composition of atoms—he had no idea what an atom is really like. But he did realize that the different properties shown by elements such as hydrogen and oxygen can be explained by assuming that hydrogen atoms are not the same as oxygen atoms.

The second hypothesis suggests that, in order to form a certain compound, we need not only atoms of the right kinds of elements, but specific numbers of these

---

[†]John Dalton (1766–1844). English chemist, mathematician, and philosopher. In addition to the atomic theory, he also formulated several gas laws and gave the first detailed description of color blindness, from which he suffered. Dalton was described as an indifferent experimenter, and singularly wanting in the language and power of illustration. His only recreation was lawn bowling on Thursday afternoons. Perhaps it was the sight of those wooden balls that provided him with the idea of the atomic theory.

Figure 2.1 *(a) According to Dalton's atomic theory, atoms of the same element are identical, but atoms of one element are different from atoms of other elements. (b) Compounds formed from atoms of elements X and Y. In this case, the ratio of the atoms of element X to the atoms of element Y is 2:1.*

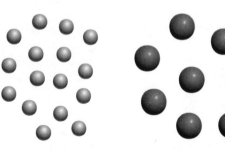

Atoms of element X

Atoms of element Y

Compounds of elements X and Y

(a)

(b)

Carbon monoxide $\dfrac{O}{C} = \dfrac{\bullet}{\bullet} = \dfrac{1}{1}$

Figure 2.2 *An illustration of the law of multiple proportions.*

Carbon dioxide $\dfrac{O}{C} = \dfrac{\bullet\ \bullet}{\bullet} = \dfrac{2}{1}$

Ratio of oxygen in carbon monoxide to oxygen in carbon dioxide: 1:2

atoms as well. This idea is an extension of a law published in 1799 by Joseph Proust,[†] a French chemist. Proust's **law of definite proportions** states that *different samples of the same compound always contain its constituent elements in the same proportion by mass.* Thus, if we were to analyze samples of carbon dioxide gas obtained from different sources, we would find in each sample the same ratio by mass of carbon to oxygen. It stands to reason, then, that if the ratio of the masses of different elements in a given compound is fixed, the ratio of the atoms of these elements in the compound also must be constant.

Dalton's second hypothesis supports another important law, the **law of multiple proportions.** According to the law, *if two elements can combine to form more than one compound, the masses of one element that combine with a fixed mass of the other element are in ratios of small whole numbers.* Dalton's theory explains the law of multiple proportions quite simply: Different compounds made up of the same elements differ in the number of atoms of each kind that combine. For example, carbon forms two stable compounds with oxygen, namely, carbon monoxide and carbon dioxide. Modern measurement techniques indicate that one atom of carbon combines with one atom of oxygen in carbon monoxide and with two atoms of oxygen in carbon dioxide. Thus, the ratio of oxygen in carbon monoxide to oxygen in carbon dioxide is 1:2. This result is consistent with the law of multiple proportions (Figure 2.2).

Dalton's third hypothesis is another way of stating the **law of conservation of mass,**[‡] which is that *matter can be neither created nor destroyed.* Because matter is made of atoms that are unchanged in a chemical reaction, it follows that mass must be conserved as well. Dalton's brilliant insight into the nature of matter was the main stimulus for the rapid progress of chemistry during the nineteenth century.

2.2 The Structure of the Atom

On the basis of Dalton's atomic theory, we can define an **atom** as *the basic unit of an element that can enter into chemical combination.* Dalton imagined an atom that was both extremely small and indivisible. However, a series of investigations that began in the 1850s and extended into the twentieth century clearly demonstrated that atoms actually possess internal structure; that is, they are made up of even

---

[†]Joseph Louis Proust (1754–1826). French chemist. Proust was the first person to isolate sugar from grapes.

[‡]According to Albert Einstein, mass and energy are alternate aspects of a single entity called *mass-energy.* Chemical reactions usually involve a gain or loss of heat and other forms of energy. Thus when energy is lost in a reaction, for example, mass is also lost. Except for nuclear reactions (see Chapter 23), however, changes of mass in chemical reactions are too small to detect. Therefore, for all practical purposes mass is conserved.

Figure 2.3 *A cathode ray tube with an electric field perpendicular to the direction of the cathode rays and an external magnetic field. The symbols N and S denote the north and south poles of the magnet. The cathode rays will strike the end of the tube at A in the presence of a magnetic field, at C in the presence of an electric field, and at B when there are no external fields present or when the effects of the electric field and magnetic field cancel each other.*

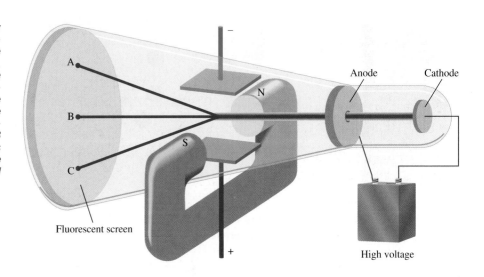

Fluorescent screen

Anode   Cathode

High voltage

smaller particles, which are called *subatomic particles.* This research led to the discovery of three such particles—electrons, protons, and neutrons.

The Electron

Animation: Cathode
Ray Tube
Online Learning Center,
Animations

In the 1890s many scientists became caught up in the study of **radiation,** *the emission and transmission of energy through space in the form of waves.* Information gained from this research contributed greatly to our understanding of atomic structure. One device used to investigate this phenomenon was a cathode ray tube, the forerunner of the television tube (Figure 2.3). It is a glass tube from which most of the air has been evacuated. When the two metal plates are connected to a high-voltage source, the negatively charged plate, called the *cathode,* emits an invisible ray. The cathode ray is drawn to the positively charged plate, called the *anode,* where it passes through a hole and continues traveling to the other end of the tube. When the ray strikes the specially coated surface, it produces a strong fluorescence, or bright light.

In some experiments two electrically charged plates and a magnet were added to the *outside* of the cathode ray tube (see Figure 2.3). When the magnetic field is on and the electric field is off, the cathode ray strikes point A. When only the electric field is on, the ray strikes point C. When both the magnetic and the electric fields are off or when they are both on but balanced so that they cancel each other's influence, the ray strikes point B. According to electromagnetic theory, a moving charged body behaves like a magnet and can interact with electric and magnetic fields through which it passes. Because the cathode ray is attracted by the plate bearing positive charges and repelled by the plate bearing negative charges, it must consist of negatively charged particles. We know these *negatively charged particles* as **electrons.** Figure 2.4 shows the effect of a bar magnet on the cathode ray.

Electrons are normally associated with atoms. However, they can also be studied individually.

An English physicist, J. J. Thomson,[†] used a cathode ray tube and his knowledge of electromagnetic theory to determine the ratio of electric charge to the mass of an individual electron. The number he came up with was -1.76×10^8 C/g, where C stands for *coulomb,* which is the unit of electric charge. Thereafter, in a series of experiments

---

[†]Joseph John Thomson (1856–1940). British physicist who received the Nobel Prize in Physics in 1906 for discovering the electron.

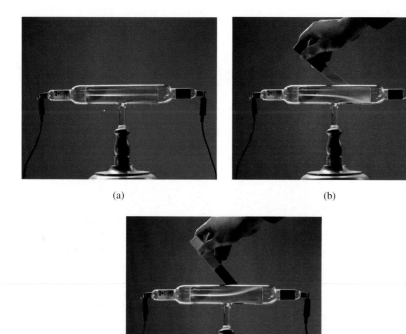

(a)   (b)

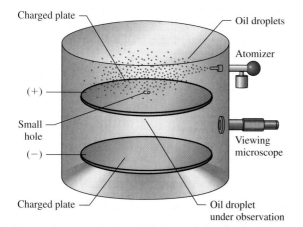

(c)

Figure 2.4 (a) A cathode ray produced in a discharge tube travels from left to right. The ray itself is invisible, but the fluorescence of a zinc sulfide coating on the glass causes it to appear green. (b) The cathode ray is bent downward when the south pole of the bar magnet is brought toward it. (c) When the polarity of the magnet is reversed, the ray bends in the opposite direction.

carried out between 1908 and 1917, R. A. Millikan[†] succeeded in measuring the charge of the electron with great precision. His work proved that the charge on each electron was exactly the same. In his experiment, Millikan examined the motion of single tiny drops of oil that picked up static charge from ions in the air. He suspended the charged drops in air by applying an electric field and followed their motions through a microscope (Figure 2.5). Using his knowledge of electrostatics, Millikan

Animation: Millikan Oil Drop
Online Learning Center, Animations

[†]Robert Andrews Millikan (1868–1953). American physicist who was awarded the Nobel Prize in Physics in 1923 for determining the charge of the electron.

Charged plate

Oil droplets

Atomizer

(+)

Small hole

(−)

Viewing microscope

Charged plate

Oil droplet under observation

Figure 2.5 Schematic diagram of Millikan's oil drop experiment.

found the charge of an electron to be -1.6022×10^{-19} C. From these data he calculated the mass of an electron:

$$\text{mass of an electron} = \frac{\text{charge}}{\text{charge/mass}}$$
$$= \frac{-1.6022 \times 10^{-19}\,\text{C}}{-1.76 \times 10^{8}\,\text{C/g}}$$
$$= 9.10 \times 10^{-28}\,\text{g}$$

This is an exceedingly small mass.

Radioactivity

In 1895, the German physicist Wilhelm Röntgen[†] noticed that cathode rays caused glass and metals to emit very unusual rays. This highly energetic radiation penetrated matter, darkened covered photographic plates, and caused a variety of substances to fluoresce. Because these rays could not be deflected by a magnet, they could not contain charged particles as cathode rays do. Röntgen called them X rays because their nature was not known.

Not long after Röntgen's discovery, Antoine Becquerel,[‡] a professor of physics in Paris, began to study the fluorescent properties of substances. Purely by accident, he found that exposing thickly wrapped photographic plates to a certain uranium compound caused them to darken, even without the stimulation of cathode rays. Like X rays, the rays from the uranium compound were highly energetic and could not be deflected by a magnet, but they differed from X rays because they arose spontaneously. One of Becquerel's students, Marie Curie,[§] suggested the name *radioactivity* to describe this *spontaneous emission of particles and/or radiation.* Since then, any element that spontaneously emits radiation is said to be *radioactive.*

Animation: Alpha, Beta, and Gamma Rays
Online Learning Center, Animations

Three types of rays are produced by the *decay,* or breakdown, of radioactive substances such as uranium. Two of the three are deflected by oppositely charged metal plates (Figure 2.6). ***Alpha (α) rays*** consist of *positively charged particles,* called ***α particles,*** and therefore are deflected by the positively charged plate. ***Beta (β) rays,*** or ***β particles,*** are *electrons* and are deflected by the negatively charged plate. The third type of radioactive radiation consists of high-energy rays called ***gamma (γ) rays.*** Like X rays, γ rays have no charge and are not affected by an external field.

The Proton and the Nucleus

By the early 1900s, two features of atoms had become clear: they contain electrons, and they are electrically neutral. To maintain electric neutrality, an atom must contain an equal number of positive and negative charges. Therefore, Thomson proposed that an atom could be thought of as a uniform, positive sphere of matter in which electrons

---

[†]Wilhelm Konrad Röntgen (1845–1923). German physicist who received the Nobel Prize in Physics in 1901 for the discovery of X rays.

[‡]Antoine Henri Becquerel (1852–1908). French physicist who was awarded the Nobel Prize in Physics in 1903 for discovering radioactivity in uranium.

[§]Marie (Marya Sklodowska) Curie (1867–1934). Polish-born chemist and physicist. In 1903 she and her French husband, Pierre Curie, were awarded the Nobel Prize in Physics for their work on radioactivity. In 1911, she again received the Nobel prize, this time in chemistry, for her work on the radioactive elements radium and polonium. She is one of only three people to have received two Nobel prizes in science. Despite her great contribution to science, her nomination to the French Academy of Sciences in 1911 was rejected by one vote because she was a woman! Her daughter Irene, and son-in-law Frederic Joliot-Curie, shared the Nobel Prize in Chemistry in 1935.

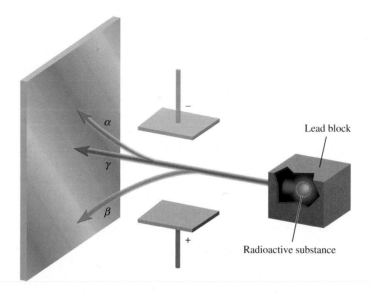

Figure 2.6 *Three types of rays emitted by radioactive elements. β rays consist of negatively charged particles (electrons) and are therefore attracted by the positively charged plate. The opposite holds true for α rays—they are positively charged and are drawn to the negatively charged plate. Because γ rays have no charge, their path is unaffected by an external electric field.*

are embedded like raisins in a cake (Figure 2.7). This so-called "plum-pudding" model was the accepted theory for a number of years.

In 1910 the New Zealand physicist Ernest Rutherford,[†] who had studied with Thomson at Cambridge University, decided to use α particles to probe the structure of atoms. Together with his associate Hans Geiger[‡] and an undergraduate named Ernest Marsden,[§] Rutherford carried out a series of experiments using very thin foils of gold and other metals as targets for α particles from a radioactive source (Figure 2.8). They

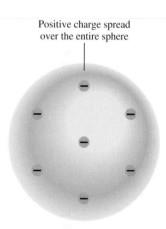

Figure 2.7 *Thomson's model of the atom, sometimes described as the "plum-pudding" model, after a traditional English dessert containing raisins. The electrons are embedded in a uniform, positively charged sphere.*

[†]Ernest Rutherford (1871–1937). New Zealand physicist. Rutherford did most of his work in England (Manchester and Cambridge universities). He received the Nobel Prize in Chemistry in 1908 for his investigations into the structure of the atomic nucleus. His often-quoted comment to his students was that "all science is either physics or stamp-collecting."

[‡]Johannes Hans Wilhelm Geiger (1882–1945). German physicist. Geiger's work focused on the structure of the atomic nucleus and on radioactivity. He invented a device for measuring radiation that is now commonly called the Geiger counter.

[§]Ernest Marsden (1889–1970). English physicist. It is gratifying to know that at times an undergraduate can assist in winning a Nobel Prize. Marsden went on to contribute significantly to the development of science in New Zealand.

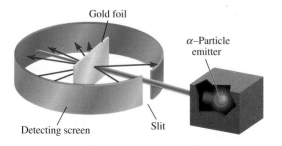

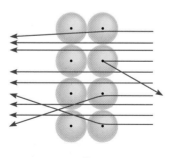

Figure 2.8 *(a) Rutherford's experimental design for measuring the scattering of α particles by a piece of gold foil. Most of the α particles passed through the gold foil with little or no deflection. A few were deflected at wide angles. Occasionally an α particle was turned back. (b) Magnified view of α particles passing through and being deflected by nuclei.*

(a)   (b)

Animation: α-Particle
Scattering
Online Learning Center,
Animations

observed that the majority of particles penetrated the foil either undeflected or with only a slight deflection. But every now and then an α particle was scattered (or deflected) at a large angle. In some instances, an α particle actually bounced back in the direction from which it had come! This was a most surprising finding, for in Thomson's model the positive charge of the atom was so diffuse that the positive α particles should have passed through the foil with very little deflection. To quote Rutherford's initial reaction when told of this discovery: "It was as incredible as if you had fired a 15-inch shell at a piece of tissue paper and it came back and hit you."

Rutherford was later able to explain the results of the α-scattering experiment in terms of a new model for the atom. According to Rutherford, most of the atom must be empty space. This explains why the majority of α particles passed through the gold foil with little or no deflection. The atom's positive charges, Rutherford proposed, are all concentrated in the **nucleus,** which is *a dense central core within the atom*. Whenever an α particle came close to a nucleus in the scattering experiment, it experienced a large repulsive force and therefore a large deflection. Moreover, an α particle traveling directly toward a nucleus would be completely repelled and its direction would be reversed.

The positively charged particles in the nucleus are called **protons.** In separate experiments, it was found that each proton carries the same *quantity* of charge as an electron and has a mass of 1.67262×10^{-24} g—about 1840 times the mass of the oppositely charged electron.

At this stage of investigation, scientists perceived the atom as follows: The mass of a nucleus constitutes most of the mass of the entire atom, but the nucleus occupies only about $1/10^{13}$ of the volume of the atom. We express atomic (and molecular) dimensions in terms of the SI unit called the *picometer (pm)*, where

$$1 \text{ pm} = 1 \times 10^{-12} \text{ m}$$

A common non-SI unit for atomic length is the angstrom (Å; 1 Å = 100 pm).

A typical atomic radius is about 100 pm, whereas the radius of an atomic nucleus is only about 5×10^{-3} pm. You can appreciate the relative sizes of an atom and its nucleus by imagining that if an atom were the size of the Houston Astrodome, the volume of its nucleus would be comparable to that of a small marble. While the protons are confined to the nucleus of the atom, the electrons are conceived of as being spread out about the nucleus at some distance from it.

Figure 2.9 *The protons and neutrons of an atom are packed in an extremely small nucleus. Electrons are shown as "clouds" around the nucleus.*

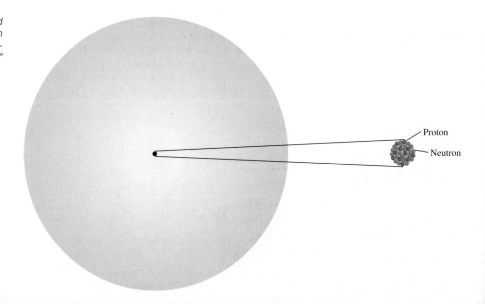

Proton

Neutron

TABLE 2.1

Mass and Charge of Subatomic Particles

Particle	Mass (g)	Charge	
		Coulomb	Charge Unit
Electron*	9.10939×10^{-28}	-1.6022×10^{-19}	-1
Proton	1.67262×10^{-24}	$+1.6022 \times 10^{-19}$	$+1$
Neutron	1.67493×10^{-24}	0	0

* More refined measurements have given us a more accurate value of an electron's mass than Millikan's.

The concept of atomic radius is useful experimentally, but it should not be inferred that atoms have well-defined boundaries or surfaces. We will learn later that the outer regions of atoms are relatively "fuzzy."

The Neutron

Rutherford's model of atomic structure left one major problem unsolved. It was known that hydrogen, the simplest atom, contains only one proton and that the helium atom contains two protons. Therefore, the ratio of the mass of a helium atom to that of a hydrogen atom should be 2:1. (Because electrons are much lighter than protons, their contribution to atomic mass can be ignored.) In reality, however, the ratio is 4:1. Rutherford and others postulated that there must be another type of subatomic particle in the atomic nucleus; the proof was provided by another English physicist, James Chadwick,[†] in 1932. When Chadwick bombarded a thin sheet of beryllium with α particles, a very high-energy radiation similar to γ rays was emitted by the metal. Later experiments showed that the rays actually consisted of a third type of subatomic particles, which Chadwick named **neutrons,** because they proved to be *electrically neutral particles having a mass slightly greater than that of protons.* The mystery of the mass ratio could now be explained. In the helium nucleus there are two protons and two neutrons, but in the hydrogen nucleus there is only one proton and no neutrons; therefore, the ratio is 4:1.

Figure 2.9 shows the location of the elementary particles (protons, neutrons, and electrons) in an atom. There are other subatomic particles, but the electron, the proton, and the neutron are the three fundamental components of the atom that are important in chemistry. Table 2.1 shows the masses and charges of these three elementary particles.

2.3 Atomic Number, Mass Number, and Isotopes

All atoms can be identified by the number of protons and neutrons they contain. The **atomic number (Z)** is *the number of protons in the nucleus of each atom of an element.* In a neutral atom the number of protons is equal to the number of electrons, so the atomic number also indicates the number of electrons present in the atom. The chemical identity of an atom can be determined solely from its atomic number. For example, the atomic number of nitrogen is 7. This means that each neutral nitrogen

[†]James Chadwick (1891–1972). British physicist. In 1935 he received the Nobel Prize in Physics for proving the existence of neutrons.

atom has 7 protons and 7 electrons. Or, viewed another way, every atom in the universe that contains 7 protons is correctly named "nitrogen."

The **mass number (A)** is *the total number of neutrons and protons present in the nucleus of an atom of an element.* Except for the most common form of hydrogen, which has one proton and no neutrons, all atomic nuclei contain both protons and neutrons. In general the mass number is given by

$$\text{mass number} = \text{number of protons} + \text{number of neutrons}$$
$$= \text{atomic number} + \text{number of neutrons}$$

The number of neutrons in an atom is equal to the difference between the mass number and the atomic number, or $(A - Z)$. For example, the mass number of fluorine is 19 and the atomic number is 9 (indicating 9 protons in the nucleus). Thus the number of neutrons in an atom of fluorine is $19 - 9 = 10$. Note that the atomic number, number of neutrons, and mass number all must be positive integers (whole numbers).

Atoms of a given element do not all have the same mass. Most elements have two or more **isotopes,** *atoms that have the same atomic number but different mass numbers.* For example, there are three isotopes of hydrogen. One, simply known as hydrogen, has one proton and no neutrons. The *deuterium* isotope contains one proton and one neutron, and *tritium* has one proton and two neutrons. The accepted way to denote the atomic number and mass number of an atom of an element (X) is as follows:

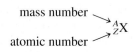

Thus, for the isotopes of hydrogen, we write

$$^1_1\text{H} \qquad ^2_1\text{H} \qquad ^3_1\text{H}$$
hydrogen deuterium tritium

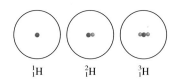

As another example, consider two common isotopes of uranium with mass numbers of 235 and 238, respectively:

$$^{235}_{92}\text{U} \qquad ^{238}_{92}\text{U}$$

The first isotope is used in nuclear reactors and atomic bombs, whereas the second isotope lacks the properties necessary for these applications. With the exception of hydrogen, which has different names for each of its isotopes, isotopes of elements are identified by their mass numbers. Thus the preceding two isotopes are called uranium-235 (pronounced "uranium two thirty-five") and uranium-238 (pronounced "uranium two thirty-eight").

The chemical properties of an element are determined primarily by the protons and electrons in its atoms; neutrons do not take part in chemical changes under normal conditions. Therefore, isotopes of the same element have similar chemistries, forming the same types of compounds and displaying similar reactivities.

Example 2.1 shows how to calculate the number of protons, neutrons, and electrons using atomic numbers and mass numbers.

Example 2.1

Give the number of protons, neutrons, and electrons in each of the following species: (a) $^{17}_8\text{O}$, (b) $^{199}_{80}\text{Hg}$, and (c) $^{200}_{80}\text{Hg}$.

(Continued)

Strategy Recall that the superscript denotes mass number and the subscript denotes atomic number. Mass number is always greater than atomic number. (The only exception is $^1_1$H, where the mass number is equal to the atomic number.)

Solution

(a) The atomic number is 8, so there are 8 protons. The mass number is 17, so the number of neutrons is $17 - 8 = 9$. The number of electrons is the same as the number of protons, that is, 8.

(b) The atomic number is 80, so there are 80 protons. The mass number is 199, so the number of neutrons is $199 - 80 = 119$. The number of electrons is 80.

(c) Here the number of protons is the same as in (b), or 80. The number of neutrons is $200 - 80 = 120$. The number of electrons is also the same as in (b), 80. The species in (b) and (c) are chemically similar isotopes of mercury.

Similar problems: 2.15, 2.16.

Practice Exercise How many protons, neutrons, and electrons are in the following isotope of copper: $^{63}_{29}$Cu?

2.4 The Periodic Table

More than half of the elements known today were discovered between 1800 and 1900. During this period, chemists noted that many elements show strong similarities to one another. Recognition of periodic regularities in physical and chemical behavior and the need to organize the large volume of available information about the structure and properties of elemental substances led to the development of the *periodic table, a chart in which elements having similar chemical and physical properties are grouped together.* Figure 2.10 shows the modern periodic table in which the elements are arranged by atomic number (shown above the element symbol) in *horizontal rows* called *periods* and in *vertical columns* known as *groups* or *families,* according to similarities in their chemical properties. Note that Elements 110–112 and 114 have recently been synthesized, although they have not yet been named.

The elements can be divided into three categories—metals, nonmetals, and metalloids. A *metal* is *a good conductor of heat and electricity* while a *nonmetal* is usually *a poor conductor of heat and electricity.* A *metalloid has properties that are intermediate between those of metals and nonmetals.* Figure 2.10 shows that the majority of known elements are metals; only 17 elements are nonmetals, and 8 elements are metalloids. From left to right across any period, the physical and chemical properties of the elements change gradually from metallic to nonmetallic.

Elements are often referred to collectively by their periodic table group number (Group 1A, Group 2A, and so on). However, for convenience, some element groups have been given special names. *The Group 1A elements (Li, Na, K, Rb, Cs, and Fr) are called alkali metals,* and *the Group 2A elements (Be, Mg, Ca, Sr, Ba, and Ra) are called alkaline earth metals. Elements in Group 7A (F, Cl, Br, I, and At) are known as halogens, and elements in Group 8A (He, Ne, Ar, Kr, Xe, and Rn) are called noble gases,* or *rare gases.*

The periodic table is a handy tool that correlates the properties of the elements in a systematic way and helps us to make predictions about chemical behavior. We will take a closer look at this keystone of chemistry in Chapter 8.

The Chemistry in Action essay on p. 53 describes the distribution of the elements on Earth and in the human body.

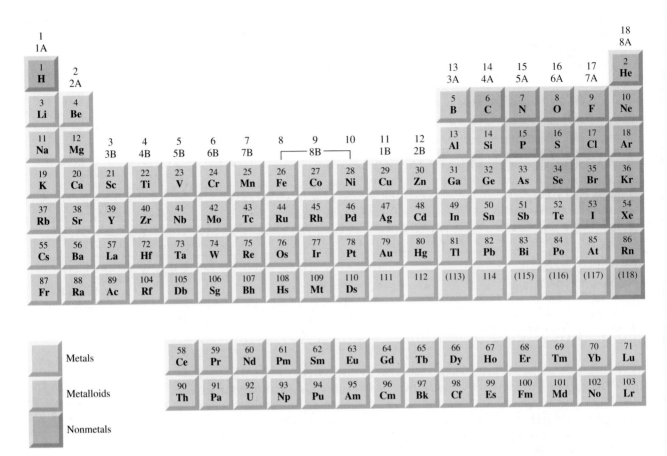

Figure 2.10 *The modern periodic table. The elements are arranged according to the atomic numbers above their symbols. With the exception of hydrogen (H), nonmetals appear at the far right of the table. The two rows of metals beneath the main body of the table are conventionally set apart to keep the table from being too wide. Actually, cerium (Ce) should follow lanthanum (La), and thorium (Th) should come right after actinium (Ac). The 1–18 group designation has been recommended by the International Union of Pure and Applied Chemistry (IUPAC) but is not yet in wide use. In this text we use the standard U.S. notation for group numbers (1A–8A and 1B–8B). Elements 113 and 115–118 have not yet been synthesized.*

2.5 Molecules and Ions

Of all the elements, only the six noble gases in Group 8A of the periodic table (He, Ne, Ar, Kr, Xe, and Rn) exist in nature as single atoms. For this reason, they are called *monatomic* (meaning a single atom) gases. Most matter is composed of molecules or ions formed by atoms.

Molecules

We will discuss the nature of chemical bonds in Chapters 9 and 10.

A *molecule* is an *aggregate of at least two atoms in a definite arrangement held together by chemical forces* (also called *chemical bonds*). A molecule may contain atoms of the same element or atoms of two or more elements joined in a fixed ratio, in accordance with the law of definite proportions stated in Section 2.1. Thus, a molecule is not necessarily a compound, which, by definition, is made up of two or more elements (see Section 1.2). Hydrogen gas, for example, is a pure element, but it consists of molecules made up of two H atoms each. Water, on the other hand, is a molecular

Distribution of Elements on Earth and in Living Systems

The majority of elements are naturally occurring. How are these elements distributed on Earth, and which are essential to living systems?

Earth's crust extends from the surface to a depth of about 40 km (about 25 mi). Because of technical difficulties, scientists have not been able to study the inner portions of Earth as easily as the crust. Nevertheless, it is believed that there is a solid core consisting mostly of iron at the center of Earth. Surrounding the core is a layer called the *mantle*, which consists of hot fluid containing iron, carbon, silicon, and sulfur.

Of the 83 elements that are found in nature, 12 make up 99.7 percent of Earth's crust by mass. They are, in decreasing order of natural abundance, oxygen (O), silicon (Si), aluminum (Al), iron (Fe), calcium (Ca), magnesium (Mg), sodium (Na),

potassium (K), titanium (Ti), hydrogen (H), phosphorus (P), and manganese (Mn). In discussing the natural abundance of the elements, we should keep in mind that (1) the elements are not evenly distributed throughout Earth's crust, and (2) most elements occur in combined forms. These facts provide the basis for most methods of obtaining pure elements from their compounds, as we will see in later chapters.

The accompanying table lists the essential elements in the human body. Of special interest are the *trace elements,* such as iron (Fe), copper (Cu), zinc (Zn), iodine (I), and cobalt (Co), which together make up about 0.1 percent of the body's mass. These elements are necessary for biological functions such as growth, transport of oxygen for metabolism, and defense against disease. There is a delicate balance in the amounts of these elements in our bodies. Too much or too little over an extended period of time can lead to serious illness, retardation, or even death.

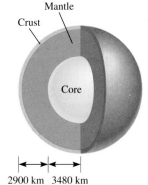

Structure of Earth's interior.

Essential Elements in the Human Body

Element	Percent by Mass*	Element	Percent by Mass*
Oxygen	65	Sodium	0.1
Carbon	18	Magnesium	0.05
Hydrogen	10	Iron	<0.05
Nitrogen	3	Cobalt	<0.05
Calcium	1.6	Copper	<0.05
Phosphorus	1.2	Zinc	<0.05
Potassium	0.2	Iodine	<0.05
Sulfur	0.2	Selenium	<0.01
Chlorine	0.2	Fluorine	<0.01

*Percent by mass *gives the mass of the element in grams present in a 100-g sample.*

(a) Natural abundance of the elements in percent by mass. For example, oxygen's abundance is 45.5 percent. This means that in a 100-g sample of Earth's crust there are, on the average, 45.5 g of the element oxygen. (b) Abundance of elements in the human body in percent by mass.

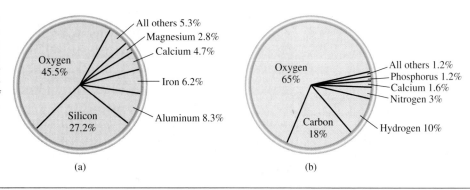

(a)

(b)

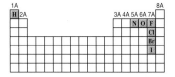

Elements that exist as diatomic molecules.

compound that contains hydrogen and oxygen in a ratio of two H atoms and one O atom. Like atoms, molecules are electrically neutral.

The hydrogen molecule, symbolized as H_2, is called a ***diatomic molecule*** because it *contains only two atoms.* Other elements that normally exist as diatomic molecules are nitrogen (N_2) and oxygen (O_2), as well as the Group 7A elements—fluorine (F_2), chlorine (Cl_2), bromine (Br_2), and iodine (I_2). Of course, a diatomic molecule can contain atoms of different elements. Examples are hydrogen chloride (HCl) and carbon monoxide (CO).

The vast majority of molecules contain more than two atoms. They can be atoms of the same element, as in ozone (O_3), which is made up of three atoms of oxygen, or they can be combinations of two or more different elements. *Molecules containing more than two atoms* are called ***polyatomic molecules.*** Like ozone, water (H_2O) and ammonia (NH_3) are polyatomic molecules.

Ions

An ***ion*** is *an atom or a group of atoms that has a net positive or negative charge.* The number of positively charged protons in the nucleus of an atom remains the same during ordinary chemical changes (called chemical reactions), but negatively charged electrons may be lost or gained. The loss of one or more electrons from a neutral atom results in a ***cation,*** *an ion with a net positive charge.* For example, a sodium atom (Na) can readily lose an electron to become sodium cation, which is represented by Na^+:

Na Atom	Na^+ Ion
11 protons	11 protons
11 electrons	10 electrons

On the other hand, an ***anion*** is *an ion whose net charge is negative* due to an increase in the number of electrons. A chlorine atom (Cl), for instance, can gain an electron

In Chapter 8 we will see why atoms of different elements gain (or lose) a specific number of electrons.

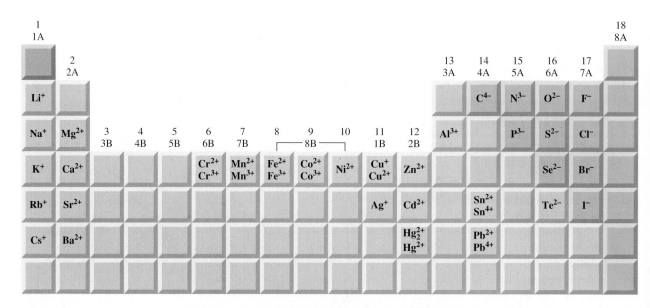

Figure 2.11 *Common monatomic ions arranged according to their positions in the periodic table. Note that the Hg_2^{2+} ion contains two atoms.*

to become the chloride ion Cl^-:

Cl Atom	Cl^- Ion
17 protons	17 protons
17 electrons	18 electrons

Sodium chloride (NaCl), ordinary table salt, is called an **ionic compound** because it is *formed from cations and anions.*

An atom can lose or gain more than one electron. Examples of ions formed by the loss or gain of more than one electron are Mg^{2+}, Fe^{3+}, S^{2-}, and N^{3-}. These ions, as well as Na^+ and Cl^-, are called **monatomic ions** because they *contain only one atom*. Figure 2.11 shows the charges of a number of monatomic ions. With very few exceptions, metals tend to form cations and nonmetals form anions.

In addition, two or more atoms can combine to form an ion that has a net positive or net negative charge. **Polyatomic ions** such as OH^- (hydroxide ion), CN^- (cyanide ion), and NH_4^+ (ammonium ion) are *ions containing more than one atom.*

2.6 Chemical Formulas

Chemists use **chemical formulas** to *express the composition of molecules and ionic compounds in terms of chemical symbols.* By composition we mean not only the elements present but also the ratios in which the atoms are combined. Here we are concerned with two types of formulas: molecular formulas and empirical formulas.

Molecular Formulas

A **molecular formula** *shows the exact number of atoms of each element in the smallest unit of a substance.* In our discussion of molecules, each example was given with its molecular formula in parentheses. Thus H_2 is the molecular formula for hydrogen, O_2 is oxygen, O_3 is ozone, and H_2O is water. The subscript numeral indicates the number of atoms of an element present. There is no subscript for O in H_2O because there is only one atom of oxygen in a molecule of water, and so the number "one" is omitted from the formula. Note that oxygen (O_2) and ozone (O_3) are allotropes of oxygen. An **allotrope** is *one of two or more distinct forms of an element.* Two allotropic forms of the element carbon—diamond and graphite—are dramatically different not only in properties but also in their relative cost.

Molecular Models Molecules are too small for us to observe directly. An effective means of visualizing them is by the use of molecular models. Two standard types of molecular models are currently in use: *ball-and-stick* models and *space-filling* models (Figure 2.12). In ball-and-stick model kits, the atoms are wooden or plastic balls with holes in them. Sticks or springs are used to represent chemical bonds. The angles they form between atoms approximate the bond angles in actual molecules. With the exception of the H atom, the balls are all the same size and each type of atom is represented by a specific color. In space-filling models, atoms are represented by truncated balls held together by snap fasteners, so that the bonds are not visible. The balls are proportional in size to atoms. The first step toward building a molecular model is writing the **structural formula**, which *shows how atoms are bonded to one another in a molecule.* For example, it is known that each of the two H atoms is bonded to an O atom in the water molecule. Therefore, the structural formula of water is H—O—H. A line connecting the two atomic symbols represents a chemical bond.

See back endpaper for color code for atoms.

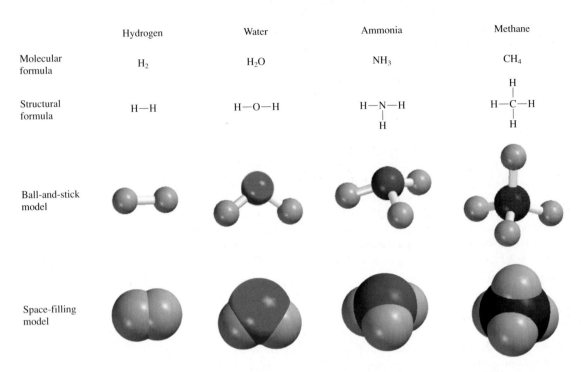

	Hydrogen	Water	Ammonia	Methane
Molecular formula	H_2	H_2O	NH_3	CH_4
Structural formula	H—H	H—O—H	H—N—H $\mid$ H	H—C—H with H above and H below
Ball-and-stick model				
Space-filling model				

Figure 2.12 *Molecular and structural formulas and molecular models of four common molecules.*

Ball-and-stick models show the three-dimensional arrangement of atoms clearly, and they are fairly easy to construct. However, the balls are not proportional to the size of atoms. Furthermore, the sticks greatly exaggerate the space between atoms in a molecule. Space-filling models are more accurate because they show the variation in atomic size. Their drawbacks are that they are time-consuming to put together and they do not show the three-dimensional positions of atoms very well. We will use both models extensively in this text.

Empirical Formulas

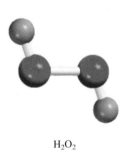

H_2O_2

The molecular formula of hydrogen peroxide, a substance used as an antiseptic and as a bleaching agent for textiles and hair, is H_2O_2. This formula indicates that each hydrogen peroxide molecule consists of two hydrogen atoms and two oxygen atoms. The ratio of hydrogen to oxygen atoms in this molecule is 2:2 or 1:1. The empirical formula of hydrogen peroxide is HO. Thus the **empirical formula** *tells us which elements are present and the simplest whole-number ratio of their atoms,* but not necessarily the actual number of atoms in a given molecule. As another example, consider the compound hydrazine (N_2H_4), which is used as a rocket fuel. The empirical formula of hydrazine is NH_2. Although the ratio of nitrogen to hydrogen is 1:2 in both the molecular formula (N_2H_4) and the empirical formula (NH_2), only the molecular formula tells us the actual number of N atoms (two) and H atoms (four) present in a hydrazine molecule.

Empirical formulas are the *simplest* chemical formulas; they are written by reducing the subscripts in molecular formulas to the smallest possible whole numbers. Molecular formulas are the *true* formulas of molecules. As we will see in Chapter 3, when chemists analyze an unknown compound, the first step is usually the determination of the compound's empirical formula.

For many molecules, the molecular formula and the empirical formula are one and the same. Some examples are water (H_2O), ammonia (NH_3), carbon dioxide (CO_2), and methane (CH_4).

Examples 2.2 and 2.3 deal with writing molecular formulas from molecular models and writing empirical formulas from molecular formulas.

Example 2.2

Write the molecular formula of methanol, an organic solvent and antifreeze, from its ball-and-stick model, shown in the margin.

Solution Refer to the labels (also see back endpapers). There are four H atoms, one C atom, and one O atom. Therefore, the molecular formula is CH_4O. However, the standard way of writing the molecular formula for methanol is CH_3OH because it shows how the atoms are joined in the molecule.

Practice Exercise Write the molecular formula of chloroform, which is used as a solvent and a cleansing agent. The ball-and-stick model of chloroform is shown in the margin.

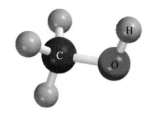

Methanol

Similar problems: 2.45, 2.46.

Example 2.3

Write the empirical formulas for the following molecules: (a) acetylene (C_2H_2), which is used in welding torches; (b) glucose ($C_6H_{12}O_6$), a substance known as blood sugar; and (c) nitrous oxide (N_2O), a gas that is used as an anesthetic gas ("laughing gas") and as an aerosol propellant for whipped creams.

Strategy Recall that to write the empirical formula, the subscripts in the molecular formula must be converted to the smallest possible whole numbers.

Solution

(a) There are two carbon atoms and two hydrogen atoms in acetylene. Dividing the subscripts by 2, we obtain the empirical formula CH.

(b) In glucose there are 6 carbon atoms, 12 hydrogen atoms, and 6 oxygen atoms. Dividing the subscripts by 6, we obtain the empirical formula CH_2O. Note that if we had divided the subscripts by 3, we would have obtained the formula $C_2H_4O_2$. Although the ratio of carbon to hydrogen to oxygen atoms in $C_2H_4O_2$ is the same as that in $C_6H_{12}O_6$ (1:2:1), $C_2H_4O_2$ is not the simplest formula because its subscripts are not in the smallest whole-number ratio.

(c) Because the subscripts in N_2O are already the smallest possible whole numbers, the empirical formula for nitrous oxide is the same as its molecular formula.

Practice Exercise Write the empirical formula for caffeine ($C_8H_{10}N_4O_2$), a stimulant found in tea and coffee.

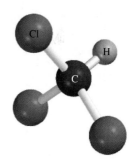

Chloroform

Similar problems: 2.43, 2.44.

Formula of Ionic Compounds

The formulas of ionic compounds are usually the same as their empirical formulas because ionic compounds do not consist of discrete molecular units. For example, a solid sample of sodium chloride (NaCl) consists of equal numbers of Na^+ and Cl^- ions arranged in a three-dimensional network (Figure 2.13). In such a compound there is a 1:1 ratio of cations to anions so that the compound is electrically neutral. As you can see in Figure 2.13, no Na^+ ion in NaCl is associated with just one particular Cl^-

Interactivity: Build an Ionic Compound
Online Learning Center, Interactives

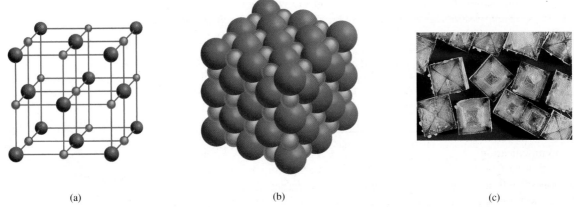

(a)   (b)   (c)

Figure 2.13 *(a) Structure of solid NaCl. (b) In reality, the cations are in contact with the anions. In both (a) and (b), the smaller spheres represent Na^+ ions and the larger spheres, Cl^- ions. (c) Crystals of NaCl.*

ion. In fact, each Na^+ ion is equally held by six surrounding Cl^- ions and vice versa. Thus NaCl is the empirical formula for sodium chloride. In other ionic compounds, the actual structure may be different, but the arrangement of cations and anions is such that the compounds are all electrically neutral. Note that the charges on the cation and anion are not shown in the formula for an ionic compound.

In order for ionic compounds to be electrically neutral, the sum of the charges on the cation and anion in each formula unit must be zero. If the charges on the cation and anion are numerically different, we apply the following rule to make the formula electrically neutral: *The subscript of the cation is numerically equal to the charge on the anion, and the subscript of the anion is numerically equal to the charge on the cation.* If the charges are numerically equal, then no subscripts are necessary. This rule follows from the fact that because the formulas of ionic compounds are empirical formulas, the subscripts must always be reduced to the smallest ratios. Let us consider some examples.

- **Potassium Bromide.** The potassium cation K^+ and the bromine anion Br^- combine to form the ionic compound potassium bromide. The sum of the charges is $+1 + (-1) = 0$, so no subscripts are necessary. The formula is KBr.

- **Zinc Iodide.** The zinc cation Zn^{2+} and the iodine anion I^- combine to form zinc iodide. The sum of the charges of one Zn^{2+} ion and one I^- ion is $+2 + (-1) = +1$. To make the charges add up to zero we multiply the -1 charge of the anion by 2 and add the subscript "2" to the symbol for iodine. Therefore the formula for zinc iodide is ZnI_2.

- **Aluminum Oxide.** The cation is Al^{3+} and the oxygen anion is O^{2-}. The following diagram helps us determine the subscripts for the compound formed by the cation and the anion:

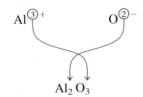

The sum of the charges is $2(+3) + 3(-2) = 0$. Thus the formula for aluminum oxide is Al_2O_3.

2.7 Naming Compounds

When chemistry was a young science and the number of known compounds was small, it was possible to memorize their names. Many of the names were derived from their physical appearance, properties, origin, or application—for example, milk of magnesia, laughing gas, limestone, caustic soda, lye, washing soda, and baking soda.

Today the number of known compounds is well over 20 million. Fortunately, it is not necessary to memorize their names. Over the years chemists have devised a clear system for naming chemical substances. The rules are accepted worldwide, facilitating communication among chemists and providing a useful way of labeling an overwhelming variety of substances. Mastering these rules now will prove beneficial almost immediately as we proceed with our study of chemistry.

To begin our discussion of chemical *nomenclature,* the naming of chemical compounds, we must first distinguish between inorganic and organic compounds. ***Organic compounds*** *contain carbon, usually in combination with elements such as hydrogen, oxygen, nitrogen, and sulfur.* All other compounds are classified as ***inorganic compounds.*** For convenience, some carbon-containing compounds, such as carbon monoxide (CO), carbon dioxide (CO_2), carbon disulfide (CS_2), compounds containing the cyanide group (CN^-), and carbonate (CO_3^{2-}) and bicarbonate (HCO_3^-) groups are considered to be inorganic compounds. Although the nomenclature of organic compounds will not be discussed until Chapter 24, we will use some organic compounds to illustrate chemical principles throughout this book.

To organize and simplify our venture into naming compounds, we can divide inorganic compounds into four categories: ionic compounds, molecular compounds, acids and bases, and hydrates.

Ionic Compounds

In Section 2.5 we learned that ionic compounds are made up of cations (positive ions) and anions (negative ions). With the important exception of the ammonium ion, NH_4^+, all cations of interest to us are derived from metal atoms. Metal cations take their names from the elements. For example:

The most reactive metals (green) and the most reactive nonmetals (blue) combine to form ionic compounds.

Element			Name of Cation
Na	sodium	Na^+	sodium ion (or sodium cation)
K	potassium	K^+	potassium ion (or potassium cation)
Mg	magnesium	Mg^{2+}	magnesium ion (or magnesium cation)
Al	aluminum	Al^{3+}	aluminum ion (or aluminum cation)

Many ionic compounds are ***binary compounds,*** or *compounds formed from just two elements.* For binary compounds, the first element named is the metal cation, followed by the nonmetallic anion. Thus NaCl is sodium chloride. The anion is named by taking the first part of the element name (chlorine) and adding "-ide." Potassium bromide (KBr), zinc iodide (ZnI_2), and aluminum oxide (Al_2O_3) are also binary compounds. Table 2.2 shows the "-ide" nomenclature of some common monatomic anions according to their positions in the periodic table.

The "-ide" ending is also used for certain anion groups containing different elements, such as hydroxide (OH^-) and cyanide (CN^-). Thus the compounds LiOH and KCN are named lithium hydroxide and potassium cyanide, respectively. These and a number of other such ionic substances are called ***ternary compounds,*** meaning *compounds consisting of three elements.* Table 2.3 lists alphabetically the names of a number of common cations and anions.

TABLE 2.2	The "-ide" Nomenclature of Some Common Monatomic Anions According to Their Positions in the Periodic Table			
	Group 4A	**Group 5A**	**Group 6A**	**Group 7A**
	C Carbide (C^{4-})*	N Nitride (N^{3-})	O Oxide (O^{2-})	F Fluoride (F^-)
	Si Silicide (Si^{4-})	P Phosphide (P^{3-})	S Sulfide (S^{2-})	Cl Chloride (Cl^-)
			Se Selenide (Se^{2-})	Br Bromide (Br^-)
			Te Telluride (Te^{2-})	I Iodide (I^-)

* The word "carbide" is also used for the anion C_2^{2-}.

TABLE 2.3	Names and Formulas of Some Common Inorganic Cations and Anions	
	Cation	**Anion**
	Aluminum (Al^{3+})	Bromide (Br^-)
	Ammonium (NH_4^+)	Carbonate (CO_3^{2-})
	Barium (Ba^{2+})	Chlorate (ClO_3^-)
	Cadmium (Cd^{2+})	Chloride (Cl^-)
	Calcium (Ca^{2+})	Chromate (CrO_4^{2-})
	Cesium (Cs^+)	Cyanide (CN^-)
	Chromium(III) or chromic (Cr^{3+})	Dichromate ($Cr_2O_7^{2-}$)
	Cobalt(II) or cobaltous (Co^{2+})	Dihydrogen phosphate ($H_2PO_4^-$)
	Copper(I) or cuprous (Cu^+)	Fluoride (F^-)
	Copper(II) or cupric (Cu^{2+})	Hydride (H^-)
	Hydrogen (H^+)	Hydrogen carbonate or bicarbonate (HCO_3^-)
	Iron(II) or ferrous (Fe^{2+})	Hydrogen phosphate (HPO_4^{2-})
	Iron(III) or ferric (Fe^{3+})	Hydrogen sulfate or bisulfate (HSO_4^-)
	Lead(II) or plumbous (Pb^{2+})	Hydroxide (OH^-)
	Lithium (Li^+)	Iodide (I^-)
	Magnesium (Mg^{2+})	Nitrate (NO_3^-)
	Manganese(II) or manganous (Mn^{2+})	Nitride (N^{3-})
	Mercury(I) or mercurous (Hg_2^{2+})*	Nitrite (NO_2^-)
	Mercury(II) or mercuric (Hg^{2+})	Oxide (O^{2-})
	Potassium (K^+)	Permanganate (MnO_4^-)
	Silver (Ag^+)	Peroxide (O_2^{2-})
	Sodium (Na^+)	Phosphate (PO_4^{3-})
	Strontium (Sr^{2+})	Sulfate (SO_4^{2-})
	Tin(II) or stannous (Sn^{2+})	Sulfide (S^{2-})
	Zinc (Zn^{2+})	Sulfite (SO_3^{2-})
		Thiocyanate (SCN^-)

* Mercury(I) exists as a pair as shown.

Certain metals, especially the *transition metals,* can form more than one type of cation. Take iron as an example. Iron can form two cations: Fe^{2+} and Fe^{3+}. An older nomenclature system that is still in limited use assigns the ending "-ous" to the cation with fewer positive charges and the ending "-ic" to the cation with more positive charges:

Fe^{2+} ferrous ion
Fe^{3+} ferric ion

The names of the compounds that these iron ions form with chlorine would thus be

$FeCl_2$ ferrous chloride
$FeCl_3$ ferric chloride

This method of naming ions has some distinct limitations. First, the "-ous" and "-ic" suffixes do not provide information regarding the actual charges of the two cations involved. Thus the ferric ion is Fe^{3+}, but the cation of copper named cupric has the formula Cu^{2+}. In addition, the "-ous" and "-ic" designations provide names for only two different elemental cations. Some metallic elements can assume three or more different positive charges in compounds. Therefore, it has become increasingly common to designate different cations with Roman numerals. This is called the Stock[†] system. In this system, the Roman numeral I indicates one positive charge, II means two positive charges, and so on. For example, manganese (Mn) atoms can assume several different positive charges:

Mn^{2+}: MnO manganese(II) oxide
Mn^{3+}: Mn_2O_3 manganese(III) oxide
Mn^{4+}: MnO_2 manganese(IV) oxide

These names are pronounced "manganese-two oxide," "manganese-three oxide," and "manganese-four oxide." Using the Stock system, we denote the ferrous ion and the ferric ion as iron(II) and iron(III), respectively; ferrous chloride becomes iron(II) chloride; and ferric chloride is called iron(III) chloride. In keeping with modern practice, we will favor the Stock system of naming compounds in this textbook.

Examples 2.4 and 2.5 illustrate how to name ionic compounds and write formulas for ionic compounds based on the information given in Figure 2.11 and Tables 2.2 and 2.3.

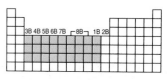

The transition metals are the elements in Groups 1B and 3B–8B (see Figure 2.10).

$FeCl_2$ (left) and $FeCl_3$ (right).

For names and symbols of the elements, see front endpapers.

Example 2.4

Name the following compounds: (a) $Cu(NO_3)_2$, (b) KH_2PO_4, and (c) NH_4ClO_3.

Strategy Our reference for the names of cations and anions is Table 2.3. Keep in mind that if a metal can form cations of different charges (see Figure 2.11), we need to use the Stock system.

Solution

(a) The nitrate ion (NO_3^-) bears one negative charge, so the copper ion must have two positive charges. Because copper forms both Cu^+ and Cu^{2+} ions, we need to use the Stock system and call the compound copper(II) nitrate.

(Continued)

[†]Alfred E. Stock (1876–1946). German chemist. Stock did most of his research in the synthesis and characterization of boron, beryllium, and silicon compounds. He was the first scientist to explore the dangers of mercury poisoning.

(b) The cation is K^+ and the anion is $H_2PO_4^-$ (dihydrogen phosphate). Because potassium only forms one type of ion (K^+), there is no need to use potassium(I) in the name. The compound is potassium dihydrogen phosphate.

(c) The cation is NH_4^+ (ammonium ion) and the anion is ClO_3^-. The compound is ammonium chlorate.

Similar problems: 2.55(b), (e), (f).

Practice Exercise Name the following compounds: (a) PbO and (b) Li_2SO_3.

Example 2.5

Write chemical formulas for the following compounds: (a) mercury(I) nitrite, (b) cesium sulfide, and (c) calcium phosphate.

Strategy We refer to Table 2.3 for the formulas of cations and anions. Recall that the Roman numerals in the Stock system provide useful information about the charges of the cation.

Solution

(a) The Roman numeral shows that the mercury ion bears a $+1$ charge. According to Table 2.3, however, the mercury(I) ion is diatomic (that is, Hg_2^{2+}) and the nitrite ion is NO_2^-. Therefore, the formula is $Hg_2(NO_2)_2$.

(b) Each sulfide ion bears two negative charges, and each cesium ion bears one positive charge (cesium is in Group 1A, as is sodium). Therefore, the formula is Cs_2S.

(c) Each calcium ion (Ca^{2+}) bears two positive charges, and each phosphate ion (PO_4^{3-}) bears three negative charges. To make the sum of the charges equal zero, we must adjust the numbers of cations and anions:

$$3(+2) + 2(-3) = 0$$

Similar problems: 2.57(a), (b), (h).

Thus the formula is $Ca_3(PO_4)_2$.

Practice Exercise Write formulas for the following ionic compounds: (a) rubidium sulfate and (b) barium hydride.

Molecular Compounds

Interactivity: Build a Covalent Compound
Online Learning Center,
Interactives

Unlike ionic compounds, molecular compounds contain discrete molecular units. They are usually composed of nonmetallic elements (see Figure 2.10). Many molecular compounds are binary compounds. Naming binary molecular compounds is similar to naming binary ionic compounds. We place the name of the first element in the formula first, and the second element is named by adding -ide to the root of the element name. Some examples are

HCl   hydrogen chloride
HBr   hydrogen bromide
SiC   silicon carbide

It is quite common for one pair of elements to form several different compounds. In these cases, confusion in naming the compounds is avoided by the use of Greek prefixes to denote the number of atoms of each element present (Table 2.4). Consider the following examples:

CO   carbon monoxide
CO_2 carbon dioxide
SO_2 sulfur dioxide
SO_3 sulfur trioxide

NO_2 nitrogen dioxide

N_2O_4 dinitrogen tetroxide

The following guidelines are helpful in naming compounds with prefixes:

- The prefix "mono-" may be omitted for the first element. For example, PCl_3 is named phosphorus trichloride, not monophosphorus trichloride. Thus the absence of a prefix for the first element usually means there is only one atom of that element present in the molecule.

- For oxides, the ending "a" in the prefix is sometimes omitted. For example, N_2O_4 may be called dinitrogen tetroxide rather than dinitrogen tetraoxide.

Exceptions to the use of Greek prefixes are molecular compounds containing hydrogen. Traditionally, many of these compounds are called either by their common, nonsystematic names or by names that do not specifically indicate the number of H atoms present:

B_2H_6 diborane

CH_4 methane

SiH_4 silane

NH_3 ammonia

PH_3 phosphine

H_2O water

H_2S hydrogen sulfide

Note that even the order of writing the elements in the formulas for hydrogen compounds is irregular. In water and hydrogen sulfide, H is written first, whereas it appears last in the other compounds.

Writing formulas for molecular compounds is usually straightforward. Thus the name arsenic trifluoride means that there are one As atom and three F atoms in each molecule, and the molecular formula is AsF_3. Note that the order of elements in the formula is the same as in its name.

TABLE 2.4

Greek Prefixes Used in Naming Molecular Compounds

Prefix	Meaning
Mono-	1
Di-	2
Tri-	3
Tetra-	4
Penta-	5
Hexa-	6
Hepta-	7
Octa-	8
Nona-	9
Deca-	10

Example 2.6

Name the following molecular compounds: (a) $SiCl_4$ and (b) P_4O_{10}.

Solution We refer to Table 2.4 for prefixes.

(a) Because there are four chlorine atoms present, the compound is silicon tetrachloride.

(b) There are four phosphorus atoms and ten oxygen atoms present, so the compound is tetraphosphorus decoxide. Note that the "a" is omitted in "deca."

Practice Exercise Name the following molecular compounds: (a) NF_3 and (b) Cl_2O_7.

Similar problems: 2.55(c), (i), (j).

Example 2.7

Write chemical formulas for the following molecular compounds: (a) carbon disulfide and (b) disilicon hexabromide.

Solution We refer to Table 2.4 for prefixes.

(a) Because there are two sulfur atoms and one carbon atom present, the formula is CS_2.

(b) There are two silicon atoms and six bromine atoms present, so the formula is Si_2Br_6.

Similar problems: 2.57(g), (j).

Practice Exercise Write chemical formulas for the following molecular compounds: (a) sulfur tetrafluoride and (b) dinitrogen pentoxide.

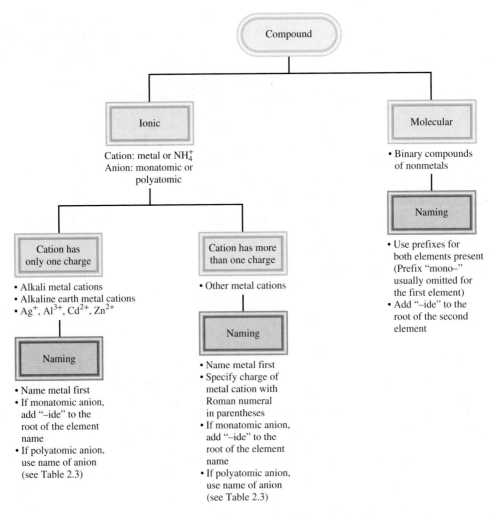

Figure 2.14 *Flowchart for naming ionic and molecular compounds.*

Figure 2.14 summarizes the steps for naming ionic and molecular compounds.

Acids and Bases

H$^+$ is equivalent to one *proton*, and is sometimes referred to that way.

Naming Acids An **acid** can be described as *a substance that yields hydrogen ions* (H^+) *when dissolved in water.* Formulas for acids contain one or more hydrogen atoms as well as an anionic group. Anions whose names end in "-ide" form acids with a "hydro-" prefix and an "-ic" ending, as shown in Table 2.5. In some cases two different names seem to be assigned to the same chemical formula.

HCl   hydrogen chloride
HCl   hydrochloric acid

The name assigned to the compound depends on its physical state. In the gaseous or pure liquid state, HCl is a molecular compound called hydrogen chloride. When it is dissolved in water, the molecules break up into H$^+$ and Cl$^-$ ions; in this state, the substance is called hydrochloric acid.

TABLE 2.5	Some Simple Acids	

Anion	Corresponding Acid
F^- (fluoride)	HF (hydrofluoric acid)
Cl^- (chloride)	HCl (hydrochloric acid)
Br^- (bromide)	HBr (hydrobromic acid)
I^- (iodide)	HI (hydroiodic acid)
CN^- (cyanide)	HCN (hydrocyanic acid)
S^{2-} (sulfide)	H_2S (hydrosulfuric acid)

Oxoacids are acids that *contain hydrogen, oxygen, and another element (the central element)*. The formulas of oxoacids are usually written with the H first, followed by the central element and then O, as illustrated by the following examples:

HNO_3 nitric acid
H_2CO_3 carbonic acid
H_2SO_4 sulfuric acid
$HClO_3$ chloric acid

Often two or more oxoacids have the same central atom but a different number of O atoms. Starting with the oxoacids whose names end with "-ic," we use the following rules to name these compounds.

1. Addition of one O atom to the "-ic" acid: The acid is called "per . . . -ic" acid. Thus adding an O atom to $HClO_3$ changes chloric acid to perchloric acid, $HClO_4$.

2. Removal of one O atom from the "-ic" acid: The acid is called "-ous" acid. Thus nitric acid, HNO_3, becomes nitrous acid, HNO_2.

3. Removal of two O atoms from the "-ic" acid: The acid is called "hypo . . . -ous" acid. Thus when $HBrO_3$ is converted to HBrO, the acid is called hypobromous acid.

The rules for naming **oxoanions**, anions of oxoacids, are as follows:

1. When all the H ions are removed from the "-ic" acid, the anion's name ends with "-ate." For example, the anion CO_3^{2-} derived from H_2CO_3 is called carbonate.

2. When all the H ions are removed from the "-ous" acid, the anion's name ends with "-ite." Thus the anion ClO_2^- derived from $HClO_2$ is called chlorite.

3. The names of anions in which one or more but not all the hydrogen ions have been removed must indicate the number of H ions present. For example, consider the anions derived from phosphoric acid:

H_3PO_4 phosphoric acid
$H_2PO_4^-$ dihydrogen phosphate
HPO_4^{2-} hydrogen phosphate
PO_4^{3-} phosphate

Note that we usually omit the prefix "mono-" when there is only one H in the anion. Figure 2.15 summarizes the nomenclature for the oxoacids and oxoanions, and Table 2.6 gives the names of the oxoacids and oxoanions that contain chlorine.

Example 2.8 deals with the nomenclature for an oxoacid and an oxoanion.

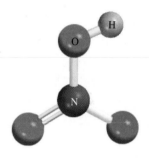

HNO_3

H_2CO_3

H_3PO_4

Figure 2.15 *Naming oxoacids and oxoanions.*

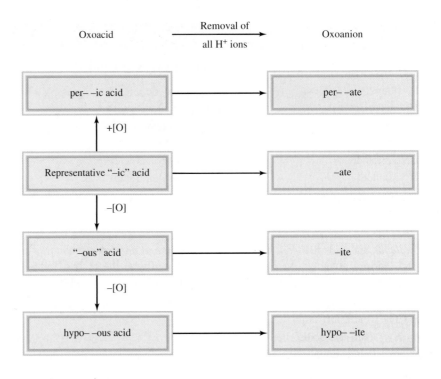

Example 2.8

Name the following oxoacid and oxoanion: (a) H_3PO_3 and (b) IO_4^-.

Solution We refer to Figure 2.15 and Table 2.6.

(a) We start with our reference acid, phosphoric acid (H_3PO_4). Because H_3PO_3 has one fewer O atom, it is called phosphorous acid.

(b) The parent acid is HIO_4. Because the acid has one more O atom than our reference iodic acid (HIO_3), it is called periodic acid. Therefore, the anion derived from HIO_4 is called periodate.

Similar problems: 2.55(h), 2.56(c).

Practice Exercise Name the following oxoacid and oxoanion: (a) HBrO and (b) HSO_4^-.

Naming Bases A **base** can be described as *a substance that yields hydroxide ions* (OH^-) *when dissolved in water.* Some examples are

NaOH   sodium hydroxide
KOH   potassium hydroxide
$Ba(OH)_2$ barium hydroxide

TABLE 2.6

Names of Oxoacids and Oxoanions That Contain Chlorine

Acid	Anion
$HClO_4$ (perchloric acid)	ClO_4^- (perchlorate)
$HClO_3$ (chloric acid)	ClO_3^- (chlorate)
$HClO_2$ (chlorous acid)	ClO_2^- (chlorite)
$HClO$ (hypochlorous acid)	ClO^- (hypochlorite)

Figure 2.16 $CuSO_4 \cdot 5H_2O$ (left) is blue; $CuSO_4$ (right) is white.

Ammonia (NH_3), a molecular compound in the gaseous or pure liquid state, is also classified as a common base. At first glance this may seem to be an exception to the definition of a base. But note that as long as a substance *yields* hydroxide ions when dissolved in water, it need not contain hydroxide ions in its structure to be considered a base. In fact, when ammonia dissolves in water, NH_3 reacts partially with water to yield NH_4^+ and OH^- ions. Thus it is properly classified as a base.

Hydrates

Hydrates are *compounds that have a specific number of water molecules attached to them.* For example, in its normal state, each unit of copper(II) sulfate has five water molecules associated with it. The systematic name for this compound is copper(II) sulfate pentahydrate, and its formula is written as $CuSO_4 \cdot 5H_2O$. The water molecules can be driven off by heating. When this occurs, the resulting compound is $CuSO_4$, which is sometimes called *anhydrous* copper(II) sulfate; "anhydrous" means that the compound no longer has water molecules associated with it (Figure 2.16). Some other hydrates are

$BaCl_2 \cdot 2H_2O$	barium chloride dihydrate
$LiCl \cdot H_2O$	lithium chloride monohydrate
$MgSO_4 \cdot 7H_2O$	magnesium sulfate heptahydrate
$Sr(NO_3)_2 \cdot 4H_2O$	strontium nitrate tetrahydrate

TABLE 2.7

Common and Systematic Names of Some Compounds

Formula	Common Name	Systematic Name
H_2O	Water	Dihydrogen monoxide
NH_3	Ammonia	Trihydrogen nitride
CO_2	Dry ice	Solid carbon dioxide
NaCl	Table salt	Sodium chloride
N_2O	Laughing gas	Dinitrogen monoxide
$CaCO_3$	Marble, chalk, limestone	Calcium carbonate
CaO	Quicklime	Calcium oxide
$Ca(OH)_2$	Slaked lime	Calcium hydroxide
$NaHCO_3$	Baking soda	Sodium hydrogen carbonate
$Na_2CO_3 \cdot 10H_2O$	Washing soda	Sodium carbonate decahydrate
$MgSO_4 \cdot 7H_2O$	Epsom salt	Magnesium sulfate heptahydrate
$Mg(OH)_2$	Milk of magnesia	Magnesium hydroxide
$CaSO_4 \cdot 2H_2O$	Gypsum	Calcium sulfate dihydrate

Familiar Inorganic Compounds

Some compounds are better known by their common names than by their systematic chemical names. Familiar examples are listed in Table 2.7 on p. 67.

Summary of Facts and Concepts

1. Modern chemistry began with Dalton's atomic theory, which states that all matter is composed of tiny, indivisible particles called atoms; that all atoms of the same element are identical; that compounds contain atoms of different elements combined in whole-number ratios; and that atoms are neither created nor destroyed in chemical reactions (the law of conservation of mass).

2. Atoms of constituent elements in a particular compound are always combined in the same proportions by mass (law of definite proportions). When two elements can combine to form more than one type of compound, the masses of one element that combine with a fixed mass of the other element are in a ratio of small whole numbers (law of multiple proportions).

3. An atom consists of a very dense central nucleus containing protons and neutrons, with electrons moving about the nucleus at a relatively large distance from it.

4. Protons are positively charged, neutrons have no charge, and electrons are negatively charged. Protons and neutrons have roughly the same mass, which is about 1840 times greater than the mass of an electron.

5. The atomic number of an element is the number of protons in the nucleus of an atom of the element; it determines the identity of an element. The mass number is the sum of the number of protons and the number of neutrons in the nucleus.

6. Isotopes are atoms of the same element with the same number of protons but different numbers of neutrons.

7. Chemical formulas combine the symbols for the constituent elements with whole-number subscripts to show the type and number of atoms contained in the smallest unit of a compound.

8. The molecular formula conveys the specific number and type of atoms combined in each molecule of a compound. The empirical formula shows the simplest ratios of the atoms combined in a molecule.

9. Chemical compounds are either molecular compounds (in which the smallest units are discrete, individual molecules) or ionic compounds (in which positive and negative ions are held together by mutual attraction). Ionic compounds are made up of cations and anions, formed when atoms lose and gain electrons, respectively.

10. The names of many inorganic compounds can be deduced from a set of simple rules. The formulas can be written from the names of the compounds.

Key Words

Acid, p. 64	Atom, p. 43	Chemical formula, p. 55	Halogens, p. 51
Alkali metals, p. 51	Atomic number (Z), p. 49	Diatomic molecule, p. 54	Hydrate, p. 67
Alkaline earth metals, p. 51	Base, p. 66	Electron, p. 44	Ion, p. 54
Allotrope, p. 55	Beta (β) particles, p. 46	Empirical formula, p. 56	Ionic compound, p. 55
Alpha (α) particles, p. 46	Beta (β) rays, p. 46	Families, p. 51	Isotope, p. 50
Alpha (α) rays, p. 46	Binary compound, p. 59	Gamma (γ) rays, p. 46	Law of conservation
Anion, p. 54	Cation, p. 54	Groups, p. 51	of mass, p. 43

Questions and Problems

Structure of the Atom
Review Questions

2.1   Define the following terms: (a) α particle, (b) β particle, (c) γ ray, (d) X ray.

2.2   Name the types of radiation known to be emitted by radioactive elements.

2.3   Compare the properties of the following: α particles, cathode rays, protons, neutrons, electrons.

2.4   What is meant by the term "fundamental particle"?

2.5   Describe the contributions of the following scientists to our knowledge of atomic structure: J. J. Thomson, R. A. Millikan, Ernest Rutherford, James Chadwick.

2.6   Describe the experimental basis for believing that the nucleus occupies a very small fraction of the volume of the atom.

Problems

2.7   The diameter of a neutral helium atom is about 1×10^2 pm. Suppose that we could line up helium atoms side by side in contact with one another. Approximately how many atoms would it take to make the distance from end to end 1 cm?

2.8   Roughly speaking, the radius of an atom is about 10,000 times greater than that of its nucleus. If an atom were magnified so that the radius of its nucleus became 2.0 cm, about the size of a marble, what would be the radius of the atom in miles? (1 mi = 1609 m.)

Atomic Number, Mass Number, and Isotopes
Review Questions

2.9   Use the helium-4 isotope to define atomic number and mass number. Why does a knowledge of atomic number enable us to deduce the number of electrons present in an atom?

2.10   Why do all atoms of an element have the same atomic number, although they may have different mass numbers?

2.11   What do we call atoms of the same elements with different mass numbers?

2.12   Explain the meaning of each term in the symbol $_Z^A X$.

Problems

2.13   What is the mass number of an iron atom that has 28 neutrons?

2.14   Calculate the number of neutrons of ^{239}Pu.

2.15   For each of the following species, determine the number of protons and the number of neutrons in the nucleus:

$$_2^3\text{He}, \,_2^4\text{He}, \,_{12}^{24}\text{Mg}, \,_{12}^{25}\text{Mg}, \,_{22}^{48}\text{Ti}, \,_{35}^{79}\text{Br}, \,_{78}^{195}\text{Pt}$$

2.16   Indicate the number of protons, neutrons, and electrons in each of the following species:

$$_7^{15}\text{N}, \,_{16}^{33}\text{S}, \,_{29}^{63}\text{Cu}, \,_{38}^{84}\text{Sr}, \,_{56}^{130}\text{Ba}, \,_{74}^{186}\text{W}, \,_{80}^{202}\text{Hg}$$

2.17   Write the appropriate symbol for each of the following isotopes: (a) Z = 11, A = 23; (b) Z = 28, A = 64.

2.18   Write the appropriate symbol for each of the following isotopes: (a) Z = 74, A = 186; (b) Z = 80, A = 201.

The Periodic Table
Review Questions

2.19   What is the periodic table, and what is its significance in the study of chemistry?

2.20   State two differences between a metal and a nonmetal.

2.21   Write the names and symbols for four elements in each of the following categories: (a) nonmetal, (b) metal, (c) metalloid.

2.22   Define, with two examples, the following terms: (a) alkali metals, (b) alkaline earth metals, (c) halogens, (d) noble gases.

Problems

2.23   Elements whose names end with *ium* are usually metals; sodium is one example. Identify a nonmetal whose name also ends with *ium*.

2.24   Describe the changes in properties (from metals to nonmetals or from nonmetals to metals) as we move (a) down a periodic group and (b) across the periodic table from left to right.

2.25 Consult a handbook of chemical and physical data (ask your instructor where you can locate a copy of the handbook) to find (a) two metals less dense than water, (b) two metals more dense than mercury, (c) the densest known solid metallic element, (d) the densest known solid nonmetallic element.

2.26 Group the following elements in pairs that you would expect to show similar chemical properties: K, F, P, Na, Cl, and N.

Molecules and Ions
Review Questions

2.27 What is the difference between an atom and a molecule?

2.28 What are allotropes? Give an example. How are allotropes different from isotopes?

2.29 Describe the two commonly used molecular models.

2.30 Give an example of each of the following: (a) a monatomic cation, (b) a monatomic anion, (c) a polyatomic cation, (d) a polyatomic anion.

Problems

2.31 Which of the following diagrams represent diatomic molecules, polyatomic molecules, molecules that are not compounds, molecules that are compounds, or an elemental form of the substance?

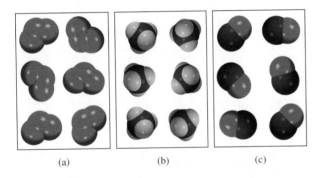

(a)   (b)   (c)

2.32 Which of the following diagrams represent diatomic molecules, polyatomic molecules, molecules that are not compounds, molecules that are compounds, or an elemental form of the substance?

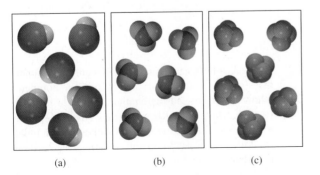

(a)   (b)   (c)

2.33 Identify the following as elements or compounds: NH_3, N_2, S_8, NO, CO, CO_2, H_2, SO_2.

2.34 Give two examples of each of the following: (a) a diatomic molecule containing atoms of the same element, (b) a diatomic molecule containing atoms of different elements, (c) polyatomic molecule containing atoms of the same element, (d) a polyatomic molecule containing atoms of different elements.

2.35 Give the number of protons and electrons in each of the following common ions: Na^+, Ca^{2+}, Al^{3+}, Fe^{2+}, I^-, F^-, S^{2-}, O^{2-}, and N^{3-}.

2.36 Give the number of protons and electrons in each of the following common ions: K^+, Mg^{2+}, Fe^{3+}, Br^-, Mn^{2+}, C^{4-}, Cu^{2+}.

Chemical Formulas
Review Questions

2.37 What does a chemical formula represent? What is the ratio of the atoms in the following molecular formulas? (a) NO, (b) NCl_3, (c) N_2O_4, (d) P_4O_6

2.38 Define molecular formula and empirical formula. What are the similarities and differences between the empirical formula and molecular formula of a compound?

2.39 Give an example of a case in which two molecules have different molecular formulas but the same empirical formula.

2.40 What does P_4 signify? How does it differ from 4P?

2.41 What is an ionic compound? How is electrical neutrality maintained in an ionic compound?

2.42 Explain why the chemical formulas of ionic compounds are usually the same as their empirical formulas.

Problems

2.43 What are the empirical formulas of the following compounds? (a) C_2N_2, (b) C_6H_6, (c) C_9H_{20}, (d) P_4O_{10}, (e) B_2H_6

2.44 What are the empirical formulas of the following compounds? (a) Al_2Br_6, (b) $Na_2S_2O_4$, (c) N_2O_5, (d) $K_2Cr_2O_7$

2.45 Write the molecular formula of glycine, an amino acid present in proteins. The color codes are: black (carbon), blue (nitrogen), red (oxygen), and gray (hydrogen).

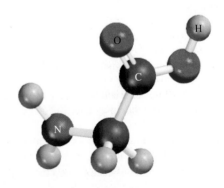

2.46 Write the molecular formula of ethanol. The color codes are: black (carbon), red (oxygen), and gray (hydrogen).

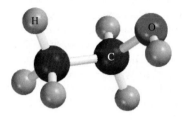

2.47 Which of the following compounds are likely to be ionic? Which are likely to be molecular? $SiCl_4$, LiF, $BaCl_2$, B_2H_6, KCl, C_2H_4

2.48 Which of the following compounds are likely to be ionic? Which are likely to be molecular? CH_4, NaBr, BaF_2, CCl_4, ICl, CsCl, NF_3

Naming Inorganic Compounds
Review Questions

2.49 What is the difference between inorganic compounds and organic compounds?

2.50 What are the four major categories of inorganic compounds?

2.51 Give an example each for a binary compound and a ternary compound.

2.52 What is the Stock system? What are its advantages over the older system of naming cations?

2.53 Explain why the formula HCl can represent two different chemical systems.

2.54 Define the following terms: acids, bases, oxoacids, oxoanions, and hydrates.

Problems

2.55 Name the following compounds: (a) KH_2PO_4, (b) K_2HPO_4, (c) HBr (gas), (d) HBr (in water), (e) Li_2CO_3, (f) $K_2Cr_2O_7$, (g) NH_4NO_2, (h) HIO_3, (i) PF_5, (j) P_4O_6, (k) CdI_2, (l) $SrSO_4$, (m) $Al(OH)_3$.

2.56 Name the following compounds: (a) KClO, (b) Ag_2CO_3, (c) HNO_2, (d) $KMnO_4$, (e) $CsClO_3$, (f) KNH_4SO_4, (g) FeO, (h) Fe_2O_3, (i) $TiCl_4$, (j) NaH, (k) Li_3N, (l) Na_2O, (m) Na_2O_2.

2.57 Write the formulas for the following compounds: (a) rubidium nitrite, (b) potassium sulfide, (c) sodium hydrogen sulfide, (d) magnesium phosphate, (e) calcium hydrogen phosphate, (f) potassium dihydrogen phosphate, (g) iodine heptafluoride, (h) ammonium sulfate, (i) silver perchlorate, (j) boron trichloride.

2.58 Write the formulas for the following compounds: (a) copper(I) cyanide, (b) strontium chlorite, (c) perbromic acid, (d) hydroiodic acid, (e) disodium ammonium phosphate, (f) lead(II) carbonate, (g) tin(II) fluoride, (h) tetraphosphorus decasulfide, (i) mercury(II) oxide, (j) mercury(I) iodide, (k) selenium hexafluoride.

Additional Problems

2.59 A sample of a uranium compound is found to be losing mass gradually. Explain what is happening to the sample.

2.60 In which one of the following pairs do the two species resemble each other most closely in chemical properties? Explain. (a) $^{1}_{1}H$ and $^{1}_{1}H^{+}$, (b) $^{14}_{7}N$ and $^{14}_{7}N^{3-}$, (c) $^{12}_{6}C$ and $^{13}_{6}C$

2.61 One isotope of a metallic element has mass number 65 and 35 neutrons in the nucleus. The cation derived from the isotope has 28 electrons. Write the symbol for this cation.

2.62 One isotope of a nonmetallic element has mass number 127 and 74 neutrons in the nucleus. The anion derived from the isotope has 54 electrons. Write the symbol for this anion.

2.63 The following table gives numbers of electrons, protons, and neutrons in atoms or ions of a number of elements. Answer the following: (a) Which of the species are neutral? (b) Which are negatively charged? (c) Which are positively charged? (d) What are the conventional symbols for all the species?

Atom or Ion of Element	A	B	C	D	E	F	G
Number of electrons	5	10	18	28	36	5	9
Number of protons	5	7	19	30	35	5	9
Number of neutrons	5	7	20	36	46	6	10

2.64 What is wrong with or ambiguous about the phrase "four molecules of NaCl"?

2.65 The following phosphorus sulfides are known: P_4S_3, P_4S_7, and P_4S_{10}. Do these compounds obey the law of multiple proportions?

2.66 Which of the following are elements, which are molecules but not compounds, which are compounds but not molecules, and which are both compounds and molecules? (a) SO_2, (b) S_8, (c) Cs, (d) N_2O_5, (e) O, (f) O_2, (g) O_3, (h) CH_4, (i) KBr, (j) S, (k) P_4, (l) LiF

2.67 What is wrong with the name (in parentheses) for each of the following compounds: (a) $BaCl_2$ (barium dichloride), (b) Fe_2O_3 [iron(II) oxide], (c) $CsNO_2$ (cesium nitrate), (d) $Mg(HCO_3)_2$ [magnesium(II) bicarbonate]?

2.68 What is wrong with the chemical formula for each of the following compounds: (a) $(NH_3)_2CO_3$ (ammonium carbonate), (b) CaOH (calcium hydroxide), (c) $CdSO_3$ (cadmium sulfide), (d) $ZnCrO_4$ (zinc dichromate)?

2.69 Fill in the blanks in the following table:

Symbol		$^{54}_{26}\text{Fe}^{2+}$			
Protons	5			79	86
Neutrons	6		16	117	136
Electrons	5		18	79	
Net charge			-3		0

2.70 (a) Which elements are most likely to form ionic compounds? (b) Which metallic elements are most likely to form cations with different charges?

2.71 Write the formula of the common ion derived from each of the following: (a) Li, (b) S, (c) I, (d) N, (e) Al, (f) Cs, (g) Mg

2.72 Which of the following symbols provides more information about the atom: ^{23}Na or $_{11}$Na? Explain.

2.73 Write the chemical formulas and names of acids that contain Group 7A elements. Do the same for elements in Groups 3A, 4A, 5A, and 6A.

2.74 Of the 113 elements known, only two are liquids at room temperature (25°C). What are they? (*Hint:* One element is a familiar metal and the other element is in Group 7A.)

2.75 For the noble gases (the Group 8A elements), $^4_2$He, $^{20}_{10}$Ne, $^{40}_{18}$Ar, $^{84}_{36}$Kr, and $^{132}_{54}$Xe, (a) determine the number of protons and neutrons in the nucleus of each atom, and (b) determine the ratio of neutrons to protons in the nucleus of each atom. Describe any general trend you discover in the way this ratio changes with increasing atomic number.

2.76 List the elements that exist as gases at room temperature. (*Hint:* Most of these elements can be found in Groups 5A, 6A, 7A, and 8A.)

2.77 The Group 1B metals, Cu, Ag, and Au, are called coinage metals. What chemical properties make them specially suitable for making coins and jewelry?

2.78 The elements in Group 8A of the periodic table are called noble gases. Can you suggest what "noble" means in this context?

2.79 The formula for calcium oxide is CaO. What are the formulas for magnesium oxide and strontium oxide?

2.80 A common mineral of barium is barytes, or barium sulfate (BaSO₄). Because elements in the same periodic group have similar chemical properties, we might expect to find some radium sulfate (RaSO₄) mixed with barytes since radium is the last member of Group 2A. However, the only source of radium compounds in nature is in uranium minerals. Why?

2.81 List five elements each that are (a) named after places, (b) named after people, (c) named after a color. (*Hint:* See Appendix 1.)

2.82 Name the only country that is named after an element. (*Hint:* This country is in South America.)

2.83 Fluorine reacts with hydrogen (H) and deuterium (D) to form hydrogen fluoride (HF) and deuterium fluoride (DF), where deuterium ($^2_1$H) is an isotope of hydrogen. Would a given amount of fluorine react with different masses of the two hydrogen isotopes? Does this violate the law of definite proportion? Explain.

2.84 Predict the formula and name of a binary compound formed from the following elements: (a) Na and H, (b) B and O, (c) Na and S, (d) Al and F, (e) F and O, (f) Sr and Cl.

2.85 Identify each of the following elements: (a) a halogen whose anion contains 36 electrons, (b) a radioactive noble gas with 86 protons, (c) a Group 6A element whose anion contains 36 electrons, (d) an alkali metal cation that contains 36 electrons, (e) a Group 4A cation that contains 80 electrons.

2.86 Write the molecular formulas for and names of the following compounds.

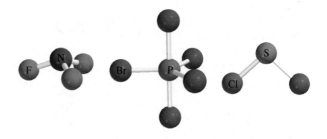

2.87 Show the locations of (a) alkali metals, (b) alkaline earth metals, (c) the halogens, and (d) the noble gases in the following outline of a periodic table. Also draw dividing lines between metals and metalloids and between metalloids and nonmetals.

2.88 Fill the blanks in the following table.

Cation	Anion	Formula	Name
			Magnesium bicarbonate
		$SrCl_2$	
Fe^{3+}	NO_2^-		
			Manganese(II) chlorate
		$SnBr_4$	
Co^{2+}	PO_4^{3-}		
Hg_2^{2+}	I^-		
		Cu_2CO_3	
			Lithium nitride
Al^{3+}	S^{2-}		

2.89 Some compounds are better known by their common names than by their systematic chemical names. Give the chemical formulas of the following substances: (a) dry ice, (b) table salt, (c) laughing gas, (d) marble (chalk, limestone), (e) quicklime, (f) slaked lime, (g) baking soda, (h) washing soda, (i) gypsum, (j) milk of magnesia.

2.90 (a) Describe Rutherford's experiment and how it led to the structure of the atom. How was he able to estimate the number of protons in a nucleus from the scattering of the α particles? (b) Consider the ^{23}Na atom. Given that the radius and mass of the nucleus are 3.04×10^{-15} m and 3.82×10^{-23} g, respectively, calculate the density of the nucleus in g/cm^3. The radius of a ^{23}Na atom is 186 pm. Calculate the density of the space occupied by the electrons in the sodium atom. Do your results support Rutherford's model of an atom? [The volume of a sphere is $(4/3)\pi r^3$, where r is the radius.]

2.91 In the following 2 × 2 crossword, each letter must be correct four ways: horizontally, vertically, diagonally, and by itself. When the puzzle is complete, the four spaces below will contain the overlapping symbols of 10 elements. Use capital letters for each square. There is only one correct solution.*

1	2
3	4

Horizontal

1–2: Two-letter symbol for a metal used in ancient times
3–4: Two-letter symbol for a metal that burns in air and is found in Group 5A

Vertical

1–3: Two-letter symbol for a metalloid
2–4: Two-letter symbol for a metal used in U.S. coins

Single Squares

1: A colorful nonmetal
2: A colorless gaseous nonmetal
3: An element that makes fireworks green
4: An element that has medicinal uses

Diagonal

1–4: Two-letter symbol for an element used in electronics
2–3: Two-letter symbol for a metal used with Zr to make wires for superconducting magnets

Answers to Practice Exercises

2.1 29 protons, 34 neutrons, and 29 electrons. **2.2** $CHCl_3$. **2.3** $C_4H_5N_2O$. **2.4** (a) Lead(II) oxide, (b) lithium sulfite. **2.5** (a) Rb_2SO_4, (b) BaH_2. **2.6** (a) Nitrogen trifluoride, (b) dichlorine heptoxide. **2.7** (a) SF_4, (b) N_2O_5. **2.8** (a) Hypobromous acid, (b) hydrogen sulfate ion.

---

*Reproduced with permission of S. J. Cyvin of the University of Trondheim (Norway). This puzzle appeared in *Chemical & Engineering News*, December 14, 1987 (p. 86) and in *Chem Matters*, October 1988.

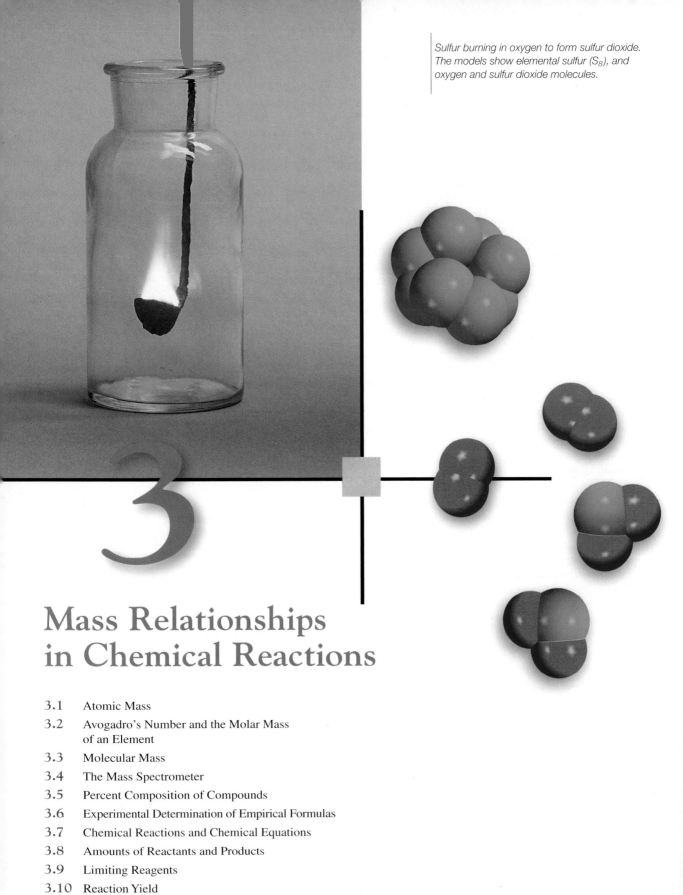

Sulfur burning in oxygen to form sulfur dioxide. The models show elemental sulfur (S_8), and oxygen and sulfur dioxide molecules.

3

Mass Relationships in Chemical Reactions

Interactive Activity Summary

1. Interactivity: Molecular Mass (3.3)
2. Interactivity: Balance the Equation (3.7)
3. Interactivity: Balancing Chemical Equations (3.7)
4. Interactivity: The Mole Method (3.8)
5. Animation: Limiting Reagent (3.9)
6. Interactivity: Limiting Reactant Game (3.9)

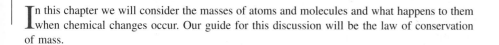

In this chapter we will consider the masses of atoms and molecules and what happens to them when chemical changes occur. Our guide for this discussion will be the law of conservation of mass.

3.1 Atomic Mass

In this chapter we will use what we have learned about chemical structure and formulas in studying the mass relationships of atoms and molecules. These relationships in turn will help us to explain the composition of compounds and the ways in which composition changes.

Section 3.4 describes a method for determining atomic mass.

The mass of an atom depends on the number of electrons, protons, and neutrons it contains. Knowledge of an atom's mass is important in laboratory work. But atoms are extremely small particles—even the smallest speck of dust that our unaided eyes can detect contains as many as 1×10^{16} atoms! Clearly we cannot weigh a single atom, but it is possible to determine the mass of one atom *relative* to another experimentally. The first step is to assign a value to the mass of one atom of a given element so that it can be used as a standard.

One atomic mass unit is also called one dalton.

By international agreement, **atomic mass** (sometimes called *atomic weight*) is *the mass of the atom in atomic mass units (amu)*. One **atomic mass unit** is defined as *a mass exactly equal to one-twelfth the mass of one carbon-12 atom.* Carbon-12 is the carbon isotope that has six protons and six neutrons. Setting the atomic mass of carbon-12 at 12 amu provides the standard for measuring the atomic mass of the other elements. For example, experiments have shown that, on average, a hydrogen atom is only 8.400 percent as massive as the carbon-12 atom. Thus, if the mass of one carbon-12 atom is exactly 12 amu, the atomic mass of hydrogen must be 0.084×12.00 amu or 1.008 amu. Similar calculations show that the atomic mass of oxygen is 16.00 amu and that of iron is 55.85 amu. Thus, although we do not know just how much an average iron atom's mass is, we know that it is approximately 56 times as massive as a hydrogen atom.

Average Atomic Mass

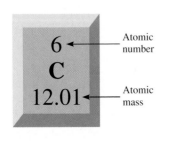

When you look up the atomic mass of carbon in a table such as the one on the inside front cover of this book, you will find that its value is not 12.00 amu but 12.01 amu. The reason for the difference is that most naturally occurring elements (including carbon) have more than one isotope. This means that when we measure the atomic mass of an element, we must generally settle for the *average* mass of the naturally occurring mixture of isotopes. For example, the natural abundances of carbon-12 and carbon-13 are 98.90 percent and 1.10 percent, respectively. The atomic mass of carbon-13 has been determined to be 13.00335 amu. Thus the average atomic mass of carbon can be calculated as follows:

$$\text{average atomic mass} \atop \text{of natural carbon} = (0.9890)(12.00000 \text{ amu}) + (0.0110)(13.00335 \text{ amu})$$
$$= 12.01 \text{ amu}$$

Note that in calculations involving percentages, we need to convert percentages to fractions. For example, 98.90 percent becomes 98.90/100, or 0.9890. Because there are many more carbon-12 atoms than carbon-13 atoms in naturally occurring carbon, the average atomic mass is much closer to 12 amu than to 13 amu.

It is important to understand that when we say that the atomic mass of carbon is 12.01 amu, we are referring to the *average* value. If carbon atoms could be examined individually, we would find either an atom of atomic mass 12.00000 amu or one of 13.00335 amu, but never one of 12.01 amu. Example 3.1 shows how to calculate the average atomic mass of an element.

Example 3.1

Copper, a metal known since ancient times, is used in electrical cables and pennies, among other things. The atomic masses of its two stable isotopes, $_{29}^{63}Cu$ (69.09 percent) and $_{29}^{65}Cu$ (30.91 percent), are 62.93 amu and 64.9278 amu, respectively. Calculate the average atomic mass of copper. The relative abundances are given in parentheses.

Strategy Each isotope contributes to the average atomic mass based on its relative abundance. Multiplying the mass of an isotope by its fractional abundance (not percent) will give the contribution to the average atomic mass of that particular isotope.

Solution First the percents are converted to fractions: 69.09 percent to 69.09/100 or 0.6909 and 30.91 percent to 30.91/100 or 0.3091. We find the contribution to the average atomic mass for each isotope, then add the contributions together to obtain the average atomic mass.

$$(0.6909)(62.93 \text{ amu}) + (0.3091)(64.9278 \text{ amu}) = 63.55 \text{ amu}$$

Check The average atomic mass should be between the two isotopic masses; therefore, the answer is reasonable. Note that because there are more $_{29}^{63}Cu$ than $_{29}^{65}Cu$ isotopes, the average atomic mass is closer to 62.93 amu than to 64.9278 amu.

Practice Exercise The atomic masses of the two stable isotopes of boron, $_{5}^{10}B$ (19.78 percent) and $_{5}^{11}B$ (80.22 percent), are 10.0129 amu and 11.0093 amu, respectively. Calculate the average atomic mass of boron.

Copper.

Similar problems: 3.5, 3.6.

The atomic masses of many elements have been accurately determined to five or six significant figures. However, for our purposes we will normally use atomic masses accurate only to four significant figures (see table of atomic masses inside the front cover). For simplicity, we will omit the word "average" when we discuss the atomic masses of the elements.

3.2 Avogadro's Number and the Molar Mass of an Element

Atomic mass units provide a relative scale for the masses of the elements. But because atoms have such small masses, no usable scale can be devised to weigh them in calibrated units of atomic mass units. In any real situation, we deal with macroscopic samples containing enormous numbers of atoms. Therefore it is convenient to have a special unit to describe a very large number of atoms. The idea of a unit to denote a particular number of objects is not new. For example, the pair (2 items), the dozen (12 items), and the gross (144 items) are all familiar units. Chemists measure atoms and molecules in moles.

In the SI system the **mole (mol)** is *the amount of a substance that contains as many elementary entities (atoms, molecules, or other particles) as there are atoms in exactly 12 g (or 0.012 kg) of the carbon-12 isotope.* The actual number of atoms in 12 g of carbon-12 is determined experimentally. This number is called **Avogadro's number** **(N_A),** in honor of the Italian scientist Amedeo Avogadro.[†] The currently accepted value is

The adjective formed from the noun "mole" is "molar."

[†]Lorenzo Romano Amedeo Carlo Avogadro di Quaregua e di Cerreto (1776–1856). Italian mathematical physicist. He practiced law for many years before he became interested in science. His most famous work, now known as Avogadro's law (see Chapter 5), was largely ignored during his lifetime, although it became the basis for determining atomic masses in the late nineteenth century.

Figure 3.1 *One mole each of several common elements. Carbon (black charcoal powder), sulfur (yellow powder), iron (as nails), copper wires, and mercury (shiny liquid metal).*

$$N_A = 6.0221367 \times 10^{23}$$

Generally, we round Avogadro's number to 6.022×10^{23}. Thus, just as one dozen oranges contains 12 oranges, 1 mole of hydrogen atoms contains 6.022×10^{23} H atoms. Figure 3.1 shows samples containing 1 mole each of several common elements.

In calculations, the units of molar mass are g/mol or kg/mol.

We have seen that 1 mole of carbon-12 atoms has a mass of exactly 12 g and contains 6.022×10^{23} atoms. This mass of carbon-12 is its ***molar mass (M),*** defined as *the mass (in grams or kilograms) of 1 mole of units* (such as atoms or molecules) of a substance. Note that the molar mass of carbon-12 (in grams) is numerically equal to its atomic mass in amu. Likewise, the atomic mass of sodium (Na) is 22.99 amu and its molar mass is 22.99 g; the atomic mass of phosphorus is 30.97 amu and its molar mass is 30.97 g; and so on. If we know the atomic mass of an element, we also know its molar mass.

Using atomic mass and molar mass, we can calculate the mass in grams of a single carbon-12 atom. From our discussion we know that 1 mole of carbon-12 atoms weighs exactly 12 grams. This enables us to write the equality

$$12.00 \text{ g carbon-12} = 1 \text{ mol carbon-12 atoms}$$

Therefore, we can write the conversion factor as

$$\frac{12.00 \text{ g carbon-12}}{1 \text{ mol carbon-12 atoms}}$$

(Note that we use the unit "mol" to represent "mole" in calculations.) Similarly, because there are 6.022×10^{23} atoms in 1 mole of carbon-12 atoms, we have

$$1 \text{ mol carbon-12 atoms} = 6.022 \times 10^{23} \text{ carbon-12 atoms}$$

and the conversion factor is

$$\frac{1 \text{ mol carbon-12 atoms}}{6.022 \times 10^{23} \text{ carbon-12 atoms}}$$

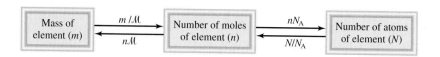

We can now calculate the mass (in grams) of 1 carbon-12 atom as follows:

$$1 \text{ carbon-12 atom} \times \frac{1 \text{ mol carbon-12 atoms}}{6.022 \times 10^{23} \text{ carbon-12 atoms}} \times \frac{12.00 \text{ g carbon-12}}{1 \text{ mol carbon-12 atoms}}$$

$$= 1.993 \times 10^{-23} \text{ g carbon-12}$$

We can use this result to determine the relationship between atomic mass units and grams. Because the mass of every carbon-12 atom is exactly 12 amu, the number of atomic mass units equivalent to 1 gram is

$$\frac{\text{amu}}{\text{gram}} = \frac{1 \text{ carbon-12 atom}}{1.993 \times 10^{-23} \text{ g}} \times \frac{12 \text{ amu}}{1 \text{ carbon-12 atom}}$$

$$= 6.022 \times 10^{23} \text{ amu/g}$$

Thus

$$1 \text{ g} = 6.022 \times 10^{23} \text{ amu}$$

and

$$1 \text{ amu} = 1.661 \times 10^{-24} \text{ g}$$

This example shows that Avogadro's number can be used to convert from the atomic mass units to mass in grams and vice versa.

The notions of Avogadro's number and molar mass enable us to carry out conversions between mass and moles of atoms and between the number of atoms and mass and to calculate the mass of a single atom. We will employ the following conversion factors in the calculations:

$$\frac{1 \text{ mol X}}{\text{molar mass of X}} \quad \text{and} \quad \frac{1 \text{ mol X}}{6.022 \times 10^{23} \text{ X atoms}}$$

The molar masses of the elements are given on the inside front cover of the book.

where X represents the symbol of an element. Figure 3.2 summarizes the relationships between the mass of an element and the number of moles of an element and between moles of an element and the number of atoms of an element. Using the proper conversion factors we can convert one quantity to another, as Examples 3.2–3.4 show.

Example 3.2

Helium (He) is a valuable gas used in industry, low-temperature research, deep-sea diving tanks, and balloons. How many moles of He atoms are in 6.46 g of He?

Strategy We are given grams of helium and asked to solve for moles of helium. What conversion factor do we need to convert between grams and moles? Arrange the appropriate conversion factor so that grams cancel and the unit moles is obtained for your answer.

Solution The conversion factor needed to convert between grams and moles is the molar mass. In the periodic table (see inside front cover) we see that the molar mass of He is 4.003 g. This can be expressed as

$$1 \text{ mol He} = 4.003 \text{ g He}$$

(Continued)

A scientific research helium balloon.

From this equality, we can write two conversion factors

$$\frac{1 \text{ mol He}}{4.003 \text{ g He}} \quad \text{and} \quad \frac{4.003 \text{ g He}}{1 \text{ mol He}}$$

The conversion factor on the left is the correct one. Grams will cancel, leaving the unit mol for the answer, that is

$$6.46 \text{ g He} \times \frac{1 \text{ mol He}}{4.003 \text{ g He}} = 1.61 \text{ mol He}$$

Thus, there are 1.61 moles of He atoms in 6.46 g of He.

Check Because the given mass (6.46 g) is larger than the molar mass of He, we expect to have more than 1 mole of He.

Similar problem: 3.15.

Practice Exercise How many moles of magnesium (Mg) are there in 87.3 g of Mg?

Zinc.

Example 3.3

Zinc (Zn) is a silvery metal that is used in making brass (with copper) and in plating iron to prevent corrosion. How many grams of Zn are in 0.356 mole of Zn?

Strategy We are trying to solve for grams of zinc. What conversion factor do we need to convert between moles and grams? Arrange the appropriate conversion factor so that moles cancel and the unit grams are obtained for your answer.

Solution The conversion factor needed to convert between moles and grams is the molar mass. In the periodic table (see inside front cover) we see the molar mass of Zn is 65.39 g. This can be expressed as

$$1 \text{ mol Zn} = 65.39 \text{ g Zn}$$

From this equality, we can write two conversion factors

$$\frac{1 \text{ mol Zn}}{65.39 \text{ g Zn}} \quad \text{and} \quad \frac{65.39 \text{ g Zn}}{1 \text{ mol Zn}}$$

The conversion factor on the right is the correct one. Moles will cancel, leaving unit of grams for the answer. The number of grams of Zn is

$$0.356 \text{ mol Zn} \times \frac{65.39 \text{ g Zn}}{1 \text{ mol Zn}} = 23.3 \text{ g Zn}$$

Thus, there are 23.3 g of Zn in 0.356 mole of Zn.

Check Does a mass of 23.3 g for 0.356 mole of Zn seem reasonable? What is the mass of 1 mole of Zn?

Similar problem: 3.16.

Practice Exercise Calculate the number of grams of lead (Pb) in 12.4 moles of lead.

Example 3.4

Sulfur (S) is a nonmetallic element that is present in coal. When coal is burned, sulfur is converted to sulfur dioxide and eventually to sulfuric acid that gives rise to the acid rain phenomenon. How many atoms are in 16.3 g of S?

(Continued)

Strategy The question asks for atoms of sulfur. We cannot convert directly from grams to atoms of sulfur. What unit do we need to convert grams of sulfur to in order to convert to atoms? What does Avogadro's number represent?

Solution We need two conversions: first from grams to moles and then from moles to number of particles (atoms). The first step is similar to Example 3.2. Because

$$1 \text{ mol S} = 32.07 \text{ g S}$$

the conversion factor is

$$\frac{1 \text{ mol S}}{32.07 \text{ g S}}$$

Avogadro's number is the key to the second step. We have

$$1 \text{ mol} = 6.022 \times 10^{23} \text{ particles (atoms)}$$

and the conversion factors are

$$\frac{6.022 \times 10^{23} \text{ S atoms}}{1 \text{ mol S}} \quad \text{and} \quad \frac{1 \text{ mol S}}{6.022 \times 10^{23} \text{ S atoms}}$$

Elemental sulfur (S_8) consists of eight S atoms joined in a ring.

The conversion factor on the left is the one we need because it has number of S atoms in the numerator. We can solve the problem by first calculating the number of moles contained in 16.3 g of S, and then calculating the number of S atoms from the number of moles of S:

$$\text{grams of S} \longrightarrow \text{moles of S} \longrightarrow \text{number of S atoms}$$

We can combine these conversions in one step as follows:

$$16.3 \text{ g S} \times \frac{1 \text{ mol S}}{32.07 \text{ g S}} \times \frac{6.022 \times 10^{23} \text{ S atoms}}{1 \text{ mol S}} = 3.06 \times 10^{23} \text{ S atoms}$$

Thus there are 3.06×10^{23} atoms of S in 16.3 g of S.

Check Should 16.3 g of S contain fewer than Avogadro's number of atoms? What mass of S would contain Avogadro's number of atoms?

Practice Exercise Calculate the number of atoms in 0.551 g of potassium (K).

Similar problems: 3.20, 3.21.

3.3 Molecular Mass

If we know the atomic masses of the component atoms, we can calculate the mass of a molecule. The ***molecular mass*** (sometimes called *molecular weight*) is *the sum of the atomic masses (in amu) in the molecule.* For example, the molecular mass of H_2O is

Interactivity: Molecular Mass
Online Learning Center, Interactives

$$2(\text{atomic mass of H}) + \text{atomic mass of O}$$

or

$$2(1.008 \text{ amu}) + 16.00 \text{ amu} = 18.02 \text{ amu}$$

In general, we need to multiply the atomic mass of each element by the number of atoms of that element present in the molecule and sum over all the elements. Example 3.5 illustrates this approach.

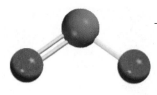

SO$_2$

Example 3.5

Calculate the molecular masses (in amu) of the following compounds: (a) sulfur dioxide (SO$_2$) and (b) caffeine (C$_8$H$_{10}$N$_4$O$_2$)

Strategy How do atomic masses of different elements combine to give the molecular mass of a compound?

Solution To calculate molecular mass, we need to sum all the atomic masses in the molecule. For each element, we multiply the atomic mass of the element by the number of atoms of that element in the molecule. We find atomic masses in the periodic table (inside front cover).

(a) There are two O atoms and one S atom in SO$_2$, so that

$$\text{molecular mass of SO}_2 = 32.07 \text{ amu} + 2(16.00 \text{ amu})$$
$$= 64.07 \text{ amu}$$

(b) There are eight C atoms, ten H atoms, four N atoms, and two O atoms in caffeine, so the molecular mass of C$_8$H$_{10}$N$_4$O$_2$ is given by

$$8(12.01 \text{ amu}) + 10(1.008 \text{ amu}) + 4(14.01 \text{ amu}) + 2(16.00 \text{ amu}) = 194.20 \text{ amu}$$

Practice Exercise What is the molecular mass of methanol (CH$_4$O)?

Similar problems: 3.23, 3.24.

From the molecular mass we can determine the molar mass of a molecule or compound. The molar mass of a compound (in grams) is numerically equal to its molecular mass (in amu). For example, the molecular mass of water is 18.02 amu, so its molar mass is 18.02 g. Note that 1 mole of water weighs 18.02 g and contains 6.022×10^{23} H$_2$O *molecules,* just as 1 mole of elemental carbon contains 6.022×10^{23} carbon *atoms.*

As Examples 3.6 and 3.7 show, a knowledge of the molar mass enables us to calculate the numbers of moles and individual atoms in a given quantity of a compound.

CH$_4$

Example 3.6

Methane (CH$_4$) is the principal component of natural gas. How many moles of CH$_4$ are present in 6.07 g of CH$_4$?

Strategy We are given grams of CH$_4$ and asked to solve for moles of CH$_4$. What conversion factor do we need to convert between grams and moles? Arrange the appropriate conversion factor so that grams cancel and the unit moles are obtained for your answer.

Solution The conversion factor needed to convert between grams and moles is the molar mass. First we need to calculate the molar mass of CH$_4$, following the procedure in Example 3.5:

$$\text{molar mass of CH}_4 = 12.01 \text{ g} + 4(1.008 \text{ g})$$
$$= 16.04 \text{ g}$$

Because

$$1 \text{ mol CH}_4 = 16.04 \text{ g CH}_4$$

Methane gas burning on a cooking range.

(Continued)

the conversion factor we need should have grams in the denominator so that the unit g will cancel, leaving the unit mol in the numerator:

$$\frac{1 \text{ mol CH}_4}{16.04 \text{ g CH}_4}$$

We now write

$$6.07 \text{ g } \cancel{CH_4} \times \frac{1 \text{ mol CH}_4}{16.04 \text{ g } \cancel{CH_4}} = 0.378 \text{ mol CH}_4$$

Thus there is 0.378 mole of CH_4 in 6.07 g of CH_4.

Check Should 6.07 g of CH_4 equal less than 1 mole of CH_4? What is the mass of 1 mole of CH_4?

Similar problem: 3.26.

Practice Exercise Calculate the number of moles of chloroform ($CHCl_3$) in 198 g of chloroform.

Example 3.7

How many hydrogen atoms are present in 25.6 g of urea [$(NH_2)_2CO$], which is used as a fertilizer, in animal feed, and in the manufacture of polymers? The molar mass of urea is 60.06 g.

Strategy We are asked to solve for atoms of hydrogen in 25.6 g of urea. We cannot convert directly from grams of urea to atoms of hydrogen. What unit do we need to obtain first before we can convert to atoms? How should Avogadro's number be used here? How many atoms of H are in 1 molecule of urea?

Solution To calculate number of H atoms, we first must convert grams of urea to number of molecules of urea. This part is similar to Example 3.4. The molecular formula of urea shows there are four H atoms in one urea molecule. We need three conversion factors: the molar mass of urea, Avogadro's number, and the number of H atoms in 1 molecule of urea. We can combine these three conversions

Urea.

grams of urea $\longrightarrow$ moles of urea $\longrightarrow$ molecules of urea $\longrightarrow$ atoms of H

into one calculation,

$$25.6 \text{ g } \cancel{(NH_2)_2CO} \times \frac{1 \text{ mol } \cancel{(NH_2)_2CO}}{60.06 \text{ g } \cancel{(NH_2)_2CO}} \times \frac{6.022 \times 10^{23} \text{ molecules } \cancel{(NH_2)_2CO}}{1 \text{ mol } \cancel{(NH_2)_2CO}}$$
$$\times \frac{4 \text{ H atoms}}{1 \text{ molecule } \cancel{(NH_2)_2CO}} = 1.03 \times 10^{24} \text{ H atoms}$$

The preceding method utilizes the ratio of molecules (urea) to atoms (hydrogen). We can also solve the problem by reading the formula as the ratio of moles of urea to moles of hydrogen using the following conversions

grams of urea $\longrightarrow$ moles of urea $\longrightarrow$ moles of H $\longrightarrow$ atoms of H

Try it.

Check Does the answer look reasonable? How many atoms of H would 60.06 g of urea contain?

Similar problems: 3.27, 3.28.

Practice Exercise How many H atoms are in 72.5 g of isopropanol (rubbing alcohol), C_3H_8O?

3.4 The Mass Spectrometer

The most direct and most accurate method for determining atomic and molecular masses is mass spectrometry, which is depicted in Figure 3.3. In a *mass spectrometer*, a gaseous sample is bombarded by a stream of high-energy electrons. Collisions between the electrons and the gaseous atoms (or molecules) produce positive ions by dislodging an electron from each atom or molecule. These positive ions (of mass *m* and charge *e*) are accelerated by two oppositely charged plates as they pass through the plates. The emerging ions are deflected into a circular path by a magnet. The radius of the path depends on the charge-to-mass ratio (that is, *e/m*). Ions of smaller *e/m* ratio trace a wider curve than those having a larger *e/m* ratio, so that ions with equal charges but different masses are separated from one another. The mass of each ion (and hence its parent atom or molecule) is determined from the magnitude of its deflection. Eventually the ions arrive at the detector, which registers a current for each type of ion. The amount of current generated is directly proportional to the number of ions, so it enables us to determine the relative abundance of isotopes.

The first mass spectrometer, developed in the 1920s by the English physicist F. W. Aston,[†] was crude by today's standards. Nevertheless, it provided indisputable evidence of the existence of isotopes—neon-20 (atomic mass 19.9924 amu and natural abundance 90.92 percent) and neon-22 (atomic mass 21.9914 amu and natural abundance 8.82 percent). When more sophisticated and sensitive mass spectrometers became available, scientists were surprised to discover that neon has a third stable isotope with an atomic mass of 20.9940 amu and natural abundance 0.257 percent (Figure 3.4). This example illustrates how very important experimental accuracy is to a quantitative science like chemistry. Early experiments failed to detect neon-21 because its natural abundance is just 0.257 percent. In other words, only 26 in 10,000 Ne atoms are neon-21. The masses of molecules can be determined in a similar manner by the mass spectrometer.

3.5 Percent Composition of Compounds

As we have seen, the formula of a compound tells us the numbers of atoms of each element in a unit of the compound. However, suppose we needed to verify the purity of a compound for use in a laboratory experiment. From the formula we could

---

[†]Francis William Aston (1877–1945). English chemist and physicist. He was awarded the Nobel Prize in Chemistry in 1922 for developing the mass spectrometer.

Figure 3.3 *Diagram showing one type of mass spectrometer.*

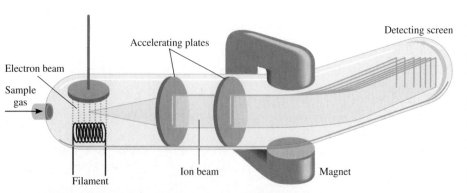

Detecting screen

Accelerating plates

Electron beam

Sample gas

Ion beam   Magnet

Filament

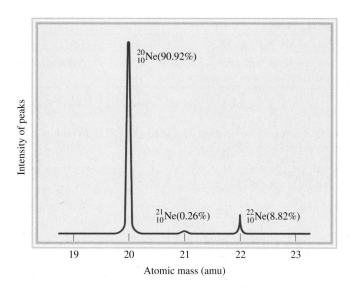

Figure 3.4 *The mass spectrum of the three isotopes of neon.*

calculate what percent of the total mass of the compound is contributed by each element. Then, by comparing the result to the percent composition obtained experimentally for our sample, we could determine the purity of the sample.

The ***percent composition by mass*** is the *percent by mass of each element in a compound.* Percent composition is obtained by dividing the mass of each element in 1 mole of the compound by the molar mass of the compound and multiplying by 100 percent. Mathematically, the percent composition of an element in a compound is expressed as

$$\text{percent composition of an element} = \frac{n \times \text{molar mass of element}}{\text{molar mass of compound}} \times 100\% \quad (3.1)$$

where n is the number of moles of the element in 1 mole of the compound. For example, in 1 mole of hydrogen peroxide (H_2O_2) there are 2 moles of H atoms and 2 moles of O atoms. The molar masses of H_2O_2, H, and O are 34.02 g, 1.008 g, and 16.00 g, respectively. Therefore, the percent composition of H_2O_2 is calculated as follows:

$$\%H = \frac{2 \times 1.008 \text{ g H}}{34.02 \text{ g } H_2O_2} \times 100\% = 5.926\%$$

$$\%O = \frac{2 \times 16.00 \text{ g O}}{34.02 \text{ g } H_2O_2} \times 100\% = 94.06\%$$

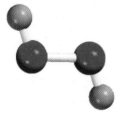

H_2O_2

The sum of the percentages is $5.926\% + 94.06\% = 99.99\%$. The small discrepancy from 100 percent is due to the way we rounded off the molar masses of the elements. If we had used the empirical formula HO for the calculation, we would have written

$$\%H = \frac{1.008 \text{ g H}}{17.01 \text{ g } H_2O_2} \times 100\% = 5.926\%$$

$$\%O = \frac{16.00 \text{ g O}}{17.01 \text{ g } H_2O_2} \times 100\% = 94.06\%$$

Because both the molecular formula and the empirical formula tell us the composition of the compound, it is not surprising that they give us the same percent composition by mass.

H_3PO_4

Example 3.8

Phosphoric acid (H_3PO_4) is a colorless, syrupy liquid used in detergents, fertilizers, toothpastes, and in carbonated beverages for a "tangy" flavor. Calculate the percent composition by mass of H, P, and O in this compound.

Strategy Recall the procedure for calculating a percentage. Assume that we have 1 mole of H_3PO_4. The percent by mass of each element (H, P, and O) is given by the combined molar mass of the atoms of the element in 1 mole of H_3PO_4 divided by the molar mass of H_3PO_4, then multiplied by 100 percent.

Solution The molar mass of H_3PO_4 is 97.99 g. The percent by mass of each of the elements in H_3PO_4 is calculated as follows:

$$\%H = \frac{3(1.008 \text{ g}) \text{ H}}{97.99 \text{ g } H_3PO_4} \times 100\% = 3.086\%$$

$$\%P = \frac{30.97 \text{ g P}}{97.99 \text{ g } H_3PO_4} \times 100\% = 31.61\%$$

$$\%O = \frac{4(16.00 \text{ g}) \text{ O}}{97.99 \text{ g } H_3PO_4} \times 100\% = 65.31\%$$

Check Do the percentages add to 100 percent? The sum of the percentages is $(3.086\% + 31.61\% + 65.31\%) = 100.01\%$. The small discrepancy from 100 percent is due to the way we rounded off.

Similar problem: 3.40.

Practice Exercise Calculate the percent composition by mass of each of the elements in sulfuric acid (H_2SO_4).

The procedure used in the example can be reversed if necessary. Given the percent composition by mass of a compound, we can determine the empirical formula of the compound (Figure 3.5). Because we are dealing with percentages and the sum of all the percentages is 100 percent, it is convenient to assume that we started with 100 g of a compound, as Example 3.9 shows.

Example 3.9

Ascorbic acid (vitamin C) cures scurvy. It is composed of 40.92 percent carbon (C), 4.58 percent hydrogen (H), and 54.50 percent oxygen (O) by mass. Determine its empirical formula.

Strategy In a chemical formula, the subscripts represent the ratio of the number of moles of each element that combine to form one mole of the compound. How can we convert from mass percent to moles? If we assume an exactly 100-g sample of the compound, do we know the mass of each element in the compound? How do we then convert from grams to moles?

Solution If we have 100 g of ascorbic acid, then each percentage can be converted directly to grams. In this sample, there will be 40.92 g of C, 4.58 g of H, and 54.50 g of O. Because the subscripts in the formula represent a mole ratio, we need to convert the grams of each element to moles. The conversion factor needed is the molar mass of each element. Let n represent the number of moles of each element so that

$$n_C = 40.92 \text{ g C} \times \frac{1 \text{ mol C}}{12.01 \text{ g C}} = 3.407 \text{ mol C}$$

$$n_H = 4.58 \text{ g H} \times \frac{1 \text{ mol H}}{1.008 \text{ g H}} = 4.54 \text{ mol H}$$

$$n_O = 54.50 \text{ g O} \times \frac{1 \text{ mol O}}{16.00 \text{ g O}} = 3.406 \text{ mol O}$$

Mass percent

↓

Moles of each element

↓

Mole ratios of elements

↓

Empirical formula

Figure 3.5 *Procedure for calculating the empirical formula of a compound from its percent compositions.*

(Continued)

Thus, we arrive at the formula $C_{3.407}H_{4.54}O_{3.406}$, which gives the identity and the mole ratios of atoms present. However, chemical formulas are written with whole numbers. Try to convert to whole numbers by dividing all the subscripts by the smallest subscript (3.406):

$$C: \frac{3.407}{3.406} \approx 1 \quad H: \frac{4.54}{3.406} = 1.33 \quad O: \frac{3.406}{3.406} = 1$$

where the $\approx$ sign means "approximately equal to." This gives $CH_{1.33}O$ as the formula for ascorbic acid. Next, we need to convert 1.33, the subscript for H, into an integer. This can be done by a trial-and-error procedure:

$$1.33 \times 1 = 1.33$$
$$1.33 \times 2 = 2.66$$
$$1.33 \times 3 = 3.99 \approx 4$$

Because 1.33×3 gives us an integer (4), we multiply all the subscripts by 3 and obtain $C_3H_4O_3$ as the empirical formula for ascorbic acid.

Check Are the subscripts in $C_3H_4O_3$ reduced to the smallest whole numbers?

Practice Exercise Determine the empirical formula of a compound having the following percent composition by mass: K: 24.75 percent; Mn: 34.77 percent; O: 40.51 percent.

The molecular formula of ascorbic acid is $C_6H_8O_6$.

Similar problems: 3.49, 3.50.

Chemists often want to know the actual mass of an element in a certain mass of a compound. For example, in the mining industry, this information will tell the scientists about the quality of the ore. Because the percent composition by mass of the elements in the substance can be readily calculated, such a problem can be solved in a rather direct way.

Example 3.10

Chalcopyrite ($CuFeS_2$) is a principal mineral of copper. Calculate the number of kilograms of Cu in 3.71×10^3 kg of chalcopyrite.

Strategy Chalcopyrite is composed of Cu, Fe, and S. The mass due to Cu is based on its percentage by mass in the compound. How do we calculate mass percent of an element?

Solution The molar masses of Cu and $CuFeS_2$ are 63.55 g and 183.5 g, respectively. The mass percent of Cu is therefore

$$\%Cu = \frac{\text{molar mass of Cu}}{\text{molar mass of } CuFeS_2} \times 100\%$$

$$= \frac{63.55 \text{ g}}{183.5 \text{ g}} \times 100\% = 34.63\%$$

To calculate the mass of Cu in a 3.71×10^3 kg sample of $CuFeS_2$, we need to convert the percentage to a fraction (that is, convert 34.63 percent to 34.63/100, or 0.3463) and write

$$\text{mass of Cu in } CuFeS_2 = 0.3463 \times (3.71 \times 10^3 \text{ kg}) = 1.28 \times 10^3 \text{ kg}$$

Check As a ball-park estimate, note that the mass percent of Cu is roughly 33 percent, so that a third of the mass should be Cu; that is, $\frac{1}{3} \times 3.71 \times 10^3$ kg $\approx 1.24 \times 10^3$ kg. This quantity is quite close to the answer.

Practice Exercise Calculate the number of grams of Al in 371 g of Al_2O_3.

Chalcopyrite.

Similar problem: 3.45.

3.6 Experimental Determination of Empirical Formulas

The fact that we can determine the empirical formula of a compound if we know the percent composition enables us to identify compounds experimentally. The procedure is as follows. First, chemical analysis tells us the number of grams of each element present in a given amount of a compound. Then we convert the quantities in grams to number of moles of each element. Finally, using the method given in Example 3.9, we find the empirical formula of the compound.

As a specific example, let us consider the compound ethanol. When ethanol is burned in an apparatus such as that shown in Figure 3.6, carbon dioxide (CO_2) and water (H_2O) are given off. Because neither carbon nor hydrogen was in the inlet gas, we can conclude that both carbon (C) and hydrogen (H) were present in ethanol and that oxygen (O) may also be present. (Molecular oxygen was added in the combustion process, but some of the oxygen may also have come from the original ethanol sample.)

The masses of CO_2 and of H_2O produced can be determined by measuring the increase in mass of the CO_2 and H_2O absorbers, respectively. Suppose that in one experiment the combustion of 11.5 g of ethanol produced 22.0 g of CO_2 and 13.5 g of H_2O. We can calculate the mass of carbon and hydrogen in the original 11.5-g sample of ethanol as follows:

$$\text{mass of C} = 22.0 \text{ g } CO_2 \times \frac{1 \text{ mol } CO_2}{44.01 \text{ g } CO_2} \times \frac{1 \text{ mol C}}{1 \text{ mol } CO_2} \times \frac{12.01 \text{ g C}}{1 \text{ mol C}}$$

$$= 6.00 \text{ g C}$$

$$\text{mass of H} = 13.5 \text{ g } H_2O \times \frac{1 \text{ mol } H_2O}{18.02 \text{ g } H_2O} \times \frac{2 \text{ mol H}}{1 \text{ mol } H_2O} \times \frac{1.008 \text{ g H}}{1 \text{ mol H}}$$

$$= 1.51 \text{ g H}$$

Thus, 11.5 g of ethanol contains 6.00 g of carbon and 1.51 g of hydrogen. The remainder must be oxygen, whose mass is

$$\begin{aligned}\text{mass of O} &= \text{mass of sample} - (\text{mass of C} + \text{mass of H}) \\ &= 11.5 \text{ g} - (6.00 \text{ g} + 1.51 \text{ g}) \\ &= 4.0 \text{ g}\end{aligned}$$

The number of moles of each element present in 11.5 g of ethanol is

$$\text{moles of C} = 6.00 \text{ g C} \times \frac{1 \text{ mol C}}{12.01 \text{ g C}} = 0.500 \text{ mol C}$$

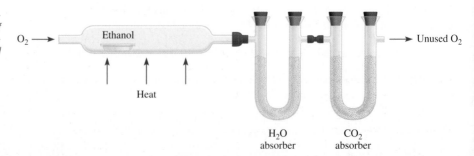

Figure 3.6 *Apparatus for determining the empirical formula of ethanol. The absorbers are substances that can retain water and carbon dioxide, respectively.*

$$\text{moles of H} = 1.51 \text{ g H} \times \frac{1 \text{ mol H}}{1.008 \text{ g H}} = 1.50 \text{ mol H}$$

$$\text{moles of O} = 4.0 \text{ g O} \times \frac{1 \text{ mol O}}{16.00 \text{ g O}} = 0.25 \text{ mol O}$$

The formula of ethanol is therefore $C_{0.50}H_{1.5}O_{0.25}$ (we round off the number of moles to two significant figures). Because the number of atoms must be an integer, we divide the subscripts by 0.25, the smallest subscript, and obtain for the empirical formula C_2H_6O.

Now we can better understand the word "empirical," which literally means "based only on observation and measurement." The empirical formula of ethanol is determined from analysis of the compound in terms of its component elements. No knowledge of how the atoms are linked together in the compound is required.

It happens that the molecular formula of ethanol is the same as its empirical formula.

Determination of Molecular Formulas

The formula calculated from percent composition by mass is always the empirical formula because the subscripts in the formula are always reduced to the smallest whole numbers. To calculate the actual, molecular formula we must know the *approximate* molar mass of the compound in addition to its empirical formula. Knowing that the molar mass of a compound must be an integral multiple of the molar mass of its empirical formula, we can use the molar mass to find the molecular formula, as Example 3.11 demonstrates.

Example 3.11

A sample of a compound contains 1.52 g of nitrogen (N) and 3.47 g of oxygen (O). The molar mass of this compound is between 90 g and 95 g. Determine the molecular formula and the accurate molar mass of the compound.

Strategy To determine the molecular formula, we first need to determine the empirical formula. How do we convert between grams and moles? Comparing the empirical molar mass to the experimentally determined molar mass will reveal the relationship between the empirical formula and molecular formula.

Solution We are given grams of N and O. Use molar mass as a conversion factor to convert grams to moles of each element. Let n represent the number of moles of each element. We write

$$n_N = 1.52 \text{ g N} \times \frac{1 \text{ mol N}}{14.01 \text{ g N}} = 0.108 \text{ mol N}$$

$$n_O = 3.47 \text{ g O} \times \frac{1 \text{ mol O}}{16.00 \text{ g O}} = 0.217 \text{ mol O}$$

Thus, we arrive at the formula $N_{0.108}O_{0.217}$, which gives the identity and the ratios of atoms present. However, chemical formulas are written with whole numbers. Try to convert to whole numbers by dividing the subscripts by the smaller subscript (0.108). After rounding off, we obtain NO_2 as the empirical formula.

The molecular formula might be the same as the empirical formula or some integral multiple of it (for example, two, three, four, or more times the empirical formula). Comparing the ratio of the molar mass to the molar mass of the empirical formula will show the integral relationship between the empirical and molecular formulas. The molar mass of the empirical formula NO_2 is

$$\text{empirical molar mass} = 14.01 \text{ g} + 2(16.00 \text{ g}) = 46.01 \text{ g}$$

(Continued)

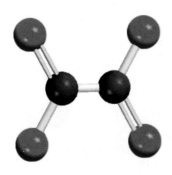

N$_2$O$_4$

Similar problems: 3.52, 3.53, 3.54.

Next, we determine the ratio between the molar mass and the empirical molar mass

$$\frac{\text{molar mass}}{\text{empirical molar mass}} = \frac{90 \text{ g}}{46.01 \text{ g}} \approx 2$$

The molar mass is twice the empirical molar mass. This means that there are two NO$_2$ units in each molecule of the compound, and the molecular formula is (NO$_2$)$_2$ or N$_2$O$_4$.

The actual molar mass of the compound is two times the empirical molar mass, that is, 2(46.01 g) or 92.02 g, which is between 90 g and 95 g.

Check Note that in determining the molecular formula from the empirical formula, we need only know the *approximate* molar mass of the compound. The reason is that the true molar mass is an integral multiple (1×, 2×, 3×, . . .) of the empirical molar mass. Therefore, the ratio (molar mass/empirical molar mass) will always be close to an integer.

Practice Exercise A sample of a compound containing boron (B) and hydrogen (H) contains 6.444 g of B and 1.803 g of H. The molar mass of the compound is about 30 g. What is its molecular formula?

3.7 Chemical Reactions and Chemical Equations

Having discussed the masses of atoms and molecules, we turn next to what happens to atoms and molecules in a ***chemical reaction,*** *a process in which a substance (or substances) is changed into one or more new substances.* To communicate with one another about chemical reactions, chemists have devised a standard way to represent them using chemical equations. A ***chemical equation*** *uses chemical symbols to show what happens during a chemical reaction.* In this section we will learn how to write chemical equations and balance them.

Writing Chemical Equations

Consider what happens when hydrogen gas (H$_2$) burns in air (which contains oxygen, O$_2$) to form water (H$_2$O). This reaction can be represented by the chemical equation

$$H_2 + O_2 \longrightarrow H_2O \tag{3.2}$$

where the "plus" sign means "reacts with" and the arrow means "to yield." Thus, this symbolic expression can be read: "Molecular hydrogen reacts with molecular oxygen to yield water." The reaction is assumed to proceed from left to right as the arrow indicates.

Equation (3.2) is not complete, however, because there are twice as many oxygen atoms on the left side of the arrow (two) as on the right side (one). To conform with the law of conservation of mass, there must be the same number of each type of atom on both sides of the arrow; that is, we must have as many atoms after the reaction ends as we did before it started. We can *balance* Equation (3.2) by placing the appropriate coefficient (2 in this case) in front of H$_2$ and H$_2$O:

When the coefficient is 1, as in the case of O$_2$, it is not shown.

$$2H_2 + O_2 \longrightarrow 2H_2O$$

This *balanced chemical equation* shows that "two hydrogen molecules can combine or react with one oxygen molecule to form two water molecules" (Figure 3.7). Because the ratio of the number of molecules is equal to the ratio of the number of moles, the equation can also be read as "2 moles of hydrogen molecules react with

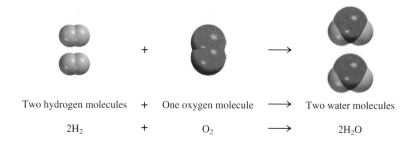

Figure 3.7 *Three ways of representing the combustion of hydrogen. In accordance with the law of conservation of mass, the number of each type of atom must be the same on both sides of the equation.*

Two hydrogen molecules   +   One oxygen molecule $\longrightarrow$ Two water molecules

$2H_2$ + O_2 $\longrightarrow$ $2H_2O$

1 mole of oxygen molecules to produce 2 moles of water molecules." We know the mass of a mole of each of these substances, so we can also interpret the equation as "4.04 g of H_2 react with 32.00 g of O_2 to give 36.04 g of H_2O." These three ways of reading the equation are summarized in Table 3.1.

We refer to H_2 and O_2 in Equation (3.2) as **reactants,** which are *the starting materials in a chemical reaction.* Water is the **product,** which is *the substance formed as a result of a chemical reaction.* A chemical equation, then, is just the chemist's shorthand description of a reaction. In a chemical equation the reactants are conventionally written on the left and the products on the right of the arrow:

$$\text{reactants} \longrightarrow \text{products}$$

To provide additional information, chemists often indicate the physical states of the reactants and products by using the letters *g*, *l*, and *s* to denote gas, liquid, and solid, respectively. For example,

$$2CO(g) + O_2(g) \longrightarrow 2CO_2(g)$$
$$2HgO(s) \longrightarrow 2Hg(l) + O_2(g)$$

The procedure for balancing chemical equations is shown on p. 92.

To represent what happens when sodium chloride (NaCl) is added to water, we write

$$NaCl(s) \xrightarrow{\text{H}_2\text{O}} NaCl(aq)$$

where *aq* denotes the aqueous (that is, water) environment. Writing H_2O above the arrow symbolizes the physical process of dissolving a substance in water, although it is sometimes left out for simplicity.

Knowing the states of the reactants and products is especially useful in the laboratory. For example, when potassium bromide (KBr) and silver nitrate ($AgNO_3$) react in an aqueous environment, a solid, silver bromide (AgBr), is formed. This reaction can be represented by the equation:

$$KBr(aq) + AgNO_3(aq) \longrightarrow KNO_3(aq) + AgBr(s)$$

TABLE 3.1

Interpretation of a Chemical Equation

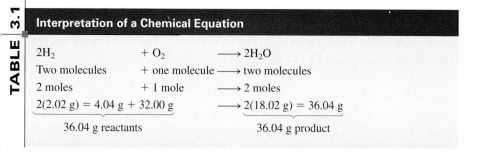

$2H_2$	$+ O_2$	$\longrightarrow 2H_2O$
Two molecules	+ one molecule	$\longrightarrow$ two molecules
2 moles	+ 1 mole	$\longrightarrow$ 2 moles
$2(2.02 \text{ g}) = 4.04 \text{ g}$	+ 32.00 g	$\longrightarrow 2(18.02 \text{ g}) = 36.04 \text{ g}$
36.04 g reactants		36.04 g product

If the physical states of reactants and products are not given, an uninformed person might try to bring about the reaction by mixing solid KBr with solid $AgNO_3$. These solids would react very slowly or not at all. Imagining the process on the microscopic level, we can understand that for a product like silver bromide to form, the Ag^+ and Br^- ions would have to come in contact with each other. However, these ions are locked in place in their solid compounds and have little mobility. (Here is an example of how we explain a phenomenon by thinking about what happens at the molecular level, as discussed in Section 1.2.)

Balancing Chemical Equations

Suppose we want to write an equation to describe a chemical reaction that we have just carried out in the laboratory. How should we go about doing it? Because we know the identities of the reactants, we can write their chemical formulas. The identities of products are more difficult to establish. For simple reactions it is often possible to guess the product(s). For more complicated reactions involving three or more products, chemists may need to perform further tests to establish the presence of specific compounds.

Interactivity: Balance the Equation
Online Learning Center, Interactives

Interactivity: Balancing Chemical Equations
Online Learning Center, Interactives

Once we have identified all the reactants and products and have written the correct formulas for them, we assemble them in the conventional sequence—reactants on the left separated by an arrow from products on the right. The equation written at this point is likely to be *unbalanced;* that is, the number of each type of atom on one side of the arrow differs from the number on the other side. In general, we can balance a chemical equation by the following steps:

1. Identify all reactants and products and write their correct formulas on the left side and right side of the equation, respectively.

2. Begin balancing the equation by trying different coefficients to make the number of atoms of each element the same on both sides of the equation. We can change the coefficients (the numbers preceding the formulas) but not the subscripts (the numbers within formulas). Changing the subscripts would change the identity of the substance. For example, $2NO_2$ means "two molecules of nitrogen dioxide," but if we double the subscripts, we have N_2O_4, which is the formula of dinitrogen tetroxide, a completely different compound.

3. First, look for elements that appear only once on each side of the equation with the same number of atoms on each side: The formulas containing these elements must have the same coefficient. Therefore, there is no need to adjust the coefficients of these elements at this point. Next, look for elements that appear only once on each side of the equation but in unequal numbers of atoms. Balance these elements. Finally, balance elements that appear in two or more formulas on the same side of the equation.

4. Check your balanced equation to be sure that you have the same total number of each type of atoms on both sides of the equation arrow.

Let's consider a specific example. In the laboratory, small amounts of oxygen gas can be prepared by heating potassium chlorate ($KClO_3$). The products are oxygen gas (O_2) and potassium chloride (KCl). From this information, we write

$$KClO_3 \longrightarrow KCl + O_2$$

(For simplicity, we omit the physical states of reactants and products.) All three elements (K, Cl, and O) appear only once on each side of the equation, but only for K and Cl do we have equal numbers of atoms on both sides. Thus $KClO_3$ and KCl must

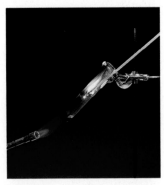

Heating potassium chlorate produces oxygen, which supports the combustion of wood splint.

have the same coefficient. The next step is to make the number of O atoms the same on both sides of the equation. Because there are three O atoms on the left and two O atoms on the right of the equation, we can balance the O atoms by placing a 2 in front of $KClO_3$ and a 3 in front of O_2.

$$2KClO_3 \longrightarrow KCl + 3O_2$$

Finally, we balance the K and Cl atoms by placing a 2 in front of KCl:

$$2KClO_3 \longrightarrow 2KCl + 3O_2 \qquad (3.3)$$

As a final check, we can draw up a balance sheet for the reactants and products where the number in parentheses indicates the number of atoms of each element:

Reactants	Products
K (2)	K (2)
Cl (2)	Cl (2)
O (6)	O (6)

Note that this equation could also be balanced with coefficients which are multiples of 2 (for $KClO_3$), 2 (for KCl), and 3 (for O_2); for example,

$$4KClO_3 \longrightarrow 4KCl + 6O_2$$

However, it is common practice to use the *simplest* possible set of whole-number coefficients to balance the equation. Equation (3.3) conforms to this convention.

Now let us consider the combustion (that is, burning) of the natural gas component ethane (C_2H_6) in oxygen or air, which yields carbon dioxide (CO_2) and water. The unbalanced equation is

$$C_2H_6 + O_2 \longrightarrow CO_2 + H_2O$$

We see that the number of atoms is not the same on both sides of the equation for any of the elements (C, H, and O). In addition, C and H appear only once on each side of the equation; O appears in two compounds on the right side (CO_2 and H_2O). To balance the C atoms, we place a 2 in front of CO_2:

$$C_2H_6 + O_2 \longrightarrow 2CO_2 + H_2O$$

To balance the H atoms, we place a 3 in front of H_2O:

$$C_2H_6 + O_2 \longrightarrow 2CO_2 + 3H_2O$$

At this stage, the C and H atoms are balanced, but the O atoms are not because there are seven O atoms on the right-hand side and only two O atoms on the left-hand side of the equation. This inequality of O atoms can be eliminated by writing $\frac{7}{2}$ in front of the O_2 on the left-hand side:

$$C_2H_6 + \tfrac{7}{2}O_2 \longrightarrow 2CO_2 + 3H_2O$$

The "logic" for using $\frac{7}{2}$ as a coefficient is that there were seven oxygen atoms on the right-hand side of the equation, but only a pair of oxygen atoms (O_2) on the left. To balance them we ask how many *pairs* of oxygen atoms are needed to equal seven

C_2H_6

oxygen atoms. Just as 3.5 pairs of shoes equal seven shoes, $\frac{7}{2}O_2$ molecules equal seven O atoms. As the following tally shows, the equation is now balanced:

Reactants	Products
C (2)	C (2)
H (6)	H (6)
O (7)	O (7)

However, we normally prefer to express the coefficients as whole numbers rather than as fractions. Therefore, we multiply the entire equation by 2 to convert $\frac{7}{2}$ to 7:

$$2C_2H_6 + 7O_2 \longrightarrow 4CO_2 + 6H_2O$$

The final tally is

Reactants	Products
C (4)	C (4)
H (12)	H (12)
O (14)	O (14)

Note that the coefficients used in balancing the last equation are the smallest possible set of whole numbers.

In Example 3.12 we will continue to practice our equation-balancing skills.

Example 3.12

When aluminum metal is exposed to air, a protective layer of aluminum oxide (Al_2O_3) forms on its surface. This layer prevents further reaction between aluminum and oxygen, and it is the reason that aluminum beverage cans do not corrode. [In the case of iron, the rust, or iron(III) oxide, that forms is too porous to protect the iron metal underneath, so rusting continues.] Write a balanced equation for the formation of Al_2O_3.

Strategy Remember that the formula of an element or compound cannot be changed when balancing a chemical equation. The equation is balanced by placing the appropriate coefficients in front of the formulas. Follow the procedure described on p. 92.

Solution The unbalanced equation is

$$Al + O_2 \longrightarrow Al_2O_3$$

In a balanced equation, the number and types of atoms on each side of the equation must be the same. We see that there is one Al atom on the reactants side and there are two Al atoms on the product side. We can balance the Al atoms by placing a coefficient of 2 in front of Al on the reactants side.

$$2Al + O_2 \longrightarrow Al_2O_3$$

There are two O atoms on the reactants side, and three O atoms on the product side of the equation. We can balance the O atoms by placing a coefficient of $\frac{3}{2}$ in front of O_2 on the reactants side.

$$2Al + \tfrac{3}{2}O_2 \longrightarrow Al_2O_3$$

This is a balanced equation. However, equations are normally balanced with the smallest set of *whole* number coefficients. Multiplying both sides of the equation by 2 gives whole number coefficients.

$$2(2Al + \tfrac{3}{2}O_2 \longrightarrow Al_2O_3)$$

(Continued)

or

$$4Al + 3O_2 \longrightarrow 2Al_2O_3$$

Check For an equation to be balanced, the number and types of atoms on each side of the equation must be the same. The final tally is

Reactants	Products
Al (4)	Al (4)
O (6)	O (6)

The equation is balanced.

Practice Exercise Balance the equation representing the reaction between iron(III) oxide, Fe_2O_3, and carbon monoxide (CO) to yield iron (Fe) and carbon dioxide (CO_2).

Similar problems: 3.59, 3.60.

3.8 Amounts of Reactants and Products

A basic question raised in the chemical laboratory is "How much product will be formed from specific amounts of starting materials (reactants)?" Or in some cases, we might ask the reverse question: "How much starting material must be used to obtain a specific amount of product?" To interpret a reaction quantitatively, we need to apply our knowledge of molar masses and the mole concept. *Stoichiometry* is *the quantitative study of reactants and products in a chemical reaction.*

Whether the units given for reactants (or products) are moles, grams, liters (for gases), or some other units, we use moles to calculate the amount of product formed in a reaction. This approach is called the *mole method,* which means simply that *the stoichiometric coefficients in a chemical equation can be interpreted as the number of moles of each substance.* For example, the combustion of carbon monoxide in air produces carbon dioxide:

Interactivity: The Mole Method
Online Learning Center, Interactives

$$2CO(g) + O_2(g) \longrightarrow 2CO_2(g)$$

The stoichiometric coefficients show that two molecules of CO react with one molecule of O_2 to form two molecules of CO_2. It follows that the relative numbers of moles are the same as the relative numbers of molecules:

$2CO(g)$	$+$	$O_2(g)$	$\longrightarrow$	$2CO_2(g)$
2 molecules		1 molecule		2 molecules
$2(6.022 \times 10^{23}$ molecules$)$		6.022×10^{23} molecules		$2(6.022 \times 10^{23}$ molecules$)$
2 mol		1 mol		1 mol

Thus this equation can also be read as "2 moles of carbon monoxide gas combine with 1 mole of oxygen gas to form 2 moles of carbon dioxide gas." In stoichiometric calculations, we say that two moles of CO are equivalent to two moles of CO_2, that is,

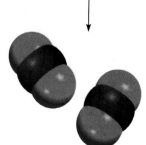

$$2 \text{ mol CO} \simeq 2 \text{ mol CO}_2$$

where the symbol $\simeq$ means "stoichiometrically equivalent to" or simply "equivalent to." The mole ratio between CO and CO_2 is 2:2 or 1:1, meaning that if 10 moles of CO are reacted, 10 moles of CO_2 will be produced. Likewise, if 0.20 mole of CO is reacted, 0.20 mole of CO_2 will be formed. This relationship enables us to write the conversion factors

$$\frac{2 \text{ mol CO}}{2 \text{ mol CO}_2} \quad \text{and} \quad \frac{2 \text{ mol CO}_2}{2 \text{ mol CO}}$$

Similarly, we have 1 mol $O_2 \simeq 2$ mol CO_2 and 2 mol CO $\simeq$ 1 mol O_2.

Let's consider a simple example in which 4.8 moles of CO react completely with O_2 to form CO_2. To calculate the amount of CO_2 produced in moles, we use the conversion factor that has CO in the denominator and write

$$\text{moles of } CO_2 \text{ produced} = 4.8 \text{ mol CO} \times \frac{1 \text{ mol } CO_2}{1 \text{ mol CO}}$$
$$= 4.8 \text{ mol } CO_2$$

Now suppose 10.7 g of CO react completely with O_2 to form CO_2. How many grams of CO_2 will be formed? To do this calculation, we note that the link between CO and CO_2 is the mole ratio from the balanced equation. So we need to first convert grams of CO to moles of CO, then to moles of CO_2, and finally to grams of CO_2. The conversion steps are

$$\text{grams of CO} \longrightarrow \text{moles of CO} \longrightarrow \text{moles of } CO_2 \longrightarrow \text{grams of } CO_2$$

First we convert 10.7 g of CO to number of moles of CO, using the molar mass of CO as the conversion factor:

$$\text{moles of CO} = 10.7 \text{ g CO} \times \frac{1 \text{ mol CO}}{28.01 \text{ g CO}}$$
$$= 0.382 \text{ mol CO}$$

Next we calculate the number of moles of CO_2 produced.

$$\text{moles of } CO_2 = 0.382 \text{ mol CO} \times \frac{2 \text{ mol } CO_2}{2 \text{ mol CO}}$$
$$= 0.382 \text{ mol } CO_2$$

Finally, we calculate the mass of CO_2 produced in grams using the molar mass of CO_2 as the conversion factor

$$\text{grams of } CO_2 = 0.382 \text{ mol } CO_2 \times \frac{44.01 \text{ g } CO_2}{1 \text{ mol } CO_2}$$
$$= 16.8 \text{ g } CO_2$$

These three separate calculations can be combined in a single step as follows:

$$\text{grams of } CO_2 = 10.7 \text{ g CO} \times \frac{1 \text{ mol CO}}{28.01 \text{ g CO}} \times \frac{1 \text{ mol } CO_2}{1 \text{ mol CO}} \times \frac{44.01 \text{ g } CO_2}{1 \text{ mol } CO_2}$$
$$= 16.8 \text{ g } CO_2$$

Figure 3.8 *Three types of stoichiometric calculations based on the mole method.*

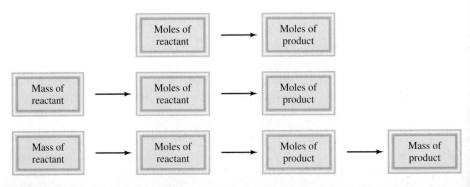

Similarly, we can calculate the mass of O_2 in grams consumed in this reaction. By using the relationship 2 mol CO $\simeq$ 1 mol O_2, we write

$$\text{grams of } O_2 = 10.7 \text{ g CO} \times \frac{1 \text{ mol CO}}{28.01 \text{ g CO}} \times \frac{1 \text{ mol } O_2}{2 \text{ mol CO}} \times \frac{32.00 \text{ g } O_2}{1 \text{ mol } O_2}$$

$$= 6.11 \text{ g } O_2$$

Figure 3.8 shows the three common types of stoichiometric calculations.

Example 3.13

All alkali metals react with water to produce hydrogen gas and the corresponding alkali metal hydroxide. A typical reaction is that between lithium and water:

$$2\text{Li}(s) + 2\text{H}_2\text{O}(l) \longrightarrow 2\text{LiOH}(aq) + \text{H}_2(g)$$

(a) How many moles of H_2 will be formed by the complete reaction of 6.23 moles of Li with water? (b) How many grams of H_2 will be formed by the complete reaction of 80.57 g of Li with water?

Lithium reacting with water to produce hydrogen gas.

(a) Strategy Looking at the balanced equation, how do we compare the amounts of Li and H_2? We can compare them based on the *mole ratio* from the balanced equation.

Solution Because the balanced equation is given in the problem, the mole ratio between Li and H_2 is known: 2 mole Li $\simeq$ 1 mol H_2. From this relationship, we have two conversion factors:

$$\frac{2 \text{ mol Li}}{1 \text{ mol } H_2} \quad \text{and} \quad \frac{1 \text{ mol } H_2}{2 \text{ mol Li}}$$

The conversion factor on the right is the correct one. Moles of Li will cancel, leaving units of "mol H_2" for the answer. We calculate moles of H_2 produced as follows:

$$\text{moles of } H_2 \text{ produced} = 6.23 \text{ mol Li} \times \frac{1 \text{ mol } H_2}{2 \text{ mol Li}} = 3.12 \text{ mol } H_2$$

Check Does the answer seem reasonable? Should the moles of H_2 produced be half the moles of Li reacted?

(b) Strategy We compare Li and H based on the *mole ratio* in the balanced equation. Before we can determine the moles of H_2 produced, we need to convert to moles of Li. What conversion factor is needed to convert from grams of Li to moles of Li? Another conversion factor is needed to convert moles of H_2 to grams of H_2.

Solution The molar mass of Li will enable us to convert from grams of Li to moles of Li. As in part (a), the balanced equation is given, so the mole ratio between Li and H_2 is known; that is, 2 mol Li $\simeq$ 1 mol H_2. Finally, the molar mass of H_2 will convert moles of H_2 to grams of H_2. This sequence is summarized as follows:

$$\text{grams of Li} \longrightarrow \text{moles of Li} \longrightarrow \text{moles of } H_2 \longrightarrow \text{grams of } H_2$$

The number of moles of Li in 80.57 g Li is

$$\text{moles of Li} = 80.57 \text{ g Li} \times \frac{1 \text{ mol Li}}{6.941 \text{ g Li}} = 11.61 \text{ mol Li}$$

(Continued)

Next, we calculate the number of moles of H_2 produced

$$\text{moles of } H_2 = 11.61 \, \cancel{\text{mol Li}} \times \frac{1 \text{ mol } H_2}{2 \, \cancel{\text{mol Li}}} = 5.805 \text{ mol } H_2$$

Finally, the amount of H_2 in grams is given by

$$\text{grams of } H_2 = 5.805 \, \cancel{\text{mol } H_2} \times \frac{2.016 \text{ g } H_2}{1 \, \cancel{\text{mol } H_2}} = 11.70 \text{ g } H_2$$

After some practice, you will find it convenient to combine all the steps in a single sequence of conversions:

$$\text{grams of } H_2 = 80.57 \, \cancel{\text{g Li}} \times \frac{1 \, \cancel{\text{mol Li}}}{6.941 \, \cancel{\text{g Li}}} \times \frac{1 \, \cancel{\text{mol } H_2}}{2 \, \cancel{\text{mol Li}}} \times \frac{2.016 \text{ g } H_2}{1 \, \cancel{\text{mol } H_2}}$$

$$= 11.70 \text{ g } H_2$$

Check Does the answer seem reasonable? Should the mass of H_2 produced be less than the mass of Li reacted? Compare the molar mass of H_2 with that of Li. Also, compare the mole ratio of H_2 and Li in the equation.

Similar problems: 3.65, 3.71.

Practice Exercise The reaction between nitric oxide (NO) and oxygen to form nitrogen dioxide (NO_2) is a key step in photochemical smog formation:

$$2NO(g) + O_2(g) \longrightarrow 2NO_2(g)$$

(a) How many moles of NO_2 are formed by the complete reaction of 0.254 mole of O_2?
(b) How many grams of NO_2 are formed by the complete reaction of 1.44 g of NO?

Example 3.14 shows another mass of reactant to mass of product calculation (see Figure 3.8).

$C_6H_{12}O_6$

Example 3.14

The food we eat is degraded, or broken down, in our bodies to provide energy for growth and function. A general overall equation for this very complex process represents the degradation of glucose ($C_6H_{12}O_6$) to carbon dioxide (CO_2) and water (H_2O):

$$C_6H_{12}O_6 + 6O_2 \longrightarrow 6CO_2 + 6H_2O$$

If 856 g of $C_6H_{12}O_6$ is consumed by a person over a certain period, what is the mass of CO_2 produced?

Strategy Looking at the balanced equation, how do we compare the amounts of $C_6H_{12}O_6$ and CO_2? We can compare them based on the *mole ratio* from the balanced equation. Starting with grams of $C_6H_{12}O_6$, how do we convert to moles of $C_6H_{12}O_6$? Once moles of CO_2 are determined using the mole ratio from the balanced equation, how do we convert to grams of CO_2?

Solution We see from the balanced equation, that 1 mol $C_6H_{12}O_6 \simeq 6$ mol CO_2. If we can convert grams to moles of $C_6H_{12}O_6$, then we can use the mole ratio to calculate moles of CO_2. Once we have moles of CO_2, we can convert to grams of CO_2. These conversions are summarized next:

$$\text{grams of } C_6H_{12}O_6 \longrightarrow \text{moles of } C_6H_{12}O_6 \longrightarrow \text{moles of } CO_2 \longrightarrow \text{grams of } CO_2$$

(Continued)

We combine all of these steps into one equation:

$$\text{mass of } CO_2 = 856 \text{ g } C_6H_{12}O_6 \times \frac{1 \text{ mol } C_6H_{12}O_6}{180.2 \text{ g } C_6H_{12}O_6} \times \frac{6 \text{ mol } CO_2}{1 \text{ mol } C_6H_{12}O_6} \times \frac{44.01 \text{ g } CO_2}{1 \text{ mol } CO_2}$$

$$= 1.25 \times 10^3 \text{ g } CO_2$$

Check Does the answer seem reasonable? Should the mass of CO_2 produced be larger than the mass of $C_6H_{12}O_6$ reacted, even though the molar mass of CO_2 is considerably less than the molar mass of $C_6H_{12}O_6$? What is the mole ratio between CO_2 and $C_6H_{12}O_6$?

Similar problem: 3.72.

Practice Exercise Methanol (CH_3OH) burns in air according to the equation

$$2CH_3OH + 3O_2 \longrightarrow 2CO_2 + 4H_2O$$

If 209 g of methanol are used up in a combustion process, what is the mass of H_2O produced?

3.9 Limiting Reagents

Animation: Limiting Reagent
Online Learning Center, Animations

When a chemist carries out a reaction, the reactants are usually not present in exact *stoichiometric amounts,* that is, *in the proportions indicated by the balanced equation.* Because the goal of a reaction is to produce the maximum quantity of a useful compound from the starting materials, frequently a large excess of one reactant is supplied to ensure that the more expensive reactant is completely converted to the desired product. Consequently, some reactant will be left over at the end of the reaction. *The reactant used up first in a reaction* is called the **limiting reagent,** because the maximum amount of product formed depends on how much of this reactant was originally present. When this reactant is used up, no more product can be formed. **Excess reagents** are the *reactants present in quantities greater than necessary to react with the quantity of the limiting reagent.*

The concept of the limiting reagent is analogous to the relationship between men and women in a dance contest at a club. If there are 14 men and only 9 women, then only 9 female/male pairs can compete. Five men will be left without partners. The number of women thus *limits* the number of men that can dance in the contest, and there is an *excess* of men.

Consider the formation of nitrogen dioxide (NO_2) from nitric oxide (NO) and oxygen:

$$2NO(g) + O_2(g) \longrightarrow 2NO_2(g)$$

Suppose initially we have 8 moles of NO and 7 moles of O_2 (Figure 3.9). One way to determine which of the two reactants is the limiting reagent is to calculate the number of moles of NO_2 obtained based on the initial quantities of NO and O_2. From the preceding definition, we see that only the limiting reagent will yield the smaller amount of the product. Starting with 8 moles of NO, we find the number of moles of NO_2 produced is

$$8 \text{ mol NO} \times \frac{2 \text{ mol } NO_2}{2 \text{ mol NO}} = 8 \text{ mol } NO_2$$

and starting with 7 moles of O_2, the number of moles of NO_2 formed is

$$7 \text{ mol } O_2 \times \frac{2 \text{ mol } NO_2}{1 \text{ mol } O_2} = 14 \text{ mol } NO_2$$

Because NO results in a smaller amount of NO_2, it must be the limiting reagent. Therefore, O_2 is the excess reagent.

Before reaction has started

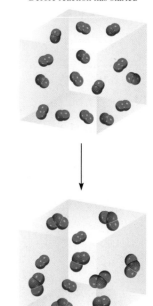

After reaction is complete

NO O_2 NO_2

Figure 3.9 *At the start of the reaction, there were eight NO molecules and seven O_2 molecules. At the end, all the NO molecules are gone and only three O_2 molecules are left. Therefore, NO is the limiting reagent and O_2 is the excess reagent. Each molecule can also be treated as one mole of the substance in this reaction.*

In stoichiometric calculations involving limiting reagents, the first step is to decide which reactant is the limiting reagent. After the limiting reagent has been identified, the rest of the problem can be solved as outlined in Section 3.8. Example 3.15 illustrates this approach.

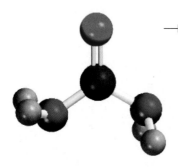

$(NH_2)_2CO$

Example 3.15

Urea [$(NH_2)_2CO$] is prepared by reacting ammonia with carbon dioxide:

$$2NH_3(g) + CO_2(g) \longrightarrow (NH_2)_2CO(aq) + H_2O(l)$$

In one process, 637.2 g of NH_3 are treated with 1142 g of CO_2. (a) Which of the two reactants is the limiting reagent? (b) Calculate the mass of $(NH_2)_2CO$ formed. (c) How much excess reagent (in grams) is left at the end of the reaction?

(a) Strategy The reactant that produces fewer moles of product is the limiting reagent because it limits the amount of product that can be formed. How do we convert from the amount of reactant to amount of product? Perform this calculation for each reactant, then compare the moles of product, $(NH_2)_2CO$, formed by the given amounts of NH_3 and CO_2 to determine which reactant is the limiting reagent.

Solution We carry out two separate calculations. First, starting with 637.2 g of NH_3, we calculate the number of moles of $(NH_2)_2CO$ that could be produced if all the NH_3 reacted according to the following conversions:

$$\text{grams of } NH_3 \longrightarrow \text{moles of } NH_3 \longrightarrow \text{moles of } (NH_2)_2CO$$

Combining these conversions in one step, we write

$$\text{moles of } (NH_2)_2CO = 637.2 \text{ g } NH_3 \times \frac{1 \text{ mol } NH_3}{17.03 \text{ g } NH_3} \times \frac{1 \text{ mol } (NH_2)_2CO}{2 \text{ mol } NH_3}$$
$$= 18.71 \text{ mol } (NH_2)_2CO$$

Second, for 1142 g of CO_2, the conversions are

$$\text{grams of } CO_2 \longrightarrow \text{moles of } CO_2 \longrightarrow \text{moles of } (NH_2)_2CO$$

The number of moles of $(NH_2)_2CO$ that could be produced if all the CO_2 reacted is

$$\text{moles of } (NH_2)_2CO = 1142 \text{ g } CO_2 \times \frac{1 \text{ mol } CO_2}{44.01 \text{ g } CO_2} \times \frac{1 \text{ mol } (NH_2)_2CO}{1 \text{ mol } CO_2}$$
$$= 25.95 \text{ mol } (NH_2)_2CO$$

It follows, therefore, that NH_3 must be the limiting reagent because it produces a smaller amount of $(NH_2)_2CO$.

(b) Strategy We determined the moles of $(NH_2)_2CO$ produced in part (a), using NH_3 as the limiting reagent. How do we convert from moles to grams?

Solution The molar mass of $(NH_2)_2CO$ is 60.06 g. We use this as a conversion factor to convert from moles of $(NH_2)_2CO$ to grams of $(NH_2)_2CO$:

$$\text{mass of } (NH_2)_2CO = 18.71 \text{ mol } (NH_2)_2CO \times \frac{60.06 \text{ g } (NH_2)_2CO}{1 \text{ mol } (NH_2)_2CO}$$
$$= 1124 \text{ g } (NH_2)_2CO$$

Check Does your answer seem reasonable? 18.71 moles of product are formed. What is the mass of 1 mole of $(NH_2)_2CO$?

(Continued)

(c) Strategy Working backward, we can determine the amount of CO_2 that reacted to produce 18.71 moles of $(NH_2)_2CO$. The amount of CO_2 left over is the difference between the initial amount and the amount reacted.

Solution Starting with 18.71 moles of $(NH_2)_2CO$, we can determine the mass of CO_2 that reacted using the mole ratio from the balanced equation and the molar mass of CO_2. The conversion steps are

$$\text{moles of } (NH_2)_2CO \longrightarrow \text{moles of } CO_2 \longrightarrow \text{grams of } CO_2$$

so that

$$\text{mass of } CO_2 \text{ reacted} = 18.71 \text{ mol } \cancel{(NH_2)_2CO} \times \frac{1 \text{ mol } \cancel{CO_2}}{1 \text{ mol } \cancel{(NH_2)_2CO}} \times \frac{44.01 \text{ g } CO_2}{1 \text{ mol } \cancel{CO_2}}$$
$$= 823.4 \text{ g } CO_2$$

The amount of CO_2 remaining (in excess) is the difference between the initial amount (1142 g) and the amount reacted (823.4 g):

$$\text{mass of } CO_2 \text{ remaining} = 1142 \text{ g} - 823.4 \text{ g} = 319 \text{ g}$$

Similar problem: 3.86.

Practice Exercise The reaction between aluminum and iron(III) oxide can generate temperatures approaching 3000°C and is used in welding metals:

$$2Al + Fe_2O_3 \longrightarrow Al_2O_3 + 2Fe$$

In one process, 124 g of Al are reacted with 601 g of Fe_2O_3. (a) Calculate the mass (in grams) of Al_2O_3 formed. (b) How much of the excess reagent is left at the end of the reaction?

Example 3.15 brings out an important point. In practice, chemists usually choose the more expensive chemical as the limiting reagent so that all or most of it will be consumed in the reaction. In the synthesis of urea, NH_3 is invariably the limiting reagent because it is much more expensive than CO_2.

Interactivity: Limiting Reactant Game
Online Learning Center, Interactives

3.10 Reaction Yield

The amount of limiting reagent present at the start of a reaction determines the **theoretical yield** of the reaction, that is, *the amount of product that would result if all the limiting reagent reacted.* The theoretical yield, then, is the *maximum* obtainable yield, predicted by the balanced equation. In practice, the **actual yield,** or *the amount of product actually obtained from a reaction,* is almost always less than the theoretical yield. There are many reasons for the difference between actual and theoretical yields. For instance, many reactions are reversible, and so they do not proceed 100 percent from left to right. Even when a reaction is 100 percent complete, it may be difficult to recover all of the product from the reaction medium (say, from an aqueous solution). Some reactions are complex in the sense that the products formed may react further among themselves or with the reactants to form still other products. These additional reactions will reduce the yield of the first reaction.

To determine how efficient a given reaction is, chemists often figure the **percent yield,** which describes *the proportion of the actual yield to the theoretical yield.* It is calculated as follows:

$$\% \text{yield} = \frac{\text{actual yield}}{\text{theoretical yield}} \times 100\% \tag{3.4}$$

CHEMISTRY IN ACTION

Chemical Fertilizers

Feeding the world's rapidly increasing population requires that farmers produce ever-larger and healthier crops. Every year they add hundreds of millions of tons of chemical fertilizers to the soil to increase crop quality and yield. In addition to carbon dioxide and water, plants need at least six elements for satisfactory growth. They are N, P, K, Ca, S, and Mg. The preparation and properties of several nitrogen- and phosphorus-containing fertilizers illustrate some of the principles introduced in this chapter.

Nitrogen fertilizers contain nitrate (NO_3^-) salts, ammonium (NH_4^+) salts, and other compounds. Plants can absorb nitrogen in the form of nitrate directly, but ammonium salts and ammonia (NH_3) must first be converted to nitrates by the action of soil bacteria. The principal raw material of nitrogen fertilizers is ammonia, prepared by the reaction between hydrogen and nitrogen:

$$3H_2(g) + N_2(g) \longrightarrow 2NH_3(g)$$

(This reaction will be discussed in detail in Chapters 13 and 14.) In its liquid form, ammonia can be injected directly into the soil.

Alternatively, ammonia can be converted to ammonium nitrate, NH_4NO_3, ammonium sulfate, $(NH_4)_2SO_4$, or ammonium hydrogen phosphate, $(NH_4)_2HPO_4$, in the following acid-base reactions:

Liquid ammonia being applied to the soil before planting.

$$NH_3(aq) + HNO_3(aq) \longrightarrow NH_4NO_3(aq)$$
$$2NH_3(aq) + H_2SO_4(aq) \longrightarrow (NH_4)_2SO_4(aq)$$
$$2NH_3(aq) + H_3PO_4(aq) \longrightarrow (NH_4)_2HPO_4(aq)$$

Percent yields may range from a fraction of 1 percent to 100 percent. Chemists strive to maximize the percent yield in a reaction. Factors that can affect the percent yield include temperature and pressure. We will study these effects later.

In Example 3.16 we will calculate the yield of an industrial process.

The frame of this bicycle is made of titanium.

Example 3.16

Titanium is a strong, lightweight, corrosion-resistant metal that is used in rockets, aircraft, jet engines, and bicycle frames. It is prepared by the reaction of titanium(IV) chloride with molten magnesium between 950°C and 1150°C:

$$TiCl_4(g) + 2Mg(l) \longrightarrow Ti(s) + 2MgCl_2(l)$$

In a certain industrial operation 3.54×10^7 g of $TiCl_4$ are reacted with 1.13×10^7 g of Mg. (a) Calculate the theoretical yield of Ti in grams. (b) Calculate the percent yield if 7.91×10^6 g of Ti are actually obtained.

(a) Strategy Because there are two reactants, this is likely to be a limiting reagent problem. The reactant that produces fewer moles of product is the limiting reagent. How do we convert from amount of reactant to amount of product? Perform this calculation for each reactant, then compare the moles of product, Ti, formed.

Solution Carry out two separate calculations to see which of the two reactants is the limiting reagent. First, starting with 3.54×10^7 g of $TiCl_4$, calculate the number of moles of Ti that could be produced if all the $TiCl_4$ reacted. The conversions are

(Continued)

Another method of preparing ammonium sulfate requires two steps:

$$2NH_3(aq) + CO_2(aq) + H_2O(l) \longrightarrow (NH_4)_2CO_3(aq) \quad (1)$$

$$(NH_4)_2CO_3(aq) + CaSO_4(aq) \longrightarrow$$
$$(NH_4)_2SO_4(aq) + CaCO_3(s) \quad (2)$$

This approach is desirable because the starting materials—carbon dioxide and calcium sulfate—are less costly than sulfuric acid. To increase the yield, ammonia is made the limiting reagent in Reaction (1) and ammonium carbonate is made the limiting reagent in Reaction (2).

The table lists the percent composition by mass of nitrogen in some common fertilizers. The preparation of urea was discussed in Example 3.15.

Percent Composition by Mass of Nitrogen in Five Common Fertilizers

Fertilizer	% N by Mass
NH_3	82.4
NH_4NO_3	35.0
$(NH_4)_2SO_4$	21.2
$(NH_4)_2HPO_4$	21.2
$(NH_2)_2CO$	46.7

Several factors influence the choice of one fertilizer over another: (1) cost of the raw materials needed to prepare the fertilizer; (2) ease of storage, transportation, and utilization; (3) percent composition by mass of the desired element; and (4) suitability of the compound, that is, whether the compound is soluble in water and whether it can be readily taken up by plants. Considering all these factors together, we find that NH_4NO_3 is the most important nitrogen-containing fertilizer in the world, even though ammonia has the highest percentage by mass of nitrogen.

Phosphorus fertilizers are derived from phosphate rock, called *fluorapatite*, $Ca_5(PO_4)_3F$. Fluorapatite is insoluble in water, so it must first be converted to water-soluble calcium dihydrogen phosphate $[Ca(H_2PO_4)_2]$:

$$2Ca_5(PO_4)_3F(s) + 7H_2SO_4(aq) \longrightarrow$$
$$3Ca(H_2PO_4)_2(aq) + 7CaSO_4(aq) + 2HF(g)$$

For maximum yield, fluorapatite is made the limiting reagent in this reaction.

The reactions we have discussed for the preparation of fertilizers all appear relatively simple, yet much effort has been expended to improve the yields by changing conditions such as temperature, pressure, and so on. Industrial chemists usually run promising reactions first in the laboratory and then test them in a pilot facility before putting them into mass production.

$$\text{grams of TiCl}_4 \longrightarrow \text{moles of TiCl}_4 \longrightarrow \text{moles of Ti}$$

so that

$$\text{moles of Ti} = 3.54 \times 10^7 \text{ g TiCl}_4 \times \frac{1 \text{ mol TiCl}_4}{189.7 \text{ g TiCl}_4} \times \frac{1 \text{ mol Ti}}{1 \text{ mol TiCl}_4}$$
$$= 1.87 \times 10^5 \text{ mol Ti}$$

Next, we calculate the number of moles of Ti formed from 1.13×10^7 g of Mg. The conversion steps are

$$\text{grams of Mg} \longrightarrow \text{moles of Mg} \longrightarrow \text{moles of Ti}$$

and we write

$$\text{moles of Ti} = 1.13 \times 10^7 \text{ g Mg} \times \frac{1 \text{ mol Mg}}{24.31 \text{ g Mg}} \times \frac{1 \text{ mol Ti}}{2 \text{ mol Mg}}$$
$$= 2.32 \times 10^5 \text{ mol Ti}$$

Therefore, $TiCl_4$ is the limiting reagent because it produces a smaller amount of Ti. The mass of Ti formed is

$$1.87 \times 10^5 \text{ mol Ti} \times \frac{47.88 \text{ g Ti}}{1 \text{ mol Ti}} = 8.95 \times 10^6 \text{ g Ti}$$

(Continued)

(b) Strategy The mass of Ti determined in part (a) is the theoretical yield. The amount given in part (b) is the actual yield of the reaction.

Solution The percent yield is given by

$$\% \text{yield} = \frac{\text{actual yield}}{\text{theoretical yield}} \times 100\%$$

$$= \frac{7.91 \times 10^6 \text{ g}}{8.95 \times 10^6 \text{ g}} \times 100\%$$

$$= 88.4\%$$

Similar problems: 3.89, 3.90.

Check Should the percent yield be less than 100 percent?

Practice Exercise Industrially, vanadium metal, which is used in steel alloys, can be obtained by reacting vanadium(V) oxide with calcium at high temperatures:

$$5Ca + V_2O_5 \longrightarrow 5CaO + 2V$$

In one process 1.54×10^3 g of V_2O_5 react with 1.96×10^3 g of Ca. (a) Calculate the theoretical yield of V. (b) Calculate the percent yield if 803 g of V are obtained.

Industrial processes usually involve huge quantities (thousands to millions of tons) of products. Thus even a slight improvement in the yield can significantly reduce the cost of production. A case in point is the manufacture of chemical fertilizers, discussed in the Chemistry in Action essay on p. 102.

Key Equations

- percent composition of an element in a compound =
$$\frac{n \times \text{molar mass of element}}{\text{molar mass of compound}} \times 100\% \qquad (3.1)$$

- $\% \text{yield} = \dfrac{\text{actual yield}}{\text{theoretical yield}} \times 100\% \qquad (3.4)$

Summary of Facts and Concepts

1. Atomic masses are measured in atomic mass units (amu), a relative unit based on a value of exactly 12 for the C-12 isotope. The atomic mass given for the atoms of a particular element is the average of the naturally occurring isotope distribution of that element. The molecular mass of a molecule is the sum of the atomic masses of the atoms in the molecule. Both atomic mass and molecular mass can be accurately determined with a mass spectrometer.

2. A mole is Avogadro's number (6.022×10^{23}) of atoms, molecules, or other particles. The molar mass (in grams) of an element or a compound is numerically equal to its mass in atomic mass units (amu) and contains Avogadro's number of atoms (in the case of elements), molecules (in the case of molecular substances), or simplest formula units (in the case of ionic compounds).

3. The percent composition by mass of a compound is the percent by mass of each element present. If we know the percent composition by mass of a compound, we

can deduce the empirical formula of the compound and also the molecular formula of the compound if the approximate molar mass is known.

4. Chemical changes, called chemical reactions, are represented by chemical equations. Substances that undergo change—the reactants—are written on the left and the substances formed—the products—appear to the right of the arrow. Chemical equations must be balanced, in accordance with the law of conservation of mass. The number of atoms of each element in the reactants must equal the number in the products.

5. Stoichiometry is the quantitative study of products and reactants in chemical reactions. Stoichiometric calculations are best done by expressing both the known and unknown quantities in terms of moles and then converting to other units if necessary. A limiting reagent is the reactant that is present in the smallest stoichiometric amount. It limits the amount of product that can be formed. The amount of product obtained in a reaction (the actual yield) may be less than the maximum possible amount (the theoretical yield). The ratio of the two multiplied by 100 percent is expressed as the percent yield.

Key Words

Actual yield, p. 101	Chemical equation, p. 90	Mole method, p. 95	Reactant, p. 91
Atomic mass, p. 76	Chemical reaction, p. 90	Molecular mass, p. 81	Stoichiometric
Atomic mass unit	Excess reagent, p. 99	Percent composition	amount, p. 99
(amu), p. 76	Limiting reagent, p. 99	by mass, p. 85	Stoichiometry, p. 95
Avogadro's number	Molar mass ($\mathcal{M}$), p. 78	Percent yield, p. 101	Theoretical yield, p. 101
(N_A), p. 77	Mole (mol), p. 77	Product, p. 91	

Questions and Problems

Atomic Mass
Review Questions

3.1 What is an atomic mass unit? Why is it necessary to introduce such a unit?

3.2 What is the mass (in amu) of a carbon-12 atom? Why is the atomic mass of carbon listed as 12.01 amu in the table on the inside front cover of this book?

3.3 Explain clearly what is meant by the statement "The atomic mass of gold is 197.0 amu."

3.4 What information would you need to calculate the average atomic mass of an element?

Problems

3.5 The atomic masses of $^{35}_{17}Cl$ (75.53 percent) and $^{37}_{17}Cl$ (24.47 percent) are 34.968 amu and 36.956 amu, respectively. Calculate the average atomic mass of chlorine. The percentages in parentheses denote the relative abundances.

3.6 The atomic masses of $^{6}_{3}Li$ and $^{7}_{3}Li$ are 6.0151 amu and 7.0160 amu, respectively. Calculate the natural abundances of these two isotopes. The average atomic mass of Li is 6.941 amu.

3.7 What is the mass in grams of 13.2 amu?

3.8 How many amu are there in 8.4 g?

Avogadro's Number and Molar Mass
Review Questions

3.9 Define the term "mole." What is the unit for mole in calculations? What does the mole have in common with the pair, the dozen, and the gross? What does Avogadro's number represent?

3.10 What is the molar mass of an atom? What are the commonly used units for molar mass?

Problems

3.11 Earth's population is about 6.5 billion. Suppose that every person on Earth participates in a process of counting identical particles at the rate of two particles per second. How many years would it take to count 6.0×10^{23} particles? Assume that there are 365 days in a year.

3.12 The thickness of a piece of paper is 0.0036 in. Suppose a certain book has an Avogadro's number of pages; calculate the thickness of the book in light-years. (*Hint:* See Problem 1.47 for the definition of light-year.)

3.13   How many atoms are there in 5.10 moles of sulfur (S)?

3.14   How many moles of cobalt (Co) atoms are there in 6.00×10^9 (6 billion) Co atoms?

3.15   How many moles of calcium (Ca) atoms are in 77.4 g of Ca?

3.16   How many grams of gold (Au) are there in 15.3 moles of Au?

3.17   What is the mass in grams of a single atom of each of the following elements? (a) Hg, (b) Ne.

3.18   What is the mass in grams of a single atom of each of the following elements? (a) As, (b) Ni.

3.19   What is the mass in grams of 1.00×10^{12} lead (Pb) atoms?

3.20   How many atoms are present in 3.14 g of copper (Cu)?

3.21   Which of the following has more atoms: 1.10 g of hydrogen atoms or 14.7 g of chromium atoms?

3.22   Which of the following has a greater mass: 2 atoms of lead or 5.1×10^{-23} mole of helium.

Molecular Mass
Problems

3.23   Calculate the molecular mass or formula mass (in amu) of each of the following substances: (a) CH_4, (b) NO_2, (c) SO_3, (d) C_6H_6, (e) NaI, (f) K_2SO_4, (g) $Ca_3(PO_4)_2$.

3.24   Calculate the molar mass of the following substances: (a) Li_2CO_3, (b) CS_2, (c) $CHCl_3$ (chloroform), (d) $C_6H_8O_6$ (ascorbic acid, or vitamin C), (e) KNO_3, (f) Mg_3N_2.

3.25   Calculate the molar mass of a compound if 0.372 mole of it has a mass of 152 g.

3.26   How many molecules of ethane (C_2H_6) are present in 0.334 g of C_2H_6?

3.27   Calculate the number of C, H, and O atoms in 1.50 g of glucose ($C_6H_{12}O_6$), a sugar.

3.28   Urea [$(NH_2)_2CO$] is used for fertilizer and many other things. Calculate the number of N, C, O, and H atoms in 1.68×10^4 g of urea.

3.29   Pheromones are a special type of compound secreted by the females of many insect species to attract the males for mating. One pheromone has the molecular formula $C_{19}H_{38}O$. Normally, the amount of this pheromone secreted by a female insect is about 1.0×10^{-12} g. How many molecules are there in this quantity?

3.30   The density of water is 1.00 g/mL at 4°C. How many water molecules are present in 2.56 mL of water at this temperature?

Mass Spectrometry
Review Questions

3.31   Describe the operation of a mass spectrometer.

3.32   Describe how you would determine the isotopic abundance of an element from its mass spectrum.

Problems

3.33   Carbon has two stable isotopes, $^{12}_6C$ and $^{13}_6C$, and fluorine has only one stable isotope, $^{19}_9F$. How many peaks would you observe in the mass spectrum of the positive ion of CF_4^+? Assume that the ion does not break up into smaller fragments.

3.34   Hydrogen has two stable isotopes, ^1_1H and ^2_1H, and sulfur has four stable isotopes, $^{32}_{16}S$, $^{33}_{16}S$, $^{34}_{16}S$, $^{36}_{16}S$. How many peaks would you observe in the mass spectrum of the positive ion of hydrogen sulfide, H_2S^+? Assume no decomposition of the ion into smaller fragments.

Percent Composition and Chemical Formulas
Review Questions

3.35   Use ammonia (NH_3) to explain what is meant by the percent composition by mass of a compound.

3.36   Describe how the knowledge of the percent composition by mass of an unknown compound can help us identify the compound.

3.37   What does the word "empirical" in empirical formula mean?

3.38   If we know the empirical formula of a compound, what additional information do we need to determine its molecular formula?

Problems

3.39   Tin (Sn) exists in Earth's crust as SnO_2. Calculate the percent composition by mass of Sn and O in SnO_2.

3.40   For many years chloroform ($CHCl_3$) was used as an inhalation anesthetic in spite of the fact that it is also a toxic substance that may cause severe liver, kidney, and heart damage. Calculate the percent composition by mass of this compound.

3.41   Cinnamic alcohol is used mainly in perfumery, particularly in soaps and cosmetics. Its molecular formula is $C_9H_{10}O$. (a) Calculate the percent composition by mass of C, H, and O in cinnamic alcohol. (b) How many molecules of cinnamic alcohol are contained in a sample of mass 0.469 g?

3.42   All of the substances listed below are fertilizers that contribute nitrogen to the soil. Which of these is the richest source of nitrogen on a mass percentage basis?
       (a) Urea, $(NH_2)_2CO$
       (b) Ammonium nitrate, NH_4NO_3
       (c) Guanidine, $HNC(NH_2)_2$
       (d) Ammonia, NH_3

3.43   Allicin is the compound responsible for the characteristic smell of garlic. An analysis of the compound gives the following percent composition by mass: C: 44.4 percent; H: 6.21 percent; S: 39.5 percent; O: 9.86 percent. Calculate its empirical formula. What is its molecular formula given that its molar mass is about 162 g?

3.44 Peroxyacylnitrate (PAN) is one of the components of smog. It is a compound of C, H, N, and O. Determine the percent composition of oxygen and the empirical formula from the following percent composition by mass: 19.8 percent C, 2.50 percent H, 11.6 percent N. What is its molecular formula given that its molar mass is about 120 g?

3.45 The formula for rust can be represented by Fe_2O_3. How many moles of Fe are present in 24.6 g of the compound?

3.46 How many grams of sulfur (S) are needed to react completely with 246 g of mercury (Hg) to form HgS?

3.47 Calculate the mass in grams of iodine (I_2) that will react completely with 20.4 g of aluminum (Al) to form aluminum iodide (AlI_3).

3.48 Tin(II) fluoride (SnF_2) is often added to toothpaste as an ingredient to prevent tooth decay. What is the mass of F in grams in 24.6 g of the compound?

3.49 What are the empirical formulas of the compounds with the following compositions? (a) 2.1 percent H, 65.3 percent O, 32.6 percent S, (b) 20.2 percent Al, 79.8 percent Cl.

3.50 What are the empirical formulas of the compounds with the following compositions? (a) 40.1 percent C, 6.6 percent H, 53.3 percent O, (b) 18.4 percent C, 21.5 percent N, 60.1 percent K.

3.51 The anticaking agent added to Morton salt is calcium silicate, $CaSiO_3$. This compound can absorb up to 2.5 times its mass of water and still remains a free-flowing powder. Calculate the percent composition of $CaSiO_3$.

3.52 The empirical formula of a compound is CH. If the molar mass of this compound is about 78 g, what is its molecular formula?

3.53 The molar mass of caffeine is 194.19 g. Is the molecular formula of caffeine $C_4H_5N_2O$ or $C_8H_{10}N_4O_2$?

3.54 Monosodium glutamate (MSG), a food-flavor enhancer, has been blamed for "Chinese restaurant syndrome," the symptoms of which are headaches and chest pains. MSG has the following composition by mass: 35.51 percent C, 4.77 percent H, 37.85 percent O, 8.29 percent N, and 13.60 percent Na. What is its molecular formula if its molar mass is about 169 g?

Chemical Reactions and Chemical Equations
Review Questions

3.55 Use the formation of water from hydrogen and oxygen to explain the following terms: chemical reaction, reactant, product.

3.56 What is the difference between a chemical reaction and a chemical equation?

3.57 Why must a chemical equation be balanced? What law is obeyed by a balanced chemical equation?

3.58 Write the symbols used to represent gas, liquid, solid, and the aqueous phase in chemical equations.

Problems

3.59 Balance the following equations using the method outlined in Section 3.7:
(a) $C + O_2 \longrightarrow CO$
(b) $CO + O_2 \longrightarrow CO_2$
(c) $H_2 + Br_2 \longrightarrow HBr$
(d) $K + H_2O \longrightarrow KOH + H_2$
(e) $Mg + O_2 \longrightarrow MgO$
(f) $O_3 \longrightarrow O_2$
(g) $H_2O_2 \longrightarrow H_2O + O_2$
(h) $N_2 + H_2 \longrightarrow NH_3$
(i) $Zn + AgCl \longrightarrow ZnCl_2 + Ag$
(j) $S_8 + O_2 \longrightarrow SO_2$
(k) $NaOH + H_2SO_4 \longrightarrow Na_2SO_4 + H_2O$
(l) $Cl_2 + NaI \longrightarrow NaCl + I_2$
(m) $KOH + H_3PO_4 \longrightarrow K_3PO_4 + H_2O$
(n) $CH_4 + Br_2 \longrightarrow CBr_4 + HBr$

3.60 Balance the following equations using the method outlined in Section 3.7:
(a) $N_2O_5 \longrightarrow N_2O_4 + O_2$
(b) $KNO_3 \longrightarrow KNO_2 + O_2$
(c) $NH_4NO_3 \longrightarrow N_2O + H_2O$
(d) $NH_4NO_2 \longrightarrow N_2 + H_2O$
(e) $NaHCO_3 \longrightarrow Na_2CO_3 + H_2O + CO_2$
(f) $P_4O_{10} + H_2O \longrightarrow H_3PO_4$
(g) $HCl + CaCO_3 \longrightarrow CaCl_2 + H_2O + CO_2$
(h) $Al + H_2SO_4 \longrightarrow Al_2(SO_4)_3 + H_2$
(i) $CO_2 + KOH \longrightarrow K_2CO_3 + H_2O$
(j) $CH_4 + O_2 \longrightarrow CO_2 + H_2O$
(k) $Be_2C + H_2O \longrightarrow Be(OH)_2 + CH_4$
(l) $Cu + HNO_3 \longrightarrow Cu(NO_3)_2 + NO + H_2O$
(m) $S + HNO_3 \longrightarrow H_2SO_4 + NO_2 + H_2O$
(n) $NH_3 + CuO \longrightarrow Cu + N_2 + H_2O$

Amounts of Reactants and Products
Review Questions

3.61 On what law is stoichiometry based? Why is it essential to use balanced equations in solving stoichiometric problems?

3.62 Describe the steps involved in the mole method.

Problems

3.63 Which of the following equations best represents the reaction shown in the diagram on page 108?
(a) $8A + 4B \longrightarrow C + D$
(b) $4A + 8B \longrightarrow 4C + 4D$
(c) $2A + B \longrightarrow C + D$

(d) 4A + 2B $\longrightarrow$ 4C + 4D

(e) 2A + 4B $\longrightarrow$ C + D

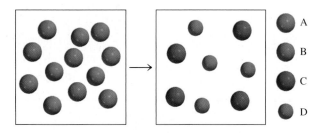

3.64 Which of the following equations best represents the reaction shown in the diagram?

(a) A + B $\longrightarrow$ C + D

(b) 6A + 4B $\longrightarrow$ C + D

(c) A + 2B $\longrightarrow$ 2C + D

(d) 3A + 2B $\longrightarrow$ 2C + D

(e) 3A + 2B $\longrightarrow$ 4C + 2D

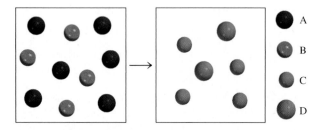

3.65 Consider the combustion of carbon monoxide (CO) in oxygen gas

$$2CO(g) + O_2(g) \longrightarrow 2CO_2(g)$$

Starting with 3.60 moles of CO, calculate the number of moles of CO_2 produced if there is enough oxygen gas to react with all of the CO.

3.66 Silicon tetrachloride ($SiCl_4$) can be prepared by heating Si in chlorine gas:

$$Si(s) + 2Cl_2(g) \longrightarrow SiCl_4(l)$$

In one reaction, 0.507 mole of $SiCl_4$ is produced. How many moles of molecular chlorine were used in the reaction?

3.67 Ammonia is a principal nitrogen fertilizer. It is prepared by the reaction between hydrogen and nitrogen.

$$3H_2(g) + N_2(g) \longrightarrow 2NH_3(g)$$

In a particular reaction, 6.0 moles of NH_3 were produced. How many moles of H_2 and how many moles of N_2 were reacted to produce this amount of NH_3?

3.68 Consider the combustion of butane (C_4H_{10}):

$$2C_4H_{10}(g) + 13O_2(g) \longrightarrow 8CO_2(g) + 10H_2O(l)$$

In a particular reaction, 5.0 moles of C_4H_{10} are reacted with an excess of O_2. Calculate the number of moles of CO_2 formed.

3.69 The annual production of sulfur dioxide from burning coal and fossil fuels, auto exhaust, and other sources is about 26 million tons. The equation for the reaction is

$$S(s) + O_2(g) \longrightarrow SO_2(g)$$

How much sulfur (in tons), present in the original materials, would result in that quantity of SO_2?

3.70 When baking soda (sodium bicarbonate or sodium hydrogen carbonate, $NaHCO_3$) is heated, it releases carbon dioxide gas, which is responsible for the rising of cookies, donuts, and bread. (a) Write a balanced equation for the decomposition of the compound (one of the products is Na_2CO_3). (b) Calculate the mass of $NaHCO_3$ required to produce 20.5 g of CO_2.

3.71 When potassium cyanide (KCN) reacts with acids, a deadly poisonous gas, hydrogen cyanide (HCN), is given off. Here is the equation:

$$KCN(aq) + HCl(aq) \longrightarrow KCl(aq) + HCN(g)$$

If a sample of 0.140 g of KCN is treated with an excess of HCl, calculate the amount of HCN formed, in grams.

3.72 Fermentation is a complex chemical process of wine making in which glucose is converted into ethanol and carbon dioxide:

$$\underset{\text{glucose}}{C_6H_{12}O_6} \longrightarrow \underset{\text{ethanol}}{2C_2H_5OH} + 2CO_2$$

Starting with 500.4 g of glucose, what is the maximum amount of ethanol in grams and in liters that can be obtained by this process? (Density of ethanol = 0.789 g/mL.)

3.73 Each copper(II) sulfate unit is associated with five water molecules in crystalline copper(II) sulfate pentahydrate ($CuSO_4 \cdot 5H_2O$). When this compound is heated in air above 100°C, it loses the water molecules and also its blue color:

$$CuSO_4 \cdot 5H_2O \longrightarrow CuSO_4 + 5H_2O$$

If 9.60 g of $CuSO_4$ are left after heating 15.01 g of the blue compound, calculate the number of moles of H_2O originally present in the compound.

3.74 For many years the recovery of gold—that is, the separation of gold from other materials—involved the use of potassium cyanide:

$$4Au + 8KCN + O_2 + 2H_2O \longrightarrow$$
$$4KAu(CN)_2 + 4KOH$$

What is the minimum amount of KCN in moles needed to extract 29.0 g (about an ounce) of gold?

3.75 Limestone ($CaCO_3$) is decomposed by heating to quicklime (CaO) and carbon dioxide. Calculate how many grams of quicklime can be produced from 1.0 kg of limestone.

3.76 Nitrous oxide (N_2O) is also called "laughing gas." It can be prepared by the thermal decomposition of ammonium nitrate (NH_4NO_3). The other product is H_2O. (a) Write a balanced equation for this reaction. (b) How many grams of N_2O are formed if 0.46 mole of NH_4NO_3 is used in the reaction?

3.77 The fertilizer ammonium sulfate [$(NH_4)_2SO_4$] is prepared by the reaction between ammonia (NH_3) and sulfuric acid:

$$2NH_3(g) + H_2SO_4(aq) \longrightarrow (NH_4)_2SO_4(aq)$$

How many kilograms of NH_3 are needed to produce 1.00×10^5 kg of $(NH_4)_2SO_4$?

3.78 A common laboratory preparation of oxygen gas is the thermal decomposition of potassium chlorate ($KClO_3$). Assuming complete decomposition, calculate the number of grams of O_2 gas that can be obtained from 46.0 g of $KClO_3$. (The products are KCl and O_2.)

Limiting Reagents
Review Questions

3.79 Define limiting reagent and excess reagent. What is the significance of the limiting reagent in predicting the amount of the product obtained in a reaction? Can there be a limiting reagent if only one reactant is present?

3.80 Give an everyday example that illustrates the limiting reagent concept.

Problems

3.81 Consider the reaction

$$2A + B \longrightarrow C$$

(a) In the diagram here that represents the reaction, which reactant, A or B, is the limiting reagent? (b) Assuming complete reaction, draw a molecular-model representation of the amounts of reactants and products left after the reaction. The atomic arrangement in C is ABA.

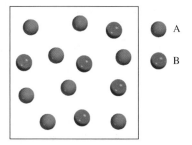

3.82 Consider the reaction

$$N_2 + 3H_2 \longrightarrow 2NH_3$$

Assuming each model represents one mole of the substance, show the number of moles of the product and the excess reagent left after the complete reaction.

3.83 Nitric oxide (NO) reacts with oxygen gas to form nitrogen dioxide (NO_2), a dark-brown gas:

$$2NO(g) + O_2(g) \longrightarrow 2NO_2(g)$$

In one experiment 0.886 mole of NO is mixed with 0.503 mole of O_2. Calculate which of the two reactants is the limiting reagent. Calculate also the number of moles of NO_2 produced.

3.84 The depletion of ozone (O_3) in the stratosphere has been a matter of great concern among scientists in recent years. It is believed that ozone can react with nitric oxide (NO) that is discharged from the high-altitude jet plane, the SST. The reaction is

$$O_3 + NO \longrightarrow O_2 + NO_2$$

If 0.740 g of O_3 reacts with 0.670 g of NO, how many grams of NO_2 will be produced? Which compound is the limiting reagent? Calculate the number of moles of the excess reagent remaining at the end of the reaction.

3.85 Propane (C_3H_8) is a component of natural gas and is used in domestic cooking and heating. (a) Balance the following equation representing the combustion of propane in air:

$$C_3H_8 + O_2 \longrightarrow CO_2 + H_2O$$

(b) How many grams of carbon dioxide can be produced by burning 3.65 moles of propane? Assume that oxygen is the excess reagent in this reaction.

3.86 Consider the reaction

$$MnO_2 + 4HCl \longrightarrow MnCl_2 + Cl_2 + 2H_2O$$

If 0.86 mole of MnO_2 and 48.2 g of HCl react, which reagent will be used up first? How many grams of Cl_2 will be produced?

Reaction Yield
Review Questions

3.87 Why is the theoretical yield of a reaction determined only by the amount of the limiting reagent?
3.88 Why is the actual yield of a reaction almost always smaller than the theoretical yield?

Problems

3.89 Hydrogen fluoride is used in the manufacture of Freons (which destroy ozone in the stratosphere) and in the production of aluminum metal. It is prepared by the reaction

$$CaF_2 + H_2SO_4 \longrightarrow CaSO_4 + 2HF$$

In one process 6.00 kg of CaF_2 are treated with an excess of H_2SO_4 and yield 2.86 kg of HF. Calculate the percent yield of HF.

3.90 Nitroglycerin ($C_3H_5N_3O_9$) is a powerful explosive. Its decomposition may be represented by

$$4C_3H_5N_3O_9 \longrightarrow 6N_2 + 12CO_2 + 10H_2O + O_2$$

This reaction generates a large amount of heat and many gaseous products. It is the sudden formation of these gases, together with their rapid expansion, that produces the explosion. (a) What is the maximum amount of O_2 in grams that can be obtained from 2.00×10^2 g of nitroglycerin? (b) Calculate the percent yield in this reaction if the amount of O_2 generated is found to be 6.55 g.

3.91 Titanium(IV) oxide (TiO_2) is a white substance produced by the action of sulfuric acid on the mineral ilmenite ($FeTiO_3$):

$$FeTiO_3 + H_2SO_4 \longrightarrow TiO_2 + FeSO_4 + H_2O$$

Its opaque and nontoxic properties make it suitable as a pigment in plastics and paints. In one process 8.00×10^3 kg of $FeTiO_3$ yielded 3.67×10^3 kg of TiO_2. What is the percent yield of the reaction?

3.92 Ethylene (C_2H_4), an important industrial organic chemical, can be prepared by heating hexane (C_6H_{14}) at 800°C:

$$C_6H_{14} \longrightarrow C_2H_4 + \text{other products}$$

If the yield of ethylene production is 42.5 percent, what mass of hexane must be reacted to produce 481 g of ethylene?

3.93 When heated, lithium reacts with nitrogen to form lithium nitride:

$$6Li(s) + N_2(g) \longrightarrow 2Li_3N(s)$$

What is the theoretical yield of Li_3N in grams when 12.3 g of Li are heated with 33.6 g of N_2? If the actual yield of Li_3N is 5.89 g, what is the percent yield of the reaction?

3.94 Disulfide dichloride (S_2Cl_2) is used in the vulcanization of rubber, a process that prevents the slippage of rubber molecules past one another when stretched. It is prepared by heating sulfur in an atmosphere of chlorine:

$$S_8(l) + 4Cl_2(g) \longrightarrow 4S_2Cl_2(l)$$

What is the theoretical yield of S_2Cl_2 in grams when 4.06 g of S_8 are heated with 6.24 g of Cl_2? If the actual yield of S_2Cl_2 is 6.55 g, what is the percent yield?

Additional Problems

3.95 The following diagram represents the products (CO_2 and H_2O) formed after the combustion of a hydrocarbon (a compound containing only C and H atoms). Write an equation for the reaction. (*Hint:* The molar mass of the hydrocarbon is about 30 g.)

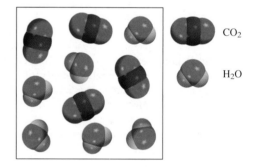

3.96 Consider the reaction of hydrogen gas with oxygen gas:

$$2H_2(g) + O_2(g) \longrightarrow 2H_2O(g)$$

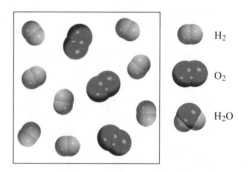

Assuming complete reaction, which of the diagrams shown on p. 111 represents the amounts of reactants and products left after the reaction?

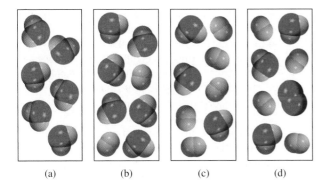

(a)   (b)   (c)   (d)

3.97 Industrially, nitric acid is produced by the Ostwald process represented by the following equations:

$$4NH_3(g) + 5O_2(g) \longrightarrow 4NO(g) + 6H_2O(l)$$
$$2NO(g) + O_2(g) \longrightarrow 2NO_2(g)$$
$$2NO_2(g) + H_2O(l) \longrightarrow HNO_3(aq) + HNO_2(aq)$$

What mass of NH_3 (in g) must be used to produce 1.00 ton of HNO_3 by the above procedure, assuming an 80 percent yield in each step? (1 ton = 2000 lb; 1 lb = 453.6 g.)

3.98 A sample of a compound of Cl and O reacts with an excess of H_2 to give 0.233 g of HCl and 0.403 g of H_2O. Determine the empirical formula of the compound.

3.99 The atomic mass of element X is 33.42 amu. A 27.22-g sample of X combines with 84.10 g of another element Y to form a compound XY. Calculate the atomic mass of Y.

3.100 How many moles of O are needed to combine with 0.212 mole of C to form (a) CO and (b) CO_2?

3.101 A research chemist used a mass spectrometer to study the two isotopes of an element. Over time, she recorded a number of mass spectra of these isotopes. On analysis, she noticed that the ratio of the taller peak (the more abundant isotope) to the shorter peak (the less abundant isotope) gradually increased with time. Assuming that the mass spectrometer was functioning normally, what do you think was causing this change?

3.102 The aluminum sulfate hydrate $[Al_2(SO_4)_3 \cdot xH_2O]$ contains 8.20 percent Al by mass. Calculate x, that is, the number of water molecules associated with each $Al_2(SO_4)_3$ unit.

3.103 Mustard gas ($C_4H_8Cl_2S$) is a poisonous gas that was used in World War I and banned afterward. It causes general destruction of body tissues, resulting in the formation of large water blisters. There is no effective antidote. Calculate the percent composition by mass of the elements in mustard gas.

3.104 The carat is the unit of mass used by jewelers. One carat is exactly 200 mg. How many carbon atoms are present in a 24-carat diamond?

3.105 An iron bar weighed 664 g. After the bar had been standing in moist air for a month, exactly one-eighth of the iron turned to rust (Fe_2O_3). Calculate the final mass of the iron bar and rust.

3.106 A certain metal oxide has the formula MO where M denotes the metal. A 39.46-g sample of the compound is strongly heated in an atmosphere of hydrogen to remove oxygen as water molecules. At the end, 31.70 g of the metal is left over. If O has an atomic mass of 16.00 amu, calculate the atomic mass of M and identify the element.

3.107 An impure sample of zinc (Zn) is treated with an excess of sulfuric acid (H_2SO_4) to form zinc sulfate ($ZnSO_4$) and molecular hydrogen (H_2). (a) Write a balanced equation for the reaction. (b) If 0.0764 g of H_2 is obtained from 3.86 g of the sample, calculate the percent purity of the sample. (c) What assumptions must you make in (b)?

3.108 One of the reactions that occurs in a blast furnace, where iron ore is converted to cast iron, is

$$Fe_2O_3 + 3CO \longrightarrow 2Fe + 3CO_2$$

Suppose that 1.64×10^3 kg of Fe are obtained from a 2.62×10^3-kg sample of Fe_2O_3. Assuming that the reaction goes to completion, what is the percent purity of Fe_2O_3 in the original sample?

3.109 Carbon dioxide (CO_2) is the gas that is mainly responsible for global warming (the greenhouse effect). The burning of fossil fuels is a major cause of the increased concentration of CO_2 in the atmosphere. Carbon dioxide is also the end product of metabolism (see Example 3.14). Using glucose as an example of food, calculate the annual human production of CO_2 in grams, assuming that each person consumes 5.0×10^2 g of glucose per day. The world's population is 6.5 billion, and there are 365 days in a year.

3.110 Carbohydrates are compounds containing carbon, hydrogen, and oxygen in which the hydrogen to oxygen ratio is 2:1. A certain carbohydrate contains 40.0 percent carbon by mass. Calculate the empirical and molecular formulas of the compound if the approximate molar mass is 178 g.

3.111 Which of the following has the greater mass: 0.72 g of O_2 or 0.0011 mole of chlorophyll ($C_{55}H_{72}MgN_4O_5$)?

3.112 Analysis of a metal chloride XCl_3 shows that it contains 67.2 percent Cl by mass. Calculate the molar mass of X and identify the element.

3.113 Hemoglobin ($C_{2952}H_{4664}N_{812}O_{832}S_8Fe_4$) is the oxygen carrier in blood. (a) Calculate its molar mass. (b) An average adult has about 5.0 L of blood. Every milliliter of blood has approximately 5.0×10^9 erythrocytes, or red blood cells, and every red blood cell has about 2.8×10^8 hemoglobin molecules. Calculate the mass of hemoglobin molecules in grams in an average adult.

3.114 Myoglobin stores oxygen for metabolic processes in muscle. Chemical analysis shows that it contains 0.34 percent Fe by mass. What is the molar mass of myoglobin? (There is one Fe atom per molecule.)

3.115 Calculate the number of cations and anions in each of the following compounds: (a) 8.38 g of KBr, (b) 5.40 g of Na_2SO_4, (c) 7.45 g of $Ca_3(PO_4)_2$.

3.116 A sample containing NaCl, Na_2SO_4, and $NaNO_3$ gives the following elemental analysis: Na: 32.08 percent; O: 36.01 percent; Cl: 19.51 percent. Calculate the mass percent of each compound in the sample.

3.117 (a) For molecules having small molecular masses, mass spectrometry can be used to identify their formulas. To illustrate this point, identify the molecule which most likely accounts for the observation of a peak in a mass spectrum at: 16 amu, 17 amu, 18 amu, and 64 amu. (b) Note that there are (among others) two likely molecules that would give rise to a peak at 44 amu, namely, C_3H_8 and CO_2. In such cases, a chemist might try to look for other peaks generated when some of the molecules break apart in the spectrometer. For example, if a chemist sees a peak at 44 amu and also one at 15 amu, which molecule is producing the 44-amu peak? Why? (c) Using the following precise atomic masses: ^1H (1.00797 amu), ^{12}C (12.00000 amu), and ^{16}O (15.99491 amu), how precisely must the masses of C_3H_8 and CO_2 be measured to distinguish between them?

3.118 Calculate the percent composition by mass of all the elements in calcium phosphate [$Ca_3(PO_4)_2$], a major component of bone.

3.119 Lysine, an essential amino acid in the human body, contains C, H, O, and N. In one experiment, the complete combustion of 2.175 g of lysine gave 3.94 g CO_2 and 1.89 g H_2O. In a separate experiment, 1.873 g of lysine gave 0.436 g NH_3. (a) Calculate the empirical formula of lysine. (b) The approximate molar mass of lysine is 150 g. What is the molecular formula of the compound?

3.120 Does 1 g of hydrogen molecules contain as many H atoms as 1 g of hydrogen atoms?

3.121 Avogadro's number has sometimes been described as a conversion factor between amu and grams. Use the fluorine atom (19.00 amu) as an example to show the relation between the atomic mass unit and the gram.

3.122 The natural abundances of the two stable isotopes of hydrogen (hydrogen and deuterium) are ^1_1H: 99.985 percent and ^2_1H: 0.015 percent. Assume that water exists as either H_2O or D_2O. Calculate the number of D_2O molecules in exactly 400 mL of water. (Density = 1.00 g/mL.)

3.123 A compound containing only C, H, and Cl was examined in a mass spectrometer. The highest mass peak seen corresponds to an ion mass of 52 amu. The most abundant mass peak seen corresponds to an ion mass of 50 amu and is about three times as intense as the peak at 52 amu. Deduce a reasonable molecular formula for the compound and explain the positions and intensities of the mass peaks mentioned. (*Hint:* Chlorine is the only element that has isotopes in comparable abundances: $^{35}_{17}Cl$: 75.5 percent; $^{35}_{17}Cl$: 24.5 percent. For H, use ^1_1H; for C, use $^{12}_6C$.)

3.124 In the formation of carbon monoxide, CO, it is found that 2.445 g of carbon combine with 3.257 g of oxygen. What is the atomic mass of oxygen if the atomic mass of carbon is 12.01 amu?

3.125 What mole ratio of molecular chlorine (Cl_2) to molecular oxygen (O_2) would result from the breakup of the compound Cl_2O_7 into its constituent elements?

3.126 Which of the following substances contains the greatest mass of chlorine? (a) 5.0 g Cl_2, (b) 60.0 g $NaClO_3$, (c) 0.10 mol KCl, (d) 30.0 g $MgCl_2$, (e) 0.50 mol Cl_2.

3.127 Potash is any potassium mineral that is used for its potassium content. Most of the potash produced in the United States goes into fertilizer. The major sources of potash are potassium chloride (KCl) and potassium sulfate (K_2SO_4). Potash production is often reported as the potassium oxide (K_2O) equivalent or the amount of K_2O that could be made from a given mineral. (a) If KCl costs $0.55 per kg, for what price (dollar per kg) must K_2SO_4 be sold in order to supply the same amount of potassium on a per dollar basis? (b) What mass (in kg) of K_2O contains the same number of moles of K atoms as 1.00 kg of KCl?

3.128 Platinum forms two different compounds with chlorine. One contains 26.7 percent Cl by mass, and the other contains 42.1 percent Cl by mass. Determine the empirical formulas of the two compounds.

3.129 Heating 2.40 g of the oxide of metal X (molar mass of X = 55.9 g/mol) in carbon monoxide (CO) yields the pure metal and carbon dioxide. The mass of the metal product is 1.68 g. From the data given, show that the simplest formula of the oxide is X_2O_3 and write a balanced equation for the reaction.

3.130 A compound X contains 63.3 percent manganese (Mn) and 36.7 percent O by mass. When X is heated, oxygen gas is evolved and a new compound Y containing 72.0 percent Mn and 28.0 percent O is formed. (a) Determine the empirical formulas of X and Y. (b) Write a balanced equation for the conversion of X to Y.

3.131 The formula of a hydrate of barium chloride is $BaCl_2 \cdot xH_2O$. If 1.936 g of the compound gives 1.864 g of anhydrous $BaSO_4$ upon treatment with sulfuric acid, calculate the value of x.

3.132 It is estimated that the day Mt. St. Helens erupted (May 18, 1980), about 4.0×10^5 tons of SO_2 were released into the atmosphere. If all the SO_2 were eventually converted to sulfuric acid, how many tons of H_2SO_4 were produced?

3.133 A mixture of $CuSO_4 \cdot 5H_2O$ and $MgSO_4 \cdot 7H_2O$ is heated until all the water is lost. If 5.020 g of the mixture gives 2.988 g of the anhydrous salts, what is the percent by mass of $CuSO_4 \cdot 5H_2O$ in the mixture?

3.134 When 0.273 g of Mg is heated strongly in a nitrogen (N_2) atmosphere, a chemical reaction occurs. The product of the reaction weighs 0.378 g. Calculate the empirical formula of the compound containing Mg and N. Name the compound.

3.135 A mixture of methane (CH_4) and ethane (C_2H_6) of mass 13.43 g is completely burned in oxygen. If the total mass of CO_2 and H_2O produced is 64.84 g, calculate the fraction of CH_4 in the mixture.

3.136 Leaded gasoline contains an additive to prevent engine "knocking." On analysis, the additive compound is found to contain carbon, hydrogen, and lead (Pb) (hence, "leaded gasoline"). When 51.36 g of this compound are burned in an apparatus such as that shown in Figure 3.6, 55.90 g of CO_2 and 28.61 g of H_2O are produced. Determine the empirical formula of the gasoline additive.

3.137 Because of its detrimental effect on the environment, the lead compound described in Problem 3.136 has been replaced in recent years by methyl *tert*-butyl ether (a compound of C, H, and O) to enhance the performance of gasoline. (As of 1999, this compound is also being phased out because of its contamination of drinking water.) When 12.1 g of the compound are burned in an apparatus like the one shown in Figure 3.6, 30.2 g of CO_2 and 14.8 g of H_2O are formed. What is the empirical formula of the compound?

3.138 Suppose you are given a cube made of magnesium (Mg) metal of edge length 1.0 cm. (a) Calculate the number of Mg atoms in the cube. (b) Atoms are spherical in shape. Therefore, the Mg atoms in the cube cannot fill all of the available space. If only 74 percent of the space inside the cube is taken up by Mg atoms, calculate the radius in picometers of a Mg atom. (The density of Mg is 1.74 g/cm^3 and the volume of a sphere of radius r is $\frac{4}{3}\pi r^3$.)

3.139 A certain sample of coal contains 1.6 percent sulfur by mass. When the coal is burned, the sulfur is converted to sulfur dioxide. To prevent air pollution, this sulfur dioxide is treated with calcium oxide (CaO) to form calcium sulfite ($CaSO_3$). Calculate the daily mass (in kilograms) of CaO needed by a power plant that uses 6.60×10^6 kg of coal per day.

3.140 Air is a mixture of many gases. However, in calculating its "molar mass" we need consider only the three major components: nitrogen, oxygen, and argon. Given that one mole of air at sea level is made up of 78.08 percent nitrogen, 20.95 percent oxygen, and 0.97 percent argon, what is the molar mass of air?

3.141 A die has an edge length of 1.5 cm. (a) What is the volume of one mole of such dice? (b) Assuming that the mole of dice could be packed in such a way that they were in contact with one another, forming stacking layers covering the entire surface of Earth, calculate the height in meters the layers would extend outward. [The radius (r) of Earth is 6371 km and the area of a sphere is $4\pi r^2$.]

3.142 The following is a crude but effective method for estimating the *order of magnitude* of Avogadro's number using stearic acid ($C_{18}H_{36}O_2$). When stearic acid is added to water, its molecules collect at the surface and form a monolayer; that is, the layer is only one molecule thick. The cross-sectional area of each stearic acid molecule has been measured to be 0.21 nm^2. In one experiment it is found that 1.4×10^{-4} g of stearic acid is needed to form a monolayer over water in a dish of diameter 20 cm. Based on these measurements, what is Avogadro's number? (The area of a circle of radius r is πr^2.)

3.143 Octane (C_8H_{18}) is a component of gasoline. Complete combustion of octane yields H_2O and CO_2. Incomplete combustion produces H_2O and CO, which not only reduces the efficiency of the engine using the fuel but is also toxic. In a certain test run, 1.000 gallon of octane is burned in an engine. The total mass of CO, CO_2, and H_2O produced is 11.53 kg. Calculate the efficiency of the process; that is, calculate the fraction of octane converted to CO_2. The density of octane is 2.650 kg/gallon.

3.144 Industrially, hydrogen gas can be prepared by reacting propane gas (C_3H_8) with steam at about 400°C. The products are carbon monoxide (CO) and hydrogen gas (H_2). (a) Write a balanced equation for the reaction. (b) How many kilograms of H_2 can be obtained from 2.84×10^3 kg of propane?

3.145 A reaction having a 90 percent yield may be considered a successful experiment. However, in the synthesis of complex molecules such as chlorophyll and many anticancer drugs, a chemist often has to carry out multiple-step synthesis. What is the overall percent yield for such a synthesis, assuming it is a 30-step reaction with a 90 percent yield at each step?

Answers to Practice Exercises

3.1 10.81 amu. **3.2** 3.59 moles. **3.3** 2.57×10^3 g. **3.4** 8.49×10^{21} K atoms. **3.5** 32.04 amu. **3.6** 1.66 moles. **3.7** 5.81×10^{24} H atoms. **3.8** H: 2.055%; S: 32.69%; O: 65.25%. **3.9** $KMnO_4$ (potassium permanganate).

3.10 196 g. **3.11** B_2H_6. **3.12** $Fe_2O_3 + 3CO \longrightarrow 2Fe + 3CO_2$. **3.13** (a) 0.508 mole, (b) 2.21 g. **3.14** 235 g. **3.15** (a) 234 g, (b) 234 g. **3.16** (a) 863 g, (b) 93.0%.

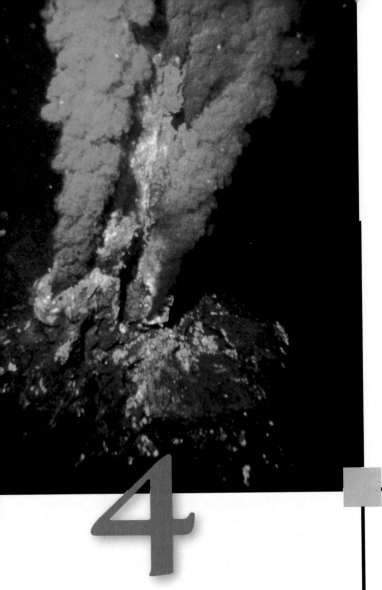

Black smokers form when superheated water (about 350°C), rich in minerals, flows out onto the ocean floor through the lava on a mid-ocean-ridge volcano. The hydrogen sulfide present converts the metals to the insoluble metal sulfides, which form a chimney-like structure. The models show hydrogen sulfide, metal ions, and a metal sulfide.

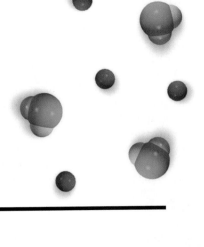

4

Reactions in Aqueous Solutions

Interactive Activity Summary

1. Animation: Strong Electrolytes, Weak Electrolytes, and Nonelectrolytes (4.1)
2. Animation: Hydration (4.1)
3. Animation: Precipitation Reactions (4.2)
4. Interactivity: Construct a Net Ionic Equation (4.2)
5. Interactivity: Acid and Base Reactions (4.3)
6. Animation: Neutralization Reactions (4.3)
7. Animation: Oxidation-Reduction Reactions (4.4)
8. Animation: Making a Solution (4.5)
9. Animation: Preparing a Solution by Dilution (4.5)

Many chemical reactions and virtually all biological processes take place in water. In this chapter we will discuss three major categories of reactions that occur in aqueous solutions: precipitation reactions, acid-base reactions, and redox reactions. In later chapters we will study the structural characteristics and properties of water—the so-called *universal solvent*—and its solutions.

4.1 General Properties of Aqueous Solutions

A *solution* is a *homogeneous mixture of two or more substances.* The **solute** is *the substance present in a smaller amount,* and the **solvent** is *the substance present in a larger amount.* A solution may be gaseous (such as air), solid (such as an alloy), or liquid (seawater, for example). In this section we will discuss only *aqueous solutions,* in which *the solute initially is a liquid or a solid and the solvent is water.*

Electrolytic Properties

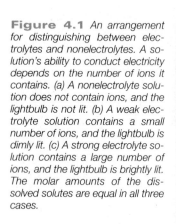

Animation: Strong Electrolytes, Weak Electrolytes, and Nonelectrolytes Online Learning Center, Animations

All solutes that dissolve in water fit into one of two categories: electrolytes and non-electrolytes. An *electrolyte* is *a substance that, when dissolved in water, results in a solution that can conduct electricity.* A *nonelectrolyte* *does not conduct electricity when dissolved in water.* Figure 4.1 shows an easy and straightforward method of distinguishing between electrolytes and nonelectrolytes. A pair of inert electrodes (copper or platinum) is immersed in a beaker of water. To light the bulb, electric current must flow from one electrode to the other, thus completing the circuit. Pure water is a very poor conductor of electricity. However, if we add a small amount of sodium chloride (NaCl), the bulb will glow as soon as the salt dissolves in the water. Solid NaCl, an ionic compound, breaks up into Na^+ and Cl^- ions when it dissolves in water. The Na^+ ions are attracted to the negative electrode and the Cl^- ions to the positive electrode. This movement sets up an electric current that is equivalent to the flow of electrons along a metal wire. Because the NaCl solution conducts electricity, we say that NaCl is an electrolyte. Pure water contains very few ions, so it cannot conduct electricity.

Comparing the lightbulb's brightness for the same molar amounts of dissolved substances helps us distinguish between strong and weak electrolytes. A characteristic of strong electrolytes is that the solute is assumed to be 100 percent dissociated into ions in solution. (By *dissociation* we mean the breaking up of the compound into cations and anions.) Thus we can represent sodium chloride dissolving in water as

$$NaCl(s) \xrightarrow{\text{H}_2\text{O}} Na^+(aq) + Cl^-(aq)$$

This equation says that all sodium chloride that enters the solution ends up as Na^+ and Cl^- ions; there are no undissociated NaCl units in solution.

Figure 4.1 *An arrangement for distinguishing between electrolytes and nonelectrolytes. A solution's ability to conduct electricity depends on the number of ions it contains. (a) A nonelectrolyte solution does not contain ions, and the lightbulb is not lit. (b) A weak electrolyte solution contains a small number of ions, and the lightbulb is dimly lit. (c) A strong electrolyte solution contains a large number of ions, and the lightbulb is brightly lit. The molar amounts of the dissolved solutes are equal in all three cases.*

(a)   (b)   (c)

Classification of Solutes in Aqueous Solution		
Strong Electrolyte	**Weak Electrolyte**	**Nonelectrolyte**
HCl	CH_3COOH	$(NH_2)_2CO$ (urea)
HNO_3	HF	CH_3OH (methanol)
$HClO_4$	HNO_2	C_2H_5OH (ethanol)
H_2SO_4*	NH_3	$C_6H_{12}O_6$ (glucose)
NaOH	$H_2O^\dagger$	$C_{12}H_{22}O_{11}$ (sucrose)
$Ba(OH)_2$		
Ionic compounds		

TABLE 4.1

* H_2SO_4 has two ionizable H^+ ions.

† Pure water is an extremely weak electrolyte.

Table 4.1 lists examples of strong electrolytes, weak electrolytes, and nonelectrolytes. Ionic compounds, such as sodium chloride, potassium iodide (KI), and calcium nitrate [$Ca(NO_3)_2$], are strong electrolytes. It is interesting to note that human body fluids contain many strong and weak electrolytes.

Water is a very effective solvent for ionic compounds. Although water is an electrically neutral molecule, it has a positive region (the H atoms) and a negative region (the O atom), or positive and negative "poles"; for this reason it is a *polar* solvent. When an ionic compound such as sodium chloride dissolves in water, the three-dimensional network of ions in the solid is destroyed. The Na^+ and Cl^- ions are separated from each other and undergo **hydration,** *the process in which an ion is surrounded by water molecules arranged in a specific manner.* Each Na^+ ion is surrounded by a number of water molecules orienting their negative poles toward the cation. Similarly, each Cl^- ion is surrounded by water molecules with their positive poles oriented toward the anion (Figure 4.2). Hydration helps to stabilize ions in solution and prevents cations from combining with anions.

Animation: Hydration
Online Learning Center,
Animations

Acids and bases are also electrolytes. Some acids, including hydrochloric acid (HCl) and nitric acid (HNO_3), are strong electrolytes. These acids are assumed to ionize completely in water; for example, when hydrogen chloride gas dissolves in water, it forms hydrated H^+ and Cl^- ions:

$$HCl(g) \xrightarrow{H_2O} H^+(aq) + Cl^-(aq)$$

In other words, *all* the dissolved HCl molecules separate into hydrated H^+ and Cl^- ions. Thus when we write HCl(*aq*), it is understood that it is a solution of only $H^+(aq)$ and $Cl^-(aq)$ ions and that there are no hydrated HCl molecules present. On the other hand, certain acids, such as acetic acid (CH_3COOH), which gives vinegar its tart flavor, do not ionize completely and are weak electrolytes. We represent the ionization of acetic acid as

$$CH_3COOH(aq) \rightleftharpoons CH_3COO^-(aq) + H^+(aq)$$

CH_3COOH

Figure 4.2 *Hydration of Na^+ and Cl^- ions.*

where CH_3COO^- is called the acetate ion. We use the term *ionization* to describe the separation of acids and bases into ions. By writing the formula of acetic acid as CH_3COOH we indicate that the ionizable proton is in the COOH group.

The ionization of acetic acid is written with a double arrow to show that it is a **reversible reaction;** that is, *the reaction can occur in both directions.* Initially, a number of CH_3COOH molecules break up into CH_3COO^- and H^+ ions. As time goes on, some of the CH_3COO^- and H^+ ions recombine into CH_3COOH molecules. Eventually, a state is reached in which the acid molecules ionize as fast as the ions recombine. Such a chemical state, in which no net change can be observed (although activity is continuous on the molecular level), is called *chemical equilibrium.* Acetic acid, then, is a weak electrolyte because its ionization in water is incomplete. By contrast, in a hydrochloric acid solution the H^+ and Cl^- ions have no tendency to recombine and form molecular HCl. We use a single arrow to represent complete ionizations.

There are different types of chemical equilibrium. We will return to this very important topic in Chapter 14.

Animation: Precipitation Reactions
Online Learning Center, Animations

4.2 Precipitation Reactions

One common type of reaction that occurs in aqueous solution is the **precipitation reaction,** which *results in the formation of an insoluble product, or precipitate.* A **precipitate** is *an insoluble solid that separates from the solution.* Precipitation reactions usually involve ionic compounds. For example, when an aqueous solution of lead nitrate $[Pb(NO_3)_2]$ is added to an aqueous solution of sodium iodide (NaI), a yellow precipitate of lead iodide (PbI_2) is formed:

$$Pb(NO_3)_2(aq) + 2NaI(aq) \longrightarrow PbI_2(s) + 2NaNO_3(aq)$$

Sodium nitrate remains in solution. Figure 4.3 shows this reaction in progress.

Solubility

How can we predict whether a precipitate will form when a compound is added to a solution or when two solutions are mixed? It depends on the **solubility** of the solute, which is defined as *the maximum amount of solute that will dissolve in a given quantity of solvent at a specific temperature.* Chemists refer to substances as soluble, slightly soluble, or insoluble in a qualitative sense. A substance is said to be soluble if a fair amount of it visibly dissolves when added to water. If not, the substance is described as slightly soluble or insoluble. All ionic compounds are strong electrolytes, but they are not equally soluble.

Table 4.2 classifies a number of common ionic compounds as soluble or insoluble. Keep in mind, however, that even insoluble compounds dissolve to a certain extent. Figure 4.4 shows several precipitates.

Example 4.1 applies the solubility rules in Table 4.2.

Figure 4.3 *Formation of yellow PbI_2 precipitate as a solution of $Pb(NO_3)_2$ is added to a solution of NaI.*

Example 4.1

Classify the following ionic compounds as soluble or insoluble: (a) silver sulfate (Ag_2SO_4), (b) calcium carbonate $(CaCO_3)$, (c) sodium phosphate (Na_3PO_4).

Strategy Although it is not necessary to memorize the solubilities of compounds, you should keep in mind the following useful rules: all ionic compounds containing alkali metal

(Continued)

TABLE 4.2

Solubility Rules for Common Ionic Compounds in Water at 25°C

Soluble Compounds	Exceptions
Compounds containing alkali metal ions (Li^+, Na^+, K^+, Rb^+, Cs^+) and the ammonium ion (NH_4^+)	
Nitrates (NO_3^-), bicarbonates (HCO_3^-), and chlorates (ClO_3^-)	
Halides (Cl^-, Br^-, I^-)	Halides of Ag^+, Hg_2^{2+}, and Pb^{2+}
Sulfates (SO_4^{2-})	Sulfates of Ag^+, Ca^{2+}, Sr^{2+}, Ba^{2+}, Hg_2^{2+}, and Pb^{2+}

Insoluble Compounds	Exceptions
Carbonates (CO_3^{2-}), phosphates (PO_4^{3-}), chromates (CrO_4^{2-}), sulfides (S^{2-})	Compounds containing alkali metal ions and the ammonium ion
Hydroxides (OH^-)	Compounds containing alkali metal ions and the Ba^{2+} ion

cations; the ammonium ion; and the nitrate, bicarbonate, and chlorate ions are soluble. For other compounds we need to refer to Table 4.2.

Solution (a) According to Table 4.2, Ag_2SO_4 is insoluble.

(b) This is a carbonate and Ca is a Group 2A metal. Therefore, $CaCO_3$ is insoluble.

(c) Sodium is an alkali metal (Group 1A) so Na_3PO_4 is soluble.

Similar problems: 4.19, 4.20.

Practice Exercise Classify the following ionic compounds as soluble or insoluble: (a) CuS, (b) $Ca(OH)_2$, (c) $Zn(NO_3)_2$.

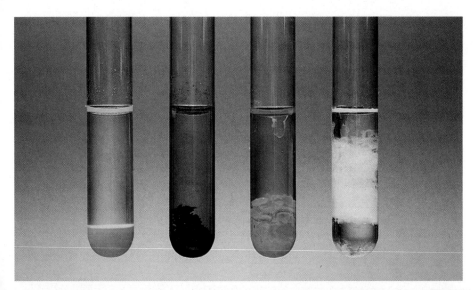

Figure 4.4 *Appearance of several precipitates. From left to right: CdS, PbS, Ni(OH)₂, Al(OH)₃.*

Figure 4.5 *The formation of BaSO₄ precipitate.*

Molecular Equations and Ionic Equations

The equation describing the precipitation of lead iodide on page 118 is called a ***molecular equation*** because *the formulas of the compounds are written as though all species existed as molecules or whole units.* A molecular equation is useful because it identifies the reagents (that is, lead nitrate and sodium iodide). If we wanted to bring about this reaction in the laboratory, the molecular equation would be the one to use. However, a molecular equation does not accurately describe what actually is happening at the microscopic level.

As pointed out earlier, when ionic compounds dissolve in water, they break apart into their component cations and anions. To be more realistic, the equations should show the dissociation of dissolved ionic compounds into ions. Therefore, returning to the reaction between sodium iodide and lead nitrate, we would write

$$Pb^{2+}(aq) + 2NO_3^-(aq) + 2Na^+(aq) + 2I^-(aq) \longrightarrow PbI_2(s) + 2Na^+(aq) + 2NO_3^-(aq)$$

The preceding equation is an example of an ***ionic equation,*** which *shows dissolved species as free ions.* An ionic equation includes ***spectator ions,*** or *ions that are not involved in the overall reaction,* in this case the Na^+ and NO_3^- ions. Spectator ions appear on both sides of the equation and are unchanged in the chemical reaction, so they can be canceled. To focus on the change that occurs, we write the ***net ionic equation,*** which *shows only the species that actually take part in the reaction:*

$$Pb^{2+}(aq) + 2I^-(aq) \longrightarrow PbI_2(s)$$

Looking at another example, we find that when an aqueous solution of barium chloride ($BaCl_2$) is added to an aqueous solution of sodium sulfate (Na_2SO_4), a white precipitate of barium sulfate ($BaSO_4$) is formed (Figure 4.5). The molecular equation for this reaction is

$$BaCl_2(aq) + Na_2SO_4(aq) \longrightarrow BaSO_4(s) + 2NaCl(aq)$$

The ionic equation for the reaction is

$$Ba^{2+}(aq) + 2Cl^-(aq) + 2Na^+(aq) + SO_4^{2-}(aq) \longrightarrow BaSO_4(s) + 2Na^+(aq) + 2Cl^-(aq)$$

Interactivity: Construct a Net Ionic Equation
Online Learning Center, Interactives

Canceling the spectator ions (Na^+ and Cl^-) on both sides of the equation gives us the net ionic equation

$$Ba^{2+}(aq) + SO_4^{2-}(aq) \longrightarrow BaSO_4(s)$$

The following steps summarize the procedure for writing ionic and net ionic equations.

1. Write a balanced molecular equation for the reaction.
2. Rewrite the equation to show the dissociated ions that form in solution. We assume that all strong electrolytes, when dissolved in solution, are completely dissociated into cations and anions. This procedure gives us the ionic equation.
3. Identify and cancel spectator ions on both sides of the equation to arrive at the net ionic equation.

These steps are applied in Example 4.2.

Example 4.2

Predict what happens when a potassium phosphate (K_3PO_4) solution is mixed with a calcium nitrate [$Ca(NO_3)_2$] solution. Write a net ionic equation for the reaction.

Strategy From the given information, it is useful to first write the unbalanced equation

$$K_3PO_4(aq) + Ca(NO_3)_2(aq) \longrightarrow ?$$

What happens when ionic compounds dissolve in water? What ions are formed from the dissociation of K_3PO_4 and $Ca(NO_3)_2$? What happens when the cations encounter the anions in solution?

Solution In solution, K_3PO_4 dissociates into K^+ and PO_4^{3-} ions and $Ca(NO_3)_2$ dissociates into Ca^{2+} and NO_3^- ions. According to Table 4.2, calcium ions (Ca^{2+}) and phosphate ions (PO_4^{3-}) will form an insoluble compound, calcium phosphate [$Ca_3(PO_4)_2$], while the other product, KNO_3, is soluble and remains in solution. Therefore, this is a precipitation reaction. The balanced molecular equation is

$$2K_3PO_4(aq) + 3Ca(NO_3)_2(aq) \longrightarrow 6KNO_3(aq) + Ca_3(PO_4)_2(s)$$

Precipitate formed by the reaction between $K_3PO_4(aq)$ and $Ca(NO_3)_2(aq)$.

To write the net ionic equation, we must first write the ionic equation, showing all the cations and anions:

$$6K^+(aq) + 2PO_4^{3-}(aq) + 3Ca^{2+}(aq) + 6NO_3^-(aq) \longrightarrow$$
$$6K^+(aq) + 6NO_3^-(aq) + Ca_3(PO_4)_2(s)$$

Canceling the spectator K^+ and NO_3^- ions, we obtain the net ionic equation

$$3Ca^{2+}(aq) + 2PO_4^{3-}(aq) \longrightarrow Ca_3(PO_4)_2(s)$$

Check Note that because we balanced the molecular equation first, the net ionic equation is balanced as to the number of atoms on each side and the number of positive and negative charges on the left-hand side is the same.

Similar problems: 4.21, 4.22.

Practice Exercise Predict the precipitate produced by mixing an $Al(NO_3)_3$ solution with a NaOH solution. Write the net ionic equation for the reaction.

The Chemistry in Action essay on p. 122 discusses some practical problems associated with precipitation reactions.

4.3 Acid-Base Reactions

Acids and bases are as familiar as aspirin and milk of magnesia although many people do not know their chemical names—acetylsalicylic acid (aspirin) and magnesium hydroxide (milk of magnesia). In addition to being the basis of many medicinal and household products, acid-base chemistry is important in industrial processes and essential in sustaining biological systems. Before we can discuss acid-base reactions, we need to know more about acids and bases themselves.

General Properties of Acids and Bases

In Section 2.7 we defined acids as substances that ionize in water to produce H^+ ions and bases as substances that ionize in water to produce OH^- ions. These definitions were formulated in the late nineteenth century by the Swedish chemist

CHEMISTRY IN ACTION

An Undesirable Precipitation Reaction

Limestone ($CaCO_3$) and dolomite ($CaCO_3 \cdot MgCO_3$), which are widespread on Earth's surface, often enter the water supply. According to Table 4.2, calcium carbonate is insoluble in water. However, in the presence of dissolved carbon dioxide (from the atmosphere), calcium carbonate is converted to soluble calcium bicarbonate [$Ca(HCO_3)_2$]:

$$CaCO_3(s) + CO_2(aq) + H_2O(l) \longrightarrow \\ Ca^{2+}(aq) + 2HCO_3^-(aq)$$

where HCO_3^- is the bicarbonate ion.

Water containing Ca^{2+} and/or Mg^{2+} ions is called *hard water,* and water that is mostly free of these ions is called *soft water.* Hard water is unsuitable for some household and industrial uses.

When water containing Ca^{2+} and HCO_3^- ions is heated or boiled, the solution reaction is reversed to produce the $CaCO_3$ precipitate

$$Ca^{2+}(aq) + 2HCO_3^-(aq) \longrightarrow \\ CaCO_3(s) + CO_2(aq) + H_2O(l)$$

and gaseous carbon dioxide is driven off:

$$CO_2(aq) \longrightarrow CO_2(g)$$

Boiler scale almost fills this hot-water pipe. The deposits consists mostly of $CaCO_3$ with some $MgCO_3$.

Solid calcium carbonate formed in this way is the main component of the scale that accumulates in boilers, water heaters, pipes, and teakettles. A thick layer of scale reduces heat transfer and decreases the efficiency and durability of boilers, pipes, and appliances. In household hot-water pipes it can restrict or totally block the flow of water. A simple method used by plumbers to remove scale deposits is to introduce a small amount of hydrochloric acid, which reacts with (and therefore dissolves) $CaCO_3$:

$$CaCO_3(s) + 2HCl(aq) \longrightarrow CaCl_2(aq) + H_2O(l) + CO_2(g)$$

In this way, $CaCO_3$ is converted to soluble $CaCl_2$.

Svante Arrhenius[†] to classify substances whose properties in aqueous solutions were well known.

Acids

- Acids have a sour taste; for example, vinegar owes its sourness to acetic acid, and lemons and other citrus fruits contain citric acid.

- Acids cause color changes in plant dyes; for example, they change the color of litmus from blue to red.

- Acids react with certain metals, such as zinc, magnesium, and iron, to produce hydrogen gas. A typical reaction is that between hydrochloric acid and magnesium:

$$2HCl(aq) + Mg(s) \longrightarrow MgCl_2(aq) + H_2(g)$$

[†]Svante August Arrhenius (1859–1927). Swedish chemist. Arrhenius made important contributions in the study of chemical kinetics and electrolyte solutions. He also speculated that life had come to Earth from other planets, a theory now known as *panspermia.* Arrhenius was awarded the Nobel Prize in Chemistry in 1903.

- Acids react with carbonates and bicarbonates, such as Na_2CO_3, $CaCO_3$, and $NaHCO_3$, to produce carbon dioxide gas (Figure 4.6). For example,

$$2HCl(aq) + CaCO_3(s) \longrightarrow CaCl_2(aq) + H_2O(l) + CO_2(g)$$
$$HCl(aq) + NaHCO_3(s) \longrightarrow NaCl(aq) + H_2O(l) + CO_2(g)$$

- Aqueous acid solutions conduct electricity.

Bases

- Bases have a bitter taste.
- Bases feel slippery; for example, soaps, which contain bases, exhibit this property.
- Bases cause color changes in plant dyes; for example, they change the color of litmus from red to blue.
- Aqueous base solutions conduct electricity.

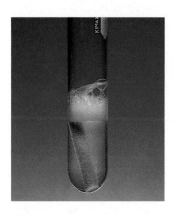

Figure 4.6 *A piece of blackboard chalk, which is mostly $CaCO_3$, reacts with hydrochloric acid.*

Brønsted Acids and Bases

Arrhenius's definitions of acids and bases are limited in that they apply only to aqueous solutions. Broader definitions were proposed by the Danish chemist Johannes Brønsted[†] in 1932; a **Brønsted acid** is *a proton donor*, and a **Brønsted base** is *a proton acceptor*. Note that Brønsted's definitions do not require acids and bases to be in aqueous solution.

Hydrochloric acid is a Brønsted acid because it donates a proton in water:

$$HCl(aq) \longrightarrow H^+(aq) + Cl^-(aq)$$

Note that the H^+ ion is a hydrogen atom that has lost its electron; that is, it is just a bare proton. The size of a proton is about 10^{-15} m, compared to a diameter of 10^{-10} m for an average atom or ion. Such an exceedingly small charged particle cannot exist as a separate entity in aqueous solution owing to its strong attraction for the negative pole (the O atom) in H_2O. Consequently, the proton exists in the hydrated form as shown in Figure 4.7. Therefore, the ionization of hydrochloric acid should be written as

$$HCl(aq) + H_2O(l) \longrightarrow H_3O^+(aq) + Cl^-(aq)$$

The *hydrated proton, H_3O^+*, is called the **hydronium ion.** This equation shows a reaction in which a Brønsted acid (HCl) donates a proton to a Brønsted base (H_2O).

Experiments show that the hydronium ion is further hydrated so that the proton may have several water molecules associated with it. Because the acidic properties of the proton are unaffected by the degree of hydration, in this text we will generally use $H^+(aq)$ to represent the hydrated proton. This notation is for convenience, but

Interactivity: Acid and Base Reactions Online Learning Center, Interactives

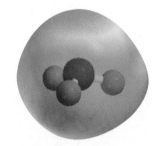

Electrostatic potential map of the H_3O^+ ion. In the rainbow color spectrum representation, the most electron-rich region is red and the most electron-poor region is blue.

[†]Johannes Nicolaus Brønsted (1879–1947). Danish chemist. In addition to his theory of acids and bases, Brønsted worked on thermodynamics and the separation of mercury into its isotopes.

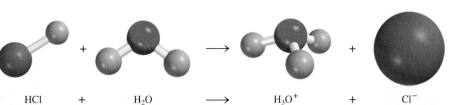

HCl + H_2O ⟶ H_3O^+ + Cl^-

Figure 4.7 *Ionization of HCl in water to form the hydronium ion and the chloride ion.*

H_3O^+ is closer to reality. Keep in mind that both notations represent the same species in aqueous solution.

Acids commonly used in the laboratory include hydrochloric acid (HCl), nitric acid (HNO_3), acetic acid (CH_3COOH), sulfuric acid (H_2SO_4), and phosphoric acid (H_3PO_4). The first three are **monoprotic acids;** that is, *each unit of the acid yields one hydrogen ion upon ionization:*

$$HCl(aq) \longrightarrow H^+(aq) + Cl^-(aq)$$
$$HNO_3(aq) \longrightarrow H^+(aq) + NO_3^-(aq)$$
$$CH_3COOH(aq) \rightleftharpoons CH_3COO^-(aq) + H^+(aq)$$

As mentioned earlier, because the ionization of acetic acid is incomplete (note the double arrows), it is a weak electrolyte. For this reason it is called a weak acid (see Table 4.1). On the other hand, HCl and HNO_3 are strong acids because they are strong electrolytes, so they are completely ionized in solution (note the use of single arrows).

Sulfuric acid (H_2SO_4) is a **diprotic acid** because *each unit of the acid gives up two H^+ ions,* in two separate steps:

$$H_2SO_4(aq) \longrightarrow H^+(aq) + HSO_4^-(aq)$$
$$HSO_4^-(aq) \rightleftharpoons H^+(aq) + SO_4^{2-}(aq)$$

H_2SO_4 is a strong electrolyte or strong acid (the first step of ionization is complete), but HSO_4^- is a weak acid or weak electrolyte, and we need a double arrow to represent its incomplete ionization.

Triprotic acids, which *yield three H^+ ions,* are relatively few in number. The best known triprotic acid is phosphoric acid, whose ionizations are

$$H_3PO_4(aq) \rightleftharpoons H^+(aq) + H_2PO_4^-(aq)$$
$$H_2PO_4^-(aq) \rightleftharpoons H^+(aq) + HPO_4^{2-}(aq)$$
$$HPO_4^{2-}(aq) \rightleftharpoons H^+(aq) + PO_4^{3-}(aq)$$

All three species (H_3PO_4, $H_2PO_4^-$, and HPO_4^{2-}) in this case are weak acids, and we use the double arrows to represent each ionization step. Anions such as $H_2PO_4^-$ and HPO_4^{2-} are found in aqueous solutions of phosphates such as NaH_2PO_4 and Na_2HPO_4.

Table 4.1 shows that sodium hydroxide (NaOH) and barium hydroxide [$Ba(OH)_2$] are strong electrolytes. This means that they are completely ionized in solution:

$$NaOH(s) \xrightarrow{H_2O} Na^+(aq) + OH^-(aq)$$
$$Ba(OH)_2(s) \xrightarrow{H_2O} Ba^{2+}(aq) + 2OH^-(aq)$$

The OH^- ion can accept a proton as follows:

$$H^+(aq) + OH^-(aq) \longrightarrow H_2O(l)$$

Thus OH^- is a Brønsted base.

Ammonia (NH_3) is classified as a Brønsted base because it can accept a H^+ ion (Figure 4.8):

$$NH_3(aq) + H_2O(l) \rightleftharpoons NH_4^+(aq) + OH^-(aq)$$

Ammonia is a weak electrolyte (and therefore a weak base) because only a small fraction of dissolved NH_3 molecules react with water to form NH_4^+ and OH^- ions.

The most commonly used strong base in the laboratory is sodium hydroxide. It is cheap and soluble. (In fact, all of the alkali metal hydroxides are soluble.) The most commonly used weak base is aqueous ammonia solution, which is sometimes

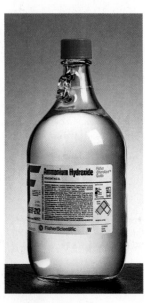

A bottle of aqueous ammonia.

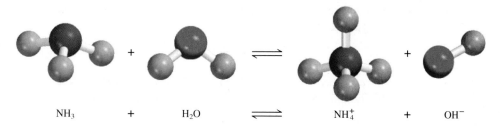

$$NH_3 \quad + \quad H_2O \quad \rightleftharpoons \quad NH_4^+ \quad + \quad OH^-$$

Figure 4.8 *Ionization of ammonia in water to form the ammonium ion and the hydroxide ion.*

erroneously called ammonium hydroxide; there is no evidence that the species NH_4OH actually exists. All of the Group 2A elements form hydroxides of the type $M(OH)_2$, where M denotes an alkaline earth metal. Of these hydroxides, only $Ba(OH)_2$ is soluble. Magnesium and calcium hydroxides are used in medicine and industry. Hydroxides of other metals, such as $Al(OH)_3$ and $Zn(OH)_2$ are insoluble and are not used as bases.

Example 4.3 classifies substances as Brønsted acids or Brønsted bases.

Example 4.3

Classify each of the following species in aqueous solution as a Brønsted acid or base: (a) HBr, (b) NO_2^-, (c) HCO_3^-.

Strategy What are the characteristics of a Brønsted acid? Does it contain at least an H atom? With the exception of ammonia, most Brønsted bases that you will encounter at this stage are anions.

Solution (a) We know that HCl is an acid. Because Br and Cl are both halogens (Group 7A), we expect HBr, like HCl, to ionize in water as follows:

$$HBr(aq) \longrightarrow H^+(aq) + Br^-(aq)$$

Therefore HBr is a Brønsted acid.

(b) In solution the nitrite ion can accept a proton from water to form nitrous acid:

$$NO_2^-(aq) + H^+(aq) \longrightarrow HNO_2(aq)$$

This property makes NO_2^- a Brønsted base.

(c) The bicarbonate ion is a Brønsted acid because it ionizes in solution as follows:

$$HCO_3^-(aq) \rightleftharpoons H^+(aq) + CO_3^{2-}(aq)$$

It is also a Brønsted base because it can accept a proton to form carbonic acid:

$$HCO_3^-(aq) + H^+(aq) \rightleftharpoons H_2CO_3(aq)$$

Comment The HCO_3^- species is said to be *amphoteric* because it possesses both acidic and basic properties. The double arrows show that this is a reversible reaction.

Similar problems: 4.31, 4.32.

Practice Exercise Classify each of the following species as a Brønsted acid or base: (a) SO_4^{2-}, (b) HI.

Acid-Base Neutralization

A *neutralization reaction* is *a reaction between an acid and a base.* Generally, aqueous acid-base reactions produce water and a *salt,* which is *an ionic compound made up of a cation other than H^+ and an anion other than OH^- or O^{2-}:*

Animation: Neutralization Reactions
Online Learning Center, Animations

$$acid + base \longrightarrow salt + water$$

All salts are strong electrolytes. The substance we know as table salt, NaCl, is a familiar example. It is a product of the acid-base reaction

$$HCl(aq) + NaOH(aq) \longrightarrow NaCl(aq) + H_2O(l)$$

Acid-base reactions generally go to completion.

However, because both the acid and the base are strong electrolytes, they are completely ionized in solution. The ionic equation is

$$H^+(aq) + Cl^-(aq) + Na^+(aq) + OH^-(aq) \longrightarrow Na^+(aq) + Cl^-(aq) + H_2O(l)$$

Therefore, the reaction can be represented by the net ionic equation

$$H^+(aq) + OH^-(aq) \longrightarrow H_2O(l)$$

Both Na^+ and Cl^- are spectator ions.

If we had started the preceding reaction with equal molar amounts of the acid and the base, at the end of the reaction we would have only a salt and no leftover acid or base. This is a characteristic of acid-base neutralization reactions.

The following are also examples of acid-base neutralization reactions, represented by molecular equations:

$$HF(aq) + KOH(aq) \longrightarrow KF(aq) + H_2O(l)$$
$$H_2SO_4(aq) + 2NaOH(aq) \longrightarrow Na_2SO_4(aq) + 2H_2O(l)$$
$$HNO_3(aq) + NH_3(aq) \longrightarrow NH_4NO_3(aq)$$

The last equation looks different because it does not show water as a product. However, if we express $NH_3(aq)$ as $NH_4^+(aq)$ and $OH^-(aq)$, as discussed earlier, then the equation becomes

$$HNO_3(aq) + NH_4^+(aq) + OH^-(aq) \longrightarrow NH_4NO_3(aq) + H_2O(l)$$

4.4 Oxidation-Reduction Reactions

Whereas acid-base reactions can be characterized as proton-transfer processes, the class of reactions called *oxidation-reduction,* or *redox, reactions* are considered *electron-transfer reactions.* Oxidation-reduction reactions are very much a part of the world around us. They range from the burning of fossil fuels to the action of household bleach. Additionally, most metallic and nonmetallic elements are obtained from their ores by the process of oxidation or reduction.

Many important redox reactions take place in water, but not all redox reactions occur in aqueous solution. Consider the formation of calcium oxide (CaO) from calcium and oxygen:

$$2Ca(s) + O_2(g) \longrightarrow 2CaO(s)$$

Calcium oxide (CaO) is an ionic compound made up of Ca^{2+} and O^{2-} ions. In this reaction, two Ca atoms give up or transfer four electrons to two O atoms (in O_2). For convenience, we can think of this process as two separate steps, one involving the loss of four electrons by the two Ca atoms and the other being the gain of four electrons by an O_2 molecule:

$$2Ca \longrightarrow 2Ca^{2+} + 4e^-$$
$$O_2 + 4e^- \longrightarrow 2O^{2-}$$

Each of these steps is called a **half-reaction,** which *explicitly shows the electrons involved in a redox reaction.* The sum of the half-reactions gives the overall reaction:

$$2Ca + O_2 + 4e^- \longrightarrow 2Ca^{2+} + 2O^{2-} + 4e^-$$

or, if we cancel the electrons that appear on both sides of the equation,

$$2Ca + O_2 \longrightarrow 2Ca^{2+} + 2O^{2-}$$

Finally, the Ca^{2+} and O^{2-} ions combine to form CaO:

$$2Ca^{2+} + 2O^{2-} \longrightarrow 2CaO$$

By convention, we do not show the charges in the formula of an ionic compound, so that calcium oxide is normally represented as CaO rather than $Ca^{2+}O^{2-}$.

The term **oxidation reaction** refers to the *half-reaction that involves loss of electrons.* Chemists originally used "oxidation" to denote the combination of elements with oxygen. However, it now has a broader meaning that includes reactions not involving oxygen. A **reduction reaction** is a *half-reaction that involves gain of electrons.* In the formation of calcium oxide, calcium is oxidized. It is said to act as a **reducing agent** because it *donates electrons* to oxygen and causes oxygen to be reduced. Oxygen is reduced and acts as an **oxidizing agent** because it *accepts electrons* from calcium, causing calcium to be oxidized. Note that the extent of oxidation in a redox reaction must be equal to the extent of reduction; that is, the number of electrons lost by a reducing agent must be equal to the number of electrons gained by an oxidizing agent.

The occurrence of electron transfer is more apparent in some redox reactions than others. When metallic zinc is added to a solution containing copper(II) sulfate ($CuSO_4$), zinc reduces Cu^{2+} by donating two electrons to it:

$$Zn(s) + CuSO_4(aq) \longrightarrow ZnSO_4(aq) + Cu(s)$$

In the process the solution loses the blue color that characterizes the presence of hydrated Cu^{2+} ions (Figure 4.9):

$$Zn(s) + Cu^{2+}(aq) \longrightarrow Zn^{2+}(aq) + Cu(s)$$

The oxidation and reduction half-reactions are

$$Zn \longrightarrow Zn^{2+} + 2e^-$$
$$Cu^{2+} + 2e^- \longrightarrow Cu$$

Similarly, metallic copper reduces silver ions in a solution of silver nitrate ($AgNO_3$):

$$Cu(s) + 2AgNO_3(aq) \longrightarrow Cu(NO_3)_2(aq) + 2Ag(s)$$

or

$$Cu(s) + 2Ag^+(aq) \longrightarrow Cu^{2+}(aq) + 2Ag(s)$$

A useful mnemonic for redox is OILRIG: Oxidation Is Loss (of electrons) and Reduction Is Gain (of electrons).

Oxidizing agents are always reduced, and reducing agents are always oxidized. This statement may be somewhat confusing, but it is simply a consequence of the definitions of the two processes.

Animation: Oxidation-Reduction Reactions
Online Learning Center, Animations

Oxidation Number

The definitions of oxidation and reduction in terms of loss and gain of electrons apply to the formation of ionic compounds such as CaO and the reduction of Cu^{2+} ions by Zn. However, these definitions do not accurately characterize the formation of hydrogen chloride (HCl) and sulfur dioxide (SO_2):

The Zn bar is in aqueous solution of CuSO$_4$

Cu^{2+} ions are converted to Cu atoms. Zn atoms enter the solution as Zn^{2+} ions.

When a piece of copper wire is placed in an aqueous AgNO$_3$ solution Cu atoms enter the solution as Cu^{2+} ions, and Ag$^+$ ions are converted to solid Ag.

Figure 4.9 *Metal displacement reactions in solution.*

$$H_2(g) + Cl_2(g) \longrightarrow 2HCl(g)$$
$$S(s) + O_2(g) \longrightarrow SO_2(g)$$

Because HCl and SO$_2$ are not ionic but molecular compounds, no electrons are actually transferred in the formation of these compounds, as they are in the case of CaO. Nevertheless, chemists find it convenient to treat these reactions as redox reactions because experimental measurements show that there is a partial transfer of electrons (from H to Cl in HCl and from S to O in SO$_2$).

To keep track of electrons in redox reactions, it is useful to assign oxidation numbers to the reactants and products. An atom's **oxidation number,** also called **oxidation state,** signifies the *number of charges the atom would have in a molecule (or an ionic compound) if electrons were transferred completely.* For example, we can rewrite the above equations for the formation of HCl and SO$_2$ as follows:

$$\overset{0}{H_2(g)} + \overset{0}{Cl_2(g)} \longrightarrow \overset{+1 \ -1}{2HCl(g)}$$
$$\overset{0}{S(s)} + \overset{0}{O_2(g)} \longrightarrow \overset{+4 \ -2}{SO_2(g)}$$

The numbers above the element symbols are the oxidation numbers. In both of the reactions shown, there is no charge on the atoms in the reactant molecules. Thus their oxidation number is zero. For the product molecules, however, it is assumed that complete electron transfer has taken place and that atoms have gained or lost electrons. The oxidation numbers reflect the number of electrons "transferred."

Oxidation numbers enable us to identify elements that are oxidized and reduced at a glance. The elements that show an increase in oxidation number—hydrogen and sulfur in the preceding examples—are oxidized. Chlorine and oxygen are reduced, so their oxidation numbers show a decrease from their initial values. Note that the sum of the oxidation numbers of H and Cl in HCl ($+1$ and -1) is zero. Likewise, if we add the charges on S ($+4$) and two atoms of O [$2 \times (-2)$], the total is zero. The reason is that the HCl and SO_2 molecules are neutral, so the charges must cancel.

We use the following rules to assign oxidation numbers:

1. In free elements (that is, in the uncombined state), each atom has an oxidation number of zero. Thus each atom in H_2, Br_2, Na, Be, K, O_2, and P_4 has the same oxidation number: zero.

2. For ions composed of only one atom (that is, monatomic ions) the oxidation number is equal to the charge on the ion. Thus Li^+ ion has an oxidation number of $+1$; Ba^{2+} ion, $+2$; Fe^{3+} ion, $+3$; I^- ion, -1; O^{2-} ion, -2; and so on. All alkali metals have an oxidation number of $+1$ and all alkaline earth metals have an oxidation number of $+2$ in their compounds. Aluminum has an oxidation number of $+3$ in all its compounds.

3. The oxidation number of oxygen in most compounds (for example, MgO and H_2O) is -2, but in hydrogen peroxide (H_2O_2) and peroxide ion (O_2^{2-}), it is -1.

4. The oxidation number of hydrogen is $+1$, except when it is bonded to metals in binary compounds. In these cases (for example, LiH, NaH, CaH_2), its oxidation number is -1.

5. Fluorine has an oxidation number of -1 in *all* its compounds. Other halogens (Cl, Br, and I) have negative oxidation numbers when they occur as halide ions in their compounds. When combined with oxygen—for example in oxoacids and oxoanions (see Section 2.7)—they have positive oxidation numbers.

6. In a neutral molecule, the sum of the oxidation numbers of all the atoms must be zero. In a polyatomic ion, the sum of oxidation numbers of all the elements in the ion must be equal to the net charge of the ion. For example, in the ammonium ion, NH_4^+, the oxidation number of N is -3 and that of H is $+1$. Thus the sum of the oxidation numbers is $-3 + 4(+1) = +1$, which is equal to the net charge of the ion.

7. Oxidation numbers do not have to be integers. For example, the oxidation number of O in the superoxide ion, O_2^-, is $-\frac{1}{2}$.

We apply the preceding rules to assign oxidation numbers in Example 4.4

Example 4.4

Assign oxidation numbers to all the elements in the following compounds and ion: (a) Li_2O, (b) HNO_3, (c) $Cr_2O_7^{2-}$.

Strategy In general we follow the rules just listed for assigning oxidation numbers. Remember that all alkali metals have an oxidation number of $+1$, and in most cases hydrogen has an oxidation number of $+1$ and oxygen has an oxidation number of -2 in their compounds.

(Continued)

Solution (a) By rule 2 we see that lithium has an oxidation number of +1 (Li^+) and oxygen's oxidation number is -2 (O^{2-}).

(b) This is the formula for nitric acid, which yields a H^+ ion and a NO_3^- ion in solution. From rule 4 we see that H has an oxidation number of +1. Thus the other group (the nitrate ion) must have a net oxidation number of -1. Oxygen has an oxidation number of -2, and if we use x to represent the oxidation number of nitrogen, then the nitrate ion can be written as

$$[N^{(x)}O_3^{(2-)}]^-$$

so that $$x + 3(-2) = -1$$

or $$x = +5$$

(c) From rule 6 we see that the sum of the oxidation numbers in the dichromate ion $Cr_2O_7^{2-}$ must be -2. We know that the oxidation number of O is -2, so all that remains is to determine the oxidation number of Cr, which we call y. The dichromate ion can be written as

$$[Cr_2^{(y)}O_7^{(2-)}]^{2-}$$

so that $$2(y) + 7(-2) = -2$$

or $$y = +6$$

Check In each case, does the sum of the oxidation numbers of all the atoms equal the net charge on the species?

Similar problems: 4.47, 4.49.

Practice Exercise Assign oxidation numbers to all the elements in the following compound and ion: (a) PF_3, (b) MnO_4^-.

Figure 4.10 shows the known oxidation numbers of the familiar elements, arranged according to their positions in the periodic table. We can summarize the content of this figure as follows:

- Metallic elements have only positive oxidation numbers, whereas nonmetallic elements may have either positive or negative oxidation numbers.

- The highest oxidation number an element in Groups 1A–7A can have is its group number. For example, the halogens are in Group 7A, so their highest possible oxidation number is +7.

- The transition metals (Groups 1B, 3B–8B) usually have several possible oxidation numbers.

Types of Redox Reactions

There are four general types of redox reactions: combination reactions, decomposition reactions, displacement reactions, and disproportionation reactions. Displacement reactions have widespread applications in industry, so we will study them in some detail.

Combination Reactions   A combination reaction can be represented by

$$A + B \longrightarrow C$$

If either A or B is an element, then the reaction is usually redox in nature. **_Combination reactions_** are reactions in which _two or more substances combine to form a single product._ Figure 4.11 on p. 132 shows some common combination reactions. For example,

$$\overset{0}{S}(s) + \overset{0}{O_2}(g) \longrightarrow \overset{+4\ -2}{SO_2}(g)$$

$$3\overset{0}{Mg}(s) + \overset{0}{N_2}(g) \longrightarrow \overset{+2\ \ -3}{Mg_3N_2}(s)$$

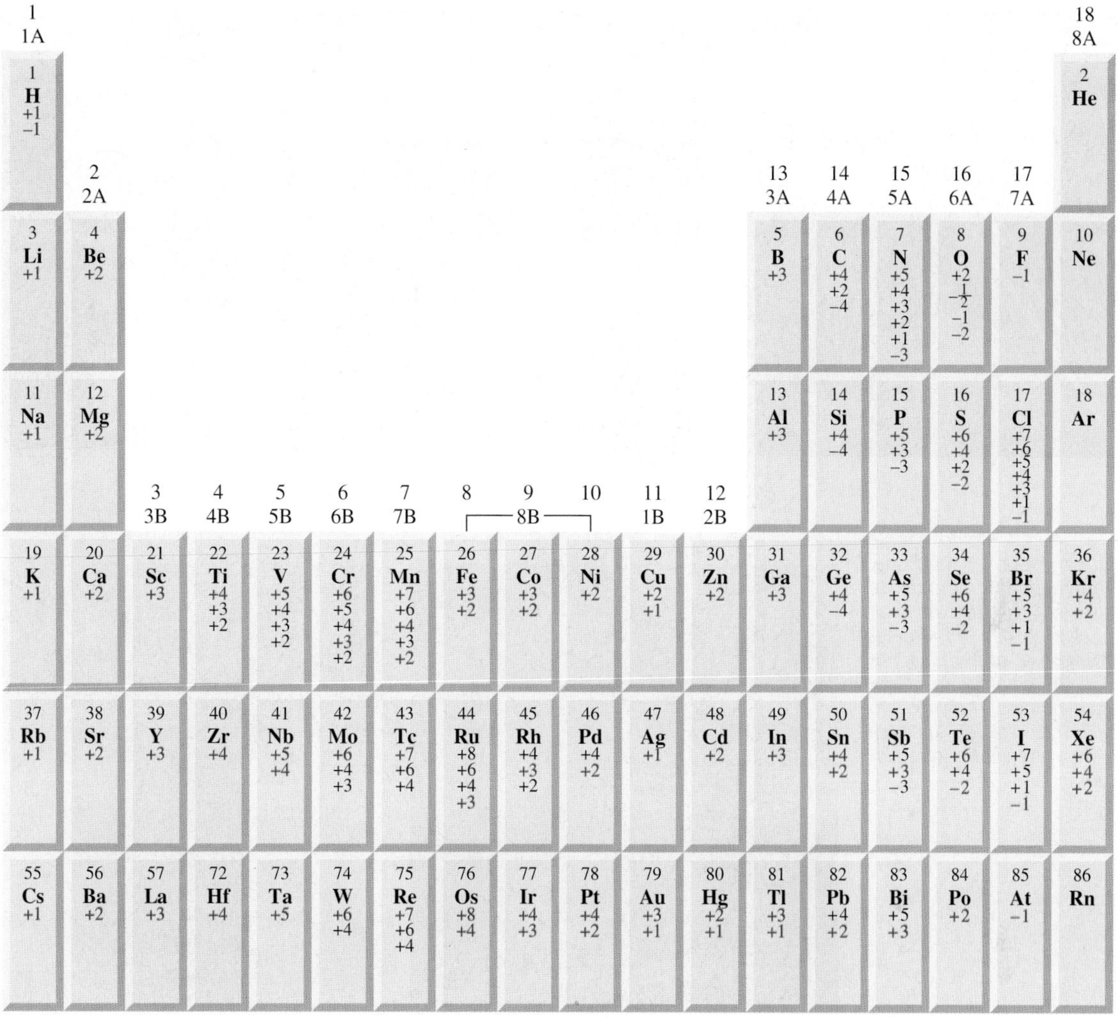

1 1A	2 2A	3 3B	4 4B	5 5B	6 6B	7 7B	8	9 8B	10	11 1B	12 2B	13 3A	14 4A	15 5A	16 6A	17 7A	18 8A
1 H +1 −1																	2 He
3 Li +1	4 Be +2											5 B +3	6 C +4 +2 −4	7 N +5 +4 +3 +2 +1 −3	8 O +2 −1 −2	9 F −1	10 Ne
11 Na +1	12 Mg +2											13 Al +3	14 Si +4 −4	15 P +5 +3 −3	16 S +6 +4 +2 −2	17 Cl +7 +6 +5 +4 +3 +1 −1	18 Ar
19 K +1	20 Ca +2	21 Sc +3	22 Ti +4 +3 +2	23 V +5 +4 +3 +2	24 Cr +6 +5 +4 +3 +2	25 Mn +7 +6 +4 +3 +2	26 Fe +3 +2	27 Co +3 +2	28 Ni +2	29 Cu +2 +1	30 Zn +2	31 Ga +3	32 Ge +4 −4	33 As +5 +3 −3	34 Se +6 +4 −2	35 Br +5 +3 +1 −1	36 Kr +4 +2
37 Rb +1	38 Sr +2	39 Y +3	40 Zr +4	41 Nb +5 +4	42 Mo +6 +4 +3	43 Tc +7 +6 +4	44 Ru +8 +6 +4 +3	45 Rh +4 +3 +2	46 Pd +4 +2	47 Ag +1	48 Cd +2	49 In +3	50 Sn +4 +2	51 Sb +5 +3 −3	52 Te +6 +4 −2	53 I +7 +5 +1 −1	54 Xe +6 +4 +2
55 Cs +1	56 Ba +2	57 La +3	72 Hf +4	73 Ta +5	74 W +6 +4	75 Re +7 +6 +4	76 Os +8 +4	77 Ir +4 +3	78 Pt +4 +2	79 Au +3 +1	80 Hg +2 +1	81 Tl +3 +1	82 Pb +4 +2	83 Bi +5 +3	84 Po +2	85 At −1	86 Rn

Figure 4.10 *The oxidation numbers of elements in their compounds. The more common oxidation numbers are in color.*

Decomposition Reactions Decomposition reactions are the opposite of combination reactions. Specifically, a ***decomposition reaction*** is *the breakdown of a compound into two or more components:*

$$C \longrightarrow A + B$$

If either A or B is an element, then the reaction is redox in nature (Figure 4.12). For example,

$$\overset{+2\ -2}{2HgO(s)} \longrightarrow \overset{0}{2Hg(l)} + \overset{0}{O_2(g)}$$

$$\overset{+5\ -2}{2KClO_3(s)} \longrightarrow \overset{-1}{2KCl(s)} + \overset{0}{3O_2(g)}$$

$$\overset{+1\ -1}{2NaH(s)} \longrightarrow \overset{0}{2Na(s)} + \overset{0}{H_2(g)}$$

Note that we show oxidation numbers only for elements that are oxidized or reduced. Thus potassium is not given an oxidation number in the decomposition of $KClO_3$.

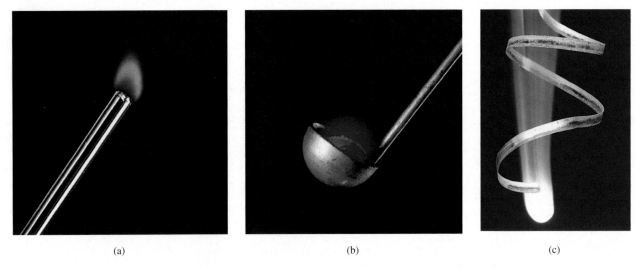

(a)   (b)   (c)

Figure 4.11 *Some simple combination redox reactions. (a) Hydrogen gas burning in air to form water. (b) Sulfur burning in air to form sulfur dioxide. (c) Magnesium burning in air to form magnesium oxide and magnesium nitride. (d) Sodium burning in chlorine to form sodium chloride. (e) Aluminum reacting with bromine to form aluminum bromide.*

(d)   (e)

Displacement Reactions In a ***displacement reaction,*** *an ion (or atom) in a compound is replaced by an ion (or atom) of another element:*

$$A + BC \longrightarrow AC + B$$

Most displacement reactions fit into one of three subcategories: hydrogen displacement, metal displacement, or halogen displacement.

1. Hydrogen Displacement.   All alkali metals and some alkaline earth metals (Ca, Sr, and Ba), which are the most reactive of the metallic elements, will displace hydrogen from cold water (Figure 4.13):

$$\overset{0}{2Na}(s) + \overset{+1}{2H_2O}(l) \longrightarrow \overset{+1\ +1}{2NaOH}(aq) + \overset{0}{H_2}(g)$$

$$\overset{0}{Ca}(s) + \overset{+1}{2H_2O}(l) \longrightarrow \overset{+2\ +1}{Ca(OH)_2}(s) + \overset{0}{H_2}(g)$$

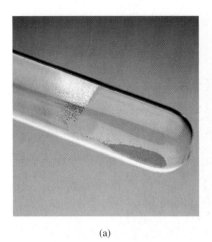
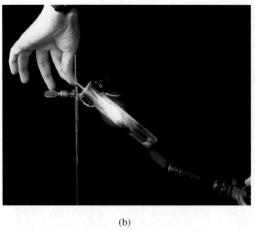

(a)   (b)

Less reactive metals, such as aluminum and iron, react with steam to give hydrogen gas:

$$\overset{0}{2Al}(s) + \overset{+1}{3H_2O}(g) \longrightarrow \overset{+3}{Al_2O_3}(s) + \overset{0}{3H_2}(g)$$

$$\overset{0}{2Fe}(s) + \overset{+1}{3H_2O}(g) \longrightarrow \overset{+3}{Fe_2O_3}(s) + \overset{0}{3H_2}(g)$$

Many metals, including those that do not react with water, are capable of displacing hydrogen from acids. For example, zinc (Zn) and magnesium (Mg) do not react with cold water but do react with hydrochloric acid, as follows:

$$\overset{0}{Zn}(s) + \overset{+1}{2HCl}(aq) \longrightarrow \overset{+2}{ZnCl_2}(aq) + \overset{0}{H_2}(g)$$

$$\overset{0}{Mg}(s) + \overset{+1}{2HCl}(aq) \longrightarrow \overset{+2}{MgCl_2}(aq) + \overset{0}{H_2}(g)$$

(a)

The ionic equations are

$$\overset{0}{Zn}(s) + \overset{+1}{2H^+}(aq) \longrightarrow \overset{+2}{Zn^{2+}}(aq) + \overset{0}{H_2}(g)$$

$$\overset{0}{Mg}(s) + \overset{+1}{2H^+}(aq) \longrightarrow \overset{+2}{Mg^{2+}}(aq) + \overset{0}{H_2}(g)$$

Figure 4.14 shows the reactions between hydrochloric acid (HCl) and iron (Fe), zinc (Zn), and magnesium (Mg). These reactions are used to prepare hydrogen gas in the laboratory. Some metals, such as copper (Cu), silver (Ag), and gold (Au), do not displace hydrogen when placed in hydrochloric acid.

2. Metal Displacement. A metal in a compound can be displaced by another metal in the elemental state. We have already seen examples of zinc replacing copper ions and copper replacing silver ions (see p. 128). Reversing the roles of the metals would result in no reaction. Thus copper metal will not displace zinc ions from zinc sulfate, and silver metal will not displace copper ions from copper nitrate.

An easy way to predict whether a metal or hydrogen displacement reaction will actually occur is to refer to an *activity series* (sometimes called the *electrochemical*

(b)

Figure 4.13 Reactions of (a) sodium (Na) and (b) calcium (Ca) with cold water. Note that the reaction is more vigorous with Na than with Ca.

(a)   (b)   (c)

Figure 4.14 *Reactions of (a) iron (Fe), (b) zinc (Zn), and (c) magnesium (Mg) with hydrochloric acid to form hydrogen gas and the metal chlorides (FeCl$_2$, ZnCl$_2$, MgCl$_2$). The reactivity of these metals is reflected in the rate of hydrogen gas evolution, which is slowest for the least reactive metal, Fe, and fastest for the most reactive metal, Mg.*

series), shown in Figure 4.15. Basically, an activity series is *a convenient summary of the results of many possible displacement reactions* similar to the ones already discussed. According to this series, any metal above hydrogen will displace it from water or from an acid, but metals below hydrogen will not react with either water or an acid. In fact, any metal listed in the series will react with any metal (in a compound) below it. For example, Zn is above Cu, so zinc metal will displace copper ions from copper sulfate.

Figure 4.15 *The activity series for metals. The metals are arranged according to their ability to displace hydrogen from water or acids. Li (lithium) is the most reactive metal, and Au (gold) is the least reactive.*

Reducing strength increases →

$$Li \rightarrow Li^+ + e^-$$
$$K \rightarrow K^+ + e^-$$
$$Ba \rightarrow Ba^{2+} + 2e^-$$
$$Ca \rightarrow Ca^{2+} + 2e^-$$
$$Na \rightarrow Na^+ + e^-$$

React with cold water to produce H$_2$

$$Mg \rightarrow Mg^{2+} + 2e^-$$
$$Al \rightarrow Al^{3+} + 3e^-$$
$$Zn \rightarrow Zn^{2+} + 2e^-$$
$$Cr \rightarrow Cr^{3+} + 3e^-$$
$$Fe \rightarrow Fe^{2+} + 2e^-$$
$$Cd \rightarrow Cd^{2+} + 2e^-$$

React with steam to produce H$_2$

$$Co \rightarrow Co^{2+} + 2e^-$$
$$Ni \rightarrow Ni^{2+} + 2e^-$$
$$Sn \rightarrow Sn^{2+} + 2e^-$$
$$Pb \rightarrow Pb^{2+} + 2e^-$$
$$H_2 \rightarrow 2H^+ + 2e^-$$
$$Cu \rightarrow Cu^{2+} + 2e^-$$

React with acids to produce H$_2$

$$Ag \rightarrow Ag^+ + e^-$$
$$Hg \rightarrow Hg^{2+} + 2e^-$$
$$Pt \rightarrow Pt^{2+} + 2e^-$$
$$Au \rightarrow Au^{3+} + 3e^-$$

Do not react with water or acids to produce H$_2$

Metal displacement reactions find many applications in metallurgical processes, the goal of which is to separate pure metals from their ores. For example, vanadium is obtained by treating vanadium(V) oxide with metallic calcium:

$$V_2O_5(s) + 5Ca(l) \longrightarrow 2V(l) + 5CaO(s)$$

Similarly, titanium is obtained from titanium(IV) chloride according to the reaction

$$TiCl_4(g) + 2Mg(l) \longrightarrow Ti(s) + 2MgCl_2(l)$$

In each case the metal that acts as the reducing agent lies above the metal that is reduced (that is, Ca is above V and Mg is above Ti) in the activity series. We will see more examples of this type of reaction in Chapter 20.

3. Halogen Displacement. Another activity series summarizes the halogens' behavior in halogen displacement reactions:

$$F_2 > Cl_2 > Br_2 > I_2$$

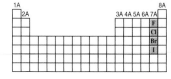

The halogens.

The power of these elements as oxidizing agents decreases as we move down Group 7A from fluorine to iodine, so molecular fluorine can replace chloride, bromide, and iodide ions in solution. In fact, molecular fluorine is so reactive that it also attacks water; thus these reactions cannot be carried out in aqueous solutions. On the other hand, molecular chlorine can displace bromide and iodide ions in aqueous solution as Figure 4.16 shows. The displacement equations are

$$\overset{0}{Cl_2}(g) + 2K\overset{-1}{Br}(aq) \longrightarrow 2K\overset{-1}{Cl}(aq) + \overset{0}{Br_2}(l)$$

$$\overset{0}{Cl_2}(g) + 2Na\overset{-1}{I}(aq) \longrightarrow 2Na\overset{-1}{Cl}(aq) + \overset{0}{I_2}(s)$$

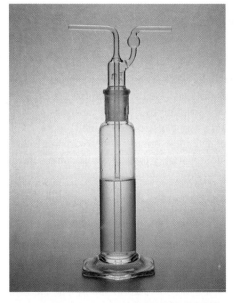

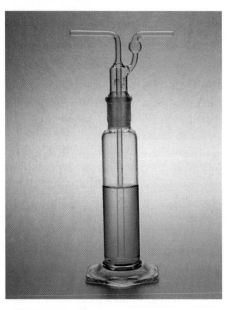

(a)   (b)

Figure 4.16 *(a) An aqueous KBr solution. (b) After chlorine gas has been bubbled through the solution, the bromide ions are all converted (oxidized) to liquid bromine, which is slightly soluble in water.*

The ionic equations are

$$\overset{0}{Cl_2}(g) + 2\overset{-1}{Br}(aq) \longrightarrow 2\overset{-1}{Cl^-}(aq) + \overset{0}{Br_2}(l)$$

$$\overset{0}{Cl_2}(g) + 2\overset{-1}{I^-}(aq) \longrightarrow 2\overset{-1}{Cl^-}(aq) + \overset{0}{I_2}(s)$$

Molecular bromine, in turn, can displace iodide ion in solution:

$$\overset{0}{Br_2}(l) + 2\overset{-1}{I^-}(aq) \longrightarrow 2\overset{-1}{Br^-}(aq) + \overset{0}{I_2}(s)$$

Reversing the roles of the halogens produces no reaction. Thus bromine cannot displace chloride ions, and iodine cannot displace bromide and chloride ions.

The halogen displacement reactions have a direct industrial application. The halogens as a group are the most reactive of the nonmetallic elements. They are all strong oxidizing agents. As a result, they are found in nature in the combined state (with metals) as halides and never as free elements. Of these four elements, chlorine is by far the most important industrial chemical. In 2002 the amount of chlorine produced in the United States was about 25 billion pounds, making chlorine the tenth-ranking industrial chemical. The annual production of bromine is only one-hundredth that of chlorine, while the amounts of fluorine and iodine produced are even less.

Recovering the halogens from their halides requires an oxidation process, which is represented by

$$2X^- \longrightarrow X_2 + 2e^-$$

where X denotes a halogen element. Seawater and natural brine (for example, underground water in contact with salt deposits) are rich sources of Cl^-, Br^-, and I^- ions. Minerals such as fluorite (CaF_2) and cryolite (Na_3AlF_6) are used to prepare fluorine. Because fluorine is the strongest oxidizing agent known, there is no way to convert F^- ions to F_2 by chemical means. The only way to carry out the oxidation is by electrolytic means, the details of which will be discussed in Chapter 19. Industrially, chlorine, like fluorine, is produced electrolytically.

Bromine is a fuming red liquid.

Bromine is prepared industrially by oxidizing Br^- ions with chlorine, which is a strong enough oxidizing agent to oxidize Br^- ions but not water:

$$2Br^-(aq) \longrightarrow Br_2(l) + 2e^-$$

One of the richest sources of Br^- ions is the Dead Sea—about 4000 parts per million (ppm) by mass of all dissolved substances in the Dead Sea is Br. Following the oxidation of Br^- ions, bromine is removed from the solution by blowing air over the solution, and the air-bromine mixture is then cooled to condense the bromine (Figure 4.17).

Iodine is also prepared from seawater and natural brine by the oxidation of I^- ions with chlorine. Because Br^- and I^- ions are invariably present in the same source, they are both oxidized by chlorine. However, it is relatively easy to separate Br_2 from I_2 because iodine is a solid that is sparingly soluble in water. The air-blowing procedure will remove most of the bromine formed but will not affect the iodine present.

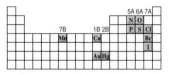

Elements that are most likely to undergo disproportionation.

Disproportionation Reaction A special type of redox reaction is the disproportionation reaction. In a ***disproportionation reaction,*** *an element in one oxidation state is simultaneously oxidized and reduced.* One reactant in a disproportionation reaction *always* contains an element that can have at least three oxidation states. The element itself is in an intermediate oxidation state; that is, both higher and lower oxidation

Figure 4.17 *The industrial manufacture of liquid bromine by oxidizing an aqueous solution containing Br^- ions with chlorine gas.*

states exist for that element in the products. The decomposition of hydrogen peroxide is an example of a disproportionation reaction:

$$\overset{-1}{2H_2O_2}(aq) \longrightarrow \overset{-2}{2H_2O}(l) + \overset{0}{O_2}(g)$$

Here the oxidation number of oxygen in the reactant (-1) both increases to zero in O_2 and decreases to -2 in H_2O. Another example is the reaction between molecular chlorine and NaOH solution:

$$\overset{0}{Cl_2}(g) + 2OH^-(aq) \longrightarrow \overset{+1}{ClO^-}(aq) + \overset{-1}{Cl^-}(aq) + H_2O(l)$$

This reaction describes the formation of household bleaching agents, for it is the hypochlorite ion (ClO^-) that oxidizes the color-bearing substances in stains, converting them to colorless compounds.

Finally, it is interesting to compare redox reactions and acid-base reactions. They are analogous in that acid-base reactions involve the transfer of protons while redox reactions involve the transfer of electrons. However, while acid-base reactions are quite easy to recognize (because they always involve an acid and a base), there is no simple procedure for identifying a redox process. The only sure way is to compare the oxidation numbers of all the elements in the reactants and products. Any change in oxidation number *guarantees* that the reaction is redox in nature.

The classification of different types of redox reactions is illustrated in Example 4.5.

Example 4.5

Classify the following redox reactions and indicate changes in the oxidation numbers of the elements:

(a) $2N_2O(g) \longrightarrow 2N_2(g) + O_2(g)$
(b) $6Li(s) + N_2(g) \longrightarrow 2Li_3N(s)$

(Continued)

CHEMISTRY IN ACTION

Breath Analyzer

Every year in the United States about 25,000 people are killed and 500,000 more are injured as a result of drunk driving. In spite of efforts to educate the public about the dangers of driving while intoxicated and stiffer penalties for drunk driving offenses, law enforcement agencies still have to devote a great deal of work to removing drunk drivers from America's roads.

The police often use a device called a breath analyzer to test drivers suspected of being drunk. The chemical basis of this device is a redox reaction. A sample of the driver's breath is drawn into the breath analyzer, where it is treated with an acidic solution of potassium dichromate. The alcohol (ethanol) in the breath is converted to acetic acid as shown in the following equation:

$$3CH_3CH_2OH \ + \ 2K_2Cr_2O_7 \ + \ 8H_2SO_4 \longrightarrow$$

ethanol   potassium dichromate (orange yellow)   sulfuric acid

$$3CH_3COOH \ + \ 2Cr_2(SO_4)_3 \ + \ 2K_2SO_4 \ + \ 11H_2O$$

acetic acid   chromium(III) sulfate (green)   potassium sulfate

In this reaction the ethanol is oxidized to acetic acid and the chromium(VI) in the orange-yellow dichromate ion is reduced to the green chromium(III) ion (see Figure 4.22). The driver's blood alcohol level can be determined readily by measuring the degree of this color change (read from a calibrated meter on the instrument). The current legal limit of blood alcohol content in most states is 0.1 percent by mass. Anything higher constitutes intoxication.

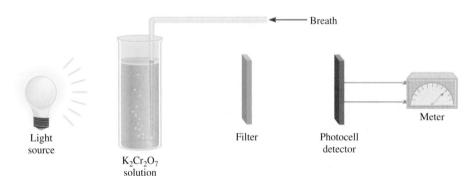

Breath

Light source

$K_2Cr_2O_7$ solution

Filter

Photocell detector

Meter

Schematic diagram of a breath analyzer. The alcohol in the driver's breath is reacted with a potassium dichromate solution. The change in the absorption of light due to the formation of chromium(III) sulfate is registered by the detector and shown on a meter, which directly displays the alcohol content in blood. The filter selects only one wavelength of light for measurement.

(c) $Ni(s) + Pb(NO_3)_2(aq) \longrightarrow Pb(s) + Ni(NO_3)_2(aq)$
(d) $2NO_2(g) + H_2O(l) \longrightarrow HNO_2(aq) + HNO_3(aq)$

Strategy Review the definitions of combination reactions, decomposition reactions, displacement reactions, and disproportionation reactions.

Solution (a) This is a decomposition reaction because one reactant is converted to two different products. The oxidation number of N changes from $+1$ to 0, while that of O changes from -2 to 0.

(b) This is a combination reaction (two reactants form a single product). The oxidation number of Li changes from 0 to $+1$ while that of N changes from 0 to -3.

(c) This is a metal displacement reaction. The Ni metal replaces (reduces) the Pb^{2+} ion. The oxidation number of Ni increases from 0 to $+2$ while that of Pb decreases from $+2$ to 0.

(d) The oxidation number of N is $+4$ in NO_2 and it is $+3$ in HNO_2 and $+5$ in HNO_3. Because the oxidation number of the *same* element both increases and decreases, this is a disproportionation reaction.

Similar problems: 4.55, 4.56.

(Continued)

Practice Exercise Identify the following redox reactions by type:

(a) $Fe + H_2SO_4 \longrightarrow FeSO_4 + H_2$
(b) $S + 3F_2 \longrightarrow SF_6$
(c) $2CuCl \longrightarrow Cu + CuCl_2$
(d) $2Ag + PtCl_2 \longrightarrow 2AgCl + Pt$

The Chemistry in Action on p. 138 describes how law enforcement makes use of a redox reaction to apprehend drunk drivers.

4.5 Concentration of Solutions

To study solution stoichiometry we must know how much of the reactants are present in a solution and also how to control the amounts of reactants used to bring about a reaction in aqueous solution.

The ***concentration of a solution*** is *the amount of solute present in a given quantity of solvent or solution.* (For this discussion we will assume the solute is a liquid or a solid and the solvent is a liquid.) The concentration of a solution can be expressed in many different ways, as we will see in Chapter 12. Here we will consider one of the most commonly used units in chemistry, ***molarity (M),*** or ***molar concentration,*** which is *the number of moles of solute in 1 liter (L) of solution.* Molarity is defined by the equation

$$M = \text{molarity} = \frac{\text{moles of solute}}{\text{liters of soln}} \tag{4.1}$$

where "soln" denotes "solution." Thus, a 1.46 molar glucose ($C_6H_{12}O_6$) solution, written 1.46 M $C_6H_{12}O_6$, contains 1.46 moles of the solute ($C_6H_{12}O_6$) in 1 L of the solution; a 0.52 molar urea [$(NH_2)_2CO$] solution, written 0.52 M $(NH_2)_2CO$, contains 0.52 mole of $(NH_2)_2CO$ (the solute) in 1 L of solution; and so on.

Of course, we do not always work with solution volumes of exactly 1 L. This is not a problem as long as we remember to convert the volume of the solution to liters. Thus, a 500-mL solution containing 0.730 mole of $C_6H_{12}O_6$ also has a concentration of 1.46 M:

$$M = \text{molarity} = \frac{0.730 \text{ mol}}{0.500 \text{ L}}$$
$$= 1.46 \text{ mol/L} = 1.46 \text{ } M$$

As you can see, the unit of molarity is moles per liter, so a 500-mL solution containing 0.730 mole of $C_6H_{12}O_6$ is equivalent to 1.46 mol/L or 1.46 M. Note that concentration, like density, is an intensive property, so its value does not depend on how much of the solution is present.

It is important to keep in mind that molarity refers only to the amount of solute originally dissolved in water and does not take into account any subsequent processes, such as the dissociation of a salt or the ionization of an acid. Both glucose and urea are nonelectrolytes, so a 1.00 M urea solution has 1.00 mole of the urea molecules in 1 L of solution. But consider what happens when a sample of

Number of moles is given by volume (L) × molarity.

Figure 4.18 *Preparing a solution of known molarity. (a) A known amount of a solid solute is transferred into the volumetric flask; then water is added through a funnel. (b) The solid is slowly dissolved by gently swirling the flask. (c) After the solid has completely dissolved, more water is added to bring the level of solution to the mark. Knowing the volume of the solution and the amount of solute dissolved in it, we can calculate the molarity of the prepared solution.*

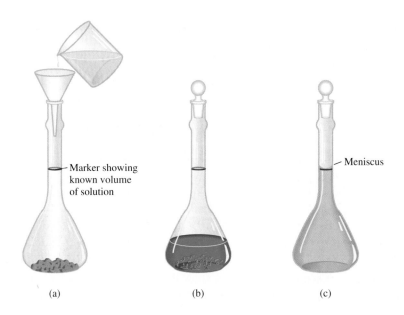

Marker showing known volume of solution

Meniscus

(a)   (b)   (c)

potassium chloride (KCl), a strong electrolyte, is dissolved in enough water to make a 1 *M* solution:

$$KCl(s) \xrightarrow{\text{H}_2\text{O}} K^+(aq) + Cl^-(aq)$$

Because KCl is a strong electrolyte, it undergoes complete dissociation in solution. Thus, a 1 *M* KCl solution contains 1 mole of K^+ ions and 1 mole of Cl^- ions, and no KCl units are present. The concentrations of the ions can be expressed as $[K^+] = 1\ M$ and $[Cl^-] = 1\ M$, where the square brackets [ ] indicate that the concentration is expressed in molarity. Similarly, in a 1 *M* barium nitrate $[Ba(NO_3)_2]$ solution

$$Ba(NO_3)_2(s) \xrightarrow{\text{H}_2\text{O}} Ba^{2+}(aq) + 2NO_3^-(aq)$$

we have $[Ba^{2+}] = 1\ M$ and $[NO_3^-] = 2\ M$ and no $Ba(NO_3)_2$ units at all.

The procedure for preparing a solution of known molarity is as follows. First, the solute is accurately weighed and transferred to a volumetric flask through a funnel (Figure 4.18). Next, water is added to the flask, which is carefully swirled to dissolve the solid. After *all* the solid has dissolved, more water is added slowly to bring the level of solution exactly to the volume mark. Knowing the volume of the solution in the flask and the quantity of compound (the number of moles) dissolved, we can calculate the molarity of the solution using Equation (4.1). Note that this procedure does not require knowing the amount of water added, as long as the volume of the final solution is known.

Example 4.6 illustrates how to prepare a solution of known molarity.

Animation: Making a Solution
Online Learning Center, Animations

Example 4.6

How many grams of potassium dichromate ($K_2Cr_2O_7$) are required to prepare a 250-mL solution whose concentration is 2.16 *M*?

Strategy How many moles of $K_2Cr_2O_7$ does a 1-L (or 1000 mL) 2.16 *M* $K_2Cr_2O_7$ solution contain? A 250-mL solution? How would you convert moles to grams?

(Continued)

A $K_2Cr_2O_7$ solution.

Solution The first step is to determine the number of moles of $K_2Cr_2O_7$ in 250 mL or 0.250 L of a 2.16 M solution:

$$\text{moles of } K_2Cr_2O_7 = 0.250 \text{ L soln} \times \frac{2.16 \text{ mol } K_2Cr_2O_7}{1 \text{ L soln}}$$

$$= 0.540 \text{ mol } K_2Cr_2O_7$$

The molar mass of $K_2Cr_2O_7$ is 294.2 g, so we write

$$\text{grams of } K_2Cr_2O_7 \text{ needed} = 0.540 \text{ mol } K_2Cr_2O_7 \times \frac{294.2 \text{ g } K_2Cr_2O_7}{1 \text{ mol } K_2Cr_2O_7}$$

$$= 159 \text{ g } K_2Cr_2O_7$$

Check As a ball-park estimate, the mass should be given by [molarity (mol/L) × volume (L) × molar mass (g/mol)] or [2 mol/L × 0.25 L × 300 g/mol] = 150 g. So the answer is reasonable.

Similar problems: 4.62, 4.63.

Practice Exercise What is the molarity of an 85.0-mL ethanol (C_2H_5OH) solution containing 1.77 g of ethanol?

Dilution of Solutions

Animation: Preparing a Solution by Dilution
Online Learning Center, Animations

Concentrated solutions are often stored in the laboratory stockroom for use as needed. Frequently we dilute these "stock" solutions before working with them. **Dilution** is *the procedure for preparing a less concentrated solution from a more concentrated one.*

Suppose that we want to prepare 1 L of a 0.400 M $KMnO_4$ solution from a solution of 1.00 M $KMnO_4$. For this purpose we need 0.400 mole of $KMnO_4$. Because there is 1.00 mole of $KMnO_4$ in 1 L of a 1.00 M $KMnO_4$ solution, there is 0.400 mole of $KMnO_4$ in 0.400 L of the same solution:

$$\frac{1.00 \text{ mol}}{1 \text{ L soln}} = \frac{0.400 \text{ mol}}{0.400 \text{ L soln}}$$

Therefore, we must withdraw 400 mL from the 1.00 M $KMnO_4$ solution and dilute it to 1000 mL by adding water (in a 1-L volumetric flask). This method gives us 1 L of the desired solution of 0.400 M $KMnO_4$.

In carrying out a dilution process, it is useful to remember that adding more solvent to a given amount of the stock solution changes (decreases) the concentration of the solution without changing the number of moles of solute present in the solution (Figure 4.19). In other words,

$$\text{moles of solute before dilution} = \text{moles of solute after dilution}$$

Two $KMnO_4$ solutions of different concentrations.

(a)   (b)

Figure 4.19 *The dilution of a more concentrated solution (a) to a less concentrated one (b) does not change the total number of solute particles (18).*

Because molarity is defined as moles of solute in one liter of solution, we see that the number of moles of solute is given by

$$\underbrace{\frac{\text{moles of solute}}{\text{liters of soln}}}_{M} \times \underbrace{\text{volume of soln (in liters)}}_{V} = \text{moles of solute}$$

or

$$MV = \text{moles of solute}$$

Because all the solute comes from the original stock solution, we can conclude that

$$\underset{\substack{\text{moles of solute} \\ \text{before dilution}}}{M_i V_i} = \underset{\substack{\text{moles of solute} \\ \text{after dilution}}}{M_f V_f} \tag{4.2}$$

where M_i and M_f are the initial and final concentrations of the solution in molarity and V_i and V_f are the initial and final volumes of the solution, respectively. Of course, the units of V_i and V_f must be the same (mL or L) for the calculation to work. To check the reasonableness of your results, be sure that $M_i > M_f$ and $V_f > V_i$.

We apply Equation (4.2) in Example 4.7.

Example 4.7

Describe how you would prepare 5.00×10^2 mL of a 1.75 M H_2SO_4 solution, starting with an 8.61 M stock solution of H_2SO_4.

Strategy Because the concentration of the final solution is less than that of the original one, this is a dilution process. Keep in mind that in dilution, the concentration of the solution decreases but the number of moles of the solute remains the same.

Solution We prepare for the calculation by tabulating our data:

$$M_i = 8.61\ M \qquad M_f = 1.75\ M$$
$$V_i = ? \qquad\quad V_f = 5.00 \times 10^2\ mL$$

Substituting in Equation (4.2),

$$(8.61\ M)(V_i) = (1.75\ M)(5.00 \times 10^2\ mL)$$
$$V_i = \frac{(1.75\ M)(5.00 \times 10^2\ mL)}{8.61\ M}$$
$$= 102\ mL$$

Thus we must dilute 102 mL of the 8.61 M H_2SO_4 solution with sufficient water to give a final volume of 5.00×10^2 mL in a 500-mL volumetric flask to obtain the desired concentration.

Check The initial volume is less than the final volume, so the answer is reasonable.

Practice Exercise How would you prepare 2.00×10^2 mL of a 0.866 M NaOH solution, starting with a 5.07 M stock solution?

Similar problems: 4.71, 4.72.

Now that we have discussed the concentration and dilution of solutions, we can examine the quantitative aspects of reactions in aqueous solution, or *solution stoichiometry*. Sections 4.6–4.8 focus on two techniques for studying solution stoichiometry: gravimetric analysis and titration. These techniques are important tools of *quantitative analysis,* which is *the determination of the amount or concentration of a substance in a sample.*

4.6 Gravimetric Analysis

Gravimetric analysis is *an analytical technique based on the measurement of mass.* One type of gravimetric analysis experiment involves the formation, isolation, and mass determination of a precipitate. Generally this procedure is applied to ionic compounds. First, a sample substance of unknown composition is dissolved in water and allowed to react with another substance to form a precipitate. Then the precipitate is filtered off, dried, and weighed. Knowing the mass and chemical formula of the precipitate formed, we can calculate the mass of a particular chemical component (that is, the anion or cation) of the original sample. Finally, from the mass of the component and the mass of the original sample, we can determine the percent composition by mass of the component in the original compound.

A reaction that is often studied in gravimetric analysis, because the reactants can be obtained in pure form, is

$$AgNO_3(aq) + NaCl(aq) \longrightarrow NaNO_3(aq) + AgCl(s)$$

The net ionic equation is

$$Ag^+(aq) + Cl^-(aq) \longrightarrow AgCl(s)$$

The precipitate is silver chloride (see Table 4.2). As an example, let us say that we wanted to determine *experimentally* the percent by mass of Cl in NaCl. First we would accurately weigh out a sample of NaCl and dissolve it in water. Next, we would add enough $AgNO_3$ solution to the NaCl solution to cause the precipitation of all the Cl^- ions present in solution as AgCl. In this procedure NaCl is the limiting reagent and $AgNO_3$ the excess reagent. The AgCl precipitate is separated from the solution by filtration, dried, and weighed. From the measured mass of AgCl, we can calculate the mass of Cl using the percent by mass of Cl in AgCl. Because this same amount of Cl was present in the original NaCl sample, we can calculate the percent by mass of Cl in NaCl. Figure 4.20 shows how this procedure is performed.

> This procedure would enable us to determine the purity of the NaCl sample.

Gravimetric analysis is a highly accurate technique, because the mass of a sample can be measured accurately. However, this procedure is applicable only to reactions that go to completion, or have nearly 100 percent yield. Thus, if AgCl were slightly soluble instead of being insoluble, it would not be possible to remove all the Cl^- ions from the NaCl solution and the subsequent calculation would be in error.

Example 4.8 shows the calculations involved in a gravimetric experiment.

Example 4.8

A 0.5662-g sample of an ionic compound containing chloride ions and an unknown metal is dissolved in water and treated with an excess of $AgNO_3$. If 1.0882 g of AgCl precipitate forms, what is the percent by mass of Cl in the original compound?

Strategy We are asked to calculate the percent by mass of Cl in the unknown sample, which is

$$\%Cl = \frac{\text{mass of Cl}}{0.5662 \text{ g sample}} \times 100\%$$

(Continued)

(a)

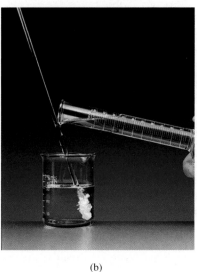
(b)

(c)

Figure 4.20 *Basic steps for gravimetric analysis. (a) A solution containing a known amount of NaCl in a beaker. (b) The precipitation of AgCl upon the addition of AgNO$_3$ solution from a measuring cylinder. In this reaction, AgNO$_3$ is the excess reagent and NaCl is the limiting reagent. (c) The solution containing the AgCl precipitate is filtered through a preweighed sintered-disk crucible, which allows the liquid (but not the precipitate) to pass through. The crucible is then removed from the apparatus, dried in an oven, and weighed again. The difference between this mass and that of the empty crucible gives the mass of the AgCl precipitate.*

The only source of Cl$^-$ ions is the original compound. These chloride ions eventually end up in the AgCl precipitate. Can we calculate the mass of the Cl$^-$ ions if we know the percent by mass of Cl in AgCl?

Solution The molar masses of Cl and AgCl are 35.45 g and 143.4 g, respectively. Therefore, the percent by mass of Cl in AgCl is given by

$$\%\text{Cl} = \frac{35.45 \text{ g Cl}}{143.4 \text{ g AgCl}} \times 100\%$$
$$= 24.72\%$$

Next we calculate the mass of Cl in 1.0882 g of AgCl. To do so we convert 24.72 percent to 0.2472 and write

$$\text{mass of Cl} = 0.2472 \times 1.0882 \text{ g}$$
$$= 0.2690 \text{ g}$$

Because the original compound also contained this amount of Cl$^-$ ions, the percent by mass of Cl in the compound is

$$\%\text{Cl} = \frac{0.2690 \text{ g}}{0.5662 \text{ g}} \times 100\%$$
$$= 47.51\%$$

Similar problem: 4.78.

Practice Exercise A sample of 0.3220 g of an ionic compound containing the bromide ion (Br$^-$) is dissolved in water and treated with an excess of AgNO$_3$. If the mass of the AgBr precipitate that forms is 0.6964 g, what is the percent by mass of Br in the original compound?

Note that gravimetric analysis does not establish the whole identity of the unknown. Thus in Example 4.8 we still do not know what the cation is. However, knowing the percent by mass of Cl greatly helps us in narrowing the possibilities. Because no two compounds containing the same anion (or cation) have the same percent composition by mass, comparison of the percent by mass obtained from gravimetric analysis with that calculated from a series of known compounds would reveal the identity of the unknown.

4.7 Acid-Base Titrations

Quantitative studies of acid-base neutralization reactions are most conveniently carried out using a technique known as titration. In **titration,** *a solution of accurately known concentration,* called a **standard solution,** *is added gradually to another solution of unknown concentration, until the chemical reaction between the two solutions is complete.* If we know the volumes of the standard and unknown solutions used in the titration, along with the concentration of the standard solution, we can calculate the concentration of the unknown solution.

Sodium hydroxide is one of the bases commonly used in the laboratory. However, it is difficult to obtain solid sodium hydroxide in a pure form because it has a tendency to absorb water from air, and its solution reacts with carbon dioxide. For these reasons, a solution of sodium hydroxide must be *standardized* before it can be used in accurate analytical work. We can standardize the sodium hydroxide solution by titrating it against an acid solution of accurately known concentration. The acid often chosen for this task is a monoprotic acid called potassium hydrogen phthalate (KHP), for which the molecular formula is $KHC_8H_4O_4$. KHP is a white, soluble solid that is commercially available in highly pure form. The reaction between KHP and sodium hydroxide is

$$KHC_8H_4O_4(aq) + NaOH(aq) \longrightarrow KNaC_8H_4O_4(aq) + H_2O(l)$$

and the net ionic equation is

$$HC_8H_4O_4^-(aq) + OH^-(aq) \longrightarrow C_8H_4O_4^{2-}(aq) + H_2O(l)$$

Potassium hydrogen phthalate.

The procedure for the titration is shown in Figure 4.21. First, a known amount of KHP is transferred to an Erlenmeyer flask and some distilled water is added to make up a solution. Next, NaOH solution is carefully added to the KHP solution from a buret until we reach the **equivalence point,** that is, *the point at which the acid has completely reacted with or been neutralized by the base.* The equivalence point is usually signaled by a sharp change in the color of an indicator in the acid solution. In acid-base titrations, **indicators** are *substances that have distinctly different colors in acidic and basic media.* One commonly used indicator is phenolphthalein, which is colorless in acidic and neutral solutions but reddish pink in basic solutions. At the equivalence point, all the KHP present has been neutralized by the added NaOH and the solution is still colorless. However, if we add just one more drop of NaOH solution from the buret, the solution will immediately turn pink because the solution is now basic. Example 4.9 illustrates such a titration.

Example 4.9

In a titration experiment, a student finds that 23.48 mL of a NaOH solution are needed to neutralize 0.5468 g of KHP. What is the concentration (in molarity) of the NaOH solution?

(Continued)

Figure 4.21 *(a) Apparatus for acid-base titration. A NaOH solution is added from the buret to a KHP solution in an Erlenmeyer flask. (b) A reddish-pink color appears when the equivalence point is reached. The color here has been intensified for visual display.*

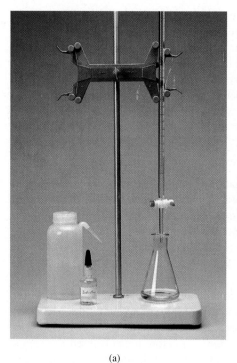
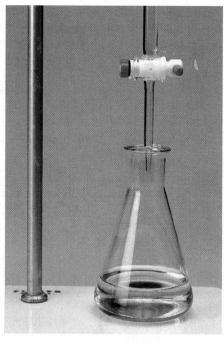

(a)   (b)

Strategy We want to determine the molarity of the NaOH solution. What is the definition of molarity?

need to find

$$\text{molarity of NaOH} = \frac{\text{mol NaOH}}{\text{L soln}}$$

want to calculate   given

The volume of NaOH solution is given in the problem. Therefore, we need to find the number of moles of NaOH to solve for molarity. From the preceding equation for the reaction between KHP and NaOH shown in the text we see that 1 mole of KHP neutralizes 1 mole of NaOH. How many moles of KHP are contained in 0.5468 g of KHP?

Solution First we calculate the number of moles of KHP consumed in the titration:

$$\text{moles of KHP} = 0.5468 \text{ g KHP} \times \frac{1 \text{ mol KHP}}{204.2 \text{ g KHP}}$$
$$= 2.678 \times 10^{-3} \text{ mol KHP}$$

Because 1 mol KHP $\simeq$ 1 mol NaOH, there must be 2.678×10^{-3} mole of NaOH in 23.48 mL of NaOH solution. Finally, we calculate the number of moles of NaOH in 1 L of the solution or the molarity as follows:

$$\text{molarity of NaOH soln} = \frac{2.678 \times 10^{-3} \text{ mol NaOH}}{23.48 \text{ mL soln}} \times \frac{1000 \text{ mL soln}}{1 \text{ L soln}}$$
$$= 0.1141 \text{ mol NaOH}/1 \text{ L soln} = 0.1141 \ M$$

Similar problems: 4.85, 4.86.

Practice Exercise How many grams of KHP are needed to neutralize 18.64 mL of a 0.1004 *M* NaOH solution?

The neutralization reaction between NaOH and KHP is one of the simplest types of acid-base neutralization known. Suppose, though, that instead of KHP, we wanted to use a diprotic acid such as H_2SO_4 for the titration. The reaction is represented by

$$2NaOH(aq) + H_2SO_4(aq) \longrightarrow Na_2SO_4(aq) + 2H_2O(l)$$

Because 2 mol NaOH $\simeq$ 1 mol H_2SO_4, we need twice as much NaOH to react completely with a H_2SO_4 solution of the *same* molar concentration and volume as a monoprotic acid like HCl. On the other hand, we would need twice the amount of HCl to neutralize a $Ba(OH)_2$ solution compared to a NaOH solution having the same concentration and volume because 1 mole of $Ba(OH)_2$ yields 2 moles of OH^- ions:

$$2HCl(aq) + Ba(OH)_2(aq) \longrightarrow BaCl_2(aq) + 2H_2O(l)$$

In calculations involving acid-base titrations, regardless of the acid or base that takes place in the reaction, keep in mind that the total number of moles of H^+ ions that have reacted at the equivalence point must be equal to the total number of moles of OH^- ions that have reacted.

Example 4.10 shows the titration of a NaOH solution with a diprotic acid.

Example 4.10

How many milliliters (mL) of a 0.610 M NaOH solution are needed to neutralize 20.0 mL of a 0.245 M H_2SO_4 solution?

Strategy We want to calculate the volume of the NaOH solution. From the definition of molarity [see Equation (4.1)], we write

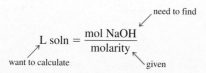

H_2SO_4 has two ionizable protons.

From the equation for the neutralization reaction just shown, we see that 1 mole of H_2SO_4 neutralizes 2 moles of NaOH. How many moles of H_2SO_4 are contained in 20.0 mL of a 0.245 M H_2SO_4 solution? How many moles of NaOH would this quantity of H_2SO_4 neutralize?

Solution First we calculate the number of moles of H_2SO_4 in a 20.0 mL solution:

$$\text{moles } H_2SO_4 = \frac{0.245 \text{ mol } H_2SO_4}{1000 \text{ mL soln}} \times 20.0 \text{ mL soln}$$
$$= 4.90 \times 10^{-3} \text{ mol } H_2SO_4$$

From the stoichiometry we see that 1 mol H_2SO_4 $\simeq$ 2 mol NaOH. Therefore, the number of moles of NaOH reacted must be $2 \times 4.90 \times 10^{-3}$ mole, or 9.80×10^{-3} mole. From the definition of molarity [see Equation (4.1)], we have

$$\text{liters of soln} = \frac{\text{moles of solute}}{\text{molarity}}$$

(Continued)

or

$$\text{volume of NaOH} = \frac{9.80 \times 10^{-3} \, \text{mol NaOH}}{0.610 \, \text{mol/L soln}}$$

$$= 0.0161 \, \text{L or } 16.1 \, \text{mL}$$

Similar problems: 4.87(b), (c).

Practice Exercise How many milliliters of a 1.28 M H_2SO_4 solution are needed to neutralize 60.2 mL of a 0.427 M KOH solution?

4.8 Redox Titrations

As mentioned earlier, redox reactions involve the transfer of electrons, and acid-base reactions involve the transfer of protons. Just as an acid can be titrated against a base, we can titrate an oxidizing agent against a reducing agent, using a similar procedure. We can, for example, carefully add a solution containing an oxidizing agent to a solution containing a reducing agent. The *equivalence point* is reached when the reducing agent is completely oxidized by the oxidizing agent.

There are not as many redox indicators as there are acid-base indicators.

Like acid-base titrations, redox titrations normally require an indicator that clearly changes color. In the presence of large amounts of reducing agent, the color of the indicator is characteristic of its reduced form. The indicator assumes the color of its oxidized form when it is present in an oxidizing medium. At or near the equivalence point, a sharp change in the indicator's color will occur as it changes from one form to the other, so the equivalence point can be readily identified.

Two common oxidizing agents are potassium dichromate ($K_2Cr_2O_7$) and potassium permanganate ($KMnO_4$). As Figure 4.22 shows, the colors of the dichromate and permanganate anions are distinctly different from those of the reduced species:

$$Cr_2O_7^{2-} \longrightarrow Cr^{3+}$$

orange yellow   green

$$MnO_4^- \longrightarrow Mn^{2+}$$

purple   light pink

Thus these oxidizing agents can themselves be used as *internal* indicator in a redox titration because they have distinctly different colors in the oxidized and reduced forms.

Figure 4.22 *Left to right: Solutions containing the MnO_4^-, Mn^{2+}, $Cr_2O_7^{2-}$, and Cr^{3+} ions.*

Redox titrations require the same type of calculations (based on the mole method) as acid-base neutralizations. The difference is that the equations and the stoichiometry tend to be more complex for redox reactions. The following is an example of a redox titration.

Example 4.11

A 16.42-mL volume of 0.1327 M KMnO$_4$ solution is needed to oxidize 25.00 mL of a FeSO$_4$ solution in an acidic medium. What is the concentration of the FeSO$_4$ solution in molarity? The net ionic equation is

$$5Fe^{2+} + MnO_4^- + 8H^+ \longrightarrow Mn^{2+} + 5Fe^{3+} + 4H_2O$$

Strategy We want to calculate the molarity of the FeSO$_4$ solution. From the definition of molarity

$$\underset{\text{want to calculate}}{\text{molarity of FeSO}_4} = \frac{\overset{\text{need to find}}{\text{mol FeSO}_4}}{\underset{\text{given}}{\text{L soln}}}$$

Addition of a KMnO$_4$ solution from a buret to a FeSO$_4$ solution.

The volume of the FeSO$_4$ solution is given in the problem. Therefore, we need to find the number of moles of FeSO$_4$ to solve for the molarity. From the net ionic equation, what is the stoichiometric equivalence between Fe^{2+} and MnO$_4^-$? How many moles of KMnO$_4$ are contained in 16.42 mL of 0.1327 M KMnO$_4$ solution?

Solution The number of moles of KMnO$_4$ in 16.42 mL of the solution is

$$\text{moles of KMnO}_4 = 16.42 \text{ mL} \times \frac{0.1327 \text{ mol KMnO}_4}{1000 \text{ mL soln}}$$
$$= 2.179 \times 10^{-3} \text{ mol KMnO}_4$$

From the net ionic equation we see that 5 mol Fe^{2+} ≏ 1 mol MnO$_4^-$. Therefore, the number of moles of FeSO$_4$ oxidized is

$$\text{moles FeSO}_4 = 2.179 \times 10^{-3} \text{ mol KMnO}_4 \times \frac{5 \text{ mol FeSO}_4}{1 \text{ mol KMnO}_4}$$
$$= 1.090 \times 10^{-2} \text{ mol FeSO}_4$$

The concentration of the FeSO$_4$ solution in moles of FeSO$_4$ per liter of solution is

$$\text{molarity of FeSO}_4 = \frac{\text{mol FeSO}_4}{\text{L soln}}$$
$$= \frac{1.090 \times 10^{-2} \text{ mol FeSO}_4}{25.00 \text{ mL soln}} \times \frac{1000 \text{ mL soln}}{1 \text{ L soln}}$$
$$= 0.4360 \ M$$

Similar problems: 4.91, 4.92.

Practice Exercise How many milliliters of a 0.206 M HI solution are needed to reduce 22.5 mL of a 0.374 M KMnO$_4$ solution according to the following equation:

$$10HI + 2KMnO_4 + 3H_2SO_4 \longrightarrow 5I_2 + 2MnSO_4 + K_2SO_4 + 8H_2O$$

The Chemistry in Action on p. 150 describes an industrial process that involves the types of reactions discussed in this chapter.

CHEMISTRY IN ACTION

Metal from the Sea

Magnesium is a valuable, lightweight metal used as a structural material as well as in alloys, in batteries, and in chemical synthesis. Although magnesium is plentiful in Earth's crust, it is cheaper to "mine" the metal from seawater. Magnesium forms the second most abundant cation in the sea (after sodium); there are about 1.3 g of magnesium in a kilogram of seawater. The process for obtaining magnesium from seawater employs all three types of reactions discussed in this chapter: precipitation, acid-base, and redox reactions.

In the first stage in the recovery of magnesium, limestone (CaCO$_3$) is heated at high temperatures to produce quicklime, or calcium oxide (CaO):

$$CaCO_3(s) \longrightarrow CaO(s) + CO_2(g)$$

When calcium oxide is treated with seawater, it forms calcium hydroxide [Ca(OH)$_2$], which is slightly soluble and ionizes to give Ca^{2+} and OH$^-$ ions:

$$CaO(s) + H_2O(l) \longrightarrow Ca^{2+}(aq) + 2OH^-(aq)$$

The surplus hydroxide ions cause the much less soluble magnesium hydroxide to precipitate:

$$Mg^{2+}(aq) + 2OH^-(aq) \longrightarrow Mg(OH)_2(s)$$

The solid magnesium hydroxide is filtered and reacted with hydrochloric acid to form magnesium chloride (MgCl$_2$):

$$Mg(OH)_2(s) + 2HCl(aq) \longrightarrow MgCl_2(aq) + 2H_2O(l)$$

Magnesium hydroxide is obtained from seawater in settling ponds at the Dow Chemical Company in Freeport, Texas.

After the water is evaporated, the solid magnesium chloride is melted in a steel cell. The molten magnesium chloride contains both Mg^{2+} and Cl$^-$ ions. In a process called *electrolysis*, an electric current is passed through the cell to reduce the Mg^{2+} ions and oxidize the Cl$^-$ ions. The half-reactions are

$$Mg^{2+} + 2e^- \longrightarrow Mg$$
$$2Cl^- \longrightarrow Cl_2 + 2e^-$$

The overall reaction is

$$MgCl_2(l) \longrightarrow Mg(l) + Cl_2(g)$$

This is how magnesium metal is produced. The chlorine gas generated can be converted to hydrochloric acid and recycled through the process.

Key Equations

- molarity $(M) = \dfrac{\text{moles of solute}}{\text{liters of soln}}$ (4.1)   Calculating molarity.

- $M_i V_i = M_f V_f$ (4.2)   Dilution of solution.

Summary of Facts and Concepts

1. Aqueous solutions are electrically conducting if the solutes are electrolytes. If the solutes are nonelectrolytes, the solutions do not conduct electricity.
2. Three major categories of chemical reactions that take place in aqueous solution are precipitation reactions, acid-base reactions, and oxidation-reduction reactions.
3. From general rules about solubilities of ionic compounds, we can predict whether a precipitate will form in a reaction.

4. Arrhenius acids ionize in water to give H^+ ions, and Arrhenius bases ionize in water to give OH^- ions. Brønsted acids donate protons, and Brønsted bases accept protons.

5. The reaction of an acid and a base is called neutralization.

6. In redox reactions, oxidation and reduction always occur simultaneously. Oxidation is characterized by the loss of electrons, reduction by the gain of electrons.

7. Oxidation numbers help us keep track of charge distribution and are assigned to all atoms in a compound or ion according to specific rules. Oxidation can be defined as an increase in oxidation number; reduction can be defined as a decrease in oxidation number.

8. Many redox reactions can be subclassified as combination, decomposition, displacement, or disproportionation reactions.

9. The concentration of a solution is the amount of solute present in a given amount of solution. Molarity expresses concentration as the number of moles of solute in 1 L of solution.

10. Adding a solvent to a solution, a process known as dilution, decreases the concentration (molarity) of the solution without changing the total number of moles of solute present in the solution.

11. Gravimetric analysis is a technique for determining the identity of a compound and/or the concentration of a solution by measuring mass. Gravimetric experiments often involve precipitation reactions.

12. In acid-base titration, a solution of known concentration (say, a base) is added gradually to a solution of unknown concentration (say, an acid) with the goal of determining the unknown concentration. The point at which the reaction in the titration is complete is called the equivalence point.

13. Redox titrations are similar to acid-base titrations. The point at which the oxidation-reduction reaction is complete is called the equivalence point.

Key Words

Activity series, p. 133
Aqueous solution, p. 116
Brønsted acid, p. 123
Brønsted base, p. 123
Combination reaction, p. 130
Concentration of a solution, p. 139
Decomposition reaction, p. 131
Dilution, p. 141
Diprotic acid, p. 124
Displacement reaction, p. 132

Disproportionation reaction, p. 136
Electrolyte, p. 116
Equivalence point, p. 145
Gravimetric analysis, p. 143
Half-reaction, p. 127
Hydration, p. 117
Hydronium ion, p. 123
Indicator, p. 145
Ionic equation, p. 120
Molar concentration, p. 139
Molarity (M), p. 139
Molecular equation, p. 120

Monoprotic acid, p. 124
Net ionic equation, p. 120
Neutralization reaction, p. 125
Nonelectrolyte, p. 116
Oxidation number, p. 128
Oxidation state, p. 128
Oxidation reaction, p. 127
Oxidation-reduction reaction, p. 126
Oxidizing agent, p. 127
Precipitate, p. 118
Precipitation reaction, p. 118
Quantitative analysis, p. 142

Redox reaction, p. 126
Reducing agent, p. 127
Reduction reaction, p. 127
Reversible reaction, p. 118
Salt, p. 125
Solubility, p. 118
Solute, p. 116
Solution, p. 116
Solvent, p. 116
Spectator ion, p. 120
Standard solution, p. 145
Titration, p. 145
Triprotic acid, p. 124

Questions and Problems

Properties of Aqueous Solutions
Review Questions

4.1 Define solute, solvent, and solution by describing the process of dissolving a solid in a liquid.

4.2 What is the difference between a nonelectrolyte and an electrolyte? Between a weak electrolyte and a strong electrolyte?

4.3 Describe hydration. What properties of water enable its molecules to interact with ions in solution?

4.4 What is the difference between the following symbols in chemical equations: $\longrightarrow$ and $\rightleftharpoons$?

4.5 Water is an extremely weak electrolyte and therefore cannot conduct electricity. Why are we often cautioned not to operate electrical appliances when our hands are wet?

4.6 Lithium fluoride (LiF) is a strong electrolyte. What species are present in $LiF(aq)$?

Problems

4.7 The aqueous solutions of three compounds are shown in the diagram. Identify each compound as a nonelectrolyte, a weak electrolyte, and a strong electrolyte.

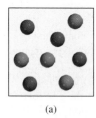  

(a)   (b)   (c)

4.8 Which of the following diagrams best represents the hydration of NaCl when dissolved in water? The Cl^- ion is larger in size than the Na^+ ion.

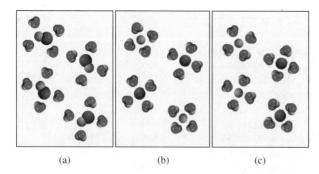

(a)   (b)   (c)

4.9 Identify each of the following substances as a strong electrolyte, weak electrolyte, or nonelectrolyte: (a) H_2O, (b) KCl, (c) HNO_3, (d) CH_3COOH, (e) $C_{12}H_{22}O_{11}$.

4.10 Identify each of the following substances as a strong electrolyte, weak electrolyte, or nonelectrolyte: (a) $Ba(NO_3)_2$, (b) Ne, (c) NH_3, (d) NaOH.

4.11 The passage of electricity through an electrolyte solution is caused by the movement of (a) electrons only, (b) cations only, (c) anions only, (d) both cations and anions.

4.12 Predict and explain which of the following systems are electrically conducting: (a) solid NaCl, (b) molten NaCl, (c) an aqueous solution of NaCl.

4.13 You are given a water-soluble compound X. Describe how you would determine whether it is an electrolyte or a nonelectrolyte. If it is an electrolyte, how would you determine whether it is strong or weak?

4.14 Explain why a solution of HCl in benzene does not conduct electricity but in water it does.

Precipitation Reactions
Review Questions

4.15 What is the difference between an ionic equation and a molecular equation?

4.16 What is the advantage of writing net ionic equations?

Problems

4.17 Two aqueous solutions of $AgNO_3$ and NaCl are mixed. Which of the following diagrams best represents the mixture?

(a)   (b)   (c)   (d)

$Na^+(aq)$	$Ag^+(aq)$	$Na^+(aq)$	
$Cl^-(aq)$	$Cl^-(aq)$	$NO_3^-(aq)$	
$Ag^+(aq)$			$AgCl(s)$
$NO_3^-(aq)$	$NaNO_3(s)$	$AgCl(s)$	$NaNO_3(s)$

4.18 Two aqueous solutions of KOH and $MgCl_2$ are mixed. Which of the following diagrams best represents the mixture?

 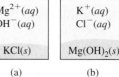 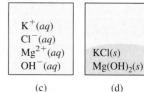

(a)   (b)   (c)   (d)

$Mg^{2+}(aq)$	$K^+(aq)$	$K^+(aq)$	
$OH^-(aq)$	$Cl^-(aq)$	$Cl^-(aq)$	
		$Mg^{2+}(aq)$	$KCl(s)$
$KCl(s)$	$Mg(OH)_2(s)$	$OH^-(aq)$	$Mg(OH)_2(s)$

4.19 Characterize the following compounds as soluble or insoluble in water: (a) $Ca_3(PO_4)_2$, (b) $Mn(OH)_2$, (c) $AgClO_3$, (d) K_2S.

4.20 Characterize the following compounds as soluble or insoluble in water: (a) $CaCO_3$, (b) $ZnSO_4$, (c) $Hg(NO_3)_2$, (d) $HgSO_4$, (e) NH_4ClO_4.

4.21 Write ionic and net ionic equations for the following reactions:

(a) $AgNO_3(aq) + Na_2SO_4(aq) \longrightarrow$
(b) $BaCl_2(aq) + ZnSO_4(aq) \longrightarrow$
(c) $(NH_4)_2CO_3(aq) + CaCl_2(aq) \longrightarrow$

4.22 Write ionic and net ionic equations for the following reactions:

(a) $Na_2S(aq) + ZnCl_2(aq) \longrightarrow$
(b) $K_3PO_4(aq) + 3Sr(NO_3)_2(aq) \longrightarrow$
(c) $Mg(NO_3)_2(aq) + 2NaOH(aq) \longrightarrow$

4.23 Which of the following processes will likely result in a precipitation reaction? (a) Mixing a $NaNO_3$ solution with a $CuSO_4$ solution. (b) Mixing a $BaCl_2$ solution with a K_2SO_4 solution. Write a net ionic equation for the precipitation reaction.

4.24 With reference to Table 4.2, suggest one method by which you might separate (a) K^+ from Ag^+, (b) Ba^{2+} from Pb^{2+}, (c) NH_4^+ from Ca^{2+}, (d) Ba^{2+} from Cu^{2+}. All cations are assumed to be in aqueous solution, and the common anion is the nitrate ion.

Acid-Base Reactions
Review Questions

4.25 List the general properties of acids and bases.

4.26 Give Arrhenius's and Brønsted's definitions of an acid and a base. Why are Brønsted's definitions more useful in describing acid-base properties?

4.27 Give an example of a monoprotic acid, a diprotic acid, and a triprotic acid.

4.28 What are the characteristics of an acid-base neutralization reaction?

4.29 What factors qualify a compound as a salt? Specify which of the following compounds are salts: CH_4, NaF, NaOH, CaO, $BaSO_4$, HNO_3, NH_3, KBr?

4.30 Identify the following as a weak or strong acid or base: (a) NH_3, (b) H_3PO_4, (c) LiOH, (d) HCOOH (formic acid), (e) H_2SO_4, (f) HF, (g) $Ba(OH)_2$.

Problems

4.31 Identify each of the following species as a Brønsted acid, base, or both: (a) HI, (b) CH_3COO^-, (c) $H_2PO_4^-$, (d) HSO_4^-.

4.32 Identify each of the following species as a Brønsted acid, base, or both: (a) PO_4^{3-}, (b) ClO_2^-, (c) NH_4^+, (d) HCO_3^-.

4.33 Balance the following equations and write the corresponding ionic and net ionic equations (if appropriate):
(a) $HBr(aq) + NH_3(aq) \longrightarrow$
(b) $Ba(OH)_2(aq) + H_3PO_4(aq) \longrightarrow$
(c) $HClO_4(aq) + Mg(OH)_2(s) \longrightarrow$

4.34 Balance the following equations and write the corresponding ionic and net ionic equations (if appropriate):
(a) $CH_3COOH(aq) + KOH(aq) \longrightarrow$
(b) $H_2CO_3(aq) + NaOH(aq) \longrightarrow$
(c) $HNO_3(aq) + Ba(OH)_2(aq) \longrightarrow$

Oxidation-Reduction Reactions
Review Questions

4.35 Give an example of a combination redox reaction, a decomposition redox reaction, and a displacement redox reaction.

4.36 All combustion reactions are redox reactions. True or false? Explain.

4.37 What is an oxidation number? How is it used to identify redox reactions? Explain why, except for ionic compounds, oxidation number does not have any physical significance.

4.38 (a) Without referring to Figure 4.10, give the oxidation numbers of the alkali and alkaline earth metals in their compounds. (b) Give the highest oxidation numbers that the Groups 3A–7A elements can have.

4.39 How is the activity series organized? How is it used in the study of redox reactions?

4.40 Use the following reaction to define redox reaction, half-reaction, oxidizing agent, reducing agent:

$$4Na(s) + O_2(g) \longrightarrow 2Na_2O(s)$$

4.41 Is it possible to have a reaction in which oxidation occurs and reduction does not? Explain.

4.42 What is the requirement for an element to undergo disproportionation reactions? Name five common elements that are likely to take part in such reactions.

Problems

4.43 For the complete redox reactions given below, (i) break down each reaction into its half-reactions; (ii) identify the oxidizing agent; (iii) identify the reducing agent.
(a) $2Sr + O_2 \longrightarrow 2SrO$
(b) $2Li + H_2 \longrightarrow 2LiH$
(c) $2Cs + Br_2 \longrightarrow 2CsBr$
(d) $3Mg + N_2 \longrightarrow Mg_3N_2$

4.44 For the complete redox reactions given below, write the half-reactions and identify the oxidizing and reducing agents:
(a) $4Fe + 3O_2 \longrightarrow 2Fe_2O_3$
(b) $Cl_2 + 2NaBr \longrightarrow 2NaCl + Br_2$
(c) $Si + 2F_2 \longrightarrow SiF_4$
(d) $H_2 + Cl_2 \longrightarrow 2HCl$

4.45 Arrange the following species in order of increasing oxidation number of the sulfur atom: (a) H_2S, (b) S_8, (c) H_2SO_4, (d) S^{2-}, (e) HS^-, (f) SO_2, (g) SO_3.

4.46 Phosphorus forms many oxoacids. Indicate the oxidation number of phosphorus in each of the following acids: (a) HPO_3, (b) H_3PO_2, (c) H_3PO_3, (d) H_3PO_4, (e) $H_4P_2O_7$, (f) $H_5P_3O_{10}$.

4.47 Give the oxidation number of the underlined atoms in the following molecules and ions: (a) $\underline{Cl}F$, (b) $\underline{I}F_7$, (c) $\underline{C}H_4$, (d) $\underline{C}_2H_2$, (e) $\underline{C}_2H_4$, (f) $K_2\underline{Cr}O_4$, (g) $K_2\underline{Cr}_2O_7$, (h) $K\underline{Mn}O_4$, (i) $Na\underline{H}CO_3$, (j) $\underline{Li}_2$, (k) $Na\underline{I}O_3$, (l) $K\underline{O}_2$, (m) $\underline{P}F_6^-$, (n) $K\underline{Au}Cl_4$.

4.48 Give the oxidation number for the following species: H_2, Se_8, P_4, O, U, As_4, B_{12}.

4.49 Give oxidation numbers for the underlined atoms in the following molecules and ions: (a) $\underline{Cs}_2O$, (b) $Ca\underline{I}_2$, (c) $\underline{Al}_2O_3$, (d) $H_3\underline{As}O_3$, (e) $\underline{Ti}O_2$, (f) $\underline{Mo}O_4^{2-}$, (g) $\underline{Pt}Cl_4^{2-}$, (h) $\underline{Pt}Cl_6^{2-}$, (i) $\underline{Sn}F_2$, (j) $\underline{Cl}F_3$, (k) $\underline{Sb}F_6^{-}$.

4.50 Give the oxidation numbers of the underlined atoms in the following molecules and ions: (a) $Mg_3\underline{N}_2$, (b) $Cs\underline{O}_2$, (c) $Ca\underline{C}_2$, (d) $\underline{C}O_3^{2-}$, (e) $\underline{C}_2O_4^{2-}$, (f) $Zn\underline{O}_2^{2-}$, (g) $Na\underline{B}H_4$, (h) $\underline{W}O_4^{2-}$.

4.51 Nitric acid is a strong oxidizing agent. State which of the following species is *least* likely to be produced when nitric acid reacts with a strong reducing agent such as zinc metal, and explain why: N_2O, NO, NO_2, N_2O_4, N_2O_5, NH_4^+.

4.52 Which of the following metals can react with water? (a) Au, (b) Li, (c) Hg, (d) Ca, (e) Pt.

4.53 On the basis of oxidation number considerations, one of the following oxides would not react with molecular oxygen: NO, N_2O, SO_2, SO_3, P_4O_6. Which one is it? Why?

4.54 Predict the outcome of the reactions represented by the following equations by using the activity series, and balance the equations.
(a) $Cu(s) + HCl(aq) \longrightarrow$
(b) $I_2(s) + NaBr(aq) \longrightarrow$
(c) $Mg(s) + CuSO_4(aq) \longrightarrow$
(d) $Cl_2(g) + KBr(aq) \longrightarrow$

4.55 Classify the following redox reactions:
(a) $2H_2O_2 \longrightarrow 2H_2O + O_2$
(b) $Mg + 2AgNO_3 \longrightarrow Mg(NO_3)_2 + 2Ag$
(c) $NH_4NO_2 \longrightarrow N_2 + 2H_2O$
(d) $H_2 + Br_2 \longrightarrow 2HBr$

4.56 Classify the following redox reactions:
(a) $P_4 + 10Cl_2 \longrightarrow 4PCl_5$
(b) $2NO \longrightarrow N_2 + O_2$
(c) $Cl_2 + 2KI \longrightarrow 2KCl + I_2$
(d) $3HNO_2 \longrightarrow HNO_3 + H_2O + 2NO$

Concentration of Solutions
Review Questions

4.57 Write the equation for calculating molarity. Why is molarity a convenient concentration unit in chemistry?

4.58 Describe the steps involved in preparing a solution of known molar concentration using a volumetric flask.

Problems

4.59 Calculate the mass of KI in grams required to prepare 5.00×10^2 mL of a 2.80 *M* solution.

4.60 Describe how you would prepare 250 mL of a 0.707 *M* $NaNO_3$ solution.

4.61 How many moles of $MgCl_2$ are present in 60.0 mL of 0.100 *M* $MgCl_2$ solution?

4.62 How many grams of KOH are present in 35.0 mL of a 5.50 *M* solution?

4.63 Calculate the molarity of each of the following solutions: (a) 29.0 g of ethanol (C_2H_5OH) in 545 mL of solution, (b) 15.4 g of sucrose ($C_{12}H_{22}O_{11}$) in 74.0 mL of solution, (c) 9.00 g of sodium chloride (NaCl) in 86.4 mL of solution.

4.64 Calculate the molarity of each of the following solutions: (a) 6.57 g of methanol (CH_3OH) in 1.50×10^2 mL of solution, (b) 10.4 g of calcium chloride ($CaCl_2$) in 2.20×10^2 mL of solution, (c) 7.82 g of naphthalene ($C_{10}H_8$) in 85.2 mL of benzene solution.

4.65 Calculate the volume in mL of a solution required to provide the following: (a) 2.14 g of sodium chloride from a 0.270 *M* solution, (b) 4.30 g of ethanol from a 1.50 *M* solution, (c) 0.85 g of acetic acid (CH_3COOH) from a 0.30 *M* solution.

4.66 Determine how many grams of each of the following solutes would be needed to make 2.50×10^2 mL of a 0.100 *M* solution: (a) cesium iodide (CsI), (b) sulfuric acid (H_2SO_4), (c) sodium carbonate (Na_2CO_3), (d) potassium dichromate ($K_2Cr_2O_7$), (e) potassium permanganate ($KMnO_4$).

Dilution of Solutions
Review Questions

4.67 Describe the basic steps involved in diluting a solution of known concentration.

4.68 Write the equation that enables us to calculate the concentration of a diluted solution. Give units for all the terms.

Problems

4.69 Describe how to prepare 1.00 L of 0.646 *M* HCl solution, starting with a 2.00 *M* HCl solution.

4.70 Water is added to 25.0 mL of a 0.866 *M* KNO_3 solution until the volume of the solution is exactly 500 mL. What is the concentration of the final solution?

4.71 How would you prepare 60.0 mL of 0.200 *M* HNO_3 from a stock solution of 4.00 *M* HNO_3?

4.72 You have 505 mL of a 0.125 *M* HCl solution and you want to dilute it to exactly 0.100 *M*. How much water should you add?

4.73 A 35.2-mL, 1.66 *M* $KMnO_4$ solution is mixed with 16.7 mL of 0.892 *M* $KMnO_4$ solution. Calculate the concentration of the final solution.

4.74 A 46.2-mL, 0.568 *M* calcium nitrate [$Ca(NO_3)_2$] solution is mixed with 80.5 mL of 1.396 *M* calcium nitrate solution. Calculate the concentration of the final solution.

Gravimetric Analysis
Review Questions

4.75 Describe the basic steps involved in gravimetric analysis. How does this procedure help us determine the identity of a compound or the purity of a compound if its formula is known?

4.76 Distilled water must be used in the gravimetric analysis of chlorides. Why?

Problems

4.77 If 30.0 mL of 0.150 M $CaCl_2$ is added to 15.0 mL of 0.100 M $AgNO_3$, what is the mass in grams of AgCl precipitate?

4.78 A sample of 0.6760 g of an unknown compound containing barium ions (Ba^{2+}) is dissolved in water and treated with an excess of Na_2SO_4. If the mass of the $BaSO_4$ precipitate formed is 0.4105 g, what is the percent by mass of Ba in the original unknown compound?

4.79 How many grams of NaCl are required to precipitate most of the Ag^+ ions from 2.50×10^2 mL of 0.0113 M $AgNO_3$ solution? Write the net ionic equation for the reaction.

4.80 The concentration of Cu^{2+} ions in the water (which also contains sulfate ions) discharged from a certain industrial plant is determined by adding excess sodium sulfide (Na_2S) solution to 0.800 L of the water. The molecular equation is

$$Na_2S(aq) + CuSO_4(aq) \longrightarrow Na_2SO_4(aq) + CuS(s)$$

Write the net ionic equation and calculate the molar concentration of Cu^{2+} in the water sample if 0.0177 g of solid CuS is formed.

Acid-Base Titrations
Review Questions

4.81 Describe the basic steps involved in an acid-base titration. Why is this technique of great practical value?

4.82 How does an acid-base indicator work?

4.83 A student carried out two titrations using a NaOH solution of unknown concentration in the buret. In one titration she weighed out 0.2458 g of KHP (see p. 145) and transferred it to an Erlenmeyer flask. She then added 20.00 mL of distilled water to dissolve the acid. In the other titration she weighed out 0.2507 g of KHP but added 40.00 mL of distilled water to dissolve the acid. Assuming no experimental error, would she obtain the same result for the concentration of the NaOH solution?

4.84 Would the volume of a 0.10 M NaOH solution needed to titrate 25.0 mL of a 0.10 M HNO_2 (a weak acid) solution be different from that needed to titrate 25.0 mL of a 0.10 M HCl (a strong acid) solution?

Problems

4.85 A quantity of 18.68 mL of a KOH solution is needed to neutralize 0.4218 g of KHP. What is the concentration (in molarity) of the KOH solution?

4.86 Calculate the concentration (in molarity) of a NaOH solution if 25.0 mL of the solution are needed to neutralize 17.4 mL of a 0.312 M HCl solution.

4.87 Calculate the volume in mL of a 1.420 M NaOH solution required to titrate the following solutions:
(a) 25.00 mL of a 2.430 M HCl solution
(b) 25.00 mL of a 4.500 M H_2SO_4 solution
(c) 25.00 mL of a 1.500 M H_3PO_4 solution

4.88 What volume of a 0.500 M HCl solution is needed to neutralize each of the following:
(a) 10.0 mL of a 0.300 M NaOH solution
(b) 10.0 mL of a 0.200 M $Ba(OH)_2$ solution

Redox Titrations
Review Questions

4.89 What are the similarities and differences between acid-base titrations and redox titrations?

4.90 Explain why potassium permanganate ($KMnO_4$) and potassium dichromate ($K_2Cr_2O_7$) can serve as internal indicators in redox titrations.

Problems

4.91 Iron(II) can be oxidized by an acidic $K_2Cr_2O_7$ solution according to the net ionic equation:

$$Cr_2O_7^{2-} + 6Fe^{2+} + 14H^+ \longrightarrow$$
$$2Cr^{3+} + 6Fe^{3+} + 7H_2O$$

If it takes 26.0 mL of 0.0250 M $K_2Cr_2O_7$ to titrate 25.0 mL of a solution containing Fe^{2+}, what is the molar concentration of Fe^{2+}?

4.92 The SO_2 present in air is mainly responsible for the acid rain phenomenon. Its concentration can be determined by titrating against a standard permanganate solution as follows:

$$5SO_2 + 2MnO_4^- + 2H_2O \longrightarrow$$
$$5SO_4^{2-} + 2Mn^{2+} + 4H^+$$

Calculate the number of grams of SO_2 in a sample of air if 7.37 mL of 0.00800 M $KMnO_4$ solution are required for the titration.

4.93 A sample of iron ore (containing only Fe^{2+} ions) weighing 0.2792 g was dissolved in dilute acid solution, and all the Fe(II) was converted to Fe(III) ions. The solution required 23.30 mL of 0.0194 M $K_2Cr_2O_7$ for titration. Calculate the percent by mass of iron in the ore. (*Hint:* See Problem 4.91 for the balanced equation.)

4.94 The concentration of a hydrogen peroxide solution can be conveniently determined by titration against a standardized potassium permanganate solution in an acidic medium according to the following equation:

$$2MnO_4^- + 5H_2O_2 + 6H^+ \longrightarrow$$
$$5O_2 + 2Mn^{2+} + 8H_2O$$

If 36.44 mL of a 0.01652 M $KMnO_4$ solution are required to oxidize 25.00 mL of a H_2O_2 solution, calculate the molarity of the H_2O_2 solution.

4.95 Iodate ion, IO_3^-, oxidizes SO_3^{2-} in acidic solution. The half-reaction for the oxidation is

$$SO_3^{2-} + H_2O \longrightarrow SO_4^{2-} + 2H^+ + 2e^-$$

A 100.0-mL sample of solution containing 1.390 g of KIO_3 reacts with 32.5 mL of 0.500 M Na_2SO_3. What is the final oxidation state of the iodine after the reaction has occurred?

4.96 Oxalic acid ($H_2C_2O_4$) is present in many plants and vegetables. If 24.0 mL of 0.0100 M $KMnO_4$ solution is needed to titrate 1.00 g of a sample of $H_2C_2O_4$ to the equivalence point, what is the percent by mass of $H_2C_2O_4$ in the sample? The net ionic equation is

$$2MnO_4^- + 16H^+ + 5C_2O_4^{2-} \longrightarrow$$
$$2Mn^{2+} + 10CO_2 + 8H_2O$$

4.97 A quantity of 25.0 mL of a solution containing both Fe^{2+} and Fe^{3+} ions is titrated with 23.0 mL of 0.0200 M $KMnO_4$ (in dilute sulfuric acid). As a result, all of the Fe^{2+} ions are oxidized to Fe^{3+} ions. Next, the solution is treated with Zn metal to convert all of the Fe^{3+} ions to Fe^{2+} ions. Finally, the solution containing only the Fe^{2+} ions requires 40.0 mL of the same $KMnO_4$ solution for oxidation to Fe^{3+}. Calculate the molar concentrations of Fe^{2+} and Fe^{3+} in the original solution. The net ionic equation is

$$MnO_4^- + 5Fe^{2+} + 8H^+ \longrightarrow$$
$$Mn^{2+} + 5Fe^{3+} + 4H_2O$$

4.98 Calcium oxalate (CaC_2O_4) is insoluble in water. For this reason it can be used to determine the amount of Ca^{2+} ions in fluids such as blood. The calcium oxalate isolated from blood is dissolved in acid and titrated against a standardized $KMnO_4$ solution as shown in Problem 4.96. In one test it is found that the calcium oxalate isolated from a 10.0-mL sample of blood requires 24.2 mL of 9.56×10^{-4} M $KMnO_4$ for titration. Calculate the number of milligrams of calcium per milliliter of blood.

Additional Problems

4.99 Classify the following reactions according to the types discussed in the chapter:
(a) $Cl_2 + 2OH^- \longrightarrow Cl^- + ClO^- + H_2O$
(b) $Ca^{2+} + CO_3^{2-} \longrightarrow CaCO_3$
(c) $NH_3 + H^+ \longrightarrow NH_4^+$
(d) $2CCl_4 + CrO_4^{2-} \longrightarrow$
$$2COCl_2 + CrO_2Cl_2 + 2Cl^-$$
(e) $Ca + F_2 \longrightarrow CaF_2$
(f) $2Li + H_2 \longrightarrow 2LiH$

(g) $Ba(NO_3)_2 + Na_2SO_4 \longrightarrow 2NaNO_3 + BaSO_4$
(h) $CuO + H_2 \longrightarrow Cu + H_2O$
(i) $Zn + 2HCl \longrightarrow ZnCl_2 + H_2$
(j) $2FeCl_2 + Cl_2 \longrightarrow 2FeCl_3$

4.100 Oxygen (O_2) and carbon dioxide (CO_2) are colorless and odorless gases. Suggest two chemical tests that would allow you to distinguish between these two gases.

4.101 Which of the following aqueous solutions would you expect to be the best conductor of electricity at 25°C? Explain your answer.
(a) 0.20 M NaCl
(b) 0.60 M CH_3COOH
(c) 0.25 M HCl
(d) 0.20 M $Mg(NO_3)_2$

4.102 A 5.00×10^2-mL sample of 2.00 M HCl solution is treated with 4.47 g of magnesium. Calculate the concentration of the acid solution after all the metal has reacted. Assume that the volume remains unchanged.

4.103 Calculate the volume of a 0.156 M $CuSO_4$ solution that would react with 7.89 g of zinc.

4.104 Sodium carbonate (Na_2CO_3) is available in very pure form and can be used to standardize acid solutions. What is the molarity of a HCl solution if 28.3 mL of the solution are required to react with 0.256 g of Na_2CO_3?

4.105 A 3.664-g sample of a monoprotic acid was dissolved in water. It took 20.27 mL of a 0.1578 M NaOH solution to neutralize the acid. Calculate the molar mass of the acid.

4.106 Acetic acid (CH_3COOH) is an important ingredient of vinegar. A sample of 50.0 mL of a commercial vinegar is titrated against a 1.00 M NaOH solution. What is the concentration (in M) of acetic acid present in the vinegar if 5.75 mL of the base are needed for the titration?

4.107 A 15.00-mL solution of potassium nitrate (KNO_3) was diluted to 125.0 mL, and 25.00 mL of this solution were then diluted to 1.000×10^3 mL. The concentration of the final solution is 0.00383 M. Calculate the concentration of the original solution.

4.108 When 2.50 g of a zinc strip were placed in a $AgNO_3$ solution, silver metal formed on the surface of the strip. After some time had passed, the strip was removed from the solution, dried, and weighed. If the mass of the strip was 3.37 g, calculate the mass of Ag and Zn metals present.

4.109 Calculate the mass of the precipitate formed when 2.27 L of 0.0820 M $Ba(OH)_2$ are mixed with 3.06 L of 0.0664 M Na_2SO_4.

4.110 Calculate the concentration of the acid (or base) remaining in solution when 10.7 mL of 0.211 M HNO_3 are added to 16.3 mL of 0.258 M NaOH.

4.111 (a) Describe a preparation for magnesium hydroxide [$Mg(OH)_2$] and predict its solubility. (b) Milk of magnesia contains mostly $Mg(OH)_2$ and is effective in treating acid (mostly hydrochloric acid) indigestion. Calculate the volume of a 0.035 M HCl solution (a typical acid concentration in an upset stomach) needed to react with two spoonfuls (approximately 10 mL) of milk of magnesia [at 0.080 g $Mg(OH)_2$/mL].

4.112 A 1.00-g sample of a metal X (that is known to form X^{2+} ions) was added to 0.100 L of 0.500 M H_2SO_4. After all the metal had reacted, the remaining acid required 0.0334 L of 0.500 M NaOH solution for neutralization. Calculate the molar mass of the metal and identify the element.

4.113 A quantitative definition of solubility is the number of grams of a solute that will dissolve in a given volume of water at a particular temperature. Describe an experiment that would enable you to determine the solubility of a soluble compound.

4.114 A 60.0-mL 0.513 M glucose ($C_6H_{12}O_6$) solution is mixed with 120.0 mL of 2.33 M glucose solution. What is the concentration of the final solution? Assume the volumes are additive.

4.115 An ionic compound X is only slightly soluble in water. What test would you employ to show that the compound does indeed dissolve in water to a certain extent?

4.116 A student is given an unknown that is either iron(II) sulfate or iron(III) sulfate. Suggest a chemical procedure for determining its identity. (Both iron compounds are water soluble.)

4.117 You are given a colorless liquid. Describe three chemical tests you would perform on the liquid to show that it is water.

4.118 Using the apparatus shown in Figure 4.1, a student found that a sulfuric acid solution caused the lightbulb to glow brightly. However, after the addition of a certain amount of a barium hydroxide [$Ba(OH)_2$] solution, the light began to dim even though $Ba(OH)_2$ is also a strong electrolyte. Explain.

4.119 You are given a soluble compound of unknown molecular formula. (a) Describe three tests that would show that the compound is an acid. (b) Once you have established that the compound is an acid, describe how you would determine its molar mass using a NaOH solution of known concentration. (Assume the acid is monoprotic.) (c) How would you find out whether the acid is weak or strong? You are provided with a sample of NaCl and an apparatus like that shown in Figure 4.1 for comparison.

4.120 You are given two colorless solutions, one containing NaCl and the other sucrose ($C_{12}H_{22}O_{11}$). Suggest a chemical and a physical test that would allow you to distinguish between these two solutions.

4.121 The concentration of lead ions (Pb^{2+}) in a sample of polluted water that also contains nitrate ions (NO_3^-) is determined by adding solid sodium sulfate (Na_2SO_4) to exactly 500 mL of the water. (a) Write

the molecular and net ionic equations for the reaction. (b) Calculate the molar concentration of Pb^{2+} if 0.00450 g of Na_2SO_4 was needed for the complete precipitation of Pb^{2+} ions as $PbSO_4$.

4.122 Hydrochloric acid is not an oxidizing agent in the sense that sulfuric acid and nitric acid are. Explain why the chloride ion is not a strong oxidizing agent like SO_4^{2-} and NO_3^-.

4.123 Explain how you would prepare potassium iodide (KI) by means of (a) an acid-base reaction and (b) a reaction between an acid and a carbonate compound.

4.124 Sodium reacts with water to yield hydrogen gas. Why is this reaction not used in the laboratory preparation of hydrogen?

4.125 Describe how you would prepare the following compounds: (a) $Mg(OH)_2$, (b) AgI, (c) $Ba_3(PO_4)_2$.

4.126 Someone spilled concentrated sulfuric acid on the floor of a chemistry laboratory. To neutralize the acid, would it be preferable to pour concentrated sodium hydroxide solution or spray solid sodium bicarbonate over the acid? Explain your choice and the chemical basis for the action.

4.127 Describe in each case how you would separate the cations or anions in an aqueous solution of: (a) $NaNO_3$ and $Ba(NO_3)_2$, (b) $Mg(NO_3)_2$ and KNO_3, (c) KBr and KNO_3, (d) K_3PO_4 and KNO_3, (e) Na_2CO_3 and $NaNO_3$.

4.128 The following are common household compounds: table salt (NaCl), table sugar (sucrose), vinegar (contains acetic acid), baking soda ($NaHCO_3$), washing soda ($Na_2CO_3 \cdot 10H_2O$), boric acid (H_3BO_3, used in eyewash), epsom salt ($MgSO_4 \cdot 7H_2O$), sodium hydroxide (used in drain openers), ammonia, milk of magnesia [$Mg(OH)_2$], and calcium carbonate. Based on what you have learned in this chapter, describe test(s) that would allow you to identify each of these compounds.

4.129 Sulfites (compounds containing the SO_3^{2-} ions) are used as preservatives in dried fruit and vegetables and in wine making. In an experiment to test the presence of sulfite in fruit, a student first soaked several dried apricots in water overnight and then filtered the solution to remove all solid particles. She then treated the solution with hydrogen peroxide (H_2O_2) to oxidize the sulfite ions to sulfate ions. Finally, the sulfate ions were precipitated by treating the solution with a few drops of a barium chloride ($BaCl_2$) solution. Write a balanced equation for each of the preceding steps.

4.130 A 0.8870-g sample of a mixture of NaCl and KCl is dissolved in water, and the solution is then treated with an excess of $AgNO_3$ to yield 1.913 g of AgCl. Calculate the percent by mass of each compound in the mixture.

4.131 Chlorine forms a number of oxides with the following oxidation numbers: +1, +3, +4, +6, and +7. Write a formula for each of these compounds.

4.132 A useful application of oxalic acid is the removal of rust (Fe_2O_3) from, say, bathtub rings according to the reaction

$$Fe_2O_3(s) + 6H_2C_2O_4(aq) \longrightarrow$$
$$2Fe(C_2O_4)_3^{3-}(aq) + 3H_2O + 6H^+(aq)$$

Calculate the number of grams of rust that can be removed by 5.00×10^2 mL of a 0.100 M solution of oxalic acid.

4.133 Acetylsalicylic acid ($C_9H_8O_4$) is a monoprotic acid commonly known as "aspirin." A typical aspirin tablet, however, contains only a small amount of the acid. In an experiment to determine its composition, an aspirin tablet was crushed and dissolved in water. It took 12.25 mL of 0.1466 M NaOH to neutralize the solution. Calculate the number of grains of aspirin in the tablet. (One grain = 0.0648 g.)

4.134 A 0.9157-g mixture of $CaBr_2$ and NaBr is dissolved in water, and $AgNO_3$ is added to the solution to form AgBr precipitate. If the mass of the precipitate is 1.6930 g, what is the percent by mass of NaBr in the original mixture?

4.135 The following "cycle of copper" experiment is performed in some general chemistry laboratories. The series of reactions starts with copper and ends with metallic copper. The steps are as follows: (1) A piece of copper wire of known mass is allowed to react with concentrated nitric acid [the products are copper(II) nitrate, nitrogen dioxide, and water]. (2) The copper(II) nitrate is treated with a sodium hydroxide solution to form copper(II) hydroxide precipitate. (3) On heating, copper(II) hydroxide decomposes to yield copper(II) oxide. (4) The copper(II) oxide is reacted with concentrated sulfuric acid to yield copper(II) sulfate. (5) Copper(II) sulfate is treated with an excess of zinc metal to form metallic copper. (6) The remaining zinc metal is removed by treatment with hydrochloric acid, and metallic copper is filtered, dried, and weighed. (a) Write a balanced equation for each step and classify the reactions. (b) Assuming that a student started with 65.6 g of copper, calculate the theoretical yield at each step. (c) Considering the nature of the steps, comment on why it is possible to recover most of the copper used at the start.

4.136 A 325-mL sample of solution contains 25.3 g of $CaCl_2$. (a) Calculate the molar concentration of Cl^- in this solution. (b) How many grams of Cl^- are in 0.100 L of this solution?

4.137 Hydrogen halides (HF, HCl, HBr, HI) are highly reactive compounds that have many industrial and laboratory uses. (a) In the laboratory, HF and HCl can be generated by reacting CaF_2 and NaCl with concentrated sulfuric acid. Write appropriate equations for the reactions. (*Hint:* These are not redox reactions.) (b) Why is it that HBr and HI cannot be prepared

similarly, that is, by reacting NaBr and NaI with concentrated sulfuric acid? (*Hint:* H_2SO_4 is a stronger oxidizing agent than both Br_2 and I_2.) (c) HBr can be prepared by reacting phosphorus tribromide (PBr_3) with water. Write an equation for this reaction.

4.138 Referring to the Chemistry in Action essay on page 150, answer the following questions: (a) Identify the precipitation, acid-base, and redox processes. (b) Instead of calcium oxide, why don't we simply add sodium hydroxide to seawater to precipitate magnesium hydroxide? (c) Sometimes a mineral called dolomite (a mixture of $CaCO_3$ and $MgCO_3$) is substituted for limestone to bring about the precipitation of magnesium hydroxide. What is the advantage of using dolomite?

4.139 Phosphoric acid (H_3PO_4) is an important industrial chemical used in fertilizers, in detergents, and in the food industry. It is produced by two different methods. In the *electric furnace method* elemental phosphorus (P_4) is burned in air to form P_4O_{10}, which is then reacted with water to give H_3PO_4. In the *wet process* the mineral phosphate rock [$Ca_5(PO_4)_3F$] is reacted with sulfuric acid to give H_3PO_4 (and HF and $CaSO_4$). Write equations for these processes and classify each step as precipitation, acid-base, or redox reaction.

4.140 Ammonium nitrate (NH_4NO_3) is one of the most important nitrogen-containing fertilizers. Its purity can be analyzed by titrating a solution of NH_4NO_3 with a standard NaOH solution. In one experiment a 0.2041-g sample of industrially prepared NH_4NO_3 required 24.42 mL of 0.1023 M NaOH for neutralization. (a) Write a net ionic equation for the reaction. (b) What is the percent purity of the sample?

4.141 Is the following reaction a redox reaction? Explain.

$$3O_2(g) \longrightarrow 2O_3(g)$$

4.142 What is the oxidation number of O in HFO?

4.143 Use molecular models like those in Figures 4.7 and 4.8 to represent the following acid-base reactions:

(a) $OH^- + H_3O^+ \longrightarrow 2H_2O$
(b) $NH_4^+ + NH_2^- \longrightarrow 2NH_3$

Identify the Brønsted acid and base in each case.

4.144 The alcohol content in a 10.0-g sample of blood from a driver required 4.23 mL of 0.07654 M $K_2Cr_2O_7$ for titration. Should the police prosecute the individual for drunken driving? (*Hint:* See Chemistry in Action essay on p. 138.)

4.145 On standing, a concentrated nitric acid gradually turns yellow in color. Explain. (*Hint:* Nitric acid slowly decomposes. Nitrogen dioxide is a colored gas.)

4.146 Describe the laboratory preparation for the following gases: (a) hydrogen, (b) oxygen, (c) carbon dioxide, and (d) nitrogen. Indicate the physical states of the reactants and products in each case. [*Hint:* Nitrogen can be obtained by heating ammonium nitrite (NH_4NO_2).]

4.147 Give a chemical explanation for each of the following: (a) When calcium metal is added to a sulfuric acid solution, hydrogen gas is generated. After a few minutes, the reaction slows down and eventually stops even though none of the reactants is used up. Explain. (b) In the activity series, aluminum is above hydrogen, yet the metal appears to be unreactive toward steam and hydrochloric acid. Why? (c) Sodium and potassium lie above copper in the activity series. Explain why Cu^{2+} ions in a $CuSO_4$ solution are not converted to metallic copper upon the addition of these metals. (d) A metal M reacts slowly with steam. There is no visible change when it is placed in a pale green iron(II) sulfate solution. Where should we place M in the activity series? (e) Before aluminum metal was obtained by electrolysis, it was produced by reducing its chloride ($AlCl_3$) with an active metal. What metals would you use to produce aluminum in that way?

4.148 Referring to Figure 4.18, explain why one must first dissolve the solid completely before making up the solution to the correct volume.

4.149 Use the periodic table framework in the right column to show the names and positions of two metals that can (a) displace hydrogen from cold water, (b) displace hydrogen from steam, and (c) displace hydrogen from acid. Also show two metals that can react neither with water nor acid.

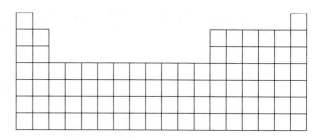

4.150 Can the following decomposition reaction be characterized as an acid-base reaction? Explain.

$$NH_4Cl(s) \longrightarrow NH_3(g) + HCl(g)$$

4.151 The recommended procedure for preparing a very dilute solution is not to weigh out a very small mass or measuring a very small volume of a stock solution. Instead, it is done by a series of dilutions. A sample of 0.8214 g of $KMnO_4$ was dissolved in water and made up to the volume in a 500-mL volumetric flask. A 2.000-mL sample of this solution was transferred to a 1000-mL volumetric flask and diluted to the mark with water. Next, 10.00 mL of the diluted solution were transferred to a 250-mL flask and diluted to the mark with water. (a) Calculate the concentration (in molarity) of the final solution. (b) Calculate the mass of $KMnO_4$ needed to directly prepare the final solution.

Answers to Practice Exercises

4.1 (a) Insoluble, (b) insoluble, (c) soluble. **4.2** $Al^{3+}(aq)$ + $3OH^-(aq) \longrightarrow Al(OH)_3(s)$. **4.3** (a) Brønsted base, (b) Brønsted acid. **4.4** (a) P: +3, F: −1; (b) Mn: +7, O: −2. **4.5** (a) Hydrogen displacement reaction, (b) combination reaction, (c) disproportionation reaction, (d) metal displacement reaction. **4.6** 0.452 *M*. **4.7** Dilute 34.2 mL of the stock solution to 200 mL. **4.8** 92.02%. **4.9** 0.3822 g. **4.10** 10.0 mL. **4.11** 204 mL.

CHEMICAL MYSTERY

Who Killed Napoleon?

After his defeat at Waterloo in 1815, Napoleon was exiled to St. Helena, a small island in the Atlantic Ocean, where he spent the last six years of his life. In the 1960s, samples of his hair were analyzed and found to contain a high level of arsenic, suggesting that he might have been poisoned. The prime suspects are the governor of St. Helena, with whom Napoleon did not get along, and the French royal family, who wanted to prevent his return to France.

Elemental arsenic is not that harmful. The commonly used poison is actually arsenic(III) oxide, As_2O_3, a white compound that dissolves in water, is tasteless, and if administered over a period of time, is hard to detect. It was once known as the "inheritance powder" because it could be added to grandfather's wine to hasten his demise so that his grandson could inherit the estate!

In 1832 the English chemist James Marsh devised a procedure for detecting arsenic. This test, which now bears Marsh's name, combines hydrogen formed by the reaction between zinc and sulfuric acid with a sample of the suspected poison. If As_2O_3 is present, it reacts with hydrogen to form a toxic gas, arsine (AsH_3). When arsine gas is heated, it decomposes to form arsenic, which is recognized by its metallic luster. The Marsh test is an effective deterrent to

Apparatus for Marsh's test. Sulfuric acid is added to zinc metal and a solution containing arsenic(III) oxide. The hydrogen produced reacts with As_2O_3 to yield arsine (AsH_3). On heating, arsine decomposes to elemental arsenic, which has a metallic appearance, and hydrogen gas.

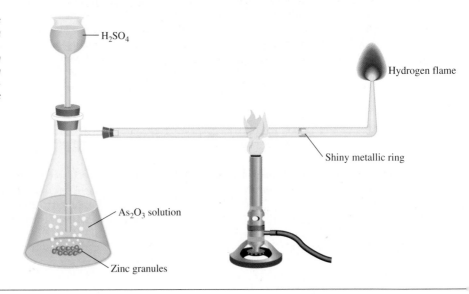

murder by As_2O_3, but it was invented too late to do Napoleon any good, if, in fact, he was a victim of deliberate arsenic poisoning.

Doubts about the conspiracy theory of Napoleon's death developed in the early 1990s, when a sample of the wallpaper from his drawing room was found to contain copper arsenate ($CuHAsO_4$), a green pigment that was commonly used at the time Napoleon lived. It has been suggested that the damp climate on St. Helena promoted the growth of molds on the wallpaper. To rid themselves of arsenic, the molds could have converted it to trimethyl arsine [$(CH_3)_3As$], which is a volatile and highly poisonous compound. Prolonged exposure to these vapors would have ruined Napoleon's health and would also account for the presence of arsenic in his body, though it may not have been the primary cause of his death. This provocative theory is supported by the fact that Napoleon's regular guests suffered from gastrointestinal disturbances and other symptoms of arsenic poisoning and that their health all seemed to improve whenever they spent hours working outdoors in the garden, their main hobby on the island.

We will probably never know whether Napoleon died from arsenic poisoning, intentional or accidental, but this exercise in historical sleuthing provides a fascinating example of the use of chemical analysis. Not only is chemical analysis used in forensic science, but it also plays an essential part in endeavors ranging from pure research to practical applications, such as quality control of commercial products and medical diagnosis.

A lock of Napoleon's hair.

Chemical Clues

1. The arsenic in Napoleon's hair was detected using a technique called *neutron activation*. When As-75 is bombarded with high-energy neutrons, it is converted to the radioactive As-76 isotope. The energy of the γ rays emitted by the radioactive isotope is characteristic of arsenic, and the intensity of the rays establishes how much arsenic is present in a sample. With this technique, as little as 5 ng (5×10^{-9} g) of arsenic can be detected in 1 g of material. (a) Write symbols for the two isotopes of As, showing mass number and atomic number. (b) Name two advantages of analyzing the arsenic content by neutron activation instead of a chemical analysis.

2. Arsenic is not an essential element for the human body. (a) Based on its position in the periodic table, suggest a reason for its toxicity. (b) In addition to hair, where else might one look for the accumulation of the element if arsenic poisoning is suspected?

3. The Marsh test for arsenic involves the following steps: (a) The generation of hydrogen gas when sulfuric acid is added to zinc. (b) The reaction of hydrogen with As(III) oxide to produce arsine. (c) Conversion of arsine to arsenic by heating. Write equations representing these steps and identify the type of the reaction in each step.

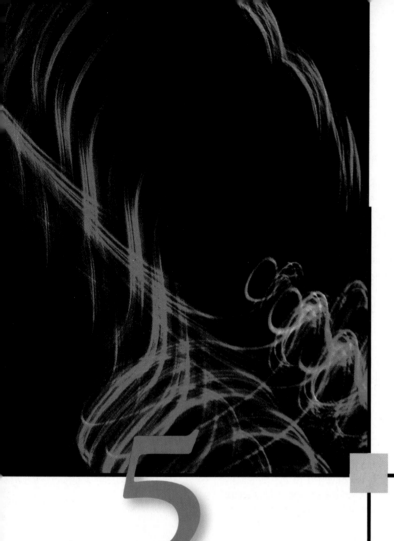

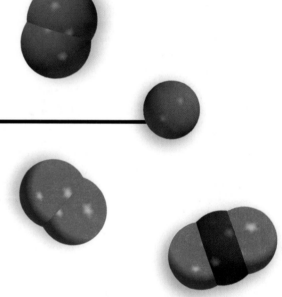

The turbulence in air created by heat from passing cars and crosswinds. This motion demonstrates the effect of heat on the motion of gases. The models show the major constituents of air: nitrogen, oxygen, and carbon dioxide molecules and an argon atom.

5

Gases

Interactive Activity Summary

1. Animation: Gas Laws (5.3)
2. Interactivity: Boyle's Law (5.3)
3. Interactivity: Volume in Gas Laws (5.3)
4. Interactivity: Primary Gas Laws (5.4)
5. Interactivity: Dalton's Law (5.6)
6. Animation: Collecting a Gas over Water (5.6)

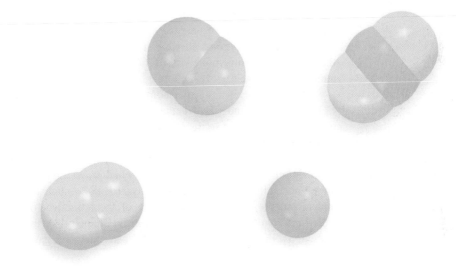

Under certain conditions of pressure and temperature, most substances can exist in any one of the three states of matter: solid, liquid, or gas. Water, for example, can be solid ice, liquid water, or steam or water vapor. The physical properties of a substance often depend on its state.

Gases, the subject of this chapter, are simpler than liquids or solids in many ways. Molecular motion in gases is totally random, and the forces of attraction between gas molecules are so small that each molecule moves freely and essentially independently of other molecules. Subjected to changes in temperature and pressure, it is easier to predict the behavior of gases. The laws that govern this behavior have played an important role in the development of the atomic theory of matter and the kinetic molecular theory of gases.

5.1 Substances That Exist as Gases

We live at the bottom of an ocean of air whose composition by volume is roughly 78 percent N_2, 21 percent O_2, and 1 percent other gases, including CO_2. Today, the chemistry of this vital mixture of gases has become a source of great interest because of the detrimental effects of environmental pollution. The chemistry of the atmosphere and polluting gases is discussed in Chapter 17. Here we will focus generally on the behavior of substances that exist as gases under normal atmospheric conditions, which are defined as 25°C and 1 atmosphere (atm) pressure.

Figure 5.1 shows the elements that are gases under normal atmospheric conditions. Note that hydrogen, nitrogen, oxygen, fluorine, and chlorine exist as gaseous diatomic molecules: H_2, N_2, O_2, F_2, and Cl_2. An allotrope of oxygen, ozone (O_3), is also a gas at room temperature. All the elements in Group 8A, the noble gases, are monatomic gases: He, Ne, Ar, Kr, Xe, and Rn.

Ionic compounds do not exist as gases at 25°C and 1 atm, because cations and anions in an ionic solid are held together by very strong electrostatic forces; that is, forces between positive and negative charges. To overcome these attractions we must apply a large amount of energy, which in practice means strongly heating the solid. Under normal conditions, all we can do is melt the solid; for example, NaCl melts at the rather high temperature of 801°C. In order to boil it, we would have to raise the temperature to well above 1000°C.

The behavior of molecular compounds is more varied. Some—for example, CO, CO_2, HCl, NH_3, and CH_4 (methane)—are gases, but the majority of molecular compounds are liquids or solids at room temperature. However, on heating they are converted to gases much more easily than ionic compounds. In other words, molecular compounds usually boil at much lower temperatures than ionic compounds do. There is no simple rule to help us determine whether a certain molecular compound is a gas under normal atmospheric conditions. To make such a determination we need to understand the nature and magnitude of the attractive forces among the molecules, called *intermolecular forces* (discussed in Chapter 11). In general, the stronger these attractions, the less likely a compound can exist as a gas at ordinary temperatures.

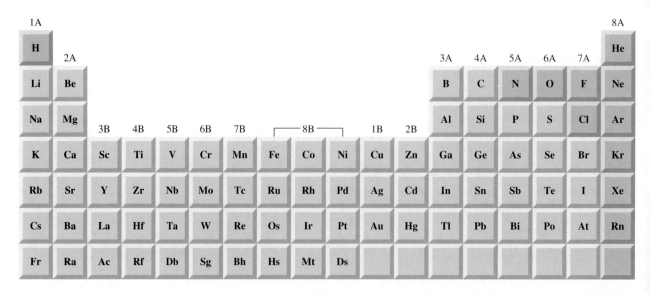

Figure 5.1 *Elements (in blue) that exist as gases at 25°C and 1 atm. The noble gases (the Group 8A elements) are monatomic; the other elements exist as diatomic molecules. Ozone (O_3) is also a gas.*

TABLE 5.1

Some Substances Found as Gases at 1 atm and 25°C

Elements	Compounds
H_2 (molecular hydrogen)	HF (hydrogen fluoride)
N_2 (molecular nitrogen)	HCl (hydrogen chloride)
O_2 (molecular oxygen)	HBr (hydrogen bromide)
O_3 (ozone)	HI (hydrogen iodide)
F_2 (molecular fluorine)	CO (carbon monoxide)
Cl_2 (molecular chlorine)	CO_2 (carbon dioxide)
He (helium)	NH_3 (ammonia)
Ne (neon)	NO (nitric oxide)
Ar (argon)	NO_2 (nitrogen dioxide)
Kr (krypton)	N_2O (nitrous oxide)
Xe (xenon)	SO_2 (sulfur dioxide)
Rn (radon)	H_2S (hydrogen sulfide)
	HCN (hydrogen cyanide)*

* The boiling point of HCN is 26°C, but it is close enough to qualify as a gas at ordinary atmospheric conditions.

A gas is a substance that is normally in the gaseous state at ordinary temperatures and pressures; a vapor is the gaseous form of any substance that is a liquid or a solid at normal temperatures and pressures. Thus, at 25°C and 1 atm pressure, we speak of water vapor and oxygen gas.

Of the gases listed in Table 5.1, only O_2 is essential for our survival. Hydrogen sulfide (H_2S) and hydrogen cyanide (HCN) are deadly poisons. Several others, such as CO, NO_2, O_3, and SO_2, are somewhat less toxic. The gases He, Ne, and Ar are chemically inert; that is, they do not react with any other substance. Most gases are colorless. Exceptions are F_2, Cl_2, and NO_2. The dark-brown color of NO_2 is sometimes visible in polluted air. All gases have the following physical characteristics:

• Gases assume the volume and shape of their containers.

• Gases are the most compressible of the states of matter.

• Gases will mix evenly and completely when confined to the same container.

• Gases have much lower densities than liquids and solids.

NO_2 gas.

5.2 Pressure of a Gas

Gases exert pressure on any surface with which they come in contact, because gas molecules are constantly in motion. We humans have adapted so well physiologically to the pressure of the air around us that we are usually unaware of it, perhaps as fish are not conscious of the water's pressure on them.

It is easy to demonstrate atmospheric pressure. One everyday example is the ability to drink a liquid through a straw. Sucking air out of the straw reduces the pressure inside the straw. The greater atmospheric pressure on the liquid pushes it up into the straw to replace the air that has been sucked out.

SI Units of Pressure

Pressure is one of the most readily measurable properties of a gas. In order to understand how we measure the pressure of a gas, it is helpful to know how the units of measurement are derived. We begin with velocity and acceleration.

Velocity is defined as the change in distance with elapsed time; that is,

$$\text{velocity} = \frac{\text{distance moved}}{\text{elapsed time}}$$

The SI unit for velocity is m/s, although we also use cm/s.

Acceleration is the change in velocity with time, or

$$\text{acceleration} = \frac{\text{change in velocity}}{\text{elapsed time}}$$

Acceleration is measured in m/s^2 (or cm/s^2).

The second law of motion, formulated by Sir Isaac Newton[†] in the late seventeenth century, defines another term, from which the units of pressure are derived, namely, *force.* According to this law,

$$\text{force} = \text{mass} \times \text{acceleration}$$

> 1 N is roughly equivalent to the force exerted by Earth's gravity on an apple.

In this context, the *SI unit of force* is the **newton (N),** where

$$1 \text{ N} = 1 \text{ kg m/s}^2$$

Finally, we define **pressure** as *force applied per unit area:*

$$\text{pressure} = \frac{\text{force}}{\text{area}}$$

The SI unit of pressure is the **pascal (Pa),**[‡] defined as *one newton per square meter:*

$$1 \text{ Pa} = 1 \text{ N/m}^2$$

Atmospheric Pressure

The atoms and molecules of the gases in the atmosphere, like those of all other matter, are subject to Earth's gravitational pull. As a consequence, the atmosphere is much denser near the surface of Earth than at high altitudes. (The air outside the pressurized cabin of an airplane at 9 km is too thin to breathe.) In fact, the density of air decreases very rapidly with increasing distance from Earth. Measurements show that about 50 percent of the atmosphere lies within 6.4 km of Earth's surface, 90 percent within 16 km, and 99 percent within 32 km. Not surprisingly the denser the air is, the greater the pressure it exerts. The force experienced by any area exposed to Earth's atmosphere is equal to *the weight of the column of air above it.* **Atmospheric pressure** is *the pressure exerted by Earth's atmosphere* (Figure 5.2). The actual value of atmospheric pressure depends on location, temperature, and weather conditions.

Does atmospheric pressure act only downward, as you might infer from its definition? Imagine what would happen, then, if you were to hold a piece of paper (with both hands) above your head. You might expect the paper to bend due to the pressure

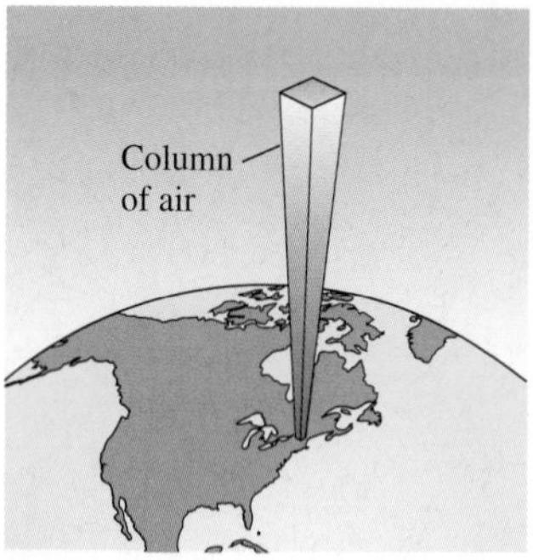

Column of air

Figure 5.2 *A column of air extending from sea level to the upper atmosphere.*

[†]Sir Isaac Newton (1642–1726). English mathematician, physicist, and astronomer. Newton is regarded by many as one of the two greatest physicists the world has known (the other is Albert Einstein). There was hardly a branch of physics to which Newton did not make a significant contribution. His book *Principia,* published in 1687, marks a milestone in the history of science.

[‡]Blaise Pascal (1623–1662). French mathematician and physicist. Pascal's work ranged widely in mathematics and physics, but his specialty was in the area of hydrodynamics (the study of the motion of fluids). He also invented a calculating machine.

of air acting on it, but this does not happen. The reason is that air, like water, is a fluid. The pressure exerted on an object in a fluid comes from all directions—downward and upward, as well as from the left and from the right. At the molecular level, air pressure results from collisions between the air molecules and any surface with which they come in contact. The magnitude of pressure depends on how often and how strongly the molecules impact the surface. It turns out that there are just as many molecules hitting the paper from the top as there are from underneath, so the paper stays flat.

How is atmospheric pressure measured? The ***barometer*** is probably the most familiar *instrument for measuring atmospheric pressure.* A simple barometer consists of a long glass tube, closed at one end and filled with mercury. If the tube is carefully inverted in a dish of mercury so that no air enters the tube, some mercury will flow out of the tube into the dish, creating a vacuum at the top (Figure 5.3). The weight of the mercury remaining in the tube is supported by atmospheric pressure acting on the surface of the mercury in the dish. ***Standard atmospheric pressure (1 atm)*** is equal to *the pressure that supports a column of mercury exactly 760 mm (or 76 cm) high at 0°C at sea level.* In other words, the standard atmosphere equals a pressure of 760 mmHg, where mmHg represents the pressure exerted by a column of mercury 1 mm high. The mmHg unit is also called the *torr,* after the Italian scientist Evangelista Torricelli,[†] who invented the barometer. Thus

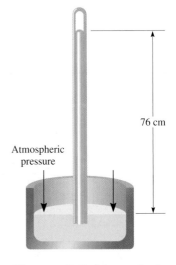

Figure 5.3 *A barometer for measuring atmospheric pressure. Above the mercury in the tube is a vacuum. The column of mercury is supported by the atmospheric pressure.*

$$1 \text{ torr} = 1 \text{ mmHg}$$

and

$$1 \text{ atm} = 760 \text{ mmHg}$$
$$= 760 \text{ torr}$$

The relation between atmospheres and pascals (see Appendix 2) is

$$1 \text{ atm} = 101,325 \text{ Pa}$$
$$= 1.01325 \times 10^5 \text{ Pa}$$

and because 1000 Pa = 1 kPa (kilopascal)

$$1 \text{ atm} = 1.01325 \times 10^2 \text{ kPa}$$

Examples 5.1 and 5.2 show the conversion from mmHg to atm and kPa.

Example 5.1

The pressure outside a jet plane flying at high altitude falls considerably below standard atmospheric pressure. Therefore, the air inside the cabin must be pressurized to protect the passengers. What is the pressure in atmospheres in the cabin if the barometer reading is 688 mmHg?

Strategy Because 1 atm = 760 mmHg, the following conversion factor is needed to obtain the pressure in atmospheres

$$\frac{1 \text{ atm}}{760 \text{ mmHg}}$$

(Continued)

[†]Evangelista Torricelli (1608–1674). Italian mathematician. Torricelli was supposedly the first person to recognize the existence of atmospheric pressure.

Solution The pressure in the cabin is given by

$$\text{pressure} = 688 \ \cancel{\text{mmHg}} \times \frac{1 \ \text{atm}}{760 \ \cancel{\text{mmHg}}}$$

$$= 0.905 \ \text{atm}$$

Similar problem: 5.13.

Practice Exercise Convert 749 mmHg to atmospheres.

Example 5.2

The atmospheric pressure in San Francisco on a certain day was 732 mmHg. What was the pressure in kPa?

Strategy Here we are asked to convert mmHg to kPa. Because

$$1 \ \text{atm} = 1.01325 \times 10^5 \ \text{Pa} = 760 \ \text{mmHg}$$

the conversion factor we need is

$$\frac{1.01325 \times 10^5 \ \text{Pa}}{760 \ \text{mmHg}}$$

Solution The pressure in kPa is

$$\text{pressure} = 732 \ \cancel{\text{mmHg}} \times \frac{1.01325 \times 10^5 \ \text{Pa}}{760 \ \cancel{\text{mmHg}}}$$

$$= 9.76 \times 10^4 \ \text{Pa}$$

$$= 97.6 \ \text{kPa}$$

Similar problem: 5.14.

Practice Exercise Convert 295 mmHg to kilopascals.

A **manometer** is *a device used to measure the pressure of gases other than the atmosphere.* The principle of operation of a manometer is similar to that of a barometer. There are two types of manometers, shown in Figure 5.4. The *closed-tube*

Figure 5.4 *Two types of manometers used to measure gas pressures. (a) Gas pressure is less than atmospheric pressure. (b) Gas pressure is greater than atmospheric pressure.*

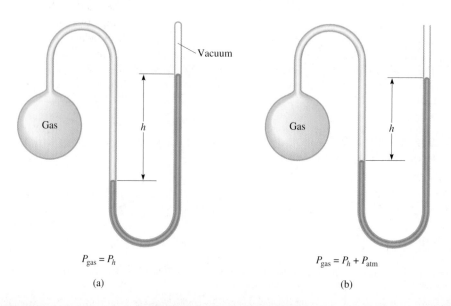

$$P_{\text{gas}} = P_h$$

(a)

$$P_{\text{gas}} = P_h + P_{\text{atm}}$$

(b)

manometer is normally used to measure pressures below atmospheric pressure [Figure 5.4(a)], whereas the *open-tube manometer* is better suited for measuring pressures equal to or greater than atmospheric pressure [Figure 5.4(b)].

Nearly all barometers and most manometers use mercury as the working fluid, despite the fact that it is a toxic substance with a harmful vapor. The reason is that mercury has a very high density (13.6 g/mL) compared with most other liquids. Because the height of the liquid in a column is inversely proportional to the liquid's density, this property enables the construction of manageably small barometers and manometers.

5.3 The Gas Laws

The gas laws we will study in this chapter are the product of countless experiments on the physical properties of gases that were carried out over several centuries. Each of these generalizations regarding the macroscopic behavior of gaseous substances represents a milestone in the history of science. Together they have played a major role in the development of many ideas in chemistry.

Animation: The Gas Laws
Online Learning Center,
Animations

The Pressure-Volume Relationship: Boyle's Law

In the seventeenth century, Robert Boyle[†] studied the behavior of gases systematically and quantitatively. In one series of studies, Boyle investigated the pressure-volume relationship of a gas sample. Typical data collected by Boyle are shown in Table 5.2. Note that as the pressure (P) is increased at constant temperature, the volume (V) occupied by a given amount of gas decreases. Compare the first data point with a pressure of 724 mmHg and a volume of 1.50 (in arbitrary unit) to the last data point with a pressure of 2250 mmHg and a volume of 0.51. Clearly there is an inverse relationship between pressure and volume of a gas at constant temperature. As the pressure is increased, the volume occupied by the gas decreases. Conversely, if the applied pressure is decreased, the volume the gas occupies increases. This relationship is now known as **Boyle's law,** which states that *the pressure of a fixed amount of gas at a constant temperature is inversely proportional to the volume of the gas.*

Interactivity: Boyle's Law
Online Learning Center,
Interactives

The apparatus used by Boyle in this experiment was very simple (Figure 5.5). In Figure 5.5(a), the pressure exerted on the gas by the mercury added to the tube is equal to atmospheric pressure. Note that the tube is open at the top and is therefore exposed to atmospheric pressure. In Figure 5.5(b) more mercury has been added, resulting in an increase in pressure on the gas sample, which is measured by the height difference (h) between the mercury levels in the tube. Note that the volume occupied by the gas

The pressure applied to a gas is equal to the gas pressure.

[†]Robert Boyle (1627–1691). British chemist and natural philosopher. Although Boyle is commonly associated with the gas law that bears his name, he made many other significant contributions in chemistry and physics. Despite the fact that Boyle was often at odds with contemporary scientists, his book *The Skeptical Chymist* (1661) influenced generations of chemists.

TABLE 5.2

Typical Pressure-Volume Relationship Obtained by Boyle						
P (mmHg)	724	869	951	998	1230	1893	2250
V (arbitrary units)	1.50	1.33	1.22	1.16	0.94	0.61	0.51
PV	1.09×10^3	1.16×10^3	1.16×10^3	1.16×10^3	1.2×10^3	1.2×10^3	1.1×10^3

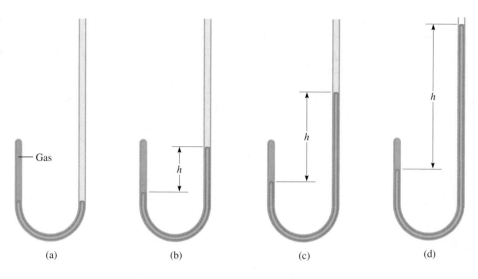

Figure 5.5 *An apparatus for studying the relationship between pressure and volume of a gas. In (a) the pressure of the gas is equal to the atmospheric pressure. The pressure exerted on the gas increases from (a) to (d) as mercury is added, and the volume of the gas decreases, as predicted by Boyle's law. The extra pressure exerted on the gas is shown by the difference in the mercury levels (h mmHg). The temperature of the gas is kept constant.*

sample has decreased with the increase in pressure. In Figures 5.5(c) and 5.5(d) the pressure is increased further by adding more mercury. The volume occupied by the gas sample continues to decrease as the pressure is increased. We can write a mathematical expression showing this inverse relationship between pressure and volume:

$$P \propto \frac{1}{V}$$

where the symbol $\propto$ means *proportional to*. We can change $\propto$ to an equals sign and write

$$P = k_1 \times \frac{1}{V} \tag{5.1a}$$

where k_1 is a constant called the *proportionality constant*. Equation (5.1a) is the mathematical expression of Boyle's law. We can rearrange Equation (5.1a) and obtain

$$PV = k_1 \tag{5.1b}$$

This form of Boyle's law says that the product of the pressure and volume of a gas at constant temperature and amount of gas is a constant. The top diagram in Figure 5.6 is a schematic representation of Boyle's law. The quantity n is the number of moles of the gas and R is a constant to be defined in Section 5.4. Thus the proportionality constant k_1 in Equations (5.1) is equal to nRT.

The concept of one quantity being proportional to another and the use of a proportionality constant can be clarified through the following analogy. The daily income of a movie theater depends on both the price of the tickets (in dollars per ticket) and the number of tickets sold. Assuming that the theater charges one price for all tickets, we write

$$\text{income} = (\text{dollar/ticket}) \times \text{number of tickets sold}$$

Because the number of tickets sold varies from day to day, the income on a given day is said to be proportional to the number of tickets sold:

$$\text{income} \propto \text{number of tickets sold}$$
$$= C \times \text{number of tickets sold}$$

where C, the proportionality constant, is the price per ticket.

Increasing or decreasing the volume of a gas
at a constant temperature

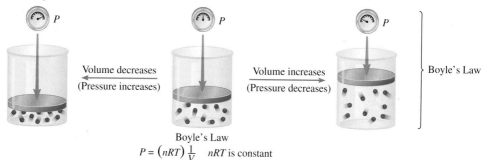

Boyle's Law

$$P = (nRT)\frac{1}{V} \quad nRT \text{ is constant}$$

Heating or cooling a gas at constant pressure

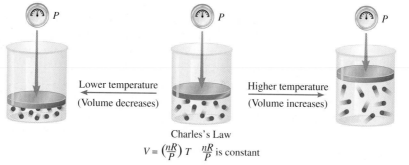

Charles's Law

$$V = \left(\frac{nR}{P}\right)T \quad \frac{nR}{P} \text{ is constant}$$

Heating or cooling a gas at constant volume

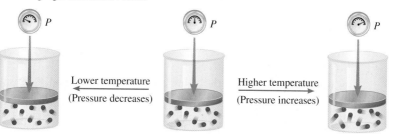

Charles's Law

$$P = \left(\frac{nR}{V}\right)T \quad \frac{nR}{V} \text{ is constant}$$

Dependence of volume on amount
of gas at constant temperature and pressure

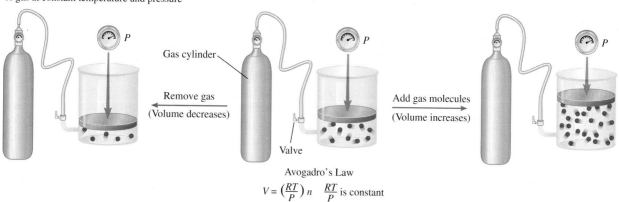

Avogadro's Law

$$V = \left(\frac{RT}{P}\right)n \quad \frac{RT}{P} \text{ is constant}$$

Figure 5.6 *Schematic illustrations of Boyle's law, Charles's law, and Avogadro's law.*

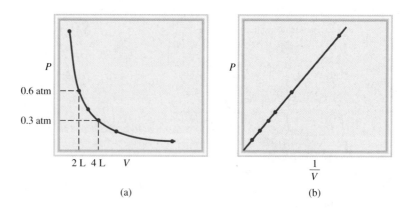

(a)   (b)

Figure 5.7 shows two conventional ways of expressing Boyle's findings graphically. Figure 5.7(a) is a graph of the equation $PV = k_1$; Figure 5.7(b) is a graph of the equivalent equation $P = k_1 \times 1/V$. Note that the latter is a linear equation of the form $y = mx + b$, where $b = 0$.

Although the individual values of pressure and volume can vary greatly for a given sample of gas, as long as the temperature is held constant and the amount of the gas does not change, P times V is always equal to the same constant. Therefore, for a given sample of gas under two different sets of conditions at constant temperature, we have

$$P_1V_1 = k_1 = P_2V_2$$

or

$$P_1V_1 = P_2V_2 \qquad (5.2)$$

where V_1 and V_2 are the volumes at pressures P_1 and P_2, respectively.

The Temperature-Volume Relationship: Charles's and Gay-Lussac's Law

Boyle's law depends on the temperature of the system remaining constant. But suppose the temperature changes: How does a change in temperature affect the volume and pressure of a gas? Let us first look at the effect of temperature on the volume of a gas. The earliest investigators of this relationship were French scientists, Jacques Charles[†] and Joseph Gay-Lussac.[‡] Their studies showed that, at constant pressure, the volume of a gas sample expands when heated and contracts when cooled (Figure 5.8). The quantitative relations involved in changes in gas temperature and volume turn out to be remarkably consistent. For example, we observe an interesting phenomenon when we study the temperature-volume relationship at various pressures. At any given pressure, the plot of volume versus temperature yields a straight line. By extending the line to zero volume, we find the intercept on the temperature axis to be −273.15°C. At any other pressure, we obtain a different straight line for the

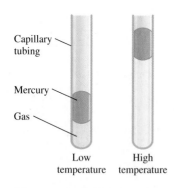

Capillary tubing

Mercury

Gas

Low temperature   High temperature

Figure 5.8 *Variation of the volume of a gas sample with temperature, at constant pressure. The pressure exerted on the gas is the sum of the atmospheric pressure and the pressure due to the weight of the mercury.*

[†]Jacques Alexandre Cesar Charles (1746–1823). French physicist. He was a gifted lecturer, an inventor of scientific apparatus, and the first person to use hydrogen to inflate balloons.

[‡]Joseph Louis Gay-Lussac (1778–1850). French chemist and physicist. Like Charles, Gay-Lussac was a balloon enthusiast. Once he ascended to an altitude of 20,000 feet to collect air samples for analysis.

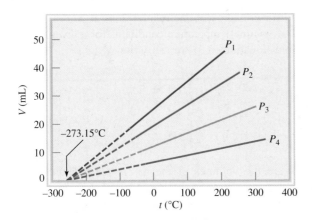

Figure 5.9 *Variation of the volume of a gas sample with temperature, at constant pressure. Each line represents the variation at a certain pressure. The pressures increase from P_1 to P_4. All gases ultimately condense (become liquids) if they are cooled to sufficiently low temperatures; the solid portions of the lines represent the temperature region above the condensation point. When these lines are extrapolated, or extended (the dashed portions), they all intersect at the point representing zero volume and a temperature of $-273.15°C$.*

volume-temperature plot, but we get the *same* zero-volume temperature intercept at $-273.15°C$ (Figure 5.9). (In practice, we can measure the volume of a gas over only a limited temperature range, because all gases condense at low temperatures to form liquids.)

In 1848 Lord Kelvin[§] realized the significance of this phenomenon. He identified $-273.15°C$ as **absolute zero,** *theoretically the lowest attainable temperature.* Then he set up an **absolute temperature scale,** now called the **Kelvin temperature scale,** with *absolute zero as the starting point* (see Section 1.7). On the Kelvin scale, one kelvin (K) is equal *in magnitude* to one degree Celsius. The only difference between the absolute temperature scale and the Celsius scale is that the zero position is shifted. Important points on the two scales match up as follows:

	Kelvin Scale	**Celsius Scale**
Absolute zero	0 K	$-273.15°C$
Freezing point of water	273.15 K	$0°C$
Boiling point of water	373.15 K	$100°C$

Under special experimental conditions, scientists have succeeded in approaching absolute zero to within a small fraction of a kelvin.

The conversion between °C and K is given on p. 20. In most calculations we will use 273 instead of 273.15 as the term relating K and °C. By convention, we use T to denote absolute (kelvin) temperature and t to indicate temperature on the Celsius scale.

The dependence of the volume of a gas on temperature is given by

$$V \propto T$$
$$V = k_2 T$$

or

$$\frac{V}{T} = k_2 \qquad (5.3)$$

where k_2 is the proportionality constant. Equation (5.3) is known as **Charles's and Gay-Lussac's law,** or simply **Charles's law,** which states that *the volume of a fixed amount of gas maintained at constant pressure is directly proportional to the absolute temperature of the gas.* Charles's law is also illustrated in Figure 5.6. We see that the proportionality constant k_2 in Equation (5.3) is equal to nR/P.

[§]William Thomson, Lord Kelvin (1824–1907). Scottish mathematician and physicist. Kelvin did important work in many branches of physics.

Just as we did for pressure-volume relationships at constant temperature, we can compare two sets of volume-temperature conditions for a given sample of gas at constant pressure. From Equation (5.3) we can write

$$\frac{V_1}{T_1} = k_2 = \frac{V_2}{T_2}$$

or
$$\frac{V_1}{T_1} = \frac{V_2}{T_2} \qquad (5.4)$$

where V_1 and V_2 are the volumes of the gas at temperatures T_1 and T_2 (both in kelvins), respectively.

Another form of Charles's law shows that at constant amount of gas and volume, the pressure of a gas is proportional to temperature

$$P \propto T$$
$$P = k_3 T$$

or
$$\frac{P}{T} = k_3 \qquad (5.5)$$

From Figure 5.6 we see that $k_3 = nR/V$. Starting with Equation (5.5), we have

$$\frac{P_1}{T_1} = k_3 = \frac{P_2}{T_2}$$

or
$$\frac{P_1}{T_1} = \frac{P_2}{T_2} \qquad (5.6)$$

where P_1 and P_2 are the pressures of the gas at temperatures T_1 and T_2, respectively.

The Volume-Amount Relationship: Avogadro's Law

Avogadro's name first appeared in Section 3.2.

The work of the Italian scientist Amedeo Avogadro complemented the studies of Boyle, Charles, and Gay-Lussac. In 1811 he published a hypothesis stating that at the same temperature and pressure, equal volumes of different gases contain the same number of molecules (or atoms if the gas is monatomic). It follows that the volume of any given gas must be proportional to the number of moles of molecules present; that is,

$$V \propto n$$
$$V = k_4 n \qquad (5.7)$$

where n represents the number of moles and k_4 is the proportionality constant. Equation (5.7) is the mathematical expression of **Avogadro's law,** which states that *at constant pressure and temperature, the volume of a gas is directly proportional to the number of moles of the gas present.* From Figure 5.6 we see that $k_4 = RT/P$.

According to Avogadro's law we see that when two gases react with each other, their reacting volumes have a simple ratio to each other. If the product is a gas, its volume is related to the volume of the reactants by a simple ratio (a fact demonstrated earlier by Gay-Lussac). For example, consider the synthesis of ammonia from molecular hydrogen and molecular nitrogen:

Interactivity: Volume in Gas Laws
Online Learning Center, Interactives

$$3H_2(g) + N_2(g) \longrightarrow 2\,NH_3(g)$$

3 mol   1 mol   2 mol

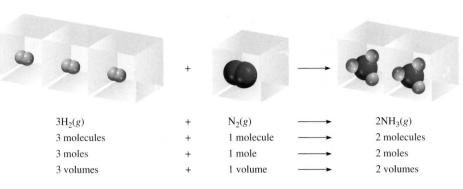

Figure 5.10 *Volume relationship of gases in a chemical reaction. The ratio of the volumes of molecular hydrogen to molecular nitrogen is 3:1, and that of ammonia (the product) to molecular hydrogen and molecular nitrogen combined (the reactants) is 2:4, or 1:2.*

$3H_2(g)$	+	$N_2(g)$ ⟶	$2NH_3(g)$
3 molecules	+	1 molecule ⟶	2 molecules
3 moles	+	1 mole ⟶	2 moles
3 volumes	+	1 volume ⟶	2 volumes

Because, at the same temperature and pressure, the volumes of gases are directly proportional to the number of moles of the gases present, we can now write

$$3H_2(g) + N_2(g) \longrightarrow 2NH_3(g)$$
$$\text{3 volumes} \quad \text{1 volume} \qquad \text{2 volumes}$$

The volume ratio of molecular hydrogen to molecular nitrogen is $3:1$, and that of ammonia (the product) to molecular hydrogen and molecular nitrogen (the reactants) combined is $2:4$, or $1:2$ (Figure 5.10).

5.4 The Ideal Gas Equation

Let us summarize the gas laws we have discussed so far:

$$\text{Boyle's law: } V \propto \frac{1}{P} \quad \text{(at constant } n \text{ and } T\text{)}$$
$$\text{Charles's law: } V \propto T \quad \text{(at constant } n \text{ and } P\text{)}$$
$$\text{Avogadro's law: } V \propto n \quad \text{(at constant } P \text{ and } T\text{)}$$

We can combine all three expressions to form a single master equation for the behavior of gases:

$$V \propto \frac{nT}{P}$$
$$V = R\frac{nT}{P}$$

or

$$PV = nRT \qquad (5.8)$$

where *R, the proportionality constant,* is called the **gas constant.** Equation (5.8), which is called the ***ideal gas equation,*** *describes the relationship among the four variables P, V, T, and n. An **ideal gas** is a hypothetical gas whose pressure-volume-temperature behavior can be completely accounted for by the ideal gas equation.* The molecules of an ideal gas do not attract or repel one another, and their volume is negligible compared with the volume of the container. Although there is no such thing in nature as an ideal gas, discrepancies in the behavior of real gases over reasonable temperature and pressure ranges do not significantly affect calculations. Thus we can safely use the ideal gas equation to solve many gas problems.

Interactivity: Primary
Gas Laws
Online Learning Center,
Interactives

Keep in mind that the ideal gas equation, unlike the gas laws discussed in Section 5.3, applies to systems that do not undergo changes in pressure, volume, temperature, and amount of a gas.

Figure 5.11 *A comparison of the molar volume at STP (which is about 22.4 L) with a basketball.*

Before we can apply the ideal gas equation to a real system, we must evaluate the gas constant R. At 0°C (273.15 K) and 1 atm pressure, many real gases behave like an ideal gas. Experiments show that under these conditions, 1 mole of an ideal gas occupies 22.414 L, which is somewhat greater than the volume of a basketball, as shown in Figure 5.11. *The conditions 0°C and 1 atm are called **standard temperature and pressure,** often abbreviated **STP.*** From Equation (5.8) we can write

The gas constant can be expressed in different units (see Appendix 2).

$$R = \frac{PV}{nT}$$
$$= \frac{(1 \text{ atm})(22.414 \text{ L})}{(1 \text{ mol})(273.15 \text{ K})}$$
$$= 0.082057 \frac{\text{L} \cdot \text{atm}}{\text{K} \cdot \text{mol}}$$
$$= 0.082057 \text{ L} \cdot \text{atm}/\text{K} \cdot \text{mol}$$

The dots between L and atm and between K and mol remind us that both L and atm are in the numerator and both K and mol are in the denominator. For most calculations, we will round off the value of R to three significant figures (0.0821 L · atm/K · mol) and use 22.41 L for the molar volume of a gas at STP.

Example 5.3 shows that if we know the quantity, volume, and temperature of a gas, we can calculate its pressure using the ideal gas equation. Unless otherwise stated, we assume that the temperatures given in °C in calculations are exact so that they do not affect the number of significant figures.

Example 5.3

Sulfur hexafluoride (SF_6) is a colorless, odorless, very unreactive gas. Calculate the pressure (in atm) exerted by 1.82 moles of the gas in a steel vessel of volume 5.43 L at 69.5°C.

Strategy The problem gives the amount of the gas and its volume and temperature. Is the gas undergoing a change in any of its properties? What equation should we use to solve for the pressure? What temperature unit should we use?

Solution Because no changes in gas properties occur, we can use the ideal gas equation to calculate the pressure. Rearranging Equation (5.8), we write

SF_6

(Continued)

$$P = \frac{nRT}{V}$$

$$= \frac{(1.82 \text{ mol})(0.0821 \text{ L} \cdot \text{atm/K} \cdot \text{mol})(69.5 + 273) \text{ K}}{5.43 \text{ L}}$$

$$= 9.42 \text{ atm}$$

Similar problem: 5.32.

Practice Exercise Calculate the volume (in liters) occupied by 2.12 moles of nitric oxide (NO) at 6.54 atm and 76°C.

By using the fact that the molar volume of a gas occupies 22.41 L at STP, we can calculate the volume of a gas at STP without using the ideal gas equation.

Example 5.4

Calculate the volume (in liters) occupied by 7.40 g of NH_3 at STP.

Strategy What is the volume of one mole of an ideal gas at STP? How many moles are there in 7.40 g of NH_3?

Solution Recognizing that 1 mole of an ideal gas occupies 22.41 L at STP and using the molar mass of NH_3 (17.03 g), we write the sequence of conversions as

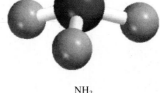

NH_3

$$\text{grams of } NH_3 \longrightarrow \text{moles of } NH_3 \longrightarrow \text{liters of } NH_3 \text{ at STP}$$

so the volume of NH_3 is given by

$$V = 7.40 \text{ g } NH_3 \times \frac{1 \text{ mol } NH_3}{17.03 \text{ g } NH_3} \times \frac{22.41 \text{ L}}{1 \text{ mol } NH_3}$$

$$= 9.74 \text{ L}$$

It is often true in chemistry, particularly in gas-law calculations, that a problem can be solved in more than one way. Here the problem can also be solved by first converting 7.40 g of NH_3 to number of moles of NH_3, and then applying the ideal gas equation ($V = nRT/P$). Try it.

Check Because 7.40 g of NH_3 is smaller than its molar mass, its volume at STP should be smaller than 22.41 L. Therefore, the answer is reasonable.

Similar problem: 5.40.

Practice Exercise What is the volume (in liters) occupied by 49.8 g of HCl at STP?

The ideal gas equation is useful for problems that do not involve changes in P, V, T, and n for a gas sample. At times, however, we need to deal with changes in pressure, volume, and temperature, or even in the amount of a gas. When conditions change, we must employ a modified form of the ideal gas equation that takes into account the initial and final conditions. We derive the modified equation as follows. From Equation (5.8),

$$R = \frac{P_1 V_1}{n_1 T_1} \text{ (before change)} \quad \text{and} \quad R = \frac{P_2 V_2}{n_2 T_2} \text{ (after change)}$$

The subscripts 1 and 2 denote the initial and final states of the gas.

Therefore

$$\frac{P_1 V_1}{n_1 T_1} = R = \frac{P_2 V_2}{n_2 T_2} \qquad (5.9)$$

If $n_1 = n_2$, as is usually the case because the amount of gas normally does not change, the equation then becomes

$$\frac{P_1V_1}{T_1} = \frac{P_2V_2}{T_2} \tag{5.10}$$

Applications of Equation (5.10) are the subject of Examples 5.5, 5.6, and 5.7.

Example 5.5

A scientific research helium balloon.

An inflated helium balloon with a volume of 0.55 L at sea level (1.0 atm) is allowed to rise to a height of 6.5 km, where the pressure is about 0.40 atm. Assuming that the temperature remains constant, what is the final volume of the balloon?

Strategy The amount of gas inside the balloon and its temperature remain constant, but both the pressure and the volume change. What gas law do you need?

Solution We start with Equation (5.10)

$$\frac{P_1V_1}{n_1T_1} = \frac{P_2V_2}{n_2T_2}$$

Because $n_1 = n_2$ and $T_1 = T_2$,

$$P_1V_1 = P_2V_2$$

which is Boyle's law [see Equation (5.2)]. The given information is tabulated:

Initial Conditions	Final Conditions
$P_1 = 1.0$ atm	$P_2 = 0.40$ atm
$V_1 = 0.55$ L	$V_2 = ?$

Therefore,

$$V_2 = V_1 \times \frac{P_1}{P_2}$$

$$= 0.55 \text{ L} \times \frac{1.0 \text{ atm}}{0.40 \text{ atm}}$$

$$= 1.4 \text{ L}$$

Similar problem: 5.19.

Check When pressure applied on the balloon is reduced (at constant temperature), the helium gas expands and the balloon's volume increases. The final volume is greater than the initial volume, so the answer is reasonable.

Practice Exercise A sample of chlorine gas occupies a volume of 946 mL at a pressure of 726 mmHg. Calculate the pressure of the gas (in mmHg) if the volume is reduced at constant temperature to 154 mL.

Example 5.6

Electric lightbulbs are usually filled with argon.

Argon is an inert gas used in lightbulbs to retard the vaporization of the tungsten filament. A certain lightbulb containing argon at 1.20 atm and 18°C is heated to 85°C at constant volume. Calculate its final pressure (in atm).

(Continued)

Strategy The temperature and pressure of argon change but the amount and volume of gas remain the same. What equation would you use to solve for the final pressure? What temperature unit should you use?

Solution Because $n_1 = n_2$ and $V_1 = V_2$, Equation (5.10) becomes

$$\frac{P_1}{T_1} = \frac{P_2}{T_2}$$

which is Charles's law [see Equation (5.6)]. Next we write

Initial Conditions	Final Conditions
$P_1 = 1.20$ atm	$P_2 = ?$
$T_1 = (18 + 273)$ K $= 291$ K	$T_2 = (85 + 273)$ K $= 358$ K

The final pressure is given by

$$P_2 = P_1 \times \frac{T_2}{T_1}$$

$$= 1.20 \text{ atm} \times \frac{358 \text{ K}}{291 \text{ K}}$$

$$= 1.48 \text{ atm}$$

Remember to convert °C to K when solving gas-law problems.

Check At constant volume, the pressure of a given amount of gas is directly proportional to its absolute temperature. Therefore the increase in pressure is reasonable.

Practice Exercise A sample of oxygen gas initially at 0.97 atm is cooled from 21°C to −68°C at constant volume. What is its final pressure (in atm)?

One practical consequence of this relationship is that automobile tire pressures should be checked only when the tires are at normal temperatures. After a long drive (especially in the summer), tires become quite hot, and the air pressure inside them rises.

Similar problem: 5.36.

Example 5.7

A small bubble rises from the bottom of a lake, where the temperature and pressure are 8°C and 6.4 atm, to the water's surface, where the temperature is 25°C and the pressure is 1.0 atm. Calculate the final volume (in mL) of the bubble if its initial volume was 2.1 mL.

Strategy In solving this kind of problem, where a lot of information is given, it is sometimes helpful to make a sketch of the situation, as shown here:

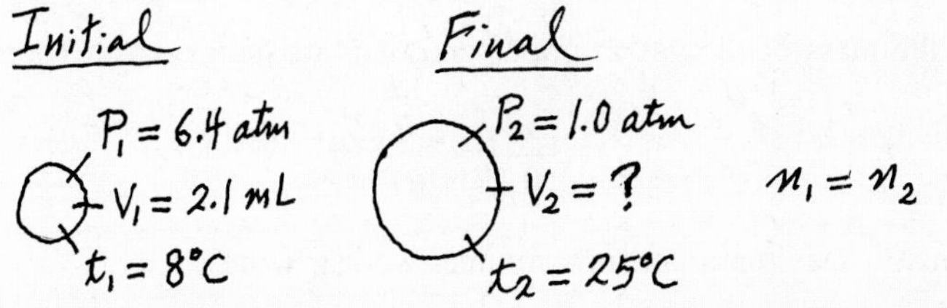

Initial

$P_1 = 6.4$ atm
$V_1 = 2.1$ mL
$t_1 = 8°C$

Final

$P_2 = 1.0$ atm
$V_2 = ?$
$t_2 = 25°C$

$n_1 = n_2$

What temperature unit should be used in the calculation?

Solution According to Equation (5.9)

$$\frac{P_1 V_1}{n_1 T_1} = \frac{P_2 V_2}{n_2 T_2}$$

(Continued)

We assume that the amount of air in the bubble remains constant, that is, $n_1 = n_2$ so that

$$\frac{P_1 V_1}{T_1} = \frac{P_2 V_2}{T_2}$$

which is Equation (5.10). The given information is summarized:

	Initial Conditions	Final Conditions
	$P_1 = 6.4$ atm	$P_2 = 1.0$ atm
	$V_1 = 2.1$ mL	$V_2 = ?$
	$T_1 = (8 + 273)$ K = 281 K	$T_2 = (25 + 273)$ K = 298 K

We can use any appropriate units for volume (or pressure) as long as we use the same units on both sides of the equation.

Rearranging Equation (5.10) gives

$$V_2 = V_1 \times \frac{P_1}{P_2} \times \frac{T_2}{T_1}$$
$$= 2.1 \text{ mL} \times \frac{6.4 \text{ atm}}{1.0 \text{ atm}} \times \frac{298 \text{ K}}{281 \text{ K}}$$
$$= 14 \text{ mL}$$

Check We see that the final volume involves multiplying the initial volume by a ratio of pressures (P_1/P_2) and a ratio of temperatures (T_2/T_1). Recall that volume is inversely proportional to pressure, and volume is directly proportional to temperature. Because the pressure decreases and temperature increases as the bubble rises, we expect the bubble's volume to increase. In fact, here the change in pressure plays a greater role in the volume change.

Similar problem: 5.35.

Practice Exercise A gas initially at 4.0 L, 1.2 atm, and 66°C undergoes a change so that its final volume and temperature are 1.7 L and 42°C. What is its final pressure? Assume the number of moles remains unchanged.

Density Calculations

If we rearrange the ideal gas equation, we can calculate the density of a gas:

$$\frac{n}{V} = \frac{P}{RT}$$

The number of moles of the gas, n, is given by

$$n = \frac{m}{\mathcal{M}}$$

where m is the mass of the gas in grams and $\mathcal{M}$ is its molar mass. Therefore

$$\frac{m}{\mathcal{M}V} = \frac{P}{RT}$$

Because density, d, is mass per unit volume, we can write

$$d = \frac{m}{V} = \frac{P\mathcal{M}}{RT} \tag{5.11}$$

Unlike molecules in condensed matter (that is, in liquids and solids), gaseous molecules are separated by distances that are large compared with their size. Consequently, the density of gases is very low under atmospheric conditions. For this reason, gas densities are usually expressed in grams per liter (g/L) rather than grams per milliliter (g/mL), as Example 5.8 shows.

Example 5.8

Calculate the density of carbon dioxide (CO_2) in grams per liter (g/L) at 0.990 atm and 55°C.

CO_2

Strategy We need Equation (5.11) to calculate gas density. Is sufficient information provided in the problem? What temperature unit should be used?

Solution To use Equation (5.11), we convert temperature to kelvins ($T = 273 + 55 = 328$ K) and use 44.01 g for the molar mass of CO_2:

$$d = \frac{P\mathcal{M}}{RT}$$

$$= \frac{(0.990 \text{ atm})(44.01 \text{ g/mol})}{(0.0821 \text{ L} \cdot \text{atm/K} \cdot \text{mol})(328 \text{ K})} = 1.62 \text{ g/L}$$

Alternatively, we can solve for the density by writing

$$\text{density} = \frac{\text{mass}}{\text{volume}}$$

Assuming that we have 1 mole of CO_2, the mass is 44.01 g. The volume of the gas can be obtained from the ideal gas equation

$$V = \frac{nRT}{P}$$

$$= \frac{(1 \text{ mol})(0.0821 \text{ L} \cdot \text{atm/K} \cdot \text{mol})(328 \text{ K})}{0.990 \text{ atm}}$$

$$= 27.2 \text{ L}$$

Therefore, the density of CO_2 is given by

$$d = \frac{44.01 \text{ g}}{27.2 \text{ L}} = 1.62 \text{ g/L}$$

Comment In units of grams per milliliter, the gas density is 1.62×10^{-3} g/mL, which is a very small number. In comparison, the density of water is 1.0 g/mL and that of gold is 19.3 g/cm^3.

Similar problem: 5.48.

Practice Exercise What is the density (in g/L) of uranium hexafluoride (UF_6) at 779 mmHg and 62°C?

The Molar Mass of a Gaseous Substance

From what we have said so far, you may have the impression that the molar mass of a substance is found by examining its formula and summing the molar masses of its component atoms. However, this procedure works only if the actual formula of the substance is known. In practice, chemists often deal with substances of unknown or only partially defined composition. If the unknown substance is gaseous, its molar mass can nevertheless be found thanks to the ideal gas equation. All that is needed is an experimentally determined density value (or mass and volume data) for the gas at a known temperature and pressure. By rearranging Equation (5.11) we get

$$\mathcal{M} = \frac{dRT}{P} \qquad (5.12)$$

182   Gases

Figure 5.12 *An apparatus for measuring the density of a gas. A bulb of known volume is filled with the gas under study at a certain temperature and pressure. First the bulb is weighed, and then it is emptied (evacuated) and weighed again. The difference in masses gives the mass of the gas. Knowing the volume of the bulb, we can calculate the density of the gas. Under atmospheric conditions,100 mL of air weigh about 0.12 g, an easily measured quantity.*

In a typical experiment, a bulb of known volume is filled with the gaseous substance under study. The temperature and pressure of the gas sample are recorded, and the total mass of the bulb plus gas sample is determined (Figure 5.12). The bulb is then evacuated (emptied) and weighed again. The difference in mass is the mass of the gas. The density of the gas is equal to its mass divided by the volume of the bulb. Once we know the density of a gas, we can calculate the molar mass of the substance using Equation (5.12). Of course, a mass spectrometer would be the ideal instrument to determine the molar mass, but not every chemist can afford one.

Example 5.9 shows the density method for molar mass determination.

Example 5.9

A chemist has synthesized a greenish-yellow gaseous compound of chlorine and oxygen and finds that its density is 7.71 g/L at 36°C and 2.88 atm. Calculate the molar mass of the compound and determine its molecular formula.

Strategy Because Equations (5.11) and (5.12) are rearrangements of each other, we can calculate the molar mass of a gas if we know its density, temperature, and pressure. The molecular formula of the compound must be consistent with its molar mass. What temperature unit should we use?

Solution From Equation (5.12)

$$\mathcal{M} = \frac{dRT}{P}$$
$$= \frac{(7.71 \text{ g/L})(0.0821 \text{ L} \cdot \text{atm/K} \cdot \text{mol})(36 + 273) \text{ K}}{2.88 \text{ atm}}$$
$$= 67.9 \text{ g/mol}$$

Alternatively, we can solve for the molar mass by writing

$$\text{molar mass of compound} = \frac{\text{mass of compound}}{\text{moles of compound}}$$

We assume that there is 1.00 L of the gas so the mass of the gas is 7.71 g. The number of moles of the gas can be obtained from the ideal gas equation

$$n = \frac{PV}{RT}$$
$$= \frac{(2.88 \text{ atm})(1.00 \text{ L})}{(0.0821 \text{ L} \cdot \text{atm/K} \cdot \text{mol})(309 \text{ K})}$$
$$= 0.1135 \text{ mol}$$

Therefore, the molar mass is given by

$$\mathcal{M} = \frac{7.71 \text{ g}}{0.1135 \text{ mol}} = 67.9 \text{ g/mol}$$

We can determine the molecular formula of the compound by trial and error, using only the knowledge of the molar masses of chlorine (35.45 g) and oxygen (16.00 g). We know that a compound containing one Cl atom and one O atom would have a molar mass of 51.45 g, which is too low, while the molar mass of a compound made up of two

ClO$_2$

(Continued)

Cl atoms and one O atom is 86.90 g, which is too high. Thus the compound must contain one Cl atom and two O atoms and have the formula ClO_2, which has a molar mass of 67.45 g.

Similar problems: 5.43, 5.47.

Practice Exercise The density of a gaseous organic compound is 3.38 g/L at 40°C and 1.97 atm. What is its molar mass?

Because Equation (5.12) is derived from the ideal gas equation, we can also calculate the molar mass of a gaseous substance using the ideal gas equation, as shown in Example 5.10.

Example 5.10

Chemical analysis of a gaseous compound showed that it contained 33.0 percent silicon (Si) and 67.0 percent fluorine (F) by mass. At 35°C, 0.210 L of the compound exerted a pressure of 1.70 atm. If the mass of 0.210 L of the compound was 2.38 g, calculate the molecular formula of the compound.

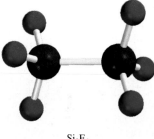

Si_2F_6

Strategy This problem can be divided into two parts. First, it asks for the empirical formula of the compound from the percent by mass of Si and F. Second, the information provided enables us to calculate the molar mass of the compound and hence determine its molecular formula. What is the relationship between empirical molar mass and molar mass calculated from the molecular formula?

Solution We follow the procedure in Example 3.9 (p. 86) to calculate the empirical formula by assuming that we have 100 g of the compound, so the percentages are converted to grams. The number of moles of Si and F are given by

$$n_{Si} = 33.0 \text{ g Si} \times \frac{1 \text{ mol Si}}{28.09 \text{ g Si}} = 1.17 \text{ mol Si}$$

$$n_F = 67.0 \text{ g F} \times \frac{1 \text{ mol F}}{19.00 \text{ g F}} = 3.53 \text{ mol F}$$

Therefore, the empirical formula is $Si_{1.17}F_{3.53}$, or SiF_3.

To calculate the molar mass of the compound, we need first to calculate the number of moles contained in 2.38 g of the compound. From the ideal gas equation

$$n = \frac{PV}{RT}$$

$$= \frac{(1.70 \text{ atm})(0.210 \text{ L})}{(0.0821 \text{ L} \cdot \text{atm/K} \cdot \text{mol})(308 \text{ K})} = 0.0141 \text{ mol}$$

Because there are 2.38 g in 0.0141 mole of the compound, the mass in 1 mole, or the molar mass, is given by

$$\mathcal{M} = \frac{2.38 \text{ g}}{0.0141 \text{ mol}} = 169 \text{ g/mol}$$

The molar mass of the empirical formula SiF_3 is 85.09 g. Recall that the ratio (molar mass/empirical molar mass) is always an integer (169/85.09 ≈ 2). Therefore, the molecular formula of the compound must be $(SiF_3)_2$ or Si_2F_6.

Similar problem: 5.49.

Practice Exercise A gaseous compound is 78.14 percent boron and 21.86 percent hydrogen. At 27°C, 74.3 mL of the gas exerted a pressure of 1.12 atm. If the mass of the gas was 0.0934 g, what is its molecular formula?

5.5 Gas Stoichiometry

In Chapter 3 we used relationships between amounts (in moles) and masses (in grams) of reactants and products to solve stoichiometry problems. When the reactants and/or products are gases, we can also use the relationships between amounts (moles, n) and volume (V) to solve such problems (Figure 5.13). Examples 5.11, 5.12, and 5.13 show how the gas laws are used in these calculations.

Figure 5.13 *Stoichiometric calculations involving gases.*

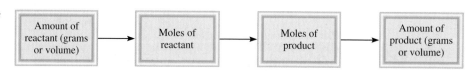

| Amount of reactant (grams or volume) | → | Moles of reactant | → | Moles of product | → | Amount of product (grams or volume) |

The reaction of calcium carbide (CaC₂) with water produces acetylene, a flammable gas.

Similar problem: 5.26.

Example 5.11

Calculate the volume of O_2 (in liters) at STP required for the complete combustion of 7.64 L of acetylene (C_2H_2) at STP:

$$2C_2H_2(g) + 5O_2(g) \longrightarrow 4CO_2(g) + 2H_2O(l)$$

Strategy Note that the temperature and pressure of O_2 and C_2H_2 are the same. Which gas law do we need to relate the volume of the gases to the moles of gases?

Solution According to Avogadro's law, at the same temperature and pressure, the number of moles of gases are directly related to their volumes. From the equation we have 5 mol $O_2 \simeq$ 2 mol C_2H_2; therefore, we can also write 5 L $O_2 \simeq$ 2 L C_2H_2. The volume of O_2 that will react with 7.64 L C_2H_2 is given by

$$\text{volume of } O_2 = 7.64 \text{ L } C_2H_2 \times \frac{5 \text{ L } O_2}{2 \text{ L } C_2H_2}$$
$$= 19.1 \text{ L}$$

Practice Exercise Assuming no change in temperature and pressure, calculate the volume of O_2 (in liters) required for the complete combustion of 14.9 L of butane (C_4H_{10}):

$$2C_4H_{10}(g) + 13O_2(g) \longrightarrow 8CO_2(g) + 10H_2O(l)$$

Example 5.12

Sodium azide (NaN_3) is used in some automobile air bags. The impact of a collision triggers the decomposition of NaN_3 as follows:

$$2NaN_3(s) \longrightarrow 2Na(s) + 3N_2(g)$$

The nitrogen gas produced quickly inflates the bag between the driver and the windshield and dashboard. Calculate the volume of N_2 generated at 80°C and 823 mmHg by the decomposition of 60.0 g of NaN_3.

(Continued)

Strategy From the balanced equation we see that 2 mol $NaN_3 \simeq$ 3 mol N_2 so the conversion factor between NaN_3 and N_2 is

$$\frac{3 \text{ mol } N_2}{2 \text{ mol } NaN_3}$$

Because the mass of NaN_3 is given, we can calculate the number of moles of NaN_3 and hence the number of moles of N_2 produced. Finally, we can calculate the volume of N_2 using the ideal gas equation.

Solution First we calculate the number of moles of N_2 produced by 60.0 g NaN_3 using the following sequence of conversions

$$\text{grams of } NaN_3 \longrightarrow \text{moles of } NaN_3 \longrightarrow \text{moles of } N_2$$

so that

$$\text{moles of } N_2 = 60.0 \text{ g } NaN_3 \times \frac{1 \text{ mol } NaN_3}{65.02 \text{ g } NaN_3} \times \frac{3 \text{ mol } N_2}{2 \text{ mol } NaN_3}$$

$$= 1.38 \text{ mol } N_2$$

The volume of 1.38 moles of N_2 can be obtained by using the ideal gas equation:

$$V = \frac{nRT}{P} = \frac{(1.38 \text{ mol})(0.0821 \text{ L} \cdot \text{atm/K} \cdot \text{mol})(80 + 273 \text{ K})}{(823/760) \text{ atm}}$$

$$= 36.9 \text{ L}$$

An air bag can protect the driver in an automobile collision.

Similar problem: 5.60.

Practice Exercise The equation for the metabolic breakdown of glucose ($C_6H_{12}O_6$) is the same as the equation for the combustion of glucose in air:

$$C_6H_{12}O_6(s) + 6O_2(g) \longrightarrow 6CO_2(g) + 6H_2O(l)$$

Calculate the volume of CO_2 produced at 37°C and 1.00 atm when 5.60 g of glucose is used up in the reaction.

Example 5.13

Aqueous lithium hydroxide solution is used to purify air in spacecrafts and submarines because it absorbs carbon dioxide, which is an end product of metabolism, according to the equation

$$2LiOH(aq) + CO_2(g) \longrightarrow Li_2CO_3(aq) + H_2O(l)$$

The pressure of carbon dioxide inside the cabin of a submarine having a volume of 2.4×10^5 L is 7.9×10^{-3} atm at 312 K. A solution of lithium hydroxide (LiOH) of negligible volume is introduced into the cabin. Eventually the pressure of CO_2 falls to 1.2×10^{-4} atm. How many grams of lithium carbonate are formed by this process?

The air in submerged submarines and space vehicles needs to be purified continously.

Strategy How do we calculate the number of moles of CO_2 reacted from the drop in CO_2 pressure? What is the conversion factor between CO_2 and Li_2CO_3?

Solution First we calculate the number of moles of CO_2 consumed in the reaction. The drop in CO_2 pressure, which is $(7.9 \times 10^{-3} \text{ atm}) - (1.2 \times 10^{-4} \text{ atm})$, or 7.8×10^{-3} atm, corresponds to the consumption of CO_2. Using the ideal gas equation, we write

(Continued)

$$n = \frac{PV}{RT}$$

$$= \frac{(7.8 \times 10^{-3} \text{ atm})(2.4 \times 10^5 \text{ L})}{(0.0821 \text{ L} \cdot \text{atm/K} \cdot \text{mol})(312 \text{ K})} = 73 \text{ mol}$$

From the chemical equation we see that 1 mol $CO_2 \cong$ 1 mol Li_2CO_3, so the amount of Li_2CO_3 formed is also 73 moles. Then, with the molar mass of Li_2CO_3 (73.89 g), we calculate its mass:

Similar problem: 5.99.

$$\text{mass of } Li_2CO_3 \text{ formed} = 73 \text{ mol } Li_2CO_3 \times \frac{73.89 \text{ g } Li_2CO_3}{1 \text{ mol } Li_2CO_3}$$

$$= 5.4 \times 10^3 \text{ g } Li_2CO_3$$

Practice Exercise A 2.14-L sample of hydrogen chloride (HCl) gas at 2.61 atm and 28°C is completely dissolved in 668 mL of water to form hydrochloric acid solution. Calculate the molarity of the acid solution. Assume no change in volume.

5.6 Dalton's Law of Partial Pressures

Thus far we have concentrated on the behavior of pure gaseous substances, but experimental studies very often involve mixtures of gases. For example, for a study of air pollution, we may be interested in the pressure-volume-temperature relationship of a sample of air, which contains several gases. In this case, and all cases involving mixtures of gases, the total gas pressure is related to *partial pressures,* that is, *the pressures of individual gas components in the mixture.* In 1801 Dalton formulated a law, now known as *Dalton's law of partial pressures,* which states that *the total pressure of a mixture of gases is just the sum of the pressures that each gas would exert if it were present alone.* Figure 5.14 illustrates Dalton's law.

Consider a case in which two gases, A and B, are in a container of volume *V.* The pressure exerted by gas A, according to the ideal gas equation, is

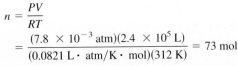

Interactivity: Dalton's Law
Online Learning Center, Interactives

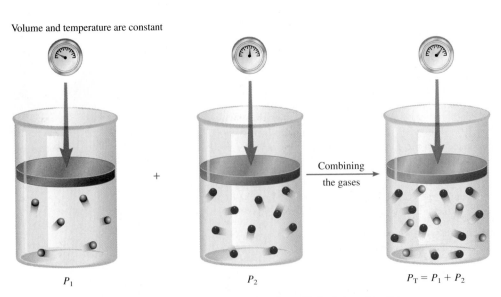

Volume and temperature are constant

P_1 + P_2 Combining the gases → $P_T = P_1 + P_2$

Figure 5.14 *Schematic illustration of Dalton's law of partial pressures.*

$$P_A = \frac{n_A RT}{V}$$

where n_A is the number of moles of A present. Similarly, the pressure exerted by gas B is

$$P_B = \frac{n_B RT}{V}$$

In a mixture of gases A and B, the total pressure P_T is the result of the collisions of both types of molecules, A and B, with the walls of the container. Thus, according to Dalton's law,

$$\begin{aligned} P_T &= P_A + P_B \\ &= \frac{n_A RT}{V} + \frac{n_B RT}{V} \\ &= \frac{RT}{V}(n_A + n_B) \\ &= \frac{nRT}{V} \end{aligned}$$

where n, the total number of moles of gases present, is given by $n = n_A + n_B$, and P_A and P_B are the partial pressures of gases A and B, respectively. For a mixture of gases, then, P_T depends only on the total number of moles of gas present, not on the nature of the gas molecules.

In general, the total pressure of a mixture of gases is given by

$$P_T = P_1 + P_2 + P_3 + \cdots$$

where $P_1, P_2, P_3, \ldots$ are the partial pressures of components 1, 2, 3, ... To see how each partial pressure is related to the total pressure, consider again the case of a mixture of two gases A and B. Dividing P_A by P_T, we obtain

$$\begin{aligned} \frac{P_A}{P_T} &= \frac{n_A RT/V}{(n_A + n_B)RT/V} \\ &= \frac{n_A}{n_A + n_B} \\ &= X_A \end{aligned}$$

where X_A is called the mole fraction of A. The **mole fraction** is *a dimensionless quantity that expresses the ratio of the number of moles of one component to the number of moles of all components present.* In general, the mole fraction of component i in a mixture is given by

$$X_i = \frac{n_i}{n_T} \tag{5.13}$$

where n_i and n_T are the number of moles of component i and the total number of moles present, respectively. The mole fraction is always smaller than 1. We can now express the partial pressure of A as

$$P_A = X_A P_T$$

Similarly,

$$P_B = X_B P_T$$

Note that the sum of the mole fractions for a mixture of gases must be unity. If only two components are present, then

$$X_A + X_B = \frac{n_A}{n_A + n_B} + \frac{n_B}{n_A + n_B} = 1$$

If a system contains more than two gases, then the partial pressure of the ith component is related to the total pressure by

$$P_i = X_i P_T \qquad (5.14)$$

How are partial pressures determined? A manometer can measure only the total pressure of a gaseous mixture. To obtain the partial pressures, we need to know the mole fractions of the components, which would involve elaborate chemical analyses. The most direct method of measuring partial pressures is using a mass spectrometer. The relative intensities of the peaks in a mass spectrum are directly proportional to the amounts, and hence to the mole fractions, of the gases present.

From mole fractions and total pressure, we can calculate the partial pressures of individual components, as Example 5.14 shows. A direct application of Dalton's law of partial pressures to scuba diving is discussed in the Chemistry in Action essay on p. 192.

Example 5.14

A mixture of gases contains 4.46 moles of neon (Ne), 0.74 mole of argon (Ar), and 2.15 moles of xenon (Xe). Calculate the partial pressures of the gases if the total pressure is 2.00 atm at a certain temperature.

Strategy What is the relationship between the partial pressure of a gas and the total gas pressure? How do we calculate the mole fraction of a gas?

Solution According to Equation (5.14), the partial pressure of Ne (P_{Ne}) is equal to the product of its mole fraction (X_{Ne}) and the total pressure (P_T)

$$\overset{\text{want to calculate}}{P_{Ne}} = \overset{\text{need to find}}{X_{Ne}} \overset{\text{given}}{P_T}$$

Using Equation (5.13), we calculate the mole fraction of Ne as follows:

$$X_{Ne} = \frac{n_{Ne}}{n_{Ne} + n_{Ar} + n_{Xe}} = \frac{4.46 \text{ mol}}{4.46 \text{ mol} + 0.74 \text{ mol} + 2.15 \text{ mol}} = 0.607$$

Therefore

$$P_{Ne} = X_{Ne} P_T$$
$$= 0.607 \times 2.00 \text{ atm}$$
$$= 1.21 \text{ atm}$$

Similarly,

$$P_{Ar} = X_{Ar} P_T$$
$$= 0.10 \times 2.00 \text{ atm}$$
$$= 0.20 \text{ atm}$$

(Continued)

and
$$P_{Xe} = X_{Xe}P_T$$
$$= 0.293 \times 2.00 \text{ atm}$$
$$= 0.586 \text{ atm}$$

Check Make sure that the sum of the partial pressures is equal to the given total pressure; that is, $(1.21 + 0.20 + 0.586) \text{ atm} = 2.00 \text{ atm}$.

Similar problem: 5.63.

Practice Exercise A sample of natural gas contains 8.24 moles of methane (CH_4), 0.421 mole of ethane (C_2H_6), and 0.116 mole of propane (C_3H_8). If the total pressure of the gases is 1.37 atm, what are the partial pressures of the gases?

Dalton's law of partial pressures is useful for calculating volumes of gases collected over water. For example, when potassium chlorate ($KClO_3$) is heated, it decomposes to KCl and O_2:

Animation: Collecting a Gas over Water
Online Learning Center, Animations

$$2KClO_3(s) \longrightarrow 2KCl(s) + 3O_2(g)$$

The oxygen gas can be collected over water, as shown in Figure 5.15. Initially, the inverted bottle is completely filled with water. As oxygen gas is generated, the gas bubbles rise to the top and displace water from the bottle. This method of collecting a gas is based on the assumptions that the gas does not react with water and that it is not appreciably soluble in it. These assumptions are valid for oxygen gas, but not for gases such as NH_3, which dissolves readily in water. The oxygen gas collected in this way is not pure, however, because water vapor is also present in the bottle. The total gas pressure is equal to the sum of the pressures exerted by the oxygen gas and the water vapor:

$$P_T = P_{O_2} + P_{H_2O}$$

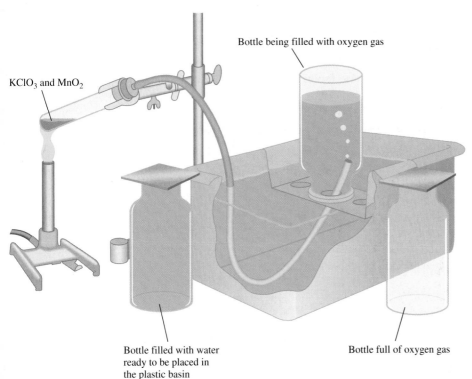

Bottle being filled with oxygen gas

$KClO_3$ and MnO_2

Bottle filled with water ready to be placed in the plastic basin

Bottle full of oxygen gas

Figure 5.15 *An apparatus for collecting gas over water. The oxygen generated by heating potassium chlorate (KClO₃) in the presence of a small amount of manganese dioxide (MnO₂), which speeds up the reaction, is bubbled through water and collected in a bottle as shown. Water originally present in the bottle is pushed into the trough by the oxygen gas.*

Figure 5.16 *The pressure of water vapor as a function of temperature. Note that at the boiling point of water (100°C) the pressure is 760 mmHg, which is exactly equal to 1 atm.*

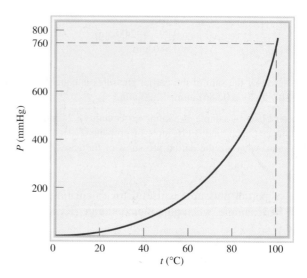

Consequently, we must allow for the pressure caused by the presence of water vapor when we calculate the amount of O_2 generated. Table 5.3 shows the pressure of water vapor at various temperatures. These data are plotted in Figure 5.16.

Example 5.15 shows how to use Dalton's law to calculate the amount of a gas collected over water.

TABLE 5.3

Pressure of Water Vapor at Various Temperatures

Temperature (°C)	Water Vapor Pressure (mmHg)
0	4.58
5	6.54
10	9.21
15	12.79
20	17.54
25	23.76
30	31.82
35	42.18
40	55.32
45	71.88
50	92.51
55	118.04
60	149.38
65	187.54
70	233.7
75	289.1
80	355.1
85	433.6
90	525.76
95	633.90
100	760.00

Example 5.15

Oxygen gas generated by the decomposition of potassium chlorate is collected as shown in Figure 5.15. The volume of oxygen collected at 24°C and atmospheric pressure of 762 mmHg is 128 mL. Calculate the mass (in grams) of oxygen gas obtained. The pressure of the water vapor at 24°C is 22.4 mmHg.

Strategy To solve for the mass of O_2 generated, we must first calculate the partial pressure of O_2 in the mixture. What gas law do we need? How do we convert pressure of O_2 gas to mass of O_2 in grams?

Solution From Dalton's law of partial pressures we know that

$$P_T = P_{O_2} + P_{H_2O}$$

Therefore

$$\begin{aligned} P_{O_2} &= P_T - P_{H_2O} \\ &= 762 \text{ mmHg} - 22.4 \text{ mmHg} \\ &= 740 \text{ mmHg} \end{aligned}$$

From the ideal gas equation we write

$$PV = nRT = \frac{m}{\mathcal{M}}RT$$

where m and $\mathcal{M}$ are the mass of O_2 collected and the molar mass of O_2, respectively. Rearranging the equation we obtain

(Continued)

$$m = \frac{PV\mathcal{M}}{RT} = \frac{(740/760)\text{atm}(0.128\text{ L})(32.00\text{ g/mol})}{(0.0821\text{ L}\cdot\text{atm/K}\cdot\text{mol})(273 + 24)\text{ K}}$$
$$= 0.164\text{ g}$$

Similar problem: 5.68.

Practice Exercise Hydrogen gas generated when calcium metal reacts with water is collected as shown in Figure 5.15. The volume of gas collected at 30°C and pressure of 988 mmHg is 641 mL. What is the mass (in grams) of the hydrogen gas obtained? The pressure of water vapor at 30°C is 31.82 mmHg.

5.7 The Kinetic Molecular Theory of Gases

The gas laws help us to predict the behavior of gases, but they do not explain what happens at the molecular level to cause the changes we observe in the macroscopic world. For example, why does a gas expand on heating?

In the nineteenth century, a number of physicists, notably Ludwig Boltzmann[†] and James Clerk Maxwell,[‡] found that the physical properties of gases can be explained in terms of the motion of individual molecules. This molecular movement is a form of *energy*, which we define as the capacity to do work or to produce change. In mechanics, *work* is defined as force times distance. Because energy can be measured as work, we can write

$$\text{energy} = \text{work done}$$
$$= \text{force} \times \text{distance}$$

The *joule (J)*[§] is *the SI unit of energy*

$$1\text{ J} = 1\text{ kg m}^2/\text{s}^2$$
$$= 1\text{ N m}$$

Alternatively, energy can be expressed in kilojoules (kJ):

$$1\text{ kJ} = 1000\text{ J}$$

As we will see in Chapter 6, there are many different kinds of energy. **Kinetic energy (KE)** is the type of energy expended by a moving object, or *energy of motion*.

The findings of Maxwell, Boltzmann, and others resulted in *a number of generalizations about gas behavior* that have since been known as the **kinetic molecular theory of gases,** or simply the *kinetic theory of gases*. Central to the kinetic theory are the following assumptions:

1. A gas is composed of molecules that are separated from each other by distances far greater than their own dimensions. The molecules can be considered to be "points"; that is, they possess mass but have negligible volume.

[†]Ludwig Eduard Boltzmann (1844–1906). Austrian physicist. Although Boltzmann was one of the greatest theoretical physicists of all time, his work was not recognized by other scientists in his own lifetime. Suffering from poor health and great depression, he committed suicide in 1906.

[‡]James Clerk Maxwell (1831–1879). Scottish physicist. Maxwell was one of the great theoretical physicists of the nineteenth century; his work covered many areas in physics, including kinetic theory of gases, thermodynamics, and electricity and magnetism.

[§]James Prescott Joule (1818–1889). English physicist. As a young man, Joule was tutored by John Dalton. He is most famous for determining the mechanical equivalent of heat, the conversion between mechanical energy and thermal energy.

Scuba Diving and the Gas Laws

Scuba diving is an exhilarating sport, and, thanks in part to the gas laws, it is also a safe activity for trained individuals who are in good health. ("Scuba" is an acronym for self-contained underwater breathing apparatus.) Two applications of the gas laws to this popular pastime are the development of guidelines for returning safely to the surface after a dive and the determination of the proper mix of gases to prevent a potentially fatal condition during a dive.

A typical dive might be 40 to 65 ft, but dives to 90 ft are not uncommon. Because seawater has a slightly higher density than fresh water—about 1.03 g/mL, compared with 1.00 g/mL—the pressure exerted by a column of 33 ft of seawater is equivalent to 1 atm pressure. Pressure increases with increasing depth, so at a depth of 66 ft the pressure of the water will be 2 atm, and so on.

What would happen if a diver rose to the surface from a depth of, say, 20 ft rather quickly without breathing? The total decrease in pressure for this change in depth would be (20 ft/33 ft) × 1 atm, or 0.6 atm. When the diver reached the surface, the volume of air trapped in the lungs would have increased by a factor of (1 + 0.6) atm/1 atm, or 1.6 times. This sudden expansion of air can fatally rupture the membranes of the lungs. Another serious possibility is that an *air embolism* might develop. As air expands in the lungs, it is forced into tiny blood vessels called capillaries. The presence of air bubbles in these vessels can block normal blood flow to the brain. As a result, the diver might lose consciousness before reaching the surface. The only cure for an air embolism is recompression. For this painful process, the victim is placed in a chamber filled with compressed air. Here bubbles in the blood are slowly squeezed down to harmless size over the course of several hours to a day. To avoid these unpleasant complications, divers know they must ascend slowly, pausing at certain points to give their bodies time to adjust to the falling pressure.

Our second example is a direct application of Dalton's law. Oxygen gas is essential for our survival, so it is hard to believe that an excess of oxygen could be harmful. Nevertheless, the toxicity of too much oxygen is well established. For example, newborn infants placed in oxygen tents often sustain damage to the retinal tissue, which can cause partial or total blindness.

Our bodies function best when oxygen gas has a partial pressure of about 0.20 atm, as it does in the air we breathe. The oxygen partial pressure is given by

$$P_{O_2} = X_{O_2}P_T = \frac{n_{O_2}}{n_{O_2} + n_{N_2}}P_T$$

where P_T is the total pressure. However, because volume is directly proportional to the number of moles of gas present (at constant temperature and pressure), we can now write

2. Gas molecules are in constant motion in random directions, and they frequently collide with one another. Collisions among molecules are perfectly elastic. In other words, energy can be transferred from one molecule to another as a result of a collision. Nevertheless, the total energy of all the molecules in a system remains the same.

3. Gas molecules exert neither attractive nor repulsive forces on one another.

4. The average kinetic energy of the molecules is proportional to the temperature of the gas in kelvins. Any two gases at the same temperature will have the same average kinetic energy. The average kinetic energy of a molecule is given by

$$\overline{KE} = \tfrac{1}{2}m\overline{u^2}$$

where m is the mass of the molecule and u is its speed. The horizontal bar denotes an average value. The quantity $\overline{u^2}$ is called mean square speed; it is the average of the square of the speeds of all the molecules:

$$\overline{u^2} = \frac{u_1^2 + u_2^2 + \cdots + u_N^2}{N}$$

where N is the number of molecules.

$$P_{O_2} = \frac{V_{O_2}}{V_{O_2} + V_{N_2}} P_T$$

Thus the composition of air is 20 percent oxygen gas and 80 percent nitrogen gas by volume. When a diver is submerged, the pressure of the water on the diver is greater than atmospheric pressure. The air pressure inside the body cavities (for example, lungs, sinuses) must be the same as the pressure of the surrounding water; otherwise they would collapse. A special valve automatically adjusts the pressure of the air breathed from a scuba tank to ensure that the air pressure equals the water pressure at all times. For example, at a depth where the total pressure is 2.0 atm, the oxygen content in air should be reduced to 10 percent by volume to maintain the same partial pressure of 0.20 atm; that is,

$$P_{O_2} = 0.20 \text{ atm} = \frac{V_{O_2}}{V_{O_2} + V_{N_2}} \times 2.0 \text{ atm}$$

$$\frac{V_{O_2}}{V_{O_2} + V_{N_2}} = \frac{0.20 \text{ atm}}{2.0 \text{ atm}} = 0.10 \text{ or } 10\%$$

Although nitrogen gas may seem to be the obvious choice to mix with oxygen gas, there is a serious problem with it. When the partial pressure of nitrogen gas exceeds 1 atm, enough of the gas dissolves in the blood to cause a condition known as *nitrogen narcosis*. The effects on the diver resemble those associated with alcohol intoxication. Divers suffering from nitrogen narcosis

A scuba diver.

have been known to do strange things, such as dancing on the sea floor and chasing sharks. For this reason, helium is often used to dilute oxygen gas. An inert gas, helium is much less soluble in blood than nitrogen and produces no narcotic effects.

Assumption 4 enables us to write

$$\overline{KE} \propto T$$
$$\tfrac{1}{2}m\overline{u^2} \propto T$$
$$\tfrac{1}{2}m\overline{u^2} = CT \tag{5.15}$$

where C is the proportionality constant and T is the absolute temperature.

According to the kinetic molecular theory, gas pressure is the result of collisions between molecules and the walls of their container. It depends on the frequency of collision per unit area and on how "hard" the molecules strike the wall. The theory also provides a molecular interpretation of temperature. According to Equation (5.15), the absolute temperature of a gas is a measure of the average kinetic energy of the molecules. In other words, the absolute temperature is an index of the random motion of the molecules—the higher the temperature, the more energetic the molecules. Because it is related to the temperature of the gas sample, random molecular motion is sometimes referred to as thermal motion.

Application to the Gas Laws

Although the kinetic theory of gases is based on a rather simple model, the mathematical details involved are very complex. However, on a qualitative basis, it is possible to use the theory to account for the general properties of substances in the gaseous state. The following examples illustrate the range of its utility.

- **Compressibility of Gases.** Because molecules in the gas phase are separated by large distances (assumption 1), gases can be compressed easily to occupy less volume.

- **Boyle's Law.** The pressure exerted by a gas results from the impact of its molecules on the walls of the container. The collision rate, or the number of molecular collisions with the walls per second, is proportional to the number density (that is, number of molecules per unit volume) of the gas. Decreasing the volume of a given amount of gas increases its number density and hence its collision rate. For this reason, the pressure of a gas is inversely proportional to the volume it occupies; as volume decreases, pressure increases and vice versa.

- **Charles's Law.** Because the average kinetic energy of gas molecules is proportional to the sample's absolute temperature (assumption 4), raising the temperature increases the average kinetic energy. Consequently, molecules will collide with the walls of the container more frequently and with greater impact if the gas is heated, and thus the pressure increases. The volume of gas will expand until the gas pressure is balanced by the constant external pressure (see Figure 5.8).

- **Avogadro's Law.** We have shown that the pressure of a gas is directly proportional to both the density and the temperature of the gas. Because the mass of the gas is directly proportional to the number of moles (n) of the gas, we can represent density by n/V. Therefore

$$P \propto \frac{n}{V} T$$

For two gases, 1 and 2, we write

$$P_1 \propto \frac{n_1 T_1}{V_1} = C \frac{n_1 T_1}{V_1}$$
$$P_2 \propto \frac{n_2 T_2}{V_2} = C \frac{n_2 T_2}{V_2}$$

where C is the proportionality constant. Thus, for two gases under the same conditions of pressure, volume, and temperature (that is, when $P_1 = P_2$, $T_1 = T_2$, and $V_1 = V_2$), it follows that $n_1 = n_2$, which is a mathematical expression of Avogadro's law.

- **Dalton's Law of Partial Pressures.** If molecules do not attract or repel one another (assumption 3), then the pressure exerted by one type of molecule is unaffected by the presence of another gas. Consequently, the total pressure is given by the sum of individual gas pressures.

Another way of stating Avogadro's law is that at the same pressure and temperature, equal volumes of gases, whether they are the same or different gases, contain equal numbers of molecules.

Distribution of Molecular Speeds

The kinetic theory of gases enables us to investigate molecular motion in more detail. Suppose we have a large number of gas molecules, say, 1 mole, in a container. As long as we hold the temperature constant, the average kinetic energy and the mean-square speed will remain unchanged as time passes. As you might expect, the motion of the molecules is totally random and unpredictable. At a given instant, how many molecules are moving at a particular speed? To answer this question Maxwell analyzed the behavior of gas molecules at different temperatures.

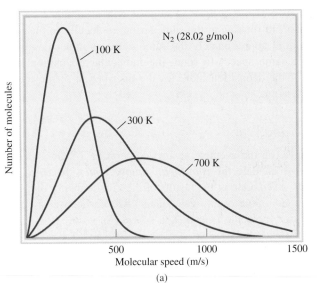

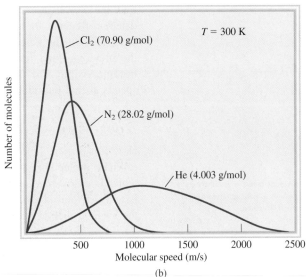

Figure 5.17 *(a) The distribution of speeds for nitrogen gas at three different temperatures. At the higher temperatures, more molecules are moving at faster speeds. (b) The distribution of speeds for three gases at 300 K. At a given temperature, the lighter molecules are moving faster, on the average.*

Figure 5.17(a) shows typical *Maxwell speed distribution curves* for nitrogen gas at three different temperatures. At a given temperature, the distribution curve tells us the number of molecules moving at a certain speed. The peak of each curve represents the *most probable speed,* that is, the speed of the largest number of molecules. Note that the most probable speed increases as temperature increases (the peak shifts toward the right). Furthermore, the curve also begins to flatten out with increasing temperature, indicating that larger numbers of molecules are moving at greater speed. Figure 5.17(b) shows the speed distributions of three gases at the *same* temperature. The difference in the curves can be explained by noting that lighter molecules move faster, on average, than heavier ones.

The distribution of molecular speeds can be demonstrated with the apparatus shown in Figure 5.18. A beam of atoms (or molecules) exits from an oven at a known temperature and passes through a pinhole (to collimate the beam). Two circular plates mounted on the same shaft are rotated by a motor. The first plate is called the "chopper" and the second is the detector. The purpose of the chopper is to allow small bursts of atoms (or molecules) to pass through it whenever the slit is aligned with the beam. Within each burst, the faster-moving molecules will reach the detector earlier

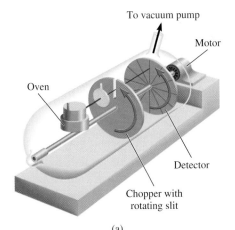

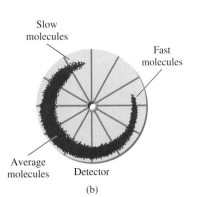

Figure 5.18 *(a) Apparatus for studying molecular speed distribution at a certain temperature. The vacuum pump causes the molecules to travel from left to right as shown. (b) The spread of the deposit on the detector gives the range of molecular speeds, and the density of the deposit is proportional to the fraction of molecules moving at different speeds.*

than the slower-moving ones. Eventually, a layer of deposit will accumulate on the detector. Because the two plates are rotating at the same speed, molecules in the next burst will hit the detector plate at approximately the same place as molecules from the previous burst having the same speed. In time, the molecular deposition will become visible. The density of the deposition indicates the distribution of molecular speeds at that particular temperature.

Root-Mean-Square Speed

How fast does a molecule move, on the average, at any temperature T? One way to estimate molecular speed is to calculate the **root-mean-square (rms) speed (u_{rms})**, which is *an average molecular speed*. One of the results of the kinetic theory of gases is that the total kinetic energy of a mole of any gas equals $\frac{3}{2}RT$. Earlier we saw that the average kinetic energy of one molecule is $\frac{1}{2}m\overline{u^2}$ and so we can write

$$N_A \left(\tfrac{1}{2}m\overline{u^2} \right) = \tfrac{3}{2}RT$$

The kinetic theory of gases treats molecules as hard spheres without internal structure.

where N_A is Avogadro's number. Because $N_A m = \mathcal{M}$, the above equation can be rearranged to give

$$\overline{u^2} = \frac{3RT}{\mathcal{M}}$$

Taking the square root of both sides gives

$$\sqrt{\overline{u^2}} = u_{rms} = \sqrt{\frac{3RT}{\mathcal{M}}} \tag{5.16}$$

Equation (5.16) shows that the root-mean-square speed of a gas increases with the square root of its temperature (in kelvins). Because $\mathcal{M}$ appears in the denominator, it follows that the heavier the gas, the more slowly its molecules move. If we substitute 8.314 J/K · mol for R (see Appendix 2) and convert the molar mass to kg/mol, then u_{rms} will be calculated in meters per second (m/s). This procedure is illustrated in Example 5.16.

Example 5.16

Calculate the root-mean-square speeds of helium atoms and nitrogen molecules in m/s at 25°C.

Strategy To calculate the root-mean-square speed we need Equation (5.16). What units should we use for R and $\mathcal{M}$ so that u_{rms} will be expressed in m/s?

Solution To calculate u_{rms}, the units of R should be 8.314 J/K · mol and, because 1 J = 1 kg m²/s², the molar mass must be in kg/mol. The molar mass of He is 4.003 g/mol, or 4.003×10^{-3} kg/mol. From Equation (5.16),

$$u_{rms} = \sqrt{\frac{3RT}{\mathcal{M}}}$$

$$= \sqrt{\frac{3(8.314 \text{ J/K} \cdot \text{mol})(298 \text{ K})}{4.003 \times 10^{-3} \text{ kg/mol}}}$$

$$= \sqrt{1.86 \times 10^6 \text{ J/kg}}$$

(Continued)

Using the conversion factor $1\text{ J} = 1\text{ kg m}^2/\text{s}^2$ we get

$$u_{rms} = \sqrt{1.86 \times 10^6 \text{ kg m}^2/\text{kg} \cdot \text{s}^2}$$
$$= \sqrt{1.86 \times 10^6 \text{ m}^2/\text{s}^2}$$
$$= 1.36 \times 10^3 \text{ m/s}$$

The procedure is the same for N_2, the molar mass of which is 28.02 g/mol, or 2.802×10^{-2} kg/mol so that we write

$$u_{rms} = \sqrt{\frac{3(8.314 \text{ J/K} \cdot \text{mol})(298 \text{ K})}{2.802 \times 10^{-2} \text{ kg/mol}}}$$
$$= \sqrt{2.65 \times 10^5 \text{ m}^2/\text{s}^2}$$
$$= 515 \text{ m/s}$$

Check Because He is a lighter gas, we expect it to move faster, on average, than N_2. A quick way to check the answers is to note that the ratio of the two u_{rms} values ($1.36 \times 10^3/515 \approx 2.6$) should be equal to the square root of the ratios of the molar masses of N_2 to He, that is, $\sqrt{28/4} \approx 2.6$.

Similar problems: 5.77, 5.78.

Practice Exercise Calculate the root-mean-square speed of molecular chlorine in m/s at 20°C.

The calculation in Example 5.16 has an interesting relationship to the composition of Earth's atmosphere. Unlike Jupiter, Earth does not have appreciable amounts of hydrogen or helium in its atmosphere. Why is this the case? A smaller planet than Jupiter, Earth has a weaker gravitational attraction for these lighter molecules. A fairly straightforward calculation shows that to escape Earth's gravitational field, a molecule must possess an escape velocity equal to or greater than 1.1×10^4 m/s. Because the average speed of helium is considerably greater than that of molecular nitrogen or molecular oxygen, more helium atoms escape from Earth's atmosphere into outer space. Consequently, only a trace amount of helium is present in our atmosphere. On the other hand, Jupiter, with a mass about 320 times greater than that of Earth, retains both heavy and light gases in its atmosphere.

The Chemistry in Action essay on p. 198 describes a fascinating phenomenon involving gases at extremely low temperatures.

Jupiter. The interior of this massive planet consists mainly of hydrogen.

Gas Diffusion

A direct demonstration of random motion is provided by *diffusion, the gradual mixing of molecules of one gas with molecules of another by virtue of their kinetic properties.* Diffusion always proceeds from a region of higher concentration to one of lower concentration. Despite the fact that molecular speeds are very great, the diffusion process takes a relatively long time to complete. For example, when a bottle of concentrated ammonia solution is opened at one end of a lab bench, it takes some time before a person at the other end of the bench can smell it. The reason is that a molecule experiences numerous collisions while moving from one end of the bench to the other, as shown in Figure 5.19. Thus, diffusion of gases always happens gradually, and not instantly as molecular speeds seem to suggest. Furthermore, because the root-mean-square speed of a light gas is greater than that of a heavier gas (see Example 5.16), a lighter gas will diffuse through a certain space more quickly than will a heavier gas. Figure 5.20 illustrates gaseous diffusion.

Figure 5.19 *The path traveled by a single gas molecule. Each change in direction represents a collision with another molecule.*

CHEMISTRY IN ACTION

Super Cold Atoms

What happens to a gas when cooled to nearly absolute zero? More than 70 years ago, Albert Einstein, extending work by the Indian physicist Satyendra Nath Bose, predicted that at extremely low temperatures gaseous atoms of certain elements would "merge" or "condense" to form a single entity and a new form of matter. Unlike ordinary gases, liquids, and solids, this supercooled substance, which was named the *Bose-Einstein condensate (BEC),* would contain no individual atoms because the original atoms would overlap one another, leaving no space in between.

Einstein's hypothesis inspired an international effort to produce the BEC. But, as sometimes happens in science, the necessary technology was not available until fairly recently, and so early investigations were fruitless. Lasers, which use a process based on another of Einstein's ideas, were not designed specifically for BEC research, but they became a critical tool for this work.

Finally, in 1995, physicists found the evidence they had sought for so long. A team at the University of Colorado was the first to report success. They created a BEC by cooling a sample of gaseous rubidium (Rb) atoms to about 1.7×10^{-7} K using a technique called "laser cooling," a process in which a laser light is directed at a beam of atoms, hitting them head on and dramatically slowing them down. The Rb atoms were further cooled in an "optical molasses" produced by the intersection of six lasers. The slowest, coolest atoms were trapped in a magnetic field while the faster-moving, "hotter" atoms escaped, thereby removing more energy from the gas. Under these conditions, the kinetic energy of the trapped atoms was virtually zero, which accounts for the extremely low temperature of the gas. At this point the Rb atoms formed the condensate, just as Einstein had predicted. Although this BEC was invisible to the naked eye (it measured only 5×10^{-3} cm across), the scientists were able to capture its image on a computer screen by focusing another laser beam on it. The laser caused the BEC to break up after about 15 seconds, but that was long enough to record its existence.

The figure shows the Maxwell velocity distribution[†] of the Rb atoms at this temperature. The colors indicate the number of atoms having velocity specified by the two horizontal axes. The blue and white portions represent atoms that have merged to form the BEC.

Within weeks of the Colorado team's discovery, a group of scientists at Rice University, using similar techniques, succeeded in producing a BEC with lithium atoms and in 1998 scientists at the Massachusetts Institute of Technology were able to produce a BEC with hydrogen atoms. Since then, many advances have been made in understanding the properties of the BEC in general and experiments are being extended to molecular systems. It is expected that studies of the BEC will shed light on atomic properties that are still not fully understood (see Chapter 7) and on the mechanism of superconductivity (see the Chemistry in Action essay on this topic in Chapter 11). An additional benefit might be the development of better lasers. Other applications will depend on further study of the BEC itself. Nevertheless, the discovery of a new form of matter has to be one of the foremost scientific achievements of the twentieth century.

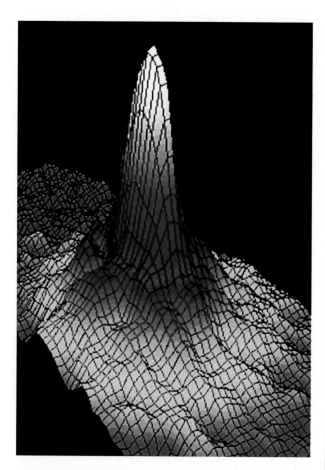

Maxwell velocity distribution of Rb atoms at about 1.7×10^{-7} K. The velocity increases from the center (zero) outward along the two axes. The red color represents the lowest number of Rb atoms and the white color the highest. The average speed in the white region is about 0.5 mm/s.

[†]Velocity distribution differs from speed distribution in that velocity has both magnitude and direction. Thus velocity can have both positive and negative values but speed can have only zero or positive values.

Figure 5.20 *A demonstration of gas diffusion. NH_3 gas (from a bottle containing aqueous ammonia) combines with HCl gas (from a bottle containing hydrochloric acid) to form solid NH_4Cl. Because NH_3 is lighter and therefore diffuses faster, solid NH_4Cl first appears nearer the HCl bottle (on the right).*

5.8 Deviation from Ideal Behavior

The gas laws and the kinetic molecular theory assume that molecules in the gaseous state do not exert any force, either attractive or repulsive, on one another. The other assumption is that the volume of the molecules is negligibly small compared with that of the container. A gas that satisfies these two conditions is said to exhibit *ideal behavior.*

Although we can assume that real gases behave like an ideal gas, we cannot expect them to do so under all conditions. For example, without intermolecular forces, gases could not condense to form liquids. The important question is: Under what conditions will gases most likely exhibit nonideal behavior?

Figure 5.21 shows PV/RT plotted against P for three real gases and an ideal gas at a given temperature. This graph provides a test of ideal gas behavior. According to the ideal gas equation (for 1 mole of gas), PV/RT equals 1, regardless of the actual gas pressure. (When $n = 1$, $PV = nRT$ becomes $PV = RT$, or $PV/RT = 1$.) For real gases, this is true only at moderately low pressures (≤ 5 atm); significant deviations occur as pressure increases. Attractive forces operate among molecules at relatively short distances. At atmospheric pressure, the molecules in a gas are far apart and the attractive forces are negligible. At high pressures, the density of the gas increases; the molecules are much closer to one another. Intermolecular forces can then be significant enough to affect the motion of the molecules, and the gas will not behave ideally.

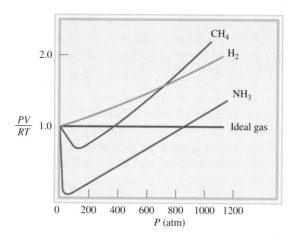

Figure 5.21 *Plot of PV/RT versus P of 1 mole of a gas at 0°C. For 1 mole of an ideal gas, PV/RT is equal to 1, no matter what the pressure of the gas is. For real gases, we observe various deviations from ideality at high pressures. At very low pressures, all gases exhibit ideal behavior; that is, their PV/RT values all converge to 1 as P approaches zero.*

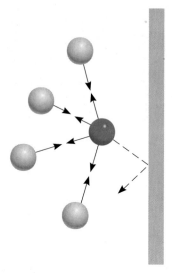

Figure 5.22 *Effect of inter-molecular forces on the pressure exerted by a gas. The speed of a molecule that is moving toward the container wall (red sphere) is reduced by the attractive forces exerted by its neighbors (gray spheres). Consequently, the impact this molecule makes with the wall is not as great as it would be if no in-termolecular forces were present. In general, the measured gas pressure is lower than the pressure the gas would exert if it behaved ideally.*

Another way to observe the nonideal behavior of gases is to lower the temperature. Cooling a gas decreases the molecules' average kinetic energy, which in a sense deprives molecules of the drive they need to break from their mutual attraction.

To study real gases accurately, then, we need to modify the ideal gas equation, taking into account intermolecular forces and finite molecular volumes. Such an analysis was first made by the Dutch physicist J. D. van der Waals[†] in 1873. Besides being mathematically simple, van der Waals' treatment provides us with an interpretation of real gas behavior at the molecular level.

Consider the approach of a particular molecule toward the wall of a container (Figure 5.22). The intermolecular attractions exerted by its neighbors tend to soften the impact made by this molecule against the wall. The overall effect is a lower gas pressure than we would expect for an ideal gas. Van der Waals suggested that the pressure exerted by an ideal gas, P_{ideal}, is related to the experimentally measured pressure, P_{real}, by the equation

$$P_{ideal} = P_{real} + \frac{an^2}{V^2}$$

$$\uparrow \qquad \uparrow$$

observed   correction
pressure   term

where a is a constant and n and V are the number of moles and volume of the gas, respectively. The correction term for pressure (an^2/V^2) can be understood as follows. The intermolecular interaction that gives rise to nonideal behavior depends on how frequently any two molecules approach each other closely. The number of such "encounters" increases with the square of the number of molecules per unit volume, $(n/V)^2$, because the presence of each of the two molecules in a particular region is proportional to n/V. The quantity P_{ideal} is the pressure we would measure if there were no intermolecular attractions, and so a is just a proportionality constant.

Another correction concerns the volume occupied by the gas molecules. In the ideal gas equation, V represents the volume of the container. However, each molecule does occupy a finite, although small, intrinsic volume, so the effective volume of the gas becomes $(V - nb)$, where n is the number of moles of the gas and b is a constant. The term nb represents the volume occupied by n moles of the gas.

Having taken into account the corrections for pressure and volume, we can rewrite the ideal gas equation as follows:

$$\left(P + \frac{an^2}{V^2}\right)(V - nb) = nRT \tag{5.17}$$

corrected   corrected
pressure   volume

Equation (5.17), *relating P, V, T, and n for a nonideal gas,* is known as the **van der Waals equation**. The van der Waals constants a and b are selected to give the best possible agreement between Equation (5.17) and observed behavior of a particular gas.

Table 5.4 lists the values of a and b for a number of gases. The value of a indicates how strongly molecules of a given type of gas attract one another. We see that

---

[†]Johannes Diderck van der Waals (1837–1923). Dutch physicist. Van der Waals received the Nobel Prize in Physics in 1910 for his work on the properties of gases and liquids.

helium atoms have the weakest attraction for one another, because helium has the smallest a value. There is also a rough correlation between molecular size and b. Generally, the larger the molecule (or atom), the greater b is, but the relationship between b and molecular (or atomic) size is not a simple one.

Example 5.17 compares the pressure of a gas calculated using the ideal gas equation and the van der Waals equation.

Example 5.17

Given that 3.50 moles of NH_3 occupy 5.20 L at 47°C, calculate the pressure of the gas (in atm) using (a) the ideal gas equation and (b) the van der Waals equation.

Strategy To calculate the pressure of NH_3 using the ideal gas equation, we proceed as in Example 5.3. What corrections are made to the pressure and volume terms in the van der Waals equation?

Solution (a) We have the following data:

$$V = 5.20 \text{ L}$$
$$T = (47 + 273) \text{ K} = 320 \text{ K}$$
$$n = 3.50 \text{ mol}$$
$$R = 0.0821 \text{ L} \cdot \text{atm/K} \cdot \text{mol}$$

Substituting these values in the ideal gas equation, we write

$$P = \frac{nRT}{V}$$
$$= \frac{(3.50 \text{ mol})(0.0821 \text{ L} \cdot \text{atm/K} \cdot \text{mol})(320 \text{ K})}{5.20 \text{ L}}$$
$$= 17.7 \text{ atm}$$

(b) We need Equation (5.17). It is convenient to first calculate the correction terms in Equation (5.17) separately. From Table 5.4, we have

$$a = 4.17 \text{ atm} \cdot \text{L}^2/\text{mol}^2$$
$$b = 0.0371 \text{ L/mol}$$

so that the correction terms for pressure and volume are

$$\frac{an^2}{V^2} = \frac{(4.17 \text{ atm} \cdot \text{L}^2/\text{mol}^2)(3.50 \text{ mol})^2}{(5.20 \text{ L})^2} = 1.89 \text{ atm}$$
$$nb = (3.50 \text{ mol})(0.0371 \text{ L/mol}) = 0.130 \text{ L}$$

Finally, substituting these values in the van der Waals equation, we have

$$(P + 1.89 \text{ atm})(5.20 \text{ L} - 0.130 \text{ L}) = (3.50 \text{ mol})(0.0821 \text{ L} \cdot \text{atm/K} \cdot \text{mol})(320 \text{ K})$$
$$P = 16.2 \text{ atm}$$

Check Based on your understanding of nonideal gas behavior, is it reasonable that the pressure calculated using the van der Waals equation should be smaller than that using the ideal gas equation? Why?

Similar problem: 5.85.

Practice Exercise Using the data shown in Table 5.4, calculate the pressure exerted by 4.37 moles of molecular chlorine confined in a volume of 2.45 L at 38°C. Compare the pressure with that calculated using the ideal gas equation.

TABLE 5.4

Van der Waals Constants of Some Common Gases

Gas	a $\left(\dfrac{\text{atm} \cdot \text{L}^2}{\text{mol}^2}\right)$	b $\left(\dfrac{\text{L}}{\text{mol}}\right)$
He	0.034	0.0237
Ne	0.211	0.0171
Ar	1.34	0.0322
Kr	2.32	0.0398
Xe	4.19	0.0266
H_2	0.244	0.0266
N_2	1.39	0.0391
O_2	1.36	0.0318
Cl_2	6.49	0.0562
CO_2	3.59	0.0427
CH_4	2.25	0.0428
CCl_4	20.4	0.138
NH_3	4.17	0.0371
H_2O	5.46	0.0305

Key Equations

- $P_1V_1 = P_2V_2$ (5.2)   Boyle's law. For calculating pressure or volume changes.

- $\dfrac{V_1}{T_1} = \dfrac{V_2}{T_2}$ (5.4)   Charles's law. For calculating temperature or volume changes.

- $\dfrac{P_1}{T_1} = \dfrac{P_2}{T_2}$ (5.6)   Charles's law. For calculating temperature or pressure changes.

- $V = k_4 n$ (5.7)   Avogadro's law. Constant P and T.

- $PV = nRT$ (5.8)   Ideal gas equation.

- $\dfrac{P_1V_1}{T_1} = \dfrac{P_2V_2}{T_2}$ (5.10)   For calculating changes in pressure, temperature, or volume when n is constant.

- $d = \dfrac{P\mathcal{M}}{RT}$ (5.11)   For calculating density or molar mass.

- $X_i = \dfrac{n_i}{n_T}$ (5.13)   Definition of mole fraction.

- $P_i = X_i P_T$ (5.14)   Dalton's law of partial pressures. For calculating partial pressures.

- $\overline{KE} = \tfrac{1}{2}m\overline{u^2} = CT$ (5.15)   Relating the average kinetic energy of a gas to its absolute temperature.

- $u_{rms} = \sqrt{\dfrac{3RT}{\mathcal{M}}}$ (5.16)   For calculating the root-mean-square speed of gas molecules.

- $\left(P + \dfrac{an^2}{V^2}\right)(V - nb) = nRT$ (5.17)   van der Waals equation. For calculating the pressure of a nonideal gas.

Summary of Facts and Concepts

1. At 25°C and 1 atm, a number of elements and molecular compounds exist as gases. Ionic compounds are solids rather than gases under atmospheric conditions.
2. Gases exert pressure because their molecules move freely and collide with any surface with which they make contact. Units of gas pressure include millimeters of mercury (mmHg), torr, pascals, and atmospheres. One atmosphere equals 760 mmHg, or 760 torr.
3. The pressure-volume relationships of ideal gases are governed by Boyle's law: Volume is inversely proportional to pressure (at constant T and n).
4. The temperature-volume relationships of ideal gases are described by Charles's and Gay-Lussac's law: Volume is directly proportional to temperature (at constant P and n).
5. Absolute zero (-273.15°C) is the lowest theoretically attainable temperature. The Kelvin temperature scale takes 0 K as absolute zero. In all gas law calculations, temperature must be expressed in kelvins.
6. The amount-volume relationships of ideal gases are described by Avogadro's law: Equal volumes of gases contain equal numbers of molecules (at the same T and P).
7. The ideal gas equation, $PV = nRT$, combines the laws of Boyle, Charles, and Avogadro. This equation describes the behavior of an ideal gas.
8. Dalton's law of partial pressures states that each gas in a mixture of gases exerts the same pressure that it would if it were alone and occupied the same volume.
9. The kinetic molecular theory, a mathematical way of describing the behavior of gas molecules, is based on the following assumptions: Gas molecules are separated by

distances far greater than their own dimensions, they possess mass but have negligible volume, they are in constant motion, and they frequently collide with one another. The molecules neither attract nor repel one another.

10. A Maxwell speed distribution curve shows how many gas molecules are moving at various speeds at a given temperature. As temperature increases, more molecules move at greater speeds.

11. Gas diffusion demonstrates random molecular motion.

12. The van der Waals equation is a modification of the ideal gas equation that takes into account the nonideal behavior of real gases. It corrects for the fact that real gas molecules do exert forces on each other and that they do have volume. The van der Waals constants are determined experimentally for each gas.

Key Words

Absolute temperature scale, p. 173
Absolute zero, p. 173
Atmospheric pressure, p. 166
Avogadro's law, p. 174
Barometer, p. 167
Boyle's law, p. 169
Charles's and Gay-Lussac's law, p. 173
Charles's law, p. 173

Dalton's law of partial pressures, p. 186
Diffusion, p. 197
Gas constant, p. 175
Ideal gas, p. 175
Ideal gas equation, p. 175
Joule (J), p. 191
Kelvin temperature scale, p. 173
Kinetic energy (KE), p. 191

Kinetic molecular theory of gases, p. 191
Manometer, p. 168
Mole fraction, p. 187
Newton (N), p. 166
Partial pressures, p. 186
Pascal (Pa), p. 166
Pressure, p. 166
Root-mean-square (rms) speed (u_{rms}), p. 196

Standard atmospheric pressure (1 atm), p. 167
Standard temperature and pressure (STP), p. 176
van der Waals equation, p. 200

Questions and Problems

Substances That Exist as Gases
Review Questions

5.1 Name five elements and five compounds that exist as gases at room temperature.

5.2 List the physical characteristics of gases.

Pressure of a Gas
Review Questions

5.3 Define pressure and give the common units for pressure.

5.4 Describe how a barometer and a manometer are used to measure gas pressure.

5.5 Why is mercury a more suitable substance to use in a barometer than water?

5.6 Explain why the height of mercury in a barometer is independent of the cross-sectional area of the tube. Would the barometer still work if the tubing were tilted at an angle, say 15° (see Figure 5.3)?

5.7 Would it be easier to drink water with a straw on top of Mt. Everest or at the foot? Explain.

5.8 Is the atmospheric pressure in a mine that is 500 m below sea level greater or less than 1 atm?

5.9 What is the difference between a gas and a vapor? At 25°C, which of the following substances in the gas phase should be properly called a gas and which should be called a vapor: molecular nitrogen (N_2), mercury?

5.10 If the maximum distance that water may be brought up a well by a suction pump is 34 ft (10.3 m), how is it possible to obtain water and oil from hundreds of feet below the surface of Earth?

5.11 Why is it that if the barometer reading falls in one part of the world, it must rise somewhere else?

5.12 Why do astronauts have to wear protective suits when they are on the surface of the moon?

Problems

5.13 Convert 562 mmHg to atm.

5.14 The atmospheric pressure at the summit of Mt. McKinley is 606 mmHg on a certain day. What is the pressure in atm and in kPa?

The Gas Laws
Review Questions

5.15 State the following gas laws in words and also in the form of an equation: Boyle's law, Charles's law,

Avogadro's law. In each case, indicate the conditions under which the law is applicable, and give the units for each quantity in the equation.

5.16 Explain why a helium weather balloon expands as it rises in the air. Assume that the temperature remains constant.

Problems

5.17 A gaseous sample of a substance is cooled at constant pressure. Which of the following diagrams best represents the situation if the final temperature is (a) above the boiling point of the substance and (b) below the boiling point but above the freezing point of the substance?

(a)   (b)   (c)   (d)

5.18 Consider the following gaseous sample in a cylinder fitted with a movable piston. Initially there are *n* moles of the gas at temperature *T*, pressure *P*, and volume *V*.

Choose the cylinder that correctly represents the gas after each of the following changes. (1) The pressure on the piston is tripled at constant *n* and *T*. (2) The temperature is doubled at constant *n* and *P*. (3) *n* moles of another gas are added at constant *T* and *P*. (4) *T* is halved and pressure on the piston is reduced to a quarter of its original value.

(a)   (b)   (c)

5.19 A gas occupying a volume of 725 mL at a pressure of 0.970 atm is allowed to expand at constant temperature until its pressure reaches 0.541 atm. What is its final volume?

5.20 At 46°C a sample of ammonia gas exerts a pressure of 5.3 atm. What is the pressure when the volume of the

gas is reduced to one-tenth (0.10) of the original value at the same temperature?

5.21 The volume of a gas is 5.80 L, measured at 1.00 atm. What is the pressure of the gas in mmHg if the volume is changed to 9.65 L? (The temperature remains constant.)

5.22 A sample of air occupies 3.8 L when the pressure is 1.2 atm. (a) What volume does it occupy at 6.6 atm? (b) What pressure is required in order to compress it to 0.075 L? (The temperature is kept constant.)

5.23 A 36.4-L volume of methane gas is heated from 25°C to 88°C at constant pressure. What is the final volume of the gas?

5.24 Under constant-pressure conditions a sample of hydrogen gas initially at 88°C and 9.6 L is cooled until its final volume is 3.4 L. What is its final temperature?

5.25 Ammonia burns in oxygen gas to form nitric oxide (NO) and water vapor. How many volumes of NO are obtained from one volume of ammonia at the same temperature and pressure?

5.26 Molecular chlorine and molecular fluorine combine to form a gaseous product. Under the same conditions of temperature and pressure it is found that one volume of Cl_2 reacts with three volumes of F_2 to yield two volumes of the product. What is the formula of the product?

The Ideal Gas Equation
Review Questions

5.27 List the characteristics of an ideal gas.
5.28 Write the ideal gas equation and also state it in words. Give the units for each term in the equation.
5.29 What are standard temperature and pressure (STP)? What is the significance of STP in relation to the volume of 1 mole of an ideal gas?
5.30 Why is the density of a gas much lower than that of a liquid or solid under atmospheric conditions? What units are normally used to express the density of gases?

Problems

5.31 A sample of nitrogen gas kept in a container of volume 2.3 L and at a temperature of 32°C exerts a pressure of 4.7 atm. Calculate the number of moles of gas present.

5.32 Given that 6.9 moles of carbon monoxide gas are present in a container of volume 30.4 L, what is the pressure of the gas (in atm) if the temperature is 62°C?

5.33 What volume will 5.6 moles of sulfur hexafluoride (SF_6) gas occupy if the temperature and pressure of the gas are 128°C and 9.4 atm?

5.34 A certain amount of gas at 25°C and at a pressure of 0.800 atm is contained in a glass vessel. Suppose that the vessel can withstand a pressure of 2.00 atm. How high can you raise the temperature of the gas without bursting the vessel?

5.35 A gas-filled balloon having a volume of 2.50 L at 1.2 atm and 25°C is allowed to rise to the stratosphere (about 30 km above the surface of Earth), where the temperature and pressure are $-23°C$ and 3.00×10^{-3} atm, respectively. Calculate the final volume of the balloon.

5.36 The temperature of 2.5 L of a gas initially at STP is raised to 250°C at constant volume. Calculate the final pressure of the gas in atm.

5.37 The pressure of 6.0 L of an ideal gas in a flexible container is decreased to one-third of its original pressure, and its absolute temperature is decreased by one-half. What is the final volume of the gas?

5.38 A gas evolved during the fermentation of glucose (wine making) has a volume of 0.78 L at 20.1°C and 1.00 atm. What was the volume of this gas at the fermentation temperature of 36.5°C and 1.00 atm pressure?

5.39 An ideal gas originally at 0.85 atm and 66°C was allowed to expand until its final volume, pressure, and temperature were 94 mL, 0.60 atm, and 45°C, respectively. What was its initial volume?

5.40 Calculate the volume (in liters) of 88.4 g of CO_2 at STP.

5.41 A gas at 772 mmHg and 35.0°C occupies a volume of 6.85 L. Calculate its volume at STP.

5.42 Dry ice is solid carbon dioxide. A 0.050-g sample of dry ice is placed in an evacuated 4.6-L vessel at 30°C. Calculate the pressure inside the vessel after all the dry ice has been converted to CO_2 gas.

5.43 At STP, 0.280 L of a gas weighs 0.400 g. Calculate the molar mass of the gas.

5.44 At 741 torr and 44°C, 7.10 g of a gas occupy a volume of 5.40 L. What is the molar mass of the gas?

5.45 Ozone molecules in the stratosphere absorb much of the harmful radiation from the sun. Typically, the temperature and pressure of ozone in the stratosphere are 250 K and 1.0×10^{-3} atm, respectively. How many ozone molecules are present in 1.0 L of air under these conditions?

5.46 Assuming that air contains 78 percent N_2, 21 percent O_2, and 1 percent Ar, all by volume, how many molecules of each type of gas are present in 1.0 L of air at STP?

5.47 A 2.10-L vessel contains 4.65 g of a gas at 1.00 atm and 27.0°C. (a) Calculate the density of the gas in grams per liter. (b) What is the molar mass of the gas?

5.48 Calculate the density of hydrogen bromide (HBr) gas in grams per liter at 733 mmHg and 46°C.

5.49 A certain anesthetic contains 64.9 percent C, 13.5 percent H, and 21.6 percent O by mass. At 120°C and 750 mmHg, 1.00 L of the gaseous compound weighs 2.30 g. What is the molecular formula of the compound?

5.50 A compound has the empirical formula SF_4. At 20°C, 0.100 g of the gaseous compound occupies a volume of 22.1 mL and exerts a pressure of 1.02 atm. What is the molecular formula of the gas?

Gas Stoichiometry
Problems

5.51 Consider the formation of nitrogen dioxide from nitric oxide and oxygen:

$$2NO(g) + O_2(g) \longrightarrow 2NO_2(g)$$

If 9.0 L of NO are reacted with excess O_2 at STP, what is the volume in liters of the NO_2 produced?

5.52 Methane, the principal component of natural gas, is used for heating and cooking. The combustion process is

$$CH_4(g) + 2O_2(g) \longrightarrow CO_2(g) + 2H_2O(l)$$

If 15.0 moles of CH_4 are reacted, what is the volume of CO_2 (in liters) produced at 23.0°C and 0.985 atm?

5.53 When coal is burned, the sulfur present in coal is converted to sulfur dioxide (SO_2), which is responsible for the acid rain phenomenon.

$$S(s) + O_2(g) \longrightarrow SO_2(g)$$

If 2.54 kg of S are reacted with oxygen, calculate the volume of SO_2 gas (in mL) formed at 30.5°C and 1.12 atm.

5.54 In alcohol fermentation, yeast converts glucose to ethanol and carbon dioxide:

$$C_6H_{12}O_6(s) \longrightarrow 2C_2H_5OH(l) + 2CO_2(g)$$

If 5.97 g of glucose are reacted and 1.44 L of CO_2 gas are collected at 293 K and 0.984 atm, what is the percent yield of the reaction?

5.55 A compound of P and F was analyzed as follows: Heating 0.2324 g of the compound in a 378-cm^3 container turned all of it to gas, which had a pressure of 97.3 mmHg at 77°C. Then the gas was mixed with calcium chloride solution, which turned all of the F to 0.2631 g of CaF_2. Determine the molecular formula of the compound.

5.56 A quantity of 0.225 g of a metal M (molar mass = 27.0 g/mol) liberated 0.303 L of molecular hydrogen (measured at 17°C and 741 mmHg) from an excess of hydrochloric acid. Deduce from these data the corresponding equation and write formulas for the oxide and sulfate of M.

5.57 What is the mass of the solid NH_4Cl formed when 73.0 g of NH_3 are mixed with an equal mass of HCl? What is the volume of the gas remaining, measured at 14.0°C and 752 mmHg? What gas is it?

5.58 Dissolving 3.00 g of an impure sample of calcium carbonate in hydrochloric acid produced 0.656 L of carbon dioxide (measured at 20.0°C and 792 mmHg). Calculate the percent by mass of calcium carbonate in the sample. State any assumptions.

5.59 Calculate the mass in grams of hydrogen chloride produced when 5.6 L of molecular hydrogen measured at STP react with an excess of molecular chlorine gas.

5.60 Ethanol (C_2H_5OH) burns in air:

$$C_2H_5OH(l) + O_2(g) \longrightarrow CO_2(g) + H_2O(l)$$

Balance the equation and determine the volume of air in liters at 35.0°C and 790 mmHg required to burn 227 g of ethanol. Assume that air is 21.0 percent O_2 by volume.

Dalton's Law of Partial Pressures
Review Questions

5.61 State Dalton's law of partial pressures and explain what mole fraction is. Does mole fraction have units?

5.62 A sample of air contains only nitrogen and oxygen gases whose partial pressures are 0.80 atm and 0.20 atm, respectively. Calculate the total pressure and the mole fractions of the gases.

Problems

5.63 A mixture of gases contains 0.31 mol CH_4, 0.25 mol C_2H_6, and 0.29 mol C_3H_8. The total pressure is 1.50 atm. Calculate the partial pressures of the gases.

5.64 A 2.5-L flask at 15°C contains a mixture of N_2, He, and Ne at partial pressures of 0.32 atm for N_2, 0.15 atm for He, and 0.42 atm for Ne. (a) Calculate the total pressure of the mixture. (b) Calculate the volume in liters at STP occupied by He and Ne if the N_2 is removed selectively.

5.65 Dry air near sea level has the following composition by volume: N_2, 78.08 percent; O_2, 20.94 percent; Ar, 0.93 percent; CO_2, 0.05 percent. The atmospheric pressure is 1.00 atm. Calculate (a) the partial pressure of each gas in atm and (b) the concentration of each gas in moles per liter at 0°C. (*Hint:* Because volume is proportional to the number of moles present, mole fractions of gases can be expressed as ratios of volumes at the same temperature and pressure.)

5.66 A mixture of helium and neon gases is collected over water at 28.0°C and 745 mmHg. If the partial pressure of helium is 368 mmHg, what is the partial pressure of neon? (Vapor pressure of water at 28°C = 28.3 mmHg.)

5.67 A piece of sodium metal reacts completely with water as follows:

$$2Na(s) + 2H_2O(l) \longrightarrow 2NaOH(aq) + H_2(g)$$

The hydrogen gas generated is collected over water at 25.0°C. The volume of the gas is 246 mL measured at 1.00 atm. Calculate the number of grams of sodium used in the reaction. (Vapor pressure of water at 25°C = 0.0313 atm.)

5.68 A sample of zinc metal reacts completely with an excess of hydrochloric acid:

$$Zn(s) + 2HCl(aq) \longrightarrow ZnCl_2(aq) + H_2(g)$$

The hydrogen gas produced is collected over water at 25.0°C using an arrangement similar to that shown in Figure 5.15. The volume of the gas is 7.80 L, and the pressure is 0.980 atm. Calculate the amount of zinc metal in grams consumed in the reaction. (Vapor pressure of water at 25°C = 23.8 mmHg.)

5.69 Helium is mixed with oxygen gas for deep-sea divers. Calculate the percent by volume of oxygen gas in the mixture if the diver has to submerge to a depth where the total pressure is 4.2 atm. The partial pressure of oxygen is maintained at 0.20 atm at this depth.

5.70 A sample of ammonia (NH_3) gas is completely decomposed to nitrogen and hydrogen gases over heated iron wool. If the total pressure is 866 mmHg, calculate the partial pressures of N_2 and H_2.

Kinetic Molecular Theory of Gases
Review Questions

5.71 What are the basic assumptions of the kinetic molecular theory of gases?

5.72 How does the kinetic molecular theory explain Boyle's law, Charles's law, Avogadro's law, and Dalton's law of partial pressures?

5.73 What does the Maxwell speed distribution curve tell us? Does Maxwell's theory work for a sample of 200 molecules? Explain.

5.74 Write the expression for the root-mean-square speed for a gas at temperature T. Define each term in the equation and show the units that are used in the calculation.

5.75 Which of the following statements is correct? (a) Heat is produced by the collision of gas molecules against one another. (b) When a gas is heated, the molecules collide with one another more often.

5.76 Uranium hexafluoride (UF_6) is a much heavier gas than helium, yet at a given temperature, the average kinetic energies of the samples of the two gases are the same. Explain.

Problems

5.77 Compare the root-mean-square speeds of O_2 and UF_6 at 65°C.

5.78 The temperature in the stratosphere is −23°C. Calculate the root-mean-square speeds of N_2, O_2, and O_3 molecules in this region.

5.79 The average distance traveled by a molecule between successive collisions is called *mean free path*. For a given amount of a gas, how does the mean free path of a gas depend on (a) density, (b) temperature at constant volume, (c) pressure at constant temperature, (d) volume at constant temperature, and (e) size of the atoms?

5.80 At a certain temperature the speeds of six gaseous molecules in a container are 2.0 m/s, 2.2 m/s, 2.6 m/s, 2.7 m/s, 3.3 m/s, and 3.5 m/s. Calculate the root-mean-square speed and the average speed of the molecules. These two average values are close to each other, but the root-mean-square value is always the larger of the two. Why?

Deviation from Ideal Behavior

Review Questions

5.81 Cite two pieces of evidence to show that gases do not behave ideally under all conditions.

5.82 Under what set of conditions would a gas be expected to behave most ideally? (a) High temperature and low pressure, (b) high temperature and high pressure, (c) low temperature and high pressure, (d) low temperature and low pressure.

5.83 Write the van der Waals equation for a real gas. Explain the corrective terms for pressure and volume.

5.84 (a) A real gas is introduced into a flask of volume V. Is the corrected volume of the gas greater or less than V? (b) Ammonia has a larger a value than neon does (see Table 5.4). What can you conclude about the relative strength of the attractive forces between molecules of ammonia and between atoms of neon?

Problems

5.85 Using the data shown in Table 5.4, calculate the pressure exerted by 2.50 moles of CO_2 confined in a volume of 5.00 L at 450 K. Compare the pressure with that predicted by the ideal gas equation.

5.86 At 27°C, 10.0 moles of a gas in a 1.50-L container exert a pressure of 130 atm. Is this an ideal gas?

Additional Problems

5.87 Discuss the following phenomena in terms of the gas laws: (a) the pressure increase in an automobile tire on a hot day, (b) the "popping" of a paper bag, (c) the expansion of a weather balloon as it rises in the air, (d) the loud noise heard when a lightbulb shatters.

5.88 Under the same conditions of temperature and pressure, which of the following gases would behave most ideally: Ne, N_2, or CH_4? Explain.

5.89 Nitroglycerin, an explosive compound, decomposes according to the equation

$$4C_3H_5(NO_3)_3(s) \longrightarrow$$
$$12CO_2(g) + 10H_2O(g) + 6N_2(g) + O_2(g)$$

Calculate the total volume of gases when collected at 1.2 atm and 25°C from 2.6×10^2 g of nitroglycerin. What are the partial pressures of the gases under these conditions?

5.90 The empirical formula of a compound is CH. At 200°C, 0.145 g of this compound occupies 97.2 mL at a pressure of 0.74 atm. What is the molecular formula of the compound?

5.91 When ammonium nitrite (NH_4NO_2) is heated, it decomposes to give nitrogen gas. This property is used to inflate some tennis balls. (a) Write a balanced equation for the reaction. (b) Calculate the quantity (in grams) of NH_4NO_2 needed to inflate a tennis ball to a volume of 86.2 mL at 1.20 atm and 22°C.

5.92 The percent by mass of bicarbonate (HCO_3^-) in a certain Alka-Seltzer product is 32.5 percent. Calculate the volume of CO_2 generated (in mL) at 37°C and 1.00 atm when a person ingests a 3.29-g tablet. (*Hint:* The reaction is between HCO_3^- and HCl acid in the stomach.)

5.93 The boiling point of liquid nitrogen is −196°C. On the basis of this information alone, do you think nitrogen is an ideal gas?

5.94 In the metallurgical process of refining nickel, the metal is first combined with carbon monoxide to form tetracarbonylnickel, which is a gas at 43°C:

$$Ni(s) + 4CO(g) \longrightarrow Ni(CO)_4(g)$$

This reaction separates nickel from other solid impurities. (a) Starting with 86.4 g of Ni, calculate the pressure of $Ni(CO)_4$ in a container of volume 4.00 L. (Assume the above reaction goes to completion.) (b) At temperatures above 43°C, the pressure of the gas is observed to increase much more rapidly than predicted by the ideal gas equation. Explain.

5.95 The partial pressure of carbon dioxide varies with seasons. Would you expect the partial pressure in the Northern Hemisphere to be higher in the summer or winter? Explain.

5.96 A healthy adult exhales about 5.0×10^2 mL of a gaseous mixture with each breath. Calculate the number of molecules present in this volume at 37°C and 1.1 atm. List the major components of this gaseous mixture.

5.97 Sodium bicarbonate ($NaHCO_3$) is called baking soda because when heated, it releases carbon dioxide gas, which is responsible for the rising of cookies, doughnuts, and bread. (a) Calculate the volume (in liters) of CO_2 produced by heating 5.0 g of $NaHCO_3$ at 180°C and 1.3 atm. (b) Ammonium bicarbonate (NH_4HCO_3) has also been used for the same purpose. Suggest one advantage and one disadvantage of using NH_4HCO_3 instead of $NaHCO_3$ for baking.

5.98 A barometer having a cross-sectional area of 1.00 cm^2 at sea level measures a pressure of 76.0 cm of mercury. The pressure exerted by this column of mercury is equal to the pressure exerted by all the air on 1 cm^2 of Earth's surface. Given that the density of mercury is 13.6 g/mL and the average radius of Earth is 6371 km, calculate the total mass of Earth's atmosphere in kilograms. (*Hint:* The surface area of a sphere is $4\pi r^2$ where r is the radius of the sphere.)

5.99 Some commercial drain cleaners contain a mixture of sodium hydroxide and aluminum powder. When the mixture is poured down a clogged drain, the following reaction occurs:

$$2NaOH(aq) + 2Al(s) + 6H_2O(l) \longrightarrow$$
$$2NaAl(OH)_4(aq) + 3H_2(g)$$

The heat generated in this reaction helps melt away obstructions such as grease, and the hydrogen gas released stirs up the solids clogging the drain. Calculate the volume of H_2 formed at 23°C and 1.00 atm if 3.12 g of Al are treated with an excess of NaOH.

5.100 The volume of a sample of pure HCl gas was 189 mL at 25°C and 108 mmHg. It was completely dissolved in about 60 mL of water and titrated with a NaOH solution; 15.7 mL of the NaOH solution were required to neutralize the HCl. Calculate the molarity of the NaOH solution.

5.101 Propane (C_3H_8) burns in oxygen to produce carbon dioxide gas and water vapor. (a) Write a balanced equation for this reaction. (b) Calculate the number of liters of carbon dioxide measured at STP that could be produced from 7.45 g of propane.

5.102 Consider the following apparatus. Calculate the partial pressures of helium and neon after the stopcock is open. The temperature remains constant at 16°C.

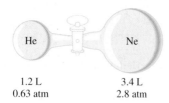

He   Ne

1.2 L   3.4 L
0.63 atm   2.8 atm

5.103 Nitric oxide (NO) reacts with molecular oxygen as follows:

$$2NO(g) + O_2(g) \longrightarrow 2NO_2(g)$$

Initially NO and O_2 are separated as shown here. When the valve is opened, the reaction quickly goes to completion. Determine what gases remain at the end and calculate their partial pressures. Assume that the temperature remains constant at 25°C.

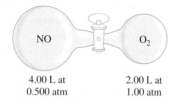

NO O_2

4.00 L at   2.00 L at
0.500 atm   1.00 atm

5.104 Consider the apparatus shown here. When a small amount of water is introduced into the flask by squeezing the bulb of the medicine dropper, water is squirted upward out of the long glass tubing. Explain this observation. (*Hint:* Hydrogen chloride gas is soluble in water.)

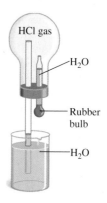

HCl gas

H_2O

Rubber bulb

H_2O

5.105 Describe how you would measure, by either chemical or physical means, the partial pressures of a mixture of gases of the following composition: (a) CO_2 and H_2, (b) He and N_2.

5.106 A certain hydrate has the formula $MgSO_4 \cdot xH_2O$. A quantity of 54.2 g of the compound is heated in an oven to drive off the water. If the steam generated exerts a pressure of 24.8 atm in a 2.00-L container at 120°C, calculate x.

5.107 A mixture of Na_2CO_3 and $MgCO_3$ of mass 7.63 g is reacted with an excess of hydrochloric acid. The CO_2 gas generated occupies a volume of 1.67 L at 1.24 atm and 26°C. From these data, calculate the percent composition by mass of Na_2CO_3 in the mixture.

5.108 The following apparatus can be used to measure atomic and molecular speed. Suppose that a beam of metal atoms is directed at a rotating cylinder in a vacuum. A small opening in the cylinder allows the atoms to strike a target area. Because the cylinder is rotating, atoms traveling at different speeds will strike the target at different positions. In time, a layer of the metal will deposit on the target area, and the variation in its thickness is found to correspond to Maxwell's speed distribution. In one experiment it is found that at 850°C some bismuth (Bi) atoms struck the target at a point 2.80 cm from the spot directly opposite the slit. The diameter of the cylinder is 15.0 cm and it is rotating at 130 revolutions per second. (a) Calculate the speed (m/s) at which the target is moving. (*Hint:* The circumference of a circle is given by $2\pi r$, where r is the radius.) (b) Calculate the time (in seconds) it takes for the target to travel 2.80 cm. (c) Determine the speed of the Bi atoms. Compare your result in (c) with the u_{rms} of Bi at 850°C. Comment on the difference.

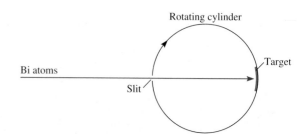

Rotating cylinder

Bi atoms

Slit

Target

5.109 If 10.00 g of water are introduced into an evacuated flask of volume 2.500 L at 65°C, calculate the mass of water vaporized. (*Hint:* Assume that the volume of the remaining liquid water is negligible; the vapor pressure of water at 65°C is 187.5 mmHg.)

5.110 Commercially, compressed oxygen is sold in metal cylinders. If a 120-L cylinder is filled with oxygen to a pressure of 132 atm at 22°C, what is the mass of O_2 present? How many liters of O_2 gas at 1.00 atm and 22°C could the cylinder produce? (Assume ideal behavior.)

5.111 The shells of hard-boiled eggs sometimes crack due to the rapid thermal expansion of the shells at high temperatures. Suggest another reason why the shells may crack.

5.112 Ethylene gas (C_2H_4) is emitted by fruits and is known to be responsible for their ripening. Based on this information, explain why a bunch of bananas ripens faster in a closed paper bag than in a bowl.

5.113 About 8.0×10^6 tons of urea [$(NH_2)_2CO$] are used annually as a fertilizer. The urea is prepared at 200°C and under high-pressure conditions from carbon dioxide and ammonia (the products are urea and steam). Calculate the volume of ammonia (in liters) measured at 150 atm needed to prepare 1.0 ton of urea.

5.114 Some ballpoint pens have a small hole in the main body of the pen. What is the purpose of this hole?

5.115 The gas laws are vitally important to scuba divers. The pressure exerted by 33 ft of seawater is equivalent to 1 atm pressure. (a) A diver ascends quickly to the surface of the water from a depth of 36 ft without exhaling gas from his lungs. By what factor will the volume of his lungs increase by the time he reaches the surface? Assume that the temperature is constant. (b) The partial pressure of oxygen in air is about 0.20 atm. (Air is 20 percent oxygen by volume.) In deep-sea diving, the composition of air the diver breathes must be changed to maintain this partial pressure. What must the oxygen content (in percent by volume) be when the total pressure exerted on the diver is 4.0 atm? (At constant temperature and pressure, the volume of a gas is directly proportional to the number of moles of gases.) (*Hint:* See Chemistry in Action essay on p. 192.)

5.116 Nitrous oxide (N_2O) can be obtained by the thermal decomposition of ammonium nitrate (NH_4NO_3). (a) Write a balanced equation for the reaction. (b) In a certain experiment, a student obtains 0.340 L of the gas at 718 mmHg and 24°C. If the gas weighs 0.580 g, calculate the value of the gas constant.

5.117 Two vessels are labeled A and B. Vessel A contains NH_3 gas at 70°C, and vessel B contains Ne gas at the same temperature. If the average kinetic energy of NH_3 is 7.1×10^{-21} J/molecule, calculate the mean-square speed of Ne atoms in m^2/s^2.

5.118 Which of the following molecules has the largest *a* value: CH_4, F_2, C_6H_6, Ne?

5.119 The following procedure is a simple though somewhat crude way to measure the molar mass of a gas. A liquid of mass 0.0184 g is introduced into a syringe like the one shown here by injection through the rubber tip using a hypodermic needle. The syringe is then transferred to a temperature bath heated to 45°C, and the liquid vaporizes. The final volume of the vapor (measured by the outward movement of the plunger) is 5.58 mL and the atmospheric pressure is 760 mmHg. Given that the compound's empirical formula is CH_2, determine the molar mass of the compound.

Rubber tip

5.120 In 1995 a man suffocated as he walked by an abandoned mine in England. At that moment there was a sharp drop in atmospheric pressure due to a change in the weather. Suggest what might have caused the man's death.

5.121 Acidic oxides such as carbon dioxide react with basic oxides like calcium oxide (CaO) and barium oxide (BaO) to form salts (metal carbonates). (a) Write equations representing these two reactions. (b) A student placed a mixture of BaO and CaO of combined mass 4.88 g in a 1.46-L flask containing carbon dioxide gas at 35°C and 746 mmHg. After the reactions were complete, she found that the CO_2 pressure had dropped to 252 mmHg. Calculate the percent composition by mass of the mixture. Assume volumes of the solids are negligible.

5.122 (a) What volume of air at 1.0 atm and 22°C is needed to fill a 0.98-L bicycle tire to a pressure of 5.0 atm at the same temperature? (Note that the 5.0 atm is the gauge pressure, which is the difference between the pressure in the tire and atmospheric pressure. Before filling, the pressure in the tire was 1.0 atm.) (b) What is the total pressure in the tire when the gauge pressure reads 5.0 atm? (c) The tire is pumped by filling the cylinder of a hand pump with air at 1.0 atm and then, by compressing the gas in the cylinder, adding all the air in the pump to the air in the tire. If the volume of the pump is 33 percent of the tire's volume, what is the gauge pressure in the tire after three full strokes of the pump? Assume constant temperature.

5.123 The running engine of an automobile produces carbon monoxide (CO), a toxic gas, at the rate of about 188 g CO per hour. A car is left idling in a poorly ventilated garage that is 6.0 m long, 4.0 m wide, and

2.2 m high at 20°C. (a) Calculate the rate of CO production in moles per minute. (b) How long would it take to build up a lethal concentration of CO of 1000 ppmv (parts per million by volume)?

5.124 Interstellar space contains mostly hydrogen atoms at a concentration of about 1 atom/cm³. (a) Calculate the pressure of the H atoms. (b) Calculate the volume (in liters) that contains 1.0 g of H atoms. The temperature is 3 K.

5.125 Atop Mt. Everest, the atmospheric pressure is 210 mmHg and the air density is 0.426 kg/m³. (a) Calculate the air temperature, given that the molar mass of air is 29.0 g/mol. (b) Assuming no change in air composition, calculate the percent decrease in oxygen gas from sea level to the top of Mt. Everest.

5.126 Relative humidity is defined as the ratio (expressed as a percentage) of the partial pressure of water vapor in the air to the equilibrium vapor pressure (see Table 5.3) at a given temperature. On a certain summer day in North Carolina the partial pressure of water vapor in the air is 3.9×10^3 Pa at 30°C. Calculate the relative humidity.

5.127 Under the same conditions of temperature and pressure, why does one liter of moist air weigh less than one liter of dry air? In weather forecasts, an oncoming low-pressure front usually means imminent rainfall. Explain.

5.128 Air entering the lungs ends up in tiny sacs called alveoli. It is from the alveoli that oxygen diffuses into the blood. The average radius of the alveoli is 0.0050 cm and the air inside contains 14 percent oxygen. Assuming that the pressure in the alveoli is 1.0 atm and the temperature is 37°C, calculate the number of oxygen molecules in one of the alveoli. (*Hint:* The volume of a sphere of radius r is $\frac{4}{3}\pi r^3$.)

5.129 A student breaks a thermometer and spills most of the mercury (Hg) onto the floor of a laboratory that measures 15.2 m long, 6.6 m wide, and 2.4 m high. (a) Calculate the mass of mercury vapor (in grams) in the room at 20°C. The vapor pressure of mercury at 20°C is 1.7×10^{-6} atm. (b) Does the concentration of mercury vapor exceed the air quality regulation of 0.050 mg Hg/m³ of air? (c) One way to treat small quantities of spilled mercury is to spray sulfur powder over the metal. Suggest a physical and a chemical reason for this action.

5.130 Nitrogen forms several gaseous oxides. One of them has a density of 1.33 g/L measured at 764 mmHg and 150°C. Write the formula of the compound.

5.131 Nitrogen dioxide (NO_2) cannot be obtained in a pure form in the gas phase because it exists as a mixture of NO_2 and N_2O_4. At 25°C and 0.98 atm, the density of this gas mixture is 2.7 g/L. What is the partial pressure of each gas?

5.132 The Chemistry in Action essay on p. 198 describes the cooling of rubidium vapor to 1.7×10^{-7} K. Calculate the root-mean-square speed and average kinetic energy of a Rb atom at this temperature.

5.133 Lithium hydride reacts with water as follows:

$$LiH(s) + H_2O(l) \longrightarrow LiOH(aq) + H_2(g)$$

During World War II, U.S. pilots carried LiH tablets. In the event of a crash landing at sea, the LiH would react with the seawater and fill their life belts and lifeboats with hydrogen gas. How many grams of LiH are needed to fill a 4.1-L life belt at 0.97 atm and 12°C?

5.134 The atmosphere on Mars is composed mainly of carbon dioxide. The surface temperature is 220 K and the atmospheric pressure is about 6.0 mmHg. Taking these values as Martian "STP," calculate the molar volume in liters of an ideal gas on Mars.

5.135 Venus's atmosphere is composed of 96.5 percent CO_2, 3.5 percent N_2, and 0.015 percent SO_2 by volume. Its standard atmospheric pressure is 9.0×10^6 Pa. Calculate the partial pressures of the gases in pascals.

5.136 A student tries to determine the volume of a bulb like the one shown on p. 182. These are her results: Mass of the bulb filled with dry air at 23°C and 744 mmHg = 91.6843 g; mass of evacuated bulb = 91.4715 g. Assume the composition of air is 78 percent N_2, 21 percent O_2, and 1 percent argon. What is the volume (in milliliters) of the bulb? (*Hint:* First calculate the average molar mass of air, as shown in Problem 3.140.)

5.137 Apply your knowledge of the kinetic theory of gases to the following situations. (a) Two flasks of volumes V_1 and V_2 ($V_2 > V_1$) contain the same number of helium atoms at the same temperature. (i) Compare the root-mean-square (rms) speeds and average kinetic energies of the helium (He) atoms in the flasks. (ii) Compare the frequency and the force with which the He atoms collide with the walls of their containers. (b) Equal numbers of He atoms are placed in two flasks of the same volume at temperatures T_1 and T_2 ($T_2 > T_1$). (i) Compare the rms speeds of the atoms in the two flasks. (ii) Compare the frequency and the force with which the He atoms collide with the walls of their containers. (c) Equal numbers of He and neon (Ne) atoms are placed in two flasks of the same volume, and the temperature of both gases is 74°C. Comment on the validity of the following statements: (i) The rms speed of He is equal to that of Ne. (ii) The average kinetic energies of the two gases are equal. (iii) The rms speed of each He atom is 1.47×10^3 m/s.

5.138 It has been said that every breath we take, on average, contains molecules that were once exhaled by Wolfgang Amadeus Mozart (1756–1791). The following calculations demonstrate the validity of this statement. (a) Calculate the total number of molecules in the atmosphere. (*Hint:* Use the result in Problem 5.98 and 29.0 g/mol as the molar mass of air.) (b) Assuming the volume of every breath (inhale or exhale) is 500 mL, calculate the number of molecules exhaled in each breath at 37°C, which is the body temperature. (c) If Mozart's lifespan was exactly 35 years, what is the number of molecules he exhaled in that period? (Given that an average person breathes 12 times per minute.) (d) Calculate the fraction of molecules in the atmosphere that was exhaled by Mozart. How many of Mozart's molecules do we breathe in with every inhale of air? Round off your answer to one significant figure. (e) List three important assumptions in these calculations.

5.139 Referring to Figure 5.21, explain the following: (a) Why do the curves dip below the horizontal line labeled ideal gas at low pressures and then why do they arise above the horizontal line at high pressures? (b) Why do the curves all converge to 1 at very low pressures? (c) Each curve intercepts the horizontal line labeled ideal gas. Does it mean that at that point the gas behaves ideally?

5.140 Estimate the distance (in nanometers) between molecules of water vapor at 100°C and 1.0 atm. Assume ideal behavior. Repeat the calculation for liquid water at 100°C, given that the density of water is 0.96 g/cm^3 at that temperature. Comment on your results. (Assume water molecule to be a sphere with a diameter of 0.3 nm.) (Hint: First calculate the number density of water molecules. Next, convert the number density to linear density, that is, number of molecules in one direction.)

5.141 Which of the noble gases would not behave ideally under any circumstance? Why?

5.142 A relation known as the barometric formula is useful for estimating the change in atmospheric pressure with altitude. The formula is given by $P = P_0 e^{-gMh/RT}$, where P and P_0 are the pressures at height h and sea level, respectively, g is the acceleration due to gravity (9.8 m/s^2), M is the average molar mass of air (29.0 g/mol), and R is the gas constant. Calculate the atmospheric pressure in atm at a height of 5.0 km, assuming the temperature is constant at 5°C and $P_0 = 1.0$ atm.

5.143 A 5.72-g sample of graphite was heated with 68.4 g of O$_2$ in a 8.00-L flask. The reaction that took place was

$$C(graphite) + O_2(g) \longrightarrow CO_2(g)$$

After the reaction was complete, the temperature in the flask was 182°C. What was the total pressure inside the flask?

5.144 A 6.11-g sample of a Cu-Zn alloy reacts with HCl acid to produce hydrogen gas. If the hydrogen gas has

a volume of 1.26 L at 22°C and 728 mmHg, what is the percent of Zn in the alloy? (Hint: Cu does not react with HCl.)

5.145 Graham's law of gas diffusion states that at the same temperature and pressure, the rates of diffusion of gases are inversely proportional to the square roots of their molar masses. Thus, for gases 1 and 2, we have

$$\frac{r_1}{r_2} = \sqrt{\frac{M_2}{M_1}}$$

where r_1 and r_2 are the rates of diffusion of the gases and M_1 and M_2 are the molar masses, respectively. Based on your knowledge of the kinetic theory of gases, derive Graham's law.

5.146 Referring to Figure 5.17, we see that the maximum of each speed distribution plot is called the most probable speed (u_{mp}) because it is the speed possessed by the largest number of molecules. It is given by $u_{mp} = \sqrt{2RT/M}$. (a) Compare u_{mp} with u_{rms} for nitrogen at 25°C. (b) The following diagram shows the Maxwell speed distribution curves for an ideal gas at two different temperatures T_1 and T_2. Calculate the value of T_2.

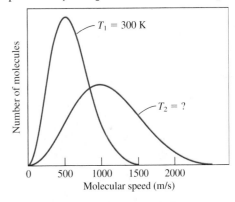

5.147 A stockroom supervisor measured the contents of a partially filled 25.0-gallon acetone drum on a day when the temperature was 18.0°C and atmospheric pressure was 750 mmHg, and found that 15.4 gallons of the solvent remained. After tightly sealing the drum, an assistant dropped the drum while carrying it upstairs to the organic laboratory. The drum was dented and its internal volume was decreased to 20.4 gallons. What is the total pressure inside the drum after the accident? The vapor pressure of acetone at 18.0°C is 400 mmHg. (Hint: At the time the drum was sealed, the pressure inside the drum, which is equal to the sum of the pressures of air and acetone, was equal to the atmospheric pressure.)

Answers to Practice Exercises

5.1 0.986 atm. 5.2 39.3 kPa. 5.3 9.29 L. 5.4 30.6 L. 5.5 4.46 × 10^3 mmHg. 5.6 0.68 atm. 5.7 2.6 atm. 5.8 13.1 g/L. 5.9 44.1 g/mol. 5.10 B$_2$H$_6$. 5.11 96.9 L. 5.12 4.75 L.

5.13 0.338 M. 5.14 CH$_4$: 1.29 atm; C$_2$H$_6$: 0.0657 atm; C$_3$H$_8$: 0.0181 atm. 5.15 0.0653 g. 5.16 321 m/s. 5.17 30.0 atm; 45.5 atm using the ideal gas equation.

CHEMICAL MYSTERY

Out of Oxygen[†]

In September 1991 four men and four women entered the world's largest glass bubble, known as Biosphere II, to test the idea that humans could design and build a totally self-contained ecosystem, a model for some future colony on another planet. Biosphere II (Earth is considered Biosphere I) was a 3-acre mini-world, complete with a tropical rain forest, savanna, marsh, desert, and working farm that was intended to be fully self-sufficient. This unique experiment was to continue for 2 to 3 years, but almost immediately there were signs that the project could be in jeopardy.

Soon after the bubble had been sealed, sensors inside the facility showed that the concentration of oxygen in Biosphere II's atmosphere had fallen from its initial level of 21 percent (by volume), while the amount of carbon dioxide had risen from a level of 0.035 percent (by volume), or 350 ppm (parts per million). Alarmingly, the oxygen level continued to fall at a rate of about 0.5 percent a month and the level of carbon dioxide kept rising, forcing the crew to turn on electrically powered chemical scrubbers, similar to those on submarines, to remove some of the excess CO_2. Gradually the CO_2 level stabilized around 4000 ppm, which is high but not dangerous. The loss of oxygen did not stop, though. By January 1993— 16 months into the experiment—the oxygen concentration had dropped to 14 percent, which is equivalent to the O_2 concentration in air at an elevation of 4360 m (14,300 ft). The crew began having trouble performing normal tasks. For their safety it was necessary to pump pure oxygen into Biosphere II.

With all the plants present in Biosphere II, the production of oxygen should have been greater as a consequence of photosynthesis. Why had the oxygen concentration declined to such a low level? A small part of the loss was blamed on unusually cloudy weather, which had slowed down plant growth. The possibility that iron in the soil was reacting with oxygen to form iron(III) oxide or rust was ruled out along with several other explanations for lack of evidence. The most plausible hypothesis was that microbes (microorganisms) were using oxygen to metabolize the excess organic matter that had been added to the soils to promote plant growth. This turned out to be the case.

Identifying the cause of oxygen depletion raised another question. Metabolism produces carbon dioxide. Based on the amount of oxygen consumed by the microbes, the CO_2 level should have been at 40,000 ppm, 10 times what was measured. What happened to the excess gas? After ruling out leakage to the outside world and reactions between CO_2 with compounds in the soils and in water, scientists found that the concrete inside Biosphere II was consuming large amounts of CO_2!

Concrete is a mixture of sand and gravel held together by a binding agent which is a mixture of calcium silicate hydrates and calcium hydroxide. The calcium hydroxide is the key ingredient in the CO_2 mystery. Carbon dioxide diffuses into the porous structure of concrete, then reacts with calcium hydroxide to form calcium carbonate and water:

$$Ca(OH)_2(s) + CO_2(g) \longrightarrow CaCO_3(s) + H_2O(l)$$

Under normal conditions, this reaction goes on slowly. But CO_2 concentrations in Biosphere II were much higher than normal, so the reaction proceeded much faster. In fact, in just over

[†]Adapted with permission from "Biosphere II: Out of Oxygen," by Joe Alper, CHEM MATTERS, February, 1995, p. 8. Copyright 1995 American Chemical Society.

Vegetation in Biosphere II.

2 years, $CaCO_3$ had accumulated to a depth of more than 2 cm in Biosphere II's concrete. Some 10,000 m^2 of exposed concrete was hiding 500,000 to 1,500,000 moles of CO_2.

The water produced in the reaction between $Ca(OH)_2$ and CO_2 created another problem: CO_2 also reacts with water to form carbonic acid (H_2CO_3), and hydrogen ions produced by the acid promote the corrosion of the reinforcing iron bars in the concrete, thereby weakening its structure. This situation was dealt with effectively by painting all concrete surfaces with an impermeable coating.

In the meantime the decline in oxygen (and hence also the rise in carbon dioxide) slowed, perhaps because there was now less organic matter in the soils and also because new lights in the agricultural areas may have boosted photosynthesis. The project was terminated prematurely and, as of 1996, the facility was transformed into a science education and research center.

The Biosphere II experiment is an interesting project from which we can learn a lot about Earth and its inhabitants. If nothing else, it has shown us how complex Earth's ecosystems are and how difficult it is to mimic nature, even on a small scale.

Chemical Clues

1. What solution would you use in a chemical scrubber to remove carbon dioxide?

2. Photosynthesis converts carbon dioxide and water to carbohydrates and oxygen gas, while metabolism is the process by which carbohydrates react with oxygen to form carbon dioxide and water. Using glucose ($C_6H_{12}O_6$) to represent carbohydrates, write equations for these two processes.

3. Why was diffusion of O_2 from Biosphere II to the outside world not considered a possible cause for the depletion in oxygen?

4. Carbonic acid is a diprotic acid. Write equations for the stepwise ionization of the acid in water.

5. What are the factors to consider in choosing a planet on which to build a structure like Biosphere II?

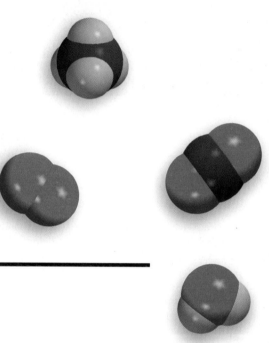

The analysis of particles formed from burning methane in a flame is performed with a visible laser. The models show methane and oxygen molecules and the combustion products carbon dioxide and water molecules.

Thermochemistry

Interactive Activity Summary

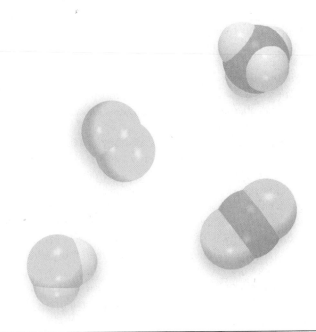

Every chemical reaction obeys two fundamental laws: the law of conservation of mass and the law of conservation of energy. We discussed the mass relationships between reactants and products in Chapter 3; here we will look at the energy changes that accompany chemical reactions.

6.1 The Nature of Energy and Types of Energy

"Energy" is a much-used term that represents a rather abstract concept. For instance, when we feel tired, we might say we haven't any *energy;* and we read about the need to find alternatives to nonrenewable *energy* sources. Unlike matter, energy is known and recognized by its effects. It cannot be seen, touched, smelled, or weighed.

Energy is usually defined as *the capacity to do work.* In Chapter 5 we defined work as "force × distance," but we will soon see that there are other kinds of work. All forms of energy are capable of doing work (that is, of exerting a force over a distance), but not all of them are equally relevant to chemistry. The energy contained in tidal waves, for example, can be harnessed to perform useful work, but the relationship between tidal waves and chemistry is minimal. Chemists define

Kinetic energy was introduced in Chapter 5.

work as *directed energy change resulting from a process.* Kinetic energy—the energy produced by a moving object—is one form of energy that is of particular interest to chemists. Others include radiant energy, thermal energy, chemical energy, and potential energy.

Radiant energy, or *solar energy, comes from the sun* and is Earth's primary energy source. Solar energy heats the atmosphere and Earth's surface, stimulates the growth of vegetation through the process known as photosynthesis, and influences global climate patterns.

Thermal energy is *the energy associated with the random motion of atoms and molecules.* In general, thermal energy can be calculated from temperature measurements. The more vigorous the motion of the atoms and molecules in a sample of matter, the hotter the sample is and the greater its thermal energy. However, we need to distinguish carefully between thermal energy and temperature. A cup of coffee at 70°C has a higher temperature than a bathtub filled with warm water at 40°C, but much more thermal energy is stored in the bathtub water because it has a much larger volume and greater mass than the coffee and therefore more water molecules and more molecular motion.

Chemical energy is *stored within the structural units of chemical substances;* its quantity is determined by the type and arrangement of constituent atoms. When substances participate in chemical reactions, chemical energy is released, stored, or converted to other forms of energy.

Potential energy is *energy available by virtue of an object's position.* For instance, because of its altitude, a rock at the top of a cliff has more potential energy and will make a bigger splash if it falls into the water below than a similar rock located partway down the cliff. Chemical energy can be considered a form of potential energy because it is associated with the relative positions and arrangements of atoms within a given substance.

As the water falls over the dam, its potential energy is converted to kinetic energy. Use of this energy to generate electricity is called hydroelectric power.

All forms of energy can be converted (at least in principle) from one form to another. We feel warm when we stand in sunlight because radiant energy is converted to thermal energy on our skin. When we exercise, chemical energy stored in our bodies is used to produce kinetic energy. When a ball starts to roll downhill, its potential energy is converted to kinetic energy. You can undoubtedly think of many other examples. Although energy can assume many different forms that are interconvertible, scientists have concluded that energy can be neither destroyed nor created. When one form of energy disappears, some other form of energy (of equal magnitude) must appear, and vice versa. This principle is summarized by the **law of conservation of energy:** *the total quantity of energy in the universe is assumed constant.*

6.2 Energy Changes in Chemical Reactions

Often the energy changes that take place during chemical reactions are of as much practical interest as the mass relationships we discussed in Chapter 3. For example, combustion reactions involving fuels such as natural gas and oil are carried out in daily life more for the thermal energy they release than for their products, which are water and carbon dioxide.

Almost all chemical reactions absorb or produce (release) energy, generally in the form of heat. It is important to understand the distinction between thermal energy and heat. **Heat** is *the transfer of thermal energy between two bodies that are at different temperatures.* Thus we often speak of the "heat flow" from a hot object to a cold one. Although the term "heat" by itself implies the transfer of energy, we customarily talk of "heat absorbed" or "heat released" when describing the energy changes that occur during a process. **Thermochemistry** is *the study of heat change in chemical reactions.*

To analyze energy changes associated with chemical reactions we must first define the **system,** or the *specific part of the universe that is of interest to us.* For chemists, systems usually include substances involved in chemical and physical changes. For example, in an acid-base neutralization experiment, the system may be a beaker containing 50 mL of HCl to which 50 mL of NaOH is added. The **surroundings** are *the rest of the universe outside the system.*

There are three types of systems. An **open system** *can exchange mass and energy, usually in the form of heat with its surroundings.* For example, an open system may consist of a quantity of water in an open container, as shown in Figure 6.1(a). If we close the flask, as in Figure 6.1(b), so that no water vapor can escape from or condense into the container, we create a **closed system,** which *allows the transfer of energy (heat) but not mass.* By placing the water in a totally insulated container, we can construct an **isolated system,** which *does not allow the transfer of either mass or energy,* as shown in Figure 6.1(c).

The combustion of hydrogen gas in oxygen is one of many chemical reactions that release considerable quantities of energy (Figure 6.2):

$$2H_2(g) + O_2(g) \longrightarrow 2H_2O(l) + \text{energy}$$

In this case, we label the reacting mixture (hydrogen, oxygen, and water molecules) the *system* and the rest of the universe the *surroundings.* Because energy cannot be

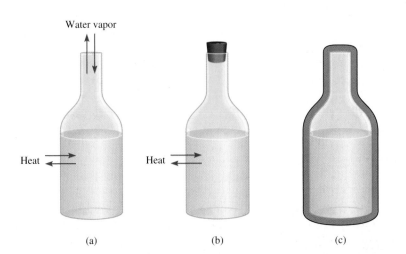

Water vapor

Heat

Heat

(a)   (b)   (c)

Figure 6.1 *Three systems represented by water in a flask: (a) an open system, which allows the exchange of both energy and mass with surroundings; (b) a closed system, which allows the exchange of energy but not mass; and (c) an isolated system, which allows neither energy nor mass to be exchanged (here the flask is enclosed by a vacuum jacket).*

Figure 6.2 *The Hindenburg disaster. The Hindenburg, a German airship filled with hydrogen gas, was destroyed in a spectacular fire at Lakehurst, New Jersey, in 1937.*

Exo- comes from the Greek word meaning "outside"; *endo-* means "within."

On heating, HgO decomposes to give Hg and O_2.

created or destroyed, any energy lost by the system must be gained by the surroundings. Thus the heat generated by the combustion process is transferred from the system to its surroundings. This reaction is an example of an **exothermic process,** which is *any process that gives off heat—that is, transfers thermal energy to the surroundings.* Figure 6.3(a) shows the energy change for the combustion of hydrogen gas.

Now consider another reaction, the decomposition of mercury(II) oxide (HgO) at high temperatures:

$$energy + 2HgO(s) \longrightarrow 2Hg(l) + O_2(g)$$

This reaction is an **endothermic process,** *in which heat has to be supplied to the system* (that is, to HgO) *by the surroundings* [Figure 6.3(b)].

From Figure 6.3 you can see that in exothermic reactions, the total energy of the products is less than the total energy of the reactants. The difference is the heat supplied by the system to the surroundings. Just the opposite happens in endothermic reactions. Here, the difference between the energy of the products and the energy of the reactants is equal to the heat supplied to the system by the surroundings.

Figure 6.3 *(a) An exothermic process. (b) An endothermic process. Parts (a) and (b) are not drawn to the same scale; that is, the heat released in the formation of H_2O from H_2 and O_2 is not equal to the heat absorbed in the decomposition of HgO.*

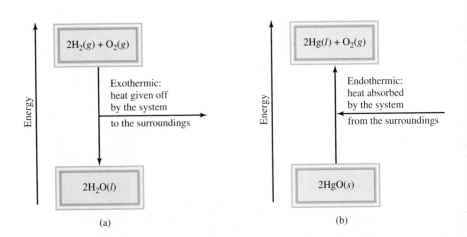

6.3 Introduction to Thermodynamics

Thermochemistry is part of a broader subject called ***thermodynamics,*** which is *the scientific study of the interconversion of heat and other kinds of energy.* The laws of thermodynamics provide useful guidelines for understanding the energetics and directions of processes. In this section we will concentrate on the first law of thermodynamics, which is particularly relevant to the study of thermochemistry. We will continue our discussion of thermodynamics in Chapter 18.

In thermodynamics, we study changes in the ***state of a system,*** which is defined by *the values of all relevant macroscopic properties, for example, composition, energy, temperature, pressure, and volume.* Energy, pressure, volume, and temperature are said to be ***state functions***—*properties that are determined by the state of the system, regardless of how that condition was achieved.* In other words, when the state of a system changes, the magnitude of change in any state function depends only on the initial and final states of the system and not on how the change is accomplished.

The state of a given amount of a gas is specified by its volume, pressure, and temperature. Consider a gas at 2 atm, 300 K, and 1 L (the initial state). Suppose a process is carried out at constant temperature such that the gas pressure decreases to 1 atm. According to Boyle's law, its volume must increase to 2 L. The final state then corresponds to 1 atm, 300 K, and 2 L. The change in volume (ΔV) is

The Greek letter *delta*, Δ, symbolizes change. We use Δ in this text always to mean final − initial.

$$\Delta V = V_f - V_i$$
$$= 2\,\text{L} - 1\,\text{L}$$
$$= 1\,\text{L}$$

where V_i and V_f denote the initial and final volume, respectively. No matter how we arrive at the final state (for example, the pressure of the gas can be increased first and then decreased to 1 atm), the change in volume is always 1 L. Thus the volume of a gas is a state function. In a similar manner we can show that pressure and temperature are also state functions.

Energy is another state function. Using potential energy as an example, we find that the net increase in gravitational potential energy when we go from the same starting point to the top of a mountain is always the same, regardless of how we get there (Figure 6.4).

Recall that an object possesses potential energy by virtue of its position or chemical composition.

The First Law of Thermodynamics

The ***first law of thermodynamics,*** which is based on the law of conservation of energy, states that *energy can be converted from one form to another, but cannot be created or destroyed.*[†] How do we know this is so? It would be impossible to prove the validity

Interactivity:
Conservation of Energy
Online Learning Center,
Interactives

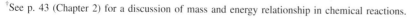

[†]See p. 43 (Chapter 2) for a discussion of mass and energy relationship in chemical reactions.

Figure 6.4 *The gain in gravitational potential energy that occurs when a person climbs from the base to the top of a mountain is independent of the path taken.*

of the first law of thermodynamics if we had to determine the total energy content of the universe. Even determining the total energy content of 1 g of iron, say, would be extremely difficult. Fortunately, we can test the validity of the first law by measuring only the *change* in the internal energy of a system between its *initial state* and its *final state* in a process. The change in internal energy ΔE is given by

$$\Delta E = E_f - E_i$$

where E_i and E_f are the internal energies of the system in the initial and final states, respectively.

The internal energy of a system has two components: kinetic energy and potential energy. The kinetic energy component consists of various types of molecular motion and the movement of electrons within molecules. Potential energy is determined by the attractive interactions between electrons and nuclei and by repulsive interactions between electrons and between nuclei in individual molecules, as well as by interaction between molecules. It is impossible to measure all these contributions accurately, so we cannot calculate the total energy of a system with any certainty. Changes in energy, on the other hand, can be determined experimentally.

Consider the reaction between 1 mole of sulfur and 1 mole of oxygen gas to produce 1 mole of sulfur dioxide:

$$S(s) + O_2(g) \longrightarrow SO_2(g)$$

In this case our system is composed of the reactant molecules S and O_2 and the product molecules SO_2. We do not know the internal energy content of either the reactant molecules or the product molecules, but we can accurately measure the *change* in energy content, ΔE, given by

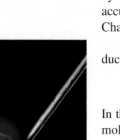

Sulfur burning in air to form SO_2.

$\Delta E = E(\text{product}) - E(\text{reactants})$
  $= $ energy content of 1 mol $SO_2(g)$ − energy content of [1 mol $S(s)$ + 1 mol $O_2(g)$]

We find that this reaction gives off heat. Therefore, the energy of the product is less than that of the reactants, and ΔE is negative.

Interpreting the release of heat in this reaction to mean that some of the chemical energy contained in the molecules has been converted to thermal energy, we conclude that the transfer of energy from the system to the surroundings does not change the total energy of the universe. That is, the sum of the energy changes must be zero:

$$\Delta E_{sys} + \Delta E_{surr} = 0$$

or

$$\Delta E_{sys} = -\Delta E_{surr}$$

where the subscripts "sys" and "surr" denote system and surroundings, respectively. Thus, if one system undergoes an energy change ΔE_{sys}, the rest of the universe, or the surroundings, must undergo a change in energy that is equal in magnitude but opposite in sign ($-\Delta E_{surr}$); energy gained in one place must have been lost somewhere else. Furthermore, because energy can be changed from one form to another, the energy lost by one system can be gained by another system in a different form. For example, the energy lost by burning oil in a power plant may ultimately turn up in our homes as electrical energy, heat, light, and so on.

In chemistry, we are normally interested in the energy changes associated with the system (which may be a flask containing reactants and products), not with its surroundings. Therefore, a more useful form of the first law is

We use lowercase letters (such as w and q) to represent thermodynamic quantities that are not state functions.

$$\Delta E = q + w \tag{6.1}$$

TABLE 6.1

Sign Conventions for Work and Heat	
Process	**Sign**
Work done by the system on the surroundings	−
Work done on the system by the surroundings	+
Heat absorbed by the system from the surroundings (endothermic process)	+
Heat absorbed by the surroundings from the system (exothermic process)	−

(We drop the subscript "sys" for simplicity.) Equation (6.1) says that the change in the internal energy ΔE of a system is the sum of the heat exchange q between the system and the surroundings and the work done w on (or by) the system. The sign conventions for q and w are as follows: q is positive for an endothermic process and negative for an exothermic process and w is positive for work done on the system by the surroundings and negative for work done by the system on the surroundings. We can think of the first law of thermodynamics as an energy balance sheet, much like a money balance sheet kept in a bank that does currency exchange. You can withdraw or deposit money in either of two different currencies (like energy change due to heat exchange and work done). However, the value of your bank account depends only on the net amount of money left in it after these transactions, not on which currency you used.

For convenience, we sometimes omit the word "internal" when discussing the energy of a system.

Equation (6.1) may seem abstract, but it is actually quite logical. If a system loses heat to the surroundings or does work on the surroundings, we would expect its internal energy to decrease because they are energy-depleting processes. For this reason, both q and w are negative. Conversely, if heat is added to the system or if work is done on the system, then the internal energy of the system would increase. In this case, both q and w are positive. Table 6.1 summarizes the sign conventions for q and w.

Work and Heat

We have seen that work can be defined as force F multiplied by distance d:

$$w = Fd \tag{6.2}$$

In thermodynamics, work has a broader meaning that includes mechanical work (for example, a crane lifting a steel beam), electrical work (a battery supplying electrons to light the bulb of a flashlight), and surface work (blowing up a soap bubble). In this section we will concentrate on mechanical work; in Chapter 19 we will discuss the nature of electrical work.

A useful example of mechanical work is the expansion of a gas (Figure 6.5). Suppose that a gas is in a cylinder fitted with a weightless, frictionless movable piston,

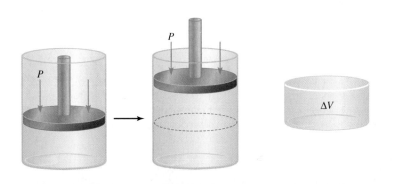

Figure 6.5 *The expansion of a gas against a constant external pressure (such as atmospheric pressure). The gas is in a cylinder fitted with a weightless movable piston. The work done is given by* $-P\Delta V$.

at a certain temperature, pressure, and volume. As it expands, the gas pushes the piston upward against a constant opposing external atmospheric pressure P. The work done by the gas on the surroundings is

$$w = -P\Delta V \tag{6.3}$$

where ΔV, the change in volume, is given by $V_f - V_i$. The minus sign in Equation (6.3) takes care of the convention for w. For gas expansion, $\Delta V > 0$, so $-P\Delta V$ is a negative quantity. For gas compression (work done on the system), $\Delta V < 0$, and $-P\Delta V$ is a positive quantity.

Equation (6.3) derives from the fact that pressure × volume can be expressed as (force/area) × volume; that is,

$$P \times V = \underbrace{\frac{F}{d^2}}_{\text{pressure}} \times \underbrace{d^3}_{\text{volume}} = Fd = w$$

where F is the opposing force and d has the dimension of length, d^2 has the dimensions of area, and d^3 has the dimensions of volume. Thus the product of pressure and volume is equal to force times distance, or work. You can see that for a given increase in volume (that is, for a certain value of ΔV), the work done depends on the magnitude of the external, opposing pressure P. If P is zero (that is, if the gas is expanding against a vacuum), the work done must also be zero. If P is some positive, nonzero value, then the work done is given by $-P\Delta V$.

According to Equation (6.3), the units for work done by or on a gas are liters atmospheres. To express the work done in the more familiar unit of joules, we use the conversion factor (see Appendix 2).

$$1 \text{ L} \cdot \text{atm} = 101.3 \text{ J}$$

Example 6.1

A certain gas expands in volume from 2.0 L to 6.0 L at constant temperature. Calculate the work done by the gas if it expands (a) against a vacuum and (b) against a constant pressure of 1.2 atm.

Strategy A simple sketch of the situation is helpful here:

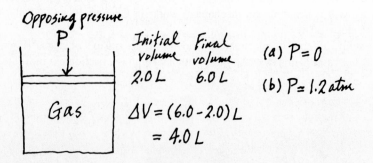

The work done in gas expansion is equal to the product of the external, opposing pressure and the change in volume. What is the conversion factor between L · atm and J?

(Continued)

Solution

(a) Because the external pressure is zero, no work is done in the expansion.

$$w = -P\Delta V$$
$$= -(0)(6.0 - 2.0)\text{ L}$$
$$= 0$$

(b) The external, opposing pressure is 1.2 atm, so

$$w = -P\Delta V$$
$$= -(1.2 \text{ atm})(6.0 - 2.0)\text{ L}$$
$$= -4.8 \text{ L} \cdot \text{atm}$$

To convert the answer to joules, we write

$$w = -4.8 \text{ L} \cdot \text{atm} \times \frac{101.3 \text{ J}}{1 \text{ L} \cdot \text{atm}}$$
$$= -4.9 \times 10^2 \text{ J}$$

Check Because this is gas expansion (work is done by the system on the surroundings), the work done has a negative sign.

Similar problems: 6.15, 6.16.

Practice Exercise A gas expands from 264 mL to 971 mL at constant temperature. Calculate the work done (in joules) by the gas if it expands (a) against a vacuum and (b) against a constant pressure of 4.00 atm.

Example 6.1 shows that work is not a state function. Although the initial and final states are the same in (a) and (b), the amount of work done is different because the external, opposing pressures are different. We *cannot* write $\Delta w = w_f - w_i$ for a change. Work done depends not only on the initial state and final state, but also on how the process is carried out, that is, on the path.

Because temperature is kept constant, you can use Boyle's law to show that the final pressure is the same in (a) and (b).

The other component of internal energy is q, heat. Like work, heat is not a state function. Suppose that we raise the temperature of 100.0 g of water initially at 20.0°C and 1 atm to 30.0°C and 1 atm. What is the heat transferred to the water for this process? We do not know the answer because the process is not specified. One way to raise the temperature is to heat the water using a Bunsen burner or electrically using an immersion heater. In either case we can calculate the heat transferred to be 4184 J.[†]

Alternatively, we can bring about the temperature increase by stirring the water with a magnetic stirring bar until the desired temperature is reached as a result of friction. The heat transferred in this case is zero. Or we could first raise the temperature of water from 20°C to 25°C by direct heating, and then stir the bar to bring it up to 30°C. In each case q is somewhere between zero and 4184 J. This simple example shows that heat associated with a given process, like work, depends on how the process is carried out; that is, we *cannot* write $\Delta q = q_f - q_i$. It is important to note that although neither heat nor work is a state function, their sum $(q + w)$ is equal to

---

[†]The heat transferred to water is $q = ms\Delta t$, where m is the mass of water in grams, s the specific heat of water (4.184 J/g · °C), and Δt the temperature change. Thus $q = (100.0 \text{ g})(4.184 \text{ J/g} \cdot °\text{C})(10°\text{C}) = 4184 \text{ J}$. Specific heat will be discussed in Section 6.5.

CHEMISTRY IN ACTION

Making Snow and Inflating a Bicycle Tire

Many phenomena in everyday life can be explained by the first law of thermodynamics. Here we will discuss two examples of interest to lovers of the outdoors.

Making Snow

If you are an avid downhill skier, you have probably skied on artificial snow. How is this stuff made in quantities large enough to meet the needs of skiers on snowless days? The secret of snowmaking is in the equation $\Delta E = q + w$. A snowmaking machine contains a mixture of compressed air and water vapor at about 20 atm. Because of the large difference in pressure between the tank and the outside atmosphere, when the mixture is sprayed into the atmosphere it expands so rapidly that, as a good approximation, no heat exchange occurs between the system (air and water) and its surroundings; that is, $q = 0$. (In thermodynamics, such a process is called an *adiabatic process*.) Thus we write

$$\Delta E = q + w = w$$

Because the system does work on the surroundings, w is a negative quantity, and there is a decrease in the system's energy.

Kinetic energy is part of the total energy of the system. In Section 5.7 we saw that the average kinetic energy of a gas is directly proportional to the absolute temperature [Equation (5.15)]. It follows, therefore, that the change in energy ΔE is given by

$$\Delta E = C\Delta T$$

where C is the proportionality constant. Because ΔE is negative, ΔT must also be negative, and it is this cooling effect (or the decrease in the kinetic energy of the water molecules) that is responsible for the formation of snow. Although we need only water to form snow, the presence of air, which also cools on expansion, helps to lower the temperature of the water vapor.

Inflating a Bicycle Tire

If you have ever pumped air into a bicycle tire, you probably noticed a warming effect at the valve stem. This phenomenon, too, can be explained by the first law of thermodynamics. The action of the pump compresses the air inside the pump and the tire. The process is rapid enough to be treated as approximately adiabatic, so that $q = 0$ and $\Delta E = w$. Because work is done on the gas in this case (it is being compressed), w is positive, and there is an increase in energy. Hence, the temperature of the system increases also, according to the equation

$$\Delta E = C\Delta T$$

A snowmaking machine in operation.

ΔE and, as we saw earlier, E is a state function. Thus if changing the path from the initial state to the final state increases the value of q, it will decrease the value of w by the same amount and vice versa.

In summary, heat and work are not state functions because they are not properties of a system. They manifest themselves only during a process (during a change). Thus their values depend on the path of the process and vary accordingly.

Example 6.2

The work done when a gas is compressed in a cylinder like that shown in Figure 6.5 is 462 J. During this process, there is a heat transfer of 128 J from the gas to the surroundings. Calculate the energy change for this process.

Strategy Compression is work done on the gas, so what is the sign for w? Heat is released by the gas to the surroundings. Is this an endothermic or exothermic process? What is the sign for q?

Solution To calculate the energy change of the gas, we need Equation (6.1). Work of compression is positive and because heat is released by the gas, q is negative. Therefore we have

$$\Delta E = q + w$$
$$= -128 \text{ J} + 462 \text{ J}$$
$$= 334 \text{ J}$$

As a result, the energy of the gas increases by 334 J.

Similar problems: 6.17, 6.18.

Practice Exercise A gas expands and does P-V work on the surroundings equal to 279 J. At the same time, it absorbs 216 J of heat from the surroundings. What is the change in energy of the system?

6.4 Enthalpy of Chemical Reactions

Our next step is to see how the first law of thermodynamics can be applied to processes carried out under different conditions. Specifically, we will consider a situation in which the volume of the system is kept constant and one in which the pressure applied on the system is kept constant.

If a chemical reaction is run at constant volume, then $\Delta V = 0$ and no P-V work will result from this change. From Equation (6.1) it follows that

$$\Delta E = q - P\Delta V$$
$$= q_v \tag{6.4}$$

We add the subscript "v" to remind us that this is a constant-volume process. This equality may seem strange at first, for we showed earlier that q is not a state function. The process is carried out under constant-volume conditions, however, so that the heat change can have only a specific value, which is equal to ΔE.

Enthalpy

Constant-volume conditions are often inconvenient and sometimes impossible to achieve. Most reactions occur under conditions of constant pressure (usually atmospheric pressure). If such a reaction results in a net increase in the number of moles of a gas, then the system does work on the surroundings (expansion). This follows from the fact that for the gas formed to enter the atmosphere, it must push the surrounding air back. Conversely, if more gas molecules are consumed than are produced, work is done on the system by the surroundings (compression). Finally, no work is done if there is no net change in the number of moles of gases from reactants to products.

In general, for a constant-pressure process we write

$$\Delta E = q + w$$
$$= q_p - P\Delta V$$

or
$$q_p = \Delta E + P\Delta V \tag{6.5}$$

where the subscript "p" denotes constant-pressure condition.

We now introduce a new thermodynamic function of a system called **enthalpy (H),** which is defined by the equation

$$H = E + PV \tag{6.6}$$

where E is the internal energy of the system and P and V are the pressure and volume of the system, respectively. Because E and PV have energy units, enthalpy also has energy units. Furthermore, E, P, and V are all state functions, that is, the changes in $(E + PV)$ depend only on the initial and final states. It follows, therefore, that the change in H, or ΔH, also depends only on the initial and final states. Thus H is a state function.

For any process, the change in enthalpy according to Equation (6.6) is given by

$$\Delta H = \Delta E + \Delta(PV) \tag{6.7}$$

If the pressure is held constant, then

$$\Delta H = \Delta E + P\Delta V \tag{6.8}$$

Comparing Equation (6.8) with Equation (6.5), we see that for a constant-pressure process, $q_p = \Delta H$. Again, although q is not a state function, the heat change at constant pressure is equal to ΔH because the "path" is defined and therefore it can have only a specific value.

In Section 6.5 we will discuss ways to measure heat changes at constant volume and constant pressure.

We now have two quantities—ΔE and ΔH—that can be associated with a reaction. If the reaction occurs under constant-volume conditions, then the heat change, q_v, is equal to ΔE. On the other hand, when the reaction is carried out at constant pressure, the heat change, q_p, is equal to ΔH.

Enthalpy of Reactions

Because most reactions are constant-pressure processes, we can equate the heat change in these cases to the change in enthalpy. For any reaction of the type

$$\text{reactants} \longrightarrow \text{products}$$

we define the change in enthalpy, called the **enthalpy of reaction, ΔH,** as *the difference between the enthalpies of the products and the enthalpies of the reactants:*

$$\Delta H = H(\text{products}) - H(\text{reactants}) \tag{6.9}$$

The enthalpy of reaction can be positive or negative, depending on the process. For an endothermic process (heat absorbed by the system from the surroundings), ΔH is positive (that is, $\Delta H > 0$). For an exothermic process (heat released by the system to the surroundings), ΔH is negative (that is, $\Delta H < 0$).

An analogy for enthalpy change is a change in the balance in your bank account. Suppose your initial balance is \$100. After a transaction (deposit or withdrawal), the change in your bank balance, ΔX, is given by

This analogy assumes that you will not overdraw your bank account. The enthalpy of a substance *cannot* be negative.

$$\Delta X = X_{\text{final}} - X_{\text{initial}}$$

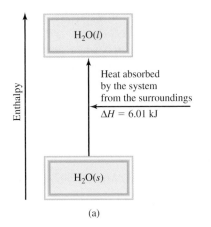

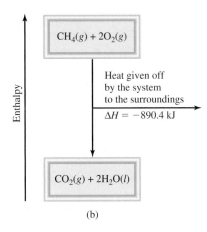

(a)   (b)

Figure 6.6 *(a) Melting 1 mole of ice at 0°C (an endothermic process) results in an enthalpy increase in the system of 6.01 kJ. (b) Burning 1 mole of methane in oxygen gas (an exothermic process) results in an enthalpy decrease in the system of 890.4 kJ.*

where X represents the bank balance. If you deposit \$80 into your account, then $\Delta X = \$180 - \$100 = \$80$. This corresponds to an endothermic reaction. (The balance increases and so does the enthalpy of the system.) On the other hand, a withdrawal of \$60 means $\Delta X = \$40 - \$100 = -\$60$. The negative sign of ΔX means your balance has decreased. Similarly, a negative value of ΔH reflects a decrease in enthalpy of the system as a result of an exothermic process. The difference between this analogy and Equation (6.9) is that while you always know your exact bank balance, there is no way to know the enthalpies of individual products and reactants. In practice, we can only measure the *difference* in their values.

Now let us apply the idea of enthalpy changes to two common processes, the first involving a physical change, the second a chemical change.

Thermochemical Equations

At 0°C and a pressure of 1 atm, ice melts to form liquid water. Measurements show that for every mole of ice converted to liquid water under these conditions, 6.01 kilojoules (kJ) of heat energy are absorbed by the system (ice). Because the pressure is constant, the heat change is equal to the enthalpy change, ΔH. Furthermore, this is an endothermic process, as expected for the energy-absorbing change of melting ice (Figure 6.6a). Therefore, ΔH is a positive quantity. The equation for this physical change is

Animation: Heat Flow
Online Learning Center,
Animations

$$H_2O(s) \longrightarrow H_2O(l) \qquad \Delta H = 6.01 \text{ kJ/mol}$$

The "per mole" in the unit for ΔH means that this is the enthalpy change *per mole of the reaction (or process) as it is written*, that is, when 1 mole of ice is converted to 1 mole of liquid water.

As another example, consider the combustion of methane (CH_4), the principal component of natural gas:

$$CH_4(g) + 2O_2(g) \longrightarrow CO_2(g) + 2H_2O(l) \quad \Delta H = -890.4 \text{ kJ/mol}$$

From experience we know that burning natural gas releases heat to the surroundings, so it is an exothermic process. Under constant-pressure condition this heat change is equal to enthalpy change and ΔH must have a negative sign (Figure 6.6b). Again, the per mole of reaction unit for ΔH means that when 1 mole of CH_4 reacts with 2 moles of O_2 to yield 1 mole of CO_2 and 2 moles of liquid H_2O, 890.4 kJ of heat are released to the surroundings.

Methane gas burning from a Bunsen burner.

The equations for the melting of ice and the combustion of methane are examples of ***thermochemical equations,*** which *show the enthalpy changes as well as the mass relationships.* It is essential to specify a balanced equation when quoting the enthalpy change of a reaction. The following guidelines are helpful in writing and interpreting thermochemical equations:

1. When writing thermochemical equations, we must always specify the physical states of all reactants and products, because they help determine the actual enthalpy changes. For example, in the equation for the combustion of methane, if we show water vapor rather than liquid water as a product,

$$CH_4(g) + 2O_2(g) \longrightarrow CO_2(g) + 2H_2O(g) \qquad \Delta H = -802.4 \text{ kJ/mol}$$

the enthalpy change is -802.4 kJ rather than -890.4 kJ because 88.0 kJ are needed to convert 2 moles of liquid water to water vapor; that is,

$$2H_2O(l) \longrightarrow 2H_2O(g) \qquad \Delta H = 88.0 \text{ kJ/mol}$$

Keep in mind that H is an extensive property.

2. If we multiply both sides of a thermochemical equation by a factor n, then ΔH must also change by the same factor. Thus, for the melting of ice, if $n = 2$, we have

$$2H_2O(s) \longrightarrow 2H_2O(l) \quad \Delta H = 2(6.01 \text{ kJ/mol}) = 12.0 \text{ kJ/mol}$$

3. When we reverse an equation, we change the roles of reactants and products. Consequently, the magnitude of ΔH for the equation remains the same, but its sign changes. For example, if a reaction consumes thermal energy from its surroundings (that is, if it is endothermic), then the reverse reaction must release thermal energy back to its surroundings (that is, it must be exothermic) and the enthalpy change expression must also change its sign. Thus, reversing the melting of ice and the combustion of methane, the thermochemical equations become

$$H_2O(l) \longrightarrow H_2O(s) \qquad \Delta H = -6.01 \text{ kJ/mol}$$
$$CO_2(g) + 2H_2O(l) \longrightarrow CH_4(g) + 2O_2(g) \qquad \Delta H = 890.4 \text{ kJ/mol}$$

and what was an endothermic process becomes exothermic, and vice versa.

Example 6.3

Given the thermochemical equation

$$SO_2(g) + \tfrac{1}{2}O_2(g) \longrightarrow SO_3(g) \qquad \Delta H = -99.1 \text{ kJ/mol}$$

calculate the heat evolved when 74.6 g of SO_2 (molar mass = 64.07 g/mol) is converted to SO_3.

Strategy The thermochemical equation shows that for every mole of SO_2 burned, 99.1 kJ of heat are given off (note the negative sign). Therefore, the conversion factor is

$$\frac{-99.1 \text{ kJ}}{1 \text{ mol } SO_2}$$

(Continued)

How many moles of SO_2 are in 74.6 g of SO_2? What is the conversion factor between grams and moles?

Solution We need to first calculate the number of moles of SO_2 in 74.6 g of the compound and then find the number of kilojoules produced from the exothermic reaction. The sequence of conversions is as follows:

$$\text{grams of } SO_2 \longrightarrow \text{moles of } SO_2 \longrightarrow \text{kilojoules of heat generated}$$

Therefore, the heat produced is given by

$$74.6 \text{ g } SO_2 \times \frac{1 \text{ mol } SO_2}{64.07 \text{ g } SO_2} \times \frac{-99.1 \text{ kJ}}{1 \text{ mol } SO_2} = -115 \text{ kJ}$$

Check Because 74.6 g is greater than the molar mass of SO_2, we expect the heat released to be larger than -99.1 kJ. The negative sign indicates that this is an exothermic reaction.

Similar problem: 6.26.

Practice Exercise Calculate the heat evolved when 266 g of white phosphorus (P_4) burns in air according to the equation

$$P_4(s) + 5O_2(g) \longrightarrow P_4O_{10}(s) \qquad \Delta H = -3013 \text{ kJ/mol}$$

A Comparison of ΔH and ΔE

What is the relationship between ΔH and ΔE for a process? To find out, let us consider the reaction between sodium metal and water:

$$2Na(s) + 2H_2O(l) \longrightarrow 2NaOH(aq) + H_2(g) \qquad \Delta H = -367.5 \text{ kJ/mol}$$

This thermochemical equation says that when two moles of sodium react with an excess of water, 367.5 kJ of heat are given off. Note that one of the products is hydrogen gas, which must push back air to enter the atmosphere. Consequently, some of the energy produced by the reaction is used to do work of pushing back a volume of air (ΔV) against atmospheric pressure (P) (Figure 6.7). To calculate the change in internal energy, we rearrange Equation (6.8) as follows:

$$\Delta E = \Delta H - P\Delta V$$

Sodium reacting with water to form hydrogen gas.

If we assume the temperature to be 25°C and ignore the small change in the volume of the solution, we can show that the volume of 1 mole of H_2 gas at 1.0 atm and 298 K is 24.5 L, so that $-P\Delta V = -24.5$ L · atm or -2.5 kJ. Finally,

1 L · atm = 101.3 J

$$\Delta E = -367.5 \text{ kJ/mol} - 2.5 \text{ kJ/mol}$$
$$= -370.0 \text{ kJ/mol}$$

(a)

P

Air + water vapor + H_2 gas

(b)

Figure 6.7 (a) A beaker of water inside a cylinder fitted with a movable piston. The pressure inside is equal to the atmospheric pressure. (b) As the sodium metal reacts with water, hydrogen gas pushes the piston upward (doing work on the surroundings) until the pressure inside is again equal to that outside.

For reactions that do not result in a change in the number of moles of gases from reactants to products, $\Delta E = \Delta H$.

This calculation shows that ΔE and ΔH are approximately the same. The reason ΔH is smaller than ΔE in magnitude is that some of the internal energy released is used to do gas expansion work, so less heat is evolved. For reactions that do not involve gases, ΔV is usually very small and so ΔE is practically the same as ΔH.

Another way to calculate the internal energy change of a gaseous reaction is to assume ideal gas behavior and constant temperature. In this case,

$$
\begin{aligned}
\Delta E &= \Delta H - \Delta(PV) \\
&= \Delta H - \Delta(nRT) \\
&= \Delta H - RT\Delta n
\end{aligned}
\tag{6.10}
$$

where Δn is defined as

$$\Delta n = \text{number of moles of product gases} - \text{number of moles of reactant gases}$$

Carbon monoxide burns in air to form carbon dioxide.

Example 6.4

Calculate the change in internal energy when 2 moles of CO are converted to 2 moles of CO_2 at 1 atm and 25°C:

$$2CO(g) + O_2(g) \longrightarrow 2CO_2(g) \qquad \Delta H = -566.0 \text{ kJ/mol}$$

Strategy We are given the enthalpy change, ΔH, for the reaction and are asked to calculate the change in internal energy, ΔE. Therefore we need Equation (6.10). What is the change in the number of moles of gases? ΔH is given in kilojoules, so what units should we use for R?

Solution From the chemical equation we see that 3 moles of gases are converted to 2 moles of gases so that

$$
\begin{aligned}
\Delta n &= \text{number of moles of product gas} - \text{number of moles of reactant gases} \\
&= 2 - 3 \\
&= -1
\end{aligned}
$$

Using 8.314 J/K · mol for R and $T = 298$ K in Equation (6.10), we write

$$
\begin{aligned}
\Delta E &= \Delta H - RT\Delta n \\
&= -566.0 \text{ kJ/mol} - (8.314 \text{ J/K} \cdot \text{mol})\left(\frac{1 \text{ kJ}}{1000 \text{ J}}\right)(298 \text{ K})(-1) \\
&= -563.5 \text{ kJ/mol}
\end{aligned}
$$

Check Knowing that the reacting gaseous system undergoes a compression (3 moles to 2 moles), is it reasonable to have $\Delta H > \Delta E$ in magnitude?

Similar problem: 6.27.

Practice Exercise What is ΔE for the formation of 1 mole of CO at 1 atm and 25°C?

$$C(\text{graphite}) + \tfrac{1}{2}O_2(g) \longrightarrow CO(g) \qquad \Delta H = -110.5 \text{ kJ/mol}$$

6.5 Calorimetry

In the laboratory, heat changes in physical and chemical processes are measured with a *calorimeter,* a closed container designed specifically for this purpose. Our discussion of **calorimetry,** *the measurement of heat changes,* will depend on an understanding of specific heat and heat capacity, so let us consider them first.

Specific Heat and Heat Capacity

The *specific heat (s)* of a substance is *the amount of heat required to raise the temperature of one gram of the substance by one degree Celsius.* The *heat capacity (C)* of a substance is *the amount of heat required to raise the temperature of a given quantity of the substance by one degree Celsius.* Specific heat is an intensive property, whereas heat capacity is an extensive property. The relationship between the heat capacity and specific heat of a substance is

$$C = ms \qquad (6.11)$$

where m is the mass of the substance in grams. For example, the specific heat of water is $4.184 \text{ J/g} \cdot {}^\circ\text{C}$, and the heat capacity of 60.0 g of water is

$$(60.0 \text{ g})(4.184 \text{ J/g} \cdot {}^\circ\text{C}) = 251 \text{ J/}^\circ\text{C}$$

Note that specific heat has the units $\text{J/g} \cdot {}^\circ\text{C}$ and heat capacity has the units $\text{J/}^\circ\text{C}$. Table 6.2 shows the specific heat of some common substances.

If we know the specific heat and the amount of a substance, then the change in the sample's temperature (Δt) will tell us the amount of heat (q) that has been absorbed or released in a particular process. The equations for calculating the heat change are given by

$$q = ms\Delta t \qquad (6.12)$$

$$q = C\Delta t \qquad (6.13)$$

where Δt is the temperature change:

$$\Delta t = t_{\text{final}} - t_{\text{initial}}$$

The sign convention for q is the same as that for enthalpy change; q is positive for endothermic processes and negative for exothermic processes.

TABLE 6.2 The Specific Heats of Some Common Substances	
Substance	Specific Heat (J/g·°C)
Al	0.900
Au	0.129
C (graphite)	0.720
C (diamond)	0.502
Cu	0.385
Fe	0.444
Hg	0.139
H_2O	4.184
C_2H_5OH (ethanol)	2.46

Example 6.5

A 466-g sample of water is heated from 8.50°C to 74.60°C. Calculate the amount of heat absorbed (in kilojoules) by the water.

Strategy We know the quantity of water and the specific heat of water. With this information and the temperature rise, we can calculate the amount of heat absorbed (q).

Solution Using Equation (6.12), we write

$$\begin{aligned}
q &= ms\Delta t \\
&= (466 \text{ g})(4.184 \text{ J/g} \cdot {}^\circ\text{C})(74.60{}^\circ\text{C} - 8.50{}^\circ\text{C}) \\
&= 1.29 \times 10^5 \text{ J} \times \frac{1 \text{ kJ}}{1000 \text{ J}} \\
&= 129 \text{ kJ}
\end{aligned}$$

Check The units g and °C cancel, and we are left with the desired unit kJ. Because heat is absorbed by the water from the surroundings, it has a positive sign.

Similar problem: 6.34.

Practice Exercise An iron bar of mass 869 g cools from 94°C to 5°C. Calculate the heat released (in kilojoules) by the metal.

Figure 6.8 *A constant-volume bomb calorimeter. The bomb is filled with oxygen gas before it is placed in the bucket. The sample is ignited electrically, and the heat produced by the reaction can be accurately determined by measuring the temperature increase in the known amount of surrounding water.*

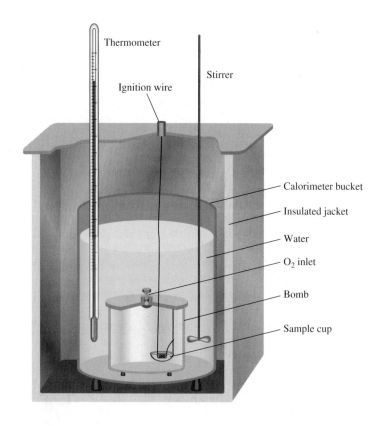

Figure 6.8 *A constant-volume bomb calorimeter. The bomb is filled with oxygen gas before it is placed in the bucket. The sample is ignited electrically, and the heat produced by the reaction can be accurately determined by measuring the temperature increase in the known amount of surrounding water.*

Constant-Volume Calorimetry

"Constant volume" refers to the volume of the bomb, which does not change during the reaction. Note that the bomb remains intact after the measurement. The term "bomb calorimeter" connotes the explosive nature of the reaction (on a small scale) in the presence of excess oxygen gas.

Heat of combustion is usually measured by placing a known mass of a compound in a steel container called a *constant-volume bomb calorimeter,* which is filled with oxygen at about 30 atm of pressure. The closed bomb is immersed in a known amount of water, as shown in Figure 6.8. The sample is ignited electrically, and the heat produced by the combustion reaction can be calculated accurately by recording the rise in temperature of the water. The heat given off by the sample is absorbed by the water and the bomb. The special design of the calorimeter allows us to assume that no heat (or mass) is lost to the surroundings during the time it takes to make measurements. Therefore we can call the bomb and the water in which it is submerged an isolated system. Because no heat enters or leaves the system throughout the process, the heat change of the system (q_{system}) must be zero and we can write

$$q_{system} = q_{cal} + q_{rxn}$$
$$= 0 \qquad (6.14)$$

where q_{cal} and q_{rxn} are the heat changes for the calorimeter and the reaction, respectively. Thus

$$q_{rxn} = -q_{cal} \qquad (6.15)$$

Note that C_{cal} comprises both the bomb and the surrounding water.

To calculate q_{cal}, we need to know the heat capacity of the calorimeter (C_{cal}) and the temperature rise, that is

$$q_{cal} = C_{cal}\Delta t \qquad (6.16)$$

The quantity C_{cal} is calibrated by burning a substance with an accurately known heat of combustion. For example, it is known that the combustion of 1 g of benzoic acid

(C_6H_5COOH) releases 26.42 kJ of heat. If the temperature rise is 4.673°C, then the heat capacity of the calorimeter is given by

$$C_{cal} = \frac{q_{cal}}{\Delta t}$$

$$= \frac{26.42 \text{ kJ}}{4.673°C} = 5.654 \text{ kJ/°C}$$

Once C_{cal} has been determined, the calorimeter can be used to measure the heat of combustion of other substances.

Note that because reactions in a bomb calorimeter occur under constant-volume rather than constant-pressure conditions, the heat changes *do not* correspond to the enthalpy change ΔH (see Section 6.4). It is possible to correct the measured heat changes so that they correspond to ΔH values, but the corrections usually are quite small so we will not concern ourselves with the details here. Finally, it is interesting to note that the energy contents of food and fuel (usually expressed in calories where 1 cal = 4.184 J) are measured with constant-volume calorimeters.

Example 6.6

A quantity of 1.435 g of naphthalene ($C_{10}H_8$), a pungent-smelling substance used in moth repellents, was burned in a constant-volume bomb calorimeter. Consequently, the temperature of the water rose from 20.28°C to 25.95°C. If the heat capacity of the bomb plus water was 10.17 kJ/°C, calculate the heat of combustion of naphthalene on a molar basis; that is, find the molar heat of combustion.

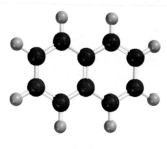

$C_{10}H_8$

Strategy Knowing the heat capacity and the temperature rise, how do we calculate the heat absorbed by the calorimeter? What is the heat generated by the combustion of 1.435 g of naphthalene? What is the conversion factor between grams and moles of naphthalene?

Solution The heat absorbed by the bomb and water is equal to the product of the heat capacity and the temperature change. From Equation (6.16), assuming no heat is lost to the surroundings, we write

$$q_{cal} = C_{cal}\Delta t$$
$$= (10.17 \text{ kJ/°C})(25.95°C - 20.28°C)$$
$$= 57.66 \text{ kJ}$$

Because $q_{sys} = q_{cal} + q_{rxn} = 0$, $q_{cal} = -q_{rxn}$. The heat change of the reaction is -57.66 kJ. This is the heat released by the combustion of 1.435 g of $C_{10}H_8$; therefore, we can write the conversion factor as

$$\frac{-57.66 \text{ kJ}}{1.435 \text{ g } C_{10}H_8}$$

The molar mass of naphthalene is 128.2 g, so the heat of combustion of 1 mole of naphthalene is

$$\text{molar heat of combustion} = \frac{-57.66 \text{ kJ}}{1.435 \text{ g } C_{10}H_8} \times \frac{128.2 \text{ g } C_{10}H_8}{1 \text{ mol } C_{10}H_8}$$
$$= -5.151 \times 10^3 \text{ kJ/mol}$$

Check Knowing that the combustion reaction is exothermic and that the molar mass of naphthalene is much greater than 1.4 g, is the answer reasonable? Under the reaction conditions, can the heat change (-57.66 kJ) be equated to the enthalpy change of the reaction?

Similar problem: 6.37.

Practice Exercise A quantity of 1.922 g of methanol (CH_3OH) was burned in a constant-volume bomb calorimeter. Consequently, the temperature of the water rose by 4.20°C. If the heat capacity of the bomb plus water was 10.4 kJ/°C, calculate the molar heat of combustion of methanol.

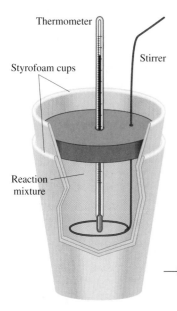

Figure   6.9 *A constant-pressure calorimeter made of two Styrofoam coffee cups. The outer cup helps to insulate the reacting mixture from the surroundings. Two solutions of known volume containing the reactants at the same temperature are carefully mixed in the calorimeter. The heat produced or absorbed by the reaction can be determined by measuring the temperature change.*

Constant-Pressure Calorimetry

A simpler device than the constant-volume calorimeter is the constant-pressure calorimeter, which is used to determine the heat changes for noncombustion reactions. A crude constant-pressure calorimeter can be constructed from two Styrofoam coffee cups, as shown in Figure 6.9. This device measures the heat effects of a variety of reactions, such as acid-base neutralization, as well as the heat of solution and heat of dilution. Because the pressure is constant, the heat change for the process (q_{rxn}) is equal to the enthalpy change (ΔH). As in the case of a constant-volume calorimeter, we treat the calorimeter as an isolated system. Furthermore, we neglect the small heat capacity of the coffee cups in our calculations. Table 6.3 lists some reactions that have been studied with the constant-pressure calorimeter.

Example 6.7

A lead pellet having a mass of 26.47 g at 89.98°C was placed in a constant-pressure calorimeter of negligible heat capacity containing 100.0 mL of water. The water temperature rose from 22.50°C to 23.17°C. What is the specific heat of the lead pellet?

Strategy A sketch of the initial and final situation is as follows:

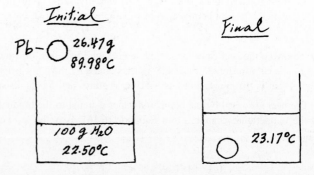

We know the masses of water and the lead pellet as well as the initial and final temperatures. Assuming no heat is lost to the surroundings, we can equate the heat lost by the

(Continued)

TABLE 6.3	Heats of Some Typical Reactions Measured at Constant Pressure		
Type of Reaction	**Example**		**ΔH (kJ/mol)**
Heat of neutralization	$HCl(aq) + NaOH(aq) \longrightarrow NaCl(aq) + H_2O(l)$		-56.2
Heat of ionization	$H_2O(l) \longrightarrow H^+(aq) + OH^-(aq)$		56.2
Heat of fusion	$H_2O(s) \longrightarrow H_2O(l)$		6.01
Heat of vaporization	$H_2O(l) \longrightarrow H_2O(g)$		44.0^*
Heat of reaction	$MgCl_2(s) + 2Na(l) \longrightarrow 2NaCl(s) + Mg(s)$		-180.2

*Measured at 25°C. At 100°C, the value is 40.79 kJ.

lead pellet to the heat gained by the water. Knowing the specific heat of water, we can then calculate the specific heat of lead.

Solution Treating the calorimeter as an isolated system (no heat lost to the surroundings), we write

$$q_{Pb} + q_{H_2O} = 0$$

or

$$q_{Pb} = -q_{H_2O}$$

The heat gained by the water is given by

$$q_{H_2O} = ms\Delta t$$

where m and s are the mass and specific heat and $\Delta t = t_{final} - t_{initial}$. Therefore,

$$q_{H_2O} = (100.0 \text{ g})(4.184 \text{ J/g} \cdot {}^\circ\text{C})(23.17{}^\circ\text{C} - 22.50{}^\circ\text{C})$$
$$= 280.3 \text{ J}$$

Because the heat lost by the lead pellet is equal to the heat gained by the water, so $q_{Pb} = -280.3$ J. Solving for the specific heat of Pb, we write

$$q_{Pb} = ms\Delta t$$
$$-280.3 \text{ J} = (26.47 \text{ g})(s)(23.17{}^\circ\text{C} - 89.98{}^\circ\text{C})$$
$$s = 0.158 \text{ J/g} \cdot {}^\circ\text{C}$$

Similar problem: 6.82.

Practice Exercise A 30.14-g stainless steel ball bearing at 117.82°C is placed in a constant-pressure calorimeter containing 120.0 mL of water at 18.44°C. If the specific heat of the ball bearing is 0.474 J/g · °C, calculate the final temperature of the water. Assume the calorimeter to have negligible heat capacity.

Example 6.8

A quantity of 1.00×10^2 mL of 0.500 M HCl was mixed with 1.00×10^2 mL of 0.500 M NaOH in a constant-pressure calorimeter of negligible heat capacity. The initial temperature of the HCl and NaOH solutions was the same, 22.50°C, and the final temperature of the mixed solution was 25.86°C. Calculate the heat change for the neutralization reaction on a molar basis

$$\text{NaOH}(aq) + \text{HCl}(aq) \longrightarrow \text{NaCl}(aq) + \text{H}_2\text{O}(l)$$

Assume that the densities and specific heats of the solutions are the same as for water (1.00 g/mL and 4.184 J/g · °C, respectively).

Strategy Because the temperature rose, the neutralization reaction is exothermic. How do we calculate the heat absorbed by the combined solution? What is the heat of the reaction? What is the conversion factor for expressing the heat of reaction on a molar basis?

Solution Assuming no heat is lost to the surroundings, $q_{sys} = q_{soln} + q_{rxn} = 0$, so $q_{rxn} = -q_{soln}$, where q_{soln} is the heat absorbed by the combined solution. Because the density of the solution is 1.00 g/mL, the mass of a 100-mL solution is 100 g. Thus

$$q_{soln} = ms\Delta t$$
$$= (1.00 \times 10^2 \text{ g} + 1.00 \times 10^2 \text{ g})(4.184 \text{ J/g} \cdot {}^\circ\text{C})(25.86{}^\circ\text{C} - 22.50{}^\circ\text{C})$$
$$= 2.81 \times 10^3 \text{ J}$$
$$= 2.81 \text{ kJ}$$

(Continued)

CHEMISTRY IN ACTION

Fuel Values of Foods and Other Substances

The food we eat is broken down, or metabolized, in stages by a group of complex biological molecules called enzymes. Most of the energy released at each stage is captured for function and growth. One interesting aspect of metabolism is that the overall change in energy is the same as it is in combustion. For example, the total enthalpy change for the conversion of glucose ($C_6H_{12}O_6$) to carbon dioxide and water is the same whether we burn the substance in air or digest it in our bodies:

$$C_6H_{12}O_6(s) + 6O_2(g) \longrightarrow 6CO_2(g) + 6H_2O(l)$$
$$\Delta H = -2801 \text{ kJ/mol}$$

The important difference between metabolism and combustion is that the latter is usually a one-step, high-temperature process. Consequently, much of the energy released by combustion is lost to the surroundings.

Various foods have different compositions and hence different energy contents. The energy content of food is generally measured in calories. The *calorie (cal)* is a non-SI unit of energy that is equivalent to 4.184 J:

$$1 \text{ cal} = 4.184 \text{ J}$$

In the context of nutrition, however, the calorie we speak of (sometimes called a "big calorie") is actually equal to a *kilocalorie*; that is,

$$1 \text{ Cal} = 1000 \text{ cal} = 4184 \text{ J}$$

Note the use of a capital "C" to represent the "big calorie."

The bomb calorimeter described in Section 6.5 is ideally suited for measuring the energy content, or "fuel value," of foods. Fuel values are just the enthalpies of combustion (see table). In order to be analyzed in a bomb calorimeter, food must be dried first because most foods contain a considerable amount of water. Because the composition of particular foods is often not known, fuel values are expressed in terms of kJ/g rather than kJ/mol.

Fuel Values of Foods and Some Common Fuels

Substance	$\Delta H_{combustion}$ (kJ/g)
Apple	−2
Beef	−8
Beer	−1.5
Bread	−11
Butter	−34
Cheese	−18
Eggs	−6
Milk	−3
Potatoes	−3
Charcoal	−35
Coal	−30
Gasoline	−34
Kerosene	−37
Natural gas	−50
Wood	−20

Nutrition Facts

Serving Size 6 cookies (28g)
Servings Per Container about 11

Amount Per Serving

Calories 120   Calories from Fat 30

	% Daily Value*
Total Fat 4g	6%
Saturated Fat 0.5g	4%
Polyunsaturated Fat 0g	
Monounsaturated Fat 1g	
Cholesterol 5mg	2%
Sodium 105mg	4%
Total Carbohydrate 20g	7%
Dietary Fiber Less than 1gram	2%
Sugars 7g	
Protein 2g	

The labels on food packages reveal the calorie content of the food inside.

Because $q_{rxn} = -q_{soln}$, $q_{rxn} = -2.81$ kJ.

From the molarities given, the number of moles of both HCl and NaOH in 1.00×10^2 mL solution is

$$\frac{0.500 \text{ mol}}{1 \text{ L}} \times 0.100 \text{ L} = 0.0500 \text{ mol}$$

(Continued)

Therefore, the heat of neutralization when 1.00 mole of HCl reacts with 1.00 mole of NaOH is

$$\text{heat of neutralization} = \frac{-2.81 \text{ kJ}}{0.0500 \text{ mol}} = -56.2 \text{ kJ/mol}$$

Check Is the sign consistent with the nature of the reaction? Under the reaction condition, can the heat change be equated to the enthalpy change?

Similar problem: 6.38.

Practice Exercise A quantity of 4.00×10^2 mL of 0.600 M HNO$_3$ is mixed with 4.00×10^2 mL of 0.300 M Ba(OH)$_2$ in a constant-pressure calorimeter of negligible heat capacity. The initial temperature of both solutions is the same at 18.46°C. What is the final temperature of the solution? (Use the result in Example 6.8 for your calculation.)

6.6 Standard Enthalpy of Formation and Reaction

So far we have learned that we can determine the enthalpy change that accompanies a reaction by measuring the heat absorbed or released (at constant pressure). From Equation (6.9) we see that ΔH can also be calculated if we know the actual enthalpies of all reactants and products. However, as mentioned earlier, there is no way to measure the *absolute* value of the enthalpy of a substance. Only values *relative* to an arbitrary reference can be determined. This problem is similar to the one geographers face in expressing the elevations of specific mountains or valleys. Rather than trying to devise some type of "absolute" elevation scale (perhaps based on distance from the center of Earth?), by common agreement all geographic heights and depths are expressed relative to sea level, an arbitrary reference with a defined elevation of "zero" meters or feet. Similarly, chemists have agreed on an arbitrary reference point for enthalpy.

The "sea level" reference point for all enthalpy expressions is called the **standard enthalpy of formation (ΔH_f°),** which is defined as *the heat change that results when 1 mole of a compound is formed from its elements at a pressure of 1 atm.* Elements are said to be in the **standard state** at *1 atm,* hence the term "standard enthalpy." The superscript "°" represents standard-state conditions (1 atm), and the subscript "f" stands for formation. Although the standard state does not specify a temperature, we will always use ΔH_f° values measured at 25°C.

Table 6.4 lists the standard enthalpies of formation for a number of elements and compounds. (For a more complete list of ΔH_f° values, see Appendix 3.) By convention, *the standard enthalpy of formation of any element in its most stable form is zero.* Take the element oxygen as an example. Molecular oxygen (O$_2$) is more stable than the other allotropic form of oxygen, ozone (O$_3$), at 1 atm and 25°C. Thus we can write $\Delta H_f^\circ(\text{O}_2) = 0$, but $\Delta H_f^\circ(\text{O}_3) \neq 0$. Similarly, graphite is a more stable allotropic form of carbon than diamond at 1 atm and 25°C, so we have $\Delta H_f^\circ(\text{C, graphite}) = 0$ and $\Delta H_f^\circ(\text{C, diamond}) \neq 0$.

The importance of the standard enthalpies of formation is that once we know their values, we can readily calculate the **standard enthalpy of reaction, ΔH_{rxn}°,** defined as *the enthalpy of a reaction carried out at 1 atm.* For example, consider the hypothetical reaction

$$a\text{A} + b\text{B} \longrightarrow c\text{C} + d\text{D}$$

Graphite (top) and diamond (bottom).

TABLE 6.4

Standard Enthalpies of Formation of Some Inorganic Substances at 25°C

Substance	ΔH_f° (kJ/mol)	Substance	ΔH_f° (kJ/mol)
$Ag(s)$	0	$H_2O_2(l)$	−187.6
$AgCl(s)$	−127.0	$Hg(l)$	0
$Al(s)$	0	$I_2(s)$	0
$Al_2O_3(s)$	−1669.8	$HI(g)$	25.9
$Br_2(l)$	0	$Mg(s)$	0
$HBr(g)$	−36.2	$MgO(s)$	−601.8
$C(graphite)$	0	$MgCO_3(s)$	−1112.9
$C(diamond)$	1.90	$N_2(g)$	0
$CO(g)$	−110.5	$NH_3(g)$	−46.3
$CO_2(g)$	−393.5	$NO(g)$	90.4
$Ca(s)$	0	$NO_2(g)$	33.85
$CaO(s)$	−635.6	$N_2O_4(g)$	9.66
$CaCO_3(s)$	−1206.9	$N_2O(g)$	81.56
$Cl_2(g)$	0	$O(g)$	249.4
$HCl(g)$	−92.3	$O_2(g)$	0
$Cu(s)$	0	$O_3(g)$	142.2
$CuO(s)$	−155.2	$S(rhombic)$	0
$F_2(g)$	0	$S(monoclinic)$	0.30
$HF(g)$	−271.6	$SO_2(g)$	−296.1
$H(g)$	218.2	$SO_3(g)$	−395.2
$H_2(g)$	0	$H_2S(g)$	−20.15
$H_2O(g)$	−241.8	$ZnO(s)$	−348.0
$H_2O(l)$	−285.8		

where a, b, c, and d are stoichiometric coefficients. For this reaction ΔH_{rxn}° is given by

$$\Delta H_{rxn}^\circ = [c\Delta H_f^\circ(C) + d\Delta H_f^\circ(D)] - [a\Delta H_f^\circ(A) + b\Delta H_f^\circ(B)] \qquad (6.17)$$

We can generalize Equation (6.17) as:

$$\Delta H_{rxn}^\circ = \Sigma n\Delta H_f^\circ(\text{products}) - \Sigma m\Delta H_f^\circ(\text{reactants}) \qquad (6.18)$$

where m and n denote the stoichiometric coefficients for the reactants and products, and Σ (sigma) means "the sum of." Note that in calculations, the stoichiometric coefficients are just numbers without units.

In order to use Equation (6.17) to calculate ΔH_{rxn}° we must know the ΔH_f° values of the compounds that take part in the reaction. To determine these values we can apply the direct method or the indirect method.

The Direct Method

This method of measuring ΔH_f° works for compounds that can be readily synthesized from their elements. Suppose we want to know the enthalpy of formation of carbon dioxide. We must measure the enthalpy of the reaction when carbon (graphite) and molecular oxygen in their standard states are converted to carbon dioxide in its standard state:

$$C(graphite) + O_2(g) \longrightarrow CO_2(g) \quad \Delta H^\circ_{rxn} = -393.5 \text{ kJ/mol}$$

We know from experience that this combustion easily goes to completion. Thus, from Equation (6.17) we can write

$$\Delta H^\circ_{rxn} = \Delta H^\circ_f(CO_2, g) - [\Delta H^\circ_f(C, graphite) + \Delta H^\circ_f(O_2, g)]$$
$$= -393.5 \text{ kJ/mol}$$

Because both graphite and O_2 are stable allotropic forms of the elements, it follows that $\Delta H^\circ_f(C, graphite)$ and $\Delta H^\circ_f(O_2, g)$ are zero. Therefore

$$\Delta H^\circ_{rxn} = \Delta H^\circ_f(CO_2, g) = -393.5 \text{ kJ/mol}$$

or

$$\Delta H^\circ_f(CO_2, g) = -393.5 \text{ kJ/mol}$$

Note that arbitrarily assigning zero ΔH°_f for each element in its most stable form at the standard state does not affect our calculations in any way. Remember, in thermochemistry we are interested only in enthalpy *changes* because they can be determined experimentally whereas the absolute enthalpy values cannot. The choice of a zero "reference level" for enthalpy makes calculations easier to handle. Again referring to the terrestrial altitude analogy, we find that Mt. Everest is 8708 ft higher than Mt. McKinley. This difference in altitude is unaffected by the decision to set sea level at 0 ft or at 1000 ft.

Other compounds that can be studied by the direct method are SF_6, P_4O_{10}, and CS_2. The equations representing their syntheses are

$$S(rhombic) + 3F_2(g) \longrightarrow SF_6(g)$$
$$P_4(white) + 5O_2(g) \longrightarrow P_4O_{10}(s)$$
$$C(graphite) + 2S(rhombic) \longrightarrow CS_2(l)$$

Note that S(rhombic) and P(white) are the most stable allotropes of sulfur and phosphorus, respectively, at 1 atm and 25°C, so their ΔH°_f values are zero.

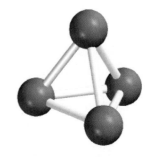

P_4

The Indirect Method

Many compounds cannot be directly synthesized from their elements. In some cases, the reaction proceeds too slowly, or side reactions produce substances other than the desired compound. In these cases ΔH°_f can be determined by an indirect approach, which is based on the Hess's law of heat summation, or simply Hess's law. **Hess's law**[†] can be stated as follows: *When reactants are converted to products, the change in enthalpy is the same whether the reaction takes place in one step or in a series of steps.* In other words, if we can break down the reaction of interest into a series of reactions for which ΔH°_{rxn} can be measured, we can calculate ΔH°_{rxn} for the overall reaction. Hess's law is based on the fact that because H is a state function, ΔH depends only on the initial and final state (that is, only on the nature of reactants and products). The enthalpy change would be the same whether the overall reaction takes place in one step or many steps.

An analogy for Hess's law is as follows. Suppose you go from the first floor to the sixth floor of a building by elevator. The gain in your gravitational potential energy

White phosphorus burns in air to form P_4O_{10}.

[†]Germain Henri Hess (1802–1850). Swiss chemist. Hess was born in Switzerland but spent most of his life in Russia. For formulating Hess's law, he is called the father of thermochemistry.

(which corresponds to the enthalpy change for the overall process) is the same whether you go directly there or stop at each floor on your way up (breaking the trip into a series of steps).

Let's say we are interested in the standard enthalpy of formation of methane (CH_4). We might represent the synthesis of CH_4 from its elements as

$$C(graphite) + 2H_2(g) \longrightarrow CH_4(g)$$

However, this reaction does not take place as written, so we cannot measure the enthalpy change directly. We must employ an indirect route, based on Hess's law. To begin with, the following reactions involving C(graphite), H_2, and CH_4 with O_2 have all been studied and the ΔH°_{rxn} values are accurately known.

(a)	$C(graphite) + O_2(g) \longrightarrow CO_2(g)$	$\Delta H^\circ_{rxn} = -393.5$ kJ/mol
(b)	$2H_2(g) + O_2(g) \longrightarrow 2H_2O(l)$	$\Delta H^\circ_{rxn} = -571.6$ kJ/mol
(c)	$CH_4(g) + 2O_2(g) \longrightarrow CO_2(g) + 2H_2O(l)$	$\Delta H^\circ_{rxn} = -890.4$ kJ/mol

Because we want to obtain one equation containing only C and H_2 as reactants and CH_4 as product, we must reverse (c) to get

Remember to reverse the sign of ΔH when you reverse an equation.

(d)	$CO_2(g) + 2H_2O(l) \longrightarrow CH_4(g) + 2O_2(g)$	$\Delta H^\circ_{rxn} = 890.4$ kJ/mol

The next step is to add Equations (a), (b), and (d):

(a)	$C(graphite) + O_2(g) \longrightarrow CO_2(g)$	$\Delta H^\circ_{rxn} = -393.5$ kJ/mol
(b)	$2H_2(g) + O_2(g) \longrightarrow 2H_2O(l)$	$\Delta H^\circ_{rxn} = -571.6$ kJ/mol
(d)	$CO_2(g) + 2H_2O(l) \longrightarrow CH_4(g) + 2O_2(g)$	$\Delta H^\circ_{rxn} = 890.4$ kJ/mol
(e)	$C(graphite) + 2H_2(g) \longrightarrow CH_4(g)$	$\Delta H^\circ_{rxn} = -74.7$ kJ/mol

As you can see, all the nonessential species (O_2, CO_2, and H_2O) cancel in this operation. Because this equation represents the synthesis of 1 mole of CH_4 from its elements, we have $\Delta H^\circ_f(CH_4) = -74.7$ kJ/mol.

The general rule in applying Hess's law is to arrange a series of chemical equations (corresponding to a series of steps) in such a way that, when added together, all species will cancel except for the reactants and products that appear in the overall reaction. This means that we want the elements on the left and the compound of interest on the right of the arrow. Further, we often need to multiply some or all of the equations representing the individual steps by the appropriate coefficients.

C_2H_2

Example 6.9

Calculate the standard enthalpy of formation of acetylene (C_2H_2) from its elements:

$$2C(graphite) + H_2(g) \longrightarrow C_2H_2(g)$$

The equations for each step and the corresponding enthalpy changes are

(a)	$C(graphite) + O_2(g) \longrightarrow CO_2(g)$	$\Delta H^\circ_{rxn} = -393.5$ kJ/mol
(b)	$H_2(g) + \frac{1}{2}O_2(g) \longrightarrow H_2O(l)$	$\Delta H^\circ_{rxn} = -285.8$ kJ/mol
(c)	$2C_2H_2(g) + 5O_2(g) \longrightarrow 4CO_2(g) + 2H_2O(l)$	$\Delta H^\circ_{rxn} = -2598.8$ kJ/mol

(Continued)

Strategy Our goal here is to calculate the enthalpy change for the formation of C_2H_2 from its elements C and H_2. The reaction does not occur directly, however, so we must use an indirect route using the information given by Equations (a), (b), and (c).

Solution Looking at the synthesis of C_2H_2, we need 2 moles of graphite as reactant. So we multiply Equation (a) by 2 to get

(d)
$$2C(\text{graphite}) + 2O_2(g) \longrightarrow 2CO_2(g) \quad \Delta H^\circ_{\text{rxn}} = 2(-393.5 \text{ kJ/mol})$$
$$= -787.0 \text{ kJ/mol}$$

Next, we need 1 mole of H_2 as a reactant and this is provided by Equation (b). Last, we need 1 mole of C_2H_2 as a product. Equation (c) has 2 moles of C_2H_2 as a reactant so we need to reverse the equation and divide it by 2:

(e)
$$2CO_2(g) + H_2O(l) \longrightarrow C_2H_2(g) + \tfrac{5}{2}O_2(g) \quad \Delta H^\circ_{\text{rxn}} = \tfrac{1}{2}(2598.8 \text{ kJ/mol})$$
$$= 1299.4 \text{ kJ/mol}$$

Adding Equations (d), (b), and (e) together, we get

$2C(\text{graphite}) + 2O_2(g) \longrightarrow 2CO_2(g)$	$\Delta H^\circ_{\text{rxn}} = -787.0 \text{ kJ/mol}$
$H_2(g) + \tfrac{1}{2}O_2(g) \longrightarrow H_2O(l)$	$\Delta H^\circ_{\text{rxn}} = -285.8 \text{ kJ/mol}$
$2CO_2(g) + H_2O(l) \longrightarrow C_2H_2(g) + \tfrac{5}{2}O_2(g)$	$\Delta H^\circ_{\text{rxn}} = 1299.4 \text{ kJ/mol}$
$2C(\text{graphite}) + H_2(g) \longrightarrow C_2H_2(g)$	$\Delta H^\circ_{\text{rxn}} = 226.6 \text{ kJ/mol}$

Therefore, $\Delta H^\circ_f = \Delta H^\circ_{\text{rxn}} = 226.6$ kJ/mol. The ΔH°_f value means that when 1 mole of C_2H_2 is synthesized from 2 moles of C(graphite) and 1 mole of H_2, 226.6 kJ of heat are absorbed by the reacting system from the surroundings. Thus this is an endothermic process.

Practice Exercise Calculate the standard enthalpy of formation of carbon disulfide (CS_2) from its elements, given that

$$C(\text{graphite}) + O_2(g) \longrightarrow CO_2(g) \qquad \Delta H^\circ_{\text{rxn}} = -393.5 \text{ kJ/mol}$$
$$S(\text{rhombic}) + O_2(g) \longrightarrow SO_2(g) \qquad \Delta H^\circ_{\text{rxn}} = -296.4 \text{ kJ/mol}$$
$$CS_2(l) + 3O_2(g) \longrightarrow CO_2(g) + 2SO_2(g) \quad \Delta H^\circ_{\text{rxn}} = -1073.6 \text{ kJ/mol}$$

An oxyacetylene torch has a high flame temperature (3000°C) and is used to weld metals.

Similar problems: 6.62, 6.63.

We can calculate the enthalpy of reactions from the values of ΔH°_f as shown in Example 6.10.

Example 6.10

Pentaborane-9, B_5H_9, is a colorless, highly reactive liquid that will burst into flame or even explode when exposed to oxygen. The reaction is

$$2B_5H_9(l) + 12O_2(g) \longrightarrow 5B_2O_3(s) + 9H_2O(l)$$

In the 1950s Pentaborane-9 was considered as a potential rocket fuel because it produces a large amount of heat per gram. However, the solid B_2O_3 formed by the combustion of B_5H_9 is an abrasive that would quickly destroy the nozzle of the rocket, and so the idea was abandoned. Calculate the kilojoules of heat released per gram of the compound reacted with oxygen. The standard enthalpy of formation of B_5H_9 is 73.2 kJ/mol.

(Continued)

CHEMISTRY IN ACTION

How a Bombardier Beetle Defends Itself

Survival techniques of insects and small animals in a fiercely competitive environment take many forms. For example, chameleons have developed the ability to change color to match their surroundings and the butterfly *Limenitis* has evolved into a form that mimics the poisonous and unpleasant-tasting monarch butterfly (*Danaus*). A less passive defense mechanism is employed by bombardier beetles (*Brachinus*), which repel predators with a "chemical spray."

The bombardier beetle has a pair of glands at the tip of its abdomen. Each gland consists of two compartments. The inner compartment contains an aqueous solution of hydroquinone and hydrogen peroxide, and the outer compartment holds a mixture of enzymes. (Enzymes are biological molecules that can speed up a reaction.) When threatened, the beetle squeezes some fluid from the inner compartment into the outer compartment, where, in the presence of the enzymes, an exothermic reaction takes place:

(a) $C_6H_4(OH)_2(aq) + H_2O_2(aq) \longrightarrow$
   hydroquinone

$$C_6H_4O_2(aq) + 2H_2O(l)$$
   quinone

To estimate the heat of reaction, let us consider the following steps:

(b) $C_6H_4(OH)_2(aq) \longrightarrow C_6H_4O_2(aq) + H_2(g)$
$$\Delta H° = 177 \text{ kJ/mol}$$
(c) $H_2O_2(aq) \longrightarrow H_2O(l) + \frac{1}{2}O_2(g)$ $\Delta H° = -94.6 \text{ kJ/mol}$
(d) $H_2(g) + \frac{1}{2}O_2(g) \longrightarrow H_2O(l)$ $\Delta H° = -286 \text{ kJ/mol}$

Recalling Hess's law, we find that the heat of reaction for (a) is simply the *sum* of those for (b), (c), and (d).

A bombardier beetle discharging a chemical spray.

Therefore, we write

$$\Delta H_a° = \Delta H_b° + \Delta H_c° + \Delta H_d°$$
$$= (177 - 94.6 - 286) \text{ kJ/mol}$$
$$= -204 \text{ kJ/mol}$$

The large amount of heat generated is sufficient to bring the mixture to its boiling point. By rotating the tip of its abdomen, the beetle can quickly discharge the vapor in the form of a fine mist toward an unsuspecting predator. In addition to the thermal effect, the quinones also act as a repellent to other insects and animals. One bombardier beetle carries enough reagents to produce 20 to 30 discharges in quick succession, each with an audible detonation.

Strategy The enthalpy of a reaction is the difference between the sum of the enthalpies of the products and the sum of the enthalpies of the reactants. The enthalpy of each species (reactant or product) is given by the product of the stoichiometric coefficient and the standard enthalpy of formation of the species.

Solution Using the $\Delta H_f°$ values in Appendix 3 and Equation (6.17), we write

$$\Delta H_{rxn}° = [5\Delta H_f°(B_2O_3) + 9\Delta H_f°(H_2O)] - [2\Delta H_f°(B_5H_9) + 12\Delta H_f°(O_2)]$$
$$= [5(-1263.6 \text{ kJ/mol}) + 9(-285.8 \text{ kJ/mol})] - [2(73.2 \text{ kJ/mol}) + 12(0 \text{ kJ/mol})]$$
$$= -9036.6 \text{ kJ/mol}$$

Looking at the balanced equation, this is the amount of heat released for every 2 moles of B_5H_9 reacted. We can use the following ratio

(Continued)

$$\frac{-9036.6 \text{ kJ}}{2 \text{ mol B}_5\text{H}_9}$$

to convert to kJ/g B_5H_9. The molar mass of B_5H_9 is 63.12 g so

$$\text{heat released per gram of B}_5\text{H}_9 = \frac{-9036.6 \text{ kJ}}{2 \text{ mol B}_5\text{H}_9} \times \frac{1 \text{ mol B}_5\text{H}_9}{63.12 \text{ g B}_5\text{H}_9}$$
$$= -71.58 \text{ kJ/g B}_5\text{H}_9$$

Check Is the negative sign consistent with the fact that B_5H_9 was considered to be used as a rocket fuel? As a quick check, we see that 2 moles of B_5H_9 weigh about 2×63 or 126 g and give off about -9×10^3 kJ of heat on combustion. Therefore, the heat given off per gram of B_5H_9 is approximately -9×10^3 kJ/126 g or -71.4 kJ/g.

Similar problems: 6.54, 6.57.

Practice Exercise Benzene (C_6H_6) burns in air to produce carbon dioxide and liquid water. Calculate the heat released (in kilojoules) per gram of the compound reacted with oxygen. The standard enthalpy of formation of benzene is 49.04 kJ/mol.

B_5H_9 is called a high-energy compound because of the large amount of energy it releases upon combustion. In general, compounds that have positive ΔH_f° values tend to release more heat as a result of combustion and to be less stable than those with negative ΔH_f° values.

6.7 Heat of Solution and Dilution

Although we have focused so far on the thermal energy effects resulting from chemical reactions, many physical processes, such as the melting of ice or the condensation of a vapor, also involve the absorption or release of heat. Enthalpy changes occur as well when a solute dissolves in a solvent or when a solution is diluted. Let us look at these two related physical processes, involving heat of solution and heat of dilution.

Heat of Solution

In the vast majority of cases, dissolving a solute in a solvent produces measurable heat change. At constant pressure, the heat change is equal to the enthalpy change. The *heat of solution,* or *enthalpy of solution, ΔH_{soln},* is *the heat generated or absorbed when a certain amount of solute dissolves in a certain amount of solvent.* The quantity ΔH_{soln} represents the difference between the enthalpy of the final solution and the enthalpies of its original components (that is, solute and solvent) before they are mixed. Thus

$$\Delta H_{soln} = H_{soln} - H_{components} \tag{6.19}$$

Neither H_{soln} nor $H_{components}$ can be measured, but their difference, ΔH_{soln}, can be readily determined in a constant-pressure calorimeter. Like other enthalpy changes, ΔH_{soln} is positive for endothermic (heat-absorbing) processes and negative for exothermic (heat-generating) processes.

Consider the heat of solution of a process in which an ionic compound is the solute and water is the solvent. For example, what happens when solid NaCl dissolves in water? In solid NaCl, the Na^+ and Cl^- ions are held together by strong positive-negative (electrostatic) forces, but when a small crystal of NaCl dissolves in water,

Figure 6.10 *The solution process for NaCl. The process can be considered to occur in two separate steps: (1) separation of ions from the crystal state to the gaseous state and (2) hydration of the gaseous ions. The heat of solution is equal to the energy changes for these two steps,* $\Delta H_{soln} = U + \Delta H_{hydr}.$

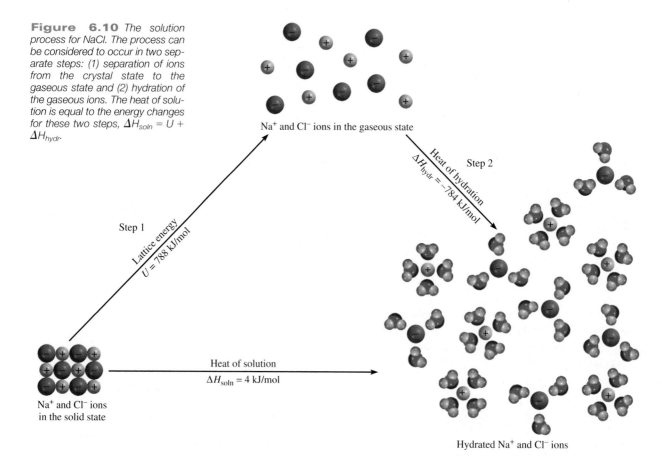

Na$^+$ and Cl$^-$ ions in the gaseous state

Step 2

Heat of hydration $\Delta H_{hydr} = -784$ kJ/mol

Step 1

Lattice energy $U = 788$ kJ/mol

Heat of solution $\Delta H_{soln} = 4$ kJ/mol

Na$^+$ and Cl$^-$ ions in the solid state

Hydrated Na$^+$ and Cl$^-$ ions

the three-dimensional network of ions breaks into its individual units. (The structure of solid NaCl is shown in Figure 2.13.) The separated Na$^+$ and Cl$^-$ ions are stabilized in solution by their interaction with water molecules (see Figure 4.2). These ions are said to be *hydrated*. In this case water plays a role similar to that of a good electrical insulator. Water molecules shield the ions (Na$^+$ and Cl$^-$) from each other and effectively reduce the electrostatic attraction that held them together in the solid state. The heat of solution is defined by the following process:

$$NaCl(s) \xrightarrow{\text{H}_2\text{O}} Na^+(aq) + Cl^-(aq) \qquad\qquad \Delta H_{soln} = ?$$

Dissolving an ionic compound such as NaCl in water involves complex interactions among the solute and solvent species. However, for the sake of analysis we can imagine that the solution process takes place in two separate steps, illustrated in Figure 6.10. First, the Na$^+$ and Cl$^-$ ions in the solid crystal are separated from each other and converted to the gaseous state:

$$\text{energy} + NaCl(s) \longrightarrow Na^+(g) + Cl^-(g)$$

The energy required to completely separate one mole of a solid ionic compound into gaseous ions is called **lattice energy** (*U*). The lattice energy of NaCl is 788 kJ/mol. In other words, we would need to supply 788 kJ of energy to break 1 mole of solid NaCl into 1 mole of Na$^+$ ions and 1 mole of Cl$^-$ ions.

Next, the "gaseous" Na$^+$ and Cl$^-$ ions enter the water and become hydrated:

$$Na^+(g) + Cl^-(g) \xrightarrow{\text{H}_2\text{O}} Na^+(aq) + Cl^-(aq) + \text{energy}$$

The word "lattice" describes arrangement in space of isolated points (occupied by ions) in a regular pattern. Lattice energy is a positive quantity.

The enthalpy change associated with the hydration process is called the **heat of hydration, ΔH_{hydr}** (heat of hydration is a negative quantity for cations and anions). Applying Hess's law, it is possible to consider ΔH_{soln} as the sum of two related quantities, lattice energy (U) and heat of hydration (ΔH_{hydr}):

$$
\begin{array}{ll}
NaCl(s) \longrightarrow Na^+(g) + Cl^-(g) & U = 788 \text{ kJ/mol} \\
Na^+(g) + Cl^-(g) \xrightarrow{H_2O} Na^+(aq) + Cl^-(aq) & \Delta H_{hydr} = -784 \text{ kJ/mol} \\
\hline
NaCl(s) \xrightarrow{H_2O} Na^+(aq) + Cl^-(aq) & \Delta H_{soln} = 4 \text{ kJ/mol}
\end{array}
$$

Therefore, when 1 mole of NaCl dissolves in water, 4 kJ of heat will be absorbed from the surroundings. We would observe this effect by noting that the beaker containing the solution becomes slightly colder. Table 6.5 lists the ΔH_{soln} of several ionic compounds. Depending on the nature of the cation and anion involved, ΔH_{soln} for an ionic compound may be either negative (exothermic) or positive (endothermic).

Heats of Solution of Some Ionic Compounds	
Compound	**ΔH_{soln} (kJ/mol)**
LiCl	−37.1
CaCl$_2$	−82.8
NaCl	4.0
KCl	17.2
NH$_4$Cl	15.2
NH$_4$NO$_3$	26.2

TABLE 6.5

Heat of Dilution

When a previously prepared solution is *diluted,* that is, when more solvent is added to lower the overall concentration of the solute, additional heat is usually given off or absorbed. The **heat of dilution** is *the heat change associated with the dilution process.* If a certain solution process is endothermic and the solution is subsequently diluted, *more* heat will be absorbed by the same solution from the surroundings. The converse holds true for an exothermic solution process—more heat will be liberated if additional solvent is added to dilute the solution. Therefore, always be cautious when working on a dilution procedure in the laboratory. Because of its highly exothermic heat of dilution, concentrated sulfuric acid (H$_2$SO$_4$) poses a particularly hazardous problem if its concentration must be reduced by mixing it with additional water. Concentrated H$_2$SO$_4$ is composed of 98 percent acid and 2 percent water by mass. Diluting it with water releases considerable amount of heat to the surroundings. This process is so exothermic that you must *never* attempt to dilute the concentrated acid by adding water to it. The heat generated could cause the acid solution to boil and splatter. The recommended procedure is to add the concentrated acid slowly to the water (while constantly stirring).

Generations of chemistry students have been reminded of the safe procedure for diluting acids by the venerable saying, "Do as you oughter, add acid to water."

Key Equations

•	$\Delta E = q + w$ (6.1)	Mathematical statement of the first law of thermodynamics.
•	$w = -P\Delta V$ (6.3)	Calculating work done in gas expansion or compression.
•	$H = E + PV$ (6.6)	Definition of enthalpy.
•	$\Delta H = \Delta E + P\Delta V$ (6.8)	Calculating enthalpy (or energy) change for a constant-pressure process.
•	$\Delta E = \Delta H - RT\Delta n$ (6.10)	Calculating enthalpy (or energy) change for a constant-temperature process.
•	$C = ms$ (6.11)	Definition of heat capacity.
•	$q = ms\Delta t$ (6.12)	Calculating heat change in terms of specific heat.
•	$q = C\Delta t$ (6.13)	Calculating heat change in terms of heat capacity.
•	$\Delta H^\circ_{rxn} = \Sigma n\Delta H^\circ_f(\text{products}) - \Sigma m\Delta H^\circ_f(\text{reactants})$ (6.18)	Calculating standard enthalpy of reaction.

Summary of Facts and Concepts

1. Energy is the capacity to do work. There are many forms of energy and they are interconvertible. The law of conservation of energy states that the total amount of energy in the universe is constant.
2. A process that gives off heat to the surroundings is exothermic; a process that absorbs heat from the surroundings is endothermic.
3. The state of a system is defined by properties such as composition, volume, temperature, and pressure. These properties are called state functions.
4. The change in a state function for a system depends only on the initial and final states of the system, and not on the path by which the change is accomplished. Energy is a state function; work and heat are not.
5. Energy can be converted from one form to another, but it cannot be created or destroyed (first law of thermodynamics). In chemistry we are concerned mainly with thermal energy, electrical energy, and mechanical energy, which is usually associated with pressure-volume work.
6. Enthalpy is a state function. A change in enthalpy ΔH is equal to $\Delta E + P\Delta V$ for a constant-pressure process.
7. The change in enthalpy (ΔH, usually given in kilojoules) is a measure of the heat of reaction (or any other process) at constant pressure.
8. Constant-volume and constant-pressure calorimeters are used to measure heat changes that occur in physical and chemical processes.
9. Hess's law states that the overall enthalpy change in a reaction is equal to the sum of enthalpy changes for individual steps in the overall reaction.
10. The standard enthalpy of a reaction can be calculated from the standard enthalpies of formation of reactants and products.
11. The heat of solution of an ionic compound in water is the sum of the lattice energy of the compound and the heat of hydration. The relative magnitudes of these two quantities determine whether the solution process is endothermic or exothermic. The heat of dilution is the heat absorbed or evolved when a solution is diluted.

Key Words

Questions and Problems

Definitions
Review Questions

6.1   Define these terms: system, surroundings, open system, closed system, isolated system, thermal energy, chemical energy, potential energy, kinetic energy, law of conservation of energy.

6.2   What is heat? How does heat differ from thermal energy? Under what condition is heat transferred from one system to another?

6.3   What are the units for energy commonly employed in chemistry?

6.4   A truck initially traveling at 60 km per hour is brought to a complete stop at a traffic light. Does this change violate the law of conservation of energy? Explain.

6.5   These are various forms of energy: chemical, heat, light, mechanical, and electrical. Suggest ways of interconverting these forms of energy.

6.6   Describe the interconversions of forms of energy occurring in these processes: (a) You throw a softball up into the air and catch it. (b) You switch on a flashlight. (c) You ride the ski lift to the top of the hill and then ski down. (d) You strike a match and let it burn down.

Energy Changes in Chemical Reactions
Review Questions

6.7   Define these terms: thermochemistry, exothermic process, endothermic process.

6.8   Stoichiometry is based on the law of conservation of mass. On what law is thermochemistry based?

6.9   Describe two exothermic processes and two endothermic processes.

6.10   Decomposition reactions are usually endothermic, whereas combination reactions are usually exothermic. Give a qualitative explanation for these trends.

First Law of Thermodynamics
Review Questions

6.11   On what law is the first law of thermodynamics based? Explain the sign conventions in the equation $\Delta E = q + w$.

6.12   Explain what is meant by a state function. Give two examples of quantities that are state functions and two that are not.

6.13   The internal energy of an ideal gas depends only on its temperature. Do a first-law analysis of this process. A sample of an ideal gas is allowed to expand at constant temperature against atmospheric pressure. (a) Does the gas do work on its surroundings? (b) Is there heat exchange between the system and the surroundings? If so, in which direction? (c) What is ΔE for the gas for this process?

6.14   Consider these changes.
(a) $Hg(l) \longrightarrow Hg(g)$
(b) $3O_2(g) \longrightarrow 2O_3(g)$
(c) $CuSO_4 \cdot 5H_2O(s) \longrightarrow CuSO_4(s) + 5H_2O(g)$
(d) $H_2(g) + F_2(g) \longrightarrow 2HF(g)$

At constant pressure, in which of the reactions is work done by the system on the surroundings? By the surroundings on the system? In which of them is no work done?

Problems

6.15   A sample of nitrogen gas expands in volume from 1.6 L to 5.4 L at constant temperature. Calculate the work done in joules if the gas expands (a) against a vacuum, (b) against a constant pressure of 0.80 atm, and (c) against a constant pressure of 3.7 atm.

6.16   A gas expands in volume from 26.7 mL to 89.3 mL at constant temperature. Calculate the work done (in joules) if the gas expands (a) against a vacuum, (b) against a constant pressure of 1.5 atm, and (c) against a constant pressure of 2.8 atm.

6.17   A gas expands and does P-V work on the surroundings equal to 325 J. At the same time, it absorbs 127 J of heat from the surroundings. Calculate the change in energy of the gas.

6.18   The work done to compress a gas is 74 J. As a result, 26 J of heat is given off to the surroundings. Calculate the change in energy of the gas.

6.19   Calculate the work done when 50.0 g of tin dissolves in excess acid at 1.00 atm and 25°C:

$$Sn(s) + 2H^+(aq) \longrightarrow Sn^{2+}(aq) + H_2(g)$$

Assume ideal gas behavior.

6.20   Calculate the work done in joules when 1.0 mole of water vaporizes at 1.0 atm and 100°C. Assume that the volume of liquid water is negligible compared with that of steam at 100°C, and ideal gas behavior.

Enthalpy of Chemical Reactions
Review Questions

6.21   Define these terms: enthalpy, enthalpy of reaction. Under what condition is the heat of a reaction equal to the enthalpy change of the same reaction?

6.22 In writing thermochemical equations, why is it important to indicate the physical state (that is, gaseous, liquid, solid, or aqueous) of each substance?

6.23 Explain the meaning of this thermochemical equation:

$$4NH_3(g) + 5O_2(g) \longrightarrow 4NO(g) + 6H_2O(g)$$
$$\Delta H = -904 \text{ kJ/mol}$$

6.24 Consider this reaction:

$$2CH_3OH(l) + 3O_2(g) \longrightarrow 4H_2O(l) + 2CO_2(g)$$
$$\Delta H = -1452.8 \text{ kJ/mol}$$

What is the value of ΔH if (a) the equation is multiplied throughout by 2, (b) the direction of the reaction is reversed so that the products become the reactants and vice versa, (c) water vapor instead of liquid water is formed as the product?

Problems

6.25 The first step in the industrial recovery of zinc from the zinc sulfide ore is roasting, that is, the conversion of ZnS to ZnO by heating:

$$2ZnS(s) + 3O_2(g) \longrightarrow 2ZnO(s) + 2SO_2(g)$$
$$\Delta H = -879 \text{ kJ/mol}$$

Calculate the heat evolved (in kJ) per gram of ZnS roasted.

6.26 Determine the amount of heat (in kJ) given off when 1.26×10^4 g of NO_2 are produced according to the equation

$$2NO(g) + O_2(g) \longrightarrow 2NO_2(g)$$
$$\Delta H = -114.6 \text{ kJ/mol}$$

6.27 Consider the reaction

$$2H_2O(g) \longrightarrow 2H_2(g) + O_2(g)$$
$$\Delta H = 483.6 \text{ kJ/mol}$$

If 2.0 moles of $H_2O(g)$ are converted to $H_2(g)$ and $O_2(g)$ against a pressure of 1.0 atm at 125°C, what is ΔE for this reaction?

6.28 Consider the reaction

$$H_2(g) + Cl_2(g) \longrightarrow 2HCl(g)$$
$$\Delta H = -184.6 \text{ kJ/mol}$$

If 3 moles of H_2 react with 3 moles of Cl_2 to form HCl, calculate the work done (in joules) against a pressure of 1.0 atm at 25°C. What is ΔE for this reaction? Assume the reaction goes to completion.

Calorimetry
Review Questions

6.29 What is the difference between specific heat and heat capacity? What are the units for these two quantities? Which is the intensive property and which is the extensive property?

6.30 Consider two metals A and B, each having a mass of 100 g and an initial temperature of 20°C. The specific heat of A is larger than that of B. Under the same heating conditions, which metal would take longer to reach a temperature of 21°C?

6.31 Define calorimetry and describe two commonly used calorimeters. In a calorimetric measurement, why is it important that we know the heat capacity of the calorimeter? How is this value determined?

6.32 Consider the following data:

Metal	Al	Cu
Mass (g)	10	30
Specific heat (J/g · °C)	0.900	0.385
Temperature (°C)	40	60

When these two metals are placed in contact, which of the following will take place?
(a) Heat will flow from Al to Cu because Al has a larger specific heat.
(b) Heat will flow from Cu to Al because Cu has a larger mass.
(c) Heat will flow from Cu to Al because Cu has a larger heat capacity.
(d) Heat will flow from Cu to Al because Cu is at a higher temperature.
(e) No heat will flow in either direction.

Problems

6.33 A piece of silver of mass 362 g has a heat capacity of 85.7 J/°C. What is the specific heat of silver?

6.34 A 6.22-kg piece of copper metal is heated from 20.5°C to 324.3°C. Calculate the heat absorbed (in kJ) by the metal.

6.35 Calculate the amount of heat liberated (in kJ) from 366 g of mercury when it cools from 77.0°C to 12.0°C.

6.36 A sheet of gold weighing 10.0 g and at a temperature of 18.0°C is placed flat on a sheet of iron weighing 20.0 g and at a temperature of 55.6°C. What is the final temperature of the combined metals? Assume that no heat is lost to the surroundings. (*Hint:* The heat gained by the gold must be equal to the heat lost by the iron. The specific heats of the metals are given in Table 6.2.)

6.37 A 0.1375-g sample of solid magnesium is burned in a constant-volume bomb calorimeter that has a heat capacity of 3024 J/°C. The temperature increases by 1.126°C. Calculate the heat given off by the burning Mg, in kJ/g and in kJ/mol.

6.38 A quantity of 2.00×10^2 mL of 0.862 M HCl is mixed with 2.00×10^2 mL of 0.431 M $Ba(OH)_2$ in a constant-pressure calorimeter of negligible heat capacity. The initial temperature of the HCl and $Ba(OH)_2$ solutions is the same at 20.48°C. For the process

$$H^+(aq) + OH^-(aq) \longrightarrow H_2O(l)$$

the heat of neutralization is -56.2 kJ/mol. What is the final temperature of the mixed solution?

Standard Enthalpy of Formation and Reaction
Review Questions

6.39 What is meant by the standard-state condition?

6.40 How are the standard enthalpies of an element and of a compound determined?

6.41 What is meant by the standard enthalpy of a reaction?

6.42 Write the equation for calculating the enthalpy of a reaction. Define all the terms.

6.43 State Hess's law. Explain, with one example, the usefulness of Hess's law in thermochemistry.

6.44 Describe how chemists use Hess's law to determine the ΔH_f° of a compound by measuring its heat (enthalpy) of combustion.

Problems

6.45 Which of the following standard enthalpy of formation values is not zero at 25°C? $Na(s)$, $Ne(g)$, $CH_4(g)$, $S_8(s)$, $Hg(l)$, $H(g)$.

6.46 The ΔH_f° values of the two allotropes of oxygen, O_2 and O_3, are 0 and 142.2 kJ/mol, respectively, at 25°C. Which is the more stable form at this temperature?

6.47 Which is the more negative quantity at 25°C: ΔH_f° for $H_2O(l)$ or ΔH_f° for $H_2O(g)$?

6.48 Predict the value of ΔH_f° (greater than, less than, or equal to zero) for these elements at 25°C: (a) $Br_2(g)$; $Br_2(l)$, (b) $I_2(g)$; $I_2(s)$.

6.49 In general, compounds with negative ΔH_f° values are more stable than those with positive ΔH_f° values. $H_2O_2(l)$ has a negative ΔH_f° (see Table 6.4). Why, then, does $H_2O_2(l)$ have a tendency to decompose to $H_2O(l)$ and $O_2(g)$?

6.50 Suggest ways (with appropriate equations) that would allow you to measure the ΔH_f° values of $Ag_2O(s)$ and $CaCl_2(s)$ from their elements. No calculations are necessary.

6.51 Calculate the heat of decomposition for this process at constant pressure and 25°C:

$$CaCO_3(s) \longrightarrow CaO(s) + CO_2(g)$$

(Look up the standard enthalpy of formation of the reactant and products in Table 6.4.)

6.52 The standard enthalpies of formation of ions in aqueous solutions are obtained by arbitrarily assigning a value of zero to H^+ ions; that is, $\Delta H_f^\circ[H^+(aq)] = 0$.
(a) For the following reaction

$$HCl(g) \xrightarrow{H_2O} H^+(aq) + Cl^-(aq)$$
$$\Delta H^\circ = -74.9 \text{ kJ/mol}$$

calculate ΔH_f° for the Cl^- ions.
(b) Given that ΔH_f° for OH^- ions is -229.6 kJ/mol, calculate the enthalpy of neutralization when 1 mole of a strong monoprotic acid (such as HCl) is titrated by 1 mole of a strong base (such as KOH) at 25°C.

6.53 Calculate the heats of combustion for the following reactions from the standard enthalpies of formation listed in Appendix 3:
(a) $2H_2(g) + O_2(g) \longrightarrow 2H_2O(l)$
(b) $2C_2H_2(g) + 5O_2(g) \longrightarrow 4CO_2(g) + 2H_2O(l)$

6.54 Calculate the heats of combustion for the following reactions from the standard enthalpies of formation listed in Appendix 3:
(a) $C_2H_4(g) + 3O_2(g) \longrightarrow 2CO_2(g) + 2H_2O(l)$
(b) $2H_2S(g) + 3O_2(g) \longrightarrow 2H_2O(l) + 2SO_2(g)$

6.55 Methanol, ethanol, and n-propanol are three common alcohols. When 1.00 g of each of these alcohols is burned in air, heat is liberated as shown by the following data: (a) methanol (CH_3OH), -22.6 kJ; (b) ethanol (C_2H_5OH), -29.7 kJ; (c) n-propanol (C_3H_7OH), -33.4 kJ. Calculate the heats of combustion of these alcohols in kJ/mol.

6.56 The standard enthalpy change for the following reaction is 436.4 kJ/mol:

$$H_2(g) \longrightarrow H(g) + H(g)$$

Calculate the standard enthalpy of formation of atomic hydrogen (H).

6.57 From the standard enthalpies of formation, calculate ΔH_{rxn}° for the reaction

$$C_6H_{12}(l) + 9O_2(g) \longrightarrow 6CO_2(g) + 6H_2O(l)$$

For $C_6H_{12}(l)$, $\Delta H_f^\circ = -151.9$ kJ/mol.

6.58 The first step in the industrial recovery of zinc from the zinc sulfide ore is roasting, that is, the conversion of ZnS to ZnO by heating:

$$2ZnS(s) + 3O_2(g) \longrightarrow 2ZnO(s) + 2SO_2(g)$$
$$\Delta H_{rxn}^{\circ} = -879 \text{ kJ/mol}$$

Calculate the heat evolved (in kJ) per gram of ZnS roasted.

6.59 Determine the amount of heat (in kJ) given off when 1.26×10^4 g of ammonia are produced according to the equation

$$N_2(g) + 3H_2(g) \longrightarrow 2NH_3(g)$$
$$\Delta H_{rxn}^{\circ} = -92.6 \text{ kJ/mol}$$

Assume that the reaction takes place under standard-state conditions at 25°C.

6.60 At 850°C, $CaCO_3$ undergoes substantial decomposition to yield CaO and CO_2. Assuming that the ΔH_f° values of the reactant and products are the same at 850°C as they are at 25°C, calculate the enthalpy change (in kJ) if 66.8 g of CO_2 are produced in one reaction.

6.61 From these data,

$$S(\text{rhombic}) + O_2(g) \longrightarrow SO_2(g)$$
$$\Delta H_{rxn}^{\circ} = -296.06 \text{ kJ/mol}$$
$$S(\text{monoclinic}) + O_2(g) \longrightarrow SO_2(g)$$
$$\Delta H_{rxn}^{\circ} = -296.36 \text{ kJ/mol}$$

calculate the enthalpy change for the transformation

$$S(\text{rhombic}) \longrightarrow S(\text{monoclinic})$$

(Monoclinic and rhombic are different allotropic forms of elemental sulfur.)

6.62 From the following data,

$$C(\text{graphite}) + O_2(g) \longrightarrow CO_2(g)$$
$$\Delta H_{rxn}^{\circ} = -393.5 \text{ kJ/mol}$$
$$H_2(g) + \tfrac{1}{2}O_2(g) \longrightarrow H_2O(l)$$
$$\Delta H_{rxn}^{\circ} = -285.8 \text{ kJ/mol}$$
$$2C_2H_6(g) + 7O_2(g) \longrightarrow 4CO_2(g) + 6H_2O(l)$$
$$\Delta H_{rxn}^{\circ} = -3119.6 \text{ kJ/mol}$$

calculate the enthalpy change for the reaction

$$2C(\text{graphite}) + 3H_2(g) \longrightarrow C_2H_6(g)$$

6.63 From the following heats of combustion,

$$CH_3OH(l) + \tfrac{3}{2}O_2(g) \longrightarrow CO_2(g) + 2H_2O(l)$$
$$\Delta H_{rxn}^{\circ} = -726.4 \text{ kJ/mol}$$
$$C(\text{graphite}) + O_2(g) \longrightarrow CO_2(g)$$
$$\Delta H_{rxn}^{\circ} = -393.5 \text{ kJ/mol}$$
$$H_2(g) + \tfrac{1}{2}O_2(g) \longrightarrow H_2O(l)$$
$$\Delta H_{rxn}^{\circ} = -285.8 \text{ kJ/mol}$$

calculate the enthalpy of formation of methanol (CH_3OH) from its elements:

$$C(\text{graphite}) + 2H_2(g) + \tfrac{1}{2}O_2(g) \longrightarrow CH_3OH(l)$$

6.64 Calculate the standard enthalpy change for the reaction

$$2Al(s) + Fe_2O_3(s) \longrightarrow 2Fe(s) + Al_2O_3(s)$$

given that

$$2Al(s) + \tfrac{3}{2}O_2(g) \longrightarrow Al_2O_3(s)$$
$$\Delta H_{rxn}^{\circ} = -1601 \text{ kJ/mol}$$
$$2Fe(s) + \tfrac{3}{2}O_2(g) \longrightarrow Fe_2O_3(s)$$
$$\Delta H_{rxn}^{\circ} = -821 \text{ kJ/mol}$$

Heat of Solution and Dilution
Review Questions

6.65 Define the following terms: enthalpy of solution, hydration, heat of hydration, lattice energy, heat of dilution.

6.66 Why is the lattice of a solid always a positive quantity? Why is the hydration of ions always a negative quantity?

6.67 Consider two ionic compounds A and B. A has a larger lattice energy than B. Which of the two compounds is more stable?

6.68 Mg^{2+} is a smaller cation than Na^+ and also carries more positive charge. Which of the two species has a larger hydration energy (in kJ/mol)? Explain.

6.69 Consider the dissolution of an ionic compound such as potassium fluoride in water. Break the process into the following steps: separation of the cations and anions in the vapor phase and the hydration of the ions in the aqueous medium. Discuss the energy changes associated with each step. How does the heat of solution of KF depend on the relative magnitudes of these two quantities? On what law is the relationship based?

6.70 Why is it dangerous to add water to a concentrated acid such as sulfuric acid in a dilution process?

Additional Problems

6.71 The convention of arbitrarily assigning a zero enthalpy value for the most stable form of each element in the standard state at 25°C is a convenient way of dealing with enthalpies of reactions. Explain why this convention cannot be applied to nuclear reactions.

6.72 Consider the following two reactions:

$$A \longrightarrow 2B \qquad \Delta H_{rxn}^{\circ} = \Delta H_1$$
$$A \longrightarrow C \qquad \Delta H_{rxn}^{\circ} = \Delta H_2$$

Determine the enthalpy change for the process

$$2B \longrightarrow C$$

6.73 The standard enthalpy change $\Delta H°$ for the thermal decomposition of silver nitrate according to the following equation is $+78.67$ kJ:

$$AgNO_3(s) \longrightarrow AgNO_2(s) + \tfrac{1}{2}O_2(g)$$

The standard enthalpy of formation of $AgNO_3(s)$ is -123.02 kJ/mol. Calculate the standard enthalpy of formation of $AgNO_2(s)$.

6.74 Hydrazine, N_2H_4, decomposes according to the following reaction:

$$3N_2H_4(l) \longrightarrow 4NH_3(g) + N_2(g)$$

(a) Given that the standard enthalpy of formation of hydrazine is 50.42 kJ/mol, calculate $\Delta H°$ for its decomposition. (b) Both hydrazine and ammonia burn in oxygen to produce $H_2O(l)$ and $N_2(g)$. Write balanced equations for each of these processes and calculate $\Delta H°$ for each of them. On a mass basis (per kg), would hydrazine or ammonia be the better fuel?

6.75 Consider the reaction

$$N_2(g) + 3H_2(g) \longrightarrow 2NH_3(g)$$
$$\Delta H°_{rxn} = -92.6 \text{ kJ/mol}$$

If 2.0 moles of N_2 react with 6.0 moles of H_2 to form NH_3, calculate the work done (in joules) against a pressure of 1.0 atm at 25°C. What is ΔE for this reaction? Assume the reaction goes to completion.

6.76 Calculate the heat released when 2.00 L of $Cl_2(g)$ with a density of 1.88 g/L react with an excess of sodium metal as 25°C and 1 atm to form sodium chloride.

6.77 Photosynthesis produces glucose, $C_6H_{12}O_6$, and oxygen from carbon dioxide and water:

$$6CO_2 + 6H_2O \longrightarrow C_6H_{12}O_6 + 6O_2$$

(a) How would you determine experimentally the $\Delta H°_{rxn}$ value for this reaction? (b) Solar radiation produces about 7.0×10^{14} kg glucose a year on Earth. What is the corresponding $\Delta H°$ change?

6.78 2.10-mole sample of crystalline acetic acid, initially at 17.0°C, is allowed to melt at 17.0°C and is then heated to 118.1°C (its normal boiling point) at 1.00 atm. The sample is allowed to vaporize at 118.1°C and is then rapidly quenched to 17.0°C, so that it recrystallizes. Calculate $\Delta H°$ for the total process as described.

6.79 Calculate the work done in joules by the reaction

$$2Na(s) + 2H_2O(l) \longrightarrow 2NaOH(aq) + H_2(g)$$

when 0.34 g of Na reacts with water to form hydrogen gas at 0°C and 1.0 atm.

6.80 You are given the following data:

$$H_2(g) \longrightarrow 2H(g) \qquad \Delta H° = 436.4 \text{ kJ/mol}$$
$$Br_2(g) \longrightarrow 2Br(g) \qquad \Delta H° = 192.5 \text{ kJ/mol}$$
$$H_2(g) + Br_2(g) \longrightarrow 2HBr(g)$$
$$\Delta H° = -72.4 \text{ kJ/mol}$$

Calculate $\Delta H°$ for the reaction

$$H(g) + Br(g) \longrightarrow HBr(g)$$

6.81 Methanol (CH_3OH) is an organic solvent and is also used as a fuel in some automobile engines. From the following data, calculate the standard enthalpy of formation of methanol:

$$2CH_3OH(l) + 3O_2(g) \longrightarrow 2CO_2(g) + 4H_2O(l)$$
$$\Delta H°_{rxn} = -1452.8 \text{ kJ/mol}$$

6.82 A 44.0-g sample of an unknown metal at 99.0°C was placed in a constant-pressure calorimeter containing 80.0 g of water at 24.0°C. The final temperature of the system was found to be 28.4°C. Calculate the specific heat of the metal. (The heat capacity of the calorimeter is 12.4 J/°C.)

6.83 A 1.00-mole sample of ammonia at 14.0 atm and 25°C in a cylinder fitted with a movable piston expands against a constant external pressure of 1.00 atm. At equilibrium, the pressure and volume of the gas are 1.00 atm and 23.5 L, respectively. (a) Calculate the final temperature of the sample. (b) Calculate q, w, and ΔE for the process. The specific heat of ammonia is 0.0258 J/g · °C.

6.84 Producer gas (carbon monoxide) is prepared by passing air over red-hot coke:

$$C(s) + \tfrac{1}{2}O_2(g) \longrightarrow CO(g)$$

Water gas (mixture of carbon monoxide and hydrogen) is prepared by passing steam over red-hot coke:

$$C(s) + H_2O(g) \longrightarrow CO(g) + H_2(g)$$

For many years, both producer gas and water gas were used as fuels in industry and for domestic cooking. The large-scale preparation of these gases was carried out alternately, that is, first producer gas, then water gas, and so on. Using thermochemical reasoning, explain why this procedure was chosen.

6.85 Compare the heat produced by the complete combustion of 1 mole of methane (CH_4) with a mole of water gas (0.50 mole H_2 and 0.50 mole CO) under the same conditions. On the basis of your answer, would you prefer methane over water gas as a fuel? Can you suggest two other reasons why methane is preferable to water gas as a fuel?

6.86 The so-called hydrogen economy is based on hydrogen produced from water using solar energy. The gas is then burned as a fuel:

$$2H_2(g) + O_2(g) \longrightarrow 2H_2O(l)$$

A primary advantage of hydrogen as a fuel is that it is nonpolluting. A major disadvantage is that it is a gas and therefore is harder to store than liquids or solids. Calculate the volume of hydrogen gas at 25°C and 1.00 atm required to produce an amount of energy equivalent to that produced by the combustion of a gallon of octane (C_8H_{18}). The density of octane is 2.66 kg/gal, and its standard enthalpy of formation is −249.9 kJ/mol.

6.87 Ethanol (C_2H_5OH) and gasoline (assumed to be all octane, C_8H_{18}) are both used as automobile fuel. If gasoline is selling for $1.20/gal, what would the price of ethanol have to be in order to provide the same amount of heat per dollar? The density and ΔH_f° of octane are 0.7025 g/mL and −249.9 kJ/mol and of ethanol are 0.7894 g/mL and −277.0 kJ/mol, respectively. 1 gal = 3.785 L.

6.88 The combustion of what volume of ethane (C_2H_6), measured at 23.0°C and 752 mmHg, would be required to heat 855 g of water from 25.0°C to 98.0°C?

6.89 If energy is conserved, how can there be an energy crisis?

6.90 The heat of vaporization of a liquid (ΔH_{vap}) is the energy required to vaporize 1.00 g of the liquid at its boiling point. In one experiment, 60.0 g of liquid nitrogen (boiling point −196°C) are poured into a Styrofoam cup containing 2.00×10^2 g of water at 55.3°C. Calculate the molar heat of vaporization of liquid nitrogen if the final temperature of the water is 41.0°C.

6.91 Explain the cooling effect experienced when ethanol is rubbed on your skin, given that

$$C_2H_5OH(l) \longrightarrow C_2H_5OH(g) \quad \Delta H^\circ = 42.2 \text{ kJ/mol}$$

6.92 For which of the following reactions does $\Delta H_{rxn}^\circ = \Delta H_f^\circ$?
(a) $H_2(g) + S(\text{rhombic}) \longrightarrow H_2S(g)$
(b) $C(\text{diamond}) + O_2(g) \longrightarrow CO_2(g)$
(c) $H_2(g) + CuO(s) \longrightarrow H_2O(l) + Cu(s)$
(d) $O(g) + O_2(g) \longrightarrow O_3(g)$

6.93 Calculate the work done (in joules) when 1.0 mole of water is frozen at 0°C and 1.0 atm. The volumes of one mole of water and ice at 0°C are 0.0180 L and 0.0196 L, respectively.

6.94 A quantity of 0.020 mole of a gas initially at 0.050 L and 20°C undergoes a constant-temperature expansion until its volume is 0.50 L. Calculate the work done (in joules) by the gas if it expands (a) against a vacuum and (b) against a constant pressure of 0.20 atm. (c) If the gas in (b) is allowed to expand unchecked until its pressure is equal to the external pressure, what would its final volume be before it stopped expanding, and what would be the work done?

6.95 Calculate the standard enthalpy of formation for diamond, given that

$$C(\text{graphite}) + O_2(g) \longrightarrow CO_2(g)$$
$$\Delta H^\circ = -393.5 \text{ kJ/mol}$$
$$C(\text{diamond}) + O_2(g) \longrightarrow CO_2(g)$$
$$\Delta H^\circ = -395.4 \text{ kJ/mol}$$

6.96 (a) For most efficient use, refrigerator freezer compartments should be fully packed with food. What is the thermochemical basis for this recommendation? (b) Starting at the same temperature, tea and coffee remain hot longer in a thermal flask than chicken noodle soup. Explain.

6.97 Calculate the standard enthalpy change for the fermentation process. (See Problem 3.72.)

6.98 Portable hot packs are available for skiers and people engaged in other outdoor activities in a cold climate. The air-permeable paper packet contains a mixture of powdered iron, sodium chloride, and other components, all moistened by a little water. The exothermic reaction that produces the heat is a very common one—the rusting of iron:

$$4Fe(s) + 3O_2(g) \longrightarrow 2Fe_2O_3(s)$$

When the outside plastic envelope is removed, O_2 molecules penetrate the paper, causing the reaction to begin. A typical packet contains 250 g of iron to warm your hands or feet for up to 4 hours. How much heat (in kJ) is produced by this reaction? (*Hint:* See Appendix 3 for ΔH_f° values.)

6.99 A person ate 0.50 pound of cheese (an energy intake of 4000 kJ). Suppose that none of the energy was stored in his body. What mass (in grams) of water would he need to perspire in order to maintain his original temperature? (It takes 44.0 kJ to vaporize 1 mole of water.)

6.100 The total volume of the Pacific Ocean is estimated to be 7.2×10^8 km^3. A medium-sized atomic bomb produces 1.0×10^{15} J of energy upon explosion. Calculate the number of atomic bombs needed to release enough energy to raise the temperature of the water in the Pacific Ocean by 1°C.

6.101 A 19.2-g quantity of dry ice (solid carbon dioxide) is allowed to sublime (evaporate) in an apparatus like the one shown in Figure 6.5. Calculate the expansion work done against a constant external pressure of 0.995 atm and at a constant temperature of 22°C. Assume that the initial volume of dry ice is negligible and that CO_2 behaves like an ideal gas.

6.102 The enthalpy of combustion of benzoic acid (C_6H_5COOH) is commonly used as the standard for calibrating constant-volume bomb calorimeters; its value has been accurately determined to be −3226.7 kJ/mol. When 1.9862 g of benzoic acid are burned in a calorimeter, the temperature rises from 21.84°C to 25.67°C. What is the heat capacity of the bomb? (Assume that the quantity of water surrounding the bomb is exactly 2000 g.)

6.103 Lime is a term that includes calcium oxide (CaO, also called quicklime) and calcium hydroxide [$Ca(OH)_2$, also called slaked lime]. It is used in the steel industry to remove acidic impurities, in air-pollution control to remove acidic oxides such as SO_2, and in water treatment. Quicklime is made industrially by heating limestone ($CaCO_3$) above 2000°C:

$$CaCO_3(s) \longrightarrow CaO(s) + CO_2(g)$$
$$\Delta H° = 177.8 \text{ kJ/mol}$$

Slaked lime is produced by treating quicklime with water:

$$CaO(s) + H_2O(l) \longrightarrow Ca(OH)_2(s)$$
$$\Delta H° = -65.2 \text{ kJ/mol}$$

The exothermic reaction of quicklime with water and the rather small specific heats of both quicklime (0.946 J/g · °C) and slaked lime (1.20 J/g · °C) make it hazardous to store and transport lime in vessels made of wood. Wooden sailing ships carrying lime would occasionally catch fire when water leaked into the hold. (a) If a 500-g sample of water reacts with an equimolar amount of CaO (both at an initial temperature of 25°C), what is the final temperature of the product, $Ca(OH)_2$? Assume that the product absorbs all of the heat released in the reaction. (b) Given that the standard enthalpies of formation of CaO and H_2O are −635.6 kJ/mol and −285.8 kJ/mol, respectively, calculate the standard enthalpy of formation of $Ca(OH)_2$.

6.104 Calcium oxide (CaO) is used to remove sulfur dioxide generated by coal-burning power stations:

$$2CaO(s) + 2SO_2(g) + O_2(g) \longrightarrow 2CaSO_4(s)$$

Calculate the enthalpy change for this process if 6.6×10^5 g of SO_2 are removed by this process every day.

6.105 Glauber's salt, sodium sulfate decahydrate ($Na_2SO_4 \cdot 10H_2O$), undergoes a phase transition (that is, melting or freezing) at a convenient temperature of about 32°C:

$$Na_2SO_4 \cdot 10H_2O(s) \longrightarrow Na_2SO_4 \cdot 10H_2O(l)$$
$$\Delta H° = 74.4 \text{ kJ/mol}$$

As a result, this compound is used to regulate the temperature in homes. It is placed in plastic bags in the ceiling of a room. During the day, the endothermic melting process absorbs heat from the surroundings, cooling the room. At night, it gives off heat as it freezes. Calculate the mass of Glauber's salt in kilograms needed to lower the temperature of air in a room by 8.2°C at 1.0 atm. The dimensions of the room are 2.80 m × 10.6 m × 17.2 m, the specific heat of air is 1.2 J/g · °C, and the molar mass of air may be taken as 29.0 g/mol.

6.106 A balloon 16 m in diameter is inflated with helium at 18°C. (a) Calculate the mass of He in the balloon, assuming ideal behavior. (b) Calculate the work done (in joules) during the inflation process if the atmospheric pressure is 98.7 kPa.

6.107 An excess of zinc metal is added to 50.0 mL of a 0.100 M $AgNO_3$ solution in a constant-pressure calorimeter like the one pictured in Figure 6.9. As a result of the reaction

$$Zn(s) + 2Ag^+(aq) \longrightarrow Zn^{2+}(aq) + 2Ag(s)$$

the temperature rises from 19.25°C to 22.17°C. If the heat capacity of the calorimeter is 98.6 J/°C, calculate the enthalpy change for the above reaction on a molar basis. Assume that the density and specific heat of the solution are the same as those for water, and ignore the specific heats of the metals.

6.108 (a) A person drinks four glasses of cold water (3.0°C) every day. The volume of each glass is 2.5×10^2 mL. How much heat (in kJ) does the body have to supply to raise the temperature of the water to 37°C, the body temperature? (b) How much heat would your body lose if you were to ingest 8.0×10^2 g of snow at 0°C to quench thirst? (The amount of heat necessary to melt snow is 6.01 kJ/mol.)

6.109 A driver's manual states that the stopping distance quadruples as the speed doubles; that is, if it takes 30 ft to stop a car moving at 25 mph then it would take 120 ft to stop a car moving at 50 mph. Justify this statement by using mechanics and the first law of thermodynamics. [Assume that when a car is stopped, its kinetic energy ($\frac{1}{2}mu^2$) is totally converted to heat.]

6.110 At 25°C the standard enthalpy of formation of HF(aq) is −320.1 kJ/mol; of OH⁻(aq), it is −229.6 kJ/mol;

of $F^-(aq)$, it is -329.1 kJ/mol; and of $H_2O(l)$, it is -285.8 kJ/mol.

(a) Calculate the standard enthalpy of neutralization of $HF(aq)$:

$$HF(aq) + OH^-(aq) \longrightarrow F^-(aq) + H_2O(l)$$

(b) Using the value of -56.2 kJ as the standard enthalpy change for the reaction

$$H^+(aq) + OH^-(aq) \longrightarrow H_2O(l)$$

calculate the standard enthalpy change for the reaction

$$HF(aq) \longrightarrow H^+(aq) + F^-(aq)$$

6.111 Why are cold, damp air and hot, humid air more uncomfortable than dry air at the same temperatures? (The specific heats of water vapor and air are approximately 1.9 J/g · °C and 1.0 J/g · °C, respectively.)

6.112 From the enthalpy of formation for CO_2 and the following information, calculate the standard enthalpy of formation for carbon monoxide (CO).

$$CO(g) + \tfrac{1}{2}O_2(g) \longrightarrow CO_2(g)$$
$$\Delta H° = -283.0 \text{ kJ/mol}$$

Why can't we obtain it directly by measuring the enthalpy of the following reaction?

$$C(graphite) + \tfrac{1}{2}O_2(g) \longrightarrow CO(g)$$

6.113 A 46-kg person drinks 500 g of milk, which has a "caloric" value of approximately 3.0 kJ/g. If only 17 percent of the energy in milk is converted to mechanical work, how high (in meters) can the person climb based on this energy intake? [*Hint:* The work done in ascending is given by *mgh*, where *m* is the mass (in kilograms), *g* the gravitational acceleration (9.8 m/s^2), and *h* the height (in meters).]

6.114 The height of Niagara Falls on the American side is 51 meters. (a) Calculate the potential energy of 1.0 g of water at the top of the falls relative to the ground level. (b) What is the speed of the falling water if all of the potential energy is converted to kinetic energy? (c) What would be the increase in temperature of the water if all the kinetic energy were converted to heat? (See Problem 6.113 for suggestions.)

6.115 In the nineteenth century two scientists named Dulong and Petit noticed that for a solid element, the product of its molar mass and its specific heat is approximately 25 J/°C. This observation, now called Dulong and Petit's law, was used to estimate the specific heat of metals. Verify the law for the metals listed in Table 6.2. The law does not apply to one of the metals. Which one is it? Why?

6.116 Determine the standard enthalpy of formation of ethanol (C_2H_5OH) from its standard enthalpy of combustion (-1367.4 kJ/mol).

6.117 Acetylene (C_2H_2) and benzene (C_6H_6) have the same empirical formula. In fact, benzene can be made from acetylene as follows:

$$3C_2H_2(g) \longrightarrow C_6H_6(l)$$

The enthalpies of combustion for C_2H_2 and C_6H_6 are -1299.4 kJ/mol and -3267.4 kJ/mol, respectively. Calculate the standard enthalpies of formation of C_2H_2 and C_6H_6 and hence the enthalpy change for the formation of C_6H_6 from C_2H_2.

6.118 Ice at 0°C is placed in a Styrofoam cup containing 361 g of a soft drink at 23°C. The specific heat of the drink is about the same as that of water. Some ice remains after the ice and soft drink reach an equilibrium temperature of 0°C. Determine the mass of ice that has melted. Ignore the heat capacity of the cup. (*Hint:* It takes 334 J to melt 1 g of ice at 0°C.)

6.119 A gas company in Massachusetts charges $1.30 for 15 ft^3 of natural gas (CH_4) measured at 20°C and 1.0 atm. Calculate the cost of heating 200 mL of water (enough to make a cup of coffee or tea) from 20°C to 100°C. Assume that only 50 percent of the heat generated by the combustion is used to heat the water; the rest of the heat is lost to the surroundings.

6.120 Calculate the internal energy of a Goodyear blimp filled with helium gas at 1.2×10^5 Pa. The volume of the blimp is 5.5×10^3 m^3. If all the energy were used to heat 10.0 tons of copper at 21°C, calculate the final temperature of the metal. (*Hint:* See Section 5.7 for help in calculating the internal energy of a gas. 1 ton $= 9.072 \times 10^5$ g.)

6.121 Decomposition reactions are usually endothermic, whereas combination reactions are usually exothermic. Give a qualitative explanation for these trends.

6.122 Acetylene (C_2H_2) can be made by reacting calcium carbide (CaC_2) with water. (a) Write an equation for the reaction. (b) What is the maximum amount of heat (in joules) that can be obtained from the combustion of acetylene, starting with 74.6 g of CaC_2?

6.123 The average temperature in deserts is high during the day but quite cool at night, whereas that in regions along the coastline is more moderate. Explain.

6.124 When 1.034 g of naphthalene ($C_{10}H_8$) are burned in a constant-volume bomb calorimeter at 298 K, 41.56 kJ of heat are evolved. Calculate ΔE and ΔH for the reaction on a molar basis.

6.125 From a thermochemical point of view, explain why a carbon dioxide fire extinguisher or water should not be used on a magnesium fire.

Answers to Practice Exercises

6.1 (a) 0, (b) -286 J. **6.2** -63 J. **6.3** -6.47×10^3 kJ. **6.4** -111.7 kJ/mol. **6.5** -34.3 kJ. **6.6** -728 kJ/mol.

6.7 21.19°C. **6.8** 22.49°C. **6.9** 87.3 kJ/mol. **6.10** -41.83 kJ/g.

CHEMICAL MYSTERY

The Exploding Tire[†]

It was supposed to be a routine job: Fix the flat tire on Harvey Smith's car. The owner of Tom's Garage, Tom Lee, gave the tire to Jerry to work on, while he went outside to pump gas. A few minutes later, Tom heard a loud bang. He rushed inside to find the tire blown to pieces, a wall collapsed, equipment damaged, and Jerry lying on the floor, unconscious and bleeding. Luckily Jerry's injury was not serious. As he lay in the hospital recovering, the mystery of the exploding tire unfolded.

The tire had gone flat when Harvey drove over a nail. Being a cautious driver, Harvey carried a can of instant tire repair in the car, so he was able to reinflate the tire and drive safely home. The can of tire repair Harvey used contained latex (natural rubber) dissolved in a liquid propellant, which is a mixture of propane (C_3H_8) and butane (C_4H_{10}). Propane and butane are gases under atmospheric conditions but exist as liquids under compression in the can. When the valve on the top of the can is pressed, it opens, releasing the pressure inside. The mixture boils, forming a latex foam which is propelled by the gases into the tire to seal the puncture while the gas reinflates the tire.

The pressure in a flat tire is approximately one atmosphere, or roughly 15 pounds per square inch (psi). Using the aerosol tire repair, Harvey reinflated his damaged tire to a pressure of 35 psi. This is called the gauge pressure, which is the pressure of the tire *above* the atmospheric pressure. Thus the total pressure in the tire was actually (15 + 35) psi, or 50 psi. One problem with using natural gases like propane and butane as propellants is that they are highly flammable. In fact, these gases can react explosively when mixed with air at a concentration of 2 percent to 9 percent by volume. Jerry was aware of the hazards of repairing Harvey's tire and took precautions to avoid an accident. First he let out the excess gas in the tire. Next he reinflated the tire to 35 psi with air. And he repeated the procedure once. Clearly, this is a dilution process intended to gradually decrease the concentrations of propane and butane. The fact that the tire exploded means that Jerry had not diluted the gases enough. But what was the source of ignition?

When Jerry found the nail hole in the tire, he used a tire reamer, a metal file-like instrument, to clean dirt and loose rubber from the hole before applying a rubber plug and liquid sealant. The last thing Jerry remembered was pulling the reamer out of the hole. The next thing he knew he was lying in the hospital, hurting all over. To solve this mystery, make use of the following clues.

†Adapted with permission from "The Exploding Tire," by Jay A. Young, CHEM MATTERS, April, 1988, p. 12. Copyright 1995 American Chemical Society.

Chemical Clues

1. Write balanced equations for the combustion of propane and butane. The products are carbon dioxide and water.

2. When Harvey inflated his flat tire to 35 psi, the composition by volume of the propane and butane gases is given by (35 psi/50 psi) × 100%, or 70 percent. When Jerry deflated the tire the first time, the pressure fell to 15 psi but the composition remained at 70 percent. Based on these facts, calculate the percent composition of propane and butane at the end of two deflation-inflation steps. Does it fall within the explosive range?

3. Given that Harvey's flat tire is a steel-belted tire, explain how the ignition of the gas mixture might have been triggered. (A steel-belted tire has two belts of steel wire for outer reinforcement and two belts of polyester cord for inner reinforcement.)

Instant flat tire repair.

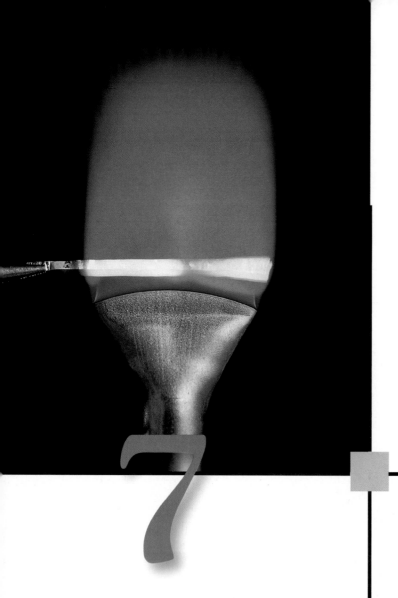

The color emitted by excited lithium atoms when a piece of platinum strip moistened with a lithium salt solution is placed in a flame. The model shows lithium atoms.

Quantum Theory and the Electronic Structure of Atoms

Interactive Activity Summary

Quantum theory enables us to predict and understand the critical role that electrons play in chemistry. In one sense, studying atoms amounts to asking the following questions:

1. How many electrons are present in a particular atom?

2. What energies do individual electrons possess?

3. Where in the atom can electrons be found?

The answers to these questions have a direct relationship to the behavior of all substances in chemical reactions, and the story of the search for answers provides a fascinating backdrop for our discussion.

7.1 From Classical Physics to Quantum Theory

Early attempts by nineteenth-century physicists to understand atoms and molecules met with only limited success. By assuming that molecules behave like rebounding balls, physicists were able to predict and explain some macroscopic phenomena, such as the pressure exerted by a gas. However, this model did not account for the stability of molecules; that is, it could not explain the forces that hold atoms together. It took a long time to realize—and an even longer time to accept—that the properties of atoms and molecules are *not* governed by the same physical laws as larger objects.

The new era in physics started in 1900 with a young German physicist named Max Planck.[†] While analyzing the data on radiation emitted by solids heated to various temperatures, Planck discovered that atoms and molecules emit energy only in certain discrete quantities, or *quanta*. Physicists had always assumed that energy is continuous and that any amount of energy could be released in a radiation process. Planck's *quantum theory* turned physics upside down. Indeed, the flurry of research that ensued altered our concept of nature forever.

Properties of Waves

To understand Planck's quantum theory, we must know something about the nature of waves. A **wave** can be thought of as a *vibrating disturbance by which energy is transmitted*. The fundamental properties of a wave are illustrated by a familiar type—water waves. Figure 7.1 shows a seagull floating on the ocean. Water waves are generated by pressure differences in various regions on the surface of water. If we carefully observe the motion of a water wave as it affects the motion of the seagull, we find that it is periodic in character; that is, the wave form repeats itself at regular intervals.

Waves are characterized by their length and height and by the number of waves that pass through a certain point in one second (Figure 7.2). **Wavelength** λ (lambda) is *the distance between identical points on successive waves*. The **frequency** ν (nu) is *the number of waves that pass through a particular point in 1 second*. In Figure 7.1, the frequency corresponds to the number of times per second that the seagull moves through a complete cycle of upward and downward motion. **Amplitude** is *the vertical distance from the midline of a wave to the peak or trough*.

Interactivity:
Wavelength, Frequency, Amplitude
Online Learning Center, Interactives

[†]Max Karl Ernst Ludwig Planck (1858–1947). German physicist. Planck received the Nobel Prize in Physics in 1918 for his quantum theory. He also made significant contributions in thermodynamics and other areas of physics.

Figure 7.1 *Properties of water waves. The distance between corresponding points on successive waves is called the wavelength, and the number of times the seagull rises up per unit of time is called the frequency. It is assumed that the seagull makes no effort to move, but simply rides up and down as the wave moves from left to right under it.*

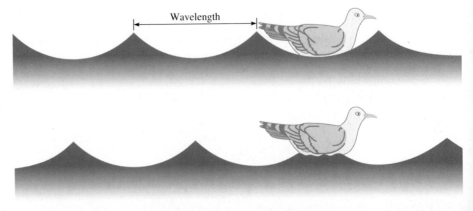

Wavelength

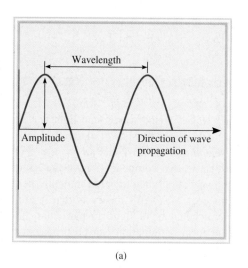

(a)

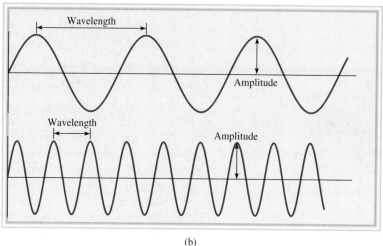

(b)

Another important property of waves is their speed, which depends on the type of wave and the nature of the medium through which the wave is traveling (for example, air, water, or a vacuum). The speed (u) of a wave is the product of its wavelength and its frequency:

$$u = \lambda \nu \qquad (7.1)$$

Figure 7.2 *(a) Wavelength and amplitude. (b) Two waves having different wavelengths and frequencies. The wavelength of the top wave is three times that of the lower wave, but its frequency is only one-third that of the lower wave. Both waves have the same amplitude.*

The inherent "sensibility" of Equation (7.1) becomes apparent if we analyze the physical dimensions involved in the three terms. The wavelength (λ) expresses the length of a wave, or distance/wave. The frequency (ν) indicates the number of these waves that pass any reference point per unit of time, or waves/time. Thus the product of these terms results in dimensions of distance/time, which is speed:

$$\frac{\text{distance}}{\text{time}} = \frac{\text{distance}}{\text{wave}} \times \frac{\text{waves}}{\text{time}}$$

Wavelength is usually expressed in units of meters, centimeters, or nanometers, and frequency is measured in hertz (Hz), where

$$1 \text{ Hz} = 1 \text{ cycle/s}$$

The word "cycle" may be left out and the frequency expressed as, for example, 25/s (read as "25 per second").

Example 7.1

Calculate the speed of a wave whose wavelength and frequency are 17.4 cm and 87.4 Hz, respectively.

Solution Recall that 87.4 Hz is the same as 87.4/s. From Equation (7.1),

$$\begin{aligned}
u &= \lambda \nu \\
&= 17.4 \text{ cm} \times 87.4 \text{ Hz} \\
&= 17.4 \text{ cm} \times 87.4/\text{s} \\
&= 1.52 \times 10^3 \text{ cm/s}
\end{aligned}$$

Similar problem: 7.8.

(Continued)

Practice Exercise Calculate the frequency (in Hz) of a wave whose speed and wavelength are 713 m/s and 1.14 m, respectively.

Electromagnetic Radiation

There are many kinds of waves, such as water waves, sound waves, and light waves. In 1873 James Clerk Maxwell proposed that visible light consists of electromagnetic waves. According to Maxwell's theory, an ***electromagnetic wave*** *has an electric field component and a magnetic field component.* These two components have the same wavelength and frequency, and hence the same speed, but they travel in mutually perpendicular planes (Figure 7.3). The significance of Maxwell's theory is that it provides a mathematical description of the general behavior of light. In particular, his model accurately describes how energy in the form of radiation can be propagated through space as vibrating electric and magnetic fields. ***Electromagnetic radiation*** *is the emission and transmission of energy in the form of electromagnetic waves.*

Electromagnetic waves travel 3.00×10^{8} meters per second (rounded off), or 186,000 miles per second in a vacuum. This speed does differ from one medium to another, but not enough to distort our calculations significantly. By convention, we use the symbol c for the speed of electromagnetic waves, or as it is more commonly called, the *speed of light.* The wavelength of electromagnetic waves is usually given in nanometers (nm).

Sound waves and water waves are not electromagnetic waves, but X rays and radio waves are.

A more accurate value for the speed of light is given on the inside back cover of the book.

Example 7.2

The wavelength of the green light from a traffic signal is centered at 522 nm. What is the frequency of this radiation?

Strategy We are given the wavelength of an electromagnetic wave and asked to calculate its frequency. Rearranging Equation (7.1) and replacing u with c (the speed of light) gives

$$\nu = \frac{c}{\lambda}$$

Solution Because the speed of light is given in meters per second, it is convenient to first convert wavelength to meters. Recall that 1 nm = 1×10^{-9} m (see Table 1.3). We write

(Continued)

Figure 7.3 *The electric field and magnetic field components of an electromagnetic wave. These two components have the same wavelength, frequency, and amplitude, but they vibrate in two mutually perpendicular planes.*

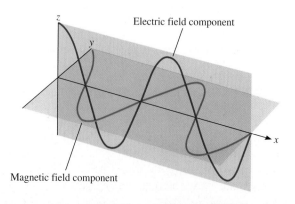

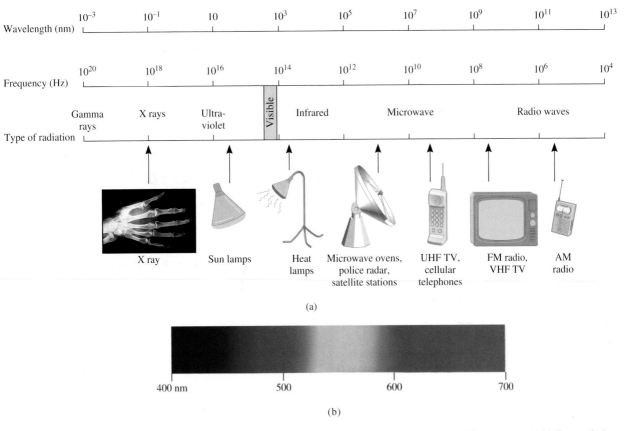

(a)

(b)

$$\lambda = 522 \text{ nm} \times \frac{1 \times 10^{-9} \text{ m}}{1 \text{ nm}} = 522 \times 10^{-9} \text{ m}$$

$$= 5.22 \times 10^{-7} \text{ m}$$

Substituting in the wavelength and the speed of light (3.00×10^8 m/s), the frequency is

$$\nu = \frac{3.00 \times 10^8 \text{ m/s}}{5.22 \times 10^{-7} \text{ m}}$$

$$= 5.75 \times 10^{14} \text{/s, or } 5.75 \times 10^{14} \text{ Hz}$$

Check The answer shows that 5.75×10^{14} waves pass a fixed point every second. This very high frequency is in accordance with the very high speed of light.

Practice Exercise What is the wavelength (in meters) of an electromagnetic wave whose frequency is 3.64×10^7 Hz?

Figure 7.4 (a) Types of electromagnetic radiation. Gamma rays have the shortest wavelength and highest frequency; radio waves have the longest wavelength and the lowest frequency. Each type of radiation is spread over a specific range of wavelengths (and frequencies). (b) Visible light ranges from a wavelength of 400 nm (violet) to 700 nm (red).

Similar problem: 7.7.

Figure 7.4 shows various types of electromagnetic radiation, which differ from one another in wavelength and frequency. The long radio waves are emitted by large antennas, such as those used by broadcasting stations. The shorter, visible light waves are produced by the motions of electrons within atoms and molecules. The shortest waves, which also have the highest frequency, are associated with γ (gamma) rays, which result from changes within the nucleus of the atom (see Chapter 2). As we will see shortly, the higher the frequency, the more energetic the radiation. Thus, ultraviolet radiation, X rays, and γ rays are high-energy radiation.

Planck's Quantum Theory

When solids are heated, they emit electromagnetic radiation over a wide range of wavelengths. The dull red glow of an electric heater and the bright white light of a tungsten lightbulb are examples of radiation from heated solids.

Measurements taken in the latter part of the nineteenth century showed that the amount of radiation energy emitted by an object at a certain temperature depends on its wavelength. Attempts to account for this dependence in terms of established wave theory and thermodynamic laws were only partially successful. One theory explained short-wavelength dependence but failed to account for the longer wavelengths. Another theory accounted for the longer wavelengths but failed for short wavelengths. It seemed that something fundamental was missing from the laws of classical physics.

Planck solved the problem with an assumption that departed drastically from accepted concepts. Classical physics assumed that atoms and molecules could emit (or absorb) any arbitrary amount of radiant energy. Planck said that atoms and molecules could emit (or absorb) energy only in discrete quantities, like small packages or bundles. Planck gave the name *quantum* to *the smallest quantity of energy that can be emitted (or absorbed) in the form of electromagnetic radiation*. The energy E of a single quantum of energy is given by

$$E = h\nu \tag{7.2}$$

where h is called *Planck's constant* and ν is the frequency of radiation. The value of Planck's constant is 6.63×10^{-34} J · s.

According to quantum theory, energy is always emitted in multiples of $h\nu$; for example, $h\nu$, $2\,h\nu$, $3\,h\nu$, . . . , but never, for example, $1.67\,h\nu$ or $4.98\,h\nu$. At the time Planck presented his theory, he could not explain why energies should be fixed or quantized in this manner. Starting with this hypothesis, however, he had no trouble correlating the experimental data for emission by solids over the *entire* range of wavelengths; they all supported the quantum theory.

The idea that energy should be quantized or "bundled" may seem strange, but the concept of quantization has many analogies. For example, an electric charge is also quantized; there can be only whole-number multiples of e, the charge of one electron. Matter itself is quantized, for the numbers of electrons, protons, and neutrons and the numbers of atoms in a sample of matter must also be integers. Our money system is based on a "quantum" of value called a penny. Even processes in living systems involve quantized phenomena. The eggs laid by hens are quantized, and a pregnant cat gives birth to an integral number of kittens, not to one-half or three-quarters of a kitten.

7.2 The Photoelectric Effect

In 1905, only five years after Planck presented his quantum theory, Albert Einstein[†] used the theory to solve another mystery in physics, the *photoelectric effect,* a phenomenon in which *electrons are ejected from the surface of certain metals exposed to light of at least a certain minimum frequency,* called *the threshold*

[†]Albert Einstein (1879–1955). German-born American physicist. Regarded by many as one of the two greatest physicists the world has known (the other is Isaac Newton). The three papers (on special relativity, Brownian motion, and the photoelectric effect) that he published in 1905 while employed as a technical assistant in the Swiss patent office in Berne have profoundly influenced the development of physics. He received the Nobel Prize in Physics in 1921 for his explanation of the photoelectric effect.

frequency (Figure 7.5). The number of electrons ejected was proportional to the intensity (or brightness) of the light, but the energies of the ejected electrons were not. Below the threshold frequency no electrons were ejected no matter how intense the light.

The photoelectric effect could not be explained by the wave theory of light. Einstein, however, made an extraordinary assumption. He suggested that a beam of light is really a stream of particles. These *particles of light* are now called **photons.** Using Planck's quantum theory of radiation as a starting point, Einstein deduced that each photon must possess energy E, given by the equation

$$E = h\nu$$

where ν is the frequency of light. Electrons are held in a metal by attractive forces, and so removing them from the metal requires light of a sufficiently high frequency (which corresponds to sufficiently high energy) to break them free. Shining a beam of light onto a metal surface can be thought of as shooting a beam of particles— photons—at the metal atoms. If the frequency of photons is such that $h\nu$ is exactly equal to the energy that binds the electrons in the metal, then the light will have just enough energy to knock the electrons loose. If we use light of a higher frequency, then not only will the electrons be knocked loose, but they will also acquire some kinetic energy. This situation is summarized by the equation

$$h\nu = KE + BE \tag{7.3}$$

where KE is the kinetic energy of the ejected electron and BE is the binding energy of the electron in the metal. Rewriting Equation (7.3) as

$$KE = h\nu - BE$$

shows that the more energetic the photon (that is, the higher its frequency), the greater the kinetic energy of the ejected electron.

Now consider two beams of light having the same frequency (which is greater than the threshold frequency) but different intensities. The more intense beam of light consists of a larger number of photons; consequently, it ejects more electrons from the metal's surface than the weaker beam of light. Thus the more intense the light, the greater the number of electrons emitted by the target metal; the higher the frequency of the light, the greater the kinetic energy of the ejected electrons.

The margin note reads: This equation has the same form as Equation (7.2) because, as we will see shortly, electromagnetic radiation is emitted as well as absorbed in the form of photons.

Example 7.3

Calculate the energy (in joules) of (a) a photon with a wavelength of 5.00×10^4 nm (infrared region) and (b) a photon with a wavelength of 5.00×10^{-2} nm (X ray region).

Strategy In both (a) and (b) we are given the wavelength of a photon and asked to calculate its energy. We need to convert the wavelength into frequency using Equation (7.1) and then use Equation (7.2) to calculate the energy. Planck's constant is given in the text and also on the back inside cover.

Solution (a) Because

$$E = h\nu \quad \text{and} \quad \nu = \frac{c}{\lambda}$$

(Continued)

Incident light

Metal

Voltage source   Meter

Figure 7.5 *An apparatus for studying the photoelectric effect. Light of a certain frequency falls on a clean metal surface. Ejected electrons are attracted toward the positive electrode. The flow of electrons is registered by a detecting meter.*

then

$$E = h\frac{c}{\lambda}$$

$$= \frac{(6.63 \times 10^{-34}\,\text{J} \cdot \text{s})(3.00 \times 10^8\,\text{m/s})}{(5.00 \times 10^4\,\text{nm})\dfrac{1 \times 10^{-9}\,\text{m}}{1\,\text{nm}}}$$

$$= 3.98 \times 10^{-21}\,\text{J}$$

This is the energy of a single photon with a 5.00×10^4 nm wavelength.

(b) Following the same procedure as in (a), we can show that the energy of the photon that has a wavelength of 5.00×10^{-2} nm is 3.98×10^{-15} J.

Check Because the energy of a photon increases with decreasing wavelength, we see that an "X-ray" photon is 1×10^6, or a million times, more energetic than an "infrared" photon.

Similar problem: 7.15.

Practice Exercise The energy of a photon is 5.87×10^{-20} J. What is its wavelength (in nanometers)?

Einstein's theory of light posed a dilemma for scientists. On the one hand, it explains the photoelectric effect satisfactorily. On the other hand, the particle theory of light is not consistent with the known wave behavior of light. The only way to resolve the dilemma is to accept the idea that light possesses *both* particlelike and wavelike properties. Depending on the experiment, light behaves either as a wave or as a stream of particles. This concept was totally alien to the way physicists had thought about matter and radiation, and it took a long time for them to accept it. We will see in Section 7.4 that a dual nature (particles and waves) is not unique to light but is characteristic of all matter, including electrons.

7.3 Bohr's Theory of the Hydrogen Atom

Einstein's work paved the way for the solution of yet another nineteenth-century "mystery" in physics: the emission spectra of atoms.

Emission Spectra

Animation: Emission
Spectra
Online Learning Center,
Animations

Ever since the seventeenth century, when Newton showed that sunlight is composed of various color components that can be recombined to produce white light, chemists and physicists have studied the characteristics of *emission spectra*, that is, *either continuous or line spectra of radiation emitted by substances.* The emission spectrum of a substance can be seen by energizing a sample of material either with thermal energy or with some other form of energy (such as a high-voltage electrical discharge if the substance is gaseous). A "red-hot" or "white-hot" iron bar freshly removed from a high-temperature source produces a characteristic glow. This visible glow is the portion of its emission spectrum that is sensed by eye. The warmth of the same iron bar represents another portion of its emission spectrum—the infrared region. A feature common to the emission spectra of the sun and of a heated solid is that both are continuous; that is, all wavelengths of visible light are represented in the spectra (see the visible region in Figure 7.4).

The emission spectra of atoms in the gas phase, on the other hand, do not show a continuous spread of wavelengths from red to violet; rather, the atoms produce bright lines in different parts of the visible spectrum. These **line spectra** are *the light emission*

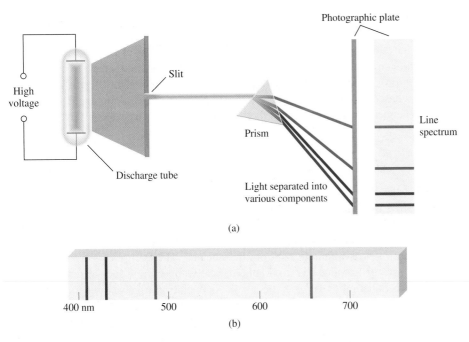

Figure 7.6 (a) An experimental arrangement for studying the emission spectra of atoms and molecules. The gas under study is in a discharge tube containing two electrodes. As electrons flow from the negative electrode to the positive electrode, they collide with the gas. This collision process eventually leads to the emission of light by the atoms (or molecules). The emitted light is separated into its components by a prism. Each component color is focused at a definite position, according to its wavelength, and forms a colored image of the slit on the photographic plate. The colored images are called spectral lines. (b) The line emission spectrum of hydrogen atoms in the visible region.

only at specific wavelengths. Figure 7.6 is a schematic diagram of a discharge tube that is used to study emission spectra, and Figure 7.7 shows the color emitted by hydrogen atoms in a discharge tube.

Every element has a unique emission spectrum. The characteristic lines in atomic spectra can be used in chemical analysis to identify unknown atoms, much as fingerprints are used to identify people. When the lines of the emission spectrum of a known element exactly match the lines of the emission spectrum of an unknown sample, the identity of the sample is established. Although the utility of this procedure was recognized some time ago in chemical analysis, the origin of these lines was unknown until early in the twentieth century. Figure 7.8 shows the emission spectra of several elements.

Emission Spectrum of the Hydrogen Atom

In 1913, not too long after Planck's and Einstein's discoveries, a theoretical explanation of the emission spectrum of the hydrogen atom was presented by the Danish physicist Niels Bohr.[†] Bohr's treatment is very complex and is no longer considered to be correct in all its details. Thus, we will concentrate only on his important assumptions and final results, which do account for the special lines.

When Bohr first tackled this problem, physicists already knew that the atom contains electrons and protons. They thought of an atom as an entity in which electrons whirled around the nucleus in circular orbits at high velocities. This was an appealing model because it resembled the motions of the planets around the sun. In the hydrogen atom, it was believed that the electrostatic attraction between the positive "solar" proton and the negative "planetary" electron pulls the electron inward and that this force is balanced exactly by the outward acceleration due to the circular motion of the electron.

Bohr's model of the atom included the idea of electrons moving in circular orbits, but he imposed a rather severe restriction: The single electron in the hydrogen atom

When a high voltage is applied between the forks, some of the sodium ions in the pickle are converted to sodium atoms in an excited state. These atoms emit the characteristic yellow light as they relax to the ground state.

[†]Niels Henrik David Bohr (1885–1962). Danish physicist. One of the founders of modern physics, he received the Nobel Prize in Physics in 1922 for his theory explaining the spectrum of the hydrogen atom.

could be located only in certain orbits. Because each orbit has a particular energy associated with it, the energies associated with electron motion in the permitted orbits must be fixed in value, or *quantized*. Bohr attributed the emission of radiation by an energized hydrogen atom to the electron dropping from a higher-energy orbit to a lower one and giving up a quantum of energy (a photon) in the form of light (Figure 7.9). Using arguments based on electrostatic interaction and Newton's laws of motion, Bohr showed that the energies that the electron in the hydrogen atom can possess are given by

$$E_n = -R_H\left(\frac{1}{n^2}\right) \qquad (7.4)$$

where R_H, the Rydberg[†] constant, has the value 2.18×10^{-18} J. The number n is an integer called the principal quantum number; it has the values $n = 1, 2, 3, \ldots$.

The negative sign in Equation (7.4) is an arbitrary convention, signifying that the energy of the electron in the atom is *lower* than the energy of a *free electron,* which is an electron that is infinitely far from the nucleus. The energy of a free electron is arbitrarily assigned a value of zero. Mathematically, this corresponds to setting n equal to infinity in Equation (7.4), so that $E_\infty = 0$. As the electron gets closer to the nucleus (as n decreases), E_n becomes larger in absolute value, but also more negative. The most negative value, then, is reached when $n = 1$, which corresponds to the most stable energy state. We call this the **ground state,** or the **ground level,** which refers to *the lowest energy state of a system* (which is an atom in our discussion). The stability of the electron diminishes for $n = 2, 3, \ldots$. Each of these levels is called an **excited state,** or **excited level,** which is *higher in energy than the ground state.* A hydrogen

Figure 7.7 *Color emitted by hydrogen atoms in a discharge tube. The color observed results from the combination of the colors emitted in the visible spectrum.*

[†]Johannes Robert Rydberg (1854–1919). Swedish physicist. Rydberg's major contribution to physics was his study of the line spectra of many elements.

Figure 7.8 *The emission spectra of various elements.*

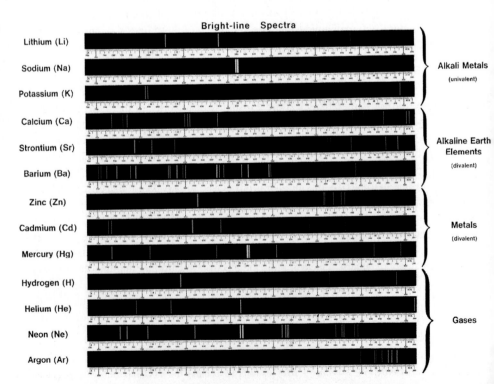

electron for which n is greater than 1 is said to be in an excited state. The radius of each circular orbit in Bohr's model depends on n^2. Thus, as n increases from 1 to 2 to 3, the orbit radius increases very rapidly. The higher the excited state, the farther away the electron is from the nucleus (and the less tightly it is held by the nucleus).

Bohr's theory enables us to explain the line spectrum of the hydrogen atom. Radiant energy absorbed by the atom causes the electron to move from a lower-energy state (characterized by a smaller n value) to a higher-energy state (characterized by a larger n value). Conversely, radiant energy (in the form of a photon) is emitted when the electron moves from a higher-energy state to a lower-energy state. The quantized movement of the electron from one energy state to another is analogous to the movement of a tennis ball either up or down a set of stairs (Figure 7.10). The ball can be on any of several steps but never between steps. The journey from a lower step to a higher one is an energy-requiring process, whereas movement from a higher step to a lower step is an energy-releasing process. The quantity of energy involved in either type of change is determined by the distance between the beginning and ending steps. Similarly, the amount of energy needed to move an electron in the Bohr atom depends on the difference in energy levels between the initial and final states.

To apply Equation (7.4) to the emission process in a hydrogen atom, let us suppose that the electron is initially in an excited state characterized by the principal quantum number n_i. During emission, the electron drops to a lower energy state characterized by the principal quantum number n_f (the subscripts i and f denote the initial and final states, respectively). This lower energy state may be either a less excited state or the ground state. The difference between the energies of the initial and final states is

$$\Delta E = E_f - E_i$$

From Equation (7.4),

$$E_f = -R_H\left(\frac{1}{n_f^2}\right)$$

and

$$E_i = -R_H\left(\frac{1}{n_i^2}\right)$$

Therefore

$$\Delta E = \left(\frac{-R_H}{n_f^2}\right) - \left(\frac{-R_H}{n_i^2}\right)$$

$$= R_H\left(\frac{1}{n_i^2} - \frac{1}{n_f^2}\right)$$

Because this transition results in the emission of a photon of frequency ν and energy $h\nu$, we can write

$$\Delta E = h\nu = R_H\left(\frac{1}{n_i^2} - \frac{1}{n_f^2}\right) \tag{7.5}$$

When a photon is emitted, $n_i > n_f$. Consequently the term in parentheses is negative and ΔE is negative (energy is lost to the surroundings). When energy is absorbed, $n_i < n_f$ and the term in parentheses is positive, so ΔE is positive. Each spectral line in the emission spectrum corresponds to a particular transition in a hydrogen atom. When we study a large number of hydrogen atoms, we observe all possible transitions and hence the corresponding spectral lines. The brightness of a spectral line depends on how many photons of the same wavelength are emitted.

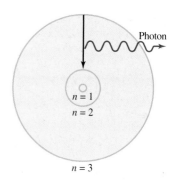

Figure 7.9 The emission process in an excited hydrogen atom, according to Bohr's theory. An electron originally in a higher-energy orbit (n = 3) falls back to a lower-energy orbit (n = 2). As a result, a photon with energy hν is given off. The value of hν is equal to the difference in energies of the two orbits occupied by the electron in the emission process. For simplicity, only three orbits are shown.

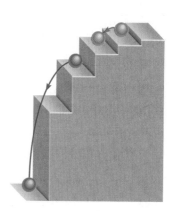

Figure 7.10 A mechanical analogy for the emission processes. The ball can rest on any step but not between steps.

TABLE 7.1	The Various Series in Atomic Hydrogen Emission Spectrum			
	Series	n_f	n_i	**Spectrum Region**
	Lyman	1	2, 3, 4, . . .	Ultraviolet
	Balmer	2	3, 4, 5, . . .	Visible and ultraviolet
	Paschen	3	4, 5, 6, . . .	Infrared
	Brackett	4	5, 6, 7, . . .	Infrared

The emission spectrum of hydrogen includes a wide range of wavelengths from the infrared to the ultraviolet. Table 7.1 lists the series of transitions in the hydrogen spectrum; they are named after their discoverers. The Balmer series was particularly easy to study because a number of its lines fall in the visible range.

Figure 7.9 shows a single transition. However, it is more informative to express transitions as shown in Figure 7.11. Each horizontal line represents an allowed energy level for the electron in a hydrogen atom. The energy levels are labeled with their principal quantum numbers.

Example 7.4 illustrates the use of Equation (7.5).

Example 7.4

What is the wavelength of a photon (in nanometers) emitted during a transition from the $n_i = 5$ state to the $n_f = 2$ state in the hydrogen atom?

(Continued)

Figure 7.11 *The energy levels in the hydrogen atom and the various emission series. Each energy level corresponds to the energy associated with an allowed energy state for an orbit, as postulated by Bohr and shown in Figure 7.9. The emission lines are labeled according to the scheme in Table 7.1.*

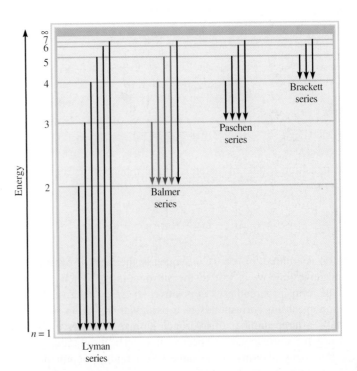

Strategy We are given the initial and final states in the emission process. We can calculate the energy of the emitted photon using Equation (7.5). Then from Equations (7.2) and (7.1) we can solve for the wavelength of the photon. The value of Rydberg's constant is given in the text.

Solution From Equation (7.5) we write

$$\Delta E = R_H \left(\frac{1}{n_i^2} - \frac{1}{n_f^2} \right)$$

$$= 2.18 \times 10^{-18} \, J \left(\frac{1}{5^2} - \frac{1}{2^2} \right)$$

$$= -4.58 \times 10^{-19} \, J$$

The negative sign indicates that this is energy associated with an emission process. To calculate the wavelength, we will omit the minus sign for ΔE because the wavelength of the photon must be positive. Because $\Delta E = h\nu$ or $\nu = \Delta E/h$, we can calculate the wavelength of the photon by writing

The negative sign is in accord with our convention that energy is given off to the surroundings.

$$\lambda = \frac{c}{\nu}$$

$$= \frac{ch}{\Delta E}$$

$$= \frac{(3.00 \times 10^8 \, m/s)(6.63 \times 10^{-34} \, J \cdot s)}{4.58 \times 10^{-19} \, J}$$

$$= 4.34 \times 10^{-7} \, m$$

$$= 4.34 \times 10^{-7} \, m \times \left(\frac{1 \, nm}{1 \times 10^{-9} \, m} \right) = 434 \, nm$$

Check The wavelength is in the visible region of the electromagnetic region (see Figure 7.4). This is consistent with the fact that because $n_f = 2$, this transition gives rise to a spectral line in the Balmer series (see Figure 7.6).

Similar problems: 7.31, 7.32.

Practice Exercise What is the wavelength (in nanometers) of a photon emitted during a transition from $n_i = 6$ to $n_f = 4$ state in the H atom?

The Chemistry in Action essays on p. 272 and p. 274 discuss atomic emission and lasers.

7.4 The Dual Nature of the Electron

Physicists were both mystified and intrigued by Bohr's theory. They questioned why the energies of the hydrogen electron are quantized. Or, phrasing the question in a more concrete way, Why is the electron in a Bohr atom restricted to orbiting the nucleus at certain fixed distances? For a decade no one, not even Bohr himself, had a logical explanation. In 1924 Louis de Broglie[†] provided a solution to this puzzle. De Broglie reasoned that if light waves can behave like a stream of particles (photons), then perhaps particles such as electrons can possess wave properties.

[†]Louis Victor Pierre Raymond Duc de Broglie (1892–1977). French physicist. Member of an old and noble family in France, he held the title of a prince. In his doctoral dissertation, he proposed that matter and radiation have the properties of both wave and particle. For this work, de Broglie was awarded the Nobel Prize in Physics in 1929.

CHEMISTRY IN ACTION

Element from the Sun

S cientists know that our sun and other stars contain certain elements. How was this information obtained?

In the early nineteenth century, the German physicist Josef Fraunhofer studied the emission spectrum of the sun and noticed certain dark lines at specific wavelengths. We interpret the appearance of these lines by supposing that originally a continuous band of color was radiated and that, as the emitted light moves outward from the sun, some of the radiation is reabsorbed at those wavelengths by the atoms in space. These dark lines are therefore absorption lines. For atoms, the emission and absorption of light occur at the same wavelengths, but they differ in appearance—colored lines for emission and dark lines for absorption. By matching the absorption lines in the emission spectra of distant stars with the emission spectra of known elements, scientists have been able to deduce the types of elements present in those stars.

In 1868 the French physicist Pierre Janssen detected a new dark line in the solar emission spectrum that did not match the emission lines of known elements. The name helium (from the Greek helios, meaning the sun) was given to the element responsible for the absorption line. Twenty-seven years later, helium was discovered on Earth by the British chemist William Ramsay in a mineral of uranium. On Earth, the only source of helium is through radioactive decay processes—α particles emitted during nuclear decay are eventually converted to helium atoms.

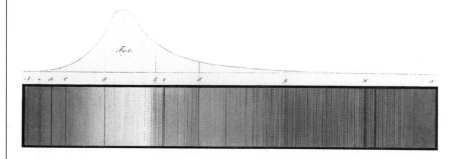

Fraunhofer's original drawing, showing the dark absorption lines in the sun's emission spectrum.

According to de Broglie, an electron bound to the nucleus behaves like a *standing wave.* Standing waves can be generated by plucking, say, a guitar string (Figure 7.12). The waves are described as standing, or stationary, because they do not travel along the string. Some points on the string, called **nodes,** do not move at all; that is, *the amplitude of the wave at these points is zero.* There is a node at each end, and there may be nodes between the ends. The greater the frequency of vibration, the shorter the wavelength of the standing wave and the greater the number of nodes. As Figure 7.12 shows, there can be only certain wavelengths in any of the allowed motions of the string.

De Broglie argued that if an electron does behave like a standing wave in the hydrogen atom, the length of the wave must fit the circumference of the orbit exactly

Figure 7.12 *The standing waves generated by plucking a guitar string. Each dot represents a node. The length of the string (l) must be equal to a whole number times one-half the wavelength (λ/2).*

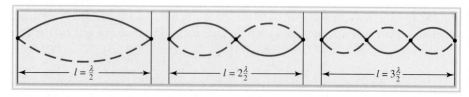

$$l = \frac{\lambda}{2} \qquad l = 2\frac{\lambda}{2} \qquad l = 3\frac{\lambda}{2}$$

(Figure 7.13). Otherwise the wave would partially cancel itself on each successive orbit. Eventually the amplitude of the wave would be reduced to zero, and the wave would not exist.

The relation between the circumference of an allowed orbit ($2\pi r$) and the wavelength (λ) of the electron is given by

$$2\pi r = n\lambda \qquad (7.6)$$

where r is the radius of the orbit, λ is the wavelength of the electron wave, and $n = 1, 2, 3, \ldots$. Because n is an integer, it follows that r can have only certain values as n increases from 1 to 2 to 3 and so on. And because the energy of the electron depends on the size of the orbit (or the value of r), its value must be quantized.

De Broglie's reasoning led to the conclusion that waves can behave like particles and particles can exhibit wavelike properties. De Broglie deduced that the particle and wave properties are related by the expression

$$\lambda = \frac{h}{mu} \qquad (7.7)$$

where λ, m, and u are the wavelengths associated with a moving particle, its mass, and its velocity, respectively. Equation (7.7) implies that a particle in motion can be treated as a wave, and a wave can exhibit the properties of a particle. Note that the left side of Equation (7.7) involves the wavelike property of wavelength, whereas the right side makes references to mass, a distinctly particlelike property.

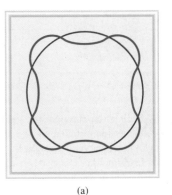

(a)

(b)

Figure 7.13 (a) The circumference of the orbit is equal to an integral number of wavelengths. This is an allowed orbit. (b) The circumference of the orbit is not equal to an integral number of wavelengths. As a result, the electron wave does not close in on itself. This is a nonallowed orbit.

Example 7.5

Calculate the wavelength of the "particle" in the following two cases: (a) The fastest serve in tennis is about 140 miles per hour, or 63 m/s. Calculate the wavelength associated with a 6.0×10^{-2}-kg tennis ball traveling at this speed. (b) Calculate the wavelength associated with an electron (9.1094×10^{-31} kg) moving at 63 m/s.

Strategy We are given the mass and the speed of the particle in (a) and (b) and asked to calculate the wavelength so we need Equation (7.7). Note that because the units of Planck's constants are J · s, m and u must be in kg and m/s (1 J = 1 kg m^2/s^2), respectively.

Solution (a) Using Equation (7.7) we write

$$\lambda = \frac{h}{mu}$$
$$= \frac{6.63 \times 10^{-34} \text{ J} \cdot \text{s}}{(6.0 \times 10^{-2} \text{ kg}) \times 63 \text{ m/s}}$$
$$= 1.8 \times 10^{-34} \text{ m}$$

Comment This is an exceedingly small wavelength considering that the size of an atom itself is on the order of 1×10^{-10} m. For this reason, the wave properties of a tennis ball cannot be detected by any existing measuring device.

(Continued)

CHEMISTRY IN ACTION

Laser—The Splendid Light

*L*aser is an acronym for light amplification by stimulated emission of radiation. It is a special type of emission that involves either atoms or molecules. Since the discovery of laser in 1960, it has been used in numerous systems designed to operate in the gas, liquid, and solid states. These systems emit radiation with wavelengths ranging from infrared through visible and ultraviolet. The advent of laser has truly revolutionized science, medicine, and technology.

Ruby laser was the first known laser. Ruby is a deep-red mineral containing corundum, Al_2O_3, in which some of the Al^{3+} ions have been replaced by Cr^{3+} ions. A flashlamp is used to

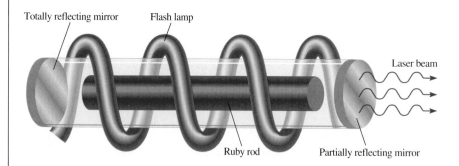

Totally reflecting mirror   Flash lamp

Laser beam

Ruby rod   Partially reflecting mirror

The emission of laser light from a ruby laser.

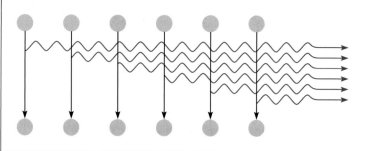

The stimulated emission of one photon by another photon in a cascade event that leads to the emission of laser light. The synchronization of the light waves produces an intensely penetrating laser beam.

(b) In this case,

$$\lambda = \frac{h}{mu}$$

$$= \frac{6.63 \times 10^{-34} \, J \cdot s}{(9.1094 \times 10^{-31} \, kg) \times 63 \, m/s}$$

$$= 1.2 \times 10^{-5} \, m$$

Similar problems: 7.40, 7.41.

Comment This wavelength (1.2×10^{-5} m or 1.2×10^4 nm) is in the infrared region. This calculation shows that only electrons (and other submicroscopic particles) have measurable wavelengths.

Practice Exercise Calculate the wavelength (in nanometers) of a H atom (mass = 1.674×10^{-27} kg) moving at 7.00×10^2 cm/s.

Example 7.5 shows that although de Broglie's equation can be applied to diverse systems, the wave properties become observable only for submicroscopic objects. This

excite the chromium atoms to a higher energy level. The excited atoms are unstable, so at a given instant some of them will return to the ground state by emitting a photon in the red region of the spectrum. The photon bounces back and forth many times between mirrors at opposite ends of the laser tube. This photon can stimulate the emission of photons of exactly the same wavelength from other excited chromium atoms; these photons in turn can stimulate the emission of more photons, and so on. Because the light waves are *in phase*—that is, their maxima and minima coincide—the photons enhance one another, increasing their power with each passage between the mirrors. One of the mirrors is only partially reflecting, so that when the light reaches a certain intensity it emerges from the mirror as a laser beam. Depending on the mode of operation, the laser light may be emitted in pulses (as in the ruby laser case) or in continuous waves.

Laser light is characterized by three properties: It is intense, it has precisely known wavelength and hence energy, and it is coherent. By *coherent* we mean that the light waves are all in phase. The applications of lasers are quite numerous. Their high intensity and ease of focus make them suitable for doing eye surgery, for drilling holes in metals and welding, and for carrying out nuclear fusion. The fact that they are highly directional and have precisely known wavelengths makes them very useful for telecommunications. Lasers are also used in isotope separation, in holography (three-dimensional photography), in compact disc players, and in supermarket scanners. Lasers have played an important role in the spectroscopic investigation of molecular properties and of many chemical and biological processes. Laser lights are increasingly being used to probe the details of chemical reactions (see Chapter 13).

State-of-the-art lasers used in the research laboratory of Dr. A. H. Zewail at the California Institute of Technology.

distinction is due to the smallness of Planck's constant, h, which appears in the numerator in Equation (7.7).

Shortly after de Broglie introduced his equation, Clinton Davisson[†] and Lester Germer[‡] in the United States and G. P. Thomson[§] in England demonstrated that electrons do indeed possess wavelike properties. By directing a beam of electrons through a thin piece of gold foil, Thomson obtained a set of concentric rings on a screen, similar to the pattern observed when X rays (which are waves) were used. Figure 7.14 shows such a pattern for aluminum.

The Chemistry in Action essay on p. 276 describes electron microscopy.

[†]Clinton Joseph Davisson (1881–1958). American physicist. He and G. P. Thomson shared the Nobel Prize in Physics in 1937 for demonstrating wave properties of electrons.

[‡]Lester Halbert Germer (1896–1972). American physicist. Discoverer (with Davisson) of the wave properties of electrons.

[§]George Paget Thomson (1892–1975). English physicist. Son of J. J. Thomson, he received the Nobel Prize in Physics in 1937, along with Clinton Davisson, for demonstrating wave properties of electrons.

Electron Microscopy

The electron microscope is an extremely valuable application of the wavelike properties of electrons because it produces images of objects that cannot be seen with the naked eye or with light microscopes. According to the laws of optics, it is impossible to form an image of an object that is smaller than half the wavelength of the light used for the observation. Because the range of visible light wavelengths starts at around 400 nm, or 4×10^{-5} cm, we cannot see anything smaller than 2×10^{-5} cm. In principle, we can see objects on the atomic and molecular scale by using X rays, whose wavelengths range from about 0.01 nm to 10 nm. However, X rays cannot be focused, so they do not produce well-formed images. Electrons, on the other hand, are charged particles, which can be focused in the same way the image on a TV screen is focused, that is, by applying an electric field or a magnetic field. According to Equation (7.7), the wavelength of an electron is inversely proportional to its velocity. By accelerating electrons to very high velocities, we can obtain wavelengths as short as 0.004 nm.

A different type of electron microscope, called the *scanning tunneling microscope (STM),* makes use of another quantum mechanical property of the electron to produce an image of the atoms on the surface of a sample. Because of its extremely small mass, an electron is able to move or "tunnel" through an energy barrier (instead of going over it). The STM consists of a tungsten metal needle with a very fine point, the source of the tunneling electrons. A voltage is maintained between the needle and the surface of the sample to induce electrons to tunnel through space to the sample. As the needle moves over the sample, at a distance of a few atomic diameters from the surface, the tunneling current is measured. This current decreases with increasing distance from the sample. By using a feedback loop, the vertical position of the tip can be adjusted to a constant distance from the surface. The extent of these adjustments, which profile the sample, is recorded and displayed as a three-dimensional false-colored image.

Both the electron microscope and the STM are among the most powerful tools in chemical and biological research.

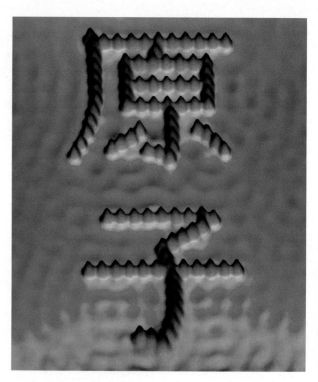

STM image of iron atoms arranged to display the Chinese characters for atom on a copper surface.

An electron micrograph showing a normal red blood cell and a sickled red blood cell from the same person.

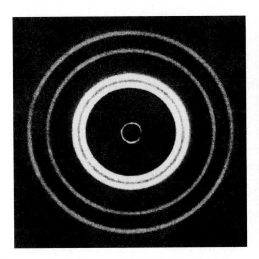 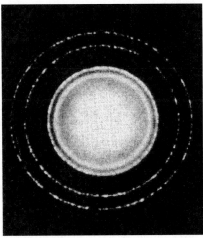

Figure 7.14 *Left: X-ray diffraction pattern of aluminum foil. Right: Electron diffraction of aluminum foil. The similarity of these two patterns shows that electrons can behave like X rays and display wave properties.*

7.5 Quantum Mechanics

The spectacular success of Bohr's theory was followed by a series of disappointments. Bohr's approach did not account for the emission spectra of atoms containing more than one electron, such as atoms of helium and lithium. Nor did it explain why extra lines appear in the hydrogen emission spectrum when a magnetic field is applied. Another problem arose with the discovery that electrons are wavelike: How can the "position" of a wave be specified? We cannot define the precise location of a wave because a wave extends in space.

To describe the problem of trying to locate a subatomic particle that behaves like a wave, Werner Heisenberg[†] formulated what is now known as the ***Heisenberg uncertainty principle:*** *it is impossible to know simultaneously both the momentum p* (defined as mass times velocity) *and the position of a particle with certainty.* Stated mathematically,

$$\Delta x \Delta p \geq \frac{h}{4\pi} \qquad (7.8)$$

where Δx and Δp are the uncertainties in measuring the position and momentum, respectively. Equation (7.8) says that if we make the measurement of the momentum of a particle more precise (that is, if we make Δp a small quantity), our knowledge of the position will become correspondingly less precise (that is, Δx will become larger). Similarly, if the position of the particle is known more precisely, then its momentum measurement must be less precise. Applying the Heisenberg uncertainty principle to the hydrogen atom, we see that in reality the electron does not orbit the nucleus in a well-defined path, as Bohr thought. If it did, we could determine precisely both the position of the electron (from the radius of the orbit) and its momentum (from its kinetic energy) at the same time, a violation of the uncertainty principle.

To be sure, Bohr made a significant contribution to our understanding of atoms, and his suggestion that the energy of an electron in an atom is quantized remains

In reality, Bohr's theory accounted for the observed emission spectra of He^+ and Li^{2+} ions, as well as that of hydrogen. However, all three systems have one feature in common—each contains a single electron. Thus the Bohr model worked successfully only for the hydrogen atom and for "hydrogenlike ions."

The ≥ sign means that the product $\Delta x \Delta p$ can be greater than or equal to $h/4\pi$, but it can never be smaller than $h/4\pi$.

[†]Werner Karl Heisenberg (1901–1976). German physicist. One of the founders of modern quantum theory, Heisenberg received the Nobel Prize in Physics in 1932.

unchallenged. But his theory did not provide a complete description of electronic behavior in atoms. In 1926 the Austrian physicist Erwin Schrödinger,[†] using a complicated mathematical technique, formulated an equation that describes the behavior and energies of submicroscopic particles in general, an equation analogous to Newton's laws of motion for macroscopic objects. The *Schrödinger equation* requires advanced calculus to solve, and we will not discuss it here. It is important to know, however, that the equation incorporates both particle behavior, in terms of mass m, and wave behavior, in terms of a *wave function* ψ (psi), which depends on the location in space of the system (such as an electron in an atom).

The wave function itself has no direct physical meaning. However, the probability of finding the electron in a certain region in space is proportional to the square of the wave function, ψ^2. The idea of relating ψ^2 to probability stemmed from a wave theory analogy. According to wave theory, the intensity of light is proportional to the square of the amplitude of the wave, or ψ^2. The most likely place to find a photon is where the intensity is greatest, that is, where the value of ψ^2 is greatest. A similar argument associates ψ^2 with the likelihood of finding an electron in regions surrounding the nucleus.

Schrödinger's equation began a new era in physics and chemistry, for it launched a new field, *quantum mechanics* (also called *wave mechanics*). We now refer to the developments in quantum theory from 1913—the time Bohr presented his analysis for the hydrogen atom—to 1926 as "old quantum theory."

The Quantum Mechanical Description of the Hydrogen Atom

The Schrödinger equation specifies the possible energy states the electron can occupy in a hydrogen atom and identifies the corresponding wave functions (ψ). These energy states and wave functions are characterized by a set of quantum numbers (to be discussed shortly), with which we can construct a comprehensive model of the hydrogen atom.

Although quantum mechanics tells us that we cannot pinpoint an electron in an atom, it does define the region where the electron might be at a given time. The concept of **electron density** *gives the probability that an electron will be found in a particular region of an atom.* The square of the wave function, ψ^2, defines the distribution of electron density in three-dimensional space around the nucleus. Regions of high electron density represent a high probability of locating the electron, whereas the opposite holds for regions of low electron density (Figure 7.15).

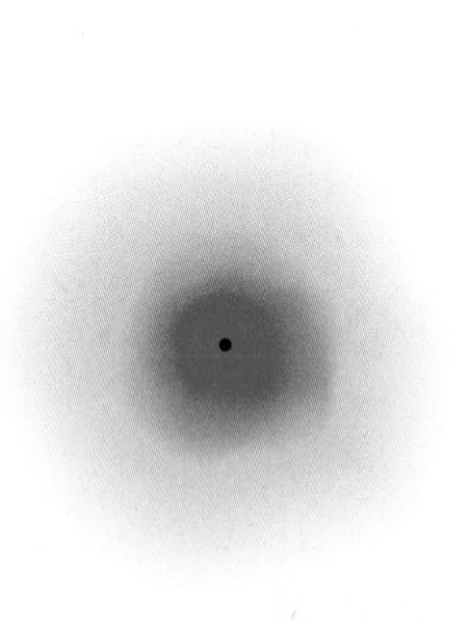

To distinguish the quantum mechanical description of an atom from Bohr's model, we speak of an atomic orbital, rather than an orbit. An **atomic orbital** can be thought of as *the wave function of an electron in an atom.* When we say that an electron is in a certain orbital, we mean that the distribution of the electron density or the probability of locating the electron in space is described by the square of the wave function associated with that orbital. An atomic orbital, therefore, has a characteristic energy, as well as a characteristic distribution of electron density.

The Schrödinger equation works nicely for the simple hydrogen atom with its one proton and one electron, but it turns out that it cannot be solved exactly for any atom containing more than one electron! Fortunately, chemists and physicists have learned to get around this kind of difficulty by approximation. For example, although

Figure 7.15 *A representation of the electron density distribution surrounding the nucleus in the hydrogen atom. It shows a high probability of finding the electron closer to the nucleus.*

[†]Erwin Schrödinger (1887–1961). Austrian physicist. Schrödinger formulated wave mechanics, which laid the foundation for modern quantum theory. He received the Nobel Prize in Physics in 1933.

the behavior of electrons in **many-electron atoms** (that is, *atoms containing two or more electrons*) is not the same as in the hydrogen atom, we assume that the difference is probably not too great. Thus we can use the energies and wave functions obtained from the hydrogen atom as good approximations of the behavior of electrons in more complex atoms. In fact, this approach provides fairly reliable descriptions of electronic behavior in many-electron atoms.

Although the helium atom has only two electrons, in quantum mechanics it is regarded as a many-electron atom.

7.6 Quantum Numbers

In quantum mechanics, three **quantum numbers** are required to *describe the distribution of electrons in hydrogen and other atoms*. These numbers are derived from the mathematical solution of the Schrödinger equation for the hydrogen atom. They are called the *principal quantum number,* the *angular momentum quantum number,* and the *magnetic quantum number.* These quantum numbers will be used to describe atomic orbitals and to label electrons that reside in them. A fourth quantum number—the *spin quantum number*—describes the behavior of a specific electron and completes the description of electrons in atoms.

The Principal Quantum Number (n)

The principal quantum number (n) can have integral values 1, 2, 3, and so forth; it corresponds to the quantum number in Equation (7.4). In a hydrogen atom, the value of n determines the energy of an orbital. As we will see shortly, this is not the case for a many-electron atom. The principal quantum number also relates to the average distance of the electron from the nucleus in a particular orbital. The larger n is, the greater the average distance of an electron in the orbital from the nucleus and therefore the larger the orbital.

Equation (7.4) holds only for the hydrogen atom.

The Angular Momentum Quantum Number (ℓ)

The angular momentum quantum number (ℓ) tells us the "shape" of the orbitals (see Section 7.7). The values of ℓ depend on the value of the principal quantum number, n. For a given value of n, ℓ has possible integral values from 0 to ($n - 1$). If $n = 1$, there is only one possible value of ℓ; that is, $\ell = n - 1 = 1 - 1 = 0$. If $n = 2$, there are two values of ℓ, given by 0 and 1. If $n = 3$, there are three values of ℓ, given by 0, 1, and 2. The value of ℓ is generally designated by the letters $s, p, d, \ldots$ as follows:

ℓ	0	1	2	3	4	5
Name of orbital	s	p	d	f	g	h

Thus if $\ell = 0$, we have an s orbital; if $\ell = 1$, we have a p orbital; and so on.

The unusual sequence of letters ($s, p,$ and d) has a historical origin. Physicists who studied atomic emission spectra tried to correlate the observed spectral lines with the particular energy states involved in the transitions. They noted that some of the lines were **s**harp; some were rather spread out, or **d**iffuse; and some were very strong and hence referred to as **p**rincipal lines. Subsequently, the initial letters of each adjective were assigned to those energy states. However, after the letter d and starting with the letter f (for **f**undamental), the orbital designations follow alphabetical order.

Remember that the "2" in 2s refers to the value of n and the "s" symbolizes the value of ℓ.

A collection of orbitals with the same value of n is frequently called a shell. One or more orbitals with the same n and ℓ values are referred to as a subshell. For example, the shell with $n = 2$ is composed of two subshells, $\ell = 0$ and 1 (the allowed values for $n = 2$). These subshells are called the $2s$ and $2p$ subshells where 2 denotes the value of n, and s and p denote the values of ℓ.

The Magnetic Quantum Number (m_ℓ)

The magnetic quantum number (m_ℓ) describes the orientation of the orbital in space (to be discussed in Section 7.7). Within a subshell, the value of m_ℓ depends on the value of the angular momentum quantum number, ℓ. For a certain value of ℓ, there are $(2\ell + 1)$ integral values of m_ℓ as follows:

$$-\ell, (-\ell + 1), \ldots 0, \ldots (+\ell - 1), +\ell$$

If $\ell = 0$, then $m_\ell = 0$. If $\ell = 1$, then there are $[(2 \times 1) + 1]$, or three values of m_ℓ, namely, -1, 0, and 1. If $\ell = 2$, there are $[(2 \times 2) + 1]$, or five values of m_ℓ, namely, -2, -1, 0, 1, and 2. The number of m_ℓ values indicates the number of orbitals in a subshell with a particular ℓ value.

To conclude our discussion of these three quantum numbers, let us consider a situation in which $n = 2$ and $\ell = 1$. The values of n and ℓ indicate that we have a $2p$ subshell, and in this subshell we have *three* $2p$ orbitals (because there are three values of m_ℓ, given by -1, 0, and 1).

The Electron Spin Quantum Number (m_s)

Experiments on the emission spectra of hydrogen and sodium atoms indicated that lines in the emission spectra could be split by the application of an external magnetic field. The only way physicists could explain these results was to assume that electrons act like tiny magnets. If electrons are thought of as spinning on their own axes, as Earth does, their magnetic properties can be accounted for. According to electromagnetic theory, a spinning charge generates a magnetic field, and it is this motion that causes an electron to behave like a magnet. Figure 7.16 shows the two possible spinning motions of an electron, one clockwise and the other counterclockwise. To take the electron spin into account, it is necessary to introduce a fourth quantum number, called the electron spin quantum number (m_s), which has a value of $+\frac{1}{2}$ or $-\frac{1}{2}$.

Conclusive proof of electron spin was provided by Otto Stern[†] and Walther Gerlach[‡] in 1924. Figure 7.17 shows the basic experimental arrangement. A beam of gaseous atoms generated in a hot furnace passes through a nonhomogeneous magnetic field. The interaction between an electron and the magnetic field causes the atom to be deflected from its straight-line path. Because the spinning motion is completely random, the electrons in half of the atoms will be spinning in one direction, and those atoms will be deflected in one way; the electrons in the other half of the atoms will be spinning in the opposite direction, and those atoms will be deflected in the other direction. Thus, two spots of equal intensity are observed on the detecting screen.

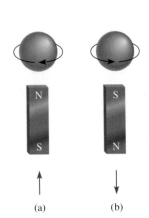

Figure 7.16 *The (a) clockwise and (b) counterclockwise spins of an electron. The magnetic fields generated by these two spinning motions are analogous to those from the two magnets. The upward and downward arrows are used to denote the direction of spin.*

[†]Otto Stern (1888–1969). German physicist. He made important contributions to the study of magnetic properties of atoms and the kinetic theory of gases. Stern was awarded the Nobel Prize in Physics in 1943.
[‡]Walther Gerlach (1889–1979). German physicist. Gerlach's main area of research was in quantum theory.

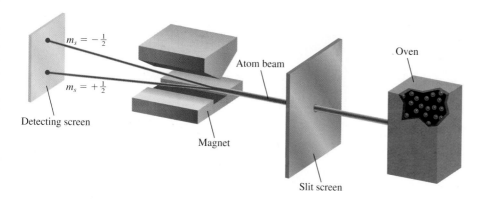

7.7 Atomic Orbitals

Table 7.2 shows the relation between quantum numbers and atomic orbitals. We see that when $\ell = 0$, $(2\ell + 1) = 1$ and there is only one value of m_ℓ, thus we have an s orbital. When $\ell = 1$, $(2\ell + 1) = 3$, so there are three values of m_ℓ or three p orbitals, labeled p_x, p_y, and p_z. When $\ell = 2$, $(2\ell + 1) = 5$ and there are five values of m_ℓ, and the corresponding five d orbitals are labeled with more elaborate subscripts. In the following sections we will consider the s, p, and d orbitals separately.

Interactivity: Orbital Shapes and Energy
Online Learning Center, Interactives

s Orbitals. One of the important questions we ask when studying the properties of atomic orbitals is, What are the shapes of the orbitals? Strictly speaking, an orbital does not have a well-defined shape because the wave function characterizing the orbital extends from the nucleus to infinity. In that sense, it is difficult to say what an orbital looks like. On the other hand, it is certainly convenient to think of orbitals as having specific shapes, particularly in discussing the formation of chemical bonds between atoms, as we will do in Chapters 9 and 10.

That the wave function for an orbital theoretically has no outer limit as one moves outward from the nucleus raises interesting philosophical questions regarding the sizes of atoms. Chemists have agreed on an operational definition of atomic size, as we will see in later chapters.

Although in principle an electron can be found anywhere, we know that most of the time it is quite close to the nucleus. Figure 7.18(a) shows the distribution of electron density in a hydrogen $1s$ orbital moving outward from the nucleus. As you can see, the electron density falls off rapidly as the distance from the nucleus increases. Roughly speaking, there is about a 90 percent probability of finding the electron within a sphere of radius 100 pm (1 pm = 1×10^{-12} m) surrounding the

		TABLE 7.2 Relation Between Quantum Numbers and Atomic Orbitals			
n	ℓ	m_ℓ	Number of Orbitals	Atomic Orbital Designations
1	0	0	1	$1s$
2	0	0	1	$2s$
	1	$-1, 0, 1$	3	$2p_x$, $2p_y$, $2p_z$
3	0	0	1	$3s$
	1	$-1, 0, 1$	3	$3p_x$, $3p_y$, $3p_z$
	2	$-2, -1, 0, 1, 2$	5	$3d_{xy}$, $3d_{yz}$, $3d_{xz}$, $3d_{x^2-y^2}$, $3d_{z^2}$
$\vdots$	$\vdots$	$\vdots$	$\vdots$	$\vdots$

An s subshell has one orbital, a p subshell has three orbitals, and a d subshell has five orbitals.

Figure 7.18 *(a) Distribution of electron density in the hydrogen 1s orbital. The electron density falls off rapidly as the distance from the nucleus increases. (b) Boundary surface diagram of the hydrogen 1s orbital. (c) A more realistic way of viewing electron density distribution is to divide the 1s orbital into successive spherical thin shells. A plot of the probability of finding the electron in each shell, called radial probability, as a function of distance shows a maximum at 52.9 pm from the nucleus. Interestingly, this is equal to the radius of the innermost orbit in the Bohr model.*

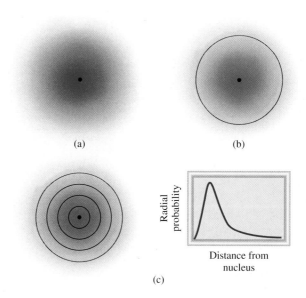

(a)   (b)

(c)

nucleus. Thus, we can represent the 1s orbital by drawing a **boundary surface diagram** that *encloses about 90 percent of the total electron density in an orbital,* as shown in Figure 7.18(b). A 1s orbital represented in this manner is merely a sphere.

Figure 7.19 shows boundary surface diagrams for the 1s, 2s, and 3s hydrogen atomic orbitals. All s orbitals are spherical in shape but differ in size, which increases as the principal quantum number increases. Although the details of electron density variation within each boundary surface are lost, there is no serious disadvantage. For us the most important features of atomic orbitals are their shapes and *relative* sizes, which are adequately represented by boundary surface diagrams.

p Orbitals. It should be clear that the p orbitals start with the principal quantum number $n = 2$. If $n = 1$, then the angular momentum quantum number ℓ can assume only the value of zero; therefore, there is only a 1s orbital. As we saw earlier, when $\ell = 1$, the magnetic quantum number m_ℓ can have values of -1, 0, 1. Starting with $n = 2$ and $\ell = 1$, we therefore have three 2p orbitals: $2p_x$, $2p_y$, and $2p_z$ (Figure 7.20). The letter subscripts indicate the axes along which the orbitals are oriented. These three p orbitals are identical in size, shape, and energy; they differ from one another only in orientation. Note, however, that there is no simple relation between the values of m_ℓ and the x, y, and z directions. For our purpose, you need only remember that because there are three possible values of m_ℓ, there are three p orbitals with different orientations.

The boundary surface diagrams of p orbitals in Figure 7.20 show that each p orbital can be thought of as two lobes on opposite sides of the nucleus. Like s orbitals, p orbitals increase in size from 2p to 3p to 4p orbital and so on.

d Orbitals and Other Higher-Energy Orbitals. When $\ell = 2$, there are five values of m_ℓ, which correspond to five d orbitals. The lowest value of n for a d orbital is 3. Because ℓ can never be greater than $n - 1$, when $n = 3$ and $\ell = 2$, we have five 3d orbitals ($3d_{xy}$, $3d_{yz}$, $3d_{xz}$, $3d_{x^2-y^2}$, and $3d_{z^2}$), shown in Figure 7.21. As in the case of the p orbitals, the different orientations of the d orbitals correspond to the different values of m_ℓ, but again there is no direct correspondence between a given orientation and a particular m_ℓ value. All the 3d orbitals in an atom are identical in energy. The d orbitals for which n is greater than 3 (4d, 5d, . . .) have similar shapes.

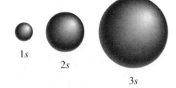

1s

2s

3s

Figure 7.19 *Boundary surface diagrams of the hydrogen 1s, 2s, and 3s orbitals. Each sphere contains about 90 percent of the total electron density. All s orbitals are spherical. Roughly speaking, the size of an orbital is proportional to n^2, where n is the principal quantum number.*

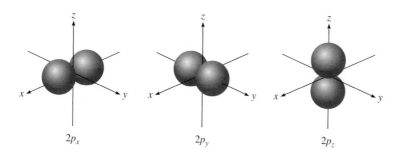

Figure 7.20 *The boundary surface diagrams of the three 2p orbitals. These orbitals are identical in shape and energy, but their orientations are different. The p orbitals of higher principal quantum numbers have a similar shape.*

Orbitals having higher energy than d orbitals are labeled f, g, ... and so on. The f orbitals are important in accounting for the behavior of elements with atomic numbers greater than 57, but their shapes are difficult to represent. In general chemistry we are not concerned with orbitals having ℓ values greater than 3 (the g orbitals and beyond).

Examples 7.6 and 7.7 illustrate the labeling of orbitals with quantum numbers and the calculation of total number of orbitals associated with a given principal quantum number.

Example 7.6

List the values of n, ℓ, and m_ℓ for orbitals in the $4d$ subshell.

Strategy What are the relationships among n, ℓ, and m_ℓ? What do "4" and "d" represent in $4d$?

Solution As we saw earlier, the number given in the designation of the subshell is the principal quantum number, so in this case $n = 4$. The letter designates the type of orbital. Because we are dealing with d orbitals, $\ell = 2$. The values of m_ℓ can vary from $-\ell$ to ℓ. Therefore, m_ℓ can be -2, -1, 0, 1, or 2.

Check The values of n and ℓ are fixed for $4d$, but m_ℓ can have any one of the five values, which correspond to the five d orbitals.

Similar problem: 7.55.

Practice Exercise Give the values of the quantum numbers associated with the orbitals in the $3p$ subshell.

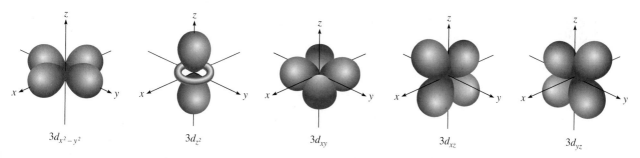

Figure 7.21 *Boundary surface diagrams of the five 3d orbitals. Although the 3d$_{z^2}$ orbital looks different, it is equivalent to the other four orbitals in all other respects. The d orbitals of higher principal quantum numbers have similar shapes.*

Example 7.7

What is the total number of orbitals associated with the principal quantum number $n = 3$?

Strategy To calculate the total number of orbitals for a given n value, we need to first write the possible values of ℓ. We then determine how many m_ℓ values are associated with each value of ℓ. The total number of orbitals is equal to the sum of all the m_ℓ values.

Solution For $n = 3$, the possible values of ℓ are 0, 1, and 2. Thus there is one $3s$ orbital ($n = 3$, $\ell = 0$, and $m_\ell = 0$); there are three $3p$ orbitals ($n = 3$, $\ell = 1$, and $m_\ell = -1, 0, 1$); there are five $3d$ orbitals ($n = 3$, $\ell = 2$, and $m_\ell = -2, -1, 0, 1, 2$). The total number of orbitals is $1 + 3 + 5 = 9$.

Similar problem: 7.60.

Check The total number of orbitals for a given value of n is n^2. So here we have $3^2 = 9$. Can you prove the validity of this relationship?

Practice Exercise What is the total number of orbitals associated with the principal quantum number $n = 4$?

The Energies of Orbitals

Now that we have some understanding of the shapes and sizes of atomic orbitals, we are ready to inquire into their relative energies and look at how energy levels affect the actual arrangement of electrons in atoms.

According to Equation (7.4), the energy of an electron in a hydrogen atom is determined solely by its principal quantum number. Thus the energies of hydrogen orbitals increase as follows (Figure 7.22):

$$1s < 2s = 2p < 3s = 3p = 3d < 4s = 4p = 4d = 4f < \cdots$$

Although the electron density distributions are different in the $2s$ and $2p$ orbitals, hydrogen's electron has the same energy whether it is in the $2s$ orbital or a $2p$ orbital. The $1s$ orbital in a hydrogen atom corresponds to the most stable condition, the ground state. An electron residing in this orbital is most strongly held by the nucleus because it is closest to the nucleus. An electron in the $2s$, $2p$, or higher orbitals in a hydrogen atom is in an excited state.

The energy picture is more complex for many-electron atoms than for hydrogen. The energy of an electron in such an atom depends on its angular momentum quantum

Figure 7.22 *Orbital energy levels in the hydrogen atom. Each short horizontal line represents one orbital. Orbitals with the same principal quantum number (n) all have the same energy.*

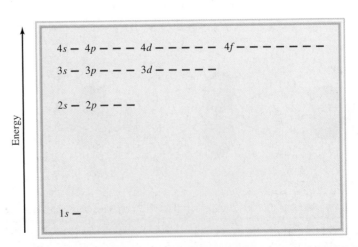

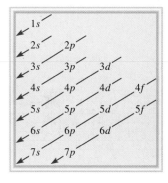

Figure 7.23 *Orbital energy levels in a many-electron atom. Note that the energy level depends on both n and ℓ values.*

number as well as on its principal quantum number (Figure 7.23). For many-electron atoms, the 3*d* energy level is very close to the 4*s* energy level. The total energy of an atom, however, depends not only on the sum of the orbital energies but also on the energy of repulsion between the electrons in these orbitals (each orbital can accommodate up to two electrons, as we will see in Section 7.8). It turns out that the total energy of an atom is lower when the 4*s* subshell is filled before a 3*d* subshell. Figure 7.24 depicts the order in which atomic orbitals are filled in a many-electron atom. We will consider specific examples in Section 7.8.

7.8 Electron Configuration

The four quantum numbers n, ℓ, m_ℓ, and m_s enable us to label completely an electron in any orbital in any atom. In a sense, we can regard the set of four quantum numbers as the "address" of an electron in an atom, somewhat in the same way that a street address, city, state, and postal ZIP code specify the address of an individual. For example, the four quantum numbers for a 2*s* orbital electron are $n = 2$, $\ell = 0$, $m_\ell = 0$, and $m_s = +\frac{1}{2}$ or $-\frac{1}{2}$. It is inconvenient to write out all the individual quantum numbers, and so we use the simplified notation (n, ℓ, m_ℓ, m_s). For the preceding example, the quantum numbers are either $(2, 0, 0, +\frac{1}{2})$ or $(2, 0, 0, -\frac{1}{2})$. The value of m_s has no effect on the energy, size, shape, or orientation of an orbital, but it determines how electrons are arranged in an orbital.

Example 7.8 shows how quantum numbers of an electron in an orbital are assigned.

Figure 7.24 *The order in which atomic subshells are filled in a many-electron atom. Start with the 1s orbital and move downward, following the direction of the arrows. Thus the order goes as follows: 1s < 2s < 2p < 3s < 3p < 4s < 3d < ....*

Animation: Electron Configurations
Online Learning Center, Animations

Example 7.8

Write the four quantum numbers for an electron in a 3*p* orbital.

Strategy What do the "3" and "*p*" designate in 3*p*? How many orbitals (values of m_ℓ) are there in a 3*p* subshell? What are the possible values of electron spin quantum number?

Solution To start with, we know that the principal quantum number n is 3 and the angular momentum quantum number ℓ must be 1 (because we are dealing with a *p* orbital).

(Continued)

For $\ell = 1$, there are three values of m_ℓ given by -1, 0, and 1. Because the electron spin quantum number m_s can be either $+\frac{1}{2}$ or $-\frac{1}{2}$, we conclude that there are six possible ways to designate the electron using the (n, ℓ, m_ℓ, m_s) notation:

$$(3, 1, -1, +\tfrac{1}{2}) \qquad\qquad (3, 1, -1, -\tfrac{1}{2})$$
$$(3, 1, 0, +\tfrac{1}{2}) \qquad\qquad (3, 1, 0, -\tfrac{1}{2})$$
$$(3, 1, 1, +\tfrac{1}{2}) \qquad\qquad (3, 1, 1, -\tfrac{1}{2})$$

Similar problem: 7.56.

Check In these six designations we see that the values of n and ℓ are constant, but the values of m_ℓ and m_s can vary.

Practice Exercise Write the four quantum numbers for an electron in a $5p$ orbital.

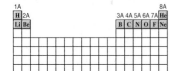

The hydrogen atom is a particularly simple system because it contains only one electron. The electron may reside in the $1s$ orbital (the ground state), or it may be found in some higher-energy orbital (an excited state). For many-electron atoms, however, we must know the ***electron configuration*** of the atom, that is, *how the electrons are distributed among the various atomic orbitals,* in order to understand electronic behavior. We will use the first 10 elements (hydrogen to neon) to illustrate the rules for writing electron configurations for atoms in the *ground state.* (Section 7.9 will describe how these rules can be applied to the remainder of the elements in the periodic table.) For this discussion, recall that the number of electrons in an atom is equal to its atomic number Z.

Figure 7.22 indicates that the electron in a ground-state hydrogen atom must be in the $1s$ orbital, so its electron configuration is $1s^1$:

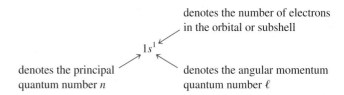

The electron configuration can also be represented by an *orbital diagram* that shows the spin of the electron (see Figure 7.16):

$$\text{H} \quad \boxed{\uparrow}$$
$$1s^1$$

Remember that the direction of electron spin has no effect on the energy of the electron.

The upward arrow denotes one of the two possible spinning motions of the electron. (Alternatively, we could have represented the electron with a downward arrow.) The box represents an atomic orbital.

The Pauli Exclusion Principle

Interactivity: Pauli
Exclusion Principle
Online Learning Center,
Interactives

For many-electron atoms we use the ***Pauli*[†] *exclusion principle*** to determine electron configurations. This principle states that *no two electrons in an atom can have the same four quantum numbers.* If two electrons in an atom should have the same n, ℓ, and m_ℓ values (that is, these two electrons are in the *same* atomic orbital), then they

---

[†]Wolfgang Pauli (1900–1958). Austrian physicist. One of the founders of quantum mechanics, Pauli was awarded the Nobel Prize in Physics in 1945.

must have different values of m_s. In other words, only two electrons may occupy the same atomic orbital, and these electrons must have opposite spins. Consider the helium atom, which has two electrons. The three possible ways of placing two electrons in the $1s$ orbital are as follows:

He ⬛[↑↑] ⬛[↓↓] ⬛[↑↓]

$1s^2$ $1s^2$ $1s^2$

(a)   (b)   (c)

Diagrams (a) and (b) are ruled out by the Pauli exclusion principle. In (a), both electrons have the same upward spin and would have the quantum numbers $(1, 0, 0, +\frac{1}{2})$; in (b), both electrons have downward spins and would have the quantum numbers $(1, 0, 0, -\frac{1}{2})$. Only the configuration in (c) is physically acceptable, because one electron has the quantum numbers $(1, 0, 0, +\frac{1}{2})$ and the other has $(1, 0, 0, -\frac{1}{2})$. Thus the helium atom has the following configuration:

He ⬛[↑↓]

$1s^2$

Note that $1s^2$ is read "one s two," not "one s squared."

> Electrons that have opposite spins are said to be paired. In helium, $m_s = +\frac{1}{2}$ for one electron; $m_s = -\frac{1}{2}$ for the other.

Diamagnetism and Paramagnetism

The Pauli exclusion principle is one of the fundamental principles of quantum mechanics. It can be tested by a simple observation. If the two electrons in the $1s$ orbital of a helium atom had the same, or parallel, spins (↑↑ or ↓↓), their net magnetic fields would reinforce each other [Figure 7.25(a)]. Such an arrangement would make the helium gas paramagnetic. **Paramagnetic** substances are those that *contain net unpaired spins and are attracted by a magnet.* On the other hand, if the electron spins are paired, or antiparallel to each other (↑↓ or ↓↑), the magnetic effects cancel out [Figure 7.25(b)]. **Diamagnetic** substances *do not contain net unpaired spins and are slightly repelled by a magnet.*

Measurements of magnetic properties provide the most direct evidence for specific electron configurations of elements. Advances in instrument design during the last 30 years or so enable us to determine the number of unpaired electrons in an atom. By experiment we find that the helium atom in its ground state has no net magnetic field. Therefore, the two electrons in the $1s$ orbital must be paired in accord with the Pauli exclusion principle and the helium gas is diamagnetic. A useful rule to keep

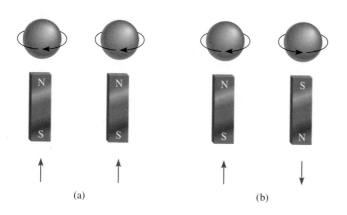

Figure 7.25 *The (a) parallel and (b) antiparallel spins of two electrons. In (a) the two magnetic fields reinforce each other. In (b) the two magnetic fields cancel each other.*

(a)   (b)

in mind is that any atom with an *odd* number of electrons will always contain one or more unpaired spins because we need an even number of electrons for complete pairing. On the other hand, atoms containing an even number of electrons may or may not contain unpaired spins. We will see the reason for this behavior shortly.

As another example, consider the lithium atom ($Z = 3$) which has three electrons. The third electron cannot go into the $1s$ orbital because it would inevitably have the same four quantum numbers as one of the first two electrons. Therefore, this electron "enters" the next (energetically) higher orbital, which is the $2s$ orbital (see Figure 7.23). The electron configuration of lithium is $1s^2 2s^1$, and its orbital diagram is

$$\text{Li} \quad \boxed{\uparrow\downarrow} \quad \boxed{\uparrow}$$
$$\qquad\quad 1s^2 \qquad 2s^1$$

The lithium atom contains one unpaired electron and the lithium metal is therefore paramagnetic.

The Shielding Effect in Many-Electron Atoms

Experimentally we find that the $2s$ orbital lies at a lower energy level than the $2p$ orbital in a many-electron atom. Why? In comparing the electron configurations of $1s^2 2s^1$ and $1s^2 2p^1$, we note that, in both cases, the $1s$ orbital is filled with two electrons. Figure 7.26 shows the radial probability plots for the $1s$, $2s$, and $2p$ orbitals. Because the $2s$ and $2p$ orbitals are larger than the $1s$ orbital, an electron in either of these orbitals will spend more time away from the nucleus than an electron in the $1s$ orbital. Thus, we can speak of a $2s$ or $2p$ electron being partly "shielded" from the attractive force of the nucleus by the $1s$ electrons. The important consequence of the shielding effect is that it *reduces* the electrostatic attraction between the protons in the nucleus and the electron in the $2s$ or $2p$ orbital.

The manner in which the electron density varies as we move from the nucleus outward depends on the type of orbital. Although a $2s$ electron spends most of its time (on average) slightly farther from the nucleus than a $2p$ electron, the electron density near the nucleus is actually greater for the $2s$ electron (see the small maximum for the $2s$ orbital in Figure 7.26). For this reason, the $2s$ orbital is said to be more "penetrating" than the $2p$ orbital. Therefore, a $2s$ electron is less shielded by the $1s$ electrons and is more strongly held by the nucleus. In fact, for the same principal quantum number n, the penetrating power decreases as the angular momentum quantum number ℓ increases, or

$$s > p > d > f > \cdots$$

Because the stability of an electron is determined by the strength of its attraction to the nucleus, it follows that a $2s$ electron will be lower in energy than a $2p$ electron. To put it another way, less energy is required to remove a $2p$ electron than a $2s$ electron because a $2p$ electron is not held quite as strongly by the nucleus. The hydrogen atom has only one electron and, therefore, is without such a shielding effect.

Continuing our discussion of atoms of the first 10 elements, we go next to beryllium ($Z = 4$). The ground-state electron configuration of beryllium is $1s^2 2s^2$, or

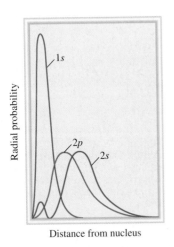

Radial probability / Distance from nucleus

Figure 7.26 *Radial probability plots for the 1s, 2s, and 2p orbitals. The 1s electrons effectively shield both the 2s and 2p electrons from the nucleus. The 2s orbital is more penetrating than the 2p orbital.*

$$\text{Be} \quad \boxed{\uparrow\downarrow} \quad \boxed{\uparrow\downarrow}$$
$$\qquad\quad 1s^2 \qquad 2s^2$$

Beryllium is diamagnetic, as we would expect.

The electron configuration of boron ($Z = 5$) is $1s^2 2s^2 2p^1$, or

B $1s^2$ $2s^2$ $2p^1$

Note that the unpaired electron can be in the $2p_x$, $2p_y$, or $2p_z$ orbital. The choice is completely arbitrary because the three p orbitals are equivalent in energy. As the diagram shows, boron is paramagnetic.

Hund's Rule

The electron configuration of carbon ($Z = 6$) is $1s^2 2s^2 2p^2$. The following are different ways of distributing two electrons among three p orbitals:

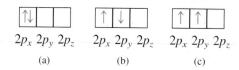

$2p_x\ 2p_y\ 2p_z$	$2p_x\ 2p_y\ 2p_z$	$2p_x\ 2p_y\ 2p_z$
(a)	(b)	(c)

None of the three arrangements violates the Pauli exclusion principle, so we must determine which one will give the greatest stability. The answer is provided by **Hund's rule,**[†] which states that *the most stable arrangement of electrons in subshells is the one with the greatest number of parallel spins.* The arrangement shown in (c) satisfies this condition. In both (a) and (b) the two spins cancel each other. Thus the orbital diagram for carbon is

C $1s^2$ $2s^2$ $2p^2$

Qualitatively, we can understand why (c) is preferred to (a). In (a), the two electrons are in the same $2p_x$ orbital, and their proximity results in a greater mutual repulsion than when they occupy two separate orbitals, say $2p_x$ and $2p_y$. The choice of (c) over (b) is more subtle but can be justified on theoretical grounds. The fact that carbon atoms contain two unpaired electrons is in accord with Hund's rule.

The electron configuration of nitrogen ($Z = 7$) is $1s^2 2s^2 2p^3$:

N $1s^2$ $2s^2$ $2p^3$

Again, Hund's rule dictates that all three $2p$ electrons have spins parallel to one another; the nitrogen atom contains three unpaired electrons.

The electron configuration of oxygen ($Z = 8$) is $1s^2 2s^2 2p^4$. An oxygen atom has two unpaired electrons:

O $1s^2$ $2s^2$ $2p^4$

[†]Frederick Hund (1896–1997). German physicist. Hund's work was mainly in quantum mechanics. He also helped to develop the molecular orbital theory of chemical bonding.

The electron configuration of fluorine $(Z = 9)$ is $1s^2 2s^2 2p^5$. The nine electrons are arranged as follows:

F   ⇅   ⇅   ⇅ ⇅ ↑
    $1s^2$ $2s^2$ $2p^5$

The fluorine atom has one unpaired electron.

In neon $(Z = 10)$, the $2p$ subshell is completely filled. The electron configuration of neon is $1s^2 2s^2 2p^6$, and *all* the electrons are paired, as follows:

Ne   ⇅   ⇅   ⇅ ⇅ ⇅
    $1s^2$ $2s^2$ $2p^6$

The neon gas should be diamagnetic, and experimental observation bears out this prediction.

General Rules for Assigning Electrons to Atomic Orbitals

Based on the preceding examples we can formulate some general rules for determining the maximum number of electrons that can be assigned to the various subshells and orbitals for a given value of n:

Interactivity: Orbital
Filling Rules
Online Learning Center,
Interactives

1. Each shell or principal level of quantum number n contains n subshells. For example, if $n = 2$, then there are two subshells (two values of ℓ) of angular momentum quantum numbers 0 and 1.

2. Each subshell of quantum number ℓ contains $(2\ell + 1)$ orbitals. For example, if $\ell = 1$, then there are three p orbitals.

3. No more than two electrons can be placed in each orbital. Therefore, the maximum number of electrons is simply twice the number of orbitals that are employed.

4. A quick way to determine the maximum number of electrons that an atom can have in a principal level n is to use the formula $2n^2$.

Examples 7.9 and 7.10 illustrate the procedure for calculating the number of electrons in orbitals and labeling electrons with the four quantum numbers.

Example 7.9

What is the maximum number of electrons that can be present in the principal level for which $n = 3$?

Strategy We are given the principal quantum number (n) so we can determine all the possible values of the angular momentum quantum number (ℓ). The preceding rule shows that the number of orbitals for each value of ℓ is $(2\ell + 1)$. Thus we can determine the total number of orbitals. How many electrons can each orbital accommodate?

Solution When $n = 3$, $\ell = 0$, 1, and 2. The number of orbitals for each value of ℓ is given by

(Continued)

Value of ℓ	Number of Orbitals $(2\ell + 1)$
0	1
1	3
2	5

The total number of orbitals is nine. Because each orbital can accommodate two electrons, the maximum number of electrons that can reside in the orbitals is 2×9, or 18.

Check If we use the formula (n^2) in Example 7.7, we find that the total number of orbitals is 3^2 and the total number of electrons is $2(3^2)$ or 18. In general, the number of electrons in a given principal energy level n is $2n^2$.

Similar problems: 7.62, 7.63.

Practice Exercise Calculate the total number of electrons that can be present in the principal level for which $n = 4$.

Example 7.10

An oxygen atom has a total of eight electrons. Write the four quantum numbers for each of the eight electrons in the ground state.

Strategy We start with $n = 1$ and proceed to fill orbitals in the order shown in Figure 7.24. For each value of n we determine the possible values of ℓ. For each value of ℓ, we assign the possible values of m_ℓ. We can place electrons in the orbitals according to the Pauli exclusion principle and Hund's rule.

Solution We start with $n = 1$, so $\ell = 0$, a subshell corresponding to the $1s$ orbital. This orbital can accommodate a total of two electrons. Next, $n = 2$, and ℓ may be either 0 or 1. The $\ell = 0$ subshell contains one $2s$ orbital, which can accommodate two electrons. The remaining four electrons are placed in the $\ell = 1$ subshell, which contains three $2p$ orbitals. The orbital diagram is

$$\text{O} \quad \boxed{\uparrow\downarrow} \quad \boxed{\uparrow\downarrow} \quad \boxed{\uparrow\downarrow}\,\boxed{\uparrow}\,\boxed{\uparrow}$$
$$\qquad\quad 1s^2 \qquad 2s^2 \qquad 2p^4$$

The results are summarized in the following table:

Electron	n	ℓ	m_ℓ	m_s	Orbital
1	1	0	0	$+\frac{1}{2}$	$1s$
2	1	0	0	$-\frac{1}{2}$	
3	2	0	0	$+\frac{1}{2}$	$2s$
4	2	0	0	$-\frac{1}{2}$	
5	2	1	-1	$+\frac{1}{2}$	
6	2	1	0	$+\frac{1}{2}$	$2p_x, 2p_y, 2p_z$
7	2	1	1	$+\frac{1}{2}$	
8	2	1	1	$-\frac{1}{2}$	

Of course, the placement of the eighth electron in the orbital labeled $m_\ell = 1$ is completely arbitrary. It would be equally correct to assign it to $m_\ell = 0$ or $m_\ell = -1$.

Similar problem: 7.85.

Practice Exercise Write a complete set of quantum numbers for each of the electrons in boron (B).

7.9 The Building-Up Principle

Here we will extend the rules used in writing electron configurations for the first 10 elements to the rest of the elements. This process is based on the Aufbau principle. The **Aufbau principle** dictates that *as protons are added one by one to the nucleus to build up the elements, electrons are similarly added to the atomic orbitals.* Through this process we gain a detailed knowledge of the ground-state electron configurations of the elements. As we will see later, knowledge of electron configurations helps us to understand and predict the properties of the elements; it also explains why the periodic table works so well.

The German word "Aufbau" means "building up."

Table 7.3 gives the ground-state electron configurations of elements from H ($Z = 1$) through Mt ($Z = 109$). The electron configurations of all elements except hydrogen and helium are represented by a **noble gas core,** which *shows in brackets the noble gas element that most nearly precedes the element being considered,* followed by the symbol for the highest filled subshells in the outermost shells. Notice that the electron configurations of the highest filled subshells in the outermost shells for the elements sodium ($Z = 11$) through argon ($Z = 18$) follow a pattern similar to those of lithium ($Z = 3$) through neon ($Z = 10$).

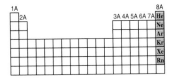

The noble gases.

As mentioned in Section 7.7, the $4s$ subshell is filled before the $3d$ subshell in a many-electron atom (see Figure 7.24). Thus the electron configuration of potassium ($Z = 19$) is $1s^2 2s^2 2p^6 3s^2 3p^6 4s^1$. Because $1s^2 2s^2 2p^6 3s^2 3p^6$ is the electron configuration of argon, we can simplify the electron configuration of potassium by writing [Ar]$4s^1$, where [Ar] denotes the "argon core." Similarly, we can write the electron configuration of calcium ($Z = 20$) as [Ar]$4s^2$. The placement of the outermost electron in the $4s$ orbital (rather than in the $3d$ orbital) of potassium is strongly supported by experimental evidence. The following comparison also suggests that this is the correct configuration. The chemistry of potassium is very similar to that of lithium and sodium, the first two alkali metals. The outermost electron of both lithium and sodium is in an s orbital (there is no ambiguity in assigning their electron configurations); therefore, we expect the last electron in potassium to occupy the $4s$ rather than the $3d$ orbital.

The elements from scandium ($Z = 21$) to copper ($Z = 29$) are transition metals. **Transition metals** either *have incompletely filled d subshells or readily give rise to cations that have incompletely filled d subshells.* Consider the first transition metal series, from scandium through copper. In this series additional electrons are placed in the $3d$ orbitals, according to Hund's rule. However, there are two irregularities. The electron configuration of chromium ($Z = 24$) is [Ar]$4s^1 3d^5$ and not [Ar]$4s^2 3d^4$, as we might expect. A similar break in the pattern is observed for copper, whose electron configuration is [Ar]$4s^1 3d^{10}$ rather than [Ar]$4s^2 3d^9$. The reason for these irregularities is that a slightly greater stability is associated with the half-filled ($3d^5$) and completely filled ($3d^{10}$) subshells. Electrons in the same subshell (in this case, the d orbitals) have equal energy but different spatial distributions. Consequently, their shielding of one another is relatively small, and the electrons are more strongly attracted by the nucleus when they have the $3d^5$ configuration. According to Hund's rule, the orbital diagram for Cr is

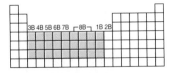

The transition metals.

$$\text{Cr} \quad [\text{Ar}] \quad \boxed{\uparrow} \qquad \boxed{\uparrow \;|\; \uparrow \;|\; \uparrow \;|\; \uparrow \;|\; \uparrow}$$
$$\qquad\qquad\qquad\quad 4s^1 \qquad\qquad\quad 3d^5$$

Thus, Cr has a total of six unpaired electrons. The orbital diagram for copper is

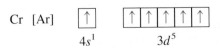

$$\text{Cu} \quad [\text{Ar}] \quad \boxed{\uparrow} \qquad \boxed{\uparrow\downarrow \;|\; \uparrow\downarrow \;|\; \uparrow\downarrow \;|\; \uparrow\downarrow \;|\; \uparrow\downarrow}$$
$$\qquad\qquad\qquad\quad 4s^1 \qquad\qquad\qquad 3d^{10}$$

TABLE 7.3

The Ground-State Electron Configurations of the Elements*

Atomic Number	Symbol	Electron Configuration	Atomic Number	Symbol	Electron Configuration	Atomic Number	Symbol	Electron Configuration
1	H	$1s^1$	38	Sr	$[Kr]5s^2$	75	Re	$[Xe]6s^24f^{14}5d^5$
2	He	$1s^2$	39	Y	$[Kr]5s^24d^1$	76	Os	$[Xe]6s^24f^{14}5d^6$
3	Li	$[He]2s^1$	40	Zr	$[Kr]5s^24d^2$	77	Ir	$[Xe]6s^24f^{14}5d^7$
4	Be	$[He]2s^2$	41	Nb	$[Kr]5s^14d^4$	78	Pt	$[Xe]6s^14f^{14}5d^9$
5	B	$[He]2s^22p^1$	42	Mo	$[Kr]5s^14d^5$	79	Au	$[Xe]6s^14f^{14}5d^{10}$
6	C	$[He]2s^22p^2$	43	Tc	$[Kr]5s^24d^5$	80	Hg	$[Xe]6s^24f^{14}5d^{10}$
7	N	$[He]2s^22p^3$	44	Ru	$[Kr]5s^14d^7$	81	Tl	$[Xe]6s^24f^{14}5d^{10}6p^1$
8	O	$[He]2s^22p^4$	45	Rh	$[Kr]5s^14d^8$	82	Pb	$[Xe]6s^24f^{14}5d^{10}6p^2$
9	F	$[He]2s^22p^5$	46	Pd	$[Kr]4d^{10}$	83	Bi	$[Xe]6s^24f^{14}5d^{10}6p^3$
10	Ne	$[He]2s^22p^6$	47	Ag	$[Kr]5s^14d^{10}$	84	Po	$[Xe]6s^24f^{14}5d^{10}6p^4$
11	Na	$[Ne]3s^1$	48	Cd	$[Kr]5s^24d^{10}$	85	At	$[Xe]6s^24f^{14}5d^{10}6p^5$
12	Mg	$[Ne]3s^2$	49	In	$[Kr]5s^24d^{10}5p^1$	86	Rn	$[Xe]6s^24f^{14}5d^{10}6p^6$
13	Al	$[Ne]3s^23p^1$	50	Sn	$[Kr]5s^24d^{10}5p^2$	87	Fr	$[Rn]7s^1$
14	Si	$[Ne]3s^23p^2$	51	Sb	$[Kr]5s^24d^{10}5p^3$	88	Ra	$[Rn]7s^2$
15	P	$[Ne]3s^23p^3$	52	Te	$[Kr]5s^24d^{10}5p^4$	89	Ac	$[Rn]7s^26d^1$
16	S	$[Ne]3s^23p^4$	53	I	$[Kr]5s^24d^{10}5p^5$	90	Th	$[Rn]7s^26d^2$
17	Cl	$[Ne]3s^23p^5$	54	Xe	$[Kr]5s^24d^{10}5p^6$	91	Pa	$[Rn]7s^25f^26d^1$
18	Ar	$[Ne]3s^23p^6$	55	Cs	$[Xe]6s^1$	92	U	$[Rn]7s^25f^36d^1$
19	K	$[Ar]4s^1$	56	Ba	$[Xe]6s^2$	93	Np	$[Rn]7s^25f^46d^1$
20	Ca	$[Ar]4s^2$	57	La	$[Xe]6s^25d^1$	94	Pu	$[Rn]7s^25f^6$
21	Sc	$[Ar]4s^23d^1$	58	Ce	$[Xe]6s^24f^15d^1$	95	Am	$[Rn]7s^25f^7$
22	Ti	$[Ar]4s^23d^2$	59	Pr	$[Xe]6s^24f^3$	96	Cm	$[Rn]7s^25f^76d^1$
23	V	$[Ar]4s^23d^3$	60	Nd	$[Xe]6s^24f^4$	97	Bk	$[Rn]7s^25f^9$
24	Cr	$[Ar]4s^13d^5$	61	Pm	$[Xe]6s^24f^5$	98	Cf	$[Rn]7s^25f^{10}$
25	Mn	$[Ar]4s^23d^5$	62	Sm	$[Xe]6s^24f^6$	99	Es	$[Rn]7s^25f^{11}$
26	Fe	$[Ar]4s^23d^6$	63	Eu	$[Xe]6s^24f^7$	100	Fm	$[Rn]7s^25f^{12}$
27	Co	$[Ar]4s^23d^7$	64	Gd	$[Xe]6s^24f^75d^1$	101	Md	$[Rn]7s^25f^{13}$
28	Ni	$[Ar]4s^23d^8$	65	Tb	$[Xe]6s^24f^9$	102	No	$[Rn]7s^25f^{14}$
29	Cu	$[Ar]4s^13d^{10}$	66	Dy	$[Xe]6s^24f^{10}$	103	Lr	$[Rn]7s^25f^{14}6d^1$
30	Zn	$[Ar]4s^23d^{10}$	67	Ho	$[Xe]6s^24f^{11}$	104	Rf	$[Rn]7s^25f^{14}6d^2$
31	Ga	$[Ar]4s^23d^{10}4p^1$	68	Er	$[Xe]6s^24f^{12}$	105	Db	$[Rn]7s^25f^{14}6d^3$
32	Ge	$[Ar]4s^23d^{10}4p^2$	69	Tm	$[Xe]6s^24f^{13}$	106	Sg	$[Rn]7s^25f^{14}6d^4$
33	As	$[Ar]4s^23d^{10}4p^3$	70	Yb	$[Xe]6s^24f^{14}$	107	Bh	$[Rn]7s^25f^{14}6d^5$
34	Se	$[Ar]4s^23d^{10}4p^4$	71	Lu	$[Xe]6s^24f^{14}5d^1$	108	Hs	$[Rn]7s^25f^{14}6d^6$
35	Br	$[Ar]4s^23d^{10}4p^5$	72	Hf	$[Xe]6s^24f^{14}5d^2$	109	Mt	$[Rn]7s^25f^{14}6d^7$
36	Kr	$[Ar]4s^23d^{10}4p^6$	73	Ta	$[Xe]6s^24f^{14}5d^3$	110	Ds	$[Rn]7s^25f^{14}6d^8$
37	Rb	$[Kr]5s^1$	74	W	$[Xe]6s^24f^{14}5d^4$			

*The symbol [He] is called the helium core and represents $1s^2$. [Ne] is called the neon core and represents $1s^22s^22p^6$. [Ar] is called the argon core and represents [Ne]$3s^23p^6$. [Kr] is called the krypton core and represents [Ar]$4s^23d^{10}4p^6$. [Xe] is called the xenon core and represents [Kr]$5s^24d^{10}5p^6$. [Rn] is called the radon core and represents [Xe]$6s^24f^{14}5d^{10}6p^6$.

Again, extra stability is gained in this case by having the 3d subshell completely filled.

For elements Zn ($Z = 30$) through Kr ($Z = 36$), the 4s and 4p subshells fill in a straightforward manner. With rubidium ($Z = 37$), electrons begin to enter the $n = 5$ energy level.

The electron configurations in the second transition metal series [yttrium ($Z = 39$) to silver ($Z = 47$)] are also irregular, but we will not be concerned with the details here.

The sixth period of the periodic table begins with cesium ($Z = 55$) and barium ($Z = 56$), whose electron configurations are [Xe]$6s^1$ and [Xe]$6s^2$, respectively. Next we come to lanthanum ($Z = 57$). From Figure 7.24 we would expect that after filling the 6s orbital we would place the additional electrons in 4f orbitals. In reality, the energies of the 5d and 4f orbitals are very close; in fact, for lanthanum 4f is slightly higher in energy than 5d. Thus lanthanum's electron configuration is [Xe]$6s^2 5d^1$ and not [Xe]$6s^2 4f^1$.

Following lanthanum are the 14 elements known as the **lanthanides**, or **rare earth series** [cerium ($Z = 58$) to lutetium ($Z = 71$)]. The rare earth metals *have incompletely filled 4f subshells or readily give rise to cations that have incompletely filled 4f subshells.* In this series, the added electrons are placed in 4f orbitals. After the 4f subshell is completely filled, the next electron enters the 5d subshell of lutetium. Note that the electron configuration of gadolinium ($Z = 64$) is [Xe]$6s^2 4f^7 5d^1$ rather than [Xe]$6s^2 4f^8$. Like chromium, gadolinium gains extra stability by having a half-filled subshell ($4f^7$).

The third transition metal series, including lanthanum and hafnium ($Z = 72$) and extending through gold ($Z = 79$), is characterized by the filling of the 5d subshell. The 6s and 6p subshells are filled next, which takes us to radon ($Z = 86$).

The *last row of elements* is the **actinide series**, which starts at thorium ($Z = 90$). *Most of these elements are not found in nature but have been synthesized.*

With few exceptions, you should be able to write the electron configuration of any element, using Figure 7.24 as a guide. Elements that require particular care are the transition metals, the lanthanides, and the actinides. As we noted earlier, at larger values of the principal quantum number n, the order of subshell filling may reverse from one element to the next. Figure 7.27 groups the elements according to the type of subshell in which the outermost electrons are placed.

Figure 7.27 *Classification of groups of elements in the periodic table according to the type of subshell being filled with electrons.*

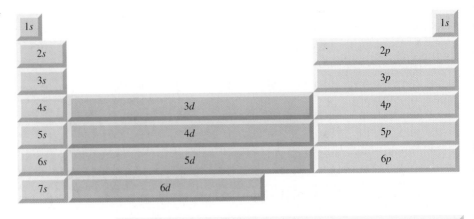

Example 7.11

Write the ground-state electron configurations for (a) sulfur (S) and (b) palladium (Pd), which is diamagnetic.

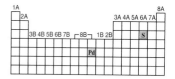

(a) Strategy How many electrons are in the S ($Z = 16$) atom? We start with $n = 1$ and proceed to fill orbitals in the order shown in Figure 7.24. For each value of ℓ, we assign the possible values of m_ℓ. We can place electrons in the orbitals according to the Pauli exclusion principle and Hund's rule and then write the electron configuration. The task is simplified if we use the noble-gas core preceding S for the inner electrons.

Solution Sulfur has 16 electrons. The noble gas core in this case is [Ne]. (Ne is the noble gas in the period preceding sulfur.) [Ne] represents $1s^2 2s^2 2p^6$. This leaves us 6 electrons to fill the $3s$ subshell and partially fill the $3p$ subshell. Thus the electron configuration of S is $1s^2 2s^2 2p^6 3s^2 3p^4$ or $[\text{Ne}]3s^2 3p^4$.

(b) Strategy We use the same approach as that in (a). What does it mean to say that Pd is a diamagnetic element?

Solution Palladium has 46 electrons. The noble-gas core in this case is [Kr]. (Kr is the noble gas in the period preceding palladium.) [Kr] represents

$$1s^2 2s^2 2p^6 3s^2 3p^6 4s^2 3d^{10} 4p^6$$

The remaining 10 electrons are distributed among the $4d$ and $5s$ orbitals. The three choices are (1) $4d^{10}$, (2) $4d^9 5s^1$, and (3) $4d^8 5s^2$. Because palladium is diamagnetic, all the electrons are paired and its electron configuration must be

$$1s^2 2s^2 2p^6 3s^2 3p^6 4s^2 3d^{10} 4p^6 4d^{10}$$

or simply $[\text{Kr}]4d^{10}$. The configurations in (2) and (3) both represent paramagnetic elements.

Check To confirm the answer, write the orbital diagrams for (1), (2), and (3).

Similar problems: 7.91, 7.92.

Practice Exercise Write the ground-state electron configuration for phosphorus (P).

Key Equations

- $u = \lambda \nu$ (7.1) — Relating speed of a wave to its wavelength and frequency.

- $E = h\nu$ (7.2) — Relating energy of a quantum (and of a photon) to the frequency.

- $E_n = -R_H\left(\dfrac{1}{n^2}\right)$ (7.4) — Energy of an electron in the nth state in a hydrogen atom.

- $\Delta E = h\nu = R_H\left(\dfrac{1}{n_i^2} - \dfrac{1}{n_f^2}\right)$ (7.5) — Energy of a photon emitted as the electron undergoes a transition from the n_i level to the n_f level.

- $\lambda = \dfrac{h}{mu}$ (7.7) — Relating wavelength of a particle to its mass m and velocity u.

- $\Delta x \Delta p \geq \dfrac{h}{4\pi}$ (7.8) — Calculating the uncertainty in the position or in the momentum of a particle.

Summary of Facts and Concepts

1. The quantum theory developed by Planck successfully explains the emission of radiation by heated solids. The quantum theory states that radiant energy is emitted by atoms and molecules in small discrete amounts (quanta), rather than over a continuous range. This behavior is governed by the relationship $E = h\nu$, where E is the energy of the radiation, h is Planck's constant, and ν is the frequency of the radiation. Energy is always emitted in whole-number multiples of $h\nu$ ($1\ h\nu$, $2\ h\nu$, $3\ h\nu$, ...).

2. Using quantum theory, Einstein solved another mystery of physics—the photo-electric effect. Einstein proposed that light can behave like a stream of particles (photons).

3. The line spectrum of hydrogen, yet another mystery to nineteenth-century physicists, was also explained by applying the quantum theory. Bohr developed a model of the hydrogen atom in which the energy of its single electron is quantized—limited to certain energy values determined by an integer, the principal quantum number.

4. An electron in its most stable energy state is said to be in the ground state, and an electron at an energy level higher than its most stable state is said to be in an excited state. In the Bohr model, an electron emits a photon when it drops from a higher-energy state (an excited state) to a lower-energy state (the ground state or another, less excited state). The release of specific amounts of energy in the form of photons accounts for the lines in the hydrogen emission spectrum.

5. De Broglie extended Einstein's wave-particle description of light to all matter in motion. The wavelength of a moving particle of mass m and velocity u is given by the de Broglie equation $\lambda = h/mu$.

6. The Schrödinger equation describes the motions and energies of submicroscopic particles. This equation launched quantum mechanics and a new era in physics.

7. The Schrödinger equation tells us the possible energy states of the electron in a hydrogen atom and the probability of its location in a particular region surrounding the nucleus. These results can be applied with reasonable accuracy to many-electron atoms.

8. An atomic orbital is a function (ψ) that defines the distribution of electron density (ψ^2) in space. Orbitals are represented by electron density diagrams or boundary surface diagrams.

9. Four quantum numbers characterize each electron in an atom: the principal quantum number n identifies the main energy level, or shell, of the orbital; the angular momentum quantum number ℓ indicates the shape of the orbital; the magnetic quantum number m_ℓ specifies the orientation of the orbital in space; and the electron spin quantum number m_s indicates the direction of the electron's spin on its own axis.

10. The single s orbital for each energy level is spherical and centered on the nucleus. The three p orbitals present at $n = 2$ and higher; each has two lobes, and the pairs of lobes are arranged at right angles to one another. Starting with $n = 3$, there are five d orbitals, with more complex shapes and orientations.

11. The energy of the electron in a hydrogen atom is determined solely by its principal quantum number. In many-electron atoms, the principal quantum number and the angular momentum quantum number together determine the energy of an electron.

12. No two electrons in the same atom can have the same four quantum numbers (the Pauli exclusion principle).

13. The most stable arrangement of electrons in a subshell is the one that has the greatest number of parallel spins (Hund's rule). Atoms with one or more unpaired electron spins are paramagnetic. Atoms in which all electrons are paired are diamagnetic.

14. The Aufbau principle provides the guideline for building up the elements. The periodic table classifies the elements according to their atomic numbers and thus also by the electronic configurations of their atoms.

Key Words

Questions and Problems

Quantum Theory and Electromagnetic Radiation
Review Questions

7.1   What is a wave? Explain the following terms associated with waves: wavelength, frequency, amplitude.

7.2   What are the units for wavelength and frequency of electromagnetic waves? What is the speed of light in meters per second and miles per hour?

7.3   List the types of electromagnetic radiation, starting with the radiation having the longest wavelength and ending with the radiation having the shortest wavelength.

7.4   Give the high and low wavelength values that define the visible region of the electromagnetic spectrum.

7.5   Briefly explain Planck's quantum theory and explain what a quantum is. What are the units for Planck's constant?

7.6   Give two everyday examples that illustrate the concept of quantization.

Problems

7.7   (a) What is the wavelength (in nanometers) of light having a frequency of 8.6×10^{13} Hz? (b) What is the frequency (in Hz) of light having a wavelength of 566 nm?

7.8   (a) What is the frequency of light having a wavelength of 456 nm? (b) What is the wavelength (in nanometers) of radiation having a frequency of 2.45×10^9 Hz? (This is the type of radiation used in microwave ovens.)

7.9   The average distance between Mars and Earth is about 1.3×10^8 miles. How long would it take TV pictures transmitted from the *Viking* space vehicle on Mars' surface to reach Earth? (1 mile = 1.61 km.)

7.10 How many minutes would it take a radio wave to travel from the planet Venus to Earth? (Average distance from Venus to Earth = 28 million miles.)

7.11 The SI unit of time is the second, which is defined as 9,192,631,770 cycles of radiation associated with a certain emission process in the cesium atom. Calculate the wavelength of this radiation (to three significant figures). In which region of the electromagnetic spectrum is this wavelength found?

7.12 The SI unit of length is the meter, which is defined as the length equal to 1,650,763.73 wavelengths of the light emitted by a particular energy transition in krypton atoms. Calculate the frequency of the light to three significant figures.

The Photoelectric Effect
Review Questions

7.13 Explain what is meant by the photoelectric effect.

7.14 What are photons? What role did Einstein's explanation of the photoelectric effect play in the development of the particle-wave interpretation of the nature of electromagnetic radiation?

Problems

7.15 A photon has a wavelength of 624 nm. Calculate the energy of the photon in joules.

7.16 The blue color of the sky results from the scattering of sunlight by air molecules. The blue light has a frequency of about 7.5×10^{14} Hz. (a) Calculate the wavelength, in nm, associated with this radiation, and (b) calculate the energy, in joules, of a single photon associated with this frequency.

7.17 A photon has a frequency of 6.0×10^4 Hz. (a) Convert this frequency into wavelength (nm). Does this frequency fall in the visible region? (b) Calculate the energy (in joules) of this photon. (c) Calculate the energy (in joules) of 1 mole of photons all with this frequency.

7.18 What is the wavelength, in nm, of radiation that has an energy content of 1.0×10^3 kJ/mol? In which region of the electromagnetic spectrum is this radiation found?

7.19 When copper is bombarded with high-energy electrons, X rays are emitted. Calculate the energy (in joules) associated with the photons if the wavelength of the X rays is 0.154 nm.

7.20 A particular form of electromagnetic radiation has a frequency of 8.11×10^{14} Hz. (a) What is its wavelength in nanometers? In meters? (b) To what region of the electromagnetic spectrum would you assign it? (c) What is the energy (in joules) of one quantum of this radiation?

Bohr's Theory of the Hydrogen Atom
Review Questions

7.21 What are emission spectra? How do line spectra differ from continuous spectra?

7.22 What is an energy level? Explain the difference between ground state and excited state.

7.23 Briefly describe Bohr's theory of the hydrogen atom and how it explains the appearance of an emission spectrum. How does Bohr's theory differ from concepts of classical physics?

7.24 Explain the meaning of the negative sign in Equation (7.4).

Problems

7.25 Explain why elements produce their own characteristic colors when they emit photons?

7.26 Some copper compounds emit green light when they are heated in a flame. How would you determine whether the light is of one wavelength or a mixture of two or more wavelengths?

7.27 Is it possible for a fluorescent material to emit radiation in the ultraviolet region after absorbing visible light? Explain your answer.

7.28 Explain how astronomers are able to tell which elements are present in distant stars by analyzing the electromagnetic radiation emitted by the stars.

7.29 Consider the following energy levels of a hypothetical atom:

E_4 _____ -1.0×10^{-19} J
E_3 _____ -5.0×10^{-19} J
E_2 _____ -10×10^{-19} J
E_1 _____ -15×10^{-19} J

(a) What is the wavelength of the photon needed to excite an electron from E_1 to E_4? (b) What is the energy (in joules) a photon must have in order to excite an electron from E_2 to E_3? (c) When an electron drops from the E_3 level to the E_1 level, the atom is said to undergo emission. Calculate the wavelength of the photon emitted in this process.

7.30 The first line of the Balmer series occurs at a wavelength of 656.3 nm. What is the energy difference between the two energy levels involved in the emission that results in this spectral line?

7.31 Calculate the wavelength (in nanometers) of a photon emitted by a hydrogen atom when its electron drops from the $n = 5$ state to the $n = 3$ state.

7.32 Calculate the frequency (Hz) and wavelength (nm) of the emitted photon when an electron drops from the $n = 4$ to the $n = 2$ level in a hydrogen atom.

7.33 Careful spectral analysis shows that the familiar yellow light of sodium lamps (such as street lamps) is made up of photons of two wavelengths, 589.0 nm and 589.6 nm. What is the difference in energy (in joules) between photons with these wavelengths?

7.34 An electron in the hydrogen atom makes a transition from an energy state of principal quantum numbers n_i to the $n = 2$ state. If the photon emitted has a wavelength of 434 nm, what is the value of n_i?

Particle-Wave Duality
Review Questions

7.35 Explain the statement, Matter and radiation have a "dual nature."

7.36 How does de Broglie's hypothesis account for the fact that the energies of the electron in a hydrogen atom are quantized?

7.37 Why is Equation (7.7) meaningful only for submicroscopic particles, such as electrons and atoms, and not for macroscopic objects?

7.38 Does a baseball in flight possess wave properties? If so, why can we not determine its wave properties?

Problems

7.39 Thermal neutrons are neutrons that move at speeds comparable to those of air molecules at room temperature. These neutrons are most effective in initiating a nuclear chain reaction among ^{235}U isotopes. Calculate the wavelength (in nm) associated with a beam of neutrons moving at 7.00×10^2 m/s. (Mass of a neutron = 1.675×10^{-27} kg.)

7.40 Protons can be accelerated to speeds near that of light in particle accelerators. Estimate the wavelength (in nm) of such a proton moving at 2.90×10^8 m/s. (Mass of a proton = 1.673×10^{-27} kg.)

7.41 What is the de Broglie wavelength, in cm, of a 12.4-g hummingbird flying at 1.20×10^2 mph? (1 mile = 1.61 km.)

7.42 What is the de Broglie wavelength (in nm) associated with a 2.5-g Ping-Pong ball traveling 35 mph?

Quantum Mechanics
Review Questions

7.43 What are the inadequacies of Bohr's theory?

7.44 What is the Heisenberg uncertainty principle? What is the Schrödinger equation?

7.45 What is the physical significance of the wave function?

7.46 How is the concept of electron density used to describe the position of an electron in the quantum mechanical treatment of an atom?

7.47 What is an atomic orbital? How does an atomic orbital differ from an orbit?

7.48 Describe the characteristics of an s orbital, a p orbital, and a d orbital. Which of the following orbitals do not exist: $1p$, $2s$, $2d$, $3p$, $3d$, $3f$, $4g$?

7.49 Why is a boundary surface diagram useful in representing an atomic orbital?

7.50 Describe the four quantum numbers used to characterize an electron in an atom.

7.51 Which quantum number defines a shell? Which quantum numbers define a subshell?

7.52 Which of the four quantum numbers (n, ℓ, m_ℓ, m_s) determine (a) the energy of an electron in a hydrogen atom and in a many-electron atom, (b) the size of an orbital, (c) the shape of an orbital, (d) the orientation of an orbital in space?

Problems

7.53 An electron in a certain atom is in the $n = 2$ quantum level. List the possible values of ℓ and m_ℓ that it can have.

7.54 An electron in an atom is in the $n = 3$ quantum level. List the possible values of ℓ and m_ℓ that it can have.

7.55 Give the values of the quantum numbers associated with the following orbitals: (a) $2p$, (b) $3s$, (c) $5d$.

7.56 Give the values of the four quantum numbers of an electron in the following orbitals: (a) $3s$, (b) $4p$, (c) $3d$.

7.57 Discuss the similarities and differences between a $1s$ and a $2s$ orbital.

7.58 What is the difference between a $2p_x$ and a $2p_y$ orbital?

7.59 List all the possible subshells and orbitals associated with the principal quantum number n, if $n = 5$.

7.60 List all the possible subshells and orbitals associated with the principal quantum number n, if $n = 6$.

7.61 Calculate the total number of electrons that can occupy (a) one s orbital, (b) three p orbitals, (c) five d orbitals, (d) seven f orbitals.

7.62 What is the total number of electrons that can be held in all orbitals having the same principal quantum number n?

7.63 Determine the maximum number of electrons that can be found in each of the following subshells: $3s$, $3d$, $4p$, $4f$, $5f$.

7.64 Indicate the total number of (a) p electrons in N ($Z = 7$); (b) s electrons in Si ($Z = 14$); and (c) $3d$ electrons in S ($Z = 16$).

7.65 Make a chart of all allowable orbitals in the first four principal energy levels of the hydrogen atom. Designate each by type (for example, s, p) and indicate how many orbitals of each type there are.

7.66 Why do the $3s$, $3p$, and $3d$ orbitals have the same energy in a hydrogen atom but different energies in a many-electron atom?

7.67 For each of the following pairs of hydrogen orbitals, indicate which is higher in energy: (a) $1s$, $2s$; (b) $2p$, $3p$; (c) $3d_{xy}$, $3d_{yz}$; (d) $3s$, $3d$; (e) $4f$, $5s$.

7.68 Which orbital in each of the following pairs is lower in energy in a many-electron atom? (a) $2s$, $2p$; (b) $3p$, $3d$; (c) $3s$, $4s$; (d) $4d$, $5f$.

Atomic Orbitals
Review Questions

7.69 Describe the shapes of s, p, and d orbitals. How are these orbitals related to the quantum numbers n, ℓ, and m_ℓ?

7.70 List the hydrogen orbitals in increasing order of energy.

Electron Configuration
Review Questions

7.71 What is electron configuration? Describe the roles that the Pauli exclusion principle and Hund's rule play in writing the electron configuration of elements.

7.72 Explain the meaning of the symbol $4d^6$.

7.73 Explain the meaning of diamagnetic and paramagnetic. Give an example of an element that is diamagnetic and one that is paramagnetic. What does it mean when we say that electrons are paired?

7.74 What is meant by the term "shielding of electrons" in an atom? Using the Li atom as an example, describe the effect of shielding on the energy of electrons in an atom.

7.75 Define the following terms and give an example of each: transition metals, lanthanides, actinides.

7.76 Explain why the ground-state electron configurations of Cr and Cu are different from what we might expect.

7.77 Explain what is meant by a noble gas core. Write the electron configuration of a xenon core.

7.78 Comment on the correctness of the following statement: The probability of finding two electrons with the same four quantum numbers in an atom is zero.

Problems

7.79 Indicate which of the following sets of quantum numbers in an atom are unacceptable and explain why: (a) $(1, 0, \frac{1}{2}, \frac{1}{2})$, (b) $(3, 0, 0, +\frac{1}{2})$, (c) $(2, 2, 1, +\frac{1}{2})$, (d) $(4, 3, -2, +\frac{1}{2})$, (e) $(3, 2, 1, 1)$.

7.80 The ground-state electron configurations listed here are incorrect. Explain what mistakes have been made in each and write the correct electron configurations.

Al: $1s^2 2s^2 2p^4 3s^2 3p^3$

B: $1s^2 2s^2 2p^5$

F: $1s^2 2s^2 2p^6$

7.81 The atomic number of an element is 73. Is this element diamagnetic or paramagnetic?

7.82 Indicate the number of unpaired electrons present in each of the following atoms: B, Ne, P, Sc, Mn, Se, Kr, Fe, Cd, I, Pb.

7.83 Write the ground-state electron configurations for the following elements: B, V, Ni, As, I, Au.

7.84 Write the ground-state electron configurations for the following elements: Ge, Fe, Zn, Ni, W, Tl.

7.85 The electron configuration of a neutral atom is $1s^2 2s^2 2p^6 3s^2$. Write a complete set of quantum numbers for each of the electrons. Name the element.

7.86 Which of the following species has the most unpaired electrons? S^+, S, or S^-. Explain how you arrive at your answer.

The Aufbau Principle

Review Questions

7.87 State the Aufbau principle and explain the role it plays in classifying the elements in the periodic table.

7.88 Describe the characteristics of the following groups of elements: transition metals, lanthanides, actinides.

7.89 What is the noble gas core? How does it simplify the writing of electron configurations?

7.90 What are the group and period of the element osmium?

Problems

7.91 Use the Aufbau principle to obtain the ground-state electron configuration of selenium.

7.92 Use the Aufbau principle to obtain the ground-state electron configuration of technetium.

Additional Problems

7.93 When a compound containing cesium ion is heated in a Bunsen burner flame, photons with an energy of 4.30×10^{-19} J are emitted. What color is the cesium flame?

7.94 Discuss the current view of the correctness of the following statements. (a) The electron in the hydrogen atom is in an orbit that never brings it closer than 100 pm to the nucleus. (b) Atomic absorption spectra result from transitions of electrons from lower to higher energy levels. (c) A many-electron atom behaves somewhat like a solar system that has a number of planets.

7.95 Distinguish carefully between the following terms: (a) wavelength and frequency, (b) wave properties and particle properties, (c) quantization of energy and continuous variation in energy.

7.96 What is the maximum number of electrons in an atom that can have the following quantum numbers? Specify the orbitals in which the electrons would be found. (a) $n = 2$, $m_s = +\frac{1}{2}$; (b) $n = 4$, $m_\ell = +1$; (c) $n = 3$, $\ell = 2$; (d) $n = 2$, $\ell = 0$, $m_s = -\frac{1}{2}$; (e) $n = 4$, $\ell = 3$, $m_\ell = -2$.

7.97 Identify the following individuals and their contributions to the development of quantum theory: Bohr, de Broglie, Einstein, Planck, Heisenberg, Schrödinger.

7.98 What properties of electrons are used in the operation of an electron microscope?

7.99 In a photoelectric experiment a student uses a light source whose frequency is greater than that needed to eject electrons from a certain metal. However, after continuously shining the light on the same area of the metal for a long period of time the student notices that the maximum kinetic energy of ejected electrons begins to decrease, even though the frequency of the light is held constant. How would you account for this behavior?

7.100 A certain pitcher's fastballs have been clocked at about 100 mph. (a) Calculate the wavelength of a 0.141-kg baseball (in nm) at this speed. (b) What is the wavelength of a hydrogen atom at the same speed? (1 mile = 1609 m.)

7.101 Considering only the ground-state electron configuration, are there more diamagnetic or paramagnetic elements? Explain.

7.102 A ruby laser produces radiation of wavelength 633 nm in pulses whose duration is 1.00×10^{-9} s. (a) If the laser produces 0.376 J of energy per pulse, how many photons are produced in each pulse? (b) Calculate the power (in watts) delivered by the laser per pulse. (1 W = 1 J/s.)

7.103 A 368-g sample of water absorbs infrared radiation at 1.06×10^4 nm from a carbon dioxide laser. Suppose all the absorbed radiation is converted to heat. Calculate the number of photons at this wavelength required to raise the temperature of the water by 5.00°C.

7.104 Photodissociation of water

$$H_2O(l) + h\nu \longrightarrow H_2(g) + \tfrac{1}{2}O_2(g)$$

has been suggested as a source of hydrogen. The ΔH°_{rxn} for the reaction, calculated from thermochemical data, is 285.8 kJ per mole of water decomposed. Calculate the maximum wavelength (in nm) that would provide the necessary energy. In principle, is it feasible to use sunlight as a source of energy for this process?

7.105 Spectral lines of the Lyman and Balmer series do not overlap. Verify this statement by calculating the longest wavelength associated with the Lyman series and the shortest wavelength associated with the Balmer series (in nm).

7.106 Only a fraction of the electrical energy supplied to a tungsten lightbulb is converted to visible light. The rest of the energy shows up as infrared radiation (that is, heat). A 75-W lightbulb converts 15.0 percent of the energy supplied to it into visible light (assume the wavelength to be 550 nm). How many photons are emitted by the lightbulb per second? (1 W = 1 J/s.)

7.107 Certain sunglasses have small crystals of silver chloride (AgCl) incorporated in the lenses. When the lenses are exposed to light of the appropriate wavelength, the following reaction occurs:

$$AgCl \longrightarrow Ag + Cl$$

The Ag atoms formed produce a uniform gray color that reduces the glare. If ΔH for the preceding reaction is 248 kJ/mol, calculate the maximum wavelength of light that can induce this process.

7.108 The He^+ ion contains only one electron and is therefore a hydrogenlike ion. Calculate the wavelengths, in increasing order, of the first four transitions in the Balmer series of the He^+ ion. Compare these wavelengths with the same transitions in a H atom. Comment on the differences. (The Rydberg constant for He^+ is 8.72×10^{-18} J.)

7.109 Ozone (O_3) in the stratosphere absorbs the harmful radiation from the sun by undergoing decomposition: $O_3 \longrightarrow O + O_2$. (a) Referring to Table 6.3, calculate the $\Delta H°$ for this process. (b) Calculate the maximum wavelength of photons (in nm) that possess this energy to cause the decomposition of ozone photochemically.

7.110 The retina of a human eye can detect light when radiant energy incident on it is at least 4.0×10^{-17} J. For light of 600-nm wavelength, how many photons does this correspond to?

7.111 An electron in an excited state in a hydrogen atom can return to the ground state in two different ways: (a) via a direct transition in which a photon of wavelength λ_1 is emitted and (b) via an intermediate excited state reached by the emission of a photon of wavelength λ_2. This intermediate excited state then decays to the ground state by emitting another photon of wavelength λ_3. Derive an equation that relates λ_1 to λ_2 and λ_3.

7.112 A photoelectric experiment was performed by separately shining a laser at 450 nm (blue light) and a laser at 560 nm (yellow light) on a clean metal surface and measuring the number and kinetic energy of the ejected electrons. Which light would generate more electrons? Which light would eject electrons with greater kinetic energy? Assume that the same amount of energy is delivered to the metal surface by each laser and that the frequencies of the laser lights exceed the threshold frequency.

7.113 Draw the shapes (boundary surfaces) of the following orbitals: (a) $2p_y$, (b) $3d_{z^2}$, (c) $3d_{x^2-y^2}$. (Show coordinate axes in your sketches.)

7.114 The electron configurations described in this chapter all refer to gaseous atoms in their ground states. An atom may absorb a quantum of energy and promote one of its electrons to a higher-energy orbital. When this happens, we say that the atom is in an excited state. The electron configurations of some excited atoms are given. Identify these atoms and write their ground-state configurations:
(a) $1s^1 2s^1$
(b) $1s^2 2s^2 2p^2 3d^1$
(c) $1s^2 2s^2 2p^6 4s^1$
(d) $[Ar]4s^1 3d^{10} 4p^4$
(e) $[Ne]3s^2 3p^4 3d^1$

7.115 Draw orbital diagrams for atoms with the following electron configurations:
(a) $1s^2 2s^2 2p^5$
(b) $1s^2 2s^2 2p^6 3s^2 3p^3$
(c) $1s^2 2s^2 2p^6 3s^2 3p^6 4s^2 3d^7$

7.116 If Rutherford and his coworkers had used electrons instead of alpha particles to probe the structure of the nucleus (see Chapter 2), what might have they discovered?

7.117 Scientists have found interstellar hydrogen atoms with quantum number n in the hundreds. Calculate the wavelength of light emitted when a hydrogen atom undergoes a transition from $n = 236$ to $n = 235$. In what region of the electromagnetic spectrum does this wavelength fall?

7.118 Calculate the wavelength of a helium atom whose speed is equal to the root-mean-square speed at 20°C.

7.119 Ionization energy is the minimum energy required to remove an electron from an atom. It is usually expressed in units of kJ/mol, that is, the energy in kilojoules required to remove one mole of electrons from one mole of atoms. (a) Calculate the ionization energy for the hydrogen atom. (b) Repeat the calculation, assuming in this second case that the electrons are removed from the $n = 2$ state.

7.120 An electron in a hydrogen atom is excited from the ground state to the $n = 4$ state. Comment on the correctness of the following statements (true or false).
(a) $n = 4$ is the first excited state.
(b) It takes more energy to ionize (remove) the electron from $n = 4$ than from the ground state.
(c) The electron is farther from the nucleus (on average) in $n = 4$ than in the ground state.
(d) The wavelength of light emitted when the electron drops from $n = 4$ to $n = 1$ is longer than that from $n = 4$ to $n = 2$.
(e) The wavelength the atom absorbs in going from $n = 1$ to $n = 4$ is the same as that emitted as it goes from $n = 4$ to $n = 1$.

7.121 The ionization energy of a certain element is 412 kJ/mol (see Problem 7.119). However, when the atoms of this element are in the first excited state, the ionization energy is only 126 kJ/mol. Based on this information, calculate the wavelength of light emitted in a transition from the first excited state to the ground state.

7.122 Alveoli are the tiny sacs of air in the lungs (see Problem 5.128) whose average diameter is 5.0×10^{-5} m. Consider an oxygen molecule (5.3×10^{-26} kg) trapped within a sac. Calculate the uncertainty in the velocity of the oxygen molecule. (*Hint:* The maximum uncertainty in the position of the molecule is given by the diameter of the sac.)

7.123 How many photons at 660 nm must be absorbed to melt 5.0×10^2 g of ice? On average, how many H_2O molecules does one photon convert from ice to water? (*Hint:* It takes 334 J to melt 1 g of ice at 0°C.)

7.124 Shown below are portions of orbital diagrams representing the ground-state electron configurations of certain elements. Which of them violate the Pauli exclusion principle? Hund's rule?

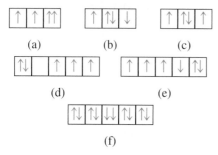

(a)   (b)   (c)

(d)   (e)

(f)

7.125 The UV light that is responsible for tanning the skin falls in the 320- to 400-nm region. Calculate the total energy (in joules) absorbed by a person exposed to this radiation for 2.0 h, given that there are 2.0×10^{16} photons hitting Earth's surface per square centimeter per second over a 80-nm (320 nm to 400 nm) range and that the exposed body area is 0.45 m². Assume that only half of the radiation is absorbed and the other half is reflected by the body. (*Hint:* Use an average wavelength of 360 nm in calculating the energy of a photon.)

7.126 The sun is surrounded by a white circle of gaseous material called the corona, which becomes visible during a total eclipse of the sun. The temperature of the corona is in the millions of degrees Celsius, which is high enough to break up molecules and remove some or all of the electrons from atoms. One way astronomers have been able to estimate the temperature of the corona is by studying the emission lines of ions of certain elements. For example, the emission spectrum of Fe^{14+} ions has been recorded and analyzed. Knowing that it takes 3.5×10^4 kJ/mol to convert Fe^{13+} to Fe^{14+}, estimate the temperature of the sun's corona. (*Hint:* The average kinetic energy of one mole of a gas is $\frac{3}{2}RT$.)

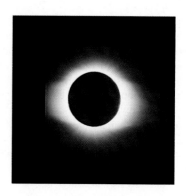

7.127 In 1996 physicists created an anti-atom of hydrogen. In such an atom, which is the antimatter equivalent of an ordinary atom, the electrical charges of all the component particles are reversed. Thus the nucleus of an anti-atom is made of an anti-proton, which has the same mass as a proton but bears a negative charge, while the electron is replaced by an anti-electron (also called positron) with the same mass as an electron, but bearing a positive charge. Would you expect the energy levels, emission spectra, and atomic orbitals of an antihydrogen atom to be different from those of a hydrogen atom? What would happen if an anti-atom of hydrogen collided with a hydrogen atom?

7.128 Use Equation (5.16) to calculate the de Broglie wavelength of a N_2 molecule at 300 K.

7.129 When an electron makes a transition between energy levels of a hydrogen atom, there are no restrictions on the initial and final values of the principal quantum number n. However, there is a quantum mechanical rule that restricts the initial and final values of the orbital angular momentum ℓ. This is the *selection rule*, which states that $\Delta \ell = \pm 1$, that is, in a transition, the value of ℓ can only increase or decrease by one. According to this rule, which of the following transitions are allowed: (a) $1s \rightarrow 2s$, (b) $2p \rightarrow 1s$, (c) $1s \rightarrow 3d$, (d) $3d \rightarrow 4f$, (e) $4d \rightarrow 3s$?

7.130 In an electron microscope, electrons are accelerated by passing them through a voltage difference. The kinetic energy thus acquired by the electrons is equal to the voltage times the charge on the electron. Thus a voltage difference of 1 volt imparts a kinetic energy of 1.602×10^{-19} volt-coulomb or 1.602×10^{-19} J. Calculate the wavelength associated with electrons accelerated by 5.00×10^3 volts.

7.131 A microwave oven operating at 1.22×10^8 nm is used to heat 150 mL of water (roughly the volume of a tea cup) from 20°C to 100°C. Calculate the number of photons needed if 92.0 percent of microwave energy is converted to the thermal energy of water.

7.132 The radioactive Co-60 isotope is used in nuclear medicine to treat certain types of cancer. Calculate the

wavelength and frequency of an emitted gamma particle having the energy of 1.29×10^{11} J/mol.

7.133 For hydrogenlike ions, that is, ions containing only one
electron, Equation (7.4) is modified as follows: $E_n = -R_H Z^2 (1/n^2)$, where Z is the atomic number of the parent atom. The figure here represents the emission spec-
trum of such a hydrogenlike ion in the gas phase. All
the lines result from the electronic transitions from the
excited states to the $n = 2$ state. (a) What electronic
transitions correspond to lines B and C? (b) If the wavelength of line C is 27.1 nm, calculate the wavelengths of
lines A and B. (c) Calculate the energy needed to
remove the electron from the ion in the $n = 4$ state.
(d) What is the physical significance of the continuum?

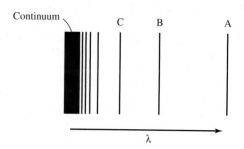

Answers to Practice Exercises

7.1 625 Hz. **7.2** 8.24 m. **7.3** 3.39×10^3 nm. **7.4** 2.63×10^3 nm. **7.5** 56.6 nm. **7.6** $n = 3, \ell = 1, m_\ell = -1, 0, 1$. **7.7** 16. **7.8** $(5, 1, -1, +\frac{1}{2}), (5, 1, 0, +\frac{1}{2}), (5, 1, 1, +\frac{1}{2}), (5, 1, -1, -\frac{1}{2}), (5, 1, 0, -\frac{1}{2}), (5, 1, 1, -\frac{1}{2})$. **7.9** 32.

7.10 $(1, 0, 0, +\frac{1}{2}), (1, 0, 0, -\frac{1}{2}), (2, 0, 0, +\frac{1}{2}), (2, 0, 0, -\frac{1}{2}), (2, 1, -1, +\frac{1}{2})$. There are 5 other acceptable ways to write
the quantum numbers for the last electron.
7.11 $[\text{Ne}]3s^2 3p^3$.

ELEMENTS

		wt.				wt.
⊙	Hydrogen.	1	⊕	Strontian		46
⊖	Azote	5	✳	Barytes		68
●	Carbon	54	Ⓘ	Iron		50
○	Oxygen	7	Ⓩ	Zinc		56
⊘	Phosphorus	9	Ⓒ	Copper		56
⊕	Sulphur	13	Ⓛ	Lead		90
◉	Magnesia	20	Ⓢ	Silver		190
⊖	Lime	24	Ⓖ	Gold		190
⦶	Soda	28	Ⓟ	Platina		190
⦷	Potash	42	⊛	Mercury		167

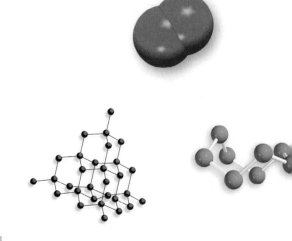

John Dalton's chart of elements, compiled in the early nineteenth century. Today 113 elements are known. The models show the following elements: hydrogen, carbon (diamond), oxygen, sulfur, phosphorus, and iron.

8

Periodic Relationships Among the Elements

Interactive Activity Summary

1. Animation: Atomic and Ionic Radius (8.3)
2. Interactivity: Atomic Radii (8.3)
3. Interactivity: Attraction of Nucleus (8.3)
4. Interactivity: Ionic Radii (8.3)
5. Interactivity: Ionization Energy (8.4)

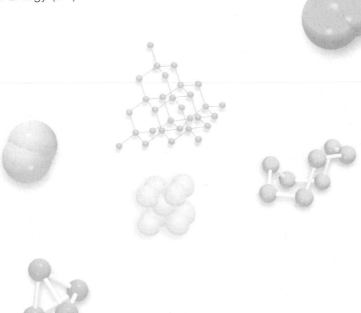

Many of the chemical properties of the elements can be understood in terms of their electron configurations. Because electrons fill atomic orbitals in a fairly regular fashion, it is not surprising that elements with similar electron configurations, such as sodium and potassium, behave similarly in many respects and that, in general, the properties of the elements exhibit observable trends. Chemists in the nineteenth century recognized periodic trends in the physical and chemical properties of elements, long before quantum theory came onto the scene. Although these chemists were not aware of the existence of electrons and protons, their efforts to systematize the chemistry of the elements were remarkably successful. Their main sources of information were the atomic masses of the elements and other known physical and chemical properties.

8.1 Development of the Periodic Table

In the nineteenth century, when chemists had only a vague idea of atoms and molecules and did not know of the existence of electrons and protons, they devised the periodic table using their knowledge of atomic masses. Accurate measurements of the atomic masses of many elements had already been made. Arranging elements according to their atomic masses in a periodic table seemed logical to those chemists, who felt that chemical behavior should somehow be related to atomic mass.

In 1864 the English chemist John Newlands[†] noticed that when the elements were arranged in order of atomic mass, every eighth element had similar properties. Newlands referred to this peculiar relationship as the *law of octaves*. However, this "law" turned out to be inadequate for elements beyond calcium, and Newlands's work was not accepted by the scientific community.

In 1869 the Russian chemist Dmitri Mendeleev[‡] and the German chemist Lothar Meyer[§] independently proposed a much more extensive tabulation of the elements based on the regular, periodic recurrence of properties. Mendeleev's classification system was a great improvement over Newlands's for two reasons. First, it grouped the elements together more accurately, according to their properties. Equally important, it made possible the prediction of the properties of several elements that had not yet been discovered. For example, Mendeleev proposed the existence of an unknown element that he called eka-aluminum and predicted a number of its properties. (*Eka* is a Sanskrit word meaning "first"; thus eka-aluminum would be the first element under aluminum in the same group.) When gallium was discovered four years later, its properties matched the predicted properties of eka-aluminum remarkably well:

	Eka-Aluminum (Ea)	Gallium (Ga)
Atomic mass	68 amu	69.9 amu
Melting point	Low	30.15°C
Density	5.9 g/cm^3	5.94 g/cm^3
Formula of oxide	Ea_2O_3	Ga_2O_3

Appendix 1 explains the names and symbols of the elements.

Mendeleev's periodic table included 66 known elements. By 1900, some 30 more had been added to the list, filling in some of the empty spaces. Figure 8.1 charts the discovery of the elements chronologically.

Although this periodic table was a celebrated success, the early versions had some glaring inconsistencies. For example, the atomic mass of argon (39.95 amu) is greater than that of potassium (39.10 amu). If elements were arranged solely according to increasing atomic mass, argon would appear in the position occupied by potassium in our modern periodic table (see the inside front cover). But no chemist would place argon, an inert gas, in the same group as lithium and sodium, two very reactive metals. This and other discrepancies suggested that some fundamental property other than atomic mass must be the basis of periodicity. This property turned out to be associated with atomic number, a concept unknown to Mendeleev and his contemporaries.

[†]John Alexander Reina Newlands (1838–1898). English chemist. Newlands's work was a step in the right direction in the classification of the elements. Unfortunately, because of its shortcomings, he was subjected to much criticism, and even ridicule. At one meeting he was asked if he had ever examined the elements according to the order of their initial letters! Nevertheless, in 1887 Newlands was honored by the Royal Society of London for his contribution.

[‡]Dmitri Ivanovich Mendeleev (1836–1907). Russian chemist. His work on the periodic classification of elements is regarded by many as the most significant achievement in chemistry in the nineteenth century.

[§]Julius Lothar Meyer (1830–1895). German chemist. In addition to his contribution to the periodic table, Meyer also discovered the chemical affinity of hemoglobin for oxygen.

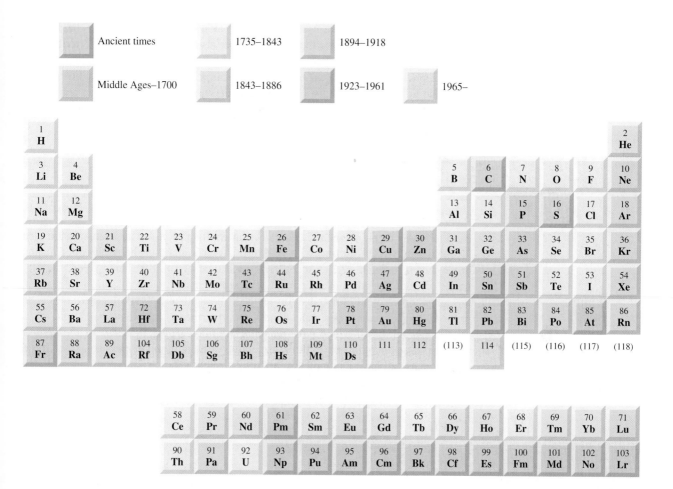

Figure 8.1 *A chronological chart of the discovery of the elements. To date, 113 elements have been identified.*

Using data from α-scattering experiments (see Section 2.2), Rutherford estimated the number of positive charges in the nucleus of a few elements, but the significance of these numbers was overlooked for several more years. In 1913 a young English physicist, Henry Moseley,[†] discovered a correlation between what he called *atomic number* and the frequency of X rays generated by bombarding an element with high-energy electrons. Moseley noticed that the frequencies of X rays emitted from the elements could be correlated by the equation

$$\sqrt{v} = a(Z - b)$$

where v is the frequency of the emitted X rays and a and b are constants that are the same for all the elements. Thus, from the square root of the measured frequency of the X rays emitted, we can determine the atomic number of the element.

With a few exceptions, Moseley found that atomic number increases in the same order as atomic mass. For example, calcium is the twentieth element in order of increasing atomic mass, and it has an atomic number of 20. The discrepancies that had puzzled earlier scientists now made sense. The atomic number of argon is 18 and that of potassium is 19, so potassium should follow argon in the periodic table.

[†]Henry Gwyn-Jeffreys Moseley (1887–1915). English physicist. Moseley discovered the relationship between X-ray spectra and atomic number. A lieutenant in the Royal Engineers, he was killed in action at the age of 28 during the British campaign in Gallipoli, Turkey.

A modern periodic table usually shows the atomic number along with the element symbol. As you already know, the atomic number also indicates the number of electrons in the atoms of an element. Electron configurations of elements help to explain the recurrence of physical and chemical properties. The importance and usefulness of the periodic table lie in the fact that we can use our understanding of the general properties and trends within a group or a period to predict with considerable accuracy the properties of any element, even though that element may be unfamiliar to us.

8.2 Periodic Classification of the Elements

Figure 8.2 shows the periodic table together with the outermost ground-state electron configurations of the elements. (The electron configurations of the elements are also given in Table 7.3.) Starting with hydrogen, we see that subshells are filled in the order shown in Figure 7.24. According to the type of subshell being filled, the elements can be divided into categories—the representative elements, the noble gases, the transition elements (or transition metals), the lanthanides, and the actinides. The ***representative elements*** (also called *main group elements*) are *the elements in Groups 1A through 7A, all of which have incompletely filled s or p subshells of the highest principal quantum number.* With the exception of helium, the *noble gases* (the Group 8A elements) all have a completely filled p subshell. (The electron configurations are $1s^2$ for helium and ns^2np^6 for the other noble gases, where n is the principal quantum number for the outermost shell.)

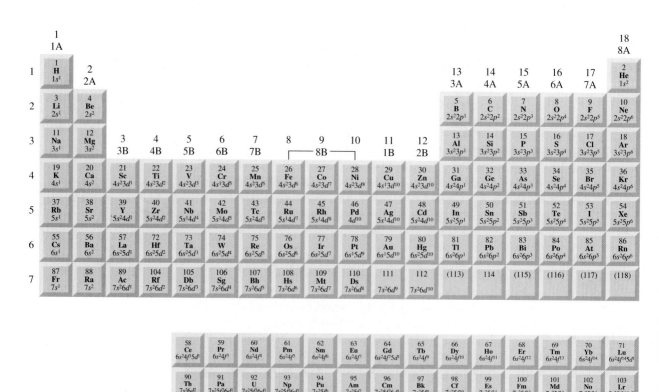

Figure 8.2 *The ground-state electron configurations of the elements. For simplicity, only the configurations of the outer electrons are shown.*

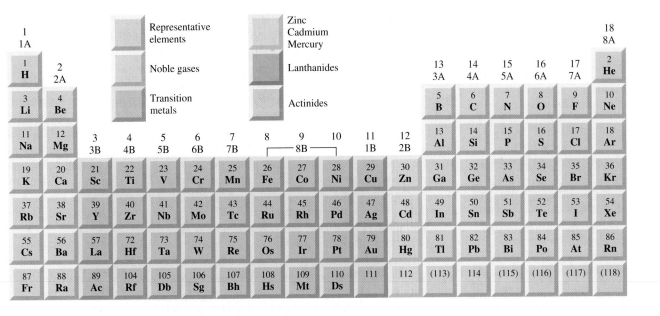

1 1A																		18 8A
1 H	2 2A											13 3A	14 4A	15 5A	16 6A	17 7A	2 He
3 Li	4 Be												5 B	6 C	7 N	8 O	9 F	10 Ne
11 Na	12 Mg	3 3B	4 4B	5 5B	6 6B	7 7B	8 ⟶ 8B ⟵	9	10	11 1B	12 2B	13 Al	14 Si	15 P	16 S	17 Cl	18 Ar
19 K	20 Ca	21 Sc	22 Ti	23 V	24 Cr	25 Mn	26 Fe	27 Co	28 Ni	29 Cu	30 Zn	31 Ga	32 Ge	33 As	34 Se	35 Br	36 Kr
37 Rb	38 Sr	39 Y	40 Zr	41 Nb	42 Mo	43 Tc	44 Ru	45 Rh	46 Pd	47 Ag	48 Cd	49 In	50 Sn	51 Sb	52 Te	53 I	54 Xe
55 Cs	56 Ba	57 La	72 Hf	73 Ta	74 W	75 Re	76 Os	77 Ir	78 Pt	79 Au	80 Hg	81 Tl	82 Pb	83 Bi	84 Po	85 At	86 Rn
87 Fr	88 Ra	89 Ac	104 Rf	105 Db	106 Sg	107 Bh	108 Hs	109 Mt	110 Ds	111	112	(113)	114	(115)	(116)	(117)	(118)

58 Ce	59 Pr	60 Nd	61 Pm	62 Sm	63 Eu	64 Gd	65 Tb	66 Dy	67 Ho	68 Er	69 Tm	70 Yb	71 Lu
90 Th	91 Pa	92 U	93 Np	94 Pu	95 Am	96 Cm	97 Bk	98 Cf	99 Es	100 Fm	101 Md	102 No	103 Lr

Figure 8.3 *Classification of the elements. Note that the Group 2B elements are often classified as transition metals even though they do not exhibit the characteristics of the transition metals.*

The transition metals are the elements in Groups 1B and 3B through 8B, which have incompletely filled *d* subshells, or readily produce cations with incompletely filled *d* subshells. (These metals are sometimes referred to as the *d*-block transition elements.) The nonsequential numbering of the transition metals in the periodic table (that is, 3B–8B, followed by 1B–2B) acknowledges a correspondence between the outer electron configurations of these elements and those of the representative elements. For example, scandium and gallium both have three outer electrons. However, because they are in different types of atomic orbitals, they are placed in different groups (3B and 3A). The metals iron (Fe), cobalt (Co), and nickel (Ni) do not fit this classification and are all placed in Group 8B. The Group 2B elements, Zn, Cd, and Hg, are neither representative elements nor transition metals. There is no special name for this group of metals. It should be noted that the designation of A and B groups is not universal. In Europe the practice is to use B for representative elements and A for transition metals, which is just the opposite of the American convention. The International Union of Pure and Applied Chemistry (IUPAC) has recommended numbering the columns sequentially with Arabic numerals 1 through 18 (see Figure 8.2). The proposal has sparked much controversy in the international chemistry community, and its merits and drawbacks will be deliberated for some time to come. In this text we will adhere to the American designation.

The lanthanides and actinides are sometimes called *f*-block transition elements because they have incompletely filled *f* subshells. Figure 8.3 distinguishes the groups of elements discussed here.

A clear pattern emerges when we examine the electron configurations of the elements in a particular group. The electron configurations for Groups 1A and 2A are

For the representative elements, the valence electrons are simply those electrons at the highest principal energy level n.

TABLE 8.1

Electron Configurations of Group 1A and Group 2A Elements

Group 1A	Group 2A
Li [He]$2s^1$	Be [He]$2s^2$
Na [Ne]$3s^1$	Mg [Ne]$3s^2$
K [Ar]$4s^1$	Ca [Ar]$4s^2$
Rb [Kr]$5s^1$	Sr [Kr]$5s^2$
Cs [Xe]$6s^1$	Ba [Xe]$6s^2$
Fr [Rn]$7s^1$	Ra [Rn]$7s^2$

shown in Table 8.1. All members of the Group 1A alkali metals have similar outer electron configurations; each has a noble gas core and an ns^1 outer electron. Similarly, the Group 2A alkaline earth metals have a noble gas core and an outer electron configuration of ns^2. *The outer electrons of an atom, which are the ones involved in chemical bonding,* are often called **valence electrons.** The similarity of the outer electron configurations (that is, they have the same number and type of valence electrons) is what makes the elements in the same group resemble one another in chemical behavior. This observation holds true for the other representative elements. Thus, for instance, the halogens (the Group 7A elements) all have outer electron configurations of ns^2np^5, and they have very similar properties. We must be careful, however, in predicting properties for Groups 3A through 7A. For example, the elements in Group 4A all have the same outer electron configuration, ns^2np^2, but there is some variation in chemical properties among these elements: Carbon is a nonmetal, silicon and germanium are metalloids, and tin and lead are metals.

As a group, the noble gases behave very similarly. With the exception of krypton and xenon, the rest of these elements are totally inert chemically. The reason is that these elements all have completely filled outer ns and np subshells, a condition that represents great stability. Although the outer electron configuration of the transition metals is not always the same within a group and there is no regular pattern in the change of the electron configuration from one metal to the next in the same period, all transition metals share many characteristics that set them apart from other elements. The reason is that these metals all have an incompletely filled d subshell. Likewise, the lanthanide (and the actinide) elements resemble one another because they have incompletely filled f subshells.

Example 8.1

An atom of a certain element has 15 electrons. Without consulting a periodic table, answer the following questions: (a) What is the ground-state electron configuration of the element? (b) How should the element be classified? (c) Is the element diamagnetic or paramagnetic?

Strategy (a) We refer to the building-up principle discussed in Section 7.9 and start writing the electron configuration with principal quantum number $n = 1$ and continuing upward until all the electrons are accounted for. (b) What are the electron configuration characteristics of representative elements? transition elements? noble gases? (c) Examine the pairing scheme of the electrons in the outermost shell. What determines whether an element is diamagnetic or paramagnetic?

Solution (a) We know that for $n = 1$ we have a $1s$ orbital (2 electrons); for $n = 2$ we have a $2s$ orbital (2 electrons) and three $2p$ orbitals (6 electrons); for $n = 3$ we have a $3s$ orbital (2 electrons). The number of electrons left is $15 - 12 = 3$ and these three electrons are placed in the $3p$ orbitals. The electron configuration is $1s^2 2s^2 2p^6 3s^2 3p^3$.

(b) Because the $3p$ subshell is not completely filled, this is a representative element. Based on the information given, we cannot say whether it is a metal, a nonmetal, or a metalloid.

(c) According to Hund's rule, the three electrons in the $3p$ orbitals have parallel spins (three unpaired electrons). Therefore, the element is paramagnetic.

Check For (b), note that a transition metal possesses an incompletely filled d subshell and a noble gas has a completely filled outer shell. For (c), recall that if the atoms of an element contain an odd number of electrons, then the element must be paramagnetic.

Practice Exercise An atom of a certain element has 20 electrons. (a) Write the ground-state electron configuration of the element, (b) classify the element, (c) determine whether the element is diamagnetic or paramagnetic.

Similar problem: 8.20.

Representing Free Elements in Chemical Equations

Having classified the elements according to their ground-state electron configurations, we can now look at the way chemists represent metals, metalloids, and nonmetals as free elements in chemical equations. Because metals do not exist in discrete molecular units, we always use their empirical formulas in chemical equations. The empirical formulas are the same as the symbols that represent the elements. For example, the empirical formula for iron is Fe, the same as the symbol for the element.

For nonmetals there is no single rule. Carbon, for example, exists as an extensive three-dimensional network of atoms, and so we use its empirical formula (C) to represent elemental carbon in chemical equations. But hydrogen, nitrogen, oxygen, and the halogens exist as diatomic molecules, and so we use their molecular formulas (H_2, N_2, O_2, F_2, Cl_2, Br_2, I_2) in equations. The stable form of phosphorus is molecular (P_4), and so we use P_4. For sulfur, chemists often use the empirical formula (S) in chemical equations, rather than S_8, which is the stable form. Thus, instead of writing the equation for the combustion of sulfur as

$$S_8(s) + 8O_2(g) \longrightarrow 8SO_2(g)$$

we usually write

$$S(s) + O_2(g) \longrightarrow SO_2(g)$$

All the noble gases are monatomic species; thus we use their symbols: He, Ne, Ar, Kr, Xe, and Rn. The metalloids, like the metals, all have complex three-dimensional networks, and we represent them, too, with their empirical formulas, that is, their symbols: B, Si, Ge, and so on.

Note that these two equations for the combustion of sulfur have identical stoichiometry. This correspondence should not be surprising, because both equations describe the same chemical system. In both cases, a number of sulfur atoms react with twice as many oxygen atoms.

Electron Configurations of Cations and Anions

Because many ionic compounds are made up of monatomic anions and cations, it is helpful to know how to write the electron configurations of these ionic species. Just as for neutral atoms, we use the Pauli exclusion principle and Hund's rule in writing the ground-state electron configurations of cations and anions. We will group the ions in two categories for discussion.

Ions Derived from Representative Elements Ions formed from atoms of most representative elements have the noble-gas outer-electron configuration of ns^2np^6. In the formation of a cation from the atom of a representative element, one or more electrons are removed from the highest occupied n shell. Following are the electron configurations of some atoms and their corresponding cations:

Na: $[Ne]3s^1$ Na^+: $[Ne]$
Ca: $[Ar]4s^2$ Ca^{2+}: $[Ar]$
Al: $[Ne]3s^23p^1$ Al^{3+}: $[Ne]$

Note that each ion has a stable noble gas configuration.

In the formation of an anion, one or more electrons are added to the highest partially filled n shell. Consider the following examples:

H: $1s^1$ H^-: $1s^2$ or $[He]$
F: $1s^22s^22p^5$ F^-: $1s^22s^22p^6$ or $[Ne]$
O: $1s^22s^22p^4$ O^{2-}: $1s^22s^22p^6$ or $[Ne]$
N: $1s^22s^22p^3$ N^{3-}: $1s^22s^22p^6$ or $[Ne]$

All of these anions also have stable noble gas configurations. Notice that F^-, Na^+, and Ne (and Al^{3+}, O^{2-}, and N^{3-}) have the same electron configuration. They are said to be **isoelectronic** because they *have the same number of electrons, and hence the same ground-state electron configuration.* Thus H^- and He are also isoelectronic.

Cations Derived from Transition Metals In Section 7.9 we saw that in the first-row transition metals (Sc to Cu), the $4s$ orbital is always filled before the $3d$ orbitals. Consider manganese, whose electron configuration is $[Ar]4s^2 3d^5$. When the Mn^{2+} ion is formed, we might expect the two electrons to be removed from the $3d$ orbitals to yield $[Ar]4s^2 3d^3$. In fact, the electron configuration of Mn^{2+} is $[Ar]3d^5$! The reason is that the electron-electron and electron-nucleus interactions in a neutral atom can be quite different from those in its ion. Thus, whereas the $4s$ orbital is always filled before the $3d$ orbital in Mn, electrons are removed from the $4s$ orbital in forming Mn^{2+} because the $3d$ orbital is more stable than the $4s$ orbital in transition metal ions. Therefore, when a cation is formed from an atom of a transition metal, electrons are always removed first from the ns orbital and then from the $(n-1)d$ orbitals.

Keep in mind that most transition metals can form more than one cation and that frequently the cations are not isoelectronic with the preceding noble gases.

Bear in mind that the order of electron filling does not determine or predict the order of electron removal for transition metals.

8.3 Periodic Variation in Physical Properties

As we have seen, the electron configurations of the elements show a periodic variation with increasing atomic number. Consequently, there are also periodic variations in physical and chemical behavior. In this section and the next two, we will examine some physical properties of elements that are in the same group or period and additional properties that influence the chemical behavior of the elements. First, let's look at the concept of effective nuclear charge, which has a direct bearing on atomic size and on the tendency for ionization.

Effective Nuclear Charge

In Chapter 7, we discussed the shielding effect that electrons close to the nucleus have on outer-shell electrons in many-electron atoms. The presence of shielding electrons reduces the electrostatic attraction between the positively charged protons in the nucleus and the outer electrons. Moreover, the repulsive forces between electrons in a many-electron atom further offset the attractive force exerted by the nucleus. The concept of effective nuclear charge enables us to account for the effects of shielding on periodic properties.

Consider, for example, the helium atom, which has the ground-state electron configuration $1s^2$. Helium's two protons give the nucleus a charge of $+2$, but the full attractive force of this charge on the two $1s$ electrons is partially offset by electron-electron repulsion. Consequently we say that the $1s$ electrons shield each other from the nucleus. The effective nuclear charge (Z_{eff}), which is the charge felt by an electron, is given by

$$Z_{eff} = Z - \sigma$$

where Z is the actual nuclear charge (that is, the atomic number of the element) and σ (sigma) is called the *shielding constant* (also called the *screening constant*). The shielding constant is greater than zero but smaller than Z.

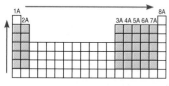

The increase in effective nuclear charge from left to right across a period and from bottom to top in a group for representative elements.

One way to illustrate electron shielding is to consider the amounts of energy required to remove the two electrons from a helium atom. Measurements show that it takes 2373 kJ of energy to remove the first electron from 1 mole of He atoms and 5251 kJ of energy to remove the remaining electron from 1 mole of He$^+$ ions. The reason it takes so much more energy to remove the second electron is that with only one electron present, there is no shielding, and the electron feels the full effect of the +2 nuclear charge.

For atoms with three or more electrons, the electrons in a given shell are shielded by electrons in inner shells (that is, shells closer to the nucleus) but not by electrons in outer shells. Thus, in a lithium atom, whose electron configuration is $1s^2 2s^1$, the 2s electron is shielded by the two 1s electrons, but the 2s electron does not have a shielding effect on the 1s electrons. In addition, filled inner shells shield outer electrons more effectively than electrons in the same subshell shield each other.

See Figure 7.26 for radial probability plots of 1s and 2s orbitals.

Atomic Radius

A number of physical properties, including density, melting point, and boiling point, are related to the sizes of atoms, but atomic size is difficult to define. As we saw in Chapter 7, the electron density in an atom extends far beyond the nucleus, but we normally think of atomic size as the volume containing about 90 percent of the total electron density around the nucleus. When we must be even more specific, we define the size of an atom in terms of its *atomic radius,* which is *one-half the distance between the two nuclei in two adjacent metal atoms.*

For atoms linked together to form an extensive three-dimensional network, atomic radius is simply one-half the distance between the nuclei in two neighboring atoms [Figure 8.4(a)]. For elements that exist as simple diatomic molecules, the atomic radius is one-half the distance between the nuclei of the two atoms in a particular molecule [Figure 8.4(b)].

Figure 8.5 shows the atomic radii of many elements according to their positions in the periodic table, and Figure 8.6 plots the atomic radii of these elements against their atomic numbers. Periodic trends are clearly evident. In studying the trends, bear in mind that the atomic radius is determined to a large extent by the strength of the attraction between the nucleus and the outer-shell electrons. The larger the effective nuclear charge, the stronger the hold of the nucleus on these electrons, and the smaller the atomic radius. Consider the second-period elements from Li to F, for example. Moving from left to right, we find that the number of electrons in the inner shell ($1s^2$) remains constant while the nuclear charge increases. The electrons that are added to counterbalance the increasing nuclear charge are ineffective in shielding one another. Consequently, the effective nuclear charge increases steadily while the principal quantum number remains constant ($n = 2$). For example, the outer 2s electron in lithium is shielded from the nucleus (which has three protons) by the two 1s electrons. As an approximation, we assume that the shielding effect of the two 1s electrons is to cancel two positive charges in the nucleus. Thus the 2s electron only feels the attraction of one proton in the nucleus; the effective nuclear charge is +1. In beryllium ($1s^2 2s^2$), each of the 2s electrons is shielded by the inner two 1s electrons, which cancel two of the four positive charges in the nucleus. Because the 2s electrons do not shield each other as effectively, the net result is that the effective nuclear charge of each 2s electron is greater than +1. Thus as the effective nuclear charge increases, the atomic radius decreases steadily from lithium to fluorine.

Within a group of elements we find that atomic radius increases with increasing atomic number. For the alkali metals in Group 1A, the outermost electron resides in the *ns* orbital. Because orbital size increases with the increasing principal quantum

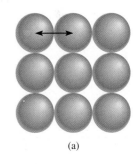

(a)

(b)

Figure 8.4 (a) In metals such as beryllium, the atomic radius is defined as one-half the distance between the nuclei of two adjacent atoms. (b) For elements that exist as diatomic molecules, such as iodine, the radius of the atom is defined as one-half the distance between the nuclei.

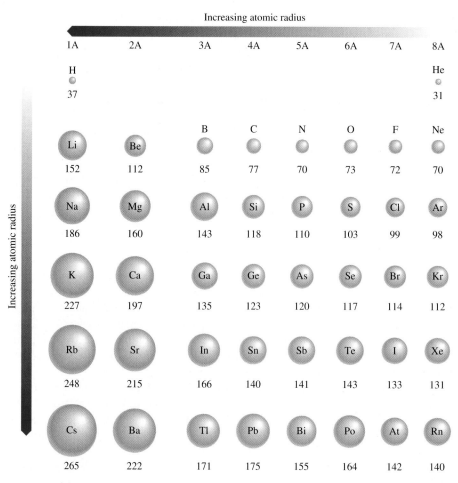

Figure 8.5 *Atomic radii (in picometers) of representative elements according to their positions in the periodic table. Note that there is no general agreement on the size of atomic radii. We focus only on the trends in atomic radii, not on their precise values.*

number n, the size of the metal atoms increases from Li to Cs. We can apply the same reasoning to the elements in other groups.

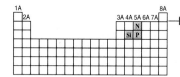

Example 8.2

Referring to a periodic table, arrange the following atoms in order of increasing atomic radius: P, Si, N.

Strategy What are the trends in atomic radii in a periodic group and in a particular period? Which of the preceding elements are in the same group? in the same period?

Solution From Figure 8.1 we see that N and P are in the same group (Group 5A). Therefore, the radius of N is smaller than that of P (atomic radius increases as we go down a group). Both Si and P are in the third period, and Si is to the left of P. Therefore, the radius of P is smaller than that of Si (atomic radius decreases as we move from left to right across a period). Thus the order of increasing radius is N < P < Si.

Practice Exercise Arrange the following atoms in order of decreasing radius: C, Li, Be.

Similar problems: 8.37, 8.38.

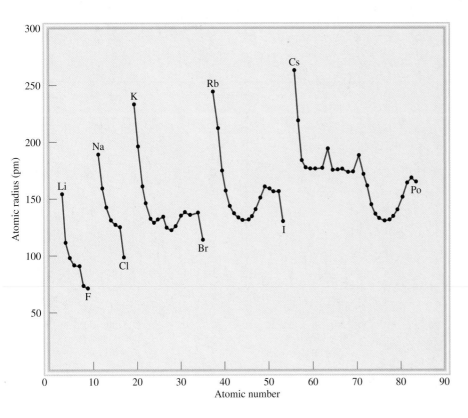

Figure 8.6 *A plot of atomic radii (in picometers) of elements against their atomic numbers.*

Ionic Radius

Ionic radius is *the radius of a cation or an anion.* It can be measured by X-ray diffraction (see Chapter 11). Ionic radius affects the physical and chemical properties of an ionic compound. For example, the three-dimensional structure of an ionic compound depends on the relative sizes of its cations and anions.

When a neutral atom is converted to an ion, we expect a change in size. If the atom forms an anion, its size (or radius) increases, because the nuclear charge remains the same but the repulsion resulting from the additional electron(s) enlarges the domain of the electron cloud. On the other hand, removing one or more electrons from an atom reduces electron-electron repulsion but the nuclear charge remains the same, so the electron cloud shrinks, and the cation is smaller than the atom. Figure 8.7 shows the changes in size that result when alkali metals are converted to cations and halogens are converted to anions; Figure 8.8 shows the changes in size that occur when a lithium atom reacts with a fluorine atom to form a LiF unit.

Figure 8.9 shows the radii of ions derived from the familiar elements, arranged according to elements' positions in the periodic table. We can see parallel trends between atomic radii and ionic radii. For example, from top to bottom both the atomic radius and the ionic radius increase within a group. For ions derived from elements in different groups, a size comparison is meaningful only if the ions are isoelectronic. If we examine isoelectronic ions, we find that cations are smaller than anions. For example, Na^+ is smaller than F^-. Both ions have the same number of electrons, but Na ($Z = 11$) has more protons than F ($Z = 9$). The larger effective nuclear charge of Na^+ results in a smaller radius.

Focusing on isoelectronic cations, we see that the radii of *tripositive ions* (ions that bear three positive charges) are smaller than those of *dipositive ions* (ions that

Interactivity: Ionic Radii
Online Learning Center,
Interactives

Interactivity: Attraction
of Nucleus
Online Learning Center,
Interactives

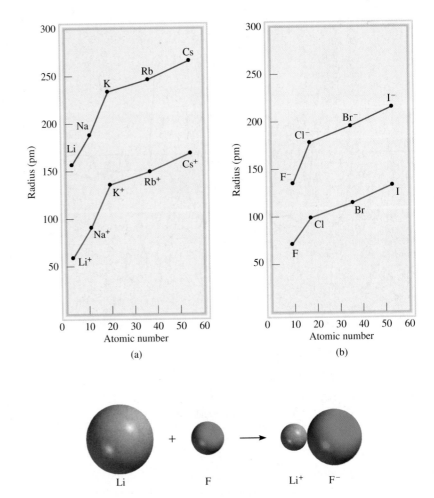

Figure 8.7 *Comparison of atomic radii with ionic radii. (a) Alkali metals and alkali metal cations. (b) Halogens and halide ions.*

Figure 8.8 *Changes in the sizes of Li and F when they react to form LiF.*

bear two positive charges), which in turn are smaller than *unipositive ions* (ions that bear one positive charge). This trend is nicely illustrated by the sizes of three isoelectronic ions in the third period: Al^{3+}, Mg^{2+}, and Na^+ (see Figure 8.9). The Al^{3+} ion has the same number of electrons as Mg^{2+}, but it has one more proton. Thus the electron cloud in Al^{3+} is pulled inward more than that in Mg^{2+}. The smaller radius of Mg^{2+} compared with that of Na^+ can be similarly explained. Turning to isoelectronic anions, we find that the radius increases as we go from ions with uninegative charge $(-)$ to those with dinegative charge $(2-)$, and so on. Thus the oxide ion is larger than the fluoride ion because oxygen has one fewer proton than fluorine; the electron cloud is spread out more in O^{2-}.

Example 8.3

For each of the following pairs, indicate which one of the two species is larger: (a) N^{3-} or F^-; (b) Mg^{2+} or Ca^{2+}; (c) Fe^{2+} or Fe^{3+}.

Strategy In comparing ionic radii, it is useful to classify the ions into three categories: (1) isoelectronic ions, (2) ions that carry the same charges and are generated from atoms

(Continued)

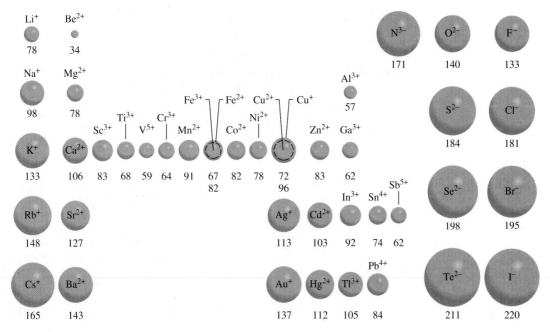

Figure 8.9 *The radii (in picometers) of ions of familiar elements arranged according to the elements' positions in the periodic table.*

of the same periodic group, and (3) ions carry different charges but are generated from the same atom. In case (1), ions carrying a greater negative charge are always larger; in case (2), ions from atoms having a greater atomic number are always larger; in case (3), ions having a smaller positive charge are always larger.

Solution (a) N^{3-} and F^- are isoelectronic anions, both containing 10 electrons. Because N^{3-} has only seven protons and F^- has nine, the smaller attraction exerted by the nucleus on the electrons results in a larger N^{3-} ion.

(b) Both Mg and Ca belong to Group 2A (the alkaline earth metals). Thus Ca^{2+} ion is larger than Mg^{2+} because Ca's valence electrons are in a larger shell ($n = 4$) than are Mg's ($n = 3$).

(c) Both ions have the same nuclear charge, but Fe^{2+} has one more electron (24 electrons compared to 23 electrons for Fe^{3+}) and hence greater electron-electron repulsion. The radius of Fe^{2+} is larger.

Similar problems: 8.43, 8.45.

Practice Exercise Select the smaller ion in each of the following pairs: (a) K^+, Li^+; (b) Au^+, Au^{3+}; (c) P^{3-}, N^{3-}.

Variation of Physical Properties Across a Period and Within a Group

From left to right across a period there is a transition from metals to metalloids to nonmetals. Consider the third-period elements from sodium to argon (Figure 8.10). Sodium, the first element in the third period, is a very reactive metal, whereas chlorine, the second-to-last element of that period, is a very reactive nonmetal. In between, the elements show a gradual transition from metallic properties to nonmetallic properties. Sodium, magnesium, and aluminum all have extensive three-dimensional atomic networks, which are held together by forces characteristic of the metallic state. Silicon is a metalloid; it has a giant three-dimensional structure in which the Si atoms are held together very strongly. Starting with phosphorus, the

Figure 8.10 *The third-period elements. The photograph of argon, which is a colorless, odorless gas, shows the color emitted by the gas from a discharge tube.*

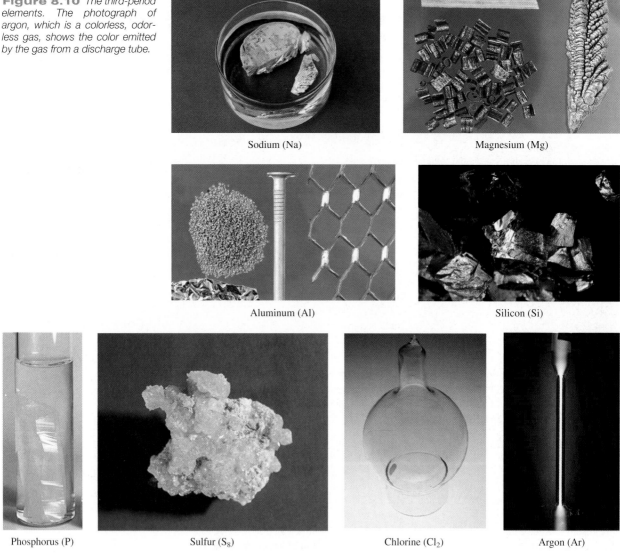

Sodium (Na)

Magnesium (Mg)

Aluminum (Al)

Silicon (Si)

Phosphorus (P)

Sulfur (S_8)

Chlorine (Cl_2)

Argon (Ar)

elements exist in simple, discrete molecular units (P_4, S_8, Cl_2, and Ar) that have low melting points and boiling points.

Within a periodic group the physical properties vary more predictably, especially if the elements are in the same physical state. For example, the melting points of argon and xenon are $-189.2°C$ and $-111.9°C$, respectively. We can estimate the melting point of the intermediate element krypton by taking the average of these two values as follows:

$$\text{melting point of Kr} = \frac{[(-189.2°C) + (-111.9°C)]}{2} = -150.6°C$$

This value is quite close to the actual melting point of $-156.6°C$.

The Chemistry in Action essay on p. 319 illustrates one interesting application of periodic group properties.

CHEMISTRY IN ACTION

The Third Liquid Element?

Of the 113 known elements, 11 are gases under atmospheric conditions. Six of these are the Group 8A elements (the noble gases He, Ne, Ar, Kr, Xe, and Rn), and the other five are hydrogen (H_2), nitrogen (N_2), oxygen (O_2), fluorine (F_2), and chlorine (Cl_2). Curiously, only two elements are liquids at 25°C: mercury (Hg) and bromine (Br_2).

We do not know the properties of all the known elements because some of them have never been prepared in quantities large enough for investigation. In these cases we must rely on periodic trends to predict their properties. What are the chances, then, of discovering a third liquid element?

Let us look at francium (Fr), the last member of Group 1A, to see if it might be a liquid at 25°C. All of francium's isotopes are radioactive. The most stable isotope is francium-223, which has a half-life of 21 minutes. (*Half-life* is the time it takes for one-half of the nuclei in any given amount of a radioactive substance to disintegrate.) This short half-life means that only very small traces of francium could possibly exist on Earth. And although it is feasible to prepare francium in the laboratory, no weighable quantity of the element has been prepared or isolated. Thus we know very little about francium's physical and chemical properties. Yet we can use the group periodic trends to predict some of those properties.

Take francium's melting point as an example. The plot shows how the melting points of the alkali metals vary with atomic

number. From lithium to sodium, the melting point drops 81.4°; from sodium to potassium, 34.6°; from potassium to rubidium, 24°; from rubidium to cesium, 11°. On the basis of this trend, we can predict that the change from cesium to francium would be about 5°. If so, the melting point of francium would be about 25°C, which would make it a liquid under atmospheric conditions.

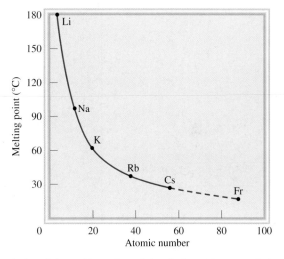

A plot of the melting points of the alkali metals versus their atomic numbers. By extrapolation, the melting point of francium should be 23°C.

8.4 Ionization Energy

Not only is there a correlation between electron configuration and physical properties, but a close correlation also exists between electron configuration (a microscopic property) and chemical behavior (a macroscopic property). As we will see throughout this book, the chemical properties of any atom are determined by the configuration of the atom's valence electrons. The stability of these outermost electrons is reflected directly in the atom's ionization energies. *Ionization energy* is *the minimum energy (in kJ/mol) required to remove an electron from a gaseous atom in its ground state*. In other words, ionization energy is the amount of energy in kilojoules needed to strip 1 mole of electrons from 1 mole of gaseous atoms. Gaseous atoms are specified in this definition because an atom in the gas phase is virtually uninfluenced by its neighbors and so there are no intermolecular forces (that is, forces between molecules) to take into account when measuring ionization energy.

The magnitude of ionization energy is a measure of how "tightly" the electron is held in the atom. The higher the ionization energy, the more difficult it is to remove the electron. For a many-electron atom, the amount of energy required to remove the first electron from the atom in its ground state,

Interactivity: Ionization Energy
Online Learning Center, Interactives

$$\text{energy} + X(g) \longrightarrow X^+(g) + e^-$$
(8.1)

TABLE 8.2

		The Ionization Energies (kJ/mol) of the First 20 Elements					
Z	Element	First	Second	Third	Fourth	Fifth	Sixth
1	H	1,312					
2	He	2,373	5,251				
3	Li	520	7,300	11,815			
4	Be	899	1,757	14,850	21,005		
5	B	801	2,430	3,660	25,000	32,820	
6	C	1,086	2,350	4,620	6,220	38,000	47,261
7	N	1,400	2,860	4,580	7,500	9,400	53,000
8	O	1,314	3,390	5,300	7,470	11,000	13,000
9	F	1,680	3,370	6,050	8,400	11,000	15,200
10	Ne	2,080	3,950	6,120	9,370	12,200	15,000
11	Na	495.9	4,560	6,900	9,540	13,400	16,600
12	Mg	738.1	1,450	7,730	10,500	13,600	18,000
13	Al	577.9	1,820	2,750	11,600	14,800	18,400
14	Si	786.3	1,580	3,230	4,360	16,000	20,000
15	P	1,012	1,904	2,910	4,960	6,240	21,000
16	S	999.5	2,250	3,360	4,660	6,990	8,500
17	Cl	1,251	2,297	3,820	5,160	6,540	9,300
18	Ar	1,521	2,666	3,900	5,770	7,240	8,800
19	K	418.7	3,052	4,410	5,900	8,000	9,600
20	Ca	589.5	1,145	4,900	6,500	8,100	11,000

is called the *first ionization energy* (I_1). In Equation (8.1), X represents an atom of any element and e^- is an electron. The second ionization energy (I_2) and the third ionization energy (I_3) are shown in the following equations:

$$\text{energy} + X^+(g) \longrightarrow X^{2+}(g) + e^- \quad \text{second ionization}$$
$$\text{energy} + X^{2+}(g) \longrightarrow X^{3+}(g) + e^- \quad \text{third ionization}$$

The pattern continues for the removal of subsequent electrons.

When an electron is removed from an atom, the repulsion among the remaining electrons decreases. Because the nuclear charge remains constant, more energy is needed to remove another electron from the positively charged ion. Thus, ionization energies always increase in the following order:

$$I_1 < I_2 < I_3 < \cdots$$

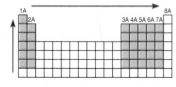

The increase in first ionization energy from left to right across a period and from bottom to top in a group for representative elements.

Table 8.2 lists the ionization energies of the first 20 elements. Ionization is always an endothermic process. By convention, energy absorbed by atoms (or ions) in the ionization process has a positive value. Thus ionization energies are all positive quantities. Figure 8.11 shows the variation of the first ionization energy with atomic number. The plot clearly exhibits the periodicity in the stability of the most loosely held electron. Note that, apart from small irregularities, the first ionization energies of elements in a period increase with increasing atomic number. This trend is due to the increase in effective nuclear charge from left to right (as in the case of atomic radii variation). A larger effective nuclear charge means a more tightly held outer electron, and hence

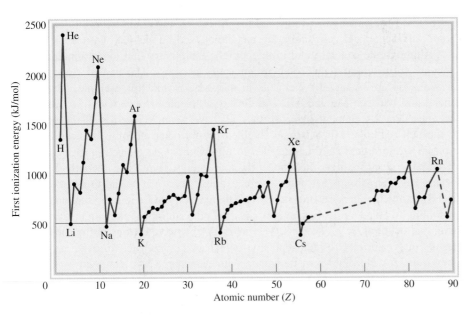

a higher first ionization energy. A notable feature of Figure 8.11 is the peaks, which correspond to the noble gases. The high ionization energies of the noble gases, stemming from their stable ground-state electron configurations, account for the fact that most of them are chemically unreactive. In fact, helium ($1s^2$) has the highest first ionization energy of all the elements.

At the bottom of the graph in Figure 8.11 are the Group 1A elements (the alkali metals) which have the lowest first ionization energies. Each of these metals has one valence electron (the outermost electron configuration is ns^1), which is effectively shielded by the completely filled inner shells. Consequently, it is energetically easy to remove an electron from the atom of an alkali metal to form a unipositive ion (Li^+, Na^+, K^+, . . .). Significantly, the electron configurations of these cations are isoelectronic with those noble gases just preceding them in the periodic table.

The Group 2A elements (the alkaline earth metals) have higher first ionization energies than the alkali metals do. The alkaline earth metals have two valence electrons (the outermost electron configuration is ns^2). Because these two s electrons do not shield each other well, the effective nuclear charge for an alkaline earth metal atom is larger than that for the preceding alkali metal. Most alkaline earth compounds contain dipositive ions (Mg^{2+}, Ca^{2+}, Sr^{2+}, Ba^{2+}). The Be^{2+} ion is isoelectronic with Li^+ and with He, Mg^{2+} is isoelectronic with Na^+ and with Ne, and so on.

As Figure 8.11 shows, metals have relatively low ionization energies compared to nonmetals. The ionization energies of the metalloids generally fall between those of metals and nonmetals. The difference in ionization energies suggests why metals always form cations and nonmetals form anions in ionic compounds. (The only important nonmetallic cation is the ammonium ion, NH_4^+.) For a given group, ionization energy decreases with increasing atomic number (that is, as we move down the group). Elements in the same group have similar outer electron configurations. However, as the principal quantum number n increases, so does the average distance of a valence electron from the nucleus. A greater separation between the electron and the nucleus means a weaker attraction, so that it becomes increasingly easier to remove the first electron as we go from element to element down a group. Thus the metallic character of the elements within a group increases from top to bottom. This trend is particularly noticeable for elements in Groups 3A to 7A. For example, in Group 4A, carbon is a nonmetal, silicon and germanium are metalloids, and tin and lead are metals.

Although the general trend in the periodic table is for first ionization energies to increase from left to right, some irregularities do exist. The first exception occurs between Group 2A and 3A elements in the same period (for example, between Be and B and between Mg and Al). The Group 3A elements have lower first ionization energies than 2A elements because they all have a single electron in the outermost p subshell (ns^2np^1), which is well shielded by the inner electrons and the ns^2 electrons. Therefore, less energy is needed to remove a single p electron than to remove a paired s electron from the same principal energy level. The second irregularity occurs between Groups 5A and 6A (for example, between N and O and between P and S). In the Group 5A elements (ns^2np^3) the p electrons are in three separate orbitals according to Hund's rule. In Group 6A (ns^2np^4) the additional electron must be paired with one of the three p electrons. The proximity of two electrons in the same orbital results in greater electrostatic repulsion, which makes it easier to ionize an atom of the Group 6A element, even though the nuclear charge has increased by one unit. Thus the ionization energies for Group 6A elements are lower than those for Group 5A elements in the same period.

Example 8.4 compares the ionization energies of some elements.

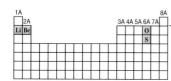

Example 8.4

(a) Which atom should have a smaller first ionization energy: oxygen or sulfur? (b) Which atom should have a higher second ionization energy: lithium or beryllium?

Strategy (a) First ionization energy decreases as we go down a group because the outermost electron is farther away from the nucleus and feels less attraction. (b) Removal of the outermost electron requires less energy if it is shielded by a filled inner shell.

Solution (a) Oxygen and sulfur are members of Group 6A. They have the same valence electron configuration (ns^2np^4), but the $3p$ electron in sulfur is farther from the nucleus and experiences less nuclear attraction than the $2p$ electron in oxygen. Thus, we predict that sulfur should have a smaller first ionization energy.

(b) The electron configurations of Li and Be are $1s^22s^1$ and $1s^22s^2$, respectively. The second ionization energy is the minimum energy required to remove an electron from a gaseous unipositive ion in its ground state. For the second ionization process we write

$$\text{Li}^+(g) \longrightarrow \text{Li}^{2+}(g) + e^-$$
$$\qquad 1s^2 \qquad\qquad 1s^1$$
$$\text{Be}^+(g) \longrightarrow \text{Be}^{2+}(g) + e^-$$
$$\quad 1s^22s^1 \qquad\qquad 1s^2$$

Because $1s$ electrons shield $2s$ electrons much more effectively than they shield each other, we predict that it should be easier to remove a $2s$ electron from Be^+ than to remove a $1s$ electron from Li^+.

Check Compare your result with the data shown in Table 8.2. In (a), is your prediction consistent with the fact that the metallic character of the elements increases as we move down a periodic group? In (b), does your prediction account for the fact that alkali metals form $+1$ ions while alkaline earth metals form $+2$ ions?

Similar problem: 8.55.

Practice Exercise (a) Which of the following atoms should have a larger first ionization energy: N or P? (b) Which of the following atoms should have a smaller second ionization energy: Na or Mg?

8.5 Electron Affinity

Another property that greatly influences the chemical behavior of atoms is their ability to accept one or more electrons. This property is called **electron affinity,** which is *the negative of the energy change that occurs when an electron is accepted by an atom in the gaseous state to form an anion.*

$$X(g) + e^- \longrightarrow X^-(g) \tag{8.2}$$

Consider the process in which a gaseous fluorine atom accepts an electron:

$$F(g) + e^- \longrightarrow F^-(g) \qquad \Delta H = -328 \text{ kJ/mol}$$

The electron affinity of fluorine is therefore assigned a value of +328 kJ/mol. The more positive is the electron affinity of an element, the greater is the affinity of an atom of the element to accept an electron. Another way of viewing electron affinity is to think of it as the energy that must be supplied to remove an electron from the anion. For fluorine, we write

$$F^-(g) \longrightarrow F(g) + e^- \qquad \Delta H = +328 \text{ kJ/mol}$$

Thus a large positive electron affinity means that the negative ion is very stable (that is, the atom has a great tendency to accept an electron), just as a high ionization energy of an atom means that the electron in the atom is very stable.

Experimentally, electron affinity is determined by removing the additional electron from an anion. In contrast to ionization energies, however, electron affinities are difficult to measure because the anions of many elements are unstable. Table 8.3 shows the electron affinities of some representative elements and the noble gases, and Figure 8.12 plots the electron affinities of the first 56 elements versus atomic number. The overall trend is an increase in the tendency to accept electrons (electron affinity values become more positive) from left to right across a period. The electron

Electron affinity is positive if the reaction is exothermic and negative if the reaction is endothermic.

TABLE 8.3 Electron Affinities (kJ/mol) of Some Representative Elements and the Noble Gases*

1A	2A	3A	4A	5A	6A	7A	8A
H							He
73							<0
Li	Be	B	C	N	O	F	Ne
60	≤0	27	122	0	141	328	<0
Na	Mg	Al	Si	P	S	Cl	Ar
53	≤0	44	134	72	200	349	<0
K	Ca	Ga	Ge	As	Se	Br	Kr
48	2.4	29	118	77	195	325	<0
Rb	Sr	In	Sn	Sb	Te	I	Xe
47	4.7	29	121	101	190	295	<0
Cs	Ba	Tl	Pb	Bi	Po	At	Rn
45	14	30	110	110	?	?	<0

* The electron affinities of the noble gases, Be, and Mg have not been determined experimentally, but are believed to be close to zero or negative.

Figure 8.12 *A plot of electron affinity against atomic number for the first 56 elements.*

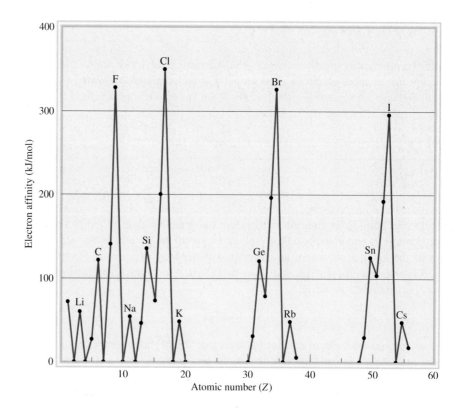

affinities of metals are generally lower than those of nonmetals. The values vary little within a given group. The halogens (Group 7A) have the highest electron affinity values. This is not surprising when we realize that by accepting an electron, each halogen atom assumes the stable electron configuration of the noble gas immediately to its right. For example, the electron configuration of F^- is $1s^2 2s^2 2p^6$, or [Ne]; for Cl^- it is $[Ne]3s^2 3p^6$ or [Ar]; and so on. Calculations show that the noble gases all have electron affinities of less than zero. Thus the anions of these gases, if formed, would be inherently unstable.

The electron affinity of oxygen has a positive value (141 kJ/mol), which means that the process

$$O(g) + e^- \longrightarrow O^-(g) \qquad \Delta H = -141 \text{ kJ/mol}$$

is favorable (exothermic). On the other hand, the electron affinity of the O^- ion is highly negative (-780 kJ/mol), which means the process

$$O^-(g) + e^- \longrightarrow O^{2-}(g) \qquad \Delta H = 780 \text{ kJ/mol}$$

is endothermic even though the O^{2-} ion is isoelectronic with the noble gas Ne. This process is unfavorable in the gas phase because the resulting increase in electron-electron repulsion outweighs the stability gained by achieving a noble gas configuration. However, note that O^{2-} is common in ionic compounds (for example, Li_2O and MgO); in solids, the O^{2-} ion is stabilized by the neighboring cations. We will study the stability of ionic compounds in Chapter 9.

Example 8.5 shows why the alkaline earth metals do not have a great tendency to accept electrons.

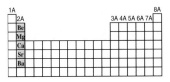

Example 8.5

Why are the electron affinities of the alkaline earth metals, shown in Table 8.3, either negative or small positive values?

Strategy What are the electron configurations of alkaline earth metals? Would the added electron to such an atom be held strongly by the nucleus?

Solution The valence electron configuration of the alkaline earth metals is ns^2, where n is the highest principal quantum number. For the process

$$\underset{ns^2}{M(g)} + e^- \longrightarrow \underset{ns^2 np^1}{M^-(g)}$$

where M denotes a member of the Group 2A family, the extra electron must enter the np subshell, which is effectively shielded by the two ns electrons (the ns electrons are more penetrating than the np electrons) and the inner electrons. Consequently, alkaline earth metals have little tendency to pick up an extra electron.

Similar problem: 8.62.

Practice Exercise Is it likely that Ar will form the anion Ar^-?

8.6 Variation in Chemical Properties of the Representative Elements

Ionization energy and electron affinity help chemists understand the types of reactions that elements undergo and the nature of the elements' compounds. On a conceptual level, these two measures are related in a simple way: Ionization energy indexes the attraction of an atom for its own electrons, whereas electron affinity expresses the attraction of an atom for an additional electron from some other source. Together they give us insight into the general attraction of an atom for electrons. With these concepts we can survey the chemical behavior of the elements systematically, paying particular attention to the relationship between chemical properties and electron configuration.

We have seen that the metallic character of the elements *decreases* from left to right across a period and *increases* from top to bottom within a group. On the basis of these trends and the knowledge that metals usually have low ionization energies while nonmetals usually have high electron affinities, we can frequently predict the outcome of a reaction involving some of these elements.

General Trends in Chemical Properties

Before we study the elements in individual groups, let us look at some overall trends. We have said that elements in the same group resemble one another in chemical behavior because they have similar outer electron configurations. This statement, although correct in the general sense, must be applied with caution. Chemists have long known that the first member of each group (the element in the second period from lithium to fluorine) differs from the rest of the members of the same group. Lithium, for example, exhibits many, but not all, of the properties characteristic of the alkali metals. Similarly, beryllium is a somewhat atypical member of Group 2A, and so on. The difference can be attributed to the unusually small size of the first element in each group (see Figure 8.5).

Another trend in the chemical behavior of the representative elements is the diagonal relationship. *Diagonal relationships* are *similarities between pairs of elements*

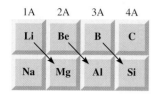

Figure 8.13 *Diagonal relationships in the periodic table.*

in different groups and periods of the periodic table. Specifically, the first three members of the second period (Li, Be, and B) exhibit many similarities to those elements located diagonally below them in the periodic table (Figure 8.13). The reason for this phenomenon is the closeness of the charge densities of their cations. (*Charge density* is the charge of an ion divided by its volume.) Cations with comparable charge densities react similarly with anions and therefore form the same type of compounds. Thus the chemistry of lithium resembles that of magnesium in some ways; the same holds for beryllium and aluminum and for boron and silicon. Each of these pairs is said to exhibit a diagonal relationship. We will see a number of examples of this relationship later.

Bear in mind that a comparison of the properties of elements in the same group is most valid if we are dealing with elements of the same type with respect to their metallic character. This guideline applies to the elements in Groups 1A and 2A, which are all metals, and to the elements in Groups 7A and 8A, which are all nonmetals. In Groups 3A through 6A, where the elements change either from nonmetals to metals or from nonmetals to metalloids, it is natural to expect greater variation in chemical properties even though the members of the same group have similar outer electron configurations.

Now let us take a closer look at the chemical properties of the representative elements and the noble gases. (We will consider the chemistry of the transition metals in Chapter 22.)

Hydrogen $(1s^1)$ There is no totally suitable position for hydrogen in the periodic table. Traditionally hydrogen is shown in Group 1A, but it really could be a class by itself. Like the alkali metals, it has a single s valence electron and forms a unipositive ion (H^+), which is hydrated in solution. On the other hand, hydrogen also forms the hydride ion (H^-) in ionic compounds such as NaH and CaH_2. In this respect, hydrogen resembles the halogens, all of which form uninegative ions (F^-, Cl^-, Br^-, and I^-) in ionic compounds. Ionic hydrides react with water to produce hydrogen gas and the corresponding metal hydroxides:

$$2NaH(s) + 2H_2O(l) \longrightarrow 2NaOH(aq) + H_2(g)$$
$$CaH_2(s) + 2H_2O(l) \longrightarrow Ca(OH)_2(s) + 2H_2(g)$$

Of course, the most important compound of hydrogen is water, which forms when hydrogen burns in air:

$$2H_2(g) + O_2(g) \longrightarrow 2H_2O(l)$$

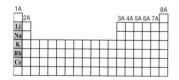

Group 1A Elements $(ns^1, n \geq 2)$ Figure 8.14 shows the Group 1A elements, the alkali metals. All of these elements have low ionization energies and therefore a great tendency to lose the single valence electron. In fact, in the vast majority of their compounds they are unipositive ions. These metals are so reactive that they are never found in the pure state in nature. They react with water to produce hydrogen gas and the corresponding metal hydroxide:

$$2M(s) + 2H_2O(l) \longrightarrow 2MOH(aq) + H_2(g)$$

where M denotes an alkali metal. When exposed to air, they gradually lose their shiny appearance as they combine with oxygen gas to form oxides. Lithium forms lithium oxide (containing the O^{2-} ion):

$$4Li(s) + O_2(g) \longrightarrow 2Li_2O(s)$$

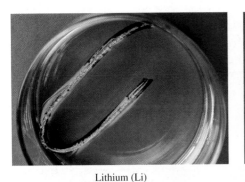

Lithium (Li)   Sodium (Na)

Figure 8.14 *The Group 1A elements: the alkali metals. Francium (not shown) is radioactive.*

Potassium (K)   Rubidium (Rb)   Cesium (Cs)

The other alkali metals all form oxides and *peroxides* (containing the O_2^{2-} ion). For example,

$$2Na(s) + O_2(g) \longrightarrow Na_2O_2(s)$$

Potassium, rubidium, and cesium also form *superoxides* (containing the O_2^- ion):

$$K(s) + O_2(g) \longrightarrow KO_2(s)$$

The reason that different types of oxides are formed when alkali metals react with oxygen has to do with the stability of the oxides in the solid state. Because these oxides are all ionic compounds, their stability depends on how strongly the cations and anions attract one another. Lithium tends to form predominantly lithium oxide because this compound is more stable than lithium peroxide. The formation of other alkali metal oxides can be explained similarly.

Group 2A Elements ($ns^2, n \geq 2$) Figure 8.15 shows the Group 2A elements. As a group, the alkaline earth metals are somewhat less reactive than the alkali metals. Both the first and the second ionization energies decrease from beryllium to barium. Thus the tendency is to form M^{2+} ions (where M denotes an alkaline earth metal atom), and hence the metallic character increases from top to bottom. Most beryllium compounds (BeH_2 and beryllium halides, such as $BeCl_2$) and some magnesium compounds (MgH_2, for example) are molecular rather than ionic in nature.

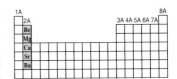

The reactivities of alkaline earth metals with water vary quite markedly. Beryllium does not react with water; magnesium reacts slowly with steam; calcium, strontium, and barium are reactive enough to attack cold water:

$$Ba(s) + 2H_2O(l) \longrightarrow Ba(OH)_2(aq) + H_2(g)$$

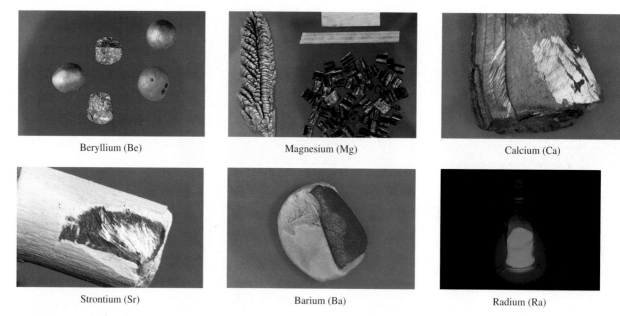

Beryllium (Be)   Magnesium (Mg)   Calcium (Ca)

Strontium (Sr)   Barium (Ba)   Radium (Ra)

Figure 8.15 *The Group 2A elements: the alkaline earth metals.*

The reactivities of the alkaline earth metals toward oxygen also increase from Be to Ba. Beryllium and magnesium form oxides (BeO and MgO) only at elevated temperatures, whereas CaO, SrO, and BaO form at room temperature.

Magnesium reacts with acids in aqueous solution, liberating hydrogen gas:

$$Mg(s) + 2H^+(aq) \longrightarrow Mg^{2+}(aq) + H_2(g)$$

Calcium, strontium, and barium also react with aqueous acid solutions to produce hydrogen gas. However, because these metals also attack water, two different reactions will occur simultaneously.

The chemical properties of calcium and strontium provide an interesting example of periodic group similarity. Strontium-90, a radioactive isotope, is a major product of an atomic bomb explosion. If an atomic bomb is exploded in the atmosphere, the strontium-90 formed will eventually settle on land and water, and it will reach our bodies via a relatively short food chain. For example, if cows eat contaminated grass and drink contaminated water, they will pass along strontium-90 in their milk. Because calcium and strontium are chemically similar, Sr^{2+} ions can replace Ca^{2+} ions in our bones. Constant exposure of the body to the high-energy radiation emitted by the strontium-90 isotopes can lead to anemia, leukemia, and other chronic illnesses.

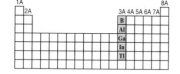

Group 3A Elements $(ns^2np^1, n \geq 2)$ The first member of Group 3A, boron, is a metalloid; the rest are metals (Figure 8.16). Boron does not form binary ionic compounds and is unreactive toward oxygen gas and water. The next element, aluminum, readily forms aluminum oxide when exposed to air:

$$4Al(s) + 3O_2(g) \longrightarrow 2Al_2O_3(s)$$

Aluminum that has a protective coating of aluminum oxide is less reactive than elemental aluminum. Aluminum forms only tripositive ions. It reacts with hydrochloric acid as follows:

$$2Al(s) + 6H^+(aq) \longrightarrow 2Al^{3+}(aq) + 3H_2(g)$$

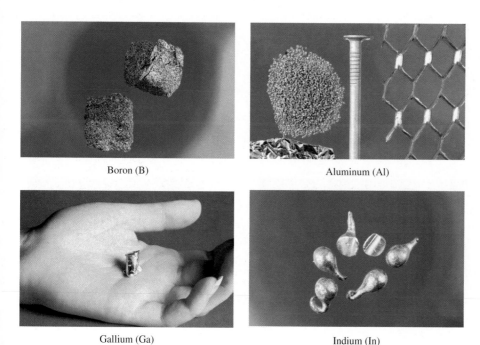

Boron (B)

Aluminum (Al)

Gallium (Ga)

Indium (In)

The other Group 3A metallic elements form both unipositive and tripositive ions. Moving down the group, we find that the unipositive ion becomes more stable than the tripositive ion.

The metallic elements in Group 3A also form many molecular compounds. For example, aluminum reacts with hydrogen to form AlH_3, which resembles BeH_2 in its properties. (Here is an example of the diagonal relationship.) Thus, from left to right across the periodic table, we are seeing a gradual shift from metallic to nonmetallic character in the representative elements.

Group 4A Elements $(ns^2np^2, n \geq 2)$ The first member of Group 4A, carbon, is a nonmetal, and the next two members, silicon and germanium, are metalloids (Figure 8.17). The metallic elements of this group, tin and lead, do not react with water, but they do react with acids (hydrochloric acid, for example) to liberate hydrogen gas:

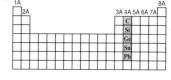

$$Sn(s) + 2H^+(aq) \longrightarrow Sn^{2+}(aq) + H_2(g)$$
$$Pb(s) + 2H^+(aq) \longrightarrow Pb^{2+}(aq) + H_2(g)$$

The Group 4A elements form compounds in both the +2 and +4 oxidation states. For carbon and silicon, the +4 oxidation state is the more stable one. For example, CO_2 is more stable than CO, and SiO_2 is a stable compound, but SiO does not exist under normal conditions. As we move down the group, however, the trend in stability is reversed. In tin compounds the +4 oxidation state is only slightly more stable than the +2 oxidation state. In lead compounds the +2 oxidation state is unquestionably the more stable one. The outer electron configuration of lead is $6s^26p^2$, and lead tends to lose only the $6p$ electrons (to form Pb^{2+}) rather than both the $6p$ and $6s$ electrons (to form Pb^{4+}).

Group 5A Elements $(ns^2np^3, n \geq 2)$ In Group 5A, nitrogen and phosphorus are nonmetals, arsenic and antimony are metalloids, and bismuth is a metal (Figure 8.18). Thus we expect a greater variation in properties within the group.

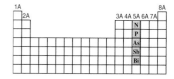

Carbon (graphite)   Carbon (diamond)   Silicon (Si)

Germanium (Ge)   Tin (Sn)   Lead (Pb)

Figure 8.17 *The Group 4A elements.*

Elemental nitrogen is a diatomic gas (N_2). It forms a number of oxides (NO, N_2O, NO_2, N_2O_4, and N_2O_5), of which only N_2O_5 is a solid; the others are gases. Nitrogen has a tendency to accept three electrons to form the nitride ion, N^{3-} (thus achieving the electron configuration $1s^2 2s^2 2p^6$, which is isoelectronic with neon). Most metallic nitrides (Li_3N and Mg_3N_2, for example) are ionic compounds. Phosphorus exists as P_4 molecules. It forms two solid oxides with the formulas P_4O_6 and P_4O_{10}. The important oxoacids HNO_3 and H_3PO_4 are formed when the following oxides react with water:

$$N_2O_5(s) + H_2O(l) \longrightarrow 2HNO_3(aq)$$
$$P_4O_{10}(s) + 6H_2O(l) \longrightarrow 4H_3PO_4(aq)$$

Arsenic, antimony, and bismuth have extensive three-dimensional structures. Bismuth is a far less reactive metal than those in the preceding groups.

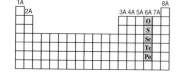

Group 6A Elements ($ns^2 np^4$, $n \geq 2$) The first three members of Group 6A (oxygen, sulfur, and selenium) are nonmetals, and the last two (tellurium and polonium) are metalloids (Figure 8.19). Oxygen is a diatomic gas; elemental sulfur and selenium have the molecular formulas S_8 and Se_8, respectively; tellurium and polonium have more extensive three-dimensional structures. (Polonium is a radioactive element that is difficult to study in the laboratory.) Oxygen has a tendency to accept two electrons to form the oxide ion (O^{2-}) in many ionic compounds. Sulfur, selenium, and tellurium also form dinegative anions (S^{2-}, Se^{2-}, and Te^{2-}). The elements in this group (especially oxygen) form a large number of molecular compounds with nonmetals. The important compounds of sulfur are SO_2, SO_3, and H_2S. Sulfuric acid is formed when sulfur trioxide reacts with water:

$$SO_3(g) + H_2O(l) \longrightarrow H_2SO_4(aq)$$

Nitrogen (N$_2$)

White and red phosphorus (P)

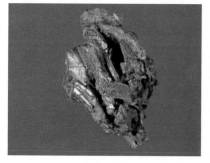

Arsenic (As)

Antimony (Sb)

Bismuth (Bi)

Sulfur (S$_8$)

Selenium (Se$_8$)

Tellurium (Te)

Figure 8.19 *The Group 6A elements sulfur, selenium, and tellurium. Molecular oxygen is a colorless, odorless gas. Polonium (not shown) is radioactive.*

Figure 8.20 *The Group 7A elements chlorine, bromine, and iodine. Fluorine is a greenish-yellow gas that attacks ordinary glassware. Astatine is radioactive.*

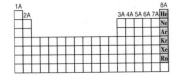

Group 7A Elements (ns^2np^5, $n \geq 2$) All the halogens are nonmetals with the general formula X_2, where X denotes a halogen element (Figure 8.20). Because of their great reactivity, the halogens are never found in the elemental form in nature. (The last member of Group 7A, astatine, is a radioactive element. Little is known about its properties.) Fluorine is so reactive that it attacks water to generate oxygen:

$$2F_2(g) + 2H_2O(l) \longrightarrow 4HF(aq) + O_2(g)$$

Actually the reaction between molecular fluorine and water is quite complex; the products formed depend on reaction conditions. The reaction shown above is one of several possible changes.

The halogens have high ionization energies and large positive electron affinities. Anions derived from the halogens (F^-, Cl^-, Br^-, and I^-) are called *halides*. They are isoelectronic with the noble gases immediately to their right in the periodic table. For example, F^- is isoelectronic with Ne, Cl^- with Ar, and so on. The vast majority of the alkali metal halides and alkaline earth metal halides are ionic compounds. The halogens also form many molecular compounds among themselves (such as ICl and BrF_3) and with nonmetallic elements in other groups (such as NF_3, PCl_5, and SF_6). The halogens react with hydrogen to form hydrogen halides:

$$H_2(g) + X_2(g) \longrightarrow 2HX(g)$$

When this reaction involves fluorine, it is explosive, but it becomes less and less violent as we substitute chlorine, bromine, and iodine. The hydrogen halides dissolve in water to form hydrohalic acids. Hydrofluoric acid (HF) is a weak acid (that is, it is a weak electrolyte), but the other hydrohalic acids (HCl, HBr, and HI) are all strong acids (strong electrolytes).

Group 8A Elements (ns^2np^6, $n \geq 2$) All noble gases exist as monatomic species (Figure 8.21). Their atoms have completely filled outer ns and np subshells, which give them great stability. (Helium is $1s^2$.) The Group 8A ionization energies are among the highest of all elements, and these gases have no tendency to accept extra electrons. For years these elements were called inert gases, and rightly so. Until 1963 no one had been able to prepare a compound containing any of these elements. The British chemist Neil Bartlett[†] shattered chemists' long-held views of these elements

[†]Neil Bartlett (1932–   ). English chemist. Bartlett's work is mainly in the preparation and study of compounds with unusual oxidation states and in solid-state chemistry.

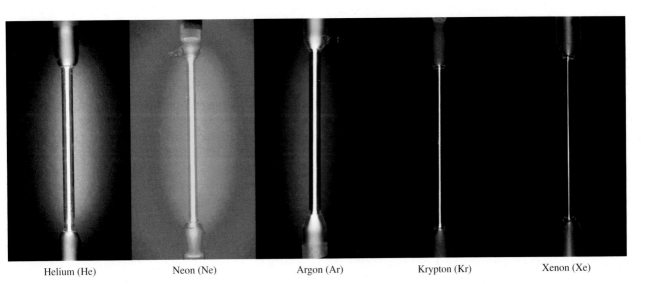

| Helium (He) | Neon (Ne) | Argon (Ar) | Krypton (Kr) | Xenon (Xe) |

Figure 8.21 *All noble gases are colorless and odorless. These pictures show the colors emitted by the gases from a discharge tube.*

when he exposed xenon to platinum hexafluoride, a strong oxidizing agent, and brought about the following reaction (Figure 8.22):

$$Xe(g) + PtF_6(g) \longrightarrow XePtF_6(s)$$

Since then, a number of xenon compounds (XeF_4, XeO_3, XeO_4, $XeOF_4$) and a few krypton compounds (KrF_2, for example) have been prepared (Figure 8.23). Despite the immense interest in the chemistry of the noble gases, however, their compounds do not have any commercial applications, and they are not involved in natural biological processes. No compounds of helium, neon, and argon are known.

In 2000, chemists prepared a compound containing argon (HArF), which is stable only at very low temperatures.

Comparison of Group 1A and Group 1B Elements

When we compare the Group 1A elements (alkali metals) and the Group 1B elements (copper, silver, and gold), we arrive at an interesting conclusion. Although the metals in these two groups have similar outer electron configurations, with one electron in the outermost *s* orbital, their chemical properties are quite different.

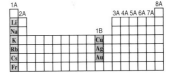

(a)

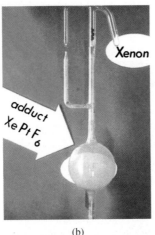
(b)

Figure 8.22 *(a) Xenon gas (colorless) and PtF_6 (red gas) separated from each other. (b) When the two gases are allowed to mix, a yellow-orange solid compound is formed.*

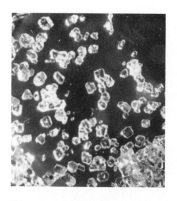

Figure 8.23 *XeF₄ crystals.*

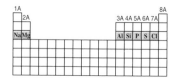

The first ionization energies of Cu, Ag, and Au are 745 kJ/mol, 731 kJ/mol, and 890 kJ/mol, respectively. Because these values are considerably larger than those of the alkali metals (see Table 8.2), the Group 1B elements are much less reactive. The higher ionization energies of the Group 1B elements result from incomplete shielding of the nucleus by the inner *d* electrons (compared with the more effective shielding of the completely filled noble gas cores). Consequently the outer *s* electrons of these elements are more strongly attracted by the nucleus. In fact, copper, silver, and gold are so unreactive that they are usually found in the uncombined state in nature. The inertness and rarity of these metals make them valuable in the manufacture of coins and in jewelry. For this reason, these metals are also called "coinage metals." The difference in chemical properties between the Group 2A elements (the alkaline earth metals) and the Group 2B metals (zinc, cadmium, and mercury) can be explained in a similar way.

Properties of Oxides Across a Period

One way to compare the properties of the representative elements across a period is to examine the properties of a series of similar compounds. Because oxygen combines with almost all elements, we will compare the properties of oxides of the third-period elements to see how metals differ from metalloids and nonmetals. Some elements in the third period (P, S, and Cl) form several types of oxides, but for simplicity we will consider only those oxides in which the elements have the highest oxidation number. Table 8.4 lists a few general characteristics of these oxides. We observed earlier that oxygen has a tendency to form the oxide ion. This tendency is greatly favored when oxygen combines with metals that have low ionization energies, namely, those in Groups 1A and 2A, plus aluminum. Thus Na_2O, MgO, and Al_2O_3 are ionic compounds, as indicated by their high melting points and boiling points. They have extensive three-dimensional structures in which each cation is surrounded by a specific number of anions, and vice versa. As the ionization energies of the elements increase from left to right, so does the molecular nature of the oxides that are formed. Silicon is a metalloid; its oxide (SiO_2) also has a huge three-dimensional network, although no ions are present. The oxides of phosphorus, sulfur, and chlorine are molecular compounds composed of small discrete units. The weak attractions among these molecules result in relatively low melting points and boiling points.

Most oxides can be classified as acidic or basic depending on whether they produce acids or bases when dissolved in water or react as acids or bases in certain processes. Some oxides are **amphoteric,** which means that they *display both acidic and basic properties.* The first two oxides of the third period, Na_2O and MgO, are basic oxides. For example, Na_2O reacts with water to form the base sodium hydroxide:

$$Na_2O(s) + H_2O(l) \longrightarrow 2NaOH(aq)$$

TABLE 8.4

Some Properties of Oxides of the Third-Period Elements

	Na₂O	MgO	Al₂O₃	SiO₂	P₄O₁₀	SO₃	Cl₂O₇
Type of compound	←——— Ionic ———→			←——— Molecular ———→			
Structure	←—— Extensive three-dimensional ——→			←—— Discrete ——→ molecular units			
Melting point (°C)	1275	2800	2045	1610	580	16.8	−91.5
Boiling point (°C)	?	3600	2980	2230	?	44.8	82
Acid-base nature	Basic	Basic	Amphoteric	←————— Acidic ————→			

Magnesium oxide is quite insoluble; it does not react with water to any appreciable extent. However, it does react with acids in a manner that resembles an acid-base reaction:

$$MgO(s) + 2HCl(aq) \longrightarrow MgCl_2(aq) + H_2O(l)$$

Note that the products of this reaction are a salt ($MgCl_2$) and water, the usual products of an acid-base neutralization.

Aluminum oxide is even less soluble than magnesium oxide; it too does not react with water. However, it shows basic properties by reacting with acids:

$$Al_2O_3(s) + 6HCl(aq) \longrightarrow 2AlCl_3(aq) + 3H_2O(l)$$

It also exhibits acidic properties by reacting with bases:

$$Al_2O_3(s) + 2NaOH(aq) + 3H_2O(l) \longrightarrow 2NaAl(OH)_4(aq)$$

Note that this acid-base neutralization produces a salt but no water.

Thus Al_2O_3 is classified as an amphoteric oxide because it has properties of both acids and bases. Other amphoteric oxides are ZnO, BeO, and Bi_2O_3.

Silicon dioxide is insoluble and does not react with water. It has acidic properties, however, because it reacts with very concentrated bases:

$$SiO_2(s) + 2NaOH(aq) \longrightarrow Na_2SiO_3(aq) + H_2O(l)$$

For this reason, concentrated aqueous, strong bases such as $NaOH(aq)$ should not be stored in Pyrex glassware, which is made of SiO_2.

The remaining third-period oxides are acidic. They react with water to form phosphoric acid (H_3PO_4), sulfuric acid (H_2SO_4), and perchloric acid ($HClO_4$):

$$P_4O_{10}(s) + 6H_2O(l) \longrightarrow 4H_3PO_4(aq)$$
$$SO_3(g) + H_2O(l) \longrightarrow H_2SO_4(aq)$$
$$Cl_2O_7(l) + H_2O(l) \longrightarrow 2HClO_4(aq)$$

Certain oxides such as CO and NO are neutral; that is, they do not react with water to produce an acidic or basic solution. In general, oxides containing nonmetallic elements are not basic.

This brief examination of oxides of the third-period elements shows that as the metallic character of the elements decreases from left to right across the period, their oxides change from basic to amphoteric to acidic. Metallic oxides are usually basic, and most oxides of nonmetals are acidic. The intermediate properties of the oxides (as shown by the amphoteric oxides) are exhibited by elements whose positions are intermediate within the period. Note also that because the metallic character of the elements increases from top to bottom within a group of representative elements, we would expect oxides of elements with higher atomic numbers to be more basic than the lighter elements. This is indeed the case.

Example 8.6

Classify the following oxides as acidic, basic, or amphoteric: (a) Rb_2O, (b) BeO, (c) As_2O_5.

Strategy What type of elements form acidic oxides? basic oxides? amphoteric oxides?

Solution (a) Because rubidium is an alkali metal, we would expect Rb_2O to be a basic oxide.

(Continued)

CHEMISTRY IN ACTION

Discovery of the Noble Gases

In the late 1800s John William Strutt, Third Baron of Rayleigh, who was a professor of physics at the Cavendish Laboratory in Cambridge, England, accurately determined the atomic masses of a number of elements, but he obtained a puzzling result with nitrogen. One of his methods of preparing nitrogen was by the thermal decomposition of ammonia:

$$2NH_3(g) \longrightarrow N_2(g) + 3H_2(g)$$

Another method was to start with air and remove from it oxygen, carbon dioxide, and water vapor. Invariably, the nitrogen from air was a little denser (by about 0.5 percent) than the nitrogen from ammonia.

Lord Rayleigh's work caught the attention of Sir William Ramsay, a professor of chemistry at the University College, London. In 1898 Ramsay passed nitrogen, which he had obtained from air by Rayleigh's procedure, over red-hot magnesium to convert it to magnesium nitride:

$$3Mg(s) + N_2(g) \longrightarrow Mg_3N_2(s)$$

After all of the nitrogen had reacted with magnesium, Ramsay was left with an unknown gas that would not combine with anything.

With the help of Sir William Crookes, the inventor of the discharge tube, Ramsay and Lord Rayleigh found that the emission spectrum of the gas did not match any of the known elements. The gas was a new element! They determined its atomic mass to be 39.95 amu and called it argon, which means "the lazy one" in Greek.

Once argon had been discovered, other noble gases were quickly identified. Also in 1898 Ramsay isolated helium from uranium ores (see Chemistry in Action essay on p. 272). From the atomic masses of helium and argon, their lack of chemical reactivity, and what was then known about the periodic table, Ramsay was convinced that there were other unreactive gases and that they were all members of one periodic group. He and his student Morris Travers set out to find the unknown gases. They used a refrigeration machine to first produce liquid air. Applying a technique called *fractional distillation,* they then allowed the liquid air to warm up gradually and collected components that boiled off at different temperatures. In this manner they analyzed and identified three new elements—neon, krypton, and xenon—in only three months. Three new elements in three months is a record that may never be broken!

The discovery of the noble gases helped to complete the periodic table. Their atomic masses suggested that these elements should be placed to the right of the halogens. The apparent discrepancy with the position of argon was resolved by Moseley, as discussed in the chapter.

Finally, the last member of the noble gases, radon, was discovered by the German chemist Frederick Dorn in 1900. A radioactive element and the heaviest elemental gas known, radon's discovery not only completed the Group 8A elements, but also advanced our understanding about the nature of radioactive decay and transmutation of elements.

Lord Rayleigh and Ramsay both won Nobel Prizes in 1904 for the discovery of argon. Lord Rayleigh received the prize in physics and Ramsay's award was in chemistry.

Sir William Ramsay (1852–1916).

(b) Beryllium is an alkaline earth metal. However, because it is the first member of Group 2A, we expect that it may differ somewhat from the other members of the group. In the text we saw that Al_2O_3 is amphoteric. Because beryllium and aluminum exhibit a diagonal relationship, BeO may resemble Al_2O_3 in properties. It turns out that BeO is also an amphoteric oxide.

(c) Because arsenic is a nonmetal, we expect As_2O_5 to be an acidic oxide.

Similar problem: 8.72.

Practice Exercise Classify the following oxides as acidic, basic, or amphoteric: (a) ZnO, (b) P_4O_{10}, (c) CaO.

Summary of Facts and Concepts

1. Nineteenth-century chemists developed the periodic table by arranging elements in the increasing order of their atomic masses. Discrepancies in early versions of the periodic table were resolved by arranging the elements in order of their atomic numbers.
2. Electron configuration determines the properties of an element. The modern periodic table classifies the elements according to their atomic numbers, and thus also by their electron configurations. The configuration of the valence electrons directly affects the properties of the atoms of the representative elements.
3. Periodic variations in the physical properties of the elements reflect differences in atomic structure. The metallic character of elements decreases across a period from metals through the metalloids to nonmetals and increases from top to bottom within a particular group of representative elements.
4. Atomic radius varies periodically with the arrangement of the elements in the periodic table. It decreases from left to right and increases from top to bottom.
5. Ionization energy is a measure of the tendency of an atom to resist the loss of an electron. The higher the ionization energy, the stronger the attraction between the nucleus and an electron. Electron affinity is a measure of the tendency of an atom to gain an electron. The more positive the electron affinity, the greater the tendency for the atom to gain an electron. Metals usually have low ionization energies, and nonmetals usually have high electron affinities.
6. Noble gases are very stable because their outer ns and np subshells are completely filled. The metals among the representative elements (in Groups 1A, 2A, and 3A) tend to lose electrons until their cations become isoelectronic with the noble gases that precede them in the periodic table. The nonmetals in Groups 5A, 6A, and 7A tend to accept electrons until their anions become isoelectronic with the noble gases that follow them in the periodic table.

Key Words

Amphoteric oxide, p. 334
Atomic radius, p. 313
Diagonal relationship, p. 325
Electron affinity, p. 323
Ionic radius, p. 315
Ionization energy, p. 319
Isoelectronic, p. 312
Representative elements, p. 308
Valence electrons, p. 310

Questions and Problems

Development of the Periodic Table
Review Questions

8.1 Briefly describe the significance of Mendeleev's periodic table.

8.2 What is Moseley's contribution to the modern periodic table?

8.3 Describe the general layout of a modern periodic table.

8.4 What is the most important relationship among elements in the same group in the periodic table?

Periodic Classification of the Elements
Review Questions

8.5 Which of the following elements are metals, nonmetals, or metalloids? As, Xe, Fe, Li, B, Cl, Ba, P, I, Si.

8.6 Compare the physical and chemical properties of metals and nonmetals.

8.7 Draw a rough sketch of a periodic table (no details are required). Indicate regions where metals, nonmetals, and metalloids are located.

8.8 What is a representative element? Give names and symbols of four representative elements.

8.9 Without referring to a periodic table, write the name and give the symbol for an element in each of the following groups: 1A, 2A, 3A, 4A, 5A, 6A, 7A, 8A, transition metals.

8.10 Indicate whether the following elements exist as atomic species, molecular species, or extensive three-dimensional structures in their most stable states at 25°C and 1 atm and write the molecular or empirical formula for each one: phosphorus, iodine, magnesium, neon, carbon, sulfur, cesium, and oxygen.

8.11 You are given a dark shiny solid and asked to determine whether it is iodine or a metallic element. Suggest a nondestructive test that would enable you to arrive at the correct answer.

8.12 What are valence electrons? For representative elements, the number of valence electrons of an element is equal to its group number. Show that this is true for the following elements: Al, Sr, K, Br, P, S, C.

8.13 Write the outer electron configurations for the (a) alkali metals, (b) alkaline earth metals, (c) halogens, (d) noble gases.

8.14 Use the first-row transition metals (Sc to Cu) as an example to illustrate the characteristics of the electron configurations of transition metals.

8.15 How does the electron configuration of ions derived from representative elements give them stability?

8.16 What do we mean when we say that two ions or an atom and an ion are isoelectronic?

8.17 What is wrong with the statement "The atoms of element X are isoelectronic with the atoms of element Y"?

8.18 Give three examples of first-row transition metal (Sc to Cu) ions whose electron configurations are represented by the argon core.

Problems

8.19 In the periodic table, the element hydrogen is sometimes grouped with the alkali metals (as in this book) and sometimes with the halogens. Explain why hydrogen can resemble the Group 1A and the Group 7A elements.

8.20 A neutral atom of a certain element has 17 electrons. Without consulting a periodic table, (a) write the ground-state electron configuration of the element, (b) classify the element, (c) determine whether this element is diamagnetic or paramagnetic.

8.21 Group the following electron configurations in pairs that would represent similar chemical properties of their atoms:
(a) $1s^22s^22p^63s^2$
(b) $1s^22s^22p^3$
(c) $1s^22s^22p^63s^23p^64s^23d^{10}4p^6$
(d) $1s^22s^2$
(e) $1s^22s^22p^6$
(f) $1s^22s^22p^63s^23p^3$

8.22 Group the following electron configurations in pairs that would represent similar chemical properties of their atoms:
(a) $1s^22s^22p^5$
(b) $1s^22s^1$
(c) $1s^22s^22p^6$
(d) $1s^22s^22p^63s^23p^5$
(e) $1s^22s^22p^63s^23p^64s^1$
(f) $1s^22s^22p^63s^23p^64s^23d^{10}4p^6$

8.23 Without referring to a periodic table, write the electron configuration of elements with the following atomic numbers: (a) 9, (b) 20, (c) 26, (d) 33. Classify the elements.

8.24 Specify the group of the periodic table in which each of the following elements is found: (a) $[Ne]3s^1$, (b) $[Ne]3s^23p^3$, (c) $[Ne]3s^23p^6$, (d) $[Ar]4s^23d^8$.

8.25 A M^{2+} ion derived from a metal in the first transition metal series has four electrons in the $3d$ subshell. What element might M be?

8.26 A metal ion with a net $+3$ charge has five electrons in the $3d$ subshell. Identify the metal.

8.27 Write the ground-state electron configurations of the following ions: (a) Li^+, (b) H^-, (c) N^{3-}, (d) F^-, (e) S^{2-}, (f) Al^{3+}, (g) Se^{2-}, (h) Br^-, (i) Rb^+, (j) Sr^{2+}, (k) Sn^{2+}, (l) Te^{2-}, (m) Ba^{2+}, (n) Pb^{2+}, (o) In^{3+}, (p) Tl^+, (q) Tl^{3+}.

8.28 Write the ground-state electron configurations of the following ions, which play important roles in biochemical processes in our bodies: (a) Na^+, (b) Mg^{2+}, (c) Cl^-, (d) K^+, (e) Ca^{2+}, (f) Fe^{2+}, (g) Cu^{2+}, (h) Zn^{2+}.

8.29 Write the ground-state electron configurations of the following transition metal ions: (a) Sc^{3+}, (b) Ti^{4+}, (c) V^{5+}, (d) Cr^{3+}, (e) Mn^{2+}, (f) Fe^{2+}, (g) Fe^{3+}, (h) Co^{2+}, (i) Ni^{2+}, (j) Cu^+, (k) Cu^{2+}, (l) Ag^+, (m) Au^+, (n) Au^{3+}, (o) Pt^{2+}.

8.30 Name the ions with +3 charges that have the following electron configurations: (a) $[Ar]3d^3$, (b) $[Ar]$, (c) $[Kr]4d^6$, (d) $[Xe]4f^{14}5d^6$.

8.31 Which of the following species are isoelectronic with each other? C, Cl^-, Mn^{2+}, B^-, Ar, Zn, Fe^{3+}, Ge^{2+}.

8.32 Group the species that are isoelectronic: Be^{2+}, F^-, Fe^{2+}, N^{3-}, He, S^{2-}, Co^{3+}, Ar.

Periodic Variation in Physical Properties
Review Questions

8.33 Define atomic radius. Does the size of an atom have a precise meaning?

8.34 How does atomic radius change (a) from left to right across a period and (b) from top to bottom in a group?

8.35 Define ionic radius. How does the size of an atom change when it is converted to (a) an anion and (b) a cation?

8.36 Explain why, for isoelectronic ions, the anions are larger than the cations.

Problems

8.37 On the basis of their positions in the periodic table, select the atom with the larger atomic radius in each of the following pairs: (a) Na, Cs; (b) Be, Ba; (c) N, Sb; (d) F, Br; (e) Ne, Xe.

8.38 Arrange the following atoms in order of decreasing atomic radius: Na, Al, P, Cl, Mg.

8.39 Which is the largest atom in Group 4A?

8.40 Which is the smallest atom in Group 7A?

8.41 Why is the radius of the lithium atom considerably larger than the radius of the hydrogen atom?

8.42 Use the second period of the periodic table as an example to show that the size of atoms decreases as we move from left to right. Explain the trend.

8.43 Indicate which one of the two species in each of the following pairs is smaller: (a) Cl or Cl^-; (b) Na or Na^+; (c) O^{2-} or S^{2-}; (d) Mg^{2+} or Al^{3+}; (e) Au^+ or Au^{3+}.

8.44 List the following ions in order of increasing ionic radius: N^{3-}, Na^+, F^-, Mg^{2+}, O^{2-}.

8.45 Explain which of the following cations is larger, and why: Cu^+ or Cu^{2+}.

8.46 Explain which of the following anions is larger, and why: Se^{2-} or Te^{2-}.

8.47 Give the physical states (gas, liquid, or solid) of the representative elements in the fourth period (K, Ca, Ga, Ge, As, Se, Br) at 1 atm and 25°C.

8.48 The boiling points of neon and krypton are −245.9°C and −152.9°C, respectively. Using these data, estimate the boiling point of argon.

Ionization Energy
Review Questions

8.49 Define ionization energy. Ionization energy measurements are usually made when atoms are in the gaseous state. Why? Why is the second ionization energy always greater than the first ionization energy for any element?

8.50 Sketch the outline of the periodic table and show group and period trends in the first ionization energy of the elements. What types of elements have the highest ionization energies and what types the lowest ionization energies?

Problems

8.51 Arrange the following in order of increasing first ionization energy: Na, Cl, Al, S, and Cs.

8.52 Arrange the following in order of increasing first ionization energy: F, K, P, Ca, and Ne.

8.53 Use the third period of the periodic table as an example to illustrate the change in first ionization energies of the elements as we move from left to right. Explain the trend.

8.54 In general, ionization energy increases from left to right across a given period. Aluminum, however, has a lower ionization energy than magnesium. Explain.

8.55 The first and second ionization energies of K are 419 kJ/mol and 3052 kJ/mol, and those of Ca are 590 kJ/mol and 1145 kJ/mol, respectively. Compare their values and comment on the differences.

8.56 Two atoms have the electron configurations $1s^22s^22p^6$ and $1s^22s^22p^63s^1$. The first ionization energy of one is 2080 kJ/mol, and that of the other is 496 kJ/mol. Match each ionization energy with one of the given electron configurations. Justify your choice.

8.57 A hydrogenlike ion is an ion containing only one electron. The energies of the electron in a hydrogenlike ion are given by

$$E_n = -(2.18 \times 10^{-18} \text{ J})Z^2\left(\frac{1}{n^2}\right)$$

where n is the principal quantum number and Z is the atomic number of the element. Calculate the ionization energy (in kJ/mol) of the He^+ ion.

8.58 Plasma is a state of matter consisting of positive gaseous ions and electrons. In the plasma state, a mercury atom could be stripped of its 80 electrons and therefore would exist as Hg^{80+}. Use the equation in Problem 8.57 to calculate the energy required for the last ionization step, that is,

$$Hg^{79+}(g) \longrightarrow Hg^{80+}(g) + e^-$$

Electron Affinity
Review Questions

8.59 (a) Define electron affinity. (b) Electron affinity measurements are made with gaseous atoms. Why? (c) Ionization energy is always a positive quantity, whereas electron affinity may be either positive or negative. Explain.

8.60 Explain the trends in electron affinity from aluminum to chlorine (see Table 8.3).

Problems

8.61 Arrange the elements in each of the following groups in increasing order of the most positive electron affinity: (a) Li, Na, K; (b) F, Cl, Br, I.

8.62 Specify which of the following elements you would expect to have the greatest electron affinity: He, K, Co, S, Cl.

8.63 Considering their electron affinities, do you think it is possible for the alkali metals to form an anion like M^-, where M represents an alkali metal?

8.64 Explain why alkali metals have a greater affinity for electrons than alkaline earth metals.

Variation in Chemical Properties of the Representative Elements
Review Questions

8.65 What is meant by the diagonal relationship? Name two pairs of elements that show this relationship.

8.66 Which elements are more likely to form acidic oxides? Basic oxides? Amphoteric oxides?

Problems

8.67 Use the alkali metals and alkaline earth metals as examples to show how we can predict the chemical properties of elements simply from their electron configurations.

8.68 Based on your knowledge of the chemistry of the alkali metals, predict some of the chemical properties of francium, the last member of the group.

8.69 As a group, the noble gases are very stable chemically (only Kr and Xe are known to form compounds). Why?

8.70 Why are Group 1B elements more stable than Group 1A elements even though they seem to have the same outer electron configuration, ns^1, where n is the principal quantum number of the outermost shell?

8.71 How do the chemical properties of oxides change from left to right across a period? From top to bottom within a particular group?

8.72 Write balanced equations for the reactions between each of the following oxides and water: (a) Li_2O, (b) CaO, (c) SO_3.

8.73 Write formulas for and name the binary hydrogen compounds of the second-period elements (Li to F).

Describe how the physical and chemical properties of these compounds change from left to right across the period.

8.74 Which oxide is more basic, MgO or BaO? Why?

Additional Problems

8.75 State whether each of the following properties of the representative elements generally increases or decreases (a) from left to right across a period and (b) from top to bottom within a group: metallic character, atomic size, ionization energy, acidity of oxides.

8.76 With reference to the periodic table, name (a) a halogen element in the fourth period, (b) an element similar to phosphorus in chemical properties, (c) the most reactive metal in the fifth period, (d) an element that has an atomic number smaller than 20 and is similar to strontium.

8.77 Write equations representing the following processes:
(a) The electron affinity of S^-.
(b) The third ionization energy of titanium.
(c) The electron affinity of Mg^{2+}.
(d) The ionization energy of O^{2-}.

8.78 Arrange the following isoelectronic species in order of (a) increasing ionic radius and (b) increasing ionization energy: O^{2-}, F^-, Na^+, Mg^{2+}.

8.79 Write the empirical (or molecular) formulas of compounds that the elements in the third period (sodium to chlorine) should form with (a) molecular oxygen and (b) molecular chlorine. In each case indicate whether you would expect the compound to be ionic or molecular in character.

8.80 Element M is a shiny and highly reactive metal (melting point 63°C), and element X is a highly reactive nonmetal (melting point −7.2°C). They react to form a compound with the empirical formula MX, a colorless, brittle white solid that melts at 734°C. When dissolved in water or when in the molten state, the substance conducts electricity. When chlorine gas is bubbled through an aqueous solution containing MX, a reddish-brown liquid appears and Cl^- ions are formed. From these observations, identify M and X. (You may need to consult a handbook of chemistry for the melting-point values.)

8.81 Match each of the elements on the right with its description on the left:
(a) A dark-red liquid   Calcium (Ca)
(b) A colorless gas that burns   Gold (Au)
    in oxygen gas   Hydrogen (H_2)
(c) A reactive metal that attacks   Argon (Ar)
    water   Bromine (Br_2)
(d) A shiny metal that is used in
    jewelry
(e) An inert gas

8.82 Arrange the following species in isoelectronic pairs: O^+, Ar, S^{2-}, Ne, Zn, Cs^+, N^{3-}, As^{3+}, N, Xe.

8.83 In which of the following are the species written in decreasing order by size of radius? (a) Be, Mg, Ba, (b) N^{3-}, O^{2-}, F^-, (c) Tl^{3+}, Tl^{2+}, Tl^+.

8.84 Which of the following properties show a clear periodic variation? (a) first ionization energy, (b) molar mass of the elements, (c) number of isotopes of an element, (d) atomic radius.

8.85 When carbon dioxide is bubbled through a clear calcium hydroxide solution, the solution appears milky. Write an equation for the reaction and explain how this reaction illustrates that CO_2 is an acidic oxide.

8.86 You are given four substances: a fuming red liquid, a dark metallic-looking solid, a pale-yellow gas, and a yellow-green gas that attacks glass. You are told that these substances are the first four members of Group 7A, the halogens. Name each one.

8.87 For each pair of elements listed below, give three properties that show their chemical similarity: (a) sodium and potassium and (b) chlorine and bromine.

8.88 Name the element that forms compounds, under appropriate conditions, with every other element in the periodic table except He, Ne, and Ar.

8.89 Explain why the first electron affinity of sulfur is 200 kJ/mol but the second electron affinity is −649 kJ/mol.

8.90 The H^- ion and the He atom have two 1s electrons each. Which of the two species is larger? Explain.

8.91 Predict the products of the following oxides with water: Na_2O, BaO, CO_2, N_2O_5, P_4O_{10}, SO_3. Write an equation for each of the reactions. Specify whether the oxides are acidic, basic, or amphoteric.

8.92 Write the formulas and names of the oxides of the second-period elements (Li to N). Identify the oxides as acidic, basic, or amphoteric.

8.93 State whether each of the following elements is a gas, a liquid, or a solid under atmospheric conditions. Also state whether it exists in the elemental form as atoms, as molecules, or as a three-dimensional network: Mg, Cl, Si, Kr, O, I, Hg, Br.

8.94 What factors account for the unique nature of hydrogen?

8.95 The air in a manned spacecraft or submarine needs to be purified of exhaled carbon dioxide. Write equations for the reactions between carbon dioxide and (a) lithium oxide (Li_2O), (b) sodium peroxide (Na_2O_2), and (c) potassium superoxide (KO_2).

8.96 The formula for calculating the energies of an electron in a hydrogenlike ion is given in Problem 8.57. This equation cannot be applied to many-electron atoms. One way to modify it for the more complex atoms is to replace Z with $(Z - \sigma)$, where Z is the atomic number and σ is a positive dimensionless quantity called the shielding constant. Consider the helium atom as an example. The physical significance of σ is that it represents the extent of shielding that the two 1s electrons exert on each other. Thus the quantity $(Z - \sigma)$ is appropriately called the "effective nuclear charge." Calculate the value of σ if the first ionization energy of helium is 3.94×10^{-18} J per atom. (Ignore the minus sign in the given equation in your calculation.)

8.97 Why do noble gases have negative electron affinity values?

8.98 The atomic radius of K is 216 pm and that of K^+ is 133 pm. Calculate the percent decrease in volume that occurs when $K(g)$ is converted to $K^+(g)$. [The volume of a sphere is $(\frac{4}{3}) \pi r^3$, where r is the radius of the sphere.]

8.99 The atomic radius of F is 72 pm and that of F^- is 136 pm. Calculate the percent increase in volume that occurs when $F(g)$ is converted to $F^-(g)$. (See Problem 8.98 for the volume of a sphere.)

8.100 A technique called photoelectron spectroscopy is used to measure the ionization energy of atoms. A sample is irradiated with UV light, and electrons are ejected from the valence shell. The kinetic energies of the ejected electrons are measured. Because the energy of the UV photon and the kinetic energy of the ejected electron are known, we can write

$$hv = IE + \tfrac{1}{2}mu^2$$

where v is the frequency of the UV light, and m and u are the mass and velocity of the electron, respectively. In one experiment the kinetic energy of the ejected electron from potassium is found to be 5.34×10^{-19} J using a UV source of wavelength 162 nm. Calculate the ionization energy of potassium. How can you be sure that this ionization energy corresponds to the electron in the valence shell (that is, the most loosely held electron)?

8.101 Referring to the Chemistry in Action essay on p. 336, answer the following questions. (a) Why did it take so long to discover the first noble gas (argon) on Earth? (b) Once argon had been discovered, why did it take relatively little time to discover the rest of the noble gases? (c) Why was helium not isolated by the fractional distillation of liquid air?

8.102 The energy needed for the following process is 1.96×10^4 kJ/mol:

$$Li(g) \longrightarrow Li^{3+}(g) + 3e^-$$

If the first ionization energy of lithium is 520 kJ/mol, calculate the second ionization energy of lithium, that is, the energy required for the process

$$Li^+(g) \longrightarrow Li^{2+}(g) + e^-$$

(Hint: You need the equation in Problem 8.57.)

8.103 An element X reacts with hydrogen gas at 200°C to form compound Y. When Y is heated to a higher temperature, it decomposes to the element X and hydrogen gas in the ratio of 559 mL of H_2 (measured at STP) for 1.00 g of X reacted. X also combines with chlorine to form a compound Z, which contains 63.89 percent by mass of chlorine. Deduce the identity of X.

8.104 A student is given samples of three elements, X, Y, and Z, which could be an alkali metal, a member of Group 4A, and a member of Group 5A. She makes the following observations: Element X has a metallic luster and conducts electricity. It reacts slowly with hydrochloric acid to produce hydrogen gas. Element Y is a light-yellow solid that does not conduct electricity. Element Z has a metallic luster and conducts electricity. When exposed to air, it slowly forms a white powder. A solution of the white powder in water is basic. What can you conclude about the elements from these observations?

8.105 Using the following boiling-point data and the procedure in the Chemistry in Action essay on p. 319, estimate the boiling point of francium:

metal	Li	Na	K	Rb	Cs
boiling point (°C)	1347	882.9	774	688	678.4

8.106 What is the electron affinity of the Na^+ ion?

8.107 The ionization energies of sodium (in kJ/mol), starting with the first and ending with the eleventh, are 495.9, 4560, 6900, 9540, 13,400, 16,600, 20,120, 25,490, 28,930, 141,360, 170,000. Plot the log of ionization energy (y axis) versus the number of ionization (x axis); for example, log 495.9 is plotted versus 1 (labeled I_1, the first ionization energy), log 4560 is plotted versus 2 (labeled I_2, the second ionization energy), and so on. (a) Label I_1 through I_{11} with the electrons in orbitals such as $1s$, $2s$, $2p$, and $3s$. (b) What can you deduce about electron shells from the breaks in the curve?

8.108 Experimentally, the electron affinity of an element can be determined by using a laser light to ionize the anion of the element in the gas phase:

$$X^-(g) + h\nu \longrightarrow X(g) + e^-$$

Referring to Table 8.3, calculate the photon wavelength (in nanometers) corresponding to the electron affinity for chlorine. In what region of the electromagnetic spectrum does this wavelength fall?

8.109 Explain, in terms of their electron configurations, why Fe^{2+} is more easily oxidized to Fe^{3+} than Mn^{2+} to Mn^{3+}.

8.110 The standard enthalpy of atomization of an element is the energy required to convert one mole of an element in its most stable form at 25°C to one mole of monatomic gas. Given that the standard enthalpy of atomization for sodium is 108.4 kJ/mol, calculate the energy in kilojoules required to convert one mole of sodium metal at 25°C to one mole of gaseous Na^+ ions.

8.111 Write the formulas and names of the hydrides of the following second-period elements: Li, C, N, O, F. Predict their reactions with water.

8.112 Based on knowledge of the electronic configuration of titanium, state which of the following compounds of titanium is unlikely to exist: K_3TiF_6, $K_2Ti_2O_5$, $TiCl_3$, K_2TiO_4, K_2TiF_6.

8.113 Name an element in Group 1A or Group 2A that is an important constituent of each of the following substances: (a) remedy for acid indigestion, (b) coolant in nuclear reactors, (c) Epsom salt, (d) baking powder, (e) gunpowder, (f) a light alloy, (g) fertilizer that also neutralizes acid rain, (h) cement, and (i) grit for icy roads. You may need to ask your instructor about some of the items.

8.114 In halogen displacement reactions a halogen element can be generated by oxidizing its anions with a halogen element that lies above it in the periodic table. This means that there is no way to prepare elemental fluorine, because it is the first member of Group 7A. Indeed, for years the only way to prepare elemental fluorine was to oxidize F^- ions by electrolytic means. Then, in 1986, a chemist reported that by reacting potassium hexafluoromanganate(IV) (K_2MnF_6) with antimony pentafluoride (SbF_5) at 150°C, he had generated elemental fluorine. Balance the following equation representing the reaction:

$$K_2MnF_6 + SbF_5 \longrightarrow KSbF_6 + MnF_3 + F_2$$

8.115 Write a balanced equation for the preparation of (a) molecular oxygen, (b) ammonia, (c) carbon dioxide, (d) molecular hydrogen, (e) calcium oxide. Indicate the physical state of the reactants and products in each equation.

8.116 Write chemical formulas for oxides of nitrogen with the following oxidation numbers: +1, +2, +3, +4, +5. (*Hint:* There are *two* oxides of nitrogen with +4 oxidation number.)

8.117 Most transition metal ions are colored. For example, a solution of $CuSO_4$ is blue. How would you show that the blue color is due to the hydrated Cu^{2+} ions and not the SO_4^{2-} ions?

8.118 In general, atomic radius and ionization energy have opposite periodic trends. Why?

8.119 Explain why the electron affinity of nitrogen is approximately zero, while the elements on either side, carbon and oxygen, have substantial positive electron affinities.

8.120 Consider the halogens chlorine, bromine, and iodine. The melting point and boiling point of chlorine are −101.0°C and −34.6°C while those of iodine are 113.5°C and 184.4°C, respectively. Thus chlorine is a gas and iodine is a solid under room conditions.

Estimate the melting point and boiling point of bromine. Compare your values with those from a handbook of chemistry.

8.121 While it is possible to determine the second, third, and higher ionization energies of an element, the same cannot usually be done with the electron affinities of an element. Explain.

8.122 The only confirmed compound of radon is radon fluoride, RnF. One reason that it is difficult to study the chemistry of radon is that all isotopes of radon are radioactive so it is dangerous to handle the substance. Can you suggest another reason why there are so few known radon compounds? (*Hint:* Radioactive decays are exothermic processes.)

8.123 Little is known of the chemistry of astatine, the last member of Group 7A. Describe the physical characteristics that you would expect this halogen to have. Predict the products of the reaction between sodium astatide (NaAt) and sulfuric acid. (*Hint:* Sulfuric acid is an oxidizing agent.)

8.124 As discussed in the chapter, the atomic mass of argon is greater than that of potassium. This observation created a problem in the early development of the periodic table because it meant that argon should be placed after potassium. (a) How was this difficulty resolved? (b) From the following data, calculate the average atomic masses of argon and potassium: Ar-36 (35.9675 amu; 0.337 percent), Ar-38 (37.9627 amu; 0.063 percent), Ar-40 (39.9624 amu; 99.60 percent); K-39 (38.9637 amu; 93.258 percent), K-40 (39.9640 amu; 0.0117 percent), K-41 (40.9618 amu; 6.730 percent).

8.125 Calculate the maximum wavelength of light (in nanometers) required to ionize a single sodium atom.

8.126 Predict the atomic number and ground-state electron configuration of the next member of the alkali metals after francium.

8.127 Why do elements that have high ionization energies also have more positive electron affinities? Which group of elements would be an exception to this generalization?

8.128 The first four ionization energies of an element are approximately 738 kJ/mol, 1450 kJ/mol, 7.7×10^3 kJ/mol, and 1.1×10^4 kJ/mol. To which periodic group does this element belong? Why?

8.129 Some chemists think that helium should properly be called "helon." Why? What does the ending in helium (-ium) suggest?

8.130 (a) The formula of the simplest hydrocarbon is CH_4 (methane). Predict the formulas of the simplest compounds formed between hydrogen and the following elements: silicon, germanium, tin, and lead. (b) Sodium hydride (NaH) is an ionic compound. Would you expect rubidium hydride (RbH) to be more or less ionic than NaH? (c) Predict the reaction between radium (Ra) and water. (d) When exposed to air, aluminum forms a tenacious oxide (Al_2O_3) coating that protects the metal from corrosion. Which metal in Group 2A would you expect to exhibit similar properties? Why?

8.131 Match each of the elements on the right with its description on the left:
(a) A pale yellow gas that reacts with water.
(b) A soft metal that reacts with water to produce hydrogen.
(c) A metalloid that is hard and has a high melting point.
(d) A colorless, odorless gas.
(e) A metal that is more reactive than iron, but does not corrode in air.

Nitrogen (N_2)
Boron (B)
Aluminum (Al)
Fluorine (F_2)
Sodium (Na)

8.132 Write an account on the importance of the periodic table. Pay particular attention to the significance of the position of an element in the table and how the position relates to the chemical and physical properties of the element.

8.133 On the same graph, plot the effective nuclear charge (shown in parentheses) and atomic radius (see Figure 8.5) versus atomic number for the second-period elements: Li(1.30), Be(1.95), B(2.60), C(3.25), N(3.90), O(4.55), F(5.20), Ne(5.85). Comment on the trends.

8.134 One allotropic form of an element X is a colorless crystalline solid. The reaction of X with an excess amount of oxygen produces a colorless gas. This gas dissolves in water to yield an acidic solution. Choose one of the following elements that matches X: (a) sulfur, (b) phosphorus, (c) carbon, (d) boron, and (e) silicon.

8.135 When magnesium metal is burned in air, it forms two products A and B. A reacts with water to form a basic solution. B reacts with water to form a similar solution as that of A plus a gas with a pungent odor. Identify A and B and write equations for the reactions. (*Hint:* See Chemistry in Action on p. 336.)

Answers to Practice Exercises

8.1 (a) $1s^22s^22p^63s^23p^64s^2$, (b) it is a representative element, (c) diamagnetic. **8.2** Li > Be > C. **8.3** (a) Li$^+$, (b) Au^{3+}, (c) N^{3-}. **8.4** (a) N, (b) Mg. **8.5** No. **8.6** (a) amphoteric, (b) acidic, (c) basic.

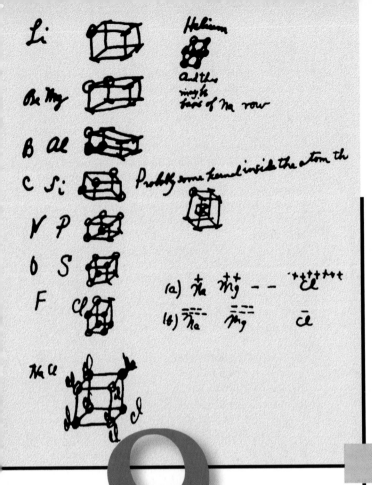

Lewis first sketched his idea about the octet rule on the back of an envelope. The models show water, ammonia, methane, ethylene, and acetylene molecules.

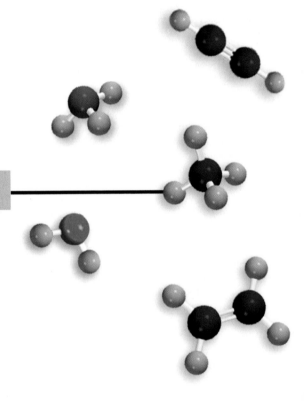

Chemical Bonding I: Basic Concepts

Interactive Activity Summary

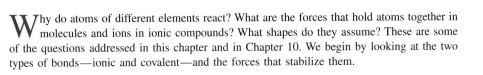

W hy do atoms of different elements react? What are the forces that hold atoms together in molecules and ions in ionic compounds? What shapes do they assume? These are some of the questions addressed in this chapter and in Chapter 10. We begin by looking at the two types of bonds—ionic and covalent—and the forces that stabilize them.

9.1 Lewis Dot Symbols

The development of the periodic table and concept of electron configuration gave chemists a rationale for molecule and compound formation. This explanation, formulated by Gilbert Lewis,[†] is that atoms combine in order to achieve a more stable electron configuration. Maximum stability results when an atom is isoelectronic with a noble gas.

When atoms interact to form a chemical bond, only their outer regions are in contact. For this reason, when we study chemical bonding, we are concerned primarily with the valence electrons of the atoms. To keep track of valence electrons in a chemical reaction, and to make sure that the total number of electrons does not change, chemists use a system of dots devised by Lewis and called Lewis dot symbols. A *Lewis dot symbol consists of the symbol of an element and one dot for each valence electron in an atom of the element.* Figure 9.1 shows the Lewis dot symbols for the representative elements and the noble gases. Note that, except for helium, the number of valence electrons each atom has is the same as the group number of the element. For example, Li is a Group 1A element and has one dot for one valence electron; Be, a Group 2A element, has two valence electrons (two dots); and so on. Elements in the same group have similar outer electron configurations and hence similar Lewis dot symbols. The transition metals, lanthanides, and actinides all have incompletely filled inner shells, and in general, we cannot write simple Lewis dot symbols for them.

In this chapter we will learn to use electron configurations and the periodic table to predict the type of bond atoms will form, as well as the number of bonds an atom of a particular element can form and the stability of the product.

[†]Gilbert Newton Lewis (1875–1946). American chemist. Lewis made many important contributions in the areas of chemical bonding, thermodynamics, acids and bases, and spectroscopy. Despite the significance of Lewis's work, he was never awarded a Nobel Prize.

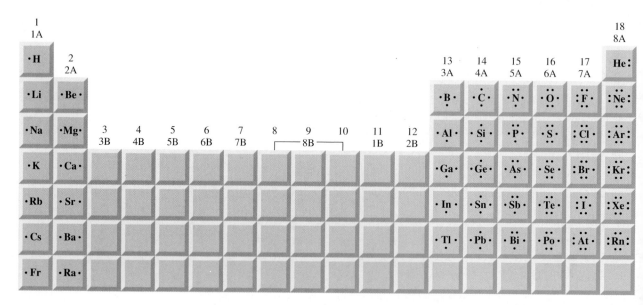

Figure 9.1 *Lewis dot symbols for the representative elements and the noble gases. The number of unpaired dots corresponds to the number of bonds an atom of the element can form in a compound.*

9.2 The Ionic Bond

In Chapter 8 we saw that atoms of elements with low ionization energies tend to form cations, while those with high electron affinities tend to form anions. As a rule, the elements most likely to form cations in ionic compounds are the alkali metals and alkaline earth metals, and the elements most likely to form anions are the halogens and oxygen. Consequently, a wide variety of ionic compounds combine a Group 1A or Group 2A metal with a halogen or oxygen. An **ionic bond** is *the electrostatic force that holds ions together in an ionic compound.* Consider, for example, the reaction between lithium and fluorine to form lithium fluoride, a poisonous white powder used in lowering the melting point of solders and in manufacturing ceramics. The electron configuration of lithium is $1s^2 2s^1$, and that of fluorine is $1s^2 2s^2 2p^5$. When lithium and fluorine atoms come in contact with each other, the outer $2s^1$ valence electron of lithium is transferred to the fluorine atom. Using Lewis dot symbols, we represent the reaction like this:

Interactivity: Ionic Bonds
Online Learning Center,
Interactives

$$\cdot \text{Li} \; + \; :\overset{\cdot\cdot}{\underset{\cdot\cdot}{\text{F}}}\cdot \longrightarrow \text{Li}^+ \; :\overset{\cdot\cdot}{\underset{\cdot\cdot}{\text{F}}}:^- \quad \text{(or LiF)} \tag{9.1}$$
$$1s^2 2s^1 \quad 1s^2 2s^2 2p^5 \qquad 1s^2 \;\; 1s^2 2s^2 2p^6$$

For convenience, imagine that this reaction occurs in separate steps—first the ionization of Li:

$$\cdot \text{Li} \longrightarrow \text{Li}^+ + e^-$$

and then the acceptance of an electron by F:

$$:\overset{\cdot\cdot}{\underset{\cdot\cdot}{\text{F}}}\cdot \; + e^- \longrightarrow :\overset{\cdot\cdot}{\underset{\cdot\cdot}{\text{F}}}:^-$$

Next, imagine the two separate ions joining to form a LiF unit:

$$\text{Li}^+ + :\overset{\cdot\cdot}{\underset{\cdot\cdot}{\text{F}}}:^- \longrightarrow \text{Li}^+ :\overset{\cdot\cdot}{\underset{\cdot\cdot}{\text{F}}}:^-$$

Note that the sum of these three equations is

$$\cdot \text{Li} + :\overset{\cdot\cdot}{\underset{\cdot\cdot}{\text{F}}}\cdot \longrightarrow \text{Li}^+ :\overset{\cdot\cdot}{\underset{\cdot\cdot}{\text{F}}}:^-$$

which is the same as Equation (9.1). The ionic bond in LiF is the electrostatic attraction between the positively charged lithium ion and the negatively charged fluoride ion. The compound itself is electrically neutral.

Many other common reactions lead to the formation of ionic bonds. For instance, calcium burns in oxygen to form calcium oxide:

$$2\text{Ca}(s) + \text{O}_2(g) \longrightarrow 2\text{CaO}(s)$$

Assuming that the diatomic O_2 molecule first splits into separate oxygen atoms (we will look at the energetics of this step later), we can represent the reaction with Lewis symbols:

$$\cdot \text{Ca} \cdot \; + \; \cdot \overset{\cdot\cdot}{\text{O}} \cdot \longrightarrow \text{Ca}^{2+} \; :\overset{\cdot\cdot}{\underset{\cdot\cdot}{\text{O}}}:^{2-}$$
$$[\text{Ar}]4s^2 \quad 1s^2 2s^2 2p^4 \qquad [\text{Ar}] \quad [\text{Ne}]$$

There is a transfer of two electrons from the calcium atom to the oxygen atom. Note that the resulting calcium ion (Ca^{2+}) has the argon electron configuration, the oxide ion (O^{2-}) is isoelectronic with neon, and the compound (CaO) is electrically neutral.

Lithium fluoride. Industrially, LiF (like most other ionic compounds) is obtained by purifying minerals containing the compound.

We normally write the empirical formulas of ionic compounds without showing the charges. The + and − are shown here to emphasize the transfer of electrons.

In many cases, the cation and the anion in a compound do not carry the same charges. For instance, when lithium burns in air to form lithium oxide (Li_2O), the balanced equation is

$$4Li(s) + O_2(g) \longrightarrow 2Li_2O(s)$$

Using Lewis dot symbols, we write

$$2 \cdot Li + \cdot \ddot{O} \cdot \longrightarrow 2Li^+ \quad :\ddot{O}:^{2-} \text{ (or } Li_2O)$$
$$ 1s^22s^1 \quad 1s^22s^22p^4 \qquad [He] \quad [Ne]$$

In this process, the oxygen atom receives two electrons (one from each of the two lithium atoms) to form the oxide ion. The Li^+ ion is isoelectronic with helium.

When magnesium reacts with nitrogen at elevated temperatures, a white solid compound, magnesium nitride (Mg_3N_2), forms:

$$3Mg(s) + N_2(g) \longrightarrow Mg_3N_2(s)$$

or

$$3 \cdot Mg \cdot + 2 \cdot \ddot{N} \cdot \longrightarrow 3Mg^{2+} \quad 2 :\ddot{N}:^{3-} \text{ (or } Mg_3N_2)$$
$$[Ne]3s^2 \quad 1s^22s^22p^3 \qquad [Ne] \quad\quad [Ne]$$

The reaction involves the transfer of six electrons (two from each Mg atom) to two nitrogen atoms. The resulting magnesium ion (Mg^{2+}) and the nitride ion (N^{3-}) are both isoelectronic with neon. Because there are three $+2$ ions and two -3 ions, the charges balance and the compound is electrically neutral.

In Example 9.1, we apply the Lewis dot symbols to study the formation of an ionic compound.

The mineral corundum (Al_2O_3).

Example 9.1

Use Lewis dot symbols to show the formation of aluminum oxide (Al_2O_3).

Strategy We use electroneutrality as our guide in writing formulas for ionic compounds, that is, the total positive charges on the cations must be equal to the total negative charges on the anions.

Solution According to Figure 9.1, the Lewis dot symbols of Al and O are

$$\cdot Al \cdot \qquad \cdot \ddot{O} \cdot$$

Because aluminum tends to form the cation (Al^{3+}) and oxygen the anion (O^{2-}) in ionic compounds, the transfer of electrons is from Al to O. There are three valence electrons in each Al atom; each O atom needs two electrons to form the O^{2-} ion, which is isoelectronic with neon. Thus the simplest neutralizing ratio of Al^{3+} to O^{2-} is 2:3; two Al^{3+} ions have a total charge of $+6$, and three O^{2-} ions have a total charge of -6. So the empirical formula of aluminum oxide is Al_2O_3, and the reaction is

$$2 \cdot Al \cdot + 3 \cdot \ddot{O} \cdot \longrightarrow 2Al^{3+} \quad 3 :\ddot{O}:^{2-} \text{ (or } Al_2O_3)$$
$$[Ne]3s^23p^1 \quad 1s^22s^22p^4 \qquad [Ne] \quad\quad [Ne]$$

(Continued)

Check Make sure that the number of valence electrons (24) is the same on both sides of the equation. Are the subscripts in Al_2O_3 reduced to the smallest possible whole numbers?

Similar problems: 9.17, 9.18.

Practice Exercise Use Lewis dot symbols to represent the formation of barium hydride.

9.3 Lattice Energy of Ionic Compounds

We can predict which elements are likely to form ionic compounds based on ionization energy and electron affinity, but how do we evaluate the stability of an ionic compound? Ionization energy and electron affinity are defined for processes occurring in the gas phase, but at 1 atm and 25°C all ionic compounds are solids. The solid state is a very different environment because each cation in a solid is surrounded by a specific number of anions, and vice versa. Thus the overall stability of a solid ionic compound depends on the interactions of all these ions and not merely on the interaction of a single cation with a single anion. A quantitative measure of the stability of any ionic solid is its **lattice energy,** defined as *the energy required to completely separate one mole of a solid ionic compound into gaseous ions.*

The Born-Haber Cycle for Determining Lattice Energies

Lattice energy cannot be measured directly. However, if we know the structure and composition of an ionic compound, we can calculate the compound's lattice energy by using **Coulomb's**[†] **law,** which states that *the potential energy (E) between two ions is directly proportional to the product of their charges and inversely proportional to the distance of separation between them.* For a single Li^+ ion and a single F^- ion separated by distance r, the potential energy of the system is given by

$$E \propto \frac{Q_{Li^+}Q_{F^-}}{r}$$
$$= k\frac{Q_{Li^+}Q_{F^-}}{r} \tag{9.2}$$

Because energy = force × distance, Coulomb's law can also be stated as
$$F = k\frac{Q_{Li} \cdot Q_F}{r^2}$$
where F is the force between the ions.

where Q_{Li^+} and Q_{F^-} are the charges on the Li^+ and F^- ions and k is the proportionality constant. Because Q_{Li^+} is positive and Q_{F^-} is negative, E is a negative quantity, and the formation of an ionic bond from Li^+ and F^- is an exothermic process. Consequently, energy must be supplied to reverse the process (in other words, the lattice energy of LiF is positive), and so a bonded pair of Li^+ and F^- ions is more stable than separate Li^+ and F^- ions.

We can also determine lattice energy indirectly, by assuming that the formation of an ionic compound takes place in a series of steps. This procedure, known as the **Born-Haber cycle,** *relates lattice energies of ionic compounds to ionization energies, electron affinities, and other atomic and molecular properties.* It is based on Hess's

[†]Charles Augustin de Coulomb (1736–1806). French physicist. Coulomb did research in electricity and magnetism and applied Newton's inverse square law to electricity. He also invented a torsion balance.

law (see Section 6.6). Developed by Max Born[‡] and Fritz Haber,[§] the Born-Haber cycle defines the various steps that precede the formation of an ionic solid. We will illustrate its use to find the lattice energy of lithium fluoride.

Consider the reaction between lithium and fluorine:

$$Li(s) + \tfrac{1}{2}F_2(g) \longrightarrow LiF(s)$$

Interactivity: Born-Haber Cycle for Lithium Fluoride Online Learning Center, Interactives

The standard enthalpy change for this reaction is -594.1 kJ/mol. (Because the reactants and product are in their standard states, that is, at 1 atm, the enthalpy change is also the standard enthalpy of formation for LiF.) Keeping in mind that the sum of enthalpy changes for the steps is equal to the enthalpy change for the overall reaction (-594.1 kJ/mol), we can trace the formation of LiF from its elements through five separate steps. The process may not occur exactly this way, but this pathway enables us to analyze the energy changes of ionic compound formation, with the help of Hess's law.

1. Convert solid lithium to lithium vapor (the direct conversion of a solid to a gas is called sublimation):

$$Li(s) \longrightarrow Li(g) \qquad\qquad \Delta H_1^\circ = 155.2 \text{ kJ/mol}$$

The energy of sublimation for lithium is 155.2 kJ/mol.

2. Dissociate $\tfrac{1}{2}$ mole of F_2 gas into separate gaseous F atoms:

The F atoms in a F_2 molecule are held together by a covalent bond. The energy required to break this bond is called the bond energy (Section 9.10).

$$\tfrac{1}{2}F_2(g) \longrightarrow F(g) \qquad\qquad \Delta H_2^\circ = 75.3 \text{ kJ/mol}$$

The energy needed to break the bonds in 1 mole of F_2 molecules is 150.6 kJ. Here we are breaking the bonds in half a mole of F_2, so the enthalpy change is 150.6/2, or 75.3, kJ.

3. Ionize 1 mole of gaseous Li atoms (see Table 8.3):

$$Li(g) \longrightarrow Li^+(g) + e^- \qquad\qquad \Delta H_3^\circ = 520 \text{ kJ/mol}$$

This process corresponds to the first ionization of lithium.

4. Add 1 mole of electrons to 1 mole of gaseous F atoms. As discussed on page 323, the energy change for this process is just the opposite of electron affinity (see Table 8.3):

$$F(g) + e^- \longrightarrow F^-(g) \qquad\qquad \Delta H_4^\circ = -328 \text{ kJ/mol}$$

5. Combine 1 mole of gaseous Li^+ and 1 mole of F^- to form 1 mole of solid LiF:

$$Li^+(g) + F^-(g) \longrightarrow LiF(s) \qquad\qquad \Delta H_5^\circ = ?$$

The reverse of step 5,

$$\text{energy} + LiF(s) \longrightarrow Li^+(g) + F^-(g)$$

[‡]Max Born (1882–1970). German physicist. Born was one of the founders of modern physics. His work covered a wide range of topics. He received the Nobel Prize in Physics in 1954 for his interpretation of the wave function for particles.

[§]Fritz Haber (1868–1934). German chemist. Haber's process for synthesizing ammonia from atmospheric nitrogen kept Germany supplied with nitrates for explosives during World War I. He also did work on gas warfare. In 1918 Haber received the Nobel Prize in Chemistry.

defines the lattice energy of LiF. Thus the lattice energy must have the same magnitude as ΔH_5° but an opposite sign. Although we cannot determine ΔH_5° directly, we can calculate its value by the following procedure.

1.	$Li(s) \longrightarrow Li(g)$	$\Delta H_1^{\circ} = 155.2$ kJ/mol
2.	$\frac{1}{2}F_2(g) \longrightarrow F(g)$	$\Delta H_2^{\circ} = 75.3$ kJ/mol
3.	$Li(g) \longrightarrow Li^+(g) + e^-$	$\Delta H_3^{\circ} = 520$ kJ/mol
4.	$F(g) + e^- \longrightarrow F^-(g)$	$\Delta H_4^{\circ} = -328$ kJ/mol
5.	$Li^+(g) + F^-(g) \longrightarrow LiF(s)$	$\Delta H_5^{\circ} = ?$

$$Li(s) + \tfrac{1}{2}F_2(g) \longrightarrow LiF(s) \qquad \Delta H_{\text{overall}}^{\circ} = -594.1 \text{ kJ/mol}$$

According to Hess's law, we can write

$$\Delta H_{\text{overall}}^{\circ} = \Delta H_1^{\circ} + \Delta H_2^{\circ} + \Delta H_3^{\circ} + \Delta H_4^{\circ} + \Delta H_5^{\circ}$$

or

$$-594.1 \text{ kJ/mol} = 155.2 \text{ kJ/mol} + 75.3 \text{ kJ/mol} + 520 \text{ kJ/mol} - 328 \text{ kJ/mol} + \Delta H_5^{\circ}$$

Hence

$$\Delta H_5^{\circ} = -1017 \text{ kJ/mol}$$

and the lattice energy of LiF is $+1017$ kJ/mol.

Figure 9.2 summarizes the Born-Haber cycle for LiF. Steps 1, 2, and 3 all require the input of energy. On the other hand, steps 4 and 5 release energy. Because ΔH_5° is a large negative quantity, the lattice energy of LiF is a large positive quantity, which accounts for the stability of solid LiF. The greater the lattice energy, the more stable the ionic compound. Keep in mind that lattice energy is *always* a positive quantity because the separation of ions in a solid into ions in the gas phase is, by Coulomb's law, an endothermic process.

Table 9.1 lists the lattice energies and the melting points of several common ionic compounds. There is a rough correlation between lattice energy and melting point. The larger the lattice energy, the more stable the solid and the more tightly held the ions. It takes more energy to melt such a solid, and so the solid has a higher melting point than one with a smaller lattice energy. Note that $MgCl_2$, Na_2O, and MgO have

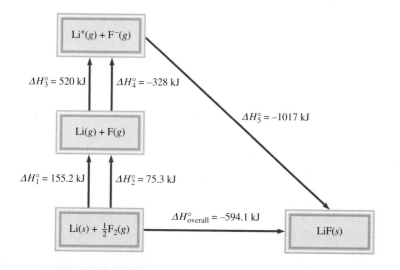

Figure 9.2 *The Born-Haber cycle for the formation of 1 mole of solid LiF.*

TABLE 9.1

Lattice Energies and Melting Points of Some Alkali Metal and Alkaline Earth Metal Halides and Oxides

Compound	Lattice Energy (kJ/mol)	Melting Point (°C)
LiF	1017	845
LiCl	828	610
LiBr	787	550
LiI	732	450
NaCl	788	801
NaBr	736	750
NaI	686	662
KCl	699	772
KBr	689	735
KI	632	680
$MgCl_2$	2527	714
Na_2O	2570	Sub*
MgO	3890	2800

* Na_2O sublimes at 1275°C.

unusually high lattice energies. The first of these ionic compounds has a doubly charged cation (Mg^{2+}) and the second a doubly charged anion (O^{2-}); in the third compound there is an interaction between two doubly charged species (Mg^{2+} and O^{2-}). The coulombic attractions between two doubly charged species, or between a doubly charged ion and a singly charged ion, are much stronger than those between singly charged anions and cations.

Lattice Energy and the Formulas of Ionic Compounds

Because lattice energy is a measure of the stability of ionic compounds, its value can help us explain the formulas of these compounds. Consider magnesium chloride as an example. We have seen that the ionization energy of an element increases rapidly as successive electrons are removed from its atom. For example, the first ionization energy of magnesium is 738 kJ/mol, and the second ionization energy is 1450 kJ/mol, almost twice the first. We might ask why, from the standpoint of energy, magnesium does not prefer to form unipositive ions in its compounds. Why doesn't magnesium chloride have the formula MgCl (containing the Mg^+ ion) rather than $MgCl_2$ (containing the Mg^{2+} ion)? Admittedly, the Mg^{2+} ion has the noble gas configuration [Ne], which represents stability because of its completely filled shells. But the stability gained through the filled shells does not, in fact, outweigh the energy input needed to remove an electron from the Mg^+ ion. The reason the formula is $MgCl_2$ lies in the extra stability gained by the formation of solid magnesium chloride. The lattice energy of $MgCl_2$ is 2527 kJ/mol, which is more than enough to compensate for the energy needed to remove the first two electrons from a Mg atom (738 kJ/mol + 1450 kJ/mol = 2188 kJ/mol).

What about sodium chloride? Why is the formula for sodium chloride NaCl and not $NaCl_2$ (containing the Na^{2+} ion)? Although Na^{2+} does not have the noble gas electron configuration, we might expect the compound to be $NaCl_2$ because Na^{2+} has a higher charge and therefore the hypothetical $NaCl_2$ should have a greater lattice

CHEMISTRY IN ACTION

Sodium Chloride— A Common and Important Ionic Compound

We are all familiar with sodium chloride as table salt. It is a typical ionic compound, a brittle solid with a high melting point (801°C) that conducts electricity in the molten state and in aqueous solution. The structure of solid NaCl is shown in Figure 2.13.

One source of sodium chloride is rock salt, which is found in subterranean deposits often hundreds of meters thick. It is also obtained from seawater or brine (a concentrated NaCl solution) by solar evaporation. Sodium chloride also occurs in nature as the mineral *halite*.

Sodium chloride is used more often than any other material in the manufacture of inorganic chemicals. World consumption of this substance is about 150 million tons per year. The major use of sodium chloride is in the production of other essential inorganic chemicals such as chlorine gas, sodium hydroxide, sodium metal, hydrogen gas, and sodium carbonate. It is also used to melt ice and snow on highways and roads. However,

because sodium chloride is harmful to plant life and promotes corrosion of cars, its use for this purpose is of considerable environmental concern.

Solar evaporation process for obtaining sodium chloride.

Underground rock salt mining.

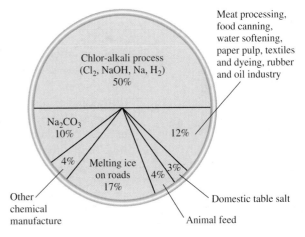

Uses of sodium chloride.

energy. Again the answer lies in the balance between energy input (that is, ionization energies) and the stability gained from the formation of the solid. The sum of the first two ionization energies of sodium is

$$496 \text{ kJ/mol} + 4560 \text{ kJ/mol} = 5056 \text{ kJ/mol}$$

The compound $NaCl_2$ does not exist, but if we assume a value of 2527 kJ/mol as its lattice energy (same as that for $MgCl_2$), we see that the energy yield would be far too small to compensate for the energy required to produce the Na^{2+} ion.

353

What has been said about the cations applies also to the anions. In Section 8.5 we observed that the electron affinity of oxygen is 141 kJ/mol, meaning that the following process releases energy (and is therefore favorable):

$$O(g) + e^- \longrightarrow O^-(g)$$

As we would expect, adding another electron to the O^- ion

$$O^-(g) + e^- \longrightarrow O^{2-}(g)$$

would be unfavorable because of the increase in electrostatic repulsion. Indeed, the electron affinity of O^- is negative. Yet compounds containing the oxide ion (O^{2-}) do exist and are very stable, whereas compounds containing the O^- ion are not known. Again, the high lattice energy resulting from the presence of O^{2-} ions in compounds such as Na_2O or MgO far outweighs the energy needed to produce the O^{2-} ion.

9.4 The Covalent Bond

Animation: Ionic Versus Covalent Bonding
Online Learning Center, Animations

Although the concept of molecules goes back to the seventeenth century, it was not until early in the twentieth century that chemists began to understand how and why molecules form. The first major breakthrough was Gilbert Lewis's suggestion that a chemical bond involves electron sharing by atoms. He depicted the formation of a chemical bond in H_2 as

$$H \cdot + \cdot H \longrightarrow H : H$$

This type of electron pairing is an example of a **covalent bond,** *a bond in which two electrons are shared by two atoms.* **Covalent compounds** *are compounds that contain only covalent bonds.* For the sake of simplicity, the shared pair of electrons is often represented by a single line. Thus the covalent bond in the hydrogen molecule can be written as H—H. In a covalent bond, each electron in a shared pair is attracted to the nuclei of both atoms. This attraction holds the two atoms in H_2 together and is responsible for the formation of covalent bonds in other molecules.

This discussion applies only to representative elements. Remember that for these elements, the number of valence electrons is equal to the group number (Groups 1A–7A).

Covalent bonding between many-electron atoms involves only the valence electrons. Consider the fluorine molecule, F_2. The electron configuration of F is $1s^22s^22p^5$. The $1s$ electrons are low in energy and stay near the nucleus most of the time. For this reason they do not participate in bond formation. Thus each F atom has seven valence electrons (the $2s$ and $2p$ electrons). According to Figure 9.1, there is only one unpaired electron on F, so the formation of the F_2 molecule can be represented as follows:

$$:\overset{..}{F}\cdot \; + \; \cdot \overset{..}{F}: \; \longrightarrow \; :\overset{..}{F}:\overset{..}{F}: \quad \text{or} \quad :\overset{..}{F}-\overset{..}{F}:$$

Note that only two valence electrons participate in the formation of F_2. The other, nonbonding electrons, are called **lone pairs**—*pairs of valence electrons that are not involved in covalent bond formation.* Thus each F in F_2 has three lone pairs of electrons:

$$\text{lone pairs} \longrightarrow :\overset{..}{F}-\overset{..}{F}: \longleftarrow \text{lone pairs}$$

The structures we use to represent covalent compounds, such as H_2 and F_2, are called Lewis structures. A **Lewis structure** is *a representation of covalent bonding in which shared electron pairs are shown either as lines or as pairs of dots between two atoms, and lone pairs are shown as pairs of dots on individual atoms.* Only valence electrons are shown in a Lewis structure.

Let us consider the Lewis structure of the water molecule. Figure 9.1 shows the Lewis dot symbol for oxygen with two unpaired dots or two unpaired electrons, so we expect that O might form two covalent bonds. Because hydrogen has only one electron, it can form only one covalent bond. Thus the Lewis structure for water is

$$\text{H}\!:\!\overset{..}{\underset{..}{\text{O}}}\!:\!\text{H} \qquad \text{or} \qquad \text{H}\!-\!\overset{..}{\underset{..}{\text{O}}}\!-\!\text{H}$$

In this case, the O atom has two lone pairs. The hydrogen atom has no lone pairs because its only electron is used to form a covalent bond.

In the F_2 and H_2O molecules, the F and O atoms achieve the stable noble gas configuration by sharing electrons:

$$8e^-\ \ 8e^- \qquad\qquad 2e^-\ \ 8e^-\ \ 2e^-$$

The formation of these molecules illustrates the **octet rule,** formulated by Lewis: *An atom other than hydrogen tends to form bonds until it is surrounded by eight valence electrons.* In other words, a covalent bond forms when there are not enough electrons for each individual atom to have a complete octet. By sharing electrons in a covalent bond, the individual atoms can complete their octets. The requirement for hydrogen is that it attain the electron configuration of helium, or a total of two electrons.

The octet rule works mainly for elements in the second period of the periodic table. These elements have only $2s$ and $2p$ subshells, which can hold a total of eight electrons. When an atom of one of these elements forms a covalent compound, it can attain the noble gas electron configuration [Ne] by sharing electrons with other atoms in the same compound. Later, we will discuss a number of important exceptions to the octet rule that give us further insight into the nature of chemical bonding.

Atoms can form different types of covalent bonds. In a **single bond,** *two atoms are held together by one electron pair.* Many compounds are held together by **multiple bonds,** that is, bonds formed when *two atoms share two or more pairs of electrons.* If *two atoms share two pairs of electrons,* the covalent bond is called a **double bond.** Double bonds are found in molecules of carbon dioxide (CO_2) and ethylene (C_2H_4):

$$8e^-\ \ 8e^-\ \ 8e^- \qquad\qquad\qquad 8e^-\ \ 8e^-$$

A **triple bond** arises when *two atoms share three pairs of electrons,* as in the nitrogen molecule (N_2):

$$8e^-\ \ 8e^-$$

Interactivity: Covalent Bonds
Online Learning Center, Interactives

Shortly you will be introduced to the rules for writing proper Lewis structures. Here we simply want to become familiar with the language associated with them.

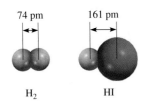

74 pm   161 pm

H₂   HI

Figure 9.3 *Bond length (in pm) in H₂ and HI.*

The acetylene molecule (C_2H_2) also contains a triple bond, in this case between two carbon atoms:

$$H(:C :::C:)H \quad \text{or} \quad H—C≡C—H$$

$$8e^- \quad 8e^-$$

Note that in ethylene and acetylene all the valence electrons are used in bonding; there are no lone pairs on the carbon atoms. In fact, with the exception of carbon monoxide, stable molecules containing carbon do not have lone pairs on the carbon atoms.

Multiple bonds are shorter than single covalent bonds. **Bond length** is defined as the *distance between the nuclei of two covalently bonded atoms in a molecule* (Figure 9.3). Table 9.2 shows some experimentally determined bond lengths. For a given pair of atoms, such as carbon and nitrogen, triple bonds are shorter than double bonds, which, in turn, are shorter than single bonds. The shorter multiple bonds are also more stable than single bonds, as we will see later.

Comparison of the Properties of Covalent and Ionic Compounds

Ionic and covalent compounds differ markedly in their general physical properties because of differences in the nature of their bonds. There are two types of attractive forces in covalent compounds. The first type is the force that holds the atoms together in a molecule. A quantitative measure of this attraction is given by bond energy, to be discussed in Section 9.10. The second type of attractive force operates *between* molecules and is called an *intermolecular force*. Because intermolecular forces are usually quite weak compared with the forces holding atoms together within a molecule, molecules of a covalent compound are not held together tightly. Consequently covalent compounds are usually gases, liquids, or low-melting solids. On the other hand, the electrostatic forces holding ions together in an ionic compound are usually very strong, so ionic compounds are solids at room temperature and have high melting

If intermolecular forces are weak, it is relatively easy to break up aggregates of molecules to form liquids (from solids) and gases (from liquids).

TABLE 9.2

Average Bond Lengths of Some Common Single, Double, and Triple Bonds

Bond Type	Bond Length (pm)
C—H	107
C—O	143
C=O	121
C—C	154
C=C	133
C≡C	120
C—N	143
C=N	138
C≡N	116
N—O	136
N=O	122
O—H	96

TABLE 9.3

Comparison of Some General Properties of an Ionic Compound and a Covalent Compound

Property	NaCl	CCl₄
Appearance	White solid	Colorless liquid
Melting point (°C)	801	−23
Molar heat of fusion* (kJ/mol)	30.2	2.5
Boiling point (°C)	1413	76.5
Molar heat of vaporization* (kJ/mol)	600	30
Density (g/cm³)	2.17	1.59
Solubility in water	High	Very low
Electrical conductivity		
Solid	Poor	Poor
Liquid	Good	Poor

* Molar heat of fusion and molar heat of vaporization are the amounts of heat needed to melt 1 mole of the solid and to vaporize 1 mole of the liquid, respectively.

points. Many ionic compounds are soluble in water, and the resulting aqueous solutions conduct electricity, because the compounds are strong electrolytes. Most covalent compounds are insoluble in water, or if they do dissolve, their aqueous solutions generally do not conduct electricity, because the compounds are nonelectrolytes. Molten ionic compounds conduct electricity because they contain mobile cations and anions; liquid or molten covalent compounds do not conduct electricity because no ions are present. Table 9.3 compares some of the general properties of a typical ionic compound, sodium chloride, with those of a covalent compound, carbon tetrachloride (CCl_4).

Figure 9.4 *Electrostatic potential map of the HF molecule. The electron distribution varies according to the colors of the rainbow. The most electron-rich region is red; the most electron-poor region is blue.*

9.5 Electronegativity

A covalent bond, as we have said, is the sharing of an electron pair by two atoms. In a molecule like H_2, in which the atoms are identical, we expect the electrons to be equally shared—that is, the electrons spend the same amount of time in the vicinity of each atom. However, in the covalently bonded HF molecule, the H and F atoms do not share the bonding electrons equally because H and F are different atoms:

$$\text{H}\!-\!\ddot{\underset{\cdot\cdot}{\text{F}}}\!:$$

Hydrogen fluoride is a clear, fuming liquid that boils at 19.8°C. It is used to make refrigerants and to prepare hydrofluoric acid.

The bond in HF is called a ***polar covalent bond,*** or simply a *polar bond,* because *the electrons spend more time in the vicinity of one atom than the other.* Experimental evidence indicates that in the HF molecule the electrons spend more time near the F atom. We can think of this unequal sharing of electrons as a partial electron transfer or a shift in electron density, as it is more commonly described, from H to F (Figure 9.4). This "unequal sharing" of the bonding electron pair results in a relatively greater electron density near the fluorine atom and a correspondingly lower electron density near hydrogen. The HF bond and other polar bonds can be thought of as being intermediate between a (nonpolar) covalent bond, in which the sharing of electrons is exactly equal, and an ionic bond, in which the *transfer of the electron(s) is nearly complete.*

A property that helps us distinguish a nonpolar covalent bond from a polar covalent bond is ***electronegativity,*** *the ability of an atom to attract toward itself the electrons in a chemical bond.* Elements with high electronegativity have a greater tendency to attract electrons than do elements with low electronegativity. As we might expect, electronegativity is related to electron affinity and ionization energy. Thus an atom such as fluorine, which has a high electron affinity (tends to pick up electrons easily) and a high ionization energy (does not lose electrons easily), has a high electronegativity. On the other hand, sodium has a low electron affinity, a low ionization energy, and a low electronegativity.

Electronegativity is a relative concept, meaning that an element's electronegativity can be measured only in relation to the electronegativity of other elements. Linus Pauling[†] devised a method for calculating *relative* electronegativities of most elements. These values are shown in Figure 9.5. A careful examination of this chart reveals trends and relationships among electronegativity values of different elements.

Electronegativity values have no units.

[†]Linus Carl Pauling (1901–1994). American chemist. Regarded by many as the most influential chemist of the twentieth century, Pauling did research in a remarkably broad range of subjects, from chemical physics to molecular biology. Pauling received the Nobel Prize in Chemistry in 1954 for his work on protein structure, and the Nobel Peace Prize in 1962. He is the only person to be the sole recipient of two Nobel Prizes.

Increasing electronegativity

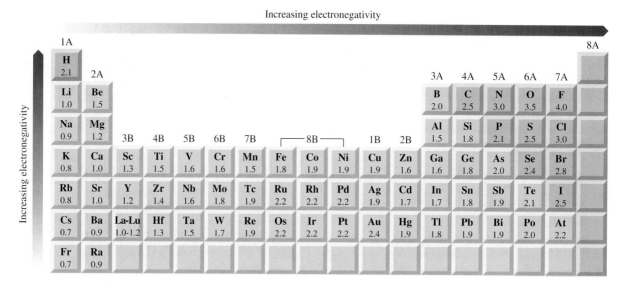

Increasing electronegativity

Figure 9.5 *The electronega-tivities of common elements. The color codes are: green (metals), blue (nonmetals), gray (metalloids).*

In general, electronegativity increases from left to right across a period in the periodic table, as the metallic character of the elements decreases. Within each group, electronegativity decreases with increasing atomic number, and increasing metallic character. Note that the transition metals do not follow these trends. The most electronegative elements—the halogens, oxygen, nitrogen, and sulfur—are found in the upper right-hand corner of the periodic table, and the least electronegative elements (the alkali and alkaline earth metals) are clustered near the lower left-hand corner. These trends are readily apparent on a graph, as shown in Figure 9.6.

Atoms of elements with widely different electronegativities tend to form ionic bonds (such as those that exist in NaCl and CaO compounds) with each other because the atom of the less electronegative element gives up its electron(s) to the atom of the more electronegative element. An ionic bond generally joins an atom of a metallic element and an atom of a nonmetallic element. Atoms of elements with comparable electronegativities tend to form polar covalent bonds with each other because the shift in electron density is usually small. Most covalent bonds involve atoms of nonmetallic

Figure 9.6 *Variation of elec-tronegativity with atomic number. The halogens have the highest electronegativities, and the alkali metals the lowest.*

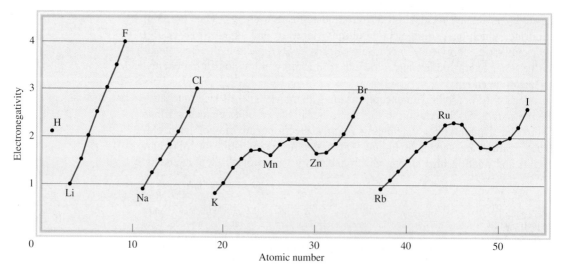

elements. Only atoms of the same element, which have the same electronegativity, can be joined by a pure covalent bond. These trends and characteristics are what we would expect, given our knowledge of ionization energies and electron affinities.

There is no sharp distinction between a polar bond and an ionic bond, but the following rule is helpful in distinguishing between them. An ionic bond forms when the electronegativity difference between the two bonding atoms is 2.0 or more. This rule applies to most but not all ionic compounds. Sometimes chemists use the quantity *percent ionic character* to describe the nature of a bond. A purely ionic bond would have 100 percent ionic character, although no such bond is known, whereas a nonpolar or purely covalent bond has 0 percent ionic character.

Electronegativity and electron affinity are related but different concepts. Both indicate the tendency of an atom to attract electrons. However, electron affinity refers to an isolated atom's attraction for an additional electron, whereas electronegativity signifies the ability of an atom in a chemical bond (with another atom) to attract the shared electrons. Furthermore, electron affinity is an experimentally measurable quantity, whereas electronegativity is an estimated number that cannot be measured.

Example 9.2 shows how a knowledge of electronegativity can help us determine whether a chemical bond is covalent or ionic.

> An ionic bond generally involves an atom of a metallic element and an atom of a nonmetallic element, whereas a covalent bond generally involves two atoms of nonmetallic elements.

Example 9.2

Classify the following bonds as ionic, polar covalent, or covalent: (a) the bond in HCl, (b) the bond in KF, and (c) the CC bond in H_3CCH_3.

Strategy We follow the 2.0 rule of electronegativity difference and look up the values in Figure 9.5.

Solution (a) The electronegativity difference between H and Cl is 0.9, which is appreciable but not large enough (by the 2.0 rule) to qualify HCl as an ionic compound. Therefore, the bond between H and Cl is polar covalent.

(b) The electronegativity difference between K and F is 3.2, which is well above the 2.0 mark; therefore, the bond between K and F is ionic.

(c) The two C atoms are identical in every respect—they are bonded to each other and each is bonded to three other H atoms. Therefore, the bond between them is purely covalent.

Practice Exercise Which of the following bonds is covalent, which is polar covalent, and which is ionic? (a) the bond in CsCl, (b) the bond in H_2S, (c) the NN bond in H_2NNH_2.

The most electronegative elements are the nonmetals (Groups 5A–7A) and the least electronegative elements are the alkali and alkaline earth metals (Group 1A–2A). Beryllium, the first member of Group 2A, forms mostly covalent compounds.

Similar problems: 9.39, 9.40.

Electronegativity and Oxidation Number

In Chapter 4 we introduced the rules for assigning oxidation numbers of elements in their compounds. The concept of electronegativity is the basis for these rules. In essence, oxidation number refers to the number of charges an atom would have if electrons were transferred completely to the more electronegative of the bonded atoms in a molecule.

Consider the NH_3 molecule, in which the N atom forms three single bonds with the H atoms. Because N is more electronegative than H, electron density will be shifted from H to N. If the transfer were complete, each H would donate an electron to N, which would have a total charge of -3 while each H would have a charge of $+1$. Thus we assign an oxidation number of -3 to N and an oxidation number of $+1$ to H in NH_3.

Oxygen usually has an oxidation number of -2 in its compounds, except in hydrogen peroxide (H_2O_2), whose Lewis structure is

$$H-\overset{..}{\underset{..}{O}}-\overset{..}{\underset{..}{O}}-H$$

A bond between identical atoms makes no contribution to the oxidation number of those atoms because the electron pair of that bond is *equally* shared. Because H has an oxidation number of $+1$, each O atom has an oxidation number of -1.

Can you see now why fluorine always has an oxidation number of -1? It is the most electronegative element known, and it *always* forms a single bond in its compounds. Therefore, it would bear a -1 charge if electron transfer were complete.

9.6 Writing Lewis Structures

Interactivity: Lewis Dot Structure
Online Learning Center, Interactives

Although the octet rule and Lewis structures do not present a complete picture of covalent bonding, they do help to explain the bonding scheme in many compounds and account for the properties and reactions of molecules. For this reason, you should practice writing Lewis structures of compounds. The basic steps are as follows:

1. Write the skeletal structure of the compound, using chemical symbols and placing bonded atoms next to one another. For simple compounds, this task is fairly easy. For more complex compounds, we must either be given the information or make an intelligent guess about it. In general, the least electronegative atom occupies the central position. Hydrogen and fluorine usually occupy the terminal (end) positions in the Lewis structure.

2. Count the total number of valence electrons present, referring, if necessary, to Figure 9.1. For polyatomic anions, add the number of negative charges to that total. (For example, for the CO_3^{2-} ion we add two electrons because the $2-$ charge indicates that there are two more electrons than are provided by the atoms.) For polyatomic cations, we subtract the number of positive charges from this total. (Thus, for NH_4^+ we subtract one electron because the $1+$ charge indicates a loss of one electron from the group of atoms.)

3. Draw a single covalent bond between the central atom and each of the surrounding atoms. Complete the octets of the atoms bonded to the central atom. (Remember that the valence shell of a hydrogen atom is complete with only two electrons.) Electrons belonging to the central or surrounding atoms must be shown as lone pairs if they are not involved in bonding. The total number of electrons to be used is that determined in step 2.

4. After completing steps 1–3, if the central atom has fewer than eight electrons, try adding double or triple bonds between the surrounding atoms and the central atom, using lone pairs from the surrounding atoms to complete the octet of the central atom.

Examples 9.3, 9.4, and 9.5 illustrate the four-step procedure for writing Lewis structures of compounds and an ion.

NF$_3$ is a colorless, odorless, unreactive gas.

Example 9.3

Write the Lewis structure for nitrogen trifluoride (NF_3) in which all three F atoms are bonded to the N atom.

Solution We follow the preceding procedure for writing Lewis structure.

(Continued)

Step 1: The N atom is less electronegative than F, so the skeletal structure of NF_3 is

$$F \quad N \quad F$$
$$F$$

Step 2: The outer-shell electron configurations of N and F are $2s^2 2p^3$ and $2s^2 2p^5$, respectively. Thus there are $5 + (3 \times 7)$, or 26, valence electrons to account for in NF_3.

Step 3: We draw a single covalent bond between N and each F, and complete the octets for the F atoms. We place the remaining two electrons on N:

$$:\ddot{F}-\ddot{N}-\ddot{F}:$$
$$:\ddot{F}:$$

Because this structure satisfies the octet rule for all the atoms, step 4 is not required.

Check Count the valence electrons in NF_3 (in bonds and in lone pairs). The result is 26, the same as the total number of valence electrons on three F atoms ($3 \times 7 = 21$) and one N atom (5).

Similar problem: 9.45.

Practice Exercise Write the Lewis structure for carbon disulfide (CS_2).

Example 9.4

Write the Lewis structure for nitric acid (HNO_3) in which the three O atoms are bonded to the central N atom and the ionizable H atom is bonded to one of the O atoms.

Solution We follow the procedure already outlined for writing Lewis structure.

Step 1: The skeletal structure of HNO_3 is

$$O \quad N \quad O \quad H$$
$$O$$

HNO_3 is a strong electrolyte.

Step 2: The outer-shell electron configurations of N, O, and H are $2s^2 2p^3$, $2s^2 2p^4$, and $1s^1$, respectively. Thus there are $5 + (3 \times 6) + 1$, or 24, valence electrons to account for in HNO_3.

Step 3: We draw a single covalent bond between N and each of the three O atoms and between one O atom and the H atom. Then we fill in electrons to comply with the octet rule for the O atoms:

$$:\ddot{O}-N-\ddot{O}-H$$
$$:\ddot{O}:$$

Step 4: We see that this structure satisfies the octet rule for all the O atoms but not for the N atom. The N atom has only six electrons. Therefore, we move a lone pair from one of the end O atoms to form another bond with N. Now the octet rule is also satisfied for the N atom:

$$\ddot{O}=N-\ddot{O}-H$$
$$:\ddot{O}:$$

(Continued)

Similar problem: 9.45.

Check Make sure that all the atoms (except H) satisfy the octet rule. Count the valence electrons in HNO_3 (in bonds and in lone pairs). The result is 24, the same as the total number of valence electrons on three O atoms ($3 \times 6 = 18$), one N atom (5), and one H atom (1).

Practice Exercise Write the Lewis structure for formic acid (HCOOH).

Example 9.5

Write the Lewis structure for the carbonate ion (CO_3^{2-}).

Solution We follow the preceding procedure for writing Lewis structures and note that this is an anion with two negative charges.

Step 1: We can deduce the skeletal structure of the carbonate ion by recognizing that C is less electronegative than O. Therefore, it is most likely to occupy a central position as follows:

O

O   C   O

Step 2: The outer-shell electron configurations of C and O are $2s^2 2p^2$ and $2s^2 2p^4$, respectively, and the ion itself has two negative charges. Thus the total number of electrons is $4 + (3 \times 6) + 2$, or 24.

Step 3: We draw a single covalent bond between C and each O and comply with the octet rule for the O atoms:

$$:\overset{..}{\underset{..}{O}}:$$
$$:\overset{..}{\underset{..}{O}}-\overset{|}{C}-\overset{..}{\underset{..}{O}}:$$

This structure shows all 24 electrons.

Step 4: Although the octet rule is satisfied for the O atoms, it is not for the C atom. Therefore we move a lone pair from one of the O atoms to form another bond with C. Now the octet rule is also satisfied for the C atom:

$$\left[:\overset{..}{\underset{..}{O}}-\overset{\overset{\displaystyle :O:}{\|}}{C}-\overset{..}{\underset{..}{O}}: \right]^{2-}$$

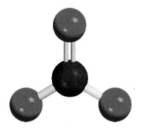 CO_3^{2-}

We use the brackets to indicate that the -2 charge is on the whole molecule.

Check Make sure that all the atoms satisfy the octet rule. Count the valence electrons in CO_3^{2-} (in chemical bonds and in lone pairs). The result is 24, the same as the total number of valence electrons on three O atoms ($3 \times 6 = 18$), one C atom (4), and two negative charges (2).

Similar problem: 9.44.

Practice Exercise Write the Lewis structure for the nitrite ion (NO_2^-).

9.7 Formal Charge and Lewis Structure

By comparing the number of electrons in an isolated atom with the number of electrons that are associated with the same atom in a Lewis structure, we can determine the distribution of electrons in the molecule and draw the most plausible Lewis structure. The bookkeeping procedure is as follows: In an isolated atom, the number of electrons associated with the atom is simply the number of valence electrons. (As usual, we need not be concerned with the inner electrons.) In a molecule, electrons associated with the atom are the nonbonding electrons plus the electrons in the bonding pair(s) between the atom and other atom(s). However, because electrons are shared in a bond, we must divide the electrons in a bonding pair equally between the atoms forming the bond. An atom's *formal charge* is *the electrical charge difference between the valence electrons in an isolated atom and the number of electrons assigned to that atom in a Lewis structure.*

To assign the number of electrons on an atom in a Lewis structure, we proceed as follows:

- All the atom's nonbonding electrons are assigned to the atom.
- We break the bond(s) between the atom and other atom(s) and assign half of the bonding electrons to the atom.

Let us illustrate the concept of formal charge using the ozone molecule (O_3). Proceeding by steps, as we did in Examples 9.3 and 9.4, we draw the skeletal structure of O_3 and then add bonds and electrons to satisfy the octet rule for the two end atoms:

$$:\overset{..}{\underset{..}{O}}-\overset{..}{O}-\overset{..}{\underset{..}{O}}:$$

You can see that although all available electrons are used, the octet rule is not satisfied for the central atom. To remedy this, we convert a lone pair on one of the end atoms to a second bond between that end atom and the central atom, as follows:

$$\overset{..}{\underset{..}{O}}=\overset{..}{O}-\overset{..}{\underset{..}{O}}:$$

Liquid ozone below its boiling point ($-111.3°C$). Ozone is a toxic, light-blue gas with a pungent odor.

The formal charge on each atom in O_3 can now be calculated according to the following scheme:

$$\overset{..}{\underset{..}{O}}\lessgtr\overset{..}{O}\lessgtr\overset{..}{\underset{..}{O}}:$$

Valence e^-	6	6	6
e^- assigned to atom	6	5	7
Difference (formal charge)	0	+1	−1

where the wavy red lines denote the breaking of the bonds. Note that the breaking of a single bond results in the transfer of an electron, the breaking of a double bond results in a transfer of two electrons to each of the bonding atoms, and so on. Thus the formal charges of the atoms in O_3 are

$$\overset{..}{\underset{..}{O}}=\overset{..}{\overset{+}{O}}-\overset{..}{\underset{..}{O}}:^-$$

For single positive and negative charges, we normally omit the numeral 1.

When you write formal charges, these rules are helpful:

1. For molecules, the sum of the formal charges must add up to zero because molecules are electrically neutral species. (This rule applies, for example, to the O_3 molecule.)

2. For cations, the sum of the formal charges must equal the positive charge.

3. For anions, the sum of the formal charges must equal the negative charge.

Keep in mind that formal charges do not represent actual charge separation within the molecule. In the O_3 molecule, for example, there is no evidence that the central atom bears a net $+1$ charge or that one of the end atoms bears a -1 charge. Writing these charges on the atoms in the Lewis structure merely helps us keep track of the valence electrons in the molecule.

Example 9.6

Write formal charges for the carbonate ion.

Solution The Lewis structure for the carbonate ion was developed in Example 9.5:

$$\left[\begin{array}{c} :\overset{..}{O}: \\ \overset{..}{O}\text{—}C\text{—}\overset{..}{O}: \end{array} \right]^{2-}$$

The formal charges on the atoms can be calculated using the given procedure.

The C atom: The C atom has four valence electrons and there are no nonbonding electrons on the atom in the Lewis structure. The breaking of the double bond and two single bonds results in the transfer of four electrons to the C atom. Therefore, the formal charge is $4 - 4 = 0$.

The O atom in C=O: The O atom has six valence electrons and there are four nonbonding electrons on the atom. The breaking of the double bond results in the transfer of two electrons to the O atom. Here the formal charge is $6 - 4 - 2 = 0$.

The O atom in C—O: This atom has six nonbonding electrons and the breaking of the single bond transfers another electron to it. Therefore, the formal charge is $6 - 6 - 1 = -1$.

Thus the Lewis structure for CO_3^{2-} with formal charges is

$$\begin{array}{c} :\overset{..}{O}: \\ \| \\ ^{-}:\overset{..}{O}\text{—}C\text{—}\overset{..}{O}:^{-} \end{array}$$

Check Note that the sum of the formal charges is -2, the same as the charge on the carbonate ion.

Practice Exercise Write formal charges for the nitrite ion (NO_2^-).

Similar problem: 9.46.

Sometimes there is more than one acceptable Lewis structure for a given species. In such cases, we can often select the most plausible Lewis structure by using formal charges and the following guidelines:

- For molecules, a Lewis structure in which there are no formal charges is preferable to one in which formal charges are present.

- Lewis structures with large formal charges ($+2$, $+3$, and/or -2, -3, and so on) are less plausible than those with small formal charges.

- Among Lewis structures having similar distributions of formal charges, the most plausible structure is the one in which negative formal charges are placed on the more electronegative atoms.

Example 9.7 shows how formal charges facilitate the choice of the correct Lewis structure for a molecule.

Example 9.7

Formaldehyde (CH_2O), a liquid with a disagreeable odor, traditionally has been used to preserve laboratory specimens. Draw the most likely Lewis structure for the compound.

Strategy A plausible Lewis structure should satisfy the octet rule for all the elements, except H, and have the formal charges (if any) distributed according to electronegativity guidelines.

Solution The two possible skeletal structures are

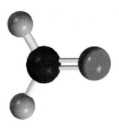

CH_2O

```
              H
  H  C  O  H      C  O
              H
     (a)         (b)
```

First we draw the Lewis structures for each of these possibilities

```
    ..  +
    :.  ..            H
  H—C=O—H              \
                        C=O
                       /
                      H
     (a)              (b)
```

To show the formal charges, we follow the procedure given in Example 9.6. In (a) the C atom has a total of five electrons (one lone pair plus three electrons from the breaking of a single and a double bond). Because C has four valence electrons, the formal charge on the atom is $4 - 5 = -1$. The O atom has a total of five electrons (one lone pair and three electrons from the breaking of a single and a double bond). Because O has six valence electrons, the formal charge on the atom is $6 - 5 = +1$. In (b) the C atom has a total of four electrons from the breaking of two single bonds and a double bond, so its formal charge is $4 - 4 = 0$. The O atom has a total of six electrons (two lone pairs and two electrons from the breaking of the double bond). Therefore, the formal charge on the atom is $6 - 6 = 0$. Although both structures satisfy the octet rule, (b) is the more likely structure because it carries no formal charges.

Check In each case make sure that the total number of valence electrons is 12. Can you suggest two other reasons why (a) is less plausible?

Practice Exercise Draw the most reasonable Lewis structure of a molecule that contains a N atom, a C atom, and an H atom.

Similar problem: 9.47.

9.8 The Concept of Resonance

Our drawing of the Lewis structure for ozone (O_3) satisfied the octet rule for the central atom because we placed a double bond between it and one of the two end O atoms. In fact, we can put the double bond at either end of the molecule, as shown by these two equivalent Lewis structures:

```
  ..   ..+  ..          ..    ..+  ..
  O=O—O:⁻        ⁻:O—O=O
  ..   ..                ..
```

However, neither one of these two Lewis structures accounts for the known bond lengths in O_3.

We would expect the O—O bond in O_3 to be longer than the O=O bond because double bonds are known to be shorter than single bonds. Yet experimental evidence

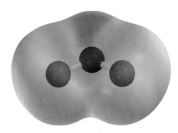

Electrostatic potential map of O_3. The electron density is evenly distributed between the two end O atoms.

shows that both oxygen-to-oxygen bonds are equal in length (128 pm). We resolve this discrepancy by using *both* Lewis structures to represent the ozone molecule:

$$\overset{..}{O}=\overset{..}{\underset{..}{O}}-\overset{..}{\underset{..}{O}}:^- \longleftrightarrow {}^-:\overset{..}{\underset{..}{O}}-\overset{..}{\underset{..}{O}}=\overset{..}{\underset{..}{O}}$$

Each of these structures is called a resonance structure. A ***resonance structure,*** then, is *one of two or more Lewis structures for a single molecule that cannot be represented accurately by only one Lewis structure.* The double-headed arrow indicates that the structures shown are resonance structures.

Interactivity: Resonance
Online Learning Center,
Interactives

The term ***resonance*** itself means *the use of two or more Lewis structures to represent a particular molecule.* Like the medieval European traveler to Africa who described a rhinoceros as a cross between a griffin and a unicorn, two familiar but imaginary animals, we describe ozone, a real molecule, in terms of two familiar but nonexistent structures.

A common misconception about resonance is the notion that a molecule such as ozone somehow shifts quickly back and forth from one resonance structure to the other. Keep in mind that *neither* resonance structure adequately represents the actual molecule, which has its own unique, stable structure. "Resonance" is a human invention, designed to address the limitations in these simple bonding models. To extend the animal analogy, a rhinoceros is a distinct creature, not some oscillation between mythical griffin and unicorn!

The carbonate ion provides another example of resonance:

$$
\underset{{}^-:\overset{..}{\underset{..}{O}}-\overset{\overset{\displaystyle :O:}{\|}}{C}-\overset{..}{\underset{..}{O}}:^-}{} \longleftrightarrow \underset{\overset{..}{O}=C-\overset{..}{\underset{..}{O}}:^-}{\overset{:\overset{..}{O}:^-}{|}} \longleftrightarrow \underset{{}^-:\overset{..}{\underset{..}{O}}-C=\overset{..}{O}}{\overset{:\overset{..}{O}:^-}{|}}
$$

According to experimental evidence, all carbon-to-oxygen bonds in CO_3^{2-} are equivalent. Therefore, the properties of the carbonate ion are best explained by considering its resonance structures together.

The concept of resonance applies equally well to organic systems. A good example is the benzene molecule (C_6H_6):

The hexagonal structure of benzene was first proposed by the German chemist August Kekulé (1829–1896).

If one of these resonance structures corresponded to the actual structure of benzene, there would be two different bond lengths between adjacent C atoms, one characteristic of the single bond and the other of the double bond. In fact, the distance between all adjacent C atoms in benzene is 140 pm, which is shorter than a C—C bond (154 pm) and longer than a C=C bond (133 pm).

A simpler way of drawing the structure of the benzene molecule and other compounds containing the "benzene ring" is to show only the skeleton and not the carbon and hydrogen atoms. By this convention the resonance structures are represented by

Note that the C atoms at the corners of the hexagon and the H atoms are all omitted, although they are understood to exist. Only the bonds between the C atoms are shown.

Remember this important rule for drawing resonance structures: The positions of electrons, but not those of atoms, can be rearranged in different resonance structures. In other words, the same atoms must be bonded to one another in all the resonance structures for a given species.

Example 9.8 illustrates the procedure for drawing resonance structures of a molecule.

Example 9.8

Draw resonance structures (including formal charges) for the nitrate ion, NO_3^-, which has the following skeletal arrangement:

$$O$$
$$O \quad N \quad O$$

Strategy We follow the procedure used for drawing Lewis structures and calculating formal charges in Examples 9.5 and 9.6.

Solution Just as in the case of the carbonate ion, we can draw three equivalent resonance structures for the nitrate ion:

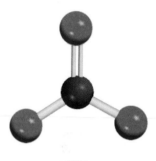

NO_3^-

$$:\overset{..}{O}:^- \qquad\qquad :\overset{..}{O}: \qquad\qquad :\overset{..}{O}:^-$$
$$\overset{..}{O}=\overset{+}{N}-\overset{..}{\underset{..}{O}}:^- \longleftrightarrow {}^-:\overset{..}{\underset{..}{O}}-\overset{+}{N}-\overset{..}{\underset{..}{O}}:^- \longleftrightarrow {}^-:\overset{..}{\underset{..}{O}}-\overset{+}{N}=\overset{..}{O}$$

Check Because N has five valence electrons and each O has six valence electrons and there is a net negative charge, the total number of valence electrons is $5 + (3 \times 6) + 1 = 24$, the same as the number of valence electrons in the NO_3^- ion.

Similar problems: 9.51, 9.56.

Practice Exercise Draw resonance structures for the nitrite ion (NO_2^-).

9.9 Exceptions to the Octet Rule

As mentioned earlier, the octet rule applies mainly to the second-period elements. Exceptions to the octet rule fall into three categories characterized by an incomplete octet, an odd number of electrons, or more than eight valence electrons around the central atom.

Interactivity: Octet Rule
Exceptions
Online Learning Center,
Interactives

The Incomplete Octet

In some compounds the number of electrons surrounding the central atom in a stable molecule is fewer than eight. Consider, for example, beryllium, which is a Group 2A (and a second-period) element. The electron configuration of beryllium is $1s^2 2s^2$; it has two valence electrons in the $2s$ orbital. In the gas phase, beryllium hydride (BeH_2) exists as discrete molecules. The Lewis structure of BeH_2 is

Beryllium, unlike the other Group 2A elements, forms mostly covalent compounds of which BeH_2 is an example.

$$H—Be—H$$

As you can see, only four electrons surround the Be atom, and there is no way to satisfy the octet rule for beryllium in this molecule.

Elements in Group 3A, particularly boron and aluminum, also tend to form compounds in which they are surrounded by fewer than eight electrons. Take boron as an example. Because its electron configuration is $1s^2 2s^2 2p^1$, it has a total of three valence electrons. Boron reacts with the halogens to form a class of compounds having the general formula BX_3, where X is a halogen atom. Thus, in boron trifluoride there are only six electrons around the boron atom:

$$: \ddot{F} :$$
$$|$$
$$: \ddot{F} - B$$
$$|$$
$$: \ddot{F} :$$

The following resonance structures all contain a double bond between B and F and satisfy the octet rule for boron:

$$
\begin{array}{ccccc}
: \ddot{F} : & & : \ddot{F} :^+ & & : \ddot{F} : \\
| & & \| & & | \\
^+\!F\!\!=\!\!B^- & \longleftrightarrow & : \ddot{F} - B^- & \longleftrightarrow & : \ddot{F} - B^- \\
| & & | & & \| \\
: \ddot{F} : & & : \ddot{F} : & & : \ddot{F} :^+
\end{array}
$$

The fact that the B—F bond length in BF_3 (130.9 pm) is shorter than a single bond (137.3 pm) lends support to the resonance structures even though in each case the negative formal charge is placed on the B atom and the positive formal charge on the F atom.

Although boron trifluoride is stable, it readily reacts with ammonia. This reaction is better represented by using the Lewis structure in which boron has only six valence electrons around it:

$$
\begin{array}{ccccccc}
: \ddot{F} : & H & & & : \ddot{F} : & H \\
| & | & & & | & | \\
: \ddot{F} - B & + & : N - H & \longrightarrow & : \ddot{F} - B^- - N^+ - H \\
| & | & & & | & | \\
: \ddot{F} : & H & & & : \ddot{F} : & H
\end{array}
$$

It seems that the properties of BF_3 are best explained by all four resonance structures.

The B—N bond in the above compound is different from the covalent bonds discussed so far in the sense that both electrons are contributed by the N atom. This type of bond is called a **coordinate covalent bond** (also referred to as a *dative bond*), defined as *a covalent bond in which one of the atoms donates both electrons*. Although the properties of a coordinate covalent bond do not differ from those of a normal covalent bond (because all electrons are alike no matter what their source), the distinction is useful for keeping track of valence electrons and assigning formal charges.

Odd-Electron Molecules

Some molecules contain an *odd* number of electrons. Among them are nitric oxide (NO) and nitrogen dioxide (NO_2):

$$\dot{N}\!\!=\!\!\ddot{O} \qquad \ddot{O}\!\!=\!\!N^+\!\!-\!\!\ddot{O}:^-$$

Because we need an even number of electrons for complete pairing (to reach eight), the octet rule clearly cannot be satisfied for all the atoms in any of these molecules.

Odd-electron molecules are sometimes called *radicals*. Many radicals are highly reactive. The reason is that there is a tendency for the unpaired electron to form a

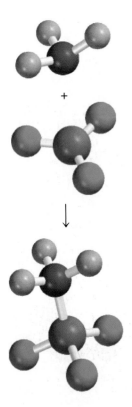

+

↓

$NH_3 + BF_3 \longrightarrow H_3N{-}BF_3$

covalent bond with an unpaired electron on another molecule. For example, when two nitrogen dioxide molecules collide, they form dinitrogen tetroxide in which the octet rule is satisfied for both the N and O atoms:

The Expanded Octet

Atoms of the second-period elements cannot have more than eight valence electrons around the central atom, but atoms of elements in and beyond the third period of the periodic table form some compounds in which more than eight electrons surround the central atom. In addition to the $3s$ and $3p$ orbitals, elements in the third period also have $3d$ orbitals that can be used in bonding. These orbitals allow an atom to form an *expanded octet*. One compound in which there is an expanded octet is sulfur hexafluoride, a very stable compound. The electron configuration of sulfur is $[Ne]3s^23p^4$. In SF_6, each of sulfur's six valence electrons forms a covalent bond with a fluorine atom, so there are twelve electrons around the central sulfur atom:

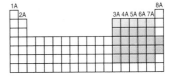

Yellow: second-period elements cannot have an expanded octet. Blue: third-period elements and beyond can have an expanded octet. Green: the noble gases usually have only an expanded octet.

In Chapter 10 we will see that these 12 electrons, or six bonding pairs, are accommodated in six orbitals that originate from the one $3s$, the three $3p$, and two of the five $3d$ orbitals. Sulfur also forms many compounds in which it obeys the octet rule. In sulfur dichloride, for instance, S is surrounded by only eight electrons:

Sulfur dichloride is a toxic, foul-smelling, cherry-red liquid (boiling point: 59°C).

Examples 9.9–9.11 concern compounds that do not obey the octet rule.

Example 9.9

Draw the Lewis structure for aluminum triiodide (AlI_3).

Strategy We follow the procedures used in Examples 9.5 and 9.6 to draw the Lewis structure and calculate formal charges.

Solution The outer-shell electron configurations of Al and I are $3s^23p^1$ and $5s^25p^5$, respectively. The total number of valence electrons is $3 + 3 \times 7$ or 24. Because Al is less electronegative than I, it occupies a central position and forms three bonds with the I atoms:

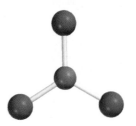

AlI_3 has a tendency to dimerize or form two units as Al_2I_6.

(Continued)

Note that there are no formal charges on the Al and I atoms.

Check Although the octet rule is satisfied for the I atoms, there are only six valence electrons around the Al atom. Thus AlI_3 is an example of the incomplete octet.

Practice Exercise Draw the Lewis structure for BeF_2.

Similar problem: 9.62.

Example 9.10

Draw the Lewis structure for phosphorus pentafluoride (PF_5), in which all five F atoms are bonded to the central P atom.

Strategy Note that P is a third-period element. We follow the procedures given in Examples 9.5 and 9.6 to draw the Lewis structure and calculate formal charges.

Solution The outer-shell electron configurations for P and F are $3s^2 3p^3$ and $2s^2 2p^5$, respectively, and so the total number of valence electrons is $5 + (5 \times 7)$, or 40. Phosphorus, like sulfur, is a third-period element, and therefore it can have an expanded octet. The Lewis structure of PF_5 is

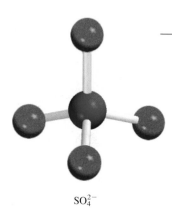

PF$_5$ is a reactive gaseous compound.

Note that there are no formal charges on the P and F atoms.

Check Although the octet rule is satisfied for the F atoms, there are 10 valence electrons around the P atom, giving it an expanded octet.

Similar problem: 9.64.

Practice Exercise Draw the Lewis structure for arsenic pentafluoride (AsF_5).

Example 9.11

Draw a Lewis structure for the sulfate ion (SO_4^{2-}) in which all four O atoms are bonded to the central S atom.

Strategy Note that S is a third-period element. We follow the procedures given in Examples 9.5 and 9.6 to draw the Lewis structure and calculate formal charges.

Solution The outer-shell electron configurations of S and O are $3s^2 3p^4$ and $2s^2 2p^4$, respectively.

Step 1: The skeletal structure of (SO_4^{2-}) is

$$\text{O}$$
$$\text{O} \quad \text{S} \quad \text{O}$$
$$\text{O}$$

Step 2: Both O and S are Group 6A elements and so have six valence electrons each. Including the two negative charges, we must therefore account for a total of $6 + (4 \times 6) + 2$, or 32, valence electrons in SO_4^{2-}.

Step 3: We draw a single covalent bond between all the bonding atoms:

SO_4^{2-}

(Continued)

Next we show formal charges on the S and O atoms:

$$\overset{\displaystyle :\overset{..}{\underset{..}{O}}:^-}{\underset{\displaystyle :\overset{..}{\underset{..}{O}}:_-}{^-:\overset{..}{\underset{..}{O}}-\overset{|}{\underset{|}{S^{2+}}}-\overset{..}{\underset{..}{O}}:^-}}$$

Check One of six other equivalent structures for SO_4^{2-} is as follows:

$$\overset{\displaystyle :\overset{..}{O}:}{\underset{\displaystyle :\overset{..}{O}:}{^-:\overset{..}{\underset{..}{O}}\overset{\|}{-}\overset{\|}{S}\overset{\|}{-}\overset{..}{\underset{..}{O}}:^-}}$$

This structure involves an expanded octet on S but may be considered more plausible because it bears fewer formal charges. However, detailed theoretical calculation shows that the most likely structure is the one that satisfies the octet rule, even though it has greater formal charge separations. The general rule for elements in the third period and beyond is that a resonance structure that obeys the octet rule is preferred over one that involves an expanded octet but bears fewer formal charges.

Practice Exercise Draw the Lewis structure of sulfuric acid (H_2SO_4).

Similar problem: 9.85.

A final note about the expanded octet: In drawing Lewis structures of compounds containing a central atom from the third period and beyond, sometimes we find that the octet rule is satisfied for all the atoms but there are still valence electrons left to place. In such cases, the extra electrons should be placed as lone pairs on the central atom. Example 9.12 shows this approach.

Example 9.12

Draw a Lewis structure of the noble gas compound xenon tetrafluoride (XeF_4) in which all F atoms are bonded to the central Xe atom.

Strategy Note that Xe is a fifth-period element. We follow the procedures in Examples 9.5 and 9.6 for drawing the Lewis structure and calculating formal charges.

Solution *Step 1:* The skeletal structure of XeF_4 is

F   F
Xe
F   F

XeF_4

Step 2: The outer-shell electron configurations of Xe and F are $5s^25p^6$ and $2s^22p^5$, respectively, and so the total number of valence electrons is $8 + (4 \times 7)$ or 36.

Step 3: We draw a single covalent bond between all the bonding atoms. The octet rule is satisfied for the F atoms, each of which has three lone pairs. The sum of the lone pair electrons on the four F atoms (4×6) and the four bonding pairs (4×2) is 32. Therefore, the remaining four electrons are shown as two lone pairs on the Xe atom:

(Continued)

CHEMISTRY IN ACTION

Just Say NO

Nitric oxide (NO), the simplest nitrogen oxide, is an odd-electron molecule, and therefore it is paramagnetic. A colorless gas (boiling point: $-152°C$), NO can be prepared in the laboratory by reacting sodium nitrite ($NaNO_2$) with a reducing agent such as Fe^{2+} in an acidic medium.

$$NO_2^-(aq) + Fe^{2+}(aq) + 2H^+(aq) \longrightarrow$$
$$NO(g) + Fe^{3+}(aq) + H_2O(l)$$

Environmental sources of nitric oxide include the burning of fossil fuels containing nitrogen compounds and the reaction between nitrogen and oxygen inside the automobile engine at high temperatures

$$N_2(g) + O_2(g) \longrightarrow 2NO(g)$$

Lightning also contributes to the atmospheric concentration of NO. Exposed to air, nitric oxide quickly forms brown nitrogen dioxide gas:

$$2NO(g) + O_2(g) \longrightarrow 2NO_2(g)$$

Nitrogen dioxide is a major component of smog.

About 18 years ago scientists studying muscle relaxation discovered that our bodies produce nitric oxide for use as a neurotransmitter. (A *neurotransmitter* is a small molecule that serves to facilitate cell-to-cell communications.) Since then, it has been detected in at least a dozen cell types in various parts of the body. Cells in the brain, the liver, the pancreas, the gastrointestinal tract, and the blood vessels can synthesize nitric oxide. This molecule also functions as a cellular toxin to kill harmful bacteria. And that's not all: In 1996 it was reported that NO binds to hemoglobin, the oxygen-carrying protein in the blood. No doubt it helps to regulate blood pressure.

Colorless nitric oxide gas is produced by the action of Fe^{2+} on an acidic sodium nitrite solution. The gas is bubbled through water and immediately reacts with oxygen to form the brown NO_2 gas when exposed to air.

The discovery of the biological role of nitric oxide has shed light on how nitroglycerin ($C_3H_5N_3O_9$) works as a drug. Nitroglycerin tablets are commonly prescribed for heart patients to relieve the pain (*angina pectoris*) caused by a brief interference in the flow of blood to the heart. It is now believed that nitroglycerin produces nitric oxide, which causes the muscles to relax and allows the arteries to dilate.

That NO evolved as a messenger molecule is entirely appropriate. Nitric oxide is small and so can diffuse quickly from cell to cell. It is a stable molecule but under certain circumstances it is highly reactive, which accounts for its protective function. The enzyme that brings about muscle relaxation contains iron for which nitric oxide has a high affinity. It is the binding of NO to the iron that activates the enzyme. Nevertheless, in the cell, where biological effectors are typically very large molecules, the pervasive effects of one of the smallest known molecules are unprecedented.

We see that the Xe atom has an expanded octet. There are no formal charges on the Xe and F atoms.

Similar problem: 9.63.

Practice Exercise Write the Lewis structure of sulfur tetrafluoride (SF_4).

9.10 Bond Energy

A measure of the stability of a molecule is its ***bond energy,*** which is *the enthalpy change required to break a particular bond in 1 mole of gaseous molecules.* (Bond energies in solids and liquids are affected by neighboring molecules.) The experimentally determined bond energy of the diatomic hydrogen molecule, for example, is

$$H_2(g) \longrightarrow H(g) + H(g) \qquad \Delta H° = 436.4 \text{ kJ/mol}$$

This equation tells us that breaking the covalent bonds in 1 mole of gaseous H_2 molecules requires 436.4 kJ of energy. For the less stable chlorine molecule,

$$Cl_2(g) \longrightarrow Cl(g) + Cl(g) \qquad \Delta H° = 242.7 \text{ kJ/mol}$$

Bond energies can also be directly measured for diatomic molecules containing unlike elements, such as HCl,

$$HCl(g) \longrightarrow H(g) + Cl(g) \qquad \Delta H° = 431.9 \text{ kJ/mol}$$

as well as for molecules containing double and triple bonds:

$$O_2(g) \longrightarrow O(g) + O(g) \qquad \Delta H° = 498.7 \text{ kJ/mol}$$
$$N_2(g) \longrightarrow N(g) + N(g) \qquad \Delta H° = 941.4 \text{ kJ/mol}$$

The Lewis structure of O_2 is Ö—Ö

Measuring the strength of covalent bonds in polyatomic molecules is more complicated. For example, measurements show that the energy needed to break the first O—H bond in H_2O is different from that needed to break the second O—H bond:

$$H_2O(g) \longrightarrow H(g) + OH(g) \qquad \Delta H° = 502 \text{ kJ/mol}$$
$$OH(g) \longrightarrow H(g) + O(g) \qquad \Delta H° = 427 \text{ kJ/mol}$$

In each case, an O—H bond is broken, but the first step is more endothermic than the second. The difference between the two $\Delta H°$ values suggests that the second O—H bond itself undergoes change, because of the changes in chemical environment.

Now we can understand why the bond energy of the same O—H bond in two different molecules such as methanol (CH_3OH) and water (H_2O) will not be the same: their environments are different. Thus for polyatomic molecules we speak of the *average* bond energy of a particular bond. For example, we can measure the energy of the O—H bond in 10 different polyatomic molecules and obtain the average O—H bond energy by dividing the sum of the bond energies by 10. Table 9.4 lists the average bond energies of a number of diatomic and polyatomic molecules. As stated earlier, triple bonds are stronger than double bonds, which, in turn, are stronger than single bonds.

Use of Bond Energies in Thermochemistry

A comparison of the thermochemical changes that take place during a number of reactions (Chapter 6) reveals a strikingly wide variation in the enthalpies of different reactions. For example, the combustion of hydrogen gas in oxygen gas is fairly exothermic:

$$H_2(g) + \tfrac{1}{2}O_2(g) \longrightarrow H_2O(l) \qquad \Delta H° = -285.8 \text{ kJ/mol}$$

On the other hand, the formation of glucose ($C_6H_{12}O_6$) from water and carbon dioxide, best achieved by photosynthesis, is highly endothermic:

$$6CO_2(g) + 6H_2O(l) \longrightarrow C_6H_{12}O_6(s) + 6O_2(g) \qquad \Delta H° = 2801 \text{ kJ/mol}$$

We can account for such variations by looking at the stability of individual reactant and product molecules. After all, most chemical reactions involve the making and breaking of bonds. Therefore, knowing the bond energies and hence the stability of molecules tells us something about the thermochemical nature of reactions that molecules undergo.

TABLE 9.4 Some Bond Energies of Diatomic Molecules* and Average Bond Energies for Bonds in Polyatomic Molecules

Bond	Bond Energy (kJ/mol)	Bond	Bond Energy (kJ/mol)
H—H	436.4	C—S	255
H—N	393	C=S	477
H—O	460	N—N	193
H—S	368	N=N	418
H—P	326	N≡N	941.4
H—F	568.2	N—O	176
H—Cl	431.9	N—P	209
H—Br	366.1	O—O	142
H—I	298.3	O=O	498.7
C—H	414	O—P	502
C—C	347	O=S	469
C=C	620	P—P	197
C≡C	812	P=P	489
C—N	276	S—S	268
C=N	615	S=S	352
C≡N	891	F—F	156.9
C—O	351	Cl—Cl	242.7
C=O†	745	Br—Br	192.5
C—P	263	I—I	151.0

* Bond energies for diatomic molecules (in color) have more significant figures than bond energies for bonds in polyatomic molecules because the bond energies of diatomic molecules are directly measurable quantities and not averaged over many compounds.

† The C=O bond energy in CO_2 is 799 kJ/mol.

In many cases, it is possible to predict the approximate enthalpy of reaction by using the average bond energies. Because energy is always required to break chemical bonds and chemical bond formation is always accompanied by a release of energy, we can estimate the enthalpy of a reaction by counting the total number of bonds broken and formed in the reaction and recording all the corresponding energy changes. The enthalpy of reaction in the *gas phase* is given by

$$\Delta H° = \Sigma BE(\text{reactants}) - \Sigma BE(\text{products})$$
$$= \text{total energy input} - \text{total energy released} \qquad (9.3)$$

where BE stands for average bond energy and Σ is the summation sign. As written, Equation (9.3) takes care of the sign convention for $\Delta H°$. Thus, if the total energy input is greater than the total energy released, $\Delta H°$ is positive and the reaction is endothermic. On the other hand, if more energy is released than absorbed, $\Delta H°$ is negative and the reaction is exothermic (Figure 9.7). If reactants and products are all diatomic molecules, then Equation (9.3) will yield accurate results because the bond energies of diatomic molecules are accurately known. If some or all of the reactants and products are polyatomic molecules, Equation (9.3) will yield only approximate results because the bond energies used will be averages.

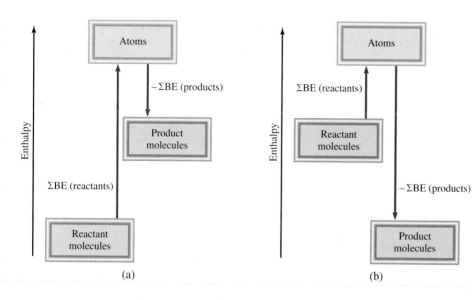

Figure 9.7 Bond energy changes in (a) an endothermic reaction and (b) an exothermic reaction.

For diatomic molecules, Equation (9.3) is equivalent to Equation (6.17), so the results obtained from these two equations should correspond, as Example 9.13 illustrates.

Example 9.13

Use Equation (9.3) to calculate the enthalpy of reaction for the process

$$H_2(g) + Cl_2(g) \longrightarrow 2HCl(g)$$

Compare your result with that obtained using Equation (6.17).

Strategy Keep in mind that bond breaking is an energy absorbing (endothermic) process and bond making is an energy releasing (exothermic) process. Therefore, the overall energy change is the difference between these two opposing processes, as described by Equation (9.3).

Solution We start by counting the number of bonds broken and the number of bonds formed and the corresponding energy changes. This is best done by creating a table:

Type of bonds broken	Number of bonds broken	Bond energy (kJ/mol)	Energy change (kJ/mol)
H—H (H_2)	1	436.4	436.4
Cl—Cl (Cl_2)	1	242.7	242.7

Type of bonds formed	Number of bonds formed	Bond energy (kJ/mol)	Energy change (kJ/mol)
H—Cl (HCl)	2	431.9	863.8

Next, we obtain the total energy input and total energy released:

$$\text{total energy input} = 436.4 \text{ kJ/mol} + 242.7 \text{ kJ/mol} = 679.1 \text{ kJ/mol}$$
$$\text{total energy released} = 863.8 \text{ kJ/mol}$$

Using Equation (9.3), we write

$$\Delta H° = 679.1 \text{ kJ/mol} - 863.8 \text{ kJ/mol} = -184.7 \text{ kJ/mol}$$

(Continued)

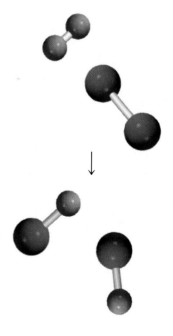

Refer to Table 9.4 for bond energies of these diatomic molecules.

Alternatively, we can use Equation (6.17) and the data in Appendix 3 to calculate the enthalpy of reaction:

$$\Delta H° = 2\Delta H_f°(HCl) - [\Delta H_f°(H_2) + \Delta H_f°(Cl_2)]$$
$$= (2)(-92.3 \text{ kJ/mol}) - 0 - 0$$
$$= -184.6 \text{ kJ/mol}$$

Check Because the reactants and products are all diatomic molecules, we expect the results of Equations (9.3) and (6.17) to be the same. The small discrepancy here is due to different ways of rounding off.

Similar problem: 9.104.

Practice Exercise Calculate the enthalpy of the reaction

$$H_2(g) + F_2(g) \longrightarrow 2HF(g)$$

using (a) Equation (9.3) and (b) Equation (6.17).

Example 9.14 uses Equation (9.3) to estimate the enthalpy of a reaction involving a polyatomic molecule.

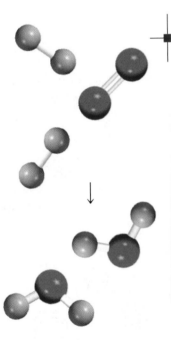

Example 9.14

Estimate the enthalpy change for the combustion of hydrogen gas:

$$2H_2(g) + O_2(g) \longrightarrow 2H_2O(g)$$

Strategy We basically follow the same procedure as that in Example 9.13. Note, however, that H_2O is a polyatomic molecule, and so we need to use the average bond energy value for the O—H bond.

Solution We construct the following table:

Type of bonds broken	Number of bonds broken	Bond energy (kJ/mol)	Energy change (kJ/mol)
H—H (H_2)	2	436.4	872.8
O=O (O_2)	1	498.7	498.7
Type of bonds formed	Number of bonds formed	Bond energy (kJ/mol)	Energy change (kJ/mol)
O—H (H_2O)	4	460	1840

Next, we obtain the total energy input and total energy released:

$$\text{total energy input} = 872.8 \text{ kJ/mol} + 498.7 \text{ kJ/mol} = 1371.5 \text{ kJ/mol}$$
$$\text{total energy released} = 1840 \text{ kJ/mol}$$

Using Equation (9.3), we write

$$\Delta H° = 1371.5 \text{ kJ/mol} - 1840 \text{ kJ/mol} = -469 \text{ kJ/mol}$$

This result is only an estimate because the bond energy of O—H is an average quantity. Alternatively, we can use Equation (6.17) and the data in Appendix 3 to calculate the enthalpy of reaction:

$$\Delta H° = 2\Delta H_f°(H_2O) - [2\Delta H_f°(H_2) + \Delta H_f°(O_2)]$$
$$= 2(-241.8 \text{ kJ/mol}) - 0 - 0$$
$$= -483.6 \text{ kJ/mol}$$

(Continued)

Check Note that the estimated value based on average bond energies is quite close to the value calculated using ΔH_f° data. In general, Equation (9.3) works best for reactions that are either quite endothermic or quite exothermic, that is, reactions for which $\Delta H_{rxn}^\circ > 100$ kJ/mol or for which $\Delta H_{rxn}^\circ < -100$ kJ/mol.

Similar problem: 9.72.

Practice Exercise For the reaction

$$H_2(g) + C_2H_4(g) \longrightarrow C_2H_6(g)$$

(a) Estimate the enthalpy of reaction, using the bond energy values in Table 9.4.
(b) Calculate the enthalpy of reaction, using standard enthalpies of formation. (ΔH_f° for H_2, C_2H_4, and C_2H_6 are 0, 52.3 kJ/mol, and −84.7 kJ/mol, respectively.)

Key Equation

- $\Delta H^\circ = \Sigma BE(\text{reactants}) - \Sigma BE(\text{products})$ (9.3)   Calculating enthalpy change of a reaction from bond energies.

Summary of Facts and Concepts

1. A Lewis dot symbol shows the number of valence electrons possessed by an atom of a given element. Lewis dot symbols are useful mainly for the representative elements.
2. The elements most likely to form ionic compounds have low ionization energies (such as the alkali metals and the alkaline earth metals, which form cations) or high electron affinities (such as the halogens and oxygen, which form anions).
3. An ionic bond is the product of the electrostatic forces of attraction between positive and negative ions. An ionic compound consists of a large network of ions in which positive and negative charges are balanced. The structure of a solid ionic compound maximizes the net attractive forces among the ions.
4. Lattice energy is a measure of the stability of an ionic solid. It can be calculated by means of the Born-Haber cycle, which is based on Hess's law.
5. In a covalent bond, two electrons (one pair) are shared by two atoms. In multiple covalent bonds, two or three pairs of electrons are shared by two atoms. Some covalently bonded atoms also have lone pairs, that is, pairs of valence electrons that are not involved in bonding. The arrangement of bonding electrons and lone pairs around atoms in a molecule is represented by a Lewis structure.
6. The octet rule predicts that atoms form enough covalent bonds to surround themselves with eight electrons each. When one atom in a covalently bonded pair donates two electrons to the bond, the Lewis structure can include the formal charge on each atom as a means of keeping track of the valence electrons. There are exceptions to the octet rule, particularly for covalent beryllium compounds, elements in Group 3A, and elements in the third period and beyond in the periodic table.
7. Electronegativity is a measure of an atom's ability to attract electrons in a chemical bond.
8. For some molecules or polyatomic ions, two or more Lewis structures based on the same skeletal structure satisfy the octet rule and appear chemically reasonable. Taken together, such resonance structures represent the molecule or ion more accurately than any single Lewis structure does.
9. The strength of a covalent bond is measured in terms of its bond energy. Bond energies can be used to estimate the enthalpy of reactions.

Key Words

Bond energy, p. 372	Covalent bond, p. 354	Lattice energy, p. 349	Polar covalent bond, p. 357
Bond length, p. 356	Covalent compound, p. 354	Lewis dot symbol, p. 346	Resonance, p. 366
Born-Haber cycle, p. 349	Double bond, p. 355	Lewis structure, p. 355	Resonance structure, p. 366
Coordinate covalent	Electronegativity, p. 357	Lone pair, p. 354	Single bond, p. 355
bond, p. 368	Formal charge, p. 363	Multiple bond, p. 355	Triple bond, p. 355
Coulomb's law, p. 349	Ionic bond, p. 347	Octet rule, p. 355	

Questions and Problems

Lewis Dot Symbols
Review Questions

9.1   What is a Lewis dot symbol? To what elements does the symbol mainly apply?

9.2   Use the second member of each group from Group 1A to Group 7A to show that the number of valence electrons on an atom of the element is the same as its group number.

9.3   Without referring to Figure 9.1, write Lewis dot symbols for atoms of the following elements: (a) Be, (b) K, (c) Ca, (d) Ga, (e) O, (f) Br, (g) N, (h) I, (i) As, (j) F.

9.4   Write Lewis dot symbols for the following ions: (a) Li^+, (b) Cl^-, (c) S^{2-}, (d) Sr^{2+}, (e) N^{3-}.

9.5   Write Lewis dot symbols for the following atoms and ions: (a) I, (b) I^-, (c) S, (d) S^{2-}, (e) P, (f) P^{3-}, (g) Na, (h) Na^+, (i) Mg, (j) Mg^{2+}, (k) Al, (l) Al^{3+}, (m) Pb, (n) Pb^{2+}.

The Ionic Bond
Review Questions

9.6   Explain what an ionic bond is.

9.7   Explain how ionization energy and electron affinity determine whether atoms of elements will combine to form ionic compounds.

9.8   Name five metals and five nonmetals that are very likely to form ionic compounds. Write formulas for compounds that might result from the combination of these metals and nonmetals. Name these compounds.

9.9   Name one ionic compound that contains only non-metallic elements.

9.10 Name one ionic compound that contains a polyatomic cation and a polyatomic anion (see Table 2.3).

9.11 Explain why ions with charges greater than 3 are seldom found in ionic compounds.

9.12 The term "molar mass" was introduced in Chapter 3. What is the advantage of using the term "molar mass" when we discuss ionic compounds?

9.13 In which of the following states would NaCl be electrically conducting? (a) solid, (b) molten (that is, melted), (c) dissolved in water. Explain your answers.

9.14 Beryllium forms a compound with chlorine that has the empirical formula $BeCl_2$. How would you determine whether it is an ionic compound? (The compound is not soluble in water.)

Problems

9.15 An ionic bond is formed between a cation A^+ and an anion B^-. How would the energy of the ionic bond [see Equation (9.2)] be affected by the following changes? (a) doubling the radius of A^+, (b) tripling the charge on A^+, (c) doubling the charges on A^+ and B^-, (d) decreasing the radii of A^+ and B^- to half their original values.

9.16 Give the empirical formulas and names of the compounds formed from the following pairs of ions: (a) Rb^+ and I^-, (b) Cs^+ and SO_4^{2-}, (c) Sr^{2+} and N^{3-}, (d) Al^{3+} and S^{2-}.

9.17 Use Lewis dot symbols to show the transfer of electrons between the following atoms to form cations and anions: (a) Na and F, (b) K and S, (c) Ba and O, (d) Al and N.

9.18 Write the Lewis dot symbols of the reactants and products in the following reactions. (First balance the equations.)
(a) Sr + Se $\longrightarrow$ SrSe
(b) Ca + H_2 $\longrightarrow$ CaH_2
(c) Li + N_2 $\longrightarrow$ Li_3N
(d) Al + S $\longrightarrow$ Al_2S_3

9.19 For each of the following pairs of elements, state whether the binary compound they form is likely to be ionic or covalent. Write the empirical formula and name of the compound: (a) I and Cl, (b) Mg and F.

9.20 For each of the following pairs of elements, state whether the binary compound they form is likely to be ionic or covalent. Write the empirical formula and name of the compound: (a) B and F, (b) K and Br.

Lattice Energy of Ionic Compounds
Review Questions

9.21 What is lattice energy and what role does it play in the stability of ionic compounds?

9.22 Explain how the lattice energy of an ionic compound such as KCl can be determined using the Born-Haber cycle. On what law is this procedure based?

9.23 Specify which compound in the following pairs of ionic compounds has the higher lattice energy: (a) KCl or MgO, (b) LiF or LiBr, (c) Mg_3N_2 or NaCl. Explain your choice.

9.24 Compare the stability (in the solid state) of the following pairs of compounds: (a) LiF and LiF_2 (containing the Li^{2+} ion), (b) Cs_2O and CsO (containing the O^- ion), (c) $CaBr_2$ and $CaBr_3$ (containing the Ca^{3+} ion).

Problems

9.25 Use the Born-Haber cycle outlined in Section 9.3 for LiF to calculate the lattice energy of NaCl. [The heat of sublimation of Na is 108 kJ/mol and $\Delta H_f^\circ(NaCl) = -411$ kJ/mol. Energy needed to dissociate $\frac{1}{2}$ mole of Cl_2 into Cl atoms = 121.4 kJ.]

9.26 Calculate the lattice energy of calcium chloride given that the heat of sublimation of Ca is 121 kJ/mol and $\Delta H_f^\circ(CaCl_2) = -795$ kJ/mol. (See Tables 8.2 and 8.3 for other data.)

The Covalent Bond
Review Questions

9.27 What is Lewis's contribution to our understanding of the covalent bond?

9.28 Use an example to illustrate each of the following terms: lone pairs, Lewis structure, the octet rule, bond length.

9.29 What is the difference between a Lewis dot symbol and a Lewis structure?

9.30 How many lone pairs are on the underlined atoms in these compounds? H$\underline{Br}$, H$_2\underline{S}$, $\underline{C}H_4$

9.31 Compare single, double, and triple bonds in a molecule, and give an example of each. For the same bonding atoms, how does the bond length change from single bond to triple bond?

9.32 Compare the properties of ionic compounds and covalent compounds.

Electronegativity and Bond Type
Review Questions

9.33 Define electronegativity, and explain the difference between electronegativity and electron affinity. Describe in general how the electronegativities of the elements change according to position in the periodic table.

9.34 What is a polar covalent bond? Name two compounds that contain one or more polar covalent bonds.

Problems

9.35 List the following bonds in order of increasing ionic character: the lithium-to-fluorine bond in LiF, the potassium-to-oxygen bond in K_2O, the nitrogen-to-nitrogen bond in N_2, the sulfur-to-oxygen bond in SO_2, the chlorine-to-fluorine bond in ClF_3.

9.36 Arrange the following bonds in order of increasing ionic character: carbon to hydrogen, fluorine to hydrogen, bromine to hydrogen, sodium to chlorine, potassium to fluorine, lithium to chlorine.

9.37 Four atoms are arbitrarily labeled D, E, F, and G. Their electronegativities are as follows: D = 3.8, E = 3.3, F = 2.8, and G = 1.3. If the atoms of these elements form the molecules DE, DG, EG, and DF, how would you arrange these molecules in order of increasing covalent bond character?

9.38 List the following bonds in order of increasing ionic character: cesium to fluorine, chlorine to chlorine, bromine to chlorine, silicon to carbon.

9.39 Classify the following bonds as ionic, polar covalent, or covalent, and give your reasons: (a) the CC bond in H_3CCH_3, (b) the KI bond in KI, (c) the NB bond in H_3NBCl_3, (d) the CF bond in CF_4.

9.40 Classify the following bonds as ionic, polar covalent, or covalent, and give your reasons: (a) the SiSi bond in $Cl_3SiSiCl_3$, (b) the SiCl bond in $Cl_3SiSiCl_3$, (c) the CaF bond in CaF_2, (d) the NH bond in NH_3.

Lewis Structure and the Octet Rule
Review Questions

9.41 Summarize the essential features of the Lewis octet rule. The octet rule applies mainly to the second-period elements. Explain.

9.42 Explain the concept of formal charge. Do formal charges represent actual separation of charges?

Problems

9.43 Write Lewis structures for the following molecules and ions: (a) NCl_3, (b) OCS, (c) H_2O_2, (d) CH_3COO^-, (e) CN^-, (f) $CH_3CH_2NH_3^+$.

9.44 Write Lewis structures for the following molecules and ions: (a) OF_2, (b) N_2F_2, (c) Si_2H_6, (d) OH^-, (e) CH_2ClCOO^-, (f) $CH_3NH_3^+$.

9.45 Write Lewis structures for the following molecules: (a) ICl, (b) PH_3, (c) P_4 (each P is bonded to three other P atoms), (d) H_2S, (e) N_2H_4, (f) $HClO_3$, (g) $COBr_2$ (C is bonded to O and Br atoms).

9.46 Write Lewis structures for the following ions: (a) O_2^{2-}, (b) C_2^{2-}, (c) NO^+, (d) NH_4^+. Show formal charges.

9.47. The following Lewis structures are incorrect. Explain what is wrong with each one and give a correct Lewis structure for the molecule. (Relative positions of atoms are shown correctly.)

(a) $H-C\equiv\overset{..}{N}$

(b) $H=C=C=H$

(c) $\overset{..}{\underset{..}{O}}-Sn-\overset{..}{\underset{..}{O}}$

(d) $:\overset{..}{\underset{..}{F}}\diagdown_{\underset{|}{B}}\diagup\overset{..}{\underset{..}{F}}:$
    $:\overset{..}{\underset{..}{F}}:$

(e) $H-\overset{..}{\underset{..}{O}}=\overset{..}{\underset{..}{F}}:$

(f) $\overset{\textstyle H}{\diagdown}\overset{..}{\underset{..}{C}}-\overset{..}{\underset{..}{F}}:$
    $\overset{.}{\underset{..}{O}}.$

(g) $:\overset{..}{F}\diagdown_{\underset{|}{N}}\diagup\overset{..}{F}:$
    $:\overset{..}{\underset{..}{F}}:$

9.48 The skeletal structure of acetic acid shown below is correct, but some of the bonds are wrong. (a) Identify the incorrect bonds and explain what is wrong with them. (b) Write the correct Lewis structure for acetic acid.

$$\begin{array}{ccc} H & :O: \\ | & | \\ H=C-C-\overset{..}{\underset{..}{O}}-H \\ | \\ H \end{array}$$

The Concept of Resonance
Review Questions

9.49 Define bond length, resonance, and resonance structure. What are the rules for writing resonance structures?

9.50 Is it possible to "trap" a resonance structure of a compound for study? Explain.

Problems

9.51 Write Lewis structures for the following species, including all resonance forms, and show formal charges: (a) HCO_2^-, (b) $CH_2NO_2^-$. Relative positions of the atoms are as follows:

$$\begin{array}{cccccc} & O & & H & & O \\ H & C & & & C & N \\ & O & & H & & O \end{array}$$

9.52 Draw three resonance structures for the chlorate ion, ClO_3^-. Show formal charges.

9.53 Write three resonance structures for hydrazoic acid, HN_3. The atomic arrangement is HNNN. Show formal charges.

9.54 Draw two resonance structures for diazomethane, CH_2N_2. Show formal charges. The skeletal structure of the molecule is

$$\begin{array}{ccc} H \\ & C & N & N \\ H \end{array}$$

9.55 Draw three reasonable resonance structures for the OCN^- ion. Show formal charges.

9.56 Draw three resonance structures for the molecule N_2O in which the atoms are arranged in the order NNO. Indicate formal charges.

Exceptions to the Octet Rule
Review Questions

9.57 Why does the octet rule not hold for many compounds containing elements in the third period of the periodic table and beyond?

9.58 Give three examples of compounds that do not satisfy the octet rule. Write a Lewis structure for each.

9.59 Because fluorine has seven valence electrons $(2s^2 2p^5)$, seven covalent bonds in principle could form around the atom. Such a compound might be FH_7 or FCl_7. These compounds have never been prepared. Why?

9.60 What is a coordinate covalent bond? Is it different from a normal covalent bond?

Problems

9.61 The AlI_3 molecule has an incomplete octet around Al. Draw three resonance structures of the molecule in which the octet rule is satisfied for both the Al and the I atoms. Show formal charges.

9.62 In the vapor phase, beryllium chloride consists of discrete $BeCl_2$ molecules. Is the octet rule satisfied for Be in this compound? If not, can you form an octet around Be by drawing another resonance structure? How plausible is this structure?

9.63 Of the noble gases, only Kr, Xe, and Rn are known to form a few compounds with O and/or F. Write Lewis structures for the following molecules: (a) XeF_2, (b) XeF_4, (c) XeF_6, (d) $XeOF_4$, (e) XeO_2F_2. In each case Xe is the central atom.

9.64 Write a Lewis structure for $SbCl_5$. Does this molecule obey the octet rule?

9.65 Write Lewis structures for SeF_4 and SeF_6. Is the octet rule satisfied for Se?

9.66 Write Lewis structures for the reaction

$$AlCl_3 + Cl^- \longrightarrow AlCl_4^-$$

What kind of bond joins Al and Cl in the product?

Bond Energy
Review Questions

9.67 What is bond energy? Bond energies of polyatomic molecules are average values, whereas those of diatomic molecules can be accurately determined. Why?

9.68 Explain why the bond energy of a molecule is usually defined in terms of a gas-phase reaction. Why are bond-breaking processes always endothermic and bond-forming processes always exothermic?

Problems

9.69 From the following data, calculate the average bond energy for the N—H bond:

$$NH_3(g) \longrightarrow NH_2(g) + H(g) \quad \Delta H° = 435 \text{ kJ/mol}$$
$$NH_2(g) \longrightarrow NH(g) + H(g) \quad \Delta H° = 381 \text{ kJ/mol}$$
$$NH(g) \longrightarrow N(g) + H(g) \quad \Delta H° = 360 \text{ kJ/mol}$$

9.70 For the reaction

$$O(g) + O_2(g) \longrightarrow O_3(g) \quad \Delta H° = -107.2 \text{ kJ/mol}$$

Calculate the average bond energy in O_3.

9.71 The bond energy of $F_2(g)$ is 156.9 kJ/mol. Calculate $\Delta H_f°$ for $F(g)$.

9.72 For the reaction

$$2C_2H_6(g) + 7O_2(g) \longrightarrow 4CO_2(g) + 6H_2O(g)$$

(a) Predict the enthalpy of reaction from the average bond energies in Table 9.4.
(b) Calculate the enthalpy of reaction from the standard enthalpies of formation (see Appendix 3) of the reactant and product molecules, and compare the result with your answer for part (a).

Additional Problems

9.73 Classify the following substances as ionic compounds or covalent compounds containing discrete molecules: CH_4, KF, CO, $SiCl_4$, $BaCl_2$.

9.74 Which of the following are ionic compounds? Which are covalent compounds? RbCl, PF_5, BrF_3, KO_2, CI_4

9.75 Match each of the following energy changes with one of the processes given: ionization energy, electron affinity, bond energy, and standard enthalpy of formation.
(a) $F(g) + e^- \longrightarrow F^-(g)$
(b) $F_2(g) \longrightarrow 2F(g)$
(c) $Na(g) \longrightarrow Na^+(g) + e^-$
(d) $Na(s) + \frac{1}{2}F_2(g) \longrightarrow NaF(s)$

9.76 The formulas for the fluorides of the third-period elements are NaF, MgF_2, AlF_3, SiF_4, PF_5, SF_6, and ClF_3. Classify these compounds as covalent or ionic.

9.77 Use ionization energy (see Table 8.2) and electron affinity values (see Table 8.3) to calculate the energy change (in kJ/mol) for the following reactions:
(a) $Li(g) + I(g) \longrightarrow Li^+(g) + I^-(g)$
(b) $Na(g) + F(g) \longrightarrow Na^+(g) + F^-(g)$
(c) $K(g) + Cl(g) \longrightarrow K^+(g) + Cl^-(g)$

9.78 Describe some characteristics of an ionic compound such as KF that would distinguish it from a covalent compound such as benzene (C_6H_6).

9.79 Write Lewis structures for BrF_3, ClF_5, and IF_7. Identify those in which the octet rule is not obeyed.

9.80 Write three reasonable resonance structures for the azide ion N_3^- in which the atoms are arranged as NNN. Show formal charges.

9.81 The amide group plays an important role in determining the structure of proteins:

Draw another resonance structure for this group. Show formal charges.

9.82 Give an example of an ion or molecule containing Al that (a) obeys the octet rule, (b) has an expanded octet, and (c) has an incomplete octet.

9.83 Draw four reasonable resonance structures for the PO_3F^{2-} ion. The central P atom is bonded to the three O atoms and to the F atom. Show formal charges.

9.84 Attempts to prepare the compounds listed here as stable species under atmospheric conditions have failed. Suggest possible reasons for the failure. CF_2, LiO_2, $CsCl_2$, PI_5

9.85 Draw reasonable resonance structures for the following ions: (a) HSO_4^-, (b) PO_4^{3-}, (c) HSO_3^-, (d) SO_3^{2-}. (*Hint:* See comment on p. 371.)

9.86 Are the following statements true or false? (a) Formal charges represent actual separation of charges. (b) $\Delta H_{rxn}°$ can be estimated from the bond energies of reactants and products. (c) All second-period elements obey the octet rule in their compounds. (d) The resonance structures of a molecule can be separated from one another.

9.87 A rule for drawing plausible Lewis structures is that the central atom is invariably less electronegative than the surrounding atoms. Explain why this is so.

9.88 Using the following information and the fact that the average C—H bond energy is 414 kJ/mol, estimate the standard enthalpy of formation of methane (CH_4).

$$C(s) \longrightarrow C(g) \quad \Delta H_{rxn}° = 716 \text{ kJ/mol}$$
$$2H_2(g) \longrightarrow 4H(g) \quad \Delta H_{rxn}° = 872.8 \text{ kJ/mol}$$

9.89 Based on energy considerations, which of the following reactions will occur more readily?
(a) $Cl(g) + CH_4(g) \longrightarrow CH_3Cl(g) + H(g)$
(b) $Cl(g) + CH_4(g) \longrightarrow CH_3(g) + HCl(g)$
(*Hint:* Refer to Table 9.4, and assume that the average bond energy of the C—Cl bond is 338 kJ/mol.)

9.90 Which of the following molecules has the shortest nitrogen-to-nitrogen bond? Explain. N_2H_4, N_2O, N_2, N_2O_4

9.91 Most organic acids can be represented as RCOOH, where COOH is the carboxyl group and R is the rest of the molecule. (For example, R is CH_3 in acetic acid, CH_3COOH). (a) Draw a Lewis structure for the carboxyl group. (b) Upon ionization, the carboxyl group is converted to the carboxylate group, COO^-. Draw resonance structures for the carboxylate group.

9.92 Which of the following species are isoelectronic? NH_4^+, C_6H_6, CO, CH_4, N_2, $B_3N_3H_6$

9.93 The following species have been detected in interstellar space: (a) CH, (b) OH, (c) C_2, (d) HNC, (e) HCO.

Draw Lewis structures for these species and indicate whether they are diamagnetic or paramagnetic.

9.94 The amide ion, NH_2^-, is a Brønsted base. Represent the reaction between the amide ion and water.

9.95 Draw Lewis structures for the following organic molecules: (a) tetrafluoroethylene (C_2F_4), (b) propane (C_3H_8), (c) butadiene ($CH_2CHCHCH_2$), (d) propyne (CH_3CCH), (e) benzoic acid (C_6H_5COOH). (To draw C_6H_5COOH, replace a H atom in benzene with a COOH group.)

9.96 The triiodide ion (I_3^-) in which the I atoms are arranged in a straight line is stable, but the corresponding F_3^- ion does not exist. Explain.

9.97 Compare the bond energy of F_2 with the energy change for the following process:

$$F_2(g) \longrightarrow F^+(g) + F^-(g)$$

Which is the preferred dissociation for F_2, energetically speaking?

9.98 Methyl isocyanate (CH_3NCO) is used to make certain pesticides. In December 1984, water leaked into a tank containing this substance at a chemical plant, producing a toxic cloud that killed thousands of people in Bhopal, India. Draw Lewis structures for CH_3NCO, showing formal charges.

9.99 The chlorine nitrate molecule ($ClONO_2$) is believed to be involved in the destruction of ozone in the Antarctic stratosphere. Draw a plausible Lewis structure for this molecule.

9.100 Several resonance structures for the molecule CO_2 are shown below. Explain why some of them are likely to be of little importance in describing the bonding in this molecule.

(a) $\overset{..}{O}=C=\overset{..}{O}$

(b) $:O\equiv\overset{+}{C}-\overset{..\,-}{O}:$

(c) $:\overset{+}{O}\equiv\overset{\,\,-}{C}\;\;\overset{..}{O}:$

(d) $\overset{-\,..}{:O}-\overset{2+}{C}-\overset{..\,-}{O}:$

9.101 For each of the following organic molecules draw a Lewis structure in which the carbon atoms are bonded to each other by single bonds: (a) C_2H_6, (b) C_4H_{10}, (c) C_5H_{12}. For (b) and (c), show only structures in which each C atom is bonded to no more than two other C atoms.

9.102 Draw Lewis structures for the following chlorofluorocarbons (CFCs), which are partly responsible for the depletion of ozone in the stratosphere: (a) $CFCl_3$, (b) CF_2Cl_2, (c) CHF_2Cl, (d) CF_3CHF_2.

9.103 Draw Lewis structures for the following organic molecules. In each there is one $C=C$ bond, and the rest of the carbon atoms are joined by $C-C$ bonds. C_2H_3F, C_3H_6, C_4H_8

9.104 Calculate $\Delta H°$ for the reaction

$$H_2(g) + I_2(g) \longrightarrow 2HI(g)$$

using (a) Equation (9.3) and (b) Equation (6.17), given that $\Delta H_f°$ for $I_2(g)$ is 61.0 kJ/mol.

9.105 Draw Lewis structures for the following organic molecules: (a) methanol (CH_3OH); (b) ethanol (CH_3CH_2OH); (c) tetraethyllead [$Pb(CH_2CH_3)_4$], which is used in "leaded gasoline"; (d) methylamine (CH_3NH_2), which is used in tanning; (e) mustard gas ($ClCH_2CH_2SCH_2CH_2Cl$), a poisonous gas used in World War I; (f) urea [$(NH_2)_2CO$], a fertilizer; and (g) glycine (NH_2CH_2COOH), an amino acid.

9.106 Write Lewis structures for the following four isoelectronic species: (a) CO, (b) NO^+, (c) CN^-, (d) N_2. Show formal charges.

9.107 Oxygen forms three types of ionic compounds in which the anions are oxide (O^{2-}), peroxide (O_2^{2-}), and superoxide (O_2^-). Draw Lewis structures of these ions.

9.108 Comment on the correctness of the statement, "All compounds containing a noble gas atom violate the octet rule."

9.109 Write three resonance structures for (a) the cyanate ion (NCO^-) and (b) the isocyanate ion (CNO^-). In each case, rank the resonance structures in order of increasing importance.

9.110 (a) From the following data calculate the bond energy of the F_2^- ion.

$$\begin{array}{ll} F_2(g) \longrightarrow 2F(g) & \Delta H°_{rxn} = 156.9 \text{ kJ/mol} \\ F^-(g) \longrightarrow F(g) + e^- & \Delta H°_{rxn} = 333 \text{ kJ/mol} \\ F_2^-(g) \longrightarrow F_2(g) + e^- & \Delta H°_{rxn} = 290 \text{ kJ/mol} \end{array}$$

(b) Explain the difference between the bond energies of F_2 and F_2^-.

9.111 The resonance concept is sometimes described by analogy to a mule, which is a cross between a horse and a donkey. Compare this analogy with the one used in this chapter, that is, the description of a rhinoceros as a cross between a griffin and a unicorn. Which description is more appropriate? Why?

9.112 What are the other two reasons for choosing (b) in Example 9.7?

9.113 In the Chemistry in Action essay on p. 372, nitric oxide is said to be one of about ten of the smallest stable molecules known. Based on what you have learned in the course so far, write all the diatomic molecules you know, give their names, and show their Lewis structures.

9.114 The N—O bond distance in nitric oxide is 115 pm, which is intermediate between a triple bond (106 pm) and a double bond (120 pm). (a) Draw two resonance structures for NO and comment on their relative importance. (b) Is it possible to draw a resonance structure having a triple bond between the atoms?

9.115 Although nitrogen dioxide (NO_2) is a stable compound, there is a tendency for two such molecules to combine to form dinitrogen tetroxide (N_2O_4). Why? Draw four resonance structures of N_2O_4, showing formal charges.

9.116 Another possible skeletal structure for the CO_3^{2-} (carbonate) ion besides the one presented in Example 9.5 is O C O O. Why would we not use this structure to represent CO_3^{2-}?

9.117 Draw a Lewis structure for nitrogen pentoxide (N_2O_5) in which each N is bonded to three O atoms.

9.118 In the gas phase, aluminum chloride exists as a dimer (a unit of two) with the formula Al_2Cl_6. Its skeletal structure is given by

$$\begin{array}{ccc} Cl & Cl & Cl \\ \diagdown & \diagup \diagdown & \diagup \\ & Al \quad Al & \\ \diagup & \diagdown \diagup & \diagdown \\ Cl & Cl & Cl \end{array}$$

Complete the Lewis structure and indicate the coordinate covalent bonds in the molecule.

9.119 The hydroxyl radical (OH) plays an important role in atmospheric chemistry. It is highly reactive and has a tendency to combine with a H atom from other compounds, causing them to break up. Thus OH is sometimes called a "detergent" radical because it helps to clean up the atmosphere. (a) Write the Lewis structure for the radical. (b) Refer to Table 9.4 and explain why the radical has a high affinity for H atoms. (c) Estimate the enthalpy change for the following reaction:

$$OH(g) + CH_4(g) \longrightarrow CH_3(g) + H_2O(g)$$

(d) The radical is generated when sunlight hits water vapor. Calculate the maximum wavelength (in nanometers) required to break an O—H bond in H_2O.

9.120 Experiments show that it takes 1656 kJ/mol to break all the bonds in methane (CH_4) and 4006 kJ/mol to break all the bonds in propane (C_3H_8). Based on these data, calculate the average bond energy of the C—C bond.

9.121 Draw three resonance structures of sulfur dioxide (SO_2). Indicate the most plausible structure(s). (*Hint:* See Example 9.11.)

9.122 Vinyl chloride (C_2H_3Cl) differs from ethylene (C_2H_4) in that one of the H atoms is replaced with a Cl atom. Vinyl chloride is used to prepare poly(vinyl chloride), which is an important polymer used in pipes. (a) Draw the Lewis structure of vinyl chloride. (b) The repeating unit in poly(vinyl chloride) is —CH_2—$CHCl$—. Draw a portion of the molecule showing three such repeating units. (c) Calculate the enthalpy change when 1.0×10^3 kg of vinyl chloride forms poly(vinyl chloride).

9.123 In 1998 scientists using a special type of electron microscope were able to measure the force needed to break a *single* chemical bond. If 2.0×10^{-9} N was needed to break a C—Si bond, estimate the bond energy in kJ/mol. Assume that the bond had to be stretched by a distance of 2 Å (2×10^{-10} m) before it is broken.

9.124 The American chemist Robert S. Mulliken suggested a different definition for the electronegativity (EN) of an element, given by

$$EN = \frac{IE + EA}{2}$$

where IE is the first ionization energy and EA the electron affinity of the element. Calculate the electronegativities of O, F, and Cl using the above equation. Compare the electronegativities of these elements on the Mulliken and Pauling scale. (To convert to the Pauling scale, divide each EN value by 230 kJ/mol.)

9.125 Among the common inhaled anesthetics are:
halothane: $CF_3CHClBr$
enflurane: $CHFClCF_2OCHF_2$
isoflurane: $CF_3CHClOCHF_2$
methoxyflurane: $CHCl_2CF_2OCH_3$
Draw Lewis structures of these molecules.

9.126 A student in your class claims that magnesium oxide actually consists of Mg^+ and O^- ions, not Mg^{2+} and O^{2-} ions. Suggest some experiments one could do to show that your classmate is wrong.

Answers to Practice Exercises

9.1 $\cdot Ba \cdot \; + 2 \cdot H \longrightarrow Ba^{2+} \; 2H:^- \quad$ (or BaH_2)
$\;\;[Xe]6s^2 \quad 1s^1 \qquad [Xe] \; [He]$

9.2 (a) Ionic, (b) polar covalent, (c) covalent.

9.3 $\ddot{S}=C=\ddot{S}$ **9.4** $H—\overset{\overset{\ddot{}}{\ddot{O}}}{\underset{}{C}}—\ddot{O}—H$ **9.5** $\left[\ddot{O}=N—\ddot{O}: \right]^-$

9.6 $\ddot{O}=N—\ddot{O}:^-$ **9.7** $H—C\equiv N:$

9.8 $\ddot{O}=N—\ddot{O}:^- \longleftrightarrow {}^-:\ddot{O}—N=\ddot{O}$

9.9 $:\ddot{F}—Be—\ddot{F}:$

9.10 $\begin{array}{c} :\ddot{F}: \\ :\ddot{F}—As \end{array}$ with $\ddot{F}:$ and $:\ddot{F}:$ (pentafluoride structure)

9.11 $H—\ddot{O}—\overset{\overset{:O:}{\|}}{\underset{\underset{:O:}{\|}}{S}}—\ddot{O}—H$

9.12 $\begin{array}{c} :\ddot{F} \quad \ddot{F}: \\ S \\ :\ddot{F} \quad \ddot{F}: \end{array}$

9.13 (a) -543.1 kJ/mol, (b) -543.2 kJ/mol.

9.14 (a) -119 kJ/mol, (b) -137.0 kJ/mol.

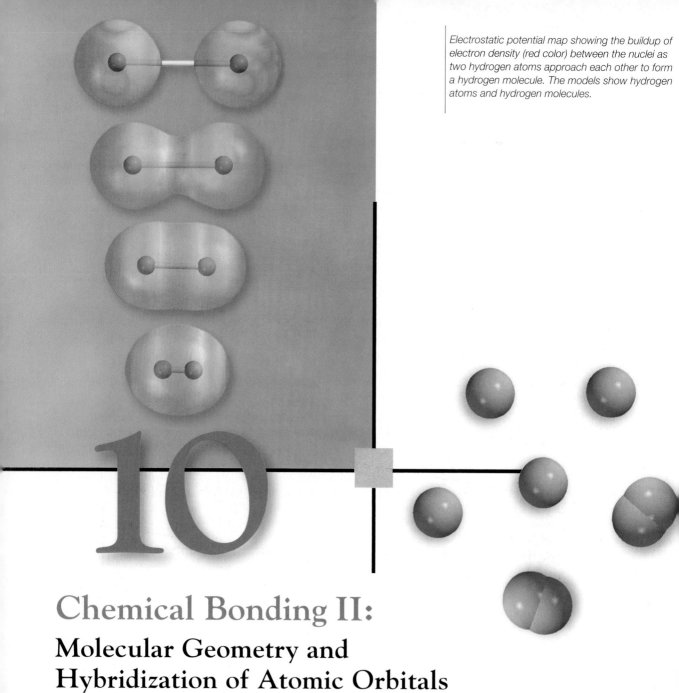

Electrostatic potential map showing the buildup of electron density (red color) between the nuclei as two hydrogen atoms approach each other to form a hydrogen molecule. The models show hydrogen atoms and hydrogen molecules.

10

Chemical Bonding II:
Molecular Geometry and Hybridization of Atomic Orbitals

Interactive Activity Summary

1. Animation: VSEPR (10.1)
2. Interactivity: Determining Molecular Shape (10.1)
3. Animation: Polarity of Molecules (10.2)
4. Interactivity: Molecular Polarity (10.2)
5. Animation: Hybridization (10.4)
6. Interactivity: Determining Orbital Hybridization (10.4)
7. Animation: Sigma and Pi Bonds (10.5)
8. Interactivity: Energy Levels—Homonuclear Diatomic Molecules (10.7)

In Chapter 9 we discussed bonding in terms of the Lewis theory. Here we will study the shape, or geometry, of molecules. Geometry has an important influence on the physical and chemical properties of molecules, such as melting point, boiling point, and reactivity. We will see that we can predict the shapes of molecules with considerable accuracy using a simple method based on Lewis structures.

The Lewis theory of chemical bonding, although useful and easy to apply, does not tell us how and why bonds form. A proper understanding of bonding comes from quantum mechanics. Therefore, in the second part of this chapter, we will apply quantum mechanics to the study of the geometry and stability of molecules.

10.1 Molecular Geometry

Molecular geometry is the three-dimensional arrangement of atoms in a molecule. A molecule's geometry affects its physical and chemical properties, such as melting point, boiling point, density, and the types of reactions it undergoes. In general, bond lengths and bond angles must be determined by experiment. However, there is a simple procedure that enables us to predict with considerable success the overall geometry of a molecule or ion if we know the number of electrons surrounding a central atom in its Lewis structure. The basis of this approach is the assumption that electron pairs in the valence shell of an atom repel one another. The **valence shell** is *the outermost electron-occupied shell of an atom; it holds the electrons that are usually involved in bonding.* In a covalent bond, a pair of electrons, often called the *bonding pair,* is responsible for holding two atoms together. However, in a polyatomic molecule, where there are two or more bonds between the central atom and the surrounding atoms, the repulsion between electrons in different bonding pairs causes them to remain as far apart as possible. The geometry that the molecule ultimately assumes (as defined by the positions of all the atoms) minimizes the repulsion. This approach to the study of molecular geometry is called the **valence-shell electron-pair repulsion (VSEPR) model,** because *it accounts for the geometric arrangements of electron pairs around a central atom in terms of the electrostatic repulsion between electron pairs.*

Two general rules govern the use of the VSEPR model:

1. As far as electron-pair repulsion is concerned, double bonds and triple bonds can be treated like single bonds. This approximation is good for qualitative purposes. However, you should realize that in reality multiple bonds are "larger" than single bonds; that is, because there are two or three bonds between two atoms, the electron density occupies more space.

2. If a molecule has two or more resonance structures, we can apply the VSEPR model to any one of them. Formal charges are usually not shown.

With this model in mind, we can predict the geometry of molecules (and ions) in a systematic way. For this purpose, it is convenient to divide molecules into two categories, according to whether or not the central atom has lone pairs.

Molecules in Which the Central Atom Has No Lone Pairs

For simplicity we will consider molecules that contain atoms of only two elements, A and B, of which A is the central atom. These molecules have the general formula AB_x, where x is an integer 2, 3, ... (If $x = 1$, we have the diatomic molecule AB, which is linear by definition.) In the vast majority of cases, x is between 2 and 6.

Table 10.1 shows five possible arrangements of electron pairs around the central atom A. As a result of mutual repulsion, the electron pairs stay as far from one another as possible. Note that the table shows arrangements of the electron pairs but not the positions of the atoms that surround the central atom. Molecules in which the central atom has no lone pairs have one of these five arrangements of bonding pairs. Using Table 10.1 as a reference, let us take a close look at the geometry of molecules with the formulas AB_2, AB_3, AB_4, AB_5, and AB_6.

The term "central atom" means an atom that is not a terminal atom in a polyatomic molecule.

VSEPR is pronounced "vesper."

Animation: VSEPR
Online Learning Center,
Animations

Interactivity: Determining
Molecular Shape
Online Learning Center,
Interactives

TABLE 10.1

Arrangement of Electron Pairs About a Central Atom (A) in a Molecule and Geometry of Some Simple Molecules and Ions in Which the Central Atom Has No Lone Pairs

Number of Electron Pairs	Arrangement of Electron Pairs*	Molecular Geometry*	Examples
2	180° :—A—: Linear	B—A—B Linear	$BeCl_2$, $HgCl_2$
3	120° Trigonal planar	Trigonal planar	BF_3
4	109.5° Tetrahedral	Tetrahedral	CH_4, NH_4^+
5	90° 120° Trigonal bipyramidal	Trigonal bipyramidal	PCl_5
6	90° 90° Octahedral	Octahedral	SF_6

* The colored lines are used only to show the overall shapes; they do not represent bonds.

AB₂: Beryllium Chloride (BeCl₂) The Lewis structure of beryllium chloride in the gaseous state is

$$:\overset{..}{\underset{..}{Cl}}—Be—\overset{..}{\underset{..}{Cl}}:$$

Because the bonding pairs repel each other, they must be at opposite ends of a straight line in order for them to be as far apart as possible. Thus, the ClBeCl angle is predicted to be 180°, and the molecule is linear (see Table 10.1). The "ball-and-stick" model of $BeCl_2$ is

The blue and gold spheres are for atoms in general.

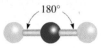

AB$_3$: Boron Trifluoride (BF$_3$) Boron trifluoride contains three covalent bonds, or bonding pairs. In the most stable arrangement, the three BF bonds point to the corners of an equilateral triangle with B in the center of the triangle:

According to Table 10.1, the geometry of BF_3 is *trigonal planar* because the three end atoms are at the corners of an equilateral triangle which is planar:

Planar

Thus, each of the three FBF angles is 120°, and all four atoms lie in the same plane.

AB$_4$: Methane (CH$_4$) The Lewis structure of methane is

$$H-\overset{\overset{\displaystyle H}{|}}{\underset{\underset{\displaystyle H}{|}}{C}}-H$$

Because there are four bonding pairs, the geometry of CH_4 is tetrahedral (see Table 10.1). A *tetrahedron* has four sides (the prefix *tetra* means "four"), or faces, all of which are equilateral triangles. In a tetrahedral molecule, the central atom (C in this case) is located at the center of the tetrahedron and the other four atoms are at the corners. The bond angles are all 109.5°.

Tetrahedral

AB$_5$: Phosphorus Pentachloride (PCl$_5$) The Lewis structure of phosphorus pentachloride (in the gas phase) is

The only way to minimize the repulsive forces among the five bonding pairs is to arrange the PCl bonds in the form of a trigonal bipyramid (see Table 10.1). A trigonal bipyramid can be generated by joining two tetrahedrons along a common triangular base:

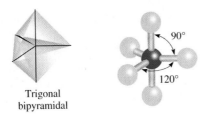

Trigonal
bipyramidal

The central atom (P in this case) is at the center of the common triangle with the surrounding atoms positioned at the five corners of the trigonal bipyramid. The atoms that are above and below the triangular plane are said to occupy *axial* positions, and those that are in the triangular plane are said to occupy *equatorial* positions. The angle between any two equatorial bonds is 120°; that between an axial bond and an equatorial bond is 90°, and that between the two axial bonds is 180°.

AB_6: Sulfur Hexafluoride (SF_6) The Lewis structure of sulfur hexafluoride is

$$\begin{array}{c} :\ddot{F}: \\ :\ddot{F}\diagdown\ |\ \diagup\ddot{F}: \\ \diagup\overset{\displaystyle S}{}\diagdown \\ :\ddot{F}\diagup\ |\ \diagdown\ddot{F}: \\ :\ddot{F}: \end{array}$$

The most stable arrangement of the six SF bonding pairs is in the shape of an octahedron, shown in Table 10.1. An octahedron has eight sides (the prefix *octa* means "eight"). It can be generated by joining two square pyramids on a common base. The central atom (S in this case) is at the center of the square base and the surrounding atoms are at the six corners. All bond angles are 90° except the one made by the bonds between the central atom and the pairs of atoms that are diametrically opposite each other. That angle is 180°. Because the six bonds are equivalent in an octahedral molecule, we cannot use the terms "axial" and "equatorial" as in a trigonal bipyramidal molecule.

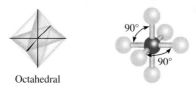

Octahedral

Molecules in Which the Central Atom Has One or More Lone Pairs

Determining the geometry of a molecule is more complicated if the central atom has both lone pairs and bonding pairs. In such molecules there are three types of repulsive forces—those between bonding pairs, those between lone pairs, and those between a bonding pair and a lone pair. In general, according to the VSEPR model, the repulsive forces decrease in the following order:

lone-pair vs. lone-pair > lone-pair vs. bonding- > bonding-pair vs. bonding-
repulsion   pair repulsion   pair repulsion

Electrons in a bond are held by the attractive forces exerted by the nuclei of the two bonded atoms. These electrons have less "spatial distribution" than lone pairs; that is, they take up less space than lone-pair electrons, which are associated with only one particular atom. Because lone-pair electrons in a molecule occupy more space, they experience greater repulsion from neighboring lone pairs and bonding pairs. To keep track of the total number of bonding pairs and lone pairs, we designate molecules with lone pairs as AB_xE_y, where A is the central atom, B is a surrounding atom, and E is a lone pair on A. Both x and y are integers; $x = 2, 3, \ldots$, and $y = 1, 2, \ldots$. Thus the values of x and y indicate the number of surrounding atoms and number of lone pairs on the central atom, respectively. The simplest such molecule would be a triatomic molecule with one lone pair on the central atom and the formula is AB_2E.

As the following examples show, in most cases the presence of lone pairs on the central atom makes it difficult to predict the bond angles accurately.

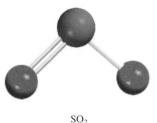

SO₂

AB_2E: Sulfur Dioxide (SO_2) The Lewis structure of sulfur dioxide is

$$\ddot{O}=\overset{\cdot\cdot}{S}-\ddot{O}:$$

Because VSEPR treats double bonds as though they were single, the SO_2 molecule can be viewed as consisting of three electron pairs on the central S atom. Of these, two are bonding pairs and one is a lone pair. In Table 10.1 we see that the overall arrangement of three electron pairs is trigonal planar. But because one of the electron pairs is a lone pair, the SO_2 molecule has a "bent" shape.

Because the lone-pair versus bonding-pair repulsion is greater than the bonding-pair versus bonding-pair repulsion, the two sulfur-to-oxygen bonds are pushed together slightly and the OSO angle is less than 120°.

AB_3E: Ammonia (NH_3) The ammonia molecule contains three bonding pairs and one lone pair:

$$H-\overset{\cdot\cdot}{N}-H$$
$$|$$
$$H$$

As Table 10.1 shows, the overall arrangement of four electron pairs is tetrahedral. But in NH_3 one of the electron pairs is a lone pair, so the geometry of NH_3 is trigonal pyramidal (so called because it looks like a pyramid, with the N atom at the apex). Because the lone pair repels the bonding pairs more strongly, the three NH bonding pairs are pushed closer together:

Thus the HNH angle in ammonia is smaller than the ideal tetrahedral angle of 109.5° (Figure 10.1).

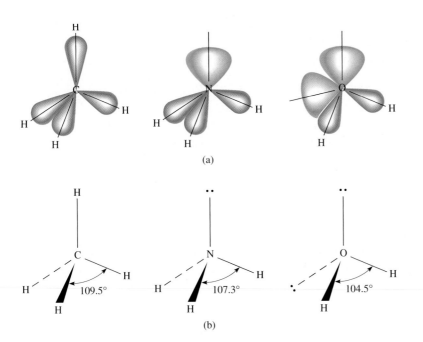

AB_2E_2: Water (H_2O) A water molecule contains two bonding pairs and two lone pairs:

$$H—\overset{..}{\underset{..}{O}}—H$$

The overall arrangement of the four electron pairs in water is tetrahedral, the same as in ammonia. However, unlike ammonia, water has two lone pairs on the central O atom. These lone pairs tend to be as far from each other as possible. Consequently, the two OH bonding pairs are pushed toward each other, and we predict an even greater deviation from the tetrahedral angle than in NH_3. As Figure 10.1 shows, the HOH angle is 104.5°. The geometry of H_2O is bent:

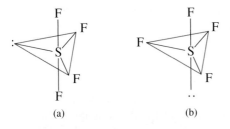

AB_4E: Sulfur Tetrafluoride (SF_4) The Lewis structure of SF_4 is

$$\begin{array}{c} :\overset{..}{F} \quad \overset{..}{F}: \\ \diagdown \diagup \\ S \\ \diagup \diagdown \\ :\overset{..}{F} \quad \overset{..}{F}: \end{array}$$

The central sulfur atom has five electron pairs whose arrangement, according to Table 10.1, is trigonal bipyramidal. In the SF_4 molecule, however, one of the electron pairs is a lone pair, so the molecule must have one of the following geometries:

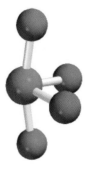

SF_4

Figure 10.2 *The geometry of CH₃OH.*

In (a) the lone pair occupies an equatorial position, and in (b) it occupies an axial position. The axial position has three neighboring pairs at 90° and one at 180°, while the equatorial position has two neighboring pairs at 90° and two more at 120°. The repulsion is smaller for (a), and indeed (a) is the structure observed experimentally. This shape is sometimes described as a distorted tetrahedron (or seesaw if you turn the structure 90° to the right to view it). The angle between the axial F atoms and S is 173°, and that between the equatorial F atoms and S is 102°.

Table 10.2 shows the geometries of simple molecules in which the central atom has one or more lone pairs, including some that we have not discussed.

Geometry of Molecules with More Than One Central Atom

So far we have discussed the geometry of molecules having only one central atom. The overall geometry of molecules with more than one central atom is difficult to define in most cases. Often we can only describe the shape around each of the central atoms. For example, consider methanol, CH_3OH, whose Lewis structure is shown below:

$$H-\overset{\overset{\displaystyle H}{|}}{\underset{\underset{\displaystyle H}{|}}{C}}-\overset{..}{\underset{..}{O}}-H$$

The two central (nonterminal) atoms in methanol are C and O. We can say that the three CH and the CO bonding pairs are tetrahedrally arranged about the C atom. The HCH and OCH bond angles are approximately 109°. The O atom here is like the one in water in that it has two lone pairs and two bonding pairs. Therefore, the HOC portion of the molecule is bent, and the angle HOC is approximately equal to 105° (Figure 10.2).

Guidelines for Applying the VSEPR Model

Having studied the geometries of molecules in two categories (central atoms with and without lone pairs), let us consider some rules for applying the VSEPR model to all types of molecules:

1. Write the Lewis structure of the molecule, considering only the electron pairs around the central atom (that is, the atom that is bonded to more than one other atom).

2. Count the number of electron pairs around the central atom (bonding pairs and lone pairs). Treat double and triple bonds as though they were single bonds. Refer to Table 10.1 to predict the overall arrangement of the electron pairs.

3. Use Tables 10.1 and 10.2 to predict the geometry of the molecule.

4. In predicting bond angles, note that a lone pair repels another lone pair or a bonding pair more strongly than a bonding pair repels another bonding pair. Remember that in general there is no easy way to predict bond angles accurately when the central atom possesses one or more lone pairs.

The VSEPR model generates reliable predictions of the geometries of a variety of molecular structures. Chemists use the VSEPR approach because of its simplicity. Although there are some theoretical concerns about whether "electron-pair repulsion" actually determines molecular shapes, the assumption that it does leads to useful (and

TABLE 10.2

Geometry of Simple Molecules and Ions in Which the Central Atom Has One or More Lone Pairs

Class of molecule	Total number of electron pairs	Number of bonding pairs	Number of lone pairs	Arrangement of electron pairs*	Geometry	Examples
AB_2E	3	2	1	Trigonal planar	Bent	SO_2
AB_3E	4	3	1	Tetrahedral	Trigonal pyramidal	NH_3
AB_2E_2	4	2	2	Tetrahedral	Bent	H_2O
AB_4E	5	4	1	Trigonal bipyramidal	Distorted tetrahedron (or seesaw)	SF_4
AB_3E_2	5	3	2	Trigonal bipyramidal	T-shaped	ClF_3
AB_2E_3	5	2	3	Trigonal bipyramidal	Linear	I_3^-
AB_5E	6	5	1	Octahedral	Square pyramidal	BrF_5
AB_4E_2	6	4	2	Octahedral	Square planar	XeF_4

* The colored lines are used to show the overall shape, not bonds.

generally reliable) predictions. We need not ask more of any model at this stage in the study of chemistry. Example 10.1 illustrates the application of VSEPR.

Example 10.1

Use the VSEPR model to predict the geometry of the following molecules and ions: (a) AsH_3, (b) OF_2, (c) $AlCl_4^-$, (d) I_3^-, (e) C_2H_4.

Strategy The sequence of steps in determining molecular geometry is as follows:

draw Lewis $\longrightarrow$ find arrangement of $\longrightarrow$ find arrangement $\longrightarrow$ determine geometry
structure   electron pairs   of bonding pairs   based on bonding pairs

Solution (a) The Lewis structure of AsH_3 is

$$H\text{—}\overset{..}{\underset{|}{As}}\text{—}H$$
$$H$$

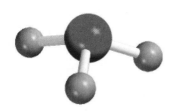

AsH₃

There are four electron pairs around the central atom; therefore, the electron pair arrangement is tetrahedral (see Table 10.1). Recall that the geometry of a molecule is determined only by the arrangement of atoms (in this case the As and H atoms). Thus removing the lone pair leaves us with three bonding pairs and a trigonal pyramidal geometry, like NH_3. We cannot predict the HAsH angle accurately, but we know that it is less than 109.5° because the repulsion of the bonding electron pairs in the As—H bonds by the lone pair on As is greater than the repulsion between the bonding pairs.

(b) The Lewis structure of OF_2 is

$$:\overset{..}{\underset{..}{F}}\text{—}\overset{..}{\underset{..}{O}}\text{—}\overset{..}{\underset{..}{F}}:$$

OF₂

There are four electron pairs around the central atom; therefore, the electron pair arrangement is tetrahedral (see Table 10.1). Recall that the geometry of a molecule is determined only by the arrangement of atoms (in this case the O and F atoms). Thus removing the two lone pairs leaves us with two bonding pairs and a bent geometry, like H_2O. We cannot predict the FOF angle accurately, but we know that it must be less than 109.5° because the repulsion of the bonding electron pairs in the O—F bonds by the lone pairs on O is greater than the repulsion between the bonding pairs.

(c) The Lewis structure of $AlCl_4^-$ is

$$\left[\begin{array}{c} :\overset{..}{\underset{..}{Cl}}: \\ | \\ :\overset{..}{\underset{..}{Cl}}\text{—}Al\text{—}\overset{..}{\underset{..}{Cl}}: \\ | \\ :\overset{..}{\underset{..}{Cl}}: \end{array}\right]^-$$

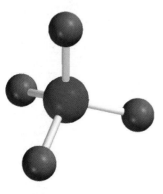

AlCl₄⁻

There are four electron pairs around the central atom; therefore, the electron pair arrangement is tetrahedral. Because there are no lone pairs present, the arrangement of the bonding pairs is the same as the electron pair arrangement. Therefore, $AlCl_4^-$ has a tetrahedral geometry and the ClAlCl angles are all 109.5°.

(d) The Lewis structure of I_3^- is

$$\left[:\overset{..}{\underset{..}{I}}\text{—}\overset{..}{\underset{..}{I}}\text{—}\overset{..}{\underset{..}{I}}:\right]^-$$

I₃⁻

(Continued)

There are five electron pairs around the central I atom; therefore, the electron pair arrangement is trigonal bipyramidal. Of the five electron pairs, three are lone pairs and two are bonding pairs. Recall that the lone pairs preferentially occupy the equatorial positions in a trigonal bipyramid (see Table 10.2). Thus removing the lone pairs leaves us with a linear geometry for I_3^-, that is, all three I atoms lie in a straight line.

(e) The Lewis structure of C_2H_4 is

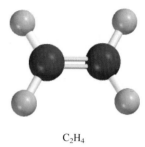

C_2H_4

The C=C bond is treated as though it were a single bond in the VSEPR model. Because there are three electron pairs around each C atom and there are no lone pairs present, the arrangement around each C atom has a trigonal planar shape like BF_3, discussed earlier. Thus the predicted bond angles in C_2H_4 are all 120°.

Comment (1) The I_3^- ion is one of the few structures for which the bond angle (180°) can be predicted accurately even though the central atom contains lone pairs. (2) In C_2H_4, all six atoms lie in the same plane. The overall planar geometry is not predicted by the VSEPR model, but we will see why the molecule prefers to be planar later. In reality, the angles are close, but not equal, to 120° because the bonds are not all equivalent.

Similar problems: 10.7, 10.8, 10.9.

Practice Exercise Use the VSEPR model to predict the geometry of (a) $SiBr_4$, (b) CS_2, and (c) NO_3^-.

10.2 Dipole Moments

In Section 9.4 we learned that hydrogen fluoride is a covalent compound with a polar bond. There is a shift of electron density from H to F because the F atom is more electronegative than the H atom (see Figure 9.4). The shift of electron density is symbolized by placing a crossed arrow (⊢⟶) above the Lewis structure to indicate the direction of the shift. For example,

$$\overset{\longmapsto}{H-\ddot{\underset{..}{F}}:}$$

The consequent charge separation can be represented as

$$\overset{\delta+ \quad \delta-}{H-\ddot{\underset{..}{F}}:}$$

where δ (delta) denotes a partial charge. This separation of charges can be confirmed in an electric field (Figure 10.3). When the field is turned on, HF molecules orient their negative ends toward the positive plate and their positive ends toward the negative plate. This alignment of molecules can be detected experimentally.

A quantitative measure of the polarity of a bond is its *dipole moment (μ)*, which is *the product of the charge Q and the distance r between the charges:*

$$\mu = Q \times r \qquad\qquad (10.1)$$

Figure 10.3 *Behavior of polar molecules (a) in the absence of an external electric field and (b) when the electric field is turned on. Nonpolar molecules are not affected by an electric field.*

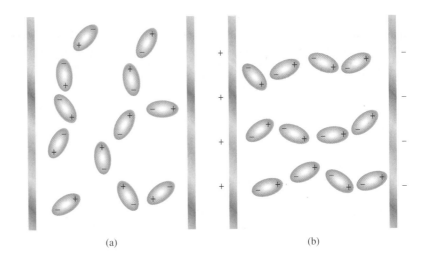

(a)   (b)

In a diatomic molecule like HF, the charge *Q* is equal to $\delta+$ and $\delta-$.

To maintain electrical neutrality, the charges on both ends of an electrically neutral diatomic molecule must be equal in magnitude and opposite in sign. However, in Equation (10.1), Q refers only to the magnitude of the charge and not to its sign, so μ is always positive. Dipole moments are usually expressed in debye units (D), named for Peter Debye.[†] The conversion factor is

$$1 \text{ D} = 3.336 \times 10^{-30} \text{ C m}$$

where C is coulomb and m is meter.

Diatomic molecules containing atoms of *different* elements (for example, HCl, CO, and NO) *have dipole moments* and are called **polar molecules.** Diatomic molecules containing atoms of the *same* element (for example, H_2, O_2, and F_2) are examples of **nonpolar molecules** because they *do not have dipole moments.* For a molecule made up of three or more atoms both the polarity of the bonds and the molecular geometry determine whether there is a dipole moment. Even if polar bonds are present, the molecule will not necessarily have a dipole moment. Carbon dioxide (CO_2), for example, is a triatomic molecule, so its geometry is either linear or bent:

Animation: Polarity of Molecules
Online Learning Center, Animations

Each carbon-to-oxygen bond is polar, with the electron density shifted toward the more electronegative oxygen atom. However, the linear geometry of the molecule results in the cancellation of the two bond moments.

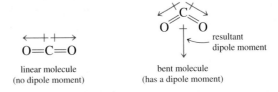

O=C=O

linear molecule
(no dipole moment)

resultant
dipole moment

bent molecule
(has a dipole moment)

The arrows show the shift of electron density from the less electronegative carbon atom to the more electronegative oxygen atom. In each case, the dipole moment of the entire molecule is made up of two *bond moments,* that is, individual dipole moments in the polar C=O bonds. The bond moment is a *vector quantity,* which means that it has both magnitude and direction. The measured dipole moment is equal to the vector sum of the bond moments. The two bond moments in CO_2 are equal in magnitude. Because they point in opposite directions in a linear CO_2 molecule, the

Interactivity: Molecular Polarity
Online Learning Center, Interactives

[†]Peter Joseph William Debye (1884–1966). American chemist and physicist of Dutch origin. Debye made many significant contributions in the study of molecular structure, polymer chemistry, X-ray analysis, and electrolyte solution. He was awarded the Nobel Prize in Chemistry in 1936.

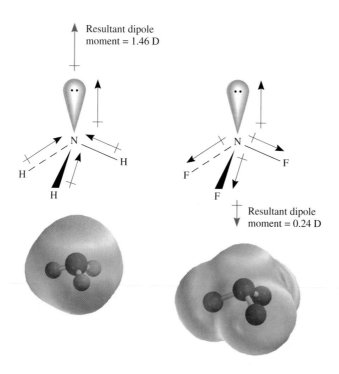

Figure 10.4 *Bond moments and resultant dipole moments in NH_3 and NF_3. The electrostatic potential maps show the electron density distributions in these molecules.*

sum or resultant dipole moment would be zero. On the other hand, if the CO_2 molecule were bent, the two bond moments would partially reinforce each other, so that the molecule would have a dipole moment. Experimentally it is found that carbon dioxide has no dipole moment. Therefore, we conclude that the carbon dioxide molecule is linear. The linear nature of carbon dioxide has been confirmed through other experimental measurements.

The VSEPR model predicts that CO_2 is a linear molecule.

Next let us consider the NH_3 and NF_3 molecules shown in Figure 10.4. In both cases the central N atom has a lone pair, whose charge density is away from the N atom. From Figure 9.5 we know that N is more electronegative than H, and F is more electronegative than N. For this reason, the shift of electron density in NH_3 is toward N and so contributes a larger dipole moment, whereas the NF bond moments are directed away from the N atom and so together they offset the contribution of the lone pair to the dipole moment. Thus the resultant dipole moment in NH_3 is larger than that in NF_3.

Dipole moments can be used to distinguish between molecules that have the same formula but different structures. For example, the following molecules both exist; they have the same molecular formula ($C_2H_2Cl_2$), the same number and type of bonds, but different molecular structures:

resultant dipole moment

cis-dichloroethylene
$\mu = 1.89$ D

trans-dichloroethylene
$\mu = 0$

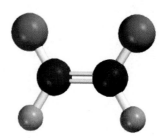

cis-dichloroethylene

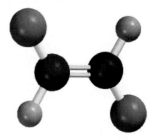

trans-dichloroethylene

Because *cis*-dichloroethylene is a polar molecule but *trans*-dichloroethylene is not, they can readily be distinguished by a dipole moment measurement. Additionally, as

CHEMISTRY IN ACTION

Microwave Ovens—Dipole Moments at Work

In the last 20 years the microwave oven has become a ubiquitous appliance. Microwave technology enables us to thaw and cook food much more rapidly than conventional appliances do. How do microwaves heat food so quickly?

In Chapter 7 we saw that microwaves are a form of electromagnetic radiation (see Figure 7.3). Microwaves are generated by a magnetron, which was invented during World War II when radar technology was being developed. The magnetron is a hollow cylinder encased in a horseshoe-shaped magnet. In the center of the cylinder is a cathode rod. The walls of the cylinder act as an anode. When heated, the cathode emits electrons that travel toward the anode. The magnetic field forces

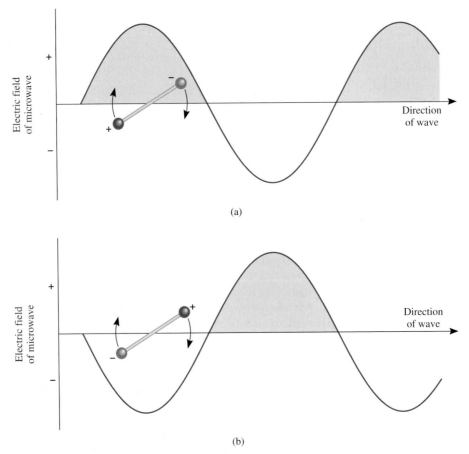

Interaction between the electric field component of the microwave and a polar molecule. (a) The negative end of the dipole follows the propagation of the wave (the positive region) and rotates in a clockwise direction. (b) If, after the molecule has rotated to the new position the radiation has also moved along to its next cycle, the positive end of the dipole will move into the negative region of the wave while the negative end will be pushed up. Thus the molecule will rotate faster. No such interaction can occur with nonpolar molecules.

the electrons to move in a circular path. This motion of charged particles generates microwaves, which are adjusted to a frequency of 2.45 GHz (2.45×10^9 Hz) for cooking. A "waveguide" directs the microwaves into the cooking compartment. Rotating fan blades reflect the microwaves to all parts of the oven.

The cooking action in a microwave oven results from the interaction between the electric field component of the radiation with the polar molecules—mostly water—in food. All molecules rotate at room temperature. If the frequency of the radiation and that of the molecular rotation are equal, energy can be transferred from microwave to the polar molecule. As a result, the molecule will rotate faster. This is what happens in a gas. In the condensed state (for example, in food), a molecule cannot execute the free rotation. Nevertheless, it still experiences a torque (a force that causes rotation) that tends to align its dipole moment with the oscillating field of the microwave. Consequently, there is friction between the molecules, which appears as heat in the food.

The reason that a microwave oven can cook food so fast is that the radiation is not absorbed by nonpolar molecules and can therefore reach different parts of food at the same time.

(Depending on the amount of water present, microwaves can penetrate food to a depth of several inches.) In a conventional oven, heat can affect the center of foods only by conduction (that is, by transfer of heat from hot air molecules to cooler molecules in food in a layer-by-layer fashion), which is a very slow process.

The following points are relevant to the operation of a microwave oven. Plastics and Pyrex glasswares do not contain polar molecules and are therefore not affected by microwave radiation. (Styrofoam and certain plastics cannot be used in microwaves because they melt from the heat of the food.) Metals, however, reflect microwaves, thereby shielding the food and possibly returning enough energy to the microwave emitter to overload it. Because microwaves can induce a current in the metal, this action can lead to sparks jumping between the container and the bottom or walls of the oven. Finally, although water molecules in ice are locked in position and therefore cannot rotate, we routinely thaw food in a microwave oven. The reason is that at room temperature a thin film of liquid water quickly forms on the surface of frozen food and the mobile molecules in that film can absorb the radiation to start the thawing process.

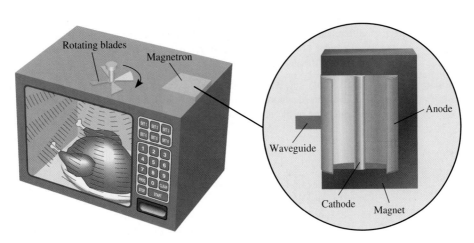

A microwave oven. The microwaves generated by the magnetron are reflected to all parts of the oven by the rotating fan blades.

TABLE 10.3

Dipole Moments of Some Polar Molecules		
Molecule	**Geometry**	**Dipole Moment (D)**
HF	Linear	1.92
HCl	Linear	1.08
HBr	Linear	0.78
HI	Linear	0.38
H_2O	Bent	1.87
H_2S	Bent	1.10
NH_3	Trigonal pyramidal	1.46
SO_2	Bent	1.60

we will see in the next chapter, the strength of intermolecular forces is partially determined by whether molecules possess a dipole moment. Table 10.3 lists the dipole moments of several polar molecules.

Example 10.2 shows how we can predict whether a molecule possesses a dipole moment if we know its molecular geometry.

Example 10.2

Predict whether each of the following molecules has a dipole moment: (a) IBr, (b) BF_3 (trigonal planar), (c) CH_2Cl_2 (tetrahedral).

Strategy Keep in mind that the dipole moment of a molecule depends on both the difference in electronegativities of the elements present and its geometry. A molecule can have polar bonds (if the bonded atoms have different electronegativities), but it may not possess a dipole moment if it has a highly symmetrical geometry.

Solution (a) Because IBr (iodine bromide) is diatomic, it has a linear geometry. Bromine is more electronegative than iodine (see Figure 9.5), so IBr is polar with bromine at the negative end.

$$\overset{\longmapsto}{I\!-\!Br}$$

Thus the molecule does have a dipole moment.

(b) Because fluorine is more electronegative than boron, each B—F bond in BF_3 (boron trifluoride) is polar and the three bond moments are equal. However, the symmetry of a trigonal planar shape means that the three bond moments exactly cancel one another:

An analogy is an object that is pulled in the directions shown by the three bond moments. If the forces are equal, the object will not move. Consequently, BF_3 has no dipole moment; it is a nonpolar molecule.

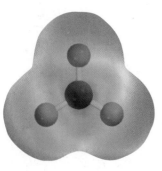

Electrostatic potential map shows that the electron density is symmetrically distributed in the BF_3 molecule.

(Continued)

(c) The Lewis structure of CH_2Cl_2 (methylene chloride) is

$$
\begin{array}{c}
Cl \\
| \\
H-C-H \\
| \\
Cl
\end{array}
$$

This molecule is similar to CH_4 in that it has an overall tetrahedral shape. However, because not all the bonds are identical, there are three different bond angles: HCH, HCCl, and ClCCl. These bond angles are close to, but not equal to, 109.5°. Because chlorine is more electronegative than carbon, which is more electronegative than hydrogen, the bond moments do not cancel and the molecule possesses a dipole moment:

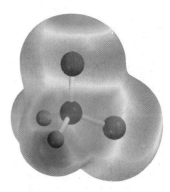

Electrostatic potential map of CH_2Cl_2. The electron density is shifted toward the electronegative Cl atoms.

Thus CH_2Cl_2 is a polar molecule.

Practice Exercise Does the $AlCl_3$ molecule have a dipole moment?

Similar problems: 10.21, 10.22, 10.23.

10.3 Valence Bond Theory

The VSEPR model, based largely on Lewis structures, provides a relatively simple and straightforward method for predicting the geometry of molecules. But as we noted earlier, the Lewis theory of chemical bonding does not clearly explain why chemical bonds exist. Relating the formation of a covalent bond to the pairing of electrons was a step in the right direction, but it did not go far enough. For example, the Lewis theory describes the single bond between the H atoms in H_2 and that between the F atoms in F_2 in essentially the same way—as the pairing of two electrons. Yet these two molecules have quite different bond energies and bond lengths (436.4 kJ/mol and 74 pm for H_2 and 150.6 kJ/mol and 142 pm for F_2). These and many other facts cannot be explained by the Lewis theory. For a more complete explanation of chemical bond formation we look to quantum mechanics. In fact, the quantum mechanical study of chemical bonding also provides a means for understanding molecular geometry.

At present, two quantum mechanical theories are used to describe covalent bond formation and the electronic structure of molecules. *Valence bond (VB) theory* assumes that the electrons in a molecule occupy atomic orbitals of the individual atoms. It enables us to retain a picture of individual atoms taking part in the bond formation. The second theory, called *molecular orbital (MO) theory,* assumes the formation of molecular orbitals from the atomic orbitals. Neither theory perfectly explains all aspects of bonding, but each has contributed something to our understanding of many observed molecular properties.

Let us start our discussion of valence bond theory by considering the formation of a H_2 molecule from two H atoms. The Lewis theory describes the H—H bond in terms of the pairing of the two electrons on the H atoms. In the framework of valence bond theory, the covalent H—H bond is formed by the *overlap* of the two $1s$ orbitals in the H atoms. By overlap, we mean that the two orbitals share a common region in space.

Figure 10.5 *Change in potential energy of two H atoms with their distance of separation. At the point of minimum potential energy, the H_2 molecule is in its most stable state and the bond length is 74 pm. The spheres represent the 1s orbitals.*

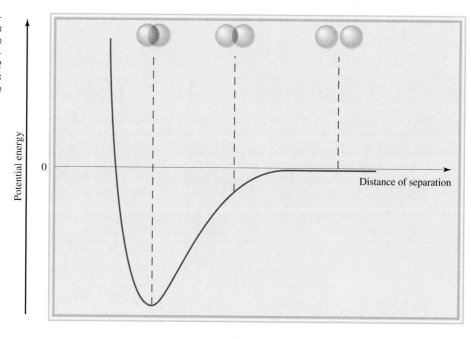

Recall that an object has potential energy by virtue of its position.

What happens to two H atoms as they move toward each other and form a bond? Initially, when the two atoms are far apart, there is no interaction. We say that the potential energy of this system (that is, the two H atoms) is zero. As the atoms approach each other, each electron is attracted by the nucleus of the other atom; at the same time, the electrons repel each other, as do the nuclei. While the atoms are still separated, attraction is stronger than repulsion, so that the potential energy of the system *decreases* (that is, it becomes negative) as the atoms approach each other (Figure 10.5). This trend continues until the potential energy reaches a minimum value. At this point, when the system has the lowest potential energy, it is most stable. This condition corresponds to substantial overlap of the 1s orbitals and the formation of a stable H_2 molecule. If the distance between nuclei were to decrease further, the potential energy would rise steeply and finally become positive as a result of the increased electron-electron and nuclear-nuclear repulsions. In accord with the law of conservation of energy, the decrease in potential energy as a result of H_2 formation must be accompanied by a release of energy. Experiments show that as a H_2 molecule is formed from two H atoms, heat is given off. The converse is also true. To break a H—H bond, energy must be supplied to the molecule. Figure 10.6 is another way of viewing the formation of an H_2 molecule.

Thus valence bond theory gives a clearer picture of chemical bond formation than the Lewis theory does. Valence bond theory states that a stable molecule forms from reacting atoms when the potential energy of the system has decreased to a minimum; the Lewis theory ignores energy changes in chemical bond formation.

The orbital diagram of the F atom is shown on p. 290.

The concept of overlapping atomic orbitals applies equally well to diatomic molecules other than H_2. Thus a stable F_2 molecule forms when the 2p orbitals (containing the unpaired electrons) in the two F atoms overlap to form a covalent bond. Similarly, the formation of the HF molecule can be explained by the overlap of the 1s orbital in H with the 2p orbital in F. In each case, VB theory accounts for the changes in potential energy as the distance between the reacting atoms changes. Because the orbitals involved are not the same kind in all cases, we can see why the bond energies and bond lengths in H_2, F_2, and HF might be different. As we stated

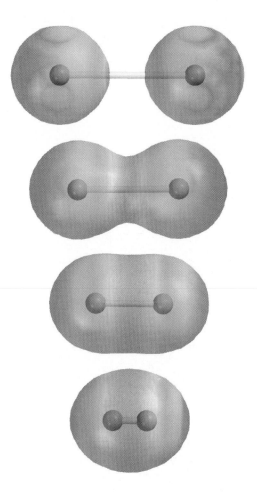

Figure 10.6 *Top to bottom: As two H atoms approach each other, their 1s orbitals begin to interact and each electron begins to feel the attraction of the other proton. Gradually, the electron density builds up in the region between the two nuclei (red color). Eventually, a stable H_2 molecule is formed when the internuclear distance is 74 pm.*

earlier, Lewis theory treats *all* covalent bonds the same way and offers no explanation for the differences among covalent bonds.

10.4 Hybridization of Atomic Orbitals

The concept of atomic orbital overlap should apply also to polyatomic molecules. However, a satisfactory bonding scheme must account for molecular geometry. We will discuss three examples of VB treatment of bonding in polyatomic molecules.

sp^3 Hybridization

Consider the CH_4 molecule. Focusing only on the valence electrons, we can represent the orbital diagram of C as

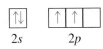

Because the carbon atom has two unpaired electrons (one in each of the two $2p$ orbitals), it can form only two bonds with hydrogen in its ground state. Although the

Animation: Hybridization
Online Learning Center,
Animations

Interactivity: Determining
Orbital Hybridization
Online Learning Center,
Interactives

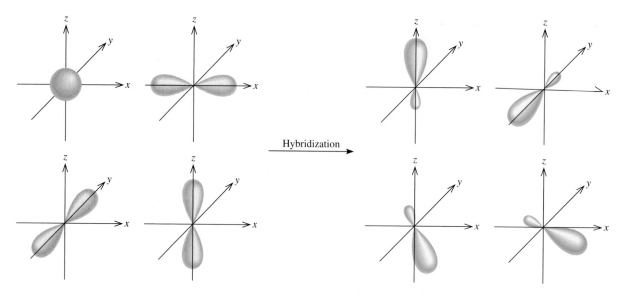

Figure 10.7 *Formation of sp^3 hybrid orbitals.*

species CH_2 is known, it is very unstable. To account for the four C—H bonds in methane, we can try to promote (that is, energetically excite) an electron from the $2s$ orbital to the $2p$ orbital:

Now there are four unpaired electrons on C that could form four C—H bonds. However, the geometry is wrong, because three of the HCH bond angles would have to be 90° (remember that the three $2p$ orbitals on carbon are mutually perpendicular), and yet *all* HCH angles are 109.5°.

To explain the bonding in methane, VB theory uses hypothetical **hybrid orbitals,** which are *atomic orbitals obtained when two or more nonequivalent orbitals of the same atom combine in preparation for covalent bond formation.* **Hybridization** is the term applied to *the mixing of atomic orbitals in an atom (usually a central atom) to generate a set of hybrid orbitals.* We can generate four equivalent hybrid orbitals for carbon by mixing the $2s$ orbital and the three $2p$ orbitals:

sp^3 orbitals

Because the new orbitals are formed from one s and three p orbitals, they are called sp^3 hybrid orbitals. Figure 10.7 shows the shape and orientations of the sp^3 orbitals. These four hybrid orbitals are directed toward the four corners of a regular tetrahedron. Figure 10.8 shows the formation of four covalent bonds between the carbon sp^3 hybrid orbitals and the hydrogen $1s$ orbitals in CH_4. Thus CH_4 has a tetrahedral shape, and all the HCH angles are 109.5°. Note that although energy is required to bring about hybridization, this input is more than compensated for by the energy released upon the formation of C—H bonds. (Recall that bond formation is an exothermic process.)

The following analogy is useful for understanding hybridization. Suppose that we have a beaker of a red solution and three beakers of blue solutions and that the volume

sp^3 is pronounced "s-p three."

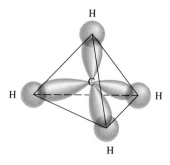

Figure 10.8 *Formation of four bonds between the carbon sp^3 hybrid orbitals and the hydrogen $1s$ orbitals in CH_4.*

of each is 50 mL. The red solution corresponds to one 2s orbital, the blue solutions represent three 2p orbitals, and the four equal volumes symbolize four separate orbitals. By mixing the solutions we obtain 200 mL of a purple solution, which can be divided into four 50-mL portions (that is, the hybridization process generates four sp^3 orbitals). Just as the purple color is made up of the red and blue components of the original solutions, the sp^3 hybrid orbitals possess both s and p orbital characteristics.

Another example of sp^3 hybridization is ammonia (NH_3). Table 10.1 shows that the arrangement of four electron pairs is tetrahedral, so that the bonding in NH_3 can be explained by assuming that N, like C in CH_4, is sp^3-hybridized. The ground-state electron configuration of N is $1s^2 2s^2 2p^3$, so that the orbital diagram for the sp^3 hybridized N atom is

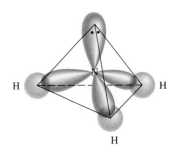

Figure 10.9 The N atom in NH_3 is sp^3-hybridized. Three sp^3 hybrid orbitals form bonds with the H atoms. The fourth is occupied by nitrogen's lone pair.

sp^3 orbitals

Three of the four hybrid orbitals form covalent N—H bonds, and the fourth hybrid orbital accommodates the lone pair on nitrogen (Figure 10.9). Repulsion between the lone-pair electrons and electrons in the bonding orbitals decreases the HNH bond angles from 109.5° to 107.3°.

It is important to understand the relationship between hybridization and the VSEPR model. We use hybridization to describe the bonding scheme only when the arrangement of electron pairs has been predicted using VSEPR. If the VSEPR model predicts a tetrahedral arrangement of electron pairs, then we assume that one s and three p orbitals are hybridized to form four sp^3 hybrid orbitals. The following are examples of other types of hybridization.

sp Hybridization

The beryllium chloride ($BeCl_2$) molecule is predicted to be linear by VSEPR. The orbital diagram for the valence electrons in Be is

2s   2p

We know that in its ground state Be does not form covalent bonds with Cl because its electrons are paired in the 2s orbital. So we turn to hybridization for an explanation of Be's bonding behavior. First we promote a 2s electron to a 2p orbital, resulting in

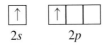

2s   2p

Now there are two Be orbitals available for bonding, the 2s and 2p. However, if two Cl atoms were to combine with Be in this excited state, one Cl atom would share a 2s electron and the other Cl would share a 2p electron, making two nonequivalent BeCl bonds. This scheme contradicts experimental evidence. In the actual $BeCl_2$ molecule, the two BeCl bonds are identical in every respect. Thus the 2s and 2p orbitals must be mixed, or hybridized, to form two equivalent sp hybrid orbitals:

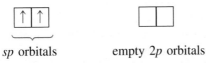

sp orbitals   empty 2p orbitals

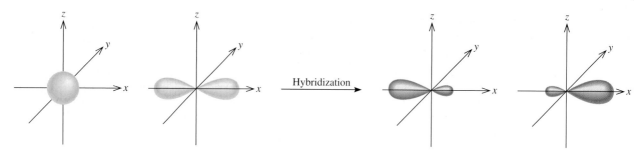

Figure 10.10 *Formation of sp hybrid orbitals.*

Figure 10.10 shows the shape and orientation of the *sp* orbitals. These two hybrid orbitals lie on the same line, the *x*-axis, so that the angle between them is 180°. Each of the BeCl bonds is then formed by the overlap of a Be *sp* hybrid orbital and a Cl 3*p* orbital, and the resulting $BeCl_2$ molecule has a linear geometry (Figure 10.11).

sp^2 Hybridization

Next we will look at the BF_3 (boron trifluoride) molecule, known to have planar geometry based on VSEPR. Considering only the valence electrons, the orbital diagram of B is

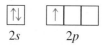

$2s$ $2p$

First, we promote a 2*s* electron to an empty 2*p* orbital:

$2s$ $2p$

sp² is pronounced "s-p two."

Mixing the 2*s* orbital with the two 2*p* orbitals generates three sp^2 hybrid orbitals:

sp^2 orbitals   empty 2*p* orbital

These three sp^2 orbitals lie in the same plane, and the angle between any two of them is 120° (Figure 10.12). Each of the BF bonds is formed by the overlap of a boron sp^2 hybrid orbital and a fluorine 2*p* orbital (Figure 10.13). The BF_3 molecule is planar with all the FBF angles equal to 120°. This result conforms to experimental findings and also to VSEPR predictions.

You may have noticed an interesting connection between hybridization and the octet rule. Regardless of the type of hybridization, an atom starting with one *s* and three *p* orbitals would still possess four orbitals, enough to accommodate a total of eight electrons in a compound. For elements in the second period of the periodic table, eight is the maximum number of electrons that an atom of any of these elements can accommodate in the valence shell. It is for this reason that the octet rule is usually obeyed by the second-period elements.

Figure 10.11 *The linear geometry of $BeCl_2$ can be explained by assuming that Be is sp-hybridized. The two sp hybrid orbitals overlap with the two chlorine 3p orbitals to form two covalent bonds.*

The situation is different for an atom of a third-period element. If we use only the 3*s* and 3*p* orbitals of the atom to form hybrid orbitals in a molecule, then the octet rule applies. However, in some molecules the same atom may use one or more 3*d* orbitals, in addition to the 3*s* and 3*p* orbitals, to form hybrid orbitals. In these cases the octet rule does not hold. We will see specific examples of the participation of the 3*d* orbital in hybridization shortly.

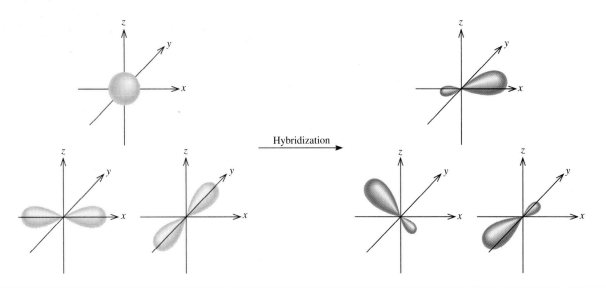

Hybridization

Figure 10.12 *Formation of sp^2 hybrid orbitals.*

To summarize our discussion of hybridization, we note that

- The concept of hybridization is not applied to isolated atoms. It is a theoretical model used only to explain covalent bonding.

- Hybridization is the mixing of at least two nonequivalent atomic orbitals, for example, *s* and *p* orbitals. Therefore, a hybrid orbital is not a pure atomic orbital. Hybrid orbitals and pure atomic orbitals have very different shapes.

- The number of hybrid orbitals generated is equal to the number of pure atomic orbitals that participate in the hybridization process.

- Hybridization requires an input of energy; however, the system more than recovers this energy during bond formation.

- Covalent bonds in polyatomic molecules and ions are formed by the overlap of hybrid orbitals, or of hybrid orbitals with unhybridized ones. Therefore, the hybridization bonding scheme is still within the framework of valence bond theory; electrons in a molecule are assumed to occupy hybrid orbitals of the individual atoms.

Table 10.4 summarizes *sp*, sp^2, and sp^3 hybridization (as well as other types that we will discuss shortly).

Procedure for Hybridizing Atomic Orbitals

Before going on to discuss the hybridization of *d* orbitals, let us specify what we need to know in order to apply hybridization to bonding in polyatomic molecules in general. In essence, hybridization simply extends Lewis theory and the VSEPR model. To assign a suitable state of hybridization to the central atom in a molecule, we must have some idea about the geometry of the molecule. The steps are as follows:

1. Draw the Lewis structure of the molecule.

2. Predict the overall arrangement of the electron pairs (both bonding pairs and lone pairs) using the VSEPR model (see Table 10.1).

3. Deduce the hybridization of the central atom by matching the arrangement of the electron pairs with those of the hybrid orbitals shown in Table 10.4.

Example 10.3 illustrates this procedure.

Figure 10.13 *The sp^2 hybrid orbitals of boron overlap with the 2p orbitals of fluorine. The BF_3 molecule is planar, and all the FBF angles are 120°.*

TABLE 10.4

Important Hybrid Orbitals and Their Shapes

Pure Atomic Orbitals of the Central Atom	Hybridization of the Central Atom	Number of Hybrid Orbitals	Shape of Hybrid Orbitals	Examples
s, p	sp	2	Linear	$BeCl_2$
s, p, p	sp^2	3	Trigonal planar	BF_3
s, p, p, p	sp^3	4	Tetrahedral	CH_4, NH_4^+
s, p, p, p, d	sp^3d	5	Trigonal bipyramidal	PCl_5
s, p, p, p, d, d	sp^3d^2	6	Octahedral	SF_6

Example 10.3

Determine the hybridization state of the central (underlined) atom in each of the following molecules: (a) $\underline{Be}H_2$, (b) $\underline{Al}I_3$, and (c) $\underline{P}F_3$. Describe the hybridization process and determine the molecular geometry in each case.

Strategy The steps for determining the hybridization of the central atom in a molecule are:

draw Lewis structure
of the molecule $\longrightarrow$

use VSEPR to determine the
electron pair arrangement $\longrightarrow$
surrounding the central
atom (Table 10.1)

use Table 10.4 to
determine the
hybridization state of
the central atom

Solution (a) The ground-state electron configuration of Be is $1s^22s^2$ and the Be atom has two valence electrons. The Lewis structure of BeH_2 is

$$H-Be-H$$

BeH_2

There are two bonding pairs around Be; therefore, the electron pair arrangement is linear. We conclude that Be uses sp hybrid orbitals in bonding with H, because sp orbitals have a linear arrangement (see Table 10.4). The hybridization process can be imagined as follows. First we draw the orbital diagram for the ground state of Be:

$2s$ $2p$

By promoting a $2s$ electron to the $2p$ orbital, we get the excited state:

$2s$ $2p$

The $2s$ and $2p$ orbitals then mix to form two hybrid orbitals:

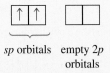

sp orbitals   empty $2p$
orbitals

The two Be—H bonds are formed by the overlap of the Be sp orbitals with the $1s$ orbitals of the H atoms. Thus BeH_2 is a linear molecule.

(b) The ground-state electron configuration of Al is $[Ne]3s^23p^1$. Therefore, the Al atom has three valence electrons. The Lewis structure of AlI_3 is

There are three pairs of electrons around Al; therefore, the electron pair arrangement is trigonal planar. We conclude that Al uses sp^2 hybrid orbitals in bonding with I because sp^2 orbitals have a trigonal planar arrangement (see Table 10.4). The orbital diagram of the ground-state Al atom is

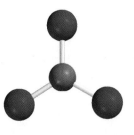

AlI_3

(Continued)

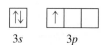

By promoting a 3s electron into the 3p orbital we obtain the following excited state:

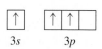

The 3s and two 3p orbitals then mix to form three sp^2 hybrid orbitals:

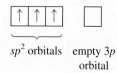

sp^2 orbitals   empty 3p
orbital

The sp^2 hybrid orbitals overlap with the 5p orbitals of I to form three covalent Al—I bonds. We predict that the AlI$_3$ molecule is trigonal planar and all the IAlI angles are 120°.

(c) The ground-state electron configuration of P is [Ne]$3s^2 3p^3$. Therefore, P atom has five valence electrons. The Lewis structure of PF$_3$ is

$$:\ddot{F}—\overset{\displaystyle \cdot\cdot}{P}—\ddot{F}:$$
$$|$$
$$:\ddot{F}:$$

PF$_3$

There are four pairs of electrons around P; therefore, the electron pair arrangement is tetrahedral. We conclude that P uses sp^3 hybrid orbitals in bonding to F, because sp^3 orbitals have a tetrahedral arrangement (see Table 10.4). The hybridization process can be imagined to take place as follows. The orbital diagram of the ground-state P atom is

By mixing the 3s and 3p orbitals, we obtain four sp^3 hybrid orbitals.

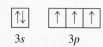

sp^3 orbitals

As in the case of NH$_3$, one of the sp^3 hybrid orbitals is used to accommodate the lone pair on P. The other three sp^3 hybrid orbitals form covalent P—F bonds with the 2p orbitals of F. We predict the geometry of the molecule to be trigonal pyramidal; the FPF angle should be somewhat less than 109.5°.

Similar problems: 10.33, 10.34.

Practice Exercise Determine the hybridization state of the underlined atoms in the following compounds: (a) $\underline{Si}Br_4$ and (b) $\underline{B}Cl_3$.

Hybridization of s, p, and d Orbitals

We have seen that hybridization neatly explains bonding that involves s and p orbitals. For elements in the third period and beyond, however, we cannot always account for molecular geometry by assuming that only s and p orbitals hybridize. To understand the formation of molecules with trigonal bipyramidal and octahedral geometries, for instance, we must include d orbitals in the hybridization concept.

Consider the SF_6 molecule as an example. In Section 10.1 we saw that this molecule has octahedral geometry, which is also the arrangement of the six electron pairs. Table 10.4 shows that the S atom is sp^3d^2-hybridized in SF_6. The ground-state electron configuration of S is $[Ne]3s^23p^4$:

Because the $3d$ level is quite close in energy to the $3s$ and $3p$ levels, we can promote $3s$ and $3p$ electrons to two of the $3d$ orbitals:

Mixing the $3s$, three $3p$, and two $3d$ orbitals generates six sp^3d^2 hybrid orbitals:

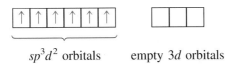

sp^3d^2 orbitals   empty $3d$ orbitals

sp^3d^2 is pronounced "s-p three d two."

The six S—F bonds are formed by the overlap of the hybrid orbitals of the S atom with the $2p$ orbitals of the F atoms. Because there are 12 electrons around the S atom, the octet rule is violated. The use of d orbitals in addition to s and p orbitals to form an expanded octet (see Section 9.9) is an example of *valence-shell expansion*. Second-period elements, unlike third-period elements, do not have $2d$ energy levels, so they can never expand their valence shells. (Recall that when $n = 2$, $l = 0$ and 1. Thus we can only have $2s$ and $2p$ orbitals.) Hence atoms of second-period elements can never be surrounded by more than eight electrons in any of their compounds.

Example 10.4 deals with valence-shell expansion in a third-period element.

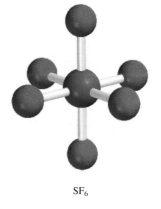

SF_6

Example 10.4

Describe the hybridization state of phosphorus in phosphorus pentabromide (PBr_5).

Strategy Follow the same procedure shown in Example 10.3.

Solution The ground-state electron configuration of P is $[Ne]3s^23p^3$. Therefore, the P atom has five valence electrons. The Lewis structure of PBr_5 is

$$\ddot{:}\ddot{Br} \diagdown \underset{\underset{:\ddot{Br}:}{|}}{\overset{\overset{:\ddot{Br}:}{|}}{P}}\!\!-\!\!\ddot{Br}:$$
$$:\ddot{Br}$$

There are five pairs of electrons around P; therefore, the electron pair arrangement is trigonal bipyramidal. We conclude that P uses sp^3d hybrid orbitals in bonding to Br, because sp^3d hybrid orbitals have a trigonal bipyramidal arrangement (see Table 10.4). The hybridization process can be imagined as follows. The orbital diagram of the ground-state P atom is

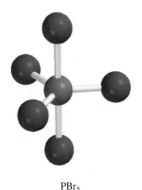

PBr_5

(Continued)

Ground state

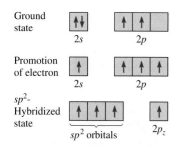

2s   2p

Promotion of electron

2s   2p

sp^2-Hybridized state

sp^2 orbitals $2p_z$

Figure 10.14 *The sp^2 hybridization of a carbon atom. The 2s orbital is mixed with only two 2p orbitals to form three equivalent sp^2 hybrid orbitals. This process leaves an electron in the unhybridized orbital, the $2p_z$ orbital.*

Similar problem: 10.42.

3s   3p   3d

Promoting a 3s electron into a 3d orbital results in the following excited state:

3s   3p   3d

Mixing the one 3s, three 3p, and one 3d orbitals generates five sp^3d hybrid orbitals:

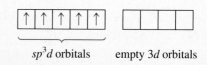

sp^3d orbitals   empty 3d orbitals

These hybrid orbitals overlap the 4p orbitals of Br to form five covalent P—Br bonds. Because there are no lone pairs on the P atom, the geometry of PBr_5 is trigonal bipyramidal.

Practice Exercise Describe the hybridization state of Se in SeF_6.

10.5 Hybridization in Molecules Containing Double and Triple Bonds

Animation: Sigma and Pi Bonds
Online Learning Center, Animations

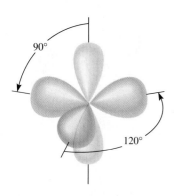

90°

120°

Figure 10.15 *Each carbon atom in the C_2H_4 molecule has three sp^2 hybrid orbitals (green) and one unhybridized $2p_z$ orbital (gray), which is perpendicular to the plane of the hybrid orbitals.*

The concept of hybridization is useful also for molecules with double and triple bonds. Consider the ethylene molecule, C_2H_4, as an example. In Example 10.1 we saw that C_2H_4 contains a carbon-carbon double bond and has planar geometry. Both the geometry and the bonding can be understood if we assume that each carbon atom is sp^2-hybridized. Figure 10.14 shows orbital diagrams of this hybridization process. We assume that only the $2p_x$ and $2p_y$ orbitals combine with the 2s orbital, and that the $2p_z$ orbital remains unchanged. Figure 10.15 shows that the $2p_z$ orbital is perpendicular to the plane of the hybrid orbitals. Now how do we account for the bonding of the C atoms? As Figure 10.16(a) shows, each carbon atom uses the three sp^2 hybrid orbitals to form two bonds with the two hydrogen 1s orbitals and one bond with the sp^2 hybrid orbital of the adjacent C atom. In addition, the two unhybridized $2p_z$ orbitals of the C atoms form another bond by overlapping sideways [Figure 10.16(b)].

A distinction is made between the two types of covalent bonds in C_2H_4. The three bonds formed by each C atom in Figure 10.16(a) are all *sigma bonds (σ bonds)*, *covalent bonds formed by orbitals overlapping end-to-end, with the electron density concentrated between the nuclei of the bonding atoms*. The second type is called a *pi bond (π bond)*, which is defined as *a covalent bond formed by sideways overlapping orbitals with electron density concentrated above and below the plane of the nuclei of the bonding atoms*. The two C atoms form a pi bond as shown in Figure 10.16(b). It is this pi bond formation that gives ethylene its planar geometry. Figure 10.17 is yet another way of looking at the planar C_2H_4 molecule and the formation of the pi bond. Although we normally represent the carbon-carbon double bond as C=C (as in a Lewis structure), it is important to keep in mind that the two bonds are different types: One is a sigma bond and the other is a pi bond. In fact, the bond energies of the carbon-carbon pi and sigma bonds are about 270 kJ/mol and 350 kJ/mol, respectively.

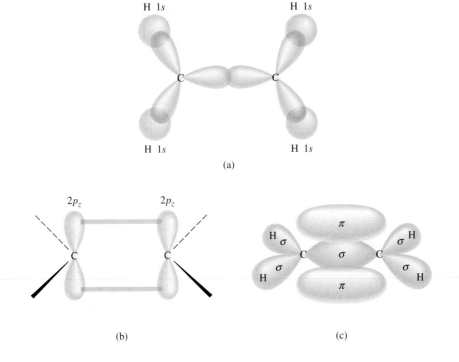

(a)

(b)   (c)

Figure 10.16 *Bonding in ethylene, C_2H_4. (a) Top view of the sigma bonds between carbon atoms and between carbon and hydrogen atoms. All the atoms lie in the same plane, making C_2H_4 a planar molecule. (b) Side view showing how the two $2p_z$ orbitals on the two carbon atoms overlap, leading to the formation of a pi bond. (c) The interactions in (a) and (b) lead to the formation of the sigma bonds and the pi bond in ethylene. Note that the pi bond lies above and below the plane of the molecule.*

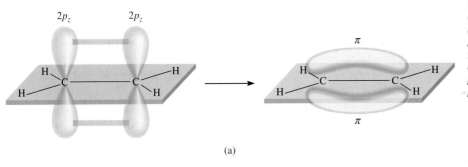

(a)

Figure 10.17 *(a) Another view of pi bond formation in the C_2H_4 molecule. Note that all six atoms are in the same plane. It is the overlap of the $2p_z$ orbitals that causes the molecule to assume a planar structure. (b) Electrostatic potential map of C_2H_4.*

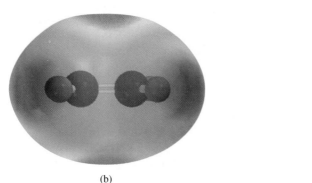

(b)

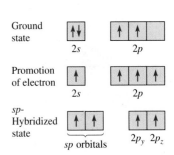

Figure 10.18 *The sp hybridization of a carbon atom. The 2s orbital is mixed with only one 2p orbital to form two sp hybrid orbitals. This process leaves an electron in each of the two unhybridized 2p orbitals, namely, the $2p_y$ and $2p_z$ orbitals.*

The acetylene molecule (C_2H_2) contains a carbon-carbon triple bond. Because the molecule is linear, we can explain its geometry and bonding by assuming that each C atom is *sp*-hybridized by mixing the 2s with the $2p_x$ orbital (Figure 10.18). As Figure 10.19 shows, the two *sp* hybrid orbitals of each C atom form one sigma bond with a hydrogen 1s orbital and another sigma bond with the other C atom. In

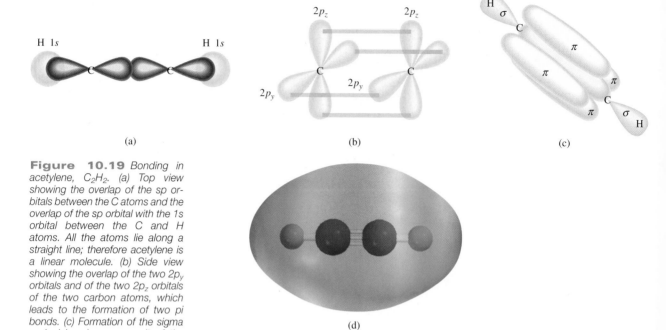

Figure 10.19 *Bonding in acetylene, C_2H_2. (a) Top view showing the overlap of the sp orbitals between the C atoms and the overlap of the sp orbital with the 1s orbital between the C and H atoms. All the atoms lie along a straight line; therefore acetylene is a linear molecule. (b) Side view showing the overlap of the two $2p_y$ orbitals and of the two $2p_z$ orbitals of the two carbon atoms, which leads to the formation of two pi bonds. (c) Formation of the sigma and pi bonds as a result of the interactions in (a) and (b). (d) Electrostatic potential map of C_2H_2.*

(d)

addition, two pi bonds are formed by the sideways overlap of the unhybridized $2p_y$ and $2p_z$ orbitals. Thus the C≡C bond is made up of one sigma bond and two pi bonds.

The following rule helps us predict hybridization in molecules containing multiple bonds: If the central atom forms a double bond, it is sp^2-hybridized; if it forms two double bonds or a triple bond, it is sp-hybridized. Note that this rule applies only to atoms of the second-period elements. Atoms of third-period elements and beyond that form multiple bonds present a more complicated picture and will not be dealt with here.

Example 10.5

Describe the bonding in the formaldehyde molecule whose Lewis structure is

$$\begin{array}{c} H \\ \diagdown \\ C=\ddot{O}\colon \\ \diagup \\ H \end{array}$$

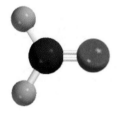

CH_2O

Assume that the O atom is sp^2-hybridized.

Strategy Follow the procedure shown in Example 10.3.

Solution There are three pairs of electrons around the C atom; therefore, the electron pair arrangement is trigonal planar. (Recall that a double bond is treated as a single bond in the VSEPR model.) We conclude that C uses sp^2 hybrid orbitals in bonding, because sp^2 hybrid orbitals have a trigonal planar arrangement (see Table 10.4). We can imagine the hybridization processes for C and O as follows:

(Continued)

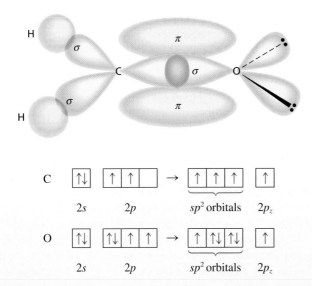

Figure 10.20 *Bonding in the formaldehyde molecule. A sigma bond is formed by the overlap of the sp^2 hybrid orbital of carbon and the sp^2 hybrid orbital of oxygen; a pi bond is formed by the overlap of the $2p_z$ orbitals of the carbon and oxygen atoms. The two lone pairs on oxygen are placed in the other two sp^2 orbitals of oxygen.*

Carbon has one electron in each of the three sp^2 orbitals, which are used to form sigma bonds with the H atoms and the O atom. There is also an electron in the $2p_z$ orbital, which forms a pi bond with oxygen. Oxygen has two electrons in two of its sp^2 hybrid orbitals. These are the lone pairs on oxygen. Its third sp^2 hybrid orbital with one electron is used to form a sigma bond with carbon. The $2p_z$ orbital (with one electron) overlaps with the $2p_z$ orbital of C to form a pi bond (Figure 10.20).

Similar problems: 10.39, 10.41.

Practice Exercise Describe the bonding in the hydrogen cyanide molecule, HCN. Assume that N is *sp*-hybridized.

10.6 Molecular Orbital Theory

Valence bond theory is one of the two quantum mechanical approaches that explain bonding in molecules. It accounts, at least qualitatively, for the stability of the covalent bond in terms of overlapping atomic orbitals. Using the concept of hybridization, valence bond theory can explain molecular geometries predicted by the VSEPR model. However, the assumption that electrons in a molecule occupy atomic orbitals of the individual atoms can only be an approximation, because each bonding electron in a molecule must be in an orbital that is characteristic of the molecule as a whole.

In some cases, valence bond theory cannot satisfactorily account for observed properties of molecules. Consider the oxygen molecule, whose Lewis structure is

$$\ddot{O}\!=\!\ddot{O}$$

According to this description, all the electrons in O_2 are paired and oxygen should therefore be diamagnetic. But experiments have shown that the oxygen molecule has two unpaired electrons (Figure 10.21). This finding suggests a fundamental deficiency in valence bond theory, one that justifies searching for an alternative bonding approach that accounts for the properties of O_2 and other molecules that do not match the predictions of valence bond theory.

Magnetic and other properties of molecules are sometimes better explained by another quantum mechanical approach called *molecular orbital (MO) theory*. Molecular orbital theory describes covalent bonds in terms of **molecular orbitals,** which *result from interaction of the atomic orbitals of the bonding atoms and are associated with*

Figure 10.21 *Liquid oxygen caught between the poles of a magnet, because the O_2 molecules are paramagnetic.*

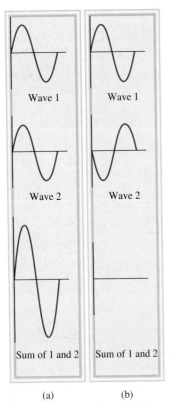

Figure 10.22 *Constructive interference (a) and destructive interference (b) of two waves of the same wavelength and amplitude.*

The two electrons in the sigma molecular orbital are paired. The Pauli exclusion principle applies to molecules as well as to atoms.

Figure 10.23 *(a) Energy levels of bonding and antibonding molecular orbitals in the H₂ molecule. Note that the two electrons in the σ_{1s} orbital must have opposite spins in accord with the Pauli exclusion principle. Keep in mind that the higher the energy of the molecular orbital, the less stable the electrons in that molecular orbital. (b) Constructive and destructive interactions between the two hydrogen 1s orbitals lead to the formation of a bonding and an antibonding molecular orbital. In the bonding molecular orbital, there is a buildup between the nuclei of electron density, which acts as a negatively charged "glue" to hold the positively charged nuclei together.*

the entire molecule. The difference between a molecular orbital and an atomic orbital is that an atomic orbital is associated with only one atom.

Bonding and Antibonding Molecular Orbitals

According to MO theory, the overlap of the 1s orbitals of two hydrogen atoms leads to the formation of two molecular orbitals: one bonding molecular orbital and one antibonding molecular orbital. A **bonding molecular orbital** has *lower energy and greater stability than the atomic orbitals from which it was formed.* An **antibonding molecular orbital** has *higher energy and lower stability than the atomic orbitals from which it was formed.* As the names "bonding" and "antibonding" suggest, placing electrons in a bonding molecular orbital yields a stable covalent bond, whereas placing electrons in an antibonding molecular orbital results in an unstable bond.

In the bonding molecular orbital the electron density is greatest between the nuclei of the bonding atoms. In the antibonding molecular orbital, on the other hand, the electron density decreases to zero between the nuclei. We can understand this distinction if we recall that electrons in orbitals have wave characteristics. A property unique to waves allows waves of the same type to interact in such a way that the resultant wave has either an enhanced amplitude or a diminished amplitude. In the former case, we call the interaction *constructive interference;* in the latter case, it is *destructive interference* (Figure 10.22).

The formation of bonding molecular orbitals corresponds to constructive interference (the increase in amplitude is analogous to the buildup of electron density between the two nuclei). The formation of antibonding molecular orbitals corresponds to destructive interference (the decrease in amplitude is analogous to the decrease in electron density between the two nuclei). The constructive and destructive interactions between the two 1s orbitals in the H₂ molecule, then, lead to the formation of a sigma bonding molecular orbital (σ_{1s}) and a sigma antibonding molecular orbital $\sigma_{1s}^{\star}$:

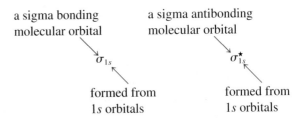

where the star denotes an antibonding molecular orbital.

In a **sigma molecular orbital** (bonding or antibonding) *the electron density is concentrated symmetrically around a line between the two nuclei of the bonding atoms.* Two electrons in a sigma molecular orbital form a sigma bond (see Section 10.5). Remember that a single covalent bond (such as H—H or F—F) is almost always a sigma bond.

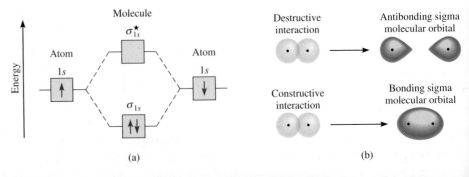

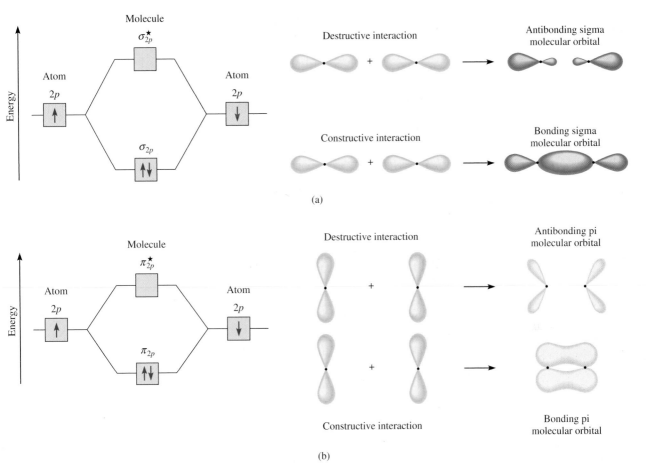

(a)

(b)

Figure 10.23 shows the *molecular orbital energy level diagram*—that is, the relative energy levels of the orbitals produced in the formation of the H_2 molecule—and the constructive and destructive interactions between the two $1s$ orbitals. Notice that in the antibonding molecular orbital there is a *node* between the nuclei that signifies zero electron density. The nuclei are repelled by each other's positive charges, rather than held together. Electrons in the antibonding molecular orbital have higher energy (and less stability) than they would have in the isolated atoms. On the other hand, electrons in the bonding molecular orbital have less energy (and hence greater stability) than they would have in the isolated atoms.

Although we have used the hydrogen molecule to illustrate molecular orbital formation, the concept is equally applicable to other molecules. In the H_2 molecule we consider only the interaction between $1s$ orbitals; with more complex molecules we need to consider additional atomic orbitals as well. Nevertheless, for all s orbitals, the process is the same as for $1s$ orbitals. Thus, the interaction between two $2s$ or $3s$ orbitals can be understood in terms of the molecular orbital energy level diagram and the formation of bonding and antibonding molecular orbitals shown in Figure 10.23.

For p orbitals, the process is more complex because they can interact with each other in two different ways. For example, two $2p$ orbitals can approach each other end-to-end to produce a sigma bonding and a sigma antibonding molecular orbital, as shown in Figure 10.24(a). Alternatively, the two p orbitals can overlap sideways to generate a bonding and an antibonding pi molecular orbital [Figure 10.24(b)].

Figure 10.24 *Two possible interactions between two equivalent p orbitals and the corresponding molecular orbitals. (a) When the p orbitals overlap end-to-end, a sigma bonding and a sigma antibonding molecular orbital form. (b) When the p orbitals overlap side-to-side, a pi bonding and a pi antibonding molecular orbital form. Normally, a sigma bonding molecular orbital is more stable than a pi bonding molecular orbital, because side-to-side interaction leads to a smaller overlap of the p orbitals than does end-to-end interaction. We assume that the $2p_x$ orbitals take part in the sigma molecular orbital formation. The $2p_y$ and $2p_z$ orbitals can interact to form only π molecular orbitals. The behavior shown in (b) represents the interaction between the $2p_y$ orbitals or the $2p_z$ orbitals.*

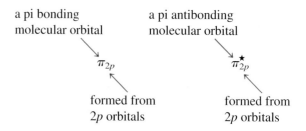

In a ***pi molecular orbital*** (bonding or antibonding), *the electron density is concentrated above and below a line joining the two nuclei of the bonding atoms.* Two electrons in a pi molecular orbital form a pi bond (see Section 10.5). A double bond is almost always composed of a sigma bond and a pi bond; a triple bond is always a sigma bond plus two pi bonds.

10.7 Molecular Orbital Configurations

To understand properties of molecules, we must know how electrons are distributed among molecular orbitals. The procedure for determining the electron configuration of a molecule is analogous to the one we use to determine the electron configurations of atoms (see Section 7.8).

Rules Governing Molecular Electron Configuration and Stability

In order to write the electron configuration of a molecule, we must first arrange the molecular orbitals in order of increasing energy. Then we can use the following guidelines to fill the molecular orbitals with electrons. The rules also help us understand the stabilities of the molecular orbitals.

1. The number of molecular orbitals formed is always equal to the number of atomic orbitals combined.

2. The more stable the bonding molecular orbital, the less stable the corresponding antibonding molecular orbital.

3. The filling of molecular orbitals proceeds from low to high energies. In a stable molecule, the number of electrons in bonding molecular orbitals is always greater than that in antibonding molecular orbitals because we place electrons first in the lower-energy bonding molecular orbitals.

4. Like an atomic orbital, each molecular orbital can accommodate up to two electrons with opposite spins in accordance with the Pauli exclusion principle.

5. When electrons are added to molecular orbitals of the same energy, the most stable arrangement is predicted by Hund's rule; that is, electrons enter these molecular orbitals with parallel spins.

6. The number of electrons in the molecular orbitals is equal to the sum of all the electrons on the bonding atoms.

Hydrogen and Helium Molecules

Later in this section we will study molecules formed by atoms of the second-period elements. Before we do, it will be instructive to predict the relative stabilities of the simple species H_2^+, H_2, He_2^+, and He_2, using the energy-level diagrams shown in

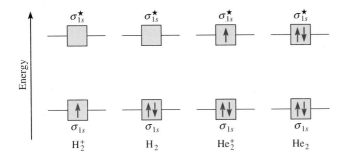

Figure 10.25 *Energy levels of the bonding and antibonding molecular orbitals in H_2^+, H_2, He_2^+, and He_2. In all these species, the molecular orbitals are formed by the interaction of two 1s orbitals.*

Figure 10.25. The σ_{1s} and $\sigma_{1s}^{\star}$ orbitals can accommodate a maximum of four electrons. The total number of electrons increases from one for H_2^+ to four for He_2. The Pauli exclusion principle stipulates that each molecular orbital can accommodate a maximum of two electrons with opposite spins. We are concerned only with the ground-state electron configurations in these cases.

To evaluate the stabilities of these species we determine their ***bond order,*** defined as

$$\text{bond order} = \frac{1}{2}\left(\begin{array}{c}\text{number of electrons} \\ \text{in bonding MOs}\end{array} - \begin{array}{c}\text{number of electrons} \\ \text{in antibonding MOs}\end{array}\right) \quad (10.2)$$

The bond order indicates the strength of a bond. For example, if there are two electrons in the bonding molecular orbital and none in the antibonding molecular orbital, the bond order is one, which means that there is one covalent bond and that the molecule is stable. Note that the bond order can be a fraction, but a bond order of zero (or a negative value) means the bond has no stability and the molecule cannot exist. Bond order can be used only qualitatively for purposes of comparison. For example, a bonding sigma molecular orbital with two electrons and a bonding pi molecular orbital with two electrons would each have a bond order of one. Yet, these two bonds must differ in bond strength (and bond length) because of the differences in the extent of atomic orbital overlap.

We are ready now to make predictions about the stability of H_2^+, H_2, He_2^+, and He_2 (see Figure 10.25). The H_2^+ molecular ion has only one electron in the σ_{1s} orbital. Because a covalent bond consists of two electrons in a bonding molecular orbital, H_2^+ has only half of one bond, or a bond order of $\frac{1}{2}$. Thus, we predict that the H_2^+ molecule may be a stable species. The electron configuration of H_2^+ is written as $(\sigma_{1s})^1$.

The H_2 molecule has two electrons, both of which are in the σ_{1s} orbital. According to our scheme, two electrons equal one full bond; therefore, the H_2 molecule has a bond order of one, or one full covalent bond. The electron configuration of H_2 is $(\sigma_{1s})^2$.

As for the He_2^+ molecular ion, we place the first two electrons in the σ_{1s} orbital and the third electron in the $\sigma_{1s}^{\star}$ orbital. Because the antibonding molecular orbital is destabilizing, we expect He_2^+ to be less stable than H_2. Roughly speaking, the instability resulting from the electron in the $\sigma_{1s}^{\star}$ orbital is balanced by one of the σ_{1s} electrons. The bond order is $\frac{1}{2}(2 - 1) = \frac{1}{2}$ and the overall stability of He_2^+ is similar to that of the H_2^+ molecule. The electron configuration of He_2^+ is $(\sigma_{1s})^2(\sigma_{1s}^{\star})^1$.

In He_2 there would be two electrons in the σ_{1s} orbital and two electrons in the $\sigma_{1s}^{\star}$ orbital, so the molecule would have a bond order of zero and no net stability. The electron configuration of He_2 would be $(\sigma_{1s})^2(\sigma_{1s}^{\star})^2$.

To summarize, we can arrange our examples in order of decreasing stability:

$$H_2 > H_2^+, He_2^+ > He_2$$

The quantitative measure of the strength of a bond is bond energy (Section 9.10).

The superscript in $(\sigma_{1s})^1$ indicates that there is one electron in the sigma bonding molecular orbital.

We know that the hydrogen molecule is a stable species. Our simple molecular orbital method predicts that H_2^+ and He_2^+ also possess some stability, because both have bond orders of $\frac{1}{2}$. Indeed, their existence has been confirmed by experiment. It turns out that H_2^+ is somewhat more stable than He_2^+, because there is only one electron in the hydrogen molecular ion and therefore it has no electron-electron repulsion. Furthermore, H_2^+ also has less nuclear repulsion than He_2^+. Our prediction about He_2 is that it would have no stability, but in 1993 He_2 gas was found to exist. The "molecule" is extremely unstable and has only a transient existence under specially created conditions.

Homonuclear Diatomic Molecules of Second-Period Elements

Interactivity: Energy Levels—Homonuclear Diatomic Molecules Online Learning Center, Interactives

We are now ready to study the ground-state electron configuration of molecules containing second-period elements. We will consider only the simplest case, that of **homonuclear diatomic molecules,** or *diatomic molecules containing atoms of the same elements.*

Figure 10.26 shows the molecular orbital energy level diagram for the first member of the second period, Li_2. These molecular orbitals are formed by the overlap of $1s$ and $2s$ orbitals. We will use this diagram to build up all the diatomic molecules, as we will see shortly.

The situation is more complex when the bonding also involves p orbitals. Two p orbitals can form either a sigma bond or a pi bond. Because there are three p orbitals for each atom of a second-period element, we know that one sigma and two pi molecular orbitals will result from the constructive interaction. The sigma molecular orbital is formed by the overlap of the $2p_x$ orbitals along the internuclear axis, that is, the x-axis. The $2p_y$ and $2p_z$ orbitals are perpendicular to the x-axis, and they will overlap

Figure 10.26 *Molecular orbital energy level diagram for the Li_2 molecule. The six electrons in Li_2 (Li's electron configuration is $1s^2 2s^1$) are in the σ_{1s}, $\sigma_{1s}^\star$, and σ_{2s} orbitals. Since there are two electrons each in σ_{1s} and $\sigma_{1s}^\star$ (just as in He_2), there is no net bonding or antibonding effect. Therefore, the single covalent bond in Li_2 is formed by the two electrons in the bonding molecular orbital σ_{2s}. Note that although the antibonding orbital ($\sigma_{1s}^\star$) has higher energy and is thus less stable than the bonding orbital (σ_{1s}), this antibonding orbital has less energy and greater stability than the σ_{2s} bonding orbital.*

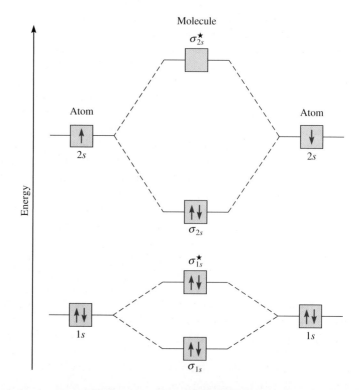

Molecule

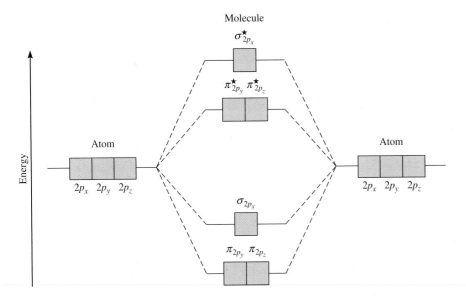

Figure 10.27 *General molecular orbital energy level diagram for the second-period homonuclear diatomic molecules Li_2, Be_2, B_2, C_2, and N_2. For simplicity, the σ_{1s} and σ_{2s} orbitals have been omitted. Note that in these molecules the σ_{2p_x} orbital is higher in energy than either the π_{2p_y} or the π_{2p_z} orbitals. This means that electrons in the σ_{2p_x} orbitals are less stable than those in π_{2p_y} and π_{2p_z}. For O_2 and F_2, the σ_{2p_x} orbital is lower in energy than π_{2p_y} and π_{2p_z}.*

sideways to give two pi molecular orbitals. The molecular orbitals are called σ_{2p_x}, π_{2p_y}, and π_{2p_z} orbitals, where the subscripts indicate which atomic orbitals take part in forming the molecular orbitals. As shown in Figure 10.24, overlap of the two p orbitals is normally greater in a σ molecular orbital than in a π molecular orbital, so we would expect the former to be lower in energy. However, the energies of molecular orbitals actually increase as follows:

$$\sigma_{1s} < \sigma_{1s}^{\star} < \sigma_{2s} < \sigma_{2s}^{\star} < \pi_{2p_y} = \pi_{2p_z} < \sigma_{2p_x} < \pi_{2p_y}^{\star} = \pi_{2p_z}^{\star} < \sigma_{2p_x}^{\star}$$

The inversion of the σ_{2p_x} orbital and the π_{2p_y} and π_{2p_z} orbitals is due to the interaction between the $2s$ orbital on one atom with the $2p$ orbital on the other. In MO terminology, we say there is mixing between these orbitals. The condition for mixing is that the $2s$ and $2p$ orbitals must be close in energy. This condition is met for the lighter molecules B_2, C_2, and N_2 with the result that the σ_{2p_x} orbital is raised in energy relative to the π_{2p_y} and π_{2p_z} orbitals as already shown. The mixing is less pronounced for O_2 and F_2 so the σ_{2p_x} orbital lies lower in energy than the π_{2p_y} and π_{2p_z} orbitals in these molecules.

With these concepts and Figure 10.27, which shows the order of increasing energies for $2p$ molecular orbitals, we can write the electron configurations and predict the magnetic properties and bond orders of second-period homonuclear diatomic molecules. We will consider a few examples.

The Lithium Molecule (Li_2)

The electron configuration of Li is $1s^2 2s^1$, so Li_2 has a total of six electrons. According to Figure 10.26, these electrons are placed (two each) in the σ_{1s}, $\sigma_{1s}^{\star}$, and σ_{2s} molecular orbitals. The electrons of σ_{1s} and $\sigma_{1s}^{\star}$ make no net contribution to the bonding in Li_2. Thus the electron configuration of the molecular orbitals in Li_2 is $(\sigma_{1s})^2(\sigma_{1s}^{\star})^2(\sigma_{2s})^2$. Since there are two more electrons in the bonding molecular orbitals than in antibonding orbitals, the bond order is 1 [see Equation (10.2)]. We conclude that the Li_2 molecule is stable, and because it has no unpaired electron spins, it should be diamagnetic. Indeed, diamagnetic Li_2 molecules are known to exist in the vapor phase.

The Carbon Molecule (C_2)

The carbon atom has the electron configuration $1s^2 2s^2 2p^2$; thus there are 12 electrons in the C_2 molecule. From the bonding scheme for Li_2, we place four additional carbon electrons in the π_{2p_y} and π_{2p_z} orbitals. Therefore, C_2 has the electron configuration

$$(\sigma_{1s})^2(\sigma_{1s}^\star)^2(\sigma_{2s})^2(\sigma_{2s}^\star)^2(\pi_{2p_y})^2(\pi_{2p_z})^2$$

Its bond order is 2, and the molecule has no unpaired electrons. Again, diamagnetic C_2 molecules have been detected in the vapor state. Note that the double bonds in C_2 are both pi bonds because of the four electrons in the two pi molecular orbitals. In most other molecules, a double bond is made up of a sigma bond and a pi bond.

The Oxygen Molecule (O_2)

As we stated earlier, valence bond theory does not account for the magnetic properties of the oxygen molecule. To show the two unpaired electrons on O_2, we need to draw an alternative to the resonance structure present on p. 415:

$$\cdot \overset{\displaystyle ..}{\underset{\displaystyle ..}{O}}-\overset{\displaystyle ..}{\underset{\displaystyle ..}{O}}\cdot$$

This structure is unsatisfactory on at least two counts. First, it implies the presence of a single covalent bond, but experimental evidence strongly suggests that there is a double bond in this molecule. Second, it places seven valence electrons around each oxygen atom, a violation of the octet rule.

The ground-state electron configuration of O is $1s^2 2s^2 2p^4$; thus there are 16 electrons in O_2. Using the order of increasing energies of the molecular orbitals discussed above, we write the ground-state electron configuration of O_2 as

TABLE 10.5

Properties of Homonuclear Diatomic Molecules of the Second-Period Elements*

	Li_2	B_2	C_2	N_2	O_2	F_2	
$\sigma_{2p_x}^\star$	☐	☐	☐	☐	☐	☐	$\sigma_{2p_x}^\star$
$\pi_{2p_y}^\star, \pi_{2p_z}^\star$	☐ ☐	☐ ☐	☐ ☐	☐ ☐	↑ ↑	↑↓ ↑↓	$\pi_{2p_y}^\star, \pi_{2p_z}^\star$
σ_{2p_x}	☐	☐	☐	↑↓	↑↓ ↑↓	↑↓ ↑↓	π_{2p_y}, π_{2p_z}
π_{2p_y}, π_{2p_z}	☐ ☐	↑ ↑	↑↓ ↑↓	↑↓ ↑↓	↑↓	↑↓	σ_{2p_x}
$\sigma_{2s}^\star$	☐	↑↓	↑↓	↑↓	↑↓	↑↓	$\sigma_{2s}^\star$
σ_{2s}	↑↓	↑↓	↑↓	↑↓	↑↓	↑↓	σ_{2s}
Bond order	1	1	2	3	2	1	
Bond length (pm)	267	159	131	110	121	142	
Bond energy (kJ/mol)	104.6	288.7	627.6	941.4	498.7	156.9	
Magnetic properties	Diamagnetic	Paramagnetic	Diamagnetic	Diamagnetic	Paramagnetic	Diamagnetic	

* For simplicity the σ_{1s} and $\sigma_{1s}^\star$ orbitals are omitted. These two orbitals hold a total of four electrons. Remember that for O_2 and F_2, σ_{2p_x} is lower in energy than π_{2p_y} and π_{2p_z}.

$$(\sigma_{1s})^2(\sigma_{1s}^{\star})^2(\sigma_{2s})^2(\sigma_{2s}^{\star})^2(\sigma_{2p_x})^2(\pi_{2p_y})^2(\pi_{2p_z})^2(\pi_{2p_y}^{\star})^1(\pi_{2p_z}^{\star})^1$$

According to Hund's rule, the last two electrons enter the $\pi_{2p_y}^{\star}$ and $\pi_{2p_z}^{\star}$ orbitals with parallel spins. Ignoring the σ_{1s} and σ_{2s} orbitals (because their net effects on bonding are zero), we calculate the bond order of O_2 using Equation (10.2):

$$\text{bond order} = \tfrac{1}{2}(6 - 2) = 2$$

Therefore, the O_2 molecule has a bond order of 2 and oxygen is paramagnetic, a prediction that corresponds to experimental observations.

Table 10.5 summarizes the general properties of the stable diatomic molecules of the second period.

Example 10.6 shows how MO theory can help predict molecular properties of ions.

Example 10.6

The N_2^+ ion can be prepared by bombarding the N_2 molecule with fast-moving electrons. Predict the following properties of N_2^+: (a) electron configuration, (b) bond order, (c) magnetic properties, and (d) bond length relative to the bond length of N_2 (is it longer or shorter?).

Strategy From Table 10.5 we can deduce the properties of ions generated from the homonuclear molecules. How does the stability of a molecule depend on the number of electrons in bonding and antibonding molecular orbitals? From what molecular orbital is an electron removed to form the N_2^+ ion from N_2? What properties determine whether a species is diamagnetic or paramagnetic?

Solution From Table 10.5 we can deduce the properties of ions generated from the homonuclear diatomic molecules.

(a) Because N_2^+ has one fewer electron than N_2, its electron configuration is

$$(\sigma_{1s})^2(\sigma_{1s}^{\star})^2(\sigma_{2s})^2(\sigma_{2s}^{\star})^2(\pi_{2p_y})^2(\pi_{2p_z})^2(\sigma_{2p_x})^1$$

(b) The bond order of N_2^+ is found by using Equation (10.2):

$$\text{bond order} = \tfrac{1}{2}(9 - 4) = 2.5$$

(c) N_2^+ has one unpaired electron, so it is paramagnetic.

(d) Because the electrons in the bonding molecular orbitals are responsible for holding the atoms together, N_2^+ should have a weaker and, therefore, longer bond than N_2. (In fact, the bond length of N_2^+ is 112 pm, compared with 110 pm for N_2.)

Check Because an electron is removed from a bonding molecular orbital, we expect the bond order to decrease. The N_2^+ ion has an odd number of electrons (13), so it should be paramagnetic.

Similar problems: 10.57, 10.58.

Practice Exercise Which of the following species has a longer bond length: F_2 or F_2^-?

10.8 Delocalized Molecular Orbitals

So far we have discussed chemical bonding only in terms of electron pairs. However, the properties of a molecule cannot always be explained accurately by a single structure. A case in point is the O_3 molecule, discussed in Section 9.8. There we overcame the dilemma by introducing the concept of resonance. In this section we will tackle the problem in another way—by applying the molecular orbital approach. As in

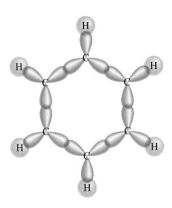

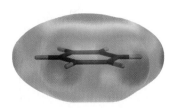

Electrostatic potential map of benzene shows the electron density (red color) above and below the plane of the molecule. For simplicity, only the framework of the molecule is shown.

Section 9.8, we will use the benzene molecule and the carbonate ion as examples. Note that in discussing the bonding of polyatomic molecules or ions, it is convenient to determine first the hybridization state of the atoms present (a valence bond approach), followed by the formation of appropriate molecular orbitals.

The Benzene Molecule

Benzene (C_6H_6) is a planar hexagonal molecule with carbon atoms situated at the six corners. All carbon-carbon bonds are equal in length and strength, as are all carbon-hydrogen bonds, and the CCC and HCC angles are all 120°. Therefore, each carbon atom is sp^2-hybridized; it forms three sigma bonds with two adjacent carbon atoms and a hydrogen atom (Figure 10.28). This arrangement leaves an unhybridized $2p_z$ orbital on each carbon atom, perpendicular to the plane of the benzene molecule, or *benzene ring*, as it is often called. So far the description resembles the configuration of ethylene (C_2H_4), discussed in Section 10.5, except that in this case there are six unhybridized $2p_z$ orbitals in a cyclic arrangement.

Because of their similar shape and orientation, each $2p_z$ orbital overlaps two others, one on each adjacent carbon atom. According to the rules listed on p. 418, the interaction of six $2p_z$ orbitals leads to the formation of six pi molecular orbitals, of which three are bonding and three antibonding. A benzene molecule in the ground state therefore has six electrons in the three pi bonding molecular orbitals, two electrons with paired spins in each orbital (Figure 10.29).

Unlike the pi bonding molecular orbitals in ethylene, those in benzene form ***delocalized molecular orbitals,*** *which are not confined between two adjacent bonding atoms, but actually extend over three or more atoms.* Therefore, electrons residing in any of these orbitals are free to move around the benzene ring. For this reason, the structure of benzene is sometimes represented as

in which the circle indicates that the pi bonds between carbon atoms are not confined to individual pairs of atoms; rather, the pi electron densities are evenly distributed throughout the benzene molecule. The carbon and hydrogen atoms are not shown in the simplified diagram.

We can now state that each carbon-to-carbon linkage in benzene contains a sigma bond and a "partial" pi bond. The bond order between any two adjacent carbon atoms is therefore between 1 and 2. Thus molecular orbital theory offers an alternative to the resonance approach, which is based on valence bond theory. (The resonance structures of benzene are shown on p. 366.)

Top view   Side view

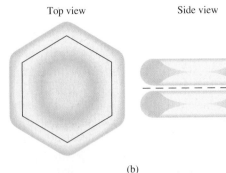

(a)   (b)

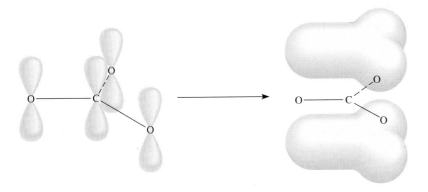

Figure 10.30 *Bonding in the carbonate ion. The carbon atom forms three sigma bonds with the three oxygen atoms. In addition, the $2p_z$ orbitals of the carbon and oxygen atoms overlap to form delocalized molecular orbitals, so that there is also a partial pi bond between the carbon atom and each of the three oxygen atoms.*

The Carbonate Ion

Cyclic compounds like benzene are not the only ones with delocalized molecular orbitals. Let's look at bonding in the carbonate ion (CO_3^{2-}). VSEPR predicts a trigonal planar geometry for the carbonate ion, like that for BF_3. The planar structure of the carbonate ion can be explained by assuming that the carbon atom is sp^2-hybridized. The C atom forms sigma bonds with three O atoms. Thus the unhybridized $2p_z$ orbital of the C atom can simultaneously overlap the $2p_z$ orbitals of all three O atoms (Figure 10.30). The result is a delocalized molecular orbital that extends over all four nuclei in such a way that the electron densities (and hence the bond orders) in the carbon-to-oxygen bonds are all the same. Molecular orbital theory therefore provides an acceptable alternative explanation of the properties of the carbonate ion as compared with the resonance structures of the ion shown on p. 366.

We should note that molecules with delocalized molecular orbitals are generally more stable than those containing molecular orbitals extending over only two atoms. For example, the benzene molecule, which contains delocalized molecular orbitals, is chemically less reactive (and hence more stable) than molecules containing "localized" C=C bonds, such as ethylene.

Key Equations

- $\mu = Q \times r$ (10.1)   Expressing dipole moment in terms of charge (Q) and distance of separation (r) between charges.

- bond order $= \dfrac{1}{2}\left(\begin{array}{l}\text{number of electrons} \\ \text{in bonding MOs}\end{array} - \begin{array}{l}\text{number of elecrons} \\ \text{in antibonding MOs}\end{array}\right)$ (10.2)

Summary of Facts and Concepts

1. The VSEPR model for predicting molecular geometry is based on the assumption that valence-shell electron pairs repel one another and tend to stay as far apart as possible.
2. According to the VSEPR model, molecular geometry can be predicted from the number of bonding electron pairs and lone pairs. Lone pairs repel other pairs more forcefully than bonding pairs do and thus distort bond angles from the ideal geometry.
3. Dipole moment is a measure of the charge separation in molecules containing atoms of different electronegativities. The dipole moment of a molecule is the

CHEMISTRY IN ACTION

Buckyball, Anyone?

In 1985 chemists at Rice University in Texas used a high-powered laser to vaporize graphite in an effort to create unusual molecules believed to exist in interstellar space. Mass spectrometry revealed that one of the products was an unknown species with the formula C_{60}. Because of its size and the fact that it is pure carbon, this molecule has an exotic shape, which the researchers worked out using paper, scissors, and tape. Subsequent spectroscopic and X-ray measurements confirmed that C_{60} is shaped like a hollow sphere with a carbon atom at each of the 60 vertices. Geometrically, buckyball (short for "buckminsterfullerene") is the most symmetrical molecule known. In spite of its unique features, however, its bonding scheme is straightforward. Each carbon is sp^2-hybridized, and there are extensive delocalized molecular orbitals over the entire structure.

The discovery of buckyball generated tremendous interest within the scientific community. Here was a new allotrope of carbon with an intriguing geometry and unknown properties to investigate. Since 1985 chemists have created a whole class of *fullerenes*, with 70, 76, and even larger numbers of carbon atoms. Moreover, buckyball has been found to be a natural component of soot, and the fullerenes C_{60} and C_{70} turned up in a rock sample from northwestern Russia.

Buckyball and its heavier members represent a whole new concept in molecular architecture with far-reaching implications. Studies have shown that the fullerenes and their compounds can act as high-temperature superconductors and lubricants, as well as catalysts. One fascinating discovery, made in 1991 by Japanese scientists, was the identification of structural relatives of buckyball. These molecules are hundreds of nanometers long with a tubular shape and an internal cavity about 15 nanometers in diameter. Dubbed "buckytubes" or

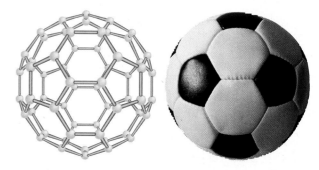

The geometry of a buckyball C_{60} (left) resembles a soccer ball (right). Scientists arrived at this structure by fitting together paper cutouts of enough hexagons and pentagons to accommodate 60 carbon atoms at the points where they intersect.

"nanotubes" (because of their size), these molecules have two distinctly different structures. One is a single sheet of graphite that is capped at both ends with a kind of truncated buckyball. The other is a scroll-like tube having anywhere from 2 to 30 graphite-like layers. Buckytubes are several times stronger than steel wires of similar dimensions and one day they might be used to make ultralight bicycles, rocket motor casings, and tennis racquets. They could also serve as casting molds for very thin metal wires to be used in microscopic integrated circuits or as "bottles" for storing molecules.

In the first biological application of buckyball, chemists at the University of California at San Francisco and Santa Barbara made a discovery in 1993 that could help in designing drugs to treat AIDS. The human immunodeficiency virus (HIV) that causes AIDS reproduces by synthesizing a long protein chain, which is cut into smaller segments by an enzyme called HIV-protease. One way to stop AIDS, then, might be to inactivate the enzyme. When the chemists reacted a water-soluble

resultant of whatever bond moments are present. Information about molecular geometry can be obtained from dipole moment measurements.

4. There are two quantum mechanical explanations for covalent bond formation: valence bond theory and molecular orbital theory. In valence bond theory, hybridized atomic orbitals are formed by the combination and rearrangement of orbitals from the same atom. The hybridized orbitals are all of equal energy and electron density, and the number of hybridized orbitals is equal to the number of pure atomic orbitals that combine.

5. Valence-shell expansion can be explained by assuming hybridization of *s*, *p*, and *d* orbitals.

6. In *sp* hybridization, the two hybrid orbitals lie in a straight line; in sp^2 hybridization, the three hybrid orbitals are directed toward the corners of a triangle;

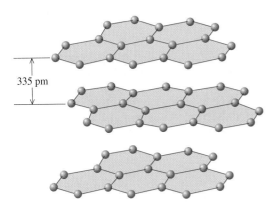

335 pm

Graphite is made up of layers of six-membered rings of carbon.

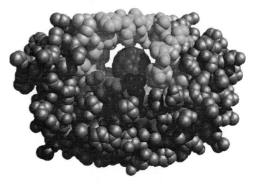

Computer-generated model of the binding of a buckyball derivative to the site of HIV-protease that normally attaches to a protein needed for the reproduction of HIV. The buckyball structure (purple color) fits tightly into the active site, thus preventing the enzyme from carrying out its function.

The structure of a buckytube that consists of a single layer of carbon atoms. Note that the truncated buckyball "cap," which has been separated from the rest of the buckytube in this view, has a different structure than the graphite-like cylindrical portion of the tube. Chemists have devised ways to open the cap in order to place other molecules inside the tube.

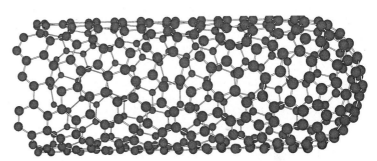

derivative of buckyball with HIV-protease, they found that it binds to the portion of the enzyme that would ordinarily cleave the reproductive protein, thereby preventing the HIV virus from reproducing. Consequently the virus could no longer infect the human cells they had grown in the laboratory. The buckyball compound itself is not a suitable drug for use against AIDS because of potential side effects and delivery difficulties, but it does provide a model for the development of such drugs.

in sp^3 hybridization, the four hybrid orbitals are directed toward the corners of a tetrahedron; in sp^3d hybridization, the five hybrid orbitals are directed toward the corners of a trigonal bipyramid; in sp^3d^2 hybridization, the six hybrid orbitals are directed toward the corners of an octahedron.

7. In an sp^2-hybridized atom (for example, carbon), the one unhybridized p orbital can form a pi bond with another p orbital. A carbon-carbon double bond consists of a sigma bond and a pi bond. In an sp-hybridized carbon atom, the two unhybridized p orbitals can form two pi bonds with two p orbitals on another atom (or atoms). A carbon-carbon triple bond consists of one sigma bond and two pi bonds.

8. Molecular orbital theory describes bonding in terms of the combination and rearrangement of atomic orbitals to form orbitals that are associated with the molecule as a whole.

9. Bonding molecular orbitals increase electron density between the nuclei and are lower in energy than individual atomic orbitals. Antibonding molecular orbitals have a region of zero electron density between the nuclei, and an energy level higher than that of the individual atomic orbitals.

10. We write electron configurations for molecular orbitals as we do for atomic orbitals, filling in electrons in the order of increasing energy levels. The number of molecular orbitals always equals the number of atomic orbitals that were combined. The Pauli exclusion principle and Hund's rule govern the filling of molecular orbitals.

11. Molecules are stable if the number of electrons in bonding molecular orbitals is greater than that in antibonding molecular orbitals.

12. Delocalized molecular orbitals, in which electrons are free to move around a whole molecule or group of atoms, are formed by electrons in p orbitals of adjacent atoms. Delocalized molecular orbitals are an alternative to resonance structures in explaining observed molecular properties.

Key Words

Antibonding molecular orbital, p. 416	Dipole moment (μ), p. 395	Pi bond (π bond), p. 412	Valence-shell electron-pair repulsion (VSEPR) model, p. 386
Bond order, p. 419	Homonuclear diatomic molecule, p. 420	Pi molecular orbital, p. 418	
Bonding molecular orbital, p. 416	Hybrid orbital, p. 404	Polar molecule, p. 396	
Delocalized molecular orbital, p. 424	Hybridization, p. 404	Sigma bond (σ bond), p. 412	
	Molecular orbital, p. 415	Sigma molecular orbital, p. 416	
	Nonpolar molecule, p. 396	Valence shell, p. 386	

Questions and Problems

Molecular Geometry
Review Questions

10.1 How is the geometry of a molecule defined and why is the study of molecular geometry important?

10.2 Sketch the shape of a linear triatomic molecule, a trigonal planar molecule containing four atoms, a tetrahedral molecule, a trigonal bipyramidal molecule, and an octahedral molecule. Give the bond angles in each case.

10.3 How many atoms are directly bonded to the central atom in a tetrahedral molecule, a trigonal bipyramidal molecule, and an octahedral molecule?

10.4 Discuss the basic features of the VSEPR model. Explain why the magnitude of repulsion decreases in the following order: lone pair-lone pair > lone pair-bonding pair > bonding pair-bonding pair.

10.5 In the trigonal bipyramidal arrangement, why does a lone pair occupy an equatorial position rather than an axial position?

10.6 The geometry of CH_4 could be square planar, with the four H atoms at the corners of a square and the C atom at the center of the square. Sketch this geometry and compare its stability with that of a tetrahedral CH_4 molecule.

Problems

10.7 Predict the geometries of the following species using the VSEPR method: (a) PCl_3, (b) $CHCl_3$, (c) SiH_4, (d) $TeCl_4$.

10.8 Predict the geometries of the following species: (a) $AlCl_3$, (b) $ZnCl_2$, (c) $ZnCl_4^{2-}$.

10.9 Predict the geometry of the following molecules and ion using the VSEPR model: (a) CBr_4, (b) BCl_3, (c) NF_3, (d) H_2Se, (e) NO_2^-.

10.10 Predict the geometry of the following molecules and ion using the VSEPR model: (a) CH_3I, (b) ClF_3, (c) H_2S, (d) SO_3, (e) SO_4^{2-}.

10.11 Predict the geometry of the following molecules using the VSEPR method: (a) $HgBr_2$, (b) N_2O (arrangement of atoms is NNO), (c) SCN^- (arrangement of atoms is SCN).

10.12 Predict the geometries of the following ions: (a) NH_4^+, (b) NH_2^-, (c) CO_3^{2-}, (d) ICl_2^-, (e) ICl_4^-, (f) AlH_4^-, (g) $SnCl_5^-$, (h) H_3O^+, (i) BeF_4^{2-}.

10.13 Describe the geometry around each of the three central atoms in the CH_3COOH molecule.

10.14 Which of the following species are tetrahedral? $SiCl_4$, SeF_4, XeF_4, CI_4, $CdCl_4^{2-}$

Dipole Moments
Review Questions

10.15 Define dipole moment. What are the units and symbol for dipole moment?

10.16 What is the relationship between the dipole moment and bond moment? How is it possible for a molecule to have bond moments and yet be nonpolar?

10.17 Explain why an atom cannot have a permanent dipole moment.

10.18 The bonds in beryllium hydride (BeH_2) molecules are polar, and yet the dipole moment of the molecule is zero. Explain.

Problems

10.19 Referring to Table 10.3, arrange the following molecules in order of increasing dipole moment: H_2O, H_2S, H_2Te, H_2Se.

10.20 The dipole moments of the hydrogen halides decrease from HF to HI (see Table 10.3). Explain this trend.

10.21 List the following molecules in order of increasing dipole moment: H_2O, CBr_4, H_2S, HF, NH_3, CO_2.

10.22 Does the molecule OCS have a higher or lower dipole moment than CS_2?

10.23 Which of the following molecules has a higher dipole moment?

(a)   (b)

10.24 Arrange the following compounds in order of increasing dipole moment:

(a)   (b)   (c)   (d)

Valence Bond Theory
Review Questions

10.25 What is valence bond theory? How does it differ from the Lewis concept of chemical bonding?

10.26 Use valence bond theory to explain the bonding in Cl_2 and HCl. Show how the atomic orbitals overlap when a bond is formed.

10.27 Draw a potential energy curve for the bond formation in F_2.

Hybridization
Review Questions

10.28 What is the hybridization of atomic orbitals? Why is it impossible for an isolated atom to exist in the hybridized state?

10.29 How does a hybrid orbital differ from a pure atomic orbital? Can two $2p$ orbitals of an atom hybridize to give two hybridized orbitals?

10.30 What is the angle between the following two hybrid orbitals on the same atom? (a) sp and sp hybrid orbitals, (b) sp^2 and sp^2 hybrid orbitals, (c) sp^3 and sp^3 hybrid orbitals

10.31 How would you distinguish between a sigma bond and a pi bond?

10.32 Which of the following pairs of atomic orbitals of adjacent nuclei can overlap to form a sigma bond? Which overlap to form a pi bond? Which cannot overlap (no bond)? Consider the x-axis to be the internuclear axis, that is, the line joining the nuclei of the two atoms. (a) $1s$ and $1s$, (b) $1s$ and $2p_x$, (c) $2p_x$ and $2p_y$, (d) $3p_y$ and $3p_y$, (e) $2p_x$ and $2p_x$, (f) $1s$ and $2s$

Problems

10.33 Describe the bonding scheme of the AsH_3 molecule in terms of hybridization.

10.34 What is the hybridization state of Si in SiH_4 and in $H_3Si—SiH_3$?

10.35 Describe the change in hybridization (if any) of the Al atom in the following reaction:

$$AlCl_3 + Cl^- \longrightarrow AlCl_4^-$$

10.36 Consider the reaction

$$BF_3 + NH_3 \longrightarrow F_3B—NH_3$$

Describe the changes in hybridization (if any) of the B and N atoms as a result of this reaction.

10.37 What hybrid orbitals are used by nitrogen atoms in the following species? (a) NH_3, (b) $H_2N—NH_2$, (c) NO_3^-

10.38 What are the hybrid orbitals of the carbon atoms in the following molecules?
(a) $H_3C—CH_3$
(b) $H_3C—CH=CH_2$
(c) $CH_3—C\equiv C—CH_2OH$
(d) $CH_3CH=O$
(e) CH_3COOH

10.39   Specify which hybrid orbitals are used by carbon atoms in the following species: (a) CO, (b) CO_2, (c) CN^-.

10.40   What is the hybridization state of the central N atom in the azide ion, N_3^-? (Arrangement of atoms: NNN.)

10.41   The allene molecule $H_2C=C=CH_2$ is linear (the three C atoms lie on a straight line). What are the hybridization states of the carbon atoms? Draw diagrams to show the formation of sigma bonds and pi bonds in allene.

10.42   Describe the hybridization of phosphorus in PF_5.

10.43   How many sigma bonds and pi bonds are there in each of the following molecules?

(a)   (b)   (c)

10.44   How many pi bonds and sigma bonds are there in the tetracyanoethylene molecule?

Molecular Orbital Theory
Review Questions

10.45   What is molecular orbital theory? How does it differ from valence bond theory?

10.46   Define the following terms: bonding molecular orbital, antibonding molecular orbital, pi molecular orbital, sigma molecular orbital.

10.47   Sketch the shapes of the following molecular orbitals: σ_{1s}, $\sigma_{1s}^{\star}$, π_{2p}, and $\pi_{2p}^{\star}$. How do their energies compare?

10.48   Explain the significance of bond order. Can bond order be used for quantitative comparisons of the strengths of chemical bonds?

Problems

10.49   Explain in molecular orbital terms the changes in H—H internuclear distance that occur as the molecular H_2 is ionized first to H_2^+ and then to H_2^{2+}.

10.50   The formation of H_2 from two H atoms is an energetically favorable process. Yet statistically there is less than a 100 percent chance that any two H atoms will undergo the reaction. Apart from energy considerations, how would you account for this observation based on the electron spins in the two H atoms?

10.51   Draw a molecular orbital energy level diagram for each of the following species: He_2, HHe, He_2^+. Compare their relative stabilities in terms of bond orders. (Treat HHe as a diatomic molecule with three electrons.)

10.52   Arrange the following species in order of increasing stability: Li_2, Li_2^+, Li_2^-. Justify your choice with a molecular orbital energy level diagram.

10.53   Use molecular orbital theory to explain why the Be_2 molecule does not exist.

10.54   Which of these species has a longer bond, B_2 or B_2^+? Explain in terms of molecular orbital theory.

10.55   Acetylene (C_2H_2) has a tendency to lose two protons (H^+) and form the carbide ion (C_2^{2-}), which is present in a number of ionic compounds, such as CaC_2 and MgC_2. Describe the bonding scheme in the C_2^{2-} ion in terms of molecular orbital theory. Compare the bond order in C_2^{2-} with that in C_2.

10.56   Compare the Lewis and molecular orbital treatments of the oxygen molecule.

10.57   Explain why the bond order of N_2 is greater than that of N_2^+, but the bond order of O_2 is less than that of O_2^+.

10.58   Compare the relative stability of the following species and indicate their magnetic properties (that is, diamagnetic or paramagnetic): O_2, O_2^+, O_2^- (superoxide ion), O_2^{2-} (peroxide ion).

10.59   Use molecular orbital theory to compare the relative stabilities of F_2 and F_2^+.

10.60   A single bond is almost always a sigma bond, and a double bond is almost always made up of a sigma bond and a pi bond. There are very few exceptions to this rule. Show that the B_2 and C_2 molecules are examples of the exceptions.

Delocalized Molecular Orbitals
Review Questions

10.61   How does a delocalized molecular orbital differ from a molecular orbital such as that found in H_2 or C_2H_4? What do you think are the minimum conditions (for example, number of atoms and types of orbitals) for forming a delocalized molecular orbital?

10.62   In Chapter 9 we saw that the resonance concept is useful for dealing with species such as the benzene molecule and the carbonate ion. How does molecular orbital theory deal with these species?

Problems

10.63   Both ethylene (C_2H_4) and benzene (C_6H_6) contain the C=C bond. The reactivity of ethylene is greater than that of benzene. For example, ethylene readily reacts with molecular bromine, whereas benzene is normally quite inert toward molecular bromine and many other compounds. Explain this difference in reactivity.

10.64 Explain why the symbol on the left is a better representation of benzene molecules than that on the right.

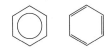

10.65 Determine which of these molecules has a more delocalized orbital and justify your choice.

(*Hint:* Both molecules contain two benzene rings. In naphthalene, the two rings are fused together. In biphenyl, the two rings are joined by a single bond, around which the two rings can rotate.)

10.66 Nitryl fluoride (FNO_2) is very reactive chemically. The fluorine and oxygen atoms are bonded to the nitrogen atom. (a) Write a Lewis structure for FNO_2. (b) Indicate the hybridization of the nitrogen atom. (c) Describe the bonding in terms of molecular orbital theory. Where would you expect delocalized molecular orbitals to form?

10.67 Describe the bonding in the nitrate ion NO_3^- in terms of delocalized molecular orbitals.

10.68 What is the state of hybridization of the central O atom in O_3? Describe the bonding in O_3 in terms of delocalized molecular orbitals.

Additional Problems

10.69 Which of the following species is not likely to have a tetrahedral shape? (a) $SiBr_4$, (b) NF_4^+, (c) SF_4, (d) $BeCl_4^{2-}$, (e) BF_4^-, (f) $AlCl_4^-$

10.70 Draw the Lewis structure of mercury(II) bromide. Is this molecule linear or bent? How would you establish its geometry?

10.71 Sketch the bond moments and resultant dipole moments for the following molecules: H_2O, PCl_3, XeF_4, PCl_5, SF_6.

10.72 Although both carbon and silicon are in Group 4A, very few Si=Si bonds are known. Account for the instability of silicon-to-silicon double bonds in general. (*Hint:* Compare the atomic radii of C and Si in Figure 8.5. What effect would the larger size have on pi bond formation?)

10.73 Predict the geometry of sulfur dichloride (SCl_2) and the hybridization of the sulfur atom.

10.74 Antimony pentafluoride, SbF_5, reacts with XeF_4 and XeF_6 to form ionic compounds, $XeF_3^+SbF_6^-$ and $XeF_5^+SbF_6^-$. Describe the geometries of the cations and anion in these two compounds.

10.75 Draw Lewis structures and give the other information requested for the following molecules: (a) BF_3. Shape: planar or nonplanar? (b) ClO_3^-. Shape: planar or nonplanar? (c) H_2O. Show the direction of the resultant dipole moment. (d) OF_2. Polar or nonpolar molecule? (e) NO_2. Estimate the ONO bond angle.

10.76 Predict the bond angles for the following molecules: (a) $BeCl_2$, (b) BCl_3, (c) CCl_4, (d) CH_3Cl, (e) Hg_2Cl_2 (arrangement of atoms: ClHgHgCl), (f) $SnCl_2$, (g) H_2O_2, (h) SnH_4.

10.77 Briefly compare the VSEPR and hybridization approaches to the study of molecular geometry.

10.78 Describe the hybridization state of arsenic in arsenic pentafluoride (AsF_5).

10.79 Draw Lewis structures and give the other information requested for the following: (a) SO_3. Polar or nonpolar molecule? (b) PF_3. Polar or nonpolar molecule? (c) F_3SiH. Show the direction of the resultant dipole moment. (d) SiH_3^-. Planar or pyramidal shape? (e) Br_2CH_2. Polar or nonpolar molecule?

10.80 Which of the following molecules are linear? ICl_2^-, IF_2^+, OF_2, SnI_2, $CdBr_2$

10.81 Draw the Lewis structure for the $BeCl_4^{2-}$ ion. Predict its geometry and describe the hybridization state of the Be atom.

10.82 The N_2F_2 molecule can exist in either of the following two forms:

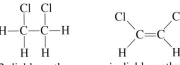

(a) What is the hybridization of N in the molecule?
(b) Which structure has a dipole moment?

10.83 Cyclopropane (C_3H_6) has the shape of a triangle in which a C atom is bonded to two H atoms and two other C atoms at each corner. Cubane (C_8H_8) has the shape of a cube in which a C atom is bonded to one H atom and three other C atoms at each corner. (a) Draw Lewis structures of these molecules. (b) Compare the CCC angles in these molecules with those predicted for an sp^3-hybridized C atom. (c) Would you expect these molecules to be easy to make?

10.84 The compound 1,2-dichloroethane ($C_2H_4Cl_2$) is nonpolar, while *cis*-dichloroethylene ($C_2H_2Cl_2$) has a dipole moment:

<figure>
```
    Cl  Cl
    |   |
H — C — C — H
    |   |
    H   H
1,2-dichloroethane
```

```
Cl        Cl
  \      /
   C = C
  /      \
 H        H
cis-dichloroethylene
```
</figure>

The reason for the difference is that groups connected by a single bond can rotate with respect to each other, but no rotation occurs when a double bond connects the groups. On the basis of bonding considerations, explain why rotation occurs in 1,2-dichloroethane but not in *cis*-dichloroethylene.

10.85 Does the following molecule have a dipole moment?

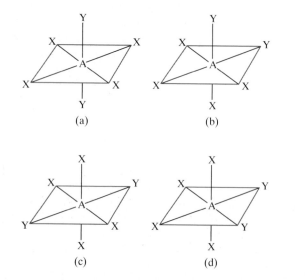

(*Hint:* See the answer to Problem 10.41.)

10.86 So-called greenhouse gases, which contribute to global warming, have a dipole moment or can be bent or distorted into shapes that have a dipole moment. Which of the following gases are greenhouse gases? N_2, O_2, O_3, CO, CO_2, NO_2, N_2O, CH_4, $CFCl_3$

10.87 The bond angle of SO_2 is very close to 120°, even though there is a lone pair on S. Explain.

10.88 3′-azido-3′-deoxythymidine, commonly known as AZT, is one of the drugs used to treat acquired immune deficiency syndrome (AIDS). What are the hybridization states of the C and N atoms in this molecule?

10.89 The following molecules (AX_4Y_2) all have octahedral geometry. Group the molecules that are equivalent to each other.

(a)   (b)

(c)   (d)

10.90 The compounds carbon tetrachloride (CCl_4) and silicon tetrachloride ($SiCl_4$) are similar in geometry and hybridization. However, CCl_4 does not react with water but $SiCl_4$ does. Explain the difference in their chemical reactivities. (*Hint:* The first step of the reaction is believed to be the addition of a water molecule to the Si atom in $SiCl_4$.)

10.91 Write the ground-state electron configuration for B_2. Is the molecule diamagnetic or paramagnetic?

10.92 What are the hybridization states of the C and N atoms in this molecule?

10.93 Use molecular orbital theory to explain the difference between the bond energies of F_2 and F_2^- (see Problem 9.110).

10.94 Referring to the Chemistry in Action on p. 398, answer the following questions: (a) If you wanted to cook a roast (beef or lamb), would you use a microwave oven or a conventional oven? (b) Radar is a means of locating an object by measuring the time for the echo of a microwave from the object to return to the source and the direction from which it returns. Would radar work if oxygen, nitrogen, and carbon dioxide were polar molecules? (c) In early tests of radar at the English Channel during World War II, the results were inconclusive even though there was no equipment malfunction. Why? (*Hint:* The weather is often foggy in the region.)

10.95 The geometries discussed in this chapter all lend themselves to fairly straightforward elucidation of bond angles. The exception is the tetrahedron, because its bond angles are hard to visualize. Consider the CCl_4 molecule, which has a tetrahedral geometry and is nonpolar. By equating the bond moment of a particular C—Cl bond to the resultant bond moments of the other three C—Cl bonds in opposite directions, show that the bond angles are all equal to 109.5°.

10.96 Referring to Table 9.4, explain why the bond energy for Cl_2 is greater than that for F_2. (*Hint:* The bond lengths of F_2 and Cl_2 are 142 pm and 199 pm, respectively.)

10.97 Use molecular orbital theory to explain the bonding in the azide ion (N_3^-). (Arrangement of atoms is NNN.)

10.98 The ionic character of the bond in a diatomic molecule can be estimated by the formula

$$\frac{\mu}{ed} \times 100\%$$

where μ is the experimentally measured dipole moment (in C m), e the electronic charge, and d the bond length in meters. (The quantity ed is the hypothetical dipole moment for the case in which the transfer of an electron from the less electronegative to the more electronegative atom is complete.) Given that the dipole moment and bond length of HF are 1.92 D and 91.7 pm, respectively, calculate the percent ionic character of the molecule.

10.99 Only one of the following two molecules containing C and H atoms is known to exist. Which one is it? Explain your choice.

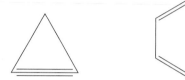

The C atoms occupy the apexes and the H atoms are not shown.

10.100 Greenhouse gases absorb (and trap) outgoing infared radiation (heat) from Earth and contribute to global warming. The molecule of a greenhouse gas either possesses a permanent dipole moment or has a changing dipole moment during its vibrational motions. Consider three of the vibrational modes of carbon dioxide

$$\overset{\leftarrow}{O}=C=\vec{O} \qquad \vec{O}=\overset{\leftarrow}{C}=\vec{O} \qquad \overset{\uparrow}{O}=C=\overset{\uparrow}{O}$$
$$\downarrow$$

where the arrows indicate the movement of the atoms. (During a complete cycle of vibration, the atoms move toward one extreme position and then reverse their direction to the other extreme position.) Which of the preceding vibrations are responsible for CO_2 to behave as a greenhouse gas? Which of the following molecules can act as a greenhouse gas: N_2, O_2, CO, NO_2, and N_2O?

10.101 Aluminum trichloride ($AlCl_3$) is an electron-deficient molecule. It has a tendency to form a dimer (a molecule made of two $AlCl_3$ units):

$$AlCl_3 + AlCl_3 \longrightarrow Al_2Cl_6$$

(a) Draw a Lewis structure for the dimer. (b) Describe the hybridization state of Al in $AlCl_3$ and Al_2Cl_6. (c) Sketch the geometry of the dimer. (d) Do these molecules possess a dipole moment?

10.102 Assume that the third-period element phosphorus forms a diatomic molecule, P_2, in an analogous way as nitrogen does to form N_2. (a) Write the electronic configuration for P_2. Use $[Ne_2]$ to represent the electron configuration for the first two periods. (b) Calculate its bond order. (c) What are its magnetic properties (diamagnetic or paramagnetic)?

10.103 Progesterone is a hormone responsible for female sex characteristics. In the usual shorthand structure, each point where lines meet represent a C atom, and most H atoms are not shown. Draw the complete structure of the molecule, showing all C and H atoms. Indicate which C atoms are sp^2- and sp^3-hybridized.

10.104 The molecules *cis*-dichloroethylene and *trans*-dichloroethylene shown on p. 397 can be interconverted by heating or irradiation. (a) Starting with *cis*-dichloroethylene, show that rotating the C=C bond by 180° will break only the pi bond but will leave the sigma bond intact. Explain the formation of *trans*-dichloroethylene from this process. (Treat the rotation as two, stepwise 90° rotations.) (b) Account for the difference in the bond energies for the pi bond (about 270 kJ/mol) and the sigma bond (about 350 kJ/mol). (c) Calculate the longest wavelength of light needed to bring about this conversion.

Answers to Practice Exercises

10.1 (a) Tetrahedral, (b) linear, (c) trigonal planar. **10.2** No. **10.3** (a) sp^3, (b) sp^2. **10.4** sp^3d^2. **10.5** The C atom is sp-hybridized. It forms a sigma bond with the H atom and another sigma bond with the N atom. The two unhybridized p orbitals on the C atom are used to form two pi bonds with the N atom. The lone pair on the N atom is placed in the sp orbital. **10.6** F_2^-.

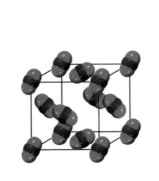

11

Intermolecular Forces and Liquids and Solids

Interactive Activity Summary

1. Animation: Packing Spheres (11.4)
2. Animation: Equilibrium Vapor Pressure (11.8)

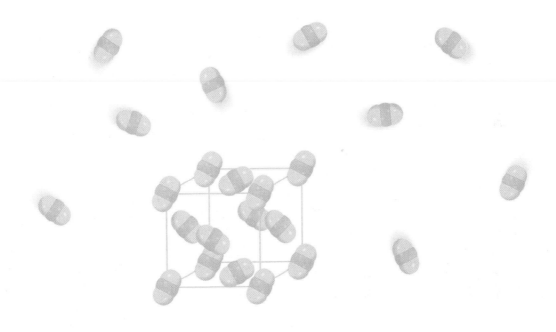

Although we live immersed in a mixture of gases that make up Earth's atmosphere, we are more familiar with the behavior of liquids and solids because they are more visible. Every day we use water and other liquids for drinking, bathing, cleaning, and cooking, and we handle, sit upon, and wear solids.

Molecular motion is more restricted in liquids than in gases; and in solids, the atoms and molecules are packed even more tightly together. In fact, in a solid they are held in well-defined positions and are capable of little free motion relative to one another. In this chapter we will examine the structure of liquids and solids and discuss some of the fundamental properties of these two states of matter.

11.1 The Kinetic Molecular Theory of Liquids and Solids

In Chapter 5 we used the kinetic molecular theory to explain the behavior of gases in terms of the constant, random motion of gas molecules. In gases, the distances between molecules are so great (compared with their diameters) that at ordinary temperatures and pressures (say, 25°C and 1 atm), there is no appreciable interaction between the molecules. Because there is a great deal of empty space in a gas—that is, space that is not occupied by molecules—gases can be readily compressed. The lack of strong forces between molecules also allows a gas to expand to fill the volume of its container. Furthermore, the large amount of empty space explains why gases have very low densities under normal conditions.

Liquids and solids are quite a different story. The principal difference between the condensed states (liquids and solids) and the gaseous state is the distance between molecules. In a liquid, the molecules are so close together that there is very little empty space. Thus liquids are much more difficult to compress than gases, and they are also much denser under normal conditions. Molecules in a liquid are held together by one or more types of attractive forces, which will be discussed in the next section. A liquid also has a definite volume, because molecules in a liquid do not break away from the attractive forces. The molecules can, however, move past one another freely, and so a liquid can flow, can be poured, and assumes the shape of its container.

In a solid, molecules are held rigidly in position with virtually no freedom of motion. Many solids are characterized by long-range order; that is, the molecules are arranged in regular configurations in three dimensions. There is even less empty space in a solid than in a liquid. Thus solids are almost incompressible and possess definite shape and volume. With very few exceptions (water being the most important), the density of the solid form is higher than that of the liquid form for a given substance. It is not uncommon for two states of a substance to coexist. An ice cube (solid) floating in a glass of water (liquid) is a familiar example. Chemists refer to the different states of a substance that are present in a system as phases. A **phase** is *a homogeneous part of the system in contact with other parts of the system but separated from them by a well-defined boundary.* Thus, our glass of ice water contains both the solid phase and the liquid phase of water. In this chapter we will use the term "phase" when talking about changes of state involving one substance, as well as systems containing more than one phase of a substance. Table 11.1 summarizes some of the characteristic properties of the three phases of matter.

TABLE 11.1 Characteristic Properties of Gases, Liquids, and Solids

State of Matter	Volume/Shape	Density	Compressibility	Motion of Molecules
Gas	Assumes the volume and shape of its container	Low	Very compressible	Very free motion
Liquid	Has a definite volume but assumes the shape of its container	High	Only slightly compressible	Slide past one another freely
Solid	Has a definite volume and shape	High	Virtually incompressible	Vibrate about fixed positions

11.2 Intermolecular Forces

Intermolecular forces are *attractive forces between molecules.* Intermolecular forces are responsible for the nonideal behavior of gases described in Chapter 5. They exert even more influence in the condensed phases of matter—liquids and solids. As the temperature of a gas drops, the average kinetic energy of its molecules decreases. Eventually, at a sufficiently low temperature, the molecules no longer have enough energy to break away from the attraction of neighboring molecules. At this point, the molecules aggregate to form small drops of liquid. This transition from the gaseous to the liquid phase is known as *condensation.*

Figure 11.1 *Molecules that have a permanent dipole moment tend to align with opposite polarities in the solid phase for maximum attractive interaction.*

In contrast to intermolecular forces, ***intramolecular forces*** *hold atoms together in a molecule.* (Chemical bonding, discussed in Chapters 9 and 10, involves intramolecular forces.) Intramolecular forces stabilize individual molecules, whereas intermolecular forces are primarily responsible for the bulk properties of matter (for example, melting point and boiling point).

Generally, intermolecular forces are much weaker than intramolecular forces. It usually requires much less energy to evaporate a liquid than to break the bonds in the molecules of the liquid. For example, it takes about 41 kJ of energy to vaporize 1 mole of water at its boiling point; but about 930 kJ of energy are necessary to break the two O—H bonds in 1 mole of water molecules. The boiling points of substances often reflect the strength of the intermolecular forces operating among the molecules. At the boiling point, enough energy must be supplied to overcome the attractive forces among molecules before they can enter the vapor phase. If it takes more energy to separate molecules of substance A than of substance B because A molecules are held together by stronger intermolecular forces, then the boiling point of A is higher than that of B. The same principle applies also to the melting points of the substances. In general, the melting points of substances increase with the strength of the intermolecular forces.

To discuss the properties of condensed matter, we must understand the different types of intermolecular forces. *Dipole-dipole, dipole-induced dipole,* and *dispersion forces* make up what chemists commonly refer to as ***van der Waals forces,*** after the Dutch physicist Johannes van der Waals (see Section 5.8). Ions and dipoles are attracted to one another by electrostatic forces called *ion-dipole forces,* which are *not* van der Waals forces. *Hydrogen bonding* is a particularly strong type of dipole-dipole interaction. Because only a few elements can participate in hydrogen bond formation, it is treated as a separate category. Depending on the phase of a substance, the nature of chemical bonds, and the types of elements present, more than one type of interaction may contribute to the total attraction between molecules, as we will see below.

Dipole-Dipole Forces

Dipole-dipole forces are *attractive forces between polar molecules,* that is, between molecules that possess dipole moments (see Section 10.2). Their origin is electrostatic, and they can be understood in terms of Coulomb's law. The larger the dipole moment, the greater the force. Figure 11.1 shows the orientation of polar molecules in a solid. In liquids, polar molecules are not held as rigidly as in a solid, but they tend to align in a way that, on average, maximizes the attractive interaction.

Ion-Dipole Forces

Coulomb's law also explains ***ion-dipole forces,*** which *attract an ion (either a cation or an anion) and a polar molecule to each other* (Figure 11.2). The strength of this interaction depends on the charge and size of the ion and on the magnitude of the dipole

Figure 11.2 *Two types of ion-dipole interaction.*

Figure 11.3 *Ion-dipole inter-action between Mg^{2+} and Na^+ ions and a water molecule.*

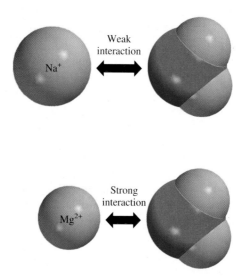

moment and size of the molecule. The charges on cations are generally more concentrated, because cations are usually smaller than anions. Therefore, a cation interacts more strongly with dipoles than does an anion having a charge of the same magnitude.

Hydration, discussed in Section 4.1, is one example of ion-dipole interaction. Heat of hydration (see p. 245) is the result of the favorable interaction between the cations and anions of an ionic compound with water. Figure 11.3 shows the ion-dipole interaction between the Na^+ and Mg^{2+} ions with a water molecule, which has a large dipole moment (1.87 D). Because the Mg^{2+} ion has a higher charge and a smaller ionic radius (78 pm) than that of the Na^+ ion (98 pm), it interacts more strongly with water molecules. (In reality, each ion is surrounded by a number of water molecules in solution.) Consequently, the heats of hydration for the Na^+ and Mg^{2+} ions are -405 kJ/mol and -1926 kJ/mol, respectively.[†] Similar differences exist for anions of different charges and sizes.

Dispersion Forces

What attractive interaction occurs in nonpolar substances? To learn the answer to this question, consider the arrangement shown in Figure 11.4. If we place an ion or a polar molecule near an atom (or a nonpolar molecule), the electron distribution of the atom (or molecule) is distorted by the force exerted by the ion or the polar molecule, resulting in a kind of dipole. The dipole in the atom (or nonpolar molecule) is said to be an ***induced dipole*** because *the separation of positive and negative charges in the atom (or nonpolar molecule) is due to the proximity of an ion or a polar molecule.* The attractive interaction between an ion and the induced dipole is called *ion-induced dipole interaction,* and the attractive interaction between a polar molecule and the induced dipole is called *dipole-induced dipole interaction.*

The likelihood of a dipole moment being induced depends not only on the charge on the ion or the strength of the dipole but also on the *polarizability* of the atom or molecule—that is, the ease with which the electron distribution in the atom (or molecule) can be distorted. Generally, the larger the number of electrons and the more diffuse the electron cloud in the atom or molecule, the greater its polarizability. By *diffuse cloud* we mean an electron cloud that is spread over an appreciable volume, so that the electrons are not held tightly by the nucleus.

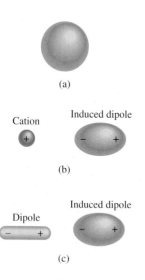

Figure 11.4 *(a) Spherical charge distribution in a helium atom. (b) Distortion caused by the approach of a cation. (c) Distortion caused by the approach of a dipole.*

[†]Heats of hydration of individual ions cannot be measured directly, but they can be reliably estimated.

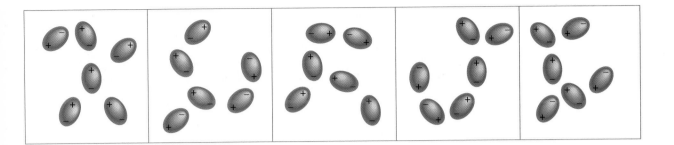

Figure 11.5 *Induced dipoles interacting with each other. Such patterns exist only momentarily; new arrangements are formed in the next instant. This type of interaction is responsible for the condensation of nonpolar gases.*

Polarizability allows gases containing atoms or nonpolar molecules (for example, He and N_2) to condense. In a helium atom the electrons are moving at some distance from the nucleus. At any instant it is likely that the atom has a dipole moment created by the specific positions of the electrons. This dipole moment is called an *instantaneous dipole* because it lasts for just a tiny fraction of a second. In the next instant the electrons are in different locations and the atom has a new instantaneous dipole, and so on. Averaged over time (that is, the time it takes to make a dipole moment measurement), however, the atom has no dipole moment because the instantaneous dipoles all cancel one another. In a collection of He atoms, an instantaneous dipole of one He atom can induce a dipole in each of its nearest neighbors (Figure 11.5). At the next moment, a different instantaneous dipole can create temporary dipoles in the surrounding He atoms. The important point is that this kind of interaction produces **dispersion forces,** *attractive forces that arise as a result of temporary dipoles induced in atoms or molecules.* At very low temperatures (and reduced atomic speeds), dispersion forces are strong enough to hold He atoms together, causing the gas to condense. The attraction between nonpolar molecules can be explained similarly.

A quantum mechanical interpretation of temporary dipoles was provided by Fritz London[†] in 1930. London showed that the magnitude of this attractive interaction is directly proportional to the polarizability of the atom or molecule. As we might expect, dispersion forces may be quite weak. This is certainly true for helium, which has a boiling point of only 4.2 K, or $-269°C$. (Note that helium has only two electrons, which are tightly held in the $1s$ orbital. Therefore, the helium atom has a low polarizability.)

Dispersion forces, which are also called London forces, usually increase with molar mass because molecules with larger molar mass tend to have more electrons, and dispersion forces increase in strength with the number of electrons. Furthermore, larger molar mass often means a bigger atom whose electron distribution is more easily disturbed because the outer electrons are less tightly held by the nuclei. Table 11.2 compares the melting points of similar substances that consist of nonpolar molecules. As expected, the melting point increases as the number of electrons in the molecule increases. Because these are all nonpolar molecules, the only attractive intermolecular forces present are the dispersion forces.

In many cases, dispersion forces are comparable to or even greater than the dipole-dipole forces between polar molecules. For a dramatic illustration, let us compare the boiling points of $CH_3F(-78.4°C)$ and $CCl_4(76.5°C)$. Although CH_3F has a dipole moment of 1.8 D, it boils at a much lower temperature than CCl_4, a nonpolar molecule. CCl_4 boils at a higher temperature simply because it contains more electrons. As a result, the dispersion forces between CCl_4 molecules are stronger than the

For simplicity we use the term "intermolecular forces" for both atoms and molecules.

TABLE 11.2

Melting Points of Similar Nonpolar Compounds

Compound	Melting Point (°C)
CH_4	-182.5
CF_4	-150.0
CCl_4	-23.0
CBr_4	90.0
CI_4	171.0

[†]Fritz London (1900–1954). German physicist. London was a theoretical physicist whose major work was on superconductivity in liquid helium.

dispersion forces plus the dipole-dipole forces between CH_3F molecules. (Keep in mind that dispersion forces exist among species of all types, whether they are neutral or bear a net charge and whether they are polar or nonpolar.)

Example 11.1 shows that if we know the kind of species present, we can readily determine the types of intermolecular forces that exist between the species.

Example 11.1

What type(s) of intermolecular forces exist between the following pairs: (a) HBr and H_2S, (b) Cl_2 and CBr_4, (c) I_2 and NO_3^-, (d) NH_3 and C_6H_6?

Strategy Classify the species into three categories: ionic, polar (possessing a dipole moment), and nonpolar. Keep in mind that dispersion forces exist between *all* species.

Solution (a) Both HBr and H_2S are polar molecules

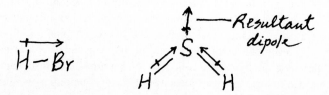

Therefore, the intermolecular forces present are dipole-dipole forces, as well as dispersion forces.

(b) Both Cl_2 and CBr_4 are nonpolar, so there are only dispersion forces between these molecules.

(c) I_2 is a homonuclear diatomic molecule and therefore nonpolar, so the forces between it and the ion NO_3^- are ion-induced dipole forces and dispersion forces.

(d) NH_3 is polar, and C_6H_6 is nonpolar. The forces are dipole-induced dipole forces and dispersion forces.

Similar problem: 11.10.

Practice Exercise Name the type(s) of intermolecular forces that exists between molecules (or basic units) in each of the following species: (a) LiF, (b) CH_4, (c) SO_2.

The Hydrogen Bond

Normally, the boiling points of a series of similar compounds containing elements in the same periodic group increase with increasing molar mass. This increase in boiling point is due to the increase in dispersion forces for molecules with more electrons. Hydrogen compounds of Group 4A follow this trend, as Figure 11.6 shows. The lightest compound, CH_4, has the lowest boiling point, and the heaviest compound, SnH_4, has the highest boiling point. However, hydrogen compounds of the elements

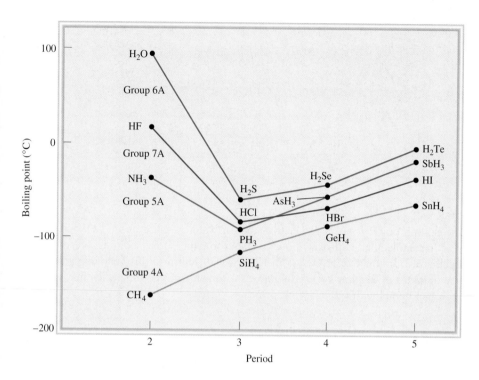

Figure 11.6 *Boiling points of the hydrogen compounds of Groups 4A, 5A, 6A, and 7A elements. Although normally we expect the boiling point to increase as we move down a group, we see that three compounds (NH_3, H_2O, and HF) behave differently. The anomaly can be explained in terms of intermolecular hydrogen bonding.*

in Groups 5A, 6A, and 7A do not follow this trend. In each of these series, the lightest compound (NH_3, H_2O, and HF) has the highest boiling point, contrary to our expectations based on molar mass. This observation must mean that there are stronger intermolecular attractions in NH_3, H_2O, and HF, compared to other molecules in the same groups. In fact, this particularly strong type of intermolecular attraction is called the **hydrogen bond,** which is *a special type of dipole-dipole interaction between the hydrogen atom in a polar bond, such as N—H, O—H, or F—H, and an electronegative O, N, or F atom.* The interaction is written

$$A—H \cdots B \qquad \text{or} \qquad A—H \cdots A$$

A and B represent O, N, or F; A—H is one molecule or part of a molecule and B is a part of another molecule; and the dotted line represents the hydrogen bond. The three atoms usually lie in a straight line, but the angle AHB (or AHA) can deviate as much as 30° from linearity. Note that the O, N, and F atoms all possess at least one lone pair that can interact with the hydrogen atom in hydrogen bonding.

The average energy of a hydrogen bond is quite large for a dipole-dipole interaction (up to 40 kJ/mol). Thus, hydrogen bonds have a powerful effect on the structures and properties of many compounds. Figure 11.7 shows several examples of hydrogen bonding.

The strength of a hydrogen bond is determined by the coulombic interaction between the lone-pair electrons of the electronegative atom and the hydrogen nucleus. For example, fluorine is more electronegative than oxygen, and so we would expect a stronger hydrogen bond to exist in liquid HF than in H_2O. In the liquid phase, the HF molecules form zigzag chains:

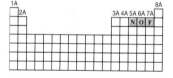

The three most electronegative elements that take part in hydrogen bonding.

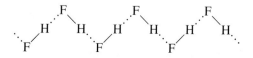

Figure 11.7 *Hydrogen bonding in water, ammonia, and hydrogen fluoride. Solid lines represent covalent bonds, and dotted lines represent hydrogen bonds.*

The boiling point of HF is lower than that of water because each H_2O takes part in *four* intermolecular hydrogen bonds. Therefore, the forces holding the molecules together are stronger in H_2O than in HF. We will return to this very important property of water in Section 11.3. Example 11.2 shows the type of species that can form hydrogen bonds with water.

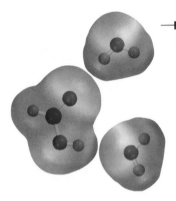

HCOOH forms hydrogen bonds with two H_2O molecules.

Example 11.2

Which of the following can form hydrogen bonds with water? CH_3OCH_3, CH_4, F^-, HCOOH, Na^+.

Strategy A species can form hydrogen bonds with water if it contains one of the three electronegative elements (F, O, or N) or it has an H atom bonded to one of these three elements.

Solution There are no electronegative elements (F, O, or N) in either CH_4 or Na^+. Therefore, only CH_3OCH_3, F^-, and HCOOH can form hydrogen bonds with water.

Check Note that HCOOH (formic acid) can form hydrogen bonds with water in two different ways.

Practice Exercise Which of the following species are capable of hydrogen bonding among themselves? (a) H_2S, (b) C_6H_6, (c) CH_3OH.

Similar problem: 11.12.

The intermolecular forces discussed so far are all attractive in nature. Keep in mind, though, that molecules also exert repulsive forces on one another. Thus when two molecules approach each other, the repulsion between the electrons and between the nuclei in the molecules comes into play. The magnitude of the repulsive force rises very steeply as the distance separating the molecules in a condensed phase decreases. This is the reason that liquids and solids are so hard to compress. In these phases, the molecules are already in close contact with one another, and so they greatly resist being compressed further.

11.3 Properties of Liquids

Intermolecular forces give rise to a number of structural features and properties of liquids. In this section we will look at two such phenomena associated with liquids in general: surface tension and viscosity. Then we will discuss the structure and properties of water.

Surface Tension

Molecules within a liquid are pulled in all directions by intermolecular forces; there is no tendency for them to be pulled in any one way. However, molecules at the surface are pulled downward and sideways by other molecules, but not upward away from the surface (Figure 11.8). These intermolecular attractions thus tend to pull the molecules into the liquid and cause the surface to tighten like an elastic film. Because there is little or no attraction between polar water molecules and, say, the nonpolar wax molecules on a freshly waxed car, a drop of water assumes the shape of a small round bead, because a sphere minimizes the surface area of a liquid. The waxy surface of a wet apple also produces this effect (Figure 11.9).

A measure of the elastic force in the surface of a liquid is surface tension. The **surface tension** is *the amount of energy required to stretch or increase the surface of a liquid by a unit area* (for example, by 1 cm^2). Liquids that have strong intermolecular forces also have high surface tensions. Thus, because of hydrogen bonding, water has a considerably greater surface tension than most other liquids.

Another example of surface tension is *capillary action*. Figure 11.10(a) shows water rising spontaneously in a capillary tube. A thin film of water adheres to the wall of the glass tube. The surface tension of water causes this film to contract, and as it does, it pulls the water up the tube. Two types of forces bring about capillary action. One is **cohesion,** which is *the intermolecular attraction between like*

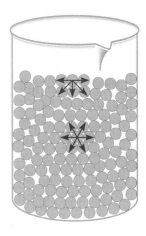

Figure 11.8 *Intermolecular forces acting on a molecule in the surface layer of a liquid and in the interior region of the liquid.*

Surface tension enables the water strider to "walk" on water.

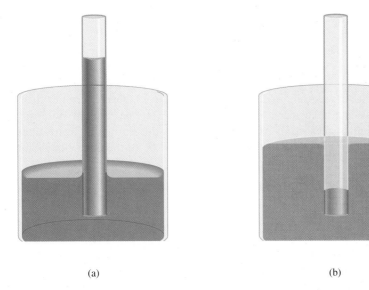

(a)   (b)

Figure 11.10 *(a) When adhesion is greater than cohesion, the liquid (for example, water) rises in the capillary tube. (b) When cohesion is greater than adhesion, as it is for mercury, a depression of the liquid in the capillary tube results. Note that the meniscus in the tube of water is concave, or rounded downward, whereas that in the tube of mercury is convex, or rounded upward.*

Figure 11.9 *Water beads on an apple which has a waxy surface.*

TABLE 11.3

Viscosity of Some Common Liquids at 20°C

Liquid	Viscosity $(N\ s/m^2)$*
Acetone (C_3H_6O)	3.16×10^{-4}
Benzene (C_6H_6)	6.25×10^{-4}
Blood	4×10^{-3}
Carbon tetrachloride (CCl_4)	9.69×10^{-4}
Ethanol (C_2H_5OH)	1.20×10^{-3}
Diethyl ether ($C_2H_5OC_2H_5$)	2.33×10^{-4}
Glycerol ($C_3H_8O_3$)	1.49
Mercury (Hg)	1.55×10^{-3}
Water (H_2O)	1.01×10^{-3}

* The SI units of viscosity are newton-second per meter squared.

molecules (in this case, the water molecules). The second force, called **adhesion,** is *an attraction between unlike molecules,* such as those in water and in the sides of a glass tube. If adhesion is stronger than cohesion, as it is in Figure 11.10(a), the contents of the tube will be pulled upward. This process continues until the adhesive force is balanced by the weight of the water in the tube. This action is by no means universal among liquids, as Figure 11.10(b) shows. In mercury, cohesion is greater than the adhesion between mercury and glass, so that when a capillary tube is dipped in mercury, the result is a depression or lowering, at the mercury level—that is, the height of the liquid in the capillary tube is below the surface of the mercury.

Viscosity

The expression "slow as molasses in January" owes its truth to another physical property of liquids called viscosity. **Viscosity** is *a measure of a fluid's resistance to flow.* The greater the viscosity, the more slowly the liquid flows. The viscosity of a liquid usually decreases as temperature increases; thus hot molasses flows much faster than cold molasses.

Liquids that have strong intermolecular forces have higher viscosities than those that have weak intermolecular forces (Table 11.3). Water has a higher viscosity than many other liquids because of its ability to form hydrogen bonds. Interestingly, the viscosity of glycerol is significantly higher than that of all the other liquids listed in Table 11.3. Glycerol has the structure

$$CH_2—OH$$
$$CH—OH$$
$$CH_2—OH$$

Glycerol is a clear, odorless, syrupy liquid used to make explosives, ink, and lubricants.

Like water, glycerol can form hydrogen bonds. Each glycerol molecule has three —OH groups that can participate in hydrogen bonding with other glycerol molecules. Furthermore, because of their shape, the molecules have a great tendency to become entangled rather than to slip past one another as the molecules of less viscous liquids do. These interactions contribute to its high viscosity.

The Structure and Properties of Water

Water is so common a substance on Earth that we often overlook its unique nature. All life processes involve water. Water is an excellent solvent for many ionic compounds, as well as for other substances capable of forming hydrogen bonds with water.

As Table 6.2 shows, water has a high specific heat. The reason is that to raise the temperature of water (that is, to increase the average kinetic energy of water molecules), we must first break the many intermolecular hydrogen bonds. Thus, water can absorb a substantial amount of heat while its temperature rises only slightly. The converse is also true: Water can give off much heat with only a slight decrease in its temperature. For this reason, the huge quantities of water that are present in our lakes and oceans can effectively moderate the climate of adjacent land areas by absorbing heat in the summer and giving off heat in the winter, with only small changes in the temperature of the body of water.

The most striking property of water is that its solid form is less dense than its liquid form: ice floats at the surface of liquid water. The density of almost all other substances is greater in the solid state than in the liquid state (Figure 11.11).

To understand why water is different, we have to examine the electronic structure of the H_2O molecule. As we saw in Chapter 9, there are two pairs of nonbonding electrons, or two lone pairs, on the oxygen atom:

Although many compounds can form intermolecular hydrogen bonds, the difference between H_2O and other polar molecules, such as NH_3 and HF, is that each oxygen atom can form *two* hydrogen bonds, the same as the number of lone electron pairs on the oxygen atom. Thus, water molecules are joined together in an extensive three-dimensional network in which each oxygen atom is approximately tetrahedrally bonded to four hydrogen atoms, two by covalent bonds and two by hydrogen bonds. This equality in the number of hydrogen atoms and lone pairs is not characteristic of NH_3 or HF or, for that matter, of any other molecule capable of forming hydrogen bonds. Consequently, these other molecules can form rings or chains, but not three-dimensional structures.

The highly ordered three-dimensional structure of ice (Figure 11.12) prevents the molecules from getting too close to one another. But consider what happens when ice melts. At the melting point, a number of water molecules have enough kinetic energy

If water did not have the ability to form hydrogen bonds, it would be a gas at room temperature.

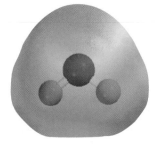

Electrostatic potential map of water.

Figure 11.11 *Left: Ice cubes float on water. Right: Solid benzene sinks to the bottom of liquid benzene.*

Figure 11.12 *The three-dimensional structure of ice. Each O atom is bonded to four H atoms. The covalent bonds are shown by short solid lines and the weaker hydrogen bonds by long dotted lines between O and H. The empty space in the structure accounts for the low density of ice.*

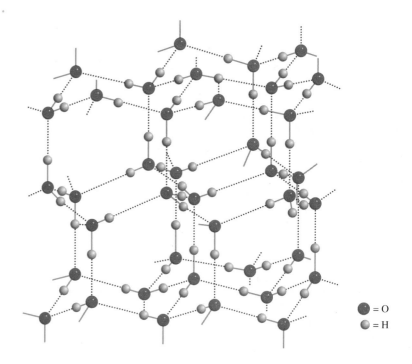

● = O
○ = H

to pull free of the intermolecular hydrogen bonds. These molecules become trapped in the cavities of the three-dimensional structure, which is broken down into smaller clusters. As a result, there are more molecules per unit volume in liquid water than in ice. Thus, because density = mass/volume, the density of water is greater than that of ice. With further heating, more water molecules are released from intermolecular hydrogen bonding, so that the density of water tends to increase with rising temperature just above the melting point. Of course, at the same time, water expands as it is being heated so that its density is decreased. These two processes—the trapping of free water molecules in cavities and thermal expansion—act in opposite directions. From 0°C to 4°C, the trapping prevails and water becomes progressively denser. Beyond 4°C, however, thermal expansion predominates and the density of water decreases with increasing temperature (Figure 11.13).

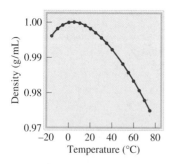

Figure 11.13 *Plot of density versus temperature for liquid water. The maximum density of water is reached at 4°C. The density of ice at 0°C is about 0.92 g/cm³.*

11.4 Crystal Structure

Solids can be divided into two categories: crystalline and amorphous. Ice is a **crystalline solid,** which *possesses rigid and long-range order; its atoms, molecules, or ions occupy specific positions.* The arrangement of such particles in a crystalline solid is such that the net attractive intermolecular forces are at their maximum. The forces responsible for the stability of a crystal can be ionic forces, covalent bonds, van der Waals forces, hydrogen bonds, or a combination of these forces. *Amorphous solids* such as glass lack a well-defined arrangement and long-range molecular order. We will discuss them in Section 11.7. In this section we will concentrate on the structure of crystalline solids.

A **unit cell** is *the basic repeating structural unit of a crystalline solid.* Figure 11.14 shows a unit cell and its extension in three dimensions. Each sphere represents an atom, ion, or molecule and is called a *lattice point*. In many crystals, the lattice point does not

CHEMISTRY IN ACTION

Why Do Lakes Freeze from the Top Down?

The fact that ice is less dense than water has a profound ecological significance. Consider, for example, the temperature changes in the fresh water of a lake in a cold climate. As the temperature of the water near the surface drops, the density of this water increases. The colder water then sinks toward the bottom, while warmer water, which is less dense, rises to the top. This normal convection motion continues until the temperature throughout the water reaches 4°C. Below this temperature, the density of water begins to decrease with decreasing temperature (see Figure 11.13), so that it no longer sinks. On further cooling, the water begins to freeze at the surface. The ice layer formed does not sink because it is less dense than the liquid; it even acts as a thermal insulator for the water below it. Were ice heavier, it would sink to the bottom of the lake and eventually the water would freeze upward. Most living organisms in the body of water could not survive being frozen in ice. Fortunately, lake water does not freeze upward from the bottom. This unusual property of water makes the sport of ice fishing possible.

Ice fishing. The ice layer that forms on the surface of a lake insulates the water beneath and maintains a high enough temperature to sustain aquatic life.

actually contain such a particle. Rather, there may be several atoms, ions, or molecules identically arranged about each lattice point. For simplicity, however, we can assume that each lattice point is occupied by an atom. This is certainly the case with most metals. Every crystalline solid can be described in terms of one of the seven types of unit cells shown in Figure 11.15. The geometry of the cubic unit cell is particularly simple because all sides and all angles are equal. Any of the unit cells, when repeated in space in all three dimensions, forms the lattice structure characteristic of a crystalline solid.

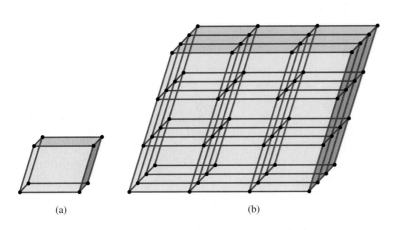

(a)   (b)

Figure 11.14 *(a) A unit cell and (b) its extension in three dimensions. The black spheres represent either atoms or molecules.*

Figure 11.15 *The seven types of unit cells. Angle α is defined by edges b and c, angle β by edges a and c, and angle γ by edges a and b.*

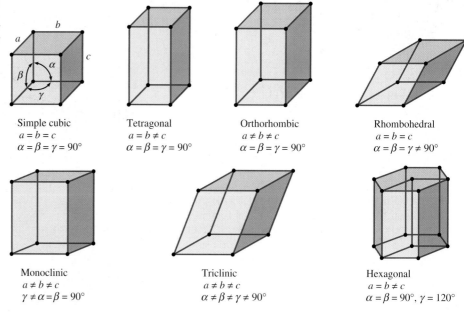

Simple cubic
$a = b = c$
$\alpha = \beta = \gamma = 90°$

Tetragonal
$a = b \neq c$
$\alpha = \beta = \gamma = 90°$

Orthorhombic
$a \neq b \neq c$
$\alpha = \beta = \gamma = 90°$

Rhombohedral
$a = b = c$
$\alpha = \beta = \gamma \neq 90°$

Monoclinic
$a \neq b \neq c$
$\gamma \neq \alpha = \beta = 90°$

Triclinic
$a \neq b \neq c$
$\alpha \neq \beta \neq \gamma \neq 90°$

Hexagonal
$a = b \neq c$
$\alpha = \beta = 90°, \gamma = 120°$

Packing Spheres

We can understand the general geometric requirements for crystal formation by considering the different ways of packing a number of identical spheres (Ping-Pong balls, for example) to form an ordered three-dimensional structure. The way the spheres are arranged in layers determines what type of unit cell we have.

In the simplest case, a layer of spheres can be arranged as shown in Figure 11.16(a). The three-dimensional structure can be generated by placing a layer above and below this layer in such a way that spheres in one layer are directly over the spheres in the layer below it. This procedure can be extended to generate many, many layers, as in the case of a crystal. Focusing on the sphere labeled with an "*x*," we see that it is in contact with four spheres in its own layer, one sphere in the layer above, and one sphere in the layer below. Each sphere in this arrangement is said to have a *coordination number* of 6 because it has six immediate neighbors. The **coordination number** is defined as *the number of atoms (or ions) surrounding an atom (or ion) in a crystal lattice*. Its value gives us a measure of how tightly the spheres are packed together—the larger the coordination number, the closer the spheres are to each other. The basic, repeating unit in the array of spheres described above is called a *simple cubic cell* (scc) [Figure 11.16(b)].

Figure 11.16 *Arrangement of identical spheres in a simple cubic cell. (a) Top view of one layer of spheres. (b) Definition of a simple cubic cell. (c) Since each sphere is shared by eight unit cells and there are eight corners in a cube, there is the equivalent of one complete sphere inside a simple cubic unit cell.*

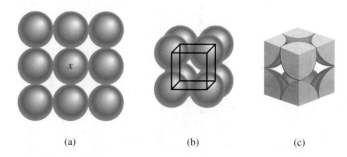

(a)   (b)   (c)

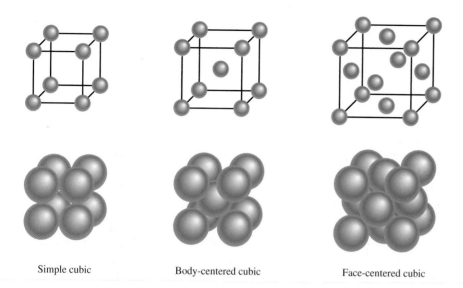

Simple cubic   Body-centered cubic   Face-centered cubic

Figure 11.17 *Three types of cubic cells. In reality, the spheres representing atoms, molecules, or ions are in contact with one another in these cubic cells.*

The other types of cubic cells are the *body-centered cubic cell* (bcc) and the *face-centered cubic cell* (fcc) (Figure 11.17). A body-centered cubic arrangement differs from a simple cube in that the second layer of spheres fits into the depressions of the first layer and the third layer into the depressions of the second layer (Figure 11.18). The coordination number of each sphere in this structure is 8 (each sphere is in contact with four spheres in the layer above and four spheres in the layer below). In the face-centered cubic cell, there are spheres at the center of each of the six faces of the cube, in addition to the eight corner spheres.

Because every unit cell in a crystalline solid is adjacent to other unit cells, most of a cell's atoms are shared by neighboring cells. For example, in all types of cubic cells, each corner atom belongs to eight unit cells [Figure 11.19(a)]; a face-centered atom is shared by two unit cells [Figure 11.19(b)]. Because each corner sphere is shared by eight unit cells and there are eight corners in a cube, there will be the equivalent of only one complete sphere inside a simple cubic unit cell [see Figure 11.16(c)]. A body-centered cubic cell contains the equivalent of two complete spheres, one in the center and eight shared corner spheres, as shown in Figure 11.18(c). A face-centered cubic cell contains four complete spheres—three from the six face-centered atoms and one from the eight shared corner spheres.

Closest Packing

Clearly there is more empty space in the simple cubic and body-centered cubic cells than in the face-centered cubic cell. **Closest packing,** *the most efficient arrangement of spheres,* starts with the structure shown in Figure 11.20(a), which we call layer A.

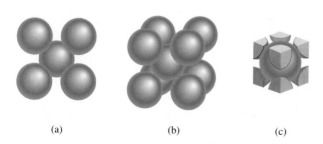

(a)   (b)   (c)

Figure 11.18 *Arrangement of identical spheres in a body-centered cube. (a) Top view. (b) Definition of a body-centered cubic unit cell. (c) There is the equivalent of two complete spheres inside a body-centered cubic unit cell.*

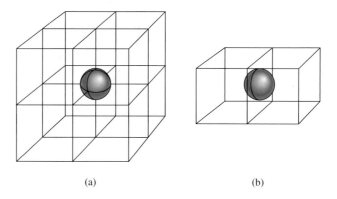

(a)   (b)

Focusing on the only enclosed sphere, we see that it has six immediate neighbors in that layer. In the second layer (which we call layer B), spheres are packed into the depressions between the spheres in the first layer so that all the spheres are as close together as possible [Figure 11.20(b)].

There are two ways that a third-layer sphere may cover the second layer to achieve closest packing. The spheres may fit into the depressions so that each third-layer sphere is directly over a first-layer sphere [Figure 11.20(c)]. Because there is no difference between the arrangement of the first and third layers, we also call the third layer layer A. Alternatively, the third-layer spheres may fit into the depressions that lie directly over the depressions in the first layer [Figure 11.20(d)]. In this case, we

These oranges are in a closest packed arrangement.

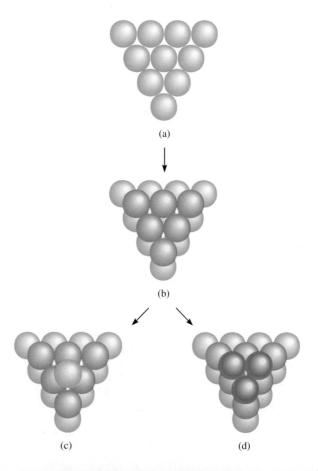

(a)

(b)

(c)   (d)

Figure 11.20 *(a) In a close-packed layer, each sphere is in contact with six others. (b) Spheres in the second layer fit into the depressions between the first-layer spheres. (c) In the hexagonal close-packed structure, each third-layer sphere is directly over a first-layer sphere. (d) In the cubic close-packed structure, each third-layer sphere fits into a depression that is directly over a depression in the first layer.*

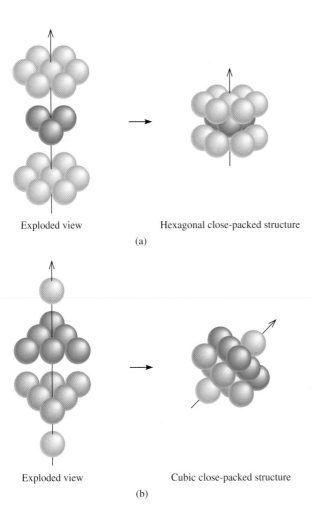

Exploded view   Hexagonal close-packed structure

(a)

Exploded view   Cubic close-packed structure

(b)

Figure 11.21 *Exploded views of (a) a hexagonal close-packed structure and (b) a cubic close-packed structure. The arrow is tilted to show the face-centered cubic unit cell more clearly. Note that this arrangement is the same as the face-centered unit cell.*

call the third layer layer C. Figure 11.21 shows the "exploded views" and the structures resulting from these two arrangements. The ABA arrangement is known as the *hexagonal close-packed (hcp) structure,* and the ABC arrangement is the *cubic close-packed (ccp) structure,* which corresponds to the face-centered cube already described. Note that in the hcp structure, the spheres in every other layer occupy the same vertical position (ABABAB. . .), while in the ccp structure, the spheres in every fourth layer occupy the same vertical position (ABCABCA. . .). In both structures, each sphere has a coordination number of 12 (each sphere is in contact with six spheres in its own layer, three spheres in the layer above, and three spheres in the layer below). Both the hcp and ccp structures represent the most efficient way of packing identical spheres in a unit cell, and there is no way to increase the coordination number to beyond 12.

Many metals and noble gases, which are monatomic, form crystals with hcp or ccp structures. For example, magnesium, titanium, and zinc crystallize with their atoms in a hcp array, while aluminum, nickel, and silver crystallize in the ccp arrangement. All solid noble gases have the ccp structure except helium, which crystallizes in the hcp structure. It is natural to ask why a series of related substances, such as the transition metals or the noble gases, would form different crystal structures. The answer lies in the relative stability of a particular crystal structure, which is governed by intermolecular forces. Thus magnesium metal has the hcp structure because this arrangement of Mg atoms results in the greatest stability of the solid.

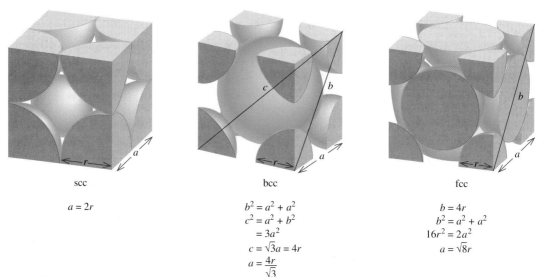

Figure 11.22 *The relationship between the edge length (a) and radius (r) of atoms in the simple cubic cell (scc), body-centered cubic cell (bcc), and face-centered cubic cell (fcc).*

Figure 11.22 summarizes the relationship between the atomic radius r and the edge length a of a simple cubic cell, a body-centered cubic cell, and a face-centered cubic cell. This relationship can be used to determine the atomic radius of a sphere if the density of the crystal is known, as Example 11.3 shows.

Example 11.3

Gold (Au) crystallizes in a cubic close-packed structure (the face-centered cubic unit cell) and has a density of 19.3 g/cm³. Calculate the atomic radius of gold in picometers.

Strategy We want to calculate the radius of a gold atom. For a face-centered cubic unit cell, the relationship between radius (r) and edge length (a), according to Figure 11.22, is $a = \sqrt{8}r$. Therefore, to determine r of a Au atom, we need to find a. The volume of a cube is $V = a^3$ or $a = \sqrt[3]{V}$. Thus if we can determine the volume of the unit cell, we can calculate a. We are given the density in the problem.

$$\underset{\text{given}}{\nearrow}\text{density} = \frac{\overset{\text{need to find}}{\nwarrow}\text{mass}}{\underset{\text{want to calculate}}{\searrow}\text{volume}}$$

The sequence of steps is summarized as follows:

$$\begin{array}{c}\text{density of}\\\text{unit cell}\end{array} \longrightarrow \begin{array}{c}\text{volume of}\\\text{unit cell}\end{array} \longrightarrow \begin{array}{c}\text{edge length}\\\text{of unit cell}\end{array} \longrightarrow \begin{array}{c}\text{radius of}\\\text{Au atom}\end{array}$$

Solution

Step 1: We know the density, so in order to determine the volume, we find the mass of the unit cell. Each unit cell has eight corners and six faces. The total number of atoms within such a cell, according to Figure 11.19, is

$$\left(8 \times \frac{1}{8}\right) + \left(6 \times \frac{1}{2}\right) = 4$$

(Continued)

The mass of a unit cell in grams is

$$m = \frac{4 \text{ atoms}}{1 \text{ unit cell}} \times \frac{1 \text{ mol}}{6.022 \times 10^{23} \text{ atoms}} \times \frac{197.0 \text{ g Au}}{1 \text{ mol Au}}$$
$$= 1.31 \times 10^{-21} \text{ g/unit cell}$$

From the definition of density ($d = m/V$), we calculate the volume of the unit cell as follows:

$$V = \frac{m}{d} = \frac{1.31 \times 10^{-21} \text{ g}}{19.3 \text{ g/cm}^3} = 6.79 \times 10^{-23} \text{ cm}^3$$

Remember that density is an intensive property, so that it is the same for one unit cell and 1 cm³ of the substance.

Step 2: Because volume is length cubed, we take the cubic root of the volume of the unit cell to obtain the edge length (a) of the cell

$$a = \sqrt[3]{V}$$
$$= \sqrt[3]{6.79 \times 10^{-23} \text{ cm}^3}$$
$$= 4.08 \times 10^{-8} \text{ cm}$$

Step 3: From Figure 11.22 we see that the radius of an Au sphere (r) is related to the edge length by

$$a = \sqrt{8}\, r$$

Therefore

$$r = \frac{a}{\sqrt{8}} = \frac{4.08 \times 10^{-8} \text{ cm}}{\sqrt{8}}$$
$$= 1.44 \times 10^{-8} \text{ cm}$$
$$= 1.44 \times 10^{-8} \text{ cm} \times \frac{1 \times 10^{-2} \text{ m}}{1 \text{ cm}} \times \frac{1 \text{ pm}}{1 \times 10^{-12} \text{ m}}$$
$$= 144 \text{ pm}$$

Similar problem: 11.39.

Practice Exercise When silver crystallizes, it forms face-centered cubic cells. The unit cell edge length is 408.7 pm. Calculate the density of silver.

11.5 X-Ray Diffraction by Crystals

Virtually all we know about crystal structure has been learned from X-ray diffraction studies. *X-ray diffraction* refers to *the scattering of X rays by the units of a crystalline solid.* The scattering, or diffraction, patterns produced are used to deduce the arrangement of particles in the solid lattice.

In Section 10.6 we discussed the interference phenomenon associated with waves (see Figure 10.21). Because X rays are one form of electromagnetic radiation, and therefore waves, we would expect them to exhibit such behavior under suitable conditions. In 1912 the German physicist Max von Laue[†] correctly suggested that, because the wavelength of X rays is comparable in magnitude to the distances between lattice points in a crystal, the lattice should be able to *diffract*

[†]Max Theodor Felix von Laue (1879–1960). German physicist. Von Laue received the Nobel Prize in Physics in 1914 for his discovery of X-ray diffraction.

Figure 11.23 *Arrangement for obtaining the X-ray diffraction pattern of a crystal. The shield prevents the strong undiffracted X rays from damaging the photographic plate.*

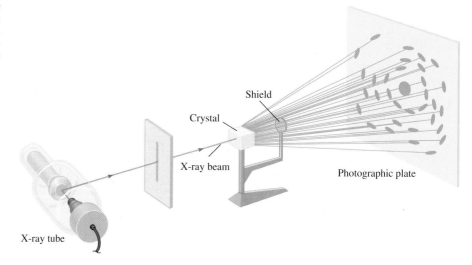

X rays. An X-ray diffraction pattern is the result of interference in the waves associated with X rays.

Figure 11.23 shows a typical X-ray diffraction setup. A beam of X rays is directed at a mounted crystal. Atoms in the crystal absorb some of the incoming radiation and then reemit it; the process is called the *scattering of X rays.*

To understand how a diffraction pattern may be generated, consider the scattering of X rays by atoms in two parallel planes (Figure 11.24). Initially, the two incident rays are *in phase* with each other (their maxima and minima occur at the same positions). The upper wave is scattered, or reflected, by an atom in the first layer, while the lower wave is scattered by an atom in the second layer. In order for these two scattered waves to be in phase again, the extra distance traveled by the lower wave must be an integral multiple of the wavelength (λ) of the X ray; that is,

$$BC + CD = 2d\sin\theta = n\lambda \qquad n = 1, 2, 3, \ldots \qquad (11.1)$$

Figure 11.24 *Reflection of X rays from two layers of atoms. The lower wave travels a distance $2d\sin\theta$ longer than the upper wave does. For the two waves to be in phase again after reflection, it must be true that $2d\sin\theta = n\lambda$, where λ is the wavelength of the X ray and $n = 1, 2, 3, \ldots$. The sharply defined spots in Figure 11.23 are observed only if the crystal is large enough to consist of hundreds of parallel layers.*

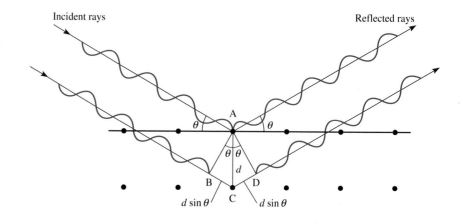

where θ is the angle between the X rays and the plane of the crystal and d is the distance between adjacent planes. Equation (11.1) is known as the Bragg equation after William H. Bragg[†] and Sir William L. Bragg.[‡] The reinforced waves produce a dark spot on a photographic film for each value of θ that satisfies the Bragg equation.

Example 11.4 illustrates the use of Equation (11.1).

Reinforced waves are waves that have interacted constructively (see Figure 10.22).

Example 11.4

X rays of wavelength 0.154 nm strike an aluminum crystal; the rays are reflected at an angle of 19.3°. Assuming that $n = 1$, calculate the spacing between the planes of aluminum atoms (in pm) that is responsible for this angle of reflection. The conversion factor is obtained from 1 nm = 1000 pm.

Strategy This is an application of Equation (11.1).

Solution Converting the wavelength to picometers and using the angle of reflection (19.3°), we write

$$d = \frac{n\lambda}{2 \sin \theta} = \frac{\lambda}{2 \sin \theta}$$

$$= \frac{0.154 \text{ nm} \times \dfrac{1000 \text{ pm}}{1 \text{ nm}}}{2 \sin 19.3°}$$

$$= 233 \text{ pm}$$

Similar problems: 11.47, 11.48.

Practice Exercise X rays of wavelength 0.154 nm are diffracted from a crystal at an angle of 14.17°. Assuming that $n = 1$, calculate the distance (in pm) between layers in the crystal.

The X-ray diffraction technique offers the most accurate method for determining bond lengths and bond angles in molecules in the solid state. Because X rays are scattered by electrons, chemists can construct an electron-density contour map from the diffraction patterns by using a complex mathematical procedure. Basically, an *electron-density contour map* tells us the relative electron densities at various locations in a molecule. The densities reach a maximum near the center of each atom. In this manner, we can determine the positions of the nuclei and hence the geometric parameters of the molecule.

11.6 Types of Crystals

The structures and properties of crystals, such as melting point, density, and hardness, are determined by the kinds of forces that hold the particles together. We can classify any crystal as one of four types: ionic, covalent, molecular, or metallic.

[†]William Henry Bragg (1862–1942). English physicist. Bragg's work was mainly in X-ray crystallography. He shared the Nobel Prize in Physics with his son Sir William Bragg in 1915.

[‡]Sir William Lawrence Bragg (1890–1972). English physicist. Bragg formulated the fundamental equation for X-ray diffraction and shared the Nobel Prize in Physics with his father in 1915.

564 pm

Figure 11.25 *Relation between the radii of Na$^+$ and Cl$^-$ ions and the unit cell dimensions. Here the cell edge length is equal to twice the sum of the two ionic radii.*

These giant potassium dihydrogen phosphate crystals were grown in the laboratory. The largest one weighs 701 lb!

Figure 11.26 *Crystal structures of (a) CsCl, (b) ZnS, and (c) CaF$_2$. In each case, the cation is the smaller sphere.*

Ionic Crystals

Ionic crystals have two important characteristics: (1) They are composed of charged species and (2) anions and cations are generally quite different in size. Knowing the radii of the ions is helpful in understanding the structure and stability of these compounds. There is no way to measure the radius of an individual ion, but sometimes it is possible to come up with a reasonable estimate. For example, if we know the radius of I$^-$ in KI is about 216 pm, we can determine the radius of K$^+$ ion in KI, and from that, the radius of Cl$^-$ in KCl, and so on. The ionic radii in Figure 8.9 are average values derived from many different compounds. Let us consider the NaCl crystal, which has a face-centered cubic lattice (see Figure 2.13). Figure 11.25 shows that the edge length of the unit cell of NaCl is twice the sum of the ionic radii of Na$^+$ and Cl$^-$. Using the values given in Figure 8.9, we calculate the edge length to be 2(95 + 181) pm, or 552 pm. But the edge length shown in Figure 11.25 was determined by X-ray diffraction to be 564 pm. The discrepancy between these two values tells us that the radius of an ion actually varies slightly from one compound to another.

Figure 11.26 shows the crystal structures of three ionic compounds: CsCl, ZnS, and CaF$_2$. Because Cs$^+$ is considerably larger than Na$^+$, CsCl has the simple cubic lattice. ZnS has the *zincblende* structure, which is based on the face-centered cubic lattice. If the S^{2-} ions occupy the lattice points, the Zn^{2+} ions are located one-fourth of the distance along each body diagonal. Other ionic compounds that have the zincblende structure include CuCl, BeS, CdS, and HgS. CaF$_2$ has the *fluorite* structure. The Ca^{2+} ions occupy the lattice points, and each F$^-$ ion is tetrahedrally surrounded by four Ca^{2+} ions. The compounds SrF$_2$, BaF$_2$, BaCl$_2$, and PbF$_2$ also have the fluorite structure.

Examples 11.5 and 11.6 show how to calculate the number of ions in and the density of a unit cell.

Example 11.5

How many Na$^+$ and Cl$^-$ ions are in each NaCl unit cell?

Solution NaCl has a structure based on a face-centered cubic lattice. As Figure 2.13 shows, one whole Na$^+$ ion is at the center of the unit cell, and there are twelve Na$^+$ ions at the edges. Because each edge Na$^+$ ion is shared by four unit cells, the total number of Na$^+$ ions is $1 + (12 \times \frac{1}{4}) = 4$. Similarly, there are six Cl$^-$ ions at the face centers and eight Cl$^-$ ions at the corners. Each face-centered ion is shared by two unit cells, and each corner ion is shared by eight unit cells (see Figure 11.19), so the total number of Cl$^-$ ions

(Continued)

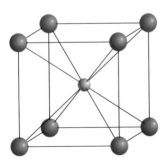

(a)

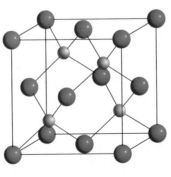

(b)

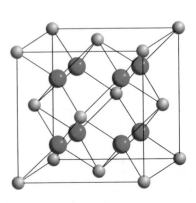

(c)

is $(6 \times \frac{1}{2}) + (8 \times \frac{1}{8}) = 4$. Thus there are four Na^+ ions and four Cl^- ions in each NaCl unit cell. Figure 11.27 shows the portions of the Na^+ and Cl^- ions *within* a unit cell.

Similar problem: 11.41.

Practice Exercise How many atoms are in a body-centered cube, assuming that all atoms occupy lattice points?

Example 11.6

The edge length of the NaCl unit cell is 564 pm. What is the density of NaCl in g/cm^3?

Strategy To calculate the density, we need to know the mass of the unit cell. The volume can be calculated from the given edge length because $V = a^3$. How many Na^+ and Cl^- ions are in a unit cell? What is the total mass in amu? What are the conversion factors between amu and g and between pm and cm?

Solution From Example 11.5 we see that there are four Na^+ ions and four Cl^- ions in each unit cell. So the total mass (in amu) of a unit cell is

$$\text{mass} = 4(22.99 \text{ amu} + 35.45 \text{ amu}) = 233.8 \text{ amu}$$

Converting amu to grams, we write

$$233.8 \text{ amu} \times \frac{1 \text{ g}}{6.022 \times 10^{23} \text{ amu}} = 3.882 \times 10^{-22} \text{ g}$$

The volume of the unit cell is $V = a^3 = (564 \text{ pm})^3$. Converting pm^3 to cm^3, the volume is given by

$$V = (564 \text{ pm})^3 \times \left(\frac{1 \times 10^{-12} \text{ m}}{1 \text{ pm}}\right)^3 \times \left(\frac{1 \text{ cm}}{1 \times 10^{-2} \text{ m}}\right)^3 = 1.794 \times 10^{-22} \text{ cm}^3$$

Finally, from the definition of density

$$\text{density} = \frac{\text{mass}}{\text{volume}} = \frac{3.882 \times 10^{-22} \text{ g}}{1.794 \times 10^{-22} \text{ cm}^3}$$
$$= 2.16 \text{ g/cm}^3$$

Similar problem: 11.42.

Practice Exercise Copper crystallizes in a face-centered cubic lattice (the Cu atoms are at the lattice points only). If the density of the metal is 8.96 g/cm^3, what is the unit cell edge length in pm?

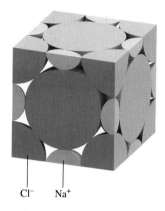

Figure 11.27 *Portions of Na^+ and Cl^- ions within a face-centered cubic unit cell.*

Cl^- Na^+

Most ionic crystals have high melting points, an indication of the strong cohesive forces holding the ions together. A measure of the stability of ionic crystals is the lattice energy (see Section 9.3); the higher the lattice energy, the more stable the compound. These solids do not conduct electricity because the ions are fixed in position. However, in the molten state (that is, when melted) or dissolved in water, the ions are free to move and the resulting liquid is electrically conducting.

Covalent Crystals

In covalent crystals, atoms are held together in an extensive three-dimensional network entirely by covalent bonds. Well-known examples are the two allotropes of carbon: diamond and graphite (see Figure 8.17). In diamond, each carbon atom is sp^3-hybridized; it is bonded to four other atoms (Figure 11.28). The strong covalent

Figure 11.28 *(a) The structure of diamond. Each carbon is tetrahedrally bonded to four other carbon atoms. (b) The structure of graphite. The distance between successive layers is 335 pm.*

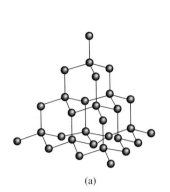

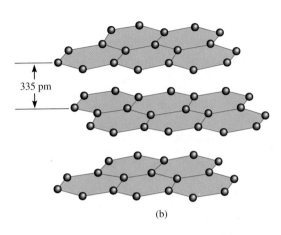

335 pm

(a)

(b)

The central electrode in flashlight batteries is made of graphite.

Quartz.

bonds in three dimensions contribute to diamond's unusual hardness (it is the hardest material known) and very high melting point (3550°C). In graphite, carbon atoms are arranged in six-membered rings. The atoms are all sp^2-hybridized; each atom is covalently bonded to three other atoms. The remaining unhybridized $2p$ orbital is used in pi bonding. In fact, each layer of graphite has the kind of delocalized molecular orbital that is present in benzene (see Section 10.8). Because electrons are free to move around in this extensively delocalized molecular orbital, graphite is a good conductor of electricity in directions along the planes of carbon atoms. The layers are held together by weak van der Waals forces. The covalent bonds in graphite account for its hardness; however, because the layers can slide over one another, graphite is slippery to the touch and is effective as a lubricant. It is also used in pencils and in ribbons made for computer printers and typewriters.

Another covalent crystal is quartz (SiO_2). The arrangement of silicon atoms in quartz is similar to that of carbon in diamond, but in quartz there is an oxygen atom between each pair of Si atoms. Because Si and O have different electronegativities, the Si—O bond is polar. Nevertheless, SiO_2 is similar to diamond in many respects, such as hardness and high melting point (1610°C).

Molecular Crystals

In a molecular crystal, the lattice points are occupied by molecules, and the attractive forces between them are van der Waals forces and/or hydrogen bonding. An example of a molecular crystal is solid sulfur dioxide (SO_2), in which the predominant attractive force is a dipole-dipole interaction. Intermolecular hydrogen bonding is mainly responsible for maintaining the three-dimensional lattice of ice (see Figure 11.12). Other examples of molecular crystals are I_2, P_4, and S_8.

In general, except in ice, molecules in molecular crystals are packed together as closely as their size and shape allow. Because van der Waals forces and hydrogen bonding are generally quite weak compared with covalent and ionic bonds, molecular crystals are more easily broken apart than ionic and covalent crystals. Indeed, most molecular crystals melt at temperatures below 100°C.

Sulfur.

Metallic Crystals

In a sense, the structure of metallic crystals is the simplest because every lattice point in a crystal is occupied by an atom of the same metal. Metallic crystals are generally body-centered cubic, face-centered cubic, or hexagonal close-packed (Figure 11.29). Consequently, metallic elements are usually very dense.

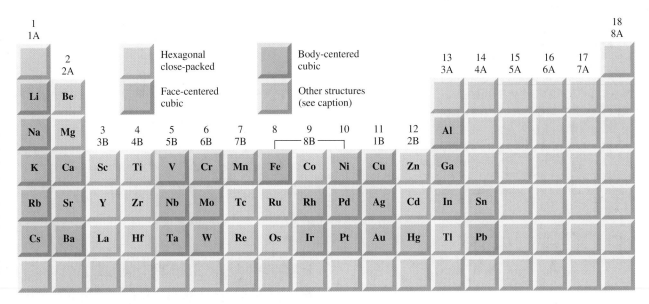

Figure 11.29 *Crystal structures of metals. The metals are shown in their positions in the periodic table. Mn has a cubic structure, Ga an orthorhombic structure, In and Sn a tetragonal structure, and Hg a rhombohedral structure (see Figure 11.15).*

The bonding in metals is quite different from that in other types of crystals. In a metal, the bonding electrons are delocalized over the entire crystal. In fact, metal atoms in a crystal can be imagined as an array of positive ions immersed in a sea of delocalized valence electrons (Figure 11.30). The great cohesive force resulting from delocalization is responsible for a metal's strength. The mobility of the delocalized electrons makes metals good conductors of heat and electricity.

Table 11.4 summarizes the properties of the four different types of crystals discussed.

TABLE 11.4

Types of Crystals and General Properties

Type of Crystal	Force(s) Holding the Units Together	General Properties	Examples
Ionic	Electrostatic attraction	Hard, brittle, high melting point, poor conductor of heat and electricity	NaCl, LiF, MgO, $CaCO_3$
Covalent	Covalent bond	Hard, high melting point, poor conductor of heat and electricity	C (diamond),[†] SiO_2 (quartz)
Molecular*	Dispersion forces, dipole-dipole forces, hydrogen bonds	Soft, low melting point, poor conductor of heat and electricity	Ar, CO_2, I_2, H_2O, $C_{12}H_{22}O_{11}$ (sucrose)
Metallic	Metallic bond	Soft to hard, low to high melting point, good conductor of heat and electricity	All metallic elements; for example, Na, Mg, Fe, Cu

* Included in this category are crystals made up of individual atoms.

† Diamond is a good thermal conductor.

CHEMISTRY IN ACTION

High-Temperature Superconductors

Metals such as copper and aluminum are good conductors of electricity, but they do possess some electrical resistance. In fact, up to about 20 percent of electrical energy may be lost in the form of heat when cables made of these metals are used to transmit electricity. Wouldn't it be marvelous if we could produce cables that possessed no electrical resistance?

Actually it has been known for over 80 years that certain metals and alloys, when cooled to very low temperatures (around the boiling point of liquid helium, or 4 K), lose their resistance totally. However, it is not practical to use these substances, called superconductors, for transmission of electric power because the cost of maintaining electrical cables at such

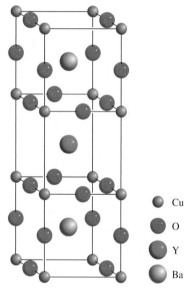

Cu
O
Y
Ba

Crystal structure of $YBa_2Cu_3O_x$ (x = 6 or 7). Because some of the O atom sites are vacant, the formula is not constant.

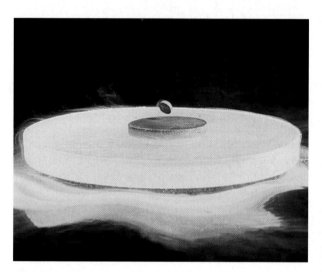

The levitation of a magnet above a high-temperature superconductor immersed in liquid nitrogen.

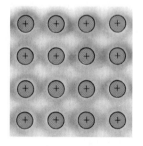

Figure 11.30 *A cross section of a metallic crystal. Each circled positive charge represents the nucleus and inner electrons of a metal atom. The gray area surrounding the positive metal ions indicates the mobile sea of electrons.*

11.7 Amorphous Solids

Solids are most stable in crystalline form. However, if a solid is formed rapidly (for example, when a liquid is cooled quickly), its atoms or molecules do not have time to align themselves and may become locked in positions other than those of a regular crystal. The resulting solid is said to be *amorphous*. **Amorphous solids,** such as glass, *lack a regular three-dimensional arrangement of atoms*. In this section, we will discuss briefly the properties of glass.

Glass is one of civilization's most valuable and versatile materials. It is also one of the oldest—glass articles date back as far as 1000 B.C. **Glass** commonly refers to *an optically transparent fusion product of inorganic materials that has cooled to a rigid state without crystallizing*. By fusion product we mean that the glass is formed by mixing molten silicon dioxide (SiO_2), its chief component, with

460

low temperatures is prohibitive and would far exceed the savings from more efficient electricity transmission.

In 1986 two physicists in Switzerland discovered a new class of materials that are superconducting at around 30 K. Although 30 K is still a very low temperature, the improvement over the 4 K range was so dramatic that their work generated immense interest and triggered a flurry of research activity. Within months, scientists synthesized compounds that are superconducting around 95 K, which is well above the boiling point of liquid nitrogen (77 K). The figure shows the crystal structure of one of these compounds, a mixed oxide of yttrium, barium, and copper with the formula $YBa_2Cu_3O_x$ (where $x = 6$ or 7). The accompanying figure shows a magnet being levitated above such a superconductor, which is immersed in liquid nitrogen.

There is good reason to be enthusiastic about these materials. Because liquid nitrogen is quite cheap (a liter of liquid nitrogen costs *less* than a liter of milk), we can envision electrical power being transmitted over hundreds of miles with no loss of energy. The levitation effect can be used to construct fast, quiet trains that glide over (but are not in contact with) the tracks. Superconductors can also be used to build superfast computers, called supercomputers, whose speeds are limited by how fast electric current flows. Furthermore, the enormous magnetic fields that can be created in superconductors will result in more powerful particle accelerators, efficient devices for nuclear fusion, and more accurate magnetic resonance imaging techniques for medical use.

Despite their promise, we are still a long way from seeing the commercial use of high-temperature superconductors. A number of technical problems remain, and so far scientists have not been able to make durable wires out of these materials in

large quantities. Nevertheless, the payoff is so enormous that high-temperature superconductivity is one of the most actively researched areas in physics and chemistry today.

An experimental levitation train that operates on superconducting material at the temperature of liquid helium.

compounds such as sodium oxide (Na_2O), boron oxide (B_2O_3), and certain transition metal oxides for color and other properties. In some respects glass behaves more like a liquid than a solid. X-ray diffraction studies show that glass lacks long-range periodic order.

There are about 800 different types of glass in common use today. Figure 11.31 shows two-dimensional schematic representations of crystalline quartz and amorphous quartz glass. Table 11.5 shows the composition and properties of quartz, Pyrex, and soda-lime glass.

The color of glass is due largely to the presence of metal ions (as oxides). For example, green glass contains iron(III) oxide, Fe_2O_3, or copper(II) oxide, CuO; yellow glass contains uranium(IV) oxide, UO_2; blue glass contains cobalt(II) and copper(II) oxides, CoO and CuO; and red glass contains small particles of gold and copper. Note that most of the ions mentioned here are derived from the transition metals.

Figure 11.31 *The two-dimensional representation of (a) crystalline quartz and (b) non-crystalline quartz glass. The small spheres represent silicon. In reality, the structure of quartz is three-dimensional. Each Si atom is tetrahedrally bonded to four O atoms.*

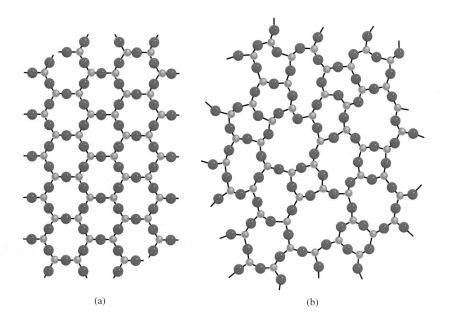

(a)   (b)

TABLE 11.5

Composition and Properties of Three Types of Glass

Name	Composition	Properties and Uses
Pure quartz glass	100% SiO_2	Low thermal expansion, transparent to wide range of wavelengths. Used in optical research.
Pyrex glass	SiO_2, 60–80% B_2O_3, 10–25% Al_2O_3, small amount	Low thermal expansion; transparent to visible and infrared, but not to UV, radiation. Used mainly in laboratory and household cooking glassware.
Soda-lime glass	SiO_2, 75% Na_2O, 15% CaO, 10%	Easily attacked by chemicals and sensitive to thermal shocks. Transmits visible light, but absorbs UV radiation. Used mainly in windows and bottles.

11.8 Phase Changes

The discussions in Chapter 5 and in this chapter have given us an overview of the properties of the three phases of matter: gas, liquid, and solid. **Phase changes,** *transformations from one phase to another,* occur when energy (usually in the form of heat) is added or removed. Phase changes are physical changes characterized by changes in molecular order; molecules in the solid phase have the greatest order, and those in the gas phase have the greatest randomness. Keeping in mind the relationship between energy change and the increase or decrease in molecular order will help us understand the nature of these physical changes.

Liquid-Vapor Equilibrium

Molecules in a liquid are not fixed in a rigid lattice. Although they lack the total freedom of gaseous molecules, these molecules are in constant motion. Because liquids are denser than gases, the collision rate among molecules is much higher in the liquid

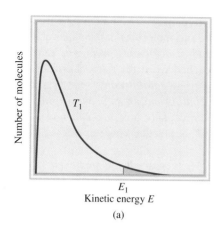
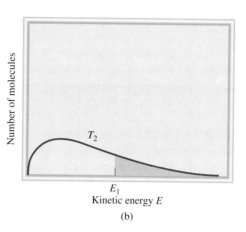

(a)

(b)

Figure 11.32 *Kinetic energy distribution curves for molecules in a liquid (a) at a temperature T_1 and (b) at a higher temperature T_2. Note that at the higher temperature the curve flattens out. The shaded areas represent the number of molecules possessing kinetic energy equal to or greater than a certain kinetic energy E_1. The higher the temperature, the greater the number of molecules with high kinetic energy.*

phase than in the gas phase. When the molecules in a liquid have sufficient energy to escape from the surface a phase change occurs. *Evaporation,* or *vaporization,* is *the process in which a liquid is transformed into a gas.*

How does evaporation depend on temperature? Figure 11.32 shows the kinetic energy distribution of molecules in a liquid at two different temperatures. As we can see, the higher the temperature, the greater the kinetic energy, and hence more molecules are leaving the liquid.

Vapor Pressure When a liquid evaporates, its gaseous molecules exert a vapor pressure. Consider the apparatus shown in Figure 11.33. Before the evaporation process starts, the mercury levels in the U-shaped manometer tube are equal. As soon as some molecules leave the liquid, a vapor phase is established. The vapor pressure is measurable only when a fair amount of vapor is present. The process of evaporation does not continue indefinitely, however. Eventually, the mercury levels stabilize and no further changes are seen.

What happens at the molecular level during evaporation? In the beginning, the traffic is only one way: Molecules are moving from the liquid to the empty space. Soon the molecules in the space above the liquid establish a vapor phase. As the concentration of molecules in the vapor phase increases, some molecules *condense,* that is, they return to the liquid phase. *Condensation, the change from the gas phase to the liquid phase,* occurs because a molecule strikes the liquid surface and becomes trapped by intermolecular forces in the liquid.

The difference between a gas and a vapor is explained on p. 165.

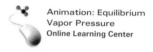

Animation: Equilibrium
Vapor Pressure
Online Learning Center

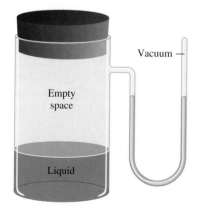
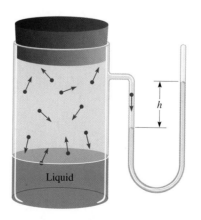

(a)

(b)

Figure 11.33 *Apparatus for measuring the vapor pressure of a liquid (a) before the evaporation begins and (b) at equilibrium, when no further change is evident. In (b) the number of molecules leaving the liquid is equal to the number of molecules returning to the liquid. The difference in the mercury levels (h) gives the equilibrium vapor pressure of the liquid at the specified temperature.*

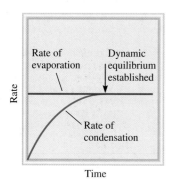

Figure 11.34 *Comparison of the rates of evaporation and condensation at constant temperature.*

The rate of evaporation is constant at any given temperature, and the rate of condensation increases with the increasing concentration of molecules in the vapor phase. A state of **dynamic equilibrium,** in which *the rate of a forward process is exactly balanced by the rate of the reverse process,* is reached when the rates of condensation and evaporation become equal (Figure 11.34). The **equilibrium vapor pressure** is *the vapor pressure measured when a dynamic equilibrium exists between condensation and evaporation.* We often use the simpler term "vapor pressure" when we talk about the equilibrium vapor pressure of a liquid. This practice is acceptable as long as we know the meaning of the abbreviated term.

It is important to note that the equilibrium vapor pressure is the *maximum* vapor pressure of a liquid at a given temperature and that it is constant at a constant temperature. (It is independent of the amount of liquid as long as there is some liquid present.) From the foregoing discussion we expect the vapor pressure of a liquid to increase with temperature. Plots of vapor pressure versus temperature for three different liquids in Figure 11.35 confirm this expectation.

Molar Heat of Vaporization and Boiling Point

A measure of the strength of intermolecular forces in a liquid is the **molar heat of vaporization (ΔH_{vap}),** defined as *the energy* (usually in kilojoules) *required to vaporize 1 mole of a liquid.* The molar heat of vaporization is directly related to the strength of intermolecular forces that exist in the liquid. If the intermolecular attraction is strong, it takes a lot of energy to free the molecules from the liquid phase. Consequently, the liquid has a relatively low vapor pressure and a high molar heat of vaporization.

The quantitative relationship between the vapor pressure P of a liquid and the absolute temperature T is given by the Clausius[†]-Clapeyron[‡] equation

$$\ln P = -\frac{\Delta H_{vap}}{RT} + C \tag{11.2}$$

[†]Rudolf Julius Emanuel Clausius (1822–1888). German physicist. Clausius's work was mainly in electricity, kinetic theory of gases, and thermodynamics.

[‡]Benoit Paul Emile Clapeyron (1799–1864). French engineer. Clapeyron made contributions to the thermodynamic aspects of steam engines.

Figure 11.35 *The increase in vapor pressure with temperature for three liquids. The normal boiling points of the liquids (at 1 atm) are shown on the horizontal axis.*

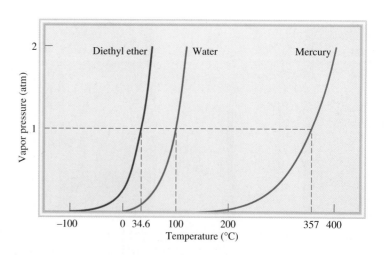

TABLE 11.6

Molar Heats of Vaporization for Selected Liquids		
Substance	**Boiling Point* (°C)**	**ΔH_{vap} (kJ/mol)**
Argon (Ar)	−186	6.3
Benzene (C_6H_6)	80.1	31.0
Ethanol (C_2H_5OH)	78.3	39.3
Diethyl ether ($C_2H_5OC_2H_5$)	34.6	26.0
Mercury (Hg)	357	59.0
Methane (CH_4)	−164	9.2
Water (H_2O)	100	40.79

* Measured at 1 atm.

where ln is the natural logarithm, R is the gas constant (8.314 J/K · mol), and C is a constant. The Clausius-Clapeyron equation has the form of the linear equation $y = mx + b$:

$$\ln P = \left(-\frac{\Delta H_{vap}}{R}\right)\left(\frac{1}{T}\right) + C$$
$$\updownarrow \qquad \updownarrow \quad \updownarrow \quad \updownarrow$$
$$y = \qquad m \quad x \; + \; b$$

By measuring the vapor pressure of a liquid at different temperatures (see Figure 11.35) and plotting ln P versus $1/T$, we determine the slope, which is equal to $-\Delta H_{vap}/R$. (ΔH_{vap} is assumed to be independent of temperature.) This is the method used to determine heats of vaporization (Table 11.6). Figure 11.36 shows plots of ln P versus $1/T$ for water and diethylether. Note that the straight line for water has a steeper slope because water has a larger ΔH_{vap}.

If we know the values of ΔH_{vap} and P of a liquid at one temperature, we can use the Clausius-Clapeyron equation to calculate the vapor pressure of the liquid at a different temperature. At temperatures T_1 and T_2, the vapor pressures are P_1 and P_2. From Equation (11.2) we can write

$$\ln P_1 = -\frac{\Delta H_{vap}}{RT_1} + C \tag{11.3}$$

$$\ln P_2 = -\frac{\Delta H_{vap}}{RT_2} + C \tag{11.4}$$

Subtracting Equation (11.4) from Equation (11.3) we obtain

$$\ln P_1 - \ln P_2 = -\frac{\Delta H_{vap}}{RT_1} - \left(-\frac{\Delta H_{vap}}{RT_2}\right)$$
$$= \frac{\Delta H_{vap}}{R}\left(\frac{1}{T_2} - \frac{1}{T_1}\right)$$

Hence

$$\ln \frac{P_1}{P_2} = \frac{\Delta H_{vap}}{R}\left(\frac{1}{T_2} - \frac{1}{T_1}\right)$$
$$= \frac{\Delta H_{vap}}{R}\left(\frac{T_1 - T_2}{T_1T_2}\right) \tag{11.5}$$

Example 11.7 illustrates the use of Equation (11.5).

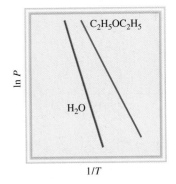

Figure 11.36 Plots of ln P versus 1/T for water and diethyl ether. The slope in each case is equal to $-\Delta H_{vap}/R$.

$C_2H_5OC_2H_5$

Example 11.7

Diethyl ether is a volatile, highly flammable organic liquid that is used mainly as a solvent. The vapor pressure of diethyl ether is 401 mmHg at 18°C. Calculate its vapor pressure at 32°C.

Strategy We are given the vapor pressure of diethyl ether at one temperature and asked to find the pressure at another temperature. Therefore, we need Equation (11.5).

Solution Table 11.6 tells us that $\Delta H_{vap} = 26.0$ kJ/mol. The data are

$$P_1 = 401 \text{ mmHg} \qquad P_2 = ?$$
$$T_1 = 18°C = 291 \text{ K} \qquad T_2 = 32°C = 305 \text{ K}$$

From Equation (11.5) we have

$$\ln \frac{401}{P_2} = \frac{26{,}000 \text{ J/mol}}{8.314 \text{ J/K} \cdot \text{mol}} \left[\frac{291 \text{ K} - 305 \text{ K}}{(291 \text{ K})(305 \text{ K})} \right]$$
$$= -0.493$$

Taking the antilog of both sides (see Appendix 4), we obtain

$$\frac{401}{P_2} = e^{-0.493} = 0.611$$

Hence

$$P_2 = 656 \text{ mmHg}$$

Check We expect the vapor pressure to be greater at the higher temperature. Therefore, the answer is reasonable.

Similar problem: 11.86.

Practice Exercise The vapor pressure of ethanol is 100 mmHg at 34.9°C. What is its vapor pressure at 63.5°C? (ΔH_{vap} for ethanol is 39.3 kJ/mol.)

A practical way to demonstrate the molar heat of vaporization is by rubbing an alcohol such as ethanol (C_2H_5OH) or isopropanol (C_3H_7OH), or rubbing alcohol, on your hands. These alcohols have a lower ΔH_{vap} than water, so that the heat from your hands is enough to increase the kinetic energy of the alcohol molecules and evaporate them. As a result of the loss of heat, your hands feel cool. This process is similar to perspiration, which is one of the means by which the human body maintains a constant temperature. Because of the strong intermolecular hydrogen bonding that exists in water, a considerable amount of energy is needed to vaporize the water in perspiration from the body's surface. This energy is supplied by the heat generated in various metabolic processes.

You have already seen that the vapor pressure of a liquid increases with temperature. Every liquid has a temperature at which it begins to boil. The *boiling point* is *the temperature at which the vapor pressure of a liquid is equal to the external pressure*. The *normal* boiling point of a liquid is the temperature at which it boils when the external pressure is 1 atm.

At the boiling point, bubbles form within the liquid. When a bubble forms, the liquid originally occupying that space is pushed aside, and the level of the liquid in the container is forced to rise. The pressure exerted *on* the bubble is largely atmospheric pressure, plus some *hydrostatic pressure* (that is, pressure due to the presence of liquid). The pressure *inside* the bubble is due solely to the vapor pressure of the liquid. When the vapor pressure becomes equal to the external pressure, the bubble rises to the surface of the liquid and bursts. If the vapor pressure in the bubble were lower than the external pressure, the bubble would collapse before it could rise. We can thus conclude that the boiling point of a liquid depends on the external pressure. (We usually ignore the small contribution due to the hydrostatic pressure.) For example, at 1 atm, water boils at 100°C, but if the pressure is reduced to 0.5 atm, water boils at only 82°C.

Because the boiling point is defined in terms of the vapor pressure of the liquid, we expect the boiling point to be related to the molar heat of vaporization: The higher ΔH_{vap}, the higher the boiling point. The data in Table 11.6 roughly confirm our prediction. Ultimately, both the boiling point and ΔH_{vap} are determined by the strength of intermolecular forces. For example, argon (Ar) and methane (CH_4), which have weak dispersion forces, have low boiling points and small molar heats of vaporization. Diethyl ether ($C_2H_5OC_2H_5$) has a dipole moment, and the dipole-dipole forces account for its moderately high boiling point and ΔH_{vap}. Both ethanol (C_2H_5OH) and water have strong hydrogen bonding, which accounts for their high boiling points and large ΔH_{vap} values. Strong metallic bonding causes mercury to have the highest boiling point and ΔH_{vap} of this group of liquids. Interestingly, the boiling point of benzene, which is nonpolar, is comparable to that of ethanol. Benzene has a high polarizability due to the distribution of its electrons in the delocalized pi molecular orbitals, and the dispersion forces among benzene molecules can be as strong as or even stronger than dipole-dipole forces and/or hydrogen bonds.

Critical Temperature and Pressure The opposite of evaporation is condensation. In principle, a gas can be made to liquefy by either one of two techniques. By cooling a sample of gas we decrease the kinetic energy of its molecules, so that eventually molecules aggregate to form small drops of liquid. Alternatively, we can apply pressure to the gas. Compression reduces the average distance between molecules so that they are held together by mutual attraction. Industrial liquefaction processes combine these two methods.

Every substance has a ***critical temperature (T_c),*** *above which its gas phase cannot be made to liquefy, no matter how great the applied pressure.* This is also *the highest temperature at which a substance can exist as a liquid.* Putting it another way, above the critical temperature there is no fundamental distinction between a liquid and a gas—we simply have a fluid. ***Critical pressure (P_c)*** *is the minimum pressure that must be applied to bring about liquefaction at the critical temperature.* The existence of the critical temperature can be qualitatively explained as follows. Intermolecular attraction is a finite quantity for any given substance and it is independent of temperature. Below T_c, this force is sufficiently strong to hold the molecules together (under some appropriate pressure) in a liquid. Above T_c, molecular motion becomes so energetic that the molecules can break away from this attraction. Figure 11.37 shows what happens when sulfur hexafluoride is heated above its critical temperature (45.5°C) and then cooled down to below 45.5°C.

Table 11.7 lists the critical temperatures and critical pressures of a number of common substances. The critical temperature of a substance reflects the strength of its intermolecular forces. Benzene, ethanol, mercury, and water, which have strong

Intermolecular forces are independent of temperature; the kinetic energy of molecules increases with temperature.

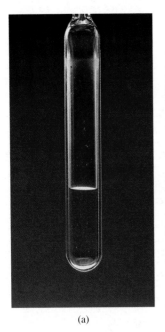
(a)

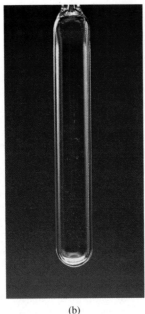
(b)

(c)

(d)

Figure 11.37 *The critical phenomenon of sulfur hexafluoride. (a) Below the critical temperature the clear liquid phase is visible. (b) Above the critical temperature the liquid phase has disappeared. (c) The substance is cooled just below its critical temperature. The fog represents the condensation of vapor. (d) Finally, the liquid phase reappears.*

"Fusion" refers to the process of melting. Thus a "fuse" breaks an electrical circuit when a metallic strip melts due to the heat generated by excessively high electrical current.

intermolecular forces, also have high critical temperatures compared with the other substances listed in the table.

Liquid-Solid Equilibrium

The transformation of liquid to solid is called *freezing*, and the reverse process is called *melting*, or *fusion*. The **melting point** of a solid or the **freezing point** of a liquid is *the temperature at which solid and liquid phases coexist in equilibrium.* The *normal* melting (or freezing) point of a substance is the temperature at which a

TABLE 11.7

Critical Temperatures and Critical Pressures of Selected Substances		
Substance	T_c **(°C)**	P_c **(atm)**
Ammonia (NH_3)	132.4	111.5
Argon (Ar)	−186	6.3
Benzene (C_6H_6)	288.9	47.9
Carbon dioxide (CO_2)	31.0	73.0
Ethanol (C_2H_5OH)	243	63.0
Diethyl ether ($C_2H_5OC_2H_5$)	192.6	35.6
Mercury (Hg)	1462	1036
Methane (CH_4)	−83.0	45.6
Molecular hydrogen (H_2)	−239.9	12.8
Molecular nitrogen (N_2)	−147.1	33.5
Molecular oxygen (O_2)	−118.8	49.7
Sulfur hexafluoride (SF_6)	45.5	37.6
Water (H_2O)	374.4	219.5

substance melts (or freezes) at 1 atm pressure. We generally omit the word "normal" when the pressure is at 1 atm.

The most familiar liquid-solid equilibrium is that of water and ice. At 0°C and 1 atm, the dynamic equilibrium is represented by

$$\text{ice} \rightleftharpoons \text{water}$$

A practical illustration of this dynamic equilibrium is provided by a glass of ice water. As the ice cubes melt to form water, some of the water between ice cubes may freeze, thus joining the cubes together. This is not a true dynamic equilibrium; because the glass is not kept at 0°C, all the ice cubes will eventually melt away.

Because molecules are more strongly held in the solid phase than in the liquid phase, heat is required to bring about the solid-liquid phase transition. Looking at the heating curve shown in Figure 11.38, we see that when a solid is heated, its temperature increases gradually until point A is reached. At this point, the solid begins to melt. During the melting period (A ⟶ B), the first flat portion of the curve in Figure 11.38, heat is being absorbed by the system, yet its temperature remains constant. The heat helps the molecules to overcome the attractive forces in the solid. Once the sample has melted completely (point B), the heat absorbed increases the average kinetic energy of the liquid molecules, and the liquid temperature rises (B ⟶ C). The vaporization process (C ⟶ D) can be explained similarly. The temperature remains constant during the period when the increased kinetic energy is used to overcome the cohesive forces in the liquid. When all molecules are in the gas phase, the temperature rises again.

Molar heat of fusion (ΔH_{fus}) is *the energy* (usually in kilojoules) *required to melt 1 mole of a solid.* Table 11.8 shows the molar heats of fusion for the substances listed in Table 11.6. A comparison of the data in the two tables shows that for each substance ΔH_{fus} is smaller than ΔH_{vap}. This is consistent with the fact that molecules in a liquid are still fairly closely packed together, so that some energy is needed to bring about the rearrangement from solid to liquid. On the other hand, when a liquid evaporates, its molecules become completely separated from one another and considerably more energy is required to overcome the attractive force.

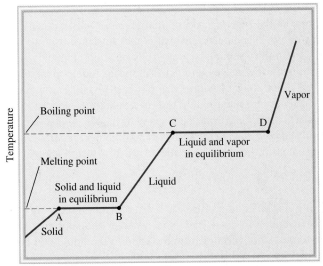

Figure 11.38 *A typical heating curve, from the solid phase through the liquid phase to the gas phase of a substance. Because ΔH_{fus} is smaller than ΔH_{vap}, a substance melts in less time than it takes to boil. This explains why AB is shorter than CD. The steepness of the solid, liquid, and vapor heating lines is determined by the specific heat of the substance in each state.*

TABLE 11.8

Molar Heats of Fusion for Selected Substances		
Substance	**Melting Point* (°C)**	**ΔH_{fus} (kJ/mol)**
Argon (Ar)	−190	1.3
Benzene (C_6H_6)	5.5	10.9
Ethanol (C_2H_5OH)	−117.3	7.61
Diethyl ether ($C_2H_5OC_2H_5$)	−116.2	6.90
Mercury (Hg)	−39	23.4
Methane (CH_4)	−183	0.84
Water (H_2O)	0	6.01

* Measured at 1 atm.

As we would expect, *cooling* a substance has the opposite effect of heating it. If we remove heat from a gas sample at a steady rate, its temperature decreases. As the liquid is being formed, heat is given off by the system, because its potential energy is decreasing. For this reason, the temperature of the system remains constant over the condensation period (D ⟶ C). After all the vapor has condensed, the temperature of the liquid begins to drop. Continued cooling of the liquid finally leads to freezing (B ⟶ A).

The phenomenon known as **supercooling** refers to the situation in which *a liquid can be temporarily cooled to below its freezing point*. Supercooling occurs when heat is removed from a liquid so rapidly that the molecules literally have no time to assume the ordered structure of a solid. A supercooled liquid is unstable; gentle stirring or the addition to it of a small "seed" crystal of the same substance will cause it to solidify quickly.

Solid-Vapor Equilibrium

Solids, too, undergo evaporation and, therefore, possess a vapor pressure. Consider the following dynamic equilibrium:

$$\text{solid} \rightleftharpoons \text{vapor}$$

Sublimation is *the process in which molecules go directly from the solid into the vapor phase*. **Deposition** is the reverse process, that is, *molecules make the transition from vapor to solid directly*. Naphthalene, which is the substance used to make mothballs, has a fairly high (equilibrium) vapor pressure for a solid (1 mmHg at 53°C); thus its pungent vapor quickly permeates an enclosed space. Iodine also sublimes. At room temperature, the violet color of iodine vapor is easily visible in a closed container.

Because molecules are more tightly held in a solid, the vapor pressure of a solid is generally much less than that of the corresponding liquid. **Molar heat of sublimation (ΔH_{sub})** of a substance is *the energy* (usually in kilojoules) *required to sublime 1 mole of a solid*. It is equal to the sum of the molar heats of fusion and vaporization:

$$\Delta H_{sub} = \Delta H_{fus} + \Delta H_{vap} \tag{11.6}$$

Equation (11.6) is an illustration of Hess's law (see Section 6.6). The enthalpy, or heat change, for the overall process is the same whether the substance changes directly from the solid to the vapor form or from the solid to the liquid and then to the vapor. Note that Equation (11.6) holds only if all the phase changes occur at the *same* temperature. If not, the equation can be used only as an approximation.

Solid iodine in equilibrium with its vapor.

Figure 11.39 summarizes the types of phase changes discussed in this section. When a substance is heated, its temperature will rise and eventually it will undergo a phase transition. To calculate the total energy change for such a process we must include all of the steps, shown in Example 11.8.

Example 11.8

Calculate the amount of energy (in kilojoules) needed to heat 346 g of liquid water from 0°C to 182°C. Assume that the specific heat of water is 4.184 J/g · °C over the entire liquid range and that the specific heat of steam is 1.99 J/g · °C.

Strategy The heat change (q) at each stage is given by $q = ms\Delta t$, where m is the mass of water, s is the specific heat, and Δt is the temperature change. If there is a phase change, such as vaporization, then q is given by $n\Delta H_{vap}$, where n is the number of moles of water.

Solution The calculation can be broken down in three steps.

Step 1: Heating water from 0°C to 100°C
    Using Equation (6.12) we write

$$\begin{aligned} q_1 &= ms\,\Delta t \\ &= (346\ \text{g})(4.184\ \text{J/g}\cdot{}^\circ\text{C})(100^\circ\text{C} - 0^\circ\text{C}) \\ &= 1.45 \times 10^5\ \text{J} \\ &= 145\ \text{kJ} \end{aligned}$$

Step 2: Evaporating 346 g of water at 100°C (a phase change)
    In Table 11.6 we see $\Delta H_{vap} = 40.79$ kJ/mol for water, so

$$\begin{aligned} q_2 &= 346\ \text{g H}_2\text{O} \times \frac{1\ \text{mol H}_2\text{O}}{18.02\ \text{g H}_2\text{O}} \times \frac{40.79\ \text{kJ}}{1\ \text{mol H}_2\text{O}} \\ &= 783\ \text{kJ} \end{aligned}$$

Step 3: Heating steam from 100°C to 182°C

$$\begin{aligned} q_3 &= ms\,\Delta t \\ &= (346\ \text{g})(1.99\ \text{J/g}\cdot{}^\circ\text{C})(182^\circ\text{C} - 100^\circ\text{C}) \\ &= 5.65 \times 10^4\ \text{J} \\ &= 56.5\ \text{kJ} \end{aligned}$$

The overall energy required is given by

$$\begin{aligned} q_{overall} &= q_1 + q_2 + q_3 \\ &= 145\ \text{kJ} + 783\ \text{kJ} + 56.5\ \text{kJ} \\ &= 985\ \text{kJ} \end{aligned}$$

Check All the qs have a positive sign, which is consistent with the fact that heat is absorbed to raise the temperature from 0°C to 182°C.

Practice Exercise Calculate the heat released when 68.0 g of steam at 124°C is converted to water at 45°C.

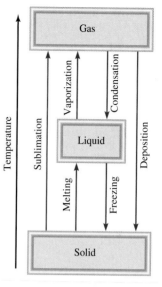

Figure 11.39 *The various phase changes that a substance can undergo.*

Similar problem: 11.78.

11.9 Phase Diagrams

The overall relationships among the solid, liquid, and vapor phases are best represented in a single graph known as a phase diagram. A **_phase diagram_** summarizes *the conditions at which a substance exists as a solid, liquid, or gas.* In this section we will briefly discuss the phase diagrams of water and carbon dioxide.

Figure 11.40 *(a) The phase diagram of water. Each solid line between two phases specifies the conditions of pressure and temperature under which the two phases can exist in equilibrium. The point at which all three phases can exist in equilibrium (0.006 atm and 0.01°C) is called the triple point. (b) This phase diagram tells us that increasing the pressure on ice lowers its melting point and that increasing the pressure of liquid water raises its boiling point.*

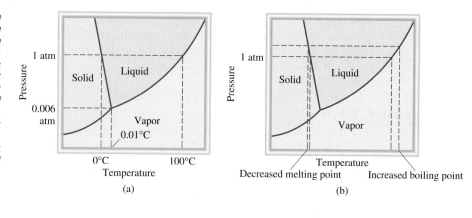

(a)

(b)

Decreased melting point   Increased boiling point

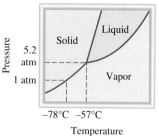

Figure 11.41 *The phase diagram of carbon dioxide. Note that the solid-liquid boundary line has a positive slope. The liquid phase is not stable below 5.2 atm, so that only the solid and vapor phases can exist under atmospheric conditions.*

Water

Figure 11.40(a) shows the phase diagram of water. The graph is divided into three regions, each of which represents a pure phase. The line separating any two regions indicates conditions under which these two phases can exist in equilibrium. For example, the curve between the liquid and vapor phases shows the variation of vapor pressure with temperature. (Compare this curve with Figure 11.35.) The other two curves similarly indicate conditions for equilibrium between ice and liquid water and between ice and water vapor. (Note that the solid-liquid boundary line has a negative slope.) The point at which all three curves meet is called the ***triple point,*** which is *the only condition under which all three phases can be in equilibrium with one another.* For water, this point is at 0.01°C and 0.006 atm.

Phase diagrams enable us to predict changes in the melting point and boiling point of a substance as a result of changes in the external pressure; we can also anticipate directions of phase transitions brought about by changes in temperature and pressure. The normal melting point and boiling point of water at 1 atm are 0°C and 100°C, respectively. What would happen if melting and boiling were carried out at some other pressure? Figure 11.40(b) shows that increasing the pressure above 1 atm will raise the boiling point and lower the melting point. A decrease in pressure will lower the boiling point and raise the melting point.

Carbon Dioxide

The phase diagram of carbon dioxide (Figure 11.41) is generally similar to that of water, with one important exception—the slope of the curve between solid and liquid is positive. In fact, this holds true for almost all other substances. Water behaves differently because ice is *less* dense than liquid water. The triple point of carbon dioxide is at 5.2 atm and −57°C.

An interesting observation can be made about the phase diagram in Figure 11.41. As you can see, the entire liquid phase lies well above atmospheric pressure; therefore, it is impossible for solid carbon dioxide to melt at 1 atm. Instead, when solid CO_2 is heated to −78°C at 1 atm, it sublimes. In fact, solid carbon dioxide is called dry ice because it looks like ice and *does not melt* (Figure 11.42). Because of this property, dry ice is useful as a refrigerant.

Figure 11.42 *Under atmospheric conditions, solid carbon dioxide does not melt; it only sublimes. The cold carbon dioxide gas causes nearby water vapor to condense and form a fog.*

CHEMISTRY IN ACTION

Hard-Boiling an Egg on a Mountaintop, Pressure Cookers, and Ice Skating

Phase equilibria are affected by external pressure. Depending on atmospheric conditions, the boiling point and freezing point of water may deviate appreciably from 100°C and 0°C, respectively, as we see below.

Hard-Boiling an Egg on a Mountaintop

Suppose you have just scaled Pike's Peak in Colorado. To help regain your strength following the strenuous work, you decide to hard-boil an egg and eat it. To your surprise, water seems to boil more quickly than usual, but after 10 minutes in boiling water, the egg is still not cooked. A little knowledge of phase equilibria could have saved you the disappointment of cracking open an uncooked egg (especially if it is the only egg you brought with you). The summit of Pike's Peak is 14,000 ft above sea level. At this altitude, the atmospheric pressure is only about 0.6 atm. From Figure 11.40(b), we see that the boiling point of water decreases with decreasing pressure, so at the lower pressure water will boil at about 86°C. However, it is not the boiling action but the amount of heat delivered to the egg that does the actual cooking, and the amount of heat delivered is proportional to the temperature of the water. For this reason, it would take considerably longer, perhaps 30 minutes, to hard-cook your egg.

Pressure Cookers

The effect of pressure on boiling point also explains why pressure cookers save time in the kitchen. A pressure cooker is a sealed container that allows steam to escape only when it exceeds a certain pressure. The pressure above the water in the cooker is the sum of the atmospheric pressure and the pressure of the steam. Consequently, the water in the pressure cooker will boil at a higher temperature than 100°C and the food in it will be hotter and cook faster.

Ice Skating

Let us now turn to the ice-water equilibrium. The negative slope of the solid-liquid curve means that the melting point of ice decreases with increasing external pressure, as shown in Figure 11.40(b). This phenomenon helps to make ice skating possible. Because skates have very thin runners, a 130-lb person can exert a pressure equivalent to 500 atm on the ice. (Remember that pressure is defined as force per unit area.) Consequently, at a temperature lower than 0°C, the ice under the skates melts and the film of water formed under the runner facilitates the movement of the skater over ice. Calculations show that the melting point of ice decreases by 7.4×10^{-3}°C when the pressure increases by 1 atm. Thus, when the pressure exerted on the ice by the skater is 500 atm, the melting point falls to $-(500 \times 7.4 \times 10^{-3})$, or -3.7°C. Actually, it turns out that friction between the blades and the ice is the major cause for melting the ice. This explains why it is possible to skate outdoors even when the temperature drops below -20°C.

The pressure exerted by the skater on ice lowers its melting point, and the film of water formed under the blades acts as a lubricant between the skate and the ice.

CHEMISTRY IN ACTION

Liquid Crystals

Ordinarily, there is a sharp distinction between the highly ordered state of a crystalline solid and the more random molecular arrangement of liquids. Crystalline ice and liquid water, for example, differ from each other in this respect. One class of substances, however, tends so greatly toward an ordered arrangement that a melting crystal first forms a milky liquid, called the *paracrystalline state,* with characteristically crystalline properties. At higher temperatures, this milky fluid changes sharply into a clear liquid that behaves like an ordinary liquid. Such substances are known as *liquid crystals.*

Molecules that exhibit liquid crystallinity are usually long and rodlike. An important class of liquid crystals is called thermotropic liquid crystals, which form when the solid is heated. The two common structures of thermotropic liquid crystals are nematic and smectic. In smectic liquid crystals, the long axes of the molecules are perpendicular to the plane of the layers. The layers are free to slide over one another so that the substance has the mechanical properties of a two-dimensional solid. Nematic liquid crystals are less ordered. Although the molecules in nematic liquid crystals are aligned with their long axes parallel to one another, they are not separated into layers.

Thermotropic liquid crystals have many applications in science, technology, and medicine. The familiar black-and-white displays in timepieces and calculators are based on the properties of these substances. Transparent aligning agents made of tin oxide (SnO_2) applied to the lower and upper inside surfaces of the liquid crystal cell preferentially orient the molecules in the nematic phase by 90° relative to each other. In this way, the molecules become "twisted" through the liquid crystal phase. When properly adjusted, this twist rotates the plane of polarization by 90° and allows the light to pass through the two polarizers (arranged at 90° to each other). When an electric field

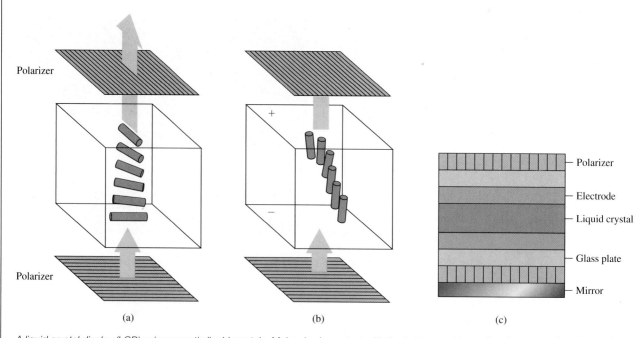

A liquid crystal display (LCD) using nematic liquid crystals. Molecules in contact with the bottom and top cell surfaces are aligned at right angles to one another. (a) The extent of twist in the molecular orientation between the surfaces is adjusted so as to rotate the plane of polarized light by 90°, allowing it to pass through the top polarizer. Consequently, the cell appears clear. (b) When the electric field is on, molecules orient along the direction of the field, the plane of polarized light can no longer pass through the top polarizer, and the cell appears black. (c) A cross section of a LCD such as that used in watches and calculators.

is applied, the nematic molecules experience a torque (a torsion or rotation) that forces them to align along the direction of the field. Now the incident polarized light cannot pass through the top polarizer. In watches and calculators, a mirror is placed under the bottom polarizer. In the absence of an electric field, the reflected light goes through both polarizers and the cell looks clear from the top. When the electric field is turned on, the incident light from the top cannot pass through the bottom polarizer to reach the reflector and the cell becomes dark. Typically a few volts are applied across a nematic layer about 10 μm thick (1 μm = 10^{-6} m). The response time for molecules to align and relax when the electric field is turned on and off is in the ms range (1 ms = 10^{-3} s).

Another type of thermotropic liquid crystals is called cholesteric liquid crystals. The color of cholesteric liquid crystals changes with temperature and therefore they are suitable for use as sensitive thermometers. In metallurgy, for example, they are used to detect metal stress, heat sources, and conduction paths. Medically, the temperature of the body at specific sites can be determined with the aid of liquid crystals. This technique has become an important diagnostic tool in treating infection and tumor growth (for example, breast tumors). Because localized infections and tumors increase metabolic rate and hence temperature in the affected tissues, a thin film of liquid crystal can help a physician see whether an infection or tumor is present by responding to a temperature difference with a change of color.

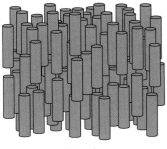

Nematic

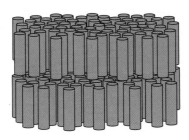

Smectic

The alignment of molecules in two types of liquid crystals. Nematic liquid crystals behave like a one-dimensional solid and smectic liquid crystals behave like a two-dimensional solid.

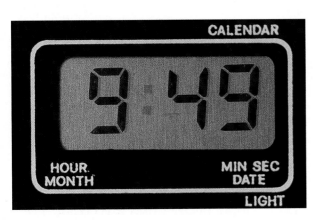

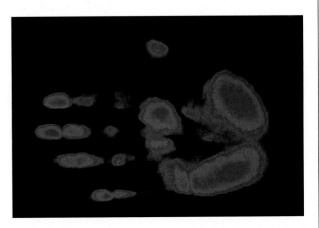

A liquid crystal thermogram. The red color represents the highest temperature and the blue color the lowest temperature.

Key Equations

- $2d \sin \theta = n\lambda$ (11.1)   Bragg equation for calculating the distance between planes of atoms in a crystal lattice.

- $\ln P = -\dfrac{\Delta H_{vap}}{RT} + C$ (11.2)   Clausius-Clapeyron equation for determining ΔH_{vap} of a liquid.

- $\ln \dfrac{P_1}{P_2} = \dfrac{\Delta H_{vap}}{R}\left(\dfrac{T_1 - T_2}{T_1 T_2}\right)$ (11.5)   For calculating ΔH_{vap}, vapor pressure, or boiling point of a liquid.

- $\Delta H_{sub} = \Delta H_{fus} + \Delta H_{vap}$ (11.6)   Application of Hess's law.

Summary of Facts and Concepts

1. All substances exist in one of three states: gas, liquid, or solid. The major difference between the condensed state and the gaseous state is the distance separating molecules.
2. Intermolecular forces act between molecules or between molecules and ions. Generally, these attractive forces are much weaker than bonding forces.
3. Dipole-dipole forces and ion-dipole forces attract molecules with dipole moments to other polar molecules or ions.
4. Dispersion forces are the result of temporary dipole moments induced in ordinarily nonpolar molecules. The extent to which a dipole moment can be induced in a molecule is called its polarizability. The term "van der Waals forces" refers to dipole-dipole, dipole-induced dipole, and dispersion forces.
5. Hydrogen bonding is a relatively strong dipole-dipole interaction between a polar bond containing a hydrogen atom and an electronegative O, N, or F atom. Hydrogen bonds between water molecules are particularly strong.
6. Liquids tend to assume a geometry that minimizes surface area. Surface tension is the energy needed to expand a liquid surface area; strong intermolecular forces lead to greater surface tension.
7. Viscosity is a measure of the resistance of a liquid to flow; it decreases with increasing temperature.
8. Water molecules in the solid state form a three-dimensional network in which each oxygen atom is covalently bonded to two hydrogen atoms and is hydrogen-bonded to two hydrogen atoms. This unique structure accounts for the fact that ice is less dense than liquid water, a property that allows life to survive under the ice in ponds and lakes in cold climates.
9. Water is also ideally suited for its ecological role by its high specific heat, another property imparted by its strong hydrogen bonding. Large bodies of water are able to moderate Earth's climate by giving off and absorbing substantial amounts of heat with only small changes in the water temperature.
10. All solids are either crystalline (with a regular structure of atoms, ions, or molecules) or amorphous (without a regular structure). Glass is an example of an amorphous solid.
11. The basic structural unit of a crystalline solid is the unit cell, which is repeated to form a three-dimensional crystal lattice. X-ray diffraction has provided much of our knowledge about crystal structure.
12. The four types of crystals and the forces that hold their particles together are ionic crystals, held together by ionic bonding; covalent crystals, covalent bonding; molecular

crystals, van der Waals forces and/or hydrogen bonding; and metallic crystals, metallic bonding.

13. A liquid in a closed vessel eventually establishes a dynamic equilibrium between evaporation and condensation. The vapor pressure over the liquid under these conditions is the equilibrium vapor pressure, which is often referred to simply as "vapor pressure."

14. At the boiling point, the vapor pressure of a liquid equals the external pressure. The molar heat of vaporization of a liquid is the energy required to vaporize one mole of the liquid. It can be determined by measuring the vapor pressure of the liquid as a function of temperature and using the Clausius-Clapeyron equation [Equation (11.2)]. The molar heat of fusion of a solid is the energy required to melt one mole of the solid.

15. For every substance there is a temperature, called the critical temperature, above which its gas phase cannot be made to liquefy.

16. The relationships among the phases of a single substance are illustrated by a phase diagram, in which each region represents a pure phase and the boundaries between the regions show the temperatures and pressures at which the two phases are in equilibrium. At the triple point, all three phases are in equilibrium.

Key Words

Adhesion, p. 444	Deposition, p. 470	Intermolecular	Phase changes, p. 462
Amorphous solid, p. 460	Dipole-dipole	forces, p. 437	Phase diagram, p. 471
Boiling point, p. 466	forces, p. 437	Intramolecular forces, p. 437	Sublimation, p. 470
Closest packing, p. 449	Dispersion forces, p. 439	Ion-dipole forces, p. 437	Supercooling, p. 470
Cohesion, p. 443	Dynamic equilibrium, p. 464	Melting point, p. 468	Surface tension, p. 443
Condensation, p. 463	Equilibrium vapor	Molar heat of fusion	Triple point, p. 472
Coordination	pressure, p. 464	(ΔH_{fus}), p. 469	Unit cell, p. 446
number, p. 448	Evaporation, p. 463	Molar heat of sublimation	van der Waals
Critical pressure (P_c), p. 467	Freezing point, p. 468	(ΔH_{sub}), p. 470	forces, p. 437
Critical temperature	Glass, p. 460	Molar heat of vaporization	Vaporization, p. 463
(T_c), p. 467	Hydrogen bond, p. 441	(ΔH_{vap}), p. 464	Viscosity, p. 444
Crystalline solid, p. 446	Induced dipole, p. 438	Phase, p. 436	X-ray diffraction, p. 453

Questions and Problems

Intermolecular Forces

Review Questions

11.1 Give an example for each type of intermolecular forces. (a) dipole-dipole interaction, (b) dipole-induced dipole interaction, (c) ion-dipole interaction, (d) dispersion forces, (e) van der Waals forces

11.2 Explain the term "polarizability." What kind of molecules tend to have high polarizabilities? What is the relationship between polarizability and intermolecular forces?

11.3 Explain the difference between a temporary dipole moment and the permanent dipole moment.

11.4 Give some evidence that all atoms and molecules exert attractive forces on one another.

11.5 What physical properties should you consider in comparing the strength of intermolecular forces in solids and in liquids?

11.6 Which elements can take part in hydrogen bonding? Why is hydrogen unique in this kind of interaction?

Problems

11.7 The compounds Br_2 and ICl have the same number of electrons, yet Br_2 melts at $-7.2°C$ and ICl melts at $27.2°C$. Explain.

11.8   If you lived in Alaska, which of the following natural gases would you keep in an outdoor storage tank in winter? Explain why. methane (CH_4), propane (C_3H_8), or butane (C_4H_{10})

11.9   The binary hydrogen compounds of the Group 4A elements and their boiling points are: CH_4, $-162°C$; SiH_4, $-112°C$; GeH_4, $-88°C$; and SnH_4, $-52°C$. Explain the increase in boiling points from CH_4 to SnH_4.

11.10 List the types of intermolecular forces that exist between molecules (or basic units) in each of the following species: (a) benzene (C_6H_6), (b) CH_3Cl, (c) PF_3, (d) NaCl, (e) CS_2.

11.11 Ammonia is both a donor and an acceptor of hydrogen in hydrogen-bond formation. Draw a diagram showing the hydrogen bonding of an ammonia molecule with two other ammonia molecules.

11.12 Which of the following species are capable of hydrogen-bonding among themselves? (a) C_2H_6, (b) HI, (c) KF, (d) BeH_2, (e) CH_3COOH

11.13 Arrange the following in order of increasing boiling point: RbF, CO_2, CH_3OH, CH_3Br. Explain your reasoning.

11.14 Diethyl ether has a boiling point of $34.5°C$, and 1-butanol has a boiling point of $117°C$:

H—C—C—O—C—C—H   H—C—C—C—C—OH

diethyl ether   1-butanol

Both of these compounds have the same numbers and types of atoms. Explain the difference in their boiling points.

11.15 Which member of each of the following pairs of substances would you expect to have a higher boiling point? (a) O_2 and Cl_2, (b) SO_2 and CO_2, (c) HF and HI

11.16 Which substance in each of the following pairs would you expect to have the higher boiling point? Explain why. (a) Ne or Xe, (b) CO_2 or CS_2, (c) CH_4 or Cl_2, (d) F_2 or LiF, (e) NH_3 or PH_3

11.17 Explain in terms of intermolecular forces why (a) NH_3 has a higher boiling point than CH_4 and (b) KCl has a higher melting point than I_2.

11.18 What kind of attractive forces must be overcome in order to (a) melt ice, (b) boil molecular bromine, (c) melt solid iodine, and (d) dissociate F_2 into F atoms?

11.19 The following compounds have the same molecular formulas (C_4H_{10}). Which one would you expect to have a higher boiling point?

11.20 Explain the difference in the melting points of the following compounds:

NO$_2$ NO$_2$

OH

OH

m.p. 45°C   m.p. 115°C

(*Hint:* Only one of the two can form intramolecular hydrogen bonds.)

Properties of Liquids
Review Questions

11.21 Explain why liquids, unlike gases, are virtually incompressible.

11.22 What is surface tension? What is the relationship between intermolecular forces and surface tension? How does surface tension change with temperature?

11.23 Despite the fact that stainless steel is much denser than water, a stainless-steel razor blade can be made to float on water. Why?

11.24 Use water and mercury as examples to explain adhesion and cohesion.

11.25 A glass can be filled slightly above the rim with water. Explain why the water does not overflow.

11.26 Draw diagrams showing the capillary action of (a) water and (b) mercury in three tubes of different radii.

11.27 What is viscosity? What is the relationship between intermolecular forces and viscosity?

11.28 Why does the viscosity of a liquid decrease with increasing temperature?

11.29 Why is ice less dense than water?

11.30 Outdoor water pipes have to be drained or insulated in winter in a cold climate. Why?

Problems

11.31 Predict which of the following liquids has greater surface tension: ethanol (C_2H_5OH) or dimethyl ether (CH_3OCH_3).

11.32 Predict the viscosity of ethylene glycol relative to that of ethanol and glycerol (see Table 11.3).

$$CH_2—OH$$
$$|$$
$$CH_2—OH$$
ethylene glycol

Crystal Structure
Review Questions

11.33 Define the following terms: crystalline solid, lattice point, unit cell, coordination number, closest packing.

11.34 Describe the geometries of the following cubic cells: simple cubic, body-centered cubic, face-centered cubic. Which of these structures would give the highest density for the same type of atoms? Which the lowest?

11.35 Classify the solid states in terms of crystal types of the elements in the third period of the periodic table. Predict the trends in their melting points and boiling points.

11.36 The melting points of the oxides of the third-period elements are given in parentheses: Na_2O (1275°C), MgO (2800°C), Al_2O_3 (2045°C), SiO_2 (1610°C), P_4O_{10} (580°C), SO_3 (16.8°C), Cl_2O_7 (−91.5°C). Classify these solids in terms of crystal types.

Problems

11.37 What is the coordination number of each sphere in (a) a simple cubic cell, (b) a body-centered cubic cell, and (c) a face-centered cubic cell? Assume the spheres are all the same.

11.38 Calculate the number of spheres that would be found within a simple cubic, body-centered cubic, and face-centered cubic cells. Assume that the spheres are the same.

11.39 Metallic iron crystallizes in a cubic lattice. The unit cell edge length is 287 pm. The density of iron is 7.87 g/cm³. How many iron atoms are within a unit cell?

11.40 Barium metal crystallizes in a body-centered cubic lattice (the Ba atoms are at the lattice points only). The unit cell edge length is 502 pm, and the density of the metal is 3.50 g/cm³. Using this information, calculate Avogadro's number. [*Hint:* First calculate the volume (in cm³) occupied by 1 mole of Ba atoms in the unit cells. Next calculate the volume (in cm³) occupied by one Ba atom in the unit cell. Assume that 68% of the unit cell is occupied by Ba atoms.]

11.41 Vanadium crystallizes in a body-centered cubic lattice (the V atoms occupy only the lattice points). How many V atoms are present in a unit cell?

11.42 Europium crystallizes in a body-centered cubic lattice (the Eu atoms occupy only the lattice points). The density of Eu is 5.26 g/cm³. Calculate the unit cell edge length in pm.

11.43 Crystalline silicon has a cubic structure. The unit cell edge length is 543 pm. The density of the solid is 2.33 g/cm³. Calculate the number of Si atoms in one unit cell.

11.44 A face-centered cubic cell contains 8 X atoms at the corners of the cell and 6 Y atoms at the faces. What is the empirical formula of the solid?

X-Ray Diffraction of Crystals
Review Questions

11.45 Define X-ray diffraction. What are the typical wavelengths (in nanometers) of X rays (see Figure 7.4).

11.46 Write the Bragg equation. Define every term and describe how this equation can be used to measure interatomic distances.

Problems

11.47 When X rays of wavelength 0.090 nm are diffracted by a metallic crystal, the angle of first-order diffraction ($n = 1$) is measured to be 15.2°. What is the distance (in pm) between the layers of atoms responsible for the diffraction?

11.48 The distance between layers in a NaCl crystal is 282 pm. X rays are diffracted from these layers at an angle of 23.0°. Assuming that $n = 1$, calculate the wavelength of the X rays in nm.

Types of Crystals
Review Questions

11.49 Describe and give examples of the following types of crystals: (a) ionic crystals, (b) covalent crystals, (c) molecular crystals, (d) metallic crystals.

11.50 Why are metals good conductors of heat and electricity? Why does the ability of a metal to conduct electricity decrease with increasing temperature?

Problems

11.51 A solid is hard, brittle, and electrically nonconducting. Its melt (the liquid form of the substance) and an aqueous solution containing the substance conduct electricity. Classify the solid.

11.52 A solid is soft and has a low melting point (below 100°C). The solid, its melt, and an aqueous solution containing the substance are all nonconductors of electricity. Classify the solid.

11.53   A solid is very hard and has a high melting point. Neither the solid nor its melt conducts electricity. Classify the solid.

11.54   Which of the following are molecular solids and which are covalent solids? Se_8, HBr, Si, CO_2, C, P_4O_6, SiH_4

11.55   Classify the solid state of the following substances as ionic crystals, covalent crystals, molecular crystals, or metallic crystals: (a) CO_2, (b) B_{12}, (c) S_8, (d) KBr, (e) Mg, (f) SiO_2, (g) LiCl, (h) Cr.

11.56   Explain why diamond is harder than graphite. Why is graphite an electrical conductor but diamond is not?

Amorphous Solids
Review Questions

11.57   What is an amorphous solid? How does it differ from crystalline solid?

11.58   Define glass. What is the chief component of glass? Name three types of glass.

Phase Changes
Review Questions

11.59   What is a phase change? Name all possible changes that can occur among the vapor, liquid, and solid phases of a substance.

11.60   What is the equilibrium vapor pressure of a liquid? How is it measured and how does it change with temperature?

11.61   Use any one of the phase changes to explain what is meant by dynamic equilibrium.

11.62   Define the following terms: (a) molar heat of vaporization, (b) molar heat of fusion, (c) molar heat of sublimation. What are their units?

11.63   How is the molar heat of sublimation related to the molar heats of vaporization and fusion? On what law are these relationships based?

11.64   What can we learn about the intermolecular forces in a liquid from the molar heat of vaporization?

11.65   The greater the molar heat of vaporization of a liquid, the greater its vapor pressure. True or false?

11.66   Define boiling point. How does the boiling point of a liquid depend on external pressure? Referring to Table 5.3, what is the boiling point of water when the external pressure is 187.5 mmHg?

11.67   As a liquid is heated at constant pressure, its temperature rises. This trend continues until the boiling point of the liquid is reached. No further rise in temperature of the liquid can be induced by heating. Explain.

11.68   What is critical temperature? What is the significance of critical temperature in liquefaction of gases?

11.69   What is the relationship between intermolecular forces in a liquid and the liquid's boiling point and critical temperature? Why is the critical temperature of water greater than that of most other substances?

11.70   How do the boiling points and melting points of water and carbon tetrachloride vary with pressure? Explain any difference in behavior of these two substances.

11.71   Why is solid carbon dioxide called dry ice?

11.72   The vapor pressure of a liquid in a closed container depends on which of the following? (a) the volume above the liquid, (b) the amount of liquid present, (c) temperature, (d) intermolecular forces between the molecules in the liquid

11.73   Referring to Figure 11.35, estimate the boiling points of diethyl ether, water, and mercury at 0.5 atm.

11.74   Wet clothes dry more quickly on a hot, dry day than on a hot, humid day. Explain.

11.75   Which of the following phase transitions gives off more heat? (a) 1 mole of steam to 1 mole of water at 100°C, or (b) 1 mole of water to 1 mole of ice at 0°C

11.76   A beaker of water is heated to boiling by a Bunsen burner. Would adding another burner raise the boiling point of water? Explain.

Problems

11.77   Calculate the amount of heat (in kJ) required to convert 74.6 g of water to steam at 100°C.

11.78   How much heat (in kJ) is needed to convert 866 g of ice at −10°C to steam at 126°C? (The specific heats of ice and steam are 2.03 J/g · °C and 1.99 J/g · °C, respectively.)

11.79   How is the rate of evaporation of a liquid affected by (a) temperature, (b) the surface area of a liquid exposed to air, (c) intermolecular forces?

11.80   The molar heats of fusion and sublimation of molecular iodine are 15.27 kJ/mol and 62.30 kJ/mol, respectively. Estimate the molar heat of vaporization of liquid iodine.

11.81   The following compounds, listed with their boiling points, are liquid at −10°C: butane, −0.5°C; ethanol, 78.3°C; toluene, 110.6°C. At −10°C, which of these liquids would you expect to have the highest vapor pressure? Which the lowest? Explain.

11.82   Freeze-dried coffee is prepared by freezing brewed coffee and then removing the ice component with a vacuum pump. Describe the phase changes taking place during these processes.

11.83   A student hangs wet clothes outdoors on a winter day when the temperature is −15°C. After a few hours, the clothes are found to be fairly dry. Describe the phase changes in this drying process.

11.84 Steam at 100°C causes more serious burns than water at 100°C. Why?

11.85 Vapor pressure measurements at several different temperatures are shown below for mercury. Determine graphically the molar heat of vaporization for mercury.

t (°C)	200	250	300	320	340
P (mmHg)	17.3	74.4	246.8	376.3	557.9

11.86 The vapor pressure of benzene, C_6H_6, is 40.1 mmHg at 7.6°C. What is its vapor pressure at 60.6°C? The molar heat of vaporization of benzene is 31.0 kJ/mol.

11.87 The vapor pressure of liquid X is lower than that of liquid Y at 20°C, but higher at 60°C. What can you deduce about the relative magnitude of the molar heats of vaporization of X and Y?

11.88 Estimate the molar heat of vaporization of a liquid whose vapor pressure doubles when the temperature is raised from 85°C to 95°C.

Phase Diagrams
Review Questions

11.89 What is a phase diagram? What useful information can be obtained from study of a phase diagram?

11.90 Explain how water's phase diagram differs from those of most substances. What property of water causes the difference?

Problems

11.91 The blades of ice skates are quite thin, so that the pressure exerted on ice by a skater can be substantial. Explain how this fact enables a person to skate on ice.

11.92 A length of wire is placed on top of a block of ice. The ends of the wire extend over the edges of the ice, and a heavy weight is attached to each end. It is found that the ice under the wire gradually melts, so that the wire slowly moves through the ice block. At the same time, the water above the wire refreezes. Explain the phase changes that accompany this phenomenon.

11.93 The boiling point and freezing point of sulfur dioxide are −10°C and −72.7°C (at 1 atm), respectively. The triple point is −75.5°C and 1.65×10^{-3} atm, and its critical point is at 157°C and 78 atm. On the basis of this information, draw a rough sketch of the phase diagram of SO_2.

11.94 A phase diagram of water is shown at the end of this problem. Label the regions. Predict what would happen as a result of the following changes: (a) Starting at A, we raise the temperature at constant pressure. (b) Starting at C, we lower the temperature at constant pressure. (c) Starting at B, we lower the pressure at constant temperature.

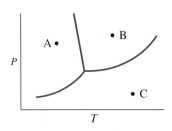

Additional Problems

11.95 Name the kinds of attractive forces that must be overcome in order to (a) boil liquid ammonia, (b) melt solid phosphorus (P_4), (c) dissolve CsI in liquid HF, (d) melt potassium metal.

11.96 Which of the following properties indicates very strong intermolecular forces in a liquid? (a) very low surface tension, (b) very low critical temperature, (c) very low boiling point, (d) very low vapor pressure

11.97 At −35°C, liquid HI has a higher vapor pressure than liquid HF. Explain.

11.98 Based on the following properties of elemental boron, classify it as one of the crystalline solids discussed in Section 11.6: high melting point (2300°C), poor conductor of heat and electricity, insoluble in water, very hard substance.

11.99 Referring to Figure 11.41, determine the stable phase of CO_2 at (a) 4 atm and −60°C and (b) 0.5 atm and −20°C.

11.100 Which of the following substances has the highest polarizability? CH_4, H_2, CCl_4, SF_6, H_2S

11.101 A CO_2 fire extinguisher is located on the outside of a building in Massachusetts. During the winter months, one can hear a sloshing sound when the extinguisher is gently shaken. In the summertime there is often no sound when it is shaken. Explain. Assume that the extinguisher has no leaks and that it has not been used.

11.102 What is the vapor pressure of mercury at its normal boiling point (357°C)?

11.103 A flask of water is connected to a powerful vacuum pump. When the pump is turned on, the water begins to boil. After a few minutes, the same water begins to freeze. Eventually, the ice disappears. Explain what happens at each step.

11.104 The liquid-vapor boundary line in the phase diagram of any substance always stops abruptly at a certain point. Why?

11.105 The interionic distance of several alkali halide crystals are:

NaCl	NaBr	NaI	KCl	KBr	KI
282 pm	299 pm	324 pm	315 pm	330 pm	353 pm

Plot lattice energy versus the reciprocal interionic distance. How would you explain the plot in terms of the dependence of lattice energy on distance of separation between ions? What law governs this interaction? (For lattice energies, see Table 9.1.)

11.106 Which has a greater density, crystalline SiO_2 or amorphous SiO_2? Why?

11.107 A student is given four solid samples labeled W, X, Y, and Z. All have a metallic luster. She is told that the solids could be gold, lead sulfide, mica (which is quartz, or SiO_2), and iodine. The results of her investigations are: (a) W is a good electrical conductor; X, Y, and Z are poor electrical conductors. (b) When the solids are hit with a hammer, W flattens out, X shatters into many pieces, Y is smashed into a powder, and Z is not affected. (c) When the solids are heated with a Bunsen burner, Y melts with some sublimation, but X, W, and Z do not melt. (d) In treatment with 6 M HNO_3, X dissolves; there is no effect on W, Y, or Z. On the basis of these test results, identify the solids.

11.108 Which of the following statements are false? (a) Dipole-dipole interactions between molecules are greatest if the molecules possess only temporary dipole moments. (b) All compounds containing hydrogen atoms can participate in hydrogen-bond formation. (c) Dispersion forces exist between all atoms, molecules, and ions. (d) The extent of ion-induced dipole interaction depends only on the charge on the ion.

11.109 The diagram below shows a kettle of boiling water on a stove. Identify the phases in regions A and B.

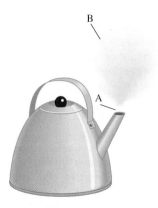

11.110 The south pole of Mars is covered with dry ice, which partly sublimes during the summer. The CO_2 vapor recondenses in the winter when the temperature drops to 150 K. Given that the heat of sublimation of CO_2 is 25.9 kJ/mol, calculate the atmospheric pressure on the surface of Mars. [*Hint:*

Use Figure 11.41 to determine the normal sublimation temperature of dry ice and Equation (11.5), which also applies to sublimations.]

11.111 The properties of gases, liquids, and solids differ in a number of respects. How would you use the kinetic molecular theory (see Section 5.7) to explain the following observations? (a) Ease of compressibility decreases from gas to liquid to solid. (b) Solids retain a definite shape, but gases and liquids do not. (c) For most substances, the volume of a given amount of material increases as it changes from solid to liquid to gas.

11.112 Select the substance in each pair that should have the higher boiling point. In each case identify the principal intermolecular forces involved and account briefly for your choice. (a) K_2S or $(CH_3)_3N$, (b) Br_2 or $CH_3CH_2CH_2CH_3$

11.113 A small drop of oil in water assumes a spherical shape. Explain. (*Hint:* Oil is made up of nonpolar molecules, which tend to avoid contact with water.)

11.114 Under the same conditions of temperature and density, which of the following gases would you expect to behave less ideally: CH_4, SO_2? Explain.

11.115 The fluorides of the second-period elements and their melting points are: LiF, 845°C; BeF_2, 800°C; BF_3, −126.7°C; CF_4, −184°C; NF_3, −206.6°C; OF_2, −223.8°C; F_2, −219.6°C. Classify the type(s) of intermolecular forces present in each compound.

11.116 The standard enthalpy of formation of gaseous molecular iodine is 62.4 kJ/mol. Use this information to calculate the molar heat of sublimation of molecular iodine at 25°C.

11.117 The distance between Li^+ and Cl^- is 257 pm in solid LiCl and 203 pm in a LiCl unit in the gas phase. Explain the difference in the bond lengths.

11.118 Heat of hydration, that is, the heat change that occurs when ions become hydrated in solution, is largely due to ion-dipole interactions. The heats of hydration for the alkali metal ions are Li^+, −520 kJ/mol; Na^+, −405 kJ/mol; K^+, −321 kJ/mol. Account for the trend in these values.

11.119 If water were a linear molecule, (a) would it still be polar, and (b) would the water molecules still be able to form hydrogen bonds with one another?

11.120 Calculate the $\Delta H°$ for the following processes at 25°C: (a) $Br_2(l) \longrightarrow Br_2(g)$ and (b) $Br_2(g) \longrightarrow 2Br(g)$. Comment on the relative magnitudes of these $\Delta H°$ values in terms of the forces involved in each case. {*Hint:* See Table 9.4, and given that $\Delta H_f°$ $[Br_2(g)] = 30.7$ kJ/mol.}

11.121 Which liquid would you expect to have a greater viscosity, water or diethyl ether? The structure of diethyl ether is shown in Problem 11.14.

11.122 A beaker of water is placed in a closed container. Predict the effect on the vapor pressure of the water when (a) its temperature is lowered, (b) the volume of the container is doubled, (c) more water is added to the beaker.

11.123 Ozone (O_3) is a strong oxidizing agent that can oxidize all the common metals except gold and platinum. A convenient test for ozone is based on its action on mercury. When exposed to ozone, mercury becomes dull looking and sticks to glass tubing (instead of flowing freely through it). Write a balanced equation for the reaction. What property of mercury is altered by its interaction with ozone?

11.124 A sample of limestone ($CaCO_3$) is heated in a closed vessel until it is partially decomposed. Write an equation for the reaction and state how many phases are present.

11.125 Silicon used in computer chips must have an impurity level below 10^{-9} (that is, fewer than one impurity atom for every 10^9 Si atoms). Silicon is prepared by the reduction of quartz (SiO_2) with coke (a form of carbon made by the destructive distillation of coal) at about 2000°C:

$$SiO_2(s) + 2C(s) \longrightarrow Si(l) + 2CO(g)$$

Next, solid silicon is separated from other solid impurities by treatment with hydrogen chloride at 350°C to form gaseous trichlorosilane ($SiCl_3H$):

$$Si(s) + 3HCl(g) \longrightarrow SiCl_3H(g) + H_2(g)$$

Finally, ultrapure Si can be obtained by reversing the above reaction at 1000°C:

$$SiCl_3H(g) + H_2(g) \longrightarrow Si(s) + 3HCl(g)$$

(a) Trichlorosilane has a vapor pressure of 0.258 atm at −2°C. What is its normal boiling point? Is trichlorosilane's boiling point consistent with the type of intermolecular forces that exist among its molecules? (The molar heat of vaporization of trichlorosilane is 28.8 kJ/mol.) (b) What types of crystals do Si and SiO_2 form? (c) Silicon has a diamond crystal structure (see Figure 11.28). Each cubic unit cell (edge length $a = 543$ pm) contains eight Si atoms. If there are 1.0×10^{13} boron atoms per cubic centimeter in a sample of pure silicon, how many Si atoms are there for every B atom in the sample? Does this sample satisfy the 10^{-9} purity requirement for the electronic grade silicon?

11.126 Carbon and silicon belong to Group 4A of the periodic table and have the same valence electron configuration (ns^2np^2). Why does silicon dioxide (SiO_2) have a much higher melting point than carbon dioxide (CO_2)?

11.127 A pressure cooker is a sealed container that allows steam to escape when it exceeds a predetermined pressure. How does this device reduce the time needed for cooking?

11.128 A 1.20-g sample of water is injected into an evacuated 5.00-L flask at 65°C. What percentage of the water will be vapor when the system reaches equilibrium? Assume ideal behavior of water vapor and that the volume of liquid water is negligible. The vapor pressure of water at 65°C is 187.5 mmHg.

11.129 What are the advantages of cooking the vegetable broccoli with steam instead of boiling it in water?

11.130 A quantitative measure of how efficiently spheres pack into unit cells is called *packing efficiency,* which is the percentage of the cell space occupied by the spheres. Calculate the packing efficiencies of a simple cubic cell, a body-centered cubic cell, and a face-centered cubic cell. (*Hint:* Refer to Figure 11.22 and use the relationship that the volume of a sphere is $\frac{4}{3}\pi r^3$, where r is the radius of the sphere.)

11.131 Provide an explanation for each of the following phenomena: (a) Solid argon (m.p. −189.2°C; b.p. −185.7°C) can be prepared by immersing a flask containing argon gas in liquid nitrogen (b.p. −195.8°C) until it liquefies and then connecting the flask to a vacuum pump. (b) The melting point of cyclohexane (C_6H_{12}) increases with increasing pressure exerted on the solid cyclohexane. (c) Certain high-altitude clouds contain water droplets at −10°C. (d) When a piece of dry ice is added to a beaker of water, fog forms above the water.

11.132 Argon crystallizes in the face-centered cubic arrangement at 40 K. Given that the atomic radius of argon is 191 pm, calculate the density of solid argon.

11.133 A chemistry instructor performed the following mystery demonstration. Just before the students arrived in class, she heated some water to boiling in an Erlenmeyer flask. She then removed the flask from the flame and closed the flask with a rubber stopper. After the class commenced, she held the flask in front of the students and announced that she could make the water boil simply by rubbing an ice cube on the outside walls of the flask. To the amazement of everyone, it worked. Give an explanation for this phenomenon.

11.134 Given the phase diagram of carbon below, answer the following questions: (a) How many triple points are there and what are the phases that can coexist at each triple point? (b) Which has a higher density, graphite or diamond? (c) Synthetic diamond can be made from graphite. Using the phase diagram, how would you go about making diamond?

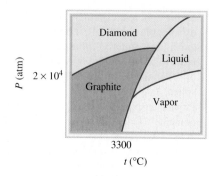

11.135 Swimming coaches sometimes suggest that a drop of alcohol (ethanol) placed in an ear plugged with water "draws out the water." Explain this action from a molecular point of view.

11.136 Use the concept of intermolecular forces to explain why the far end of a walking cane rises when one raises the handle.

11.137 Why do citrus growers spray their trees with water to protect them from freezing?

11.138 What is the origin of dark spots on the inner glass walls of an old tungsten lightbulb? What is the purpose of filling these lightbulbs with argon gas?

11.139 The compound dichlorodifluoromethane (CCl_2F_2) has a normal boiling point of $-30°C$, a critical temperature of $112°C$, and a corresponding critical pressure of 40 atm. If the gas is compressed to 18 atm at $20°C$, will the gas condense? Your answer should be based on a graphical interpretation.

11.140 A student heated a beaker of cold water (on a tripod) with a Bunsen burner. When the gas is ignited, she noticed that there was water condensed on the outside of the beaker. Explain what happened.

11.141 A sample of water shows the following behavior as it is heated at a constant rate:

If twice the mass of water has the same amount of heat transferred to it, which of the following graphs best describes the temperature variation? Note that the scales for all the graphs are the same.

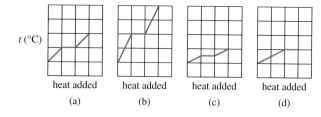

(Used with permission from the *Journal of Chemical Education*, Vol. 79, No. 7, 2002, pp. 889–895; © 2002, Division of Chemical Education, Inc.)

Answers to Practice Exercises

11.1 (a) Ionic and dispersion forces, (b) dispersion forces, (c) dipole-dipole and dispersion forces. **11.2** Only (c).

11.3 10.50 g/cm^3. **11.4** 315 pm. **11.5** Two. **11.6** 361 pm. **11.7** 369 mmHg. **11.8** 173 kJ.

A sugar cube dissolving in water. The properties of a solution are markedly different from those of its solvent. The solubility of sugar molecules in water is mainly due to hydrogen bond formations between the solute and the solvent. The models show glucose (a common sugar) and water molecules.

12

Physical Properties of Solutions

Interactive Activity Summary

1. Animation: Dissolution of an Ionic and a Covalent Compound (12.2)
2. Interactivity: Test Solution with Electrolytes (12.7)

Most chemical reactions take place, not between pure solids, liquids, or gases, but among ions and molecules dissolved in water or other solvents. In Chapters 5 and 11, we looked at the properties of gases, liquids, and solids. In this chapter we examine the properties of solutions, concentrating mainly on the role of intermolecular forces in solubility and other physical properties of solutions.

12.1 Types of Solutions

In Section 4.1 we noted that a solution is a homogeneous mixture of two or more substances. Because this definition places no restriction on the nature of the substances involved, we can distinguish six types of solutions, depending on the original states (solid, liquid, or gas) of the solution components. Table 12.1 gives examples of each type.

Our focus in this chapter will be on solutions involving at least one liquid component—that is, gas-liquid, liquid-liquid, and solid-liquid solutions. And, perhaps not too surprisingly, the liquid solvent in most of the solutions we will study is water.

Chemists also characterize solutions by their capacity to dissolve a solute. A *saturated solution contains the maximum amount of a solute that will dissolve in a given solvent at a specific temperature.* An **unsaturated solution** *contains less solute than it has the capacity to dissolve.* A third type, a ***supersaturated solution,*** *contains more solute than is present in a saturated solution.* Supersaturated solutions are not very stable. In time, some of the solute will come out of a supersaturated solution as crystals. ***Crystallization*** *is the process in which dissolved solute comes out of solution and forms crystals* (Figure 12.1). Note that both precipitation and crystallization describe the

TABLE 12.1

Types of Solutions			
Component 1	**Component 2**	**State of Resulting Solution**	**Examples**
Gas	Gas	Gas	Air
Gas	Liquid	Liquid	Soda water (CO$_2$ in water)
Gas	Solid	Solid	H$_2$ gas in palladium
Liquid	Liquid	Liquid	Ethanol in water
Solid	Liquid	Liquid	NaCl in water
Solid	Solid	Solid	Brass (Cu/Zn), solder (Sn/Pb)

Figure 12.1 *In a supersaturated sodium acetate solution (left), sodium acetate crystals rapidly form when a small seed crystal is added.*

separation of excess solid substance from a supersaturated solution. However, solids formed by the two processes differ in appearance. We normally think of precipitates as being made up of small particles, whereas crystals may be large and well formed.

12.2 A Molecular View of the Solution Process

The intermolecular attractions that hold molecules together in liquids and solids also play a central role in the formation of solutions. When one substance (the solute) dissolves in another (the solvent), particles of the solute disperse throughout the solvent. The solute particles occupy positions that are normally taken by solvent molecules. The ease with which a solute particle replaces a solvent molecule depends on the relative strengths of three types of interactions:

- solvent-solvent interaction
- solute-solute interaction
- solvent-solute interaction

For simplicity, we can imagine the solution process taking place in three distinct steps (Figure 12.2). Step 1 is the separation of solvent molecules, and step 2 entails the separation of solute molecules. These steps require energy input to break attractive intermolecular forces; therefore, they are endothermic. In step 3 the solvent and solute molecules mix. This process can be exothermic or endothermic. The heat of solution ΔH_{soln} is given by

$$\Delta H_{soln} = \Delta H_1 + \Delta H_2 + \Delta H_3$$

If the solute-solvent attraction is stronger than the solvent-solvent attraction and solute-solute attraction, the solution process is favorable, or exothermic ($\Delta H_{soln} < 0$). If the solute-solvent interaction is weaker than the solvent-solvent and solute-solute interactions, then the solution process is endothermic ($\Delta H_{soln} > 0$).

You may wonder why a solute dissolves in a solvent at all if the attraction for its own molecules is stronger than the solute-solvent attraction. The solution process, like all physical and chemical processes, is governed by two factors. One is energy, which

In Section 6.6 we discussed the solution process from a macroscopic point of view.

Animation: Dissolution of an Ionic and a Covalent Compound
Online Learning Center

This equation is an application of Hess's law.

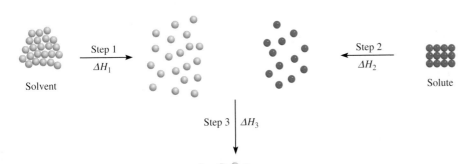

Step 1 ΔH_1 Step 2 ΔH_2

Solvent   Solute

Step 3 ΔH_3

Solution

Figure 12.2 *A molecular view of the solution process portrayed as taking place in three steps: First the solvent and solute molecules are separated (steps 1 and 2). Then the solvent and solute molecules mix (step 3).*

determines whether a solution process is exothermic or endothermic. The second factor is an inherent tendency toward disorder in all natural events. In much the same way that a deck of new playing cards becomes mixed up after it has been shuffled a few times, when solute and solvent molecules mix to form a solution, there is an increase in randomness, or disorder. In the pure state, the solvent and solute possess a fair degree of order, characterized by the more or less regular arrangement of atoms, molecules, or ions in three-dimensional space. Much of this order is destroyed when the solute dissolves in the solvent (see Figure 12.2). Therefore, the solution process is accompanied by an increase in disorder. It is the increase in disorder of the system that favors the solubility of any substance, even if the solution process is endothermic.

Solubility is a measure of how much solute will dissolve in a solvent at a specific temperature. The saying "like dissolves like" is helpful in predicting the solubility of a substance in a given solvent. What this expression means is that two substances with intermolecular forces of similar type and magnitude are likely to be soluble in each other. For example, both carbon tetrachloride (CCl_4) and benzene (C_6H_6) are nonpolar liquids. The only intermolecular forces present in these substances are dispersion forces (see Section 11.2). When these two liquids are mixed, they readily dissolve in each other, because the attraction between CCl_4 and C_6H_6 molecules is comparable in magnitude to the forces between CCl_4 molecules and between C_6H_6 molecules. Two liquids are said to be *miscible* if *they are completely soluble in each other in all proportions.* Alcohols such as methanol, ethanol, and 1,2-ethylene glycol are miscible with water because they can form hydrogen bonds with water molecules:

CH_3OH

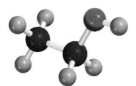

C_2H_5OH

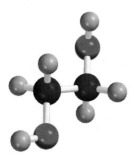

$CH_2(OH)CH_2(OH)$

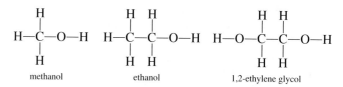

methanol   ethanol   1,2-ethylene glycol

The rules given in Table 4.2 (p. 119) enable us to predict the solubility of a particular ionic compound in water. When sodium chloride dissolves in water, the ions are stabilized in solution by hydration, which involves ion-dipole interaction. In general, we predict that ionic compounds should be much more soluble in polar solvents, such as water, liquid ammonia, and liquid hydrogen fluoride, than in nonpolar solvents, such as benzene and carbon tetrachloride. Because the molecules of nonpolar solvents lack a dipole moment, they cannot effectively solvate the Na^+ and Cl^- ions. (*Solvation* is *the process in which an ion or a molecule is surrounded by solvent molecules arranged in a specific manner.* The process is called *hydration* when the solvent is water.) The predominant intermolecular interaction between ions and nonpolar compounds is ion-induced dipole interaction, which is much weaker than ion-dipole interaction. Consequently, ionic compounds usually have extremely low solubility in nonpolar solvents.

Example 12.1 illustrates how to predict solubility based on a knowledge of the intermolecular forces in the solute and the solvent.

Example 12.1

Predict the relative solubilities in the following cases: (a) Bromine (Br_2) in benzene (C_6H_6, $\mu = 0$ D) and in water ($\mu = 1.87$ D), (b) KCl in carbon tetrachloride (CCl_4, $\mu = 0$ D) and in liquid ammonia (NH_3, $\mu = 1.46$ D), (c) formaldehyde (CH_2O) in carbon disulfide (CS_2, $\mu = 0$) and in water.

(Continued)

Strategy In predicting solubility, remember the saying: Like dissolves like. A nonpolar solute will dissolve in a nonpolar solvent; ionic compounds will generally dissolve in polar solvents due to favorable ion-dipole interaction; solutes that can form hydrogen bonds with the solvent will have high solubility in the solvent.

Solution (a) Br_2 is a nonpolar molecule and therefore should be more soluble in C_6H_6, which is also nonpolar, than in water. The only intermolecular forces between Br_2 and C_6H_6 are dispersion forces.

(b) KCl is an ionic compound. For it to dissolve, the individual K^+ and Cl^- ions must be stabilized by ion-dipole interaction. Because CCl_4 has no dipole moment, KCl should be more soluble in liquid NH_3, a polar molecule with a large dipole moment.

(c) Because CH_2O is a polar molecule and CS_2 (a linear molecule) is nonpolar,

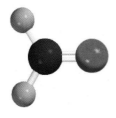

CH_2O

the forces between molecules of CH_2O and CS_2 are dipole-induced dipole and dispersion. On the other hand, CH_2O can form hydrogen bonds with water, so it should be more soluble in that solvent.

Similar problem: 12.11.

Practice Exercise Is iodine (I_2) more soluble in water or in carbon disulfide (CS_2)?

12.3 Concentration Units

Quantitative study of a solution requires knowing its *concentration*, that is, the amount of solute present in a given amount of solution. Chemists use several different concentration units, each of which has advantages as well as limitations. Let us examine the four most common units of concentration: percent by mass, mole fraction, molarity, and molality.

Types of Concentration Units

Percent by Mass The **percent by mass** (also called *percent by weight* or *weight percent*) is *the ratio of the mass of a solute to the mass of the solution, multiplied by 100 percent:*

$$\text{percent by mass of solute} = \frac{\text{mass of solute}}{\text{mass of solute } + \text{ mass of solvent}} \times 100\%$$

$$= \frac{\text{mass of solute}}{\text{mass of soln}} \times 100\% \qquad (12.1)$$

The percent by mass has no units because it is a ratio of two similar quantities.

Example 12.2

A sample of 0.892 g of potassium chloride (KCl) is dissolved in 54.6 g of water. What is the percent by mass of KCl in the solution?

(Continued)

Strategy We are given the mass of a solute dissolved in a certain amount of solvent. Therefore, we can calculate the mass percent of KCl using Equation (12.1).

Solution We write

$$\text{percent by mass of KCl} = \frac{\text{mass of solute}}{\text{mass of soln}} \times 100\%$$

$$= \frac{0.892 \text{ g}}{0.892 \text{ g} + 54.6 \text{ g}} \times 100\%$$

$$= 1.61\%$$

Similar problem: 12.15.

Practice Exercise A sample of 6.44 g of naphthalene ($C_{10}H_8$) is dissolved in 80.1 g of benzene (C_6H_6). Calculate the percent by mass of naphthalene in this solution.

Mole Fraction (X) The mole fraction was introduced in Section 5.6. The mole fraction of a component of a solution, say, component A, is written X_A and is defined as

$$\text{mole fraction of component A} = X_A = \frac{\text{moles of A}}{\text{sum of moles of all components}}$$

The mole fraction has no units, because it too is a ratio of two similar quantities.

For calculations involving molarity, see Example 4.6.

Molarity (M) In Section 4.5 molarity was defined as the number of moles of solute in 1 L of solution; that is,

$$\text{molarity} = \frac{\text{moles of solute}}{\text{liters of soln}}$$

Thus, the units of molarity are mol/L.

Molality (m) *Molality* is *the number of moles of solute dissolved in 1 kg (1000 g) of solvent*—that is,

$$\text{molality} = \frac{\text{moles of solute}}{\text{mass of solvent (kg)}} \tag{12.2}$$

For example, to prepare a 1 molal, or 1 m, sodium sulfate (Na_2SO_4) aqueous solution, we need to dissolve 1 mole (142.0 g) of the substance in 1000 g (1 kg) of water. Depending on the nature of the solute-solvent interaction, the final volume of the solution will be either greater or less than 1000 mL. It is also possible, though very unlikely, that the final volume could be equal to 1000 mL.

Example 12.3 shows how to calculate the molality of a solution.

Example 12.3

Calculate the molality of a sulfuric acid solution containing 24.4 g of sulfuric acid in 198 g of water. The molar mass of sulfuric acid is 98.08 g.

Strategy To calculate the molality of a solution, we need to know the number of moles of solute and the mass of the solvent in kilograms.

(Continued)

H_2SO_4

Solution The definition of molality (m) is

$$m = \frac{\text{moles of solute}}{\text{mass of solvent (kg)}}$$

First, we find the number of moles of sulfuric acid in 24.4 g of the acid, using its molar mass as the conversion factor.

$$\text{moles of } H_2SO_4 = 24.4 \text{ g } H_2SO_4 \times \frac{1 \text{ mol } H_2SO_4}{98.09 \text{ g } H_2SO_4}$$

$$= 0.249 \text{ mol } H_2SO_4$$

The mass of water is 198 g, or 0.198 kg. Therefore,

$$m = \frac{0.249 \text{ mol } H_2SO_4}{0.198 \text{ kg } H_2O}$$

$$= 1.26 \, m$$

Similar problem: 12.17.

Practice Exercise What is the molality of a solution containing 7.78 g of urea $[(NH_2)_2CO]$ in 203 g of water?

Comparison of Concentration Units

The choice of a concentration unit is based on the purpose of the experiment. For instance, the mole fraction is not used to express the concentrations of solutions for titrations and gravimetric analyses, but it is appropriate for calculating partial pressures of gases (see Section 5.6) and for dealing with vapor pressures of solutions (to be discussed later in this chapter).

The advantage of molarity is that it is generally easier to measure the volume of a solution, using precisely calibrated volumetric flasks, than to weigh the solvent, as we saw in Section 4.5. For this reason, molarity is often preferred over molality. On the other hand, molality is independent of temperature, because the concentration is expressed in number of moles of solute and mass of solvent. The volume of a solution typically increases with increasing temperature, so that a solution that is 1.0 M at 25°C may become 0.97 M at 45°C because of the increase in volume. This concentration dependence on temperature can significantly affect the accuracy of an experiment. Therefore it is sometimes preferable to use molality instead of molarity.

Percent by mass is similar to molality in that it is independent of temperature. Furthermore, because it is defined in terms of ratio of mass of solute to mass of solution, we do not need to know the molar mass of the solute in order to calculate the percent by mass.

Sometimes it is desirable to convert one concentration unit of a solution to another; for example, the same solution may be employed for different experiments that require different concentration units for calculations. Suppose we want to express the concentration of a 0.396 m glucose ($C_6H_{12}O_6$) solution in molarity. We know there is 0.396 mole of glucose in 1000 g of the solvent and we need to determine the volume of this solution to calculate molarity. First, we calculate the mass of the solution from the molar mass of glucose:

$$\left(0.396 \text{ mol } C_6H_{12}O_6 \times \frac{180.2 \text{ g}}{1 \text{ mol } C_6H_{12}O_6}\right) + 1000 \text{ g } H_2O \text{ soln} = 1071 \text{ g}$$

The next step is to experimentally determine the density of the solution, which is found to be 1.16 g/mL. We can now calculate the volume of the solution in liters by writing

$$
\begin{aligned}
\text{volume} &= \frac{\text{mass}}{\text{density}} \\
&= \frac{1071 \text{ g}}{1.16 \text{ g/mL}} \times \frac{1 \text{ L}}{1000 \text{ mL}} \\
&= 0.923 \text{ L}
\end{aligned}
$$

Finally, the molarity of the solution is given by

$$
\begin{aligned}
\text{molarity} &= \frac{\text{moles of solute}}{\text{liters of soln}} \\
&= \frac{0.396 \text{ mol}}{0.923 \text{ L}} \\
&= 0.429 \text{ mol/L} = 0.429 \ M
\end{aligned}
$$

As you can see, the density of the solution serves as a conversion factor between molality and molarity.

Examples 12.4 and 12.5 show concentration unit conversions.

CH$_3$OH

Example 12.4

The density of a 2.45 M aqueous solution of methanol (CH$_3$OH) is 0.976 g/mL. What is the molality of the solution? The molar mass of methanol is 32.04 g.

Strategy To calculate the molality, we need to know the number of moles of methanol and the mass of solvent in kilograms. We assume 1 L of solution, so the number of moles of methanol is 2.45 mol.

$$
m = \frac{\text{moles of solute}}{\text{mass of solvent (kg)}}
$$

want to calculate   given   need to find

Solution Our first step is to calculate the mass of water in one liter of the solution, using density as a conversion factor. The total mass of 1 L of a 2.45 M solution of methanol is

$$
1 \text{ L soln} \times \frac{1000 \text{ mL soln}}{1 \text{ L soln}} \times \frac{0.976 \text{ g}}{1 \text{ mL soln}} = 976 \text{ g}
$$

Because this solution contains 2.45 moles of methanol, the amount of water (solvent) in the solution is

$$
\begin{aligned}
\text{mass of H}_2\text{O} &= \text{mass of soln} - \text{mass of solute} \\
&= 976 \text{ g} - \left(2.45 \text{ mol CH}_3\text{OH} \times \frac{32.04 \text{ g CH}_3\text{OH}}{1 \text{ mol CH}_3\text{OH}} \right) \\
&= 898 \text{ g}
\end{aligned}
$$

(Continued)

The molality of the solution can be calculated by converting 898 g to 0.898 kg:

$$\text{molality} = \frac{2.45 \text{ mol CH}_3\text{OH}}{0.898 \text{ kg H}_2\text{O}}$$

$$= 2.73 \, m$$

Similar problems: 12.18(a), 12.19.

Practice Exercise Calculate the molality of a 5.86 M ethanol (C_2H_5OH) solution whose density is 0.927 g/mL.

Example 12.5

Calculate the molality of a 35.4 percent (by mass) aqueous solution of phosphoric acid (H_3PO_4). The molar mass of phosphoric acid is 98.00 g.

Strategy In solving this type of problem, it is convenient to assume that we start with a 100.0 g of the solution. If the mass of phosphoric acid is 35.4 percent, or 35.4 g, the percent by mass and mass of water must be $100.0\% - 35.4\% = 64.6\%$ and 64.6 g.

Solution From the known molar mass of phosphoric acid, we can calculate the molality in two steps, as shown in Example 12.3. First we calculate the number of moles of phosphoric acid in 35.4 g of the acid

$$\text{moles of H}_3\text{PO}_4 = 35.4 \text{ g H}_3\text{PO}_4 \times \frac{1 \text{ mol H}_3\text{PO}_4}{97.99 \text{ g H}_3\text{PO}_4}$$

$$= 0.361 \text{ mol H}_3\text{PO}_4$$

The mass of water is 64.6 g, or 0.0646 kg. Therefore, the molality is given by

$$\text{molality} = \frac{0.361 \text{ mol H}_3\text{PO}_4}{0.0646 \text{ kg H}_2\text{O}}$$

$$= 5.59 \, m$$

Similar problem: 12.18(b).

H_3PO_4

Practice Exercise Calculate the molality of a 44.6 percent (by mass) aqueous solution of sodium chloride.

12.4 The Effect of Temperature on Solubility

Recall that solubility is defined as the maximum amount of a solute that will dissolve in a given quantity of solvent *at a specific temperature*. Temperature affects the solubility of most substances. In this section we will consider the effects of temperature on the solubility of solids and gases.

Solid Solubility and Temperature

Figure 12.3 shows the temperature dependence of the solubility of some ionic compounds in water. In most but certainly not all cases, the solubility of a solid substance increases with temperature. However, there is no clear correlation between the sign of ΔH_{soln} and the variation of solubility with temperature. For example, the solution process of $CaCl_2$ is exothermic, and that of NH_4NO_3 is endothermic. But the solubility of both compounds increases with increasing temperature. In general, the effect of temperature on solubility is best determined experimentally.

Figure 12.3 *Temperature dependence of the solubility of some ionic compounds in water.*

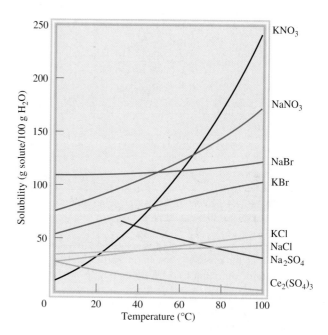

Fractional Crystallization The dependence of the solubility of a solid on temperature varies considerably, as Figure 12.3 shows. The solubility of $NaNO_3$, for example, increases sharply with temperature, while that of NaBr changes very little. This wide variation provides a means of obtaining pure substances from mixtures. *Fractional crystallization* is *the separation of a mixture of substances into pure components on the basis of their differing solubilities.*

Suppose we have a sample of 90 g of KNO_3 that is contaminated with 10 g of NaCl. To purify the KNO_3 sample, we dissolve the mixture in 100 mL of water at 60°C and then gradually cool the solution to 0°C. At this temperature the solubilities of KNO_3 and NaCl are 12.1 g/100 g H_2O and 34.2 g/100 g H_2O, respectively. Thus (90 − 12) g, or 78 g, of KNO_3 will crystallize out of the solution, but all of the NaCl will remain dissolved (Figure 12.4). In this manner, we can obtain about 90 percent of the original amount of KNO_3 in pure form. The KNO_3 crystals can be separated from the solution by filtration.

Many of the solid inorganic and organic compounds that are used in the laboratory were purified by fractional crystallization. Generally the method works best if the compound to be purified has a steep solubility curve, that is, if it is considerably more soluble at high temperatures than at low temperatures. Otherwise, much of it will remain dissolved as the solution is cooled. Fractional crystallization also works well if the amount of impurity in the solution is relatively small.

Gas Solubility and Temperature

The solubility of gases in water usually decreases with increasing temperature (Figure 12.5). When water is heated in a beaker, you can see bubbles of air forming on the side of the glass before the water boils. As the temperature rises, the dissolved air molecules begin to "boil out" of the solution long before the water itself boils.

The reduced solubility of molecular oxygen in hot water has a direct bearing on *thermal pollution*—that is, the heating of the environment (usually waterways) to temperatures that are harmful to its living inhabitants. It is estimated that every year in the United States some 100,000 billion gallons of water are used for industrial cooling, mostly in electric power and nuclear power production. This process heats the water, which is then returned to the rivers and lakes from which it was taken. Ecologists have become

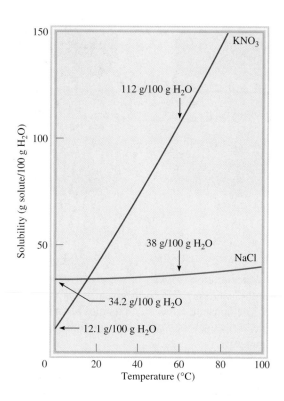

Figure 12.4 *The solubilities of KNO₃ and NaCl at 0°C and 60°C. The difference in temperature dependence enables us to isolate one of these compounds from a solution containing both of them, through fractional crystallization.*

increasingly concerned about the effect of thermal pollution on aquatic life. Fish, like all other cold-blooded animals, have much more difficulty coping with rapid temperature fluctuation in the environment than humans do. An increase in water temperature accelerates their rate of metabolism, which generally doubles with each 10°C rise. The speedup of metabolism increases the fish's need for oxygen at the same time that the supply of oxygen decreases because of its lower solubility in heated water. Effective ways to cool power plants while doing only minimal damage to the biological environment are being sought.

On the lighter side, a knowledge of the variation of gas solubility with temperature can improve one's performance in a popular recreational sport—fishing. On a hot summer day, an experienced fisherman usually picks a deep spot in the river or lake to cast the bait. Because the oxygen content is greater in the deeper, cooler region, most fish will be found there.

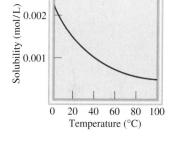

Figure 12.5 *Dependence on temperature of the solubility of O₂ gas in water. Note that the solubility decreases as temperature increases. The pressure of the gas over the solution is 1 atm.*

12.5 The Effect of Pressure on the Solubility of Gases

For all practical purposes, external pressure has no influence on the solubilities of liquids and solids, but it does greatly affect the solubility of gases. The quantitative relationship between gas solubility and pressure is given by **Henry's[†] law,** which states that *the solubility of a gas in a liquid is proportional to the pressure of the gas over the solution:*

$$c \propto P$$
$$c = kP \qquad (12.3)$$

[†]William Henry (1775–1836). English chemist. Henry's major contribution to science was his discovery of the law describing the solubility of gases, which now bears his name.

Figure 12.6 *A molecular interpretation of Henry's law. When the partial pressure of the gas over the solution increases from (a) to (b), the concentration of the dissolved gas also increases according to Equation (12.3).*

(a)

(b)

Each gas has a different k value at a given temperature.

Here c is the molar concentration (mol/L) of the dissolved gas; P is the pressure (in atm) of the gas over the solution; and, for a given gas, k is a constant that depends only on temperature. The constant k has the units mol/L · atm. You can see that when the pressure of the gas is 1 atm, c is *numerically* equal to k. If several gases are present, P is the partial pressure.

Henry's law can be understood qualitatively in terms of the kinetic molecular theory. The amount of gas that will dissolve in a solvent depends on how frequently the gas molecules collide with the liquid surface and become trapped by the condensed phase. Suppose we have a gas in dynamic equilibrium with a solution [Figure 12.6(a)]. At every instant, the number of gas molecules entering the solution is equal to the number of dissolved molecules moving into the gas phase. If the partial pressure of the gas is greater [Figure 12.6(b)], more molecules dissolve in the liquid because more molecules are striking the surface of the liquid. This process continues until the concentration of the solution is again such that the number of molecules leaving the solution per second equals the number entering the solution. Because of the higher concentration of molecules in both the gas and solution phases, this number is greater in (b) than in (a), where the partial pressure is lower.

A practical demonstration of Henry's law is the effervescence of a soft drink when the cap of the bottle is removed. Before the beverage bottle is sealed, it is pressurized with a mixture of air and CO_2 saturated with water vapor. Because of the high partial pressure of CO_2 in the pressurizing gas mixture, the amount dissolved in the soft drink is many times the amount that would dissolve under normal atmospheric conditions. When the cap is removed, the pressurized gases escape, eventually the pressure in the bottle falls to atmospheric pressure, and the amount of CO_2 remaining in the beverage is determined only by the normal atmospheric partial pressure of CO_2, 0.0003 atm. The excess dissolved CO_2 comes out of solution, causing the effervescence.

Example 12.6 applies Henry's law to nitrogen gas.

The effervescence of a soft drink. The bottle was shaken before being opened to dramatize the escape of CO_2.

Example 12.6

The solubility of nitrogen gas at 25°C and 1 atm is 6.8×10^{-4} mol/L. What is the concentration of nitrogen dissolved in water under atmospheric conditions? The partial pressure of nitrogen gas in the atmosphere is 0.78 atm.

(Continued)

Strategy The given solubility enables us to calculate Henry's law constant (k), which can then be used to determine the concentration of the solution.

Solution The first step is to calculate the quantity k in Equation (12.3):

$$c = kP$$
$$6.8 \times 10^{-4} \text{ mol/L} = k \, (1 \text{ atm})$$
$$k = 6.8 \times 10^{-4} \text{ mol/L} \cdot \text{atm}$$

Therefore, the solubility of nitrogen gas in water is

$$c = (6.8 \times 10^{-4} \text{ mol/L} \cdot \text{atm})(0.78 \text{ atm})$$
$$= 5.3 \times 10^{-4} \text{ mol/L}$$
$$= 5.3 \times 10^{-4} \, M$$

The decrease in solubility is the result of lowering the pressure from 1 atm to 0.78 atm.

Check The ratio of the concentrations $[(5.3 \times 10^{-4} \, M/6.8 \times 10^{-4} \, M) = 0.78]$ should be equal to the ratio of the pressures (0.78 atm/1.0 atm = 0.78).

Similar problem: 12.37.

Practice Exercise Calculate the molar concentration of oxygen in water at 25°C for a partial pressure of 0.22 atm. The Henry's law constant for oxygen is 1.3×10^{-3} mol/L · atm.

Most gases obey Henry's law, but there are some important exceptions. For example, if the dissolved gas *reacts* with water, higher solubilities can result. The solubility of ammonia is much higher than expected because of the reaction

$$NH_3 + H_2O \rightleftharpoons NH_4^+ + OH^-$$

Carbon dioxide also reacts with water, as follows:

$$CO_2 + H_2O \rightleftharpoons H_2CO_3$$

Another interesting example is the dissolution of molecular oxygen in blood. Normally, oxygen gas is only sparingly soluble in water (see Practice Exercise in Example 12.6). However, its solubility in blood is dramatically greater because of the high content of hemoglobin (Hb) molecules. Each hemoglobin molecule can bind up to four oxygen molecules, which are eventually delivered to the tissues for use in metabolism:

$$Hb + 4O_2 \rightleftharpoons Hb(O_2)_4$$

It is this process that accounts for the high solubility of molecular oxygen in blood. The Chemistry in Action essay on p. 500 explains a natural disaster with Henry's law.

12.6 Colligative Properties of Nonelectrolyte Solutions

Colligative properties (or collective properties) are *properties that depend only on the number of solute particles in solution and not on the nature of the solute particles.* These properties are bound together by a common origin—they all depend on the number of solute particles present, regardless of whether they are atoms, ions, or molecules. The colligative properties are vapor-pressure lowering, boiling-point elevation, freezing-point

CHEMISTRY IN ACTION

The Killer Lake

Disaster struck swiftly and without warning. On August 21, 1986, Lake Nyos in Cameroon, a small nation on the west coast of Africa, suddenly belched a dense cloud of carbon dioxide. Speeding down a river valley, the cloud asphyxiated over 1700 people and many livestock.

How did this tragedy happen? Lake Nyos is stratified into layers that do not mix. A boundary separates the freshwater at the surface from the deeper, denser solution containing dissolved minerals and gases, including CO_2. The CO_2 gas comes from springs of carbonated groundwater that percolate upward into the bottom of the volcanically formed lake. Given the high water pressure at the bottom of the lake, the concentration of CO_2 gradually accumulated to a dangerously high level, in accordance with Henry's law. What triggered the release of CO_2 is not known for certain. It is believed that an earthquake, landslide, or even strong winds may have upset the delicate balance within the lake, creating waves that overturned the water layers. When the deep water rose, dissolved CO_2 came out of solution, just as a soft drink fizzes when the bottle is uncapped. Being heavier than air, the CO_2 traveled close to the ground and literally smothered an entire village 15 miles away.

Now, more than 18 years after the incident, scientists are concerned that the CO_2 concentration at the bottom of Lake Nyos is again reaching saturation level. To prevent a recurrence of the earlier tragedy, an attempt has been made to pump up the deep water, thus releasing the dissolved CO_2. In addition to being costly, this approach is controversial because it might disturb the waters near the bottom of the lake, leading to an uncontrollable release of CO_2 to the surface. In the meantime, a natural time bomb is ticking away.

Deep waters in Lake Nyos are pumped to the surface to remove dissolved CO_2 gas.

depression, and osmotic pressure. For our discussion of colligative properties of no electrolyte solutions it is important to keep in mind that we are talking about relative dilute solutions, that is, solutions whose concentrations are $\leq 0.2\ M$.

Vapor-Pressure Lowering

To review the concept of equilibrium vapor pressure as it applies to pure liquids, see Section 11.8.

If a solute is **nonvolatile** (that is, it *does not have a measurable vapor pressure*), t vapor pressure of its solution is always less than that of the pure solvent. Thus t relationship between solution vapor pressure and solvent vapor pressure depends (the concentration of the solute in the solution. This relationship is expressed t **Raoult's[†] law,** which states that *the partial pressure of a solvent over a solution, P is given by the vapor pressure of the pure solvent, P_1°, times the mole fraction of th solvent in the solution, X_1:*

$$P_1 = X_1 P_1^\circ \qquad (12.$$

[†]François Marie Raoult (1830–1901). French chemist. Raoult's work was mainly in solution properties a electrochemistry.

In a solution containing only one solute, $X_1 = 1 - X_2$, where X_2 is the mole fraction of the solute. Equation (12.4) can therefore be rewritten as

$$P_1 = (1 - X_2)P_1^\circ$$

or

$$P_1 = P_1^\circ - X_2 P_1^\circ$$

so that

$$P_1^\circ - P_1 = \Delta P = X_2 P_1^\circ \qquad (12.5)$$

We see that the *decrease* in vapor pressure, ΔP, is directly proportional to the solute concentration (measured in mole fraction).

Example 12.7 illustrates the use of Raoult's law [Equation (12.5)].

Example 12.7

Calculate the vapor pressure of a solution made by dissolving 218 g of glucose (molar mass = 180.2 g/mol) in 460 mL of water at 30°C. What is the vapor-pressure lowering? The vapor pressure of pure water at 30°C is given in Table 5.3. Assume the density of the solution is 1.00 g/mL.

Strategy We need Raoult's law [Equation (12.4)] to determine the vapor pressure of a solution. Note that glucose is a nonvolatile solute.

Solution The vapor pressure of a solution (P_1) is

$C_6H_{12}O_6$

$$\overset{\text{need to find}}{P_1} = \underset{\text{want to calculate}}{X_1} \underset{\text{given}}{P_1^\circ}$$

First we calculate the number of moles of glucose and water in the solution:

$$n_1(\text{water}) = 460 \text{ mL} \times \frac{1.00 \text{ g}}{1 \text{ mL}} \times \frac{1 \text{ mol}}{18.02 \text{ g}} = 25.5 \text{ mol}$$

$$n_2(\text{glucose}) = 218 \text{ g} \times \frac{1 \text{ mol}}{180.2 \text{ g}} = 1.21 \text{ mol}$$

The mole fraction of water, X_1, is given by

$$X_1 = \frac{n_1}{n_1 + n_2}$$

$$= \frac{25.5 \text{ mol}}{25.5 \text{ mol} + 1.21 \text{ mol}} = 0.955$$

From Table 5.3, we find the vapor pressure of water at 30°C to be 31.82 mmHg. Therefore, the vapor pressure of the glucose solution is

$$P_1 = 0.955 \times 31.82 \text{ mmHg}$$
$$= 30.4 \text{ mmHg}$$

Finally, the vapor-pressure lowering is $(31.82 - 30.4)$ mmHg, or 1.4 mmHg.

Check We can also calculate the vapor pressure lowering by using Equation (12.5). Because the mole fraction of glucose is $(1 - 0.955)$, or 0.045, the vapor pressure lowering is given by $(0.045)(31.82$ mmHg$)$ or 1.4 mmHg.

Similar problems: 12.51, 12.52.

(Continued)

Practice Exercise Calculate the vapor pressure of a solution made by dissolving 82.4 g of urea (molar mass = 60.06 g/mol) in 212 mL of water at 35°C. What is the vapor-pressure lowering?

Why is the vapor pressure of a solution less than that of the pure solvent? As was mentioned in Section 12.2, one driving force in physical and chemical processes is an increase in disorder—the greater the disorder, the more favorable the process. Vaporization increases the disorder of a system because molecules in a vapor have less order than those in a liquid. Because a solution is more disordered than a pure solvent, the difference in disorder between a solution and a vapor is less than that between a pure solvent and a vapor. Thus solvent molecules have less of a tendency to leave a solution than to leave the pure solvent to become vapor, and the vapor pressure of a solution is less than that of the solvent.

If both components of a solution are **volatile** (that is, *have measurable vapor pressure*), the vapor pressure of the solution is the sum of the individual partial pressures. Raoult's law holds equally well in this case:

$$P_A = X_A P_A^\circ$$
$$P_B = X_B P_B^\circ$$

where P_A and P_B are the partial pressures over the solution for components A and B; P_A° and P_B° are the vapor pressures of the pure substances; and X_A and X_B are their mole fractions. The total pressure is given by Dalton's law of partial pressure (see Section 5.6):

$$P_T = P_A + P_B$$

or

$$P_T = X_A P_A^\circ + X_B P_B^\circ$$

For example, benzene and toluene are volatile components that have similar structures and therefore similar intermolecular forces:

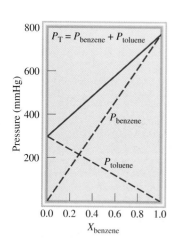

benzene   toluene

In a solution of benzene and toluene, the vapor pressure of each component obeys Raoult's law. Figure 12.7 shows the dependence of the total vapor pressure (P_T) in a benzene-toluene solution on the composition of the solution. Note that we need only express the composition of the solution in terms of the mole fraction of one component. For every value of $X_{benzene}$, the mole fraction of toluene, $X_{toluene}$, is given by $(1 - X_{benzene})$. The benzene-toluene solution is one of the few examples of an **ideal solution**, which is *any solution that obeys Raoult's law*. One characteristic of an ideal solution is that the heat of solution, ΔH_{soln}, is zero.

Most solutions do not behave ideally in this respect. Designating two volatile substances as A and B, we can consider the following two cases:

Case 1: If the intermolecular forces between A and B molecules are weaker than those between A molecules and between B molecules, then there is a greater tendency

Figure 12.7 *The dependence of the partial pressures of benzene and toluene on their mole fractions in a benzene-toluene solution ($X_{toluene} = 1 - X_{benzene}$) at 80°C. This solution is said to be ideal because the vapor pressures obey Raoult's law.*

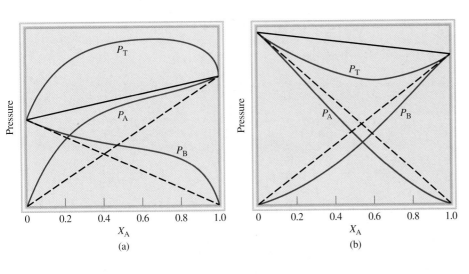

Figure 12.8 *Nonideal solutions. (a) Positive deviation occurs when P_T is greater than that predicted by Raoult's law (the solid black line). (b) Negative deviation. Here, P_T is less than that predicted by Raoult's law (the solid black line).*

for these molecules to leave the solution than in the case of an ideal solution. Consequently, the vapor pressure of the solution is greater than the sum of the vapor pressures as predicted by Raoult's law for the same concentration. This behavior gives rise to the *positive deviation* [Figure 12.8(a)]. In this case, the heat of solution is positive (that is, mixing is an endothermic process).

Case 2: If A molecules attract B molecules more strongly than they do their own kind, the vapor pressure of the solution is less than the sum of the vapor pressures as predicted by Raoult's law. Here we have a *negative deviation* [Figure 12.8(b)]. In this case, the heat of solution is negative (that is, mixing is an exothermic process).

Fractional Distillation Solution vapor pressure has a direct bearing on *fractional distillation, a procedure for separating liquid components of a solution based on their different boiling points.* Fractional distillation is somewhat analogous to fractional crystallization. Suppose we want to separate a *binary system* (a system with two components), say, benzene-toluene. Both benzene and toluene are relatively volatile, yet their boiling points are appreciably different (80.1°C and 110.6°C, respectively). When we boil a solution containing these two substances, the vapor formed is somewhat richer in the more volatile component, benzene. If the vapor is condensed in a separate container and that liquid is boiled again, a still higher concentration of benzene will be obtained in the vapor phase. By repeating this process many times, it is possible to separate benzene completely from toluene.

In practice, chemists use an apparatus like that shown in Figure 12.9 to separate volatile liquids. The round-bottomed flask containing the benzene-toluene solution is fitted with a long column packed with small glass beads. When the solution boils, the vapor condenses on the beads in the lower portion of the column, and the liquid falls back into the distilling flask. As time goes on, the beads gradually heat up, allowing the vapor to move upward slowly. In essence, the packing material causes the benzene-toluene mixture to be subjected continuously to numerous vaporization-condensation steps. At each step the composition of the vapor in the column will be richer in the more volatile, or lower boiling-point, component (in this case, benzene). The vapor that rises to the top of the column is essentially pure benzene, which is then condensed and collected in a receiving flask.

Figure 12.9 *An apparatus for small-scale fractional distillation. The fractionating column is packed with tiny glass beads. The longer the fractionating column, the more complete the separation of the volatile liquids.*

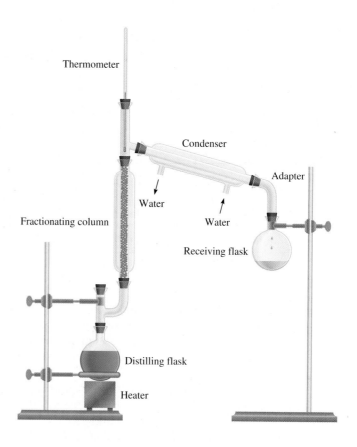

Fractional distillation is as important in industry as it is in the laboratory. The petroleum industry employs fractional distillation on a large scale to separate the components of crude oil. More will be said of this process in Chapter 24.

Boiling-Point Elevation

The boiling point of a solution is the temperature at which its vapor pressure equals the external atmospheric pressure (see Section 11.8). Because the presence of a nonvolatile solute lowers the vapor pressure of a solution, it must also affect the boiling point of the solution. Figure 12.10 shows the phase diagram of water and the changes that occur in an aqueous solution. Because at any temperature the vapor pressure of the solution is lower than that of the pure solvent regardless of temperature, the liquid-vapor curve for the solution lies below that for the pure solvent. Consequently, the dashed solution curve intersects the horizontal line that marks $P = 1$ atm at a *higher* temperature than the normal boiling point of the pure solvent. This graphical analysis shows that the boiling point of the solution is higher than that of water. The ***boiling-point elevation*** (ΔT_b) is defined as *the boiling point of the solution* (T_b) *minus the boiling point of the pure solvent* (T_b°):

$$\Delta T_b = T_b - T_b^\circ$$

Because $T_b > T_b^\circ$, ΔT_b is a positive quantity.

The value of ΔT_b is proportional to the vapor-pressure lowering, and so it is also proportional to the concentration (molality) of the solution. That is,

$$\Delta T_b \propto m$$
$$\Delta T_b = K_b m \tag{12.6}$$

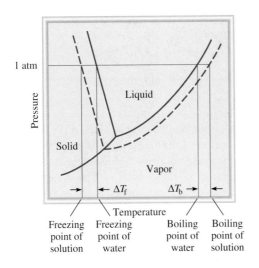

Figure 12.10 *Phase diagram illustrating the boiling-point elevation and freezing-point depression of aqueous solutions. The dashed curves pertain to the solution, and the solid curves to the pure solvent. As you can see, the boiling point of the solution is higher than that of water, and the freezing point of the solution is lower than that of water.*

where m is the molality of the solution and K_b is the *molal boiling-point elevation constant*. The units of K_b are °C/m. It is important to understand the choice of concentration unit here. We are dealing with a system (the solution) whose temperature is *not* constant, so we cannot express the concentration units in molarity because molarity changes with temperature.

Table 12.2 lists values of K_b for several common solvents. Using the boiling-point elevation constant for water and Equation (12.6), you can see that if the molality of an aqueous solution is 1.00 m, the boiling point will be 100.52°C.

Freezing-Point Depression

A nonscientist may remain forever unaware of the boiling-point elevation phenomenon, but a careful observer living in a cold climate is familiar with freezing-point depression. Ice on frozen roads and sidewalks melts when sprinkled with salts such as NaCl or $CaCl_2$. This method of thawing succeeds because it depresses the freezing point of water.

Figure 12.10 shows that lowering the vapor pressure of the solution shifts the solid-liquid curve to the left. Consequently, this line intersects the horizontal line at a temperature *lower* than the freezing point of water. The **freezing point depression** (ΔT_f) is defined as *the freezing point of the pure solvent* (T_f°) *minus the freezing point of the solution* (T_f):

De-icing of airplanes is based on freezing-point depression.

$$\Delta T_f = T_f^{\circ} - T_f$$

TABLE 12.2	Molal Boiling-Point Elevation and Freezing-Point Depression Constants of Several Common Liquids				
	Solvent	Normal Freezing Point (°C)*	K_f (°C/m)	Normal Boiling Point (°C)*	K_b (°C/m)
	Water	0	1.86	100	0.52
	Benzene	5.5	5.12	80.1	2.53
	Ethanol	−117.3	1.99	78.4	1.22
	Acetic acid	16.6	3.90	117.9	2.93
	Cyclohexane	6.6	20.0	80.7	2.79

* Measured at 1 atm.

Because $T_f^\circ > T_f$, ΔT_f is a positive quantity. Again, ΔT_f is proportional to the concentration of the solution:

$$\Delta T_f \propto m$$
$$\Delta T_f = K_f m \qquad (12.7)$$

where m is the concentration of the solute in molality units, and K_f is the *molal freezing-point depression constant* (see Table 12.2). Like K_b, K_f has the units °C/m.

A qualitative explanation of the freezing-point depression phenomenon is as follows. Freezing involves a transition from the disordered state to the ordered state. For this to happen, energy must be removed from the system. Because a solution has greater disorder than the solvent, more energy needs to be removed from it to create order than in the case of a pure solvent. Therefore, the solution has a lower freezing point than its solvent. Note that when a solution freezes, the solid that separates is the pure solvent component.

In order for boiling-point elevation to occur, the solute must be nonvolatile, but no such restriction applies to freezing-point depression. For example, methanol (CH_3OH), a fairly volatile liquid that boils at only 65°C, has sometimes been used as an antifreeze in automobile radiators.

A practical application of the freezing-point depression is described in Example 12.8.

In cold climate regions, antifreeze must be used in car radiators in winter.

Example 12.8

Ethylene glycol (EG), $CH_2(OH)CH_2(OH)$, is a common automobile antifreeze. It is water soluble and fairly nonvolatile (b.p. 197°C). Calculate the freezing point of a solution containing 651 g of this substance in 2505 g of water. Would you keep this substance in your car radiator during the summer? The molar mass of ethylene glycol is 62.01 g.

Strategy This question asks for the depression in freezing point of the solution.

$$\Delta T_f = K_f m$$

want to calculate   constant   need to find

The information given enables us to calculate the molality of the solution and we refer to Table 12.2 for the K_f of water.

Solution To solve for the molality of the solution, we need to know the number of moles of EG and the mass of the solvent in kilograms. We find the molar mass of EG, and convert the mass of the solvent to 2.505 kg, and calculate the molality as follows:

$$651 \text{ g EG} \times \frac{1 \text{ mol EG}}{62.07 \text{ g EG}} = 10.5 \text{ mol EG}$$

$$m = \frac{\text{moles of solute}}{\text{mass of solvent (kg)}}$$

$$= \frac{10.5 \text{ mol EG}}{2.505 \text{ kg H}_2\text{O}} = 4.19 \text{ mol EG/kg H}_2\text{O}$$

$$= 4.19 \ m$$

(Continued)

From Equation (12.7) and Table 12.2 we write

$$\Delta T_f = K_f m$$
$$= (1.86°C/m)(4.19\ m)$$
$$= 7.79°C$$

Because pure water freezes at 0°C, the solution will freeze at −7.79°C. We can calculate boiling-point elevation in the same way as follows:

$$\Delta T_b = K_b m$$
$$= (0.52°C/m)(4.19\ m)$$
$$= 2.2°C$$

Because the solution will boil at (100 + 2.2)°C, or 102.2°C, it would be preferable to leave the antifreeze in your car radiator in summer to prevent the solution from boiling.

Similar problems: 12.58, 12.61.

Practice Exercise Calculate the boiling point and freezing point of a solution containing 478 g of ethylene glycol in 3202 g of water.

Osmotic Pressure

Many chemical and biological processes depend on *osmosis, the selective passage of solvent molecules through a porous membrane from a dilute solution to a more concentrated one.* Figure 12.11 illustrates this phenomenon. The left compartment of the apparatus contains pure solvent; the right compartment contains a solution. The two compartments are separated by a *semipermeable membrane,* which *allows the passage of solvent molecules but blocks the passage of solute molecules.* At the start, the water levels in the two tubes are equal [see Figure 12.11(a)]. After some time, the level in the right tube begins to rise and continues to go up until equilibrium is reached, that is, until no further change can be observed. The *osmotic pressure (π)* of a solution is *the pressure required to stop osmosis.* As shown in Figure 12.11(b), this pressure can be measured directly from the difference in the final fluid levels.

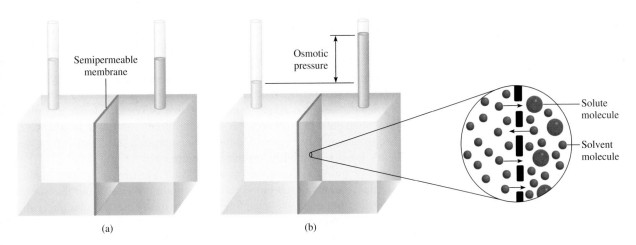

Figure 12.11 *Osmotic pressure. (a) The levels of the pure solvent (left) and of the solution (right) are equal at the start. (b) During osmosis, the level on the solution side rises as a result of the net flow of solvent from left to right. The osmotic pressure is equal to the hydrostatic pressure exerted by the column of fluid in the right tube at equilibrium. Basically the same effect occurs when the pure solvent is replaced by a more dilute solution than that on the right.*

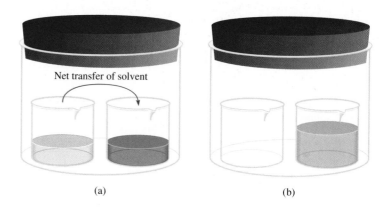

Net transfer of solvent

(a)   (b)

What causes water to move spontaneously from left to right in this case? The situation depicted in Figure 12.12 helps us understand the driving force behind osmosis. Because the vapor pressure of pure water is higher than the vapor pressure of the solution, there is a net transfer of water from the left beaker to the right one. Given enough time, the transfer will continue until no more water remains in the left beaker. A similar driving force causes water to move from the pure solvent into the solution during osmosis.

The osmotic pressure of a solution is given by

$$\pi = MRT \tag{12.8}$$

where M is the molarity of solution, R is the gas constant (0.0821 L · atm/K · mol), and T is the absolute temperature. The osmotic pressure, π, is expressed in atm. Because osmotic pressure measurements are carried out at constant temperature, we express the concentration in terms of the more convenient units of molarity rather than molality.

Like boiling-point elevation and freezing-point depression, osmotic pressure is directly proportional to the concentration of solution. This is what we would expect, because all colligative properties depend only on the number of solute particles in solution. If two solutions are of equal concentration and, hence, have the same osmotic pressure, they are said to be *isotonic*. If two solutions are of unequal osmotic pressures, the more concentrated solution is said to be *hypertonic* and the more dilute solution is described as *hypotonic* (Figure 12.13).

Although osmosis is a common and well-studied phenomenon, relatively little is known about how the semipermeable membrane stops some molecules yet allows others to pass. In some cases, it is simply a matter of size. A semipermeable membrane may have pores small enough to let only the solvent molecules through. In other cases, a different mechanism may be responsible for the membrane's selectivity—for example, the solvent's greater "solubility" in the membrane.

The osmotic pressure phenomenon manifests itself in many interesting applications. To study the contents of red blood cells, which are protected from the external environment by a semipermeable membrane, biochemists use a technique called hemolysis. The red blood cells are placed in a hypotonic solution. Because the hypotonic solution is less concentrated than the interior of the cell, water moves into the cells, as shown in the middle photo of Figure 12.13(d). The cells swell and eventually burst, releasing hemoglobin and other molecules.

Home preserving of jam and jelly provides another example of the use of osmotic pressure. A large quantity of sugar is actually essential to the preservation process

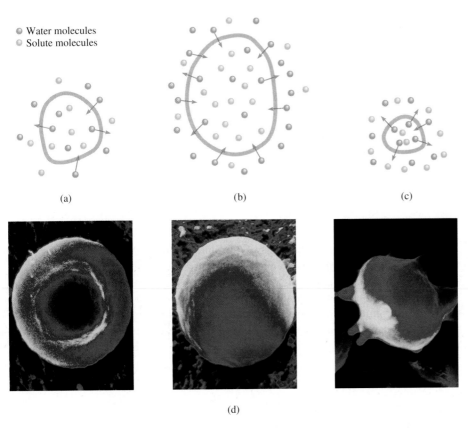

● Water molecules
○ Solute molecules

(a)   (b)   (c)

(d)

Figure 12.13 *A cell in (a) an isotonic solution, (b) a hypotonic solution, and (c) a hypertonic solution. The cell remains unchanged in (a), swells in (b), and shrinks in (c). (d) From left to right: a red blood cell in an isotonic solution, in a hypotonic solution, and in a hypertonic solution.*

because the sugar helps to kill bacteria that may cause botulism. As Figure 12.13(c) shows, when a bacterial cell is in a hypertonic (high-concentration) sugar solution, the intracellular water tends to move out of the bacterial cell to the more concentrated solution by osmosis. This process, known as *crenation,* causes the cell to shrink and, eventually, to cease functioning. The natural acidity of fruits also inhibits bacteria growth.

Osmotic pressure also is the major mechanism for transporting water upward in plants. Because leaves constantly lose water to the air, in a process called *transpiration,* the solute concentrations in leaf fluids increase. Water is pulled up through the trunk, branches, and stems of trees by osmotic pressure. Up to 10 to 15 atm pressure is necessary to transport water to the leaves at the tops of California's redwoods, which reach about 120 m in height. (The capillary action discussed in Section 11.3 is responsible for the rise of water only up to a few centimeters.)

Example 12.9 shows that an osmotic pressure measurement can be used to find the concentration of a solution.

California redwoods.

Example 12.9

The average osmotic pressure of seawater, measured in the kind of apparatus shown in Figure 12.11, is about 30.0 atm at 25°C. Calculate the molar concentration of an aqueous solution of sucrose ($C_{12}H_{22}O_{11}$) that is isotonic with seawater.

Strategy When we say the sucrose solution is isotonic with seawater, what can we conclude about the osmotic pressures of these two solutions?

(Continued)

Solution A solution of sucrose that is isotonic with seawater must have the same osmotic pressure, 30.0 atm. Using Equation (12.8).

$$\pi = MRT$$

$$M = \frac{\pi}{RT} = \frac{30.0 \text{ atm}}{(0.0821 \text{ L} \cdot \text{atm}/\text{K} \cdot \text{mol})(298 \text{ K})}$$

$$= 1.23 \text{ mol/L}$$

$$= 1.23 \ M$$

Similar problem: 12.65.

Practice Exercise What is the osmotic pressure (in atm) of a 0.884 M urea solution at 16°C?

Using Colligative Properties to Determine Molar Mass

The colligative properties of nonelectrolyte solutions provide a means of determining the molar mass of a solute. Theoretically, any of the four colligative properties is suitable for this purpose. In practice, however, only freezing-point depression and osmotic pressure are used because they show the most pronounced changes. The procedure is as follows. From the experimentally determined freezing-point depression or osmotic pressure, we can calculate the molality or molarity of the solution. Knowing the mass of the solute, we can readily determine its molar mass, as Examples 12.10 and 12.11 demonstrate.

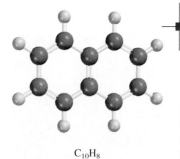

$C_{10}H_8$

Example 12.10

A 7.85-g sample of a compound with the empirical formula C_5H_4 is dissolved in 301 g of benzene. The freezing point of the solution is 1.05°C below that of pure benzene. What are the molar mass and molecular formula of this compound?

Strategy Solving this problem requires three steps. First, we calculate the molality of the solution from the depression in freezing point. Next, from the molality we determine the number of moles in 7.85 g of the compound and hence its molar mass. Finally, comparing the experimental molar mass with the empirical molar mass enables us to write the molecular formula.

Solution The sequence of conversions for calculating the molar mass of the compound is

$$\text{freezing-point} \longrightarrow \text{molality} \longrightarrow \text{number of} \longrightarrow \text{molar mass}$$
$$\text{depression} \qquad\qquad\qquad\qquad \text{moles}$$

Our first step is to calculate the molality of the solution. From Equation (12.7) and Table 12.2 we write

$$\text{molality} = \frac{\Delta T_f}{K_f} = \frac{1.05°C}{5.12°C/m} = 0.205 \ m$$

Because there is 0.205 mole of the solute in 1 kg of solvent, the number of moles of solute in 301 g, or 0.301 kg, of solvent is

$$0.301 \text{ kg} \times \frac{0.205 \text{ mol}}{1 \text{ kg}} = 0.0617 \text{ mol}$$

(Continued)

Thus the molar mass of the solute is

$$\text{molar mass} = \frac{\text{grams of compound}}{\text{moles of compound}}$$

$$= \frac{7.85 \text{ g}}{0.0617 \text{ mol}} = 127 \text{ g/mol}$$

Now we can determine the ratio

$$\frac{\text{molar mass}}{\text{empirical molar mass}} = \frac{127 \text{ g/mol}}{64 \text{ g/mol}} \approx 2$$

Therefore, the molecular formula is $(C_5H_4)_2$ or $C_{10}H_8$ (naphthalene).

Similar problem: 12.59.

Practice Exercise A solution of 0.85 g of an organic compound in 100.0 g of benzene has a freezing point of 5.16°C. What are the molality of the solution and the molar mass of the solute?

Example 12.11

A solution is prepared by dissolving 35.0 g of hemoglobin (Hb) in enough water to make up 1 L in volume. If the osmotic pressure of the solution is found to be 10.0 mmHg at 25°C, calculate the molar mass of hemoglobin.

Strategy We are asked to calculate the molar mass of Hb. The steps are similar to those outlined in Example 12.10. From the osmotic pressure of the solution, we calculate the molarity of the solution. Then, from the molarity, we determine the number of moles in 35.0 g of Hb and hence its molar mass. What units should we use for π and temperature?

Solution The sequence of conversions is as follows:

$$\text{osmotic pressure} \longrightarrow \text{molarity} \longrightarrow \text{number of moles} \longrightarrow \text{molar mass}$$

First we calculate the molarity using Equation (12.8)

$$\pi = MRT$$

$$M = \frac{\pi}{RT}$$

$$= \frac{10.0 \text{ mmHg} \times \dfrac{1 \text{ atm}}{760 \text{ mmHg}}}{(0.0821 \text{ L} \cdot \text{atm/K} \cdot \text{mol})(298 \text{ K})}$$

$$= 5.38 \times 10^{-4} M$$

The volume of the solution is 1 L, so it must contain 5.38×10^{-4} mol of Hb. We use this quantity to calculate the molar mass:

$$\text{moles of Hb} = \frac{\text{mass of Hb}}{\text{molar mass of Hb}}$$

$$\text{molar mass of Hb} = \frac{\text{mass of Hb}}{\text{moles of Hb}}$$

$$= \frac{35.0 \text{ g}}{5.38 \times 10^{-4} \text{ mol}}$$

$$= 6.51 \times 10^4 \text{ g/mol}$$

Similar problems: 12.66, 12.68.

(Continued)

Practice Exercise A 202-mL benzene solution containing 2.47 g of an organic polymer has an osmotic pressure of 8.63 mmHg at 21°C. Calculate the molar mass of the polymer.

The density of mercury is 13.6 g/mL. Therefore, 10 mmHg corresponds to a column of water 13.6 cm in height.

A pressure of 10.0 mmHg, as in Example 12.11, can be measured easily and accurately. For this reason, osmotic pressure measurements are very useful for determining the molar masses of large molecules, such as proteins. To see how much more practical the osmotic pressure technique is than freezing-point depression would be, let us estimate the change in freezing point of the same hemoglobin solution. If an aqueous solution is quite dilute, we can assume that molarity is roughly equal to molality. (Molarity would be equal to molality if the density of the aqueous solution were 1 g/mL.) Hence, from Equation (12.7) we write

$$\Delta T_f = (1.86°C/m)(5.38 \times 10^{-4}\, m)$$
$$= 1.00 \times 10^{-3}°C$$

The freezing-point depression of one-thousandth of a degree is too small a temperature change to measure accurately. For this reason, the freezing-point depression technique is more suitable for determining the molar mass of smaller and more soluble molecules, those having molar masses of 500 g or less, because the freezing-point depressions of their solutions are much greater.

12.7 Colligative Properties of Electrolyte Solutions

*Interactivity: Test Solution with Electrolytes
Online Learning Center, Interactives*

The study of colligative properties of electrolytes requires a slightly different approach than the one used for the colligative properties of nonelectrolytes. The reason is that electrolytes dissociate into ions in solution, and so one unit of an electrolyte compound separates into two or more particles when it dissolves. (Remember, it is the number of solute particles that determines the colligative properties of a solution.) For example, each unit of NaCl dissociates into two ions—Na^+ and Cl^-. Thus the colligative properties of a 0.1 *m* NaCl solution should be twice as great as those of a 0.1 *m* solution containing a nonelectrolyte, such as sucrose. Similarly, we would expect a 0.1 *m* $CaCl_2$ solution to depress the freezing point by three times as much as a 0.1 *m* sucrose solution because each $CaCl_2$ produces three ions. To account for this effect we define a quantity called the ***van't Hoff*** [†] ***factor,*** given by

$$i = \frac{\text{actual number of particles in soln after dissociation}}{\text{number of formula units initially dissolved in soln}} \qquad (12.9)$$

[†] Jacobus Hendricus van't Hoff (1852–1911). Dutch chemist. One of the most prominent chemists of his time, van't Hoff did significant work in thermodynamics, molecular structure and optical activity, and solution chemistry. In 1901 he received the first Nobel Prize in Chemistry.

TABLE 12.3	The van't Hoff Factor of 0.0500 M Electrolyte Solutions at 25°C		
	Electrolyte	***i* (Measured)**	***i* (Calculated)**
	Sucrose*	1.0	1.0
	HCl	1.9	2.0
	NaCl	1.9	2.0
	MgSO$_4$	1.3	2.0
	MgCl$_2$	2.7	3.0
	FeCl$_3$	3.4	4.0

* Sucrose is a nonelectrolyte. It is listed here for comparison only.

Thus i should be 1 for all nonelectrolytes. For strong electrolytes such as NaCl and KNO$_3$, i should be 2, and for strong electrolytes such as Na$_2$SO$_4$ and CaCl$_2$, i should be 3. Consequently, the equations for colligative properties must be modified as

$$\Delta T_b = iK_b m \qquad (12.10)$$

$$\Delta T_f = iK_f m \qquad (12.11)$$

$$\pi = iMRT \qquad (12.12)$$

Every unit of NaCl or KNO$_3$ that dissociates yields two ions ($i = 2$); every unit of Na$_2$SO$_4$ or MgCl$_2$ that dissociates produces three ions ($i = 3$).

In reality, the colligative properties of electrolyte solutions are usually smaller than anticipated because at higher concentrations, electrostatic forces come into play and bring about the formation of ion pairs. An ***ion pair*** is made up of *one or more cations and one or more anions held together by electrostatic forces.* The presence of an ion pair reduces the number of particles in solution, causing a reduction in the colligative properties (Figure 12.14). Electrolytes containing multi-charged ions such as Mg^{2+}, Al^{3+}, SO$_4^{2-}$, and PO$_4^{3-}$ have a greater tendency to form ion pairs than electrolytes such as NaCl and KNO$_3$, which are made up of singly charged ions.

Table 12.3 shows the experimentally measured values of i and those calculated assuming complete dissociation. As you can see, the agreement is close but not perfect, indicating that the extent of ion-pair formation in these solutions at that concentration is appreciable.

As Example 12.12 shows, the van't Hoff factor can be determined from colligative properties measurements.

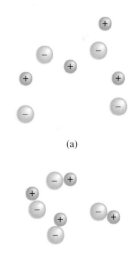

(a)

(b)

Figure 12.14 (a) Free ions and (b) ion pairs in solution. Such an ion pair bears no net charge and therefore cannot conduct electricity in solution.

Example 12.12

The osmotic pressure of a 0.010 M potassium iodide (KI) solution at 25°C is 0.465 atm. Calculate the van't Hoff factor for KI at this concentration.

Strategy Note that KI is a strong electrolyte, so we expect it to dissociate completely in solution. If so, its osmotic pressure would be

$$2(0.010\ M)(0.0821\ \text{L} \cdot \text{atm/K} \cdot \text{mol})(298\ \text{K}) = 0.489\ \text{atm}$$

(Continued)

However, the measured osmotic pressure is only 0.465 atm. The smaller than predicted osmotic pressure means that there is ion-pair formation, which reduces the number of solute particles (K^+ and I^- ions) in solution.

Solution From Equation (12.12) we have

$$i = \frac{\pi}{MRT}$$

$$= \frac{0.465 \text{ atm}}{(0.010 \, M)(0.0821 \text{ L} \cdot \text{atm/K} \cdot \text{mol})(298 \text{ K})}$$

$$= 1.90$$

Similar problem: 12.81.

Practice Exercise The freezing-point depression of a 0.100 m $MgSO_4$ solution is 0.225°C. Calculate the van't Hoff factor of $MgSO_4$ at this concentration.

The Chemistry in Action essay on p. 516 describes three physical techniques for obtaining the pure solvent (water) from a solution (seawater).

12.8 Colloids

The solutions discussed so far are true homogeneous mixtures. Now consider what happens if we add fine sand to a beaker of water and stir. The sand particles are suspended at first but then gradually settle to the bottom. This is an example of a heterogeneous mixture. Between these two extremes is an intermediate state called a colloidal suspension, or simply, a colloid. A **colloid** is *a dispersion of particles of one substance (the dispersed phase) throughout a dispersing medium made of another substance*. Colloidal particles are much larger than the normal solute molecules; they range from 1×10^3 pm to 1×10^6 pm. Also, a colloidal suspension lacks the homogeneity of an ordinary solution. The dispersed phase and the dispersing medium can be gases, liquids, solids, or a combination of different phases, as shown in Table 12.4.

A number of colloids are familiar to us. An *aerosol* consists of liquid droplets or solid particles dispersed in a gas. Examples are fog and smoke. Mayonnaise, which

TABLE 12.4

Types of Colloids

Dispersing Medium	Dispersed Phase	Name	Example
Gas	Liquid	Aerosol	Fog, mist
Gas	Solid	Aerosol	Smoke
Liquid	Gas	Foam	Whipped cream
Liquid	Liquid	Emulsion	Mayonnaise
Liquid	Solid	Sol	Milk of magnesia
Solid	Gas	Foam	Plastic foams
Solid	Liquid	Gel	Jelly, butter
Solid	Solid	Solid sol	Certain alloys (steel), gemstones (glass with dispersed metal)

is made by breaking oil into small droplets in water, is an example of *emulsion,* which consists of liquid droplets dispersed in another liquid. Milk of magnesia is an example of *sol,* a suspension of solid particles in a liquid.

One way to distinguish a solution from a colloid is by the *Tyndall*[†] *effect.* When a beam of light passes through a colloid, it is scattered by the dispersed phase (Figure 12.15). No such scattering is observed with ordinary solutions because the solute molecules are too small to interact with visible light. Another demonstration of the Tyndall effect is the scattering of sunlight by dust or smoke in the air (Figure 12.16).

Hydrophilic and Hydrophobic Colloids

Among the most important colloids are those in which the dispersing medium is water. Such colloids are divided into two categories called **hydrophilic,** or *water-loving,* and **hydrophobic,** or *water-fearing.* Hydrophilic colloids are solutions containing extremely large molecules such as proteins. In the aqueous phase, a protein like hemoglobin folds in such a way that the hydrophilic parts of the molecule, the parts that can interact favorably with water molecules by ion-dipole forces or hydrogen-bond formation, are on the outside surface (Figure 12.17).

A hydrophobic colloid normally would not be stable in water, and the particles would clump together, like droplets of oil in water merging to form a film of oil at water's surface. They can be stabilized, however, by *adsorption* of ions on their surface (Figure 12.18). (Adsorption refers to adherence onto a surface. It differs from

[†]John Tyndall (1820–1893). Irish physicist. Tyndall did important work in magnetism, and explained glacier motion.

Figure 12.15 *Three beams of white light, passing through a colloid of sulfur particles in water, change to orange, pink, and bluish-green. The colors produced depend on the size of the particles and also on the position of the viewer. The smaller the dispersed particles, the shorter (and bluer) the wavelengths.*

Figure 12.16 *Sunlight scattered by dust particles in the air.*

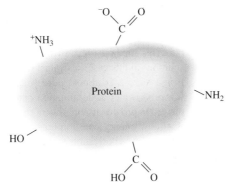

Figure 12.17 *Hydrophilic groups on the surface of a large molecule such as protein stabilizes the molecule in water. Note that all these groups can form hydrogen bonds with water.*

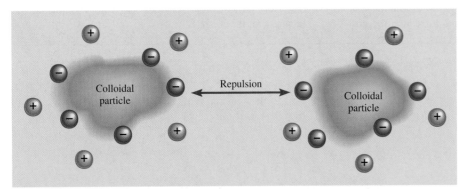

Figure 12.18 *Diagram showing the stabilization of hydrophobic colloids. Negative ions are adsorbed onto the surface and the repulsion between like charges prevents the clumping of the particles.*

CHEMISTRY IN ACTION

Desalination

O ver the centuries, scientists have sought ways of removing salts from seawater, a process called *desalination,* to augment the supply of fresh water. The ocean is an enormous and extremely complex aqueous solution. There are about 1.5×10^{21} L of seawater in the ocean, of which 3.5 percent (by mass) is dissolved material. The accompanying table lists the concentrations of seven substances that together comprise more than 99 percent of the dissolved constituents of ocean water. In an age when astronauts have landed on the moon and spectacular advances in science and medicine have been made, desalination may seem a simple enough objective. However, the technology is very costly. It is an interesting paradox that in our technological society, accomplishing something simple like desalination at a socially acceptable cost is often as difficult as achieving something complex, such as sending an astronaut to the moon.

Composition of Seawater

Ions	g/kg of Seawater
Chloride (Cl^-)	19.35
Sodium (Na^+)	10.76
Sulfate (SO_4^{2-})	2.71
Magnesium (Mg^{2+})	1.29
Calcium (Ca^{2+})	0.41
Potassium (K^+)	0.39
Bicarbonate (HCO_3^-)	0.14

Distillation

The oldest method of desalination, distillation, accounts for more than 90 percent of the approximately 500 million gallons per day capacity of the desalination systems currently in operation worldwide. The process involves vaporizing seawater and then condensing the pure water vapor. Most distillation systems use heat energy to do this. Attempts to reduce the cost of

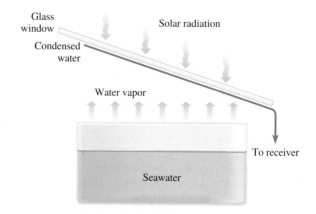

A solar still for desalinating seawater.

distillation include the use of solar radiation as the energy source. This approach is attractive because sunshine is normally more intense in arid lands, where the need for water is also greatest. However, despite intensive research and development efforts, several engineering problems persist, and "solar stills" do not yet operate on a large scale.

Freezing

Desalination by freezing has also been under development for a number of years, but it has not yet become commercially feasible. This method is based on the fact that when an aqueous solution (in this case, seawater) freezes, the solid that separates from solution is almost pure water. Thus, ice crystals from frozen seawater at desalination plants could be rinsed off and thawed to provide usable water. The main advantage of freezing is its low energy consumption, as compared with distillation. The heat of vaporization of water is 40.79 kJ/mol, whereas that of fusion is only 6.01 kJ/mol. Some scientists have even suggested that a partial solution to the water shortage in California would be to tow icebergs from the Arctic down to the West Coast. The major disadvantages of freezing are associated with the slow growth of ice crystals and with washing the salt deposits off the crystals.

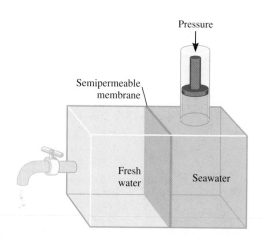

Pressure

Semipermeable
membrane

Fresh
water

Seawater

Reverse osmosis. By applying enough pressure on the solution side, fresh water can be made to flow from right to left. The semipermeable membrane allows the passage of water molecules but not of dissolved ions.

Reverse Osmosis

Both distillation and freezing involve phase changes that require considerable energy. On the other hand, desalination by reverse osmosis does not involve a phase change and is economically more desirable. *Reverse osmosis* uses high pressure to force water from a more concentrated solution to a less concentrated one through a semipermeable membrane. The osmotic pressure of seawater is about 30 atm—this is the pressure that must be applied to the saline solution in order to stop the flow of water from left to right. If the pressure on the salt solution were increased beyond 30 atm, the osmotic flow would be reversed, and fresh water would actually pass from the solution through the membrane into the left compartment. Desalination by reverse osmosis is considerably cheaper than distillation and it avoids the technical difficulties associated with freezing. The main obstacle to this method is the development of a membrane that is permeable to water but not to other dissolved substances and that can be used on a large scale for prolonged periods under high-pressure conditions. Once this problem has been solved, and present signs are encouraging, reverse osmosis could become a major desalination technique.

A small reverse-osmosis apparatus allows a person to obtain drinkable freshwater from seawater.

517

Figure 12.19 (a) A sodium stearate molecule. (b) The simplified representation of the molecule that shows a hydrophilic head and a hydrophobic tail.

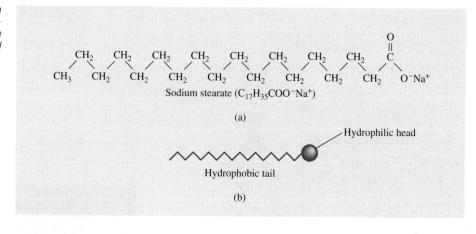

Sodium stearate ($C_{17}H_{35}COO^-Na^+$)

(a)

Hydrophilic head

Hydrophobic tail

(b)

Figure 12.20 The cleansing action of soap. (a) Grease (oily substance) is not soluble in water. (b) When soap is added to water, the nonpolar tails of soap molecules dissolve in grease. (c) Finally, the grease is removed in the form of an emulsion. Note that each oily droplet now has an ionic exterior that is hydrophilic.

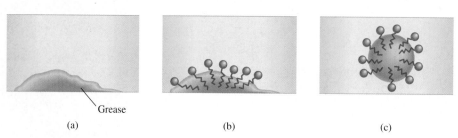

Grease

(a)   (b)   (c)

absorption in that the latter means passage to the interior of the medium.) These adsorbed ions can interact with water, thus stabilizing the colloid. At the same time, the electrostatic repulsion between the particles prevents them from clumping together. Soil particles in rivers and streams are hydrophobic particles stabilized this way. When the fresh water enters the sea, the charges on the particles are neutralized by the high-salt medium, and the particles clump together to form the silt that is seen at the mouth of the river.

Another way hydrophobic colloids can be stabilized is by the presence of other hydrophilic groups on their surfaces. Consider sodium stearate, a soap molecule that has a polar head and a long hydrocarbon tail that is nonpolar (Figure 12.19). The cleansing action of soap is the result of the dual nature of the hydrophobic tail and the hydrophilic end group. The hydrocarbon tail is readily soluble in oily substances, which are also nonpolar, while the ionic —COO^- group remains outside the oily surface. When enough soap molecules have surrounded an oil droplet, as shown in Figure 12.20, the entire system becomes stabilized in water because the exterior portion is now largely hydrophilic. This is how greasy substances are removed by the action of soap.

Key Equations

- molality (m) = $\dfrac{\text{moles of solute}}{\text{mass of solvent (kg)}}$ (12.2) Calculating the molality of a solution.

- $c = kP$ (12.3) Henry's law for calculating solubility of gases.

- $P_1 = X_1 P_1^\circ$ (12.4) Raoult's law relating the vapor pressure of a liquid to its vapor pressure in a solution.

- $\Delta P = X_2 P_1^\circ$ (12.5) Vapor pressure lowering in terms of the concentration of solution.

- $\Delta T_b = K_b m$ (12.6) Boiling-point elevation.

- $\Delta T_f = K_f m$ (12.7) Freezing-point depression.

- $\pi = MRT$ (12.8) Osmotic pressure of a solution.

- $i = \dfrac{\text{actual number of particles in soln after dissociation}}{\text{number of formula units initially dissolved in soln}}$ (12.9)

   Calculating the van't Hoff factor for an electrolyte solution.

Summary of Facts and Concepts

1. Solutions are homogeneous mixtures of two or more substances, which may be solids, liquids, or gases.
2. The ease of dissolving a solute in a solvent is governed by intermolecular forces. Energy and the disorder that results when molecules of the solute and solvent mix to form a solution are the forces driving the solution process.
3. The concentration of a solution can be expressed as percent by mass, mole fraction, molarity, and molality. The choice of units depends on the circumstances.
4. Increasing temperature usually increases the solubility of solid and liquid substances and usually decreases the solubility of gases in water.
5. According to Henry's law, the solubility of a gas in a liquid is directly proportional to the partial pressure of the gas over the solution.
6. Raoult's law states that the partial pressure of a substance A over a solution is equal to the mole fraction (X_A) of A times the vapor pressure (P_A°) of pure A. An ideal solution obeys Raoult's law over the entire range of concentration. In practice, very few solutions exhibit ideal behavior.
7. Vapor-pressure lowering, boiling-point elevation, freezing-point depression, and osmotic pressure are colligative properties of solutions; that is, they depend only on the number of solute particles that are present and not on their nature.
8. In electrolyte solutions, the interaction between ions leads to the formation of ion pairs. The van't Hoff factor provides a measure of the extent of dissociation of electrolytes in solution.
9. A colloid is a dispersion of particles (about 1×10^3 pm to 1×10^6 pm) of one substance in another substance. A colloid is distinguished from a regular solution by the Tyndall effect, which is the scattering of visible light by colloidal particles. Colloids in water are classified as hydrophilic colloids and hydrophobic colloids.

Key Words

Boiling-point elevation (ΔT_b), p. 504
Colligative properties, p. 499
Colloid, p. 514
Crystallization, p. 488
Fractional crystallization, p. 496
Fractional distillation, p. 503

Freezing-point depression (ΔT_f), p. 505
Henry's law, p. 497
Hydrophilic, p. 515
Hydrophobic, p. 515
Ideal solution, p. 502
Ion pair, p. 513
Miscible, p. 490

Molality, p. 492
Nonvolatile, p. 500
Osmosis, p. 507
Osmotic pressure (π), p. 507
Percent by mass, p. 491
Raoult's law, p. 500
Saturated solution, p. 488

Semipermeable membrane, p. 507
Solvation, p. 490
Supersaturated solution, p. 488
Unsaturated solution, p. 488
van't Hoff factor (i), p. 512
Volatile, p. 502

Questions and Problems

Types of Solutions
Review Questions

12.1   Distinguish between an unsaturated solution, a saturated solution, and a supersaturated solution.

12.2   From which type of solution listed in Question 12.1 does crystallization or precipitation occur? How does a crystal differ from a precipitate?

A Molecular View of the Solution Process
Review Questions

12.3   Briefly describe the solution process at the molecular level. Use the dissolution of a solid in a liquid as an example.

12.4   Basing your answer on intermolecular force considerations, explain what "like dissolves like" means.

12.5   What is solvation? What factors influence the extent to which solvation occurs? Give two examples of solvation; include one that involves ion-dipole interaction and one in which dispersion forces come into play.

12.6   As you know, some solution processes are endothermic and others are exothermic. Provide a molecular interpretation for the difference.

12.7   Explain why the solution process invariably leads to an increase in disorder.

12.8   Describe the factors that affect the solubility of a solid in a liquid. What does it mean to say that two liquids are miscible?

Problems

12.9   Why is naphthalene ($C_{10}H_8$) more soluble than CsF in benzene?

12.10   Explain why ethanol (C_2H_5OH) is not soluble in cyclohexane (C_6H_{12}).

12.11   Arrange the following compounds in order of increasing solubility in water: O_2, LiCl, Br_2, methanol (CH_3OH).

12.12   Explain the variations in solubility in water of the alcohols listed below:

Compound	Solubility in Water (g/100 g) at 20°C
CH_3OH	∞
CH_3CH_2OH	∞
$CH_3CH_2CH_2OH$	∞
$CH_3CH_2CH_2CH_2OH$	9
$CH_3CH_2CH_2CH_2CH_2OH$	2.7

(*Note:* ∞ means that the alcohol and water are completely miscible in all proportions.)

Concentration Units
Review Questions

12.13   Define the following concentration terms and give their units: percent by mass, mole fraction, molarity, molality. Compare their advantages and disadvantages.

12.14   Outline the steps required for conversion between molarity, molality, and percent by mass.

Problems

12.15   Calculate the percent by mass of the solute in each of the following aqueous solutions: (a) 5.50 g of NaBr in 78.2 g of solution, (b) 31.0 g of KCl in 152 g of water, (c) 4.5 g of toluene in 29 g of benzene.

12.16   Calculate the amount of water (in grams) that must be added to (a) 5.00 g of urea ($(NH_2)_2CO$) in the preparation of a 16.2 percent by mass solution, and (b) 26.2 g of $MgCl_2$ in the preparation of a 1.5 percent by mass solution.

12.17   Calculate the molality of each of the following solutions: (a) 14.3 g of sucrose ($C_{12}H_{22}O_{11}$) in 676 g of water, (b) 7.20 moles of ethylene glycol ($C_2H_6O_2$) in 3546 g of water.

12.18   Calculate the molality of each of the following aqueous solutions: (a) 2.50 M NaCl solution (density of solution = 1.08 g/mL), (b) 48.2 percent by mass KBr solution.

12.19   Calculate the molalities of the following aqueous solutions: (a) 1.22 M sugar ($C_{12}H_{22}O_{11}$) solution (density of solution = 1.12 g/mL), (b) 0.87 M NaOH solution (density of solution = 1.04 g/mL), (c) 5.24 M NaHCO$_3$ solution (density of solution = 1.19 g/mL).

12.20   For dilute aqueous solutions in which the density of the solution is roughly equal to that of the pure solvent, the molarity of the solution is equal to its molality. Show that this statement is correct for a 0.010 M aqueous urea ($(NH_2)_2CO$) solution.

12.21   The alcohol content of hard liquor is normally given in terms of the "proof," which is defined as twice the percentage by volume of ethanol (C_2H_5OH) present. Calculate the number of grams of alcohol present in 1.00 L of 75-proof gin. The density of ethanol is 0.798 g/mL.

12.22   The concentrated sulfuric acid we use in the laboratory is 98.0 percent H_2SO_4 by mass. Calculate the molality and molarity of the acid solution. The density of the solution is 1.83 g/mL.

12.23 Calculate the molarity and the molality of an NH_3 solution made up of 30.0 g of NH_3 in 70.0 g of water. The density of the solution is 0.982 g/mL.

12.24 The density of an aqueous solution containing 10.0 percent of ethanol (C_2H_5OH) by mass is 0.984 g/mL. (a) Calculate the molality of this solution. (b) Calculate its molarity. (c) What volume of the solution would contain 0.125 mole of ethanol?

The Effect of Temperature on Solubility
Review Questions

12.25 How do the solubilities of most ionic compounds in water change with temperature? With pressure?

12.26 Describe the fractional crystallization process and its application.

Problems

12.27 A 3.20-g sample of a salt dissolves in 9.10 g of water to give a saturated solution at 25°C. What is the solubility (in g salt/100 g of H_2O) of the salt?

12.28 The solubility of KNO_3 is 155 g per 100 g of water at 75°C and 38.0 g at 25°C. What mass (in grams) of KNO_3 will crystallize out of solution if exactly 100 g of its saturated solution at 75°C is cooled to 25°C?

12.29 A 50-g sample of impure $KClO_3$ (solubility = 7.1 g per 100 g H_2O at 20°C) is contaminated with 10 percent of KCl (solubility = 25.5 g per 100 g of H_2O at 20°C). Calculate the minimum quantity of 20°C water needed to dissolve all the KCl from the sample. How much $KClO_3$ will be left after this treatment? (Assume that the solubilities are unaffected by the presence of the other compound.)

Gas Solubility
Review Questions

12.30 Discuss the factors that influence the solubility of a gas in a liquid.

12.31 What is thermal pollution? Why is it harmful to aquatic life?

12.32 What is Henry's law? Define each term in the equation, and give its units. How would you account for the law in terms of the kinetic molecular theory of gases? Give two exceptions to Henry's law.

12.33 A student is observing two beakers of water. One beaker is heated to 30°C, and the other is heated to 100°C. In each case, bubbles form in the water. Are these bubbles of the same origin? Explain.

12.34 A man bought a goldfish in a pet shop. Upon returning home, he put the goldfish in a bowl of recently boiled water that had been cooled quickly. A few minutes later the fish was found dead. Explain what happened to the fish.

Problems

12.35 A beaker of water is initially saturated with dissolved air. Explain what happens when He gas at 1 atm is bubbled through the solution for a long time.

12.36 A miner working 260 m below sea level opened a carbonated soft drink during a lunch break. To his surprise, the soft drink tasted rather "flat." Shortly afterward, the miner took an elevator to the surface. During the trip up, he could not stop belching. Why?

12.37 The solubility of CO_2 in water at 25°C and 1 atm is 0.034 mol/L. What is its solubility under atmospheric conditions? (The partial pressure of CO_2 in air is 0.0003 atm.) Assume that CO_2 obeys Henry's law.

12.38 The solubility of N_2 in blood at 37°C and at a partial pressure of 0.80 atm is 5.6×10^{-4} mol/L. A deep-sea diver breathes compressed air with the partial pressure of N_2 equal to 4.0 atm. Assume that the total volume of blood in the body is 5.0 L. Calculate the amount of N_2 gas released (in liters at 37°C and 1 atm) when the diver returns to the surface of the water, where the partial pressure of N_2 is 0.80 atm.

Colligative Properties of Nonelectrolyte Solutions
Review Questions

12.39 What are colligative properties? What is the meaning of the word "colligative" in this context?

12.40 Give two examples of (a) a volatile liquid and (b) a nonvolatile liquid.

12.41 Write the equation representing Raoult's law, and express it in words.

12.42 Use a solution of benzene in toluene to explain what is meant by an ideal solution.

12.43 Write the equations relating boiling-point elevation and freezing-point depression to the concentration of the solution. Define all the terms, and give their units.

12.44 How is vapor-pressure lowering related to a rise in the boiling point of a solution?

12.45 Use a phase diagram to show the difference in freezing points and boiling points between an aqueous urea solution and pure water.

12.46 What is osmosis? What is a semipermeable membrane?

12.47 Write the equation relating osmotic pressure to the concentration of a solution. Define all the terms and specify their units.

12.48   What does it mean when we say that the osmotic pressure of a sample of seawater is 25 atm at a certain temperature?

12.49   Explain why molality is used for boiling-point elevation and freezing-point depression calculations and molarity is used in osmotic pressure calculations.

12.50   Describe how you would use freezing-point depression and osmotic pressure measurements to determine the molar mass of a compound. Why are boiling-point elevation and vapor-pressure lowering normally not used for this purpose?

Problems

12.51   A solution is prepared by dissolving 396 g of sucrose ($C_{12}H_{22}O_{11}$) in 624 g of water. What is the vapor pressure of this solution at 30°C? (The vapor pressure of water is 31.8 mmHg at 30°C.)

12.52   How many grams of sucrose ($C_{12}H_{22}O_{11}$) must be added to 552 g of water to give a solution with a vapor pressure 2.0 mmHg less than that of pure water at 20°C? (The vapor pressure of water at 20°C is 17.5 mmHg.)

12.53   The vapor pressure of benzene is 100.0 mmHg at 26.1°C. Calculate the vapor pressure of a solution containing 24.6 g of camphor ($C_{10}H_{16}O$) dissolved in 98.5 g of benzene. (Camphor is a low-volatility solid.)

12.54   The vapor pressures of ethanol (C_2H_5OH) and 1-propanol (C_3H_7OH) at 35°C are 100 mmHg and 37.6 mmHg, respectively. Assume ideal behavior and calculate the partial pressures of ethanol and 1-propanol at 35°C over a solution of ethanol in 1-propanol, in which the mole fraction of ethanol is 0.300.

12.55   The vapor pressure of ethanol (C_2H_5OH) at 20°C is 44 mmHg, and the vapor pressure of methanol (CH_3OH) at the same temperature is 94 mmHg. A mixture of 30.0 g of methanol and 45.0 g of ethanol is prepared (and can be assumed to behave as an ideal solution). (a) Calculate the vapor pressure of methanol and ethanol above this solution at 20°C. (b) Calculate the mole fraction of methanol and ethanol in the vapor above this solution at 20°C. (c) Suggest a method for separating the two components of the solution.

12.56   How many grams of urea [$(NH_2)_2CO$] must be added to 450 g of water to give a solution with a vapor pressure 2.50 mmHg less than that of pure water at 30°C? (The vapor pressure of water at 30°C is 31.8 mmHg.)

12.57   What are the boiling point and freezing point of a 2.47 m solution of naphthalene in benzene? (The boiling point and freezing point of benzene are 80.1°C and 5.5°C, respectively.)

12.58   An aqueous solution contains the amino acid glycine (NH_2CH_2COOH). Assuming that the acid does not ionize in water, calculate the molality of the solution if it freezes at −1.1°C.

12.59   Pheromones are compounds secreted by the females of many insect species to attract males. One of these compounds contains 80.78 percent C, 13.56 percent H, and 5.66 percent O. A solution of 1.00 g of this pheromone in 8.50 g of benzene freezes at 3.37°C. What are the molecular formula and molar mass of the compound? (The normal freezing point of pure benzene is 5.50°C.)

12.60   The elemental analysis of an organic solid extracted from gum arabic (a gummy substance used in adhesives, inks, and pharmaceuticals) showed that it contained 40.0 percent C, 6.7 percent H, and 53.3 percent O. A solution of 0.650 g of the solid in 27.8 g of the solvent diphenyl gave a freezing-point depression of 1.56°C. Calculate the molar mass and molecular formula of the solid. (K_f for diphenyl is 8.00°C/m.)

12.61   How many liters of the antifreeze ethylene glycol [$CH_2(OH)CH_2(OH)$] would you add to a car radiator containing 6.50 L of water if the coldest winter temperature in your area is −20°C? Calculate the boiling point of this water-ethylene glycol mixture. (The density of ethylene glycol is 1.11 g/mL.)

12.62   A solution is prepared by condensing 4.00 L of a gas, measured at 27°C and 748 mmHg pressure, into 58.0 g of benzene. Calculate the freezing point of this solution.

12.63   The molar mass of benzoic acid (C_6H_5COOH) determined by measuring the freezing-point depression in benzene is twice what we would expect for the molecular formula, $C_7H_6O_2$. Explain this apparent anomaly.

12.64   A solution of 2.50 g of a compound having the empirical formula C_6H_5P in 25.0 g of benzene is observed to freeze at 4.3°C. Calculate the molar mass of the solute and its molecular formula.

12.65   What is the osmotic pressure (in atm) of a 1.36 M aqueous solution of urea [$(NH_2)_2CO$] at 22.0°C?

12.66   A solution containing 0.8330 g of a polymer of unknown structure in 170.0 mL of an organic solvent was found to have an osmotic pressure of 5.20 mmHg at 25°C. Determine the molar mass of the polymer.

12.67   A quantity of 7.480 g of an organic compound is dissolved in water to make 300.0 mL of solution. The solution has an osmotic pressure of 1.43 atm at 27°C. The analysis of this compound shows that it contains 41.8 percent C, 4.7 percent H, 37.3 percent O, and 16.3 percent N. Calculate the molecular formula of the compound.

12.68 A solution of 6.85 g of a carbohydrate in 100.0 g of water has a density of 1.024 g/mL and an osmotic pressure of 4.61 atm at 20.0°C. Calculate the molar mass of the carbohydrate.

Colligative Properties of Electrolyte Solutions
Review Questions

12.69 Why is the discussion of the colligative properties of electrolyte solutions more involved than that of non-electrolyte solutions?

12.70 What are ion pairs? What effect does ion-pair formation have on the colligative properties of a solution? How does the ease of ion-pair formation depend on (a) charges on the ions, (b) size of the ions, (c) nature of the solvent (polar versus nonpolar), (d) concentration?

12.71 Indicate which compound in each of the following pairs is more likely to form ion pairs in water: (a) NaCl or Na_2SO_4, (b) $MgCl_2$ or $MgSO_4$, (c) LiBr or KBr.

12.72 What is the van't Hoff factor? What information does it provide?

Problems

12.73 Which of the following aqueous solutions has (a) the higher boiling point, (b) the higher freezing point, and (c) the lower vapor pressure: 0.35 m $CaCl_2$ or 0.90 m urea? Explain. Assume complete dissociation.

12.74 Consider two aqueous solutions, one of sucrose ($C_{12}H_{22}O_{11}$) and the other of nitric acid (HNO_3). Both solutions freeze at −1.5°C. What other properties do these solutions have in common?

12.75 Arrange the following solutions in order of decreasing freezing point: 0.10 m Na_3PO_4, 0.35 m NaCl, 0.20 m $MgCl_2$, 0.15 m $C_6H_{12}O_6$, 0.15 m CH_3COOH.

12.76 Arrange the following aqueous solutions in order of decreasing freezing point, and explain your reasoning: 0.50 m HCl, 0.50 m glucose, 0.50 m acetic acid.

12.77 What are the normal freezing points and boiling points of the following solutions? (a) 21.2 g NaCl in 135 mL of water and (b) 15.4 g of urea in 66.7 mL of water

12.78 At 25°C the vapor pressure of pure water is 23.76 mmHg and that of seawater is 22.98 mmHg. Assuming that seawater contains only NaCl, estimate its molal concentration.

12.79 Both NaCl and $CaCl_2$ are used to melt ice on roads and sidewalks in winter. What advantages do these substances have over sucrose or urea in lowering the freezing point of water?

12.80 A 0.86 percent by mass solution of NaCl is called "physiological saline" because its osmotic pressure is equal to that of the solution in blood cells. Calculate the osmotic pressure of this solution at normal body temperature (37°C). Note that the density of the saline solution is 1.005 g/mL.

12.81 The osmotic pressure of 0.010 M solutions of $CaCl_2$ and urea at 25°C are 0.605 atm and 0.245 atm, respectively. Calculate the van't Hoff factor for the $CaCl_2$ solution.

12.82 Calculate the osmotic pressure of a 0.0500 M $MgSO_4$ solution at 25°C. (*Hint:* See Table 12.3.)

Colloids
Review Questions

12.83 What are colloids? Referring to Table 12.4, why is there no colloid in which both the dispersed phase and the dispersing medium are gases?

12.84 Describe how hydrophilic and hydrophobic colloids are stabilized in water.

Additional Problems

12.85 Lysozyme is an enzyme that cleaves bacterial cell walls. A sample of lysozyme extracted from egg white has a molar mass of 13,930 g. A quantity of 0.100 g of this enzyme is dissolved in 150 g of water at 25°C. Calculate the vapor-pressure lowering, the depression in freezing point, the elevation in boiling point, and the osmotic pressure of this solution. (The vapor pressure of water at 25°C is 23.76 mmHg.)

12.86 Solutions A and B have osmotic pressures of 2.4 atm and 4.6 atm, respectively, at a certain temperature. What is the osmotic pressure of a solution prepared by mixing equal volumes of A and B at the same temperature?

12.87 A cucumber placed in concentrated brine (salt water) shrivels into a pickle. Explain.

12.88 Two liquids A and B have vapor pressures of 76 mmHg and 132 mmHg, respectively, at 25°C. What is the total vapor pressure of the ideal solution made up of (a) 1.00 mole of A and 1.00 mole of B and (b) 2.00 moles of A and 5.00 moles of B?

12.89 Calculate the van't Hoff factor of Na_3PO_4 in a 0.40 m solution whose freezing point is −2.6°C.

12.90 A 262-mL sample of a sugar solution containing 1.22 g of the sugar has an osmotic pressure of 30.3 mmHg at 35°C. What is the molar mass of the sugar?

12.91 Consider the three mercury manometers shown in the diagram on p. 524. One of them has 1 mL of water on top of the mercury, another has 1 mL of a 1 *m* urea solution on top of the mercury, and the third one has 1 mL of a 1 *m* NaCl solution placed on top of the mercury. Which of these solutions is in the tube labeled X, which is in Y, and which is in Z?

12.92 A forensic chemist is given a white powder for analysis. She dissolves 0.50 g of the substance in 8.0 g of benzene. The solution freezes at 3.9°C. Can the chemist conclude that the compound is cocaine $(C_{17}H_{21}NO_4)$? What assumptions are made in the analysis?

12.93 "Time-release" drugs have the advantage of releasing the drug to the body at a constant rate so that the drug concentration at any time is not too high as to have harmful side effects or too low as to be ineffective. A schematic diagram of a pill that works on this basis is shown below. Explain how it works.

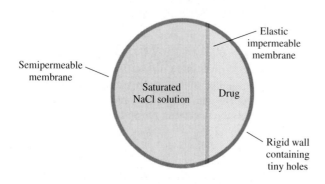

12.94 A solution of 1.00 g of anhydrous aluminum chloride, $AlCl_3$, in 50.0 g of water freezes at −1.11°C. Does the molar mass determined from this freezing point agree with that calculated from the formula? Why?

12.95 Explain why reverse osmosis is (theoretically) more desirable as a desalination method than distillation or

freezing. What minimum pressure must be applied to seawater at 25°C in order for reverse osmosis to occur? (Treat seawater as a 0.70 *M* NaCl solution.)

12.96 What masses of sodium chloride, magnesium chloride, sodium sulfate, calcium chloride, potassium chloride, and sodium bicarbonate are needed to produce 1 L of artificial seawater for an aquarium? The required ionic concentrations are $[Na^+]$ = 2.56 *M*, $[K^+]$ = 0.0090 *M*, $[Mg^{2+}]$ = 0.054 *M*, $[Ca^{2+}]$ = 0.010 *M*, $[HCO_3^-]$ = 0.0020 *M*, $[Cl^-]$ = 2.60 *M*, $[SO_4^{2-}]$ = 0.051 *M*.

12.97 A protein has been isolated as a salt with the formula $Na_{20}P$ (this notation means that there are 20 Na^+ ions associated with a negatively charged protein P^{20-}). The osmotic pressure of a 10.0-mL solution containing 0.225 g of the protein is 0.257 atm at 25.0°C. (a) Calculate the molar mass of the protein from these data. (b) Calculate the actual molar mass of the protein.

12.98 A nonvolatile organic compound Z was used to make up two solutions. Solution A contains 5.00 g of Z dissolved in 100 g of water, and solution B contains 2.31 g of Z dissolved in 100 g of benzene. Solution A has a vapor pressure of 754.5 mmHg at the normal boiling point of water, and solution B has the same vapor pressure at the normal boiling point of benzene. Calculate the molar mass of Z in solutions A and B and account for the difference.

12.99 Hydrogen peroxide with a concentration of 3.0 percent (3.0 g of H_2O_2 in 100 mL of solution) is sold in drugstores for use as an antiseptic. For a 10.0-mL 3.0 percent H_2O_2 solution, calculate (a) the oxygen gas produced (in liters) at STP when the compound undergoes complete decomposition and (b) the ratio of the volume of O_2 collected to the initial volume of the H_2O_2 solution.

12.100 State which of the alcohols listed in Problem 12.12 you would expect to be the best solvent for each of the following substances, and explain why: (a) I_2, (b) KBr, (c) $CH_3CH_2CH_2CH_2CH_3$.

12.101 Before a carbonated beverage bottle is sealed, it is pressurized with a mixture of air and carbon dioxide. (a) Explain the effervescence that occurs when the cap of the bottle is removed. (b) What causes the fog to form near the mouth of the bottle right after the cap is removed?

12.102 Iodine (I_2) is only sparingly soluble in water (left photo). Yet upon the addition of iodide ions (for example, from KI), iodine is converted to the triiodide ion, which readily dissolves (right photo):

$$I_2(s) + I^-(aq) \rightleftharpoons I_3^-(aq)$$

Describe the change in solubility of I_2 in terms of the change in intermolecular forces.

12.103 Two beakers, one containing a 50-mL aqueous 1.0 *M* glucose solution and the other a 50-mL aqueous 2.0 *M* glucose solution, are placed under a tightly sealed bell jar at room temperature. What are the volumes in these two beakers at equilibrium?

12.104 In the apparatus shown below, what will happen if the membrane is (a) permeable to both water and the Na^+ and Cl^- ions, (b) permeable to water and Na^+ ions but not to Cl^- ions, (c) permeable to water but not to Na^+ and Cl^- ions?

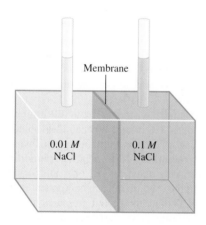

12.105 Explain why it is essential that fluids used in intravenous injections have approximately the same osmotic pressure as blood.

12.106 Concentrated hydrochloric acid is usually available at a concentration of 37.7 percent by mass. What is its molar concentration? (The density of the solution is 1.19 g/mL.)

12.107 Explain each of the following statements: (a) The boiling point of seawater is higher than that of pure water. (b) Carbon dioxide escapes from the solution when the cap is removed from a carbonated soft-drink bottle. (c) Molal and molar concentrations of dilute aqueous solutions are approximately equal. (d) In discussing the colligative properties of a solution (other than osmotic pressure), it is preferable to express the concentration in units of molality rather than in molarity. (e) Methanol (b.p. 65°C) is useful as an antifreeze, but it should be removed from the car radiator during the summer season.

12.108 A mixture of NaCl and sucrose ($C_{12}H_{22}O_{11}$) of combined mass 10.2 g is dissolved in enough water to make up a 250 mL solution. The osmotic pressure of the solution is 7.32 atm at 23°C. Calculate the mass percent of NaCl in the mixture.

12.109 A 1.32-g sample of a mixture of cyclohexane (C_6H_{12}) and naphthalene ($C_{10}H_8$) is dissolved in 18.9 g of benzene (C_6H_6). The freezing point of the solution is 2.2°C. Calculate the mass percent of the mixture. (See Table 12.2 for constants.)

12.110 How does each of the following affect the solubility of an ionic compound? (a) lattice energy, (b) solvent (polar versus nonpolar), (c) enthalpies of hydration of cation and anion

12.111 A solution contains two volatile liquids A and B. Complete the following table, in which the symbol ⟷ indicates attractive intermolecular forces.

Attractive Forces	Deviation from Raoult's Law	ΔH_{soln}
A ⟷ A, B ⟷ B > A ⟷ B		
	Negative	
		Zero

12.112 The concentration of commercially available concentrated sulfuric acid is 98.0 percent by mass, or 18 *M*. Calculate the density and the molality of the solution.

12.113 The concentration of commercially available concentrated nitric acid is 70.0 percent by mass, or 15.9 *M*. Calculate the density and the molality of the solution.

12.114 A mixture of ethanol and 1-propanol behaves ideally at 36°C and is in equilibrium with its vapor. If the mole fraction of ethanol in the solution is 0.62, calculate its mole fraction in the vapor phase at this temperature. (The vapor pressures of pure ethanol and 1-propanol at 36°C are 108 mmHg and 40.0 mmHg, respectively.)

12.115 For ideal solutions, the volumes are additive. This means that if 5 mL of A and 5 mL of B form an ideal solution, the volume of the solution is 10 mL. Provide a molecular interpretation for this observation. When 500 mL of ethanol (C_2H_5OH) are mixed with 500 mL of water, the final volume is less than 1000 mL. Why?

12.116 Ammonia (NH_3) is very soluble in water, but nitrogen trichloride (NCl_3) is not. Explain.

12.117 Aluminum sulfate [$Al_2(SO_4)_3$] is sometimes used in municipal water treatment plants to remove undesirable particles. Explain how this process works.

12.118 Acetic acid is a weak acid that ionizes in solution as follows:

$$CH_3COOH(aq) \rightleftharpoons CH_3COO^-(aq) + H^+(aq)$$

If the freezing point of a 0.106 m CH_3COOH solution is $-0.203°C$, calculate the percent of the acid that has undergone ionization.

12.119 Making mayonnaise involves beating oil into small droplets in water, in the presence of egg yolk. What is the purpose of the egg yolk? (*Hint:* Egg yolk contains lecithins, which are molecules with a polar head and a long nonpolar hydrocarbon tail.)

12.120 Acetic acid is a polar molecule and can form hydrogen bonds with water molecules. Therefore, it has a high solubility in water. Yet acetic acid is also soluble in benzene (C_6H_6), a nonpolar solvent that lacks the ability to form hydrogen bonds. A solution of 3.8 g of CH_3COOH in 80 g C_6H_6 has a freezing point of 3.5°C. Calculate the molar mass of the solute and suggest what its structure might be. (*Hint:* Acetic acid molecules can form hydrogen bonds between themselves.)

12.121 A 2.6-L sample of water contains 192 μg of lead. Does this concentration of lead exceed the safety limit of 0.050 ppm of lead per liter of drinking water? [*Hint:* 1 $\mu g = 1 \times 10^{-6}$ g. Parts per million (ppm) is defined as (mass of component/mass of solution) $\times 10^6$.]

12.122 Fishes in the Antarctic Ocean swim in water at about $-2°C$. (a) To prevent their blood from freezing, what must be the concentration (in molality) of the blood? Is this a reasonable physiological concentration? (b) In recent years scientists have discovered a special type of protein in these fishes' blood which, although present in quite low concentrations (≤ 0.001 m), has the ability to prevent the blood from freezing. Suggest a mechanism for its action.

12.123 As we know, if a soft drink can is shaken and then opened, the drink escapes violently. However, if after shaking the can we tap it several times with a metal spoon, no such "explosion" of the drink occurs. Why?

12.124 Why are ice cubes (for example, those you see in the trays in the freezer of a refrigerator) cloudy inside?

12.125 Using Henry's law and the ideal gas equation to prove the statement that the volume of a gas that dissolves in a given amount of solvent is *independent* of the pressure of the gas. (*Hint:* Henry's law can be modified as $n = kP$, where n is the number of moles of the gas dissolved in the solvent.)

12.126 At 27°C, the vapor pressure of pure water is 23.76 mmHg and that of an urea solution is 22.98 mmHg. Calculate the molality of solution.

12.127 An example of the positive deviation shown in Figure 12.8(a) is a solution made of acetone (CH_3COCH_3) and carbon disulfide (CS_2). (a) Draw Lewis structures of these molecules. Explain the deviation from ideal behavior in terms of intermolecular forces. (b) A solution composed of 0.60 mole of acetone and 0.40 mole of carbon disulfide has a vapor pressure of 615 mmHg at 35.2°C. What would be the vapor pressure if the solution behaved ideally? The vapor pressure of the pure solvents at the same temperature are: acetone: 349 mmHg; carbon disulfide: 501 mmHg. (c) Predict the sign of ΔH_{soln}.

12.128 Liquids A (molar mass 100 g/mol) and B (molar mass 110 g/mol) form an ideal solution. At 55°C, A has a vapor pressure of 95 mmHg and B has a vapor pressure of 42 mmHg. A solution is prepared by mixing equal masses of A and B. (a) Calculate the mole fraction of each component in the solution. (b) Calculate the partial pressures of A and B over the solution at 55°C. (c) Suppose that some of the vapor described in (b) is condensed to a liquid. Calculate the mole fraction of each component in this liquid and the vapor pressure of each component above this liquid at 55°C.

Answers to Practice Exercises

12.1 Carbon disulfide. **12.2** 7.44 percent. **12.3** 0.638 m. **12.4** 8.92 m. **12.5** 13.8 m. **12.6** 2.9×10^{-4} M. **12.7** 37.8 mmHg; 4.4 mmHg. **12.8** T_b: 101.3°C; T_f: -4.48°C. **12.9** 21.0 atm. **12.10** 0.066 m and 1.3×10^2 g/mol. **12.11** 2.60×10^4 g. **12.12** 1.21.

CHEMICAL MYSTERY

The Wrong Knife[†]

Dr. Thomas Noguchi, the renowned Los Angeles coroner, was performing an autopsy on a young man in his twenties who had been stabbed to death. A Los Angeles Police Department homicide detective entered the room, carrying a brown bag that held the fatal weapon. "Do you want to take a look at it?" he asked.

"No," Dr. Noguchi said. "I'll tell *you* exactly what it looks like."

Dr. Noguchi wasn't showing off. He wanted to demonstrate an important forensic technique to the pathology residents who were observing the autopsy. The traditional method of measuring a knife was to pour barium sulfate ($BaSO_4$) solution into the wound and X ray it. Dr. Noguchi thought he had found a better way.

He lit a little Bunsen burner and melted some Wood's metal over it while the detective and the residents watched. (Wood's metal is an alloy of bismuth, lead, tin, and cadmium that has a low melting point of 71°C.) Then he selected a wound in the victim's chest above the location of the liver and poured the liquid metal into it. The metal slid down through the wound into the punctured liver. When it was cool he removed an exact mold of the tip of the murder weapon. He added the length of this tip to the distance between the liver and the skin surface of the chest. Then he said to the homicide detective, "It's a knife five and a half inches long, one inch wide and one sixteenth of an inch thick."

The detective smiled and reached into his bag. "Sorry, Dr. Noguchi." He pulled out a much smaller pocketknife, only about three inches in length.

"That's the wrong knife," Dr. Noguchi said at once.

"Oh, now, come on," the detective said. "We found the knife that killed him right at the scene."

"You don't have the murder weapon," Dr. Noguchi insisted.

The detective didn't believe him. But two days later police found a blood-stained knife in a trash can two blocks from the crime scene. That weapon was exactly five and a half inches long, one inch wide, and one sixteenth of an inch thick. And the blood on its blade matched the victim's.

It turned out to be the murder weapon. The pocketknife the police discovered at the scene had been used by the victim in self-defense. And two knives indicated a knife fight. Was it part of a gang war? The police investigated and found out that the victim was a member of a gang that was at war with another gang. By interrogating members of the rival gang, they eventually identified the murderer.

[†]Adapted with the permission of Simon & Schuster from "Coroner," by Thomas T. Noguchi, M.D., Copyright 1984 by Thomas Noguchi and Joseph DiMona.

Composition of Wood's Metal*

Component	Melting Point (°C)
Bismuth (50%)	271
Cadmium (12.5%)	321
Lead (25%)	328
Tin (12.5%)	232

* The components are shown in percent by mass, and the melting point is that of the pure metal.

Chemical Clues

1. What is the function of the $BaSO_4$ solution as a traditional method for measuring a knife wound in a homicide victim's body? Describe a medical application of $BaSO_4$.

2. As the table shows, the melting points of the pure metals are much higher than that of Wood's metal. What phenomenon accounts for its low melting point?

3. Wood's metal is used in automatic sprinklers in the ceilings of hotels and stores. Explain how such a sprinkling system works.

4. The melting point of an alloy can be altered by changing the composition. Certain organic materials have also been developed for the same purpose. Shown below is a simplified diagram of the pop-up thermometer used in cooking turkeys. Describe how this thermometer works.

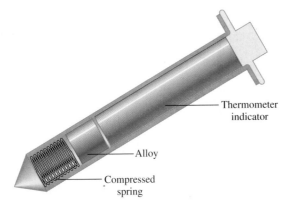

A pop-up thermometer used for cooking turkeys.

A hot platinum wire glows when held over a concentrated ammonia solution. The oxidation of ammonia to produce nitric oxide and water, catalyzed by platinum, is highly exothermic. This reaction is the first step toward the synthesis of nitric acid. The models show ammonia, oxygen, nitric oxide, and water molecules.

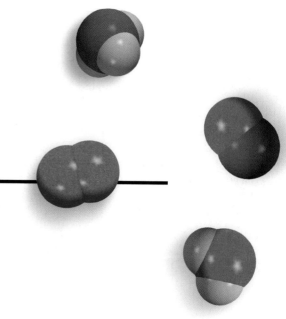

13

Chemical Kinetics

Appendix 1

Derivation of the Names of Elements*

Element	Symbol	Atomic No.	Atomic Mass[†]	Date of Discovery	Discoverer and Nationality[‡]	Derivation
Actinium	Ac	89	(227)	1899	A. Debierne (Fr.)	Gr. *aktis*, beam or ray
Aluminum	Al	13	26.98	1827	F. Woehler (Ge.)	Alum, the aluminum compound in which it was discovered; derived from L. *alumen*, astringent taste
Americium	Am	95	(243)	1944	A. Ghiorso (USA) R. A. James (USA) G. T. Seaborg (USA) S. G. Thompson (USA)	The Americas
Antimony	Sb	51	121.8	Ancient		L. *antimonium* (*anti*, opposite of; *monium*, isolated condition), so named because it is a tangible (metallic) substance which combines readily; symbol L. *stibium*, mark
Argon	Ar	18	39.95	1894	Lord Raleigh (GB) Sir William Ramsay (GB)	Gr. *argos*, inactive
Arsenic	As	33	74.92	1250	Albertus Magnus (Ge.)	Gr. *aksenikon*, yellow pigment; L. *arsenicum*, orpiment; the Greeks once used arsenic trisulfide as a pigment
Astatine	At	85	(210)	1940	D. R. Corson (USA) K. R. MacKenzie (USA) E. Segre (USA)	Gr. *astatos*, unstable
Barium	Ba	56	137.3	1808	Sir Humphry Davy (GB)	barite, a heavy spar, derived from Gr. *barys*, heavy
Berkelium	Bk	97	(247)	1950	G. T. Seaborg (USA) S. G. Thompson (USA) A. Ghiorso (USA)	Berkeley, Calif.
Beryllium	Be	4	9.012	1828	F. Woehler (Ge.) A. A. B. Bussy (Fr.)	Fr. L. *beryl*, sweet

(Continued)

Source: Reprinted with permission from "The Elements and Derivation of Their Names and Symbols," G. P. Dinga, *Chemistry* **41** (2), 20–22 (1968). Copyright by the American Chemical Society.

* At the time this table was drawn up, only 103 elements were known to exist.

† The atomic masses given here correspond to the 1961 values of the Commission on Atomic Weights. Masses in parentheses are those of the most stable or most common isotopes.

‡ The abbreviations are (Ar.) Arabic; (Au.) Austrian; (Du.) Dutch; (Fr.) French; (Ge.) German; (GB) British; (Gr.) Greek; (H.) Hungarian; (I.) Italian; (L.) Latin; (P.) Polish; (R.) Russian; (Sp.) Spanish; (Swe.) Swedish; (USA) American.

Element	Symbol	Atomic No.	Atomic Mass[†]	Date of Discovery	Discoverer and Nationality[‡]	Derivation
Bismuth	Bi	83	209.0	1753	Claude Geoffroy (Fr.)	Ge. *bismuth*, probably a distortion of *weisse masse* (white mass) in which it was found
Boron	B	5	10.81	1808	Sir Humphry Davy (GB) J. L. Gay-Lussac (Fr.) L. J. Thenard (Fr.)	The compound borax, derived from Ar. *buraq*, white
Bromine	Br	35	79.90	1826	A. J. Balard (Fr.)	Gr. *bromos*, stench
Cadmium	Cd	48	112.4	1817	Fr. Stromeyer (Ge.)	Gr. *kadmia*, earth; L. *cadmia*, calamine (because it is found along with calamine)
Calcium	Ca	20	40.08	1808	Sir Humphry Davy (GB)	L. *calx*, lime
Californium	Cf	98	(249)	1950	G. T. Seaborg (USA) S. G. Thompson (USA) A. Ghiorso (USA) K. Street, Jr. (USA)	California
Carbon	C	6	12.01	Ancient		L. *carbo*, charcoal
Cerium	Ce	58	140.1	1803	J. J. Berzelius (Swe.) William Hisinger (Swe.) M. H. Klaproth (Ge.)	Asteroid Ceres
Cesium	Cs	55	132.9	1860	R. Bunsen (Ge.) G. R. Kirchhoff (Ge.)	L. *caesium*, blue (cesium was discovered by its spectral lines, which are blue)
Chlorine	Cl	17	35.45	1774	K. W. Scheele (Swe.)	Gr. *chloros*, light green
Chromium	Cr	24	52.00	1797	L. N. Vauquelin (Fr.)	Gr. *chroma*, color (because it is used in pigments)
Cobalt	Co	27	58.93	1735	G. Brandt (Ge.)	Ge. *Kobold*, goblin (because the ore yielded cobalt instead of the expected metal, copper, it was attributed to goblins)
Copper	Cu	29	63.55	Ancient		L. *cuprum*, copper, derived from *cyprium*, Island of Cyprus, the main source of ancient copper
Curium	Cm	96	(247)	1944	G. T. Seaborg (USA) R. A. James (USA) A. Ghiorso (USA)	Pierre and Marie Curie
Dysprosium	Dy	66	162.5	1886	Lecoq de Boisbaudran (Fr.)	Gr. *dysprositos*, hard to get at
Einsteinium	Es	99	(254)	1952	A. Ghiorso (USA)	Albert Einstein
Erbium	Er	68	167.3	1843	C. G. Mosander (Swe.)	Ytterby, Sweden, where many rare earths were discovered
Europium	Eu	63	152.0	1896	E. Demarcay (Fr.)	Europe

(Continued)

Element	Symbol	Atomic No.	Atomic Mass[†]	Date of Discovery	Discoverer and Nationality[‡]	Derivation
Fermium	Fm	100	(253)	1953	A. Ghiorso (USA)	Enrico Fermi
Fluorine	F	9	19.00	1886	H. Moissan (Fr.)	Mineral fluorspar, from L. *fluere*, flow (because fluorspar was used as a flux)
Francium	Fr	87	(223)	1939	Marguerite Perey (Fr.)	France
Gadolinium	Gd	64	157.3	1880	J. C. Marignac (Fr.)	Johan Gadolin, Finnish rare earth chemist
Gallium	Ga	31	69.72	1875	Lecoq de Boisbaudran (Fr.)	L. *Gallia*, France
Germanium	Ge	32	72.59	1886	Clemens Winkler (Ge.)	L. *Germania*, Germany
Gold	Au	79	197.0	Ancient		L. *aurum*, shining dawn
Hafnium	Hf	72	178.5	1923	D. Coster (Du.) G. von Hevesey (H.)	L. *Hafnia*, Copenhagen
Helium	He	2	4.003	1868	P. Janssen (spectr) (Fr.) Sir William Ramsay (isolated) (GB)	Gr. *helios*, sun (because it was first discovered in the sun's spectrum)
Holmium	Ho	67	164.9	1879	P. T. Cleve (Swe.)	L. *Holmia*, Stockholm
Hydrogen	H	1	1.008	1766	Sir Henry Cavendish (GB)	Gr. *hydro*, water; *genes*, forming (because it produces water when burned with oxygen)
Indium	In	49	114.8	1863	F. Reich (Ge.) T. Richter (Ge.)	Indigo, because of its indigo blue lines in the spectrum
Iodine	I	53	126.9	1811	B. Courtois (Fr.)	Gr. *iodes*, violet
Iridium	Ir	77	192.2	1803	S. Tennant (GB)	L. *iris*, rainbow
Iron	Fe	26	55.85	Ancient		L. *ferrum*, iron
Krypton	Kr	36	83.80	1898	Sir William Ramsay (GB) M. W. Travers (GB)	Gr. *kryptos*, hidden
Lanthanum	La	57	138.9	1839	C. G. Mosander (Swe.)	Gr. *lanthanein*, concealed
Lawrencium	Lr	103	(257)	1961	A. Ghiorso (USA) T. Sikkeland (USA) A. E. Larsh (USA) R. M. Latimer (USA)	E. O. Lawrence (USA), inventor of the cyclotron
Lead	Pb	82	207.2	Ancient		Symbol, L. *plumbum*, lead, meaning heavy
Lithium	Li	3	6.941	1817	A. Arfvedson (Swe.)	Gr. *lithos*, rock (because it occurs in rocks)
Lutetium	Lu	71	175.0	1907	G. Urbain (Fr.) C. A. von Welsbach (Au.)	*Luteria*, ancient name for Paris
Magnesium	Mg	12	24.31	1808	Sir Humphry Davy (GB)	*Magnesia*, a district in Thessaly; possibly derived from L. *magnesia*
Manganese	Mn	25	54.94	1774	J. G. Gahn (Swe.)	L. *magnes*, magnet

(Continued)

Element	Symbol	Atomic No.	Atomic Mass[†]	Date of Discovery	Discoverer and Nationality[‡]	Derivation
Mendelevium	Md	101	(256)	1955	A. Ghiorso (USA) G. R. Choppin (USA) G. T. Seaborg (USA) B. G. Harvey (USA) S. G. Thompson (USA)	Mendeleev, Russian chemist who prepared the periodic chart and predicted properties of undiscovered elements
Mercury	Hg	80	200.6	Ancient		Symbol, L. *hydrargyrum,* liquid silver
Molybdenum	Mo	42	95.94	1778	G. W. Scheele (Swe.)	Gr. *molybdos,* lead
Neodymium	Nd	60	144.2	1885	C. A. von Welsbach (Au.)	Gr. *neos,* new; *didymos,* twin
Neon	Ne	10	20.18	1898	Sir William Ramsay (GB) M. W. Travers (GB)	Gr. *neos,* new
Neptunium	Np	93	(237)	1940	E. M. McMillan (USA) P. H. Abelson (USA)	Planet Neptune
Nickel	Ni	28	58.69	1751	A. F. Cronstedt (Swe.)	Swe. *kopparnickel,* false copper; also Ge. *nickel,* referring to the devil that prevented copper from being extracted from nickel ores
Niobium	Nb	41	92.91	1801	Charles Hatchett (GB)	Gr. *Niobe,* daughter of Tantalus (niobium was considered identical to tantalum, named after *Tantalus,* until 1884)
Nitrogen	N	7	14.01	1772	Daniel Rutherford (GB)	Fr. *nitrogene,* derived from L. *nitrum,* native soda, or Gr. *nitron,* native soda, and Gr. *genes,* forming
Nobelium	No	102	(253)	1958	A. Ghiorso (USA) T. Sikkeland (USA) J. R. Walton (USA) G. T. Seaborg (USA)	Alfred Nobel
Osmium	Os	76	190.2	1803	S. Tennant (GB)	Gr. *osme,* odor
Oxygen	O	8	16.00	1774	Joseph Priestley (GB) C. W. Scheele (Swe.)	Fr. *oxygene,* generator of acid, derived from Gr. *oxys,* acid, and L. *genes,* forming (because it was once thought to be a part of all acids)
Palladium	Pd	46	106.4	1803	W. H. Wollaston (GB)	Asteroid Pallas
Phosphorus	P	15	30.97	1669	H. Brandt (Ge.)	Gr. *phosphoros,* light bearing
Platinum	Pt	78	195.1	1735 1741	A. de Ulloa (Sp.) Charles Wood (GB)	Sp. *platina,* silver

(Continued)

Element	Symbol	Atomic No.	Atomic Mass[†]	Date of Discovery	Discoverer and Nationality[‡]	Derivation
Plutonium	Pu	94	(242)	1940	G. T. Seaborg (USA) E. M. McMillan (USA) J. W. Kennedy (USA) A. C. Wahl (USA)	Planet Pluto
Polonium	Po	84	(210)	1898	Marie Curie (P.)	Poland
Potassium	K	19	39.10	1807	Sir Humphry Davy (GB)	Symbol, L. *kalium*, potash
Praseodymium	Pr	59	140.9	1885	C. A. von Welsbach (Au.)	Gr. *prasios*, green; *didymos*, twin
Promethium	Pm	61	(147)	1945	J. A. Marinsky (USA) L. E. Glendenin (USA) C. D. Coryell (USA)	Gr. mythology, *Prometheus*, the Greek Titan who stole fire from heaven
Protactinium	Pa	91	(231)	1917	O. Hahn (Ge.) L. Meitner (Au.)	Gr. *protos*, first; *actinium* (because it distintegrates into actinium)
Radium	Ra	88	(226)	1898	Pierre and Marie Curie (Fr.; P.)	L. *radius*, ray
Radon	Rn	86	(222)	1900	F. E. Dorn (Ge.)	Derived from radium
Rhenium	Re	75	186.2	1925	W. Noddack (Ge.) I. Tacke (Ge.) Otto Berg (Ge.)	L. *Rhenus*, Rhine
Rhodium	Rh	45	102.9	1804	W. H. Wollaston (GB)	Gr. *rhodon*, rose (because some of its salts are rose-colored)
Rubidium	Rb	37	85.47	1861	R. W. Bunsen (Ge.) G. Kirchhoff (Ge.)	L. *rubidus*, dark red (discovered with the spectroscope, its spectrum shows red lines)
Ruthenium	Ru	44	101.1	1844	K. K. Klaus (R.)	L. *Ruthenia*, Russia
Samarium	Sm	62	150.4	1879	Lecoq de Boisbaurdran (Fr.)	Samarskite, after Samarski, a Russian engineer
Scandium	Sc	21	44.96	1879	L. F. Nilson (Swe.)	Scandinavia
Selenium	Se	34	78.96	1817	J. J. Berzelius (Swe.)	Gr. *selene*, moon (because it resembles tellurium, named for the earth)
Silicon	Si	14	28.09	1824	J. J. Berzelius (Swe.)	L. *silex, silicis,* flint
Silver	Ag	47	107.9	Ancient		Symbol, L. *argentum*, silver
Sodium	Na	11	22.99	1807	Sir Humphry Davy (GB)	L. *sodanum*, headache remedy; symbol, L. *natrium*, soda
Strontium	Sr	38	87.62	1808	Sir Humphry Davy (GB)	Strontian, Scotland, derived from mineral strontionite

(Continued)

Element	Symbol	Atomic No.	Atomic Mass[†]	Date of Discovery	Discoverer and Nationality[‡]	Derivation
Sulfur	S	16	32.07	Ancient		L. *sulphurium* (Sanskrit, *sulvere*)
Tantalum	Ta	73	180.9	1802	A. G. Ekeberg (Swe.)	Gr. mythology, *Tantalus,* because of difficulty in isolating it
Technetium	Tc	43	(99)	1937	C. Perrier (I.)	Gr. *technetos,* artificial (because it was the first artificial element)
Tellurium	Te	52	127.6	1782	F. J. Müller (Au.)	L. *tellus,* earth
Terbium	Tb	65	158.9	1843	C. G. Mosander (Swe.)	Ytterby, Sweden
Thallium	Tl	81	204.4	1861	Sir William Crookes (GB)	Gr. *thallos,* a budding twig (because its spectrum shows a bright green line)
Thorium	Th	90	232.0	1828	J. J. Berzelius (Swe.)	Mineral thorite, derived from *Thor,* Norse god of war
Thulium	Tm	69	168.9	1879	P. T. Cleve (Swe.)	*Thule,* early name for Scandinavia
Tin	Sn	50	118.7	Ancient		Symbol, L. *stannum,* tin
Titanium	Ti	22	47.88	1791	W. Gregor (GB)	Gr. giants, the Titans, and L. titans, giant deities
Tungsten	W	74	183.9	1783	J. J. and F. de Elhuyar (Sp.)	Swe. *tung sten,* heavy stone; symbol, wolframite, a mineral
Uranium	U	92	238.0	1789 1841	M. H. Klaproth (Ge.) E. M. Peligot (Fr.)	Planet Uranus
Vanadium	V	23	50.94	1801 1830	A. M. del Rio (Sp.) N. G. Sefstrom (Swe.)	*Vanadis,* Norse goddess of love and beauty
Xenon	Xe	54	131.3	1898	Sir William Ramsay (GB) M. W. Travers (GB)	Gr. *xenos,* stranger
Ytterbium	Yb	70	173.0	1907	G. Urbain (Fr.)	Ytterby, Sweden
Yttrium	Y	39	88.91	1843	C. G. Mosander (Swe.)	Ytterby, Sweden
Zinc	Zn	30	65.39	1746	A. S. Marggraf (Ge.)	Ge. *zink,* of obscure origin
Zirconium	Zr	40	91.22	1789	M. H. Klaproth (Ge.)	Zircon, in which it was found, derived from *Ar. zargum,* gold color

Appendix 2

Units for the Gas Constant

In this appendix we will see how the gas constant R can be expressed in units J/K · mol. Our first step is to derive a relationship between atm and pascal. We start with

$$\begin{aligned} \text{pressure} &= \frac{\text{force}}{\text{area}} \\ &= \frac{\text{mass} \times \text{acceleration}}{\text{area}} \\ &= \frac{\text{volume} \times \text{density} \times \text{acceleration}}{\text{area}} \\ &= \text{length} \times \text{density} \times \text{acceleration} \end{aligned}$$

By definition, the standard atmosphere is the pressure exerted by a column of mercury exactly 76 cm high of density 13.5951 g/cm^3, in a place where acceleration due to gravity is 980.665 cm/s^2. However, to express pressure in N/m^2 it is necessary to write

$$\begin{aligned} \text{density of mercury} &= 1.35951 \times 10^4 \, \text{kg/m}^3 \\ \text{acceleration due to gravity} &= 9.80665 \, \text{m/s}^2 \end{aligned}$$

The standard atmosphere is given by

$$\begin{aligned} 1 \, \text{atm} &= (0.76 \, \text{m Hg})(1.35951 \times 10^4 \, \text{kg/m}^3)(9.80665 \, \text{m/s}^2) \\ &= 101{,}325 \, \text{kg m/m}^2 \cdot \text{s}^2 \\ &= 101{,}325 \, \text{N/m}^2 \\ &= 101{,}325 \, \text{Pa} \end{aligned}$$

From Section 5.5 we see that the gas constant R is given by 0.082057 L · atm/K · mol. Using the conversion factors

$$\begin{aligned} 1 \, \text{L} &= 1 \times 10^{-3} \, \text{m}^3 \\ 1 \, \text{atm} &= 101{,}325 \, \text{N/m}^2 \end{aligned}$$

we write

$$\begin{aligned} R &= \left(0.082057 \, \frac{\text{L atm}}{\text{K mol}}\right)\left(\frac{1 \times 10^{-3} \, \text{m}^3}{1 \, \text{L}}\right)\left(\frac{101{,}325 \, \text{N/m}^2}{1 \, \text{atm}}\right) \\ &= 8.314 \, \frac{\text{N m}}{\text{K mol}} \\ &= 8.314 \, \frac{\text{J}}{\text{K mol}} \end{aligned}$$

and

$$\begin{aligned} 1 \, \text{L} \cdot \text{atm} &= (1 \times 10^{-3} \, \text{m}^3)(101{,}325 \, \text{N/m}^2) \\ &= 101.3 \, \text{N m} \\ &= 101.3 \, \text{J} \end{aligned}$$

Appendix 3

Thermodynamic Data at 1 atm and 25°C*

Inorganic Substances			
Substance	ΔH_f° (kJ/mol)	ΔG_f° (kJ/mol)	S° (J/K · mol)
Ag(s)	0	0	42.7
$Ag^+(aq)$	105.9	77.1	73.9
AgCl(s)	−127.0	−109.7	96.1
AgBr(s)	−99.5	−95.9	107.1
AgI(s)	−62.4	−66.3	114.2
$AgNO_3(s)$	−123.1	−32.2	140.9
Al(s)	0	0	28.3
$Al^{3+}(aq)$	−524.7	−481.2	−313.38
$Al_2O_3(s)$	−1669.8	−1576.4	50.99
As(s)	0	0	35.15
$AsO_4^{3-}(aq)$	−870.3	−635.97	−144.77
$AsH_3(g)$	171.5		
$H_3AsO_4(s)$	−900.4		
Au(s)	0	0	47.7
$Au_2O_3(s)$	80.8	163.2	125.5
AuCl(s)	−35.2		
$AuCl_3(s)$	−118.4		
B(s)	0	0	6.5
$B_2O_3(s)$	−1263.6	−1184.1	54.0
$H_3BO_3(s)$	−1087.9	−963.16	89.58
$H_3BO_3(aq)$	−1067.8	−963.3	159.8
Ba(s)	0	0	66.9
$Ba^{2+}(aq)$	−538.4	−560.66	12.55
BaO(s)	−558.2	−528.4	70.3
$BaCl_2(s)$	−860.1	−810.66	125.5
$BaSO_4(s)$	−1464.4	−1353.1	132.2
$BaCO_3(s)$	−1218.8	−1138.9	112.1
Be(s)	0	0	9.5
BeO(s)	−610.9	−581.58	14.1
$Br_2(l)$	0	0	152.3
$Br^-(aq)$	−120.9	102.8	80.7
HBr(g)	−36.2	−53.2	198.48
C(graphite)	0	0	5.69
C(diamond)	1.90	2.87	2.4
CO(g)	−110.5	−137.3	197.9
$CO_2(g)$	−393.5	−394.4	213.6
$CO_2(aq)$	−412.9	−386.2	121.3
$CO_3^{2-}(aq)$	−676.3	−528.1	−53.1

(Continued)

* The thermodynamic quantities of ions are based on the reference states that $\Delta H_f^\circ[H^+(aq)] = 0$, $\Delta G_f^\circ[H^+(aq)] = 0$, and $S^\circ[H^+(aq)] = 0$

Substance	ΔH_f° (kJ/mol)	ΔG_f° (kJ/mol)	S° (J/K · mol)
$HCO_3^-(aq)$	−691.1	−587.1	94.98
$H_2CO_3(aq)$	−699.7	−623.2	187.4
$CS_2(g)$	115.3	65.1	237.8
$CS_2(l)$	87.3	63.6	151.0
$HCN(aq)$	105.4	112.1	128.9
$CN^-(aq)$	151.0	165.69	117.99
$(NH_2)_2CO(s)$	−333.19	−197.15	104.6
$(NH_2)_2CO(aq)$	−319.2	−203.84	173.85
$Ca(s)$	0	0	41.6
$Ca^{2+}(aq)$	−542.96	−553.0	−55.2
$CaO(s)$	−635.6	−604.2	39.8
$Ca(OH)_2(s)$	−986.6	−896.8	83.4
$CaF_2(s)$	−1214.6	−1161.9	68.87
$CaCl_2(s)$	−794.96	−750.19	113.8
$CaSO_4(s)$	−1432.69	−1320.3	106.69
$CaCO_3(s)$	−1206.9	−1128.8	92.9
$Cd(s)$	0	0	51.46
$Cd^{2+}(aq)$	−72.38	−77.7	−61.09
$CdO(s)$	−254.6	−225.06	54.8
$CdCl_2(s)$	−389.1	−342.59	118.4
$CdSO_4(s)$	−926.17	−820.2	137.2
$Cl_2(g)$	0	0	223.0
$Cl^-(aq)$	−167.2	−131.2	56.5
$HCl(g)$	−92.3	−95.27	187.0
$Co(s)$	0	0	28.45
$Co^{2+}(aq)$	−67.36	−51.46	155.2
$CoO(s)$	−239.3	−213.38	43.9
$Cr(s)$	0	0	23.77
$Cr^{2+}(aq)$	−138.9		
$Cr_2O_3(s)$	−1128.4	−1046.8	81.17
$CrO_4^{2-}(aq)$	−863.16	−706.26	38.49
$Cr_2O_7^{2-}(aq)$	−1460.6	−1257.29	213.8
$Cs(s)$	0	0	82.8
$Cs^+(aq)$	−247.69	−282.0	133.05
$Cu(s)$	0	0	33.3
$Cu^+(aq)$	51.88	50.2	40.6
$Cu^{2+}(aq)$	64.39	64.98	−99.6
$CuO(s)$	−155.2	−127.2	43.5
$Cu_2O(s)$	−166.69	−146.36	100.8
$CuCl(s)$	−134.7	−118.8	91.6
$CuCl_2(s)$	−205.85	?	?
$CuS(s)$	−48.5	−49.0	66.5
$CuSO_4(s)$	−769.86	−661.9	113.39
$F_2(g)$	0	0	203.34
$F^-(aq)$	−329.1	−276.48	−9.6
$HF(g)$	−271.6	−270.7	173.5
$Fe(s)$	0	0	27.2
$Fe^{2+}(aq)$	−87.86	−84.9	−113.39

(Continued)

Substance	ΔH_f° (kJ/mol)	ΔG_f° (kJ/mol)	S° (J/K · mol)
$Fe^{3+}(aq)$	−47.7	−10.5	−293.3
$FeO(s)$	−272.0	−255.2	60.8
$Fe_2O_3(s)$	−822.2	−741.0	90.0
$Fe(OH)_2(s)$	−568.19	−483.55	79.5
$Fe(OH)_3(s)$	−824.25	?	?
$H(g)$	218.2	203.2	114.6
$H_2(g)$	0	0	131.0
$H^+(aq)$	0	0	0
$OH^-(aq)$	−229.94	−157.30	−10.5
$H_2O(g)$	−241.8	−228.6	188.7
$H_2O(l)$	−285.8	−237.2	69.9
$H_2O_2(l)$	−187.6	−118.1	?
$Hg(l)$	0	0	77.4
$Hg^{2+}(aq)$		−164.38	
$HgO(s)$	−90.7	−58.5	72.0
$HgCl_2(s)$	−230.1		
$Hg_2Cl_2(s)$	−264.9	−210.66	196.2
$HgS(s)$	−58.16	−48.8	77.8
$HgSO_4(s)$	−704.17		
$Hg_2SO_4(s)$	−741.99	−623.92	200.75
$I_2(s)$	0	0	116.7
$I^-(aq)$	55.9	51.67	109.37
$HI(g)$	25.9	1.30	206.3
$K(s)$	0	0	63.6
$K^+(aq)$	−251.2	−282.28	102.5
$KOH(s)$	−425.85		
$KCl(s)$	−435.87	−408.3	82.68
$KClO_3(s)$	−391.20	−289.9	142.97
$KClO_4(s)$	−433.46	−304.18	151.0
$KBr(s)$	−392.17	−379.2	96.4
$KI(s)$	−327.65	−322.29	104.35
$KNO_3(s)$	−492.7	−393.1	132.9
$Li(s)$	0	0	28.0
$Li^+(aq)$	−278.46	−293.8	14.2
$Li_2O(s)$	−595.8	?	?
$LiOH(s)$	−487.2	−443.9	50.2
$Mg(s)$	0	0	32.5
$Mg^{2+}(aq)$	−461.96	−456.0	−117.99
$MgO(s)$	−601.8	−569.6	26.78
$Mg(OH)_2(s)$	−924.66	−833.75	63.1
$MgCl_2(s)$	−641.8	−592.3	89.5
$MgSO_4(s)$	−1278.2	−1173.6	91.6
$MgCO_3(s)$	−1112.9	−1029.3	65.69
$Mn(s)$	0	0	31.76
$Mn^{2+}(aq)$	−218.8	−223.4	−83.68
$MnO_2(s)$	−520.9	−466.1	53.1
$N_2(g)$	0	0	191.5
$N_3^-(aq)$	245.18	?	?

(Continued)

Substance	ΔH_f° (kJ/mol)	ΔG_f° (kJ/mol)	S° (J/K · mol)
$NH_3(g)$	−46.3	−16.6	193.0
$NH_4^+(aq)$	−132.80	−79.5	112.8
$NH_4Cl(s)$	−315.39	−203.89	94.56
$NH_3(aq)$	−80.3	−26.5	111.3
$N_2H_4(l)$	50.4		
$NO(g)$	90.4	86.7	210.6
$NO_2(g)$	33.85	51.8	240.46
$N_2O_4(g)$	9.66	98.29	304.3
$N_2O(g)$	81.56	103.6	219.99
$HNO_2(aq)$	−118.8	−53.6	
$HNO_3(l)$	−173.2	−79.9	155.6
$NO_3^-(aq)$	−206.57	−110.5	146.4
$Na(s)$	0	0	51.05
$Na^+(aq)$	−239.66	−261.87	60.25
$Na_2O(s)$	−415.89	−376.56	72.8
$NaCl(s)$	−411.0	−384.0	72.38
$NaI(s)$	−288.0		
$Na_2SO_4(s)$	−1384.49	−1266.8	149.49
$NaNO_3(s)$	−466.68	−365.89	116.3
$Na_2CO_3(s)$	−1130.9	−1047.67	135.98
$NaHCO_3(s)$	−947.68	−851.86	102.09
$Ni(s)$	0	0	30.1
$Ni^{2+}(aq)$	−64.0	−46.4	159.4
$NiO(s)$	−244.35	−216.3	38.58
$Ni(OH)_2(s)$	−538.06	−453.1	79.5
$O(g)$	249.4	230.1	160.95
$O_2(g)$	0	0	205.0
$O_3(aq)$	−12.09	16.3	110.88
$O_3(g)$	142.2	163.4	237.6
$P(white)$	0	0	44.0
$P(red)$	−18.4	13.8	29.3
$PO_4^{3-}(aq)$	−1284.07	−1025.59	−217.57
$P_4O_{10}(s)$	−3012.48		
$PH_3(g)$	9.25	18.2	210.0
$HPO_4^{2-}(aq)$	−1298.7	−1094.1	−35.98
$H_2PO_4^-(aq)$	−1302.48	−1135.1	89.1
$Pb(s)$	0	0	64.89
$Pb^{2+}(aq)$	1.6	24.3	21.3
$PbO(s)$	−217.86	−188.49	69.45
$PbO_2(s)$	−276.65	−218.99	76.57
$PbCl_2(s)$	−359.2	−313.97	136.4
$PbS(s)$	−94.3	−92.68	91.2
$PbSO_4(s)$	−918.4	−811.2	147.28
$Pt(s)$	0	0	41.84
$PtCl_4^{2-}(aq)$	−516.3	−384.5	175.7
$Rb(s)$	0	0	69.45
$Rb^+(aq)$	−246.4	−282.2	124.27
$S(rhombic)$	0	0	31.88

(Continued)

Substance	ΔH_f° (kJ/mol)	ΔG_f° (kJ/mol)	S° (J/K · mol)
S(monoclinic)	0.30	0.10	32.55
$SO_2(g)$	−296.4	−300.4	248.5
$SO_3(g)$	−395.2	−370.4	256.2
$SO_3^{2-}(aq)$	−624.25	−497.06	43.5
$SO_4^{2-}(aq)$	−907.5	−741.99	17.15
$H_2S(g)$	−20.15	−33.0	205.64
$HSO_3^-(aq)$	−627.98	−527.3	132.38
$HSO_4^-(aq)$	−885.75	−752.87	126.86
$H_2SO_4(l)$	−811.3	?	?
$SF_6(g)$	−1096.2	?	?
Se(s)	0	0	42.44
$SeO_2(s)$	−225.35		
$H_2Se(g)$	29.7	15.90	218.9
Si(s)	0	0	18.70
$SiO_2(s)$	−859.3	−805.0	41.84
Sr(s)	0	0	54.39
$Sr^{2+}(aq)$	−545.5	−557.3	39.33
$SrCl_2(s)$	−828.4	−781.15	117.15
$SrSO_4(s)$	−1444.74	−1334.28	121.75
$SrCO_3(s)$	−1218.38	−1137.6	97.07
W(s)	0	0	33.47
$WO_3(s)$	−840.3	−763.45	83.26
$WO_4^-(aq)$	−1115.45		
Zn(s)	0	0	41.6
$Zn^{2+}(aq)$	−152.4	−147.2	106.48
ZnO(s)	−348.0	−318.2	43.9
$ZnCl_2(s)$	−415.89	−369.26	108.37
ZnS(s)	−202.9	−198.3	57.7
$ZnSO_4(s)$	−978.6	−871.6	124.7

Organic Substances

Substance	Formula	ΔH_f° (kJ/mol)	ΔG_f° (kJ/mol)	S° (J/K · mol)
Acetic acid(l)	CH_3COOH	−484.2	−389.45	159.8
Acetaldehyde(g)	CH_3CHO	−166.35	−139.08	264.2
Acetone(l)	CH_3COCH_3	−246.8	−153.55	198.7
Acetylene(g)	C_2H_2	226.6	209.2	200.8
Benzene(l)	C_6H_6	49.04	124.5	172.8
Ethanol(l)	C_2H_5OH	−276.98	−174.18	161.0
Ethane(g)	C_2H_6	−84.7	−32.89	229.5
Ethylene(g)	C_2H_4	52.3	68.1	219.5
Formic acid(l)	HCOOH	−409.2	−346.0	129.0
Glucose(s)	$C_6H_{12}O_6$	−1274.5	−910.56	212.1
Methane(g)	CH_4	−74.85	−50.8	186.2
Methanol(l)	CH_3OH	−238.7	−166.3	126.8
Sucrose(s)	$C_{12}H_{22}O_{11}$	−2221.7	−1544.3	360.2

Mathematical Operations

Logarithms

Common Logarithms

The concept of the logarithms is an extension of the concept of exponents, which is discussed in Chapter 1. The *common,* or base-10, logarithm of any number is the power to which 10 must be raised to equal the number. The following examples illustrate this relationship:

Logarithm	Exponent
$\log 1 = 0$	$10^0 = 1$
$\log 10 = 1$	$10^1 = 10$
$\log 100 = 2$	$10^2 = 100$
$\log 10^{-1} = -1$	$10^{-1} = 0.1$
$\log 10^{-2} = -2$	$10^{-2} = 0.01$

In each case the logarithm of the number can be obtained by inspection.

Because the logarithms of numbers are exponents, they have the same properties as exponents. Thus, we have

Logarithm	Exponent
$\log AB = \log A + \log B$	$10^A \times 10^B = 10^{A+B}$
$\log \dfrac{A}{B} = \log A - \log B$	$\dfrac{10^A}{10^B} = 10^{A-B}$

Furthermore, $\log A^n = n \log A$.

Now suppose we want to find the common logarithm of 6.7×10^{-4}. On most electronic calculators, the number is entered first and then the log key is punched. This operation gives us

$$\log 6.7 \times 10^{-4} = -3.17$$

Note that there are as many digits *after* the decimal point as there are significant figures in the original number. The original number has two significant figures and the "17" in -3.17 tells us that the log has two significant figures. The "3" in -3.17 serves only to locate the decimal point in the number 6.7×10^{-4}. Other examples are

Number	Common Logarithm
62	1.79
0.872	-0.0595
1.0×10^{-7}	-7.00

Sometimes (as in the case of pH calculations) it is necessary to obtain the number whose logarithm is known. This procedure is known as taking the antilogarithm; it is simply the reverse of taking the logarithm of a number. Suppose in a certain calculation we have $pH = 1.46$ and are asked to calculate $[H^+]$. From the definition of pH ($pH = -\log [H^+]$) we can write

$$[H^+] = 10^{-1.46}$$

Many calculators have a key labeled $\log^{-1}$ or INV log to obtain antilogs. Other calculators have a 10^x or y^x key (where x corresponds to -1.46 in our example and y is 10 for base-10 logarithm). Therefore, we find that $[H^+] = 0.035$ *M*.

Natural Logarithms

Logarithms taken to the base e instead of 10 are known as natural logarithms (denoted by ln or $\log_e$); e is equal to 2.7183. The relationship between common logarithms and natural logarithms is as follows:

$$\log 10 = 1 \qquad\qquad 10^1 = 10$$
$$\ln 10 = 2.303 \qquad e^{2.303} = 10$$

Thus

$$\ln x = 2.303 \log x$$

To find the natural logarithm of 2.27, say, we first enter the number on the electronic calculator and then punch the ln key to get

$$\ln 2.27 = 0.820$$

If no ln key is provided, we can proceed as follows:

$$2.303 \log 2.27 = 2.303 \times 0.356$$
$$= 0.820$$

Sometimes we may be given the natural logarithm and asked to find the number it represents. For example

$$\ln x = 59.7$$

On many calculators, we simply enter the number and punch the e key:

$$e^{59.7} = 8 \times 10^{25}$$

The Quadratic Equation

A quadratic equation takes the form

$$ax^2 + bx + c = 0$$

If coefficients a, b, and c are known, then x is given by

$$x = \frac{-b \pm \sqrt{b^2 - 4ac}}{2a}$$

Suppose we have the following quadratic equation:

$$2x^2 + 5x - 12 = 0$$

Solving for x, we write

$$x = \frac{-5 \pm \sqrt{(5)^2 - 4(2)(-12)}}{2(2)}$$
$$= \frac{-5 \pm \sqrt{25 + 96}}{4}$$

Therefore

$$x = \frac{-5 + 11}{4} = \frac{3}{2}$$

and

$$x = \frac{-5 - 11}{4} = -4$$

Glossary*

A

absolute temperature scale. A temperature scale that uses the absolute zero of temperature as the lowest temperature. (5.3)

absolute zero. Theoretically the lowest attainable temperature. (5.3)

acceptor impurities. Impurities that can accept electrons from semiconductors. (20.3)

accuracy. The closeness of a measurement to the true value of the quantity that is measured. (1.8)

acid. A substance that yields hydrogen ions (H^+) when dissolved in water. (2.7)

acid ionization constant (K_a). The equilibrium constant for the acid ionization. (15.5)

actinide series. Elements that have incompletely filled $5f$ subshells or readily give rise to cations that have incompletely filled $5f$ subshells. (7.9)

activated complex. The species temporarily formed by the reactant molecules as a result of the collision before they form the product. (13.4)

activation energy (E_a). The minimum amount of energy required to initiate a chemical reaction. (13.4)

activity series. A summary of the results of many possible displacement reactions. (4.4)

actual yield. The amount of product actually obtained in a reaction. (3.10)

addition reaction. A reaction in which one molecule adds to another. (24.2)

adhesion. Attraction between unlike molecules. (11.3)

alcohol. An organic compound containing the hydroxyl group —OH. (24.4)

aldehydes. Compounds with a carbonyl functional group and the general formula RCHO, where R is an H atom, an alkyl, or an aromatic group. (24.4)

aliphatic hydrocarbons. Hydrocarbons that do not contain the benzene group or the benzene ring. (24.2)

alkali metals. The Group 1A elements (Li, Na, K, Rb, Cs, and Fr). (2.4)

alkaline earth metals. The Group 2A elements (Be, Mg, Ca, Sr, Ba, and Ra). (2.4)

alkanes. Hydrocarbons having the general formula C_nH_{2n+2}, where $n = 1,2,\ldots$. (24.2)

alkenes. Hydrocarbons that contain one or more carbon-carbon double bonds. They

have the general formula C_nH_{2n}, where $n = 2,3,\ldots$. (24.2)

alkynes. Hydrocarbons that contain one or more carbon-carbon triple bonds. They have the general formula C_nH_{2n-2}, where $n = 2,3,\ldots$. (24.2)

allotropes. Two or more forms of the same element that differ significantly in chemical and physical properties. (2.6)

alloy. A solid solution composed of two or more metals, or of a metal or metals with one or more nonmetals. (20.2)

alpha particles. See alpha rays.

alpha (α) rays. Helium ions with a positive charge of $+2$. (2.2)

amalgam. An alloy of mercury with another metal or metals. (20.2)

amines. Organic bases that have the functional group —NR_2, where R may be H, an alkyl group, or an aromatic group. (24.4)

amino acids. A compound that contains at least one amino group and at least one carboxyl group. (25.3)

amorphous solid. A solid that lacks a regular three-dimensional arrangement of atoms or molecules. (11.7)

amphoteric oxide. An oxide that exhibits both acidic and basic properties. (8.6)

amplitude. The vertical distance from the middle of a wave to the peak or trough. (7.1)

anion. An ion with a net negative charge. (2.5)

anode. The electrode at which oxidation occurs. (19.2)

antibonding molecular orbital. A molecular orbital that is of higher energy and lower stability than the atomic orbitals from which it was formed. (10.6)

aqueous solution. A solution in which the solvent is water. (4.1)

aromatic hydrocarbon. A hydrocarbon that contains one or more benzene rings. (24.1)

atmospheric pressure. The pressure exerted by Earth's atmosphere. (5.2)

atom. The basic unit of an element that can enter into chemical combination. (2.2)

atomic mass. The mass of an atom in atomic mass units. (3.1)

atomic mass unit (amu). A mass exactly equal to $\frac{1}{12}$th the mass of one carbon-12 atom. (3.1)

atomic number (Z). The number of protons in the nucleus of an atom. (2.3)

atomic orbital. The wave function (Ψ) of an electron in an atom. (7.5)

atomic radius. One-half the distance between the two nuclei in two adjacent atoms of the same element in a metal. For elements that exist as diatomic units, the atomic radius is one-half the distance between the nuclei of the two atoms in a particular molecule. (8.3)

Aufbau principle. As protons are added one by one to the nucleus to build up the elements, electrons similarly are added to the atomic orbitals. (7.9)

Avogadro's law. At constant pressure and temperature, the volume of a gas is directly proportional to the number of moles of the gas present. (5.3)

Avogadro's number (N_A). 6.022×10^{23}; the number of particles in a mole. (3.2)

B

band theory. Delocalized electrons move freely through "bands" formed by overlapping molecular orbitals. (20.3)

barometer. An instrument that measures atmospheric pressure. (5.2)

base. A substance that yields hydroxide ions (OH^-) when dissolved in water. (2.7)

base ionization constant (K_b). The equilibrium constant for the base ionization. (15.6)

battery. A galvanic cell, or a series of combined galvanic cells, that can be used as a source of direct electric current at a constant voltage. (19.6)

beta particles. See beta rays.

beta (β) rays. Electrons. (2.2)

bimolecular reaction. An elementary step that involves two molecules. (13.5)

binary compounds. Compounds formed from just two elements. (2.7)

boiling point. The temperature at which the vapor pressure of a liquid is equal to the external atmospheric pressure. (11.8)

boiling-point elevation (ΔT_b). The boiling point of the solution (T_b) minus the boiling point of the pure solvent (T_b°). (12.6)

bond energy. The enthalpy change required to break a bond in a mole of gaseous molecules. (9.10)

bond length. The distance between the nuclei of two bonded atoms in a molecule. (9.4)

---

* The number in parentheses is the number of the section in which the term first appears.

bond order. The difference between the numbers of electrons in bonding molecular orbitals and antibonding molecular orbitals, divided by two. (10.7)

bonding molecular orbital. A molecular orbital that is of lower energy and greater stability than the atomic orbitals from which it was formed. (10.6)

Born-Haber cycle. The cycle that relates lattice energies of ionic compounds to ionization energies, electron affinities, heats of sublimation and formation, and bond energies. (9.3)

boundary surface diagram. Diagram of the region containing a substantial amount of the electron density (about 90 percent) in an orbital. (7.7)

Boyle's law. The volume of a fixed amount of gas maintained at constant temperature is inversely proportional to the gas pressure. (5.3)

breeder reactor. A nuclear reactor that produces more fissionable materials than it uses. (23.5)

Brønsted acid. A substance capable of donating a proton. (4.3)

Brønsted base. A substance capable of accepting a proton. (4.3)

buffer solution. A solution of (a) a weak acid or base and (b) its salt; both components must be present. The solution has the ability to resist changes in pH upon the addition of small amounts of either acid or base. (16.3)

C

calorimetry. The measurement of heat changes. (6.5)

carbides. Ionic compounds containing the C_2^{2-} or C^{4-} ion. (21.3)

carboxylic acids. Acids that contain the carboxyl group —COOH. (24.4)

catalyst. A substance that increases the rate of a chemical reaction without itself being consumed. (13.6)

catenation. The ability of the atoms of an element to form bonds with one another. (21.3)

cathode. The electrode at which reduction occurs. (19.2)

cation. An ion with a net positive charge. (2.5)

cell voltage. Difference in electrical potential between the anode and the cathode of a galvanic cell. (19.2)

Charles and Gay-Lussac's law. See Charles's law.

Charles's law. The volume of a fixed amount of gas maintained at constant pressure is directly proportional to the absolute temperature of the gas. (5.3)

chelating agent. A substance that forms complex ions with metal ions in solution. (22.3)

chemical energy. Energy stored within the structural units of chemical substances. (6.1)

chemical equation. An equation that uses chemical symbols to show what happens during a chemical reaction. (3.7)

chemical equilibrium. A state in which the rates of the forward and reverse reactions are equal. (14.1)

chemical formula. An expression showing the chemical composition of a compound in terms of the symbols for the atoms of the elements involved. (2.6)

chemical kinetics. The area of chemistry concerned with the speeds, or rates, at which chemical reactions occur. (13.1)

chemical property. Any property of a substance that cannot be studied without converting the substance into some other substance. (1.6)

chemical reaction. A process in which a substance (or substances) is changed into one or more new substances. (3.7)

chemistry. The study of matter and the changes it undergoes. (1.1)

chiral. Compounds or ions that are not super-imposable with their mirror images. (22.4)

chlo-alkali process. The production of chlorine gas by the electrolysis of aqueous NaCl solution. (21.6)

closed system. A system that enables the exchange of energy (usually in the form of heat) but not mass with its surroundings. (6.2)

closest packing. The most efficient arrangements for packing atoms, molecules, or ions in a crystal. (11.4)

cohesion. The intermolecular attraction between like molecules. (11.3)

colligative properties. Properties of solutions that depend on the number of solute particles in solution and not on the nature of the solute particles. (12.6)

colloid. A dispersion of particles of one substance (the dispersed phase) throughout a dispersing medium made of another substance. (12.8)

combination reaction. A reaction in which two or more substances combine to form a single product. (4.4)

common ion effect. The shift in equilibrium caused by the addition of a compound having an ion in common with the dissolved substances. (16.2)

complex ion. An ion containing a central metal cation bonded to one or more molecules or ions. (16.10)

compound. A substance composed of atoms of two or more elements chemically united in fixed proportions. (1.4)

concentration of a solution. The amount of solute present in a given quantity of solvent or solution. (4.5)

condensation. The phenomenon of going from the gaseous state to the liquid state. (11.8)

condensation reaction. A reaction in which two smaller molecules combine to form a larger molecule. Water is invariably one of the products of such a reaction. (24.4)

conductor. Substance capable of conducting electric current. (20.3)

conjugate acid-base pair. An acid and its conjugate base or a base and its conjugate acid. (15.1)

coordinate covalent bond. A bond in which the pair of electrons is supplied by one of the two bonded atoms; also called a dative bond. (9.9)

coordination compound. A neutral species containing one or more complex ions. (22.3)

coordination number. In a crystal lattice it is defined as the number of atoms (or ions) surrounding an atom (or ion) (11.4). In coordination compounds it is defined as the number of donor atoms surrounding the central metal atom in a complex. (22.3)

copolymer. A polymer containing two or more different monomers. (25.2)

corrosion. The deterioration of metals by an electrochemical process. (19.7)

Coulomb's law. The potential energy between two ions is directly proportional to the product of their charges and inversely proportional to the distance between them. (9.3)

covalent bond. A bond in which two electrons are shared by two atoms. (9.4)

covalent compounds. Compounds containing only covalent bonds. (9.4)

critical mass. The minimum mass of fissionable material required to generate a self-sustaining nuclear chain reaction. (23.5)

critical pressure. The minimum pressure necessary to bring about liquefaction at the critical temperature. (11.8)

critical temperature. The temperature above which a gas will not liquefy. (11.8)

crystal field splitting (Δ). The energy difference between two sets of d orbitals in a metal atom when ligands are present. (22.5)

crystalline solid. A solid that possesses rigid and long-range order; its atoms, molecules, or ions occupy specific positions. (11.4)

crystallization. The process in which dissolved solute comes out of solution and forms crystals. (12.1)

cyanides. Compounds containing the CN^- ion. (21.3)

cycloalkanes. Alkanes whose carbon atoms are joined in rings. (24.2)

D

Dalton's law of partial pressures. The total pressure of a mixture of gases is just the sum of the pressures that each gas would exert if it were present alone. (5.6)

decomposition reaction. The breakdown of a compound into two or more components. (4.4)

delocalized molecular orbitals. Molecular orbitals that are not confined between two adjacent bonding atoms but actually extend over three or more atoms. (10.8)

denatured protein. Protein that does not exhibit normal biological activities. (25.3)

density. The mass of a substance divided by its volume. (1.6)

deoxyribonucleic acids (DNA). A type of nucleic acid. (25.4)

deposition. The process in which the molecules go directly from the vapor into the solid phase. (11.8)

diagonal relationship. Similarities between pairs of elements in different groups and periods of the periodic table. (8.6)

diamagnetic. Repelled by a magnet; a diamagnetic substance contains only paired electrons. (7.8)

diatomic molecule. A molecule that consists of two atoms. (2.5)

diffusion. The gradual mixing of molecules of one gas with the molecules of another by virtue of their kinetic properties. (5.7)

dilution. A procedure for preparing a less concentrated solution from a more concentrated solution. (4.5)

dipole moment (μ). The product of charge and the distance between the charges in a molecule. (10.2)

dipole-dipole forces. Forces that act between polar molecules. (11.2)

diprotic acid. Each unit of the acid yields two hydrogen ions upon ionization. (4.3)

dispersion forces. The attractive forces that arise as a result of temporary dipoles induced in the atoms or molecules; also called London forces. (11.2)

displacement reaction. An atom or an ion in a compound is replaced by an atom of another element. (4.4)

disproportionation reaction. A reaction in which an element in one oxidation state is both oxidized and reduced. (4.4)

donor atom. The atom in a ligand that is bonded directly to the metal atom. (22.3)

donor impurities. Impurities that provide conduction electrons to semiconductors. (20.3)

double bond. Two atoms are held together by two pairs of electrons. (9.4)

dynamic equilibrium. The condition in which the rate of a forward process is exactly balanced by the rate of a reverse process. (11.8)

E

electrochemistry. The branch of chemistry that deals with the interconversion of electrical energy and chemical energy. (19.1)

electrolysis. A process in which electrical energy is used to cause a nonspontaneous chemical reaction to occur. (19.8)

electrolyte. A substance that, when dissolved in water, results in a solution that can conduct electricity. (4.1)

electrolytic cell. An apparatus for carrying out electrolysis. (19.8)

electromagnetic radiation. The emission and transmission of energy in the form of electromagnetic waves. (7.1)

electromagnetic wave. A wave that has an electric field component and a mutually perpendicular magnetic field component. (7.1)

electromotive force (emf) (E). The voltage difference between electrodes. (19.2)

electron. A subatomic particle that has a very low mass and carries a single negative electric charge. (2.2)

electron affinity. The negative of the energy change when an electron is accepted by an atom in the gaseous state to form an anion. (8.5)

electron configuration. The distribution of electrons among the various orbitals in an atom or molecule. (7.8)

electron density. The probability that an electron will be found at a particular region in an atomic orbital. (7.5)

electronegativity. The ability of an atom to attract electrons toward itself in a chemical bond. (9.5)

element. A substance that cannot be separated into simpler substances by chemical means. (1.4)

elementary steps. A series of simple reactions that represent the progress of the overall reaction at the molecular level. (13.5)

emission spectra. Continuous or line spectra emitted by substances. (7.3)

empirical formula. An expression showing the types of elements present and the simplest ratios of the different kinds of atoms. (2.6)

enantiomers. Optical isomers, that is, compounds and their nonsuperimposable mirror images. (22.4)

endothermic processes. Processes that absorb heat from the surroundings. (6.2)

end point. The pH at which the indicator changes color. (16.5)

energy. The capacity to do work or to produce change. (6.1)

enthalpy (H). A thermodynamic quantity used to describe heat changes taking place at constant pressure. (6.4)

enthalpy of reaction (ΔH_{rxn}). The difference between the enthalpies of the products and the enthalpies of the reactants. (6.4)

enthalpy of solution (ΔH_{soln}). The heat generated or absorbed when a certain amount of solute is dissolved in a certain amount of solvent. (6.7)

entropy (S). A direct measure of the randomness or disorder of a system. (18.3)

enzyme. A biological catalyst. (13.6)

equilibrium constant (K). A number equal to the ratio of the equilibrium concentrations of products to the equilibrium concentrations of reactants, each raised to the power of its stoichiometric coefficient. (14.1)

equilibrium vapor pressure. The vapor pressure measured under dynamic equilibrium of condensation and evaporation at some temperature. (11.8)

equivalence point. The point at which the acid has completely reacted with or been neutralized by the base. (4.7)

esters. Compounds that have the general formula R'COOR, where R' can be H or an alkyl group or an aromatic group and R is an alkyl group or an aromatic group. (24.4)

ether. An organic compound containing the R—O—R' linkage, where R and R' are alkyl and/or aromatic groups. (24.4)

evaporation. The process in which a liquid is transformed into a gas; also called vaporization. (11.8)

excess reagents. One or more reactants present in quantities greater than necessary to react with the quantity of the limiting reagent. (3.9)

excited state (or level). A state that has higher energy than the ground state. (7.3)

exothermic processes. Processes that give off heat to the surroundings. (6.2)

extensive property. A property that depends on how much matter is being considered. (1.6)

F

family. The elements in a vertical column of the periodic table. (2.4)

Faraday. Charge contained in 1 mole of electrons, equivalent to 96,485.3 coulombs. (19.4)

ferromagnetic. Attracted by a magnet. The unpaired spins in a ferromagnetic substance are aligned in a common direction. (20.2)

first law of thermodynamics. Energy can be converted from one form to another, but cannot be created or destroyed. (6.3)

first-order reaction. A reaction whose rate depends on reactant concentration raised to the first power. (13.3)

formal charge. The difference between the valence electrons in an isolated atom and the number of electrons assigned to that atom in a Lewis structure. (9.7)

formation constant (K_f). The equilibrium constant for the complex ion formation. (16.10)

fractional crystallization. The separation of a mixture of substances into pure components on the basis of their different solubilities. (12.4)

fractional distillation. A procedure for separating liquid components of a solution that is based on their different boiling points. (12.6)

free energy (G). The energy available to do useful work. (18.5)

freezing point. The temperature at which the solid and liquid phases of a substance coexist at equilibrium. (11.8)

freezing point depression (ΔT_f). The freezing point of the pure solvent (T_f°) minus the freezing point of the solution (T_f). (12.6)

frequency (ν). The number of waves that pass through a particular point per unit time. (7.1)

fuel cell. A galvanic cell that requires a continuous supply of reactants to keep functioning. (19.6)

functional group. That part of a molecule characterized by a special arrangement of atoms that is largely responsible for the chemical behavior of the parent molecule. (24.1)

G

galvanic cell. The experimental apparatus for generating electricity through the use of a spontaneous redox reaction. (19.2)

gamma (γ) rays. High-energy radiation. (2.2)

gas constant (R). The constant that appears in the ideal gas equation. It is usually expressed as 0.08206 L · atm/K · mol, or 8.314 J/K · mol. (5.4)

geometric isomers. Compounds with the same type and number of atoms and the same chemical bonds but different spatial arrangements; such isomers cannot be interconverted without breaking a chemical bond. (22.4)

Gibbs free energy. See free energy.

glass. The optically transparent fusion product of inorganic materials that has cooled to a rigid state without crystallizing. (11.7)

gravimetric analysis. An experimental procedure that involves the measurement of mass. (4.6)

greenhouse effect. Carbon dioxide and other gases' influence on Earth's temperature. (17.5)

ground state (or level). The lowest energy state of a system. (7.3)

group. The elements in a vertical column of the periodic table. (2.4)

H

half-cell reactions. Oxidation and reduction reactions at the electrodes. (19.2)

Half-life ($t_{\frac{1}{2}}$). The time required for the concentration of a reactant to decrease to half of its initial concentration. (13.3)

half-reaction. A reaction that explicitly shows electrons involved in either oxidation or reduction. (4.4)

halogens. The nonmetallic elements in Group 7A (F, Cl, Br, I, and At). (2.4)

heat. Transfer of energy between two bodies that are at different temperatures. (6.2)

heat capacity (C). The amount of heat required to raise the temperature of a given quantity of the substance by one degree Celsius. (6.5)

heat of dilution. The heat change associated with the dilution process. (6.7)

heat of hydration (ΔH_{hydr}). The heat change associated with the hydration process. (6.7)

heat of solution. See enthalpy of solution.

Heisenberg uncertainty principle. It is impossible to know simultaneously both the momentum and the position of a particle with certainty. (7.5)

Henry's law. The solubility of a gas in a liquid is proportional to the pressure of the gas over the solution. (12.5)

Hess's law. When reactants are converted to products, the change in enthalpy is the same whether the reaction takes place in one step or in a series of steps. (6.6)

heterogeneous equilibrium. An equilibrium state in which the reacting species are not all in the same phase. (14.2)

heterogeneous mixture. The individual components of a mixture remain physically separated and can be seen as separate components. (1.4)

homogeneous equilibrium. An equilibrium state in which all reacting species are in the same phase. (14.2)

homogeneous mixture. The composition of a mixture, after sufficient stirring, is the same throughout the solution. (1.4)

homonuclear diatomic molecule. A diatomic molecule containing atoms of the same element. (10.7)

homopolymer. A polymer that is made from only one type of monomer. (25.2)

Hund's rule. The most stable arrangement of electrons in subshells is the one with the greatest number of parallel spins. (7.8)

hybrid orbitals. Atomic orbitals obtained when two or more nonequivalent orbitals of the same atom combine. (10.4)

hybridization. The process of mixing the atomic orbitals in an atom (usually the central atom) to generate a set of new atomic orbitals. (10.4)

hydrates. Compounds that have a specific number of water molecules attached to them. (2.7)

hydration. A process in which an ion or a molecule is surrounded by water molecules arranged in a specific manner. (4.1)

hydrocarbons. Compounds made up only of carbon and hydrogen. (24.1)

hydrogen bond. A special type of dipole-dipole interaction between the hydrogen atom bonded to an atom of a very electronegative element (F, N, O) and another atom of one of the three electronegative elements. (11.2)

hydrogenation. The addition of hydrogen, especially to compounds with double and triple carbon-carbon bonds. (21.2)

hydronium ion. The hydrated proton, H_3O^+. (4.3)

hydrophilic. Water-liking. (12.8)

hydrophobic. Water-fearing. (12.8)

hypothesis. A tentative explanation for a set of observations. (1.3)

I

ideal gas. A hypothetical gas whose pressure-volume-temperature behavior can be completely accounted for by the ideal gas equation. (5.4)

ideal gas equation. An equation expressing the relationships among pressure, volume, temperature, and amount of gas ($PV = nRT$, where R is the gas constant). (5.4)

ideal solution. Any solution that obeys Raoult's law. (12.6)

indicators. Substances that have distinctly different colors in acidic and basic media. (4.7)

induced dipole. The separation of positive and negative charges in a neutral atom (or a nonpolar molecule) caused by the proximity of an ion or a polar molecule. (11.2)

inert complex. A complex ion that undergoes very slow ligand exchange reactions. (22.6)

inorganic compounds. Compounds other than organic compounds. (2.7)

insulator. A substance incapable of conducting electricity. (20.3)

intensive property. A property that does not depend on how much matter is being considered. (1.6)

intermediate. A species that appears in the mechanism of the reaction (that is, the elementary steps) but not in the overall balanced equation. (13.5)

intermolecular forces. Attractive forces that exist among molecules. (11.2)

International System of Units (SI). A system of units based on metric units. (1.7)

intramolecular forces. Forces that hold atoms together in a molecule. (11.2)

ion. An atom or a group of atoms that has a net positive or negative charge. (2.5)

ion pair. One or more cations and one or more anions held together by electrostatic forces. (12.7)

ionic bond. The electrostatic force that holds ions together in an ionic compound. (9.2)

ionic compound. Any neutral compound containing cations and anions. (2.5)

ionic equation. An equation that shows dissolved species as free ions. (4.2)

ionic radius. The radius of a cation or an anion as measured in an ionic compound. (8.3)

ionization energy. The minimum energy required to remove an electron from an isolated atom (or an ion) in its ground state. (8.4)

ion pair. A species made up of at least one cation and at least one anion held together by electrostatic forces. (12.7)

ion-dipole forces. Forces that operate between an ion and a dipole. (11.2)

ion-product constant. Product of hydrogen ion concentration and hydroxide ion concentration (both in molarity) at a particular temperature. (15.2)

ionosphere. The uppermost layer of the atmosphere. (17.1)

isoelectronic. Ions, or atoms and ions, that possess the same number of electrons, and hence the same ground-state electron configuration, are said to be isoelectronic. (8.2)

isolated system. A system that does not allow the transfer of either mass or energy to or from its surroundings. (6.2)

isotopes. Atoms having the same atomic number but different mass numbers. (2.3)

J

Joule (J). Unit of energy given by newtons × meters. (5.7)

K

kelvin. The SI base unit of temperature. (1.7)

Kelvin temperature scale. See absolute temperature scale.

ketones. Compounds with a carbonyl functional group and the general formula RR′CO, where R and R′ are alkyl and/or aromatic groups. (24.4)

kinetic energy (KE). Energy available because of the motion of an object. (5.7)

kinetic molecular theory of gases. Treatment of gas behavior in terms of the random motion of molecules. (5.7)

L

labile complex. Complexes that undergo rapid ligand exchange reactions. (22.6)

lanthanide (rare earth) series. Elements that have incompletely filled $4f$ subshells or readily give rise to cations that have incompletely filled $4f$ subshells. (7.9)

lattice energy. The energy required to completely separate one mole of a solid ionic compound into gaseous ions. (6.7, 9.3)

law. A concise verbal or mathematical statement of a relationship between phenomena that is always the same under the same conditions. (1.3)

law of conservation of energy. The total quantity of energy in the universe is constant. (6.1)

law of conservation of mass. Matter can be neither created nor destroyed. (2.1)

law of definite proportions. Different samples of the same compound always contain its constituent elements in the same proportions by mass. (2.1)

law of mass action. For a reversible reaction at equilibrium and a constant temperature, a certain ratio of reactant and product concentrations has a constant value, K (the equilibrium constant). (14.1)

law of multiple proportions. If two elements can combine to form more than one type of compound, the masses of one element that combine with a fixed mass of the other element are in ratios of small whole numbers. (2.1)

Le Châtelier's principle. If an external stress is applied to a system at equilibrium, the system will adjust itself in such a way as to partially offset the stress as the system reaches a new equilibrium position. (14.5)

Lewis acid. A substance that can accept a pair of electrons. (15.12)

Lewis base. A substance that can donate a pair of electrons. (15.12)

Lewis dot symbol. The symbol of an element with one or more dots that represent the number of valence electrons in an atom of the element. (9.1)

Lewis structure. A representation of covalent bonding using Lewis symbols. Shared electron pairs are shown either as lines or as pairs of dots between two atoms, and lone pairs are shown as pairs of dots on individual atoms. (9.4)

ligand. A molecule or an ion that is bonded to the metal ion in a complex ion. (22.3)

limiting reagent. The reactant used up first in a reaction. (3.9)

line spectra. Spectra produced when radiation is absorbed or emitted by substances only at some wavelengths. (7.3)

liter. The volume occupied by one cubic decimeter. (1.7)

lone pairs. Valence electrons that are not involved in covalent bond formation. (9.4)

M

macroscopic properties. Properties that can be measured directly. (1.7)

manometer. A device used to measure the pressure of gases. (5.2)

many-electron atoms. Atoms that contain two or more electrons. (7.5)

mass. A measure of the quantity of matter contained in an object. (1.6)

mass defect. The difference between the mass of an atom and the sum of the masses of its protons, neutrons, and electrons. (23.2)

mass number (A). The total number of neutrons and protons present in the nucleus of an atom. (2.3)

matter. Anything that occupies space and possesses mass. (1.4)

melting point. The temperature at which solid and liquid phases coexist in equilibrium. (11.8)

mesosphere. A region between the stratosphere and the ionosphere. (17.1)

metalloid. An element with properties intermediate between those of metals and nonmetals. (2.4)

metals. Elements that are good conductors of heat and electricity and have the tendency to form positive ions in ionic compounds. (2.4)

metallurgy. The science and technology of separating metals from their ores and of compounding alloys. (20.2)

microscopic properties. Properties that cannot be measured directly without the aid of a microscope or other special instrument. (1.7)

mineral. A naturally occurring substance with a range of chemical composition. (20.1)

miscible. Two liquids that are completely soluble in each other in all proportions are said to be miscible. (12.2)

mixture. A combination of two or more substances in which the substances retain their identity. (1.4)

moderator. A substance that can reduce the kinetic energy of neutrons. (23.5)

molality. The number of moles of solute dissolved in one kilogram of solvent. (12.3)

molar concentration. See molarity.

molar heat of fusion (ΔH_{fus}). The energy (in kilojoules) required to melt one mole of a solid. (11.8)

molar heat of sublimation (ΔH_{sub}). The energy (in kilojoules) required to sublime one mole of a solid. (11.8)

molar heat of vaporization (ΔH_{vap}). The energy (in kilojoules) required to vaporize one mole of a liquid. (11.8)

molar mass ($\mathcal{M}$). The mass (in grams or kilograms) of one mole of atoms, molecules, or other particles. (3.2)

molar solubility. The number of moles of solute in one liter of a saturated solution (mol/L). (16.6)

molarity (M). The number of moles of solute in one liter of solution. (4.5)

mole (mol). The amount of substance that contains as many elementary entities (atoms, molecules, or other particles) as there are atoms in exactly 12 grams (or 0.012 kilograms) of the carbon-12 isotope. (3.2)

mole fraction. Ratio of the number of moles of one component of a mixture to the total number of moles of all components in the mixture. (5.6)

mole method. An approach for determining the amount of product formed in a reaction. (3.8)

molecular equations. Equations in which the formulas of the compounds are written as though all species existed as molecules or whole units. (4.2)

molecular formula. An expression showing the exact numbers of atoms of each element in a molecule. (2.6)

molecular mass. The sum of the atomic masses (in amu) present in the molecule. (3.3)

molecular orbital. An orbital that results from the interaction of the atomic orbitals of the bonding atoms. (10.6)

molecularity of a reaction. The number of molecules reacting in an elementary step. (13.5)

molecule. An aggregate of at least two atoms in a definite arrangement held together by special forces. (2.5)

monatomic ion. An ion that contains only one atom. (2.5)

monomer. The single repeating unit of a polymer. (25.2)

monoprotic acid. Each unit of the acid yields one hydrogen ion upon ionization. (4.3)

multiple bonds. Bonds formed when two atoms share two or more pairs of electrons. (9.4)

N

Nernst equation. The relation between the emf of a galvanic cell and the standard emf and the concentrations of the oxidizing and reducing agents. (19.5)

net ionic equation. An equation that indicates only the ionic species that actually take part in the reaction. (4.2)

neutralization reaction. A reaction between an acid and a base. (4.3)

neutron. A subatomic particle that bears no net electric charge. Its mass is slightly greater than a proton's. (2.2)

newton (N). The SI unit for force. (5.2)

nitrogen fixation. The conversion of molecular nitrogen into nitrogen compounds. (17.1)

noble gas core. The electron configuration of the noble gas element that most nearly precedes the element being considered. (7.9)

noble gases. Nonmetallic elements in Group 8A (He, Ne, Ar, Kr, Xe, and Rn). (2.4)

node. The point at which the amplitude of the wave is zero. (7.4)

nonelectrolyte. A substance that, when dissolved in water, gives a solution that is not electrically conducting. (4.1)

nonmetals. Elements that are usually poor conductors of heat and electricity. (2.4)

nonpolar molecule. A molecule that does not possess a dipole moment. (10.2)

nonvolatile. Does not have a measurable vapor pressure. (12.6)

n-**type semiconductors.** Semiconductors that contain donor impurities. (20.3)

nuclear binding energy. The energy required to break up a nucleus into its protons and neutrons. (23.2)

nuclear chain reaction. A self-sustaining sequence of nuclear fission reactions. (23.5)

nuclear fission. A heavy nucleus (mass number > 200) divides to form smaller nuclei of intermediate mass and one or more neutrons. (23.5)

nuclear fusion. The combining of small nuclei into larger ones. (23.6)

nuclear transmutation. The change undergone by a nucleus as a result of bombardment by neutrons or other particles. (23.1)

nucleic acids. High molar mass polymers that play an essential role in protein synthesis. (25.4)

nucleotide. The repeating unit in each strand of a DNA molecule which consists of a base-deoxyribose-phosphate linkage. (25.4)

nucleus. The central core of an atom. (2.2)

O

octet rule. An atom other than hydrogen tends to form bonds until it is surrounded by eight valence electrons. (9.4)

open system. A system that can exchange mass and energy (usually in the form of heat) with its surroundings. (6.2)

optical isomers. Compounds that are nonsuperimposable mirror images. (22.4)

orbital. See atomic orbital and molecular orbital.

ore. The material of a mineral deposit in a sufficiently concentrated form to allow economical recovery of a desired metal. (20.1)

organic chemistry. The branch of chemistry that deals with carbon compounds. (24.1)

organic compounds. Compounds that contain carbon, usually in combination with elements such as hydrogen, oxygen, nitrogen, and sulfur. (2.7)

osmosis. The net movement of solvent molecules through a semipermeable membrane from a pure solvent or from a dilute solution to a more concentrated solution. (12.6)

osmotic pressure (π). The pressure required to stop osmosis. (12.6)

overvoltage. The difference between the electrode potential and the actual voltage required to cause electrolysis. (19.8)

oxidation number. The number of charges an atom would have in a molecule if electrons were transferred completely in the direction indicated by the difference in electronegativity. (4.4)

oxidation reaction. The half-reaction that involves the loss of electrons. (4.4)

oxidation-reduction reaction. A reaction that involves the transfer of electron(s) or the change in the oxidation state of reactants. (4.4)

oxidation state. See oxidation number.

oxidizing agent. A substance that can accept electrons from another substance or increase the oxidation numbers in another substance. (4.4)

oxoacid. An acid containing hydrogen, oxygen, and another element (the central element). (2.7)

oxoanion. An anion derived from an oxoacid. (2.7)

P

paramagnetic. Attracted by a magnet. A paramagnetic substance contains one or more unpaired electrons. (7.8)

partial pressure. Pressure of one component in a mixture of gases. (5.6)

pascal (Pa). A pressure of one newton per square meter ($1 N/m^2$). (5.2)

Pauli exclusion principle. No two electrons in an atom can have the same four quantum numbers. (7.8)

percent by mass. The ratio of the mass of a solute to the mass of the solution, multiplied by 100%. (12.3)

percent composition by mass. The percent by mass of each element in a compound. (3.5)

percent ionization. Ratio of ionized acid concentration at equilibrium to the initial concentration of acid. (15.5)

percent yield. The ratio of actual yield to theoretical yield, multiplied by 100%. (3.10)

period. A horizontal row of the periodic table. (2.4)

periodic table. A tabular arrangement of the elements. (2.4)

pH. The negative logarithm of the hydrogen ion concentration. (15.3)

phase. A homogeneous part of a system in contact with other parts of the system but separated from them by a well-defined boundary. (11.1)

phase change. Transformation from one phase to another. (11.8)

phase diagram. A diagram showing the conditions at which a substance exists as a solid, liquid, or vapor. (11.9)

photochemical smog. Formation of smog by the reactions of automobile exhaust in the presence of sunlight. (17.7)

photoelectric effect. A phenomenon in which electrons are ejected from the surface of certain metals exposed to light of at least a certain minimum frequency. (7.2)

photon. A particle of light. (7.2)

physical equilibrium. An equilibrium in which only physical properties change. (14.1)

physical property. Any property of a substance that can be observed without transforming the substance into some other substance. (1.6)

pi bond (π). A covalent bond formed by sideways overlapping orbitals; its electron density is concentrated above and below the plane of the nuclei of the bonding atoms. (10.5)

pi molecular orbital. A molecular orbital in which the electron density is concentrated above and below the line joining the two nuclei of the bonding atoms. (10.6)

plasma. A gaseous mixture of positive ions and electrons. (23.6)

polar covalent bond. In such a bond, the electrons spend more time in the vicinity of one atom than the other. (9.5)

polar molecule. A molecule that possesses a dipole moment. (10.2)

polarimeter. The instrument for measuring the rotation of polarized light by optical isomers. (22.4)

polyatomic ion. An ion that contains more than one atom. (2.5)

polyatomic molecule. A molecule that consists of more than two atoms. (2.5)

polymer. A compound distinguished by a high molar mass, ranging into thousands and millions of grams, and made up of many repeating units. (25.1)

positron. A particle that has the same mass as the electron, but bears a +1 charge. (23.1)

potential energy. Energy available by virtue of an object's position. (6.1)

precipitate. An insoluble solid that separates from the solution. (4.2)

precipitation reaction. A reaction that results in the formation of a precipitate. (4.2)

precision. The closeness of agreement of two or more measurements of the same quantity. (1.8)

pressure. Force applied per unit area. (5.2)

product. The substance formed as a result of a chemical reaction. (3.7)

protein. Polymers of amino acids. (25.3)

proton. A subatomic particle having a single positive electric charge. The mass of a proton is about 1840 times that of an electron. (2.2)

p-type semiconductors. Semiconductors that contain acceptor impurities. (20.3)

pyrometallurgy. Metallurgical processes that are carried out at high temperatures. (20.2)

Q

qualitative. Consisting of general observations about the system. (1.3)

qualitative analysis. The determination of the types of ions present in a solution. (16.11)

quantitative. Comprising numbers obtained by various measurements of the system. (1.3)

quantitative analysis. The determination of the amount of substances present in a sample. (4.5)

quantum. The smallest quantity of energy that can be emitted (or absorbed) in the form of electromagnetic radiation. (7.1)

quantum numbers. Numbers that describe the distribution of electrons in hydrogen and other atoms. (7.6)

R

racemic mixture. An equimolar mixture of the two enantiomers. (22.4)

radiant energy. Energy transmitted in the form of waves. (6.1)

radiation. The emission and transmission of energy through space in the form of particles and/or waves. (2.2)

radical. Any neutral fragment of a molecule containing an unpaired electron. (23.8)

radioactive decay series. A sequence of nuclear reactions that ultimately result in the formation of a stable isotope. (23.3)

radioactivity. The spontaneous breakdown of an atom by emission of particles and/or radiation. (2.2)

Raoult's law. The partial pressure of the solvent over a solution is given by the product of the vapor pressure of the pure solvent and the mole fraction of the solvent in the solution. (12.6)

rare earth series. See lanthanide series.

rate constant (k). Constant of proportionality between the reaction rate and the concentrations of reactants. (13.1)

rate law. An expression relating the rate of a reaction to the rate constant and the concentrations of the reactants. (13.2)

rate-determining step. The slowest step in the sequence of steps leading to the formation of products. (13.5)

reactants. The starting substances in a chemical reaction. (3.7)

reaction mechanism. The sequence of elementary steps that leads to product formation. (13.5)

reaction order. The sum of the powers to which all reactant concentrations appearing in the rate law are raised. (13.2)

reaction quotient (Q). A number equal to the ratio of product concentrations to reactant concentrations, each raised to the power of its stoichiometric coefficient at some point other than equilibrium. (14.4)

reaction rate. The change in the concentration of reactant or product with time. (13.1)

redox reaction. A reaction in which there is either a transfer of electrons or a change in the oxidation numbers of the substances taking part in the reaction. (4.4)

reducing agent. A substance that can donate electrons to another substance or decrease the oxidation numbers in another substance. (4.4)

reduction reaction. The half-reaction that involves the gain of electrons. (4.4)

representative elements. Elements in Groups 1A through 7A, all of which have incompletely filled s or p subshell of highest principal quantum number. (8.2)

resonance. The use of two or more Lewis structures to represent a particular molecule. (9.8)

resonance structure. One of two or more alternative Lewis structures for a molecule that cannot be described fully with a single Lewis structure. (9.8)

reversible reaction. A reaction that can occur in both directions. (4.1)

ribonucleic acid (RNA). A form of nucleic acid. (25.4)

root-mean-square (rms) speed (u_{rms}). A measure of the average molecular speed at a given temperature. (5.7)

S

salt. An ionic compound made up of a cation other than H^+ and an anion other than OH^- or O^{2-}. (4.3)

salt hydrolysis. The reaction of the anion or cation, or both, of a salt with water. (15.10)

saponification. Soapmaking. (24.4)

saturated hydrocarbons. Hydrocarbons that contain the maximum number of hydrogen atoms that can bond with the number of carbon atoms present. (24.2)

saturated solution. At a given temperature, the solution that results when the maximum amount of a substance has dissolved in a solvent. (12.1)

scientific method. A systematic approach to research. (1.3)

second law of thermodynamics. The entropy of the universe increases in a spontaneous process and remains unchanged in an equilibrium process. (18.4)

second-order reaction. A reaction whose rate depends on reactant concentration raised to the second power or on the concentrations of two different reactants, each raised to the first power. (13.3)

semiconductors. Elements that normally cannot conduct electricity, but can have their conductivity greatly enhanced either by raising the temperature or by adding certain impurities. (20.3)

semipermeable membrane. A membrane that enables solvent molecules to pass through, but blocks the movement of solute molecules. (12.6)

sigma bond (σ). A covalent bond formed by orbitals overlapping end-to-end; its electron density is concentrated between the nuclei of the bonding atoms. (10.5)

sigma molecular orbital. A molecular orbital in which the electron density is concentrated around a line between the two nuclei of the bonding atoms. (10.6)

significant figures. The number of meaningful digits in a measured or calculated quantity. (1.8)

single bond. Two atoms are held together by one electron pair. (9.4)

solubility. The maximum amount of solute that can be dissolved in a given quantity of solvent at a specific temperature. (4.2, 16.6)

solubility product (K_{sp}). The product of the molar concentrations of the constituent ions, each raised to the power of its stoichiometric coefficient in the equilibrium equation. (16.6)

solute. The substance present in smaller amount in a solution. (4.1)

solution. A homogeneous mixture of two or more substances. (4.1)

solvation. The process in which an ion or a molecule is surrounded by solvent molecules arranged in a specific manner. (12.2)

solvent. The substance present in larger amount in a solution. (4.1)

specific heat (s). The amount of heat energy required to raise the temperature of one gram of a substance by one degree Celsius. (6.5)

spectator ions. Ions that are not involved in the overall reaction. (4.2)

spectrochemical series. A list of ligands arranged in increasing order of their abilities to split the d-orbital energy levels. (22.5)

standard atmospheric pressure (1 atm). The pressure that supports a column of mercury exactly 76 cm high at 0°C at sea level. (5.2)

standard emf ($E°$). The difference of the standard reduction potential of the substance that undergoes reduction and the standard reduction potential of the substance that undergoes oxidation. (19.3)

standard enthalpy of formation ($\Delta H_f°$). The heat change that results when one mole of a compound is formed from its elements in their standard states. (6.6)

standard enthalpy of reaction ($\Delta H_{rxn}°$). The enthalpy change when the reaction is carried out under standard-state conditions. (6.6)

standard entropy of reaction ($\Delta S_{rxn}°$). The entropy change when the reaction is carried out under standard-state conditions. (18.4)

standard free-energy of reaction ($\Delta G_{rxn}°$). The free-energy change when the reaction is carried out under standard-state conditions. (18.5)

standard free-energy of formation ($\Delta G_f°$). The free-energy change when 1 mole of a compound is synthesized from its elements in their standard states. (18.5)

standard reduction potential. The voltage measured as a reduction reaction occurs at the electrode when all solutes are 1 M and all gases are at 1 atm. (19.3)

standard solution. A solution of accurately known concentration. (4.7)

standard state. The condition of 1 atm of pressure. (6.6)

standard temperature and pressure (STP). 0°C and 1 atm. (5.4)

state function. A property that is determined by the state of the system. (6.3)

state of a system. The values of all pertinent macroscopic variables (for example, composition, volume, pressure, and temperature) of a system. (6.3)

stereoisomers. Compounds that are made up of the same types and numbers of atoms bonded together in the same sequence but with different spatial arrangements. (22.4)

stoichiometric amounts. The exact molar amounts of reactants and products that appear in the balanced chemical equation. (3.9)

stoichiometry. The quantitative study of reactants and products in a chemical reaction. (3.8)

stratosphere. The region of the atmosphere extending upward from the troposphere to about 50 km from Earth. (17.1)

strong acids. Strong electrolytes which are assumed to ionize completely in water. (15.4)

strong bases. Strong electrolytes which are assumed to ionize completely in water. (15.4)

structural formula. A chemical formula that shows how atoms are bonded to one another in a molecule. (2.6)

structural isomers. Molecules that have the same molecular formula but different structures. (24.2)

sublimation. The process in which molecules go directly from the solid into the vapor phase. (11.8)

substance. A form of matter that has a definite or constant composition (the number and type of basic units present) and distinct properties. (1.4)

substitution reaction. A reaction in which an atom or group of atoms replaces an atom or groups of atoms in another molecule. (24.3)

supercooling. Cooling of a liquid below its freezing point without forming the solid. (11.8)

supersaturated solution. A solution that contains more of the solute than is present in a saturated solution. (12.1)

surface tension. The amount of energy required to stretch or increase the surface of a liquid by a unit area. (11.3)

surroundings. The rest of the universe outside a system. (6.2)

system. Any specific part of the universe that is of interest to us. (6.2)

T

termolecular reaction. An elementary step that involves three molecules. (13.5)

ternary compounds. Compounds consisting of three elements. (2.7)

theoretical yield. The amount of product predicted by the balanced equation when all of the limiting reagent has reacted. (3.10)

theory. A unifying principle that explains a body of facts and the laws that are based on them. (1.3)

thermal energy. Energy associated with the random motion of atoms and molecules. (6.1)

thermochemical equation. An equation that shows both the mass and enthalpy relations. (6.4)

thermochemistry. The study of heat changes in chemical reactions. (6.2)

thermodynamics. The scientific study of the interconversion of heat and other forms of energy. (6.3)

thermonuclear reactions. Nuclear fusion reactions that occur at very high temperatures. (23.6)

thermosphere. The region of the atmosphere in which the temperature increases continuously with altitude. (17.1)

third law of thermodynamics. The entropy of a perfect crystalline substance is zero at the absolute zero of temperature. (18.4)

titration. The gradual addition of a solution of accurately known concentration to another solution of unknown concentration until the chemical reaction between the two solutions is complete. (4.7)

tracers. Isotopes, especially radioactive isotopes, that are used to trace the path of the atoms of an element in a chemical or biological process. (23.7)

transition metals. Elements that have incompletely filled d subshells or readily give rise to cations that have incompletely filled d subshells. (7.9)

transition state. See activated complex.

transuranium elements. Elements with atomic numbers greater than 92. (23.4)

triple bond. Two atoms are held together by three pairs of electrons. (9.4)

triple point. The point at which the vapor, liquid, and solid states of a substance are in equilibrium. (11.9)

triprotic acid. Each unit of the acid yields three protons upon ionization. (4.3)

troposphere. The layer of the atmosphere which contains about 80 percent of the total mass of air and practically all of the atmosphere's water vapor. (17.1)

U

unimolecular reaction. An elementary step in which only one reacting molecule participates. (13.5)

unit cell. The basic repeating unit of the arrangement of atoms, molecules, or ions in a crystalline solid. (11.4)

unsaturated hydrocarbons. Hydrocarbons that contain carbon-carbon double bonds or carbon-carbon triple bonds. (24.2)

unsaturated solution. A solution that contains less solute than it has the capacity to dissolve. (12.1)

V

valence electrons. The outer electrons of an atom, which are those involved in chemical bonding. (8.2)

valence shell. The outermost electron-occupied shell of an atom, which holds the electrons that are usually involved in bonding. (10.1)

valence-shell electron-pair repulsion (VSEPR) model. A model that accounts for the geometrical arrangements of shared and unshared electron pairs around a central atom in terms of the repulsions between electron pairs. (10.1)

van der Waals equation. An equation that describes the P, V, and T of a nonideal gas. (5.8)

van der Waals forces. The dipole-dipole, dipole-induced dipole, and dispersion forces. (11.2)

van't Hoff factor. The ratio of actual number of particles in solution after dissociation to the number of formula units initially dissolved in solution. (12.7)

vaporization. The escape of molecules from the surface of a liquid; also called evaporation. (11.8)

viscosity. A measure of a fluid's resistance to flow. (11.3)

volatile. Has a measurable vapor pressure. (12.6)

volume. It is the length cubed. (1.6)

W

wave. A vibrating disturbance by which energy is transmitted. (7.1)

wavelength (λ). The distance between identical points on successive waves. (7.1)

weak acids. Weak electrolytes that ionize only to a limited extent in water. (15.4)

weak bases. Weak electrolytes that ionize only to a limited extent in water. (15.4)

weight. The force that gravity exerts on an object. (1.7)

work. Directed energy change resulting from a process. (6.1)

X

X-ray diffraction. The scattering of X rays by the units of a regular crystalline solid. (11.5)

Answers

to Even-Numbered Problems

Chapter 1

1.4 (a) Hypothesis. (b) Law. (c) Theory. **1.12** (a) Physical change. (b) Chemical change. (c) Physical change. (d) Chemical change. (e) Physical change. **1.14** (a) K. (b) Sn. (c) Cr. (d) B. (e) Ba. (f) Pu. (g) S. (h) Ar. (i) Hg. **1.16** (a) Homogeneous mixture. (b) Element. (c) Compound. (d) Homogeneous mixture. (e) Heterogeneous mixture. (f) Homogeneous mixture. (g) Heterogeneous mixture. **1.22** 13.9 g. **1.24** (a) 41°C. (b) 11.3°F. (c) 1.1×10^4°F. (d) 233°C. **1.26** (a) -196°C. (b) -269°C. (c) 328°C. **1.30** (a) 0.0152. (b) 0.0000000778. **1.32** (a) 1.8×10^{-2}. (b) 1.14×10^{10}. (c) -5×10^4. (d) 1.3×10^3. **1.34** (a) One. (b) Three. (c) Three. (d) Four. (e) Two or three. (f) One. (g) One or two. **1.36** (a) 1.28. (b) 3.18×10^{-3} mg. (c) 8.14×10^7 dm. **1.38** (a) 1.10×10^8 mg. (b) 6.83×10^{-5} m^3. (c) 7.2×10^3 L. (d) 6.24×10^{-8} lb. **1.40** 3.1557×10^7 s. **1.42** (a) 81 in/s. (b) 1.2×10^2 m/min. (c) 7.4 km/h. **1.44** 88 km/h. **1.46** 3.7×10^{-3} g Pb. **1.48** (a) 1.85×10^{-7} m. (b) 1.4×10^{17} s. (c) 7.12×10^{-5} m^3. (d) 8.86×10^4 L. **1.50** 6.25×10^{-4} g/cm^3. **1.52** (a) Chemical. (b) Chemical. (c) Physical. (d) Physical. (e) Chemical. **1.54** 2.6 g/cm^3. **1.56** 0.882 cm. **1.58** 767 mph. **1.60** Liquid must be less dense than ice; temperature below 0°C. **1.62** 2.3×10^3 cm^3. **1.64** 6.3¢. **1.66** 73°S. **1.68** (a) 8.6×10^3 L air/day. (b) 0.018 L CO/day. **1.70** 5.5×10^{10} L seawater. **1.72** 7.0×10^{20} L. **1.74** 9.0×10^1 lb; 41 kg. **1.76** O: 4.0×10^4 g; C: 1.1×10^4 g; H: 6.2×10^3 g; N: 2×10^3 g; Ca: 9.9×10^2 g; P: 7.4×10^2 g. **1.78** 4.6×10^2°C; 8.6×10^2°F. **1.80** 9.0×10^{11}. **1.82** 5.4×10^{22} Fe atoms. **1.84** 30 times. **1.86** 1.450×10^{-2} mm. **1.88** 1.3×10^3 mL. **1.90** 2.5 nm. **1.92** (a) $\$3.06 \times 10^{-3}$/L. (b) 5.5¢.

Chapter 2

2.8 0.12 mi. **2.14** 145. **2.16** N(7,8,7); S(16,17,16); Cu(29,34,29); Sr(38,46,38); Ba(56,74,56); W(74,112,74); Hg(80,122,80). **2.18** (a) $^{186}_{76}$W. (b) $^{201}_{80}$Hg. **2.24** (a) Metallic character increases down a group. (b) Metallic character decreases from left to right. **2.26** F and Cl; Na and K; P and N. **2.32** (a) Diatomic molecule and compound. (b) Polyatomic molecule and compound. (c) Polyatomic molecule and element. **2.34** (a) H$_2$ and F$_2$. (b) HCl and CO. (c) S$_8$ and P$_4$. (d) H$_2$O and C$_{12}$H$_{22}$O$_{11}$ (sucrose). **2.36** (protons, electrons): K$^+$(19,18); Mg^{2+}(12,10); Fe^{3+}(26,23); Br$^-$(35,36); Mn^{2+}(25,23); C^{4-}(6,10); Cu^{2+}(29,27). **2.44** (a) AlBr$_3$. (b) NaSO$_2$. (c) N$_2$O$_5$. (d) K$_2$Cr$_2$O$_7$. **2.46** C$_2$H$_6$O. **2.48** Ionic: NaBr, BaF$_2$, CsCl. Molecular: CH$_4$, CCl$_4$, ICl, NF$_3$. **2.56** (a) Potassium hypochlorite. (b) Silver carbonate. (c) Nitrous acid. (d) Potassium permanganate. (e) Cesium chlorate. (f) Potassium ammonium sulfate. (g) Iron(II) oxide. (h) Iron(III) oxide. (i) Titanium(IV) chloride. (j) Sodium hydride. (k) Lithium nitride. (l) Sodium oxide. (m) Sodium peroxide. **2.58** (a) CuCN. (b) Sr(ClO$_2$)$_2$. (c) HBrO$_4$. (d) HI. (e) Na$_2$(NH$_4$)PO$_4$. (f) PbCO$_3$. (g) SnF$_2$. (h) P$_4$S$_{10}$. (i) HgO. (j) Hg$_2$I$_2$. (k) SeF$_6$. **2.60** C-12 and C-13. **2.62** I$^-$. **2.64** NaCl is an ionic compound. **2.66** Element: (b), (c), (e), (f), (g), (j), (k). Molecules: (b), (f), (g), (k). Compounds: (i), (l). Compounds and molecules: (a), (d), (h). **2.68** (a) (NH$_4$)$_2$CO$_3$. (b) Ca(OH)$_2$. (c) CdS. (d) ZnCr$_2$O$_7$. **2.70** (a) Ionic compounds formed between metallic and nonmetallic elements. (b) Transition metals. **2.72** ^{23}Na. **2.74** Hg and Br$_2$. **2.76** H$_2$, N$_2$, O$_2$, F$_2$, Cl$_2$, He, Ne, Ar, Kr, Xe, Rn. **2.78** Unreactive. He, Ne, and Ar are chemically inert. **2.80** Ra is a radioactive decay product of U-238. **2.82** Argentina. **2.84** (a) NaH, sodium hydride. (b) B$_2$O$_3$, diboron trioxide. (c) Na$_2$S, sodium sulfide. (d) AlF$_3$, aluminum fluoride. (e) OF$_2$, oxygen difluoride. (f) SrCl$_2$, strontium chloride. **2.86** NF$_3$ (nitrogen trifluoride), PBr$_5$ (phosphorus pentabromide), SCl$_2$ (sulfur dichloride). **2.88** 1st row: Mg^{2+}, HCO$_3^-$, Mg(HCO$_3$)$_2$. 2nd row: Sr^{2+}, Cl$^-$, strontium chloride. 3rd row: Fe(NO$_2$)$_3$, Iron(III) nitrite. 4th row: Mn^{2+}, ClO$_3^-$, Mn(ClO$_3$)$_2$. 5th row: Sn^{4+}, Br$^-$, tin(IV) bromide. 6th row: Co$_3$(PO$_4$)$_2$, cobalt(II) phosphate. 7th row: Hg$_2$I$_2$, mercury(I) iodide. 8th row: Cu$^+$, CO$_3^{2-}$, copper(I) carbonate. 9th row: Li$^+$, N^{3-}, Li$_3$N. 10th row: Al$_2$S$_3$, aluminum sulfide. **2.90** (b) Density of nucleus: 3.24×10^{14} g/cm^3; density of space occupied by electrons: 3.71×10^{-4} g/cm^3. The results support Rutherford's model.

Chapter 3

3.6 92.5%. **3.8** 5.1×10^{24} amu. **3.12** 5.8×10^3 light yr. **3.14** 9.96×10^{-15} mol Co. **3.16** 3.01×10^3 g Au. **3.18** (a) 1.244×10^{-22} g/As atom. (b) 9.746×10^{-23} g/Ni atom. **3.20** 2.98×10^{22} Cu atoms. **3.22** Pb. **3.24** (a) 73.89 g. (b) 76.15 g. (c) 119.37 g. (d) 176.12 g. (e) 101.11 g. (f) 100.95 g. **3.26** 6.69×10^{21} C$_2$H$_6$ molecules. **3.28** N: 3.37×10^{26} atoms; C: 1.69×10^{26} atoms; O: 1.69×10^{26} atoms; H: 6.74×10^{26} atoms. **3.30** 8.56×10^{22} molecules. **3.34** 7. **3.40** C: 10.06%; H: 0.8442%; Cl: 89.07%. **3.42** NH$_3$. **3.44** C$_2$H$_3$NO$_5$. **3.46** 39.3 g S. **3.48** 5.97 g F. **3.50** (a) CH$_2$O. (b) KCN. **3.52** C$_6$H$_6$. **3.54** C$_5$H$_8$O$_4$NNa. **3.60** (a) 2N$_2$O$_5 \longrightarrow$ 2N$_2$O$_4$ + O$_2$. (b) 2KNO$_3 \longrightarrow$ 2KNO$_2$ + O$_2$. (c) NH$_4$NO$_3 \longrightarrow$ N$_2$O + 2H$_2$O. (d) NH$_4$NO$_2 \longrightarrow$ N$_2$ + 2H$_2$O. (e) 2NaHCO$_3 \longrightarrow$ Na$_2$CO$_3$ + H$_2$O + CO$_2$. (f) P$_4$O$_{10}$ + 6H$_2$O $\longrightarrow$ 4H$_3$PO$_4$. (g) 2HCl + CaCO$_3 \longrightarrow$ CaCl$_2$ + H$_2$O + CO$_2$. (h) 2Al + 3H$_2$SO$_4 \longrightarrow$ Al$_2$(SO$_4$)$_3$ + 3H$_2$. (i) CO$_2$ + 2KOH $\longrightarrow$ K$_2$CO$_3$ + H$_2$O. (j) CH$_4$ + 2O$_2 \longrightarrow$ CO$_2$ + 2H$_2$O. (k) Be$_2$C + 4H$_2$O $\longrightarrow$ 2Be(OH)$_2$ + CH$_4$. (l) 3Cu + 8HNO$_3 \longrightarrow$ 3Cu(NO$_3$)$_2$ + 2NO + 4H$_2$O. (m) S + 6HNO$_3 \longrightarrow$ H$_2$SO$_4$ + 6NO$_2$ + 2H$_2$O. (n) 2NH$_3$ + 3CuO $\longrightarrow$ 3Cu + N$_2$ + 3H$_2$O. **3.64** (d). **3.66** 1.01 mol. **3.68** 20 mol. **3.70** (a) 2NaHCO$_3 \longrightarrow$ Na$_2$CO$_3$ + CO$_2$ + H$_2$O. (b) 78.3 g. **3.72** 255.9 g; 0.324 L. **3.74** 0.294 mol. **3.76** (a) NH$_4$NO$_3 \longrightarrow$ N$_2$O + 2H$_2$O. (b) 20 g N$_2$O. **3.78** 18.0 g. **3.82** 6 mol NH$_3$; 1 mol H$_2$. **3.84** O$_3$; 0.709 g NO$_2$; 6.9×10^{-3} mol NO. **3.86** HCl; 23.4 g. **3.90** (a) 7.05 g. (b) 92.9%. **3.92** 3.47×10^3 g. **3.94** 8.55 g; 76.6%. **3.96** (b). **3.98** Cl$_2$O$_7$. **3.100** (a) 0.212 mol. (b) 0.424 mol. **3.102** 18. **3.104** 2.4×10^{23} atoms. **3.106** 65.4 amu; Zn. **3.108** 89.6%. **3.110** CH$_2$O; C$_6$H$_{12}$O$_6$. **3.112** 51.8 g/mol; Cr. **3.114** 1.6×10^4 g/mol. **3.116** NaCl: 32.17%; Na$_2$SO$_4$: 20.09%; NaNO$_3$: 47.75%. **3.118** Ca: 38.76%; P: 19.97%; O: 41.27%. **3.120** Yes. **3.122** 2.01×10^{21} molecules. **3.124** 16.00 amu. **3.126** (e). **3.128** PtCl$_2$; PtCl$_4$. **3.130** (a) Mn$_3$O$_4$. (b) 3MnO$_2 \longrightarrow$ Mn$_3$O$_4$ + O$_2$. **3.132** 6.1×10^5 tons. **3.134** Mg$_3$N$_2$ (magnesium nitride). **3.136** PbC$_8$H$_{20}$. **3.138** (a) 4.3×10^{22} atoms. (b) 1.6×10^2 pm. **3.140** 28.97 g/mol. **3.142** 3.1×10^{23} molecules/mol. **3.144** (a) C$_3$H$_8$ + 3H$_2$O $\longrightarrow$ 3CO + 7H$_2$. (b) 9.09×10^2 kg.

Chapter 4

4.8 (c). **4.10** (a) Strong electrolyte. (b) Nonelectrolyte. (c) Weak electrolyte. (d) Strong electrolyte. **4.12** (b) and (c). **4.14** HCl does not ionize in benzene. **4.18** (b). **4.20** (a) Insoluble. (b) Soluble. (c) Soluble. (d) Insoluble. (e) Soluble. **4.24** (a) Add chloride ions. (b) Add hydroxide ions. (c) Add carbonate ions. (d) Add sulfate ions. **4.32** (a) Brønsted base. (b) Brønsted base. (c) Brønsted acid. (d) Brønsted base and Brønsted acid. **4.34** (a) $CH_3COOH + K^+ + OH^- \longrightarrow K^+ + CH_3COO^- + H_2O$; $CH_3COOH + OH^- \longrightarrow CH_3COO^- + H_2O$. (b) $H_2CO_3 + 2Na^+ + 2OH^- \longrightarrow 2Na^+ + CO_3^{2-} + 2H_2O$; $H_2CO_3 + 2OH^- \longrightarrow CO_3^{2-} + 2H_2O$. (c) $2H^+ + 2NO_3^- + Ba^{2+} + 2OH^- \longrightarrow Ba^{2+} + 2NO_3^- + 2H_2O$; $2H^+ + 2OH^- \longrightarrow 2H_2O$. **4.44** (a) $Fe \longrightarrow Fe^{3+} + 3e^-$; $O_2 + 4e^- \longrightarrow 2O^{2-}$. Oxidizing agent: O_2; reducing agent: Fe. (b) $2Br^- \longrightarrow Br_2 + 2e^-$; $Cl_2 + 2e^- \longrightarrow 2Cl^-$. Oxidizing agent: Cl_2; reducing agent: Br^-. (c) $Si \longrightarrow Si^{4+} + 4e^-$; $F_2 + 2e^- \longrightarrow 2F^-$. Oxidizing agent: F_2; reducing agent: Si. (d) $H_2 \longrightarrow 2H^+ + 2e^-$; $Cl_2 + 2e^- \longrightarrow 2Cl^-$. Oxidizing agent: Cl_2; reducing agent: H_2. **4.46** (a) +5. (b) +1. (c) +3. (d) +5. (e) +5. (f) +5. **4.48** All are zero. **4.50** (a) −3. (b) −$\frac{1}{2}$. (c) −1. (d) +4. (e) +3. (f) −2. (g) +3. (h) +6. **4.52** Li and Ca. **4.54** (a) No reaction. (b) No reaction. (c) $Mg + CuSO_4 \longrightarrow MgSO_4 + Cu$. (d) $Cl_2 + 2KBr \longrightarrow Br_2 + 2KCl$. **4.56** (a) Combination. (b) Decomposition. (c) Displacement. (d) Disproportionation. **4.60** Dissolve 15.0 g $NaNO_3$ in enough water to make up 250 mL. **4.62** 10.8 g. **4.64** (a) 1.37 M. (b) 0.426 M. (c) 0.716 M. **4.66** (a) 6.50 g. (b) 2.45 g. (c) 2.65 g. (d) 7.36 g. (e) 3.95 g. **4.70** 0.0433 M. **4.72** 126 mL. **4.74** 1.09 M. **4.78** 35.72%. **4.80** 2.31×10^{-4} M. **4.86** 0.217 M. **4.88** (a) 6.00 mL. (b) 8.00 mL. **4.92** 9.45×10^{-3} g. **4.94** 0.06020 M. **4.96** 5.40%. **4.98** 0.231 mg. **4.100** (i) Only oxygen supports combustion. (ii) Only CO_2 reacts with $Ca(OH)_2$ to form $CaCO_3$ (white precipitate). **4.102** 1.26 M. **4.104** 0.171 M. **4.106** 0.115 M. **4.108** Ag: 1.25 g; Zn: 2.12 g. **4.110** 0.0722 M NaOH. **4.112** 24.0 g/mol; Mg. **4.114** 1.73 M. **4.116** Only Fe(II) is oxidized by $KMnO_4$ solution and can therefore change the purple color to colorless. **4.118** Ions are removed as the $BaSO_4$ precipitate. **4.120** (a) Conductivity test. (b) Only NaCl reacts with $AgNO_3$ to form AgCl precipitate. **4.122** The Cl^- ion cannot accept any electrons. **4.124** Reaction is too violent. **4.126** Use sodium bicarbonate: $HCO_3^- + H^+ \longrightarrow H_2O + CO_2$. NaOH is a caustic substance and unsafe to use in this manner. **4.128** (a) Conductivity. Reaction with $AgNO_3$ to form AgCl. (b) Soluble in water. Nonelectrolyte. (c) Possesses properties of acids. (d) Soluble. Reacts with acids to give CO_2. (e) Soluble, strong electrolyte. Reacts with acids to give CO_2. (f) Weak electrolyte and weak acid. (g) Soluble in water. Reacts with NaOH to produce $Mg(OH)_2$ precipitate. (h) Strong electrolyte and strong base. (i) Characteristic odor. Weak electrolyte and weak base. (j) Insoluble. Reacts with acids. (k) Insoluble. Reacts with acids to produce CO_2. **4.130** NaCl: 43.97%; KCl: 56.03%. **4.132** 1.33 g. **4.134** 55.80%. **4.136** (a) 1.40 M. (b) 4.96 g. **4.138** (a) Precipitation: $Mg^{2+} + 2OH^- \longrightarrow Mg(OH)_2$; acid-base: $Mg(OH)_2 + 2HCl \longrightarrow MgCl_2 + 2H_2O$; redox: $MgCl_2 \longrightarrow Mg + Cl_2$. (b) NaOH is more expensive than CaO. (c) Dolomite provides additional Mg. **4.140** (a) $NH_4^+ + OH^- \longrightarrow NH_3 + H_2O$. (b) 97.99%. **4.142** Zero. **4.144** 0.224%. **4.146** (a) $Zn + H_2SO_4 \longrightarrow ZnSO_4 + H_2$. (b) $2KClO_3 \longrightarrow 2KCl + 3O_2$. (c) $Na_2CO_3 + 2HCl \longrightarrow 2NaCl + CO_2 + H_2O$. (d) $NH_4NO_2 \longrightarrow N_2 + 2H_2O$. **4.148** Because the volume depends on the amount of solid dissolved. **4.150** Yes.

Chapter 5

5.14 0.797 atm; 80.8 kPa. **5.18** (1) b. (2) a. (3) c. (4) a. **5.20** 53 atm. **5.22** (a) 0.69 L. (b) 61 atm. **5.24** 1.3×10^2 K. **5.26** ClF_3.

5.32 6.2 atm. **5.34** 745 K. **5.36** 1.9 atm. **5.38** 0.82 L. **5.40** 45.1 L. **5.42** 6.1×10^{-3} atm. **5.44** 35.0 g/mol. **5.46** N_2: 2.1×10^{22}; O_2: 5.7×10^{21}; Ar: 3×10^{20}. **5.48** 2.98 g/L. **5.50** SF_4. **5.52** 370 L. **5.54** 88.9%. **5.56** $M + 3HCl \longrightarrow 1.5H_2 + MCl_3$; M_2O_3, $M_2(SO_4)_3$. **5.58** 2.84×10^{-2} mol CO_2; 94.7%. **5.60** 1.71×10^3 L. **5.64** (a) 0.89 atm. (b) 1.4 L. **5.66** 349 mmHg. **5.68** 19.8 g. **5.70** H_2: 650 mmHg; N_2: 217 mmHg. **5.78** N_2: 472 m/s; O_2: 441 m/s; O_3: 360 m/s. **5.80** 2.8 m/s; 2.7 m/s. Squaring favors the larger values. **5.86** No. **5.88** Ne. **5.90** C_6H_6. **5.92** 445 mL. **5.94** (a) 9.53 atm. (b) $Ni(CO)_4$ decomposes to give CO, which increases the pressure. **5.96** 1.30×10^{22} molecules; CO_2, O_2, N_2, H_2O. **5.98** 5.25×10^{18} kg. **5.100** 0.0701 M. **5.102** He: 0.16 atm; Ne: 2.0 atm. **5.104** HCl dissolves in the water, creating a partial vacuum. **5.106** 7. **5.108** (a) 61.2 m/s; (b) 4.58×10^{-4} s. (c) 328 m/s; 366 m/s. **5.110** 2.09×10^4 g; 1.58×10^4 L. **5.112** Higher partial pressure inside a paper bag. **5.114** To equalize the pressure as the amount of ink decreases. **5.116** (a) $NH_4NO_3 \longrightarrow N_2O + 2H_2O$. (b) 0.0821 L · atm/K · mol. **5.118** C_6H_6. **5.120** The low atmospheric pressure caused the harmful gases (CO, CO_2, CH_4) to flow out of the mine, and the man suffocated. **5.122** (a) 4.90 L. (b) 6.0 atm. (c) 1 atm. **5.124** (a) 5×10^{-22} atm. (b) 5×10^{20} L. **5.126** 91%. **5.128** 1.7×10^{12} molecules. **5.130** NO_2. **5.132** 7.0×10^{-3} m/s; 3.5×10^{-30} J. **5.134** 2.3×10^3 L. **5.136** 1.8×10^2 mL. **5.138** (a) 1.09×10^{44} molecules. (b) 1.18×10^{22} molecules/breath. (c) 2.60×10^{30} molecules. (d) 2.39×10^{-14}; 3×10^8 molecules. (e) Complete mixing of air; no molecules escaped to the outer atmosphere; no molecules used up during metabolism, nitrogen fixation, etc. **5.140** 3.7 nm; 0.31 nm. **5.142** 0.54 atm. **5.144** 53.4%. **5.146** (a) 421 m/s; 515 m/s. (b) 1200 K.

Chapter 6

6.16 (a) 0. (b) −9.5 J. (c) −18 J. **6.18** 48 J. **6.20** -3.1×10^3 J. **6.26** -1.57×10^4 kJ. **6.28** −553.8 kJ/mol. **6.34** 728 kJ. **6.36** 50.7°C. **6.38** 26.3°C. **6.46** O_2. **6.48** (a) $\Delta H_f^\circ[Br_2(l)] = 0$; $\Delta H_f^\circ[Br_2(g)] > 0$. (b) $\Delta H_f^\circ[I_2(s)] = 0$; $\Delta H_f^\circ[I_2(g)] > 0$. **6.50** Measure ΔH° for the formation of Ag_2O from Ag and O_2 and of $CaCl_2$ from Ca and Cl_2. **6.52** (a) −167.2 kJ/mol. (b) −56.2 kJ/mol. **6.54** (a) −1411 kJ/mol. (b) −1124 kJ/mol. **6.56** 218.2 kJ/mol. **6.58** −4.51 kJ/g. **6.60** 2.70×10^2 kJ. **6.62** −84.6 kJ/mol. **6.64** −780 kJ/mol. **6.72** $\Delta H_2 - \Delta H_1$. **6.74** (a) −336.5 kJ/mol. (b) NH_3. **6.76** −43.6 kJ. **6.78** 0. **6.80** −350.7 kJ/mol. **6.82** 0.492 J/g · °C. **6.84** The first (exothermic) reaction can be used to promote the second (endothermic) reaction. **6.86** 1.09×10^4 L. **6.88** 4.10 L. **6.90** 5.60 kJ/mol. **6.92** (a). **6.94** (a) 0. (b) −9.1 J. (c) 2.4 L; −48 J. **6.96** (a) A more fully packed freezer has a greater mass and hence a larger heat capacity. (b) Tea or coffee has a greater amount of water, which has a higher specific heat than noodles. **6.98** -1.84×10^3 kJ. **6.100** 3.0×10^9. **6.102** 5.35 kJ/°C. **6.104** -5.2×10^6 kJ. **6.106** (a) 3.4×10^5 g. (b) -2.0×10^8 J. **6.108** (a) 1.4×10^2 kJ. (b) 3.9×10^2 kJ. **6.110** (a) −65.2 kJ/mol. (b) −9.0 kJ/mol. **6.112** −110.5 kJ/mol. It will form both CO and CO_2. **6.114** (a) 0.50 J. (b) 32 m/s. (c) 0.12°C. **6.116** −277.0 kJ/mol. **6.118** 104 g. **6.120** 9.9×10^8 J; 304°C. **6.122** 1.51×10^3 kJ. **6.124** $\Delta E = -5153$ kJ/mol; $\Delta H = -5158$ kJ/mol.

Chapter 7

7.8 (a) 6.58×10^{14}/s. (b) 1.22×10^8 nm. **7.10** 2.5 min. **7.12** 4.95×10^{14}/s. **7.16** (a) 4.0×10^2 nm. (b) 5.0×10^{-19} J. **7.18** 1.2×10^2 nm (UV). **7.20** (a) 3.70×10^2 nm. (b) UV. (c) 5.38×10^{-19} J. **7.26** Use a prism. **7.28** Compare the emission spectra with those on Earth of known elements. **7.30** 3.027×10^{-19} J. **7.32** 6.17×10^{14}/s; 486 nm. **7.34** 5.

7.40 1.37×10^{-6} nm. **7.42** 1.7×10^{-23} nm. **7.54** $\ell = 2$: $m_\ell = -2$, $-1, 0, 1, 2$. $\ell = 1$: $m_\ell = -1, 0, 1$. $\ell = 0$: $m_\ell = 0$. **7.56** (a) $n = 3$, $\ell = 0$, $m_\ell = 0$. (b) $n = 4$, $\ell = 1$, $m_\ell = -1, 0, 1$. (c) $n = 3$, $\ell = 2$, $m_\ell = -2, -1, 0, 1, 2$. In all cases, $m_s = +\frac{1}{2}$ or $-\frac{1}{2}$. **7.58** Differ in orientation only. **7.60** $6s$, $6p$, $6d$, $6f$, $6g$, and $6h$. **7.62** $2n^2$. **7.64** (a) 3. (b) 6. (c) 0. **7.66** There is no shielding in a H atom. **7.68** (a) $2s < 2p$. (b) $3p < 3d$. (c) $3s < 4s$. (d) $4d < 5f$. **7.80** Al: $1s^2 2s^2 2p^6 3s^2 3p^1$. B: $1s^2 2s^2 2p^1$. F: $1s^2 2s^2 2p^5$. **7.82** B(1), Ne(0), P(3), Sc(1), Mn(5), Se(2), Kr(0), Fe(4), Cd(0), I(1), Pb(2). **7.84** Ge: $[\text{Ar}]4s^2 3d^{10} 4p^2$. Fe: $[\text{Ar}]4s^2 3d^6$. Zn: $[\text{Ar}]4s^2 3d^{10}$. Ni: $[\text{Ar}]4s^2 3d^8$. W: $[\text{Xe}]6s^2 4f^{14} 5d^4$. Tl: $[\text{Xe}]6s^2 4f^{14} 5d^{10} 6p^1$. **7.86** S^+. **7.92** $[\text{Kr}]5s^2 4d^5$. **7.94** (a) Incorrect. (b) Correct. (c) Incorrect. **7.96** (a) An e in a $2s$ and an e in each $2p$ orbital. (b) $2\ e$ each in a $4p$, a $4d$, and a $4f$ orbital. (c) $2\ e$ in each of the 5 $3d$ orbitals. (d) An e in a $2s$ orbital. (e) $2\ e$ in a f orbital. **7.98** Wave properties. **7.100** (a) 1.05×10^{-25} nm. (b) 8.86 nm. **7.102** (a) 1.20×10^{18} photons. (b) 3.76×10^8 W. **7.104** 419 nm. In principle, yes; in practice, no. **7.106** 3.0×10^{19} photons. **7.108** He^+: 164 nm, 121 nm, 109 nm, 103 nm (all in the UV region). H: 657 nm, 487 nm, 434 nm, 411 nm (all in the visible region). **7.110** 1.2×10^2 photons. **7.112** Yellow light will generate more electrons; blue light will generate electrons with greater kinetic energy. **7.114** (a) He. (b) N. (c) Na. (d) As. (e) Cl. See Table 7.3 for ground-state electron configurations. **7.116** They might have discovered the wave properties of electrons. **7.118** 7.39×10^{-2} nm. **7.120** (a) False. (b) False. (c) True. (d) False. (e) True. **7.122** 2.0×10^{-5} m/s. **7.124** (a) and (f) violate Pauli exclusion principle; (b), (d), and (e) violate Hund's rule. **7.126** 2.8×10^6 K. **7.128** 2.76×10^{-11} m. **7.130** 17.4 pm. **7.132** 0.929 pm; 3.23×10^{20}/s.

Chapter 8

8.20 (a) $1s^2 2s^2 2p^6 3s^2 3p^5$. (b) Representative. (c) Paramagnetic. **8.22** (a) and (d); (b) and (e); (c) and (f). **8.24** (a) Group 1A. (b) Group 5A. (c) Group 8A. (d) Group 8B. **8.26** Fe. **8.28** (a) [Ne]. (b) [Ne]. (c) [Ar]. (d) [Ar]. (e) [Ar]. (f) $[\text{Ar}]3d^6$. (g) $[\text{Ar}]3d^9$. (h) $[\text{Ar}]3d^{10}$. **8.30** (a) Cr^{3+}. (b) Sc^{3+}. (c) Rh^{3+}. (d) Ir^{3+}. **8.32** Be^{2+} and He; F^- and N^{3-}; Fe^{2+} and Co^{3+}; S^{2-} and Ar. **8.38** Na > Mg > Al > P > Cl. **8.40** F. **8.42** The effective nuclear charge that the outermost electrons feel increases across the period. **8.44** $\text{Mg}^{2+} < \text{Na}^+ < \text{F}^- < \text{O}^{2-} < \text{N}^{3-}$. **8.46** Te^{2-}. **8.48** $-199.4°\text{C}$. **8.52** K < Ca < P < F < Ne. **8.54** The single $3p$ electron in Al is well shielded by the $1s$, $2s$, and $3s$ electrons. **8.56** $1s^2 2s^2 2p^6$: 2080 kJ/mol. **8.58** 8.43×10^6 kJ/mol. **8.62** Cl. **8.64** The ns^1 configuration enables them to accept another electron. **8.68** Fr should be the most reactive toward water and oxygen, forming FrOH and Fr_2O and FrO_2. **8.70** The Group 1B elements have higher ionization energies due to the incomplete shielding of the inner d electrons. **8.72** (a) $\text{Li}_2\text{O} + \text{H}_2\text{O} \longrightarrow 2\text{LiOH}$. (b) $\text{CaO} + \text{H}_2\text{O} \longrightarrow \text{Ca(OH)}_2$. (c) $\text{SO}_3 + \text{H}_2\text{O} \longrightarrow \text{H}_2\text{SO}_4$. **8.74** BaO. **8.76** (a) Bromine. (b) Nitrogen. (c) Rubidium. (d) Magnesium. **8.78** (a) $\text{Mg}^{2+} < \text{Na}^+ < \text{F}^- < \text{O}^{2-}$. (b) $\text{O}^{2-} < \text{F}^- < \text{Na}^+ < \text{Mg}^{2+}$. **8.80** M is K; X is Br. **8.82** N and O^+; Ne and N^{3-}; Ar and S^{2-}; Zn and As^{3+}; Cs^+ and Xe. **8.84** (a) and (d). **8.86** Yellow-green gas: F_2; yellow gas: Cl_2; red liquid: Br_2; dark solid: I_2. **8.88** Fluorine. **8.90** H^-. **8.92** Li_2O (basic); BeO (amphoteric); B_2O_3 (acidic); CO_2 (acidic); N_2O_5 (acidic). **8.94** It forms both the H^+ and H^- ions; H^+ is a single proton. **8.96** 0.65. **8.98** 76.7%. **8.100** 418 kJ/mol. Use maximum wavelength. **8.102** 7.28×10^3 kJ/mol. **8.104** X: Sn or Pb; Y: P; Z: alkali metal. **8.106** 495.9 kJ/mol. **8.108** 343 nm (UV). **8.110** 604.3 kJ. **8.112** K_2TiO_4. **8.114** $2\text{K}_2\text{MnF}_6 + 4\text{SbF}_5 \longrightarrow 4\text{KSbF}_6 + 2\text{MnF}_3 + \text{F}_2$. **8.116** N_2O (+1), NO (+2), N_2O_3 (+3), NO_2 and N_2O_4 (+4), N_2O_5 (+5). **8.118** The larger the effective nuclear charge, the more tightly held are the electrons. The

atomic radius will be small and the ionization energy will be large. **8.120** m.p.: $6.3°\text{C}$; b.p.: $74.9°\text{C}$. **8.122** The heat generated from nuclear decay can decompose compounds. **8.124** Ar: 39.95 amu; K: 39.10 amu. **8.126** $Z = 119$; $[\text{Rn}]7s^2 5f^{14} 6d^{10} 7p^6 8s^1$. **8.128** Group 2A. **8.130** (a) SiH_4, GeH_4, SnH_4, PbH_4. (b) RbH more ionic. (c) $\text{Ra} + 2\text{H}_2\text{O} \longrightarrow \text{Ra(OH)}_2 + \text{H}_2$. (d) Be. **8.132** See chapter. **8.134** Carbon (diamond).

Chapter 9

9.16 (a) RbI, rubidium iodide. (b) Cs_2SO_4, cesium sulfate. (c) Sr_3N_2, strontium nitride. (d) Al_2S_3, aluminum sulfide.

9.18 (a) $\cdot \text{Sr} \cdot + \cdot \ddot{\text{Se}} \cdot \longrightarrow \text{Sr}^{2+} : \ddot{\text{Se}} :^{2-}$

(b) $\cdot \text{Ca} \cdot + 2\text{H} \cdot \longrightarrow \text{Ca}^{2+} 2\text{H} :^-$

(c) $3\text{Li} \cdot + \cdot \ddot{\text{N}} \cdot \longrightarrow 3\text{Li}^+ : \ddot{\text{N}} :^{3-}$

(d) $2 \cdot \text{Al} \cdot + 3 \cdot \ddot{\text{S}} \cdot \longrightarrow 2\text{Al}^{3+} 3 : \ddot{\text{S}} :^{2-}$

9.20 (a) BF_3, covalent. Boron trifluoride. (b) KBr, ionic. Potassium bromide. **9.26** 2195 kJ/mol. **9.36** C—H < Br—H < F—H < Li—Cl < Na—Cl < K—F. **9.38** Cl—Cl < Br—Cl < Si—C < Cs—F. **9.40** (a) Covalent. (b) Polar covalent. (c) Ionic. (d) Polar covalent.

9.44 (a) $: \ddot{\text{F}} - \ddot{\text{O}} - \ddot{\text{F}} :$ (b) $: \ddot{\text{F}} - \text{N} = \text{N} - \ddot{\text{F}} :$

(c) H—Si—Si—H with H's above and below each Si (d) $^- : \ddot{\text{O}} - \text{H}$

(e) H—C—C—Ö:$^-$ with H, O double bond and :Cl: below first C

(f) $\text{H} - \overset{+}{\text{N}} - \text{H}$ with H above and below and H at ends

9.46 (a) $^- : \ddot{\text{O}} - \ddot{\text{O}} :^-$ (b) $^- : \text{C} \equiv \text{C} :^-$ (c) $: \text{N} \equiv \text{O} :^+$

(d) $\text{H} - \overset{+}{\text{N}} - \text{H}$ with H above and below **9.48** H—C—C—Ö—H with H's and O double bond

9.52 $\ddot{\text{O}} = \text{Cl} - \ddot{\text{O}} :^- \longleftrightarrow {}^- : \ddot{\text{O}} - \text{Cl} = \ddot{\text{O}} \longleftrightarrow {}^- : \ddot{\text{O}} - \text{Cl} = \ddot{\text{O}}$

9.54 $\text{H} - \text{C} = \text{N} = \text{N}^- \longleftrightarrow \text{H} - \overset{+}{\text{C}} - \text{N} \equiv \text{N} :$

9.56 $^- \ddot{\text{N}} = \overset{+}{\text{N}} = \ddot{\text{O}} \longleftrightarrow : \text{N} \equiv \overset{+}{\text{N}} - \ddot{\text{O}} :^- \longleftrightarrow {}^{2-} : \ddot{\text{N}} - \overset{+}{\text{N}} \equiv \overset{+}{\text{O}} :$

9.62 $^+\ddot{\text{Cl}} = \overset{2-}{\text{Be}} = \ddot{\text{Cl}}^+$ Not plausible.

9.64 Cl—Sb—Cl with Cl above and Cl below (two) The octet rule is not obeyed.

9.66 Cl—Al—Cl with Cl above and Cl below Coordinate covalent bond.

9.70 303.0 kJ/mol. **9.72** (a) -2759 kJ/mol. (b) -2855 kJ/mol.
9.74 Ionic: $RbCl$, KO_2; covalent: PF_5, BrF_3, CI_4. **9.76** Ionic:
NaF, MgF_2, AlF_3; covalent: SiF_4, PF_5, SF_6, ClF_3. **9.78** KF:
ionic, high melting point, soluble in water, its melt and solution
conduct electricity. C_6H_6: covalent and discrete molecule,
low melting point, insoluble in water, does not conduct
electricity.

9.80 $\overset{-}{\text{N}}=\overset{+}{\text{N}}=\overset{..}{\underset{..}{\text{N}}}{}^{-} \longleftrightarrow :\text{N}\equiv\overset{+}{\text{N}}-\overset{..}{\underset{..}{\text{N}}}:^{2-} \longleftrightarrow {}^{2-}\overset{..}{\underset{..}{:\text{N}}}-\overset{+}{\text{N}}\equiv\text{N}:$

9.82 (a) $AlCl_4^-$. (b) AlF_6^{3-}. (c) $AlCl_3$. **9.84** CF_2: violates the octet
rule; LiO_2: lattice energy too low; $CsCl_2$: second ionization energy
too high to produce Cs^{2+}; PI_5: I atom too bulky to fit around P.
9.86 (a) False. (b) True. (c) False. (d) False. **9.88** -67 kJ/mol.
9.90 N_2. **9.92** NH_4^+ and CH_4; CO and N_2; $B_3N_3H_6$ and C_6H_6.

9.94 $\text{H}-\overset{..}{\underset{|}{\text{N}}}:{}^- + \text{H}-\overset{..}{\underset{..}{\text{O}}}: \longrightarrow \text{H}-\overset{|}{\underset{|}{\text{N}}}-\text{H} + {}^-:\overset{..}{\underset{..}{\text{O}}}-\text{H}$
$\qquad\quad \text{H} \qquad\quad \text{H} \qquad\qquad\quad \text{H}$

9.96 F_3^- violates the octet rule.

9.98 $CH_3-\overset{..}{\underset{..}{\text{N}}}=\text{C}=\overset{..}{\underset{..}{\text{O}}} \longleftrightarrow CH_3-\overset{+}{\text{N}}\equiv\text{C}-\overset{..}{\underset{..}{\text{O}}}:^-$

9.100 (c) No bond between C and O. (d) Large formal charges.

9.102 (a) $\text{F}-\overset{\text{Cl}}{\underset{\text{Cl}}{\text{C}}}-\text{Cl}$ (b) $\text{F}-\overset{\text{Cl}}{\underset{\text{Cl}}{\text{C}}}-\text{F}$ (c) $\text{H}-\overset{\text{F}}{\underset{\text{Cl}}{\text{C}}}-\text{F}$ (d) $\text{F}-\overset{\text{F}}{\underset{\text{F}}{\text{C}}}-\overset{\text{H}}{\underset{\text{F}}{\text{C}}}-\text{F}$

9.104 (a) -9.2 kJ/mol. (b) -9.2 kJ/mol. **9.106** (a) $^-:\text{C}\equiv\text{O}:^+$
(b) $:\text{N}\equiv\text{O}:^+$ (c) $^-:\text{C}\equiv\text{N}:$ (d) $:\text{N}\equiv\text{N}:$ **9.108** True. **9.110**
(a) 114 kJ/mol. (b) Extra electron increases repulsion between F
atoms. **9.112** Lone pair on C and negative formal charge on C.

9.114 (a) $:\text{N}=\overset{..}{\text{O}} \longleftrightarrow \overset{..}{\text{N}}=\overset{..}{\text{O}}{}^+$ (b) No.

9.116 Violates the octet rule.

9.118 $\overset{\text{Cl}}{\underset{\text{Cl}}{}}\diagdown\text{Al}\diagup\overset{\text{Cl}}{\underset{\text{Cl}}{}}\diagdown\text{Al}\diagup\overset{\text{Cl}}{\underset{\text{Cl}}{}}$ The arrows indicate coordinate
covalent bonds.

9.120 347 kJ/mol.

9.122 (a) $\overset{\text{H}}{\underset{\text{H}}{\text{C}}}=\overset{\text{H}}{\underset{\text{Cl}}{\text{C}}}$ (b) $-\overset{\text{H}}{\underset{\text{H}}{\text{C}}}-\overset{\text{H}}{\underset{\text{Cl}}{\text{C}}}-\overset{\text{H}}{\underset{\text{H}}{\text{C}}}-\overset{\text{H}}{\underset{\text{Cl}}{\text{C}}}-$ (c) -1.2×10^6 kJ.

9.124 O: 3.16; F: 4.37; Cl: 3.48. **9.126** (1) The MgO solid
containing Mg^+ and O^- ions would be paramagnetic. (2) The
lattice energy would be like NaCl (too low).

Chapter 10

10.8 (a) Trigonal planar. (b) Linear. (c) Tetrahedral.
10.10 (a) Tetrahedral. (b) T-shaped. (c) Bent. (d) Trigonal planar.
(e) Tetrahedral. **10.12** (a) Tetrahedral. (b) Bent. (c) Trigonal
planar. (d) Linear. (e) Square planar. (f) Tetrahedral. (g) Trigonal
bipyramidal. (h) Trigonal pyramidal. (i) Tetrahedral. **10.14** $SiCl_4$,
CI_4, $CdCl_4^{2-}$. **10.20** Electronegativity decreases from F to I.
10.22 Higher. **10.24** (b) $=$ (d) $<$ (c) $<$ (a). **10.34** sp^3. **10.36** B:
sp^2 to sp^3; N: remains sp^3. **10.38** From left to right. (a) sp^3. (b)
sp^3, sp^2, sp^2. (c) sp^3, sp, sp, sp^3. (d) sp^3, sp^2. (e) sp^3, sp^2. **10.40**
sp. **10.42** sp^3d. **10.44** 9 pi bonds and 9 sigma bonds. **10.50**
Electron spins must be paired in H_2. **10.52** $Li_2^- = Li_2^+ < Li_2$.
10.54 B_2^+. **10.56** MO theory predicts O_2 is paramagnetic. **10.58**
$O_2^{2-} < O_2^- < O_2 < O_2^+$. **10.60** B_2 contains a pi bond; C_2 contains
2 pi bonds. **10.64** The circle shows electron delocalization.

10.66 (a) $\overset{:\text{F}:}{\underset{..}{\text{O}}}=\overset{|}{\text{N}}-\overset{..}{\underset{..}{\text{O}}}:^- \longleftrightarrow {}^-:\overset{..}{\underset{..}{\text{O}}}-\overset{|}{\underset{+}{\text{N}}}=\overset{..}{\underset{..}{\text{O}}}$ (b) sp^2. (c) N forms

sigma bonds with F and O atoms. There is a pi molecular
orbital delocalized over N and O atoms. **10.68** sp^2. **10.70** Linear.
Dipole moment measurement. **10.72** The large size of Si results
in poor sideways overlap of p orbitals to form pi bonds.
10.74 XeF_3^+: T-shaped; XeF_5^+: square pyramidal; SbF_6^-:
octahedral. **10.76** (a) $180°$. (b) $120°$. (c) $109.5°$. (d) About
$109.5°$. (e) $180°$. (f) About $120°$. (g) About $109.5°$. (h) $109.5°$.
10.78 sp^3d. **10.80** ICl_2^- and $CdBr_2$. **10.82** (a) sp^2. (b) Molecule
on the right. **10.84** The pi bond in *cis*-dichloroethylene prevents
rotation. **10.86** O_3, CO, CO_2, NO_2, N_2O, CH_4, $CFCl_3$. **10.88** C:
all single-bonded C atoms are sp^3, the double-bonded C atoms
are sp^2; N: single-bonded N atoms are sp^3, N atoms that form
one double bond are sp^2, N atom that forms two double bonds
is sp. **10.90** Si has $3d$ orbitals so water can add to Si (valence
shell expansion). **10.92** C: sp^2; N: N atom that forms a double
bond is sp^2, the others are sp^3. **10.94** (a) Use a conventional
oven. (b) No. Polar molecules would absorb microwaves.
(c) Water molecules absorb part of microwaves. **10.96** The small
size of F results in a shorter bond and greater lone pair
repulsion. **10.98** 43.6%. **10.100** Second and third vibrations.
CO, NO_2, N_2O. **10.102** (a) $[Ne_2](\sigma_{3s})^2(\sigma_{3s}^*)^2(\pi_{3p_y})^2(\pi_{3p_z})^2(\sigma_{3p_x})^2$.
(b) 3. (c) Diamagnetic. **10.104** (a) The two $90°$ rotations will
break and make the pi bond and convert *cis*-dichloroethylene to
trans-dichloroethylene. (b) The pi bond is weaker because of the
lesser extent of sideways orbital overlap. (c) 444 nm.

Chapter 11

11.8 Methane. **11.10** (a) Dispersion forces. (b) Dispersion and
dipole-dipole forces. (c) Same as (b). (d) Dispersion and ion-ion
forces. (e) Same as (a). **11.12** (e). **11.14** Only 1-butanol can
form hydrogen bonds. **11.16** (a) Xe. (b) CS_2. (c) Cl_2. (d) LiF.
(e) NH_3. **11.18** (a) Hydrogen bond and dispersion forces.
(b) Dispersion forces. (c) Dispersion forces. (d) Covalent bond.
11.20 The compound on the left can form intramolecular
hydrogen bond. **11.32** Between ethanol and glycerol. **11.38** scc:
1; bcc: 2; fcc: 4. **11.40** 6.17×10^{23} Ba atoms/mol. **11.42** 458 pm.
11.44 XY_3. **11.48** 0.220 nm. **11.52** Molecular solid. **11.54** Molecular solids: Se_8, HBr, CO_2, P_4O_6, SiH_4. Covalent solids: Si, C.
11.56 Each C atom in diamond is covalently bonded to four other
C atoms. Graphite has delocalized electrons in two dimensions.
11.78 2.67×10^3 kJ. **11.80** 47.03 kJ/mol. **11.82** Freezing,
sublimation. **11.84** When steam condenses at $100°$C, it releases
heat equal to heat of vaporization. **11.86** 331 mmHg.
11.88 75.9 kJ/mol. **11.92** Initially ice melts because of the
increase in pressure. As the wire sinks into the ice, the water
above it refreezes. In this way, the wire moves through the ice
without cutting it in half. **11.94** (a) Ice melts. (b) Water vapor
condenses to ice. (c) Water boils. **11.96** (d). **11.98** Covalent
crystal. **11.100** CCl_4. **11.102** 760 mmHg. **11.104** It is the critical
point. **11.106** Crystalline SiO_2. **11.108** (a), (b), (d). **11.110** 8.3×10^{-3} atm. **11.112** (a) K_2S. (b) Br_2. **11.114** SO_2. It is a polar
molecule. **11.116** 62.4 kJ/mol. **11.118** Smaller ions have larger
charge densities and a greater extent of hydration. **11.120**
(a) 30.7 kJ/mol. (b) 192.5 kJ/mol. **11.122** (a) Decreases. (b) No
change. (c) No change. **11.124** $CaCO_3(s) \longrightarrow CaO(s) +$
$CO_2(g)$. Three phases. **11.126** SiO_2 is a covalent crystal. CO_2
exists as discrete molecules. **11.128** 66.8%. **11.130** scc: 52.4%;
bcc: 68.0%; fcc: 74.0%. **11.132** 1.69 g/cm^3. **11.134** (a) Two
(diamond/graphite/liquid and graphite/liquid/vapor).
(b) Diamond. (c) Apply high pressure at high temperature.
11.136 Molecules in the cane are held together by
intermolecular forces. **11.138** When the tungsten filament is
heated to a high temperature (ca. 3000°C), it sublimes and
condenses on the inside walls. The inert pressurized Ar gas
retards sublimation. **11.140** When methane burns in air, it forms

carbon dioxide and water vapor. The latter condenses on the outside of the cold beaker.

Chapter 12

12.10 Cyclohexane cannot form hydrogen bonds. **12.12** The longer chains become more nonpolar. **12.16** (a) 25.9 g. (b) 1.72×10^3 g. **12.18** (a) 2.68 m. (b) 7.82 m. **12.20** 0.010 m. **12.22** 5.0×10^2 m; 18.3 M. **12.24** (a) 2.41 m. (b) 2.13 M. (c) 0.0587 L. **12.28** 45.9 g. **12.36** CO_2 pressure is greater at the bottom of the mine. **12.38** 0.28 L. **12.52** 1.3×10^3 g. **12.54** Ethanol: 30.0 mmHg; 1-propanol: 26.3 mmHg. **12.56** 128 g. **12.58** 0.59 m. **12.60** 120 g/mol. $C_4H_8O_4$. **12.62** $-8.6°C$. **12.64** 4.3×10^2 g/mol. $C_{24}H_{20}P_4$. **12.66** 1.75×10^4 g/mol. **12.68** 343 g/mol. **12.74** Boiling point, vapor-pressure, osmotic pressure. **12.76** 0.50 m glucose > 0.50 m acetic acid > 0.50 m HCl. **12.78** 0.9420 m. **12.80** 7.6 atm. **12.82** 1.6 atm. **12.86** 3.5 atm. **12.88** (a) 104 mmHg. (b) 116 mmHg. **12.90** 2.95×10^3 g/mol. **12.92** No. **12.94** $AlCl_3$ dissociates into Al^{3+} and 3 Cl^- ions. **12.96** NaCl: 143.8 g; $MgCl_2$: 5.14 g; Na_2SO_4: 7.25 g; $CaCl_2$: 1.11 g; KCl: 0.67 g; $NaHCO_3$: 0.17 g. **12.98** The molar mass in B (248 g/mol) is twice as large as that in A (124 g/mol). A dimerization process. **12.100** (a) Last alcohol. (b) Methanol. (c) Last alcohol. **12.102** I_2-water: weak dipole–induced dipole; I_3^--water: favorable ion-dipole interaction. **12.104** (a) Same NaCl solution on both sides. (b) Only water would move from left to right. (c) Normal osmosis. **12.106** 12.3 M. **12.108** 14.2%. **12.110** (a) Decreases with lattice energy. (b) Increases with polarity of solvent. (c) Increases with enthalpy of hydration. **12.112** 1.80 g/mL. 5.0×10^2 m. **12.114** 0.815. **12.116** NH_3 can form hydrogen bonds with water. **12.118** 2.8%. **12.120** 1.2×10^2 g/mol. It forms a dimer in benzene. **12.122** (a) 1.1 m. (b) The protein prevents the formation of ice crystals. **12.124** It is due to the precipitated minerals that refract light and create an opaque appearance. **12.126** 1.9 m. **12.128** (a) $X_A = 0.524$, $X_B = 0.476$. (b) A: 50 mmHg; B: 20 mmHg. (c) $X_A = 0.71$, $X_B = 0.29$. $P_A = 67$ mmHg. $P_B = 12$ mmHg.

Chapter 13

13.6 (a) rate $= -\dfrac{1}{2}\dfrac{\Delta[H_2]}{\Delta t} = -\dfrac{\Delta[O_2]}{\Delta t} = \dfrac{1}{2}\dfrac{\Delta[H_2O]}{\Delta t}$.

(b) rate $= -\dfrac{1}{4}\dfrac{\Delta[NH_3]}{\Delta t} = -\dfrac{1}{5}\dfrac{\Delta[O_2]}{\Delta t} = \dfrac{1}{4}\dfrac{\Delta[NO]}{\Delta t} = \dfrac{1}{6}\dfrac{\Delta[H_2O]}{\Delta t}$.

13.8 (a) 0.049 M/s. (b) -0.025 M/s. **13.16** 2.4×10^{-4} M/s. **13.18** (a) Third order. (b) 0.38 M/s. **13.20** (a) 0.046 s^{-1}. (b) 0.13/M · s. **13.22** First order. 1.08×10^{-3} s^{-1}. **13.28** (a) 0.0198 s^{-1}. (b) 151 s. **13.30** 3.6 s. **13.38** 135 kJ/mol. **13.40** 641 K. **13.42** 51.0 kJ/mol. **13.52** (a) rate $= k[X_2][Y]$. (b) Reaction is zero order in Z. (c) $X_2 + Y \longrightarrow XY + X$ (slow). $X + Z \longrightarrow$ XZ (fast). **13.54** Mechanism I. **13.62** rate $= \dfrac{k_1 k_2}{k_{-1}}[E][S]$.

13.64 Temperature, energy of activation, concentration of reactants, catalyst. **13.66** 22.6 cm^2; 44.9 cm^2. The large surface area of grain dust can result in a violent explosion. **13.68** (a) Third order. (b) 0.38/M^2 · s. (c) $H_2 + 2NO \longrightarrow N_2 + H_2O + O$ (slow). $O + H_2 \longrightarrow H_2O$ (fast). **13.70** Water is present in excess so its concentration does not change appreciably. **13.72** 10.7/M · s. **13.74** 2.63 atm. **13.76** M^{-2} s^{-1}. **13.78** 56.4 min. **13.80** (b), (d), (e). **13.82** 9.8×10^{-4}. **13.84** (a) Increase. (b) Decrease. (c) Decrease. (d) Increase. **13.86** 0.0896 min^{-1}. **13.88** 1.12×10^3 min. **13.90** (a) I_2 absorbs visible light to form I atoms. (b) UV light is needed to dissociate H_2. **13.92** (a) rate $= k[X][Y]^2$. (b) $1.9 \times 10^{-2}/M^2$ · s. **13.94** Second order. $2.4 \times 10^7/M$ · s. **13.96** Because the engine is relatively cold so the exhaust gases will not fully react with the catalytic converter.

13.98 (a) Reaction has a large activation energy. (b) Activation energy is very small and orientation factor not important. **13.100** 5.7×10^5 yr. **13.102** (a) Mn^{2+}; Mn^{3+}; first step. (b) Without the catalyst, reaction would be termolecular. (c) Homogeneous. **13.104** 0.45 atm. **13.106** (a) $k_1[A] - k_2[B]$. (b) $[B] = (k_1/k_2)[A]$. **13.108** (a) 2.47×10^{-2} yr^{-1}. (b) 9.8×10^{-4}. (c) 186 yr. **13.110** (a) 3. (b) 2. (c) C $\longrightarrow$ D. (d) Exothermic. **13.112** 1.8×10^3 K. **13.114** (a) 2.5×10^{-5} M/s. (b) Same as (a). (c) 8.3×10^{-6} M. **13.116** (d).

Chapter 14

14.14 (a) A + C $\rightleftharpoons$ AC. (b) A + D $\rightleftharpoons$ AD. **14.16** 1.08×10^7. **14.18** 3.5×10^{-7}. **14.20** (a) 0.082. (b) 0.29. **14.22** 0.105; 2.05×10^{-3}. **14.24** 7.09×10^{-3}. **14.26** 3.3. **14.28** 3.56×10^{-2}. **14.30** 4.0×10^{-6}. **14.32** 5.6×10^{23}. **14.36** 0.64/M^2 · s. **14.40** $[NH_3]$ will increase and $[N_2]$ and $[H_2]$ will decrease. **14.42** NO: 0.50 atm; NO_2: 0.020 atm. **14.44** $[I] = 8.58 \times 10^{-4}$ M; $[I_2] = 0.0194$ M. **14.46** (a) 0.52. (b) $[CO_2] = 0.48$ M, $[H_2] = 0.020$ M, $[CO] = 0.075$ M, $[H_2O] = 0.065$ M. **14.48** $[H_2] = [CO_2] = 0.05$ M, $[H_2O] = [CO] = 0.11$ M. **14.54** (a) Shift position of equilibrium to the right. (b) No effect. (c) No effect. **14.56** (a) No effect. (b) No effect. (c) Shift the position of equilibrium to the left. (d) No effect. (e) To the left. **14.58** (a) To the right. (b) To the left. (c) To the right. (d) To the left. (e) No effect. **14.60** No change. **14.62** (a) More CO_2 will form. (b) No change. (c) No change. (d) Some CO_2 will combine with CaO to form $CaCO_3$. (e) Some CO_2 will react with NaOH so equilibrium will shift to the right. (f) HCl reacts with $CaCO_3$ to produce CO_2. Equilibrium will shift to the left. (g) Equilibrium will shift to the right. **14.64** (a) NO: 0.24 atm; Cl_2: 0.12 atm. (b) 0.017. **14.66** (a) No effect. (b) More CO_2 and H_2O will form. **14.68** (a) 8×10^{-44}. (b) The reaction has a very large activation energy. **14.70** (a) 1.7. (b) A: 0.69 atm, B: 0.81 atm. **14.72** 1.5×10^5. **14.74** H_2: 0.28 atm, Cl_2: 0.049 atm, HCl: 1.67 atm. **14.76** 5.0×10^1 atm. **14.78** 3.86×10^{-2}. **14.80** 3.13. **14.82** N_2: 0.860 atm; H_2: 0.366 atm; NH_3: 4.40×10^{-3} atm. **14.84** (a) 1.16. (b) 53.7%. **14.86** (a) 0.49 atm. (b) 0.23. (c) 0.037. (d) Greater than 0.037 mol. **14.88** $[H_2] = 0.070$ M, $[I_2] = 0.182$ M, $[HI] = 0.825$ M. **14.90** (c). **14.92** (a) 4.2×10^{-4}. (b) 0.83. (c) 1.1. (d) In (b): 2.3×10^3; in (c): 0.021. **14.94** 0.0231; 9.60×10^{-4}. **14.96** NO_2: 1.2 atm; N_2O_4: 0.12 atm. $K_p = 12$. **14.98** (a) The equilibrium will shift to the right. (b) To the right. (c) No change. (d) No change. (e) No change. (f) To the left. **14.100** NO_2: 0.10 atm; N_2O_4: 0.088 atm. **14.102** (a) 1.03 atm. (b) 0.39 atm. (c) 1.67 atm. (d) 0.620. **14.104** 22 mg/m^3. Yes. **14.106** Temporary dynamic equilibrium between the melting ice cubes and the freezing of the water between the ice cubes. **4.108** $[NH_3] = 0.042$ M, $[N_2] = 0.086$ M, $[H_2] = 0.26$ M.

Chapter 15

15.4 (a) NO_2^-. (b) HSO_4^-. (c) HS^-. (d) CN^-. (e) $HCOO^-$. **15.6** (a) H_2S. (b) H_2CO_3. (c) HCO_3^-. (d) H_3PO_4. (e) $H_2PO_4^-$. (f) HPO_4^{2-}. (g) H_2SO_4. (h) HSO_4^-. (i) HSO_3^-. **15.8** (a) CH_2ClCOO^-. (b) IO_4^-. (c) $H_2PO_4^-$. (d) HPO_4^{2-}. (e) PO_4^{3-}. (f) HSO_4^-. (g) SO_4^{2-}. (h) IO_3^-. (i) SO_3^{2-}. (j) NH_3. (k) HS^-. (l) S^{2-}. (m) OCl^-. **15.16** 1.6×10^{-14} M. **15.18** (a) 10.74. (b) 3.28. **15.20** (a) 6.3×10^{-6} M. (b) 1.0×10^{-16} M. (c) 2.7×10^{-6} M. **15.22** (a) Acidic. (b) Neutral. (c) Basic. **15.24** 1.98×10^{-3} mol. 0.444. **15.26** 0.118. **15.32** (1) c. (2) b and d. **15.34** (a) Strong. (b) Weak. (c) Weak. (d) Weak. (e) Strong. **15.36** (b) and (c). **15.38** No. **15.44** $[H^+] = [CH_3COO^-] = 5.8 \times 10^{-4}$ M, $[CH_3COOH] = 0.0181$ M. **15.46** 2.3×10^{-3} M. **15.48** (a) 3.5%. (b) 33%. (c) 79%. Percent ionization increases with dilution.

15.50 (a) 3.9%. (b) 0.30%. **15.54** 7.1×10^{-7}. **15.56** 1.5%.
15.62 HCl: 1.40; H_2SO_4: 1.31. **15.64** $[H^+] = [HCO_3^-] = 1.0 \times 10^{-4}\ M$, $[CO_3^{2-}] = 4.8 \times 10^{-11}\ M$. **15.68** (a) $H_2SO_4 > H_2SeO_4$.
(b) $H_3PO_4 > H_3AsO_4$. **15.70** The conjugate base of phenol can be stabilized by resonance. **15.76** (a) Neutral. (b) Basic.
(c) Acidic. (d) Acidic. **15.78** HZ < HY < HX. **15.80** 4.82.
15.82 Basic. **15.86** (a) $Al_2O_3 < BaO < K_2O$. (b) $CrO_3 < Cr_2O_3 < CrO$. **15.88** $Al(OH)_3 + OH^- \longrightarrow Al(OH)_4^-$. Lewis acid-base reaction. **15.92** $AlCl_3$ is the Lewis acid, Cl^- is the Lewis base.
15.94 CO_2 and BF_3. **15.96** 0.106 L. **15.98** No. **15.100** No, volume is the same. **15.102** CrO is basic and CrO_3 is acidic.
15.104 4.0×10^{-2}. **15.106** 7.00. **15.108** NH_3. **15.110** (a) 7.43.
(b) pD < 7.43. (c) pD + pOD = 14.87. **15.112** 1.79. **15.114** F^- reacts with HF to form HF_2^-, thereby shifting the ionization of HF to the right. **15.116** 6.80. **15.118** $[H^+] = [H_2PO_4^-] = 0.0239\ M$, $[H_3PO_4] = 0.076\ M$, $[HPO_4^{2-}] = 6.2 \times 10^{-8}\ M$, $[PO_4^{3-}] = 1.2 \times 10^{-18}\ M$. **15.120** $[Na^+] = 0.200\ M$, $[HCO_3^-] = [OH^-] = 4.6 \times 10^{-3}\ M$, $[H_2CO_3] = 2.4 \times 10^{-8}\ M$, $[H^+] = 2.2 \times 10^{-12}\ M$.
15.122 The H^+ ions convert CN^- to HCN, which escapes as a gas. **15.124** 0.25 g. **15.126** −0.20. **15.128** (a) Equilibrium will shift to the right. (b) To the left. (c) No effect. (d) To the right.
15.130 The amines are converted to their salts RNH_3^+.
15.132 1.6×10^{-4}. **15.134** 4.40. **15.136** In a basic medium, the ammonium salt is converted to the pungent-smelling ammonia.
15.138 (c). **15.140** 21 mL.

Chapter 16

16.6 (a) 11.28. (b) 9.07. **16.10** (a), (b), and (c). **16.12** 4.74 for both. (a) Is more effective because it has a higher concentration.
16.14 7.03. **16.16** 10. More effective against the acid.
16.18 (a) 4.82. (b) 4.64. **16.20** HC. **16.24** 90.1 g/mol.
16.26 0.467 M. **16.28** $[H^+] = 3.0 \times 10^{-13}\ M$, $[OH^-] = 0.0335\ M$, $[Na^+] = 0.0835\ M$, $[CH_3COO^-] = 0.0500\ M$, $[CH_3COOH] = 8.3 \times 10^{-10}\ M$. **16.30** 8.23. **16.32** (a) 11.36. (b) 9.55. (c) 8.95.
(d) 5.19. (e) 1.70. **16.36** CO_2 dissolves in water to form H_2CO_3, which neutralizes NaOH. **16.38** 5.70. **16.46** (a) 7.8×10^{-10}.
(b) 1.8×10^{-18}. **16.48** 1.80×10^{-10}. **16.50** $2.2 \times 10^{-4}\ M$.
16.52 2.3×10^{-9}. **16.54** $[Na^+] = 0.045\ M$, $[NO_3^-] = 0.076\ M$, $[Sr^{2+}] = 0.016\ M$, $[F^-] = 1.1 \times 10^{-4}\ M$. **16.56** pH greater than 2.68 and less than 8.11. **16.60** (a) 0.013 M. (b) $2.2 \times 10^{-4}\ M$.
(c) $3.3 \times 10^{-3}\ M$. **16.62** (a) $1.0 \times 10^{-5}\ M$. (b) $1.1 \times 10^{-10}\ M$.
16.64 (b), (c), (d), and (e). **16.66** (a) 0.016 M. (b) $1.6 \times 10^{-6}\ M$. **16.68** Yes. **16.72** $[Cd^{2+}] = 1.1 \times 10^{-18}\ M$, $[Cd(CN)_4^{2-}] = 4.2 \times 10^{-3}\ M$, $[CN^-] = 0.48\ M$. **16.74** $3.5 \times 10^{-5}\ M$.
16.76 (a) $Cu^{2+} + 4NH_3 \rightleftharpoons Cu(NH_3)_4^{2+}$. (b) $Ag^+ + 2CN^- \rightleftharpoons Ag(CN)_2^-$. (c) $Hg^{2+} + 4Cl^- \rightleftharpoons HgCl_4^{2-}$. **16.80** 0.011 M.
16.82 Use Cl^- ions or flame test. **16.84** From 2.51 to 4.41.
16.86 1.28 M. **16.88** $[H^+] = 3.0 \times 10^{-13}\ M$, $[OH^-] = 0.0335\ M$, $[HCOO^-] = 0.0500\ M$, $[HCOOH] = 8.8 \times 10^{-11}\ M$, $[Na^+] = 0.0835\ M$. **16.90** 9.97 g. pH = 13.04. **16.92** 6.0×10^3.
16.94 0.036 g/L. **16.96** (a) 1.37. (b) 5.97. (c) 10.24.
16.98 Original precipitate was HgI_2. In the presence of excess KI, it redissolves as HgI_4^{2-}. **16.100** 7.82–10.38. **16.102** (a) 3.60.
(b) 9.69. (c) 6.07. **16.104** (a) $MCO_3 + 2HCl \longrightarrow MCl_2 + H_2O + CO_2$. $HCl + NaOH \longrightarrow NaCl + H_2O$. (b) 197 g/mol. Ba.
16.106. 2. **16.108** (a) 12.6. (b) $8.8 \times 10^{-6}\ M$. **16.110** (a) Sulfate.
(b) Sulfide. (c) Iodide. **16.112** They are insoluble. **16.114** The ionized polyphenols have a dark color. The H^+ ions from lemon juice shift the equilibrium to the light color acid. **16.116** Yes.
16.118 (c). **16.120** (a) $1.7 \times 10^{-7}\ M$. (b) $MgCO_3$ is more soluble than $CaCO_3$. (c) 12.40. (d) $1.9 \times 10^{-8}\ M$. (e) Ca^{2+} because it is present in larger amount. **16.122** pH = 1.0, fully protonated; pH = 7.0, dipolar ion; pH = 12.0, fully ionized.

Chapter 17

17.6 3.3×10^{-4} atm. **17.8** N_2: 3.96×10^{18} kg; O_2: 1.22×10^{18} kg; CO_2: 2.63×10^{15} kg. **17.12** 3.57×10^{-19} J. **17.22** 5.2×10^6 kg. 5.6×10^{14} kJ. **17.24** The wavelength is not short enough.
17.26 434 nm. Both.

17.28
$$
\begin{array}{ccc}
& F\ \ H & F\ \ H \\
& |\ \ \ | & |\ \ \ | \\
F\text{—}C\text{—}C\text{—}Cl & & F\text{—}C\text{—}C\text{—}H \\
& |\ \ \ | & |\ \ \ | \\
& F\ \ Cl & F\ \ F
\end{array}
$$
17.40 1.3×10^{10} kg.

17.42 Ethane and propane are greenhouse gases. **17.50** 4.34.
17.58 $1.2 \times 10^{-11}\ M/s$. **17.60** (b). **17.66** 0.12%.
17.68 Endothermic. **17.70** O_2. **17.72** 5.72. **17.74** 394 nm.
17.76 It has a high activation energy. **17.78** Size of tree rings are related to CO_2 content. Age of CO_2 in ice can be determined by radiocarbon dating. **17.80** 165 kJ/mol.

Chapter 18

18.6 (a) 0.02. (b) 9×10^{-19}. (c) 2×10^{-181}. **18.10** (c) < (d) < (e) < (a) < (b). Solids have smaller entropies than gases. More complex structures have higher entropies. **18.12** (a) 47.5 J/K · mol.
(b) −12.5 J/K · mol. (c) −242.8 J/K · mol. **18.14** (a) $\Delta S < 0$.
(b) $\Delta S > 0$. (c) $\Delta S > 0$. (d) $\Delta S < 0$. **18.18** (a) −1139 kJ/mol.
(b) −140.0 kJ/mol. (c) −2935.0 kJ/mol. **18.20** (a) At all temperatures. (b) Below 111 K. **18.24** 8.0×10^1 kJ/mol.
18.26 4.572×10^2 kJ/mol. 4.5×10^{-81}. **18.28** (a) −24.6 kJ/mol.
(b) −1.10 kJ/mol. **18.30** −341 kJ/mol. **18.32** −2.87 kJ/mol. The process has a high activation energy. **18.36** 1×10^3. glucose + ATP $\longrightarrow$ glucose 6-phosphate + ADP. **18.38** (a) 0. (b) 4.0×10^4 J/mol. (c) -3.2×10^4 J/mol. (d) 6.4×10^4 J/mol.
18.40 (a) No reaction is possible because $\Delta G > 0$. (b) The reaction has a very large activation energy. (c) Reactants and products already at their equilibrium concentrations. **18.42** In all cases $\Delta H > 0$ and $\Delta S > 0$. $\Delta G < 0$ for a, = 0 for (b), and > 0 for (c). **18.44** $\Delta S > 0$. **18.46** (a) Most liquids have similar structure so the changes in entropy from liquid to vapor are similar. (b) ΔS_{vap} are larger for ethanol and water because of hydrogen bonding (there are fewer microstates in these liquids).
18.48 (a) $2CO + 2NO \longrightarrow 2CO_2 + N_2$. (b) Oxidizing agent: NO; reducing agent: CO. (c) 1×10^{121}. (d) 1.2×10^{18}. From left to right. (e) No. **18.50** 2.6×10^{-9}. **18.52** 976 K. **18.54** $\Delta S < 0$; $\Delta H < 0$. **18.56** 55 J/K · mol. **18.58** Increase in entropy of the surroundings offsets the decrease in entropy of the system.
18.60 56 J/K. **18.62** 4.5×10^5. **18.64** 4.5×10^{-75} atm.
18.66 (a) True. (b) True. (c) False. **18.68** C + CuO $\rightleftharpoons$ CO + Cu. 6.1. **18.70** Crystal structure has disorder or impurity.
18.72 (a) 7.6×10^{14}. (b) 4.1×10^{-12}. **18.74** (a) A reverse disproportionation reaction. (b) 8.2×10^{15}. Yes, a large K makes this an efficient process. (c) Less effective. **18.76** 1.8×10^{70}. Reaction has a large activation energy. **18.78** Heating the ore alone is not a feasible process. −214.3 kJ/mol.
18.80 $K_P = 36$. 981 K. No. **18.82** Mole percents: butane = 30%; isobutane = 70%. Yes. **18.84** $X_{CO} = 0.45$; $X_{CO_2} = 0.55$. Use ΔG_f° values at 25°C for 900°C. **18.86** 249 J/K. **18.88** 3×10^{-13} s.
18.90 $\Delta S_{sys} = -327$ J/K · mol, $\Delta S_{surr} = 1918$ J/K · mol, $\Delta S_{univ} = 1591$ J/K · mol. **18.92** q, w. **18.94** $\Delta H < 0$, $\Delta S < 0$, $\Delta G < 0$.

Chapter 19

19.2 (a) $Mn^{2+} + H_2O_2 + 2OH^- \longrightarrow MnO_2 + 2H_2O$.
(b) $2Bi(OH)_3 + 3SnO_2^{2-} \longrightarrow 2Bi + 3H_2O + 3SnO_3^{2-}$. (c) $Cr_2O_7^{2-} + 14H^+ + 3C_2O_4^{2-} \longrightarrow 2Cr^{3+} + 6CO_2 + 7H_2O$. (d) $2Cl^- + 2ClO_3^- + 4H^+ \longrightarrow Cl_2 + 2ClO_2 + 2H_2O$. **19.12** 2.46 V.

$Al + 3Ag^+ \longrightarrow 3Ag + Al^{3+}$. **19.14** $Cl_2(g)$ and $MnO_4^-(aq)$.
19.16 Only (a) and (d) are spontaneous. **19.18** (a) Li. (b) H_2.
(c) Fe^{2+}. (d) Br^-. **19.22** 0.368 V. **19.24** (a) -432 kJ/mol, 5×10^{75}.
(b) -104 kJ/mol, 2×10^{18}. (c) -178 kJ/mol, 1×10^{31}.
(d) -1.27×10^3 kJ/mol, 8×10^{211}. **19.26** 0.37 V, -36 kJ/mol,
2×10^6. **19.30** (a) 2.23 V, 2.23 V, -430 kJ/mol. (b) 0.02 V, 0.04 V,
-23 kJ/mol. **19.32** 0.083 V. **19.34** 0.010 V. **19.38** 1.09 V.
19.46 (b) 0.64 g. **19.48** (a) $\$2.10 \times 10^3$. (b) $\$2.46 \times 10^3$.
(c) $\$4.70 \times 10^3$. **19.50** (a) 0.14 F. (b) 0.121 F. (c) 0.10 F.
19.52 (a) $Ag^+ + e^- \longrightarrow Ag$. (b) $2H_2O \longrightarrow O_2 + 4H^+ + 4e^-$.
(c) 6.0×10^2 C. **19.54** (a) 0.589 Cu. (b) 0.133 A. **19.56** 2.3 h.
19.58 9.66×10^4 C. **19.60** 0.0710 F. **19.62** 0.156 M. $Cr_2O_7^{2-} +$
$6Fe^{2+} + 14H^+ \longrightarrow 2Cr^{3+} + 6Fe^{3+} + 7H_2O$. **19.64** 45.1%.
19.66 (a) $2MnO_4^- + 16H^+ + 5C_2O_4^{2-} \longrightarrow 2Mn^{2+} + 10CO_2 +$
$8H_2O$. (b) 5.40%. **19.68** 0.231 mg Ca^{2+}/mL blood.
19.70 (a) 0.80 V. (b) $2Ag^+ + H_2 \longrightarrow 2Ag + 2H^+$. (c) (i) 0.92 V.
(ii) 1.10 V. (d) The cell operates as a pH meter. **19.72** Fluorine
gas reacts with water. **19.74** 2.5×10^2 h. **19.76** Hg_2^{2+}.
19.78 $[Mg^{2+}] = 0.0500$ M, $[Ag^+] = 7 \times 10^{-55}$ M, 1.44 g.
19.80 (a) 0.206 L H_2. (b) 6.09×10^{23}/mol e^-. **19.82**
(a) -1356.8 kJ/mol. (b) 1.17 V. **19.84** $+3$. **19.86** 6.8 kJ/mol, 0.064.
19.88 1.4 A. **19.90** $+4$. **19.92** 1.60×10^{-19} C/e^-. **19.94** A cell
made of Li^+/Li and F_2/F^- gives the maximum voltage of 5.92 V.
Reactive oxidizing and reducing agents are hard to handle. **19.96**
2×10^{20}. **19.98** (a) $E°$ for X is negative; $E°$ for Y is positive. (b)
0.59 V. **19.100** (a) The reduction potential of O_2 is insufficient to
oxidize gold. (b) Yes. (c) $2Au + 3F_2 \longrightarrow 2AuF_3$. **19.102** $[Fe^{2+}]$
$= 0.0920$ M, $[Fe^{3+}] = 0.0680$ M. **19.104** (b) 104 A · h. The
concentration of H_2SO_4 keeps decreasing. (c) 2.01 V; $-3.88 \times$
10^5 J/mol. **19.106** (a) Unchanged. (b) Unchanged. (c) Squared.
(d) Doubled. (e) Doubled. **19.108** Stronger. **19.110** 4.4×10^2
atm. **19.112** (a) $Zn \longrightarrow Zn^{2+} + 2e^-$; $\frac{1}{2}O_2 + 2e^- \longrightarrow O^{2-}$.
1.65 V. (b) 1.63 V. (c) 4.87×10^3 kJ/kg. (d) 62 L.
19.114 -3.05 V. **19.116** 1×10^{-14}.

Chapter 20

20.12 111 h. **20.14** Roast the sulfide followed by reduction of the
oxide with coke or carbon monoxide. **20.16** (a) 8.9×10^{12} cm^3.
(b) 4.0×10^8 kg. **20.18** Iron does not need to be produced
electrolytically. **20.28** (a) $2Na + 2H_2O \longrightarrow 2NaOH + H_2$. (b)
$2NaOH + CO_2 \longrightarrow Na_2CO_3 + H_2O$. (c) $Na_2CO_3 + 2HCl \longrightarrow$
$2NaCl + CO_2 + H_2O$. (d) $NaHCO_3 + HCl \longrightarrow NaCl + CO_2 +$
H_2O. (e) $2NaHCO_3 \longrightarrow Na_2CO_3 + CO_2 + H_2O$. (f) No reaction.
20.30 5.59 L. **20.34** First react Mg with HNO_3 to form $Mg(NO_3)_2$.
On heating, $2Mg(NO_3)_2 \longrightarrow 2MgO + 4NO_2 + O_2$. **20.36** The
third electron is removed from the neon core. **20.38** Helium has a
closed-shell noble gas configuration. **20.40** (a) CaO. (b) $Ca(OH)_2$.
(c) An aqueous suspension of $Ca(OH)_2$. **20.44** 60.7 h.
20.46 (a) 1.03 V. (b) 3.32×10^4 kJ. **20.48** $4Al(NO_3)_3 \longrightarrow$
$2Al_2O_3 + 12NO_2 + 3O_2$. **20.50** Because Al_2Cl_6 dissociates to
form $AlCl_3$. **20.52** From sp^3 to sp^2. **20.54** 65.4 g/mol.
20.56 No. **20.58** (a) 1482 kJ/mol. (b) 3152.8 kJ/mol.
20.60 Magnesium reacts with nitrogen to form magnesium
nitride. **20.62** (a) Al^{3+} hydrolyzes in water to produce
H^+ ions. (b) $Al(OH)_3$ dissolves in a strong base to form
$Al(OH)_4^-$. **20.64** $CaO + 2HCl \longrightarrow CaCl_2 + H_2O$.
20.66 Electronic transitions (in the visible region) between
closely spaced energy levels. **20.68** NaF: toothpaste additive;
Li_2CO_3: to treat mental illness; $Mg(OH)_2$: antacid; $CaCO_3$:
antacid; $BaSO_4$: for X-ray diagnostic of digestive system;
$Al(OH)_2NaCO_3$: antacid. **20.70** (i) Both Li and Mg form
oxides. (ii) Like Mg, Li forms nitride. (iii) The carbonates,
fluorides, and phosphates of Li and Mg have low solubilities.
20.72 Zn.

Chapter 21

21.12 (a) Hydrogen reacts with alkali metals to form hydrides.
(b) Hydrogen reacts with oxygen to form water. **21.14** Use
palladium metal to separate hydrogen from other gases.
21.16 11 kg. **21.18** (a) $H_2 + Cl_2 \longrightarrow 2HCl$. (b) $N_2 + 3H_2 \longrightarrow$
$2NH_3$. (c) $2Li + H_2 \longrightarrow 2LiH$, $LiH + H_2O \longrightarrow LiOH + H_2$.
21.26 $:C\equiv C:^{2-}$. **21.28** (a) $2NaHCO_3 \longrightarrow Na_2CO_3 + H_2O +$
CO_2. (b) CO_2 reacts with $Ca(OH)_2$ solution to form a white
precipitate ($CaCO_3$). **21.30** On heating, the bicarbonate ion
decomposes: $2HCO_3^- \longrightarrow CO_3^{2-} + H_2O + CO_2$. Mg^{2+} ions
combines with CO_3^{2-} ions to form $MgCO_3$. **21.32** First, $2NaOH +$
$CO_2 \longrightarrow Na_2CO_3 + H_2O$. Then, $Na_2CO_3 + CO_2 + H_2O \longrightarrow$
$2NaHCO_3$. **21.34** Yes. **21.40** (a) $2NaNO_3 \longrightarrow 2NaNO_2 + O_2$.
(b) $NaNO_3 + C \longrightarrow NaNO_2 + CO$. **21.42** $2NH_3 + CO_2 \longrightarrow$
$(NH_2)_2CO + H_2O$. At high pressures. **21.44** NH_4Cl
decomposes to form NH_3 and HCl. **21.46** N is in its highest
oxidation state ($+5$) in HNO_3. **21.48** Favored reaction: $4Zn +$
$NO_3^- + 10H^+ \longrightarrow 4Zn^{2+} + NH_4^+ + 3H_2O$. **21.50** Linear.
21.52 -1168 kJ/mol. **21.54** P_4. 125 g/mol. **21.56** $P_4O_{10} + 4HNO_3$
$\longrightarrow 2N_2O_5 + 4HPO_3$. 60.4 g. **21.58** sp^3. **21.66** -198.3 kJ/mol,
6×10^{34}, 6×10^{34}. **21.68** 0; -1. **21.70** 4.4×10^{11} mol; $1.4 \times$
10^{13} g. **21.72** 79.1 g. **21.74** Cl, Br, and I atoms are too bulky
around the S atom. **21.76** 35 g. **21.78** $9H_2SO_4 + 8NaI \longrightarrow H_2S$
$+ 4I_2 + 4H_2O + 8NaHSO_4$. **21.82** $H_2SO_4 + NaCl \longrightarrow HCl +$
$NaHSO_4$. The HCl gas escapes, driving the equilibrium to the
right. **21.84** 25.3 L. **21.86** Sulfuric acid oxidizes sodium
bromide to molecular bromine. **21.88** 2.81 L. **21.90** $I_2O_5 + 5CO$
$\longrightarrow I_2 + 5CO_2$. C is oxidized; I is reduced. **21.92** (a) $SiCl_4$.
(b) F^-. (c) F. (d) CO_2. **21.94** No change. **21.96** (a) $2Na + D_2O$
$\longrightarrow 2NaOD + D_2$. (b) $2D_2O \longrightarrow 2D_2 + O_2$ (electrolysis). $D_2 +$
$Cl_2 \longrightarrow 2DCl$. (c) $Mg_3N_2 + 6D_2O \longrightarrow 3Mg(OD)_2 + 2ND_3$.
(d) $CaC_2 + 2D_2O \longrightarrow C_2D_2 + Ca(OD)_2$. (e) $Be_2C + 4D_2O \longrightarrow$
$2Be(OD)_2 + CD_4$. (f) $SO_3 + D_2O \longrightarrow D_2SO_4$. **21.98** (a) At
elevated pressure, water boils above 100°C. (b) So the water is
able to melt a larger area of sulfur deposit. (c) Sulfur deposits
are structurally weak. Conventional mining would be dangerous.
21.100 The C—D bond breaks at a slower rate.

Chapter 22

22.12 (a) $+3$. (b) 6. (c) oxalate. **22.14** (a) Na: $+1$, Mo: $+6$.
(b) Mg: $+2$, W: $+6$. (c) Fe: 0. **22.16** (a) cis-dichloro-
bis(ethylenediamine)cobalt(III). (b) pentaamminechloro-
platinum(IV) chloride. (c) pentaamminechlorocobalt(III) chloride.
22.18 (a) $[Cr(en)_2Cl_2]^+$. (b) $Fe(CO)_5$. (c) $K_2[Cu(CN)_4]$. (d)
$[Co(NH_3)_4(H_2O)Cl]Cl_2$. **22.24** (a) 2. (b) 2. **22.26** (a) Two
geometric isomers:

trans   cis

(b) Two optical isomers:

22.34 CN^- is a strong-field ligand. Absorbs near UV (blue) so appears yellow. **22.36** (a) Orange. (b) 255 kJ/mol. **22.38** $[Co(NH_3)_4Cl_2]Cl$. 2 moles. **22.42** Use $^{14}CN^-$ label (in NaCN). **22.44** First $Cu(CN)_2$ (white) is formed. It redissolves as $Cu(CN)_4^{2-}$. **22.46** 1.4×10^2. **22.48** Mn^{3+}. $3d^5$ (Cr^{3+}) is a stable electron configuration. **22.50** Ti: +3; Fe: +3. **22.52** Four Fe atoms per hemoglobin molecule. 1.6×10^4 g/mol. **22.54** (a) $[Cr(H_2O)_6]Cl_3$. (b) $[Cr(H_2O)_5Cl]Cl_2 \cdot H_2O$. (c) $[Cr(H_2O)_4Cl_2]Cl \cdot 2H_2O$. Compare electrical conductance with solutions of NaCl, $MgCl_2$, and $FeCl_3$ of the same molar concentration. **22.56** -1.8×10^2 kJ/mol; 4×10^{31}. **22.58** Iron is more abundant. **22.60** Oxyhemoglobin is low spin and therefore absorbs higher energy light. **22.62** All except Fe^{2+}, Cu^{2+}, and Co^{2+}. The colorless ions have electron configurations d^0 and d^{10}. **22.64** Dipole moment measurements. **22.66** EDTA sequesters essential metal ions (Ca^{2+}, Mg^{2+}). **22.68** 3.

Chapter 23

23.6 (a) $_{-1}^{0}\beta$. (b) $_{20}^{40}Ca$. (c) $_2^4\alpha$. (d) $_0^1n$. **23.14** (a) $_3^9Li$. (b) $_{11}^{25}Na$. (c) $_{21}^{48}Sc$. **23.16** $_{10}^{17}Ne$. (b) $_{20}^{45}Ca$. (c) $_{43}^{92}Tc$. (d) $_{80}^{195}Hg$. (e) $_{96}^{242}Cm$. **23.18** 6×10^9 kg/s. **23.20** (a) 4.55×10^{-12} J; 1.14×10^{-12} J/nucleon. (b) 2.36×10^{-10} J; 1.28×10^{-12} J/nucleon. **23.24** 0.251 d^{-1}. **23.26** 2.7 d. **23.28** $_{82}^{208}Pb$. **23.30** A: 0; B: 0.25 mole; C: 0; D: 0.75 mole. **23.34** (a) $_{34}^{80}Se + _1^2H \longrightarrow _1^1p + _{34}^{81}Se$. (b) $_4^9Be + _1^2H \longrightarrow 2_1^1p + _3^9Li$. (c) $_5^{10}B + _0^1n \longrightarrow _2^4\alpha + _3^7Li$. **23.36** $_{80}^{198}Hg + _0^1n \longrightarrow _{79}^{198}Au + _1^1p$. **23.48** IO_3^- is only formed from IO_4^-. **23.50** Incorporate Fe-59 into a person's body. After a few days isolate red blood cells and monitor radioactivity from the hemoglobin molecules. **23.52** An analogous Pauli exclusion principle for nucleons. **23.54** (a) 0.343 mCi. (b) $_{93}^{237}Np \longrightarrow _2^4\alpha + _{91}^{233}Pa$. **23.56** (a) 1.040×10^{-12} J/nucleon. (b) 1.111×10^{-12} J/nucleon. (c) 1.199×10^{-12} J/nucleon. (d) 1.410×10^{-12} J/nucleon. **23.58** $_7^{18}N \longrightarrow _8^{18}O + _{-1}^0\beta$. **23.60** Radioactive dating. **23.62** $_{83}^{209}Bi + _2^4\alpha \longrightarrow _{85}^{211}At + 2_0^1n$. (b) $_{83}^{209}Bi(\alpha,2n)_{85}^{211}At$. **23.64** The sun exerts a much greater gravity on the particles. **23.66** 2.77×10^3 yr. **23.68** (a) $_{19}^{40}K \longrightarrow _{18}^{40}Ar + _{+1}^0\beta$. (b) 3.0×10^9 yr. **23.70** (a) 5.59×10^{-15} J, 2.84×10^{-13} J. (b) 0.024 mole. (c) 4.06×10^6 kJ. **23.72** 2.7×10^{14} I-131 atoms. **23.74** 5.9×10^{23}/mol. **23.76** All except gravitational. **23.78** U-238 and Th-232. Long half-lives. **23.80** 8.3×10^{-4} nm. **23.82** $_1^3H$. **23.84** The reflected neutrons induced a nuclear chain reaction. **2.86** 2.1×10^2 g/mol.

Chapter 24

24.12 $CH_3CH_2CH_2CH_2CH_2Cl$. $CH_3CH_2CH_2CHClCH_3$. $CH_3CH_2CHClCH_2CH_3$.

24.14

24.16 (a) Alkene or cycloalkane. (b) Alkyne. (c) Alkane. (d) Like (a). (e) Alkyne. **24.18** No, too much strain. **24.20** (a) is alkane and (b) is alkene. Only an alkene reacts with a hydrogen halide and hydrogen. **24.22** -630.8 kJ/mol. **24.24** (a) cis-1,2-dichlorocylopropane. (b) trans-1,2-dichlorocylopropane. **24.26** (a) 2-methylpentane. (b) 2,3,4-trimethylhexane. (c) 3-ethylhexane. (d) 3-methyl-1,4-pentadiene. (e) 2-pentyne. (f) 3-phenyl-1-pentene.

24.28 (a) (b) (c) (d)

24.32 (a) 1,3-dichloro-4-methylbenzene. (b) 2-ethyl-1,4-dinitrobenzene. (c) 1,2,4,5-tetramethylbenzene. **24.36** (a) Ether. (b) Amine. (c) Aldehyde. (d) Ketone. (e) Carboxylic acid. (f) Alcohol. (g) Amino acid. **24.38** $HCOOH + CH_3OH \longrightarrow HCOOCH_3 + H_2O$. Methyl formate. **24.40** $(CH_3)_2CH-O-CH_3$. **24.42** (a) Ketone. (b) Ester. (c) Ether. **24.44** -174 kJ/mol. **24.46** (a), (c), (d), (f). **24.48** (a) Rubbing alcohol. (b) Vinegar. (c) Moth balls. (d) Organic synthesis. (e) Organic synthesis. (f) Antifreeze. (g) Natural gas. (h) Synthetic polymer. **24.50** (a) 3. (b) 16. (c) 6. **24.52** (a) C: 15.81 mg, H: 1.33 mg, O: 3.49 mg. (b) C_6H_6O. (c) Phenol.

24.54 Empirical and molecular formula: $C_5H_{10}O$. 88.7 g/mol.

$CH_2=CH-CH_2-O-CH_2-CH_3$. **24.56** (a) The C atoms bonded to the methyl group and the amino group and the H atom. (b) The C atoms bonded to Br. **24.58** CH_3CH_2CHO. **24.60** (a) Alcohol. (b) Ether. (c) Aldehyde. (d) Carboxylic acid. (e) Amine. **24.62** The acids in lemon juice convert the amines to the ammonium salts which have very low vapor pressures. **24.64** Methane (CH_4), ethanol (C_2H_5OH), methanol (CH_3OH), isopropanol (C_3H_7OH), ethylene glycol (CH_2OHCH_2OH), naphthalene ($C_{10}H_8$), acetic acid (CH_3COOH). **24.66** (a) 1. (b) 2. (c) 5. **24.68** Br_2 dissociates into Br atoms, which react with CH_4 to form CH_3Br and HBr.

Chapter 25

25.8 $+CH_2-CHCl-CH_2-CCl_2+$. **25.10** By an addition reaction involving styrene monomers. **25.12** (a) $CH_2=CH-CH=CH_2$. (b) $HO_2C(CH_2)_6NH_2$. **25.22** At 35°C the enzyme begins to denature. **25.28** Proteins are made of 20 amino acids. Nucleic acids are made of four building blocks (purines, pyrimidines, sugar, phosphate group) only. **25.30** C-G base pairs have three hydrogen bonds and higher boiling point; A-T base pairs have two hydrogen bonds. **25.32** Leg muscles are active, have a high metabolic rate and hence a high concentration of myoglobin. The iron content in Mb makes the meat look dark. **25.34** Insects have blood that contains no hemoglobin. It is unlikely that a human-sized insect could obtain sufficient oxygen for metabolism by diffusion. **25.36** There are four Fe atoms per hemoglobin molecule. 1.6×10^4 g/mol. **25.38** Mostly dispersion forces. **25.40** Gly-Ala-Phe-Glu-His-Gly-Ala-Leu-Val. **25.42** No. Enzymes only act on one of the two optical isomers of a compound. **25.44** 315 K.

25.46

Credits

Chapter 8

Opener: © Science & Society Picture Library; Figure 8.10—Sodium, Chlorine, Argon: © McGraw-Hill Higher Education, Inc./Photo by Ken Karp; Figure 8.10—Magnesium, Aluminum, Sulfur: © L.V. Bergman/The Bergman Collection; Figure 8.10—Silicon: © Frank Wing/Stock Boston; Figure 8.10—Phosphorous: © Albert Fenn/Time Life Science Library/MATTER; Figure 8.14—Lithium, Sodium: © McGraw-Hill Higher Education/Photo by Ken Karp; Figure 8.14—Potassium: © Albert Fenn/Time Life Science Library/MATTER; Figure 8.14—Rubidium, Cesium; Figure 8.15—Beryllium, Magnesium, Calcium, Strontium, Barium: © L.V. Bergman/The Bergman Collection; Figure 8.15—Radium: © Phil Brodatz; Figure 8.16 (all): © L.V. Bergman/The Bergman Collection; Figure 8.17—Carbon, Germanium, Lead: © McGraw-Hill Higher Education, Inc./Photo by Ken Karp; Figure 8.17—Diamond: © Courtesy Diamond Information Center; Figure 8.17—Silicon: © Frank Wing/Stock Boston; Figure 8.17—Tin: © L.V. Bergman/The Bergman Collection; Figure 8.18—Nitrogen: © Joe McNally/Wheeler Pictures; Figure 8.18—R&W Phosphorous: © Albert Fenn/Time-Life Science Library/MATTER; Figure 8.18—Arsenic, Antimony, Bismuth; Figure 8.19—Sulfur, Selenium: © L.V. Bergman/The Bergman Collection; Figure 8.19—Tellurium: © McGraw-Hill Higher Education, Inc./Photo by Ken Karp; Figure 8.20: © Joel Gordon Photography-Design Conceptions; Figure 8.21 (all): © McGraw-Hill Higher Education, Inc./Photo by Ken Karp; Figure 8.22a–b: © Neil Bartlett; Figure 8.23: © McGraw-Hill Higher Education, Inc./Photo by Ken Karp; Page 336: © Culver Pictures.

Chapter 9

Opener: © G.N Lewis/Dover Publications; Page 347: © McGraw-Hill Higher Education, Inc./Photo by Ken Karp; Page 348: © Wards Natural Science Establishment; Page 353 (bottom): © Courtesy of International Salt Company; Page 353 (top): © Liane Enkelis/Stock Boston; Page 363: © McGraw-Hill Higher Education, Inc./Photo by Ken Karp; Page 366: © Courtesy of James O. Schreck, Professor of Chemistry/University of Northern Colorado; Page 372: © McGraw-Hill Higher Education, Inc./Photo by Ken Karp.

Chapter 10

Figure 10.21: © Donald Clegg; Page 426: © F. Stuart Westmorland/Photo Researchers; Page 427: © Coordinates supplied by Riichiro Saito/University of Electrocommunications, Tokyo.

Chapter 11

Opener: © McGraw-Hill Higher Education, Inc./Photo by Ken Karp; Page 443: © Hermann Eisenbeiss/Photo Researchers; Figures 11.9, 11.11: © McGraw-Hill Higher Education, Inc./Photo by Ken Karp; Page 447: © Alan Carey/Image Works; Page 450: © Tony Mendoza/Stock Boston; Page 456: © Byron Quintard/Jacqueline McBride/Lawrence Livermore National Labs; Page 458 (top): © Grant Heilman/Grant Heilman Photography; Page 458 (bottom): L.V. Bergman/The Bergman Collection; Page 460: © Courtesy of Edmund Catalogs; Page 461: © Courtesy Railway Technical Research Institute, Tokyo, Japan; Figure 11.37a–d, Page 470, Figure 11.42: © McGraw-Hill Higher Education, Inc./Photo by Ken Karp; Page 473: © David Barnes/Stock Market; Page 475 (left): © Andrew McClenaghan/Science Photo Library/Photo Researchers; Page 475 (right): © E.R. Degginger/Color-Pic; Page 483: © McGraw-Hill Higher Education, Inc./Photo by Ken Karp; Page 484: © AFP/Corbis.

Chapter 12

Opener: © Richard Megna/Fundamental Photographs; Figure 12.1 (all), Page 498: © McGraw-Hill Higher Education, Inc./Photo by Ken Karp; Page 500: Bill Evans, U.S. Geological Survey; Page 505: © Hank Morgan/Photo Researchers; Page 506: © McGraw-Hill Higher Education, Inc./Photo by Ken Karp; Figure 12.13d (all): © David Phillips/Photo Researchers; Page 509: © John Mead/Photo Researchers; Figure 12.15: © Paul Weller; Figure 12.16: © Anna E. Zuckerman/Tom Stack & Associates; Page 517: © PŪR Drinking Water Systems, a division of Recovering Engineering, Inc.; Page 525 (both): © McGraw-Hill Higher Education, Inc./Photo by Ken Karp; Page 526: © George Holton/Photo Researchers; Page 528: © Michael Newman/PhotoEdit.

Chapter 13

Opener: © Ken Karp/McGraw-Hill Higher Education, Inc.; Figures 13.3, 13.7, Page 546: © McGraw-Hill Higher Education, Inc./Photo by Ken Karp; Page 552: © Francois Lochon/Liaison/Getty Images; Figure 13.19: © McGraw-Hill Higher Education, Inc./Photo by Ken Karp; Figure 13.23: © Courtesy of Jason Matthey; Figure 13.25: © Courtesy of General Motors Communications; Figure 13.27: Adapted from the *Journal of Molecular Biology,* Vol. 140, W.S. Bennett, Jr. and T.A. Steitz, "Structure of a Complex Between Yeast Hexokinase A and Glucose," 211–230, (1980), with permission from Elsevier.

Chapter 14

Opener: © Videodiscovery; Page 586: © McGraw-Hill Higher Education, Inc./Photo by Ken Karp; Page 594: © Collection Varin-Visage/Photo Researchers; Figures 14.6, 14.9a–b, 14.10: © McGraw-Hill Higher Education, Inc./Photo by Ken Karp; Page 613: © J.M. Boivin/Liaison/Getty Images; Page 625: © McGraw-Hill Higher Education, Inc./Photo by Stephen Frisch.

Chapter 15

Opener: © Ken Karp Photography; Figure 15.2: © McGraw-Hill Higher Education, Inc./Photo by Ken Karp; Page 634: © McGraw-Hill Higher Education, Inc./Photo by Stephen Frisch; Figure 15.9 (both): © McGraw-Hill Higher Education, Inc./Photo by Ken Karp; Figure 15.10: © Michael Melford/Wheeler Pictures; Figure 15.11: © McGraw-Hill Higher Education, Inc./Photo by Ken Karp; Page 677: © Kristen Brochmann/Fundamental Photographs.

Chapter 16

Opener: © Allan Morgan/Peter Arnold; Page 683, Figure 16.1: © McGraw-Hill Higher Education, Inc./Photo by Ken Karp; Page 688: © Professors P.P. Botta and S. Correr/Science Picture Library/Photo Researchers; Figures 16.3, 19.8: © McGraw-Hill Higher Education, Inc./Photo by Ken Karp; Page 700: © CNRI/SPL/Science Source/Photo Researchers; Pages 703, 704 (both): © McGraw-Hill Higher Education, Inc./Photo by Ken Karp; Page 706: © Runk/Schoenberger/Grant Heilman Photography; Pages 708, 711, Figures 16.10, 16.11, 16.12 (all): © McGraw-Hill Higher Education, Inc./Photo by Ken Karp; Page 719 (left): © Jody Dole/Image Bank/Getty Images; Page 719 (right): © Scientific American/A.R. Terepka; Figure 16.13a–d: © McGraw-Hill Higher Education, Inc./Photo by Stephen Frisch; Page 729 (both): © McGraw-Hill Higher Education, Inc./Photo by Ken Karp.

Chapter 17

Opener: © Corbis/Vol. 188; Figure 17.4: © E.R. Degginger/Color-Pic; Figure 17.5: © NASA; Page 738: © McGraw-Hill Higher Education, Inc./Photo by Ken Karp; Figure 17.8: National Oceanic and Atmospheric Administration—NOAA; Figure 17.9: © NASA; Page 742: © Roger Ressmeyer/Corbis Images; Figure 17.10: © E.R. Degginger/Color-Pic; Figure 17.20 (both): © Westfalen-Lippe/Landshafts-Verband; Figure 17.22: © Owen Franken; Page 751: © James A. Sugar/Corbis Images;

Figure 17.24: © Owen Franken; Figure 17.26: © Stan Ries/Index Stock Imagery; Page 753: © Barth Falkenberg/Stock Boston; Figure 17.28: © McGraw-Hill Higher Education, Inc./Photo by Ken Karp.

Chapter 18

Opener: © National Lime Association; Page 765: © McGraw-Hill Higher Education, Inc./Photo by Ken Karp; Page 767: © Matthias K. Gebbert/University of Maryland, Baltimore County/Dept. of Mathematics and Statistics; Pages 770, 782: © McGraw-Hill Higher Education, Inc./ Photo by Ken Karp.

Chapter 19

Opener: © Nathan S. Lewis, California Institute of Technology; Figures 19.2, 19.6: © McGraw-Hill Higher Education, Inc./ Photo by Ken Karp; Figure 19.12: © NASA; Figure 19.13a: © E.R. Degginger/Color-Pic; Figure 19.13b: © McGraw-Hill Higher Education, Inc./Photo by Ken Karp; Figure 19.13c: © Donald Dietz/Stock Boston; Figure 19.15: © McGraw-Hill Higher Education, Inc./Photo by Ken Karp; Figure 19.18: © McGraw-Hill Higher Education, Inc./Photo by Stephen Frisch; Pages 836, 839, 840 (both): © McGraw-Hill Higher Education, Inc./Photo by Ken Karp.

Chapter 20

Opener: © James L. Dye; Figure 20.2: © Lamont-Doherty/Dr. Bruce Heezen; Figure 20.5: © Jeff Smith; Figure 20.7: © Don Greenkennecott; Figure 20.13: © Wards Natural Science Establishment; Figure 20.14: © Aronson Photo/Stock Boston; Figure 20.15: © Wards Natural Science Establishment; Figure 20.16: © McGraw-Hill Higher Education, Inc./ Photo by Ken Karp; Figure 20.17: © Wards Natural Science Establishment; Figure 20.19: © E.R. Degginger/Color-Pic; Page 864 (both): © Courtesy of Aluminum Company of America.

Chapter 21

Opener: © NASA; Page 876: © McGraw-Hill Higher Education, Inc./Photo by Ken Karp; Figure 21.5: © Courtesy General Electric Research and Development Center; Figure 21.6: © Paul Logsdon; Page 881: © Jeff Smith; Figure 21.7: © McGraw-Hill Higher Education, Inc./Photo by Ken Karp; Figure 21.8: © Courtesy of Amax Inc.; Page 889: © Robert E. Daemmrich/Stone/ Getty Images; Page 889: © Jeff Roberson; Page 892: © McGraw-Hill Higher Education, Inc./Photo by Ken Karp; Figure 21.14: © L.V. Bergman/The Bergman Collection; Figure 21.16: © Tarus Photos/C.B. Jones; Page 895: © McGraw-Hill Higher Education, Inc./Photo by Ken Karp; Figure 21.19: © Charles Beck/Vulcan Materials Company; Figure 21.21: © Jim Brandenberg.

Chapter 22

Opener: © Al Lemme/Fritz Goro; Figure 22.4 (all): © McGraw-Hill Higher Education Inc./Photo by Ken Karp; Figures 22.5, 22.6: © Wards Natural Science Establishment; Page 922: © McGraw-Hill Higher Education, Inc./Photo by Ken Karp; Figure 22.15: © Joel Gordon Photography-Design Conceptions; Figure 22.20: © McGraw-Hill Higher Education, Inc./Photo by Ken Karp; Page 932: © University Science Books; Page 935: © McGraw-Hill Higher Education, Inc./Photo by Ken Karp; Page 940: © Mead Art Museum; Page 941: © McGraw-Hill Higher Education, Inc./ Photo by Ken Karp.

Chapter 23

Opener: © NASA; Figure 23.5: © Fermi Lab; Figure 23.11: © Pierre Kopp/Westlight/ Corbis Images; Figure 23.12: © Marvin Lazarus/Photo Researchers; Figure 23.13: © Los Alamos National Laboratories; Page 961: © U.S. Department of Energy/ Photo Researchers; Page 962: © W.J. Maeck; Figure 23.15: © Lawrence Livermore National Labs; Figure 23.16: © U.S. Navy Photo/Department of Defense; Figure 23.17: © B. Leonard Holman MD/Harvard Medical Center; Page 967: © Alexander Tsiaras/Photo Researchers; Page 969: © McGraw-Hill Higher Education, Inc./Photo by Ken Karp; Page 977: Christ and His Disciples at Emmaus by Han van Meegeren/Museum Boijmans Van Beuningen, Rotterdam.

Chapter 24

Opener: © Jean Miele/Corbis; Page 991: © E.R. Degginger/Color-Pic; Page 992: © Laura Stern & John Pinston, Courtesy of Laura Stern/U.S. Geological Survey; Page 993: © IBM Corporation-Almaden Research Center; Pages 997, 1000: © McGraw-Hill Higher Education, Inc./Photo by Ken Karp; Page 1001: © Biophoto/Photo Researchers; Page 1003: © Courtesy of American Petroleum Institute; Page 1012: © AP/Wide World Photos; Page 1013: © Ed Bock/Corbis Images.

Chapter 25

Opener: © Ken Karp Photography; Page 1017, Figure 25.2: © McGraw-Hill Higher Education, Inc./Photo by Ken Karp; Page 1018: © Richard Hutchings/Photo Researchers; Figure 25.4: © Charles Weckler/Image Bank/Getty Images; Figure 25.7: E.R. Degginger/Color-Pic; Page 1032: © Lawrence Berkeley Laboratory.

Index

A Note to the Student

For nearly all of you, CHEM 184 will be your first chemistry course at the college level; for some of you, it may be your first chemistry course at any level. The goals of the course are to introduce you to many of the fundamental concepts of chemistry, and to help you develop the skills needed to solve problems relating to these concepts. In the hope of assisting you in achieving these goals so that you will succeed in (and maybe even enjoy) this course, I have prepared the following material to supplement the textbook by Raymond Chang.

The first of the supplementary material, entitled "Main Concepts", succinctly lists the most important concepts in each of the chapters we will cover this semester. As we begin each chapter, you should take note of the concepts I have listed for that chapter. This list will tell you what I regard as being most important in that chapter, and you should focus your primary attention on mastering those concepts. Later, as you prepare for one of the inevitable exams in this course, these lists will serve as study guides to help you review what we have covered in each chapter. Whether you study for an exam by yourself or with others, you can test your comprehension of the material by seeing if you can accurately define or discuss each of these concepts.

The second part of the supplementary material, entitled "Practice Questions", presents twenty problems for each chapter. These problems, many of which were given on CHEM 184 exams in previous years, serve three purposes. First, they should give you an idea of the type of questions that might very well appear on a CHEM 184 exam this semester. Second, each question is based on a particular concept, and thus each question should help you identify which concepts from a given chapter are most likely to be covered on an exam. Third, your success or failure in answering these questions provides you valuable, pre-test feedback on which concepts you have or have not mastered.

I hope that you will use this supplementary material that I have prepared, and that it will help you to learn chemistry and to do well in this course.

Peter M. Hierl

MAIN CONCEPTS

Chapter 1: Chemistry: The Study of Change

The scientific method

- hypothesis
- law
- theory

Classification of matter

- mixture (homogeneous *vs.* heterogeneous)
- element
- compound

The three states of matter (solid, liquid, gas)

Physical and chemical properties of matter

Measurement

- SI units: base units, prefixes
- mass and weight
- volume
- density
- temperature scales

Handling numbers

- scientific notation
- significant figures
- accuracy and precision

Dimensional analysis in solving problems

Chapter 2: Atoms, Molecules, and Ions

The atomic theory

- law of definite proportions
- law of multiple proportions
- law of conservation of mass

The structure of the atom

- the electron
- radioactivity
- the proton and the nucleus
- the neutron

Atomic number, mass number, and isotopes

The periodic table

- periods and groups
- metals, nonmetals, and metalloids

Molecules and ions

Chemical formulas

- molecular formulas
- empirical formulas
- formulas of ionic compounds

Naming compounds

- ionic compounds
- molecular compounds
- acids and bases
- hydrates

Chapter 3: Mass Relationships in Chemical Reactions

Atomic mass

- atomic mass unit (amu)
- average atomic mass

Avogadro's number and the molar mass of an element

- the mole
- molar mass
- conversions

Molecular mass

The mass spectrometer

Percent composition of compounds

Empirical determination of empirical formulas

- experimental method
- determination of molecular formulas

Chemical reactions and chemical equations

- writing chemical reactions
- balancing chemical reactions

Amounts of reactants and products

- stoichiometry
- the mole method

Limiting reagents

Reaction yield

- theoretical yield
- percent yield

Chapter 4: Reactions in Aqueous Solutions

General properties of aqueous solutions

- electrolytic properties
- hydration

Precipitation Reactions

- solubility rules
- molecular equations
- net ionic equations

Acid-base reactions

- general properties of acids and bases
- Brønsted acids and bases
- monoprotic, diprotic, and polyprotic acids
- acid-base neutralization

Oxidation-reduction reactions

        – oxidizing agents and reducing agents
        – oxidation number
        – types of redux reactions
        – the activity series for metals

Concentration of solutions

        – molarity (molar concentration)
        – dilution of solutions

Gravimetric analysis

Acid-base titrations

        – equivalence point
        – chemical indicators

Chapter 5: Gases

Substances that exist as gases

Pressure of a gas

        – SI units of pressure
        – atmospheric pressure
        – barometers, manometers

The gas laws

        – Boyle's law
        – Charles's law
        – Guy-Lussac's law
        – Avogadro's law

The ideal gas equation

- concept of an ideal gas
- standard temperature and pressure (STP)
- density calculations
- molar mass of a gaseous substance

Gas stoichiometry

Dalton's Law of partial pressures

- definition of partial pressure
- definition of mole fraction

Kinetic molecular theory of gases

- fundamental assumptions of the theory
- relationship between kinetic energy and temperature
- application to the gas laws
- distribution of molecular speeds
- root-mean-square speed
- gas diffusion
- gas effusion

Deviation from ideal behavior

- compression factor, Z
- van der Waals equation of state

Chapter 6: Thermochemistry

The nature and types of energy

Energy changes in chemical reactions

     – definition of "system" and "surroundings"
     – types of systems: open, closed, isolated
     – definition of "exothermic" and "endothermic" processes

Introduction to thermodynamics

     – state of a system
     – state functions *vs.* path functions
     – first law of thermodynamics (conservation of energy)
     – work and heat

Enthalpy of chemical reactions

     – definition and physical meaning of enthalpy (H)
     – enthalpy of reaction (ΔH)
     – writing thermochemical equations
     – comparison of ΔH and ΔE

Calorimetry

     – definition of "specific heat" and "heat capacity"
     – constant volume calorimetry
     – constant pressure calorimetry

Standard enthalpy of formation and of reaction

     – standard enthalpy of formation (ΔH_f°)
     – standard enthalpy of reaction
     – direct method of determining ΔH_f°
     – indirect method of determining ΔH_f° (Hess's law)

Heat of solution and of dilution

     – heat of solution; hydration

- lattice energy
- heat of dilution

Chapter 7: Quantum Theory and the Electronic Structure of Atoms

Electromagnetic radiation

- the nature of waves (frequency, wavelength, and amplitude)
- the nature of electromagnetic radiation
- types of electromagnetic radiation
- relationship between wavelength, frequency, and speed of light

From classical physics to quantum theory

- black-body radiation (Planck's quantum hypothesis)
- the photoelectric effect (Einstein's hypothesis)

Bohr's theory of the H-atom

- emission spectra
- line spectra
- quantized energy levels

The dual nature of the electron

- de Broglie wavelength
- observation of electron diffraction

Quantum mechanics

- Heisenberg uncertainty principle

- wave mechanics and the Schrödinger equation
- atomic orbitals and the wave function
- electron density

Quantum numbers

- principal quantum number, n
- angular momentum quantum number, l
- magnetic quantum number, m_l
- electron spin quantum number, m_s

Atomic orbitals

- types of orbitals (*s, p, d, etc*)
- the energies of orbitals in one-electron atoms
- the energies of orbitals in multi-electron atoms

Electron configurations

- writing electron configurations
- the Pauli exclusion principle
- dimagnetism and paramagnetism
- the shielding effect in multi-electron atoms
- Hund's rule
- general rules for assigning electrons to atomic orbitals

The aufbau (building-up) principle

Chapter 8: Periodic Relationships Among the Elements

Development of the periodic table

Periodic classification of the elements

- representative elements
- transition metals
  - lanthanides
  - actinides
- noble gases

Electron configuration of cations and anions

- representative elements
- transition metals

Periodic variation in physical properties

- effective nuclear charge
- atomic radius; ionic radius
- ionization energy
- electron affinity

Chapter 9: Chemical Bonding I: Basic Concepts

Lewis dot symbols of the elements

The ionic bond

Lattice energies of ionic compounds

- definition
- determination of lattice energies (Born-Haber cycle)
- effect of ionic charge and of ionic radius

The covalent bond

- Lewis (dot) structures

- lone pairs (non-bonding electrons)
- octet rule
- multiple (i.e., double & triple) bonds
- comparison of ionic & covalent compounds

The polar covalent bond; electronegativity

Writing Lewis structures

Formal charge

Resonance

Exceptions to the octet rule

- odd-electron molecules
- the incomplete octet
- the expanded octet

Bond energies

Chapter 10: Chemical Bonding II: Molecular Geometry and Hybridization of Atomic Orbitals

VSEPR model

- guidelines for applying the VESPR model
- arrangement of electron pairs around the central atom
- molecular geometry

Dipole moments

- bond moments
- role of molecular geometry

   – polar and nonpolar molecules

Hybridization of atomic orbitals

   – types of hybridization
   – procedure for hybridizing atomic orbitals
   – hybrid orbitals and their shapes (Table 10.4)

Valence bond theory

   – formation of covalent bonds
   – sigma bonds and pi bonds
   – hybridization in molecules containing multiple bonds

Molecular orbital theory

   – formation of molecular orbitals
   – bonding and antibonding orbitals
   – molecular orbitals energy level diagrams
   – molecular orbital configurations
      – rules governing the filling of MO's
      – homonuclear diatomic molecules of 2nd-period elements

Delocalized molecular orbitals

Chapter 11: Intermolecular Forces and Liquids and Solids

Intermolecular Forces: various types and their characteristics

   – dipole-dipole forces
   – ion-dipole forces
   – dispersion forces

    – hydrogen bonding

Properties of liquids

    – surface tension
    – viscosity
    – properties of water

Crystal structure

    – unit cell: definition and types of
    – packing of spheres; number of nearest neighbors

X-Ray diffraction; Bragg's law

Types of crystals and their characteristics

    – ionic
    – molecular
    – covalent (network)
    – metallic

Amorphous solids

Phase changes

    – liquid-vapor equilibrium
        vapor pressure; boiling point
        Clausius-Clapeyron equation
        critical phenomena
    – liquid-solid equilibria
    – solid-vapor equilibria

Phase diagrams

Chapter 12: Physical Properties of Solutions

Types of solutions

Molecular view of the solution process

- types of molecular interactions
- solvation

Concentration units

- percent by mass
- mole fraction
- molarity
- molality

Effect of temperature on solubility of solids and of gases

Effect of pressure on solubility of gases (Henry's Law)

Colligative properties of non-electrolyte solutions

- Raoult's Law
- vapor pressure lowering
- boiling point elevation
- freezing point depression
- osmotic pressure

Colligative properties of electrolyte solutions (van't Hoff factor)

PRACTICE QUESTIONS

Chapter 1

1. Which of the following is a **homogeneous mixture?**

   A. Nitrogen gas   B. Liquid water   C. Sugar   D. Bread   E. Air

2. Which of the following is a **heterogeneous mixture?**

   A. Helium gas   B. Alcohol   C. Sugar   D. Concrete   E. Clean air

3. Which of the following is a **physical** change?

   A. a freshly cut apple turns brown
   B. when cooled, liquid water becomes ice
   C. milk turns sour on standing
   D. bread rises when baking
   E. fermentation of sugar

4. The SI prefixes **milli-** and **mega-** represent, respectively:

   A. 10^6 and 10^{-6} B. 10^{-3} and 10^6 C. 10^3 and 10^{-6}

   D. 10^{-3} and 10^9 E. 10^{-6} and 10^{-3}

5. The SI prefixes **micro-** and **kilo-** represent, respectively:

   A. 10^6 and 10^{-6} B. 10^{-3} and 10^6 C. 10^3 and 10^{-6}

   D. 10^{-3} and 10^9 E. 10^{-6} and 10^3

6. The diameter of an atom is approximately 1×10^{-8} cm. How many **nanometers** is this?

   A. 1×10^{-19} nm   B. 1×10^{-15} nm   C. 1×10^{-10} nm

   D. 1×10^{-5} nm   E. 1×10^{-1} nm

7. How many **cubic millimeters** equal one cubic meter?

   A. 10^{-9} B. 10^{-6} C. 10^3 D. 10^6 E. 10^9

8. How many **cubic centimeters** equal 1 liter?

   A. 10   B. 10^2 C. 10^3 D. 10^4 E. 10^6

9. How many **mL** in 0.0005 L?

   A. 0.5 mL   B. 5 mL   C. 0.05 mL   D. 0.000005 mL   E. 200 Ml

10. Convert 500 mL to **quarts**, given that 1L = 1.06 qt.

    A. 1.88 qt   B. 0.47 qt   C. 0.53 qt

    D. 4.7×10^5 qt   E. 5.4×10^5 qt

11. The **lowest possible temperature** is

    A. −273 K   B. −273 °C   D. −273 °F   D. 273 K   E. 0 °C

12. Liquid propane boils at −42°C. What is its boiling point on the **Kelvin scale**?

    A. 231 K   B. 256 K   C. 273 K   D. 315 K   E. 345 K

13. Many home freezers maintain a temperature of 0°F. Express this in **°C**.

    A. − 32°C   B. − 18°C   C. 0°C   D. 18°C   E. 57.6°C

14. How many **significant figures** does the result of the following operation contain?

    8.52010 x 7.9

    A. 2   B. 3   C. 4   D. 5   E. 6

15. How many significant figures does the following sum contain? **8.5201 + 1.93**

    A. 1   B. 2   C. 3   D. 4   E. 5

16. The number of **significant figures** in 7.5601×10^{-2} is

    A. 3   B. 4   C. 5   D. 6   E. 7

17. What is the **volume** of a 2.5 gram block of metal if its density is 4.75 g/cm^3?

    A. 0.53 cm^3 B. 1.9 cm^3 C. 2.5 cm^3 D. 4.75 cm^3 E. 11.9 cm^3

18. The density of mercury is about 13 g/cm^3. What would be the **mass in kilograms** (kg) of one cubic meter of mercury?

    A. 13 kg   B. 130 kg   C. 1,300 kg

    D. 13,000 kg   E. 1,300,000 kg

19. What **volume** of alcohol (density 0.800 g/mL) is needed to obtain 400 g of alcohol?

   A. 320 mL   B. 400 mL   C. 480 mL   D. 500 mL   E. 620 mL

20. The volume of a 10.0% glucose solution is 7.40 mL. Its density is 1.04 g/mL. What is the **mass** of the solution?

   A. 7.40 g   B. 7.70 g   C. 770 mg   D. 0.074 kg   E. 0.770 kg

Chapter 2

1. **J. J. Thomson** is credited with the discovery of

   A. the electron   B. the proton   C. the neutron   D. helium   E. the Beatles

2. **Rutherford's** experiment with alpha particle scattering by gold foil established that

   A. protons are not evenly distributed throughout an atom
   B. electrons have a negative charge
   C. electrons have a positive charge
   D. atoms are made of protons, neutrons, and electrons
   E. protons are 1840 times heavier than electrons

3. Atoms of the same element with **different mass numbers** are called

   A. nucleons   B. neutrons   C. allotropes   D. chemical families   E. isotopes

4. A certain element is listed as having an atomic mass of 35.5 amu. It is probably true that it contains a mixture of …

   A isomers   B. isotopes   C. ions   D. neutrons   E. allotropes

5. There are three **isotopes** of hydrogen; these differ from each other with respect to …

   A. atomic number   B. atomic mass   C. nuclear charge

                D. number of electrons   E. number of protons

6. There are only two naturally occurring isotopes of chlorine, ^{35}Cl and ^{37}Cl. The **natural abundance** of the ^{35}Cl must be about

   A. 10%   B. 25%   C. 50%   D. 75&   E. 90%

7. How many **neutrons** are there in an atom of **lead** whose mass number is 208?

   A. 82   B. 126   C. 208   D. 290   E. none of them

8. An atom of the isotope **sulfur-31** consists of how many protons, neutrons, and electrons? (p = proton, n = neutron, e = electron)

   A. 15 p, 16 n, 15 e   B. 16 p, 15 n, 16 e   C. 16 p, 31 n, 16 e

   D. 32 p, 31 n, 32 e   E. 16 p, 16 n, 15 e

9. What is the **symbol** of the ion having 12 protons and 10 electrons?

   A. Mg^{2+} B. Al^{3+} C. P^{3-} D. S^{2-} E. Cl^-

10. The elements in a **column** of the periodic table are known as

    A. metalloids   B. a period   C. noble gases   D. a group   E. nonmetals

11. Which of the following elements is most likely to be a **good conductor of electricity?**

    A. N   B. S   C. He   D. Cl   E. Fe

12. Which of the following elements is most likely to be a **poor conductor of electricity?**

    A. Li   B. Mg   C. Ru   D. Hg   E. S

13. Which of the following elements is <u>not</u> a **metalloid?**

    A. P   B. Si   C. Ge   D. As   E. Te

14. Which <u>one</u> of the following lists gives the **correct symbol** for the elements phosphorus, potassium, silver, chlorine, and sulfur in that order?

    A. K, Ag, Po, Cl, S
    B. P, Po, Ag, Cl, S
    C. Ph, K, Ag, S, Cl
    D. P, K, Si, S, Cl
    E. P, K, Ag, Cl, S

15. What is the formula for the ionic compound formed by **calcium ion** and **nitrate ion?**

    A. Ca_3N_2 B. $Ca(NO_3)_2$ C. Ca_2NO_3 D. Ca_2NO_2 E. $CaNO_3$

16. The formula for the **sulfate ion** is

    A. S^{2-} B. HSO_4^{2-} C. SO_4^- D. $S_2O_3^{2-}$ E. SO_4^{2-}

17.   The formula of the **nitrite ion** is

   A. N^- B. N^{3-} C. NO^- D. NO_2^- E. NO_3^-

18.   The **total number of atoms** in one formula unit of $(NH_4)_2S_2O_8$ is

   A. 4   B. 10   C. 15   D. 20   E. 25

19.   What is the correct formula for **copper(II) sulfate**?

   A. $CuSO_4$ B. $Cu_3(SO_4)_2$ C. Cu_2SO_3 D. $Cu(SO_4)_2$ E. $Cu(SO_3)_2$

20.   The correct name for **KHCO$_3$** is

   A. phosphorus bicarbonate
   B. phosphorus carbonate
   C. potassium carbonate
   D. potassium hydrogen carbon trioxide
   E. potassium bicarbonate

Chapter 3

1.   An atom of bromine has a mass about four times greater than that of an atom of neon. Which choice makes the correct comparison of the **relative numbers** of bromine and neon atoms in 1,000 g of each element?

   A. The number of Br and Ne atoms is the same.
   B. The are 1000 times as many Br atoms as Ne atoms.
   C. There are 1000 times as many Ne atoms as Br atoms.
   D. There are four times as many Ne atoms as Br atoms.
   E. There are four times as many Br atoms as Ne atoms.

2.   What is the **mass** of <u>one</u> copper atom?

   A. 1.055×10^{-22} g   B. 63.55 g   C. 1 amu
   D. 1.66×10^{-24} g   E. 9.476×10^{21} g

3.   Calculate the **molecular mass** of benzene, C_6H_6.

   A. 13 amu   B. 36 amu   C. 78 amu   D. 108 amu   E. 142 amu

4.   Calculate the **molecular mass** of ethyl alcohol, C_2H_5OH.

   A. 13 amu   B. 29 amu   C. 46 amu   D. 52 amu   E. 178 amu

5. Calculate the **formula mass** of potassium permanganate, $KMnO_4$.

   A. 52 amu   B. 70 amu   C. 110 amu   D. 158 amu   E. 176 amu

6. How many **moles** of copper atoms are contained in 10.0 g of copper?

   A. 0.0480   B. 0.0558   C. 0.109   D. 0.157   E. 0.221

7. How many **molecules** are in 8.0 g of O_3?

   A. 3   B. 3.6×10^{24} C. 1.0×10^{23}

   D. 3.0×10^{23} E. 6.0×10^{23}

8. How many **molecules** are in 16.0 g of O_2?

   A. 3   B. 3.6×10^{24} C. 1.0×10^{23} D. 3.0×10^{23} E. 6.0×10^{23}

9. If 0.274 moles of a substance weighs 62.5 g, what is the **molar mass** of the substance?

   A. 228 g/mol   B. 17.1 g/mol   C. 0.00438 g/mol   D. 117 g/mol   E. none of these

10. Calculate the **molecular mass** of benzene, C_6H_6.

    A. 13 amu   B. 36 amu   C. 78 amu   D. 108 amu   E. 142 amu

11. Determine the **number of moles** of aluminum in 96.7 g of Al.

    A. 0.279 mol   B. 3.58 mol   C. 7.43 mol   D. 4.21 mol   E. 6.02×10^{23} mol

12. What is the **mass** of 0.0250 mol of P_2O_5?

    A. 35.5 g   B. 5676 g   C. 0.0250 g   D. 1.51×10^{22} g   E. 3.55 g

13. How many **molecules** are in 9.0 g of H_2O?

    A. 3   B. 3.6×10^{24} C. 1.0×10^{23} D. 3.0×10^{23} E. 6.0×10^{23}

14. How many **oxygen atoms** are there in 1.0 g of $CaCO_3$?

    A. 6×10^{21} B. 1.8×10^{22} C. 6×10^{22} D. 6×10^{23} E. 1.8×10^{24}

15. What is the **percentage** (by mass) of carbon in benzene, C_6H_6?

    A. 20.1   B. 33.5   C. 50.0   D. 79.9   E. 92.3

16. Analysis of a hydrocarbon showed that it contained 11.1% hydrogen and 88.9% carbon by weight. What is its **empirical formula**?

   A. CH   B. CH_2 C. CH_3 D. C_2H_3 E. C_2H_5

17. An unknown compound has the empirical formula CH_2. A 0.050-mol sample of this compound weighs 2.80 g. What is the **molecular formula** of this compound?

   A. C_2H_4 B. C_3H_6 C. C_4H_8 D. C_5H_{10} E. C_6H_{12}

18. Ammonia reacts with diatomic oxygen to form nitric oxide and water vapor:

$$4NH_3 + 5O_2 \rightarrow 4NO + 6H_2O$$

   When 40.0 g NH_3 and 50.0 g O_2 are allowed to react, which is the **limiting reactant**?

   A. NH_3 B. O_2 C. NO   D. H_2O E. none of these

19. What is the **theoretical yield** (in g) of ammonia, NH_3, that can be obtained from 10.0 g of H_2 and 80.0 g of N_2?

$$N_2 + 3H_2 \rightarrow 2NH_3$$

   A. 28.4 g   B. 48.6 g   C. 56.7 g   D. 90.0 g   E. 97.1 g

20. How many **grams** of water could be made from 3.0 mol of H_2 and 3.0 mol of O_2? (Hint: write and balance the chemical equation.)

   A. 6.0 g   B. 48 g   C. 54 g   D. 96 g   E. 108 g

Chapter 4

1. Which of the following compounds is a **strong electrolyte**?
   A. KOH   B. N_2 C. H_2O D. C_2H_5OH (ethanol)   E. HF

2. Which of the following compounds is a **weak electrolyte**?
   A. NaOH   B. N_2 C. NaCl   D. C_2H_5OH (ethanol)   E. HF

3. Which of the following compounds is a **nonelectrolyte**?
   A. NaF   B. HCl   C. NaOH   D. C_2H_5OH (ethanol)   E. HF

4. Which one of the following compounds is a **weak acid** in aqueous solution?

   A. $HClO_4$ B. H_3PO_4 C. H_2SO_4 D. HNO_3 E. HCl

5. Identify the **major ionic species** present in a solution of Na_2CO_3.

   A. Na_2^+, CO_3^- B. Na_2^+, C^{2-}, O_3 C. Na^+, C^{4+}, O_3^{2-}

            D. Na^+, C^+, O^{2-} E. Na^+, CO_3^{2-}

6. According to the solubility rules, which one of the following is **soluble** in water?

   A. $AgBr$ B. $AgCl$ C. Ag_2CO_3 D. $AgNO_3$ E. Ag_2S

7. According to the solubility rules, which one of the following is **insoluble** in water?

   A. $NaCl$ B. $AgNO_3$ C. $FeCl_2$ D. $PbNO_3$ E. $AgCl$

8. The common constituent in **all acids** is

   A. H_2 B. H^+ C. OH^- D. H_2SO_4 E. Cl^-

9. Which choice gives the correct formula of the **salt** formed in the neutralization reaction of hydrochloric acid and calcium hydroxide?

   A. CaO B. $CaCl_2$ C. CaH_2 D. $CaCl$ E. $CaClH$

10. Which choice gives the correct formula of the **salt** formed in the neutralization reaction of hydrobromic acid and magnesium hydroxide?

    A. $MgBr$ B. Mg_2Br_3 C. Mg_3Br_2 D. Mg_2Br E. $MgBr_2$

11. Which metal will **displace hydrogen** from <u>cold water?</u>

    A. K   B. Cu   C. Al   D. Ni   E. Pb

12. Which one of the following is a **redox reaction**?

    A. $H^+(aq) + OH^-(aq) \rightarrow H_2O(l)$

    B. $2KBr(aq) + Pb(NO_3)_2(aq) \rightarrow 2KNO_3(aq) + PbBr_2(s)$

    C. $NaCl(aq) + AgNO_3(aq) \rightarrow NaNO_3(aq) + AgCl(s)$

    D. $Zn(s) + 2HCl(aq) \rightarrow ZnCl_2(aq) + H_2(g)$

E. $CO_3^{2-}(aq) + HSO_4^-(aq) \rightarrow HCO_3^-(aq) + SO_4^{2-}(aq)$

13.   What element is **oxidized** in the following reaction?

$$Cd + NiO_2 + 2H_2O \rightarrow Cd(OH)_2 + Ni(OH)_2$$

A. Cd   B. Ni   C. O   D. H   E. none of these

14.   What element is **reduced** in the following reaction?

$$Cd + NiO_2 + 2H_2O \rightarrow Cd(OH)_2 + Ni(OH)_2$$

A. Cd   B. Ni   C. O   D. H   E. none of these

15.   The **oxidation number** of C in the bicarbonate anion, HCO_3^-, is

A. +6   B. +5   C. +4   D. +3   E. none of these

16.   The **oxidation number** of N in $NaNO_3$ is

A. +6   B. +5   C. +3   D. −3   E. none of these

17.   How many **moles** of lead ions are there in a 0.50-L solution of 0.020 molar lead nitrate, $Pb(NO_3)_2$?

A. 0.0050   B. 0.010   C. 0.020   D. 0.025   E. 0.050

18.   How many **moles** of KOH are there in a 34.5 mL of 0.250 M KOH?

A. 0.00865   B. 0.00976   C. 0.0115   D. 0.0157   E. 0.0187

19.   Calculate the **molarity** of a solution that contains 37.5 g of NaOH in 750.0 mL of solution.

A. 0.75 M   B. 1.00 M   C. 1.25 M   D. 1.50 M   E. 1.75 M

20.   What **volume** of acid must you use to prepare 100 mL of 0.50 M HCl from 2.00 M HCl?

A. 25.0 mL   B. 50.0 mL   C. 100 mL   D. 200 mL   E. 400 mL

Chapter 5

1. Equal volumes of N_2 and CO at the same temperature and pressure have the same

    1. density
    2. number of molecules
    3. number of atoms

    A. 1 only   B. 2 only   C. 3 only   D. 2 and 3 only   E. 1,2 and 3

2. What **volume** of ammonia, NH_3, has the same number of <u>molecules</u> as 10.0 L of nitrogen, N_2, at the same temperature and pressure?

    A. 1.67 L   B. 2.50 L   C. 3.33 L   D. 7.50 L   E. 10.0 L

3. A sample of nitrogen gas has a volume of 32.4 L at 20^oC. The gas is heated to 220^oC at constant pressure. What is the **final volume** of nitrogen?

    A. 2.94 L   B. 19.3 L   C. 31.4 L   D. 54.5 L   E. 356 L

4. An ideal gas has a volume of 1.5 L at a pressure of 1.0 atm. What will be the **volume** of this gas if the pressure is reduced to 0.85 atm, the temperature remaining constant?

    A. 1.3 L   B. 1.5 L   C. 1.8 L   D. 2.0 L   E. 2.3 L

5. The gas pressure in an aerosol can is 1.8 atm at 25^oC. If the gas is an ideal gas, what **pressure** would develop in the can if it were heated to 475^oC?

    A. 0.095 atm   B. 0.717 atm   C. 3.26 atm   D. 4.52 atm   E. 34.2 atm

6. If the pressure on a sample of gas (constant number of moles) is tripled and the absolute temperature is quadrupled, by what factor will the **volume** of the sample change?

    A. 12   B. 3/4   C. 4/3   D. 1/3   E. 4

7. Calculate the number of **kilograms** of helium needed to inflate a balloon to a volume of 100,000 L at an atmospheric pressure of 250 mmHg and a temperature of -35^oC.

    A. 1.68 kg   B. 3.36 kg   C. 5.21 kg   D. 6.74 kg   E. 5120 kg

8. What **pressure** in atmospheres will be exerted by 2,500 g of oxygen gas (O_2) when stored at 22°C in a 40.0 L cylinder?

    A. 3.55 atm   B. 1,510 atm   C. 47.3 atm   D. 7.56×10^4 atm   E. 10.2 atm

9. An ideal gas has a volume of 1.25 L at 800 torr and 50.0°C. What would its **volume** be at STP?

    A. 1.02 L   B. 1.11 L   C. 1.21 L   D. 1.33 L   E. 1.41 L

10. How many **moles** of gas are in a sample occupying 0.500 L at 170 torr and 25°C?

    A. 0.000500   B. 0.00457   C. 0.0112   D. 0.236   E. 1.02

11. Calculate the **density** of $CO_2(g)$ at 100°C and 10.0 atm pressure.

    A. 1.44 g/L   B. 134 g/L   C. 44.0 g/L   D. 53.6 g/L   E. 14.4 g/L

12. Determine the **molar mass** of Freon-11 gas if a sample weighing 0.597 g occupies 100 cm^3 at 95°C, and 1,000 mmHg.

    A. 0.19 g/mol   B. 35.3 g/mol   C. 70.9 g/mol   D. 137 g/mol   E. 384 g/mol

13. Ammonium nitrite decomposes according to the equation

    $$NH_4NO_2(s) \rightarrow N_2(g) + 2H_2O(g)$$

    What is the **total volume of gases** produced at 1092 K and 1.00 atm pressure when 192 g of ammonium nitrite decomposes?

    A. 134 L   B. 202 L   C. 269 L   D. 403 L   E. 806 L

14. How many **liters** of oxygen gas at 153°C and 0.820 atm can be produced by the reaction of 22.4 g of $KClO_3$?

    $$2KClO_3(s) \rightarrow 2KCl(s) + 3O_2(g)$$

    A. 3.0 L   B. 0.085 L   C. 4.20 L   D. 7.79 l   E. 11.7 L

15. What **volume** of CO_2 gas at 645 torr and 800 K would be produced by the reaction of 10 g of $CaCO_3$ according to the equation?

$$CaCO_3(s) \rightarrow CaO(s) + CO_2(g)$$

A. 7.73 L   B. 22.4 L   C. 25.0 L   D. 34.8 L   E. 45.7 mL

16. If 0.200 mol of methane, CH_4, effuses through a small hole in 100 s, the **time** required for 0.200 mol of helium to pass through the hole will be

A. 10 s   B. 25 s   C. 50 s   D. 100 s   E. 200 s

17. Which statement is **false**?

A. The average kinetic energies of molecules from samples of different "ideal" gases is the same at the same temperature.

B. The molecules of an ideal gas are relatively far apart.

C. All molecules of an ideal gas have the same kinetic energy at constant temperature.

D. Molecules of a gas undergo many collisions with each other and the container walls.

E. Molecules of greater mass have a lower average speed than those of lesser mass at the same temperature.

18. If equal masses of $O_2(g)$ and $HBr(g)$ are in separate containers of equal volume and temperature, which one of the following statements is **true**?

A. The pressure in the O_2 container is greater than that in the HBr container.
B. There are more HBr molecules than O_2 molecules.
C. The average kinetic energy of O_2 molecules is greater than that of HBr molecules.
D. The average kinetic energy of HBr molecules is greater than that of O_2 molecules.
E. The pressures of both gases are the same.

19. What is the **ratio** of the average speed of SO_2 molecules to that of O_2 molecules at 298K?

A. 1:2   B. 1:1   C. 2:1   D. 1.41:1   E. 1:1.41

20. Under what conditions does a real gas **most closely follow** ideal behavior?

   A. high temperature and low pressure

   B. low temperature and high pressure

   C. high temperature and high pressure

   D. low temperature and low pressure

   E. standard temperature and pressure

Chapter 6

1. An **endothermic process** causes the <u>surroundings</u> to

   A. gain heat
   B. expand in volume
   C. lose heat
   D. increase in temperature
   E. none of the above

2. The **unit** for a joule (J) is

   A. $kg \cdot m^2/s^2$ B. $kg \cdot m/s^2$ C. $kg/m \cdot s^2$ D. $g \cdot m^2/s^2$ E. $kg \cdot m^2/s$

3. The amount of heat required to raise the temperature of 18.0 g of water $1^\circ C$ is called its

   A. enthalpy
   B. specific heat
   C. specific heat capacity
   D. molar heat capacity
   E. change in energy

4. The amount of heat required to raise the temperature of 1g of water $1^\circ C$ is called its

   A. enthalpy
   B. specific heat
   C. molar heat capacity
   D. change in energy
   E. adiabatic constant

5. How much heat is required to raise the temperature of 1,500 g of water from 25°C to 52°C? (The specific heat of water is 4.19 J/g·°C)

    A. 1,500 kJ   B. 170 kJ   C. 6.27 kJ   D. 40.5 J   E. 40.5 kJ

6. How many degrees of **temperature rise** will occur when a 25.0 g block of aluminum absorbs 10 kJ of heat? (The specific heat of Al is 0.900 J/g·°C.)

    A. 0.44°C   B. 22.5°C   C. 225°C   D. 360°C   E. 444°C

7. The molar enthalpy of fusion (melting), ΔH_{fus}, for water is 6.01 kJ/mol. How many **grams** of water can be melted by 50.0 kJ of heat?

    A. 8.32 g   B. 18.0 g   C. 89.1 g   D. 150 g   E. 221 g

8. The molar enthalpy of fusion (melting), ΔH_{fus}, for water is 6.01 kJ/mol. How much **heat** would be required to melt 10.0 kg of ice?

    A. 601 kJ   B. 1660 kJ   C. 2450 kJ   D. 3340 kJ   E. 4045 kJ

9. The sign of ΔH for the process $H_2O(s) \rightarrow H_2O(l)$ is

    A. positive, and the process is endothermic
    B. negative, and the process is endothermic
    C. positive, and the process is exothermic
    D. negative, and the process is exothermic
    E. none of the above

10. In a **bomb calorimeter**, reactions are carried out

    A. at 1 atm pressure and 25°C
    B. at STP (1 atm pressure and 0°C)
    C. at a constant pressure and 25°C
    D. at a constant pressure
    E. At a constant volume

11. To which the following reactions occurring at does the symbol $\Delta H^{\circ}_f[HNO_3(l)]$ refer?

A. $H(g) + N(g) + O_3(g) \rightarrow HNO_3(l)$

B. $1/2H_2(g) + 1/2N_2(g) + 3/2O_2(g) \rightarrow HNO_3(l)$

C. $HNO_3(l) \rightarrow 1/2H_2(g) + 1/2N_2(g) + 3/2O_2(g)$

D. $HNO_3(l) \rightarrow H(g) + N(g) + 3O(g)$

E. $H_2(g) + N_2(g) + O_3(g) \rightarrow HNO_3(l)$

12. The standard enthalpy change for the following reaction is 498.8 kJ:

$$O_2(g) \rightarrow 2O(g)$$

Calculate the **standard molar enthalpy of formation** of gaseous atomic oxygen, $O(g)$.

A. 0 kJ/mole   B. 249.4 kJ/mole   C. 498.8 kJ/mole

D. −249.4 kJ/mole   E. −498.8 kJ/mole

13. When 0.56 g of Na(s) reacts with excess $F_2(g)$ to form NaF(s), 13.8 kJ of heat are evolved at standard-state conditions. What is the **standard enthalpy of formation** (ΔH°_f) of NaF(s)?

A. 24.8 kJ/mol   B. +570 kJ/mol   C. -24.8 kJ/mol

D. -7.8 kJ/mol   E. -570 kJ/mol

14. The combustion of butane produces heat according to the equation

$$2C_4H_{10}(g) + 13O_2(g) \rightarrow 8CO_2(g) + 10H2O(l) \qquad \Delta H^{\circ}_{rxn} = -5,314 \text{ kJ}$$

What is the heat of combustion **per gram** of butane?

A. −32.5 kJ   B. −45.8 kJ   C. − 91.5 kJ   D. −2,656 kJ   E. −15,440 kJ

15. The combustion of methane produces heat according to the equation

$$CH_4(g) + 2O_2(g) \rightarrow CO_2(g) + 2H_2O(l) \qquad \Delta H^{\circ}_{rxn} = -890 \text{ kJ}$$

How much **heat** is generated by the combustion of 100 g of methane?

A. 65 kJ   B. 890 kJ   C. 5,560 kJ   D. 45,600 kJ   E. 890,000 kJ

16. The combustion of coal (i.e.,carbon) produces heat according to the equation

$$C(g) + O_2(g) \rightarrow CO_2(g) \qquad \Delta H^\circ_{rxn} = -393.5 \text{ kJ}$$

How much **heat** is generated by the combustion of 1.00 kg of coal?

A. 393.5 kJ   B. 890 kJ   C. 3,935 kJ   D. 4,5600 kJ   E. 32,800 kJ

17. Given that the molar enthalpy of formation of $H_2O(l)$ is –285.8 kJ/mol, how much **heat** is evolved from the combustion of 10.0 g $H_2(g)$?

$$2H_2(g) + O_2(g) \rightarrow 2H_2O(l)$$

A. 285.8 kJ   B. 571 kJ   C. 1430 kJ   D. 2860 kJ   E. 5710 kJ

18. Consider the following two reactions:

(1)	$A \rightarrow 2B$	$\Delta H_1 = 200 \text{ kJ}$
(2)	$A \rightarrow C$	$\Delta H_2 = 100 \text{ kJ}$

Determine the **enthalpy change, ΔH_3,** for the process

(3)	$2B \rightarrow C$

A. –300 kJ   B. –100 kJ   C. +100 kJ   D. +200 kJ   E. +300 kJ

19. Consider the following two reactions:

(1)	$A \rightarrow B$	$\Delta H_1 = -200 \text{ kJ}$
(2)	$2B \rightarrow C$	$\Delta H_2 = 100 \text{ kJ}$

Determine the **enthalpy change, ΔH_3,** for the process

(3)	$2A \rightarrow C$

A. –300 kJ   B. –100 kJ   C. +100 kJ   D. +200 kJ   E. +300 kJ

20. An ideal gas is allowed to expand at <u>constant temperature</u> from a volume of 1.0 L to 10 L against <u>a constant external pressure</u> of 0.50 atm. What is the value of **w, the work done on the gas**?

A. 4.5 J   B. − 4.5 J   C. 456 J   D. −456 J   E. 0 J

Chapter 7

1. Which type of radiation has the **lowest frequency**?

A. gamma rays   B. X-rays   C. ultraviolet

          D. visible   E. radiowaves

2. Rank the following regions of the electromagnetic spectrum in order of **increasing energy**.

          X-rays, microwaves, infrared, ultraviolet

A. X-rays, microwaves, infrared, ultraviolet

B. microwaves, ultraviolet, infrared, X-rays

C. microwaves, infrared, ultraviolet, X-rays

D. infrared, microwaves, ultraviolet, X-rays

E. infrared, ultraviolet, X-rays, microwaves

3. What is the **wavelength** of radiation that has a frequency of 2.10×10^{14} Hz?

A. 6.30×10^{22} m   B. 7.00×10^{2} nm   C. 7.00×10^{5} m

          D. 1.43×10^{-6} m   E. 3.00×10^{8} m

4. What is the **frequency** of radiation that has a wavelength of 556 nm?

A. 5.40×10^{5} Hz   B. 7.00×10^{8} Hz   C. 1.67×10^{11} Hz

          D. 5.40×10^{14} Hz   E. 5.70×10^{17} Hz

5. Calculate the **energy** (joules per particle) of light with a wavelength of 45.0 nm.

   A. 6.67×10^{15} B. 6.67×10^{11} C. 4.42×10^{-11}

              D. 4.42×10^{-15} E. 4.42×10^{-18}

6. What is the **energy in joules** of a <u>mole</u> of photons of wavelength 7.00×10^2 nm?

   A. 256 kJ   B. 1.71×10^5 J   C. 4.72×10^{-43} J

              D. 12.4 kJ   E. 2.12×10^{42} J

7. Which of the following scientists first postulated that the sharp lines in the emission spectra of elements were caused by electrons going from high energy levels to low energy levels?

   A. Einstein   B. Bohr   C. de Broglie   D. Pauli   E. Heisenberg

8. Which of the following scientists explained the photoelectric effect by postulating that light could behave like particles under certain circumstances?

   A. Einstein   B. Bohr   C. de Broglie   D. Pauli   E. Heisenberg

9. Which one of the following sets of quantum numbers is **unacceptable**?

	n	l	m_l	m_s
A.	4	3	-2	+ 1/2
B.	3	2	-3	- 1/2
C.	3	0	0	+ 1/2
D.	4	1	1	- 1/2
E.	2	0	0	+1/2

10. The **total number of atomic orbitals** in $n = 3$ shell is

    A. 1   B. 4   C. 7   D. 9   E. 12

11. The **number of atomic orbitals** in an <u>f subshell</u> is

    A. 1   B. 2   C. 3   D. 5   E. 7

12. The **maximum number of electrons** that can occupy the 5f subshell is

    A. 4   B. 6   C. 10   D. 12   E. 14

13. "No two electrons can have the same four quantum numbers" is a statement called ...

    A. the Pauli exclusion principle.

    B. Bohr's equation.

    C. Hund's rule.

    D. De Broglie's relation.

    E. Dalton's atomic theory.

14. The fact that the element carbon (in its ground state) is <u>paramagnetic</u> rather than diamagnetic can be understood in terms of ...

    A. the Pauli exclusion principle.
    B. Bohr's equation.
    C. Hund's rule.
    D. De Broglie's relation.
    E. Dalton's atomic theory.

15. The orbital diagram for a ground state **oxygen atom** is

	1s	2s	2p
A.	↑↓	↑↓	↑ ↑ ↑.
B.	↑↓	↑↓	↑↓ ↑↓ _.
C.	↑↓	↑	↑↓ ↑ _.
D.	↑↓	↑↓	↑↓ ↑ ↑.
E.	↑↓	↑↓	↑↓ ↑↓ ↑.

16. Which element has the following **electron configuration**? $1s^2 2s^2 2p^6 3s^2$

    A. Na   B. Mg   C. Al   D. Si   E. Ne

17. Which of the following is the ground state electron configuration of a **calcium atom**?

    A. $[Ne]3s^2$ B. $[Ne]3s^2 3p^6$ C. $[Ar]4s^1 3d^1$ D. $[Ar]4s^2$ E. $[Ar]3d^2$

18. Which element has the following **electron configuration**? $1s^22s^22p^63s^23p^1$

    A. Na   B. Mg   C. Al   D. Si   E. Ne

19. Which of the following is the ground state electron configuration of a **phosphorus atom**?

    A. $[Ne]3s^2$ B. $[Ne]3s^23p^3$ C. $[Ar]4s^13d^1$ D. $[Ar]4s^2$ E. $[Ar]3d^2$

20. Which of the following atoms in its ground state is **diamagnetic**?

    A F   B. Ne   C. B   D. O   E. Si

Chapter 8

1. The elements in **Group 2A** are known by what name?

   A. transition metals   B. halogens   C. alkali metals
                        D. alkaline earth metals   E. noble gases

2. The elements in **Group 8A** are known by what name?

   A. transition metals   B. halogens   C. alkali metals
                        D. alkaline earth metals   E. noble gases

3. Which of the following is the general **electron configuration** for the outermost electrons of elements in the halogen group?

   A. ns^1 B. ns^2 C. ns^2np^4 D. ns^2np^5 E. $ns^2np^6(n-1)d^6$

4. Which of the following is the general **electron configuration** for the outermost electrons of elements in the alkaline earth group?

   A. ns^1 B. ns^2 C. ns^2np^4 D. ns^2np^5 E. $ns^2np^6(n-1)d^6$

5. Which of the following is the general **electron configuration** for the outermost electrons of the alkali metal group of elements?

   A. ns^1 B. ns^2 C. ns^2np^4 D. ns^2np^5 E. $ns^2np^6(n-1)d^6$

6. Two elements which have the same valence electronic configuration ground state ns^2np^3 are

   A. O and Se   B. Ge and Pb   C. P and Sb   D. K and Mg   E. Mg and Ca

7. Which of the following elements would be expected to have chemical properties **most similar** to those of oxygen?

   A. carbon   B. nitrogen   C. fluorine   D. phosphorus   E. sulfur

8. Which element forms **stable +2 cations**?

   A. Kr   B. I   C. Se   D. Al   E. Ba

9. Which ion is **isoelectronic** with (*i.e*, has the same electron configuration as) <u>Ar</u>?

   A. Fe^{2+} B. F^- C. Br^- D. Ga^{3+} E. Ca^{2+}

10. Elements in Group 7A form <u>anions</u> whose valence electrons have the **same configuration** as neutral atoms of which group?

    A. 1A   B. 2A   C. 6A   D. 7A   E. 8A

11. A binary compound formed between nitrogen and fluorine would be expected to have the **formula**

    A. NF   B. NF_2 C. NF_3 D. NF_4 E. NF_5

12. Which element would you expect to have the <u>largest</u> **effective nuclear charge, Z_{eff}**?
    A. Li   B. C   C. O   D. Ne   E. Na

13. Which element would you expect to have the <u>smallest</u> **effective nuclear charge, Z_{eff}**?
    A. Li   B. C   C. O   D. F   E. Ne

14. Which element would you expect to have the <u>largest</u> **atomic radius** ?
    A. Li   B. C   C. O   D. Ne   E. Na

15. Which element would you expect to have the <u>smallest</u> **atomic radius** ?
    A. Li   B. C   C. O   D. Ne   E. Na

16. Which element would you expect to have the <u>lowest</u> **first ionization energy**?

    A. Li   B. C   C. O   D. Ne   E. Na

17. Which element would you expect to have the <u>highest</u> **first ionization energy**?

    A. Li   B. C   C. O   D. Ne   E. Na

18. Which element would you expect to have the <u>lowest</u> **electron affinity**?

    A. Li   B. C   C. O   D. Ne   E. Na

19. Which element would you expect to have the <u>highest</u> **electron affinity**?

    A. Li   B. C   C. O   D. Ne   E. Na

20. The **radii** of the species S, S^+, and S^- <u>decrease</u> in the following order:

    A. $S^+ > S > S^-$

    B. $S^+ > S^- > S$

    C. $S > S^- > S^+$

    D. $S > S^+ > S^-$

    E. $S^- > S > S^+$

Chapter 9

1. Which of the following compounds is most likely to be an **ionic compound**?

    A. NaF   B. CCl_4 C. NO_2 D. CO_2 E. ICl

2. Which pair of elements is most likely to form an **ionic compound**?

    A. Cl and I   B. Al and K   C. Mg and Cl   D. C and S   E. O and F

3. Which one of the following compounds is most likely to a **covalently bonded molecule**?

    A. KCl   B. $MgCl_2$ C. SF_4 D. Fe_2O_3 E. $BaSO_4$

4. Which one of the following compounds is most likely to a **covalently bonded molecule**?

    A. Rb_2S B. $SrCl_2$ C. CS_2 D. CaO   E. $MgBr_2$

5. Which of the following solids would have the **largest lattice energy**?

    A. MgO   B. NaCl   C. $SrBr_2$ D. CsI   E. $BaSO_4$

6. Which of the following solids would have the **highest melting point**?

   A. MgO   B. NaCl   C. $SrBr_2$ D. CsI   E. Fe_2O_3

7. Calculate the **energy change** for the reaction

$$K(g) + Br(g) \rightarrow K^+(g) + Br^-(g),$$

   given the following ionization energy (IE) and electron affinity (EA) values

	IE	EA
K	419 kJ/mol	48 kJ/mol
Br	1140 kJ/mol	324 kJ/mol

   A. -1,092 kJ/mol   B. -95 kJ/mol   C. 95 kJ/mol
               D. 1,092 kJ/mol   E. 1,187 kJ/mol

8. Which element has the **greatest electronegativity**?

   A. Na   B. Fe   C. Al   D. O   E. Ne

9. Which element has the **smallest electronegativity**?

   A. Na   B. Fe   C. B   D. O   E. Ne

10. Which of the following covalent bonds is the **most polar** (has the highest percent ionic character)?

   A. Si–P   B. N–O   C. C–H   D. O–H   E. C–O

11. The **Lewis structure** for phosphine, PH_3, has

   A. four bonding pairs
   B. two bonding pairs and two lone pairs
   C. three bonding pairs and one lone pair
   D. one bonding pair and thee lone pairs
   E. four lone pairs

12. The total **number of lone pairs** in the NF_3 molecule is

   A. 6   B. 8   C. 10   D. 12   E. 13

13. The total **number of lone pairs** in the N_2 molecule is

   A. 1   B. 2   C. 3   D. 5   E. 6

14. What is the **formal charge** on the nitrogen atom in HCN?

    A. −2   B. −1   C. 0   D. +1   E. +2

15. What is the **formal charge** on the oxygen atom in N_2O? (Hint: the structure is N=N=O.)

    A. 0   B. +1   C. −1   D. −2   E. +2

16. Which one of the following compounds does not follow the **octet rule**?

    A. NF_3 B. CO_2 C. NO   D. Br_2 E. CF_4

17. Which element is most likely to exhibit an **incomplete octet** in its compounds?

    A. B   B. C   C. N   D. O   E. F

18. Which element is most likely to exhibit an **expanded octet** in its compounds?

    A. O   B. S   C. N   D. Na   E. N

19. Estimate the **enthalpy change** (ΔH) for the reaction

$$H_2 + Cl_2 \rightarrow 2\ HCl,$$

given the following bond energies:

BE(H – H) = 436 kJ   BE(Cl – Cl) = 243 kJ   BE(H – Cl) = 432 kJ

    A. −247 kJ   B. −185 kJ   C. −101 kJ   D. +101 kJ   E. +185 kJ

20. Estimate the **enthalpy change** (ΔH) for the reaction

$$CH_4 + Cl_2 \rightarrow CH_3Cl + HCl,$$

given the following bond energies:

        BE(C – H) = 414 kJ   BE(C – Cl) = 326 kJ

        BE(H – Cl) = 432 kJ   BE(Cl – Cl) = 243 kJ

    A. -101 kJ   B. -109 kJ   C. +275 kJ   D. +109 kJ   E. +103 kJ

Chapter 10

1. According to the VSEPR theory, the **geometry** of the CO_2 molecule is

    A. linear   B. bent   C. trigonal planar

                 D. trigonal pyramidal   E. square planar

2. According to the VSEPR theory, the **geometry** of the SO_3 molecule is

    A. pyramidal.   B. tetrahedral.   C. trigonal planar.
                    D. see-saw   E. square planar.

3. The **arrangement of electron pairs** around the central P atom in the PH_3 molecule is

    A. linear   B. bent   C. trigonal planar
                D. trigonal pyramidal   E. tetrahedral

4. According to the VSEPR theory, the **geometry** of the PCl_3 molecule is

    A. linear   B. bent   C. trigonal planar
                D. trigonal pyramid   E. tetrahedral

5. According to the VSEPR theory, which one of the following species is **linear**?

    A. H_2S B. HCN   C. BF_3 D. H_2CO E. SO_2

6. According to VSEPR theory, which one of the following molecules has a **bent geometry**?

    A. Cl_2O B. CO_2 C. HCN   D. CCl_4 E. none

7. Which one of the following molecules has **tetrahedral geometry**?

    A. XeF_4 B. BF_3 C. AsF_5 D. CF_4 E. NH_3

8. The **bond angle** in carbon tetrachloride, CCl_4, is expected to be approximately

    A. $90\,^{\circ}$ B. $109.5\,^{\circ}$ C. $120\,^{\circ}$ D. $145\,^{\circ}$ E. $180\,^{\circ}$

9. Which one of the following molecules is **nonpolar**?

    A. NH_3 B. OF_2 C. CH_3Cl D. H_2O E. $BeCl_2$

10. Complete this sentence: "The BF_3 molecule, which has a trigonal planar geometry, has …"

    A. nonpolar bonds, and is a nonpolar molecule.
    B. nonpolar bonds, but is a polar molecule.

C. polar bonds, and is a polar molecule.
D. polar bonds, but is a nonpolar molecule.
E. ionic bonds

11.   Which one of the following molecules has a **dipole moment**?

   A. $BeCl_2$ B. Br_2 C. BF_3 D. IBr   E. CO_2

12.   Indicate the type of **hybrid orbitals** used by the central atom in ammonia, NH_3.

   A. sp   B. sp^2 C. sp^3 D. sp^3d E. sp^3d^2

13.   Indicate the type of **hybrid orbitals** used by the central atom in PCl_3.

   A. sp   B. sp^2 C. sp^3 D. sp^3d E. sp^3d^2

14.   Indicate the type of **hybrid orbitals** used by the central atom in SF_6.

   A. sp   B. sp^2 C. sp^3 D. sp^3d E. sp^3d^2

15.   What is the **hybridization** on the central atom in NO_3^-?

   A. sp   B. sp^2 C. sp^3 D. sp^3d E. sp^3d^2

16.   Which one of the following molecules has sp^3d **hybridization** at the central atom?

   A. PF_5 B. N_2O C. $BeCl_2$ D. SO_2 E. SF_6

17.   Valence bond theory describes the **bonding** in the CO molecule as

   A. three σ bonds
   B. three π bonds
   C. one σ bond and one π bond
   D. two σ bonds and one π bond
   E. one σ bond and two π bonds

18.   Valence bond theory describes the **bonding** in the N_2 molecule as

   A. three σ bonds
   B. three π bonds

C. one σ bond and one π bond
D. two σ bonds and one π bond
E. one σ bond and two π bonds

19. According to valence bond theory, the **σ bond** between the two carbon atoms in C_2H_2 arises from

A. The overlap of the 2s orbital on one C-atom with the 2s orbital on the other C-atom.
B. The overlap of the $2p_x$ orbital on one C-atom with the $2p_x$ orbital on the other C-atom.
C. The overlap of an sp hybrid orbital on one C-atom with an sp orbital on the other C-atom.
D. The overlap of the 2s orbital on one C-atom with the $2p_x$ orbital on the other C-atom.
E. The overlap of an sp^3 hybrid orbital on one C-atom with an sp^3 orbital on the other C-atom.

20. According to valence bond theory, π bonds arise from

A. The overlap of any two p atomic orbitals.
B. The end-to-end overlap of any two atomic obitals.
C. The side-by-side overlap of two atomic orbitals.
D. The constructive interference of one atomic orbital with another.
E. The destructive interference of one atomic orbital with another.

Chapter 11

1. Which of the following substances would you expect to have the **highest** melting point?

A. He   B. Ne   C. Ar   D. Kr   E. Xe

2. Which of the following substances should exhibit **hydrogen bonding** in the liquid state?

A. CH_4 B. H_2S C. HCl   D. HF   E. All of them

3. Which of the following indicates the presence of weak intermolecular forces in a liquid?

A. a low heat of vaporization
B. a high viscosity
C. a low vapor pressure

D. a high boiling point
E. none of the above.

4. Which of the following is **not true** with regard to water?

A. It has a high heat capacity
B. It has an unusually high boiling point
C. It exhibits hydrogen bonding
D. The solid is denser than the liquid
E. It is a polar molecule

5. The **number of atoms** in a <u>body-centered cubic</u> cell is

A. 1   B. 2   C. 3   D. 4   E. 8

6. The **number of nearest neighbors** (atoms that make contact) around each atom in <u>a face-centered cubic</u> lattice of a metal is

A. 2   B. 4   C. 6   D. 8   E. 12

7. The number of **nearest neighbors** around each sodium atom in a body-centered cubic cell is

A. 2   B. 4   C. 6   D. 8   E. 12

8. Which of the following, in the solid state, is classified as a **molecular** solid?

A. H_2 B. H_2O C. CH_3OH D. S_8 E. All of them

9. Which one of the following is a covalent network solid?

A. SiO_2 B. K   C. I_2 D. $CaCl_2$ E. CH_3OH

10. Which one of the following is classified as a metallic crystal?

A. CaO   B. SiO_2 C. CO_2 D. Pb   E. $KMnO_4$

11. Which of the following best describes the properties of an **ionic solid?**

A. hard, brittle
B. high melting point
C. large heat of fusion boiling point

D. poor electric conductor in the solid form, but good conductor when melted.
E. all of the above

12. An unidentified solid is brittle and has a high melting point. It does not conduct electricity. The solid is soluble in water. The substance could be …

A. I_2 B. $CaCl_2$ C. Cu   D. diamond   E. Xe

13. Which of the following would be expected to have the highest vapor pressure at room temperature?

A. ethanol bp = 78°C
B. methanol bp = 65°C
C. water bp = 100°C
D. acetone bp = 56°C

14. The molar heats of sublimation and fusion of iodine are 62.3 kJ/mol and 15.3 kJ/mol, respectively. Calculate the **molar heat of vaporization** of liquid iodine.

A. 77.6 kJ   B. 47.0 kJ   C. -47.0 kJ   D. -77.6 kJ   E. 4.07 kJ

15. The vapor pressure of ethanol is 400 mmHg at 63.5°C. Its molar heat of vaporization is 39.3 kJ/mol. What is **vapor pressure** of ethanol in mmHg at 34.9°C?

A. 1,510   B. 100   C. 200   D. 0.0099   E. 4.61

16. Acetic acid has a heat of fusion of 10.8 kJ/mol and a heat of sublimation of 35.1 kJ/mol. What is the expected value for the **heat of vaporization** of acetic acid?

A. 45.9 kJ/mol   B. 24.3 kJ/mol   C. –24.3 kJ/mol

          D. –45.9 kJ/mol   E. cannot tell from the data

17. Choose the response that lists the member of each of the following pairs that has **the higher boiling point**.

(1) H_2O or KI   (2) HF or HI   (3) Cl_2 or Br_2

A. H_2O, HF, and Cl_2
B. KI, HF, and Br_2
C. KI, HI, and Br_2

D. H_2O, HI, and Cl_2
E. KI, HF, and Cl_2

18.   Xenon has a **higher melting point** than neon because of its

A. hydrogen bonding
B. stronger London dispersion forces
C. permanent dipole moment
D. lower ionization energy
E. ionic bonding

19.   The **vapor pressure** of a liquid in a closed container depends upon

A. the amount of liquid.
B. the surface area of the liquid.
C. the volume of the container.
D. the temperature.
E. none of the above.

20.   The vapor pressure of ethanol is 108 mmHg at 34.9°C and 400 mmHg at 63.5°C. What is the **molar heat of vaporization** of ethanol in kJ/mol?

A. 15.1   B. 23.4   C. 39.3   D. 45.6   E. 98.7

Chapter 12

1.   Which response lists all the following pairs that are miscible liquids.

Pair # 1. octane (C_8H_{18}) and water
Pair # 2. acetic acid (CH_3COOH) and water
Pair # 3. octane (C_8H_{18}) and carbon tetrachloride(CCl_4)

A. 1, 3   B. 1, 2   C. 3   D. 2   E. 2, 3

2.   Which of the following gives the **molarity** of a 17.0% solution of sodium acetate, CH_3COONa (molar mass = 82.0 g/mol) in water? Given the density is 1.09 g/mL.

A. 2.26 x 10^{-6} M   B. 0.207 M   C. 2.07 M   D. 2.26 M   E. 2.72 M

3.   What is the percent $CdSO_4$ by mass in a 1.0 molal aqueous solution?

   A. 0.001 %   B. 0.10 %   C. 17.2 %   D. 20.8 %   E. 24.4 %

4.   How many **grams of water** are needed to dissolve 27.8 g of ammonium nitrate NH_4NO_3 in order to prepare a 0.452 m solution?

   A. 0.157 g   B. 36.2 g   C. 100 g   D. 769 g   E. 157 g

5.   Calculate the **molality** of a 20.0% by mass ammonium sulfate $(NH_4)_2SO_4$ solution. The density is 1.117 g/mL.

   A. 0.15 m   B. 1.51 m   C. 1.70 m   D. 1.89 m   E. 2.10 m

6.   A solution is prepared by dissolving 28.6 g of $MgCl_2$ in 180 g of water. What is the **percent by mass** of $MgCl_2$ in this solution?

   A. 11.6%   B. 13.7%   C. 15.9%   D. 18.3%   E. 23.4%

7.   A solution is prepared by dissolving 28.6 g of $MgCl_2$ in 180 g of water. What is the **mole fraction** of $MgCl_2$ in this solution?

   A. 0.0286   B. 0.0291   C. 0.0300   D. 0.0315   E. 0.0352

8.   A solution is prepared by dissolving 28.6 g of $MgCl_2$ in 180 g of water. What is the **molality** of this solution?

   A. 1.24   B. 1.44   C. 1.61   D. 1.67   E. 1.81

9.   A solution is prepared by dissolving 28.6 g of $MgCl_2$ in 180 g of water. The density of the resulting solution is 1.12 g/mL. What is the **molarity** of this solution?

   A. 1.24   B. 1.44   C. 1.61   D. 1.67   E. 1.81

10. In how many **grams of water** should 25.31 g of potassium nitrate (KNO_3) be dissolved to prepare a 0.1982 m solution?

   A. 250.0 g   B. 792 g   C. 1,000 g   D. 1,263 g   E. 7,917 g

11. The solubility of gases in water usually decreases with

    A. increasing pressure.
    B. increasing temperature.
    C. decreasing temperature.

12. The solubility of oxygen in lakes high in the Rocky Mountains is affected by the altitude. If the solubility of O_2 from the air is 2.67 x 10^{-4} M at sea level and 25° C, what is the solubility of O_2 at an elevation of 12,000 ft where the atmospheric pressure is 0.657 atm. Assume the temperature is 25° C, and that the **mole fraction** of O_2 in air is 0.209 at both 12,000 ft and at sea level.

    A. 1.75 x 10^{-4} M   B. 2.67 x 10^{-4} M   C. 3.66 x 10^{-5} M
              D. 4.06 x 10^{-4} M   E. none of the above

13. The Henry's law constant for oxygen is 3.5 x 10^{-4} mol/L-atm at 25°C. Calculate the **molar concentration** of oxygen in water at 25°C for a partial pressure of 0.22 atm.

    A. 630 M   B. 1.6 x 10^{-3} M   C. 3.5 x 10^{-4} M
              D. 7.7 x 10^{-5} M   E. none of the above

14. Consider a solution made from a nonvolatile solute and a volatile solvent. Which statement is **true**?

    A. The vapor pressure of the solution is always greater than the vapor pressure of the pure   solvent.
    B. The boiling point of the solution is always greater than the boiling point of the pure solvent.
    C. The freezing point of the solution is always greater than the freezing point of the pure solvent.

15. Calculate the freezing point of a solution made from 22.0 g of octane (C_8H_{18}) dissolved in 148.0 g of benzene. Benzene freezes at 5.50° C and its K_f value is 5.12 °C/m.

    A. -1.16 °C   B. 0.98 °C   C. 6.66 °C   D. 12.2 °C   E. 5.49 °C

16. At 25°C, pure liquid A has a vapor pressure of 400 mmHg, and pure liquid B a vapor pressure of 200 mmHg. At 25°C, what is the **total pressure** (in mmHg) of the vapor above a binary solution of A and B in which the mole fraction of A is 0.75?

    A. 100   B. 150   C. 350   D. 500   E. 600

17. Calculate the **freezing point** of a solution made from dissolving 17.0 g of dodecane ($C_{12}H_{26}$) in 200 g of cyclohexane. The normal freezing point of cyclohexane is 6.60°C, and its K_f value is 20.0°C/m.

    A. −10.0°C   B. −3.4°C   C. +3.4°C   D. +6.60°C   E. +16.6°C

18. The vapor pressure of water at 20°C is 17.5 mmHg. What is the **vapor pressure** of water over a solution prepared from 2.00×10^2 g of sucrose ($C_{12}H_{22}O_{11}$) and 3.50×10^2 g water?

    A. 0.51 mmHg   B. 16.0 mmHg   C. 17.0 mmHg
         D. 18.0 mmHg   E. 19.4 mmHg

19. Calculate the approximate **freezing point** of a solution made from 21.0 g NaCl and 1.00×10^2 g of H_2O. (K_f of water is 1.86°C/m.)

    A. 3.59°C   B. 6.68°C   C. −13.4°C   D. −6.68°C   E. −3.59°C

20. Which of the following aqueous solutions has the **lowest freezing point?** .

    A. 0.18 m KCl
    B. 0.15 m Na_2SO_4
    C. 0.12 m $Ca(NO_3)_2$
    D. pure water
    E. 0.20 m $C_2H_6O_2$ (ethylene glycol)

Answer Key to Practice Questions

Question	Chapter											
	1	2	3	4	5	6	7	8	9	10	11	12
1	E	A	D	A	E	C	E	D	A	A	E	E
2	D	A	A	E	E	A	C	E	C	C	D	D
3	B	E	C	D	D	D	D	D	C	E	A	C
4	B	B	C	B	C	B	D	B	C	D	D	D
5	E	B	D	E	D	B	E	A	A	B	B	D
6	E	B	D	D	C	E	B	C	E	A	E	B
7	E	B	C	E	D	D	B	E	C	D	D	B
8	C	B	D	B	C	D	A	E	D	B	E	D
9	A	A	A	B	B	A	B	E	E	E	A	C
10	C	D	C	E	B	E	D	E	D	D	D	D
11	B	E	B	A	E	B	E	C	C	D	E	B
12	A	E	E	D	D	B	E	D	C	C	B	A
13	B	A	D	A	E	E	A	A	B	C	D	D
14	A	E	B	B	E	B	C	E	C	E	B	B
15	D	B	E	C	A	C	D	D	A	B	B	A
16	C	E	D	B	C	E	B	E	C	A	B	C
17	A	D	C	B	C	C	D	D	A	E	B	B
18	D	D	B	A	A	B	C	D	B	E	B	C
19	D	A	C	C	E	A	B	C	B	C	D	C
20	B	E	C	A	A	D	B	E	A	C	C	B

Periodic Table of the Elements

Legend:

- 24 — Atomic number
- **Cr** — Chromium
- 52.00 — Atomic mass

1 / 1A	2 / 2A	3 / 3B	4 / 4B	5 / 5B	6 / 6B	7 / 7B	8 / 8B	9 / 8B	10 / 8B	11 / 1B	12 / 2B	13 / 3A	14 / 4A	15 / 5A	16 / 6A	17 / 7A	18 / 8A
1 **H** Hydrogen 1.008																	2 **He** Helium 4.003
3 **Li** Lithium 6.941	4 **Be** Beryllium 9.012											5 **B** Boron 10.81	6 **C** Carbon 12.01	7 **N** Nitrogen 14.01	8 **O** Oxygen 16.00	9 **F** Fluorine 19.00	10 **Ne** Neon 20.18
11 **Na** Sodium 22.99	12 **Mg** Magnesium 24.31											13 **Al** Aluminum 26.98	14 **Si** Silicon 28.09	15 **P** Phosphorus 30.97	16 **S** Sulfur 32.07	17 **Cl** Chlorine 35.45	18 **Ar** Argon 39.95
19 **K** Potassium 39.10	20 **Ca** Calcium 40.08	21 **Sc** Scandium 44.96	22 **Ti** Titanium 47.88	23 **V** Vanadium 50.94	24 **Cr** Chromium 52.00	25 **Mn** Manganese 54.94	26 **Fe** Iron 55.85	27 **Co** Cobalt 58.93	28 **Ni** Nickel 58.69	29 **Cu** Copper 63.55	30 **Zn** Zinc 65.39	31 **Ga** Gallium 69.72	32 **Ge** Germanium 72.59	33 **As** Arsenic 74.92	34 **Se** Selenium 78.96	35 **Br** Bromine 79.90	36 **Kr** Krypton 83.80
37 **Rb** Rubidium 85.47	38 **Sr** Strontium 87.62	39 **Y** Yttrium 88.91	40 **Zr** Zirconium 91.22	41 **Nb** Niobium 92.91	42 **Mo** Molybdenum 95.94	43 **Tc** Technetium (98)	44 **Ru** Ruthenium 101.1	45 **Rh** Rhodium 102.9	46 **Pd** Palladium 106.4	47 **Ag** Silver 107.9	48 **Cd** Cadmium 112.4	49 **In** Indium 114.8	50 **Sn** Tin 118.7	51 **Sb** Antimony 121.8	52 **Te** Tellurium 127.6	53 **I** Iodine 126.9	54 **Xe** Xenon 131.3
55 **Cs** Cesium 132.9	56 **Ba** Barium 137.3	57 **La** Lanthanum 138.9	72 **Hf** Hafnium 178.5	73 **Ta** Tantalum 180.9	74 **W** Tungsten 183.9	75 **Re** Rhenium 186.2	76 **Os** Osmium 190.2	77 **Ir** Iridium 192.2	78 **Pt** Platinum 195.1	79 **Au** Gold 197.0	80 **Hg** Mercury 200.6	81 **Tl** Thallium 204.4	82 **Pb** Lead 207.2	83 **Bi** Bismuth 209.0	84 **Po** Polonium (210)	85 **At** Astatine (210)	86 **Rn** Radon (222)
87 **Fr** Francium (223)	88 **Ra** Radium (226)	89 **Ac** Actinium (227)	104 **Rf** Rutherfordium (257)	105 **Db** Dubnium (260)	106 **Sg** Seaborgium (263)	107 **Bh** Bohrium (262)	108 **Hs** Hassium (265)	109 **Mt** Meitnerium (266)	110 **Ds** Darmstadtium (281)	111	112	(113)	114	(115)	(116)	(117)	(118)

Lanthanides:

58 **Ce** Cerium 140.1	59 **Pr** Praseodymium 140.9	60 **Nd** Neodymium 144.2	61 **Pm** Promethium (147)	62 **Sm** Samarium 150.4	63 **Eu** Europium 152.0	64 **Gd** Gadolinium 157.3	65 **Tb** Terbium 158.9	66 **Dy** Dysprosium 162.5	67 **Ho** Holmium 164.9	68 **Er** Erbium 167.3	69 **Tm** Thulium 168.9	70 **Yb** Ytterbium 173.0	71 **Lu** Lutetium 175.0

Actinides:

90 **Th** Thorium 232.0	91 **Pa** Protactinium (231)	92 **U** Uranium 238.0	93 **Np** Neptunium (237)	94 **Pu** Plutonium (242)	95 **Am** Americium (243)	96 **Cm** Curium (247)	97 **Bk** Berkelium (247)	98 **Cf** Californium (249)	99 **Es** Einsteinium (254)	100 **Fm** Fermium (253)	101 **Md** Mendelevium (256)	102 **No** Nobelium (254)	103 **Lr** Lawrencium (257)

Legend:
- Metals
- Metalloids
- Nonmetals

The 1–18 group designation has been recommended by the International Union of Pure and Applied Chemistry (IUPAC) but is not yet in wide use. In this text we use the standard U.S. notation for group numbers (1A–8A and 1B–8B). Elements 113 and 115–118 have not yet been synthesized. No names have been assigned for elements 111, 112, and 114.

List of the Elements with Their Symbols and Atomic Masses*

Element	Symbol	Atomic Number	Atomic Mass[†]	Element	Symbol	Atomic Number	Atomic Mass[†]
Actinium	Ac	89	(227)	Meitnerium	Mt	109	(266)
Aluminum	Al	13	26.98	Mendelevium	Md	101	(256)
Americium	Am	95	(243)	Mercury	Hg	80	200.6
Antimony	Sb	51	121.8	Molybdenum	Mo	42	95.94
Argon	Ar	18	39.95	Neodymium	Nd	60	144.2
Arsenic	As	33	74.92	Neon	Ne	10	20.18
Astatine	At	85	(210)	Neptunium	Np	93	(237)
Barium	Ba	56	137.3	Nickel	Ni	28	58.69
Berkelium	Bk	97	(247)	Niobium	Nb	41	92.91
Beryllium	Be	4	9.012	Nitrogen	N	7	14.01
Bismuth	Bi	83	209.0	Nobelium	No	102	(253)
Bohrium	Bh	107	(262)	Osmium	Os	76	190.2
Boron	B	5	10.81	Oxygen	O	8	16.00
Bromine	Br	35	79.90	Palladium	Pd	46	106.4
Cadmium	Cd	48	112.4	Phosphorus	P	15	30.97
Calcium	Ca	20	40.08	Platinum	Pt	78	195.1
Californium	Cf	98	(249)	Plutonium	Pu	94	(242)
Carbon	C	6	12.01	Polonium	Po	84	(210)
Cerium	Ce	58	140.1	Potassium	K	19	39.10
Cesium	Cs	55	132.9	Praseodymium	Pr	59	140.9
Chlorine	Cl	17	35.45	Promethium	Pm	61	(147)
Chromium	Cr	24	52.00	Protactinium	Pa	91	(231)
Cobalt	Co	27	58.93	Radium	Ra	88	(226)
Copper	Cu	29	63.55	Radon	Rn	86	(222)
Curium	Cm	96	(247)	Rhenium	Re	75	186.2
Darmstadtium	Ds	110	(281)	Rhodium	Rh	45	102.9
Dubnium	Db	105	(260)	Rubidium	Rb	37	85.47
Dysprosium	Dy	66	162.5	Ruthenium	Ru	44	101.1
Einsteinium	Es	99	(254)	Rutherfordium	Rf	104	(257)
Erbium	Er	68	167.3	Samarium	Sm	62	150.4
Europium	Eu	63	152.0	Scandium	Sc	21	44.96
Fermium	Fm	100	(253)	Seaborgium	Sg	106	(263)
Fluorine	F	9	19.00	Selenium	Se	34	78.96
Francium	Fr	87	(223)	Silicon	Si	14	28.09
Gadolinium	Gd	64	157.3	Silver	Ag	47	107.9
Gallium	Ga	31	69.72	Sodium	Na	11	22.99
Germanium	Ge	32	72.59	Strontium	Sr	38	87.62
Gold	Au	79	197.0	Sulfur	S	16	32.07
Hafnium	Hf	72	178.5	Tantalum	Ta	73	180.9
Hassium	Hs	108	(265)	Technetium	Tc	43	(99)
Helium	He	2	4.003	Tellurium	Te	52	127.6
Holmium	Ho	67	164.9	Terbium	Tb	65	158.9
Hydrogen	H	1	1.008	Thallium	Tl	81	204.4
Indium	In	49	114.8	Thorium	Th	90	232.0
Iodine	I	53	126.9	Thulium	Tm	69	168.9
Iridium	Ir	77	192.2	Tin	Sn	50	118.7
Iron	Fe	26	55.85	Titanium	Ti	22	47.88
Krypton	Kr	36	83.80	Tungsten	W	74	183.9
Lanthanum	La	57	138.9	Uranium	U	92	238.0
Lawrencium	Lr	103	(257)	Vanadium	V	23	50.94
Lead	Pb	82	207.2	Xenon	Xe	54	131.3
Lithium	Li	3	6.941	Ytterbium	Yb	70	173.0
Lutetium	Lu	71	175.0	Yttrium	Y	39	88.91
Magnesium	Mg	12	24.31	Zinc	Zn	30	65.39
Manganese	Mn	25	54.94	Zirconium	Zr	40	91.22

*All atomic masses have four significant figures. These values are recommended by the Committee on Teaching of Chemistry, International Union of Pure and Applied Chemistry.

[†]Approximate values of atomic masses for radioactive elements are given in parentheses.

Some Prefixes Used with SI Units

Tera (T)	10^{12}	Centi (c)	10^{-2}
Giga (G)	10^{9}	Milli (m)	10^{-3}
Mega (M)	10^{6}	Micro (μ)	10^{-6}
Kilo (k)	10^{3}	Nano (n)	10^{-9}
Deci (d)	10^{-1}	Pico (p)	10^{-12}

Index of Important Figures and Tables

Fundamental Constants

Avogadro's number	6.0221367×10^{23}
Electron charge (e)	1.6022×10^{-19} C
Electron mass	9.109387×10^{-28} g
Faraday constant (F)	96,485.3 C/mol e^-
Gas constant (R)	8.314 J/K · mol (0.08206 L · atm/K · mol)
Planck's constant (h)	6.6256×10^{-34} J · s
Proton mass	1.672623×10^{-24} g
Neutron mass	1.674928×10^{-24} g
Speed of light in vacuum	2.99792458×10^8 m/s

Useful Conversion Factors and Relationships

1 lb = 453.6 g

1 in = 2.54 cm (exactly)

1 mi = 1.609 km

1 km = 0.6215 mi

1 pm = 1×10^{-12} m = 1×10^{-10} cm

1 atm = 760 mmHg = 760 torr = 101,325 N/m^2 = 101,325 Pa

1 cal = 4.184 J (exactly)

1 L atm = 101.325 J

1 J = 1 C × 1 V

$$?°C = (°F - 32°F) \times \frac{5°C}{9°F}$$

$$?°F = \frac{9°F}{5°C} \times (°C) + 32°F$$

$$?K = (°C + 273.15°C)\left(\frac{1 \text{ K}}{1°C}\right)$$

Color Codes for Molecular Models

H

B

C

N

O

F

P

S

Cl

Br

I